Educating Individuals
With Disabilities

Elena L. Grigorenko, PhD, received her doctorate in general psychology from Moscow State University, Russia, in 1990, and her PhD in developmental psychology and genetics from Yale University, United States, in 1996. Currently, Dr. Grigorenko is Associate Professor of Child Studies and Psychology at Yale. Dr. Grigorenko has published more than 200 peer-reviewed articles, book chapters, and books. She has received awards for her work from five different divisions of the American Psychological Association (Divisions 1, 7, 10, 15, and 24). In 2004, she won the APA Distinguished Award for Early Career Contribution to Developmental Psychology. Dr. Grigorenko has worked with children and their families in the United States as well as in Africa (Kenya, Tanzania and Zanzibar, the Gambia, and Zambia), India, and Russia. Her research has been funded by the NIH, NSF, DOE, Cure Autism Now, the Foundation for Child Development, the American Psychological Foundation, and other federal and private sponsoring organizations. Dr. Grigorenko's current research includes studies of: (1) the cognitive and linguistic adaptation of international adoptees in the United States; (2) learning disabilities in harsh developmental environments and their relation to infection, intoxication, and poverty in Africa; (3) the genes involved in language disorders in a genetically isolated population; (4) the genes involved in learning disabilities and cognitive processing, with a special emphasis on studying minority samples in the United States; and (5) interactions between genetic and environmental risk factors for conduct problems and the role of these factors in response to interventions in juvenile detainees.

Educating Individuals With Disabilities

IDEIA 2004 and Beyond

Elena L. Grigorenko, PhD

Editor

SPRINGER PUBLISHING COMPANY

New York

Springer Publishing Company, LLC
11 West 42nd Street
New York, NY 10036
www.springerpub.com

Acquisitions Editor: Philip Laughlin
Project Manager: Julia Rosen
Cover design: Joanne E. Honigman
Composition: Apex CoVantage

08   09   10   11/   5   4   3   2   1

Library of Congress Cataloging-in-Publication Data

Educating individuals with disabilities : IDEIA 2004 and beyond / Elena L. Grigorenko, editor.
    p. cm.
  Includes bibliographical references and index.
  ISBN 978-0-8261-0356-7 (alk. paper)
  1. Children with disabilities—Education—United States.   2. Special education—United States.   3. Learning disabled children—Education—United States.   I. Grigorenko, Elena L.

LC4031.E3852 2008
371.90973—dc22   2007040609

Printed in the United States of America by Bang Printing.

Contents

PART III. FROM THE FRONT LINES

Contributors

Eric R. Arzubi, BS
Raging Knowledge Educational
   Services, Inc.
Westport, CT

Doris Luft Baker, PhD
University of Oregon
Eugene, OR

Scott K. Baker, PhD
Pacific Institutes for Research
Eugene, OR

**Catherine M. Brighton,
PhD, MEd**
University of Virginia
Charlottesville, VA

Carolyn M. Callahan, PhD
University of Virginia
Charlottesville, VA

David J. Chard, PhD
University of Oregon
Eugene, OR

Kerri Clopton, PhD
University of Northern Iowa
Cedar Falls, IA

Ronnie Detrich, PhD
Wing Institute
Oakland, CA

Susan Etscheidt, PhD
University of Northern Iowa
Cedar Falls, IA

Barbara R. Foorman, PhD
Florida State University
Tallahassee, FL
Florida Center for Reading
   Research
Tallahassee, FL

Douglas Fuchs, PhD
Vanderbilt University
Nashville, TN

Lynn S. Fuchs, PhD
Vanderbilt University
Nashville, TN

Barbara C. Gartin, EdD
The University of Arkansas
Fayetteville, AR

Michele Goyette-Ewing, PhD
Yale University
New Haven, CT

Daniel P. Hallahan, PhD
University of Virginia
Charlottesville, VA

Linda J. Hawkins, MEd
Bellevue School District
Bellevue, WA

Saylor Heidmann, MS
Albertus Magnus College
New Haven, CT

Denise Hexom, EdD
National University
Stockton, CA

Jane M. Jarvis, MA
University of Virginia
Charlottesville, VA

Asha Jitendra, PhD
Lehigh University
Bethlehem, PA

Alan S. Kaufman, PhD
Yale University
New Haven, CT

Andrea Kayne Kaufman, MEd, JD
DePaul University
Chicago, IL

Chandra Keller-Allen, MPP
George Washington University
Washington, DC

Leanne R. Ketterlin-Geller, PhD
University of Oregon
Eugene, OR

Jennifer H. Lindstrom, PhD, MEd
University of Virginia
Charlottesville, VA

Peggy McCardle, PhD, MPH
National Institute of Child
   Health and Human
   Development
Rockville, MD

Judith Menoher, EdD
National University
Redding, CA

Tonya R. Moon, PhD
University of Virginia
Charlottesville, VA

Nikki L. Murdick, PhD
Saint Louis University
St. Louis, MO

Dabie Nabuzoka, MSc, PhD
Leeds Metropolitan
   University
Leeds, UK

Jack A. Naglieri, PhD
George Mason
   University
Fairfax, VA

Bonnie A. Plummer, PhD
University of California
San Francisco, CA

Michael N. Riley, PhD
Bellevue School District
Bellevue, WA

Tanya Shuy, MA, PhD
National Institute
   for Literacy
Washington, DC

Louise Spear-Swerling, PhD
Southern Connecticut State
   University
New Haven, CT

Sherin Stahl, PhD
Yale University
New Haven, CT

Mary Stone, EdD
Nascent Group
Los Altos, CA

Elizabeth D. Tuckwiller, MS
University of Virginia
Charlottesville, VA

Mary Konya Weishaar, PhD
Southern Illinois University
Edwardsville
Edwardsville, IL

Stuart S. Yeh, MPP, PhD
University of
Minnesota
Minneapolis, MN

Rebecca O. Zumeta, MEd
Vanderbilt University
Nashville, TN

Introduction

At the beginning of the 21st century two pieces of educational legislation are coming together as the high water mark of standards-based reform in the United States: The No Child Left Behind (NCLB) Act of 2001 and the Individuals With Disabilities Educational Improvement Act (IDEIA) of 2004. The goal of NCLB is "to ensure that all children have a fair, equal, and significant opportunity to obtain a high-quality education and reach, at a minimum, proficiency on challenging State academic achievement standards and State academic assessments" (U.S. Code 6302 § 1001). This right to educational excellence was first articulated in 1983 in the National Commission on Excellence in Education's report, *A Nation at Risk*. In the past 25 years, states have launched standards-based educational reforms which have coupled the right to educational excellence with the original intent of the Elementary and Secondary Education Act (ESEA) of 1965 to ensure that all students, regardless of ethnicity or income, have access to education. These rights to educational access and excellence for children living in poverty ensured by modifications to ESEA during the past 42 years are reinforced by modifications to the right-to-education movement for individuals with disabilities in the past 37 years. The right-to-education movement represented most currently by IDEIA is important to any discussion of the poverty gap because poor students are disproportionately represented within the special education population. In addition, research conducted in the past 40 years to prevent

This work was supported by grant R305W020001, "Scaling Up Assessment-Driven Intervention Using the Internet and Handheld Computers," from the Institute of Education Sciences in the U.S. Department of Education.

learning disabilities and to intervene early with students at risk of learning disabilities can help promote learning for all disadvantaged students (Foorman, Kalinowski, & Sexton, 2007).

COMPLEMENTARY PROVISIONS OF NCLB AND IDEIA

In general, the provisions of NCLB and IDEIA work in concert to ensure high quality instruction that closes the achievement gap. Both emphasize prevention and early intervention and rely on whole-school approaches and multitiered instruction that incorporate scientifically based academic programs and positive behavioral interventions and supports. Both require highly qualified teachers, as defined by federal law as having at least a bachelor's degree and certification in the subject area they teach. Both require alignment of performance goals with states' definitions of adequate yearly progress. Both require data collection, evaluation, and progress monitoring to inform instruction. Both mandate high expectations for students with disabilities by including them in district and state accountability systems, counting the numbers participating in each assessment condition, and reporting results to the public with the same frequency as is done for nondisabled students. To help accomplish the integration of these two acts, funding may be shared, in particular the provision that up to 15% of special education funding may be used for prevention and early intervention.

CHALLENGES OF IMPLEMENTING IDEIA

NCLB and IDEIA share a common goal: a single, well-integrated system that connects general, remedial, and special education and considers the learning needs of *all* students. The chapters in this book point out the potential and the challenges of reaching this goal. A major challenge mentioned by Kaufman in chapter 2 is that any discussion of teacher quality is quickly overshadowed by the reality of the shortage of special education teachers. Weishaar in chapter 3 and Detrich in chapter 4 point out the lack of training in evidence-based practices in teacher preparation programs. Spear-Swerling in chapter 11 cites the National Council on Teacher Quality review of syllabi from 72 randomly selected education schools across the United States to explain the lack of teachers' pedagogical content knowledge (NCTQ, 2006).

Another major challenge to fully implementing IDEIA is that adult educators need to change—change what they do in some cases, such as school psychologists giving fewer IQ tests and more curriculum-based assessments or behavioral interventions—but, in all cases, change what they think about student learning. We are not going to wait for students to fail before providing supplemental services; we are going to provide additional instruction in kindergarten and in Grade 1 to prevent learning difficulties and to intervene with students at risk of learning disabilities. Under IDEIA, students' response to intervention (RTI) becomes part of the criteria for identification of a specific learning disability. Importantly, as pointed out by L. Fuchs, D. Fuchs, and Zumeta in chapter 5, RTI allows educators to distinguish between two explanations for low achievement: inadequate instruction versus disability. Another advantage of RTI, as pointed out by McCardle, Keller-Allen, and Shuy in chapter 6 and by the Bakers in chapter 10, is that it can help reduce the disproportionate representation of English language learners (ELLs) and other groups by using assessment data to inform instruction. Those who fail to respond to quality classroom and small-group interventions will be given brief evaluations to distinguish disabilities (e.g., learning disabilities versus mild mental retardation or language impairment) or to identify more serious cognitive, sensory, or behavioral/emotional impairments using the kinds of measures and procedures discussed by Naglieri and Kaufman in chapter 7, Lindstrom, Tuckwiller, and Hallahan in chapter 8, Moon, Brighton, Callahan, and Jarvis in chapter 12, and Goyette-Ewing and Stahl in chapter 18.

Fuchs et al. in chapter 5 emphasize that special education is not an outcome of the RTI process but rather an integral part of the multilayered system of interventions according to which students in the third tier of special education receive individualized instruction that enables them to return to the small-group supplemental Tier 2 or the classroom-level of Tier 1. Indeed, this goal of returning to Tiers 1 and 2 should be specified in the Individual Education Program, as mentioned by Gartin and Murdick in chapter 14, and in behavior intervention plans as discussed by Etscheidt and Clopton in chapter 15. Ideally, assessments and diagnostic tutoring provided in private practice settings would work in concert with these tiered interventions in school, as suggested by Arzubi in chapter 20. Furthermore, as Nabuzoka points out in the first chapter, school interventions should be consistent with the sociocultural context of the home and community.

MODELS OF RESPONSE TO INTERVENTION (RTI)

According to IDEIA, RTI means that a local education agency "may use a process that determines if the child responds to scientific, research-based intervention as a part of the evaluation procedures" (Pub. L. No. 108–446 § 614 [b][6][A]; § 614 [b] [2 & 3]). This legislated notion of RTI as a diagnostic system implies but is conceptually distinct from the RTI multitiered instructional model. It is useful to keep the RTI diagnostic model and RTI instructional model conceptually distinct because the former is new and has challenging measurement implications, whereas the latter has been in existence in public health (see Detrich's chapter 4) and in school reform models such as Success for All (Slavin & Madden, 2001) and direct instruction (Englemann & Bruner, 1995) for over 20 years with significant impacts (Borman, Hewes, Overman, & Brown, 2003; Denton, Foorman, & Mathes, 2003). The RTI instructional model is evident in many states' implementations of the primary-grade reading component of NCLB—Reading First. In the first 3 years of Florida's Reading First initiative (2003–2006), the implementation of an RTI instructional model in 318 elementary schools (where 72% of students qualify for free or reduced price lunch, 62% are minority, and 14% are ELLs), the percent of students identified as learning disabled at the end of kindergarten was reduced by 81% over the 3 years (Torgesen, 2007). The percent reductions for Grades 1, 2, and 3 were 67%, 53%, and 42%, respectively. The percent reductions in numbers of students reading below the 20th percentile on norm-referenced test at the end of first and second grades were significant but not as large (22.8% to 15.7% and 23.3% to 16.2%, respectively, over the 3 years), leading one to conclude that school administrators were confident that adequate interventions were in place to meet the instructional needs of seriously struggling readers. However, these administrators must subject their confidence in the interventions to empirical evaluation to make sure that gains in student achievement occur. Otherwise, the concern raised by Kaufman in chapter 2 that early interventions may *delay* special education services is warranted.

THE PROMISE OF RESPONSE TO INTERVENTION (RTI) MODELS

The promise of the RTI models is real: Substantial reductions in the number of students referred to special education because their academic performance catches up to grade-level expectations. Measurement issues for the RTI diagnostic model are discussed by Fuchs and colleagues in chapter 5, Chard, Ketterlin-Geller, and Jitendra in chapter 9, and Yeh in chapter 13. All agree that frequent assessment of student progress using curriculum-based, equated forms is essential. Adequacy of response may be evaluated by outcome on a criterion benchmark or norm-referenced test and/ or by the rate of improvement (see Fuchs and colleagues' discussion of these options in chapter 5). Tips on successful implementation of RTI instructional models are provided by Hawkins and Riley's description of the IDEIA implementation in an affluent district outside Seattle in chapter 17 and by Hexom, Menoher, Plummer, and Stone's description of working with 33 low-performing California elementary, middle, and high schools in chapter 16.

In another chapter from the front line of schools—chapter 19—Heidmann describes the RTI instructional model endorsed by the International Reading Association (IRA). The vast majority of K–12 reading teachers in the United States are members of the IRA and this model reflects what is possible within general education. According to this model, there are three tiers—a universal tier, a selective tier, and an intensive tier. The universal tier consists of 60 minutes of whole-group and small-group instruction with benchmark screening and assessment procedures used three times a year. The selective tier is time-limited to 4–6 weeks and includes 30 additional minutes of instruction (i.e., 30–45 hours). These first two tiers comprise the 90 minutes of reading instruction mandated by many states for Reading First (but see Fielding, Kerr, & Rosier, 2007, for an empirically derived rationale for at least 120 daily minutes of quality reading instruction).

The intensive tier is the hallmark of the RTI instructional model and no longer utilizes the core reading program. In this tier, a brief norm-referenced test battery of reading and spelling achievement and, possibly, vocabulary is given and diagnostic tutoring is provided that targets the student's literacy needs using evidence-based practices. Progress is monitored weekly using curriculum-based measurement. Students who remain in diagnostic tutoring after two cycles are considered learning disabled in reading and eligible for special education services. They are referred for further evaluation of mental retardation, attention-deficit/hyperactivity disorder, or communication disorders. In IRA's model, students with reading problems are not "special education" or "regular education" students. All teachers—classroom teachers and specialists—work collaboratively in the three tiers. A reading coach (a) helps select evidence-based materials that teachers will use to ensure that 80% of students in the universal tier are meeting benchmarks, (b) models lessons for teachers, and (c) teaches small groups in the selective tier. Reading specialists and special education teachers arc the diagnostic tutors at the intensive tier and conduct assessments at both the selective and intensive tiers.

CONCLUSION

In conclusion, IDEIA and NCLB bring together 40 years of segregated educational policies in the United States for students with disabilities and for students living in poverty into complementary legislation that can serve all children without requiring a label to receive supplemental instruction. The chapters in this book point out the many hurdles to overcome to realize the potential of the RTI models supported by these historic pieces of legislation. Let us move forward together in a deliberate fashion to embrace the change.

Barbara R. Foorman, PhD

REFERENCES

Borman, G. D., Hewes, G. M., Overman, L. T., & Brown, S. (2003). Comprehensive school reform and achievement: A meta-analysis. *Review of Educational Research, 73*(2), 125–230.

Denton, C., Foorman, B., & Mathes, P. (2003). Schools that "Beat the Odds": Implications for reading instruction. *Remedial and Special Education, 24,* 258–261.

Elementary and Secondary Education Act of 1965, Pub. L. No. 89–10, 79 Stat. 27 (1965).

Englemann, S., & Bruner, E. (1995). *Reading mastery I.* Chicago: SRA/McGraw-Hill.

Fielding, L., Kerr, N., & Rosier, P. (2007). *Annual growth for all students, catch-up growth for those who are behind.* Kennewick, WA: The New Foundation Press, Inc.

Foorman, B. R., Kalinowski, S. J., & Sexton, W. L. (2007). Standards-based educational reform is one important step toward reducing the achievement gap. In A. Gamoran (Ed.), *Standards-based reform and the poverty gap: Lessons from "No Child Left Behind."* Washington, DC: Brookings Institution.

Individuals With Disabilities Education Improvement Act of 2004 (IDEA), Pub. L. No. 108–446, 118 Stat 2647–2808, (2004).

National Commission on Excellence in Education. (1983). *A nation at risk.* Washington, DC: U.S. Government Printing Office.

National Council on Teacher Quality. (2006). *What education schools aren't teaching about reading and what elementary teachers aren't learning.* Washington, DC: Author.

No Child Left Behind Act of 2001, Pub. L. No. 107–110, 115 Stat.1425 (2001).

Slavin, R. E., & Madden, N. A. (2001). *One million children: Success for all.* Thousand Oaks, CA: Corwin.

Torgesen, J. K. (2007, June). *Using an RTI model to guide early reading instruction: Effects on identification rates for students with learning disabilities.* Under Report on Implementation of the RTI Model in Reading First Schools in Florida. Retrieved August 26, 2007, from www.fcrr.org

PART I

Educating Individuals With Disabilities

CHAPTER 1

Issues and Developments in Special Education

Dabie Nabuzoka

The development of educational services for individuals with disabilities has been characterized by various concerns at particular points in time as well as in different countries of various parts of the world. While priorities have differed accordingly, these concerns have largely focused on efforts aimed at understanding the characteristics of individuals with disabilities that have implications for their education, including the social and cognitive processes involved; the efficacy of various methods of teaching; and the contexts that promote the optimal functioning of such individuals. The services provided to reflect such concerns have generally come under the general term of *special education*. The individuals requiring such education have been referred to as having special educational needs (SEN). While some significant strides have been made in understanding the needs of individuals with disabilities and in the provision of special education, various issues have arisen and attained prominence in various contexts and at particular times in the history of special education. This chapter traces some of the developments that have characterized special education in selected countries as indicators of world trends. The chapter draws on material mostly from the United Kingdom and United States, reflecting experiences in the industrialized world, and also some third world countries to illustrate similarities and differences in concerns and priorities. The specific focus and issues discussed are necessarily selective, but it is hoped that this approach will provide some flavor of general concerns in the field while also being of interest to professionals in different parts of the world.

There has long been recognition that the needs of those with disabilities may differ not only amongst individuals involved but also between the various types of disabilities. Such a distinction has been reflected in the types of special education services provided in various parts of the world. However, a concern with specific difficulties in academic and learning tasks has been one of the major areas of special education in many countries. This chapter therefore mostly focuses on issues related to the education of children with learning disabilities (LD) to illustrate some of the main issues related to special education especially in the industrialized world. Though the emphasis is on provision for individuals with LD, developments related to provision for other types of disabilities are also discussed, especially as related to examples from third world countries where issues of concern may relate to most if not all types of disabilities.

One development in understanding the nature of difficulties faced by children with disabilities has been a recognition that although a term such as *learning disabilities* may suggest difficulties primarily in the academic domain, problems faced by children with such a label are not confined to that area alone. There is evidence that such people may encounter problems in their social relationships as well and that the factors that first set children with this label apart from their classmates, setting in motion the referral and diagnostic process, tend to be problems in social adjustment rather than just academic difficulties or underachievement (Nabuzoka, 2000). Such problems may also have a direct bearing on the academic functioning of the individuals concerned (Walker & Nabuzoka, 2007). This chapter therefore also mostly focuses on the psychosocial functioning and adjustment of children with LD and discusses issues related to this in the provision of special education services.

In discussing some of the developments and issues in special education, the chapter begins with the terminology used to describe and classify those children who may require special education provision. The nature of the presenting difficulties are then discussed focusing on the structure and functioning of cognitive processes on the one hand and levels of psychosocial adjustment on the other, as factors associated with educational outcomes of children with LD. This is followed by a discussion on the assessment and identification of children deemed to have special needs. This relates to both academic and general functioning of the affected children and is also associated with the definition and classification of the presenting difficulties. The contribution of the context in which education is provided to the academic functioning of children with LD is then discussed focusing on social ecological factors. This has mostly focused on the school setting as an environment in which children spend most of their educational time. However, in parts of the world where special education provision is not widely accessible through schools, provision in the community has been an alternative and even supplementary approach to school efforts, and this is discussed at some length.

Another issue discussed relates to some of the intervention strategies that have been applied to address difficulties faced by those children identified with LD. Some strategies aimed at enhancing the functioning of the children from the community settings of some countries in the third world to school settings in these and industrialized countries are discussed and evaluated. The chapter concludes by discussing some of the issues related to applied and evaluative research in special education.

TERMINOLOGY AND CLASSIFICATION

The term *learning disabilities* has acquired slightly different meanings in different parts of the world, notably as used in North America compared with Britain. It is of relatively recent origin as a category of special education. In the United States, the term can be traced back to Samuel Kirk, who proposed it at a meeting of parents in New York City in 1963. It had been used for the first time a year earlier in the first edition of his textbook *Educating Exceptional Children* (Kirk, 1962). Kirk (1963) proposed that the term should be used to denote the difficulties some children have in school-related basic skill areas (e.g., speech and language, reading, spelling, writing, math). He emphasized the need to forgo speculation about the causes of learning failure and rather to focus on identifying and treating the learning problems themselves. There then followed a number of alternative definitions of LD to reflect an increasing awareness of the plight of so-called disabled learners and of the need to identify and treat their problems (Hallahan & Kauffman, 1976). However, the tendency within the education profession has been to retain a broader definition of learning disabilities, this being consistent with the proposal by Hallahan and Kauffman (1977) that a child with a learning disability is simply one who is not achieving his or her full potential. Such a child may have any intelligence level, may have a learning problem for any number of reasons (some perceptual and some not), and may or may not have emotional problems.

One of the key components in the definitions in subsequent use was a discrepancy between a child's aptitude and his or her achievement, with underachievement being the main basis of classification to LD status by educational or school committees in most cases (MacMillan,

Gresham, & Bocian, 1998). This was largely reflected in the Individuals With Disabilities Education Act (IDEA). The more recent Individuals With Disabilities Education Improvement Act (IDEIA, 2004) provided revised parameters concerning LD diagnosis. One of the main changes to IDEIA legislation was to eliminate reliance on the Intelligence (IQ) Achievement discrepancy model as the basis for LD diagnostic decision making, while focusing on "relevant functional, developmental, and academic information." The federal regulations are considered to be fairly open-ended, thus allowing state departments of education some flexibility in establishing LD diagnostic parameters (Dombrowski et al., 2006).

In Britain, *people with learning disabilities* refers to the broader category of people with intellectual disabilities, including those who in the United States and elsewhere are referred to as "mentally retarded." The latter term is not generally in common usage in Britain except in the context of some clinical discourse and journals. The current British definition and classification of children experiencing difficulties in the academic domain was influenced by the Warnock Report of 1978. Until then, such children were classified into various separate categories that included physical, emotional, and intellectual difficulties (Pritchard, 1963). The Warnock Report recommended that the term *children with learning difficulties* be used for all children requiring special educational provision and that such learning difficulties might be described as mild, moderate, or severe. Children with particular difficulties only, such as with reading, may be described as having a "specific learning difficulty." This classification represented a move away from using several categorical *labels* toward statements of educational *needs* based on a detailed profile following an individual assessment.

These, then, are functional classifications based essentially on curricular requirements. They place more emphasis on what the child may require and less on the presenting limitations of the child. However, as pointed out by Dockrell and McShane (1993), identification of an appropriate curriculum for the child requires an understanding of the nature of the child's problems. For example, an understanding of the child's cognitive abilities is necessary when considering learning difficulties. Categorization solely on the basis of educational needs, as suggested by the Warnock Report, also tends to be too inclusive of children whose difficulties might be sensory, physical, emotional, or due to what has been referred to as "intellectual disability" or "mental handicap" (retardation). These difficulties also represent different social experiences for the children affected and such differences may not be reflected in a classification of special educational needs.

In this chapter, the term *learning disability* is used broadly to include a sense similar to that adopted in the United States (i.e., difficulties in the academic domain). This group of children includes those with Full Scale IQ (intelligence quotient) scores within one standard deviation below or above 100. These children are in most cases characterized by a discrepancy between aptitude and achievement but may be without any other apparent physical, sensory, or emotional problems. Also included are children who, in the British sense, may be described as having learning difficulties arising from intellectual deficits and associated difficulties (said to have "mental retardation" in the United States). These children have IQ scores significantly below 100 (the cut-off point being an IQ of 75) and may also have accompanying physical, sensory, or emotional problems. The wide spectrum of problems represented by these terms has often been referred to as "intellectual disability." Thus, in this chapter, the terms *learning disability* and *intellectual disability* are used interchangeably: the former to reflect difficulties in the academic domain and the latter to refer to the wider spectrum of problems. Those whose difficulties may apply to any type of disability are simply referred to as children or individuals with disabilities, or that they have special educational needs.

EXPLAINING THE NATURE OF PRESENTING DIFFICULTIES

Structure and Functioning of Cognitive Processes

A concern of many researchers and practitioners is to determine the nature of problems faced by individual children. The nature of these difficulties can be illustrated in the case of generalized intellectual disability. Intellectual disability, especially when severe, is a condition that tends to interfere with the normal course of human development in various domains. Thus, difficulties in a single area of functioning such as academic tasks in school may be related to problems in both the cognitive and social domains. This often leads to serious and chronic difficulties of adaptation for the developing child and also for his immediate family. Explaining these problems requires a conceptual framework. Clements (1987), for example, identified two major psychological theories that have been proposed to explain intellectual disability and which are seen as relevant to specific problems in the academic domain. One of these, the deviancy theory, considers those with intellectual disability to have one or more mental processes that are different from those in the normal population, and thus underlie low performance in various tasks. It emphasizes differences rather than commonalties between those affected and other members of society. The other theory is the developmental delay theory, which proposes that people with intellectual disability have the same mental processes as other people and go through the same stages of development as others—but at a slower rate.

These theoretical frameworks have guided service delivery policies in different ways. Deviancy theory is in support of the sociological model that encouraged enforced segregation (to be distinguished from the human rights model), and in support of the medical model. The medical model assumes a perspective of causation and remediation in terms of a condition within the child that needs appropriate treatment. Developmental delay theory, on the other hand, seems to be in tune with a sociological human rights model and, in so far as knowledge of developmental processes is regarded as relevant to education, with the education models. The latter models have their origins in developmental psychological theory.

Thus, a central question of concern has been whether children with LD are delayed in their development or whether they have a different developmental *pattern*. Dockrell and McShane (1993) suggest that because children with general LD display a slower rate of learning and reach a lower ceiling, this indicates some limits on the extent of cognitive development, and that upper limits on performance exist. They posed the question as to whether the learning process of children with LD was best explained by a model which invokes the same principles and mechanisms of development that apply to other children, or whether it was necessary to invoke specific differences over and above the slower rate and lower ceiling.

Two main foci of studies have been identified addressing the question of developmental difference versus delay:

- establishing the extent to which children with general LD follow a similar sequence of development to typically developing children;
- establishing the extent to which performance differences on cognitive tasks can be explained by underlying processing differences (Dockrell & McShane, 1993).

Studies investigating the similar-sequence hypothesis consider children's progress through stages, such as the Piagetian stages of cognitive development. Research support for the similar-sequence hypothesis both across large stages and within the substages is considered important. In the social domain for example, research on typically developing children has indicated some sequential order of developmental levels in interpersonal understanding (Gurucharri & Selman, 1982; Selman, 1980). Similar research on social perception of children with LD has sought to identify some developmental progression similar to that of non-LD children (Jackson, Enright, & Murdock, 1987; Nabuzoka & Smith, 1995). The concern of such research is predominantly with what stages the child has mastered and in what order.

The other perspective is to consider how the child's cognitive system processes information. A suggestion is that children with LD process information in a manner different from that of typically developing children and that this accounts for difficulties they may experience across a wide range of tasks. According to this perspective, learning disabilities are seen in terms of cognitive processes and structures that may be absent or inefficient, thereby leading to poor performance across tasks. However, Dockrell and McShane (1993) argued that processing difficulties should not necessarily imply cognitive differences. They suggested that it might be more useful to consider how the cognitive system of children with LD might function differently to account for slower rates of development.

In all, debates have focused on whether children with LD are essentially developing differently in attaining developmental milestones in various domains, or simply developing more slowly. One alternative argument is to regard these perspectives as not necessarily mutually exclusive but to consider how developmental delays may reflect the different ways in which children with LD function (Dockrell & McShane, 1993). According to maturation theory, there is a sequential progression in the maturation of cognitive skills, and a child's ability in a specific cognitive area will depend on his or her maturational status (Piaget, 1970). Children with LD have been described as having a maturation lag reflecting slowness in certain aspects of neurological development, so they are seen as not being qualitatively different from normally developing peers, but rather just developing more slowly (Koppitz, 1973). This has implications for the design of intervention programs. It suggests that the child continues to develop in the area of relative weakness and may eventually reach an adequate level of competence. As such, a more passive approach to intervention is implied in that if children develop at different rates, it would be easier to simply wait until a child has achieved readiness for the task at hand.

Psychosocial Adjustment

Although the term *learning disabilities* may suggest difficulties primarily in the academic domain, problems are not confined to that area alone. Evidence suggests that people with LD encounter problems in their social relationships as well (Bender & Smith, 1990; Kavale & Forness, 1996). It has long been recognized that the factors that first set children with this label apart from their classmates tend to be problems in social adjustment rather than just academic underachievement. It is often such factors that set in motion the referral and diagnostic process (Nabuzoka, 2000). However, although descriptions of individuals with LD have often included some social characteristics, it is only relatively recently that attention has been paid during assessment and intervention to social behaviors, especially peer-related interactions. Then, the major concern was merely on academic difficulties and how to address them. A child's general perceptual and cognitive development was the main factor related to academic success or failure. In the last few decades, however, efforts have been made to relate perceptual and cognitive development of children also to social functioning (Longman, Inglis, & Lawson, 1991; Spafford & Grosser, 1993).

There has been consistent evidence that many children with LD experience negative social relationships with significant people in their lives and even with strangers. A review of the literature by Nabuzoka (2000) indicated that these children are less well regarded by parents, teachers, other adult observers or strangers, and by peers. They also report more dissatisfaction and anxiety about their peer relations than other children. As children with LD are more likely to be regarded negatively by others and thus have negative experiences, the quality of their social relations can be said to be relatively poor. According to the social skills model of adjustment, children with LD may experience relatively more social adjustment problems as a consequence of social skills limitations or deficits, and others' responses to them (Spafford & Grosser, 1993). Such a relationship between social functioning and adjustment has also been used to explain academic achievement of such children (Walker & Nabuzoka, 2007). The social skills model of adjustment has been useful, leading to considerable progress in identifying abilities associated with socially competent performance and in developing intervention programs for fostering them (Chalmers & Townsend, 1990; Spence, 1991). Thus, for children with LD, identifying the skills that might need fostering has been considered to be an ongoing and integral part of the intervention process.

ASSESSMENT AND IDENTIFICATION OF CHILDREN WITH SPECIAL NEEDS

Professional intervention on behalf of children with developmental or learning disabilities requires an assessment of the child's level of functioning, and of the resources required to address the difficulties faced. This includes his or her emotional, social, moral, and intellectual skills, dispositions, and needs. Intervention can then include the design of an environment to respond to those needs. In the case of children experiencing difficulties in school, the assessment of the child's functional level and the nature of the educational needs is one of the key issues in special education. In this section, two types of assessments linked to the context of the child's functioning are discussed: assessment of academic and of general functioning. The first is related to learning in the context of the school while the other relates to learning in the general sense of the term as would relate to functioning in the community.

Assessment of Academic Functioning

Until recently relatively, assessment of levels of functioning of all children experiencing difficulties in school in the United Kingdom occurred in the context of "statementing" (Fisher, 2000). This is a process through which an educational psychologist, a medical doctor, and other professionals make an assessment of the functioning and special needs of a child. On the basis of this, a profile of the strengths and needs of the child is drawn up together with a recommendation as to the best form of educational placement for the child. This may be a mainstream school with resources to cater for the special needs (inclusive setting), or a separate school with more specialized resources (special school).

The statement thus provides an educational and social profile of a child with great emphasis on what he or she may require. The recommendation for and eventual placement would be in an educational environment deemed to best meet those needs identified in the assessment. In one case, for example, accessibility to a speech therapist and a range of mainstream peers may be seen as some of the key factors for recommending an inclusive mainstream school with a resource facility. The choice of a particular school to host the child would depend on the availability of the resources and support systems to meet the stated needs. In addition, links between the school and home setting may be seen as important for some children.

Statementing also implies that an assessment is made, in some way, of the suitability of a given setting to cater for the child's needs. Assessment in this sense involves several aspects aimed at informing professional interventions in response to the presenting disability. The need for *multidimensional assessment* is consistent with the ecological perspective on human development (Bronfenbrenner, 1979). This does not focus on a static categorization of the child's current level of functioning, nor on a predictive estimate of his or her potential to benefit from a fixed type of service. Rather an appraisal is required of the child's behavioral skills in relation to the developmental potential of various systems in which he or she operates.

A profile of the child's skills, dispositions, and needs must therefore be tied in to a continuum of support representing the various contexts within which he or she functions. In one given case, for example, it may therefore not be enough to identify a need for home-school liaison: It would be more appropriate to also analyze the home-care unit as an integrated microsystem that includes the child and his or her immediate caregivers. For example, addressing the presence of language problems may not be helped by a situation where the language used at school (English for example) is not frequently used in the home.

Assessment of General Functioning

In many parts of the developing world assessment of a disability would be linked to efforts aimed at enhancing the general development of the affected individual. In the case of learning disabilities, an underlying cause may be generalized intellectual disabilities. Studies of intellectual disability have often been concerned with identifying and documenting causes for the disability; the special needs created by the disability for the individual child and for his or her family; and the implications for intervention. An initial practical concern is with the assessment methods employed to identify the target children and their specific needs. However, objectivity in assessment procedures used can be difficult to demonstrate. This is particularly the case in determining general intellectual functioning, as opposed to assessment with a specific focus on the academic domain or sensory and motor functions, which tends to be relatively straightforward. From a global perspective, an issue that has implications for assessment is the extent to which intellectual disability may be amenable to universal definition, and also as a specific condition identifiable in various contexts or cultures. There are some indications that such agreement is possible at a general level. This has been demonstrated in the use of the term *mental retardation* to refer to the condition also known as intellectual disability.

The first indication has been in identification. This has mostly been from epidemiological studies. In medicine, such studies are concerned with the incidence and distribution of diseases and other factors related to health. It has been generally accepted that so-called mental retardation represents intellectual functioning that is significantly below average. One's score on an intelligence test often establishes such functioning. Epidemiological studies on siblings of children with IQs below 75, and also of various social class backgrounds, have been conducted to document the distribution patterns of intelligence test scores. Such studies appear to suggest that the most severe impairments of intellectual functioning reflect a distinct pattern of causation that is probably of an organic nature (WHO, 1985). In addition, Piagetian research that has a bearing on the universality of intellectual functioning has shown developmental patterns of the sensory-motor stage to be more closely followed in various cultures than patterns of later stages. Serpell (1988), for example, observed that at the earlier stages of development (i.e., the sensory-motor stage), major environmental demands on a child's cognitive functioning show a higher level of generalizability across cultures than the more subtle demands that feature at later stages. This probably has a lot to do with the earlier functions having more of a biological basis than the later functions that may have greater influences of social experience and learning.

The second general agreement has been in definitions put forward by international bodies such as the World Health Organization (WHO), the International Association for the Scientific Study of Mental Deficiency (IASSMD), and the International League of Societies for Persons with Mental Handicap (ILSMH, now Inclusion International). Such definitions include "marked impairment in the ability of the individual to adapt to the daily demands of the social environment" (WHO, 1985, p. 8; see also WHO, 1993). This inclusion places the criterion of intellectual disability within the social context, especially the cultural context of the child's society. Thus, it allows for variation reflecting the values and expectations of the child's local culture. At the same time, adaptability-in-context is a key element in a definition of intellectual disability applicable to most cultures.

Serpell (1988) concluded, on the basis of the above observations, that a child designated as having severe intellectual disability "may turn out to have certain common features irrespective of the definition of intelligence prevailing in his or her home's culture: organic impairment, significantly delayed attainment of certain transculturally early milestones of child development and a locally recognised failure to adapt to the local norms of social behaviour" (p. 120). The question then is as to what emphasis is put by assessors on the largely common features of functioning relative to more culturally variable criteria. Serpell and his colleagues addressed this question in a study of the criteria used by professional review teams to determine severe intellectual disability in nine third world countries. Their findings indicated some general consensus on five domains of functioning (Serpell, 1988). These domains included the following: (1) Social habits and skills; (2) Self-help/self-maintenance habits and skills; (3) Rate of learning/understanding new tasks; (4) Communication habits and skills; and (5) Physical coordination.

These domains represent aspects of functioning that have also been areas of focus in western assessment procedures (Luckasson, Coulter, Polloway, Reiss, Schalock et al., 1992). Because they represent features of every society, they were deemed to constitute "cross-culturally universal domains for the psychological assessment of severe intellectual handicap" (Serpell, 1983):

1. *Social habits and skills*—Every society has certain forms of interaction which a child of a particular age is expected to follow. It is therefore possible to specify objectively which behaviors are socially deviant and displayed by children with severe intellectual disability.

2. *Self-help/self-maintenance habits and skills*—Every society expects children of a given age-range to perform a number of routine functions for themselves in respect of such things as hygiene, feeding, and dressing. Inability to perform such functions may thus signal some difficulty.

3. *Rate of learning/understanding new tasks*—It is also common for societies to expect children to begin to learn some more specialized skills that may ultimately be linked to economic activities. This therefore is another function that may signal the presence or absence of intellectual difficulty.

4. *Communication habits and skills*—These are psychological functions that play an important role in determining a child's adaptation to the demands of social interaction and learning new tasks. Assessment of this domain generally focuses on the extent to which a child has mastered language, in speech or comprehension.

5. *Physical coordination*—a rather broad psychological and physiological function especially often impaired in children with severe intellectual disability.

While there might be some consensus on each of these domains, the particular form and specific behaviors involved differ from one culture to another. Because the manifestation of intellectual disability within a domain may differ from one context to another, this has implications for assessment and the planning and execution of activities aimed at reducing the impact of disability.

Thus, education in many parts of the world is best considered in the widest sense of the term, for which assessment needs to focus on a range of domains of psychological functioning. The need to accurately identify the target children has led to concerns with assessment methods, and especially with the extent to which the disabling condition may be amenable to universal definition. Areas of general consensus across contexts and cultures include functioning significantly below average and patterns that may have a biological basis. There is also a general consensus in placing the criterion of disability within the sociocultural context of the developing child. Intervention efforts as related to special education are therefore best seen as aimed at enhancing a child's functioning in each of these domains. A significant aspect of such efforts is the context in which intervention occurs.

THE CONTEXT FOR EDUCATION

The links between social ecological factors and learning difficulties have been recognized for some time (Empson & Nabuzoka, 2004).

Such recognition led to a series of major government-led projects in the 1970s, in particular Project Headstart in the United States (Weisberg, 1992) and the Educational Priority Areas projects in the United Kingdom. Strong links have specifically been shown to exist between social disadvantage and various types of learning and behavioral difficulties in school. For example, Maxwell (1994) found strong correlation between social disadvantage and disabilities in the intellectual/cognitive, physical, and sensory domains for pupils in various secondary schools of a British city. Studies such as this suggest the need to examine individual, familial, and community factors in the assessment of needs for children with LD (Lynn, Hampson, & Magee, 1983; Rutter, 1989). Intervention strategies that are designed would then be informed of the strengths and risk factors at various levels of a given child's environmental systems.

In recent decades with the increased attention to the contribution of social factors to the development of children with LD, the role of the context in which education is provided has come into focus. As the environment in which children spend most time, the school setting has been the focus of most studies, and within the school setting, the type of placement for individual children has also been examined (Hocutt, 1996). Here debate has focused on whether the needs of children with disabilities are best served in inclusive mainstream schools or specialized schools. While there has been a similar debate in parts of the world where special education provision is not widely accessible through schools, in such countries provision in the community has been seen as an alternative and even supplementary approach to school efforts. In this section, issues related to the debate surrounding the merits of inclusive versus specialized schools are first discussed. The theoretical basis and rationale for promoting each setting are first discussed followed by a brief overview of the evidence for their efficacy. Then related issues pertaining to community involvement are discussed at some length. This is focused on the special education efforts in the context of some developing countries, identifying parallels and similarities of concerns with those in industrialized countries.

Education in the School Context

There is a general acceptance that the extent to which the school setting may stimulate the social cognitive development of children with LD is largely mediated by its social ecology. In most cases the design of the social environment in schools is a policy issue. In Great Britain, for example, Education Acts in 1981 made provision for integration of children with special needs (including LD) into mainstream schools in England

and Wales, and also in Scotland (Morris, Watt, & Wheatley, 1995). Various models of provision have since been implemented. These range from partial integration, whereby a special unit is set up in a mainstream school, to full integration under which children with LD attend the same classes as their non-LD peers. From a social learning theory perspective, such contexts offer different levels of opportunities for children with LD to acquire so-called appropriate social skills through observation of others. At the level of policy formulation and its implementation, provision for children with LD can be said to reflect society's conceptualization of presenting problems (Acton, 1982).

According to Clements (1987), the most common response to individuals with disabilities has been to regard them as a homogeneous population, encouraging the formation of general social models to "mediate the interpretation of presenting phenomena and provide some kind of philosophical framework to guide and rationalise society's response" (p. 2). These models have included sociological, medical, and educational types, each of which has been predominant at various times in history. For example, one vein of the sociological model that grew up in the 1960s regarded people with intellectual disability as a deprived minority group for whom service provision and resource allocation were a human right to which they needed a fair share. Medical models regard intellectual disability as another illness needing professional treatment in a health context. Educational models, on the other hand, view intellectual disability from the functional perspective of learning and emphasize the need for services to be provided within an educational context, rather than a health one.

Over the years a characteristic shift in dominant models involved the medical model being replaced by an educational model linked to a human rights and sociological approach. This shift resulted in some rapid moves toward increased care and integration, and increased control of services by education and social welfare agencies rather than health agencies (Clements, 1987). The predominant social model has, to some extent, influenced the psychology of disability—exemplified in the shifting of educational policy in the United Kingdom, the United States and other parts of the world toward more inclusive placements of children with disabilities in the ordinary classroom (or at least the ordinary school). Such placements gained momentum in the late 1980s going into the 1990s. The terminology widely used then was *integration* in the United Kingdom and Europe or *mainstreaming* in the United States and other parts of the world.

Arguments in favor of inclusive education were put forward based on apparent benefits in social functioning and adjustment. In the social domain, these have focused on opportunities that inclusive settings offer children with LD including the following (Nabuzoka, 2000):

- more appropriate interactions and increased self initiations in social situations;
- the development of more complex language and communication skills; and
- decreased inappropriate play.

Thus, children with LD in an inclusive setting can acquire social skills and age-appropriate behaviors through observational learning from normally developing peers, and such contexts offer opportunities for generalization of those skills. These benefits have also been cited by parents of children with disabilities who consider inclusive programs to be more stimulating (Guralnick, 1990) and offering more positive social outcomes than segregated ones. It has also been argued that inclusive schools reduce the stigma of a segregated setting and increases the level of acceptance of children with LD by their non-LD peers. Non-LD children may not only help identify age-appropriate valid activities but also develop increased understanding of, sensitivity to, and tolerance for individual differences. In this way, non-LD children would develop and display favorable attitudes toward peers with LD, as a result of direct contact with these children.

Analysts such as Stobart (1986), pointed out that though the outcomes of such policies were couched in psychological terminology, the justification for integration was based on appeals for social justice rather than on specific psychological or even educational grounds. According to Stobart, "psychological theories have been conscripted to handle the psychological implications of this policy, which are usually construed as social, rather than academic benefits" (p. 1).

Alternative views for segregation include the argument that some children with LD may need protection from the pressures of social demands that obtain in inclusive settings. The strains of these pressures might inhibit the development or display of social skills the inclusive setting is purported to promote. One particular argument was that children with LD (and indeed other types of disabilities as well) could suffer as they could be rejected by mainstream peers. Such rejection, it was argued, is likely to arise from exposure of non-LD children to so-called negative behavioral characteristics of children with LD, thus increasing the social isolation of the latter (Gottlieb, 1981). Children with LD in mainstream settings would in this way have their self-confidence eroded and be subjected to greater anxiety.

Whatever the arguments, post-1980s saw rapid developments toward inclusive education. Evaluations of the benefits of inclusive compared to specialized schools have been rather mixed depending on the focus (Nabuzoka, 2000). Research has generally shown inclusive settings to be more beneficial than segregated settings for children with LD in terms of social and behavioral outcomes, and gains in social cognitive functioning. Such benefits may, however, not be of sufficient magnitude for the development of positive social relations for these children.

Social outcomes in terms of patterns of interaction, social networks, and acceptance appear to be only somewhat more positive for children with severe disabilities and not for those with mild to moderate disabilities. The differential effects of inclusion appear to be more marked in older than younger children, while gender may also be a factor. In addition, the degree of exposure or contact between children with LD and non-LD children seems to be significant in the social acceptance of children with LD. One outcome of lack of peer acceptance and the resultant social isolation is the increased risk of being bullied and victimized by peers. Children with LD appear particularly vulnerable in this regard. These and other difficulties related to peer acceptance constitute adjustment problems generally faced by these children in mainstream settings. The problems may be manifested in loneliness, unhappiness, and negative school attitudes, perceptions, and feelings. Functional limitations and problems in social relations, which may be highlighted in inclusive settings, may also undermine self-esteem as well as the emotional adjustment of children with LD. It has been argued that such adjustment problems need to be weighed against the benefits of inclusion.

Education in the Community

Resource and material allocations have influenced what context should be provided for education of children with disabilities. For example, the special school commands more highly specialized resources of a material and human nature than an inclusive mainstream setting. It could therefore be argued that inclusive education seems to offer a cheaper option for policy makers. In most developing countries, notably on the African continent, the issue of resource availability has had a more direct influence on the nature of special education provision available. Most countries on the African continent have significantly underdeveloped material and human resource capacities for provision of quality education for their citizens. This has resulted in the learning needs of many children being either unrecognized or unmet. Those with disabilities have been seen to have experienced the most significant levels of neglect, marginalization (Avoke, 2001; Eleweke, 1999), and disempowerment by national governments and the local schools (Mpofu, Peltzer, Shumba, Serpell, & Mogaji, 2005).

Special education provision in developing countries is best seen in the context of general service provision for individuals with disabilities. In this sense, and in recognition of the scarcity of such services, the World Health Organization (WHO) in the 1980s advocated a strategy, known as Community-Based Rehabilitation (CBR), which was seen to be more cost-effective in meeting the needs of individuals with disabilities (Helander, Mendis, & Nelson, 1984). The CBR approach advocated for measures to be taken at community level in addressing the needs of individuals with disabilities. The education of children with disabilities was seen, within this approach, as involving collaborative efforts between the local school and the community (Nabuzoka, 1991). Education was defined in a broad sense to include the acquisition of skills in various domains of functioning (Serpell, 1988), with lay people (e.g., family members, volunteers, school teachers, and community leaders, etc.) being agents of such education.

CBR was presented as an alternative or complementary approach to efforts of specialized institutions, such as special schools. In developing countries, such institutions were nonexistent or considered to be inadequate. The debate then was as to whether the needs of children with disabilities were best met in these communities (including local schools) rather than specialized centers such as special schools. Experiences with CBR, and the evaluations and research studies carried out on various projects (Finkenflügel, 1993), generally support a complementary approach (Miles, 1985; Serpell, 1986). The majority of efforts at the implementation of the CBR approach have been from the Sub-Saharan African region, followed by the South Asia and East Asia regions and only a few reports from South American countries (Finkenflügel, 2004).

The overall concept and effectiveness of CBR has been questioned over the period of nearly three decades since being introduced (Miles, 2004). In particular, problems have been identified in soliciting the participation of lay people in various communities to be agents for the education of children with disabilities (Nabuzoka, 1993). However, in terms of the overall provision of some services for such children, the approach has been positively regarded as offering hope and possibilities for children with disabilities and their families where there might have been little chance of any service at all (Finkenflügel, 2004; Nabuzoka, 1991).

INTERVENTION STRATEGIES

While there has been some debate about the most optimal context for provision of education services to children with disabilities, other concerns have focused on what skills or capabilities need to be developed in these children and the ways in which this can be achieved. Intervention strategies have therefore been developed in response to such concerns. In the social domain, for example, efforts would be directed at equipping children with skills that enhance their social adjustment. Thus, if problems faced by children with LD are associated with inappropriate behavioral dispositions, intervention could appropriately be focused on changing the children's behaviors. Where the children are characterized by low levels of interaction patterns, efforts can be made to increase their ability to initiate interactions and to promote social responsiveness. Similarly, training in social perceptual and cognitive skills can enhance understanding of children with LD, leading to more appropriate behavioral responses and, subsequently, more positive social and academic outcomes. The issues to be discussed in this section relate to such approaches and the problems associated with demonstrating the efficacy of these and a number of similar intervention efforts.

Intervention to Enhance Social Functioning in Schools

There have been various intervention strategies, based on research involving typically developing children, used to promote social interaction of children with disabilities in inclusive settings (Odom & Brown, 1993). These have included so-called teacher-mediation involving direct teacher (or support worker) modeling and reinforcement of social play. In this approach the teacher or support worker interacts with children with LD in ways designed to increase positive behaviors with peers. However, there have been some indications that involvement of adults in this manner could impede child-to-child interactions (Lewis, 1995). Another approach is so-called peer-mediation, whereby normally developing (non-LD) children are trained to interact positively with children with LD. In studies where this approach has been used, levels of social interaction of children with LD have been observed to improve (Hundert & Houghton, 1992; Sainato, Goldstein, & Strain, 1992). In both these approaches, however, there have been some problems with maintenance over time and with generalization of the observed improvements across settings.

A more effective approach involving peer mediation places the focus mainly on the normally developing peers as agents of behavior change (Odom & Brown, 1993; Odom & Strain, 1984; Strain & Odom, 1986). These peers would usually be trained in some operant techniques such as prompting and reinforcement, and are themselves prompted and reinforced for their performance with the children with disabilities. Despite the initial effects of peer-mediated approaches, however, these approaches have often shown limited generalization and maintenance effects across situations and time (Odom & Strain, 1984; Odom, Hoyson, Jamieson, & Strain, 1985). A review by Mathur and Rutherford (1991) identified subtypes of peer-mediated treatment. They concluded that these approaches demonstrate success in producing immediate, positive treatment effects, and that these effects may be generalizable. They pointed out, however, that systematic programming was required to produce lasting results.

There are a number of possible explanations for the lack of maintenance of intervention effects. One is that studies have tended to be carried out within periods of time that were too short for any lasting relationships to develop between children. Children with LD spend too little time with their non-LD peers—during playtime—and may demonstrate a newcomer pattern of shy, withdrawn behavior. Another problem has been that the differentiation between peer- and teacher-mediated interventions can at times be unclear. Mathur and Rutherford (1991) pointed out, for example, that despite labeling of interventions as peer-mediated, teachers or support workers would still be in control in most cases. A more distinctive feature would therefore be a situation where children with LD interacted with non-LD peers in the absence of adults.

Another reason for lack of maintenance of intervention effects could be the intensity of peer-mediated interventions. Most studies do not describe the intensity of the interventions, but one might assume that this is likely to be high bearing in mind the observed effects and relatively short times in which they are attained. It has also been suggested that there may be "fatigue effects" causing the lack of maintenance (Odom & Strain, 1984). It has also been pointed out that applying interventions of high intensity within clearly defined time intervals or situations could also lead to the participants learning to discriminate between situations where target behaviors are to be performed and those where they should not. This would be contrary to the goal of obtaining generalized and durable interaction. A more desirable approach would be to conduct intervention studies over much longer periods, with long baselines applied initially to allow familiarization among the children.

A study by Rønning and Nabuzoka (1993) demonstrates the differential effects of social skills training alone, social skills training with teacher prompts, and the use of non-LD peers as agents of social interactions (so-called special friends). In that study, each of these measures led to improved positive social interaction by children with LD, which in turn was associated with enhanced status among non-LD peers. Comparatively, teacher involvement in training and prompting of social interactions appeared to lead to greater increases in such behavior than did social skills training alone. There were also indications that the gain resulting from such measures could be generalized to other situations, although some doubts remained about the lasting effects of applying teacher prompts as a way of promoting social interaction. The peer-mediated special-friends approach, on the other hand, seemed effective in both increasing the social interaction of children with LD and non-LD peers and in the generalization and maintenance of such increases in interaction. In this approach, non-LD children acted as trainers for children with LD, enabling them to become more efficient partners in play. They took on the role of initiating and prompting general play behaviors of children with LD, but did not engage in the training of specific elements of social skills such as basic verbal and nonverbal skills. It would appear that some incidental learning of such skills occurs as a consequence of these efforts. This point, however, needs to be verified by more focused research.

The acquisition of specific components of social skills, as a direct result of teacher- or peer-mediated approaches, can be inferred through patterns of behavior that result from these interventions. Such skills may be demonstrated in the way children with LD become responsive to their social surroundings. One feature of increases in positive social interaction of children with LD, and resulting from peer-mediated approaches, has been that initiations for such interaction tend to be from non-LD peers. The gains for children with LD, from a functional point of view, are that they exhibit some increased capacity to respond appropriately and thereby sustain interaction with peers. This latter aspect not only suggests improved responsiveness but also reflects greater social understanding. As for taking the initiative, a number of studies have indicated that training children with disabilities to initiate interaction does not often lead to generalized or durable changes (e.g., James & Egel, 1986). As discussed earlier, behavioral skills developed solely through intensified efforts of teachers or support workers often have problems of maintenance. However, peer-mediated approaches can also suffer from a failure to encourage children with LD to initiate social interaction.

The issue of concern is really whether children with LD can benefit from such interventions unless they are proactive. What may appear to be a general lack of initiative by children with LD may in fact reflect a lack of opportunity to exhibit skills acquired for social interaction. There is some evidence that children with LD can repeat linguistic skills learned from non-LD peers in appropriate contexts on different occasions, even where interaction in the mainstream context may have been didactic (Lewis, 1995). Such evidence has, however, largely been anecdotal and there are also some suggestions that effects of this nature may strongly depend on the cognitive levels of the children with LD (Howlin, 1994). More controlled research designs are needed.

In all, a number of individualized intervention strategies have been tried with varying degrees of success. In the social domain, these include training specific social skills in the areas in which children with disabilities are perceived to have deficits. Others involve some training combined with increased opportunities for social interaction, including teacher-mediated and peer-mediated approaches. Both of these approaches have been shown to produce initial positive effects, but results have been equivocal on generalization and maintenance over time. Some evidence indicates that peer-mediated approaches are more promising if conducted in the context of natural peer group activities and over longer periods than just a few weeks.

However, there have been some suggestions that highly variable outcomes of social skills training programs for children with special needs may result from poor matching of treatment to needs (Gresham, Sugai, & Horner, 2001). It has been argued that the problem may be that social skills training programs have been based primarily on research with mainstream populations. In contrast, a number of studies have suggested that the social skills important for positive social adjustment, such as peer acceptance, may be different for children with special educational needs such as LD (Frederickson & Furnham, 2004). Specifically, there are some indications that different behaviors might be associated with peer rejection in inclusive mainstream schools for children with LD than for mainstream pupils (Frederickson & Furnham, 2004; Nabuzoka & Smith, 1993; Roberts & Zubrick, 1992). For example, Frederickson and Furnham (2004) found that more rejected British children with LD could be classified as internalizing than externalizing in contrast to a high proportion of externalizing rejected children (with none internalizing) in the sample of mainstream children. Roberts and Zubrick (1992) found that, amongst Australian pupils, sociometric rejection was predicted by peer perceptions of both academic and disruptive behavior for mainstream children. However, for children with LD only peer perceptions of disruption were related to sociometric rejection. Nabuzoka and Smith (1993) similarly reported a number of differences between peer-assessed behaviors associated with sociometric status for British children with LD and their mainstream classmates.

Frederickson and Furnham (2004) suggested that a better understanding of processes underlying the relationships between peer perceptions of special needs status, pupil behavior, and social acceptance was important in designing more effective interventions to improve the social adjustment of children with LD. Their conclusion was that social acceptance and inclusion of children with LD depends as much on mainstream peer expectations and attitudes toward their behavior as on the nature of the manifest behavior. This indicates a need for a change of focus regarding both the content and delivery of intervention programs. In particular, such programs need to address both the behavior of children with LD and the attitudes and expectation of their peers.

Interventions in the Home Community

The potential of the school setting to stimulate a child's cognitive development has in the past been contrasted with that of the home environment.
The focus on the home setting led to consideration of parents as agents for
such stimulation. Research evidence indicated the significant role that parents play in children's development. For example, a study by Tizard and
Hughes (1984) examined the relative impact of young children's interactions with adults at home compared to that in the preschool setting. They
compared children's conversations with their mothers at home to that
with teachers at school, and found that the former were richer and had
more depth and variety than the latter. Similar findings were also reported
in other studies (Clarke-Stewart & Fein, 1983). On the other hand, teachers have been found to differ from parents in using language that is more
often complex, in asking questions, and in providing more direct teaching
(Tizard, 1985). In all, studies suggest that the home setting may provide a
much more realistic stimulation of the children's language abilities.

Such findings have a number of implications for children with learning disabilities. For example, they suggest that assessments made solely in
the context of the school may underestimate capabilities of children categorized as being at risk for developmental delays. It would appear that
some skills possessed by children might be inhibited in that context but
not in the home. In addition, these findings indicate that the home setting
may be a much more effective context for intervention than it has been
credited for. Related to this is the recognition of parents as agents for
ameliorative programs. The role played by parents in the development
and education of children has long been recognized. In the 1960s, empirical studies focused on developing effective strategies for parents to utilize
in educating and managing their children. Notable in the United States
was the Portage approach developed in 1969 in Portage, Wisconsin, as an
education service for preschool children with disabilities and their families. The approach was introduced to the United Kingdom in 1976 (HM
Inspectorate, 1990). The model is based on a home visiting system with
emphasis on parents as teachers of their own children (Boyd & Bluma,
1977). The parents are in turn helped by professionals to develop their
own teaching skills (Boyd, Stauber, & Bluma, 1977).

In all, Portage projects have been positively evaluated both in the
U.S. and U.K. sites where they were implemented (Boyd et al., 1977;
HM Inspectorate, 1990). Such positive outcomes emphasize the importance of intervention and functioning in-context for children at risk for
developmental or learning disabilities. One reason may be that the home
context provides meaningful situations for exercising and application of
relevant skills for the children. However, for such programs to succeed,

assessment of both the children's functional limitations and the resource requirements of the various settings are necessary. The need for such an assessment has been demonstrated in the context of community-based rehabilitation (CBR) in less industrialized countries. This approach, similar to the Portage project, has used a model of parents and/or other caregivers as teachers of the children with disabilities.

The CBR approach, while a response to the scarcity of resources in less industrialized settings, has been seen as providing opportunities for children with special needs to learn relevant skills in-context. In addition, the strategy has been to try to pass on from the professionals to the children's families and community the skills required for addressing the needs of such children within their homes. Experiences of this approach have been characterized by both positive outcomes in terms of service delivery where there might have been little or none, and also challenges in promoting the participation of caregivers who may be family or community members. In rural communities of less developed countries, such people would often be impoverished and overworked such that one of the main tasks is to get the child to command sufficient attention in the context of the many demands for survival (Nabuzoka, 1991).

ISSUES IN APPLIED AND EVALUATIVE RESEARCH

Applied and evaluative research involves the testing and appraisal of intervention strategies and approaches. Such research on children with disabilities raises a number of methodological issues. These relate to problems inherent in evaluating the efficacy of various forms of intervention approaches and service provision such as inclusive education in mainstream schools. To demonstrate the success of programs, one needs to show that children with LD have acquired the necessary skills and/or changes in behavior and, in some cases, also in their general well-being. Service provision and intervention strategies can be evaluated in terms of educational outcomes as well as the psychosocial functioning and adjustment of the target children. There is, however, a difficulty in reaching firm conclusions about whether what is observed are effects of service provision and intervention.

In examining various methods and approaches to the education of individuals with disabilities, one major problem has been that various studies have at times come up with different findings when apparently carrying out similar investigations. Sometimes the findings directly contradict those from other studies. An example of this is the evaluation of the benefits of inclusive education in which studies have examined the amount of positive behavior by children with LD, compared with non-LD peers, in inclusive mainstream schools. Some studies have found no differences between the two groups of children while others have found children with LD to be involved in more positive behavior (Nabuzoka, 2000). Another example of equivocal findings is the amount of time spent by children with LD interacting with teachers compared with non-LD peers. Some studies have reported children with LD to interact more with teachers (Roberts, Pratt, & Leach, 1991), while others have reported less interaction (Mcintosh, Vaughn, Schumm, Haager, & Lee, 1993). A number of methodological problems possibly contribute to equivocal findings. For example, one factor related to outcomes for individuals in evaluative research may be characteristics of individuals included in samples of children chosen for study. Other factors are related more to the design of studies aimed at evaluating the type of provision and its impact. These factors will be considered in turn.

Characteristics of Individuals in Study Samples

Some of the issues and methodological problems specifically related to applied research include evaluation of the efficacy of intervention approaches aimed at individual children. There has been variation across studies with regard to the nature and type of LD, age, gender, ethnicity and culture, and quality of social relations. This has at times confused and complicated the interpretation of research results, and precluded adequate cross-study comparisons. Various studies have sought to address the possible confounding effects of sample characteristics by controlling for them. For example, some studies have focused solely on boys or girls, a specific age group, or even type of LD. These studies do provide information, but unfortunately it has only limited generalizability. In addition, while children do generally interact in groups in terms of gender, age, and possibly ethnicity, intergroup interactions undoubtedly occur. The latter have implications for outcomes in functioning and adjustment of children with LD. For example, children with LD have been observed to interact more positively with younger but not same-age children (Bryan & Perlmutter, 1979).

The nature and type of disability is a significant factor in that some descriptions of characteristics associated with problems faced by children with LD have identified subtypes of disabilities. For example, Rourke (1989) suggested two primary types: the nonverbal LD syndrome and the verbal (phonological) LD syndrome. Those with nonverbal LD are said to have poor overall social adaptation (due to social problem-solving deficits and difficulties identifying nonverbal communications) whereas those with verbal LD may not. The implications are that a lack of differentiation on this dimension is likely to lead to equivocal findings on measures of social adaptation. While some studies have sought to clarify the relative significance of verbal versus nonverbal LD on measures of social functioning, this distinction is not always made.

The age of the subjects is another important factor. For example, research has long indicated that, although children with LD may not function at similar levels as non-LD peers of the same chronological age, effects of age differences amongst similarly diagnosed LD children can be expected (e.g., Gerber & Zinkgraf, 1982).There are also some indications that the nature and severity of social problems may differ according to age. For example, it has been suggested that social emotional development of students with LD may be more impaired in adolescence and early adulthood than previously thought (Huntington & Bender, 1993). Research has also shown that deficits in social competence of students with LD are observable across the age range (Calhoun & Beattie, 1987; Sater & French, 1989). However, some of these deficits may become more acute during the preadolescent years (Mellard & Hazel, 1992), corresponding with the increasing significance of the peer group. While a number of studies have attempted to include a developmental dimension to their studies, there is still a need to incorporate this variable in many studies. In particular, there is a need for more longitudinal studies to document the developmental progression of functional and social emotional difficulties faced by individuals with LD. Such studies could follow individuals from the preschool age through middle childhood and into adolescence or even early adulthood.

Gender effects have been observed on several variables, sometimes even interacting with age. Studies on social perception have generally shown few gender differences. However, an interaction of age and gender has been observed, with younger females with LD displaying difficulty interpreting emotions while older males may be inaccurate though rapid interpreters (Holder & Kirkpatrick, 1991). Gender differences have also been observed on measures of social adjustment. Some studies on sociometric status, for example, have yielded findings indicating rejection to be particularly strong for girls with LD compared with boys with LD and non-LD girls (Kistner & Gatlin, 1989a, 1989b). There are also some suggestions that while children with LD tend to be victims of bullying significantly more than non-LD peers, girls with LD may particularly be at more risk than boys (Nabuzoka & Smith, 1993). With regard to attitudes toward peers with LD, research indicates that girls tend to have more positive attitudes than boys (Rothlisberg, Hill, & Damato, 1994; Townsend, Wilton, & Vakilirad, 1993). However, boys may develop more positive attitudes on exposure to peers with LD while attitudes of girls may remain essentially unchanged (Nabuzoka & Rønning, 1997).

These gender effects suggest that the social experiences of children with LD may vary between girls and boys. Gender differences in social functioning and adjustment have been recognized in many studies on children with LD. However, there appears to have been little effort in pursuing such differences as a specific line of inquiry. The tendency in most studies has been to focus solely on either boys or girls. Research is required, therefore, to focus more extensively on revealing the extent to which, and the manner in which, gender and LD status interact. Such research would more usefully inform the design of intervention strategies.

The ethnic characteristic of individuals studied is one variable that has received little attention in studies on the experiences of individuals with disabilities in educational settings. A number of studies have documented the disproportionate representation of ethnic minority children in LD classes, or as having conduct problems (Peagam, 1994). There are also some indications that race or ethnic minority status may be associated with the quality of interactions with others as reflected in some problems in peer relations (Gresham & Reschly, 1987; Kistner, Metzler, Gatlin, & Risi, 1993; Schwarzwald & Hoffman, 1993). For example, Gresham and Reschly (1987) examined sociometric differences between mainstreamed students with mild LD and non-LD Black and White students. They found differential patterns of acceptance between Black and White students with LD: White non-LD students had higher acceptance scores than Black non-LD students, but Black students with LD had higher acceptance scores than White students with LD. Gresham and Reschly suggested that the sample of White students with LD may have been more discrepant in terms of intellectual and academic performance than the Black sample related to same-race non-LD peers, and thus perceived more negatively. Another explanation was that there might be racial and cultural differences in how children react to mild LD in educational settings. What is clear from such findings, however, is that ethnic status may interact with LD in measures of psychosocial adjustment. Details of ethnic composition in samples as a specific variable to be examined are therefore important, especially for studies conducted in multiethnic contexts.

Another factor, related to gender and ethnicity, is the culture of the target children. Both gender and ethnicity can interact with culture to influence the psychosocial adjustment of individual children, as they both involve socialization. On the one hand, general cross-study comparisons regarding the functioning of children with disabilities from different cultures can provide useful information about the generalizability of the relationships between domains. For example, data from Zambia regarding effects of various intervention approaches on the social functioning

and adjustment of children with LD indicates the cross-cultural applicability of some intervention strategies (Rønning & Nabuzoka, 1993), and
the effects of contact on attitudes toward children with LD (Favazza
& Odom, 1997; Nabuzoka & Rønning, 1997). Such effects apparently
apply to the various cultures studied. However, this may not necessarily
mean that the specific modes of psychological adjustment are comparable
across the different cultures.

An example of specific cultural variation is social perception. Studies have generally indicated that children from different cultures can
differentiate basic expressions of emotions by the age of 3 years and
that this ability increases with age (Borke, 1973; Markham & Wang,
1996). However, there have also been cultural differences in the degree
to which children of similar age may understand emotions (Joshi &
MacLean, 1994; Markham & Wang, 1996). These differences have
been attributed to different socialization practices, so that children are
likely to perform better on emotion recognition in cultures where emphasis is put on the development of such skills. Thus, it is likely that
a child with LD and a certain level of social perceptual skills (e.g.,
recognition of emotions) may have greater problems functioning in
one culture requiring a high level of such skills and not in another.
Similarly, while a child's apparently shy behavior may be associated
with adjustment problems in Western culture, it may not necessarily
be problematic in non-Western societies, especially with regard to interactions with adults (Harkness & Super, 1982). The point is that
the definition of functional limitations in the social domain is likely
to be culture-specific. In multicultural contexts and for children with
LD, cultural variations may confound the social adjustment problems
faced and also the subsequent impact on educational achievement. For
researchers, failure to recognize cultural variability across samples can
make comparisons of findings difficult.

While children with LD may generally experience difficulties in
social relations more than non-LD children, not all children with LD
have problematic social relationships. Some research has indicated, for
example, that there is a subgroup of adolescents with LD who are not
rejected socially, but are rated as very similar to students without disabilities (Sabornie, 1990). It is likely that the children with LD who do
not have problems in social relations also interact more positively with
peers. Inconsistencies across various studies as to the social conduct
of children with LD in general could thus also be attributable to the
varying status of LD children. This suggests that studies reporting on
measures of psychosocial functioning of children with LD should indicate whether the samples included children who had problems in peer
relations.

Evaluating the Type of Provision and Its Impact

One focus of applied research on service provision for children with disabilities has been on evaluating the effects of different types of educational provision on the functioning of such children. Some of the issues and methodological problems specifically related to applied research include evaluation of the impact of service design and provision. Inclusive educational provision is an example of a service design whose impact may not be easy to assess due to number of methodological problems with research in this area. Farrell (1997) identified some of the main issues raised in the literature, and these have been further discussed by Nabuzoka (2000):

- a lack of control groups in designs;
- the range of difficulties faced by children with LD;
- the variety of provision and/or treatment; and
- the interests of researchers.

Control Groups

Research designs require control groups if so-called treatment effects are to be demonstrated. To demonstrate the effectiveness of inclusive education for children with LD, a matched group design should ideally be used. One group of children is placed in the mainstream regular school and another matched group is placed in a special school. A child in one group would be matched with another child in the other group on attributes likely to affect outcomes, such as age, gender, level of LD status, and so forth. Differences between the two groups can then be attributable to the type of provision experienced by the children.

However, such matched control group designs are virtually impossible, as there are ethical issues involved in allocating different provision to similar children solely for the purpose of research. In addition, it is difficult to match children with LD in such a way as to be certain that any two groups have the same relevant characteristics.

Range of Difficulties

Difficulties faced by children vary so much that generalizing from one study to another is difficult. If one is to compare studies, it is necessary to be absolutely sure that they were conducted on similar children. This problem is compounded by the fact that studies from different countries may use varying terminology to refer to similar groups. Lewis (1995) pointed out, for example, that children designated as having "severe learning difficulties" in the United Kingdom may be referred to as having "moderate intellectual disabilities" in Australia and New Zealand, or "moderate to severe mental retardation" in the United States. Even then, Lewis pointed out, it is not clear whether such categories represent similar groups.

Variety of Provision

It is not always easy to judge whether groups of children experienced similar or entirely different forms of service provision or intervention. In the United Kingdom, different levels of inclusive education exist both across and within education authorities. At the very minimum, a special unit may be placed in a mainstream school with children who have LD having opportunities to interact with non-LD children at playtime or at lunchtime. Another type of inclusive setting involves children with LD attending some classes with their non-LD peers but being withdrawn to a resource facility for other lessons. Sometimes terms such as *functional integration* or *social integration* have been used to distinguish situations where both groups of children take academic lessons together from situations where they come together only at playtime or lunchtime.

A third type of inclusive education involves children with disabilities taking part in all mainstream activities, both academic and social, and this has been referred to as *full inclusion.* In most cases this also requires a resource teacher or support worker being available to provide academic support to those with LD. This can have an effect on the success of inclusive education for children with LD. It has been suggested, for example, that staff can facilitate the development of friendships between children with disabilities and mainstream peers by setting up conditions that encourage interactions (Hegarty, 1987). On the other hand, and as observed by Lynas (1986), the amount of attention paid to children with LD by staff can be a source of resentment for non-LD peers. Therefore, research that evaluates and compares the efficacy of inclusive settings needs to consider the skills and sensitivity of the support staff, as well as that of regular teachers.

Objectivity of Evaluative Research

Evaluative research can suffer from a lack of objectivity especially when conducted and reported by those involved in the application of the service provision or intervention scheme. This is likely to be the case when the researchers have also been involved in the design of the scheme. It is then possible that the researchers might have a vested interest in showing that the scheme or type of service provision in question is effective. Thus, the only results that may be reported are those supportive of the pre-conceived views of the researchers. This problem is exacerbated by the reluctance of a significant number of journals to report so-called negative results. Vested interests are difficult to verify. However, to eliminate suspicion of any such possibility, studies are now generally required to report not only more detailed accounts of data gathering procedures and measures but also any steps taken to avoid bias.

SUMMARY AND CONCLUSIONS

The provision of educational services for individuals with disabilities has been characterized by various concerns at particular points in time, and in different parts of the world. Priorities have differed accordingly, especially those of third world compared to industrialized settings. However, most of the concerns have largely focused on efforts aimed at understanding the characteristics of individuals with disabilities that have implications for their education, including the social and cognitive processes involved; the efficacy of various methods of teaching; and the contexts which promote the optimal functioning of such individuals. The term *special education* has been used to refer to services provided to reflect such concerns. While some significant strides have been made in understanding the needs of individuals with disabilities and in the provision of special education, various issues have arisen and attained prominence at particular times in the history of special education. The issues discussed in this chapter, drawn mostly from concerns in the United Kingdom and United States reflecting experiences in the industrialized world, and also from some third world countries, indicate some world trends while also illustrating similarities and differences in concerns and priorities that have preoccupied professionals in different parts of the world.

One issue related to understanding the needs of those with disabilities has been the recognition that these needs may differ not only amongst individuals involved but also between the various types of disabilities. This has been reflected in the types of special education services provided in various parts of the world. However, a general concern with difficulties in academic and learning tasks has been one of the major areas of special education in many countries. Another development has been in understanding the nature of difficulties faced by children with disabilities. This has been illustrated in the recognition that problems faced by children with disabilities are not confined to the academic domain alone; they may also encounter problems in their social relationships, which may further impact on their academic functioning. Thus, the nature of the presenting difficulties has been examined by looking at the structure and functioning of cognitive processes as well as levels of psychosocial adjustment as factors associated with educational outcomes of the affected children. Social factors contribute to the academic functioning of children with disabilities through the context in which education is provided. This has mostly focused on the school setting as an environment in which children spend most of their educational time. However, in parts of the world where special education provision is not widely accessible through schools, provision in the community has been presented as supplementary, if not an alternative, to school efforts.

The assessment and identification of children with disabilities, focused on both academic and general functioning of the affected children, is also related to definition and classification of the presenting difficulties and has implications for intervention strategies applied to address difficulties faced by those children identified. The various forms of educational provision and intervention strategies aimed at enhancing the functioning of the children, from the home community to school settings in both industrialized and the third world countries, present different challenges for applied and evaluative research in special education. Some of these have been identified in this chapter but arguably a number of issues still remain to be discussed in other forums.

REFERENCES

Acton, N. (1982). The world's response to disability: Evolution of a philosophy. *Archives of Physical Medicine and Rehabilitation, 2,* 145–149.

Avoke, M. (2001). Some historical perspectives in development of special education in Ghana. *European Journal of Special Education, 16*(1), 29–40.

Bender, W.N., & Smith, J.K. (1990). Classroom behaviour of children and adolescents with learning disabilities: A meta-analysis. *Journal of Learning Disabilities, 23,* 298–305.

Borke, H. (1973). The development of empathy in Chinese and American children between three and six years of age: A cross-cultural study. *Developmental Psychology, 9,* 102–108.

Boyd, R.D., & Bluma, S.M. (1977). *Parent readings: Portage parent program.* Portage, WI: Co-operative Educational Service Agency No. 12.

Boyd, R.D., Stauber, K.A., & Bluma, S.M. (1977). *Instructor's manual: Portage parent program.* Portage, WI: Co-operative Educational Service Agency No. 12.

Bronfenbrenner, U. (1979). *The ecology of human development: Experiments by nature and design.* Cambridge, MA: Harvard University Press.

Bryan, J.H., & Perlmutter, B. (1979). Immediate impressions of LD children by female adults. *Learning Disability Quarterly, 2,* 80–88.

Calhoun, M.L., & Beattie, J. (1987). Social competence needs of mildly handicapped adolescents. *Adolescence, 22,* 555–563.

Chalmers, J.B., & Townsend, M.A.R. (1990). The effects of training in social perspective taking on socially maladjusted girls. *Child Development, 61,* 178–190.

Clarke-Stewart, K.A., & Fein, G.G. (1983). Early childhood programmes. In M.M. Haith & J.J. Campos (Eds.), *Infancy and developmental psychobiology* (Vol. 2) in P.H. Mussen (Ed.), *Handbook of child psychology* (4th ed.). New York: Wiley.

Clements, J. (1987). *Severe learning disability and psychological handicap.* Chichester: John Wiley.

Dockrell, J., & McShane, J. (1993). *Children's learning difficulties: A cognitive approach.* Oxford: Blackwell.

Dombrowski, S.C., Kamphaus, R.W., Barry, M., Brueggeman, A., Cavanagh, S., Devine, K., et al. (2006). The Solomon effect in learning disabilities diagnosis: Can we learn from history? *School Psychology Quarterly, 21*(4), 359–374.

Eleweke, C.J. (1999). The need for mandatory legislation to enhance services to people with disabilities in Nigeria. *Disability & Society, 14*(2), 227–237.

Empson, J., & Nabuzoka, D. (2004). *Atypical child development in context.* Houndmills, Basingstoke, UK: Palgrave Macmillan.

Farrell, P. (1997). The integration of children with severe learning difficulties: A review of the recent literature. *Journal of Applied Research in Intellectual Disabilities, 10*(1), 1–14.

Favazza, P.C., & Odom, S.L. (1997). Promoting positive attitudes of kindergarten-age children toward people with disabilities. *Exceptional Children, 63*, 405–418.

Finkenflügel, H. (1993). *The handicapped community: The relation between primary health care and community based rehabilitation.* Amsterdam: VU University Press.

Finkenflügel, H. (2004). *Empowered to differ: Stakeholders' influences in community-based rehabilitation.* Amsterdam: Vrije Universiteit.

Fisher, D. (2000). *Fairness and flexibility: LEA strategies to reduce the need for SEN statements.* Slough, UK: National Foundation for Educational Research.

Frederickson, N.L., & Furnham, A.F. (2004). Peer-assessed behavioural characteristics and sociometric rejection: Differences between pupils who have moderate learning difficulties and their mainstream peers. *British Journal of Educational Psychology, 74*, 391–410.

Gerber, P.J., & Zinkgraf, S.A. (1982). A comparative study of social-perceptual ability in learning disabled and nonhandicapped students. *Learning Disability Quarterly, 5*, 374–378.

Gottlieb, J. (1981). Mainstreaming: Fulfilling the promise? *American Journal of Mental Deficiency, 86*, 115–126.

Gresham, F.M., & Reschly, D.J. (1987). Sociometric differences between mildly handicapped Black and White students. *Journal of Educational Psychology, 79*, 195–197.

Gresham, F.M., Sugai, G., & Horner, R.H. (2001). Interpreting outcomes of social skills training for students with high-incidence disabilities. *Exceptional Children, 67*, 331–344.

Guralnick, M.J. (1990). Major accomplishments and future directions in early childhood mainstreaming. *Topics in Early Childhood Special Education, 10*(2), 1–17.

Gurucharri, C., & Selman, R.L. (1982). The development of interpersonal understanding during childhood, preadolescence, and adolescence: A longitudinal follow-up study. *Child Development, 53*, 924–927.

Hallahan, D.P., & Kauffman, J.M. (1976). *Introduction to learning disabilities: A psychobehavioral approach.* Englewoods Cliffs, NJ: Prentice-Hall.

Hallahan, D.P., & Kauffman, J.M. (1977). Labels, categories, behaviors: ED, LD, and EMR reconsidered. *Journal of Special Education, 11*, 139–149.

Harkness, S., & Super, C.M. (1982). Why African children are so hard to test. In L.L. Adler (Ed.), *Cross-cultural research at issue* (pp. 145–152). New York: Academic Press.

Hegarty, S. (1987). *Meeting special needs in ordinary schools.* London: Cassell.

Helander, E., Mendis, P., & Nelson, G. (1984). *Training the disabled in the community: A manual on community-based rehabilitation for developing countries.* Geneva: World Health Organization.

HM Inspectorate. (1990). *Portage projects: A survey of 13 projects funded by Education Support Grants (1987–1989).* Stanmore, Middlesex, UK: Department of Education and Science.

Hocutt, A. (1996). Effectiveness of special education: Is placement the critical factor? *The Future of Children, 6*(1), 77–102.

Holder, H.B., & Kirkpatrick, S.W. (1991). Interpretation of emotions from facial expressions in children with and without learning disabilities. *Journal of Learning Disabilities, 24,* 170–177.

Howlin, P. (1994). Special educational treatment. In M. Rutter, E. Taylor, & L. Hersov (Eds.), *Child and adolescent psychiatry: Modern approaches* (3rd ed.) (pp. 1071–1088). Oxford: Blackwell.

Hundert, J., & Houghton, A. (1992). Promoting social interaction of children with disabilities in integrated preschools: A failure to generalise. *Exceptional Children, 58,* 311–320.

Huntington, D.D., & Bender, W.N. (1993). Adolescents with learning disabilities at risk? Emotional well-being, depression, suicide. *Journal of Learning Disabilities, 26,* 159–166.

Individuals With Disabilities Education Improvement Act (IDEIA). (2004). Retrieved August 19, 2007, from www.ed.gov/about/offices/list/osers/osep/index.html

Jackson, S.C., Enright, R.D., & Murdock, J.Y. (1987). Social perception problems in adolescents with learning disabilities: Developmental lags versus perceptual deficit. *Journal of Learning Disabilities, 20,* 361–364.

James, S.D., & Egel, A.L. (1986). A direct prompting strategy for increasing reciprocal interactions between handicapped and nonhandicapped siblings. *Journal of Applied Behavior Analysis, 19,* 173–187.

Joshi, M.S., & MacLean, M. (1994). Indian and English children's understanding of the distinction between real and apparent emotion. *Child Development, 65,* 1364–1376.

Kavale, K.A., & Forness, S.R. (1996). Social skill deficits and learning disabilities: A meta-analysis. *Journal of Learning Disabilities, 29,* 226–257.

Kirk, S.A. (1962). *Educating the exceptional children.* Boston: Houghton Mifflin.

Kirk, S.A. (1963). Behavioural diagnosis and remediation of learning disabilities. In *Proceedings of the Annual Conference on Exploration into the Problems of the Perceptually Handicapped Child* (pp. 1–7). Evanston, IL: Fund for Perceptually Handicapped Children.

Kistner, J.A., & Gatlin, D. (1989a). Correlates of peer rejection among children with learning disabilities. *Learning Disability Quarterly, 12,* 133–140.

Kistner, J.A., & Gatlin, D.F. (1989b). Sociometric differences between learning-disabled and nonhandicapped students: Effects of sex and race. *Journal of Educational Psychology, 81,* 118–120.

Kistner, J., Metzler, A., Gatlin, D., & Risi, S. (1993). Classroom racial proportions and children's peer relations: Race and gender effects. *Journal of Educational Psychology, 85,* 446–452.

Koppitz, E. (1973). Special class pupils with learning disabilities: A five-year follow-up study. *Academic Therapy, 8,* 133–140.

Lewis, A. (1995). *Children's understanding of disability.* London: Routledge.

Longman, R.S., Inglis, J., & Lawson, J.S. (1991). WISC-R patterns of cognitive abilities in behavior disordered and learning disabled children. *Psychological Assessment, 3,* 239–246.

Luckasson, R., Coulter, D.L., Polloway, E.A., Reiss, S., Schalock, R.L., Snell, M.E., et al. (1992). *Mental retardation: Definition, classification and systems of supports.* Washington, DC: American Association on Mental Retardation.

Lynas, W. (1986). Pupils' attitudes to integration. *British Journal of Special Education, 13*(1), 31–33.

Lynn, R., Hampson, S., & Magee, M. (1983). Determinants of education achievement at 16+: Intelligence, personality, home background and school. *Personality and Individual Differences, 4*(5), 473–481.

MacMillan, D.L., Gresham, F.M., & Bocian, K.M. (1998). Discrepancy between definitions of learning disabilities and school practices: An empirical investigation. *Journal of Learning Disabilities, 31,* 314–326.

Markham, R., & Wang, L. (1996). Recognition of emotion by Chinese and Australian children. *Journal of Cross-Cultural Psychology, 27*, 616–643.

Mathur, S. R., & Rutherford, R. B. (1991). Peer-mediated interventions promoting social skills of children and youth with behavioural disorders. *Education and Treatment of Children, 14*, 227–242.

Maxwell, W. (1994). Special educational needs and social disadvantage in Aberdeen city school catchment zones. *Educational Research, 36*(1), 25–37.

Mcintosh, R., Vaughn, S., Schumm, J. S., Haager, D., & Lee, O. (1993). Observations of students with learning disabilities in general education classrooms. *Exceptional Children, 60*, 249–261.

Mellard, D. F., & Hazel, J. S. (1992). Social competencies as a pathway to successful life transitions. *Learning Disability Quarterly, 15*, 251–271.

Miles, M. (1985). *Where there is no rehab plan: A critique of the WHO scheme for community based rehabilitation: With suggestions for future directions.* Peshawar, NWFP, Pakistan: Mental Health Centre.

Miles, M. (2004). CBR in Africa: Between evidence and ideology. *Disability World, 24.* Retrieved on August 19, 2007, from http://www.disabilityworld.org/06-08_04/news/cbrinafrica.shtml

Morris, L., Watt, J., & Wheatley, P. (1995). Pupils with special needs: A Scottish perspective. *Journal of Learning Disabilities, 28*(7), 386–390.

Mpofu, E., Peltzer, K., Shumba, A., Serpell, R., & Mogaji, A. (2005). School psychology in Sub-Saharan Africa: Results and implications of a six-country survey. In C. L. Frisby & C. R. Reynolds (Eds.), *Comprehensive handbook of multicultural school psychology.* Hoboken, NJ: Wiley.

Nabuzoka, D. (1991). Community based rehabilitation for disabled children in Zambia: Experiences of the Kasama district project. *International Journal of Special Education, 6*(3), 321–340.

Nabuzoka, D. (1993). How to define, involve and assess the care unit? Experiences and research from a CBR programme in Zambia. In H. Finkenflügel (Ed.), *The handicapped community: The relation between primary health care and community-based rehabilitation* (pp. 73–87). Amsterdam: VU University Press.

Nabuzoka, D. (2000). *Children with learning disabilities: Social functioning and adjustment.* Oxford: BPS Blackwell.

Nabuzoka, D., & Rønning, J. A. (1997). Social acceptance of children with intellectual disabilities in an integrated school setting in Zambia: A pilot study. *International Journal of Disability, Development and Education, 44*, 105–115.

Nabuzoka, D., & Smith, P. K. (1993). Sociometric status and social behaviour of children with and without learning difficulties. *Journal of Child Psychology and Psychiatry, 34*, 1435–1448.

Nabuzoka, D., & Smith, P. K. (1995). Identification of expressions of emotions by children with and without learning disabilities. *Learning Disabilities Research and Practice, 10*, 91–101.

Odom, S. L., & Brown, W. H. (1993). Social interaction skills interventions for young children with disabilities in integrated settings. In C. Peck, S. Odom, & D. Bricker (Eds.), *Integrating young children with disabilities into community programs: Ecological perspectives on research and implementation.* Baltimore: Brookes.

Odom, S. L., Hoyson, M., Jamieson, B., & Strain, P. S. (1985). Increasing handicapped preschoolers' peer social interactions: Cross-setting and component analysis. *Journal of Applied Behaviour Analysis, 18*, 3–17.

Odom, S. L. & Strain, P. S. (1984). Peer mediated approaches to promoting children's social interaction: A review. *American Journal of Orthopsychiatry, 54*, 544–557.

Peagam, E. (1994). Special needs or educational apartheid? The emotional and behavioural difficulties of Afro-Caribbean children. *Support for Learning, 9*(1), 33–38.

Piaget, J. (1970). *The science of education and psychology of the child*. New York: Grossman.

Pritchard, D. G. (1963). *Education of the handicapped, 1760–1960*. London: Routledge & Kegan Paul.

Roberts, C., Pratt, C., & Leach, D. (1991). Classroom and playground interaction of students with and without disabilities. *Exceptional Children, 57*, 212–224.

Roberts, C., & Zubrick S. (1992). Factors influencing the social status of children with mild academic disabilities in regular classrooms. *Exceptional Children, 59*, 192–202.

Rønning, J. A., & Nabuzoka, D. (1993). Promoting social interaction and status of children with intellectual disabilities in Zambia. *Journal of Special Education, 27*, 277–305.

Rothlisberg, B. A., Hill, R., & Damato, R. C. (1994). Social acceptance by their peers of children with mental retardation. *Psychological Reports, 74*, 239–242.

Rourke, B. (1989). *Non-verbal learning disabilities: The syndrome and the model*. New York: Guilford.

Rutter, M. (1989). Intergenerational continuities and discontinuities in serious parenting difficulties. In D. Cicchetti & V. Carlson (Eds.), *Child maltreatment* (pp. 317–348). Cambridge: Cambridge University Press.

Sabornie, E. J. (1990). Extended sociometric status of adolescents with mild handicaps: A cross-categorical perspective. *Exceptionality, 1*, 197–209.

Sainato, D., Goldstein, H., & Strain, P. (1992). Effects of self-evaluation on pre-school children's use of social interaction strategies with their classmates with autism. *Journal of Applied Behavioual Analysis, 7*, 475–500.

Sater, G. M., & French, D. C. (1989). A comparison of the social competencies of learning-disabled and low-achieving elementary-aged children. *Journal of Special Education, 23*, 29–42.

Schwarzwald, J., & Hoffman, M. A. (1993). Academic status and ethnicity as determinants of social acceptance. *Journal of Cross-Cultural Psychology, 24*, 71–80.

Selman, R. L. (1980). *The growth of interpersonal understanding: Developmental and clinical analyses*. New York: Academic Press.

Serpell, R. (1983). *Cross-culturally universal domains for the assessment of severe intellectual handicap: A discussion paper*. Lusaka, Zambia: Institute for African Studies, University of Zambia.

Serpell, R. (1986). Specialised centres and the local home community: Children with disabilities need them both. *International Journal of Special Education, 1*(2), 107–127.

Serpell, R. (1988). Assessment criteria for severe intellectual disability in various cultural settings. *International Journal of Behavioural Development, 1*(1), 117–144.

Spafford, C. S., & Grosser, G. S. (1993). The social misperception syndrome in children with learning disabilities: Social causes versus neurological variables. *Journal of Learning Disabilities, 26*, 178–189, 198.

Spence, S. H. (1991). Developments in the assessment of social skills and social competence in children. *Behaviour Change, 8*, 148–166.

Stobart, G. (1986). Is integrating the handicapped psychologically defensible? *The Psychologist: Bulletin of the British Psychological Society, 39*, 1–3.

Strain, P. S., & Odom, S. L. (1986). Effective intervention for social skill development of exceptional children. *Exceptional Children, 52*, 543–551.

Tizard, B. (1985). Social relationships between adults and young children, and their impact on intellectual functioning. In R. A. Hinde, A. Perret-Clermont, & J. Stevenson-Hinde (Eds.), *Social relationships and cognitive development*. Oxford: Clarendon Press.

Tizard, B., & Hughes, M. (1984). *Young children learning: Talking and thinking at home and at school*. London: Fontana.

Townsend, M. A. R., Wilton, K. M., & Vakilirad, T. (1993). Children's attitudes toward peers with intellectual disability. *Journal of Intellectual Disability Research, 37*, 405–411.

Walker, A., & Nabuzoka, D. (2007). Academic achievement and social functioning of children with and without learning difficulties. *Educational Psychology, 27*, 635–654.

Weisberg, P. (1992). Education and enrichment approaches. In C.E. Walker & M.C. Roberts (Eds.), *Handbook of clinical child psychology* (2nd ed.) (pp. 919–932). New York: Wiley.

WHO (1985). *Mental retardation: Meeting the challenge.* Offset publication No. 86. Geneva: World Health Organization.

WHO (1993). *The ICD-10 classification of mental and behavioural disorders: Diagnostic criteria for research.* Geneva: World Health Organization.

CHAPTER 2

Policy and Law of Individuals With Disabilities Education Improvement Act of 2004

Attempting No Student With Disabilities Left Behind to the Extent Enforceable

Andrea Kayne Kaufman

Will the 2004 Individuals With Disabilities in Education Improvement Act (IDEIA), 20 U.S.C. § 1400 et. seq., improve education for students with disabilities? While there may be some improvement, the 2004 IDEIA most likely will result in three steps forward, two steps back. The 2004 IDEIA illustrates the problem with a lot of education law where there is a gap between rights and enforcement. There is no question that the 2004 IDEIA's attempt to align with the Elementary and Secondary Schools Act, 20 U.S.C. § 6301 et. seq. also known as the No Child Left Behind Act (NCLB) is a step forward in attempting to require more of schools and thus give more rights to students. Following NCLB, for example, the 2004 IDEIA now requires that the academic performance of students with disabilities be measured, the academic credentials of special education teachers be enhanced, and the surrounding issues impacting achievement of minority students be addressed. This expressed desire for rigor and accountability, however, may ring hollow when considering important ways in which 2004 IDEIA has limited enforcement and enhanced a school's ability to remove students with disabilities. While the goal of improving relations between schools and parents through mediation and resolution sessions might seem laudable, the revised attorney's fees provision makes enforcement in court prohibitive for many low-income parents in particular. Moreover, while the need to maintain safe schools is understandable, the revised discipline provisions in IDEIA 2004 make it much easier for schools to remove students with disabilities and much more difficult for parents to ensure that their child with a disability will remain in'school. Judging the law in terms of its lofty aims to support NCLB, therefore, can be misleading when there is no good way to ensure that those aims are realized.

The law and policy of the IDEIA is suggestive of the law and policy that underlie NCLB. While the 2004 version of the IDEIA keeps many of the core components of the Individuals With Disabilities in Education Act (IDEA) since its enactment in 1975 in its first manifestation as the *Education of All Handicapped Children Act,* the 2004 Amendments introduce new principles emanating directly from NCLB. The President's Commission on Excellence in Special Education submitted a report entitled, "A New Era: Revitalizing Special Education for Children and Their Families," in 2002 which formed the basis for the 2004 Amendments to the IDEIA. The President's report explicitly urged Congress in the 2004 IDEA to follow NCLB as a "blueprint," stating:

> Overall, federal, state, and local education reform efforts must extend to special education classrooms. What we discovered was that the central themes of the *No Child Left Behind Act of 2001* must become the driving force behind IDEA reauthorization. In short, we must insist on high academic standards and excellence, press for accountability for results at all levels, ensure yearly progress, empower and trust parents, support and enhance teacher quality, and encourage educational reforms based on scientifically rigorous research. In addition, we must emphasize identification and assessment methods that prevent disabilities and identify needs early and accurately, as well as implement scientifically based instructional practices. (President's Commission on Excellence in Special Education, 2002)

The 2004 IDEIA also reflects law and policy concerns about the practical limitations of enforcement. Specifically, the 2004 IDEIA addresses practical problems relating to burdensome paperwork, adversarial relationships, and ineffective discipline tools.

STATUTORY HISTORY OF IDEIA

The fundamental guarantee of a free appropriate public Education (FAPE) for all children with disabilities and the right to services in the least restrictive environment (LRE) with appropriate related services remains unchanged in the 2004 IDEIA. What has changed in the 2004 IDEIA, however, is a NCLB spin on the law with respect to Highly Qualified educators, the persistent minority achievement gap, and the need for detailed and regular reporting on adequate yearly progress. In following NCLB, it may seem that IDEIA 2004 is demanding and requiring more of schools, teachers, and administrators. While true in some respects, IDEIA 2004 has also sought to soften the administrative requirements in order to ease the burdens on schools, teachers, and administrators. Changes in the Individualized Education Program (IEP), discipline, and dispute resolution processes reflect this desire to ease the unnecessary burdens and conflict associated with implementing the statute.

IDEIA 2004 AMENDMENTS AS INFLUENCED BY NCLB

As stated, the IDEIA 2004 is significantly influenced by NCLB. The 2004 IDEIA explicitly acknowledges NCLB in its findings by stating that the education of children with disabilities can be made more effective by "coordinating this title with other local, educational service agencies, State, and Federal school improvement efforts, including improvement efforts under the *Elementary and Secondary Education Act of 1965,* in order to ensure that such children benefit from such efforts and that special education can become a service for such children and not just a place where such children are sent" 20 U.S.C. § 1400 (c)(5)(C). Interestingly, the IDEIA refers to the NCLB over 60 times (Weishaar, 2007). Moreover, significant changes and additions in the IDEIA reflect important NCLB themes in an attempt to align the two statutes.

One of the goals of the 2004 IDEIA, as influenced by NCLB, is to view special education and general education "no longer operated as separate systems. The lines between special education and general education continued to fade as all educators assume responsibility for the education of all children in the public schools" (Weishaar, 2007). Thus, if special education is to be viewed through the lens of general education, concerns about general education are now addressed in the 2004 IDEIA. Specifically in accordance with the NCLB, the IDEIA 2004 addresses new concerns about lack of "highly qualified" teachers, the minority achievement gap, the reporting of adequate yearly progress, and the rights of private school students. The inclusion and, in some cases, emphasis on these issues in the IDEIA 2004 suggest that priorities in NCLB for educating all children have now become priorities for educating all students with disabilities as well.

HIGHLY QUALIFIED TEACHERS

IDEIA 2004 specifically adopts NCLB's definition and requirement that all teachers, including special education teachers be "highly qualified" 20 U.S.C. §1401. This "Highly Qualified" mandate was included in 2004 IDEIA in order to align IDEIA with NCLB (Weber, Mawdsley, & Redfield, 2004a). The President's Commission found that "Children with disabilities require highly qualified teachers. Teachers, parents, and education officials desire better preparation, support, and professional development related to the needs of serving these children. Many educators wish they had better preparation before entering the classroom." The 2004 IDEIA findings explain that "Highly Qualified" teaching personnel are needed "in order to ensure that they [children with disabilities] have the skills and knowledge necessary" 20 U.S.C. § 1400(c)(5)(E). This follows language from the "Statement of Purpose" section of NCLB stating that the purpose of NCLB is "to ensure that all children have a fair, equal, and significant opportunity to obtain a high-quality education" 20 U.S.C. § 6301. NCLB goes on to explain that this purpose can be realized through "high quality . . . teacher preparation and training" 20 U.S.C. § 6301(1), "improving and strengthening teaching" 20 U.S.C. § 6301(6), and "significantly elevating the quality of instruction" 20 U.S.C. § 6301(10).

According to the IDEIA Section 1401(10)(B), a public elementary or secondary school teacher is "Highly Qualified" if she or he: "(1) Has obtained full state certification or passed a special education licensing exam; (2) Holds a license; (3) Has not had the licensure provisions waived; and (4) Holds at least a bachelor's degree" (20 U.S.C. §1401(10)(B)).

The NCLB specifically requires new teachers teaching multiple core subjects (i.e., English, reading or language arts, mathematics, science, foreign languages, civics and government, economics, arts, history, and geography) to either have an academic major or advanced degree in the subject areas taught or to pass a subject competency exam. Veteran teachers under NCLB may demonstrate competency based on a "high objective uniform state standard of evaluation" (HOUSSE), which may involve multiple measures of teacher competency as established by the individual State 20 U.S.C. § 6319.

After passage of NCLB, there was an intense debate as to whether special education teachers, who are not specifically mentioned in NCLB, would also be required to meet the "Highly Qualified" standards (Mandlawitz, 2007). While there are strands of the "Highly Qualified" mandates in NCLB that were adopted in 2004 IDEIA, there are practical issues that make it more difficult to apply the stringent NCLB "Highly Qualified" standards to IDEIA. For one thing, there is a "serious shortage" of special education teachers (Mandlawitz, 2007). In addition, many special education teachers act in a resource capacity and thus provide support to many core academic subjects; thus these teachers who need to be "jacks of all trades" would have difficulty meeting the very rigorous "Highly Qualified" standards of NCLB that require specific subject competency (Mandlawitz, 2007). Therefore, the IDEIA softens the requirement for special education teachers working in a resource capacity who provide assistance to students in the full range of academic subject areas. Under IDEIA, these teachers can demonstrate that they are highly qualified by any one of the following:

1. Meet either the NCLB requirements for new or veteran teachers;
2. Meet the HOUSSE option; or
3. For teachers already deemed highly qualified in math, language arts, or science, establish competence in any other core area taught not later than two years after being hired. NCLB, 20 U.S.C. §7801. (Mandlawitz, 2007)

In addition, the serious shortage of special education teachers has prompted the 2004 IDEIA and accompanying regulations to accommodate those special education teachers who have received licensure and certification through alternative means. According to the regulations, these alternatively certified special education teachers must demonstrate that they are working toward full state certification and may only teach under alternative certification for a maximum of 3 years. This compromise provision reflects a tension in the 2004 IDEIA and regulations between the desire for more Highly Qualified teachers in alignment with NCLB and the desperate need throughout the nation to fill the serious shortage of special education teachers (Mandlawitz, 2007). In order to overcome this tension, Congress noted a distinction between special education teachers who provide direct instruction in core academic subjects in contrast with special education teachers who merely provide consultative services to general education teachers. Consultation may include adjustments to the learning environment, modification of instructional methods, and curriculum adaptations. Consultative special education teachers are "Highly Qualified" if they meet requirements for all special education teachers. (Conference report accompanying IDEIA Amendments H. Rep. No. 108–177, Nov. 17, 2004, p. 171; Mandlawitz, 2007).

Following the NCLB, Congress did address, albeit obliquely, the qualifications of "Related Service Personnel" and paraprofessionals who assist special education teachers. The qualifications of these related service personnel are addressed by NCLB as well. Many special education teachers and special education students are assisted by these related service personnel and paraprofessionals to carry out the mandates of various Individual Education Program (IEPs). The Conference Committee writing the 2004 Amendments required that each State Education Agency (SEA) establish "rigorous qualifications" to recruit, hire, train and retain highly qualified related service personnel and paraprofessionals, 20 U.S.C. § 1412(a)(14)(D). Congress went on to encourage SEAs to consult with other state agencies, Local Education Agencies (LEAs), and the professional organizations representing service providers in establishing these qualifications but also stressed that states should have "flexibility" in developing these standards (Mandlawitz, 2007).

MINORITY ACHIEVEMENT GAP

One of the key purposes of NCLB was to address the minority achievement gap. NCLB explicitly states that one of its purposes is "closing the achievement gap between high and low performing children, especially the achievement gap between minority and non-minority students, and between disadvantaged children and their more advantaged peers" 20 U.S.C. § 6301(3). Similarly, in enacting the 2004 Amendments to the IDEIA, Congress was concerned about the achievement of special education students in the context of this minority achievement gap addressed in NCLB. For the first time, the IDEIA "Purposes" section has been revised to include discussions about the needs of children with limited English proficiency, the over-representation in special education of African American and other minority students, and the need for high expectations for minority students, 20 U.S.C. § 1400(c)(5)(10)-(13) (Weber et al., 2004b). Section 20 U.S.C. § 1400(c)(7)-(10) of 2004 IDEIA contains many congressional findings relating to the plight of minorities in public education. These findings address changing demographics, misidentification and labeling as special education, high dropout rates, full participation in awards, lack of minority teachers, among other issues. The NCLB's focus on reducing the minority achievement gap is also a focus in the 2004 IDEIA:

> The Federal Government must be responsive to the growing needs of an increasingly more diverse society. A more equitable allocation of resources is essential for the Federal Government to meet its responsibility to provide an equal educational opportunity for all individuals . . . (20 U.S.C. §1400(c)(7))

> Minorities and underserved persons are socially disadvantaged because of the lack of opportunities in training and educational programs, undergirded by the practices in the private sector that impede their full participation in the mainstream society. (20 U.S.C. §1400(c)(10))

In addition to the revised "Findings" section of IDEIA, this concern about minority achievement is also addressed in new definitions to the 2004 IDEIA regarding "Homeless Children," "Limited English Proficient," and "Ward of the State" 20 U.S.C. § 1401. Moreover, these definitions align with the similar definitions in NCLB, 20 U.S.C. § 6301 et. seq. These explicit references to groups who have been traditionally disenfranchised in education "make it clear that every child who is a child with a disability under the law must be provided special education and related services and receive the protections of the IDEA, regardless of socioeconomic, language, or other differences" (Mandlawitz, 2007). While the IDEA has always provided that all children with disabilities must be served, it has never explicitly mentioned these minority subgroups. Surely, this is another attempt to provide consistency between NCLB and IDEIA.

In addition, the IDEIA 2004 addresses the minority achievement gap by providing for the development of early intervention strategies for K–12 students ("with a particular emphasis on K–3") who are not currently identified as needing special education or related services, but who need additional academic and behavioral support to succeed in a general education environment, 20 U.S.C. §1413(f)(1), 34 C.F.R. § 300.226(a). This early intervention provision is designed to help minority students, who are more likely to be labeled "at risk" (Mandlawitz, 2007, p. 64). Moreover, this provision is controversial, since IDEA funds are to be used for students who are not currently identified as needing special education and related services (Mandlawitz, 2007, p. 64). Because NCLB has made it a priority to provide early instruction to address the minority achievement gap, it only makes sense that Congress would want to provide early intervention to address more broadly issues affecting minority achievement. Early intervention programs have been in place with a great deal of success in many school districts around the country. Struggling students in these programs receive various kinds of classroom interventions depending on their needs. If these strategies are not successful, students may then be referred for evaluation of special education and related services. LEAs are required to report on students served in this program for 2 years to determine if this program reduces the number of referrals for special education and related services (Mandlawitz, 2007, p. 64). While many of these early intervention programs are successful and lauded for taking a prophylactic problem-solving approach, there is also controversy about whether they delay students from getting the special education resources they need.

In addition, because Congress expressed concern about the over-identification of minority students in special education, the 2004 IDEIA requires states to develop "policies and procedures designed to prevent the inappropriate over identification or disproportionate representation by race and ethnicity of children as children with disabilities" 20 U.S.C. § 1412(a)(24).

ASSESSMENT, ADEQUATE YEARLY PROGRESS, AND DISAGGREGATED REPORTING

The NCLB has also influenced the 2004 IDEIA with respect to the NCLB stringent reporting requirements. According to Weber et al. (2004), "Numerous provisions of the Reauthorization tie to NCLB's requirements for assessment of students." This comes from a mandate of the President's Commission, stating:

> Consequently, IDEA should be revamped to require states to: (1) set ambitious goals for special education in alignment with the *No Child Left Behind Act;* (2) define "adequate yearly progress" toward goals for special education; (3) measure and report on achievement of these goals; and (4) take action when local education agencies chronically fail to make progress. (President's Commission on Excellence in Special Education, 2002)

Under NCLB, SEAs are required to report whether students are making adequate yearly progress (AYP) and to disaggregate those scores based on subgroups of students who have been traditionally disenfranchised. These subgroups include: "economically disadvantaged students; students from various racial and ethnic groups; students with disabilities; and students with limited English proficiency" 20 U.S.C. § 6311(b)(2)(C)(v)(II) (Mandlawitz, 2007, p. 50). Weber et al. explain that state performance goals must now be the same as the state's definition of AYP under NCLB, 20 U.S.C. § 1412(a)(15)(A)(ii). Under NCLB, states may develop alternate achievement standards for students with significant cognitive disabilities, as defined by each state and as indicated on students' IEPs. Students whose instruction is based on alternate achievement standards will take alternate assessments keyed to those standards, 20 U.S.C. § 1412(a)(16). Moreover, modifications for these NCLB assessments of AYP must be stated and explained in the IEP, 20 U.S.C.§ 1414(d)(1)(A)(i)(VI). There is no limit on the number of students who may take alternate assessments based on alternate standards; however, a cap of up to 1% of those scores may be used in the AYP calculation (Mandlawitz, 2007, p. 51).

Under the regulations implementing these reporting requirements, states can develop "modified achievement standards" for children with disabilities who are "not likely to achieve grade-level proficiency within the school year covered by the student's IEP" (Mandlawitz, 2007 p. 51). A cap of up to 2% of scores on assessments based on modified achievement standards may be used to determine AYP, but there is no limit on the number of students that may be assessed based on these modified standards (Mandlawitz, 2007, p. 51). The 2004 IDEIA provides for the state, or an LEA in the case of a district-wide assessment, to develop alternate assessments that are the aligned with the state's challenging academic content standards and challenging student academic achievement standards, 20 U.S.C. §1412(a)(16)(C)(ii)(I).

EXPANDED RIGHTS FOR STUDENTS IN PRIVATE SCHOOLS

One of George H. Bush's goals for education in advocating for passage of NCLB was to enhance the privatization of education (http://www. ontheissues.org/celeb/George_W__Bush_Education.htm.). Therefore, NCLB encourages privatization through a number of its provisions. For example, parents whose children attend public schools not making AYP can choose to send their children to a better-performing public school, charter school, or private school, 20 U.S.C. § 6316(b)(1)(E). In addition, NCLB encourages states to engage private tutoring companies to provide Supplemental Education Services (SES) for students in schools not meeting AYP, 20 U.S.C. § 6316(e). There have been disputes between LEAs and the United States Department of Education about whether SES are to be provided by public school teachers or by private corporations. This encouragement of privatization also occurs in other places of NCLB as well as other initiatives of the Bush administration.

The President's Commission embraces the NCLB privatization and choice provisions, stating, "Parental and student choice is an important accountability mechanism and IDEA should include options for parents to choose their child's educational setting." Thus, following this movement toward privatization in NCLB, 2004 IDEIA has expanded the rights of students with disabilities who attend private school. Before the enactment of the 2004 Amendments, the IDEA did provide services for students with disabilities who attend private school. The 2004 Amendments, however, make it easier to reach and serve these students. Previously, the IDEA placed the responsibility for finding and providing services for children with disabilities in private school on the school district where the child resides. The 2004 IDEIA, however, shifts those responsibilities to the school district where the private school or facility is located. LEAs must consult with private school representatives to actively institute a child-find process to determine the number of children with disabilities in private schools, 20 U.S.C. § 1412(a)(10)(A)(i)-(iii). There is also a new enforcement mechanism so private schools can more easily and directly redress any issues related to special education. Private schools now have the right to complain to the SEA or directly to the United States Secretary of Education, 20 U.S.C. § 1412(a)(10)(A).

ENFORCEMENT CONCERNS

The 2004 IDEIA Amendments also reflect new policy and law concerns about the efficacy of enforcement of the statute. Specifically, the 2004 IDEIA Amendments address enforcement problems articulated by many stakeholders affected by the statute relating to massive paperwork and inflexibility, the prevalence of adversarial relationships, and the ineffective discipline tools available for schools to maintain orderly safe environments for learning. In addition to aligning IDEIA with NCLB, the 2004 Amendments responded to concerns about massive paperwork and bureaucracy, discipline, and conflict resolution in order to give schools more flexibility to provide special education and related services and thus have a results-oriented rather than conflict-oriented focus.

REDUCED PAPERWORK AND BUREAUCRACY

One of the "major goals" of the 2004 IDEIA was to reduce the paperwork that had previously been required by the statute (Weber et al., 2004). The Presidential Commission criticized the 1997 IDEA "focus on compliance and bureaucratic imperatives" rather than "academic achievement and social outcomes" and thus recommended "reducing the regulatory burden" on schools. It specifically noted, "The combination of federal, state and local paperwork requirements creates a heavy burden on teachers, schools, and parents." According to the revised findings of the IDEIA, "the education of children with disabilities can be made more effective by focusing resources on teaching and learning while reducing paperwork and requirements that do not assist in improving educational results," 20 U.S.C. § 1400(c)(5)(G). According to Congress, the need for a massive reduction in paperwork was essential in order to maximize the time that students received instruction and services. Instead of just making it a goal, the 2004 IDEIA codifies the need for reduced paperwork (in the name of local flexibility) in several areas, including the elimination of short-term objectives in the IEP, delayed transition planning, and flexibility with respect to IEP team meetings.

ELIMINATION OF SHORT-TERM OBJECTIVES AND OTHER IEP CHANGES

In order to reduce paperwork, the 2004 IDEIA changes the requirement that IEPs include benchmarks on short-term objectives, except in the instance of children who take alternate assessments based on alternate achievement standards under NCLB 20 U.S.C. § 1414(d)(1)(A)(i)(I)-(II). Schools are required, however, to provide periodic updates on progress toward annual goals, 20 U.S.C. § 1414(d)(1)(A)(i)(III).

REVISED TRANSITION PLANNING

Transition planning involves a "coordinated set of activities for a student with a disability that is designed within an outcome-oriented process, which promotes movement from school to post-school activities, including post-secondary education, vocational training, integrated employment including supported employment," 20 U.S.C. § 1401(30). The 1997 version of the IDEA lowered the age in which transition planning occurred during the IEP process. The 1997 requirements were ambiguous so that some transition planning began at 14 and other planning began at 16. The 2004 IDEIA makes transition clear so that administrators are not burdened by confusing requirements and unnecessary paperwork. The 2004 IDEIA requires transition planning at the first IEP meeting after the child turns 16. The regulations allow the IEP team, however, to consider transition planning before age 16 if appropriate, 20 U.S.C. § 1414(d)(1)(A)(vii)(II).

IEP TEAM FLEXIBILITY

The 2004 IDEIA and accompanying regulations allow certain IEP team members to be excused from attendance if the LEA and parents agree that the attendance of that team member is not necessary because the matters in issue do not relate to that team member's area of expertise, 20 U.S.C. § 1414(d)(1)(c)(i). In addition, a team member may be excused from an IEP meeting even if the matters in issue relate to their area of expertise if parents and LEA agree in writing and the absent member submits written input regarding IEP development, 20 U.S.C. § 1414(d)(1)(C)(ii)-(iii). The purpose of these changes was to provide parents and administrators additional flexibility in scheduling meetings and to avoid delaying meetings if certain team members are unable to be present.

The 2004 IDEIA has also made the IEP process more flexible by allowing amendments to the IEP upon agreement by all parties without the team convening, 20 U.S.C. § 1414(d)(3)(D), and by allowing video conferences and conference calls if the parent and LEA agree, 20 U.S.C. § 1414(f). The 2004 IDEIA also improves the IEP process when students move between districts. If a student with disabilities moves to another district within the same state, the new district must honor the child's old IEP until it adopts the old IEP or develops a new one, 20 U.S.C. § 1414(d)(2)(c)(i). For out-of-state transfers, both school districts must facilitate the transfer of records, 20 U.S.C. § 1414(d)(2)(C)(ii). These changes attempt to facilitate IEP development and implementation, by eliminating useless administrative hurdles.

DISCIPLINE

A major goal of the 2004 IDEIA was to make it easier for school administrators to discipline students with disabilities. During hearings about the 2004 Amendments, it became clear that school administrators felt that because of the rigid *stay-put* provisions that made it very difficult to remove a student with disabilities, it was difficult for schools to manage students with disabilities who they perceived as sometimes disruptive and unsafe to the rest of the school community. School administrators also were concerned about issues of discipline and inequity. According to the United States Department of Education:

> The 2004 Amendments to section 615(k) of the IDEA were intended to address the needs expressed by school administrators and teachers for flexibility in order to address school safety issues balanced against the need to ensure that schools respond appropriately to a child's behavior that was caused by, or directly and substantially related to, the child's disability. The reauthorized IDEA and final regulations include provisions that address important disciplinary issues such as: the consideration of unique circumstances when determining the appropriateness of a disciplinary change in placement; expanded authority for removal of a child from his or her current placement for not more than 45 school days for inflicting a serious bodily injury at school or at a school function; the determination on a case-by-case basis as to whether a pattern of removals constitutes a change of placement; and revised standards and procedures related to a manifestation determination. (http://idea.ed.gov)

In order to give administrators more flexibility to provide what they perceive as a safe environment for all students, the statute has been significantly changed with respect to disciplinary short-term and long-term removal of students. So that the 2004 IDEIA now allows a principal to suspend a student with disabilities from school if that student violates a school rule for up to 10 school days, to the same extent that the discipline would be applied to a student without disabilities, 20 U.S.C. § 1415(k)(1)(A). Thus, for short-term removal, the stay-put provision no longer applies. This striking difference between the 1997 IDEA and the 2004 IDEIA that a principal can suspend for up to 10 days even if the misbehavior was a manifestation of the student's disability, 20 U.S.C. § 1415(k)(1)(E)(i), reflects larger concerns about a student with disabilities right to stay in school.

The 2004 Amendments and their accompanying regulations provide more discretion for school administrators to consider unique circumstances on a case-by-case basis when determining whether a change in placement is appropriate for a child with a disability who violates a code of student conduct, 20 U.S.C. 1415(k)(1)(A), 34 C.F.R. 300.530(a). Previously, it was difficult for school administration to remove a student from a school placement. The 2004 IDEIA has made it much easier. Under 2004 IDEIA, school personnel may remove a student to an interim alternative educational setting for not more than 45 school days without regard to whether the behavior is determined to be a manifestation of the child's disability, if the child: carries a weapon to or possesses a weapon at school, on school premises, or to or at a school function under the jurisdiction of an SEA or LEA; knowingly possesses or uses illegal drugs, or sells or solicits the sale of a controlled substance, while at school, on school premises, or at a school function under the jurisdiction of an SEA or an LEA; or, has inflicted serious bodily injury upon another person while at school, on school premises, or at a school function under the jurisdiction of an SEA or an LEA, 20 U.S.C. §1415(k)(1)(G)(i)-(iii). According to the statute, a "Serious Bodily Injury" occurs when it involves a "substantial risk of death; extreme physical pain; protracted and obvious disfigurement; or protracted loss or impairment of the function of a bodily member, organ or mental faculty," 20 U.S.C. §1365 (h)(4). A student with disabilities who is removed from school because of drugs, weapons, or serious bodily injury is still entitled to a functional behavior assessment and intervention so that the child's behavior will be addressed and will not recur, 20 U.S.C. § 1415(k)(1)(D)(ii). In addition to the drugs, weapons, and injury exceptions, a school administrator can also request permission from a hearing officer to remove a child from school for not more than 45 days if "maintaining the current placement of such a child is substantially likely to result in injury to the child or to others," 20

U.S.C. § 1415(k). Thus, school administrators have more ways they can remove students with disabilities from school that they perceive as posing a threat to the rest of the school community. A significant difference between 1997 IDEA and 2004 IDEIA is that these exceptions apply even if the behavior was a manifestation of the child's disability.

MANIFESTATION HEARING

If a school administrator decides to suspend and/or expel a student with disabilities for more than 10 days, a manifestation hearing must occur within 10 school days of the administrator's decision to remove the student. At the manifestation hearing, the LEA, parents, and other members of the IEP team review all relevant information in the student's file, including the child's IEP, any teacher observations, and any relevant information provided by the parents to determine:

1. If the conduct in question was caused by, or had a direct and substantial relationship to, the child's disability; or
2. If the conduct in question was the direct result of the LEA's failure to implement the IEP.

The conduct is determined to be a manifestation of the child's disability if the LEA, the parent, and relevant members of the child's IEP team determine that the conduct was precipitated by either condition described previously, 20 U.S.C. § 1415(k)(1)(E). If the misbehavior is found to be a manifestation of the child's disability, the LEA must take immediate steps to remedy the deficiencies, 34 C.F.R. § 300.530(e)(3). Moreover, if there is a determination that the conduct was a manifestation of the child's disability, the IEP team must either conduct a functional behavioral assessment and implement a behavioral intervention plan for the child or, if a behavioral intervention plan already had been developed, review the behavioral intervention plan, and modify it, as necessary, to address the behavior; the LEA must return the child to the placement from which the child was removed, unless the parent and the LEA agree to a change of placement as part of the modification of the behavioral intervention plan, 20 U.S.C. 1415(k)(1)(F), 34 C.F.R. § 300.530(f).

    The 2004 IDEIA eliminates the more lenient 1997 standard for manifestation hearings. Before IDEIA 2004, the burden was on the school district to show that the behavior resulting in a disciplinary action was not a manifestation of the child's disability before being allowed to apply the same disciplinary procedures as they use for non-disabled students. Thus, the burden of proof for the manifestation determination review has now been shifted to the parents who have to prove that the behavior was caused by or had a direct and substantial relationship to the disability. Moreover, the 1997 language requiring the IEP team to consider whether the disability impaired the child's ability to control or to understand the impact and consequences of the behavior has been deleted. Because the 2004 IDEIA makes it easier for schools to remove children for non-dangerous, non-weapon, non-drug-related behaviors, and places the burden on parents to prove the connection between behavior and disability, it clearly prefers administrative ease for schools rather than preserving the individual rights of students.

DISCIPLINE OF STUDENTS NOT YET CLASSIFIED

The 2004 IDEIA also favors school administrators when it comes to the discipline of students with disabilities who have not yet been classified as having disabilities. While "the rule remains focused on whether the LEA had knowledge that the child was a child with a disability before the behavior that led to the discipline," the basis of whether a school had such knowledge has been restricted to the following (Weber et al., 2004):

1. the parents of the child has expressed concern in writing to supervisory or administrative personnel of the appropriate educational agency, or a teacher of the child, that the child is in need of special education and related services;
2. the parent of the child has requested an evaluation of the child pursuant to Section 1414(a)(1)(B);
3. the teacher of the child, or other personnel of the local educational agency, has expressed specific concerns about a pattern of behavior demonstrated by the child, directly to the director of special education of such agency or to other supervisory personnel of the agency. 20 U.S.C. § 1415(k)(5)(B).

Thus, even if a student has a disability and acts out, he or she will not be accorded the benefits of the manifestation hearing if one of the three conditions above were not met. This is particularly troubling if the behavior at issue is the first sign that the child has a disability. These 2004 IDEIA changes, coupled with the other discipline revisions, are much more stringent than the 1997 provisions. The 2004 IDEIA places more onerous burdens on parents in favor of making it easier for school administrators to discipline and ultimately remove students with disabilities.

DUE PROCESS HEARINGS AND ALTERNATIVE DISPUTE RESOLUTION

Another concern about enforcement reflected in the 2004 IDEIA involves the inevitable conflict between parents and schools regarding IDEIA and Congress' desire to foster more constructive relationships among education stakeholders around IDEIA issues. The President's Commission makes it clear that there was concern about the proliferation of special education litigation. According to the report:

> More than one school administrator voiced concerns about the growing threats of litigation when parents and schools cannot agree on the appropriate level of special education and related services to provide. These threats create an adversarial atmosphere that severely limits the ability of parents and schools to cooperate. The threat of litigation alone has costs for teachers, students, and tax payers: the cost in attorneys in actual hearings and court actions; the cost of attorneys and staff time in preparation for cases that do not reach the dispute resolution system; and the cost of paperwork driven by districts believing that extensive records help prevent lawsuits. These costs and the dissatisfaction with the system merit serious reform. (President's Commission on Excellence in Special Education, 2002)

Therefore, the 2004 IDEIA includes extensive provisions that are designed to reduce litigation and promote constructive relationships. The provisions involve resolution sessions, mediation sessions, as well as a revised attorneys' fees mechanism.

DUE PROCESS HEARINGS

The 2004 IDEIA has addressed many of the procedural requirements of due process hearings that are technical in nature (Weber et al., 2004). For example, the notice requirements regarding due process hearings have been revised to be more comprehensive. The parent or LEA requesting a due process hearing must provide a complaint notice to the opposing party and SEA, 20 U.S.C. § 1415(b)(7). The hearing must be requested within 2 years of the date that the parent or LEA knew or should have known about the action forming the basis of the complaint, 20 U.S.C. § 1415(f)(3)(C). The only exceptions are if the state has a specific limitation period or if the parents were prevented from requesting a hearing due to a misrepresentation by the LEA, 20 U.S.C. § 1415(f)(3)(D).

If the opposing party wants to challenge the notice, it must do so within 15 days of receiving the complaint, 20 U.S.C. § 1415(c)(2). Moreover, the LEA or parent has 10 days to substantively respond to the complaint, 20 U.S.C. § 1415(c)(2). Specifically, the LEA's response must include:

1. an explanation of why the agency proposed or refused to take the action raised in the complaint;
2. a description of other options that the IEP team considered and the reasons those options were rejected;
3. a description of each evaluation procedure, assessment, record, or report the agency used as the basis for the proposed or refused action; and
4. a description of the factors that are relevant to the agency's proposal or refusal. (Weber et al., 2004b; 20 U.S.C. § 1415(c)(2))

The parent also has 10 days to respond to the LEA's complaint, 20 U.S.C. § 1415(c)(2)(B)(ii). The 2004 IDEIA gives the hearing officer less flexibility with respect to findings and therefore makes it more difficult for the challenging party to prevail. A hearing officer can only find a violation on substantive grounds based on a determination that a student did not receive a FAPE, 20 U.S.C. § 1415(f)(3)(E)(iii). Moreover, if the case alleges a procedural violation, it will only be successful if the hearing officer finds that the alleged procedural inadequacies "impeded the right" to a FAPE; "significantly impeded the parents' opportunity to participate" in the decision-making process; or deprived educational benefits, 20 U.S.C. § 1415(f)(3)(E)(iii).

ATTORNEYS' FEES

The 2004 IDEIA contains a "controversial amendment" regarding attorneys' fees (Weber et al., 2004). Previously, the 1997 IDEA provided that a court "may award reasonable attorneys' fees as part of the costs to the parents of a child with a disability who is the prevailing party," 20 U.S.C. § 1415(i)(3)(A) (Weber et al., 2004a). This provision included not only court cases but *all* special education proceedings, including due process hearings (Weber et al., 2004a). In fact, courts have held that fees are to be awarded "as a matter of course" when parents prevail, *Mitten v. Muscogee County Sch. Dist.*, 877 F. 2d 932 (11th Cir. 1989) (Weber et al., 2004).

Experts have argued that this original attorneys' fee provision enables parents to enforce the mandates of the law and ensures equity and justice for all students in need of special education and related services, especially those whose families cannot afford attorneys. For example, Weber and colleagues explain:

> The presence of an attorney is important for parents, and the availability of fees is designed to make representation easier to obtain . . . having an attorney representing the parent dramatically increases the probability that the parent will prevail in a due process hearing . . . Moreover, the guarantee of free education for all children with disabilities would be undermined if parents had to pay attorneys to achieve the results their children were entitled to under the statute. (Weber et al., 2004)

A major change in the 2004 IDEIA Amendments may jeopardize this important right that provides access to an attorney. The 2004 IDEIA has been revised so that the school district can collect attorneys' fees from the parent. Specifically under the 2004 IDEIA, the state or LEA may collect attorneys' fees against the parents' attorney as the prevailing party if the parent has filed a due process or court complaint that is "frivolous, unreasonable, or without foundation, or has continued to litigate after the litigation clearly became frivolous, unreasonable, or without foundation," 20 U.S.C. § 1415(i)(3)(B)(i)(II). This may be a strong disincentive for attorneys to represent students with disabilities and their parents, especially those low-income students and parents who cannot afford to hire an attorney. Ironically, while the 2004 IDEIA seeks to champion the mandates of NCLB to provide a more stringent education for children with disabilities, it may also undercut many of these stringent mandates by making it more difficult to enforce its provisions.

ALTERNATIVE DISPUTE RESOLUTION

The 2004 IDEIA also provides strong disincentives for litigation by encouraging two forms of alternative dispute resolution: Mediation and "Resolution Sessions." The use of alternative dispute resolution was suggested by the President's Commission, which recommended a shift in IDEIA philosophy from conflict resolution to conflict prevention. The commission specifically stated:

> IDEA should require states to develop early processes that avoid conflict and promote IEP agreements, such as IEP facilitators. Require states to make mediation available anytime it is requested and not only when a request for a hearing has been made. Permit parents and

schools to enter binding arbitration and hearing officers are trained in conflict resolution and negotiation. (President's Commission on Excellence in Special Education, 2002)

While it does not contain IEP facilitators, the 2004 IDEIA encourages facilitation through mediation and resolution sessions. The 2004 IDEIA requires that "mediation be available for all matters, including those that may arise before the filing of a due process complaint," 2004, 20 U.S.C. § 1415(e)(1). Mediation is a "method of nonbinding dispute resolution involving a neutral third party who tries to help the disputing parties reach a mutually agreeable solution" (Garner, 1999). If the parent and LEA reach an agreement during the mediation, the IDEIA requires that the parties execute a binding agreement that is enforceable in court, 20 U.S.C. § 1415(e)(2)(F)(ii)-(iii).

The 2004 IDEIA "introduces a new settlement mechanism, the 'resolution session'" (Weber et al., 2004). The "resolution session" is a mandatory meeting that occurs within 15 days of receipt of the parents' complaint and must include parents and a representative of LEA with decision-making authority, 20 U.S.C. § 1415(f)(1)(B)(i)(I)-(II). The meeting can only be avoided if the parents and LEA agree to use mediation or waive the resolution session, 20 U.S.C. §1415(f)(1)(B)(i). The meeting enables the parents to discuss the reasons for their complaint and to give the LEA a chance to resolve issues raised in the complaint, 20 U.S.C. § 1415(f)(1)(B)(i)(IV). In order to make the resolution session as nonadversarial as possible, the LEA cannot bring an attorney into the resolution session unless the parent brings an attorney, 20 U.S.C. § 1415(f)(1)(B)(i)(III). If the parties are not able to resolve their dispute within 30 days of receipt of the complaint, the due process hearing occurs and all applicable timetables resume, 20 U.S.C. § 1415(f)(1)(B)(ii). If the parties are able to resolve their conflict, however, they execute a binding agreement that is judicially enforceable, 20 U.S.C. § 1415(f)(1)(B)(iii). Unlike mediation, the parties do have 3 business days after a resolution session agreement is reached to void the agreement, 20 U.S.C. § 1415(i)(3)(D)(ii)-(iii). Thus, the 2004 IDEIA tries to promote agreement through alternative dispute resolution and making it very difficult for parents to pursue litigation.

CONCLUSION

With the 2004 IDEIA, Congress sought to ease the administrative burdens in implementing IDEIA as well as integrate key principles of NCLB. As the 2002 report from the President's Commission on Excellence in

Special Education, "A New Era: Revitalizing Special Education for Children and Families," states: "Children placed in special education are general education children first. Despite this basic fact, educators and policy-makers think about the two systems as separate." In the 2004 IDEIA, Congress sought to improve this special education law by integrating special education with general education, literally and figuratively. The 2004 IDEIA reflects a desire to have a highly qualified teaching staff for special education students as well as general education students. The 2004 IDEIA reflects a desire to have the same rigorous requirements and reporting of adequate yearly progress for special education students as general education students. The 2004 IDEIA also reflects a concern that the burdens of implementing special education law were taking time and resources away from educating special education students and general education students. Therefore, the 2004 IDEIA gives schools more flexibility when it comes to IEP requirements and discipline. The 2004 IDEIA also encourages cooperation and discourages litigation in the name of providing more resources for education for special education students and all students.

The companion desires to require more rigor on the one hand, but discourage litigation on the other, reflect a disconnect in the 2004 IDEIA and education law in general. While the goals of education statutes and regulations may be admirable, they are irrelevant if the law is not enforceable and if parents have to worry about whether their children will be thrown out of school. One hopes that the 2004 IDEIA will be interpreted in light of the recent Supreme Court decision in *Winkelman v. Parma,* 127 S. Ct. 1994; 167 L. Ed. 2d 904; 2007 U.S. LEXIS 5902, where the Court decided whether parents of a student with disabilities were entitled to bring an action pro se under the IDEA. The Supreme Court held that because parents enjoy independent rights under IDEA, they are entitled to prosecute IDEA claims on their own behalf. Writing for the majority, Justice Kennedy explained the reasoning behind the Supreme Court's holding as follows:

> The potential for injustice in this result is apparent. What is more, we find nothing in the statute to indicate that when Congress required States to provide adequate instruction to a child at no cost to parents, it intended that only some parents would be able to enforce that mandate. The statute instead takes pains to ensure that the rights of children with disabilities and parents of such children are protected. (Winkelman, 1275. Ct. 1994, 2005)

This decision emphasizes the importance of the ability to enforce rights in the context of special education law. Justice Kennedy acknowledges the painful irony and injustice in having rights that one cannot enforce.

This same irony potentially exists in the 2004 IDEIA where there is more required but less leverage with which to enforce these requirements. If, however, the law and policy of the 2004 IDEIA is construed in accordance with *Winkelman* and its mandate to achieve justice, the 2004 IDEIA will continue to provide all children with disabilities a free appropriate public education.

REFERENCES

Garner, B. A. (1999). *Black's law dictionary* (7th ed.). St. Paul, MN: West Group.

Mandlawitz, M. (2007). *What every teacher should know about IDEA 2004 laws and regulations.* Boston: Pearson.

Osborne, A. G., & Russo, C. J. (2006). *Special education and the law: A guide for practitioners.* Thousand Oaks, CA: Corwin.

President's Commission on Excellence in Special Education final report. (2002). A new era: revitalizing special education for children and their families.

Weber, M. C., Mawdsley, R., & Redfield, S. (2004a). *Special education law: Cases and materials.* Newark, NJ: LexisNexis.

Weber, M. C., Mawdsley, R., & Redfield, S. (2004b). *Special education law: Statutes and regulations.* Newark, NJ: LexisNexis.

Weishaar, M. (2007). *Case studies in special education law: No child left behind and individuals with disabilities education improvement act.* Columbus, OH: Pearson.

PART II

The Reauthorization of the Individuals With Disabilities Education Improvement Act of 2004 (IDEIA)

*Concepts and Constructs—
Old, New, and Modified*

CHAPTER 3

The Law and Reality

Understanding the Individuals With Disabilities Education Improvement Act

Mary Konya Weishaar

If you were a special education teacher in 1976 or 1995 or 2007, how would your role have changed? As you read the following scenarios, think about these factors: degree of parent involvement, connection between regular education and special education, accountability, and how the child is labeled.

Scenario 1: 1976

As I walked into the school building in September as a learning disabilities resource teacher, I reflected on how John was responding to my instruction. As a first grader, John was experiencing difficulty in reading and he struggled to sound out three-letter words. John was identified as a handicapped child with learning disabilities at a multidisciplinary staffing. The psychologist stated that John had difficulty processing through the visual modality and that visual perception skills were weak. As a result, John's individualized education program (IEP) focused on strengthening these processing disabilities. John was scheduled to work with me in the special education classroom on an individual basis three times a week for 20 minute sessions. I was well versed in how to help children strengthen weak modalities from my university training and we worked on puzzles, tangrams, putting blocks into patterns, and visual tracking exercises. I felt that these strategies would be helpful to John. I only occasionally talked with John's teacher, but she had great faith in the instruction from me, the learning disabilities specialist. At our end-of-year review, I reported that I felt John's reading skills had improved. John's parents gave permission for his initial evaluation and met with me annually to review his progress.

Scenario 2: 1995

Damien was identified as a child with a learning disability in second grade. He experienced considerable difficulty learning to sound out words. As the learning disabilities teacher in the building, I worked with Damien daily for about 30 minutes in a small group within my special education classroom. The children in this group worked on building reading skills using phonics workbooks, reading stories aloud that were on their instructional level, and completing reading homework. I learned how to teach reading during my undergraduate work at the university and I knew that focusing on skill-building would be helpful to Damien. The work was not directly connected with Damien's reading instruction in the regular education classroom, but the extra small group instruction seemed to be helping Damien. I assessed Damien's IEP progress at the end of the school year by administering assessments tied to his IEP objectives. Damien's second grade teacher came to the annual review at the end of the school year to report on his progress. Damien's parents gave written consent for his initial evaluation and were updated annually on his progress in reading in the special education program.

Scenario 3: 2007

Marian, a first grader, was experiencing difficulty in reading. Based on an early reading assessment (Dynamic Indicators of Basic Early Literacy Skills-DIBELS) administered to all children in the class, Marian was identified as one of several children who struggled with phonemic awareness. Her first grade teacher worked with this small group daily by providing additional instruction in phonemic segmentation fluency and nonsense word fluency. Most children responded positively, but Marian continued to be at risk for academic failure as evidenced by ongoing assessment data. The school-based problem-solving team determined that Marian needed more specialized intensive assistance in reading and she was referred for a special education evaluation. As a result of this evaluation and the evidence supporting her lack of response to intervention, Marian was identified as having a learning disability. As the special education teacher, I went into the first grade classroom for about an hour each day to work with children who needed additional help in reading. The first grade teacher and I worked together to plan lessons for all children in reading and I also worked with Marian within the regular education classroom, providing supplemental instruction. Marian's parents, her first grade teacher, and I met quarterly to discuss her progress in reading. Each quarter, we reviewed the evidence used to track her progress. Because of our interventions, Marian was making excellent progress in reading as evidenced by ongoing assessment and data collection.

Table 3.1 summarizes major differences between the scenarios.

TABLE 3.1   Major Differences Between Scenarios

	Scenario 1: 1976	Scenario 2: 1995	Scenario 3: 2007
Curriculum	Special instruction emphasized Processing disorder identified by school psychologist Intervention planned by special education teacher No connection with regular education	Special instruction emphasized special parallel reading curriculum Intervention planned by special education teacher No direct connection with regular education	Intervention emphasized regular education reading goals and curriculum Interventions jointly planned by special and regular education teachers
Place where intervention occurred	Special education classroom–individual assistance	Special education classroom–small group assistance	Regular education classroom–whole group/small group/individual assistance
Labeling	Child received label, then received specialized intervention	Child received label, then received specialized intervention	Child received specialized intervention, then when lack of response to intervention was documented, child received label, then intensified specialized interventions

Continued

TABLE 3.1   Major Differences Between Scenarios *(Continued)*

Account-ability	Little accountability other than teacher feeling that progress had been made and parents being informed of progress	Assessments administered annually to determine if IEP goals were met	Ongoing assessment to determine response to interventions in reading
Parent involvement	Little other than gatekeeping consents and annual update on child's progress	Little other than gatekeeping consents and annual update on child's progress	Appeared that parent had active and ongoing involvement in interventions prior to and after labeling
Language	"Handicapped child"	"Child with a disability"	Child who was "at risk for academic failure" and who needed interventions; Later identified as "child with a disability"
Teacher Training	Focus on categorical labels of children; Focus on strengthening "weak" learning modalities; Individualization means working one-to-one with a child; Diagnosis leads to intervention	More focus on academics, e.g., how to teach reading, written language, mathematics; Individualization means working in small groups to meet each child's needs; Diagnosis is meaningful, but does not lead to particular intervention	Focus on teaching and learning for all children; Focus on early intervening and increasing intensity of specialized instruction as needed; Focus on databased decision making to guide instruction; Focus on assessment to gather data about effects of teaching
Use of evidence-based approaches to teaching	Little use of evidence-based approaches to teaching	Some use of evidence-based approaches to teaching	Heavy reliance on evidence-based approaches to teaching

There has been a major shift in the manner in which we identify, teach, and track progress of children with disabilities. The scenarios above illustrate some factors in this shift. There is now closer alignment between regular education and special education goals for children with disabilities. More children with disabilities are receiving instruction within the regular education environment. Children receive special and intensive interventions early if assessment data generated within the regular education classroom indicates that a child is at risk for academic failure. Academic progress is now measured by ongoing assessment, which drives instructional decisions. Parents are involved early and more often in the education of their child. Labeling a child as having a disability is no longer viewed as a gatekeeping function to obtain specialized or intensive instructional services.

What factors contributed to the philosophical shift illustrated in these scenarios? Turnbull and Turnbull (2000) suggested that all educational issues were basically political policy and social issues that reflected and formed the underpinning for federal law. Although theories about child development and educational practice change over time, a major guiding factor is the federal law specifying how and under what circumstances children receive assistance.

Prior to 1975, there was no strong, enforceable federal law governing special education services within the public school system. In 1975, Congress passed the first comprehensive law mandating services for children with disabilities, the Education of All Handicapped Children's Act. This "right to education" law had as its primary purposes assurance that all children with disabilities received a free appropriate public education (FAPE) and were not the targets of discrimination by any public school or agency furnishing educational services. This law was later renamed Individuals With Disabilities Education Act (IDEA) in 1990 and Individuals With Disabilities Education Improvement Act (IDEIA) in 2004. Congress reviewed, revised, and amended this law several times (1978, 1986, 1990, 1997, 2004). Several significant changes in this federal law are summarized below.

1986

- Services for infants and toddlers (birth through age 3) were added.
- Parents who prevailed in a due process hearing were given the right to request and recover attorney's fees.

1990

- Language was changed to reflect *person-first*, from "handicapped child" to "child with a disability."
- As stated above, the name of the law was changed to Individuals With Disabilities Education Act.

- Two new categories of disabilities, autism and traumatic brain injury, were added.
- Transition services for students age 16 and above were mandated.
- The related service of assistive technology was added.

1997

- Discipline procedures for children with disabilities were specified.
- Emphasis was placed on the participation of general educators in the education of children with disabilities.
- The individualized education program (IEP) team had to determine the extent to which each child with a disability would participate in state and local assessments.
- All IEPs had to include measurable goals and objectives or benchmarks.
- Voluntary mediation as a means to resolve conflict was mandated.

2004

- As stated above, the name was changed to Individuals With Disabilities Education Improvement Act.
- The law was dovetailed with the No Child Left Behind Act (NCLB), primarily in the focus on outcomes for all children and highly qualified teachers.
- Procedures to discipline children with disabilities were streamlined and a statute of limitations (2 years) was put into place.
- In conflict, resolution meetings were mandated and the agreements reached in mediation and resolution meetings were legally binding.
- The identification process of learning disability was changed and could be based on lack of response to intervention, not just the traditional discrepancy between achievement and ability formulas.
- Paperwork was streamlined and IEPs could be changed without a formal IEP meeting and some participants could be excused from meeting attendance in certain circumstances.

Over the years, it is clear that the original purpose of the IDEIA has not been altered: to provide a free appropriate public education for all children with disabilities. However, the focus has shifted to outcomes for all children, which originated in a movement for school reform beginning in the 1980s.

The reform movement focusing on outcomes was reflected in legislation enacted in 1994, Goals 2000: Educate America Act. This reform movement affected change within regular education and special education by focusing on determination of goals for *all* children, assessment of progress toward those goals, and becoming accountable for the progress of *all* children. Because of this legislation, the majority of states specified state goals that closely matched national goals that reflected the federal law. School reform in regular education developed in a parallel manner with reform in special education.

With the enactment of the NCLB in 2001 and the reauthorization of the IDEIA of 2004, the lines between regular education and special education were faded by the increased emphasis on accountability and the focus on learning of *all* children. To illustrate, consider President George W. Bush's comments when signing the IDEIA in 2004.

> America's schools educate over 6 million children with disabilities. In the past, those students were too often just shuffled through the system with little expectation that they could make significant progress or succeed like their fellow classmates. Children With disabilities deserve high hopes, high expectations, and extra help . . . In the bill I sign today, we're raising expectations for the students. We're giving schools and parents the tools they need to meet them. We're applying the reforms of the No Child Left Behind Act to the Individuals with Disabilities Education Improvement Act so schools are accountable for teaching every single child . . . All students in America can learn. That's what all of us up here believe. All of us understand we have an obligation to make sure no child is left behind in America. (Bush, 2004)

Figure 3.1 shows how the general emphasis for school reform evolved over time to a focus on accountability and outcomes for all children.

PRINCIPLES OF THE IDEIA

With the reauthorization of the IDEIA, it is now commonly understood that the law is based on seven important principles (Weishaar, 2007). These seven principles are listed below, and then summarized using examples on the following pages.

- Zero Reject/Child Find
- Nondiscriminatory Assessment
- Appropriate Education and Individualized Education Program (IEP)
- Least Restrictive Environment (LRE)
- Procedural Due Process
- Parent Participation
- Right to Educational Achievement

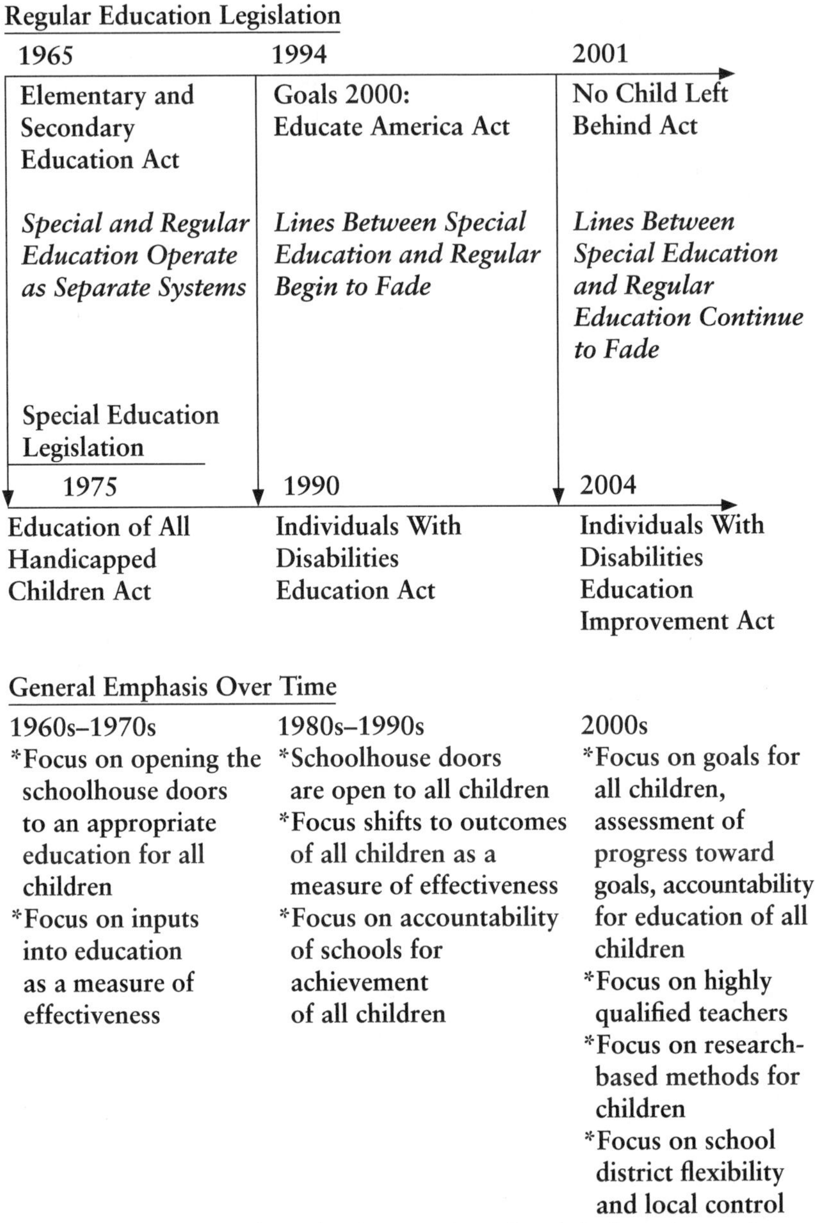

Regular Education Legislation

1965	1994	2001
Elementary and Secondary Education Act	Goals 2000: Educate America Act	No Child Left Behind Act
Special and Regular Education Operate as Separate Systems	*Lines Between Special Education and Regular Begin to Fade*	*Lines Between Special Education and Regular Education Continue to Fade*

Special Education Legislation

1975	1990	2004
Education of All Handicapped Children Act	Individuals With Disabilities Education Act	Individuals With Disabilities Education Improvement Act

General Emphasis Over Time

1960s–1970s	1980s–1990s	2000s
*Focus on opening the schoolhouse doors to an appropriate education for all children *Focus on inputs into education as a measure of effectiveness	*Schoolhouse doors are open to all children *Focus shifts to outcomes of all children as a measure of effectiveness *Focus on accountability of schools for achievement of all children	*Focus on goals for all children, assessment of progress toward goals, accountability for education of all children *Focus on highly qualified teachers *Focus on research-based methods for children *Focus on school district flexibility and local control

FIGURE 3.1   General emphasis over time: Special education and regular education.

Zero Reject/Child Find

Zero reject refers to the mandate that all children with disabilities, regardless of severity, receive a free appropriate public education (FAPE). This also includes children who have been expelled for disciplinary reasons. Historically, zero reject focused primarily on children with severe disabilities and the mandate for these children to be appropriately educated by the local school district, regardless of cost. Following is an example.

Martin was a 3-year-old child with significant disabilities. When he was a baby, his teenage father threw him against the floor in anger because he would not stop crying. This caused serious cognitive, sensory, and motor disabilities. Martin was deaf, blind, and only displayed spastic movement. He was unable to sit up, feed himself, or speak. He seemed to respond to touch by showing minimal reflex. Martin's caretaker, a foster parent, approached the local school district to provide appropriate educational services. Although Martin could not benefit from typical instruction, he was entitled to an evaluation and appropriate educational services. This was planned by his IEP team and included services from a special education teacher, and related services of occupational therapy, physical therapy, and speech therapy. Even though Martin would probably never learn to read or write, the severity of his disability or prognosis did not limit his entitlement to an individually appropriate education.

Zero reject more recently focused on exclusion of children with disabilities for disciplinary reasons. Until the 1997 reauthorization of the IDEA, school districts relied on case law, for example, *Honig v. Doe* (479 U.S. 1084, 1988) and best practice to guide decisions in disciplinary situations involving children with disabilities. In 1997, the IDEA specified detailed regulations involving discipline and these were further defined in 2004 when the IDEIA was reauthorized. Basically, a building principal can suspend a child with a disability up to and including 10 school days without involving the special education system, that is, the IEP team. Exclusions beyond 10 school days must involve the child's IEP team who determine the relationship of the behavior in question to the child's disability. If the team determines that the behavior was caused by or had a relationship to the child's disability or was the direct result of the school district's failure to implement the IEP, the behavior is a manifestation of the child's disability. If this is the case, the child must return to the current placement. Even if the behavior is not a manifestation of the child's disability, the child may not be excluded from receiving an appropriate education, although education may take place in another setting. In the case of illegal drugs, weapons, or inflicting serious bodily injury, the student can be placed for 45 school days in an interim alternative educational setting regardless of whether or not the behavior is related to the disability. Following is an example that illustrates the complexities of the law involving a high school student with a disability who had drugs at school.

Jameca was a 15-year-old 10th grade student with a learning disability in reading. She read on a third grade level, but she performed in an average manner in mathematics. Jameca was placed in special education classes for English and history. She was placed in geometry and basic chemistry within the regular education program and she received special education support for these classes during her study hall. Jameca was generally well-adjusted to high school and had two close friends. However, she was with these friends when it was discovered that she had a small amount of marijuana at school. School policy was to immediately suspend the student and hold an expulsion hearing with a likely recommendation for expulsion for the remainder of the school year. Because Jameca had an identified disability, she was suspended from school for 10 days and a functional behavioral assessment was conducted. The results of this assessment and other relevant information helped the IEP team determine services needed in a 45-day interim alternative educational setting, which consisted of placement in a day treatment facility. Jameca received the services outlined in her IEP in a different setting.

Child find focuses on identifying, locating, and evaluating children in need of special education. This mandate includes children who are homeless, attend private schools, or who are in foster care. In 2004, under the IDEIA, this mandate was expanded to include children who were advancing from grade to grade, but were in need of special education services. The following illustrates the concept of child find.

During fourth grade, Phil continued to experience difficulty in reading, writing, and spelling. He struggled every evening with homework, often working for 3 or 4 hours with his mother at his side. He failed most tests in school, but was able to make Cs and Ds by working hard and completing all homework. In kindergarten, first, second, and third grades, Phil was promoted to the next grade. However, each year became more difficult. Standardized tests given to the whole class showed that Phil functioned within the low average to below average range in most subjects. At the end of the school year, his teacher consulted with a building-based support team to determine if Phil needed further assistance. Even though Phil successfully moved from grade to grade, the team decided to refer him for a more in-depth evaluation to determine if he had a disability.

Nondiscriminatory Assessment

In general, nondiscriminatory assessment means that each child who is referred for an evaluation must receive a comprehensive, unbiased, and individualized evaluation. Included are the following principles.

- A variety of assessment strategies and instruments must be used in gathering relevant functional, developmental, and academic information about the child.
- No single instrument or strategy is used as the only criterion for identification as a student with a disability.
- Assessment instruments must be technically adequate, that is, valid and reliable, and used for the purpose for which they are intended.
- Assessments must be administered by trained professionals.
- Assessments must not discriminate on the basis of race, culture, or disability.
- Assessments should be administered in the child's native language if at all possible.
- The evaluation must be comprehensive, yield relevant information, and assess the child in relevant domains, for example, health, vision, hearing, social and emotional status, intelligence, academic performance, communication abilities, motor abilities.
- Existing evaluation data must be reviewed, including information provided by the parents, current classroom-based, local, or state assessments, and observations by teachers and related services providers.
- Parents' rights must be protected during an evaluation, including gaining informed parental consent prior to evaluation.

As an illustration of this principle, consider the following scenario.

Rosa, 3 years old, was recently adopted by Gina and Martin Martino from an orphanage in Central America. She lived in the orphanage from the age of 6 months, when she was abandoned by her mother. The Martinos knew that Rosa was delayed in her acquisition of language and that her primary language was Spanish, although English was spoken at the orphanage. Rosa was referred for a formal evaluation at her new local school district, located in a large metropolitan area in the Midwestern United States. The school district personnel met with the Martinos to explain the evaluation process and gain informed consent. A social worker met with the Martinos to gather information about Rosa's social and health history. Because Rosa's primary language was Spanish, a Spanish-speaking psychologist administered a Spanish language version of a cognitive abilities test. The speech therapist observed Rosa in a play setting to assess speech and language development. Based on this information, Rosa was determined to have a speech and language delay, and an IEP was written and implemented within the school district early childhood classroom.

One of the most significant changes in 2004 to the IDEIA was the process used in identification of a learning disability. In previous versions of this law, learning disability included, in part, significant discrepancy between ability and achievement. In the 2004 reauthorization, a child could be identified as having a learning disability if the following factors applied.

- Based on data gathered on the child's response to research-based intervention, the child does not meet approved age or grade-level academic standards.
- Data gathered shows that the child's difficulties are not due to lack of appropriate instruction in reading or math.

The following is an example of this new process for identifying learning disability.

As a first grader, June was identified as at risk in the area of reading based on results from the Dynamic Indicators of Basic Early Literacy Skills (DIBELS), which were administered to all first graders at regular intervals. June's teacher focused additional special reading strategies on June and three other first graders early in the school year. As assessment continued, data showed that June continued to fall behind in reading. By mid-year, June's teacher met with the building support team to discuss additional specialized strategies in reading. June then began working with the specialized reading teacher on a regular basis in addition to continuation of special reading strategies from her first grade teacher. Toward the end of first grade, it was apparent that June was not meeting grade-level standards in reading, so she was referred for a comprehensive individual evaluation. Her IEP team conducted the evaluation using, in part, data gathered prior to the formal referral, and determined that June exhibited a learning disability based on her lack of response to research-based interventions. June's IEP was planned and she received intensive reading assistance from the special education teacher in addition to assistance within her regular classroom. The special education teacher continued to collect data on June's progress and intensive interventions on a regular basis.

As this scenario illustrates, significant discrepancy between ability and achievement is no longer mandatory to identify a child as having a learning disability.

Appropriate Education and Individualized Education Program (IEP)

Every child with a disability is entitled to a free appropriate public education (FAPE). This means that the child receives an appropriate education that conforms to his/her IEP at public expense. The IEP is a blueprint or a plan for services to be provided to the child and it is proof of compliance that the child is receiving FAPE. The IEP is developed by a group of knowledgeable persons, including the following.

- Child's parents
- Regular education teacher (if the child is, or may be, participating in regular education)
- Special education teacher
- Professional qualified to provide or supervise special education and who is knowledgeable of resources and the general education curriculum
- Professional who can interpret the implications of evaluation results
- Other persons, or the child, as appropriate or necessary

An IEP includes the following components. Each component is described and accompanied by an example.

- Present levels of academic achievement and functional performance, which includes how the disability affects the child's involvement and progress in the general education curriculum.

Juan (15 years old) displays deficient reading skills. Juan reads on approximately a first grade level. Independently, he reads 3- or 4-letter words. His listening comprehension is age-appropriate. His writing skills are consistent with reading skills, and he is able to print his name and address with a model. In math, Juan functions close to grade level and he understands basic arithmetic operations, fractions, decimals, and geometry. Juan functions in the community independently and currently holds a job in an automotive repair shop.

- Measurable annual goals (academic and/or functional) to meet the child's needs. Note: For children who take alternate assessments aligned to alternate achievement standards, a description of benchmarks or short-term objectives is also included.

Juan will be able to read a grocery store advertisement with 100% comprehension.

Juan will itemize weekly expenditures for food and other living expenses.

- Description of how the child's progress toward the annual goals will be measured and when periodic reports on progress will be provided.

Each quarter, Juan will take the Brigance Test of Essential Skills.
Each quarter, Juan will be asked to itemize weekly living expenditures.

- Special education and related services and supplementary aids and services to be provided (based on peer-reviewed research to the greatest extent possible). Also included is a description of program modifications or supports for school personal that will be provided to help the child progress in the general education curriculum and extracurricular/nonacademic activities.

Juan will be placed in English 3 within the special education program.
Juan will receive assistance from a paraprofessional in his basic algebra and social studies classes to assist him with directions.
Reading assignments in all classes other than English will be read aloud by the special education paraprofessional.
Juan will be allowed additional time to complete tests.
Tests will be administered by the special education paraprofessional or teacher.

- Description of the extent to which the child will not participate with nondisabled children.

Because of Juan's limited reading skills, he will not participate in the regular education program for English or study hall.

- Description of individual accommodations necessary to measure performance on state- and district-wide assessments. Note: If the child cannot take regular assessments, a rationale as to why must be provided as well as a description of the alternate assessment.

Assessments will be read aloud to Juan.
Assessments will be administered in an alternate setting by a special education teacher.
Juan will be allowed extended time to complete assessments.
For reading, Juan will take an alternate reading assessment, Brigance Test of Essential Skills.

- Projected date for initiation of services and anticipated frequency, location, and duration of the services.

Learning disability services: 250 minutes per week in special education classroom; beginning September 1; ending May 30.
Individual aide services: 250 minutes for week in regular education classroom; beginning September 1; ending May 30.

- Transition services for children age 16 that includes measurable postsecondary goals based on assessments related to training, education, employment, and independent living skills and services needed to attain these goals.

Note: Juan's annual goals and services addressed transition.

In addition to these components, the IEP must reflect strengths of the child, concerns of the parent, results of the most recent evaluation, strategies to support the child's behavior (as appropriate), and the child's language and communication needs. Each IEP must be reviewed and revised on an annual basis. According to the IDEIA, it is possible to revise an IEP without holding a formal IEP meeting as long as the parent agrees not to hold the meeting.

Least Restrictive Environment (LRE)

The federal law has not significantly changed in terms of least restrictive environment since 1975. Least restrictive environment means that to the maximum extent possible, each child with a disability will be educated with children without disabilities. Each school district must maintain a continuum of services, that is, regular classroom, resource classroom, special classroom. Each child with a disability must be able to advance toward annual goals, be involved in and make progress in the general curriculum, and participate in extracurricular and nonacademic activities. As an example, consider the scenario below.

As a student with Down syndrome, Paul, a fifth grader, attended a special education class in his neighboring school district. One of Paul's annual goals focused on socialization skills with peers. Paul took a special bus to and from school daily. In November, the fifth grade boys were invited to try out for the school basketball team. Tryouts were held after school for 2 days and practice was scheduled 2 days a week after school. Paul loved basketball and wanted to try out for the team. Even though his school bus normally left right after school dismissed, the home district made arrangements for a later pick-up time so that Paul could try out for the team. Ultimately, Paul was a member of the team and the home district rearranged the bus schedule during basketball season so that Paul could attend practices and games.

Procedural Due Process

Procedural due process assures that parents' rights are protected as their child is evaluated and receives special education services. Parents are afforded many procedural safeguards, including the following examples.

- The right to review the child's school records;
- The right to participate in meetings about the child;
- The right to request an independent educational evaluation;
- The right to receive notification and give informed consent when the school district wishes to initiate or change the identification, evaluation, or placement of the child.

In addition to these procedural safeguards, parents can challenge any decision made on behalf of their child by requesting mediation or a due process hearing. Mediation is a less formal procedure when an impartial third party works with the parents and school district personnel to resolve conflict. The third party mediator facilitates resolution of the conflict, but may not impose resolution. A more formal complaint may be filed as a due process complaint. If this happens, the school district must first arrange for an informal resolution meeting with the parents and relevant members of the IEP team who have knowledge of the conflict issues. This meeting is an informal attempt by both parties to resolve the conflict. If not successful, the more formal due process hearing is scheduled. The due process hearing is conducted by a trained impartial hearing officer, who listens to both sides of the conflict, and then renders a binding decision. Both parties may be represented by legal counsel or someone with knowledge about children with disabilities. Parties may also present evidence and confront, cross-examine, and compel the attendance of witnesses. Proceedings must be recorded and made available to both parties after the hearing. If either party disagrees with the outcome, the decision may be appealed to the state for an administrative review, and, if necessary, appealed in the court system. Although lengthy and detailed, this entire process assures fairness for both parties. One major change in this process in 2004 is that the outcome of mediation or the resolution process, if achieved, is legally binding. In addition, issues in the due process hearing have a statute of limitations, that is, the issue must have occurred within 2 years before the date the parent or school district knew or should have known about the alleged action.

To understand the gravity of a due process hearing, the following example of dialogue at a due process hearing is detailed. In this example, the child's teacher is undergoing direct examination by the parent's attorney. The subject of the hearing is a 6-year-old student with autism whose parent wants him fully included in the regular first grade classroom.

Parent Attorney (to regular education teacher): Could you review Jamie's progress in kindergarten last year?

Teacher: Yes, as I understand, Jamie made good progress last year. He participated successfully in most activities. On occasion, he needed individual assistance in an activity, like cutting with scissors. Most of the time he worked well with the other children. In fact, several children wanted to work with Jamie in reading. Jamie had many friends on the playground and at lunch.

Parent Attorney: Can you help me understand why Jamie was not placed in the regular classroom this year for first grade given his obvious success in kindergarten?

Teacher: We felt that Jamie could not keep up with the pace of the class. In first grade, children quickly learn reading and writing skills. We felt that Jamie would become frustrated and give up. We were concerned about his self-concept if he could not succeed.

Parent Attorney: So you made your decision based on what you anticipated, not on Jamie's record of success in the regular education kindergarten. Did the IEP team consider adaptations and accommodations within the regular first grade classroom?

Teacher: No, we did not think anything short of a special education classroom would be successful.

One can quickly see that Jamie's IEP team did not consider a full continuum of placements for first grade and that Jamie benefited socially and academically from placement with nondisabled children. This intense questioning would continue until finished and then the school district attorney would have an opportunity to ask questions during a cross-examination. Other witnesses would be brought forward and questioned during the hearing. After the hearing concluded, the hearing officer would write a binding decision.

Parent Participation

Parents of children with disabilities are afforded the right to substantial and significant participation in their child's education. As stated in the section above, parents' rights include access to procedural safeguards that ensure participation. Ideally, parents are full and involved partners from the time the child enters school through transition of the child to post-secondary education, training, and/or work. The intent is to fully involve parents frequently and intensively in the education of a child who has a disability. Parents are often involved prior to the child's identification of a disability, during the evaluation process, planning for special education services, reviewing the child's progress, and making decisions about postsecondary transition.

Right to Educational Achievement

The right to educational achievement emerged as a principle of the IDEA during 1990 and was reinforced in the IDEIA in 2004. The focus was on several important school reform concepts:

- High expectations for *all* children and ensuring access to the general education curriculum for all children with disabilities
- Development of goals or outcomes for *all* children
- Measurement of progress toward goals for *all* children
- Schools and *all* teachers are held accountable for the education of *all* children
- Emphasis on research-based instruction for *all* children

There are many references in the IDEIA to the NCLB. The close tie between these two laws suggests that regular and special education do not operate as separate systems any longer, but focus on the education and well-being of *all* children.

Following is an example illustrating this principle.

Mary, a 16-year-old student with a mild learning disability in mathematics, was preparing to take the State Test of Achievement. This test was administered annually to all 16-year-old students throughout the state and results were used to determine if the school met overall outcomes in reading and mathematics, as defined by the state criteria for adequate yearly progress. To meet adequate yearly progress, at least 40% of all students, including students with disabilities, must meet the state standards. If this did not occur, the school would be placed on an academic warning list and have significant sanctions. When Mary took the test, she took the same test as her peers, except in mathematics, when she was allowed extended time to finish and use a calculator on all parts of the test. When results were returned, Mary met the state standards in both reading and mathematics. In addition, 41% of all students met the state standards and therefore, the school made adequate yearly progress.

ARE WE READY?

Are we, as parents, educators, school districts, and teacher-training institutions, ready for significant change in the special education system as reflected by IDEIA? We certainly are ready for some changes, but only partially ready for the most significant change. The first six principles have been in place since 1975. Although there have been some major shifts in these principles, the basic focus has not changed. These principles have served well in "opening the doors of education" for all children with disabilities. Most school districts and teachers make good faith effort to follow the principles of providing an appropriate education to all children with disabilities. Most parents are familiarized with the special education process by the local school district personnel. This is not to say that the system is perfect—it is not. However, these principles ensure that all children with disabilities receive a free appropriate public education and are not excluded or discriminated against. Overall, parents and educators are prepared for shifts within the first six principles.

The major change occurred with the addition of a seventh principle, the right to educational achievement. In the past, educators' focus has been on categorical labels or what label a child received. This label determined somewhat what would happen to the child educationally. For example, a child labeled moderately mentally retarded often would receive education to prepare him/her for independent living. A child with a learning disability often would have more choices in his/her future, depending upon specific weaknesses. For children with significant emotional disorders, education often focused on appropriate behavior, sometimes at the expense of academic achievement. In the past, educators also focused on inclusion. Inclusion was viewed as a right and some people felt that all children should be included within the regular classroom no matter what the outcome. Finally, in the past, the focus was on following procedures identified in the law. A child received appropriate services depending on the extent to which the legal procedures were followed in identifying the disability, developing the IEP, and so forth.

This new seventh principle represents a major shift in the way parents and educators think and work with children. Many people are not fully prepared for this systemic change in the education of children. The right to educational achievement is a focus on results for all children. To fully prepare for this significant change, the following changes must occur.

- Teachers must be well-versed in research-based practice. Choosing a strategy or material because "it looks or appears successful" is no longer appropriate.
- Teachers must focus on the outcomes of using any research-based strategy. Knowledge and application of research-based strategies is useless if the child does not show tangible outcomes as a result of the strategy.
- To focus on outcomes, teachers must know how to use assessment that focuses on standards, not on norms. It is essential that teachers know how to regularly assess and track children's progress.
- Teachers must know how to and practice making data-based decisions to drive teaching and instructional decisions.
- Institutions of higher education must change the manner in which they train both regular and special education teachers. Teachers should be jointly trained to work with all children, in large and small groups, using standard and specialized strategies and materials. Collaboration between teachers and how to solve problems should be a main focus in teacher training programs. Too often, regular education preservice teachers have contact with special educators in student teaching for the first time. Teacher training for regular and special education must become integrated, not parallel.
- As educators, we must listen to parents. Parents are often sidelined in education and passively defer to the so-called experts. For a true focus on the seventh principle, parents must become partners in the child's education. Parents are the true experts about their child.

If these changes do not occur, it is predicted that special education and regular education will continue on a path toward continued separation. It is also likely that more litigation will result from any school districts or educators who are ill-prepared for the focus on the educational achievement or outcomes for all children.

FINAL WORD

The IDEIA has historically been reflective of how society views children with disabilities and how they are to be educated. In 1975, the intent of the law was to mandate appropriate education for all children. This intent, to open the schoolhouse doors to all children with disabilities, has largely been successful. In more recent years, along with regular education reform, there has been a shift to focusing on outcomes for children, or results, as opposed to inputs, or resources placed into the system. No longer is a program considered successful based on the amount of resources added. Program success is now based, in part, on the outcomes that individual children met as a result of the program. Additionally, the lines between special education and regular education continue to fade, resulting in a more unified system of education for all children.

REFERENCES

Bush, G. W. (2004, December). *President's remarks at the signing of H.R. 1350: Individuals With Disabilities Education Improvement Act of 2004*. Retrieved from the White House Web site, http://www.whitehouse.gov/news/releases/2004/12/20041203–6.html

Honig v. Doe, 479 U.S. 1804 (1988).

Turnbull, H. R., & Turnbull, A. P. (2000). *Free appropriate public education: The law and children with disabilities* (6th ed.). Denver, CO: Love Publishing Co.

Weishaar, M. K. (2007). *Case studies in special education law: No Child Left Behind Act and Individuals With Disabilities Education Improvement Act*. Upper Saddle River, NJ: Prentice Hall Publishers.

CHAPTER 4

From Policy to Practice

IDEIA and Evidence-Based Practice

Ronnie Detrich

Scientific research has become a cornerstone of education policy as a result of the reauthorization of the Individuals With Disabilities Education Improvement Act (IDEIA) (2004) and the passing of the No Child Left Behind legislation (NCLB) (2001). The emphasis on scientific research reflects a significant change and will affect how educational personnel are trained and services are provided to students who are at risk of academic and behavioral difficulties as well as those students who have been qualified for special education services. This shift is part of a larger professional movement toward evidence-based practices that began in medicine and is emerging in other disciplines (Sackett, Straus, Richardson, Rosenberg, & Haynes, 2000). Education and related disciplines within psychology have been part of the discussion of evidence-based practices since the mid-1990s when the Society for the Study of School Psychology and various divisions within the American Psychological Association began developing mechanisms for validating interventions as evidence-based (Chambless et al., 1996; Kratochwill & Stoiber, 2000).

Author Note: I would like to thank Cheryl Estradié for far too many readings of this manuscript and the many helpful comments to improve it. The weaknesses remain mine. I would also like to thank Jin An for all of the technical assistance and support necessary to complete this document. This chapter would not have been completed without their tireless efforts.

Ultimately, the evidence-based practice movement is a consumer protection movement. On the face of it, the basic premise of the evidence-based movement is very simple. If practitioners use interventions that have research support to address the concerns of their consumers then benefit is more probable. While this assumption seems relatively straightforward, realizing the benefits of evidence-based practice will require resolving a great many issues. The purpose of this chapter is to review the specific policy mandates of IDEIA, describe some of the issues of the evidence-based practice movement, and discuss the implications of these policies within the context of the evidence-based practice movement.

POLICY

The discussion of the relationship between IDEIA and evidence-based practice should start with the specific language in the legislation. Within this context, the intent of IDEIA is that interventions are derived from scientifically based research (IDEIA, 2004). This is emphasized in four areas:

1. Pre-service and professional development should prepare those who work with students with disabilities with the knowledge and skills to implement scientifically based instructional practices.
2. Providing whole school approaches, scientifically based early reading programs, positive behavioral interventions and supports, and early intervening services to reduce the need to label children as disabled in order to address the learning and behavioral needs of such children.
3. In determining whether a child has a specific learning disability, a local educational agency may use a process that determines if the child responds to scientific, research-based interventions as part of the evaluation procedures.
4. Services specified in the individualized education program (IEP) are to be based on peer-reviewed research to the extent practicable.

There are several implicit assumptions in the federal policies regarding the use of evidence-based practices. The first assumption is that there is an established body of evidence-based interventions. If we accept for the moment that a body of evidence-based interventions exists, it is further assumed that educational decision makers such as superintendents, administrators, school psychologists, teachers, and curriculum committees are aware of this evidence. Finally, even if a body of evidence does indeed exist and decision makers are aware of it, it is assumed that these interventions can be directly translated from the research base to practice settings. It is likely that in many instances these assumptions are not valid in the current educational environment. The reasons this is so will be discussed throughout the rest of this chapter.

Given the weight that is placed on scientifically based research, it is important to define what counts and what does not count as research within these regulations. Anticipating such a question, scientifically based research has been defined in the regulations supporting IDEIA (Assistance to States for the Education of Children With Disabilities and Preschool Grants for Children With Disabilities, 2006) as research that involves the application of rigorous, systematic, and objective procedures to obtain reliable and valid knowledge relevant to education activities and programs; and research that:

1. Employs systematic, empirical methods that draw on observation or experiment;
2. Involves rigorous data analyses that are adequate to test the stated hypotheses and justify the general conclusions drawn;
3. Relies on measurement or observational methods that provide reliable and valid data across evaluators and observers, across multiple measurements and observations, and across studies by the same or different investigators;
4. Is evaluated using experimental or quasi-experimental designs in which individuals, entities, programs, or activities are assigned to different conditions and with appropriate controls to evaluate the effects of the condition of interest, with a preference for random assignment experiments, or other designs to the extent that those designs contain within conditions or across conditions controls.
5. Ensures that experimental studies are presented in sufficient detail and clarity to allow for replication or, at a minimum, offer the opportunity to build systematically on their findings; and
6. Has been accepted by a peer-reviewed journal or approved by a panel of independent experts through a comparably rigorous, objective, and scientific review.

This definition would appear to be an adequate definition of scientific research but there are other definitions within federal law and there are controversies regarding the definition (Eisenhart & Towne, 2003). At the heart of this controversy is the apparent emphasis on a positivistic view of science with its preference for experimental methods. The issues regarding what constitutes evidence are discussed in detail in subsequent sections.

SCOPE OF THE PROBLEM

After all of these years of research in education, one has to wonder why it was necessary to mandate scientifically based instructional practices. A second question that arises is what has been guiding instruction if educators were not taking advantage of the relevant research. In this section, some context is provided that suggests why scientifically based research was written into IDEIA (2004).

Kazdin (2000) has identified over 550 named interventions for children and adolescents. Of these, only a very small number have been empirically evaluated. Kazdin and colleagues (Kazdin, Siegel, & Bass, 1990; Weisz & Kazdin, 2003) have reported that the most preferred and common interventions in practice settings have not been evaluated.

The fact that practitioners are not using evidence-based interventions raises questions about their training. Data suggest that evidence-based interventions are not usually taught in training programs. In a survey of training directors in school psychology, 29% of the directors reported that they were not familiar with the evidence-based interventions in the survey and another 30% reported that they were somewhat familiar (Shernoff, Kratochwill, & Stoiber, 2003). In this same survey, 41% of the directors reported that the students received no exposure to the evidence-based interventions listed in the survey. If students were exposed to an intervention, it was largely through didactic course work or observation rather than direct experience (Shernoff et al., 2003). The consequence is that students in school psychology are not being prepared to implement evidence-based interventions.

In a similar survey of directors of clinical training in psychology (Crits-Christoph, Chambless, Frank, Brody, & Karp, 1995), it was reported that, on average, these programs provided any training on slightly less than half of the 25 interventions that were identified as empirically validated. Perhaps of greater concern is that the range for training in evidence-based interventions was from 0%–96%. Finally, one-fifth of the programs reported that they provided no training in 75% or more of the validated interventions. The results of these surveys are disappointing. It is likely that clinicians working in practice settings have not been informed of or trained to implement empirically validated interventions.

The situation may not be any better for teacher training. In a recent survey (Walsh, Glaser, & Wilcox, 2006) on how university teacher training programs were addressing the science of reading as defined by the National Reading Panel (National Institute of Child Health and Human Development [NICHD], 2000), 42% of the universities surveyed failed to provide any instruction in five components of good reading instruction. Another 13% addressed only one of the five components. Only 15% of the universities sampled taught all five components. The data from these three surveys are not promising if scientifically based research is to guide educators' decisions about how to deliver instruction. The policy of IDEIA may be placing a responsibility on educators for which they have not been prepared.

EVIDENCE-BASED PRACTICE

Often in the discussion of evidence-based practice, identifying interventions that are evidence-based dominates much of the discussion. Identifying evidence-based interventions is a necessary first step but is not sufficient to assure that validated interventions will be implemented or that they will have the desired effects. As described in Figure 4.1, it is also necessary to address the myriad of issues associated with implementing evidence-based practices and evaluating interventions to determine if the practices are actually effective in a specific circumstance. The survey data reported above (Crits-Christoph et al., 1995; Shernoff et al., 2003; Walsh et al., 2006) certainly suggest that identifying evidence-based interventions does not automatically lead to implementation in practice settings. The research-to-practice gap has been a frequent topic of concern for scholars interested in promoting evidence-based education (Schoenwald & Hoagwood, 2001; Shriver & Watson, 2005; Walker, 2004). Even without the research-to-practice gap, interventions validated in research settings will not automatically translate into effective practices in practice settings. There are many issues related to organizational structure and culture, training, and resource issues that must be addressed (Chorpita, 2003; Fixsen, Naoom, Blase, Friedman, & Wallace, 2005; Schaughency & Ervin, 2006). Selecting evidence-based interventions and implementing them well does not assure that they will be successful, it is necessary to evaluate the effects in the practice setting to verify that results are being achieved. Progress monitoring data can be considered to be practice-based evidence about an evidence-based practice.

The rapid spread in the use of the term *evidence-based* in psychology, education, and related disciplines has resulted in some confusion about what the term means. Evidence-based practice has been defined as "the integration of best research evidence with clinical expertise and patient values" (Sackett et al., 2000). The American Psychological Association (APA) has adopted a very similar statement as its definition (2005). The evidence-based practice movement is an effort to assure that scientific knowledge informs the practitioner's decisions regarding interventions; however, it does not minimize the decision-making responsibility of the individual practitioner. Scientific knowledge functions as a filter in the selection of interventions but clinical expertise also informs the ultimate

Identify

Evidence-based
Intervention

Evaluate   **Implement**

FIGURE 4.1   Comprehensive process for evidence-based practice.

details of the intervention. While there is some divergence of opinion about the role of manuals and strict adherence to the intervention protocol (Elliott & Mihalic, 2004), there is nothing in the Sackett et al. (2000) definition that requires strict adherence to intervention manuals and protocols. Several authors have discussed the importance of adapting educational interventions to fit local circumstances to increase the probability that the intervention will be implemented with sufficient integrity to have an impact (Albin, Lucyshyn, Horner, & Flannery, 1996; Detrich, 1999).

Federal legislation and professional movement toward evidence-based practice are two sources of influence on the evidence-based practice movement within education. A third source of influence is the ethical guidelines of most professional organizations responsible for providing services for school-age children. These organizations have embedded in their codes of ethical conduct statements regarding reliance on scientific knowledge to inform practice. APA requires its members to base their work on the "established scientific and professional knowledge of the discipline" (American Psychological Association, 2002). The National Association of School Psychology (NASP) has a number of standards relevant to basing practice on scientific research. Specifically, school psychology faculty has the responsibility to train students in research-based services, school psychologists are to use service methods that are research-based, decision making is to be primarily databased, and interventions are to be modified and discontinued as the data indicate.

Similarly, the Behavior Analyst Certification Board (BACB) has standards that emphasize the importance of evidence in the delivery of behavioral services. The BACB Guidelines for Responsible Conduct (2004) encourage behavior analysts to recommend scientifically supported treatment to clients, to collect data to assess progress, and to modify programs on the basis of data.

It is clear from the various ethical conduct codes that reliance on interventions with a scientific base is responsible, ethical behavior. Following the implementation of an evidence-based intervention, it is also responsible conduct to evaluate the impact and make changes to the program based on data. This interaction between research and practice is the heart of evidence-based practice.

In addition to the ethical standards from professional organizations, there is another form of ethical responsibility for those providing services in public school settings. That responsibility is a fiduciary responsibility. A fiduciary responsibility exists when one person or group is responsible for managing the money of a second person or group. Public instruction is largely funded by public funds and there is an implicit assumption that the money will be spent for the public good. It could be argued that those responsible for providing educational services have a fiduciary responsibility to assure that the services are a good investment by the taxpayers by being of benefit to the students. Interventions that have an evidence-base are more likely to produce positive benefits than unevaluated interventions. We know about the effects of evaluated interventions. We do not know about the effects of unevaluated interventions. The emphasis on accountability in NCLB (2001) can be viewed as part of the fiduciary responsibility.

Establishing Interventions as Evidence-Based

The broad interest in evidence-based practice is not without controversy (Norcross, Beutler, & Levant, 2006). At the center of this controversy are issues related to the nature of evidence and the process by which interventions are validated as evidence-based. Without a clear definition of evidence, there can be no process by which interventions are validated as evidence-based; however, a definition of evidence is not sufficient. There must also be a process for determining the strength of evidence across a series of studies. Figure 4.2 describes how the process works. Imagine a series of filters in which all research evidence is poured. The filter is set to eliminate studies that are not of adequate quality. Once the evidence has been filtered, it then is subjected to filtering through methods for obtaining evidence; only some evidence will make it through this filter.

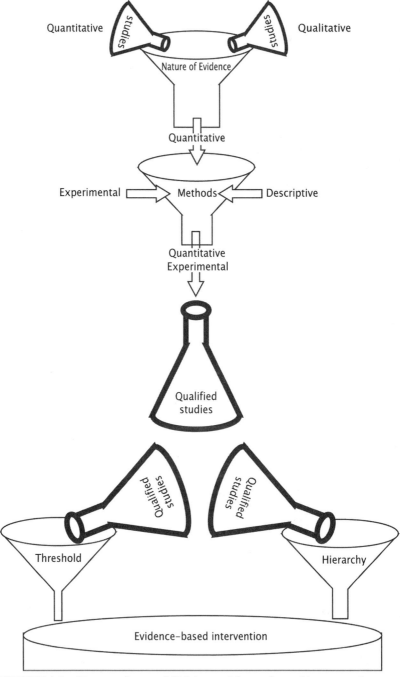

FIGURE 4.2   Process for establishing evidence-based interventions.

The research evidence that passes through these two filters results in a pool of qualified studies that are then put through a strength of evidence filter. At the end of this filtering process is a pool of evidence-based interventions. The remainder of this section will address in detail the different filters that evidence must go through in order to make statements about the evidence base of an intervention.

Nature of Evidence

Inherent in the values of evidence-based practice are the ideas that consumers should be part of the decision-making process and that information about the evidentiary status of an intervention is necessary for informed consent. Disciplines struggling with issues related to becoming more evidence-based have to answer the fundamental question regarding what counts as evidence (Drake, Latimer, Leff, McHugo, & Burns, 2004) before interventions can be meaningfully described as evidence-based. The regulations (Assistance to States for the Education of Children With Disabilities, 2006) offer one definition of scientific research and, as noted, there is controversy within the field over the adequacy of the definition (Eisenhart & Towne, 2003).

The scientific method is but one approach to knowing the world around us and is the clear preference in IDEIA (2004). Even if the scientific method is accepted as the best means for knowing, there are still many questions to be answered. The scientific method includes different types of evidence and different methods for obtaining it.

Types of Evidence

The first evidence filter concerns the nature of evidence. Evidence falls into the categories of either quantitative or qualitative evidence. Quantitative evidence reflects events that can be counted such as words read correctly per minute and can be independently verified by a second person. Qualitative evidence is a subjective measure of an event and cannot be independently verified by a second observer. Rating scales about treatment acceptability are an example of qualitative evidence. Even though a numerical rating on a Likert scale is assigned to a level of acceptability (1 = extremely unacceptable; 4 = very acceptable), the rating has no status apart from the subjective experience of the rater and the rating cannot be independently verified as true or accurate. Both types of evidence are legitimate within science with the proviso that each should be used to answer the types of questions for which they were designed (Shavelson & Towne, 2002). One of the criticisms by some researchers of the definition of scientific research used in IDEIA (Assistance to States for the Education of Children With Disabilities, 2006) is that the definition is drawn too narrowly so that only quantitative evidence is acceptable.

Methods of Obtaining Evidence

Once evidence has been put through the nature of evidence filter, the next filter is methods for obtaining evidence. The methods for obtaining evidence are categorized as either experimental or descriptive research. Experimental research systematically changes one variable at a time and then measures the impact of that change so that statements about causation (cause and effect) can be made. Systematically varying the level of difficulty of a reading passage and then measuring the number of words read correctly per minute is an example of experimental research.

Descriptive research measures the relationships between two or more variables. Monitoring a child's disruptive behavior across activities during the day is an example of descriptive research. Nothing is systematically changed to evaluate the impact but rather changes in disruptive behavior as a function of the activity are recorded. Evidence from descriptive research methods is correlational so no statements of causation can be made.

The first priority in an evidence-based approach is identifying interventions that are effective for a particular problem. The perspective in this chapter is that quantitative, experimental evidence is the best method for establishing this type of knowledge because it can directly demonstrate causal relations. If a causal relation between an intervention and a class of behaviors is not established then discussions about qualitative aspects (i.e., acceptability) of the intervention and its effects are unimportant. An ineffective intervention is unacceptable and high ratings of acceptability do not justify implementation. Descriptive methods and qualitative evidence may guide researchers to important variables that can then be evaluated experimentally but they cannot demonstrate the impact of an intervention in a causal sense. This perspective is consistent with the definition of scientific research in the regulations supporting IDEIA (Assistance to States for the Education of Children With Disabilities, 2006).

For the practitioner, there are advantages to limiting the discussion of evidence-based interventions to experimental demonstrations of impact. The primary benefit is that claims of effectiveness will be based on direct demonstrations of causal relations and are consistent with the policies in IDEIA (2004). The lack of experimental evidence does not necessarily imply that an intervention is ineffective but, perhaps, that it has not been evaluated; however, IDEIA and responsible, ethical conduct dictates that practitioners recommend interventions that have a scientific base.

Strength of Evidence

Limiting the discussion to quantitative, experimental evidence does not solve all of the problems for the practitioner. There is a large amount of experimental evidence in the professional journals and not all of it is of the same quality or consistent with respect to the findings. It is axiomatic that more than one research study is necessary to establish an intervention as evidence-based. If one study is not enough then the question becomes how many studies are required and what quality is necessary to validate an intervention as evidence-based. The challenge is how to aggregate evidence across studies so that statements about the evidentiary status of an intervention can be made. The final phase of establishing interventions as evidence-based involves filtering a body of intervention research through a set of evidence standards to determine if there is sufficient strength of evidence to validate the intervention as evidence-based. This phase of the process is represented in the bottom third of Figure 4.2. There are two approaches for determining strength of evidence: threshold and hierarchy of evidence.

The threshold approach requires a specific quantity and quality of research to validate an intervention as being evidence-based. Without a sufficient quantity or quality then it cannot be determined that there is adequate evidence about the impact of an intervention. In the threshold approach, the common standard is two randomized clinical trials showing impact to make claims that the intervention is evidence-based (Coalition for Evidence-Based Policy, 2003; Edlund, Gronseth, So, & Franklin, 2005; What Works Clearinghouse, 2006). If these strength of evidence criteria are not met, the intervention cannot be considered evidence-based even if there is a large body of research on the topic but not of the type that meets the standard. The concern with a threshold approach is that effective interventions may not be validated as evidence-based because there is insufficient research that meets the threshold criteria.

The hierarchy of evidence approach places the strength of evidence along a continuum. Within this approach, more research can be considered in the review. Essentially, there are different thresholds for different points on the continuum. For example, the Task Force on Evidence-Based Interventions in School Psychology (2003) has four levels in their classification system (Strong Evidence, Promising Evidence, Marginal/Weak Evidence, and No Evidence). The limitation with a hierarchy of evidence approach is that an intervention may be determined to be effective when, in fact, it is not. With either type of approach, there are inherent risks. One approach may be too restrictive and the other may be too inclusive.

The bias in this chapter is that some evidence, even though it may not be of a high quality is better than no evidence for the purposes of guiding decisions. Given the relative infancy of the evidence-based practice movement in education, perhaps it is better to err on the side of being too inclusive. Practitioners must make decisions about interventions every day and it is better that those decisions be based on credible, if not perfect, evidence rather than allowing other sources of information to solely influence these decisions. Waiting for research that meets the more rigorous evidentiary standards of a threshold approach will leave the practitioner with little evidence-based guidance when selecting an intervention. Relying on the current best available evidence gives the practitioner a basis for making decisions. For the practitioner it becomes necessary to understand the strength of evidence associated with a particular intervention, the standards for establishing the strength of evidence, and a willingness to revise intervention options as better evidence emerges. This approach is consistent with the definition of evidence-based practice (Sackett et al., 2000) to rely on the best available scientific evidence and is consistent with the mandates of IDEIA (2004) to base interventions on scientifically based research.

Approaches to Standards of Evidence

In the last few years, a number of different professional organizations have developed standards for determining the strength of evidence. Given that there are multiple standards, it is possible for an intervention to be validated as evidence-based by one set of standards while failing to meet criteria with a different set of standards. This highlights the difference between threshold and hierarchy approaches. For example, the What Works Clearinghouse (http://w-w-c.org/) utilizes a threshold approach that requires studies based on group designs; randomized clinical trials are necessary to validate an intervention as "meeting evidence standards." Currently, there is no place for single participant research designs in the What Works Clearinghouse evidence standards (*What Works Clearinghouse Review Process Standards,* n.d.); therefore, any intervention evaluated with single participant designs will be classified as "does not meet evidence screens." On the other hand, the same intervention reviewed with standards from the National Autism Center's National Standards Project (Wilczynski, 2006) may well meet evidentiary criteria. The differences in standards leave the practitioner with the responsibility to determine which standards were used to evaluate an intervention.

Limitations of Standards

The recent interest in evidence-based interventions in education and mental health is an excellent start but there is much work to do. At this time, there is relatively little information about which interventions are evidence-based because once standards are developed it is then necessary to filter the body of knowledge through them. Until these reviews are completed, there can be no statements about the evidentiary status for an intervention. These reviews are ongoing but it will take some time before a significant number of interventions have been evaluated with a set of standards.

An Example: The Good Behavior Game

As described above, the process for validating an intervention as evidence-based can be lengthy and complex. The understanding of this process may be facilitated with an example. The Good Behavior Game (GBG) is an intervention designed to reduce disruptive behaviors of school-age children. There are several variations of the game but all of the variations require that the group as a whole meet some behavioral criterion before any of the students can have access to special privileges. In most instances, the group is divided into teams that compete to win the game and access to the privileges. The Good Behavior Game was first described by Barrish, Saunders, and Wolf (1969) and demonstrated the efficacy of the intervention for fourth grade general education students. In subsequent years, the robustness of the effects of the GBG was demonstrated across different ages of students, different behaviors, and different settings (Fishbein & Wasik, 1981; Harris & Sherman, 1973; Medland & Stachnik, 1972; Saigh & Umar, 1983). Initially, the research evaluated the short-term impact of the GBG on disruptive behaviors but more recently researchers have been evaluating the long-term impact on a variety of social behaviors such as smoking, substance use, mental health adjustment, high school graduation, and conduct in school in subsequent years (Dolan et al., 1993; Furr-Holden, Ialongo, Anthony, Petras, & Kellam, 2004; Ialongo, Poduska, Werthamer, & Kellam, 2001; Kellam & Anthony, 1998; Storr, Ialongo, Kellam, & Anthony, 2002).

While this research gives us a knowledge base about the effects of the GBG, it is not sufficient to validate the GBG as an evidence-based intervention. To make statements about the evidentiary status of the GBG, it is necessary to evaluate the strength of the evidence regarding the GBG against a set of evidence standards. Toward this end, Stage and Quiroz (1997) completed a meta-analysis of interventions to decrease disruptive classroom behaviors in public school settings. Included in this review were group consequence programs such as the GBG. The results of this study suggest that group consequence programs have a powerful effect on disruptive behavior. While this is certainly an encouraging result, it does not definitively validate the GBG as an evidence-based intervention because the GBG was only one type of group consequence program that was evaluated, and the effects of the GBG were not evaluated separately from all group-based interventions.

The next step in validating the GBG as an evidence-based intervention was a systematic review of published research on the GBG between 1969 and 2002 (Tingstrom, Sterling-Turner, & Wilczynski, 2006). In this report, 29 studies were reviewed and it was concluded that there was sufficient evidence to warrant the use of the GBG. There are limitations to this review that warrants caution with respect to validating the intervention as an evidence-based intervention. The major limitation of the review is that the standards for including and excluding studies from the review are not described so it is not possible to know how representative the reviewed studies are. Even with this limitation, this review in conjunction with the meta-analysis described above (Stage & Quiroz, 1997) supports the conclusion there is an emerging basis for considering the GBG an evidence-based intervention.

The final stage in validating the GBG as an evidence-based intervention is for an independent organization to review a series of studies against published standards to determine if the strength of evidence of the reviewed studies is sufficient to validate the intervention as evidence-based. The GBG was reviewed (Coalition for Evidence-Based Policy, n.d.) and it was determined that the reviewed studies did meet evidence criteria to be validated as an evidence-based intervention, at least as it was implemented in the reviewed studies. The Coalition for Evidence-Based Policy reviews only randomized clinical trials and uses standards developed by the U.S. Office of Management and Budget to determine strength of evidence (United States Office of Management and Budget, n.d.). Limiting reviews to studies utilizing randomized clinical trials significantly restricts the number of studies of the GBG that can be reviewed. Most of the research on the GBG has utilized single subject designs, and were therefore not reviewed. The meta-analysis by Stage and Quiroz (1997) did include studies that utilized single subject designs, so, taken together with the review by the Coalition for Evidence-Based Policy (n.d.), the evidence from multiple sources suggests that the GBG is an evidence-based intervention and should be used in public schools to reduce disruptive behavior.

In the case of the GBG, the time lag between initial research and validation as an evidence-based intervention was very long. This is, in part, a function of the very recent rise of independent organizations developing standards and reviewing interventions. This rise has been influenced by the passage of NCLB (2001) and IDEIA (2004). One impact of the policy is that the interval between initial efficacy research and validation as an evidence-based practice should become shorter. Hoagwood, Burns, and Weisz (2002) have proposed a model for moving research more rapidly and systematically toward the validation of an intervention as evidence-based.

If the goal is to give practitioners sufficient information for decision making it will be necessary for researchers to work more systematically toward this end than has been the case historically.

IMPLEMENTING THE INTERVENTION

Much of the preceding discussion has been about what is required to identify interventions as being evidence-based; however, identifying an evidence-based intervention does not assure it will be effective in a practice setting. There are many characteristics of research that make the generalization from a research setting to a practice setting tenuous. A primary function of intervention research is to establish a causal relationship between an intervention and a class of behaviors (Johnston & Pennypacker, 1993). In order to obtain unambiguous results, researchers often impose strict subject selection criteria and carefully arrange the research environment. Participants with comorbid conditions along with the primary diagnosis are usually excluded from a study because these other conditions may moderate the impact of an intervention. Similarly, those responsible for implementing the intervention may have a higher level of training, may be supervised more closely to assure high treatment integrity, and may have a greater investment in the outcomes than their counterparts in the typical practice setting. Finally, the research setting may have many more financial and other resources available than typical practice settings. Often these differences make it difficult to directly translate efficacious research-based interventions to practice settings. Because of these differences, practitioners often view research as irrelevant, impractical, and impossible (Hoagwood, Burns, Kiser, Ringeisen, & Schoenwald, 2001; Kazdin, 2004; Schoenwald & Hoagwood, 2001; Shriver & Watson, 2005).

Much of the published research is efficacy research, which has the specific function of identifying important variables contributing to intervention effectiveness (Chorpita, 2003; Kazdin, 2004; Schoenwald & Hoagwood, 2001; Shriver & Watson, 2005). For example, the impact of a reading curriculum might be examined in a university lab school with participants selected so that any student with reading difficulties are eliminated, the instruction is provided by graduate student research assistants who are monitored to assure the reading program is implemented with integrity. Under these conditions, any positive result can be attributed to the reading program. A second type of research that is published less often is effectiveness research, which evaluates the impact of an intervention under more typical conditions (Chorpita, 2003; Kazdin, 2004; Schoenwald & Hoagwood, 2001; Shriver & Watson, 2005). Examining the impact of a reading program when implemented by public school teachers under typical conditions with students who may have reading difficulty is an example of effectiveness research. The differences between the research setting and the practice setting often result in interventions losing some impact as they move from efficacy research to effectiveness research.

The challenge for the practitioner is to select interventions that have evidentiary support under conditions similar to the conditions in which the practitioner is working. To make the determination about which intervention is most appropriate, the practitioner has to compare the characteristics of the research subjects, those responsible for implementation, and the research setting against these same characteristics for the client they are serving and the setting in which they are working. By making these comparisons, the practitioner can have greater confidence that the intervention will be effective in a specific setting.

Considerations When Selecting an Intervention

While it may seem logical to select an intervention with the strongest evidence rating, there are contextual variables that may result in selecting an intervention with a lower evidence rating (Albin et al., 1996; Ringeisen, Henderson, & Hoagwood, 2003). A lower evidence rating does not imply that an intervention is less effective but rather the strength of evidence does not meet higher evidentiary standards. For example, Lovaas (1996) has suggested that teachers implementing discrete trial procedures wear protective clothing such as bathing caps and heavy covers over arms and legs to prevent injury from physical assault. There is a growing evidence-base for discrete trial methods (Eikeseth, Smith, Jahr, & Eldevik, 2002; McEachin, Smith, & Lovaas, 1993); however, in many public school settings, these precautions are so different from the existing culture that it is unlikely that teaching staff would wear the recommended protective clothing. Without the protective clothing the risk of injury increases. This may result in teachers being unwilling to implement those elements that occasion aggressive behavior. Selectively implementing the discrete trial procedures may lower treatment integrity to such an extent that the child with autism would not benefit from the intervention.

In such a setting, an alternative may be to choose an intervention that has a lower evidence rating but has greater acceptability such as incidental teaching (Hart & Risley, 1975; Koegel & Koegel, 1995). These methods take advantage of the child's motivation and interest. This may result in lower frequencies of aggression, which reduces the need for protective clothing and may increase treatment integrity. Implementing the intervention with greater integrity may result in greater benefit for the child even though incidental teaching methods may have lower evidence ratings than discrete trial procedures.

Issues of Implementation

Once an intervention is selected, issues of training and treatment integrity become primary concerns. An evidence-based intervention will more likely be effective if it is implemented well. There is no reason to assume that those responsible for implementation will be skilled in any or all of the procedural details of an intervention. It may be necessary for the practitioner to train those responsible for implementation in the details of the procedure and then monitor to assure that there has not been drift from the protocols. Direct training of the elements of an intervention can increase treatment integrity (Sterling-Turner, Watson, & Moore, 2002), but it has been well documented that intervention without routine follow-up assessments of treatment integrity will result in declines in the accuracy of implementation (Mortenson & Witt, 1998; Noell, Witt, Gilbertson, Ranier, & Freeland, 1997; Witt, Noell, LaFleur, & Mortenson, 1997). Witt, VanDerHeyden, and Gilbertson (2004) have suggested systematically evaluating treatment integrity across four domains: problem definition and monitoring, classroom instruction and behavior management, intervention integrity, and intervention design.

Research-Informed Interventions

The requirements of IDEIA for educational practitioners to implement scientifically based interventions are in place now. It will be difficult for the practitioner to proceed because relatively few reviews validating interventions have been completed. Without easy access to reliable and relevant information, the practitioner is in the position of relying on other sources of information to select interventions, which is inconsistent with the intent of IDEIA (2004). Reliance on sources such as expert opinion is also contrary to an evidence-based practice approach because this and other alternatives to evidence have many sources of potential bias (Gambrill, 2005).

Until more interventions are validated, an alternative is to construct interventions that contain elements that are informed by the scientific principles of behavior. For example, if we are interested in increasing the language skills of young children with autism, there is a very large body of evidence to support using positive reinforcement procedures. Demonstrations of the effects of positive reinforcement on a wide variety of behaviors, including language, are readily available (Cooper, Heron, & Heward, 1987). More specifically, there are many examples of using positive reinforcement to increase language skills of individuals with autism (Koegel & Koegel, 1995). Despite the variety of procedures, there are at least two commonalities: high rates of opportunities to respond and high rates of positive reinforcement for correct responding. It would logically follow that an intervention based on these principles would more likely be effective than an intervention not based on these principles. When there are high levels of correspondence between the scientific principles of behavior and the components of an intervention, then it is safe to make claims that the specific intervention is scientifically based. This method for developing interventions is considered to be research-informed rather than evidence-based because it has not been directly evaluated. The assumption that this method will be effective is inductively derived from a large body of research. To make definitive statements about the evidence base for the intervention the evidence must be experimentally evaluated.

The Reading First initiative is a large-scale example of the research-informed approach. Reading First was authorized as part of NCLB (2001) requiring that all schools receiving Title 1 funds use scientifically based reading research to guide the selection of reading programs. The National Reading Panel (NICHD, 2000) in a thorough review of reading research identified five elements to effective reading programs: phonemic awareness, phonics, vocabulary, fluency, and reading comprehension. The Reading First guidelines require that reading programs funded through Title 1 contain all five elements making it research-informed. There is no requirement that any reading program be validated as evidence-based. Obviously, there are limits to such an approach but until the evidence base is better established, it is a reasonable approximation toward the final goal of assuring that all students are taught with evidence-based reading programs.

Modifying Evidence-Based Interventions

In the scholarly discussion of evidence-based practice, much has been made of the tension between implementing the intervention as it was validated and modifying the intervention to reflect local circumstances (Chorpita, 2003; Elliott & Mihalic, 2004; Hoagwood, Burns, & Weisz, 2002). The problem arises when the modifications to the intervention change it in ways that have not been evaluated, resulting in questions about its evidentiary status. The research-informed approach of basing the modifications on established principles of behavior maintains the scientific integrity of the intervention and is consistent with the definition of evidence-based practice (Sackett et al., 2000). Starting with the best available scientific evidence allows the practitioner to make judgments about how to arrange an intervention so that it is the best match for the individual. Relying on a research-informed approach also recognizes the realities of working with individuals in special education. The unique characteristics of each student and the living and educational settings in which they are served will almost always necessitate modifications to existing evidence-based protocols.

This research-informed approach offers advantages for the practitioner. It allows the development of interventions informed by science-based knowledge when no interventions have been validated as evidence based. Additionally, it allows the practitioner to modify an evidence-based intervention to reflect contextual variables that exist for a particular individual or family.

EVALUATING THE INTERVENTION: PROGRESS MONITORING

In a comprehensive evidence-based practice approach, evaluating the effects of an intervention or progress monitoring is the third fundamental component as described in Figure 4.1. Using evidence-based interventions increases the probability of success but it does not guarantee it. It is necessary to assess the impact of the intervention to assure that the benefits are actually achieved. As described in the codes of ethical conduct for NASP and BACB, progress monitoring is responsible, ethical behavior (BACB, 2004; NASP, 2000).

The basic principle of progress monitoring is that frequent and systematic sampling of performance is necessary to determine if progress is occurring and at what rate (Bushell & Baer, 1994; Cooper et al., 1987). Curriculum-based measurement procedures exemplify well-developed progress monitoring (Shinn, 1989). Progress monitoring data allow the practitioner, those responsible for implementation, and consumers (parents and students in special education programs) to have the same information when making programming decisions about continuing, adjusting, or discontinuing an intervention. Infrequent measures of performance are not useful for progress monitoring. For example, measuring a child's reading or math skills annually does not provide information frequently enough so that timely decisions can be made. Allowing a year to pass before making decisions increases the risk of a student not receiving any meaningful educational benefits.

The quality of decisions about the effect of an intervention is directly related to the quality of the obtained data. The methods used to assess progress must meet the standards of reliability and validity. Reliability refers to the assessment method producing consistent results across practitioners or conditions. For example, two individuals using the same method for assessing a child's reading fluency should obtain similar results. To the extent that this is true, then there is greater confidence in the obtained data. A valid instrument is one that measures what it purports to measure. In this instance, a valid measure of reading comprehension must start with the child reading a passage and then answering questions about the passage. A measure of reading comprehension that is based on someone else reading to a child is not valid because it measures listening comprehension. In an evidence-based practice approach, the quality of the data is of equal concern whether identifying, selecting, or evaluating the impact an intervention.

IDEIA IN CONTEXT OF
EVIDENCE-BASED PRACTICE

In many ways, the policy of IDEIA is visionary. The purpose of this section is to evaluate where we are currently in special education against the vision of IDEIA and the context of evidence-based practice.

Professional Development

The intent of IDEIA (2004) is that all personnel have the necessary skills and knowledge to implement scientifically based instructional practices. The assumption is that there is a body of knowledge about what constitutes scientifically based instruction. Given the relatively recent emergence of evidence-based practice in education, the reality is that there is very little agreement about what these practices are. The reviews to establish interventions as evidence based are just beginning to appear. If the surveys regarding the training of school psychologists, clinical psychologists, and reading teachers (Crits-Christoph et al., 1995; Shernoff et al., 2003; Walsh et al., 2006) are representative, then there are reasons for concern. It would appear that information about validated evidence-based interventions is not effectively disseminated to those responsible for delivering evidence-based interventions.

Similarly, the data are not encouraging regarding the quality of the training that does occur. Directors of training programs reported that most often students were exposed to evidence-based practices through didactic lectures or observation (Shernoff et al., 2003). This level of training is not likely to result in practitioners being able to implement interventions with the necessary skills to assure success. Generally, effective training requires direct coaching while the learner is acquiring the new skills and then periodic follow-up to assure that the intervention is being delivered according to the established protocols (Reid, Parsons, & Green, 1989).

Before professional development can meet the goals of IDEIA, it will be necessary to identify evidence-based interventions for academic and social domains. University training programs will have to reevaluate the way their curricula are constructed and how training is delivered. Failure to do so will leave practitioners poorly prepared to perform their responsibilities as defined by federal policy.

The situation for professionals currently working in the schools is also very difficult with respect to training. Many school districts have eliminated or significantly reduced the number of training days in an attempt to manage costs. Training often consists of brief in-services (1–2 hours), and the content of these trainings may not reflect what is known about evidence-based interventions. Even if the content is about evidence-based interventions, this approach to training does not assure that any skills have been acquired. For school districts to meet their responsibilities under IDEIA, it will be necessary for them to have easy access to information about which interventions have been validated as evidence-based. It will be equally important that they have access to individuals with the necessary competencies to provide meaningful training and that the infrastructure is organized in a way to support this training.

Early Intervention

Scientifically based interventions are the heart of services in the reauthorization of IDEIA. The assumption in the requirement to use "whole school, scientifically based early reading programs, positive behavioral interventions and supports, and early intervening services" (IDEIA, 2004) is that early intervention services will reduce the need to label children for the purposes of receiving specialized services. The emphasis on whole school functionally moves the mandate from special education policy to general education policy. Linking general education with special education represents a significant shift in the relationship between these two entities. Historically, special and general education has operated as separate systems with each having their own funding streams. To support the integration of special education and general education services, school districts are allowed to set aside 15% of their special education funds to serve general education students who are considered at risk for academic and social failure resulting in placement in special education services (Assistance to States for the Education of Children With Disabilities, 2006).

The emphasis on early intervention for at-risk students is largely influenced by the Public Health Service model of prevention (Munoz & Mrazek, 1996). One way of conceptualizing the approach is to organize services around primary, secondary, and tertiary prevention with scientific-based instruction as the cornerstone. In NCLB (2001), there are over 100 references to scientific research informing the selection of curricula and instructional practices. In this context, the policies of NCLB could be considered primary prevention. The policies of IDEIA could be considered secondary and tertiary prevention. The mechanisms in place in IDEIA (2004) for early intervention services for at-risk students are secondary prevention and for special education services are tertiary prevention.

If these services are to ultimately have impact on the number of students identified for special education, it will be necessary to have a school-wide system for monitoring the academic and social behavior of all students. Unless all students are monitored then it will not be possible to identify students requiring early intervention services. The logic of this is based on the response to intervention (RTI) approach (Brown-Chidsey & Steege, 2005). While a thorough review of RTI is beyond the scope of this chapter, the basic premise is that with frequent, systematic monitoring of student performance deficits can be identified and remediated early. This is a very different approach than has historically been the case for special education, which has been described as a "wait to fail" model (Kratochwill, Albers, & Shernoff, 2004), in which students have to experience failure before they can receive specialized services. The emphasis on progress monitoring is consistent with the model of evidence-based practice described in this chapter. In an RTI approach, students receive services based on research-based instructional methods and are then regularly assessed to assure that each student is making progress. Services are adjusted until each student is benefiting.

School-wide positive behavior support is the approach that has been most thoroughly developed in education using this prevention framework (Sugai & Horner, 2005). Using a systems perspective from the beginning, one of the requirements before initiating school-wide interventions is that at least 80% of the school staff agrees to make discipline one of the top three priorities for 3–5 years. Systematic data are collected about office referrals so that decisions can be made regarding the effectiveness of interventions. Periodically, independent reviewers evaluate the quality of the implementation to assure that the protocols are being followed (Sugai & Horner, 2005). This type of systemic approach is likely to be necessary for effective early intervention for academic problems.

Response to Intervention to Determine Eligibility

The dominant approach to identifying students with learning disabilities has been an approach that depends on a discrepancy between achievement and intellectual ability. This approach has usually required a two-year gap between a student's grade level and performance level on standardized tests to qualify students for special education. In recent years, the discrepancy model has been criticized (Fuchs, Mock, Morgan, & Young, 2003). The response to intervention approach described in IDEIA (2004) is an attempt to correct some of the difficulties inherent in the discrepancy model. As described in the preceding section, the RTI approach is a systems level intervention that involves school-wide monitoring of student performance to determine which students will require more intense interventions. In order for students to achieve greatest benefit from these more intensive interventions, federal policy requires that the interventions have a scientific research base (IDEIA, 2004). While determination for special education services is the responsibility of special educators, the responsibility for implementing scientific research-based interventions will fall to the whole school so it can be determined who is failing to respond to intervention. The first challenge to using RTI as an alternative method for determining eligibility will be to identify which interventions have the required scientific base. Once identified, the task becomes to assure that the interventions are being implemented with sufficient integrity so that valid decisions can be made. Finally, it will be necessary to establish criteria for making the determination that special education is warranted. Several models based on evaluating level and trend in performance data relative to non-risk students have been proposed (Fuchs & Fuchs, 2005).

While there is great promise in this approach, the infrastructure in most schools does not exist to support this type of approach for identifying students eligible for special education. It will be necessary for schools to have school-wide progress monitoring systems, practitioners knowledgeable about scientific research-based academic interventions, staff who are trained to implement these interventions, systems to assure treatment integrity, and mechanisms to assure that the progress monitoring data are being reviewed in a timely manner and decisions are based on these data.

Services Based on Peer-Reviewed Research

The federal policy (IDEIA, 2004) is clear that services specified in the individualized education program (IEP) are to be "based on peer review research to the maximum extent practicable." To accomplish this policy mandate, it will be necessary that those individuals responsible for developing the IEP are familiar with the peer-reviewed research. There are data to suggest that school psychologists spend approximately 1 hour per week reading the professional literature (Hosp & Reschly, 2002). If this is the case, it is unlikely that the school psychologists are sufficiently informed to assure that the services are based on the peer-reviewed research. A more promising approach is the clearinghouses (i.e., What Works Clearinghouse) that review the peer-reviewed research base and make statements about the evidentiary status of interventions. The policy in IDEIA (2004) certainly places a great responsibility on education professionals to be informed about the research base. The clearinghouses may reduce the burden on practitioners to find sufficient reading time to be informed of the peer-reviewed literature. Given the research of Kazdin and colleagues (Kazdin et al., 1990; Weisz & Kazdin, 2003), it may be optimistic to think that most professionals are aware of evidence-based interventions and have been well trained to implement them. It is also optimistic to assume that schools have the sufficient infrastructure to support these peer-reviewed interventions, which often require considerable technical skills and resources to be implemented effectively (Elliott & Mihalic, 2004).

SUMMARY

For those interested in assuring the knowledge base of educational research is effectively disseminated and implemented in public schools, the policies in IDEIA (2004) are very welcome. It may well be that these policies are more visionary rather than immediately realistic in the context of the current educational systems. It may take a decade before the full benefits of this policy are realized. The work of moving educational systems to a comprehensive evidence-based practice approach as described in this chapter will be difficult. Universities will have to change the way in which professionals are prepared; educational researchers will have to give much greater attention to how to place the research-based interventions into practice settings; school districts will have to rethink how to support educational services for all students. It will be necessary to redesign the infrastructure of public schools to train practitioners in evidence-based interventions and assure that the interventions are being implemented with integrity. The links between general education and special education will have to be made much stronger and the organizational barriers between the two eliminated. Finally, a great burden falls to the individual practitioner to be informed about the research base regarding interventions.

It has been suggested that educational innovations have a life span of 18–48 months (Latham, 1988). Latham (1988) identified a number of reasons for the short life of many educational innovations. Innovation requires great effort and often is more difficult to implement than expected, causes too much change, and takes too much time. Additionally, systems design issues may contribute to the failure of innovations to sustain. Among the design issues are that supporters of the innovation leave, personnel lack training, external funding is withdrawn, there is inadequate supervision during the transition, there is no accountability, and there are no consequences for early termination. If this holds true for IDEIA (2004), then the evidence-based approach risks being abandoned long before systemic changes are fully realized. When implementing school-wide positive behavior interventions, a 3–5 year commitment is required to train personnel and establish all of the necessary systems to assure that the interventions will be sustainable by the school without external support (Sugai & Horner, 2005). Given complexity of the systems change required to make educational systems more evidence-based, this type of commitment would seem to be the minimum necessary to produce the type of systems change envisioned in IDEIA (2004). Clearly, the work of bringing evidence-based practices to education represents an arduous and daunting endeavor. Perhaps the words of John F. Kennedy (1961) will provide inspiration, "All this will not be finished in the first hundred days. Nor will it be finished in the first thousand days, nor in the life of this administration, nor even perhaps in our lifetime on this planet. But let us begin."

REFERENCES

Albin, R. W., Lucyshyn, J. M., Horner, R. H., & Flannery, K. B. (1996). Contextual fit for behavioral support plans: A model for "goodness of fit." In L. K. Koegel, R. L. Koegel, & G. Dunlap (Eds.), *Positive behavioral support: Including people with difficult behavior in the community* (pp. 81–98). Baltimore: P. H. Brookes.

American Psychological Association. (2002, August). *Ethical principles of psychologists and code of conduct.* Retrieved December 5, 2006, from http://www.apa.org/ethics/code2002.pdf

American Psychological Association. (2005, August). *Policy statement on evidence-based practice.* Retrieved June 18, 2007, from http://www2.apa.org/practice/ebpstatement.pdf

Assistance to States for the Education of Children with Disabilities and Preschool Grants for Children with Disabilities; Final Rule, 71 Fed. Reg. 156 (2006) (to be codified at 34 C.F.R. pt. 300 and 301).

Barrish, H. H., Saunders, M., & Wolf, M. M. (1969). Good behavior game: Effects of individual contingencies for group consequences on disruptive behavior in a classroom. *Journal of Applied Behavior Analysis, 2*(2), 119–124.

Behavior Analyst Certification Board (BACB). (2004). *Behavior analyst certification board guidelines for responsible conduct for behavior analysts.* Retrieved December 5, 2006, from http://www.bacb.com/pages/download.html#guidelines

Brown-Chidsey, R., & Steege, M. W. (2005). *Response to intervention: Principles and strategies for effective practice.* New York: Guilford Press.

Bushell, D., & Baer, D. M. (1994). Measurably superior instruction means close, continual contact with the relevant outcome data: Revolutionary. In R. Gardner (Ed.), *Behavior analysis in education: Focus on measurably superior instruction* (pp. 3–10). Pacific Grove, CA: Brooks/Cole Pub. Co.

Chambless, D. L., Sanderson, W. C., Shoham, V., Johnson, S. B., Pope, K. S., Crits-Christoph, P., et al. (1996). An update on empirically validated therapies. *The Clinical Psychologist, 49*(2), 5–18.

Chorpita, B. F. (2003). The frontier of evidence-based practice. In A. E. Kazdin & J. R. Weisz (Eds.), *Evidence-based psychotherapies for children and adolescents* (pp. 42–59). New York: Guilford Press.

Coalition for Evidence-Based Policy. (n.d). *Good Behavior Game (A 1st–2nd grade class-room management strategy for decreasing aggressive/disruptive behavior)*. Retrieved August 14, 2007, from http://www.evidencebasedprograms.org/Default. aspx?tabid=154

Coalition for Evidence-Based Policy. (2003, December). *Identifying and implementing educational practices supported by rigorous evidence: A user friendly guide.* Retrieved June 18, 2007, from U.S. Department of Education Web site http://www.ed.gov/rschstat/ research/pubs/rigorousevid/index.html

Cooper, J. O., Heron, T. E., & Heward, W. L. (1987). *Applied behavior analysis.* Columbus, OH: Merrill Pub. Co.

Crits-Christoph, P., Chambless, D. L., Frank, E., Brody, C., & Karp, J. F. (1995). Training in empirically validated treatments: What are clinical psychology students learning? *Professional Psychology, Research and Practice, 26*(5), 514–522.

Detrich, R. (1999). Increasing treatment fidelity by matching interventions to contextual variables within the educational setting. *School Psychology Review, 28*(4), 608–620.

Dolan, L. J., Kellam, S. G., Brown, C. H., Werthamer-Larsson, L., Rebok, G. W., Mayer, L. S., et al. (1993). The short-term impact of two classroom-based preventive interventions on aggressive and shy behaviors and poor achievement. *Journal of Applied Developmental Psychology, 14*(3), 317–345.

Drake, R. E., Latimer, E. A., Leff, H. S., McHugo, G. J., & Burns, B. J. (2004). What is evidence? *Child and Adolescent Psychiatric Clinics of North America, 13*(4), 717–728.

Edlund, W., Gronseth, G., So, Y., & Franklin, G. (2005). *American Academy of Neurology clinical practice guideline process manual* (2004 ed.). Retrieved June 18, 2007, from http://www.aan.com/globals/axon/assets/2535.pdf

Eikeseth, S., Smith, T., Jahr, E., & Eldevik, S. (2002). Intensive behavioral treatment at school for 4- to 7-year-old children with autism: A 1-year comparison controlled study. *Behavior Modification, 26*(1), 49.

Eisenhart, M., & Towne, L. (2003). Contestation and change in national policy on "scientifically based" education research. *Educational Researcher, 32*(7), 31–38.

Elliott, D. S., & Mihalic, S. (2004). Issues in disseminating and replicating effective prevention programs. *Prevention Science, 5*(1), 47–53.

Fishbein, J. E., & Wasik, B. H. (1981). Effect of the good behavior game on disruptive library behavior. *Journal of Applied Behavior Analysis, 14*(1), 89–93.

Fixsen, D. L., Naoom, S. F., Blase, K. A., Friedman, R. M., & Wallace, F. (2005). *Implementation research: A synthesis of the literature* (FMHI Publication #231). Tampa: University of South Florida, Louis de la Parte Florida Mental Health Institute, The National Implementation Research Network.

Fuchs, D., Mock, D., Morgan, P. L., & Young, C. L. (2003). Responsiveness-to-intervention: Definitions, evidence, and implications for the learning disabilities construct. *Learning Disabilities Research & Practice, 18*(3), 157–171.

Fuchs, L. S., & Fuchs, D. (2005). Responsiveness to intervention: A blueprint for practitioners, policymakers, and parents. *Teaching Exceptional Children, 38*(1), 57–61.

Furr-Holden, C. D., Ialongo, N. S., Anthony, J. C., Petras, H., & Kellam, S. G. (2004). Developmentally inspired drug prevention: Middle school outcomes in a school-based randomized prevention trial. *Drug and Alcohol Dependence, 73*(2), 149–158.

Gambrill, E. D. (2005). *Critical thinking in clinical practice: Improving the quality of judgments and decisions* (2nd ed.). Hoboken, NJ: Wiley.

Harris, V. W., & Sherman, J. A. (1973). Use and analysis of the "good behavior game" to reduce disruptive classroom behavior. *Journal of Applied Behavior Analysis, 6*(3), 405–417.

Hart, B., & Risley, T. R. (1975). Incidental teaching of language in the preschool. *Journal of Applied Behavior Analysis, 8*, 411–420.

Hoagwood, K., Burns, B.J., Kiser, L., Ringeisen, H., & Schoenwald, S.K. (2001). Evidence-based practice in child and adolescent mental health services. *Psychiatric Services, 52*(9), 1179–1189.

Hoagwood, K., Burns, B.J., & Weisz, J.R. (2002). A profitable conjunction: From science to service in children's mental health. In B.J. Burns & K. Hoagwood (Eds.), *Community treatment for youth: Evidence-based interventions for severe emotional and behavioral disorders* (pp. 327–338). New York: Oxford University Press.

Hosp, J.L., & Reschly, D.J. (2002). Regional differences in school psychology practice. *School Psychology Review, 31*(1), 11.

Ialongo, N., Poduska, J., Werthamer, L., & Kellam, S. (2001). The distal impact of two first-grade preventive interventions on conduct problems and disorder in early adolescence. *Journal of Emotional & Behavioral Disorders, 9*(3), 146–160.

Individuals With Disabilities Education Improvement Act of 2004 (IDEIA), Pub. L. No. 108–446, 118 STAT. 2647 (2004).

Johnston, J.M., & Pennypacker, H.S. (1993). *Strategies and tactics of behavioral research* (2nd ed.). Hillsdale, NJ: L. Erlbaum Associates.

Kazdin, A.E. (2000). *Psychotherapy for children and adolescents: Directions for research and practice.* New York: Oxford University Press.

Kazdin, A.E. (2004). Evidence-based treatments: Challenges and priorities for practice and research. *Child and Adolescent Psychiatric Clinics of North America, 13*(4), 923–940, vii.

Kazdin, A.E., Siegel, T.C., & Bass, D. (1990). Drawing on clinical practice to inform research on child and adolescent psychotherapy: Survey of practitioners. *Professional Psychology: Research and Practice, 21*(3), 189–198.

Kellam, S.G., & Anthony, J.C. (1998). Targeting early antecedents to prevent tobacco smoking: Findings from an epidemiologically based randomized field trial. *American Journal of Public Health, 88*(10), 1490–1495.

Kennedy, J.F. (1961). Inaugural address. In *Encyclopædia Britannica.* Retrieved July 5, 2007, from Encyclopædia Britannica Online http://www.britannica.com/eb/article-9116922

Koegel, R.L., & Koegel, L.K. (1995). *Teaching children with autism: Strategies for initiating positive interactions and improving learning opportunities.* Baltimore: P.H. Brookes.

Kratochwill, T.R., Albers, C.A., & Shernoff, E.S. (2004). School-based interventions. *Child and Adolescent Psychiatric Clinics of North America, 13*(4), 885–903, vi–vii.

Kratochwill, T.R., & Stoiber, K.C. (2000). Empirically supported interventions and school psychology: Conceptual and practical issues: Part II. *School Psychology Quarterly, 15,* 233–253.

Latham, G. (1988). The birth and death cycles of educational innovations. *Principal, 68*(1), 41–43.

Lovaas, O.I. (1996). The UCLA young autism of service delivery. In C. Maurice, G. Green, & S.C. Luce (Eds.), *Behavioral intervention for young children with autism: A manual for parents and professionals* (pp. 241–250). Austin, TX: Pro-Ed.

McEachin, J.J., Smith, T., & Lovaas, O.I. (1993). Long-term outcome for children with autism who received early intensive behavioral treatment. *American Journal of Mental Retardation: AJMR, 97*(4), 359–372; discussion 373–391.

Medland, M.B., & Stachnik, T.J. (1972). Good-behavior game: A replication and systematic analysis. *Journal of Applied Behavior Analysis, 5*(1), 45–51.

Mortenson, B.P., & Witt, J.C. (1998). The use of weekly performance feedback to increase teacher implementation of a prereferral academic intervention. *School Psychology Review, 27*(4), 613–627.

Munoz, R.F., & Mrazek, P.J. (1996). Institute of Medicine report on prevention of mental disorders. *American Psychologist, 51*(11), 1116.

National Association of School Psychologists (NASP). (2000). *Professional conduct manual: Principles for professional ethics guidelines for the provision of school psychological services.* Retrieved December 5, 2006, from http://www.nasponline.org/standards/ProfessionalCond.pdf

National Institute of Child Health and Human Development (NICHD). (2000, Spring). *Report of the National Reading Panel. Teaching children to read: An evidence-based assessment of the scientific research literature on reading and its implications for reading instruction* (NIH Publication No. 00-4769). Washington, DC: Government Printing Office.

No Child Left Behind Act of 2001 (NCLB), Pub. L. No. 107–110, 115 Stat. 1425 (2001).

Noell, G. H., Witt, J. C., Gilbertson, D. N., Ranier, D. D., & Freeland, J. T. (1997). Increasing teacher intervention implementation in general education settings through consultation and performance feedback. *School Psychology Quarterly, 12*(1), 77–88.

Norcross, J. C., Beutler, L. E., & Levant, R. F. (2006). *Evidence-based practices in mental health: Debate and dialogue on the fundamental questions.* Washington, DC: American Psychological Association.

Reid, D. H., Parsons, M. B., & Green, C. W. (1989). *Staff management in human services: Behavioral research and application.* Springfield, IL: Thomas.

Ringeisen, H., Henderson, K., & Hoagwood, K. (2003). Context matters: Schools and the "research to practice gap" in children's mental health. *School Psychology Review, 32*(2), 153–169.

Sackett, D. L., Straus, S. E., Richardson, W. S., Rosenberg, W., & Haynes, R. B. (Eds.). (2000). *Evidence-based medicine: How to teach and practice EBM.* Edinburgh, UK: Churchill Livingstone Inc.

Saigh, P. A., & Umar, A. M. (1983). The effects of a good behavior game on the disruptive behavior of Sudanese elementary school students. *Journal of Applied Behavior Analysis, 16*(3), 339–344.

Schaughency, E., & Ervin, R. (2006). Building capacity to implement and sustain effective practices to better serve children. *School Psychology Review, 35*(2), 155–166.

Schoenwald, S. K., & Hoagwood, K. (2001). Effectiveness, transportability, and dissemination of interventions: What matters when? *Psychiatric Services, 52*(9), 1190–1197.

Shavelson, R. J., & Towne, L. (2002). *Scientific research in education.* Washington, DC: National Academy Press.

Shernoff, E. S., Kratochwill, T. R., & Stoiber, K. C. (2003). Training in evidence-based interventions (EBIs): What are school psychology programs teaching? *Journal of School Psychology, 41*(6), 467–483.

Shinn, M. R. (Ed.). (1989). *Curriculum-based measurement: Assessing special children.* New York: Guilford Press.

Shriver, M. D., & Watson, T. S. (2005). Bridging the great divide: Linking research to practice in scholarly publications. *Journal of Evidence-Based Practices for Schools, 6,* 5–18.

Stage, S. A., & Quiroz, D. R. (1997). A meta-analysis of interventions to decrease disruptive classroom behavior in public education. *School Psychology Review, 26*(3), 333–368.

Sterling-Turner, H. E., Watson, T. S., & Moore, J. W. (2002). The effects of direct training and treatment integrity on treatment outcomes in school consultation. *School Psychology Quarterly, 17*(1), 47–77.

Storr, C. L., Ialongo, N. S., Kellam, S. G., & Anthony, J. C. (2002). A randomized controlled trial of two primary school intervention strategies to prevent early onset tobacco smoking. *Drug and Alcohol Dependence, 73*(2), 149–158.

Sugai, G. M., & Horner, R. H. (2005). School-wide positive behavior supports: Achieving and sustaining effective learning environments for all students. In W. L. Heward, T. E. Heron, N. A. Neef, S. M. Peterson, D. M. Sainato, G. Cartledge, et al. (Eds.),

Focus on behavior analysis in education: Achievements, challenges, and opportunities (pp. 90–102). Upper Saddle River, NJ: Pearson/Merrill/Prentice Hall.

Task Force on Evidence-Based Interventions in School Psychology. (2003). *Procedural and coding manual for review of evidence-based interventions*. Retrieved June 5, 2007, from http://sp-ebi.org/documents/_workingfiles/EBImanual1.pdf

Tingstrom, D.H., Sterling-Turner, H.E., & Wilczynski, S.M. (2006). The good behavior game: 1969–2002. *Behavior Modification, 30*(2), 225–253.

United States Office of Management and Budget. (n.d). What constitutes strong evidence of a program effectiveness? Retrieved August 14, 2007, from http://www.whitehouse.gov/omb/part/2004_program_eval.pdf

Walker, H.M. (2004). Commentary: Use of evidence-based interventions in schools: Where we've been, where we are, and where we need to go. *School Psychology Review, 33*(3), 398–408.

Walsh, K., Glaser, D., & Wilcox, D.D. (2006, May). *What education schools aren't teaching about reading—and what elementary teachers aren't learning*. Washington, DC: National Council on Teacher Quality.

Weisz, J.R., & Kazdin, A.E. (2003). Concluding thoughts: Present and future of evidence-based psychotherapies for children and adolescents. In A.E. Kazdin & J.R. Weisz (Eds.), *Evidence-based psychotherapies for children and adolescents* (pp. 439–451). New York: Guilford Press.

What Works Clearinghouse. (2006, September). *What works clearinghouse study design classification*. Retrieved June 18, 2007, from http://www.whatworks.ed.gov/review process/studydesignclass.pdf

What Works Clearinghouse Review Process Standards. (n.d.) Retrieved June 7, 2007, from http://www.w-w-c.org/reviewprocess/standards.html

Wilczynski, S.M. (2006). *National standards project: Conceptual model for reviewing the ASD literature*. Unpublished manuscript.

Witt, J.C., Noell, G.H., LaFleur, L.H., & Mortenson, B.P. (1997). Teacher use of interventions in general education settings: Measurement and analysis of the independent variable. *Journal of Applied Behavior Analysis, 30*(4), 693.

Witt, J.C., VanDerHeyden, A.M., & Gilbertson, D. (2004). Troubleshooting behavioral interventions: A systematic process for finding and eliminating problems. *School Psychology Review, 33*(3), 363–384.

Response to Intervention

A Strategy for the Prevention and Identification of Learning Disabilities

Lynn S. Fuchs, Douglas Fuchs, and Rebecca O. Zumeta

Since passage of the Education for All Handicapped Children Act of 1975, most states, school districts, and practitioners have based their identification of learning disabilities (LD) on the presence of a discrepancy between IQ and academic achievement. This model is frequently referred to as the *discrepancy approach* to LD identification (D. Fuchs & Fuchs, 2006; D. Fuchs, Compton, Fuchs, Bryant, & Davis, in press). Under this diagnostic model, students with LD are conceptualized as having intellectual ability in the average range or above paired with unexplained low academic achievement. Over the years it has become clear that with this process, identification is often delayed until grades 3–5 because struggling students have to fall far behind in the general education curriculum before meeting classification criteria. Thus, critics often

The research described in this chapter was supported in part by Grant #H324U010004 from the U.S. Department of Education, Office of Special Education Programs, as well as Grant RO1 #HD46154–01 and Core Grant #HD15052 from the National Institute of Child Health and Human Development to Vanderbilt University. Statements do not reflect agency position or policy, and no official endorsement should be inferred.

refer to the discrepancy model as a "wait-to-fail" approach (Fuchs & Fuchs, 2007). In other words, children have to fail (repeatedly) in general education before they are recognized as having a disability and given access to more appropriate instruction in special education. In addition, students with low-average IQs often do not show a discrepancy between their IQ and achievement scores, even though their achievement is low and they clearly struggle to learn grade-level material. For these reasons, and because of various inherent measurement problems, the discrepancy approach has fallen from favor among many researchers and practitioners (Vaughn & Fuchs, 2003).

As one important indication of this dissatisfaction, the most recent reauthorization of Individuals With Disabilities Education Improvement Act in 2004 (P. L. 108–446) permits states and districts to discontinue use of the discrepancy model in favor of *response to intervention* (RTI), a tiered intervention approach that identifies struggling students with LD based on their response to high quality, evidence-based instruction (Fuchs & Fuchs, 2007). At the same time, states continue to have the option to use the discrepancy model for identification. Advantages of the RTI model include earlier identification of struggling students, a stronger focus on prevention of academic problems, and progress assessment with clear implications for academic programming (Vaughn & Fuchs, 2003). Table 5.1 provides definitions of important terms related to the discussion of RTI.

The premise behind RTI is that students are identified as having LD when their response to validated intervention is dramatically inferior to that of their peers (D. Fuchs & Fuchs, 2006). The inference is that these children who respond poorly to generally effective interventions have a disability that requires specialized treatment to produce successful learning outcomes. In this way, a central assumption is that RTI can differentiate between two explanations for low achievement: inadequate instruction versus disability. If the child responds poorly to instruction that benefits most students, then the assessment eliminates instructional quality as a viable explanation for poor academic growth, instead providing evidence of disability. Conversely, if an at-risk student responds well to intervention, then their low achievement can be attributed to lack of appropriate instruction, not a learning disability.

Virtually all RTI models are embedded within a multitier prevention system (e.g., Al Otaiba & Fuchs, 2006; L. S. Fuchs et al., 2005; McMaster, Fuchs, Fuchs, & Compton, 2005; O'Connor, 2000; Vaughn, Linan-Thompson, & Hickman, 2003; Vellutino et al., 1996). General education instruction represents primary intervention, which all typically developing students receive. Students demonstrating unsatisfactory progress in the regular classroom enter a more intensive secondary

TABLE 5.1 Glossary of Terms

Curriculum-based measurement	Frequent, standardized testing on parallel assessment forms of equivalent difficulty to quantify academic progress.
Discrepancy approach	Model for identifying students with learning disabilities on the basis of an unexplained difference between intellectual ability, as measured by IQ, and academic achievement.
Dual discrepancy	RTI method for classifying responsiveness, whereby a student's slope of improvement and final achievement level are both at least 1 standard deviation below that of peers.
False negative	Under RTI, children who score above a cut point on predictive screening, but later have academic problems; not identifying risk when it is present; Type II error.
False positive	Under RTI, children who eventually achieve academically, but score below the cut point on a predictive instrument; identification of risk when it is not present; Type I error.
Primary prevention	General education core program; all students in general education receive primary intervention in general education.
Problem solving	RTI model where interventions are tailored specifically to an individual student's needs; it is often used to support students with behavior problems.
Progress monitoring	Frequent, brief assessments administered according to standardized procedures; resulting scores are graphed in prescribed ways; educators use graphs to determine student responsiveness and design individualized programs.
Response to intervention (RTI)	Model for identifying LD using a tiered prevention system.
Secondary prevention	Structured, small group, goal-oriented, short-term instruction that uses standard treatment protocols for students who do not respond adequately to high quality general education instruction.
Standard treatment protocol	Preventative intervention model relying on interventions for specific academic problems that have been validated using randomized, controlled group research designs.
Tertiary prevention	Individualized instruction, often delivered under the auspices of special education.
Universal screening	Testing all students in a school using brief standardized assessments to identify risk in a specific area.

intervention. In most RTI research, this involves one or more rounds of small-group tutoring in which instruction is driven by an evidence-based standard protocol and specific goals for student achievement (D. Fuchs, Mock, Morgan, & Young, 2003). Students who respond poorly to the secondary intervention are understood to have demonstrated "unexpected failure," and they become candidates for the most intensive, tertiary intervention, or special education in many RTI models. Prior to moving from secondary to tertiary intervention, students undergo an abbreviated special education evaluation designed to answer questions that have arisen during primary and secondary interventions, and to determine a likely cause for the student's academic failure (Fuchs & Fuchs, in press).

In this chapter we provide an overview of the key components of RTI and offer recommendations for designing an RTI model. Then, we describe examples of research-validated forms of instruction which can be included within RTI prevention systems. In addition, we explain methods for classifying response, with a focus on progress-monitoring procedures.

COMPONENTS OF RTI AND RECOMMENDATIONS FOR AN RTI MODEL

Number of Prevention Layers

The first decision schools face when developing RTI systems is determining the number of prevention tiers. General education is always considered the first tier, and students who are targeted for preventative intervention must first show evidence of failing to respond to this universal core program. Beyond general education, however, RTI systems may include a number of tiers prior to special education. Some RTI systems incorporate general education along with a second tier of prevention. This second tier is more intensive than general education but less intensive than special education, and students must also show poor response to this second tier of prevention before special education is initiated at a third tier. Some RTI systems incorporate additional tiers of prevention to separate general and special education, with special education used as the fourth, fifth, or sixth tier (Fuchs & Fuchs, 2007). We suggest that schools employ three tiers, with only one tier separating general and special education. Figure 5.1 illustrates one such model. We make this recommendation because of the difficulty of designing more than one tier of preventative intervention that can be reliably distinguished in format, nature, style, and intensity both from general and from special education. Given this difficulty, extra tiers separating general and special education begin to resemble the intensity of special education, but serve students without a disability label. Adequate response to these extra tiers represents a shaky basis for assuming that a child does not require special education (Fuchs & Fuchs, 2007).

Primary Prevention and Universal Screening

Primary prevention, also known as Tier 1, refers to instruction that students receive in their general education classes. All students in general education receive primary intervention, with approximately 80%–85% receiving it as their sole form of instruction. These students receive all of their instruction in a general education classroom with no supplemental academic support. RTI models presuppose that Tier I instruction is evidence based, of high quality, and implemented with fidelity.

The primary intervention phase is also when universal screening for at-risk students takes place. Regardless of the number of tiers employed, a second component of RTI with which schools struggle is how students are targeted to receive prevention beyond the universal core program in general education. Some RTI systems employ one-time *universal screening,* whereby all children in a school are assessed on a brief standardized measure at the beginning of the school year. Students who score below a norm-referenced cut-point or below a performance benchmark associated with poor long-term outcome enter preventative intervention. In systems that rely on one-time universal screening to identify students who enter preventative intervention, the assumption is that low performance relative to the cut-point or the performance benchmark at the beginning of a school year constitutes evidence that the child has failed to respond to the Tier 1 universal core program during previous school years and therefore requires preventative intervention (Fuchs & Fuchs, 2007).

In other versions of RTI, universal screening is conducted to identify a subset of students who are potentially at risk for poor outcomes, and then the performance of these students is monitored for a short time to verify risk indicated from the universal screening. Only the subset of students who (a) first meet the universal screening cut-point and (b) then show poor rates of improvement over 5–8 weeks of Tier 1 general education are deemed in need of a preventative intervention.

We recommend integrating these models so that schools can rely on a combination of approaches, using a standard treatment protocol to address academic difficulties and a problem-solving approach to intervene with obvious behavioral problems. The rationale for this recommendation is that one-time universal screening at the beginning of the year may overidentify students who require secondary preventative intervention. Overidentifying students based on one-time universal screening means

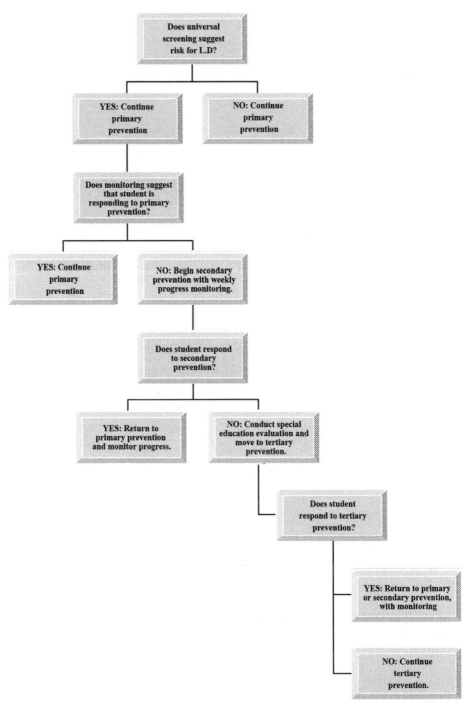

FIGURE 5.1   Typical instructional progression within an RTI system.

that schools would be pressed to deliver costly prevention to many students who do not need the services. This means that schools may water down prevention efforts due to limited resources (Compton, Fuchs, Fuchs, & Bryant, 2006).

Nature of Secondary Prevention

Two models of *secondary prevention* are prominent within responsiveness to intervention approaches. The first approach, called *problem solving,* relies on preventative interventions that are tailored to meet an individual student's needs. As reflected in the literature, these preventative interventions often conceptualize academic deficiencies as motivation problems. These interventions therefore attempt to increase student performance on skills that are already acquired, rather than designing instruction to develop new skills. Typically, the school psychologist assumes major responsibility, in collaboration with other professionals, for designing the individually tailored preventative interventions that vary in form and function across students (Fuchs & Fuchs, 2007).

A second approach to secondary prevention is to rely on *standard treatment protocols:* academic interventions that have been shown via randomized controlled studies to improve most students' achievement in a given subject area. In contrast to the problem-solving approach, standard treatment protocol is typically designed to promote the acquisition of new skills, while incorporating standard, research-validated methods for addressing behavioral and attention deficits so that instruction may proceed smoothly. Typically, standard treatment protocol for secondary intervention is more intensive than Tier 1 general education because it relies on frequent small-group tutoring by a professional teacher or a trained and supervised paraprofessional. In addition, secondary intervention attempts to ensure mastery for the majority of students (Fuchs & Fuchs, 2007). In addition, the tutoring protocols are often scripted and, in all cases, are highly prescriptive. Reliance on research-validated preventative interventions that have been shown to be highly effective for the majority of students speaks to a fundamental assumption within RTI: If the child responds inadequately to instruction that benefits most students, then the assessment eliminates instructional quality as an explanation for poor academic growth, and therefore provides evidence of a disability (Fuchs & Fuchs, 2007).

We recommend integrating the models that schools rely on a combination of approaches with a standard treatment protocol to address academic difficulties and a problem-solving approach to intervene with obvious behavioral problems. Our rationale is that standard treatment protocols have been shown to be highly effective for academic deficits. Therefore, the quality of preventative intervention does not depend on local professionals, who may have uneven training and background in instructional design. In a related way, with a standard treatment protocol, the nature of the preventative intervention to which students do and do not respond is public, clear, and represents "instruction that benefits most students." By contrast, when a problem-solving approach is applied to remedy reading or math difficulties, there is greater responsibility on collaborators within the RTI system to maintain records about the nature of a student's preventative intervention; there is more parental responsibility to judge whether an individually tailored preventative intervention is viable; and there is a weaker basis for presuming that inadequate response eliminates poor instruction as the cause for insufficient learning. Nevertheless, when dramatic behavior difficulties occur in combination with academic deficits, a problem-solving approach should be used as an attempt to resolve the behavior problem. An academic difficulty that persists despite a well-designed and functional behavioral program then requires a standard treatment protocol to build new academic skills (Fuchs & Fuchs, 2007).

Nature of Tertiary Prevention

Tertiary prevention refers to instruction that takes place in Tier 3. In most RTI models, this represents special education. Prior to entering Tier 3, students undergo an abbreviated special education evaluation to determine the nature of a suspected disability, and schools must determine how to design this multidisciplinary evaluation required by federal law for special education placement. In some RTI systems, multidisciplinary evaluations are comprehensive, with a standard battery of assessments administered to all students. In other RTI systems, multidisciplinary evaluations are specific to the questions that arise as a function of the student's participation in Tiers 1 and 2. Another dimension along which multidisciplinary evaluations differ is whether the assessment is designed to distinguish among LD, mild mental retardation, speech/language impairment, and emotional or behavior disorders as the disability underlying the lack of responsiveness. For this purpose, the following types of assessment are typically included: (a) adaptive behavior and intelligence to distinguish between LD and mild mental retardation, (b) expressive and pragmatic language to help inform distinctions between LD and language impairment, and (c) teacher rating scales, classroom observations, and parent interviews. These distinctions are warranted, of course, only if they provide utility for designing instruction and grouping students productively for instruction. Few, if any, strong studies have been conducted to assess the utility of these designations.

Pending such research findings, we recommend that the abbreviated multidisciplinary evaluation be designed to answer specific questions that arise during general education instruction and previous rounds of prevention. The multidisciplinary evaluation should include a process for distinguishing among high-incidence disabilities. Our recommendation is based on two assumptions. First, a specifically tailored, abbreviated multidisciplinary evaluation is more efficient than a full-blown evaluation and is more likely to provide useful information for designing special education programs. The second assumption is that distinctions among the high-incidence disability categories may prove helpful to special educators in formulating sensible grouping structures. If an evaluation reveals a disability, then an IEP must be developed that includes specific instructional goals related to a student's area(s) of deficit (Fuchs & Fuchs, 2007).

With respect to IEPs and special education, we note that most discussions about RTI focus on reforming general education, which is conceptualized as a research-based, multitiered system of prevention for students at-risk for academic difficulty. In these discussions, special education is rarely mentioned, except as the final outcome to be avoided. We believe that this is unfortunate because students who prove unresponsive to RTI's preventative intervention require a high quality special education tier to address their disability. Special education programs should be tailored to students' individual needs. They should include low student-teacher ratios (typically 1:1 or 1:2), extra instructional time (up to 1.5 hours per day), and use of ongoing progress monitoring (up to two times per week), to deductively build programs that empirically address student needs.

We recommend that RTI incorporate special education as an important tier that delivers the most intensive instructional programs designed formatively to address individual needs. Reform is needed to create more reasonable caseloads and paperwork demands, allowing teachers to focus on the delivery of high quality instruction. This reformed special education should be a flexible service, systematically permitting students to move in and out of this tier as their needs change in relation to the demands of the general education curriculum. This means that when needy students in Tiers 2 or 3 make adequate progress, they can return to primary intervention. Conversely, students who require additional support can move to secondary or tertiary intervention as needed. Special education has the potential to be a valuable resource for addressing the needs of students with LD if it is reformed and thoughtfully incorporated in an RTI system (Fuchs & Fuchs, 2007).

RESEARCH-VALIDATED INTERVENTIONS FOR CONDUCTING SECONDARY PREVENTION

Most of the attention in current RTI models and research has emphasized the development of instruction, identification, and assessment procedures in reading and mathematics for students in primary grades. Similar efforts in written language and science intervention are also needed. Here we briefly describe some validated protocols for conducting secondary prevention in reading and math. For additional RTI protocols, see Compton et al. (2006), L. S. Fuchs et al. (2005), and McMaster et al. (2005).

RTI in Reading

D. Fuchs et al. (in press) reported the results of a positive small-group tutoring intervention in reading for first graders. Researchers conducted weekly progress monitoring in the fall using measures of word identification fluency to identify initially low-performing first graders who were also nonresponsive to classroom instruction. The children were assigned randomly to a tutored group or a non-tutored control group. Small-group tutoring was conducted for 9 weeks during the spring semester of students' first grade year. Tutoring sessions took place outside of the classroom, four times per week, for 45 minutes per session.

The first tutoring activity was sight word recognition. The tutor presented a flash card that displayed a word; read and spelled the word; and then requested the students as a group to both say it and spell it. If a mistake was made, the tutor modeled the correct response and the group repeated it. Next, the tutor used the same procedure to present the sight words to individual students. Words missed by students were placed in a practice pile. After each student read all the words, the tutor returned to the students' respective practice piles, and asked them to read the words they initially had misread. A writing activity followed. The tutor presented a new sight word card and asked the students to read it. The tutor then turned the card over while the students wrote the word. If they did so incorrectly, the tutor again showed them the word card, turned it over, and asked them to write it once more.

The second activity was letter-sound recognition exercise. The tutor presented a picture card showing a letter and a picture of a word starting with that letter. The tutor identified the pictured object, as well as the corresponding sound and letter name. Students repeated the sound and letter name. The tutor then presented students each sound card in the set and they produced the sounds chorally. If a mistake was made, the tutor modeled the correct response and they repeated it. Students took turns identifying the letters and sounds using a similar procedure to the one used in the sight-word activity.

The third activity was decoding practice. The tutor presented a decodable word on a card, tapped each phoneme, and read the word. The tutor then asked the students to tap the sounds in the word and to "read it fast" as a group. These word cards were then presented to students individually, and they wrote the words using the same practice and correction procedure that was used in the word recognition activity.

Echo reading, choral reading, and a speed game constituted the last tutoring activity. Students reread a story from the previous session. The tutor read each line, which was repeated by the students reading as a group. If they misread a word, the tutor reread it, and they repeated it. The tutor then asked students to read the story chorally, using the same correction procedure. Next, echo reading and choral reading were conducted with a new story. Students took turns reading the new story. The first student had 30 seconds to read. If he or she misread a word or hesitated for 4 seconds, the tutor read the word, and the student repeated it. The tutor recorded how much of the story the student read on a first trial. These steps were repeated until each student read the story three times. Students had two chances to surpass their initial performance. If they read more words correctly on the second or third trial, a star was marked on their chart. Students traded their charts for a prize when their chart was full of stars.

Study results indicated that students who were tutored in this secondary intervention format significantly outperformed their peers who were not tutored on measures of word identification, word attack, and sight word fluency. Furthermore, fewer tutored students were identified as nonresponsive to instruction, suggesting that this intervention served its intended preventative function (D. Fuchs et al., in press).

RTI in Mathematics

Another study that assessed first grade RTI began by assessing the mathematics performance of children at the beginning of first grade (L.S. Fuchs et al., 2005; L.S. Fuchs, Fuchs, & Hollenbeck, 2007). Children were identified as at-risk for the development of mathematics difficulties based on their initially low performance. They were randomly assigned to tutoring (i.e., secondary prevention) and control conditions (i.e., general education without secondary prevention). Secondary prevention involved tutor-led instruction and computer practice, for a total of 40 minutes per session. Tutor-led instruction occurred in groups of 2–3 students, three times per week, each time for 40 minutes, for 20 weeks. At the end of each session, students worked individually for an additional 10 minutes on software designed to promote automatic retrieval of math facts. The tutor-led instruction (Paulsen & Fuchs, 2003) was based on the concrete-representational-abstract method for teaching math (Butler, Miller, Crehan, Babbitt, & Pierce, 2003; Cass, Cates, Smith, & Jackson, 2003; Mercer, Jordan, & Miller, 1996). This model relies on concrete objects to promote conceptual learning. Lessons followed a sequence of

17 scripted topics, and each topic included activities that relied on worksheets and manipulatives (e.g., base-10 blocks for place value instruction). Thirteen topics were each addressed with three lessons; the remaining four topics were each addressed with six lessons. Mastery of the topic was assessed each day. If every student in the group achieved mastery prior to the last day on the topic, the group moved to the next topic (a few topics required completion of all days). On the first day of each topic, students completed a cumulative review worksheet covering previous topics. During the final 10 minutes of each intervention session, students used software, *Math FLASH* (L.S. Fuchs, Hamlett, & Powell, 2003), designed to promote automatic retrieval of math facts.

Results showed that the growth of the at-risk tutored students was (a) either comparable or superior to that of their not-at-risk classmates and (b) stronger than that of at-risk children who were not tutored. Tutoring also decreased the prevalence and identification of students with math disabilities. These findings support the promise of first-grade RTI to reduce mathematics difficulty on key aspects of performance, and to serve as a test within an RTI framework for identifying learning disabilities in mathematics (L. S. Fuchs, Fuchs, & Hollenbeck, 2007).

Research has also been conducted on RTI at third grade with a specific focus on math problem solving (L. S. Fuchs, Fuchs, & Hollenbeck, 2007). Referred to as *Hot Math*, this intervention has been validated in a series of randomized controlled trials, with effects disaggregated for high-, average-, and low-performing third-grade students (e.g., D. Fuchs et al., 2003; L.S. Fuchs et al., 2004a, 2004b).

In one large-scale, multiyear ongoing study (L.S. Fuchs, 2002), researchers randomly assigned 20 general education classrooms to conventional methods for teaching math problem solving and another 40 general education classrooms to primary prevention Hot Math whole-class instruction, which occurred 2–3 times per week for 16 weeks for 25–40 minutes per session. Hot Math at the primary (whole-class) level integrated two practices to promote mathematical problem solving: explicit schema-broadening instruction and self-regulation learning strategies. Each of the four 3-week units provided instruction on skill acquisition and transfer. For the secondary prevention, students were identified at the beginning of third grade as at-risk for poor outcome, based on their initially low performances. Then, Hot Math tutoring occurred for these children in groups of 2–4 students, three times per week for 13 weeks, for 20–30 minutes each time. The instruction incorporated a stronger self-regulated learning component with tangible reinforcers, which we deem to be important in effecting learning outcomes for at-risk learners in third and first grades. The content of Hot Math tutoring mirrors the material covered in the whole-class sessions, except that more difficult concepts are targeted for review and practice, with additional use of concrete manipulatives and extra prompts to support student learning (L. S. Fuchs, Fuchs, & Hollenbeck, 2007). To date, results have shown that students who receive Hot Math are significantly less likely to experience failure in math problem-solving than students who do not receive this instruction. This controlled experimentation also indicates that RTI, which incorporates validated Hot Math intervention at primary and secondary prevention layers, may represent a promising structure for preventing and identifying math learning disabilities, specifically for word-problem deficits.

METHODS FOR CLASSIFYING RESPONSE
AND NONRESPONSE

To classify response to intervention, research provides four options. Two rely on the student's status when the secondary prevention ends. Torgesen et al. (2001) suggested that at the end of secondary prevention, any student whose performance is above the 24th percentile be deemed responsive. The idea is that the intervention has "normalized" the student's performance. A second option, which also relies on the student's status at the end of secondary prevention, employs a criterion-referenced benchmark for determining whether the intervention has made a sufficient impact to ensure long-term success. Good, Simmons, and Kame'enui (2001), for example, suggested administering curriculum-based measurement at the end of intervention and designating all students who achieve the benchmark as responsive. A third option relies on the slope of improvement during secondary prevention rather than the student's final status at the end of secondary prevention. In this way, Vellutino et al. (1996) suggested rank ordering the slopes of improvement for students who receive preventative intervention. The cut-point for distinguishing response from nonresponse is the median of those rank-ordered slopes. Finally, L. S. Fuchs and Fuchs (1998) combined the use of slope of improvement with final status for classifying response in the following way: To be deemed unresponsive, a student must demonstrate a *dual discrepancy,* whereby slope of improvement during secondary prevention and final level at the end of secondary prevention are both at least one standard deviation below that of peers.

We recommend that a dual discrepancy be used to designate unresponsiveness. Final status alone is problematic because it permits some students to be classified as unresponsive despite strong improvement during secondary prevention. That is, they begin secondary prevention far below the normalized or benchmark final criterion, and despite strong growth, they remain below the criterion at the end of intervention. Slope of improvement alone is problematic because it permits some students to be classified as unresponsive even though they complete secondary prevention meeting the normalized or benchmark performance criterion. By contrast, a dual discrepancy, which simultaneously considers slope of improvement and final status, permits the unresponsive designation only when a student (a) fails to make adequate growth during secondary prevention and (b) completes secondary prevention below the normalized or benchmark criterion. In a recent working meeting on RTI-LD classification (Fuchs, Compton, & Fuchs, 2006), dual discrepancy emerged as a tenable approach for designating unresponsiveness. It was adequately sensitive and specific with respect to future low reading performance, even as it identified students with a severe form of reading deficit with realistic prevalence rates. Additional work is required to examine how alternative methods for classifying LD within an RTI system perform, but in the meantime, dual discrepancy appears promising (Fuchs & Fuchs, 2007).

With a dual discrepancy approach, it is necessary to quantify the rate of improvement during secondary prevention. To derive a rate of improvement, *progress monitoring* is required. In addition, progress monitoring can be use to help teachers design their instruction. With progress monitoring, practitioners administer tests according to standardized procedures, graph the resulting scores in prescribed ways, quantify rates of improvement, and apply rules to the graphed scores to optimize decision making. The frequency of progress monitoring varies by prevention tier. For primary prevention teachers conduct progress monitoring for 5–8 weeks for the subset of students identified as at-risk based on universal screening. Scores are graphed, and the rate of improvement (i.e., slope of the line of best fit across the graphed scores) is compared to a goal to determine if the child is responding adequately to primary prevention. For secondary intervention, progress monitoring should take place every week *throughout* the 9–30 week program, but the goal is the same as with primary prevention; to determine whether the child is responding by calculating a slope of improvement. By contrast, within tertiary prevention, progress monitoring again occurs weekly, but the resulting data are used not only to quantify response but also to inductively formulate an individualized instructional program.

Across prevention levels, progress monitoring tools must provide schools with reliable, valid, and efficient indicators of academic competence with which to index student progress across time (Deno, 1985). *Curriculum-based measurement* (CBM) is the form of progress monitoring for which the most research has been conducted. CBM differs from most forms of classroom assessment in several ways, including three fundamental features. First, CBM is standardized so that the behaviors to be measured and the procedures for measuring those behaviors are prescribed, with documented reliability and validity. Second, CBM's focus is longer term so that testing methods and content remain constant, with equivalent weekly tests spanning much, if not all, of the school year. The reason for long-term consistency is so that progress can be monitored systematically and coherently over time. Third, CBM is fluency based so that students have a fixed amount of time to respond to the test stimuli. Thus, improvement reflects an individual's ability to perform behaviors not only with accuracy but also with ease (Fuchs & Deno, 1991).

To illustrate how CBM is used, suppose that a teacher establishes a reading goal for year-end performance as competent second-grade performance. Then, relying on established methods, the teacher identifies enough passages of equivalent, second-grade difficulty to provide weekly assessments across the school year. Each week, the teacher (or aide) administers one test by having the student read aloud from a different passage for 1 minute; the score is the number of words read correctly. Each simple, brief assessment produces an indicator of reading competence because it requires a multifaceted performance. This performance entails, for example, a reader's skill at automatically translating letters into coherent sound representations, unitizing those sound components into recognizable wholes and automatically accessing lexical representations, processing meaningful connections within and between sentences, relating text meaning to prior information, and making inferences to supply missing information (Fuchs, Fuchs, Hosp, & Jenkins, 2001). Because the CBM passage reading fluency task reflects this complex performance, it can be used to characterize overall reading expertise and to track its development in the primary grades (Biemiller, 1977–1978; Fuchs & Deno, 1991). That is, it serves as an overall indicator of reading competence.

Alternatively, CBM can be structured so that instead of assessing one behavior representing an overall indicator of academic competence, it systematically samples the various skills embedded within the annual curriculum (see L. S. Fuchs, 2004 for discussion). With either approach, each progress-monitoring test collected across the school year is of equivalent difficulty. For that reason, the scores can be graphed and directly compared to each other. Moreover, a slope can be calculated on the series of scores to quantify the rate of improvement. This strategy for characterizing progress has been shown to be more sensitive to intra-individual differences than those offered by other classroom assessments (Marston, Fuchs, & Deno, 1986).

Perhaps most importantly for tertiary prevention, studies indicate that CBM progress monitoring enhances teachers' capacity to plan programs for and effect achievement among students with serious learning problems. The methods by which CBM informs instructional planning rely on the graphed performance indicator. If a student's rate of improvement is judged to be adequate, the teacher increases the student's goal for year-end performance; if not, the teacher uses the CBM decision rules to design an individualized instructional program that meets the student's unique learning needs. Research shows that with these CBM decision rules, teachers design more varied instructional programs that are more responsive to individual needs (L. S. Fuchs, Fuchs, & Hamlett, 1989b). The programs tend to incorporate more ambitious student goals (L. S. Fuchs, Fuchs, & Hamlett, 1989a) that ultimately result in improved student outcomes.

A MODEL FOR RTI IMPLEMENTATION

In this section, we provide an example of a model school's RTI system for first grade reading and mathematics. The model we describe is based on research conducted by the National Research Center on Learning Disabilities, sponsored by the Office of Special Education Programs in the U.S. Department of Education. For specific studies, see Compton et al. (2006), D. Fuchs et al. (2006), L. S. Fuchs et al. (2005), L. S. Fuchs, Fuchs, Compton et al. (2007), and Compton, Fuchs, & Fuchs, (submitted).

Our model school uses a 3-tier RTI system that is consistent with prior recommendations in this chapter. First, Tier 2 separates general education (Tier 1) from special education (Tier 3). We consider the Tier 1 general education program at this school to be generally effective for two reasons. First, each quarter, the lead reading and math teachers observe all first-grade teachers delivering the universal core instructional program and have documented strong fidelity and implementation skill. The second form of evidence for the effectiveness of first-grade Tier 1 reading and math general education programming is based on the school's prior record of achievement. The previous year's first-grade cohort, on average, demonstrated a strong slope of improvement on both reading and mathematics measures: in reading, an average increase of 1.8 words per week on curriculum-based measurement word identification fluency (WIF); in math, an average increase of 0.50 digits per week on curriculum-based measurement computation (COMP). These figures are commensurate with recommended weekly rates of improvement for typically developing students in first grade (1.75 words per week increase in reading; 0.50 digits per week increase in math). Moreover, during the previous year, only 3 of 60 (i.e., 5%) first graders failed to achieve the end-of-year WIF benchmark and only 2 students (i.e., 3.3%) failed to achieve the end-of-year COMP benchmark.

To identify students in need of prevention, this model school provides universal screening at the beginning of the school year, coupled with 5 weeks of short-term progress monitoring for students who are below established benchmarks. Children receive preventative tutoring only when their universal screening scores are low *and* when they show poor academic growth in response to the Tier 1 universal program. All students receive universal screening in September of first grade using two alternate forms of WIF measures. Student scores are determined by averaging performance across the two forms. First graders also receive universal math screenings on two alternate forms of COMP over 2 consecutive weeks in September. Again, their scores are averaged across the two forms. In reading, students whose average WIF universal screening score is below 15 move on to weekly progress monitoring for 5 weeks. Students whose rate of weekly WIF increase (computed as slope on a line of best fit) is below 1.8 then move on to Tier 2 small-group tutoring. In math, students whose average COMP screening score is below 5 move to weekly progress monitoring for 5 weeks. Students whose rate of weekly COMP increase (computed as slope on a line of best fit) is below 0.50 then move on to Tier 2 small-group tutoring.

When students are identified for preventative tutoring (i.e., Tier 2), teachers in our model school rely on standard treatment protocols to provide intervention. In reading, students receive 45 minutes of instruction four times each week in groups of 3 students for 15 weeks. In math, students receive 30 minutes of tutoring plus 10 of computerized drill and practice on math facts, three times each week, also in groups of three students but for 20 weeks. Across reading and math, tutors are trained paraprofessionals who are observed once each week by the lead reading teacher and receive corrective feedback. Also, once each week, the lead reading teacher meets with all tutors for 1 hour to examine students' progress monitoring graphs (WIF in reading; COMP in math) and to problem solve about difficulties the tutors experience in effecting growth, in managing student behavior, and in keeping groups moving forward when a single student is not keeping pace. In reading, the tutoring sessions focus on phonological awareness, letter-sound recognition, decoding, sight word recognition, and short-story reading, with highly explicit instruction. In math, the tutoring sessions focus on number concepts, numeration, operations, basic fact strategies, story problems, and missing addends. In reading and math, self-regulated learning strategies are incorporated to increase motivation and goal-directed learning.

To determine whether students have responded to small-group tutoring, WIF and COMP are again used, in reading and math, respectively. In reading, students whose WIF slope of improvement is less than 1.8 and whose *projected* year-end WIF score is less than 30 are deemed unresponsive. In math, students whose COMP slope of improvement is less than 0.50 and whose *projected* year-end WIF score is less than 20 are deemed unresponsive. Students who meet these responsiveness criteria return to the Tier 1 universal program, but weekly progress monitoring continues. If the student fails to maintain adequate growth, a Tier 2 program can be reinitiated in a timely fashion.

Students who fail to meet the criteria in reading or math receive an abbreviated multidisciplinary evaluation. First, the school obtains written parental consent for the evaluation. Each child's evaluation is tailored to answer questions that arose during Tier 1 general education and Tier 2 tutoring and to formulate distinctions between LD, mild mental retardation, language impairment, and emotional behavior disorders. The school psychologist uses relatively brief assessments of cognitive, adaptive, behavioral, and language skills to make these distinctions.

Within our model school, special education represents a valuable and vital tier in the RTI system. Special educators incorporate formative decision making based on ongoing progress monitoring (at first grade, WIF in reading; COMP in math) to design individually tailored special education programs. The goal is to use the progress monitoring to deductively formulate a program that is effective for the student whose response to the standard treatment protocol (at Tier 2) was poor. The key distinctions between Tiers 2 and 3 are that the special educators rely on lower student-teacher ratios, provide more instructional time, and systematically use ongoing progress monitoring to deductively formulate individually tailored programs. Our model school's Tier 3 special education is also a flexible service, permitting exit and reentry as the student's needs change in relation to the demands of the general education curriculum. At first grade, students exit special education when their WIF slope of improvement exceeds 1.8 words increase per week and when their *projected* year-end performance exceeds 50 and/or when their COMP slope of improvement exceeds 0.50 digits increase per week and when their *projected* year-end performance exceeds 20. When a student exits special education, they return to Tier 2 or Tier 1, as deemed most appropriate by the school staff, and weekly progress monitoring continues. That way, when a student fails to maintain adequate growth, the school staff knows and can make data-based decisions about whether the student requires more intensive intervention within the multitier prevention system.

SUMMARY AND CONCLUSION

RTI is a promising method for preventing and identifying learning disabilities. Current research suggests that this tiered approach to prevention and early intervention can help practitioners identify and meet the needs of students at-risk for academic difficulty. Primary prevention serves all students, with universal screening and progress monitoring incorporated to identify children at-risk for academic problems. For students who do not respond adequately to primary prevention, secondary prevention is delivered to enhance academic learning. Secondary prevention is characterized by short-term, goal oriented, small group instruction, which is standardized to reflect a validated tutoring protocol. Frequent progress monitoring is conducted weekly to help teachers determine responsiveness to the secondary prevention and tutoring protocol. If students make adequate progress in secondary prevention, they return to primary intervention. If they fail to progress, they move to tertiary prevention, which is special education in most RTI models. Students in tertiary prevention receive individualized instruction that targets their specific learning needs. The individualized instruction is designed inductively, using weekly progress monitoring, with teachers making adjustments to student goals and instruction as appropriate. If the data show that a student is making adequate progress within this tier, he or she exits tertiary prevention.

REFERENCES

Al Otaiba, S., & Fuchs, D. (2006). Who are the young children for whom best practices in reading are ineffective? An experimental and longitudinal study. *Journal of Learning Disabilities, 39*(5), 414–431.

Biemiller, A. (1977–1978). Relationship between oral reading rates for letters, words, and simple text in the development of reading achievement. *Reading Research Quarterly, 13*, 223–253.

Butler, F. M., Miller, S. P., Crehan, K., Babbitt, B., & Pierce, T. (2003). Fraction instruction for students with mathematics disabilities: Comparing two teaching sequences. *Learning Disabilities Research and Practice, 18*, 99–111.

Cass, M., Cates, D., Smith, M., & Jackson, C. (2003). Effects of manipulative instruction on solving area and perimeter problems by students with learning disabilities. *Learning Disabilities Research and Practice, 18*, 112–120.

Compton, D. L., Fuchs, D., Fuchs, L. S., & Bryant, J. D. (2006). Selecting at-risk readers in first grade for early intervention: A two-year longitudinal study of decision rules and procedures. *Journal of Educational Psychology, 98*, 394–409.

Compton, D. L., Fuchs, L. S., & Fuchs, D. (submitted). *The course of reading and mathematics development in first grade: Identifying latent trajectories and early predictors.* Manuscript submitted for publication.

Deno, S. L. (1985). Curriculum-based measurement: The emerging alternative. *Exceptional Children, 52*, 219–232.

Fuchs, D., Compton, D. L., & Fuchs, L. S. (2006). *The effects of Tier 2 small-group tutoring, using a standard treatment protocol, in first grade.* Paper presented at the 2006 Pacific Coast Research Conference.

Fuchs, D., Compton, D. L., Fuchs, L. S., Bryant, J., & Davis, G. C. (in press). Making "secondary intervention" work in a three-tier responsiveness-to-intervention model: Findings from the first-grade longitudinal study at the National Research Center on Learning Disabilities. *Reading and Writing: An Interdisciplinary Journal.*

Fuchs, D., & Fuchs, L. S. (2006). Introduction to response-to-intervention: What, why, and how valid is it? *Reading Research Quarterly, 41*, 93–99.

Fuchs, D., Mock, D., Morgan, P., & Young, C. (2003). Responsiveness-to-intervention: Definitions, evidence, and implications for the learning disabilities construct. *Learning Disabilities Research and Practice, 18*(3), 157–171.

Fuchs, L. S. (2002). *Understanding/preventing math problem-solving disability* (NICHD grant #HD15052).

Fuchs, L. S. (2004). The past, present, and future of curriculum-based measurement research. *School Psychology Review, 33*, 188–192.

Fuchs, L. S., Compton, D. L., Fuchs, D., Paulsen, K., Bryant, J. D., & Hamlett, C. L. (2005). The prevention, identification, and cognitive determinants of math difficulty. *Journal of Educational Psychology, 97*, 493–513.

Fuchs, L. S., & Deno, S. L. (1991). Paradigmatic distinctions between instructionally relevant measurement models. *Exceptional Children, 57*, 488–501.

Fuchs, L. S., & Fuchs, D. (1998). Treatment validity: A unifying concept for reconceptualizing the identification of learning disabilities. *Learning Disabilities Research and Practice, 13*, 204–219.

Fuchs, L. S., & Fuchs, D. (2007). A model for implementing responsiveness-to-intervention. *Teaching Exceptional Children, 39*, 14–20.

Fuchs, L. S., & Fuchs, D. (in press). Progress monitoring within a multi-tiered prevention system: Best practices. In J. Grimes, & A. Thomas (Eds.), *Best practices in school psychology* (Vol. 5). Bethesda, MD: National Association of School Psychologists.

Fuchs, L. S., Fuchs, D., Compton, D. L., Bryant, J. D., Hamlett, C. L., & Seethaler, P. M. (2007). Mathematics screening and progress monitoring at first grade: Implications for responsiveness-to-intervention. *Exceptional Children, 73*, 311–320.

Fuchs, L. S., Fuchs, D., Finelli, R., Courey, S. J., & Hamlett, C. L. (2004b). Expanding schema-based transfer instruction to help third graders solve real-life mathematical problems. *American Educational Research Journal, 41*, 419–445.

Fuchs, L. S., Fuchs, D., & Hamlett, C. L. (1989a). Effects of alternative goal structures within curriculum-based measurement. *Exceptional Children, 55*, 429–438.

Fuchs, L. S., Fuchs, D., & Hamlett, C. L. (1989b). Effects of instrumental use of curriculum-based measurement to enhance instructional programs. *Remedial and Special Education, 10*(2), 43–52.

Fuchs, L. S., Fuchs, D., & Hollenbeck, K. (2007). Extending responsiveness-to-intervention to mathematics at first and third grades. *Learning Disabilities Research and Practice, 22*, 13–14.

Fuchs, L. S., Fuchs, D., Hosp, M., & Jenkins, J. R. (2001). Oral reading fluency as an indicator of reading competence: A theoretical, empirical, and historical analysis. *Scientific Studies of Reading, 5*, 239–256.

Fuchs, L. S., Fuchs, D., Prentice, K., Hamlett, C. L., Finelli, R., & Courey, S. J. (2004a). Enhancing mathematical problem solving among third-grade students with schema-based instruction. *Journal of Educational Psychology, 96*, 635–647.

Fuchs, L. S., Hamlett, C. L., & Powell, S. R. (2003). *Math Flash* [computer program]. Available from L. S. Fuchs, 328 Peabody, Vanderbilt University, Nashville, TN 37203.

Good, R. H., III, Simmons, D. C., & Kame'enui, E. J. (2001). The importance and decision making utility of a continuum of fluency-based indicators of foundational reading skills for third-grade high-stakes outcomes. *Scientific Studies of Reading, 5*, 257–288.

Marston, D., Fuchs, L. S., & Deno, S. L. (1986). Measuring pupil progress: A comparison of standardized achievement tests and curriculum-related measures. *Diagnostique, 11,* 71–90.

McMaster, K., Fuchs, D., Fuchs, L. S., & Compton, D. L. (2005). Responding to non-responders: An experimental field trial of identification and intervention methods. *Exceptional Children, 71*(4), 445–463.

Mercer, C. D., Jordan, L., & Miller, S. P. (1996). Constructivistic math instruction for diverse learners. *Learning Disabilities Research and Practice, 11,* 147–156.

O'Connor, R. E. (2000). Increasing the intensity of intervention in kindergarten and first grade. *Learning Disabilities Research and Practice, 15,* 43–54.

Paulsen, K., & Fuchs, L. S. (2003). *Preventing mathematics difficulties in first grade with small-group tutoring.* Available from flora.murray@vanderbilt.edu.

Torgesen, J. K., Alexander, A. W., Wagner, R. K., Rashotte, C. A., Voeller, K. K. S., & Conway, T. (2001). Intensive remedial instruction for children with severe reading disabilities: Immediate and long-term outcomes from two instructional approaches. *Journal of Learning Disabilities, 34,* 33–58.

Vaughn, S., Linan-Thompson, S., & Hickman, P. (2003). Response to instruction as a means of identifying students with reading/learning disabilities. *Exceptional Children, 69,* 391–409.

Vaughn, S. R., & Fuchs, L. S. (2003). Redefining learning disabilities as inadequate response to treatment: Rationale and assumptions. *Learning Disabilities Research and Practice, 18,* 137–146.

Vellutino, F., Scanlon, D. M., Sipay, E. R., Small, S. G., Pratt, A., Chen, R., et al. (1996). Cognitive profiles of difficult-to-remediate and readily remediated poor readers: Early intervention as a vehicle for distinguishing between cognitive and experiential deficits as basic cause of specific reading disability. *Journal of Educational Psychology, 88,* 601–638.

CHAPTER 6

Learning Disability Identification

How Does It Apply to English Language Learners?

Peggy McCardle, Chandra Keller-Allen, and Tanya Shuy

Understanding the intersection of English language learning and the existence of a learning disability (LD) among school-age children baffles practitioners and researchers alike. This chapter provides an overview of the issues pertaining to the identification of LD in students who are learning English as a second language. We review (a) the current LD identification and classification policies and practices; (b) implications of the growing population of school-age English language learners (ELLs); (c) issues with LD identification that are specific to ELLs; and (d) current research and policy changes that impact LD identification for ELLs. We conclude with a summary of what is known about ELL students and reading. Many of the same factors that predict reading success for monolingual English students also predict reading success in ELLs. Current work on interventions in both the first language and English have been shown to be effective in single studies for ELL students. With certain important modifications for ELLs, RTI holds promise not only for native

The assertions and opinions herein are those of the authors and do not purport to represent those of the National Institutes of Health, the U.S. Department of Health and Human Services, the George Washington University, or the National Institute for Literacy.

English speakers but also for ELLs. Finally, we point to areas for future research. There is a crucial need for rigorous studies addressing the education and special education needs of the growing number of ELL students in the United States.

CURRENT LEARNING DISABILITY IDENTIFICATION AND CLASSIFICATION

In order to address the unique issues that arise in the identification of LD in ELLs, it is important to consider research on the identification of LD in general. The issues raised in this research apply to the population at large and therefore provide a foundation for addressing the specific needs of all subgroups, including ELL students.

Problems with the classification and definition of LD are well documented in the research literature (Aaron, 1997; Fletcher et al., 2002; Gresham, 2002; Hoskyn & Swanson, 2000; Lyon et al., 2001; Lyon, Fletcher, & Barnes, 2003; Siegel, 1992; Stanovich, 1999; Stanovich & Siegel, 1994; Sternberg & Grigorenko, 2002; Stuebing et al., 2002; Vellutino, Scanlon, & Lyon, 2000). Several publications trace the history of the development of the definition from various perspectives: scientific, educational, and policy (e.g., Hallahan & Mercer, 2002; Kavale & Forness, 1995; and Torgesen, 1993). The definition of LD generally reflected in state laws and applied in practice prior to the 2004 reauthorization of the Individuals With Disabilities Education Act (IDEA, 1997) is still widespread, and rests largely on three assumptions: heterogeneity, exclusion, and discrepancy.

Heterogeneity

The heterogeneity assumption is that LD is domain specific and different in phenotypic definitions and intervention requirements. This is clearly not the case in actual practice. Fletcher, Lyon, Fuchs, and Barnes (2006) point out that LD cannot be considered a single overarching concept. The areas identified in the 1977 federal definition of LD (P.L. 94–142, 1975) as subgroups are neither internally consistent nor are they consistent with research findings. For instance, two categories of LD in the 1977 federal definition, oral expression and listening comprehension, are both also addressed in the speech and language category. The other five domains (basic reading, reading comprehension, math calculations, math concepts, and written expression) do not coincide with subgroups that emerge from research studies of children with learning problems (Fletcher et al., 2006). Lyon et al. (2003) noted a disproportionate focus on word identification reading disabilities but argued that this focus is motivated by the fact that word recognition deficits are a factor in 70%–80% of children identified as having LD in schools. Thus, an intervention focus on word-level reading problems has been a reasonable focus if the goal is to impact the learning of the majority of students identified with LD. In their comprehensive discussion of LD, Fletcher et al. (2006) present response to intervention (RTI) as a viable option for dealing with the heterogeneity issue. They recommend teachers monitor student progress with curriculum-based measures of achievement in word recognition, reading fluency, math and spelling. They emphasize the need to measure not only achievement but also intervention integrity and contextual factors as part of the process of LD identification. Additional research is needed to more thoroughly understand the subtypes of LD, which include disorders in reading comprehension, reading fluency, mathematics, and written expression (Fletcher et al., 2006; Lyon et al., 2003), as well as combinations of these and specific comorbidities, such as attention-deficit/hyperactivity disorder. Four Learning Disabilities Research Centers funded in 2005 by the National Institute of Child Health and Human Development (NICHD) are conducting research on the effectiveness of RTI for the identification and remediation of reading and other learning disabilities,[1] in addition to other research that is ongoing on this topic.

Exclusion

The exclusionary criteria that have traditionally been part of the definition of LD implicitly assume that children with LD commonly conceptualized as displaying unexpected underachievement, differ in their needs for intervention when compared to children who have expected low achievement due to mental retardation, sensory disorders, emotional disturbance, or are impacted by social, economic, or cultural factors (Lyon et al., 2003). For some children, this may be an appropriate assumption, such as those with mental retardation, sensory disorders, or linguistic differences whose intervention needs differ. However, the distinction is less clear for students who are disadvantaged socially and/or economically or for those who have difficulty because of inadequate instruction or lack of opportunity. This becomes important when considering services because different laws address the service needs of different populations. Students with mental retardation and emotional disturbance may be served under the Individuals With Disabilities Education Act

---

1. These centers, located in Colorado, Florida, Texas, and Maryland, are also examining the neurobiology and genetics of reading disabilities and key comorbidities such as attention-deficit disorder.

(1997 and 2004) under those specific disability categories. Students who are economically, socially, and/or culturally disadvantaged may receive services under the Title I provisions of the No Child Left Behind Act of 2001. However, those children failing to learn to read due to inadequate instruction—that is, instruction that was not sufficiently targeted to their learning needs or not sufficiently explicit to guide their learning—do not fall under any specific legislative requirement for special services. Again, RTI is a viable alternative that should enable us to miss fewer children and to deal with issues of inadequate instruction. RTI requires high quality instruction be documented as part of the early identification of unexpected underachievement.

Discrepancy

The requirement of a discrepancy between ability and achievement within the definition of LD has been a subject of great debate (Fletcher et al., 2006; Lyon et al., 2001; OSERS, 2002). The discrepancy criterion has been included in the federal definition of LD since the development of U.S. Office of Education guidance and regulations in 1977 for P.L. 94–142 (1975), and has remained unchanged until the recent passage of the Individuals With Disabilities Education Improvement Act of 2004. Even though there is little support for the validity and reliability of the discrepancy component, it has largely shaped the current conception and practice of identifying LD. The concept of unexpected underachievement in students with LD has been, in practice, translated into a discrepancy between ability, as demonstrated by intelligence testing, and achievement measures. Several empirical research studies and syntheses of bodies of research have concluded that the discrepancy criterion has, at best, weak validity and reliability (e.g., Fletcher et al., 1998; Gresham, 2002; Kavale, 2002; Lyon et al., 2001; Lyon et al., 2003; Stanovich, 1999). This research has also been summarized in the report of the President's Commission on Special Education (OSERS, 2002), and is presented briefly below.

First, there is a demonstrated confounding between students identified as having LD as a result of an aptitude-achievement discrepancy and students who are simply low achievers with no such discrepancy (Lyon et al., 2003; Stanovich, 1999). While the discrepancy criterion assumes that there is a qualitative difference between these two populations, several studies of reading have demonstrated this not to be the case. For example, two meta-analyses concluded that the discrepant and non-discrepant children did not differ significantly on variables shown to be associated with poor reading, including phonological awareness, rapid naming, verbal memory, and vocabulary (Hoskyn & Swanson, 2000; Stuebing et al., 2002). Vellutino et al. (2000) similarly concluded that "the IQ-achievement discrepancy does not reliably distinguish between disabled and non-disabled readers" (p. 235).

Second, the discrepancy criterion assumes that IQ is an adequate index of ability. As early as 1963 researchers cautioned that an IQ score at best reflects a gross estimate of current general cognitive functioning and that using it as a measure of learning potential is inappropriate (Thorndike, 1963).

Third, several researchers have demonstrated that psychometric and statistical issues inherent in comparing various scores in ability and achievement render the use of the discrepancy criterion invalid and unreliable for the purpose of identification of LD (Kavale, 2002; Lyon et al., 2001, 2003). While it has been noted that the use of regression models rather than scale scores does correct for some measurement error, the reliance on IQ-achievement discrepancy for identification purposes is still recognized as fraught with statistical issues (Francis, Fletcher, Stuebing, Lyon, Shaywitz, & Shaywitz, 2005). Francis et al. demonstrate the problems with "any psychometric approach to the identification of students as having LD that relies exclusively on observed test scores that represent the endpoints in a complex system of personal, cognitive, instructional, social, and environmental inputs" (2005, p. 99) and bring into question both the validity and reliability of these types of identification procedures.

Fourth, there is considerable variation in the policies and implementation practices of the identification of LD from state to state (MacMillan, Gresham, & Bocian, 1998; Mellard, Deshler, & Barth, 2004; Reschly & Hosp, 2004). Ambiguity in the federal definition of LD has left states free to select their own methods for determining eligibility. The lack of consistency is reflected in both policies and implementation practices for identification of and service provision to students. Students may be identified as learning disabled under a particular discrepancy definition in one state, yet may not qualify for services according to another state's definition (Lyon et al., 2001). In addition to differences in state policy, the subjectivity inherent in LD identification decisions at the school level introduces another level of variation (MacMillan et al., 1998; MacMillan & Siperstein, 2002). These disparities in state definitions and local level implementation of identification practices hinder researchers' ability to accurately collect and analyze data on the nation's population of school-age children with LD.

Fifth, the discrepancy criterion promotes a so-called wait-to-fail model. Because students must fall behind in their performance enough to show a discrepancy and in order to qualify for services under the discrepancy definition, early identification and treatment is difficult (Lyon et al., 2001; OSERS, 2002). National prevalence data indicate that the distribution of students identified as having LD is somewhat negatively skewed across the ages at which students can be served through special education (ages 3–22); the curve begins at age 7 and peaks at age 15 with 52% of students with LD in 2005 falling between the ages of 12 and 16 inclusively (using data from www.IDEAdata.org, 2005 Annual Report Table 1–7). Making students wait for intervention and instructional services until they fail has a devastating effect on all involved. The delay in identification and service is often made worse for English language learners because even more time may be spent trying to rule out the child's academic difficulties as a result of second language learning status (Zehler et al., 2003).

Finally, the discrepancy approach to the identification of LD does not provide insight or information regarding the intervention services needed by an identified child. Fuchs, Fuchs, and Speece (2002) refer to the discrepancy criterion as having low treatment validity. Identifying an IQ-achievement discrepancy tells us little if anything about the presence of a specific intrinsic disorder, nor does it provide insight into the likelihood that the student will respond to particular interventions (Lyon et al., 2001).

In summary, based on a convergence of data, there is a consensus in the scientific community that the IQ-achievement discrepancy basis for LD classification has weak validity and reliability (e.g., Aaron, 1997; Fletcher et al., 1998; Hoskyn & Swanson, 2000; Lyon et al., 2003; OSERS, 2002; Siegel, 1992; Stanovich & Siegel, 1994; Sternberg & Grigorenko, 2002; Stuebing et al., 2002). This conclusion applies to the use of IQ-achievement discrepancy for *any* student population. The IDEA reauthorization in 2004 has not changed the statutory definition of a specific learning disability, but lawmakers did add specific language pertaining to the evaluation of students with specific LD in Sec. 614(b)(6), permitting the use of an RTI approach as an alternative means of identifying students with LD (see chapter 10).

(6) Specific Learning Disabilities.

> (A) In General.—Notwithstanding section 607(b), when determining whether a child has a specific learning disability as defined in section 602, a local educational agency *shall not be required to take into consideration whether a child has a severe discrepancy between achievement and intellectual ability*[2] in oral expression, listening comprehension, written expression, basic reading skill, reading comprehension, mathematical calculation, or mathematical reasoning.

---

2. Emphases added.

(B) Additional Authority.—In determining whether a child has a specific learning disability, a local educational agency may use a process that determines if the child responds to scientific, research-based intervention as a part of the evaluation procedures described in paragraphs (2) and (3).

This change was most likely in response to the growing body of research presented in the report of the President's Commission on Excellence in Special Education (OSERS, 2002, p. 25) demonstrating the lack of validity and reliability of the discrepancy model. As states and districts have begun to change their policies and practices to include models of RTI, it will be important to track the impact of these changes. Given that the new language did not mandate that the discrepancy model be eliminated, comparisons can be made between methods if researchers and school practitioners work together.

ENGLISH LANGUAGE LEARNERS

The proportion of English language learners in the K–12 school-age population has increased from 6.7% in 1994–1995 to 10.5% in 2004–2005 (NCELA, 2006). In addition to increasing in absolute numbers, the *rate* of growth has increased exponentially each year. For example, the rate of growth in ELLs in the K–12 population between the 1994–1995 and 1995–1996 school years was 1.4% whereas the rate of growth between the 2003–2004 and 2004–2005 school years was 60.8% (NCELA, 2006). Not surprisingly, language minority students are the fastest growing subgroup of children among public school populations (McCardle, Mele-McCarthy, Cutting, Leos, & D'Emilio, 2005). As a result of the rapidly changing U.S. demographic picture, public schools are faced with multiple challenges.

One often cited challenge is how these students should be taught, that is, whether children should be educated through structured English immersion or bilingual education (e.g., Baker & Baker, this volume; Gersten & Woodward, 1994; Lesaux, 2006). There is some evidence of advantage when students can be taught in the native language while learning English (Francis, Lesaux, & August, 2006). However, the relevance of the issue of language of instruction has been diminished by the fact that in many states it is now moot. Thirty states have declared English the official language (ProEnglish, 2007; U.S. English, 2007); three of these (California [California Education Code §3.2.305]; Arizona [Arizona Revised Statutes § 15-752]; and Massachusetts [General Laws of Massachusett Title XII Chapter 71A: Section 4]) have propositions requiring that schools teach only in English, so that they must use some variant of an English immersion approach.[3] In addition, instruction in the first language is not always feasible because there is a huge variety of native languages represented among ELL students (Hopstock & Stephenson, 2003). It is time for research to focus on understanding how best to educate ELL students regardless of program type or native language. As Lesaux (2006) has aptly stated, "the research that has focused on instructional opportunities for these learners has centered on language of instruction rather than on components of effective instructional approaches and their relationship to academic outcomes" (p. 2416). Until we are able to offer equally effective instruction to all ELL students, we will not be able to successfully identify those with LD and intervene in their instruction. The 2004 reauthorization of IDEA provides an opportunity to improve LD identification for all students, including ELLs, by allowing states and localities authority to use an RTI system.

KEY ISSUES IN LD IDENTIFICATION
FOR ENGLISH LANGUAGE LEARNERS

One challenge to both general and special education is how to distinguish whether a student is struggling academically due to low language proficiency or learning difficulties (Artiles, Rueda, Salazar, & Higareda, 2002; Klingner, Artiles, & Barletta, 2006; McCardle, Mele-McCarthy, Cutting et al., 2005).[4] To address this issue, we consider several overriding factors that make this an inherently complex issue: the heterogeneity of the population; the lack of normative data on ELL students; the disproportionate representation of ELL students in special education; assessment—both the lack of linguistically and culturally appropriate assessments and the challenge of assessment for ELL students; and how the subjectivity inherent in the LD identification process impacts eligibility decisions for ELLs.

Heterogeneity of ELLs

Spanish represents the most common native language other than English in the United States; however, there are several states for which the

---

3. See also Gándara et al. (2000) for an analysis of the impact of one state's language policy (California's proposition 227) on the education of ELL students.

4. See also two special journal issues dedicated to ELL and special education: *Journal of Learning Disabilities, Vol. 39, No. 2*, March/April 2006; and *Teachers College Record, Vol. 108, No. 11*, Nov. 2006.

second most commonly spoken language is not Spanish (August & Shanahan, 2006). Kindler (2002) documented that states reported the following as the second most common language after English: Blackfoot (language of the Blackfoot Nation) in Montana, French in Maine, Hmong (a language of parts of China and Southeast Asia) in Minnesota, Ilocano (a language of the Philippines) in Hawaii, Serbo-Croatian in Vermont, and Yup'ik (an Alaska Native language) in Alaska.[5] According to a survey of district level coordinators, more than 350 different languages are represented among students designated as Limited English Proficient (LEP) in U.S. schools (Hopstock & Stephenson, 2003), and it is not uncommon to have multiple native languages represented in a single classroom. Therefore assessments and instructional approaches using English may be the most practical and feasible approach for many of these classes.

Even within speakers of the same native language, there is considerable heterogeneity among ELL students, due to differences in dialect, exposure to English at home and in the community, and language proficiency level identified by the schools. For example, the dialects spoken by Spanish speakers of Mexican heritage will differ from those from Puerto Rico, Colombia, Costa Rica, or other Spanish-speaking nations or regions. The level of English proficiency in ELL students will differ depending on whether the child speaks English at home with parents or has older siblings who speak English at home, what language predominates in the neighborhood, and so forth. We also must consider that not all ELL students may be formally designated LEP or ELL by the schools, and that even those who have been so designated bear this only as a temporary designation. Schools vary from state to state and even across districts within states as to what criteria and methods they use to assign LEP or ELL designations and to determine when those designations are no longer used (Zehler et al., 2003).

This heterogeneity of ELLs critically impacts the need for developmental trajectories. While there is ongoing work that may map the growth trajectories of Spanish-speaking ELL students, trajectories of English language learning may well differ for speakers of different native languages. Those for whom it is not feasible to provide first language support may show a different growth pattern in English and may need different types and levels of instructional support. In addition, for those classes where first language support is not feasible, teachers must nonetheless take culture into account. Such a class could easily include Vietnamese,

---

5. Note that this differs from the overall U.S. linguistic picture; nationally, the largest language groups after Spanish are Vietnamese, Hmong, Cantonese, and Korean in that order (Kindler, 2002).

Chinese, Middle Eastern, and Hispanic children, whose cultures differ in interesting ways, which could impact how students interpret teacher behavior and expectations. Clearly the heterogeneity of the ELL population presents challenges that require a great deal more research and creative approaches to assessment and instruction.

Bilingualism and Lack of Normative Data

There is a lack of normative data on the wide range of typically developing ELLs. Without normative data, we cannot effectively predict which students are at risk, identify those with LD, develop effective instructional and intervention programs, or guide teachers in how best to differentiate instruction for the wide variety of ELL students they may see in their classrooms. Understanding bilingualism and the cognitive processes associated with bilingualism are key to mapping a typical developmental trajectory for a person learning English and a second language while also attempting to learn content in the second language.

There is a body of research demonstrating cognitive advantages of bilingualism. Bialystok (2001) has studied the effects of bilingualism on cognition for over two decades. She has demonstrated that bilinguals were better at performing metalinguistic tasks requiring attentional control, although they were not better on those requiring analysis of linguistic structures. On tasks of attention and higher level processing, Martin and Bialystok (2003) found that bilingual children outperformed monolinguals, and work with older bilingual and monolingual adults revealed similar findings (Bialystok, Klein, Craik, & Viswanathan, 2004). Lesaux (2006) notes the discord between reported low academic achievement of language minority students in the United States (i.e., on the National Assessment of Educational Progress) and research showing better reading and heightened meta-linguistic awareness for bilinguals (Bialystok, 1997; Cummins, 1991). Lesaux points to possible reasons for this discrepancy:

> The disparity between the research findings suggesting bilingualism is an asset, and the reported low academic achievement of the ELLs represented in national data sets, may well reflect the samples studied in that research and the heterogeneity inherent in bilingual populations. By and large, the research that has reported heightened metalinguistic awareness has been conducted with bilinguals who are not language minority learners or who are not of low socioeconomic status. (2006, p. 2408)

There is also some more recent evidence of the value of bilingualism in learning to read. For example, Bialystok (2006) has shown that bilingual children demonstrated some benefit in learning to read in two languages, especially if those two languages share a writing system. However, the degree to which this is the case (and in fact whether for an individual child this is the case) varies not only with the languages being learned but also with the degree of language competence in each of the languages. Bialystok calls for research to address the impact of children's bilingual competence on reading. August, Calderon, Carlo, and Eakin (2006) also showed that on measures of broad reading native Spanish-speaking ELL children in grades K–2 instructed in both Spanish and English outperformed children instructed in either language alone.

However, these studies are only a beginning. We need more studies that trace language and cognitive development of various types of bilingual and ELL students over time, including the development of literacy. These studies should include both typically developing students and those who exhibit language or learning difficulties.

Disproportionate Representation

Historically, concerns have centered on the over- and underrepresentation of racial and ethnic minorities in special education (Donovan & Cross, 2002; Heller, Holtzman, & Messick, 1982; Losen & Orfield, 2002; Ortiz, 1997; Scruggs & Mastropieri, 2002). Several court cases (e.g., *Diana v. California State Board of Education,* 1970, and *Larry P. v. Riles,* 1979) have challenged boards of education based on the overrepresentation of minorities in special education (Gándara & Rumberger, 2002). In Texas in the early 1980s, Hispanics were estimated to be three times more prevalent in special education than White students in special education (Ortiz & Yates, 1983). Similarly, in the 1990s African Americans were overrepresented while Native American and Asian American students were underrepresented nationally in special education (Robertson, Kushner, Starks, & Drescher, 1994). According to more recent data, certain populations continue to be overrepresented in specific disability categories, such as the overrepresentation of African American students nationally in the categories of mental retardation and emotional disturbance (Donovan & Cross, 2002; Losen & Orfield, 2002).

Despite the plethora of theoretical and empirical literature on the disproportionate representation of racial and ethnic minorities in special education, there has been little research focused on the representation of linguistic minorities in special education. States and districts to date have not been required to report special education data by language status; therefore, the availability of data is limited.

There are two primary sources of national data on ELLs in special education: the Descriptive Study commissioned by the Office of English Language Acquisition (OELA) in the U.S. Department of Education conducted by Zehler et al. (2003) and the Civil Rights Data Collection (prior to 2004, this survey was called the Elementary and Secondary School Survey) conducted by the Office of Civil Rights, also in the U.S. Department of Education. Taken together, these two data sources offer an estimate of the prevalence of ELL learning disabled students in U.S. public schools.

Zehler et al. collected data on ELL student characteristics and services (i.e., curricular alignment, test inclusion, teacher qualifications) primarily through surveys and on-site data collection. Zehler et al. report enrollment data from a nationally representative sample of schools and school districts serving at least one ELL student. These authors also gathered information on limited English proficient students receiving special education services.

The 2000 OCR Survey (OCR, 2003) was a virtual census of the nation's 95,000 K–12 public schools. Although the survey gathered answers to only 12 questions on ELLs, 5 of which concerned ELL students with LD, the data can be disaggregated by school, district, or state. Data from Zehler et al. (2003) and the 2000 OCR survey (OCR, 2003), which was collected during the same school year, converge on the proportion of all students estimated to be in special education nationally—13.5%. The two data sources also agree that the proportion of ELL students identified for special education services is 9.2%, indicating that linguistic minority students are nationally underrepresented in special education (Zehler et al., 2003; OCR, 2003), although there is not a uniform distribution nationally. What is not clear from these reports, and thus requires further investigation, is whether (a) ELL students are truly underidentified nationally as needing special education services; (b) ELLs in special education programs are not being identified as both ELL and LD in district records, and therefore are not counted in one subpopulation; (c) there actually is a lower disability rate among those identified as ELLs; or (d) the overall lower rate of identification of ELLs is masking variability by location, first language, age, or other neighborhood, school, or student level factors, meaning under some circumstances ELLs may in fact be overidentified as LD, as suggested by the work of Artiles and his colleagues (Artiles et al., 2002, 2005).

While the OCR survey and Descriptive Study data provide a national snapshot at one point in time, there remains a paucity of research on the within-group differences that likely characterize the heterogeneity of ELLs in special education. Artiles et al. (2002, 2005) examined data from a sample of urban districts in California to unpack and disaggregate the patterns of ELL representation in special education. Artiles and colleagues found overrepresentation of ELLs in high poverty schools, especially from grade 5 through high school, in the disability categories of mental retardation, speech and language impairment, and LD (2005). They also found differences in LD identification rates depending on students' language proficiency in both their native language and English; elementary and secondary students with low proficiency in both first and second languages were overrepresented in the LD category. These findings were in districts where rapid transition to English-only classes was the norm. An added factor that sheds doubt on the accuracy of nationally aggregated special education statistics for ELL students is that, as noted by Lesaux (2006), some districts have an informal policy that students may not receive both special education services and English language instruction.

The wide variability in over- or underrepresentation depending on locality or other factors (Artiles et al., 2005) may be a function of the differences in state and district policies, procedures, and personnel. Rueda and Windmueller (2006) provide a history of the many attempts to unpack the overrepresentation of minorities in special education.

Assessment

Both large scale and individual assessments are important to the issue of the identification of LD in ELL students. First, do we have accurate statistics at the state and national level on how many ELL students are failing to achieve grade-level abilities in reading and content areas, and second can we identify accurately those individual students who have special educational needs so that we can intervene appropriately?

A key challenge for schools has been when and how to include ELL students in the required assessments of No Child Left Behind (NCLB, P.L. 107–110). NCLB requires states and local education agencies to ensure that ELLs acquire the English language, meet the same achievement standards, and receive the same academic content set by the state for all students. Language and reading instruction programs funded with federal dollars, under NCLB, must be research based, and to measure progress toward these legislated goals for ELLs, states must administer content tests in reading/language arts and math/science and submit adequate yearly progress (AYP) reports based on these standardized assessments of all students (Nixon, McCardle & Leos, 2007). Most states offer a standard set of accommodations for ELLs who need them to participate in standardized assessments. There are usually criteria in place for which accommodations ELLs may receive, based upon a needs assessment. In addition, NCLB allows an ELL student's score to be omitted from state AYP reports under specific conditions.[6] However, there is little research

---

6. For more information, see the National Center for Educational Outcomes, 2006, for state Web sites that describe available accommodations or modifications for ELLs (http://education.umn.edu/NCEO/LEP/Accommodations/StateLEPAccommPolicies.htm).

to demonstrate that these accommodations are in fact effective in leveling the playing field for ELL students in testing situations.

Francis, Rivera, Lesaux, Kieffer, and Rivera (2006) present a meta-analysis of available research on the use of accommodations for ELL students in large-scale assessments. These authors emphasize the importance of academic language, and clearly state that

> regardless of the choice of accommodations, the accommodations used during testing should match those used during classroom instruction. . . . One cannot assume that ELLs will perform better when testing in their first language. The choice . . . must take into account the students' oral proficiency and literacy in their native language, as well as the language in which they have been instructed. (p. 28)

Despite the small number of studies that actually examined the use of accommodations deemed appropriate for use with ELL students (i.e., those focused on the linguistic needs of ELL students), the authors were able to perform meta-analyses. They found that the one accommodation that appeared to have an effect on student performance was allowing students the use of English language dictionaries. Surprisingly, extra time was not helpful and in fact, those studies which combined use of English language dictionaries and extra time actually had smaller effect sizes than those with only dictionaries. The authors consider the use of extra time still an open question requiring further study. Thus, at present, the widespread use of multiple types and combinations of accommodations is not a simple, straightforward fix for the complexity of assessing ELLs and ELLs with disabilities to demonstrate AYP or content proficiency.

As noted above, while the accuracy of large-scale assessments is important, it is equally important that we have individual assessment tools that can accurately measure ELL students' language and reading abilities for diagnostic purposes. Above, in discussing heterogeneity of the ELL population, we discussed dialect. A clear example of how that comes into play in assessment is that of vocabulary. Many of the vocabulary assessments, even those in the native language, may not have been normed on a population similar to that of the ELL student being assessed. For example, ELL Spanish-speaking students in the United States should not be judged against test norms gathered in Spain. Not only do many Spanish-speaking students in the United States differ in culture, and socioeconomic status from students in Spain, but their dialects of Spanish are also different. Dialectal differences between, for example, Mexican Spanish and Spanish spoken in Spain include not only differences in pronunciation but also in vocabulary and common (colloquial) expressions. Similarly, we simply cannot take tests normed on monolingual English-speaking students and assume that they apply to ELL students. We must develop norms for assessment for ELL students within this nation, both for native language assessments and for English. Use of criterion-referenced assessments in conjunction with standardized instruments is advisable to provide some context for interpretation of these measures when they must be used.

There is general agreement in the research community that there is a paucity of linguistically and culturally appropriate assessment tools for English language learners that will adequately determine whether limited language ability in English is interfering with typical learning or is masking a learning disability (Garcia, McKoon, & August, 2006; Lesaux, 2006; MacSwan & Rolstad, 2006; McCardle, Mele-McCarthy, & Leos, 2005; Wagner, Francis, & Morris, 2005). Research and development work is severely needed in this area.

One notable effort is in the area of reading and reading disabilities. Research on assessing comprehension in second language readers has shed some light on the major issues and next steps that need to occur in this area (Francis, Rivera et al., 2006; Francis, Snow et al., 2006). Existing comprehension assessments can identify poor readers but do not isolate the determinants of poor performance. Most comprehension assessments require good decoding skills and high levels of English proficiency, including a strong academic vocabulary, which many ELL students may lack despite having adequate daily conversational abilities. The Diagnostic Assessment of Reading Comprehension (DARC) developed by August, Francis, Hsu, and Snow (2006) is a promising new measure for native Spanish speakers. The DARC instrument aims to disentangle decoding skills, language-proficiency skills, and vocabulary skills from other key skills that underlie comprehension, such as working memory and the ability to draw inferences across propositions.

Whether one can assess a student in both languages and when assessment in both languages is appropriate are not simple issues. First, in addition to a lack of appropriate assessments that can distinguish between disability and lack of language proficiency, there is a lack of comparable assessments in English and other languages. When first-language measures are available, ELL students should be assessed in their first language as well as English when the goal is to distinguish between LD and issues of English proficiency, and when assessment instruments assess the same domain of knowledge or skill at comparable levels and with comparable precision. Even when comparable assessments are available in a second language, finding qualified individuals to conduct the assessment may be challenging, depending on the local resources and variety of second languages. There is an even greater paucity of comparable assessments for students whose first language is not alphabetic. There is a critical need for research and development of linguistically and culturally appropriate assessment tools (Garcia et al., 2006; National Symposium on Learning Disabilities in English Language Learners, 2003).

Even when first language assessment instruments are available, the appropriateness of conducting first language assessments must be determined. MacSwan and Rolstad (2006) have shown the value of using natural language sampling as a more accurate means of assessing native language abilities in students who are thought to be semi-lingual or those who are thought to demonstrate low proficiency in both languages. These authors recommend against routinely assessing students in the native language using standardized assessment unless there is reason to suspect a language or learning problem. When assessing language and reading ability and the student is known to be a native speaker of a language other than English (whether formally classified by the school as LEP or ELL or not), then first language assessment should be used. However, multiple approaches/measures should be used, including natural language sampling. Language sampling must be conducted by someone with skills in language analysis and familiarity with the native language. When assessing specific content areas, it would be inappropriate to conduct an assessment in the first language if instruction has not been delivered in that language.

Impact of Subjectivity in the LD Identification Process

As noted above, much attention has focused on the inadequacy of the discrepancy formula for identifying students with LD. Recently, attention has been drawn to more subjective factors at play in the determination of disabilities (Mellard et al., 2004). These factors may include:

> the availability of other services for students who struggle to learn, the degree of involvement of the student's parents in the identification process, the student's ethnicity or SES status, the perceived role of various staff members in a school setting relative to low student achievement, and the degree to which teachers see themselves as being responsible for ensuring the success of certain low-performing students. (Mellard et al., 2004, p. 231)

MacMillan and Siperstein (2002) also conclude that subjectivity plays a major role in special education decision making. Their study found a marked difference in the samples of students identified as LD by researchers and those identified by the schools. It is possible that school level workers who are ultimately making the LD determinations for ELLs are considerably influenced by organizational and resource constraints, which differ by locality (Mellard et al., 2004), or other variable factors. Harry and Klingner (2006) shed light on the subjective culture of referral at individual schools in an ethnographic study of the special education process for linguistic and ethnic minority students. Harry and Klingner found that students' language learning needs were not typically central to the referral and eligibility determination process, even in schools where personnel involved in the process seemed knowledgeable about second language learning issues. The authors concluded that their "data . . . suggest that the referral process when applied to ELLs was variable and confused" (2006, p. 122). In addition to the subjectivity inherent in the local level decision making for LD identification of ELLs, states have taken varied approaches (or no special approach at all) to address the unique needs of ELLs being considered for LD identification (Keller-Allen, 2006), likely resulting in further variability in identification procedures and rates.

MOVING FORWARD: USING CURRENT RESEARCH TO IMPROVE LD IDENTIFICATION FOR ELLS

Recent policy changes and current research can help inform improved methods for LD identification in ELLs. In this section we provide a brief review of RTI, research on the predictive factors for English reading success in ELLs, and promising new interventions for struggling readers who are ELLs.

Response to Intervention

The recent reauthorization of IDEA in 2004 has given states and districts the option of no longer using the IQ-achievement discrepancy approach to the identification of students with LD, now allowing the use of an RTI model for identification. There is some guidance already available on RTI (e.g., National Association of State Directors of Special Education (NASDSE), 2005), and more research is underway. The International Reading Association (IRA) convened a group of education associations to discuss how best to provide helpful information to the education community about RTI. As a result they developed a set of fact sheets about RTI that include an introduction, challenges and opportunities, new and expanded roles for those typically involved in student education and the identification of LD, and other useful information. The set of fact sheets is posted on various association Web sites.[7] Fletcher et al. (2006) offers a recent, clearly detailed explanation of the potential advantages of using an RTI approach not only for identifying LD using RTI, but its potential

---

7. The International Dyslexia Association has the set downloadable in one large document, at http://www.interdys.org/npdf/rti-rev.pdf.

influence on the entire education system. Not only does RTI call for careful progress monitoring for students, but it also requires documenting the quality and intensity of instruction. To document that underachievement is indeed unexpected, it must be demonstrated there is no obvious explanation in terms of other limitations including poor instruction. (See also Chapters 5 and 10 for further discussion of RTI.)

Prediction of Reading Success or Risk

Research supported by the NICHD-Institute of Education Sciences (IES) research consortium, Development of English Literacy in Spanish Speaking Students (DELSS)[8], focused on the prediction of reading ability and risk for reading failure in ELL students, as did work of the National Panel on Language Minority Children and Youth (August & Shanahan, 2006). This work clearly indicates that many of the same cognitive skills predict reading ability in English for both monolingual and ELL students (Lesaux & Geva, 2006; Lindsey & Manis, 2005; Páez & Rinaldi, 2006).

Lindsey and Manis (Lindsey & Manis, 2005; Lindsey, Manis, & Bailey, 2003) followed a longitudinal sample of low-socioeconomic status Latino children from kindergarten through fifth grade to track developmental trends in learning over time and to attempt to predict future reading success or difficulty based on early skills. They found that the strongest beginning-of-kindergarten predictors of reading difficulty in fifth grade were Spanish letter-word identification and Spanish memory for sentences. The best predictors of reading success or failure in letter-word identification and passage comprehension in fifth grade were how well the students performed at the end of kindergarten on Spanish letter-word identification, letter names, and picture vocabulary. The authors found that many ELL students with reading comprehension problems in fifth grade needed work in decoding, oral language, and reading fluency. They found that their predictions were equally accurate whether the early phonological abilities were assessed in Spanish or English. Similarly, Geva and Genesee (2006) reported in a synthesis of research literature that early reading readiness indexes in either the first or the second language predicted language-minority students' later reading ability.

---

8. DELSS, funded jointly by the NICHD and the Institute of Education Sciences from 2000–2005, was a special initiative focused on research on the development of English reading in Spanish-speaking students in the United States, with attention to instructional approaches and the contexts that support or influence successful literacy in these students. Despite the sunset of this special initiative, both agencies continue to fund research on literacy development, instruction, and intervention with ELL students with various first language backgrounds. More information on DELSS projects and products can be found at http://www.cal.org/delss.

Lesaux and Geva (2006) found that early phonological processing skills, phonemic awareness, rapid naming, and phonological memory—the same skills that predict word level reading ability in monolingual English students—also predict English word reading in ELL students. They reported that there are similar proportions of language minority students and monolingual speakers who are classified as poor readers, and both groups exhibited difficulty with phonological awareness and word memory, and that it was these difficulties and not minority language status that underlay their early reading problems.

Oral language proficiency is quite important for reading comprehension. Limited vocabulary has been shown to be associated with low levels of reading comprehension in English; Lesaux and Geva note that ELLs with a robust vocabulary containing many high-frequency and academically relevant words are better in reading comprehension. They conclude that "for students with higher second-language proficiency, second-language reading is a function of both second-language proficiency and first language reading ability, whereas student with lower levels of second-language proficiency are less able to apply their first language reading skills to reading in a second language" (p. 65). Thus, although ELL students can master word-reading level skills while developing English oral proficiency, as they move to comprehending written English texts, the level of oral proficiency becomes an important contributor to potential reading success.

It is also important to note factors that did not predict reading ability. Hammer and Miccio (2006) studied a group of Puerto Rican preschoolers and their mothers. They found that the home literacy environments of these children from low-income homes did not predict early reading ability. Further, there were no differences in parental attitudes or practices toward early literacy experiences between first and second generation immigrant mothers. Apart from parental attitudes and home literacy practices, we know that preschool children's vocabulary and overall language ability (in any language) is an important precursor to reading development. These elements must all be considered in providing high quality, appropriately tailored literacy instruction for ELL children. It is important that we not let linguistic or racial/ethnic factors set up low expectations about reading potential.

Reading Intervention

Given the noted difficulties in identifying reading difficulties and disentangling them from broader language-learning issues, it is not unexpected that reading intervention research with ELL students has been somewhat limited. While the overarching goal the of NICHD-IES-supported DELSS research consortium was to better understand the reading development of Spanish-speaking ELL students, some of the projects within the consortium built upon their early findings by developing and testing interventions with low-achieving readers. Vaughn and colleagues have published several papers on this work (for example, Linan-Thompson, Vaughn, Prater, & Cirino, 2006; Vaughn, Cirino et al., 2006). In random-assignment experimental studies, they examined the effectiveness of a supplemental, systematic, explicit reading and oral-language intervention designed for ELL students at risk for English reading difficulties. In a modified version (in both Spanish and English) of an effective monolingual English intervention for struggling readers, students demonstrated significant gains in decoding and reading comprehension; the same comprehension gains had not been shown with monolingual English students. Modifications including story retell, the use of gestures, increased opportunities for student oral responses, and the inclusion of other sheltered-English techniques seem to have enhanced the effectiveness of the intervention (Vaughn, Linan-Thompson et al., 2006; Vaughn, Mathes et al., 2006). Despite the success of the intervention, students in both groups showed very low oral-language abilities, raising concern for longer term outcomes and signaling a need for continued intervention with additional attention to building oral language ability. This group of researchers summarized that it is clear that interventions for at-risk ELL students must integrate the foundational decoding and fluency skills with work on vocabulary, but they also hypothesized that for students whose initial reading status is very low, additional oral language support is likely to be crucial to reading success (Pollard-Duradolla, Mathes, Vaughn, Cardnas-Hagan, & Linan-Thompson, 2006).

CONCLUSION

There has been sustained attention to issues of education for ELL students since the beginning of the decade. There have been some efforts to focus this attention on the identification of LD in these students (e.g., a jointly sponsored 2003 symposium[9] and resultant special issue of *Learning Disabilities Research & Practice,* McCardle, Mele-McCarthy, Leos et al., 2005).

We know that many of the same factors that predict early reading risk or success for monolingual English-speaking children also predict reading risk or success for ELL children, and that, at least for alphabetic

---

9. The summary document, National Symposium on Learning Disabilities in English Language Learners, is available on the National Clearinghouse on English Language Acquisition at http://www.ncela.gwu.edu/oela/2003symposium_proceedings.pdf.

orthographies, such prediction can be made based on assessment in the first language, predicting to English early reading. We know that it is early phonological ability and verbal memory that seem to underlie early reading difficulties, and that linguistic minority status is not an etiologic factor for reading problems. Likewise SES and immigrant status do not explain reading problems. This does not alter the fact that ELL and language minority students will be at risk unless we give them appropriate, high quality instruction, but all children who do not receive appropriate, high quality reading instruction are at risk for reading difficulties. We also know that beginning early reading instruction at the same time that a student begins to learn to read in English is possible and can succeed. However, it is crucial that ELL students rapidly acquire English vocabulary, including academic vocabulary, and oral English proficiency to support reading comprehension.

Research has demonstrated some intervention success, as well. Vaughn and colleagues demonstrated that systematic, explicit reading and oral-language intervention that integrates the foundational decoding and fluency skills with work on vocabulary can be effective with Spanish-speaking ELL students, in either Spanish or English. However, for students whose initial reading status is very low, additional oral language support is likely to be crucial to reading success. Both identifying children who require intensive intervention and developing those interventions are areas where more research is needed.

Response to intervention, also discussed in Chapters 5 and 10, offers promise in identifying students with learning problems. RTI can target children in the early stages of learning difficulty, ensuring that they receive high quality, intensive instruction and progress monitoring, and more reliably identifying those with LD. Again it is critical to be sure that the interventions used in RTI are based on the scientific reading research. The interventions and outcomes must be documented. Although there is little question that RTI provides a useful means for identifying ELL students with LD, it is important that the interventions used are linguistically and culturally appropriate, (Klingner & Edwards, 2006) based on the scientific research, implemented effectively, allowed to continue for a sufficient amount of time, and evaluated accurately (Wilkinson, Ortiz, Robertson, & Kushner, 2006).

Clearly, there is a major commitment in the field of education generally to educating ELL students. This includes distinguishing between issues of language learning and LD, and finding optimal ways to identify ELL students with learning problems and to effectively remediate them. Determining risk status early and preventing learning difficulties is also a priority. However, despite the strong will and recent research and practice attention these topics have received, there is much more to be done. Many of the key issues identified in the research agenda that was developed as part of the 2003 National Symposium, jointly among various federal agencies and concerned associations and organizations (McCardle, Mele-McCarthy, & Leos, 2005), have not changed. That symposium was followed by two related colloquia in 2005, Improving Academic Performance Among American Indian, Alaska Native, and Native Hawaiian Students: Assessment and Identification of Learning and Learning Disabilities[10] and a follow-up colloquim on the same topic, held to inform federal agencies and policy makers (Demmert, McCardle, Mele-McCarthy, & Leos, 2006). The research agendas proposed by the 2003 National Symposium and the 2005 colloquia call for: (a) research on identification and assessment of LD and reading difficulty in ELL students; (b) the development of a description of language and learning developmental trajectories of ELLs; (c) gathering information on the individual and contextual factors affecting ELL learning outcomes; (d) research on the intersection of these ELL-specific factors with neurobiology; (e) the development of theoretical models, a classification system, and developmental benchmarks for ELLs with LD; and (f) further research on effective instruction and intervention strategies. While some work has been done in several of these areas, they remain among the key issues for today's research agenda. In 2006 and 2007, the International Reading Association and NICHD led a series of workshops cosponsored by the National Institute for Literacy, the Office of English Language Acquisition, Teachers of English to Speakers of Other Languages, and the National Association for Bilingual Education, with two goals: to produce a document of evidence-based practice guidelines,[11] and to create a research agenda. Both documents build on the report of the National Literacy Panel for Language Minority Children and Youth (August & Shanahan, 2006). Included in the research agenda are many of the issues discussed in this chapter. Also, it cannot be assumed that the attention of the research and policy communities has trickled down meaningfully to states and localities in their policies and practice. Despite a healthy amount of literature on ELLs being identified as having LD, state responses toward addressing the unique concerns are widely varied (Keller-Allen, 2006).

    In conclusion, while we have learned a great deal, there are still more questions than answers regarding ELL education and, in particular, special education. Identifying students who are in the process of learning a

---

10. The summary document for these symposia can be found on the NICHD Web site at http://www.nichd.nih.gov/publications/pubs/upload/native_american_learning_2005.pdf; two thematic issues of the *Journal of American Indian Education, Vol. 45, issues 2 & 3,* one on practice and one on research, are also based on those symposia.

11. See http://www.tesol.org/s_tesol/cat_tapestry.asp

second or additional language who have special educational needs continues to be a challenge. We have several good leads and the beginning of a coherent research agenda to address the knowledge gaps. We have promising new options for identifying students with learning difficulties and strategies for developing interventions. There is also a commitment among funders to continue to focus attention on this important and growing segment of the U.S. population, both in general and special education. With the increase in attention to RTI, there is also the promise of a closer partnership between general and special education in U.S. public schools. As we all progress in supporting and conducting the necessary research, it is important that we also recognize and act on the commitment to disseminate promising strategies and procedures in assessment, instruction, and intervention, so that the research findings, when they converge and we have confidence in their practical utility, actually find their way to implementation in classrooms and clinics.

REFERENCES

Aaron, P. G. (1997). The impending demise of the discrepancy formula. *Review of Educational Research, 67,* 461–502.

Arizona Revised Statutes § 15-752. Retrieved November 7, 2007, from http://www.azleg. state.az.us/FormatDocument.asp?inDoc=/ars/15/00752.htm&Title=15&DocType= ARS. (n.b. Section 15-753, listed as a source of exceptions in the first sentence above, provides for parental waivers.)

Artiles, A. J., Rueda, R., Salazar, J. J., & Higareda, I. (2002). English language learner representation in special education in California urban school districts. In D. J. Losen & G. Orfield (Eds.), *Racial inequity in special education* (pp. 117–136). Cambridge, MA: Harvard Education Press.

Artiles, A. J., Rueda, R., Salazar, J. J., & Higareda, I. (2005). Within-group diversity in minority disproportionate representation: English language learners in urban school districts. *Exceptional Children, 71,* 283–300.

August, D., Calderon, M., Carlo, M. & Eakin, M. N. (2006). Developing literacy in English-language learners: An examination of the impact of English-only versus bilingual instruction. In P. McCardle & E. Hoff (Eds.) *Childhood bilingualism: Research on infancy through school age.* Clevedon, UK: Multilingual Matters.

August, D., Francis, D., Hsu, H., & Snow, C. (2006). Assessing reading comprehension in bilinguals. *Elementary School Journal, 107,* 221–238.

August, D., & Shanahan, T. (Eds.). (2006). *Developing literacy in second-language learners: Report of the national literacy panel on language-minority children and youth.* Mahwah, NJ: Lawrence Erlbaum Associates.

Bialystok, E. (1997). Effects of bilingualism and biliteracy on children's emerging concepts of print. *Developmental Psychology, 33,* 429–440.

Bialystok, E. (2001). *Bilingualism in development: Language, literacy, and cognition.* New York: Cambridge University Press.

Bialystok, E. (2006). Bilingualism at school: Effect on the acquisition of literacy. In P. McCardle & E. Hoff (Eds.), *Childhood bilingualism: Research on infancy through school age.* Clevedon, UK: Multilingual Matters.

Bialystok, E., Klein, R., Craik, F.I.M., & Viswanathan, M. (2004). Bilingualism, aging, and cognitive control: Evidence from the Simon task. *Psychology and Aging, 19,* 290–303.

California Education Code §3.2.305. Retrieved November 7, 2007, from http://www.leginfo. ca.gov/cgi-bin/displaycode?section=edc&group=00001-01000&file=305-306

Cummins, J. (1991). Interdependence of first- and second- language proficiency in bilingual children. In E. Bialystok (Ed.), *Language processing in bilingual children* (pp. 70–89). Cambridge, UK: Cambridge University Press.

Demmert, W., McCardle, P. Mele-McCarthy, J., & Leos, K. (2006). Preparing Native American children for academic success: A blueprint for research. In P. McCardle & W. Demmert (Eds.) Improving academic performance among American Indian, Alaska Native, & Native Hawaiian students: Report of a national colloquium, II—The research (Special Issue). *Journal of American Indian Education, 45,* 92–106.

Diana v. California State Board of Education (1970). No. C-70, RFT, Dist. Ct. No. Cal.

Donovan, M. S., & Cross, C. T. (Eds.). (2002). *Minority students in special and gifted education.* National Research Council; Committee on Minority Representation in Special Education. Washington, DC: National Academy Press.

Fletcher, J. M., Francis, D. J., Shaywitz, S. E., Lyon, G. R., Foorman, B. R., Stuebing, K. K., et al. (1998). Intelligent testing and the discrepancy model for children with learning disabilities. *Learning Disabilities Research & Practice, 13,* 186–203.

Fletcher, J. M., Lyon, G. R., Barnes, M., Stuebing, K. K., Francis, D. J., Olson, et al. (2002). Classification of learning disabilities: An evidence-based evaluation. In R. Bradley, L. Danielson, & D. P. Hallahan (Eds.), *Identification of learning disabilities: Research to practice* (pp. 185–250). Mahwah, NJ: Lawrence Erlbaum Associates.

Fletcher, J. M., Lyon, G. R., Fuchs, L. S., & Barnes, M. A. (2006). *Learning disabilities: From identification to intervention.* New York: The Guilford Press.

Francis, D., Fletcher, J. M., Stuebing, K. K., Lyon, G. R., Shaywitz, B. A., & Shaywitz, S. E. (2005). Psychometric approaches to the identification of LD: IQ and achievement scores are not sufficient. *Journal of Learning Disabilities, 38,* 98–108.

Francis, D., Lesaux, N. K., & August, D. (2006). Language of instruction. In D. August, & T. Shanahan (Eds.), *Developing literacy in second-language learners: Report of the National Literacy Panel on Language Minority Children and Youth* (pp. 365–410). Mahwah, NJ: Lawrence Erlbaum Associates.

Francis, D., Rivera, M., Lesaux, N. K., Kieffer, M., & Rivera, H. (2006). *Research-based recommendations for the use of accommodations in large-scale assessments.* Book 3 in Practical guidelines for the education of English language learners. Center on Instruction, The RMC Research Corporation. Retrieved April 25, 2007, from http:// www.centeroninstruction.org/files/ELL3-Assessments.pdf

Francis, D., Snow, C., August, D., Carlson, C., Miller, J., & Iglesias, A. (2006). Measures of reading comprehension: A latent variable analysis of the diagnostic assessment of comprehension. *Scientific Studies of Reading, 10,* 301–322.

Fuchs, L. S., Fuchs, D., & Speece, D. L. (2002). Treatment validity as a unifying construct for identifying learning disabilities. *Learning Disability Quarterly, 25,* 33–45.

Gándara, P., Maxwell-Jolly, J., Garcia, E., Asato, J., Gutierrez, K., Stritikus, T., et al. (2000). *The initial impact of Proposition 227 on the instruction of English learners.* Santa Barbara, CA: Linguistic Minority Research Institute.

Gándara, P., & Rumberger, R. (2002). *The inequitable treatment of English learners in California's public schools.* Los Angeles, CA: UCLA's Institute for Democracy, Education, & Access (IDEA). Retrieved June 13, 2007, from http://idea.gseis.ucla.edu/ publications/williams/reports/pdfs/wws05-GandaraRumberger.pdf

Garcia, G. E., McKoon, G., & August, D. (2006). Synthesis: Language and literacy assessment. In D. August & T. Shanahan, (Eds.), *Developing literacy in second-language* learners: *Report of the national literacy panel on language-minority children and youth*. Mahwah, NJ: Lawrence Erlbaum Associates.

General Laws of Massachusett Title XII Chapter 71A: Section 4. Retrieved November 7, 2007, from http://www.mass.gov/legis/laws/mgl/71a-4.htm

Gersten, R., & Woodward, J. (1994). The language-minority student and special education: Issues, trends, and paradoxes. *Exceptional Children, 60,* 310–323.

Geva, E., & Genesee, F. (2006). First-language oral proficiency and second-language literacy. In D. August & T. Shanahan, (Eds.), *Developing literacy in second-language learners: Report of the national literacy panel on language-minority children and youth*. Mahwah, NJ: Lawrence Erlbaum Associates.

Gresham, F. M. (2002). Responsiveness to intervention: An alternative approach to the identification of learning disabilities. In R. Bradley, L. Danielson, & D. P. Hallahan (Eds.), *Identification of learning disabilities: Research to practice* (pp. 467–547). Mahwah, NJ: Lawrence Erlbaum Associates.

Hallahan, D. P., & Mercer, C. D. (2002). Learning disabilities: Historical perspectives. In R. Bradley, L. Danielson, & D. P. Hallahan (Eds.), *Identification of learning disabilities: Research to practice* (pp. 1–67). Mahwah, NJ: Lawrence Erlbaum Associates.

Hammer, C. S., & Miccio, A. W. (2006). Early language and reading development of bilingual preschoolers from low-income families. *Topics in Language Disorders, 26,* 322–337.

Harry, B., & Klingner, J. (2006). *Why are so many minority students in special education? Understanding race and disability in schools*. New York: Teachers College Press.

Heller, K. A., Holtzman, W. H., & Messick, S. (Eds.). (1982). *Placing children in special education: A strategy for equity*. Washington, DC: National Academy Press.

Hopstock, P. J., & Stephenson, T. G. (2003). *Descriptive study of services to LEP students and LEP students with disabilities: Special topic report #1: Native languages of LEP students*. Submitted to the U.S. Department of Education, Office of English Language Acquisition. Arlington, VA: Development Associates, Inc.

Hoskyn, M., & Swanson, H. L. (2000). Cognitive processing of low achievers and children with reading disabilities: A selective meta-analytic review of the published literature. *School Psychology Review, 29,* 102–120.

Individuals With Disabilities Education Act of 1997 (IDEA). (1997). 20 U.S.C. Chapter 33, as last amended by The Individuals With Disabilities Education Act Amendments of 1997 Pub.L. 105–117. Retrieved November 5, 2007, from http://www.ed.gov/offices/OSERS/Policy/IDEA/the_law.html

Individuals With Disabilities Education Improvement Act of 2004 (IDEIA), 20 U.S.C. 1414 (2004). Retrieved November 5, 2007, from http://www.nichcy.org/reauth/PL108-446.pdf

Kavale, K. A. (2002). Discrepancy models in the identification of learning disability. In R. Bradley, L. Danielson, & D. P. Hallahan (Eds.), *Identification of learning disabilities: Research to practice* (pp. 467–547). Mahwah, NJ: Lawrence Erlbaum Associates.

Kavale, K. A., & Forness, S. (1995). *The nature of learning disabilities: Critical elements of diagnosis and classification*. Mahwah, NJ: Lawrence Erlbaum Associates.

Keller-Allen, C. (2006). *English language learners with disabilities: Identification and other state policies and issues*. Alexandria, VA: National Association of State Directors of Special Education. Retrieved November 5, 2007, from http://www.projectforum.org/docs/EnglishLanguageLearnerswithDisabilities-IdentificationandOtherStatePoliciesandIssues.pdf

Kindler, A. (2002). *Survey of the states' limited English proficient students and available educational programs and services 2000–2001*. Summary report. Washington, DC: National Clearinghouse for English Language Acquisition & Language Instruction Educational Programs.

Klingner, J. K., Artiles, A. J., & Barletta, L. M. (2006). English language learners who struggle with reading: Language acquisition or LD? *Journal of Learning Disabilities, 39*, 108–128.

Klingner, J. K., & Edwards, P. A. (2006). Cultural considerations with response to intervention models. *Reading Research Quarterly, 41*, 108–117.

Larry P. v. Riles, 793 F. 2d 969 (9th Cir. 1984).

Lesaux, N. K. (2006). Building consensus: Future directions for research on English language learners at risk for learning difficulties. *Teachers College Record, 108*, 2406–2438.

Lesaux, N. K., & Geva, E. (2006). Synthesis: Development of literacy in language-minority students. In D. August & T. Shanahan, (Eds.), *Developing literacy in second-language learners: Report of the national literacy panel on language-minority children and youth*. Mahwah, NJ: Lawrence Erlbaum Associates.

Linan-Thompson, S., Vaughn, S., Prater, K., & Cirino, P. T. (2006). The response to intervention of English language learners at-risk for reading problems. *Journal of Learning Disabilities, 39*, 390–398.

Lindsey, K. A., & Manis, F. R. (2005). Development of reading skills in Spanish-speaking English-language learners: A six-year longitudinal study. International Dyslexia Association. *Perspectives, 31*, 22–26.

Lindsey, K. A., Manis, F. R., & Bailey, C. E. (2003). Prediction of first-grade reading in Spanish-speaking English-language learners. *Journal of Educational Psychology, 95*, 482–494.

Losen, D. J., & Orfield, G. (2002). *Racial inequity in special education*. Cambridge, MA: Harvard Education Press.

Lyon, G. R., Fletcher, J. M., & Barnes, M. C. (2003). Learning disabilities. In E. J. Mash & R. A. Barkley (Eds.), *Child psychopathology* (2nd ed., pp. 520–586). New York: Guilford Press.

Lyon, G. R., Fletcher, J. M., Shaywitz, S. E., Shaywitz, B. A., Torgesen, J. K., Wood, F. B., et al. (2001). Rethinking learning disabilities. In C. E. Finn, Jr., A. J. Rotherman, & C. R. Kokanson, Jr. (Eds.), *Rethinking special education for a new century* (pp. 259–287). Washington, DC: Thomas B. Fordham Foundation & The Progressive Policy Institute.

MacMillan, D. L., Gresham, F. M., & Bocian, K. M. (1998). Discrepancy between definitions of learning disabilities and school practices: An empirical investigation. *Journal of Learning Disabilities, 31*, 314–326.

MacMillan, D. L., & Siperstein, G. N. (2002). Learning disabilities as operationally defined by schools. In R. Bradley, L. Danielson, & D. P. Hallahan (Eds.), *Identification of learning disabilities: Research to practice* (pp. 287–333). Mahwah, NJ: Lawrence Erlbaum Associates.

MacSwan, J., & Rolstad, K. (2006). How language proficiency tests mislead us about language ability: Implications for English language learner placement in special education. *Teachers College Record, 108*, 2304–2328.

Martin, M. M., & Bialystok, E. (2003). *Two kinds of inhibition over the lifespan: Evidence for separate developmental trajectories*. Poster presented at the annual meeting of The Psychonomics Society, Vancouver, Canada, November 6–9.

McCardle, P., Mele-McCarthy, J., Cutting, L., Leos, K., & D'Emilio, T. (2005). Learning disabilities in English language learners: Identifying the issues. *Learning Disabilities Research & Practice, 20*, 1–5.

McCardle, P., Mele-McCarthy, J., & Leos, K. (2005). English language learners and learning disabilities: Research agenda and implications for practice. *Learning Disabilities Research & Practice, 20*, 68–78.

Mellard, D. F., Deshler, D. D., & Barth, A. (2004). LD identification: It's not simply a matter of building a better mousetrap. *Learning Disability Quarterly, 27*, 229–242.

National Association of State Directors of Special Education (NASDSE). (2005). *Response to intervention: Policy considerations and implementation.* Alexandria, VA: Author.

National Symposium on Learning Disabilities in English Language Learners: Symposium Summary. (2003). Office of Special Education and Rehabilitation Services, Office of English Language Acquisition (U.S. Department of Education) and the National Institute of Child Health and Human Development (U.S. Department of Health and Human Services. Retrieved January 30, 2005, from http://www.nichd.nih.gov/crmc/cdb/symposium_summary.pdf

Nixon, S., McCardle, P., & Leos, K. (2007). From research to practice—Implications of research on English language learning students for classroom and clinical practice. *Language Speech and Hearing Services in the Schools, 38,* 272–277.

No Child Left Behind Act of 2001 (NCLBA), Pub. L. No. 107–110, 115 Stat. 1425 (2001).

Ortiz, A.A. (1997). Learning disabilities occurring concomitantly with linguistic differences. *Journal of Learning Disabilities, 30,* 321–332.

Ortiz, A.A., & Yates, J.R. (1983). Incidence of exceptionality among Hispanics: Implications for manpower planning. *NABE: The Journal for the National Association for Bilingual Education, 7,* 41–53.

Páez, M., & Rinaldi, C. (2006). Predicting English word reading skills for Spanish-speaking students in first grade. *Topics in Language Disorders, 26,* 338–350.

Pollard-Duradolla, S.D., Mathes, P.G., Vaughn, S., Cardenas-Hagan, E., & Linan-Thompson, S. (2006). The role of oracy in developing comprehension in Spanish-speaking English language learners. *Topics in Language Disorders, 26,* 365–385.

ProEnglish. (2007). English in the 50 States. Retrieved November 7, 2007, from http://www.proenglish.org/issues/offeng/states.html

Reschly, D.J., & Hosp, J.L. (2004). State SLD identification policies and practices. *Learning Disability Quarterly, 27,* 197–213.

Robertson, P., Kushner, M. I., Starks, J., & Drescher, C. (1994). An update of participation rates of culturally and linguistically diverse students in special education: The need for a research and policy agenda. *The Bilingual Special Education Perspective, 14,* 3–9.

Rueda, R., & Windmueller, M. (2006). English language learners, LD, and overrepresentation: A multiple-level analysis. *Journal of Learning Disabilities, 39,* 99–107.

Scruggs, T.E., & Mastropieri, M.A. (2002). On babies and bathwater: Addressing the problems of identification of learning disabilities. *Learning Disability Quarterly, 25,* 155–168.

Siegel, L.S. (1992). An evaluation of the discrepancy definition of dyslexia. *Journal of Learning Disabilities, 25,* 618–629.

Stanovich, K.E. (1999). The sociopsychometrics of learning disabilities. *Journal of Learning Disabilities, 32,* 350–361.

Stanovich, K.E., & Siegel, L.S. (1994). Phenotypic performance profile of children with reading disabilities: A regression-based test of the phonological-core variable-difference model. *Journal of Educational Psychology, 86,* 24–53.

Sternberg, R.J., & Grigorenko, E.I. (2002). Difference scores in the identification of children with learning disabilities: It's time to use a different method. *Journal of School Psychology, 40,* 65–84.

Stuebing, K.K., Fletcher, J.M., LeDoux, J.M., Lyon, G.R., Shaywitz, S.E., & Shaywitz, B.A. (2002). Validity of IQ-discrepancy classifications of reading disabilities: A meta-analysis. *American Educational Research Journal, 39,* 469–518.

Thorndike, R.L. (1963). *The concepts of over and under achievement.* New York: Columbia University Bureau of Publications.

Torgesen, J.K. (1993). Variations on theory in learning disabilities. In R. Lyon, D. Gray, N. Krasnegor, & J. Kavenaugh (Eds.), *Better understanding learning disabilities: Perspectives on classification, identification, and assessment of and their implications for education and policy* (pp. 153–170). Baltimore: Brookes Publishing.

U.S. Department of Education, National Clearinghouse for English Language Acquisition & Language Instruction Educational Programs (NCELA). (2006). *The growing numbers of limited English proficient Students 1994/95–2004/05.* Retrieved June 16, 2007, from http://www.ncela.gwu.edu/policy/states/reports/statedata/2004 LEP/GrowingLEP_0405_Nov06.pdf

U.S. Department of Education, Office of Civil Rights (OCR). (2003). *OCR Elementary and Secondary School Survey.* Retrieved March 25, 2004, from http://205.207.175.84/ ocr2000r/

U.S. Department of Education, Office of Special Education and Rehabilitation Services (OSERS). (2002). *A new era: Revitalizing special education for children and their families.* Washington, DC: ED Pubs. Retrieved January 30, 2005, from http://www. ed.gov/inits/commissionsboards/whspecialeducation/reports/index.html

U.S. English. (2007). *Resource room: States with official english laws.* Retrieved November 7, 2007, from http://www.usenglish.org/inc/official/states.asp

Vaughn, S., Cirino, P.T., Linan-Thompson, S., Mathes, P.G., Carlson, C.D., Cardenas-Hagan, E., et al. (2006). Effectiveness of a Spanish intervention and an English intervention for English language learners at risk for reading problems. *American Educational Research Journal, 43,* 449–487.

Vaughn, S., Linan-Thompson, S., Mathes, P.G., Cirino, P.T., Carlson, C.D., Durodola, S.P., et al. (2006). Effectiveness of Spanish intervention for first grade English language learners at risk for reading difficulties. *Journal of Learning Disabilities, 39,* 56–73.

Vaughn, S., Mathes, P.G., Linan-Thompson, S., Cirino, P.T., Carlson, C.D., Pollard-Durodola, et al. (2006). First grade English language learners at risk for reading difficulties: Effectiveness of an English intervention. *Elementary School Journal, 107,* 153–180.

Vellutino, F.R., Scanlon, D.M., & Lyon, G.R. (2000). Differentiating between difficult-to-remediate and readily remediated poor readers. *Journal of Learning Disabilities, 33,* 223–239.

Wagner, R.K., Francis, D.J., & Morris, R.D. (2005). Identifying English language learners with learning disabilities: Key challenges and possible approaches. *Learning Disabilities Research & Practice, 20,* 6–15.

Wilkinson, C., Ortiz, A., Robertson, P., & Kushner, M. (2006). English language learners with reading-related LD: Linking data from multiple sources to make eligibility determinations. *Journal of Learning Disabilities, 39,* 129–141.

Zehler, A.M., Fleischman, H.L., Hopstock, P.J., Stephenson, T.G., Pendzick, M.L., & Sapru, S. (2003). *Descriptive study of services to LEP students and LEP students with disabilities, volume I—Research report.* Submitted to the U.S. Department of Education, Office of English Language Acquisition. Arlington, VA: Development Associates, Inc.

CHAPTER 7

IDEIA and Specific Learning Disabilities

What Role Does Intelligence Play?

Jack A. Naglieri and Alan S. Kaufman

The Individuals With Disabilities Education Improvement Act (IDEIA 2004) has had and will continue to have substantial influence on education in the United States and the practice of school psychology and related disciplines such as special education, social work, and medicine. IDEIA 2004 and the Federal Regulations that interpret the law addressed many areas of concern about educational practice. Perhaps one of the most important aspects of the law, certainly one that has gained considerable attention, involves children with specific learning disabilities (SLD). Although the law addresses new methods for dealing with these children, implementation will not be an easy task because operationalization of a law by states and practitioners requires interpretation of the law and the regulations. Counterbalancing these issues will be how state administrators, practitioners, and scholars interpret the law in relation to the practice of school psychology and related fields and particularly the science behind any methods that may be used.

This chapter focuses on the issue of identification of children with SLD. More specifically, we will examine the law and the regulations that interpret the law and examine two methods for SLD diagnosis: the assessment of basic psychological processes as a key component to a comprehensive evaluation and the use of response to intervention (RTI) for SLD determination. Our position is that both methods should be used to comprise a comprehensive service delivery model but neither alone will be sufficient to meet the demands of IDEIA 2004. We will propose explicit methods for how children with SLD can be identified and methods of incorporating the best aspects of both perspectives into a balanced practice model that maximizes diagnostic accuracy and optimizes educational outcomes for this heterogeneous population. Our position is consistent with IDEIA: When adequate attempts have been made to teach a child and little progress is found, eligibility must be determined using a comprehensive evaluation. Additionally, in order to determine if a child has SLD assessment must include reliable and valid measures of the basic psychological processes to be consistent with the definition of SLD included in IDEIA 2004.

IDEIA 2004 and Specific Learning Disabilities

IDEIA (2004) provides instructions about the identification of children with SLD that vary from specific to general. First, the law specifically states that the long-standing approach of using an ability-achievement discrepancy to determine if a child has an SLD is no longer required. Stated another way that means that ability-achievement discrepancies are allowed but not required for a diagnosis of SLD. Importantly, the law states that "the local educational agency *may* [italics added] use a process that determines if the child responds to scientific, research-based intervention as a part of the evaluation procedures" but the so-called RTI method is *not* mandated (see section 614(b)6B of IDEIA 2004). The law also describes several important components of a comprehensive evaluation. First, a variety of assessment tools and strategies must be used to gather relevant information about the child. Second, the use of any single measure or assessment as the sole criterion for determining whether a child has SLD is not permitted. Third, practitioners must use technically sound instruments to assess the relative contribution of cognitive and behavioral factors. Fourth, assessments must be selected and administered so as not to be discriminatory on the basis of race or culture, and these tests are administered in a form most likely to yield accurate information. Fifth, the measures used are valid and reliable for the purposes for which they were intended.

The Federal Regulations (U.S. Department of Education, 2006) provided important additional direction. States are not allowed to prohibit the use of a severe discrepancy between ability and achievement for SLD determination. The use of RTI in the SLD eligibility determination process was also further clarified. First, section 300.302 stated that screening to determine appropriate instructional strategies for curriculum implementation shall not be considered an evaluation for special education eligibility.

Second, RTI may be used as a part of the SLD eligibility process but "determining why a child has not responded to research-based interventions *requires* [italics added] a comprehensive evaluation" (p. 46647), and "RTI does not replace the need for a comprehensive evaluation" (p. 46648). What RTI does provide is greater assurance that (a) adequate learning experiences have been provided before initiating a comprehensive evaluation and (b) the child's failure to respond is not the result of inadequate instruction. These regulations also further clarify that those assessments used in the comprehensive evaluation "include those tailored to assess specific areas of educational need and not merely those that are designed to provide a single general intelligence quotient" (p. 43785). Despite these changes in the methodology for identifying SLD, the definition of this disorder was not changed. Section 602 of IDEIA defines an SLD as follows:

1. in general—The term *specific learning disability* means a disorder in 1 or more of the basic psychological processes involved in understanding or in using language, spoken or written, which disorder may manifest itself in the imperfect ability to listen, think, speak, read, write, spell, or do mathematical calculations.
2. disorders included—Such term includes such conditions as perceptual disabilities, brain injury, minimal brain dysfunction, dyslexia, and developmental aphasia.
3. disorders not included—Such term does not include a learning problem that is primarily the result of visual, hearing, or motor disabilities, of mental retardation, of emotional disturbance, or of environmental, cultural, or economic disadvantage.

According to the National Research Center on Learning Disabilities LD Resource Kit, SLD identification procedures need to adequately address the components in the conceptual definition in a systematic and analytical fashion to accurately identify the presence of an SLD. The identification of SLD should include a student-centered, comprehensive evaluation that insures students who have a learning disability are identified accurately. In the sections that follow we will provide our views about the role of intelligence, or the term we prefer, *basic psychological processes*, in SLD determination and instructional planning.

SLD Eligibility Issues

We have previously stated that the definition of SLD and the method used to identify children with SLD should be consistent (Hale, Kaufman, Naglieri, & Kavale, 2006; Hale, Naglieri, Kaufman & Kavale, 2004; Kavale, Kaufman, Naglieri, & Hale, 2005). IDEIA 2004 and the Federal

Regulations (2006) clearly specify that children must have a disorder in "one or more of the basic psychological processes" that is the underlying cause of an SLD. A comprehensive evaluation of the basic psychological processes unites the statutory and regulatory components of IDEIA 2004 and ensures that the methods used for identification more closely reflect the definition. Any defensible classification system would demand continuity between the statutory and regulatory definitions. Our position is that SLD assessment of basic psychological processes *must* be a part of any comprehensive evaluation if children with SLD are to be appropriately identified and that such assessments meet the technical criteria included in IDEIA 2004.

In the section that follows we will summarize the technical qualities of two measures of basic psychological processes to illustrate how cognitive assessment meets the requirements of IDEIA. We choose the Kaufman Assessment Battery for Children—Second Edition (KABC-II; A. S. Kaufman & Kaufman, 2004a) and the Cognitive Assessment System (CAS; Naglieri & Das, 1997) for inclusion here but recognize that there are other published tests that may provide useful measures of a child's processing strengths and weaknesses. Indeed, the present array of available instruments for assessing the cognitive abilities and processes of children and adolescents is unprecedented in the history of clinical assessment. Despite the fact that IQ tests have historically been devoid of theoretical foundation, from their inception in the early 1900s through the 1980s, considerable efforts have been made to conceptualize intelligence tests within theoretical frameworks. For example, the Cattell-Horn-Carroll (CHC) theory of intelligence (McGrew, 2005) is now used as a foundation for the Woodcock-Johnson III (WJ III; Woodcock, McGrew, & Mather, 2001), as well as the Stanford-Binet—Fifth Edition (Binet-5; Roid, 2003) and the Differential Abilities Scales—Second Edition (DAS-II; Elliott, 2006). Luria's neuropsychological theory provided the foundation of the Planning, Attention, Simultaneous, Successive (PASS) theory used for the CAS whereas the KABC-II is built on the dual theoretical models of Luria's theory and the CHC model. Although the Wechsler Intelligence Scale for Children—Fourth Edition (WISC-IV; Wechsler, 2003), like its predecessors, is not built on any specific theoretical foundation, the four cognitive abilities it measures have been interpreted from the perspective of CHC theory (Flanagan & Kaufman, 2004; Prifitera, Saklofske, & Weiss, 2005).

All of these instruments that were either developed or revised within the past decade provide another benefit apart from their theoretical underpinnings and excellent psychometric properties: They all yield at least four reliable and valid measures of *specific* cognitive abilities or psychological processes, in strong contrast to the historical tradition of yielding a small number of *global* scores. These specific abilities and processes can be used to help identify a child's disorder and to diagnose an SLD. Indeed, critics of IQ tests, especially those who strongly advocated the elimination of IQ tests from the SLD diagnostic process (e.g., Siegel, 1999; Stanovich, 1999), focused their attack on global IQ and on the Wechsler scales. They defended their position as if Spearman's (1904) so-called *g* theory was the predominant approach to interpreting intelligence tests and with apparent lack of awareness of the new breed of theory-based cognitive batteries that rely on a number of specific, narrow abilities and processes and *not* on a few global measures of IQ (A. S. Kaufman & Kaufman, 2001).

We are focusing on the CAS and KABC-II in this chapter because these tests were specifically developed from Luria's theory of mental processing and because these two tests yield smaller ethnic differences than differences reported for other tests of cognitive ability. Unbiased tests are especially important because IDEIA requires that assessments must be selected and administered to be non-discriminatory on the basis of race or culture. In addition, intervention research has specifically been conducted on these process-based tests, especially the CAS, but also the original version of the KABC-II (the K-ABC; A. S. Kaufman & Kaufman, 1983). However, as authors of the CAS (Naglieri & Das, 1997) and KABC-II (A. S. Kaufman & Kaufman, 2004a), respectively, we must remind readers that we are presenting *illustrations* of how to identify processing disorders and diagnose SLD with carefully developed measures of intelligence (or whatever term one chooses to use). We recognize that studies have accumulated within the CHC literature that have supported links between deficits in specific CHC abilities and difficulties in diverse areas of academic achievement—for example, deficits in lexical knowledge, listening ability, naming facility, and phonetic coding are associated with problems in reading achievement (Flanagan & Kaufman, 2004; Flanagan, Ortiz, & Alfonso, 2007; McGrew, 2005). Therefore, tests built on the CHC model, PASS theory, and Wechsler's scales are all suitable choices to serve as the main measures of cognitive abilities and processes for the identification of a processing disorder when diagnosing SLD.

We also present this discussion mindful of some important basic assumptions. First, we recognize the limitations of an IQ-achievement discrepancy and will not assume that a Full Scale score comparison to achievement should be used for diagnosis. In particular, we assume that a child with SLD will show intra-individual variability in cognitive processing, thereby making the Full Scale score a misleading representation of the strengths and weaknesses the child may have. Second, we completely agree that a variety of assessment tools and strategies must be used to make a good diagnosis and that the use of any single measure as the sole criterion for determining whether a child has SLD is not appropriate.

Comprehensive evaluation demands examination of the whole child within the greater context. Third, and finally, practitioners *must* use technically sound instruments to assess the relative contribution of cognitive and behavioral factors that are not discriminatory on the basis of race or culture and are valid and reliable for the purposes for which they were intended.

The No Child Left Behind Act of 2001 defines scientific-based research as "research that involves the application of rigorous, systematic, and objective procedures to obtain reliable and valid knowledge relevant to education activities and programs." The scientific evidence for the issues described above will be more fully explored in the sections that follow.

IDEIA REQUIREMENTS FOR AN EVALUATION

Reliability

Reliability of any score is a basic requirement for good practice because this psychometric attribute influences how scores are interpreted. Whenever a child's score is compared to any other score, reliability of the measure is critical because it reflects the "consistency of scores obtained by the same persons when they are reexamined with the same test on different occasions or with different sets of equivalent items, or under other variable examining conditions" (Anastasi & Urbina, 1997, p. 84). If a test has low reliability, then two scores can differ considerably, yet that difference would likely be related to the unreliability (that is, error) of the measure rather than a real difference in the score. Reliability estimates of test scores are used for calculation of important interpretive statistics, such as the Standard Error of Measurement, confidence intervals, and differences between scores needed for significance. Internal consistency reliabilities for the standard scores obtained from tests like the CAS, KABC-II, WISC-IV, or WJ III give practitioners guidelines for understanding how much variability in obtained scores can be attributable to errors of measurement and how much can be considered to reflect real differences. Reliability of all types of measurement, especially when SLD diagnosis is involved, must be available and the methods by which these coefficients are determined should be based on well-established principles and practices in the field.

Wechsler's scales like the DAS-II, Binet-5, KABC-II, and CAS all yield scores that have excellent reliability. For example, at ages 3–18 years, the KABC-II average internal consistency coefficients are .95 to .97 for its theory-based global scores and .88 to .93 for its five separate scales (A. S. Kaufman & Kaufman, 2004a). Similarly, the CAS Full Scale and PASS

Scales have high internal reliability (Naglieri & Das, 1997). The average reliability coefficients for the Standard Battery PASS Scales are .88 (Planning), .88 (Attention), .93 (Simultaneous), .93 (Successive), and .96 (Full Scale). These reliabilities well exceed the minimum values suggested by Bracken (1987), as do the values reported for the other tests of cognitive abilities mentioned previously, such as the WJ III and WISC-IV.

Validity

Validity is described as *"what* the test measures and *how well* it does so" (Anastasi & Urbina, 1997, p. 113) and is demonstrated through the accumulation of evidence regarding the inferences drawn from test scores. In this section we will provide evidence of validity that is particularly important for SLD diagnosis and in relation to the issues that are listed in the beginning of this chapter that are included in the IDEIA 2004. More details about validity of these two instruments can be found in the respective test manuals as well as published summaries of these tests (e.g., A. S. Kaufman, Lichtenberger, Fletcher-Janzen, & Kaufman, 2005; Naglieri, 1999, 2005). In addition, the other theory-based and well-constructed tests that have been published during the past decade have a wealth of data in support of their validity. Again, consult the test manuals for these research-based data as well as books or chapters written about the Binet-5 (Roid & Barram, 2004), WJ III (Schrank, Flanagan, Woodcock, & Mascolo, 2002), WISC-IV (Flanagan & Kaufman, 2004; Prifitera et al., 2005), and DAS-II (Elliott, 2005).

The sections that follow are generally illustrative, therefore, of the validity of currently available tests of cognitive abilities and processes. However, as noted previously, two aspects of empirical validity that are more specific to the KABC-II and CAS than to other current tests concern the reduction of ethnic differences in the scores they yield and the availability of intervention research.

To facilitate understanding of the following sections, we present a brief description of the processes derived from Luria's (1966, 1970) neuropsychological theory, as measured by the CAS and KABC-II. The CAS is a multidimensional measure of cognitive processing based on the Planning, Attention, Simultaneous, and Successive (PASS) theory of intelligence (see Naglieri & Das 1997; Naglieri, 1999, 2005). Naglieri and Das (2004) described the four PASS processes as follows.

1. *Planning* is a mental activity that provides cognitive control; use of processes, knowledge, and skills; intentionality; organization; and self-regulation. This includes self-monitoring and impulse control as well as generation, evaluation, and execution of a plan.

The essence of the construct of Planning and tests to measure it is that they provide a novel problem-solving situation for which children do not have a previously acquired strategy. This is the hallmark of the concept of executive function (Hayes, Gifford, & Ruckstuhl, 1996).

2. *Attention* is conceptualized as a mental activity that provides focused, selective cognitive activity over time and resistance to distraction. The process is involved when a person must demonstrate focused, selective, sustained, and effortful activity. This construct was conceptualized and operationalized similarly to the attention work of Schneider, Dumais, and Shiffrin (1984), and Posner and Boies (1971).

3. *Simultaneous processing* is a mental activity by which a person integrates stimuli into interrelated groups or a whole. Simultaneous processing tests typically have strong spatial aspects for this reason but can involve both nonverbal as well as verbal content as long as the cognitive demand of the task requires the integration of information. The construct of simultaneous processing is conceptually related to the examination of visual-spatial reasoning particularly found in progressive matrices tests such as those originally developed by Penrose and Raven (1936).

4. *Successive processing* is a mental activity by which the person works with stimuli in a specific serial order to form a chain-like progression. Successive processing involves both the perception of stimuli in sequence and the formation of sounds and movements in order. For this reason, successive processing is involved with recall of information in order as well as phonological analysis and the syntax of language. Successive processing has been conceptually and experimentally related to the concept of phonological analysis (Das, Naglieri, & Kirby, 1994).

The KABC-II measures the following Luria-derived processes. Each is assigned a dual name to reflect that these processes also align with Broad Abilities from the CHC theory of cognitive abilities (for more detail consult A. S. Kaufman & Kaufman, 2004a, and A. S. Kaufman et al., 2005). One additional scale is included in the KABC-II—Knowledge/Gc, which measures crystallized ability from CHC theory—but that scale is not included in the process-based global score that is featured in this chapter.

1. *Sequential/Gsm* is a measure of what Luria termed successive processing, a step-by-step approach to problem solving, and closely resembles the Sequential Processing Scale in the original K-ABC and the Successive Processing Scale in the CAS. Gsm refers to the

scale's short-term memory component as defined by CHC theory (McGrew, 2005).

2. *Simultaneous/Gv* measures Luria's notion of simultaneous processing, a gestalt-integrative approach to problem solving. This scale is an analog of the K-ABC and CAS Simultaneous Processing Scales. The "Gv" component refers to the CHC ability of visualization that is a key ability needed to solve the visual-spatial problems (McGrew, 2005).

3. *Planning/Gf* measures the frontal lobe, executive functions that are needed to solve novel problems and to develop strategies for efficiently finding the best solution to complex, abstract problems. In addition to Luria's notion of planning ability, the Planning/Gf Scale is closely aligned to the CHC notion of fluid intelligence (Gf), as defined by Horn (1989) and Carroll (1993), and to Piaget's (1972) stage of formal operational thought.

4. *Learning/Glr* reflects an integration of Luria processes, namely attention, sequential, simultaneous, and planning. This dynamic integration of processes is needed to accomplish complex tasks such as learning new information during a structured teacher-learner interaction during the administration of the KABC-II, retaining the new information for at least 30 minutes after instruction, and achieving in school. From CHC theory, this scale measures long-term retrieval of information from storage (Glr).

Relationships to Achievement

The extent to which a test of ability correlates with (or from a statistical perspective predicts) a child's level of school performance is an important indicator of that test's validity. Prediction of school achievement from a traditional IQ test has the advantage of content similarity in both measures because verbal and quantitative scales on a traditional test of ability are often very similar to tests of achievement (Naglieri & Bornstein, 2000; Naglieri & Ford, 2005). Prediction of school achievement from tests of cognitive processing that do not include achievement-like questions is particularly important because this type of predictor variable provides information about the processes, or abilities, that underlie academic success or failure. In fact, some researchers have argued the relationship between a test of ability and achievement is one of the most important aspects of validity (Brody, 1992; Naglieri & Bornstein, 2003). For this reason the relationship between measures of cognitive processing and achievement is particularly important to examine for the KABC-II and CAS. Examination of this type of validity answers the question "What relevance does a cognitive processing score have to academic performance?"

The KABC-II yields two theory-based global composites, but the one of most relevance here is the Mental Processing Index (MPI) which is derived from the Luria theoretical model and excludes measures of crystallized knowledge. The MPI correlated, on average, .68 with total achievement on the Peabody Individual Achievement Test-Revised (PIAT-R; Markwardt, 1997), .70 with total achievement on the WJ III Achievement Scale, .74 with total achievement on the Wechsler Individual Achievement Test—Second Edition (WIAT-II; The Psychological Corporation, 2001), and .74 with total achievement on the Kaufman Test of Educational Achievement—Second Edition Comprehensive Form (KTEA-II; A. S. Kaufman & Kaufman, 2004a, Tables 8–23 to 8–30; A. S. Kaufman & Kaufman, 2004b, Table 7–25). The specific processing scales also correlated substantially with total achievement on the various achievement batteries and all KABC-II scales were predictive of achievement in reading, math, written language, and oral language. For example, the four Luria-based KABC-II processing scales correlated between .52 (Sequential/Gsm) and .63 (Planning/Gf) with KTEA-II total Achievement for a representative sample 2,520 students ages 4.5 to 18 years (A. S. Kaufman & Kaufman, 2004b, Table 7–25). The Learning/Glr and Planning/Gf Scales were the best predictors of the KTEA-II Reading Composite (.56); Planning/Gf was the best predictor of Math (.59) and Oral Language (.51); and Learning/Glr was the best predictor of Written Language (.53).

Naglieri and Rojahn (2004) examined the relationships between the Planning, Attention, Simultaneous, and Successive (PASS) theory, as operationalized by the CAS, and achievement, as measured by the Woodcock-Johnson Tests of Achievement—Revised (WJ-R; Woodcock & Johnson, 1989), using a representative sample of 1,559 students aged 5–17 years. The correlation between the CAS Full Scale with the WJ-R Tests of Achievement was .71. More recently, Naglieri, Goldstein, DeLauder, and Schwebach (2006) compared the Wechsler Intelligence Scale for Children—Third Edition (WISC-III; Wechsler, 1991) to the CAS, and WJ-III Test of Achievement for a sample of children aged 6 to 16 who were referred for evaluation due to learning problems. The CAS Full Scale score correlated .83 with the WJ-III achievement scores compared to a coefficient of .63 for the WISC-III Full Scale IQ. The results suggest that when the same children took the two ability tests and those scores were correlated with the same achievement scores, both showed a strong relationship between ability and achievement, but the CAS correlated significantly higher (Naglieri et al., 2006).

These studies of the CAS and KABC-II illustrate that a cognitive approach to understanding children's intellectual variability has relevance to academic skills. Interestingly, these studies show that cognitive processes are effective for prediction of academic performance, and they also suggest that a cognitive processing approach may provide an especially important tool for predicting achievement for children who come from disadvantaged environments as well as those who have had a history of academic failure. The latter implication is based on the fact that both the CAS Full Scale and KABC-II MPI demonstrate excellent prediction of achievement based solely on problem solving and mental processing and *without* including measures of acquired knowledge.

Is Cognitive Processing Assessment Nondiscriminatory?

As the characteristics of the U.S. population continues to change, the need for fair assessment of diverse populations of children has become progressively more important. Federal law (e.g., IDEIA 2004) stipulates that assessments must be selected and administered so as to be nondiscriminatory on a racial or cultural basis. It is, therefore, critical that any measures used for evaluation be evaluated for bias. Some researchers have suggested that intelligence conceptualized on the basis of psychological processes are more appropriate for diverse populations (Das, 2002; Fagan, 2000; Naglieri, 2005). We will address the question of the validity of a test of cognitive processing for nondiscriminatory assessment on the basis of mean score differences.

Fagan (2000) and Suzuki and Valencia (1997) argued that because processing tests do not rely on test items with language and quantitative content they are more appropriate for assessment of culturally and linguistically diverse populations. Although there is considerable evidence for the validity of general intelligence (see Jensen, 1998), a multidimensional theory of cognitive processing could provide a more comprehensive view of ability (Naglieri, 2005; Sternberg, 1988). Ceci (2000) also suggested that a processing approach could allow for early detection of disabilities that predate academic failure, could have better diagnostic utility, and could provide a way to better understand children's disabilities. Although researchers have traditionally found a mean difference of about 12–15 points between African Americans and Whites on measures of IQ that include verbal, quantitative, and nonverbal tests (e.g., A. S. Kaufman & Lichtenberger, 2006; A. S. Kaufman et al., 2005, Table 6.7), results for measures of cognitive processing have been different.

CAS cognitive processing scores of 298 African American children and 1,691 White children were compared by Naglieri, Rojahn, Matto, and Aquilino (2005). Controlling for key demographic variables, regression analyses showed a CAS Full Scale mean score difference of 4.8 points in favor of White children. They also found that correlations between the

CAS scores and WJ-R Tests of Achievement were very similar for African Americans (.70) and Whites (.64). Similarly, Naglieri, Rojahn, and Matto (2007) examined the utility of the PASS theory with Hispanic children by comparing performance on the CAS of Hispanic and White children. The study showed that the two groups differed by 6.1 points using unmatched samples, 5.1 with samples matched on basic demographic variables, and 4.8 points when demographics differences were statistically controlled. They also found that the correlations between achievement and the CAS scores did not differ significantly for the Hispanic and White samples. More recently, Naglieri, Otero, DeLauder, and Matto (2007) compared scores obtained on the CAS when administered in English and Spanish to bilingual children referred for academic difficulties. The children earned similar Full Scale scores on the English and Spanish versions of the CAS that were highly correlated (r = .96), deficits in Successive processing were found for on both versions of the test, and 90% of children who had a cognitive weakness on the English version of the CAS also had the same cognitive weakness on the Spanish version of the CAS.

The original K-ABC produced ethnic differences that were far smaller than the differences associated with traditional IQ tests. At ages 2.5 to 12.5, *without* controlling for background variables, Whites (N = 1,569) scored 7 points higher than African Americans (N = 807) and 3 points higher than Hispanics (N = 160) on the global measure of mental processing—discrepancies that are considerably smaller than the differences of 16 points and 11 points, respectively, reported for the WISC-R Full Scale IQ (A. S. Kaufman & Kaufman, 1983, Tables 4.36 and 4.37). Data for the KABC-II reflect the same reduction in ethnic differences. When controlling for gender and mother's education, African American children at ages 3–18 years earned mean MPIs that were only 5 points lower than the means for White children (A. S. Kaufman & Kaufman, 2004a, Tables 8.7 and 8.8; A. S. Kaufman et al., 2005, Table 6.7). Also of interest is that the KABC-II Learning/Glr Scale, which measures the child's ability to learn and retain new information (a skill that requires an integration of Luria processes), produced very small ethnic differences. African American children scored only 1.5 to 3 points lower than White children and Hispanic children scored only 1 to 4 points lower, even though the learning tasks required language ability. Finally, Fletcher-Janzen (2003) tested 46 American Indian children on the KABC-II and retested 30 of these children on the WISC-IV about 18 months later. The children who were tested on both instruments earned an average MPI on the KABC-II that was 8.4 points higher than their mean WISC-IV Full Scale IQ (A. S. Kaufman et al., 2005, Table 6.9).

These studies on the KABC-II and CAS illustrate that assessment of basic cognitive processes yields improved consequential validity (e.g., smaller differences between groups) without loss of criterion-related validity (correlations between processing and achievement) and therefore such tests provide a fair way to assess diverse populations of children.

Do Children With Different Learning Problems Have Distinctive Profiles?

The profiles of the PASS processing scores obtained from samples of children with disabilities have been examined in several studies (see Naglieri, 2005, for a summary). The various studies have shown that differences between groups have emerged in predictable and discriminating ways. For example, children with specific reading decoding problems obtained average scores in planning, attention, and simultaneous processing but low Successive scores (Naglieri, 1999). This result is consistent with the view that reading decoding failure can be the result of a disorder in sequencing of information which is the essence of Successive processing (Das, Naglieri & Kirby, 1994). Importantly, Successive processing underlies acquisition of phonological skills. There is ample evidence that phonological skills play an important role in early reading and reading failure (Stanovich, 1988; Wagner, Torgeson & Rashotte, 1994) and that a specific cognitive processing deficit in successive processing underlies a phonological skills deficit (Das, Naglieri, & Kirby, 1994). Successive processing's involvement increases if the word is a pseudoword, and this process is even more important if the words are to be read aloud, requiring pronunciation. Related activities that involve Successive processing include speech-rate, time for naming simple short and familiar words, and short-term recall for short lists of simple words. Several studies on the relationship between PASS and reading disability have supported the hypothesis that in predicting reading disability, processes (e.g., PASS) are as important as direct measures such as phonological awareness and other tests of phonological coding (Das, Parrila, & Papadopoulos, 2000). In addition, low Sequential processing relative to Simultaneous processing for individuals with reading disabilities characterized many studies of the original K-ABC (Lichtenberger, 2001). With the KABC-II, 141 children and adolescents with reading disabilities (mean age = 13) likewise scored about 3 points higher on the Simultaneous/Gv Scale than the Sequential/Gsm Scale, as did a group of 122 individuals diagnosed with writing disabilities (A. S. Kaufman et al., 2005)

The PASS scale profiles for children with SLD are in contrast to the profiles of children diagnosed with attention-deficit/hyperactivity disorder (ADHD) who earned average scores except in Planning (Dehn, 2000; Naglieri, Goldstein, Iseman, & Schwebach, 2003; Naglieri, Salter, & Edwards, 2004). Importantly, children with anxiety disorders did not evidence significant PASS scale variability (Naglieri, Goldstein, Iseman, & Schwebach, 2003).

These studies provided evidence that measuring cognitive processes can give important information about the cognitive characteristics of children who are experiencing learning problems.

Does Assessment of Processing Have Relevance to Treatment?

Over the last 30 years, researchers have applied the PASS theory to academic remediation and instruction. The oldest of the methods is the PASS Remedial Program (PREP), which was originally developed as a cognitive remedial program (Das, Naglieri, & Kirby, 1994) and initially studied by Brailsford, Snart, and Das (1984), D. Kaufman and P. Kaufman (1979), and Krywaniuk and Das (1976). These researchers demonstrated that students could be trained to use Successive and Simultaneous processes more efficiently, which resulted in an improvement in their performance on that process; the students were also able to transfer these processes to specific reading tasks (Ashman & Conway, 1997). Further support for PREP was provided by Carlson and Das (1997), and Das, Mishra, and Pool (1995), who compared PREP to a regular reading program. In both studies, PREP groups outperformed the control groups on word attack and word identification pre- and post-treatment scores. Boden and Kirby (1995) found that a group of learning disabled children who were randomly assigned to a PREP training improved significantly in reading and decoding real and pseudowords over the control group that received regular classroom instruction. Similarly, Das, Parrila, and Papadopoulos (2000) found that children who were taught using PREP improved significantly more in pseudoword reading than did a control group. When PREP was compared to a meaning-based reading program for two carefully matched groups of first grade children the results showed a significant improvement of reading (word identification and word attack) for the PREP group and the gain in reading was greater than it was for the meaning-based control group (Parrila, Das, Kendrick, Papadopoulos, & Kirby, 1999). Specific relevance to the children's CAS profiles was also demonstrated by the fact that those children with a higher level of Successive processing at the beginning of the program benefited the most from the PREP instruction but those with the most improvement in the meaning-based program were characterized by higher level of Planning. Finally, Papadopoulos, Das, Parrila, and Kirby (2003) compared a meaning-based procedure to PREP for grade 1 children who were poor in word decoding and found that the PREP group improved significantly more in pseudoword reading compared to the meaning-based group. They also reported that those students who were difficult to remediate a year later continued to improve, showing significant gains in decoding words, when provided PREP remediation.

PREP aims to improve the use of cognitive processing strategies (e.g., Simultaneous and Successive processes) that underlie reading. The tasks in the program teach children to focus their attention on the sequential nature of many tasks, including reading. This instruction helps the children better utilize Successive processing, an important process needed in reading and decoding. The studies summarized here support the effectiveness of PREP in remediation of poor reading skills during the elementary school years, and they illustrate the connection between the PASS theory and intervention as suggested by Ashman and Conway (1997).

A second line of intervention research based on PASS theory involves Planning Strategy Instruction (PSI). The relationship between Planning from PASS and instruction has been examined in a series of studies involving both math and reading achievement. These studies have shown that children can be taught to be more strategic when they complete academic tasks and that the facilitation of plans positively impacts academic performance. The initial concept for PSI was based on the work of Cormier, Carlson, and Das (1990) and Kar, Dash, Das, and Carlson (1992). These authors demonstrated that students differentially benefited from the technique that taught them to discover the value of strategy use without being specifically instructed to do so. Importantly, children who performed poorly on measures of Planning from the CAS demonstrated significantly greater gains than those with higher Planning scores. PSI was shown to improve children's performance in math calculation in a series of research studies. Naglieri and Gottling (1995, 1997) found that children with learning disabilities who were poor in planning improved substantially more than the control group. The results obtained in a follow-up study by Naglieri and Gottling (1997) showed that teachers could integrate PSI in the regular classroom and encourage students to consider various ways to be more successful on their classroom math work. The results again showed that those children who were weak in Planning improved considerably more than those who were strong in Planning. The relationship between PSI and the PASS profiles for children with learning disabilities and mild mental impairments was studied by Naglieri and Johnson (2000). Their results showed that children with a cognitive weakness in Planning improved considerably over baseline rates, while those with no cognitive weakness improved only marginally. Similarly, children with cognitive weaknesses in Simultaneous, Successive, and Attention processing scales showed substantially lower rates of improvement. The importance of this study was that the five groups of children responded very differently to the same intervention. Stated another way, the PASS processing scores were predictive of the children's response to this math intervention (Naglieri & Johnson, 2000).

The effects of PSI on reading comprehension were reported by Haddad et al. (2003). The researchers used a sample of general education children sorted into groups based on their PASS scale profiles using the CAS. Even though the groups did not differ by CAS Full Scale scores or pretest reading comprehension scores, children with a Planning weakness benefited substantially (effect size of 1.5) from the instruction designed to encourage the use of strategies and plans. In contrast, children with no PASS weakness or a Successive weakness did not benefit as much (effect sizes of .52 and .06, respectively). These results further support previous research suggesting that the PASS profiles are relevant to instruction.

More recently, Iseman (2005) examined PSI in children with learning disabilities and ADHD. Students in the experimental group engaged in PSI designed to encourage effective strategies in mathematics. A comparison group received additional math instruction by the regular teacher. Iseman found that students with a Planning cognitive weakness in the experimental group improved considerably on math worksheets. In contrast, students with a Planning cognitive weakness in the comparison group did not improve. Students with ADHD in the experimental group with a weakness in Planning improved considerably on the worksheets. In contrast, students with ADHD in the comparison group without a cognitive weakness in Planning did not improve. Thus, individuals with cognitive weaknesses in Planning, with and without ADHD, benefited more from PSI than normal instruction (Iseman, 2005).

Two intervention studies conducted by Dr. Judy Gunnison with her students and colleagues evaluated aptitude-treatment interactions based on the distinction between Sequential and Simultaneous processing (Gunnison's studies are summarized in A. S. Kaufman & Kaufman, 1983, pp. 235–241). In the first study, Gunnison, Town, and Masunaga administered the K-ABC to 20 children with SLD. They identified 14 children with sizeable Simultaneous > Sequential discrepancies. Seven pairs of children were matched on important background variables. Both groups received 20 hours of remediation over a 10-week period. The experimental group received remediation in reading comprehension that capitalized on their strength in Simultaneous processing, using curricular methods developed by the researchers (Gunnison, Kaufman, & Kaufman, 1982). The control group was given a traditional approach to reading instruction. The experimental group earned greater gains on six of seven standardized reading subtests administered with the difference reaching statistical significance for a vocabulary subtest. In the second study (Gunnison and Moffitt), a similar methodology was used to remediate students with SLD who demonstrated Simultaneous > Sequential K-ABC profiles (two matched groups of four children, plus a third group of five SLD children who received no remediation at all). The children in the experimental group, who were remediated based on their strength in Simultaneous processing, outscored the matched control group (traditional reading instruction) on six of the seven standardized reading tests, with four of these differences reaching statistical significance (reading recognition and literal comprehension, inferential comprehension, and total comprehension). The combined experimental groups from both Gunnison studies ($N = 11$) significantly outscored the "no treatment" control group on all seven reading tests with four of the differences reaching significance.

The results of the interventions studies summarized here suggest that changing the way aptitude is conceptualized (e.g., as cognitive processing rather than traditional IQ) increases the probability that an aptitude-by-treatment interaction (ATI) is detected. Past ATI research suffered from conceptualizations of aptitudes based on the general intelligence model, which did not adequately differentiate cognitive processes that are related to instruction. The summary of studies provided here are particularly different from previous ATI research that found students with low general ability improve little, whereas those with high general ability respond more to instruction. In contrast, children with a weakness in one of the PASS processes (Planning) benefited more from instruction compared to children who had no weakness or a weakness in a different PASS process. The results of these studies also suggest that the PASS profiles, as well as the distinction between Sequential and Simultaneous processing as conceptualized on the K-ABC and KABC-II, can help predict which children will respond to a specific academic instruction and which will not. These research findings offer an important opportunity for researchers and practitioners interested in the design of instruction as suggested by Naglieri and Pickering (2003).

Conclusions on Validity

The topics covered thus far provide evidence that cognitive processes have dimensions of validity that make their assessment helpful for the diagnosis of SLD. The studies showing that measures of cognitive processing correlate strongly with achievement (even though the measure of ability does not include achievement-like content) indicate learning can be predicted from cognitive scores and that variation in processing is strongly related to variation in achievement. Evidence also shows that measuring processes yields very small differences between African American and White as well as Hispanic and White groups, and bilingual children's scores yield very similar results when administered in different languages. In addition, there is evidence that American Indian children score substantially higher on a global measure of mental processing (KABC-II MPI) than on a traditional IQ test (WISC-IV). All of these data provide evidence that measures of cognitive processes are appropriate for facilitating nonbiased assessment. The cognitive processing tasks also appear to be sensitive to the cognitive problems related to reading disability and attention deficits, a finding that is important for diagnosis and eligibility determination. Finally, research has shown that processing scores are relevant to intervention.

Detecting a Disorder in Cognitive Processing

The evidence presented in this chapter thus far provides the legal and scientific basis for using a cognitive approach as part of the evaluation used for SLD eligibility determination. Even though IDEIA 2004 specifies that the term SLD means a disorder in one or more of the basic psychological processes, these processes are neither defined by the law, nor is a method presented to determine when a child has such a disorder. In the remainder of this chapter we will articulate the role of cognitive processing in SLD diagnosis more explicitly. Our emphasis is on using measures of psychological processes that are nationally normed and carefully developed because these tools provide psychometrically defensible scores that can be used when a child's cognitive processing variability is examined. These measures of psychological processes include the CAS, which was developed from Luria-based PASS processing theory; the KABC-II, which was built on the dual theoretical foundation of Luria processes and CHC cognitive abilities; and an array of other recent, psychometrically strong, comprehensive measures of cognitive ability that have typically been based on CHC theory—namely, the WJ III, Binet-5, WISC-IV, and DAS-II.

There are also well-established psychometric methods that can be used to compare scores a child earns on a test like the KABC-II, CAS, WJ III, or WISC-IV. Perhaps the most widely used method is to compare a child's individual score to that child's average of a number of scores obtained from a test. This so-called ipsative methodology was originally proposed by Davis (1959), popularized in the 1970s by Sattler (1974) and A. S. Kaufman (1979), and modified by Silverstein (1982, 1993). This method can be used to determine when variability within a child is greater than what would be expected on the basis of unreliability of the scores. Individual scores that are significantly below the child's average are labeled as a weakness and those significantly above the child's mean described as a strength. This method has been applied to a number of tests including the WISC-IV (Naglieri & Paolitto, 2005), the CAS (Naglieri & Das, 1997), and Binet-5 (Roid & Barram, 2004). Determining if a child has significant variability relative to his or her own average score is a useful way to determine relative strengths and weaknesses but the diagnosis of an SLD requires that the child have "a disorder in one or more of the basic psychological processes." However, Naglieri (1999) and Flanagan and Kaufman (2004) cautioned that the absolute value of a relative weakness could be well within the average range and still significantly below the child's mean. In order to ensure that a child has "a disorder" in processing, numerous psychologists (e.g., Flanagan & Kaufman, 2004; Naglieri, 1999) have recommended that a child's profile should show significant variability (using the ipsative method) and that the lowest score should also fall below some normative cut-off designed to indicate what is typical or average. Therefore in comparison to a relative weakness, a cognitive weakness method uses a dual criterion based on having a low score relative to the child's mean and a low score relative to the norm group. Naglieri (1999) further suggested a disorder in one or more of the basic psychological processes could be defined as a cognitive weakness accompanied by an academic weakness (perhaps best identified using a standardized achievement test) comparable to the level of the processing scale cognitive weakness. Finding a cognitive weakness *and* an academic weakness provides evidence that contributes to the diagnosis of an SLD especially if other appropriate conditions are also met. This Consistency/Discrepancy model, graphically shown in Figure 7.1, is conceptually similar to the Hale-Fiorello Concordance-Discordance model described by Hale (2006) and Flanagan's operational definition of SLD (Flanagan et al., 2007), all of which indicate that the child has uneven abilities in cognitive processing and experiences academic failure that is commensurate with that cognitive weakness.

The Consistency/Discrepancy model was tested by Naglieri (2000), who found that children with a weakness in one or more of the basic cognitive processes of PASS earned lower scores on achievement. In fact, the more pronounced the cognitive weakness, the lower the achievement scores were. Additionally, children with a PASS cognitive weakness were more likely to have been previously identified and placed in special education. Finally, the presence of a cognitive weakness was significantly related to achievement, whereas the presence of a relative weakness was not. Naglieri's (2000) findings support the view that a cognitive processing disorder accompanied by academic failure could be used for the purpose of eligibility determination.

RTI and SLD Identification

In this chapter we have stressed the need to assess basic psychological processes as an important component of any system designed to determine if

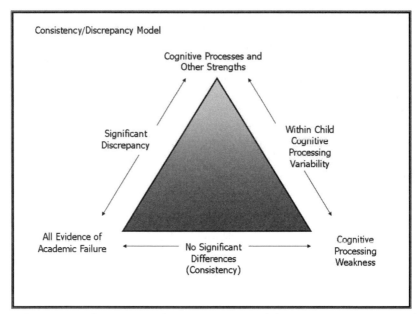

FIGURE 7.1   Consistency/Discrepancy Model.

a child has SLD. Some in the field have argued that RTI should be used for SLD classification. We think there are a number of reasons why this is both scientifically unsupported and legally disallowed.

Is RTI Scientifically Supported?

One of the advances in educational practice that is stressed with the passage of IDEIA 2004 and the current development of the regulations regarding that law is the requirement that methods be scientifically based. In plain terms, this means that there should be good research that supports a method of practice we might choose to use in the field. In order to answer the question, "Is RTI a scientifically supported method?," we went to the literature to determine if any researchers had conducted a careful study of the evidence on RTI. We will summarize the results of a study published by Fuchs, Mock, Morgan, and Young (2003), who provided a detailed description of the problem-solving model that underlies RTI and a review of the evidence of its effectiveness. In addition, we will also provide a summary of Naglieri and Crockett's (2005) examination of data provided by Marston, Muyskens, Lau, and Canter (2003) regarding their application of an RTI model.

Evidence for RTI

Fuchs et al. (2003) described the RTI approaches used in Ohio, Pennsylvania, Iowa, and Minneapolis public schools. In the first two states RTI was used as a pre-referral method and the latter used RTI as a means of eligibility determination. The science behind these programs was carefully examined, and Fuchs et al. (2003) concluded that "more needs to be understood before RTI may be viewed as a valid means of identifying students with LD" (p. 157). Why did they reach this conclusion? The details of the evidence from each of these states were carefully and thoroughly examined.

Ohio's Intervention-Based Assessment (IBA)

Ohio's IBA method combines behavioral problem-solving and collaborative consultation approaches that require clearly stating a behavioral definition of the problem, collecting baseline data, setting goals, implementing an intervention plan, and monitoring the student's progress relative to performance during baseline. Fuchs et al. (2003) cite an excellent study by Telzrow, McNamara, and Hollinger (2000), who evaluated the effectiveness of Ohio's IBA method in 329 schools and concluded that "the present study suggests that reliable implementation of problem solving approaches in schools remains elusive" (p. 458). Telzrow et al. (2000) further reported that "although problem solving consultation has considerable intuitive appeal, attributions of positive outcomes to such processes are not defensible until research confirms reliable and consistent implementation" (p. 457). Fuchs et al. (2003) concluded that evidence of reliable and consistent implementation of Ohio's IBA method was not found.

Pennsylvania's Instructional Support Teams (ISTs)

The method used in Pennsylvania employs curriculum-based assessment for academic areas and behavioral assessment for problems of behavior. This is a collaborative problem-solving approach to providing pre-referral intervention with a support teacher who assists the regular classroom teacher. Fuchs et al. (2003) referenced a secondary source (Conway & Kovaleski, 1998) to determine that ISTs' methods were implemented consistently across the state, but they caution that although the report stated that 89% of the schools achieved validation, there was no definition of the term *validation;* it was unclear what data were used to produce an index of fidelity, and no treatment integrity data were reported. Fuchs et al. (2003) also discuss Harman and Fay's IST implementation study and Kovaleski, Tucker, and Duffy's (1999) statement that the Harman-Fay study provided only indirect evidence of the utility of the processes. Fuchs et al. (2003) report that while Kovaleski et al. (1999) studied the impact of ISTs and found the students showed better progress than students in non-IST schools, "time on task, task completion and task comprehension are only indirect academic measures" (p. 162). Therefore, no evidence was provided to show that ISTs improved academic outcomes.

Iowa's Heartland Model

Heartland's problem-solving model has four levels. At level 1 the teacher works with the student's parents to try to remediate the academic or behavioral problem; at level 2 the teacher and a building-level assistance team develop a plan to implement and monitor the effectiveness of the intervention. At the third level a behavioral problem-solving method is used to refine or redesign the intervention. Finally, the fourth level involves consideration of special educational assistance. A child whose achievement is not commensurate with his or her classmates is found eligible for special education but these children are not labeled as SLD. This problem-solving approach has been implemented in Iowa for about 20 years, yet no research studies have been published in the scientific literature to support its effectiveness.

Fuchs et al. (2003) summarized research that examined the success of the Iowa model. Although there are reports that 75% of student problems were addressed without the use of special education resources, Fuchs et al. (2003) raised several important concerns. First, only a small percentage of schools actually participated (< 5%). Second, neither treatment fidelity nor consistency across settings was assessed. Third, success was not defined and no student outcome data were reported. Importantly, in the second year of the study, 34% of children were brought to the building assessment teams for a second time suggesting that many of the problems were only temporarily solved at level 1.

Minneapolis Public Schools

Minneapolis uses a four-level behavioral problem-solving method that does not require the use of IQ tests to determine eligibility. The Minneapolis problem-solving model (PSM) does require the use of standardized achievement tests and an informal or formal estimate of cognitive functioning as well as adaptive functioning where appropriate. Children who need special services are informally evaluated to determine if they have normal intellectual ability and below age-level achievement. Fuchs et al. (2003) wrote, although the Minneapolis Public Schools report that "the problem-solving model has undergone considerable evaluation" (p. 3) "we found few published or unpublished evaluations; none in peer-reviewed journals" (p. 165). Only two unpublished reports were available from the Minneapolis Public Schools. Although the first study described better reading gains for students who participated in the problem-solving model than those at schools that did not use that approach, no data were presented. The second study reported that the quality of interventions for children who participated in the problem-solving model were superior to the interventions developed for children who did not attend schools using the problem-solving model; however, the term *superior* was not operationalized. They concluded these studies yielded no evidence that children who participated in the problem-solving model made academic progress.

A third study of the Minneapolis Public Schools was reported by Marston, Muyskens, Lau, and Canter (2003). They provide considerable discussion about the beliefs underlying the application of the PSM and stated that "our program evaluation data indicate the PSM improves the assessment and decision-making processing in special education . . . [and accelerates] the learning of all students" (p. 197). This statement was made despite the fact that they had not implemented a research design that involved experimental and control groups, schools were not randomly assigned to experimental and control methods, and students were not randomly assigned to treatments. They also recognized that "all data comparing students at the problem-solving versus traditional model sites are not directly comparable given the lack of randomization and control groups" (p. 198). Moreover, they provide results without statistical tests of significance. The data they did report were reexamined by Naglieri and Crockett (2005).

Marston et al. (2003) provided the average number of words read correctly for students in general education and at the three stages involved in the PSM. These data were used to help gauge the effectiveness of their interventions. General education students were those that did not require referral to PSM. Stage 1 students needed and were given assistance but were successfully remediated and, therefore, did not advance to Stage 2. In Stage 2, students were "served by assistance teams for targeted interventions" (p. 197) and did not advance to special education assessment. Stage 3 students were evaluated for special education and "some" (Marston et al., 2003, do not specify what percentage) were found eligible.

Marston et al. (2003) argued that "a valid problem-solving decision-making system would find students at Stage 1 with higher levels and slopes than students at Stage 3" (p. 196). They reported that "as the students move through each level of the PSM, there is a decrease in words read correctly and often a lower growth rate" (p. 196). Their data did show that students in Levels 1, 2, and 3 earned lower raw scores than the general educational group, but there was little difference in the pre-post slopes. Importantly, the differences between the children in the three levels were very similar at pre- and post-time periods. This finding suggests that had the need for special education assessment been determined at the pre-intervention stage, the results would have been largely the same as if the need for assessment had been determined at the post-intervention stage. There seems to be little advantage to making children wait to fail before they are assessed when their pre- and post-intervention levels are so similar.

Naglieri and Crockett (2005) reanalyzed the CBM data using the means and SDs collected in the fall and spring and the general education group as a local norm. For each group of children at each stage and by grade, the mean raw scores were transformed to standard scores with a mean of 100 and SD of 15. This approach provided a way to compare the raw score CBM means to the general education CBM means. Their data showed that although it is true that the average number of words read correctly increased, this increase was illusory when understood from the general education reference point. That is, the median CBM raw scores for children in Stage 1 (those who improved and did not go to Stage 2) increased from fall to spring, but when these changes were calibrated in relation to the local norm using the general education sample as a reference group, the standard scores for fall and spring were nearly identical. Similarly, Stage 2 mean standard scores for fall and spring were very similar. These data indicated that although the children's raw score mean number of words read correctly increased, there was no increase when these raw score changes were compared to the local norm found for the general education children. When the changes were compared within that context, the success of the interventions provided in Stages 1 and 2 disappeared. Simply put, use of raw scores to determine that children in Levels 1 and 2 improved, and, therefore, did not move on to special education assessments, provided indications of improvement that were not corrected for normal development and were, therefore, illusory.

Fuchs et al. (2003) and Naglieri and Crockett (2005) stressed the need for data that show improvements in academic achievement as an important criterion for demonstrating the validity of RTI. Fuchs et al. (2003) concluded that there "is insufficient evidence of the effectiveness of RTI approaches in Ohio and Pennsylvania" and particularly for "Heartland's and Minneapolis's versions" (p. 166). Moreover, they stated that "the absence of such evidence weakens an important assumption among RTI advocates, namely that RTI provides feasible, timely and effective interventions" (p. 166). Finally, they write, "Proponents of RTI as an alternative means of LD identification must still prove that their problem-solving approach . . . [is] worthy of the descriptor 'scientifically based'" (p. 167).

The evidence examined by Fuchs et al. (2003) and Naglieri and Crockett (2005) suggest that there is little evidence to demonstrate the utility of RTI. Much more evidence is needed before RTI should be implemented in any school system as a way to determine if special education assessment is needed and most certainly to determine SLD eligibility. We further argue that RTI cannot be used for SLD determination because its use for that purpose would be inconsistent with the IDEIA definition of SLD—which requires identification of a psychological processing disorder—and the Federal Regulations (2006).

IDEIA, RTI, and SLD Determination

According to IDEIA and the Federal Regulations "a local educational agency *may* [emphasis added] use a process that determines if the child responds to scientific, research-based intervention as a part of the evaluation procedures." IDEIA 2004 (section B. 614.b.(5)) does state, however, that determination of eligibility for SLD shall not be determined if the child did not have appropriate instruction. In essence, then, RTI needs to be part of the identification process but should not be the sole method of identification. Naglieri (2007) further noted that according to Dr. Alexa Posny, Director of the Office of Special Education Programs, SLD identification must be accomplished using a comprehensive evaluation and that RTI results may be one component of the information used. Dr. Posny clearly stated that RTI alone is insufficient for SLD determination. This contention is consistent with the "Analysis of Comments and Changes" section that accompanies the Federal Regulations that were published August 14, 2006, which stated, "RTI is only one component of the process to identify children in need of special education and related services. Determining why a child has not responded to research-based interventions requires a comprehensive evaluation" (p. 46647) and an "RTI process does not replace the need for a comprehensive evaluation" (p. 46648).

IDEIA 2004 and the current federal regulations do clearly state that SLD eligibility must be determined using a variety of data-gathering tools and strategies. The tests and evaluation materials must be well validated and reliable, measure more than general intelligence, and help us measure competencies as well as weaknesses in abilities or achievement. A variety of measures must be used, and no single procedure can be used as the sole criterion for determining whether a child is a child with a disability or for determining an appropriate educational program. Importantly, these tests and methods are to be selected so as not to be discriminatory on the basis of race or culture. And finally, "other alternative research-based procedures for determining whether a child has SLD" are also permitted. These regulations contain a clear emphasis on use of methods that have scientific merit and that any information obtained should be interpreted by highly qualified professionals who take into consideration the context of the whole child and the environment in which the child is functioning as well as the academic, behavioral, mental health, and cognitive characteristics of the learner. At this important time in the evolution of our profession we should be sure that the important question of the presence of an SLD be made using the highest quality of procedures that include a comprehensive evaluation when attempts to help the child have been unsuccessful. In addition, the emphasis should be on the *integration* of comprehensive cognitive assessment with RTI rather than pitting one approach against the other. We refer readers to two special issues of *Psychology in the Schools* edited by Nancy Mather and Nadeen Kaufman, in which every article, by leaders in the field of SLD, address the key issue of how to best integrate assessment with RTI (Mather & Kaufman, 2006).

REFERENCES

Anastasi, A., & Urbina, S. (1997). *Psychological testing* (7th ed.). Upper Saddle River, NJ: Prentice-Hall.

Ashman, A. F., & Conway, R.N.F. (1997). *An introduction to cognitive education: Theory and applications*. London: Routledge.

Boden, C., & Kirby, J.R. (1995). Successive processing, phonological coding and the remediation of reading. *Journal of Cognitive Education, 4*, 19–31.

Bracken, B.A. (1987). Limitations of preschool instruments and standards for minimal levels of technical adequacy. *Journal of Psychoeducational Assessment, 5*, 313–326.

Brailsford, A., Snart, F., & Das, J.P. (1984). Strategy training and reading comprehension. *Journal of Learning Disabilities, 17*(5), 287–290.

Brody, N. (1992). *Intelligence*. San Diego: Academic Press.

Carlson, J., & Das, J.P. (1997). A process approach to remediating word decoding deficiencies in Chapter 1 children. *Learning Disabilities Quarterly, 20*, 93–102.

Carroll, J.B. (1993). *Human cognitive abilities: A survey of factor-analytic studies*. New York: Cambridge University Press.

Ceci, S.J. (2000). So near and yet so far: Lingering questions about the use of measures of general intelligence for college admission and employment screening. *Psychology, Public Policy, and Law, 6*, 233–252.

Conway, S.J., & Kovaleski, J.F. (1998). A model for statewide special education reform: Pennsylvania's instructional support teams. *International Journal of Educational Reform, 7*, 345–351.

Cormier, P., Carlson, J.S., & Das, J.P. (1990). Planning ability and cognitive performance: The compensatory effects of a dynamic assessment approach. *Learning and Individual Differences, 2*, 437–449.

Das, J.P. (2002). A better lo ok at intelligence. *Current Directions in Psychology, 11,* 28–32.

Das, J.P., Mishra, R.K., & Pool, J.E. (1995). An experiment on cognitive remediation or word-reading difficulty. *Journal of Learning Disabilities, 28,* 66–79.

Das, J.P., Naglieri, J.A., & Kirby, J.R. (1994). *Assessment of cognitive processes.* Boston: Allyn & Bacon.

Das, J.P., Parrila, R.K., & Papadopoulos, T.C. (2000). Cognitive education and reading disability. In A. Kozulin & Y. Rand (Eds.), *Experience of mediated learning* (pp. 276–291). Amsterdam: Pergamon.

Davis, F.B. (1959). Interpretation of differences among averages and individual test scores. *Journal of Educational Psychology, 50,* 162–170.

Dehn, M.J. (2000, April). *Cognitive assessment system performance of ADHD children.* Paper presented at the annual NASP Convention, New Orleans, LA.

Elliott, C.D. (2005). The differential ability scales. In D.P. Flanagan, & P.L. Harrison (Eds.), *Contemporary intellectual assessment: Theories, tests, and issues* (2nd ed., pp. 402–424). New York: Guilford.

Elliott, C.D. (2006). *Differential ability scales—second edition (DAS-II).* San Antonio, TX: The Psychological Corporation.

Fagan, J.R. (2000). A theory of intelligence as processing: Implications for society. *Psychology, Public Policy, and Law, 6,* 168–179.

Flanagan, D.P., & Kaufman, A.S. (2004). *Essentials of WISC-IV assessment.* New York: Wiley. (Spanish version published by Tea Ediciones of Spain, 2005.)

Flanagan, D.P., Ortiz, S.O., & Alfonso, V.C. (2007). *Essentials of cross-battery assessment* (2nd ed.). New York: Wiley.

Fletcher-Janzen, E. (2003). *A validity study of the KABC-II and the Taos Pueblo Indian children of New Mexico.* Circle Pines, MN: American Guidance Service.

Fuchs, D., Mock, D., Morgan, P, & Young, C. (2003). Responsiveness-to-intervention: Definitions, evidence, and implications for the learning disabilities construct. *Learning Disabilities Research & Practice, 18,* 157–171.

Gunnison, J., Kaufman, N.L., & Kaufman, A.S. (1982). Reading remediation based on sequential and simultaneous processing. *Academic Therapy, 17,* 297–307.

Haddad F.A., Garcia Y.E., Naglieri, J.A., Grimditch, M., McAndrews, A., & Eubanks, J. (2003). Planning facilitation and reading comprehension: Instructional relevance of the PASS theory. *Journal of Psychoeducational Assessment, 21,* 282–289.

Hale, J.B. (2006). Implementing IDEIA 2004 with the three-tier model that includes response to intervention and cognitive assessment methods. *School Psychology Forum: Research into Practice, 1,* 16–27.

Hale, J.B., Kaufman, A.S., Naglieri, J.A., & Kavale, K.A. (2006). Implementation of IDEA: Integrating response to intervention and cognitive assessment methods. *Psychology in the Schools, 43,* 753–770.

Hale, B., Naglieri, J.A., Kaufman, A.S., & Kavale, K.A. (2004). Specific learning disability classification in the new Individuals With Disabilities Education Act: The danger of good IDEIAs. *The School Psychologist, 58,* 6–13.

Hayes, S.C., Gifford, E.B, & Ruckstuhl, L.E. (1996). Relational frame theory and executive function: A behavioral approach. In G.R. Lyon & N.A. Krasnegor (Eds.), *Attention, memory and executive function* (pp. 279–306). Baltimore: Brookes.

Horn, J.L. (1989). Cognitive diversity: A framework of learning. In P.L. Ackerman, R.J. Sternberg & R. Glaser (Eds.), *Learning and individual differences* (pp. 61–116). New York: Freeman.

Individuals With Disabilities Education Improvement Act of 2004 (IDEIA). (2004). (P.L. 108–446).

Iseman, J. S. (2005). *A cognitive instructional approach to improving math calculation of children with ADHD: Application of the PASS theory.* Unpublished doctoral dissertation, George Mason University.

Jensen, A. R. (1998). *The g factor: The science of mental ability.* Westport, CT: Praeger.

Kar, B. C., Dash, U. N., Das, J. P., & Carlson, J. S. (1992). Two experiments on the dynamic assessment of planning. *Learning and Individual Differences, 5,* 13–29.

Kaufman, A. S. (1979). *Intelligent testing with the WISC-R.* New York: Wiley.

Kaufman, A. S., & Kaufman, N. L. (1983). *K-ABC interpretive manual.* Circle Pines, MN: American Guidance Service.

Kaufman, A. S., & Kaufman, N. L. (2001). Assessment of specific learning disabilities in the new millennium: Issues, conflicts, and controversies. In A. S. Kaufman & N. L. Kaufman (Eds.), *Specific learning disabilities and difficulties in children and adolescents: Psychological assessment and evaluation* (pp. 433–461). Cambridge, UK: Cambridge University Press.

Kaufman, A. S., & Kaufman, N. L. (2004a). *Kaufman assessment battery for children—second edition (K-ABC-II).* Circle Pines, MN: American Guidance Service.

Kaufman, A. S., & Kaufman, N. L. (2004b). *Kaufman test of educational achievement—second edition (K-TEA—II): Comprehensive form.* Circle Pines, MN: American Guidance Service.

Kaufman, A. S., & Lichtenberger, E. O. (2006). *Assessing adolescent and adult intelligence* (3rd ed.). New York: Wiley.

Kaufman, A. S., Lichtenberger, E. O., Fletcher-Janzen, E., & Kaufman, N. L. (2005). *Essentials of KABC-II assessment.* New York: Wiley.

Kaufman, D., & Kaufman, P. (1979). Strategy training and remedial techniques. *Journal of Learning Disabilities, 12,* 63–66.

Kavale, K. A., Kaufman, A. S., Naglieri, J. A., & Hale, J. B. (2005). Changing procedures for identifying learning disabilities: The danger of poorly supported ideas. *The School Psychologist, 59*(1), 16–25.

Krywaniuk, L. W., & Das, J. P. (1976). Cognitive strategies in native children: Analysis and intervention. *Alberta Journal of Educational Research, 22,* 271–280.

Lichtenberger, E. O. (2001). The Kaufman tests—K-ABC and KAIT. In A. S. Kaufman & N. L. Kaufman (Eds.), *Specific learning disabilities and difficulties in children and adolescents: Psychological assessment and evaluation* (pp. 97–140). Cambridge UK: Cambridge University Press.

Luria, A. R. (1966). *Higher cortical functions in man.* New York: Basic Books.

Luria, A. R. (1970). The functional organization of the brain. *Scientific American, 222,* 66–78.

Markwardt, F. C., Jr. (1997). *Peabody Individual Achievement Test* (Rev. ed.). Circle Pines, MN: American Guidance Service.

Marston, D., Muyskens, P., Lau, M., & Canter, A. (2003). Problem-solving model for decision making with high-incidence disabilities: The Minneapolis experience. *Learning Disabilities Research & Practice, 18,* 187–200.

Mather, N., & Kaufman, N. L. (Eds.) (2006). *Psychology in the schools* (Vol. 43, nos. 7–8) (Special issues—Integration of cognitive assessment and response to intervention). New York: Wiley.

McGrew, K. S. (2005). The Cattell-Horn-Carroll theory of cognitive abilities: Past, present, and future. In D. P. Flanagan & P. L. Harrison (Eds.), *Contemporary intellectual assessment: Theories, tests, and issues* (2nd ed., pp. 136–181). New York: Guilford.

Naglieri, J. A. (1999). *Essentials of CAS assessment.* New York: Wiley.

Naglieri, J. A. (2000). Can profile analysis of ability test scores work? An illustration using the PASS theory and CAS with an unselected cohort. *School Psychology Quarterly, 15,* 419–433.

Naglieri, J. A., (2005). The cognitive assessment system. In D. P. Flanagan, & P. L. Harrison (Eds.), *Contemporary intellectual assessment* (2nd ed., pp. 441–460). New York: Guilford.

Naglieri, J. A. (2007). RTI alone is not sufficient for SLD identification: Convention presentation by OSEP director Alexa Posny. *Communiqué, 35,* 53.

Naglieri, J. A., & Bornstein, B. T. (2003). Intelligence and achievement: Just how correlated are they? *Journal of Psychoeducational Assessment, 21,* 244–260.

Naglieri, J. A., & Crockett, D. (2005) Response to intervention (RTI): Is it a scientifically proven method? *NASP Communiqué, 34,* 38–39.

Naglieri, J. A., & Das, J. P. (1997). *Cognitive assessment system.* Itasca, IL: Riverside Publishing Company.

Naglieri, J. A., & Ford, D. Y. (2005). Increasing minority children's participation in gifted classes using the NNAT: A response to Lohman. *Gifted Child Quarterly, 49,* 29–36.

Naglieri, J. A., Goldstein, S., Delauder, B., & Schwebach, A. (2006). WISC-III and CAS: Which correlates higher with achievement for a clinical sample? *School Psychology Quarterly, 21,* 62–76.

Naglieri, J. A., Goldstein, S., Iseman, J. S., & Schwebach, A. (2003). Performance of children with attention deficit hyperactivity disorder and anxiety/depression on the WISC-III and cognitive assessment system (CAS). *Journal of Psychoeducational Assessment, 21,* 32–42.

Naglieri, J. A., & Gottling, S. H. (1995). A cognitive education approach to math instruction for the learning disabled: An individual study. *Psychological Reports, 76,* 1343–1354.

Naglieri, J. A., & Gottling, S. H. (1997). Mathematics instruction and PASS cognitive processes: An intervention study. *Journal of Learning Disabilities, 30,* 513–520.

Naglieri, J. A., & Johnson, D. (2000). Effectiveness of a cognitive strategy intervention to improve math calculation based on the PASS theory. *Journal of Learning Disabilities, 33,* 591–597.

Naglieri, J. A., Otero, T., DeLauder, B., & Matto, H. (2007). Bilingual Hispanic children's performance on the English and Spanish versions of the Cognitive Assessment System. *School Psychology Quarterly, 22,* 432–448.

Naglieri, J. A., & Paolitto, A. W. (2005). Ipsative comparisons of WISC-IV index scores. *Applied Neuropsychology, 12,* 208–211.

Naglieri, J. A., & Pickering, E. (2003). *Helping children learn: Intervention handouts for use in school and at home.* Baltimore: Brookes.

Naglieri, J. A., & Rojahn, J. R. (2004). Validity of the PASS theory and CAS: Correlations with achievement. *Journal of Educational Psychology, 96,* 174–181.

Naglieri, J. A., Rojahn, J., & Matto, H. (2007). Hispanic and non-Hispanic children's performance on PASS Cognitive Processes and Achievement. *Intelligence, 35,* 568–579.

Naglieri, J. A., Rojahn, J. R., Matto, H. C., & Aquilino, S. A. (2005). Black-white differences in intelligence: A study of the PASS theory and cognitive assessment system. *Journal of Psychoeducational Assessment, 23,* 146–160.

Naglieri, J. A., Salter, C. J., & Edwards, G. (2004). Assessment of ADHD and reading disabilities using the PASS theory and cognitive assessment system. *Journal of Psychoeducational Assessment, 22,* 93–105.

Papadopoulos, T. C., Das, J. P., Parrila, R. K., & Kirby, J. R. (2003). Children at risk for developing reading difficulties: A remediation study. *School Psychology International, 24*(3), 340–366.

Parrila, R. K., Das, J. P., Kendrick, M., Papadopoulos, T., & Kirby, J. (1999). Efficacy of a cognitive reading remediation program for at-risk children in Grade 1. *Developmental Disabilities Bulletin, 27,* 1–31.

Penrose, L. S., & Raven, J. C. (1936). A new series of perceptual tests: Preliminary communication. *British Journal of Medical Psychology, 16,* 97–104.

Piaget, J. (1972). Intellectual evolution from adolescence to adulthood. *Human Development, 15,* 1–12.

Posner, M. I., & Boies, S. J. (1971). Components of attention. *Psychological Review, 78,* 391–408.

Posny, A. (2007, April). *IDEIA 2004—Top ten key issues that affect school psychologists.* Featured session at the NASP April 2007 Convention.

Prifitera, A., Saklofske, D. H., & Weiss, L. G. (2005). *WISC-IV: Clinical use and interpretation.* Amsterdam: Elsevier Academic Press.

Psychological Corporation. (2001). *Wechsler individual achievement test—second edition* (WIAT-II). San Antonio, TX: The Psychological Corporation.

Roid, G. H. (2003). *Stanford-Binet intelligence scales, fifth edition, technical manual.* Itasca, IL: Riverside Publishing Company.

Roid, G. H., & Barram, R. A. (2004). *Essentials of Stanford-Binet intelligence scales (SB5) assessment.* New York: Wiley.

Sattler, J. M. (1974). *Assessment of children's intelligence* (Rev ed.). Philadelphia: Saunders.

Schneider, W., Dumais, S. T., & Shiffrin, R. M. (1984). Automatic and controlled processing and attention. In R. Parasuraman & D. R. Davies (Eds.), *Varieties of attention* (pp. 1–28). New York: Academic Press.

Schrank, F. A., Flanagan, D. P., Woodcock, R. W., & Mascolo, J. T. (2002). *Essentials of WJ III cognitive abilities assessment.* New York: Wiley.

Siegel, L. S. (1999). Issues in the definition and diagnosis of learning disabilities: A perspective on Guckenberger v. Boston University. *Journal of Learning Disabilities, 32,* 304–319.

Silverstein, A. B. (1982). Pattern analysis as simultaneous statistical inference. *Journal of Consulting and Clinical Psychology, 50,* 234–240.

Silverstein. A. B. (1993). Type I, Type II, and other types of errors in pattern analysis. *Psychological Assessment, 5,* 72–74.

Spearman, C. E. (1904). "General intelligence," objectively determined and measured. *American Journal of Psychiatry, 15,* 201–293.

Stanovich, K. E. (1988). Explaining the differences between dyslexic and the garden-variety poor reader: The phonological-core variable-difference model. *Journal of Learning Disabilities, 21,* 590–604, 612.

Stanovich, K. E. (1999). The sociopsychometrics of learning disabilities. *Journal of Learning Disabilities, 32,* 350–361.

Sternberg, R. J. (1988). *The triarchic mind: A new theory of human intelligence.* New York: Viking.

Suzuki, L. A., & Valencia, R. R. (1997). Race-Ethnicity and measured intelligence. *American Psychologist, 52,* 1103–1114.

Telzrow, C., McNamara, K., & Hollinger, C. (2000). Fidelity of problem-solving implementation and relationship to student performance. *School Psychology Review, 29,* 443–461.

U.S. Department of Education, Office of Special Education and Rehabilitative Services (2006). *Twenty-sixth annual report to Congress on the implementation of the Individuals With Disabilities Education Act.* Washington, DC: Author.

Wagner, R. K., Torgeson, J. K., & Rashotte, C. A. (1994). Development of reading-related phonological processing abilities: New evidence of bi-directional causality from a latent variable longitudinal study. *Developmental Psychology, 30,* 73–87.

Wechsler, D. (1991). *Manual for the Wechsler intelligence scale for children* (3rd ed., WISC-III). San Antonio, TX: The Psychological Corporation.

Wechsler, D. (2003). *Manual for the Wechsler intelligence scale for children* (4th ed., WISC-IV). San Antonio, TX: The Psychological Corporation.

Woodcock, R. W., & Johnson, M. B. (1989). *Woodcock-Johnson psycho-educational battery-revised*. Allen, TX: DLM/Teaching Resources.

Woodcock, R. W., McGrew, K. S., & Mather, N. (2001). *Woodcock-Johnson psycho-educational battery* (3rd ed., WJ III). Chicago: Riverside.

CHAPTER 8

Assessment and Eligibility of Students With Disabilities

Jennifer H. Lindstrom, Elizabeth D. Tuckwiller,
and Daniel P. Hallahan

The field of special education is undergoing a number of dramatic changes. And most of these changes have focused on the way in which students are found eligible for the receipt of special education services. Whereas one can broadly characterize the years immediately following the passage of P. L. 94–142, the Education of All Handicapped Children Act, in 1975, as the age of access to appropriate *instruction* and the years leading up to the amended law, the Individuals With Disabilities Education Act (IDEA) of 1990 and 1997, as the age of access to appropriate *placement,* one can characterize the years leading up to and subsequent to the Individuals With Disabilities Education Improvement Act of 2004 (IDEIA) as the age of appropriate *identification and assessment.*

Given the major thrust toward accountability in general education, as reflected in No Child Left Behind (NCLB), followed by a similar initiative in IDEIA, it is not surprising that the primary focus of researchers and policy makers has turned toward appropriately identifying students for special education and assessing the progress of students once they are in special education. It is also not surprising that, within the field of special education, the category undergoing the most change with respect to identification and assessment is that of learning disabilities. With the recent exception of autism spectrum disorders, the category of learning disabilities has undergone the largest increase since P. L. 94–142 was enacted, and for several years it has dwarfed in numbers the other special education categories and comprises over half of all students identified for special education. In this chapter, we discuss some of the major changes and issues in identification and assessment in special education, with an emphasis on the category of learning disabilities.

THE PRE-REFERRAL PROCESS

When a student exhibits difficulty in the general education classroom, educational personnel must use an array of strategic interventions designed to address the student's academic or behavioral difficulty. Since the 1970s when pre-referral intervention emerged as a component of the comprehensive evaluation process, a variety of pre-referral models have evolved across local and state educational agencies (Garcia & Ortiz, 2006). The models vary along several dimensions; however, Overton (2006) has grouped them broadly into two types—traditional and contemporary—based on the fundamental difference of how each model conceptualizes the goals of pre-referral interventions. Traditional models position pre-referral as an initial step in the process of referral for comprehensive evaluation. Contemporary models regard pre-referral intervention as an attempt to meet the student's academic and behavioral needs in the general education classroom and therefore prevent unnecessary referrals for evaluation.

Traditional Models

Traditional models of assessment position the pre-referral process as a step in the referral of the student for assessment by a multidisciplinary team (often called the teacher assistance team [TAT] or child study team) for special education services (see Figure 8.1; Overton, 2006). Traditional models of assessment do not specifically require formal intervention on the part of the general educator for struggling students. When a student is not progressing in the general curriculum, the teacher (or parent) makes a referral to a multidisciplinary team who completes a formal evaluation of the student and determines the student's eligibility for special education.

Coincident with the implementation of traditional models of pre-referral, a number of factors have occurred causing researchers, practitioners, and policy makers to question the validity of the traditional approach to pre-referral: (a) the tremendous increase in the number of students identified as learning disabled, (b) a growing dissatisfaction with using the IQ-achievement discrepancy as a method of identification of students with learning disabilities, (c) a shortage of empirical evidence

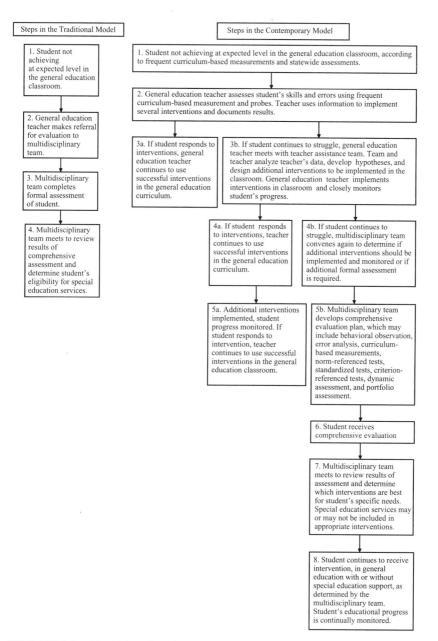

FIGURE 8.1   Traditional and contemporary models of assessment.
Adapted from *Assessing learners with special needs* by T. Overton, 2006, Upper Saddle
River, NJ: Pearson.

documenting the efficacy of traditional models of pre-referral, and (d) claims that students with learning disabilities could not be distinguished meaningfully from those with low achievement. Although some of these factors are more arguable than others, in combination they created the climate for a different way of conceptualizing pre-referral.

Contemporary Models

Under contemporary models, rather than immediately referring the struggling student to a multidisciplinary team, the general education teacher attempts to address the student's needs in the classroom. A variety of pre-referral strategies may be used including modifications to the curriculum or classroom environment, observations by neutral raters, or consultation with parents or school personnel (Overton, 2006). Furthermore, the teacher systematically collects data to measure the student's progress as different interventions are implemented. As Figure 8.1 illustrates, if these strategies work and the student demonstrates success in the classroom, there is no need for further evaluation. Furthermore, in cases where the pre-referral interventions are not successful, the teacher and other school personnel have the necessary records documenting that the student's difficulties are not due to lack of quality instruction.

Although no evidence exists with respect to whether these systematic pre-referral interventions result in more accurate identification of students with disabilities, some evidence suggests they result in fewer referrals for comprehensive evaluation for special education (Overton, 2006). For example, in one study of 34 fourth- and fifth-graders struggling to read and on the verge of referral for assessment for suspected learning disability, implementation of a pre-referral literacy intervention remediated the reading skills of 32 students, resulting in only two of the students being identified as eligible for special education (Montgomery & Moore-Brown, 2003). However, there are concerns regarding intensive pre-referral intervention, including the amount of time and effort required on the part of the general educator and the lack of understanding among general education teachers about possible intervention strategies, including when and how to implement them (Overton, 2006).

Summary

In light of the current regulations under IDEIA, professionals must conceptualize pre-referral interventions in terms of the contemporary model. Whereas the traditional model of the pre-referral process positioned pre-referral as the first step in initiating a comprehensive evaluation of the student, the contemporary model, as well as IDEIA, demands that the pre-referral process consist of a systematic series of interventions designed to meet the student's academic and/or behavioral needs in the general education classroom. Although the field of education currently lacks a clear definition of what constitutes appropriate and meaningful pre-referral intervention, school personnel are required to make adjustments in instructional delivery and/or the learning environment before referring a struggling student for evaluation.

IDENTIFYING LEARNING DISABILITIES: MODELS OF ASSESSMENT

The presence of a learning disability can affect an individual's ability to read, speak, write, spell, or do math calculations as well as recall, organize, and process information. Although most individuals with learning disabilities have average to above average intelligence, many of them find it difficult to perform tasks in the academic area(s) affected by their disability. Most experts agree that learning disabilities are the result of neurological dysfunction, and therefore, are a lifelong condition. In other words, a child will not "grow out of" a learning disability; rather he or she will need to be identified as having a learning disability and will need to receive specialized instruction in order to achieve his or her potential. In light of the prevalence of learning disabilities in the United States, the need for quick and accurate early identification as well as effective intervention is crucial.

Learning Disabilities in the United States: Facts and Figures

The estimated prevalence rate of learning disabilities in the United States varies across reports. Some sources estimate that as many as one in seven individuals or 15% of the U.S. population has some form of learning disability (WETA, 2006). However, most sources place the prevalence rates at approximately 5%–6% of the student population in the United States (Altarac & Saroha, 2007; Hallahan & Kauffman, 2006; National Research Council, 2001; U.S. Department of Education, 2006c). According to the most recent statistics available from the National Center for Education Statistics (2006), approximately 2.9 million children, ages 3–21 years, received special education services under the category Specific Learning Disabilities (SLD) in U.S. public schools during the 2003–2004 school year.

Although these numbers have remained relatively constant since 2000, throughout the 1980s and 1990s, there were significant increases in the numbers of students served under the category of SLD. During the 1980–1981 school year, approximately 1.5 million students received services under the category of SLD; by the 1990–1991 school year, the number of students receiving services had jumped to approximately 2.1 million, and throughout the 1990s, another approximately 700,000 students were identified (U.S. Department of Education, 2006c). With the exception of the autism spectrum disorders, the category of SLD has undergone the largest increase since P. L. 94–142 was enacted. Indeed, of the 6.6 million U.S. students served under IDEIA in the 2003–2004 school year nearly half of them, 2.8 million, received services under the SLD category (U.S. Department of Education, 2006c).

Defining and Identifying Learning Disabilities

Traditionally, identification of students with learning disabilities has relied on the *IQ-achievement discrepancy model* (hereafter referred to as the discrepancy model), in which a student's achievement in a specific academic area is compared to his or her overall cognitive potential, or IQ. If there is a significant discrepancy between the student's standardized achievement scores and what would be expected based on his or her standardized intelligence test scores, a student could be found eligible for special education for specific learning disability. As we noted earlier, there have been many criticisms of this model, including debate over the legitimacy of intelligence tests, the overlapping constructs measured on achievement and intelligence tests, the lack of consistency across states regarding what constitutes a significant discrepancy, and the delay between when a child first exhibits academic problems and when he or she is old enough to exhibit the discrepancy.

The Individuals With Disabilities Education Improvement Act of 2004 (IDEIA, 2004) specifically addressed these concerns regarding pre-referral intervention and comprehensive evaluation of students suspected of having learning disabilities. The model of assessment reflected in IDEIA 2004 stresses that more systematic, meticulous pre-referral interventions be employed before performing a formal assessment. Further, IDEIA 2004 requires that each state develop criteria for identifying students with specific learning disabilities that:

1. Must *not* require the use of a severe discrepancy between intellectual ability and achievement;
2. Must permit the use of a process based on the child's response to scientific, research-based intervention, and;

3. May permit the use of other alternative research-based procedures (IDEIA 2004, 34 CFR §300.307).

These additional procedures (criteria two and three above), specified by IDEIA to identify students with specific learning disabilities, have sparked much debate and confusion in the field of special education. However, policy makers claim to be justified in legislating the changes in IDEIA 2004 to address concerns regarding the overuse of the discrepancy model and the possibility that some student failures are due to poor instruction rather than student disability. The use of the discrepancy model to identify learning disabilities was never legislated as the only means by which to identify learning disabilities. Specifically, IDEA 1997 required that the comprehensive evaluation "use a variety of assessment tools . . . , [and] not use any single procedure as the sole criterion for determining eligibility" (34 CFR §300.532(g)). In spite of this, many local education agencies used the discrepancy model as the singular method for learning disability identification without regard to other possible causes of student difficulty including a lack of quality instruction or failure to provide effective interventions when students begin to fall behind (Mandlawitz, 2007). Therefore, IDEIA 2004 not only restricts states from requiring the use of the discrepancy model to identify students with specific learning disability but also permits states to employ some method in which the student's response to systematic, research-based intervention, commonly referred to as response to intervention (RTI), is documented and considered.

Response to Intervention

The theoretical foundation of RTI hails back to the initial call for pre-referral intervention in the 1970s. However, amid vague conceptions of what constituted pre-referral intervention and misunderstandings of the pre-referral process and goals, the discrepancy model emerged as the supposedly clear indicator as to whether a child had a specific learning disability. Now, concerns have sprung anew regarding the overreliance on the discrepancy model and the possibility that some students' difficulties are the product of poor instruction and lack of intervention rather than manifestations of a specific learning disability. In response to these concerns, advocates for the RTI model suggest that when a student exhibits difficulty in the general education classroom, a multitiered series of increasingly intensive interventions should be employed and the student's response measured. Only students who do not respond to the interventions at the highest tier should be considered candidates for referral for formal evaluation for special education services (see chapter 5 for a comprehensive discussion of the RTI model). Furthermore, data gathered from an RTI model cannot be used on its own to determine a child's eligibility for special education services although it can be used as one component of the comprehensive evaluation (Mandlawitz, 2007).

It bears noting, though, that despite its aforementioned virtues, the general conceptualization of RTI is currently vague and ambiguous, leaving interpretation open to state and local education agencies (Mastropieri & Scruggs, 2005). Various scholars have raised questions regarding the practical aspects of implementing RTI models in schools. For instance, how many tiers of intervention are necessary to identify students with learning disabilities accurately and efficiently? And regardless of how many tiers are chosen, we must ask from where the financial resources to implement any tier of intervention will come. Should special education or general education funding be used in general education classrooms to intervene with students who may or may not have learning disabilities (Mastropieri & Scruggs, 2005)?

Researchers have posed other significant questions of the feasibility of RTI as the preferred model for intervention and identification (D. Fuchs, L. S. Fuchs, McMaster, Yen, & Svenson, 2004; D. Fuchs, Mock, Morgan, & Young, 2003; L. S. Fuchs, 2003; Vaughn & L. S. Fuchs, 2003). How will the roles of general and special educators and educational diagnosticians change in light of the RTI model? Who is responsible for implementing each tier of intervention? How will the fidelity of implementation of interventions be measured and addressed? At what point is a student considered a non-responder and should this be standardized across local and state education agencies? How will RTI be implemented for struggling students in middle and high schools? Current RTI models and research focus almost exclusively on early education (primarily kindergarten through third grade). Even the theoretical foundation and approach to RTI vary across scholars in the field. Some suggest that RTI follow a standard protocol in which interventions shown to be effective in controlled studies are implemented in a standardized manner to help students acquire new academic skills (L. S. Fuchs & Fuchs, 2007). Others suggest that a problem-solving model approach to RTI, focused on improving student motivation and performance on already acquired skills, yields the most effective and individualized interventions possible for struggling students.

Perhaps one of the most ambiguous and, to some individuals, concerning aspects of the RTI approach to identifying learning disabilities are the questions it raises regarding the conceptualization of learning disabilities as a construct (D. Fuchs et al., 2003; Mastropieri & Scruggs, 2005). Because RTI does not employ any measure of cognitive ability, the model cannot discriminate between students who have a discrepancy between ability and achievement in a specific area (students who would be considered learning disabled according to the traditional model) and students who are generally low achievers, or have attention-related disorders, emotional and behavioral disorders, or mental retardation, many of whom would likely not respond to intervention. Because the concept of discrepancy is inextricably linked with the conceptualization of learning disabilities, Gerber (2003) suggests that the RTI model cannot be used to diagnose learning disabilities. Certainly there are those who would abolish all categorical notions of disability and thus would not regard this dilemma as a drawback to RTI, but if the eradication of learning disabilities and/or other categorical conceptualizations of disabilities are part of the agenda, this warrants its own discussion. However, if the construct of learning disabilities remains intact in the RTI model, discussions of how the RTI model can specifically improve the identification of students with learning disabilities are sorely needed (Mastropieri & Scruggs, 2005). Fuchs, Fuchs, and Zumeta (see chapter 5) provide a more in-depth discussion of RTI as an alternative method for preventing and identifying learning disabilities.

Formal Assessment

Because RTI, as a model of intervention as well as identification, remains an ambiguous and vague undertaking, most local education agencies continue to employ a combination of pre-referral interventions with the aid of the teacher assistance team, followed by a comprehensive evaluation for students who are not progressing in the general education curriculum. If the team determines that a student is in need of a comprehensive evaluation, an assessment plan is developed. Assessment plans vary in accordance with the student's individualized needs based on information gathered during the pre-intervention process (Overton, 2006).

Comprehensive evaluation of a student uses standardized, norm-referenced tests in order to compare the student's performance to the performance of same age- or grade-level peers (Overton, 2006). Traditionally, a student's scores on norm-referenced achievement tests (e.g., Woodcock-Johnson III Tests of Achievement) and processing measures (e.g., Comprehensive Test of Phonological Processing) are compared to his or her score on norm-referenced intelligence tests (e.g., Wechsler Intelligence Scale for Children, Fourth Edition). A severe discrepancy between achievement and intelligence suggests a learning disability in the academic area(s) in which achievement was unexpectedly low. Many multidisciplinary teams continue to use this IQ-achievement discrepancy model as one component of the comprehensive evaluation; although IDEIA 2004 does not allow states to *require* the severe discrepancy model, it does not prohibit them from using it as one component of the formal assessment.

Other assessments used in the comprehensive evaluation are determined based on the student's response to pre-referral intervention and specific areas of need. Components of the evaluation may include behavioral observations of the student in the classroom, error analysis to determine patterns of misunderstanding, curriculum-based measurements to assess the student's acquisition of certain skills, criterion-referenced tests (including state standards testing) to determine if a student has mastered specific content knowledge, dynamic assessment which attempts to reveal a student's potential to learn a new skill, and portfolio assessment of student's work to evaluate their growth over a specified period of time (Overton, 2006). Each of these components of the formal evaluation provides specific information regarding the student's present level of functioning and areas of difficulty. It should be noted that IDEIA 2004 gives multidisciplinary teams the latitude to diagnose a student with a learning disability based solely on substandard performance in any academic area (e.g., student scores at <16% in one or more academic areas as measured by norm-referenced tests). The constraints of the discrepancy model are no longer a factor in the identification of learning disabilities, although many teams continue to use the discrepancy model to guide their decisions about the student's eligibility.

DSM-IV-TR Criteria

Another option for establishing a student's eligibility for special education services is the use of the *Diagnostic and Statistical Manual of Mental Disorders, Fourth Edition, Text Revision (DSM-IV-TR;* American Psychiatric Association, 2000). The *DSM-IV-TR* provides diagnostic criteria for learning disorders including reading disorder, mathematics disorder, disorder of written expression, and learning disorder, not otherwise specified. However, the first criterion in each diagnostic category states that the academic skill in question, as measured by individually administered, standardized tests, is substantially below expected performance when compared to the child's age, *measured intelligence,* and educational history. Therefore, discrepancy continues to remain a feature of the *DSM-IV-TR* diagnostic criteria, suggesting that this option to establish eligibility is closely aligned with the traditional IQ-achievement discrepancy model.

Summary

Regardless of which model of assessment predominates in the evaluation of a student for special education services, whether it is primarily RTI, a formal evaluation based on standardized tests, the use of *DSM-IV-TR* criteria, or, ideally, a combination of all three, clinical judgment is a key component in the eligibility decision-making process. Every struggling student has specific and individualized needs that must be met in order for that student to succeed in the classroom. A comprehensive assessment of the student, using as much relevant information as possible, yields the most complete picture by which to make appropriate instructional programming decisions. The RTI model seeks to ensure that students have access to scientific, research-based, and differentiated instruction to facilitate their success before they are referred for evaluation for special education. When formal assessments are necessary and completed appropriately, the results generate useful and important information about what the student knows and how the student learns, as well as information about what instructional strategies may best benefit the student. Because learning disabilities are a neurological disorder that cannot (at this time) be diagnosed using brain imaging equipment, the clinical judgment of the multidisciplinary team will probably continue to play a significant role in the identification of students with learning disabilities for the foreseeable future.

IDENTIFYING ATTENTION-DEFICIT/ HYPERACTIVITY DISORDER

Although far fewer are identified as needing to receive special education services, as many as 3%–5% of the school-age population are diagnosed with attention-deficit/hyperactivity disorder (ADHD; Aaron, Joshi, Palmer, Smith, & Kirby, 2002). The diagnosis of ADHD can be challenging because many children, especially those of pre-school age, demonstrate many behaviors often associated with ADHD. Further, there is no definitive, specific assessment for ADHD, and practitioners must use a variety of assessment information to make diagnostic decisions. To properly assess a child for a potential diagnosis of ADHD, authorities agree that a practitioner skilled in the differential diagnosis of ADHD should be consulted. Typically, school and family histories as well as a medical exam and behavioral observations are used to gain a full picture of the child across school, recreational, and home environments (Hallahan & Kauffman, 2006).

ADHD in the United States: Facts and Figures

The number of children diagnosed in the United States with ADHD has been increasing. However, it is unclear if the increase in the number of diagnoses indicates an increase in pathology, more precise diagnoses, or inaccurate identification. Although most reports indicate that experts estimate 3%–5% of U.S. children as having ADHD (National Institute of Mental Health, 2006), the National Health Interview Survey (National Center for Health Statistics, 2006) indicated that from 2001–2004, 7.7% of children from the ages of 5–17 years were diagnosed as having ADHD. Because students with ADHD are served under the Other Health Impairment (OHI) category under IDEIA, it is difficult to ascertain exact numbers of students who receive special education services for ADHD. Further complicating the issue is the prevalence of comorbid disorders in students who have been diagnosed with ADHD. Of students who have a diagnosis of ADHD, 10%–30% also have a learning disability, as many as 30%–50% may have Oppositional Defiant Disorder (ODD), and still others may struggle with anxiety, depression, or bipolar disorder (NIMH, 2006). The presence of other conditions in conjunction with ADHD can make it difficult to recognize and treat the symptoms of ADHD.

Additionally, ADHD is diagnosed at different rates among males and females, although the differential prevalence rates may not be as high as is often reported in the general media. Although one can find claims that boys outnumber girls in ADHD diagnoses by as much as a 10 to 1 ratio, more accurate estimates indicate that boys are diagnosed with ADHD two to three times as often as girls (Smith, 2002). This gender bias can complicate the diagnosis of ADHD for professionals who are not well trained in the recognition and treatment of ADHD. Indeed, because ADHD is a neurobehavioral disorder, there is a large degree of clinical judgment necessary in assessing for the presence of the disorder, making it a difficult disorder to diagnose (Environmental Protection Agency, 2006). A simple familiarity with the criteria associated with the disorder is not sufficient to qualify one to diagnose ADHD; only highly trained professionals are qualified to make the diagnosis and initiate treatment for the individual.

Recognizing the Symptoms of ADHD

The *DSM-IV-TR* (2000) delineates three distinct types of ADHD: predominantly inattentive type, predominantly hyperactive-impulsive type, or combined type. Most children exhibit symptoms of both inattention and hyperactivity-impulsivity, although in some children, one pattern of behavior predominates. Symptoms of inattention in children include failure to attend to details in schoolwork or other activities, difficulty sustaining attention, difficulty listening to or following directions, losing things, and being easily distracted and forgetful. Symptoms of hyperactivity-impulsivity include fidgeting, out-of-seat behavior in school, running, climbing and talking excessively, playing loudly, interrupting others, blurting out ideas, and demonstrating difficulty awaiting turns. When completing an evaluation for ADHD, the child is assessed through a lens that considers age-appropriate expectations for behavior and academic performance.

Differentiating Between Learning Disabilities and ADHD

Two of the most common disabilities in the school-age population are learning disabilities and ADHD (Aaron et al., 2002). Frequently, students with learning disabilities, especially reading disabilities, and students with ADHD have similar academic and behavioral presentations in the classroom. It is important to be able to distinguish between students with learning disabilities and those with ADHD because the disorders are associated with different cognitive processes and often require different treatments and interventions (Aaron et al., 2002). Estimates of ADHD coexisting with learning disabilities as a comorbid disorder vary, but generally fall in the 10%–25% range (Hallahan & Kauffman, 2006).

Reading skills are especially vulnerable in children with a singular diagnosis of reading disabilities or ADHD, and particularly in children for whom both disorders are comorbid. Children with reading disabilities often struggle to read due to weak phonological processing and comprehension skills, whereas children with ADHD are more likely to be unable to sustain attention while reading and engage in off-task behavior, fragmenting their information processing and resulting in poor performance on tests of reading comprehension (Aaron et al., 2002). Therefore, the classroom presentation of students with reading disability and students with ADHD may be remarkably similar, resulting in frequent misdiagnosis and inappropriate treatment interventions. One group of researchers has suggested that by strategically incorporating listening comprehension activities with reading comprehension assessment as well as examining patterns of individual performance on continuous performance tests, a more accurate differential diagnosis of reading disability and ADHD is possible (Aaron et al., 2002)

Section 504 vs. Individualized Education Programs

IDEIA (2004) evolved from the Education for All Handicapped Children Act (1975). This federal law has been systematically revised and reauthorized, and provides funding to guarantee special education services for all students who meet the criteria for eligibility in one or more of the 13 disability categories specified in the law: autism, specific learning disability, speech or language impairments, emotional disturbance, traumatic brain injury, visual impairment, hearing impairment, deafness, mental retardation, deaf-blindness, multiple disabilities, orthopedic impairment, and other health impairment. As Table 8.1 illustrates, Section 504 of the Rehabilitation Act of 1973 is a civil rights statute, not a federal law, which prohibits schools that receive federal funding from discriminating against students with disabilities. However, Section 504 does not provide additional funding to schools to facilitate non-discrimination (deBettencourt, 2002). See Table 8.1 for a more comprehensive distinction between the two laws.

Students with ADHD may be served under IDEIA or Section 504, depending on the nature and severity of the handicaps imposed by their disability. A student with ADHD may meet the criteria for Other Health Impairment (OHI) under IDEIA due to limited alertness to curricular content or hyper-alertness to environmental stimuli which decreases alertness to educational materials. In this case, the student is served under IDEIA and is entitled to an Individualized Education Program (IEP) that demarcates specific educational strategies to provide the best instruction to the student. However, some students with ADHD do not require the more intense services guaranteed under IDEIA and may not be found eligible to receive them. This is especially true in cases in which a student's ADHD is managed through preferential seating, timing accommodations on tests, or medication (Cohen, 2006). In this case, if the student requires accommodations for the disability in the general education classroom, the student may be eligible for a 504 accommodation plan, which outlines the accommodations the student should receive in the general education setting (Overton, 2006). Although technically students with ADHD have always been eligible for services under IDEA (under the OHI category if the disability manifested in such a way that the student met the eligibility criteria), it was not until IDEA was reauthorized in 1997 that ADHD was explicitly incorporated into the definition of OHI.

Summary

There is no doubt that ADHD is a prevalent and significant disorder affecting millions of U.S. students in the educational system. The number of individuals being diagnosed with ADHD continues to rise, and the odds that at least one student in every American classroom has a diagnosis of ADHD are high. Although ADHD can be difficult to diagnose, especially if its presentation is complicated by the presence of co-morbid disorders, it is important for school professionals to understand how ADHD affects a student's ability to function in the classroom and

TABLE 8.1   Section 504 vs. IDEIA

	Section 504	IDEIA
Type of Statute	Civil rights statute prohibiting discrimination against persons with disabilities	Federal law guaranteeing free and appropriate public education for children with disabilities
Funding	No federal funding; school bears responsibility to finance accommodations	Some federal funding provided to help states pay for special education services
Provision	Prohibits exclusion from participation in or denial of benefit from any services on the basis of a disability	Establishes right to free and appropriate public education in the least restrictive environment for children with disabilities
Protected Individuals and Identification Criteria	Individuals of all ages with physical or mental impairment(s) that limit(s) a major life activity	Individuals (usually ages 3–21) who fall into any one or more of the thirteen disability categories delineated in IDEIA 2004; the disability must negatively affect student's academic performance
Parental Involvement	Parental consent is recommended but not required.	Parents must be notified before comprehensive evaluation measures are taken. Informed and written consent required
Evaluation	Evaluation information comes from multiple sources inside and/or outside of school; requires "periodic" reevaluation	Comprehensive evaluation completed by multidisciplinary team; requires reevaluation at least once every 3 years
Delivery Method	Section 504 Plan	Individualized Education Program

Note. Adapted from information in deBettencourt, L. U. (2002). "Understanding the Differences Between IDEA and Section 504," by L. U. deBettencourt, 2002, *Teaching Exceptional Children, 34*(3), pp. 16–23, and "Key Differences Between IDEA and Section 504," by S. Dickinson, 2007, retrieved May 10, 2007, from http://sdickinson.pbwiki.com/ f/IDEA%20vs%20504.pdf

engage in learning. Further, distinguishing between ADHD and learning disabilities is crucial in order to ensure that students receive the appropriate interventions and treatments in the school setting. Depending upon the severity of symptoms resulting from a diagnosis of ADHD, a student may be served with a simple 504 accommodation plan or a more specialized, detailed IEP; indeed, the most important issue is that the individual be identified properly and provided with the necessary accommodations and supports in order that he or she may achieve to the highest potential.

LEARNING DISABILITIES AND ENGLISH LANGUAGE LEARNERS

The population of non-English-speaking students enrolled in America's public schools is diverse, multicultural, multilingual, academically challenged, and growing (McCardle, Mele-McCarthy, Cutting, & D'Emilio, 2005). Although these students bring a wealth of culture, tradition, linguistic diversity, and rich heritage into their classrooms, they are also the group with the highest dropout rate, lowest achievement scores, largest mobility rate, and highest poverty (U.S. Department of Education, 2004; U.S. Department of Commerce, 2004). The challenge for non-English-speaking students, or English language learners, is not only overcoming a language barrier but also overcoming low expectations and low academic achievement. Therefore, there is a great need to better understand how to best teach these students and—an even greater challenge—to sort out how to identify and teach those who also have learning disabilities (McCardle et al., 2005). According to Baker and Baker (see chapter 10), one viable approach, which focuses on early identification and instruction to meet the academic needs of English language learners, is response to intervention.

English Language Learners/Learning Disabilities in the United States: Facts and Figures

According to the U.S. Census 2000 Brief (U.S. Department of Commerce, 2004), nearly one in five Americans speaks a language other than English at home, and the proportion of language-minority individuals in the United States grew by nearly 50% during the past decade. Given the dramatic increase in language-minority individuals in the United States over the last 10 years, it is not surprising that non-English-speaking students are the fastest growing subgroup of children among public school populations, with an annual increase of approximately 10%. Currently, there are approximately 5.5 million students attending U.S. public schools whose native or first language is not English (McCardle et al., 2005). Of the students whose native language is not English, 80% speak Spanish. Vietnamese is the second most prevalent language spoken, totaling about 4% of language-minority students. The remaining percent of language-minority students represents a total of 440 diverse languages (McCardle et al., 2005).

The increase in language-minority students in U.S. schools presents a particular challenge for the school systems because the academic achievement of students who are culturally, linguistically, and ethnically diverse has historically lagged behind that of their White, middle-class peers. The National Assessment of Educational Progress (NAEP) has demonstrated that there is a large achievement gap between minority students, many of whom are non-English-speaking students, and White students. In 2005 only 7% of English language learners in fourth grade read at the proficient or above levels, in contrast to 32% of English speaking students. Further comparisons of performance levels by race/ethnicity indicate that only 15% of Hispanic students and 18% of American Indian/Alaska Native students in fourth grade read at or above the proficient levels compared to 40% of White or Asian American students (U.S. Department of Education, National Center for Education Statistics, 2006a, 2006b). These figures are gaining increased attention as the No Child Left Behind Act (NCLB) requires all states to consider the academic achievement levels of all student groups separately, including English language learners (U.S. Government Accountability Office, 2005). Until recently, the prevalence of learning disabilities in non-English speaking children in the public school system had been unknown. Despite the fact that these estimates are somewhat compromised because neither a method for accurate identification nor a consistent definition of learning disabilities across states and school districts exists, the current figures available do offer some sense of the magnitude and complexity of this important but neglected issue (McCardle et al., 2005). National estimates reveal that English language learners are underrepresented overall in special education, meaning that a smaller percentage of these students are receiving services than would be expected, given the proportion of the overall population that they represent (U.S. Department of Education, 2006b; Zehler et al., 2003). Further complicating the picture is the fact that, whereas English language learners appear to be underrepresented overall in special education, they tend to be overrepresented in certain special education categories: speech-language impairment, mental retardation, and emotional disturbance (McCardle et al., 2005). This underscores the need for better tools and methods for accurate identification of those with special needs.

Identifying English Language Learners With Learning Disabilities: Approaches and Challenges

Distinguishing between learners with limited English proficiency and those who also have a learning disability is critical. Just as for their English speaking peers, special education law requires this distinction (Boehner & Castle, 2005). Identification of a specific learning disability is based on determination of the following criteria (IDEIA 2004, 34 CFR §300.541): (a) The child does not achieve commensurate with his/her age and ability levels in one or more of the seven areas (oral expression, listening comprehension, written expression, basic reading skill, reading comprehension, mathematical calculations, or mathematical reasoning) if provided with learning experiences appropriate for the child's age and ability levels; and (b) The team finds that a child has a severe discrepancy between achievement and intellectual ability in one or more of the seven areas. In addition, learning difficulties must not be explained by environmental variables, such as limited English proficiency or cultural differences (IDEIA, 2004).

The widespread variability across school districts in the representation of students who have limited English proficiency in special education highlights the inconsistency and lack of coherence in approaches to assessment and identification of children for special education services (Wagner, Francis, & Morris, 2005). These inconsistencies are the result of problems with the definition and identification of learning disabilities, in general, and the added complexity of the interaction between language and learning for children who are learning in a second language. For these children, it is unclear whether limited language proficiency in English is interfering with learning or is masking a learning disability, or is leading to underperformance on assessments used for identification, which are not culturally and linguistically appropriate for that purpose.

Whether to assess English language learners in English or in their native language is, in and of itself, a complex issue. Depending on levels of proficiency in the native language and in English, assessment in the native language may provide a more accurate inventory of a child's knowledge and skills but one that is less predictive for learning to read in English than is an assessment in English (Gunderson & Siegel, 2001). Assessment of English language learners in English as opposed to their native language can be problematic in that individuals may not fully understand the task instructions even if they have the competence to perform the task in English.

Ideally, English language learners would be assessed by comparable assessments in both their native language and English. Assessment in only the native language or English can give an incomplete picture of a student's knowledge, skills, and instructional needs. Comparable assessments should assess the same domain, at identical levels, and with identical precision (Wagner et al., 2005). Unfortunately, very few comparable assessments exist, and the development of high-quality native language assessments that are comparable to English language assessments is both technically and financially demanding. These problems are even more challenging when attempting to develop comparable assessments across alphabetic languages with different orthographies (e.g., Cyrillic vs. Roman), and even more complex when working with both alphabetic and nonalphabetic languages. The development of comparable native language assessments is further complicated by the fact that speakers of an identical language may have very different learning and cultural characteristics and histories, as in Spanish language speakers who are of Puerto Rican, Mexican, or Spanish origin. Even within a language and among speakers who share a common origin, dialectal variation can prove problematic, especially when those speakers will be evaluated in a cultural context in which their primary language is not the societal language and there may be a limited number of professionals who are experienced speakers of the dialect (Wagner et al., 2005).

In the case of identifying learning disabilities among students with limited English proficiency, the assessment strategy should also explicitly reflect the student's instructional history. For example, if a student has been given literacy instruction in the primary language prior to literacy instruction in English, assessment of the child's literacy skills in the primary language is likely to provide important information (Lesaux & Siegel, 2003; Lindsey, Manis, & Bailey, 2003). If the student has good phonological skills in the primary language and has developed decoding skills in that language, then failure to acquire literacy in English may be related more to the amount and quality of English literacy instruction than to a more pervasive underlying learning disability. Alternatively, if the student has not developed literacy skills in the primary language but has received adequate instruction in that language, then the likelihood of a pervasive phonological core deficit is increased as reflected in the common underlying phonological core for reading disabilities across alphabetic languages (Ziegler & Goswami, 2005).

Summary

Because appropriate classification, identification, and intervention methods have not yet been established for English language learners with learning disabilities, there are problems both in the identification and assessment of students whose native language is not English. Furthermore, identification of English language learners with learning disabilities is hindered by a lack of theory and empirical norms that can help explain the normal course of language and literacy development for English language learners and the individual, school, and social factors related to that development (Wagner et al., 2005). Without specific focus on improving the conceptualization, measurement, identification, and classification of learning disabilities in English language learners, progress toward resolving these challenges will be limited and slow given the rate of progress in the field of learning disabilities in general. Indeed, how to identify and assess this population is one of the fundamental research questions that must be answered in order to determine how best to serve them.

STUDENTS WITH DISABILITIES
AND HIGH-STAKES TESTS

Recent educational reform efforts and increased national demand for higher educational standards have led to the development of statewide assessment and accountability systems designed to measure student progress. These systems are increasingly attaching high stakes to student performance on assessments. For instance, test scores are now being used to make decisions about student graduation and grade promotion, teacher salaries, and the allocation of school resources (Bolt & Thurlow, 2004). At the same time, the need to include students with disabilities in accountability efforts has become law and a key aspect of good testing practices. In this era of educational accountability, appropriate testing and reporting of assessment results have increased in importance to educators and policy makers nationwide.

Laws Governing Participation in Statewide Assessments

The inclusion of students with disabilities in assessment is deemed critical to improve the quality of educational opportunities for these students and to provide meaningful and useful information about students' performance to the schools and communities that educate them (Elliott, McKevitt, & Kettler, 2002). Two federal laws specifically require states to administer assessments to students with disabilities: the No Child Left Behind Act of 2001 (NCLB) and the Individuals With Disabilities Education Act (IDEA), last amended in 2004. NCLB, which reauthorized the Elementary and Secondary Education Act (ESEA), was designed to improve academic achievement for all students. NCLB requires that students with disabilities be included in statewide assessments that are used to determine whether schools and districts meet state goals. Further, NCLB requires that all students, including students with disabilities, be measured against academic achievement standards established by the states. Specifically, NCLB requires annual participation in assessments in grades three through eight—and once during high school—in reading, language arts, mathematics, and science. To be deemed as making adequate yearly progress (AYP), each school must show that the school as a whole, as well as each of the designated groups, such as students with disabilities, met the state proficiency goals. Schools must also show that at least 95% of students in grades required to take the test have done so (U.S. Government Accountability Office, 2005).

Participation Policies

There are a variety of ways students with disabilities can participate in statewide assessment systems, and these can affect the way in which their scores are considered for accountability purposes (Bolt, Krentz, & Thurlow, 2002). Some students with disabilities are included in the regular test administration in the same way as most other students. Others participate with accommodations. Some take a modified test or receive non-standard test administrations, and a small percent participate in alternate assessments. Although state policy may clearly indicate the ways in which students with disabilities can participate and be included in state assessment systems, the process by which such decisions are made and the degree to which scores from these various test administrations are included in the determination of school accountability (i.e., AYP) is often unclear.

According to the National Center on Educational Outcomes's (NCEO's) 2005 analysis of states' participation and accommodation policies, the criteria cited as most frequently used to determine how students with disabilities participate in statewide assessments were: (a) IEP determined (50 states); (b) instructional relevance/instructional goals (35 states); (c) current performance/level of functioning (34 states); and (d) student needs and characteristics (26 states). Additional variables reported by states included "Level of Independence," "Content/Purpose/Nature of Assessment," and "Past Performance" (Lazarus et al., 2006, pp. 54–57). The entire report, along with additional reports on state policies, can be found on the NCEO Web site (http://www.nceo.umn.edu).

Since the passage of NCLB, public reporting of state assessment participation and performance information for students with disabilities has been tracked by the U.S. Department of Education and various other agencies, including NCEO. Under NCLB, any school accepting federal dollars must demonstrate AYP in the number of students meeting proficiency standards and publicly report statewide assessment results in a clear, timely, and useful manner (Petersen & Young, 2004; see also Yeh, chapter 13). According to results of a 2005 nationwide study conducted by the U.S. Government Accountability Office (GAO), the majority of students with disabilities were included in the regular statewide read-ing/language arts assessments (National Assessment of Educational Progress; administered in grades four and eight) in the 2003–2004 school year. Participation rates ranged from 65% (Michigan) to 99% (Missouri) across all 50 states and the District of Columbia, with the exception of Texas, where only 39% of students with disabilities participated in the NAEP assessments. A 2005 analysis of the public reporting of state as-sessment results for students with disabilities conducted by NCEO yield-ed slightly higher participation rates. NCEO summarized participation rates for eighth grade mathematics tests across states and found that dur-ing the 2004–2005 academic year, participation rates ranged from 83% (Florida) to 100% (Wyoming); 10 of the 20 states had participation rates of 95% or higher (VanGetson & Thurlow, 2007).

Accommodation Policies

NCLB redefined the role of the federal government in K–12 education. Along with mandating annual student testing in grades three through eight, NCLB stipulates that accommodations must be provided for stu-dents with disabilities as defined in IDEIA (1991; 1997; 2004). While NCLB and IDEIA have increased the participation of students with dis-abilities in statewide testing, the percentage of students who receive test-ing accommodations varies widely between states. According to results of a 2005 nationwide study conducted by the GAO, researchers found that while the majority of students with disabilities (65%–99% across all states, with the exception of Texas, where only 39% participated) were in-cluded in the regular statewide reading/language arts assessments (NAEP), the number of students with disabilities who received accommodations ranged from 58% (Florida) to 89% (Massachusetts) (U.S. Government Accountability Office, 2005).

Accommodations, and their role in high-stakes testing, are consid-ered central because they define the line for participation in which results for reports can be aggregated (Tindal, 2004). Although large organiza-tions (e.g., testing companies, state departments of education) stipulate which accommodations are allowed, the decisions about what, if any, test-ing accommodations an individual student receives are usually made by a child study team (also referred to as the IEP team), which includes general educators, special education teachers, parents, administrators, and school psychologists. Although the IEP team should be very knowledgeable about the student, research indicates that accommodation decisions often result in lowering a student's performance on the standardized test from the performance that would have been attained without the accommodation (Fuchs, Fuchs, Eaton, Hamlett, & Karns, 2000).

Accommodation Issues and Students With Disabilities

Though there is widespread agreement that accommodations are necessary for many students with disabilities to effectively participate in statewide assessments, the issue of which accommodations are appropriate is not without controversy (Bolt & Thurlow, 2004). Providing accommodations for students with sensory or physical disabilities has rarely been questioned. On the other hand, accommodations for students with cognitive or language processing disabilities (e.g., learning disabilities) have been more controversial due to commonly held beliefs that these accommodations may inappropriately change the skills tested (Phillips, 1994).

Such controversy is evident in ongoing analyses of state policies on testing accommodations. Nearly every state educational agency has developed a list of allowable accommodations for its statewide tests; however, policy analyses have pointed to limited consensus across states (Clapper, Morse, Lazarus, Thompson, & Thurlow, 2005; Lazarus, Thurlow, Lail, Eisenbraun, & Kato, 2006; Thurlow, Lazarus, Thompson, & Morse, 2005). Variability exists among the types of accommodations states allow on statewide tests as well as in the way so-called standard test administrations are defined. Additionally, state accommodation policies are continually being adapted, reflecting the fact that many of the educational agencies are uncertain about what constitutes an appropriate accommodation (Bolt & Thurlow, 2004).

Role of Accommodations on Large-Scale Assessments

A clear explanation of how accommodations are intended to function is essential in determining whether specific accommodations are valid and appropriate. Many definitions of accommodations have been posited in the testing literature. There are typically two parts to each definition (Bolt & Thurlow, 2004). First, an accommodation is commonly defined as a change in the way a test is administered under standardized conditions (Fuchs et al., 2000). Common types of accommodations that may be provided include changes in the *setting* in which the test is taken (e.g., special education classroom, study carrel), the *timing* of a test (e.g. extended time to complete the test), the *scheduling* of the test (e.g. administer the test at a time most beneficial for the student or across multiple sessions), the *presentation* of the test items (e.g., provide an audiotape or a reader, paraphrasing directions), or the way a student *responds* to the test (e.g., allowing the student to record answers directly in the test book rather than on the answer sheet).

Implicit in the second part of the definition is the notion that the accommodation is intended to facilitate the measurement goals of the

assessment (McKevitt, 2000). A variety of testing conditions can influence the degree to which students with disabilities demonstrate what
they truly know and can do. For instance, small-size print, limited testing
time, and the inability to manipulate a pencil are all potential sources of
difficulty for students with disabilities (Bolt & Thurlow, 2004). These
characteristics are frequently unrelated to what the test is intended to
measure but can understandably lower student scores. Accommodations
are intended to remove these sources of difficulty (i.e., construct irrelevant variance) and allow for the intended construct to be meaningfully
and accurately measured. This idea is commonly articulated by stating
that accommodations are intended to "level the playing field" by removing construct-irrelevant variance created by disabilities (L.S. Fuchs &
Fuchs, 2001; Sireci, Li, & Scarpati, 2003; Tindal & Fuchs, 2000).

The term *test modification* is often used interchangeably with *test
accommodation*. It is important to clarify, however, that these terms
can mean different things. The term modification is typically reserved
for those test alterations that change the construct of the test, whereas
accommodation applies to changes that aid in the measurement of
a given construct. Test changes that are commonly considered testing
accommodations (and thus, usually deemed allowable) as opposed to
modifications, are the focus of our discussion.

Although historically accommodations were often viewed as a way
to enable some students with disabilities to participate in statewide assessments, and there was often little consideration of when it was appropriate
to use a given accommodation, that approach is changing (Lazarus et al.,
2006). The 2005 NCEO analysis of states' accommodation policies revealed that the language included in accommodation policies has become
more detailed (compared to the 2003 analysis) and seeks to clarify when
and how students with disabilities participate in statewide assessments.
For instance, more states are now distinguishing between accommodations
that can be used on a math test (but not a reading test), or whether a student may take different parts of different tests, such as taking the reading
alternate assessment, the math general assessment, and the science assessment with accommodations (Lazarus et al., 2006). The results of the 2005
NCEO analysis also revealed that there continues to be wide variability
in accommodation policies across states. Current research seeking to validate accommodations remains limited (although growing), indicating that
states are continuing to struggle with how to appropriately use accommodations to enable some students with disabilities to meaningfully participate in statewide assessments. According to Thurlow, Thompson, and
Lazarus (2006), "states now seem to be honing in on the need to clarify the
purpose of the test and the construct being tested, rather than just the goal
of providing the student with access to the testing situation" (p. 662).

ggio, J., Seok, S., & Smith, S. (2006). Equity for students with high-incidence
es in statewide assessments: A technology-based solution. *Focus on Excep-
ildren, 38*(7), 1–8.
, J.K., & Moore-Brown, B.J. (2003). Last chance to become readers: Pre-
nterventions. *Leadership, 33*(2), 22–24.
r for Health Statistics (NCHS). (2006). *National health interview survey: 2006
ase.* Retrieved June 27, 2007, from http://www.cdc.gov/nchs/about/major/nhis/
6_data_release.htm
itute of Mental Health (NIMH). (2006). *Attention deficit hyperac-
isorder.* Retrieved June 27, from http://www.nimh.nih.gov/publicat/
dhdpub.pdf
arch Council (NRC). (2001). *Executive summary: LD at a glance.* Retrieved
, 2007, from http://www.ncld.org/index.php?option=content&task=view&

006). *Assessing learners with special needs: An applied approach* (5th ed.).
us, OH: Prentice Hall.
, & Young, M.D. (2004). The No Child Left Behind Act and its influence on
and future district leaders. *Journal of Law and Education, 33*(3), 343–363.
1994). High-stakes testing accommodations: Validity versus disabled rights.
Measurement in Education, 7, 93–120.
S., & Scarpati, S. (2003). *The effects of test accommodation on test perfor-
A review of the literature.* (Center for Educational Assessment Research Re-
. 485). Amherst: School of Education, University of Massachusetts.
1999). Learning disabilities as organizational pathologies. In R.J. Sternberg &
-Swerling (Eds.), *Perspectives on learning disabilities: Biological, cognitive,
al* (pp. 193–226). Boulder, CO: Westview Press.
02). *A look behind AD/HD statistics.* Retrieved June 27, 2007, from http://
kenews.duke.edu/2002/09/mm_adhdmm0902.html
., Lazarus, S.S., Thompson, S.J., & Morse, A.B. (2005). State policies on
ent participation and accommodations for students with disabilities. *The
of Special Education, 38*(4), 232–240.
L., Thompson, S.J., & Lazarus, S.S. (2006). Considerations for the
tration of tests to special needs students: Accommodations, modifications,
re. In S.M. Downing, & T. M Haladyna (Ed.), *Handbook of test development
–673). Mahwah, NJ: Lawrence Erlbaum, Inc.
004). Large-scale testing of students with disabilities. *Exceptionality, 12*(2),

Fuchs, L. (2000). *A summary of research on test changes: An empirical ba-
defining accommodations.* Lexington: Mid-South Regional Resource Center
ciplinary Human Development Institute, University of Kentucky.
ent of Commerce. (2004). *Language use and English speaking ability: 2000.*
ed May 8, 2007, from http://www.census.gov/prod/2003pubs/c2kbr-29.pdf
ent of Education, National Center for Education Statistics. (2004). *National as-
t of educational progress: The nation's report card, reading 2003 major results.*
ed May 7, 2007, from http://nces.ed.gov/nationsreportcard/reading/results2003/
ment of Education, National Center for Education Statistics. (2006a).
al assessment of educational progress. The nation's report card, reading
Retrieved May 7, 2007, from http://nces.ed.gov/nationsreportcard/pdf/
05/2006451.pdf
ment of Education, National Center for Education Statistics. (2006b).
ation in education: Elementary/secondary education.* Retrieved May 7, 2007,
tp://nces.ed.gov/programs/coe/2006/section1/indicator07.asp

Summary

To accept accommodations in testing as the solution to achieving equity in statewide assessments for students with disabilities is insufficient, if not unacceptable. The tests themselves must be designed to maximize the opportunity for all students to demonstrate what they know relative to the standards being assessed (Meyen, Poggio, Seok, & Smith, 2006). For this to occur, test items must be tailored to the knowledge level of all examinees and, subsequently, efficiently assess what the learner knows. This is particularly important given the mandates of NCLB, as merely assessing what students do not know does not inform instruction, nor does it motivate learners toward higher performance. Thus, the requirements of NCLB and IDEIA should be leveraged to provide the conditions necessary to bring about the changes needed in statewide testing to ensure that all students are able to demonstrate what they know. In chapter 13, Yeh offers several promising approaches, including changes to federal policy, that have strong potential for improving educational outcomes for all children, and especially for children with disabilities.

CONCLUSION

In this chapter, we discussed some of the major changes and issues in identification and assessment in special education, with an emphasis on the category of learning disabilities. In particular, we provided a brief overview of the special education process, from the initial stages of the pre-referral process, to the various models of formal assessment and eligibility, and ending with the role of high-stakes testing for the population of students with disabilities. Though our emphasis was primarily on the category of learning disabilities, it is clear from our discussion this is quite vast, with a great deal of overlap among students with attention-related disorders and English language learners. In fact, problems in identification, based to some degree on conceptual inconsistencies, have led some to argue that the construct of learning disabilities does not exist as a viable condition. Some have proposed that learning disabilities is, in fact, socially or organizationally constructed to serve the interests of certain elements of society rather than children (Christensen, 1999; Coles, 1987; Skrtic, 1999; see Kavale & Forness, 1998, for a review). Nevertheless, we believe many of the challenges in the identification of learning disabilities can be addressed via improvements in local implementation of state and federal criteria in the identification of learning disabilities. Practices such as strict adherence to implementing pre-referral interventions and adopting more valid assessment models should not only increase the accuracy of identifying students with learning disabilities, but also reduce the numbers of students identified, resulting in an increase in the homogeneity of identified populations.

REFERENCES

Aaron, P. G., Joshi, R. M., Palmer, H., Smith, N., & Kirby, E. (2002). Separating genuine cases of reading disability from reading deficits caused by predominantly inattentive ADHD behavior. *Journal of Learning Disabilities, 35,* 425–435.

Altarac, M., & Saroha, E. (2007). Lifetime prevalence of learning disability among U.S. children. *Pediatrics, 119,* 77–83.

American Psychiatric Association. (2000). *Diagnostic and statistical manual of mental disorders* (4th ed., Text Revision). Washington DC: American Psychiatric Press.

Boehner, J., & Castle, M. (2005). Individuals With Disabilities Education Act (IDEA) guide to "frequently asked questions." Retrieved June 10, 2005, from http://republicans. Edlabor.house.gov/archive/issues/109th/education/idea/ideafaq.pdf

Bolt, S., Krentz, J., & Thurlow, M. (2002). *Are we there yet? Accountability for the performance of students with disabilities* (Technical Report 33). Minneapolis, MN: University of Minnesota, National Center on Educational Outcomes. Retrieved May 9, 2007, from http://education.umn.edu/NCEO/OnlinePubs/ Technical33.htm

Bolt, S. E., & Thurlow, M. L. (2004). Five of the most frequently allowed testing accommodations in state policy. *Remedial & Special Education, 25*(3), 141–152.

Christensen, C. A. (1999). Learning disability: Issues of representation, power, and the medicalization of school failure. In R. J. Sternberg & L. Spear-Swerling (Eds.), *Perspectives on learning disabilities: Biological, cognitive, contextual* (pp. 227–249). Boulder, CO: Westview Press.

Clapper, A. T., Morse, A. B., Lazarus, S. S., Thompson, S. J., & Thurlow, M. L. (2005). *2003 state policies on assessment participation and accommodations for students with disabilities* (Synthesis Report 56). Minneapolis: University of Minnesota, National Center on Educational Outcomes. Retrieved May 9, 2007, from http://education. umn.edu/NCEO/OnlinePubs/Synthesis56.html

Cohen, M. (2006). *The child advocate: ADHD under IDEA.* Retrieved May 10, 2007, from http://www.childadvocate.net/adhd_and_idea.htm

Coles, G. S. (1987). *The learning mystique: A critical look at learning disabilities.* New York: Pantheon.

deBettencourt, L. U. (2002). Understanding the differences between IDEA and Section 504. *Teaching Exceptional Children, 34*(3), 16–23.

Dickinson, S. (2007). Key differences between IDEA and Section 504. Retrieved May 10, 2007, from http://sdickinson.pbwiki.com/f/IDEA%20vs%20504.pdf

Education for All Handicapped Children Act of 1975 (1975). 20 U.S.C. section 1401 *et seq.*

Elliott, S. N., McKevitt, B. C., & Kettler, R. J. (2002). Testing accommodations research and decision making: The case of "good" scores being highly valued but difficult to achieve for all students. *Measurement and Evaluation, 35,* 153–166.

Environmental Protection Agency. (2006). *Attention deficit hyperactivity disorder.* Retrieved June 27, 2007, from http://www.epa.gov/envirohealth/children/emerging_ issues/adhd.htm

Fuchs, D., Fuchs, L. S., McMaster, K. L., Yen, L., & Svenson, E. (2004). Nonresponders: How to find them? How to help them? What do they mean for special education? *Teaching Exceptional Children, 37,* 72–77.

Fuchs, D., Mock, D. Morgan, P. L., & Young, C. L. (2003) Definitions, evidence, and implications for the learni *Disabilities Research & Practice, 18,* 157–171.

Fuchs, L. S. (2003). Assessing intervention responsiveness *Learning Disabilities Research & Practice, 18,* 172

Fuchs, L. S., & Fuchs, D. (2001). Helping teachers forr decisions for students with learning disabilities. *I Practice, 16,* 174–181.

Fuchs, L. S., & Fuchs, D. (2007). A model for implement *Teaching Exceptional Children, 39*(5), 14–20.

Fuchs, L. S., Fuchs, D., Eaton, S., Hamlett, C. L., & teachers' judgments of mathematics test accommc *School Psychology Review, 29*(1), 65–85.

Garcia, S. B., & Ortiz, A. A. (2006). Preventing dispror and linguistically responsive prereferral interve *dren, 38*(4), 64–68.

Gerber, M. M. (2003, December). *Teachers are still instruction strategies for identifying children u* sented at the National Research Center on L to-Intervention Symposium, Kansas City, MO.

Gunderson, L., & Siegel, L. (2001). The evils of the us ities in first—and second—language learners. *T*

Hallahan, D. P., & Kauffman, J. M. (2006). *Exception education* (10th ed.). Boston: Pearson Educatio

Individuals With Disabilities Education Act (IDEA) law 101–476.

Individuals With Disabilities Education Act (IDEA) law 105–17.

Individual With Disabilities Education Improvement 446, Part B, 20 U. S. C. § 1400 *et seq.*

Kavale, K. A., & Forness, S. R. (1998). The poli *Disability Quarterly, 21,* 245–273.

Lazarus, S. S., Thurlow, M. L., Lail, K. E., Eisenbrau *policies on assessment participation and accon* (Synthesis Report 64). Minneapolis, MN: Ur on Educational Outcomes.

Lesaux, N. K., & Siegel, L. S. (2003). The develop English as a second language. *Developmenta*

Lindsey, K. A., Manis, F. R., & Bailey, C. E. (20(Spanish-speaking English-language learners. 482–494.

Mandlawitz, M. (2007). *What every teacher sh regulations.* Boston: Pearson Education.

Mastropieri, M. A., & Scruggs, T. E. (2005). Fea intervention: Examination of the issues ar identification of individuals with learning ties, 38,* 525–531.

McCardle, P., Mele-McCarthy, J., Cutting, L., & in English language learners: Identifying th *Practice, 20*(1), 1–5.

McKevitt, B. C. (2000, June). *The use and effec science performance assessments.* Paper ment conference of the Council for Chief

U.S. Department of Education, National Center for Education Statistics. (2006c). *Digest of education statistics, 2005* (NCES 2006–030), Chapter 2. Retrieved June 27, 2007, from http://nces.ed.gov/fastfacts/display.asp?id=4

U. S. Government Accountability Office. (July, 2005). *No child left behind act: Most students with disabilities participated in statewide assessments, but inclusion options could be improved.* Report to the Ranking Minority Member, Committee on Health, Education, Labor, and Pensions, U.S. Senate, GAO-04-734, Washington, DC.

VanGetson, G. R., & Thurlow, M. L. (2007). *Nearing the target in disaggregated subgroup reporting to the public on 2004–2005 assessment results* (Technical Report 46). Minneapolis, MN: University of Minnesota, National Center on Educational Outcomes. Retrieved May 10, 2007, from http://education.umn.edu/NCEO/OnlinePubs/Tech46/

Vaughn, S., & Fuchs, L. S. (2003). Redefining learning disabilities as inadequate response to instruction: The promise and potential problems. *Learning Disabilities Research & Practice, 18,* 137–146.

Wagner, R., Francis, D., & Morris, R. (2005). Identifying English language learners with learning disabilities: Key challenges and possible approaches. *Learning Disabilities Research & Practice, 20*(1), 6–15.

WETA. (2006). *LD basics: What is a learning disability?* Retrieved June 27, 2007, from http://www.ldonline.org/ldbasics/whatisld

Zehler, A. M., Fleischman, H. L., Hopstock, P. J., Stephenson, T. G., Pendzick, M. L., & Sapru, S. (2003). *Descriptive study of services to LEP students and LEP students with disabilities, volume I: Research report.* Submitted to the U.S. Department of Education, OELA, Arlington VA: Development Associates, Inc. Retrieved May 9, 2007, from http://www.ncela.gwu.edu/resabout/research/descriptivestudyfiles/ vol1_research_fulltxt.pdf

Ziegler, J. C., & Goswami, U. (2005). Reading acquisition, developmental dyslexia, and skilled reading across languages: A psycholinguistic grain size theory. *Psychological Bulletin, 131*(1), 3–29.

CHAPTER 9

Systems of Instruction and Assessment to Improve Mathematics Achievement for Students With Disabilities

The Potential and Promise of RTI

David J. Chard, Leanne R. Ketterlin-Geller,
and Asha Jitendra

With reauthorization of the Individuals With Disabilities Education Improvement Act (IDEIA) of 2004, educators, advocates, and parents of students with disabilities see the opportunity for dramatic changes in the manner in which their children receive instructional support. As with many of the chapters in this book, the opportunity we refer to here involves using a response to intervention (RTI) approach to simultaneously improve access and achievement for students with disabilities in the general education classroom and enhance our accuracy to identify students with specific learning disabilities. Already, there is tremendous interest and activity with regard to the procedures for implementation of RTI.

A primary challenge at this early juncture is clarifying a conceptualization of RTI that will lead to educational improvements for students with disabilities and not simply provide us with an alternative to LD identification. Indeed, we must remember that there has always been an eligibility requirement for receiving special education; if a student did not respond adequately to instructional interventions, only then were they eligible to receive special education. Or in other words, in order to receive special education, a student must have a need for special education (*Board of Education v. Rowley,* 1982). So, how will an RTI approach be different from what we already have?

Like many nascent policy changes, there is no consensus on the precise way that RTI should be implemented, and many different conceptualizations have been proposed. Some researchers have focused on RTI as a measurement framework with a secondary emphasis on the instructional interventions offered to students (Fuchs, Fuchs, & Compton, 2004; Vanderheyden, Witt, & Barnett, 2005). Others have focused more on instructional support systems with less consistency with regard to the systems of assessment that will be used to gauge progress as a result of intervention implementation. If an RTI approach is to result in improvements to the current system and not merely provide a different way to identify students with learning disabilities, schools will need guidance in establishing and sustaining a comprehensive system that supports this approach. Most research and development in RTI implementation and evaluation have taken place in early reading education. Our interest is in promoting similar efforts in mathematics. However, developing RTI models in mathematics education will be a formidable challenge.

THE CHALLENGE IN MATHEMATICS EDUCATION

Recent activities in mathematics education suggest that there is considerable concern about the status of contemporary mathematics education. The U.S. Department of Education has formed a National Mathematics Panel to evaluate the state of the research on mathematics education and to produce a statement with implications for improvement. The National Council of Teachers of Mathematics recently issued a document referred to as the *Curriculum Focal Points* (2006) to clarify and narrow their professional standards and to help teachers focus on a few core instructional standards across K–12 education. The National Research Council convened a panel of mathematicians, psychologists, and mathematics educators to develop a document designed to guide mathematics educational improvements. The resulting book *Adding It Up* (Mathematics Learning Study Committee, 2001) stimulated ongoing conversation about the steps schools must take to align instruction with the needs of students while ensuring rigorous mathematics understanding.

These recent concerns are warranted but not unprecedented. Mathematics achievement has been a concern in the United States since the late 1950s when mathematics achievement began to lag behind that of other nations. *A Nation at Risk* (National Commission on Excellence in Education, 1983) noted that we were failing to adequately develop generations of students with adequate knowledge of mathematics.

Since 1995, the *Trends in International Mathematics and Science Study* (TIMSS; Gonzales et al., 2004), which includes approximately half a million students from over 40 countries, has helped us understand the nature of mathematics development in the United States. In 1995, the United States generally performed poorly in mathematics compared to other countries. In 2003, performance for U.S. fourth graders did not show measurable improvement over their 1995 performance nor did they improve relative to their international comparators. However, the trends began to change for U.S. eighth graders as they demonstrated a 12-point scale score improvement relative to the 1995 performance and international comparisons. Similarly, the National Assessment of Educational Progress (NAEP) results indicate that overall means in mathematics have improved for most students since 1992. Overall, the longitudinal results are encouraging in some areas and disconcerting in others. The United States performance on the TIMSS still falls short of many industrialized nations though scores in general have improved somewhat in the past 15 years.

Unfortunately, while overall mathematics achievement has improved over the years, the improvements have not been uniform across student groups. Most notable for our purposes, students with disabilities are not experiencing the same kind of improvement. Additionally, mathematics achievement for other subpopulations (e.g., Latino, African American, and Native American students) despite improving, remain considerably lower than achievement rates for White and Asian/Pacific Islander students. These disparities suggest that more needs to be done to make school mathematics instruction more accessible to all students. This means schools must improve their overall instructional performance and develop systems of differentiated instruction and assessment to identify groups of students for whom the mathematics instruction is not working.

In this chapter, we describe our vision for implementation of a multitier system of instructional support for enhancing the mathematics development of students with and without disabilities in an RTI model in light of the changes in the *Individuals With Disabilities Education Improvement Act* (IDEIA, *20 USC 1400*). We begin with a discussion of the role of a strong core instructional program in preventing mathematics difficulties before they become intractable and present long-term problems for learners. Next, we identify and describe features of instructional interventions that are supported by the research literature that can enhance the mathematical development of students with learning disabilities or at-risk for failure in mathematics. Finally, we describe key assessments that would be critical to informing the implementation of the multitier instructional support system.

PREVENTING MATHEMATICS DIFFICULTIES THROUGH POWERFUL CORE INSTRUCTION

Successfully implementing an RTI model in mathematics will require a fundamental change in the relationship between general and special education (Clarke, Baker, & Chard, in press). In brief, all teachers and support personnel in a school will have to accept responsibility for the learning of all children. Rather than attributing a child's failure to a biologically based problem that teachers cannot control, it will be incumbent on the classroom teacher and other school personnel to examine the general education instruction and instructional environment to ensure that evidence-based practices are implemented that maximize the likelihood that all children will learn.

The instructional environment we refer to above includes the standards and expectations set forth by each state or national organization, the tools (i.e., media, materials) teachers use in their instruction, teachers' professional knowledge of mathematics and mathematics pedagogy, and the physical environment in which students are learning. A full discussion of each of these variables is well beyond the scope of this chapter; however, we are obliged to discuss the considerable progress being made in mathematics education as well as the areas that need further attention.

Standards and Expectations

The National Council of Teachers of Mathematics (NCTM; 1989) boldly led the education field by publishing a set of mathematical standards almost two decades ago starting a standards movement that has changed the face of U.S. education. Not surprisingly, NCTM received considerable criticism for their efforts. Many advocates for students with disabilities, in particular, noted that the standards and promoted pedagogy ignored the needs of children with disabilities. The NCTM has since revised the standards (2000) and offered more focused guidance in how to interpret and use the standards during planning and classroom instruction. Perhaps the greatest value of the standards has been in opening the conversation about what is expected in mathematics education and in guiding states to establish standards that are aligned with national and international expectations. We fully anticipate that the NCTM will continue to evaluate the standards and will be responsive to stakeholder communities (e.g., mathematicians, educators, business owners, higher education) in determining how to revise the expectations of students over time.

Pertinent to the conversation on RTI, however, the standards play a key role in our identifying which students need extra support and which students may need special education services. Because the standards serve as the primary source of learning objectives for a particular domain, like mathematics, the expectations derived from the standards become the reference point for determining which students are on track and which students are not, in light of the instruction provided. Nationwide efforts have been undertaken to ensure that teachers are knowledgeable of their state's standards in mathematics. However, just knowing the standards and the concomitant grade-level expectations will not result in instruction that maximizes student learning. Teachers also need effective professional tools to ensure that instruction is adequately supporting students' development.

Teacher Tools

The development of teachers' tools, including textbooks and supplemental materials and programs, has undergone a remarkable transformation in the past 10 years. What was once a market driven system singularly focused on teachers' collective interests, now must also reflect the available research on learning in a given domain. While there is less research on mathematics educational tools than other domains (e.g., reading), guidelines are beginning to emerge based on evidence that will enhance teachers' effectiveness. For example, as a result of the NCTM Standards (1989; 2000), there has been a shift from materials that focus largely on computation and procedural fluency to those that build procedural fluency while ensuring conceptual understanding of a particular area of mathematics and ultimately providing students with an opportunity to integrate their understanding of foundational mathematical concepts into strategic problem solving.

The *Curriculum Focal Points* recently published by NCTM (2006) go further to provide us with a clear understanding of which foundational areas need to be most heavily emphasized and at which grade level. The areas that were outlined by the NCTM *Focal Points* authors were number and operations, geometry, measurement, algebra, and data analysis, probability, and statistics. As noted in the *Focal Points*, the document serves to guard against the fragmenting of expectations and standards and focuses curricula and instruction on key areas that form the foundation of mathematical learning.

Professional tools that teachers use to teach mathematics in general education classrooms (Tier 1) should reflect the emphasis of the core foundational areas outlined in the *Focal Points*. Additionally, professional tools that would be used as part of Tier 1 instruction should contain critical elements that research indicates underlie successful mathematics knowledge and performance. For example, core instruction in the elementary grades should ensure student development of number sense. Number sense has been defined by various authors (Gersten & Chard, 1999; Kalchman, Moss, & Case, 2001) as an individual's sense of the meaning of numbers, their magnitudes, and the results that should be expected when working with numbers. Two critical components of number sense, magnitude comparison and strategic counting, are examples of foundational skills that students need to learn in order to make adequate progress in their mathematical development. For a more detailed description of these skills and their development, see Clarke et al. (in press). To effectively implement core instruction that is based on standards and that maximizes student learning, teachers should be able to draw upon well-developed professional tools that support critical areas of the domain.

A thorough review of instructional materials available for teaching mathematics is unavailable at this time due to the limited nature of the research on mathematics instruction for diverse learners. However, the U.S. Department of Education (1999) endorsed several exemplary and promising mathematics programs as being more suitable than traditional mathematics programs at emphasizing conceptually rich instruction. Expert panels reviewed and rated submitted programs on the basis of program quality, usefulness to others, and educational significance. Additionally, the review examined data showing evidence of gains in student achievement. Programs were identified as exemplary if they provided convincing evidence of effectiveness in multiple sites with multiple populations, whereas promising programs demonstrated preliminary evidence of effectiveness in different sites. Subsequent empirical studies that have included both the endorsed programs and more traditional programs have yielded mixed findings suggesting that both programs can be effective in facilitating students' mathematical development depending on the contexts of implementation (Ridgway, Zawojewski, Hoover, & Lambdin, 2002; Riordan & Noyce, 2001).

Considerable thought has also been given to critical features of mathematics instructional tools and materials. Clements (2007) laid out a finely wrought plan for conducting research on the efficacy of instructional tools and materials. Other authors have provided guidelines on selecting or creating materials that would serve teachers in their efforts to teach a wide range of learners (e.g., Chard & Jungjohann, 2006). Use of these guidelines will help teachers ensure that they are addressing the needs of children who typically can't access the general education curriculum; however, we believe that implementing well-designed materials and tools is only part of effective core instruction. Teachers must also understand students' needs in relation to their mathematical development. With sufficient pedagogical, mathematical, and developmental understanding, teachers are better equipped to ensure that a wide range of students can be successful in mathematics.

Pedagogical and Mathematical Knowledge

Recent efforts to improve mathematics instruction have called attention to the need for teachers to have the robust knowledge of mathematics and mathematical pedagogy that is needed for teaching precisely and rigorously (e.g., Ball, Hill, & Bass, 2005; Ma, 1999). This attention has fueled efforts to improve professional development in mathematics and to better understand the level of mathematics and pedagogical knowledge necessary for teachers to deliver effective instruction (Hill, Rowan, & Ball, 2005).

The concern about the adequacy of teachers' mathematical knowledge has led to a line of research focused on the type of knowledge necessary to teach mathematics effectively. It turns out that it isn't quite as simple as knowing mathematics. More than just possessing their own mathematical knowledge, *mathematical knowledge for teaching* refers to "knowledge of mathematical ideas, skills of mathematical reasoning and communication, fluency with examples and terms, and thoughtfulness about the nature of mathematical proficiency" (Ball et al., 2005, p. 17). Hill et al. found that *mathematical knowledge for teaching* predicts gains in student achievement. With this knowledge teachers are able to analyze students' errors to understand how to proceed with instruction, develop multiple illustrative representations of mathematical concepts, and how to sequence examples to guide students' thinking to increasingly sophisticated levels.

In studies of teacher knowledge, Hill and Ball (2004) demonstrated that *mathematical knowledge for teaching* was a specialized knowledge needed to answer questions that involved evaluating students' problem solving and developing representations of specific concepts or mathematical rules. Moreover, they were able to document that this specialized knowledge went beyond the generalized knowledge possessed by most mathematically literate adults. In an attempt to understand the relationship between mathematical knowledge for teaching and student outcomes, Hill et al. (2005) assessed 700 first- and third-grade teachers and their almost 3,000 students. While controlling for student socioeconomic status (SES), absenteeism, teacher credentials and experience, and average length of mathematics lessons, they found teachers' performance on an assessment of mathematical knowledge, both general and specialized, significantly predicted the size of student gain scores. Importantly, in their follow-up analyses, Hill et al. reported that the effect of teacher knowledge on student gains was similar to the effect of students' SES on students' gains. This finding suggests that teacher mathematical knowledge may mediate the widening achievement gap for disadvantaged students.

Understanding Diverse Learners' Needs

In addition to the critical need to enhance teachers' knowledge and skills in mathematics and their specialized pedagogical expertise related to teaching mathematics, we contend that teachers must understand the needs of more diverse learners and the implications of these needs for modifying instruction. For many teachers, the notion of addressing diverse learning needs conjures up images of attempting to accommodate the unique needs of 25–30 students who are all expected to meet the same state standards and grade-level expectations. Rather, we suggest that teachers be encouraged to think about the needs of diverse learners as falling into four major categories that require additional support: memory and conceptual difficulties, background knowledge deficits, linguistic and vocabulary difficulties, and strategy knowledge and use (Baker, Simmons, & Kame'enui, 1998). Each of these areas of need is briefly described below and the implications for instruction are discussed.

Memory and Conceptual Difficulties

Students with memory and conceptual difficulties experience problems remembering key principles or understanding the critical features of a particular concept. Moreover, they often attend to irrelevant features of a concept or problem. For example, in a word problem, extraneous information, which challenges students to sort relevant from irrelevant information, poses particular difficulties for some students.

These students benefit from instruction that initially introduces concepts and principles with a high degree of clarity and continues to reinforce the most significant topics. Part of this initial clear instruction involves ensuring that the knowledge being taught is relevant to the learner. Mathematics becomes relevant, and thus learned when descriptions and examples go beyond procedural application to include why we do what we do mathematically. Therefore, in planning instructional lessons, teachers should consider the following questions:

1. Are my examples of concepts, principles, and strategies thoroughly and clearly developed to avoid confusion?
2. Have I adequately supported the gradual development of knowledge and skills moving from simple to complex?
3. Where appropriate, have I included negative examples of concepts, principles, and strategies to illustrate the relevant mathematical features?
4. Am I implementing a well-planned system of review?

Background Knowledge Deficits

Students with background knowledge deficits experience a wide range of problems in learning complex mathematics. These deficits might stem from a lack of number sense typically garnered in early childhood or from inadequate teaching and learning of skills and strategies fundamental to later mathematics learning. For example, many students struggle to understand rational numbers and how operations with rational numbers differ from whole number operations. These differences depend on the strength of the learners' facility with whole number operations. Students experiencing deficits in background knowledge benefit from instruction that includes:

1. Preteaching opportunities to ensure that students will be successful with new content.
2. Assessment of background knowledge to assist teachers in planning.
3. Differentiated instruction and practice to scaffold learning.

Linguistic and Vocabulary Difficulties

Students with linguistic and vocabulary difficulties may be challenged at two levels. First, they often struggle to distinguish important symbols in mathematics that represent key concepts and principles such as the symbols for addition and multiplication, or the square root symbol. Additionally, many students are challenged by unique mathematical vocabulary. This is, in large part, because of an underdeveloped knowledge of morphemes and/or strong word recognition skills. Students with linguistic and vocabulary challenges benefit from instruction that includes:

1. Attention to defining and using mathematical symbols in a wide variety of contexts and with a high degree of precision.

2. Careful attention to the description and development of vocabulary knowledge.
3. Encouragement to use mathematical vocabulary in classroom discourse.
4. Opportunities for students to talk mathematically and receive feedback regarding their use of terminology.

Strategy Knowledge and Use

Many students, even typically developing learners, experience difficulties with strategic learning. Consequently, problem solving poses inordinate challenges as good problem solvers engage in self-talk and persist in finding a solution despite repeated failure. Not only do many students experience difficulties working through the steps of a strategy, they often do not understand which strategy to apply and when. Developing strategy knowledge and use requires:

1. Modeling important problem-solving strategies.
2. Teaching why and when to apply strategies as well as how.
3. Teaching mid-level strategies that work rather than generic problem-solving approaches.

As with any cognitive strategy, modeling requires the use of so-called think-alouds to demonstrate overtly for students how they can solve problems.

Successful RTI implementation depends on schools evaluating their core mathematics instruction and taking steps to strengthen instruction for all students. We believe strengthening mathematics instruction will include identifying effective professional tools, enhancing teachers, general and specialized mathematical knowledge, and assisting teachers to make their instruction more accessible to a wide range of learners. If these efforts are successful, it is likely that some students will continue to need more specific intervention. In the next section, we discuss features of documented effective interventions in mathematics.

FEATURES OF EFFECTIVE
MATHEMATICS INTERVENTIONS

In light of evidence-based practices that address the needs of a broad range of learners, we expect that many students with and without disabilities will be able to access core instruction that will allow them to achieve important mathematics knowledge and skills. However, there will still be students who may not respond adequately to core instruction and may need intervention and supports beyond what even well-designed classrooms can provide. Response-to-intervention models accommodate for students who do not respond to core instruction by providing more intensive intervention support. Students may need more intensive intervention due to sensory impairments; memory, processing, or attention difficulties; or self-regulation problems that require more carefully designed instruction that address their needs. Evidence on the features of these interventions is emerging. In this section, we provide a summary of the major findings from three syntheses of research on effective practices for students with mathematics difficulties that include over 50 empirical studies (Baker, Gersten, & Lee, 2002; Gersten, Chard, Baker, Jayanthi, Flojo, and Lee, in preparation; Kroesbergen & Van Luit, 2003). The interventions should target the needs of traditionally underserved groups of students who (a) have mathematical disabilities, (b) enter school with very limited knowledge of number concepts and counting procedures, (c) receive inadequate instruction in previous years of schooling and fall behind their peers, or (d) continue to experience problems regardless of motivation, quality of former mathematics instruction, and number knowledge and number sense when entering school. Next, we identify and describe exemplars of specific interventions (e.g., schema-based instruction) that are conceptually sophisticated and designed to help struggling students improve their foundational skills and understanding of the underlying mathematical ideas and principles.

The basic index of effect size used in these meta-analyses was Cohen's *d,* defined as the difference between the experimental and comparison group means divided by the pooled standard deviation. According to Cohen (1988), 0.80 is considered a large effect, 0.50 a moderate effect, and 0.20 a small effect. Positive effects were reported for (a) systematic and explicit instruction ($d = 1.19$ and 0.58 for special education students and low achieving students, respectively), (b) student think alouds ($d = 0.98$ for special education students), (c) visual and graphic depictions of problems ($d = 0.50$ for special education students), (d) peer assisted learning ($d = 0.42$ and 0.62 for special education students and low achieving students, respectively), and (e) formative assessment (ongoing) data provided to teachers ($d = 0.32$ and 0.51 for special education students and low achieving students, respectively) or students ($d = 0.33$ and 0.57 for special education students and low achieving students, respectively). In sum, students who are struggling with mathematics benefit from explicit instruction in how to use specific skills and multistep strategies. This modeling is supported by teaching students to verbalize the steps to solving problems and to use visuals in representing problems. Additionally, students benefit when their teachers receive feedback from formative assessments to inform and modify their instruction. Finally, peer-assisted learning opportunities in which students focus on problem details, observe models of proficient students' problem solving, or are guided by more proficient peers result in improved mathematics performance for struggling learners.

Many of these features have been integrated into intervention approaches that have been used successfully with a wide range of struggling learners. One example of a research-based intervention that has resulted in improved outcomes for struggling students is *Schema-Based Instruction* (SBI). SBI is a promising approach for enhancing students' mathematical problem solving abilities, with positive results for special education students and students of varying levels of academic achievement (e.g., Jitendra, DiPipi, & Perron-Jones, 2002; Jitendra, Griffin, Deatline-Buchman, & Sczesniak, in press; Jitendra et al., 1998; Jitendra, Griffin et al., 2007; Xin & Jitendra, 2006; Xin, Jitendra, & Deatline-Buchman, 2005). Research on the effectiveness of SBI using schematic diagrams as representations has resulted in an instructional program designed to teach students how to solve words problems. These word problems involve all four operations using schematic diagrams as visual representations to highlight the underlying mathematical structure of the problems and help organize important problem information (Jitendra, in press).

From schema theory, it appears that cognizance of the role of the mathematical structure (semantic structure) of a problem is critical to successful problem solution (Sweller, Chandler, Tierney, & Cooper, 1990). Schemas are domain- or context-specific knowledge structures that organize knowledge and help the learner categorize various problem types to determine the most appropriate actions needed to solve the problem (Chen, 1999; Sweller et al., 1990). Organizing problems on the basis of structural features (e.g., *compare* problem) rather than surface features (i.e., the problem's cover story) can evoke the appropriate solution strategy. For example, selecting the operation to solve for the unknown quantity in *compare* problems requires understanding that the larger set is the big number or whole and the smaller set and difference are the parts that make up the whole (Jitendra, 2002). That is, you need to add the parts if the big number or whole is not known and subtract to solve for the unknown part when the big number or whole and the other part are known. Figure 9.1 presents samples of problems (*change, group, compare*) involving additive mathematical structures and illustrates how features of the problem are mapped onto the schematic diagrams and what solution strategy (addition/subtraction) is needed to solve the problem.

The benefits of schematic diagrams as aids for organizing information in word problems for students who may have attention, organizational, and working memory problems are clear. They include reducing students' cognitive load and enhancing working memory by directing resources from creating an internal mental model to correctly setting up the math equation. Furthermore, the emphasis on essential problem schema structures (e.g., *change, group, compare*) allows teachers to directly model problem solving by representing key information in problems using

Change: The zoo tour bus is pulling into the Fairview stop. 14 people get on the bus. Now there are 35 people on the bus. How many people were on the bus before the Fairview stop?

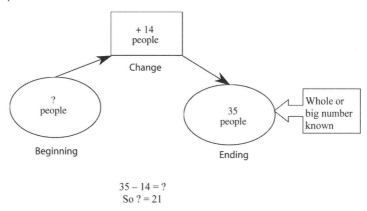

$$35 - 14 = ?$$
$$\text{So } ? = 21$$

Answer: 21 people were on the bus before the Fairview stop

Group: Last week, 79 children signed up for softball. 52 of the children have received their team shirts. How many children still need to receive their shirts?

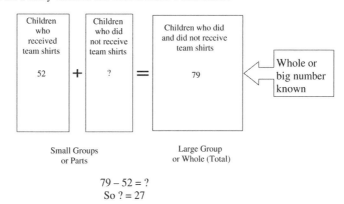

$$79 - 52 = ?$$
$$\text{So } ? = 27$$

Answer: 27 children still need to receive their team shirts

FIGURE 9.1   Schematic diagrams for change, group, and compare problems. *Change* diagram adapted from Marshall (1995, p. 133). Copyright 1995 by Cambridge University Press. Adapted by permission.

Compare: A redwood tree can grow to be 85 meters tall. A Douglas fir can grow to be 15 meters taller. How tall can the Douglas fir grow?

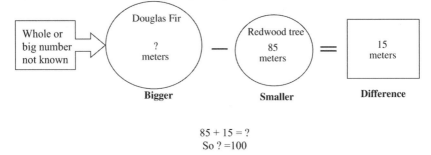

$$85 + 15 = ?$$
$$\text{So } ? = 100$$

Answer: The Douglas fir can grow to 100 meters

FIGURE 9.1   Schematic diagrams for change, group, and compare problems. *(Continued).*

schematic diagrams, explaining common rules and procedures, and analyzing students' solutions and explanations, which are crucial to enhance student understanding (Hill et al., 2005).

Features of explicit modeling of strategy steps, explanations, and elaborations using think-alouds and providing several examples are built into the program to scaffold instruction for students as they learn to solve word problems. A four-step strategy checklist (FOPS; F—Find the problem type, O—Organize the information in the problem using the diagram, P—Plan to solve the problem, S—Solve the problem) is used to help anchor students' learning. Each of the four steps is elaborated to highlight the domain-specific knowledge consistent with SBI. For example, to find the problem type (Step 1), students are prompted to examine information regarding each set (e.g., beginning, change, and ending) in the problem (e.g., *change*). In addition to schematic diagrams and explicit instruction in modeling problem solving using SBI, the approach also involves teaching metacognitive skills to transition students from teacher-mediated instruction to student self-regulation of strategy use, which is often difficult for special education students, who tend to be passive learners (Palincsar, 1986; Torgeson, 1982). In particular, student think-alouds are used to help them reflect on their understanding of the problem (e.g., "Why is this a *change* problem?"). To ensure that students engage in thinking and reasoning rather than applying rote procedures, the instructional approach requires them to justify the derived solutions using the schema features as anchors for explanations and elaborations and check the accuracy of not only the computation but also the representation.

Another component of the instructional program that follows teacher-mediated instruction and includes additional opportunities for students to focus on problem features is partner learning. A Think-Pair-Share model is used to engage students who may be struggling with the content by having them think about the problem type independently and then work with their partner to map the information in the word problem onto the schema diagram and solve it. The extended opportunities for verbalization of strategy steps during instruction serve to help students communicate orally with their peers and teachers when they share their solutions and explanations.

Finally, the program includes word problem solving measures for monitoring student progress twice a month. These measures have been validated and results from these formative assessments are used to inform instruction and practice (Jitendra, Sczesniak, & Deatline-Buchman, 2005; Leh, Jitendra, Caskie, & Griffin, 2007). By using these measures to monitor students' development of problem solving skills, teachers can modify instruction accordingly.

In this section, we have described research on features of effective interventions designed to meet the needs of students with learning disabilities and low-achievers in mathematics. Teachers who are knowledgeable of these features and are able to implement them in their interventions or select materials and programs that incorporate these features will assist students to access grade-level standards. Moreover, we illustrated these intervention features in the context of a specific intervention program. Another critically important feature of an RTI approach is assessment systems that help educators determine who needs intervention, what type of intervention they need, and whether they are making progress as a result of intervention supports. In the next section, we describe assessment systems that support the RTI approach in mathematics.

ASSESSMENT SYSTEMS IN MATHEMATICS INSTRUCTION

Assessment systems play an integral role in making informed decisions about students' instructional needs. Within a multitiered RTI model, student learning is systematically evaluated to determine (a) which students need additional instructional support to meet their learning goals, (b) what are specific problem areas within the domain for specific students, and (c) the rate in which students are learning the material. Information gained through these evaluations helps teachers design instructional programs that are aligned with the students' learning needs in relation to the outcome goals. Additionally, information about students' progress over time allows teachers to respond to students' learning needs by making adjustments to the design or delivery of the instructional program. As such, evaluation of student performance data plays a critical role in supporting student learning within an RTI framework.

Student learning can be evaluated using a variety of input mechanisms. Teachers readily have access to results from classroom-based assessments such as end-of-the-chapter tests or teacher-made tests, statewide achievement tests, and other district- or school-level tests. Although results from these tests might be appropriate for making specific instructional decisions, these tests are not useful within an RTI model. Because these assessment systems are intended for different purposes including mastery monitoring and accountability, they lack the technical qualities of assessment systems designed for evaluating and monitoring student learning over time. What is needed within an RTI framework is an integrated assessment system that is carefully designed to allow for static and fluid comparisons to a targeted outcome goal.

Static Comparisons

Static comparisons are made in relation to a criterion that is generally stable within the grade level and/or targeted domain. Making static comparisons allows teachers to evaluate student performance against a fixed standard that is associated with a specific level of proficiency of knowledge and/or skills. These standards are applied equally to all samples of behavior and are empirically grounded in research and theory. Within an RTI model, static comparisons are useful for determining students' levels of skills and knowledge as related to needed instructional services and supports.

Screening Decisions

The first step within an RTI model is identifying students who may be at-risk for failure within the domain by administering a screening test. Screening tests measure domain-specific knowledge and skills that are predictive of performance on an outcome goal. To evaluate students' risk status over time, screening tests are typically administered three times per year. As such, screening tests should efficiently measure students' knowledge and skills to provide maximum information with minimal intrusion on instructional time.

Screening results are evaluated in order to categorize students into three groups needing varying levels of instructional support, one of the tiers in a multitier model. Placement into a particular tier is based on comparing student performance on a screening measure to predetermined performance standards. Each tier is associated with a cut score on a specified performance standard or combination of standards. This cut score delimits the upper and lower score bounds for placement in the tier. By evaluating test results against these static cut scores, student performance data are used to predict future achievement within the domain. Because we want to identify the learning needs for all students in a class, all students are assessed on the same screening measure.

In order for screening assessments to work within the RTI approach, the content of the tests should be aligned with the outcome measure and the cut scores need to accurately predict future performance. Typically, screening tests are designed to predict performance on a proxy for overall achievement in the domain called an outcome measure, such as the state accountability test. Because we cannot evaluate achievement without an assessment tool of some kind, outcome measures are summative assessments that are intended to align with expectations of overall success within the domain. Early efforts in this area are promising (Chard, Clarke, Baker, Otterstedt, Braun, and Katz, 2005; Clarke & Shinn, 2004).

To develop an aligned assessment system, the content and cognitive complexity of the screening test and the outcome measure should be consistent. Proportions of items from each content domain and cognitive complexity should be consistent across the screening tests and the outcome measures. The blueprints for screening tests should be designed so that items from the five primary domains in mathematics (numbers and operations, measurement, geometry, data analysis and probability, and algebra) are sampled at the levels of cognitive complexity that match the outcome measure. The final screening measure should be evaluated for alignment by conducting an alignment analysis such as those proposed by Webb (2001).

In addition to alignment, cut scores for screening tests should accurately predict performance on the outcome measure. Because the primary purpose of administering screening tests is to determine which students might be at risk for failure in the domain, it is important to evaluate the predictive nature of the cut scores. One approach to determining if risk status accurately classifies students is to conduct logistic regression models (Hosmer & Lemeshow, 2000). Logistic regression analyses provide information about the specificity and sensitivity of the screening tests to correctly classify student risk status on the outcome measure. Because screening tests are based on accurate placement into risk categories, considering the alignment and predictive ability of these measures is essential within a multitier RTI model.

Diagnostic Assessments

The second evaluative component in an RTI model is diagnoses of students' persistent difficulties in knowledge and skills. Although a variety of measurement models (such as rule-space and general diagnostic models) are used to create diagnostic tests, most models rely on the same assumption: Students' current level of knowledge and skills are compared to the cognitive model of learning within the domain to determine misalignment resulting in persistent errors. Because the cognitive model is based on empirical evidence of learning, a static comparison is made between students' observed response patterns and the ideal response pattern to determine the areas of deficit (Tatsuoka & Tatsuoka, 1997).

Unlike screening measures, diagnostic tests are only administered to students who are identified as being at risk for failure in mathematics. Because these students often have enduring deficits that are not easily remedied by typical classroom instruction, diagnostic assessments are essential for analyzing students' domain-specific cognitive errors and misconceptions in order to design instructional interventions that are aligned with students' learning needs. Conversely, students who are on track for success typically respond adequately to high quality core instructional programs and approaches without the need of specially designed instructional programs. As such, diagnostic assessments are not necessary for these students.

Diagnosis of students' persistent misconceptions relies on carefully articulating the attributes within the cognitive model for learning (Gorin, 2007). Cognitive attributes are domain-specific knowledge and skills that are required for successfully solving content-related tasks. Attributes are specified through careful task analysis and form the basis of the assessment system. These attributes are combined to form knowledge states that explain the common deficits faced by many students when solving problems. A common method for creating diagnostic assessments is called the rule-space model (Tatsuoka & Tatsuoka, 1997). In this model, individual diagnosis of misconceptions is made by comparing the observed pattern of attribute mastery with the expected pattern that would be generated for a student within a specific knowledge state. Using Boolean algebra, the best fitting knowledge state is matched with the student's observed response pattern to make a diagnosis. Once a student's knowledge state has been diagnosed, instruction can be targeted to address the persistent errors. This step within the RTI model is necessary to design and deliver supplemental instruction that is precisely aligned with students' needs.

Fluid Comparisons

Fluid comparisons are made in relation to a criterion that changes relative to student learning. Often referred to as *individually referenced* interpretations, students' prior performance acts as the criterion against which current performance is evaluated. Making fluid comparisons allows teachers to evaluate changes in student learning over time or rates of growth. Within an RTI model, fluid comparisons are useful for determining if students are growing at an appropriate rate that will allow them to reach their goal. This evaluation may lead teachers to make adjustments in the instructional design or delivery to better meet students' learning needs.

Monitoring Progress

When evaluating students' response to instructional programs, frequent monitoring of student learning is necessary. Progress monitoring involves ongoing analysis of performance data to make decisions about students' progress toward the outcome goals. Progress monitoring involves gathering baseline data, establishing performance goals, collecting samples of performance over time, and evaluating the alignment between students' observed and anticipated growth rates given the goal. Because students' scores are compared to their own prior performance over time, an empirical database is created that can be used to design and modify instructional programs that are responsive to students' learning needs (Stecker & Fuchs, 2000).

Progress monitoring assessments efficiently measure students' knowledge and skills within the domain. Multiple parallel forms are needed to adequately monitor changes in student learning over time. Content is aligned with the expected outcome goals as either a global indicator of competence or by sampling from the curriculum. Because they may be administered as frequently as twice weekly, progress monitoring tests should be easy to administer, efficient to score, and sensitive to growth over time.

Several features of the measurement system need to be carefully analyzed in order to adequately monitor growth over time. Multiple parallel forms of the progress monitoring measures are necessary to track changes over time. Alternate forms must be comparable in order to infer that changes in scores are the result of changes in knowledge and/or skill and not variability in the measures. Item response theory modeling (IRT) is an ideal tool for creating comparable tests. Using equating designs, IRT allows items across tests to be linked to the same measurement scale without being sample dependent. As such, item parameters such as item difficulty and sensitivity do not vary with the population sampled. A common item equating design can be used to link the test items across tests and render the test scales scores comparable, enabling comparison of performance. Therefore, item-level information can be used to create equivalent forms of the same measure.

Progress monitoring assessment systems should also be evaluated on their ability to represent student growth. Although this is often assumed to be true when parallel forms are developed, progress monitoring tests should be examined for their sensitivity for detecting growth. Multilevel analyses using hierarchical linear modeling techniques can be conducted to evaluate the growth trajectories and parameters.

The sophistication of the assessment tools needed to effectively implement a multitier RTI model belies its dependence on instruction. Because RTI is based on the notion that you are measuring students' responses to evidence-based instruction that is well implemented, the assessment tools may provide spurious information if they are used to measure responses to inadequate instruction. The consequence will be the status quo for many students.

CONCLUSION

Our purpose in this chapter was to describe developments in mathematics research and development that could be realized as a result of recent statutory and regulatory changes in IDEIA (2004). Specifically, we discussed the opportunities presented by a multitiered system of instruction that can be used within a response-to-intervention approach to mathematics instruction. This system includes strengthening core mathematics instruction, designing and implementing research-based interventions, and improving the alignment between systems of instruction and assessment to benefit learning for all students. Implementing a model of instruction and assessment such as we have described in this chapter will support the changes in general and special education necessary to improve mathematics outcomes for all students.

REFERENCES

Baker, S., Gersten, R., & Lee, D. (2002). A synthesis of empirical research on teaching mathematics to low-achieving students. *Elementary School Journal, 103*(1), 51–73.

Baker, S. K., Simmons, D. C., & Kame'enui, E. J. (1995). *Vocabulary acquisition: Synthesis of the research*. (Tech. Rep. No. 13). Eugene: University of Oregon, National Center to Improve the Tools of Educators.

Baker, S., Simmons, D. C., & Kameenui, E. J. (1998). Vocabulary acquisition: Research bases. In D. C. Simmons and E. J. Kameenui (Eds.). *What reading research tells us about students with diverse learning needs: Bases and basics.* (pp. 183–218). Hilsdale, NJ: Erlbaum.

Ball, D. L., Hill, H. C., & Bass, H. (2005, Fall). Knowing mathematics for teaching. *American Educator,* 14–46.

Board of Education v. Rowley, 458 U.S. 176; 102 S. Ct. 3034; 73 L. Ed. 2d 690 (1982).

Chard, D. J., Clarke, B., Baker, S., Otterstedt, J., Braun, D., & Katz, R. (2005). Using measures of number sense to screen for difficulties in mathematics: Preliminary findings. *Assessment for Effective Intervention, 30*(2), 3–14.

Chard, D. J., & Jungjohann, K. (2006, Spring). Scaffolding instruction for success in mathematics learning. *Intersection: Mathematics educators sharing common ground.* Houston, TX: Exxon Mobil Foundation.

Chen, Z. (1999). Schema induction in children's analogical problem solving. *Journal of Educational Psychology, 91,* 703–715.

Clarke, B., Baker, S., & Chard, D. J. (in press). Best practices in mathematics intervention and assessment. In A. Thomas, & J. Grimes (Eds.), *Best practices in school psychology.* Bethesda, MD: National Association and School Psychology.

Clarke, B., & Shinn, M. R. (2004). A preliminary investigation into the identification and development of early mathematics curriculum-based measurement. *School Psychology Review, 33,* 234–248.

Clements, D. H. (2007). Curriculum research: Toward a framework for "research-based curricula." *Journal for Research in Mathematics Education, 38,* 35–70.

Cohen, J. (1988). *Statistical power analysis for the behavioral sciences* (2ⁿᵈ Ed.). Hillsdale, NJ: Erlbaum.

Fuchs, D., Fuchs, L. S., & Compton, D. L. (2004). Identifying reading disabilities by responsiveness-to-instruction: Specifying measures and criteria. *Learning Disability Quarterly, 27*, 216–228.

Gersten, R., & Chard, D. (1999). Number sense: Rethinking arithmetic instruction for students with mathematical disabilities. *Journal of Special Education, 33*(1), 18–28.

Gersten, R., Chard, D. J., Baker, S. K. Jayanthi, M., Flojo, J. R. & Lee, D. S. (in preparation). Experimental and quasi-experimental research on instructional approaches for teaching mathematics to students with learning disabilities: A research synthesis.

Gonzales, P., Guzman, J. C., Partelow, L., Pahlke, E., Jocelyn, L., Kastberg, D., et al. (2004). *Highlights from the trends in international mathematics and science study (TIMSS) 2003.* Washington, DC: National Center on Educational Statistics.

Gorin, J. S. (2007). Test design with cognition in mind. *Educational Measurement: Issues and Practice, 25*(4), 21–35.

Hill, H. C., & Ball, D. L. (2004). Learning mathematics for teaching: Results from California's mathematics professional development institutes. *Journal for Research in Mathematics Education, 35*(5), 330–351.

Hill, H. C., Rowan, B., & Ball, D. L. (2005). Effects of teachers' mathematical knowledge for teaching on student achievement. *American Educational Research Journal, 42*, 371–406.

Hosmer, D. W., & Lemeshow, S. (2000). *Applied logistic regression* (2nd ed.). Hoboken, NJ: Wiley Publishers.

Jitendra, A. K. (2002). Teaching students math problem-solving through graphic representations. *Teaching Exceptional Children, 34*, 34–38.

Jitendra, A. K. (2007). *Solving math word problems: Teaching students with learning disabilities using schema-based instruction.* Austin, TX: Pro-Ed.

Jitendra, A. K., DiPipi, C. M., & Perron-Jones, N. (2002). An exploratory study of word problem-solving instruction for middle school students with learning disabilities: An emphasis on conceptual and procedural understanding. *Journal of Special Education, 36*, 23–38.

Jitendra, A. K., Griffin, C., Deatline-Buchman, A., & Sczesniak, E. (2007). Understanding teaching and learning of mathematical word problem solving: Lessons learned from design experiments. *Journal of Educational Research.*

Jitendra, A. K., Griffin, C., Haria, P., Leh, J., Adams, A., & Kaduvetoor, A. (2007). A comparison of single and multiple strategy instruction on third grade students' mathematical problem solving. *Journal of Educational Psychology, 99*, 115–127.

Jitendra, A. K., Griffin, C., McGoey, K., Gardill, C., Bhat, P., & Riley, T. (1998). Effects of mathematical word problem solving by students at risk or with mild disabilities. *Journal of Educational Research, 91*, 345–356.

Jitendra, A. K., Sczesniak, E., & Deatline-Buchman, A. (2005). Validation of curriculum-based mathematical word problem solving tasks as indicators of mathematics proficiency for third graders. *School Psychology Review, 34*, 358–371.

Individuals with Disabilities Education Improvement Act 20 USC 1400 (2004).

Kalchman, M., Moss, J., & Case, R. (2001). Psychological models for the development of understanding: Rational numbers and functions. In S. M. Carver & D. Klahr (Eds.), *Cognition and instruction: Twenty-five years of progress* (pp. 1–38). Mahwah, NJ: Erlbaum.

Kroesbergen, E. H., & Van Luit, J. E. H. (2003). Mathematics intervention for children with special educational needs. *Remedial and Special Education, 24*(2), 97–114.

Leh, J., Jitendra, A. K., Caskie, G., & Griffin, C. (2007). An evaluation of CBM mathematics word problem solving measures for monitoring third grade students' mathematics competence. *Assessment for Effective Intervention, 32*, 90–99.

Ma, L. (1999). *Knowing and teaching elementary mathematics: Teachers' understanding of fundamental mathematics in China and the United States.* Mahwah, NJ: Lawrence Erlbaum.

Marshall, S. P. (1995). *Schemas in problem solving.* New York: Cambridge University Press.

Mathematics Learning Study Committee. (2001). *Adding it up.* Washington, DC: National Academy Press.

National Commission on Excellence in Education. (1983). *A nation at risk: The imperative for educational reform.* Washington DC: The Commission.

National Council for Teachers of Mathematics. (1989). *Principles and standards for school mathematics.* Reston, VA: NCTM.

National Council for Teachers of Mathematics. (2000). *Principles and standards for school mathematics.* Reston, VA: NCTM.

National Council for Teachers of Mathematics. (2006). *Curriculum focal points for pre-kindergarten through grade 8 mathematics: A quest for coherence.* Reston, VA: NCTM.

Palincsar A. S. (1986). Metacognitive strategy instruction. *Exceptional Children, 53,* 118–124.

Ridgway, J. E., Zawojewski, J. S., Hoover, M. N., & Lambdin, D. V. (2002). Student attainment in the connected mathematics curriculum. In S. L. Senk, & D. R. Thompson (Eds.), *Standards-based school mathematics curricula: What are they? What do students learn?* (pp. 193–224). Mahwah, NJ: Lawrence Erlbaum Associates, Inc.

Riordan, J. E., & Noyce, P. E. (2001). The impact of two standards-based mathematics curricula on student achievement in Massachusetts. *Journal for Research in Mathematics Education, 32*(4), 368–398.

Stecker, P. M., & Fuchs, L. S. (2000). Effecting superior achievement using curriculum-based measurement: The importance of individual progress monitoring. *Learning Disabilities Research and Practice, 15*(3), 128–134.

Sweller, J., Chandler, P., Tierney, P., & Cooper, M. (1990). Cognitive load as a factor in the structuring of technical material. *Journal of Experimental Psychology: General, 119,* 176–192.

Tatsuoka, K. K., & Tatsuoka, M. M. (1997). Computerized cognitive diagnostic adaptive testing: Effect of remedial instruction as empirical validation. *Journal of Educational Measurement, 34*(1), 3–20.

Torgeson, J. K. (1982). The learning disabled child as an inactive learner. *Topics in Leaning and Learning Disabilities, 2,* 45–52.

U.S. Department of Education (1999). *Exemplary and promising mathematics programs.* Jessup, MD: EdPubs. (ERIC Document Reproduction Service No. ED434033).

Vanderheyden, A. M., Witt, J. C., & Barnett, D. A. (2005). The emergence and possible futures of response to intervention. *Journal of Psychoeducational Assessment, 23,* 339–361.

Webb, N. L. (2001, April). *An analysis of the alignment between mathematics standards and assessments for three states.* Paper presented at the 83rd Annual Meeting of the American Educational Research Association, New Orleans, LA.

Xin, Y. P., & Jitendra, A. K. (2006). Teaching problem solving skills to middle school students with mathematics difficulties: Schema-based strategy instruction. In M. Montague & A. K. Jitendra (Eds.), *Teaching mathematics to middle school students with learning difficulties* (pp. 51–71). New York: Guilford Press.

Xin, Y. P., Jitendra, A. K., & Deatline-Buchman, A. (2005). Effects of mathematical word problem solving instruction on students with learning problems. *Journal of Special Education, 39,* 181–192.

CHAPTER 10

English Language Learners and Response to Intervention

Improving Quality of Instruction in General and Special Education

Scott K. Baker and Doris Luft Baker

This chapter addresses the role of instructional quality in the use of response-to-intervention (RTI) models with English language learners (ELLs). Although the use of RTI can occur across all grade levels and in multiple learning areas, we concentrate on literacy development in the elementary school settings. The reason for this focus is that research on ELLs has concentrated on early literacy development more than other areas and ages. In addition, approximately 67% of ELLs are in elementary school settings (Kindler, 2002). Thus, an RTI approach focusing on early identification and instruction to meet the academic needs of ELLs may reduce special education placement in the later grades.

RESPONSE TO INTERVENTION

In the latest reauthorization of the Individuals With Disabilities Education Improvement Act (IDEIA; http://www.nichcy.org/reauth/PL108-446. pdf), language emphasizing the quality of instruction in the identification of a learning disability (LD) has the potential to benefit educational outcomes of ELLs in both general education and special education. Current legislation states that "In determining whether a child has a specific learning disability, a local education agency may use a process that determines if the child responds to scientific, research-based intervention as a part of the evaluation procedures described in paragraphs (2) & (3)" (Section 614(b)(6)(B)). In previous versions of IDEA the language describing the role of instruction in LD determination had been indirect and nuanced. For example, an LD could not be diagnosed if the learning problem was primarily the result of "environmental, cultural, or economic disadvantage" (Section 602(30)(C)). The role of instructional quality in the context of environmental disadvantage was not addressed. This omission is noteworthy given that the conceptual basis of an LD is difficulty learning in the presence of adequate instruction and opportunity to learn (Lyon, 1994; Shaywitz & Shaywitz, 1994).

The RTI alternative in the latest authorization of IDEA states that an LD can be diagnosed only after the child has failed to make sufficient learning progress after high quality instruction and intervention has been provided. This focus on instructional quality is designed to rule out the possibility that incomplete or poor instruction has contributed to sustained poor achievement and the failure of students to make sufficient learning growth.

RTI should have a major impact on the quality of instruction in general education, *prior* to the determination of an LD. LD identification would be the culmination of an extensive process that focuses as much on features of instructional quality (e.g., explicit instruction) as on learning characteristics of the child (e.g., "a disorder in one or more of the basic psychological processes involved in understanding or in using language" that may "manifest itself in the imperfect ability to listen, think, speak, read, write, spell, or do mathematical calculations (602, 30, A).") It is not clear what steps state education agencies, local education agencies, and schools would take to validate that scientific, research-based interventions were implemented effectively for any particular child for whom it has been determined that insufficient learning had occurred and that LD was the cause. However, the new legislative language prioritizes the role of quality instruction prior to special education eligibility decisions and requires that education agencies should be responsible for documenting that quality instruction was provided.

ENGLISH-LANGUAGE LEARNERS AND ACADEMIC ACHIEVEMENT

At the outset, it is important to clarify terminology involving ELLs, because a variety of terms have been used to describe these students.

According to the National Research Council (1998), ELLs are "students who come from language backgrounds other than English and whose proficiency is not developed enough where they can profit fully from English-only instruction" (p. 15, August & Hakuta, 1997). Other terms used to describe ELLs include language minority students, second language learners, and limited English proficiency (LEP) students. *LEP* continues to be the term used by the federal government to describe and identify ELLs.

We use the term *English-language learners* because it seems to be the most preferred term and because it is considered more descriptive and less pejorative than other terms (LaCelle-Peterson & Rivera, 1994; Shanahan & August, 2007). Over 3 million ELLs attend elementary schools, representing more than 11.7% of the elementary school population. Although the vast majority of ELLs speak Spanish (79.2%) as their first language, more than 460 languages are spoken nationwide. The largest language groups after Spanish are Vietnamese (2%), Hmong (1.6%), Cantonese (1%), and Korean (1%) (Kindler, 2002).

Nationally, Hispanic students in elementary school settings represent about 17% of the elementary school age population in the United States (http://www.census.gov/population/www/socdemo/hispanic/ppl-172.html). This means that Spanish-speaking ELLs represent approximately 9.2% of the elementary school age population. Among Hispanic students in elementary schools, approximately 54% are classified as ELLs.

Low academic achievement is a critical element to determine whether a child has an LD, independent of whether a discrepancy model or an RTI model is used. Because ELLs demonstrate achievement rates that are substantially below their non-ELL peers, the causes and solutions for achievement difficulties frequently focus on these students. The National Assessment of Educational Progress has monitored the academic achievement of Hispanics nationally for many years and recently has begun to track the progress of ELLs separately. In 2005, fourth grade Hispanic students had the lowest reading scores on the NAEP, compared to other ethnic and racial groups. The gap in reading achievement between Hispanics and other ethnic groups was also apparent in eighth grade (Perie, Grigg, & Donahue, 2005), indicating that years in school did not appear to increase academic achievement for these students. The reading performance of ELLs is considerably lower than other groups, including Hispanic students overall.

DISPROPORTIONATE REPRESENTATION IN SPECIAL EDUCATION

The use of a discrepancy model in the identification of LD has been criticized on many dimensions. Regarding students from minority backgrounds generally, and ELLs specifically, a frequent criticism of the traditional disability classification procedures has resulted in a disproportionate representation of minority students, including ELLs, in special education (Klingner, Artiles, & Barletta, 2006; Rueda & Windmueller, 2006).

The National Research Council (2002) studied the percent of minority students in special education using data from the Office of Civil Rights and the Office of Special Education Programs. By far, the largest disability category is LD, which has grown consistently since 1974. In 1974, about 1.2% of students were identified as learning disabled. In 1998, 6% of students were identified as learning disabled.

It is expected that the use of a more valid approach to LD identification, such as RTI, will reduce problems associated with the disproportionate representation of ELLs and other groups of students in special education (Fuchs, Fuchs, & Zumeta, this volume; Klingner et al., 2006; National Research Council, 2002). Traditional determinations of high incidence disabilities (i.e., LD, mental retardation, and behavior disabilities) require some degree of subjective judgment in the determination process, and critics suggest that disproportionate representation occurs when inconsistent standards are applied. The inconsistent application of eligibility criteria can be particularly problematic for ELLs because of the difficulty determining whether learning problems stem from serious learning difficulties or reflect the challenges students face learning a new language (Barrera, 2006; Klingner et al., 2006; Ortiz, Wilkinson, Robertson-Courtney, & Kushner, 2006).

Drawing general conclusions about disproportionate representation, however, can be misleading. For example, since 1974 the proportion of Hispanic students identified as having mental retardation has been consistently around 1%. This is generally *below* the incidence rate for White students (National Research Council, 2002). The proportion of Hispanic students with behavior disabilities is well below 1%, which is also well below the incidence rate for White students.

Incidence rates for LD, however, present a different pattern in expected and unexpected ways. First, the rate of LD classification for Hispanic students has risen consistently since 1974, and in 1998, 6.4% of Hispanic students were classified as LD (National Research Council, 2002). Thus, in relation to the two other high incidence disability categories, LD has a much higher incidence rate. The second and more important issue in relation to disproportionate representation is that the dramatic rise in LD is also true for Black students and White students. In both groups, incidence rates are above 6%. Across the country, all three groups—Whites, Blacks, and Hispanic—have about an equal chance of being represented in special education as LD. For Native Americans, the incidence rate is somewhat greater. For Asian American students and

Pacific Islanders the chances of being identified as LD are substantially below the odds of other ethnic and racial groups.

These are overall trends, however, and the picture is much more complex when the disproportionate rates for individual states are examined. State variability is particularly acute for LD and more prominent because of the higher numbers of children served. In 2000, for example, approximately 6% of Hispanic students were identified as learning disabled, ranging from a high of 8.9% in Delaware to a low of 2.4% in Georgia (National Research Council, 2002). This variability among states prompted the National Research Council to conclude that "clearly, there is overrepresentation . . . in the LD category *in some states*" (p. 67, italics in original). What is not discussed as frequently is how problematic instruction affects special education decisions involving minority students, including ELLs.

The National Research Council (2002) concluded that improving quality of instruction should be a major part of the effort for addressing problems associated with disproportionate representation and that the focus on instructional quality needed to occur in both general and special education settings. The report does not mince words in making this point: "Current classroom practice deviates far too extensively from the knowledge of best practice to enhance outcomes for students with disabilities, and the quality of teacher preparation for both special and general education teachers with respect to instructing youngsters with disabilities is seriously inadequate. While there are indeed educators for whom this is not true—they are the exceptions" (p. 337). In the next section we describe the research evidence on some ways to improve quality of instruction for ELLs.

LITERACY INSTRUCTION WITH ELLS

A decade ago, August and Hakuta (1997) conducted a comprehensive review of educational practices with ELLs. They made the important point that remarkably little relevant instructional research had been conducted with ELLs, because investigations had concentrated on whether it is better to instruct ELLs first in their native language or in English and when is the optimal time to begin the transition to English instruction. They argued that research should shift from an exclusive focus on which language of instruction was best, to studies of components of instruction and how they work in specific locations, given a range of goals and objectives.

In 2000, the National Reading Panel synthesized research on reading instruction and identified five central instructional elements: phonemic awareness, phonics, fluency, reading comprehension, and vocabulary. These targets represent the types of components August and Hakuta (1997) suggested should characterize continuing research with ELLs. There is evidence that research with ELLs is changing to focus on these types of components.

For example, Shanahan and Beck (2006) confirmed that the available evidence, although limited in quantity and quality, indicated that core literacy components that are effective with native English speakers are effective with ELLs. Also, many of the same instructional approaches that are effective in delivering instruction with native English speakers, such as instruction that is systematic and explicit, will be effective with ELLs. In essence, systematic instruction means that the scope and sequence of the core components in reading are carefully selected to provide students with the necessary supports to understand increasingly more complex material. Explicit instruction implies that the teacher provides clear models of learning objectives for students, including students' response expectations, breaking tasks into important steps, and providing clear feedback to students on their execution of single-step and multi-step problems and learning activities.

Language of Instruction

A number of research syntheses have been conducted to address whether it is better to instruct ELLs first in their native language or in English. Francis, Lesaux, and August (2006) reviewed these syntheses and also conducted their own analysis. They concluded that although the authors of previous reviews "may disagree about the overall quality of bilingual education, they do not disagree about the overall quality of the available studies" (p. 371). Generally, the overall quality of this research is poor; problems include failure to equate experimental and control groups on important variables, nonexistent or incomplete descriptions of program characteristics, and little information about quality of program implementation (Francis et al., 2006).

The syntheses on the native language instruction have emphasized different conclusions. Green (1997), for example, emphasized the overall benefit of native-language instruction over English only instruction. The overall effect size (Cohen's d, Cohen, 1988) was 0.21. Slavin and Cheung (2004) conducted a best evidence synthesis and emphasized that the benefit of native language reading instruction may be enhanced when it is paired simultaneously with literacy instruction in English ($d = 0.33$). Francis, Lesaux, and August (2006) found that overall, native language instruction resulted in a positive impact (Hedges's $g = 0.18$, fixed effects; 0.33, random effects; Hedges, 1981) and noted the effect was strongest in those studies that paired native language instruction with English literacy instruction.

From a policy perspective, two considerations are important when thinking about the intersection of the role of language of initial literacy instruction and the role of quality instruction with ELLs. The first is that given that there are over 400 different native languages spoken in the United States, the possibility of providing high-quality native language instruction for all ELLs is remote. Overall, the student's native language is incorporated in instruction to some degree with approximately 22% of ELLs. Between 40% and 50% of ELLs attend an elementary school that provides native language instruction (Kindler, 2002). This figure, however, has decreased substantially in recent years with state policies mandating the use of English for instruction (August, 2006). Thus, many ELLs, including many Spanish-speaking ELLs, receive all of their initial literacy instruction in English. The second consideration is the role of quality of initial literacy instruction, whether students are taught to read in (a) English only, (b) their native language, or (c) both English and their native language together. One of the shortcomings of the language of instruction studies is that little attention was paid to actual instructional variables in the classroom.

One study examining language of instruction that also focused extensively on classroom instructional variables was conducted by Ramírez (1992). In this study, many instructional variables were quantified in two types of transitional bilingual education (TBE) programs and English immersion programs. In summarizing the quality of instructional opportunities for language use for ELLs across both TBE classrooms and English immersions classrooms, Ramírez concluded that

> students are limited in their opportunities to produce language and in their opportunities to produce more complex language. Direct observations reveal that teachers do most of the talking in classrooms, making about twice as many utterances as do students. Students produce language only when they are working directly with a teacher, and then only in response to teacher initiations. . . . Of major concern is that in over half of the interactions that teachers have with students, students do not produce any language as they are only listening or responding with non-verbal gestures or actions. (pp. 9–10)

Gersten and Baker (2000a, 2000b) reviewed 15 studies that described and analyzed actual practices observed during instruction and found that oral language use by ELLs in the classroom was consistently low. "Students had limited opportunities to respond to challenging, higher order thinking questions, or engage in problem-solving activities that required complex thinking skills. This was equally true when the language of instruction was English, or Spanish" (Gersten & Baker, 2000a, p. 53). The most problematic practices were (a) asking questions that required one- and two-word answers, (b) exclusive use of whole-class instruction with no opportunities for students to work in pairs or small groups, and (c) a stress on low cognitive tasks, such as copying, and on surface features of language learning, such as literal comprehension.

Reading Development With ELLs

The possibility that reading instruction fosters both reading acquisition and language development should receive more research and practice attention in school settings. Conceptually, Barrera (1983) argued that the relation between reading and language development is reciprocal, suggesting that ELLs' growth in reading was not limited by their oral language proficiency. Reading in context facilitates the development of proficiency in a second language. Anderson and Roit (1998) expressed this causal connection by suggesting that "spoken language is fleeting and inconsistent over time," while "text, by contrast, is stable and does not pass the learner by. When text is used, the learner can reread, reflect on, and reconsider the material to be learned, in its original form" (pp. 43–44). Anderson and Roit reasoned that many important language-based skills, such as the use of abstract vocabulary and the provision of extended responses, can be taught and practiced through reading activities.

A number of recent high quality studies have focused on teaching ELLs to read in English in the early grades (Denton, Anthony, Parker, & Hasbrouck, 2004; Gunn, Smolkowski, Biglan, & Black, 2002; Vaughn, Cirino et al., 2006; Vaughn, Mathes et al., 2006.) These studies, which have received favorable reviews by the What Works Clearinghouse (http://www.whatworks.ed.gov/), have focused on ELLs in grades 1–5 with reading problems (i.e., reading at least 1 year below grade level or scoring in the lowest quartile on standardized tests). In an RTI context, these would be students for whom progress would be monitored regularly. In two of the four studies (Gunn et al., 2002; Vaughn, Cirino et al., 2006), the intervention had a positive impact at the end of the study as well as 1 or 2 years after the intervention was terminated. On measures of reading, effect sizes (i.e., Cohen's d) ranged from 0.25 to 0.89. On measures of English language development, however, results were inconsistent (http://www.whatworks.ed.gov/).

The reading instruction in these studies was systematic and focused, taking between 30 and 50 minutes to implement per day. Intense small group instruction was a central feature, following the principles of direct and explicit instruction in the major areas of reading identified by the National Reading Panel (2000). Homogeneous groups were used, based on reading skill. In a study by Vaughn, Linan-Thompson, and Hickman (2003), students were regrouped frequently based on the progress they were making according to ongoing assessments.

Explicit instruction was the centerpiece in these studies, around which multiple additional instructional variables were integrated. The most important of these instructional variables included frequent opportunities for students to respond to questions, frequent opportunities for students to practice reading both words and sentences, and immediate feedback from teachers to students regarding the accuracy of student responses. The pacing of instruction was generally fast, with highly engaging activities of short duration to help keep students focused. Although the pace was rapid, the emphasis on student comprehension and understanding was high. In these settings, the teachers asked frequent questions to make sure ELLs were demonstrating evidence of their understanding.

Regarding reading instruction specifically with ELLs with LD, Maldonado (1994) examined the effectiveness of teaching literacy skills in both Spanish and in English. Twenty second and third grade students with LD were randomly assigned to literacy instruction in both Spanish and English traditional special education instruction. In the traditional condition, reading instruction was primarily in English, with a 45-minute period of ESL. The National Literacy Panel (Francis et al., 2006) indicated that there were significant problems with the reporting of the findings, but concluded that the most likely impact was that the effect size was large and favored students receiving both English and Spanish reading instruction. This is a potentially important finding because for ELLs with LD this is the only study to demonstrate that early literacy instruction in two languages is possible for a group of students for whom this level of complex learning might be expected to be particularly challenging.

A second study was conducted with ELLs with LD, this one attempting to improve language and reading skills in the students' primary language, Spanish (Echevarria, 1995). The program was a reading intervention called *instructional conversations* (Saunders, 1999; Saunders & Goldenberg, 1999), which is designed to engage students in academic language during reading instruction and to build comprehension skills. The intervention was implemented with five Spanish-speaking ELLs with LD. In an alternating treatment design, all five students received treatment and control reading instruction. The control condition was reading lessons using the basal program.

The results were complex. Gersten and Baker (2000a, 2000b) analyzed the data and found that oral retell was better in the instructional conversation group ($d = 0.25$) but the number of idea units and literal recall was better in the control (basal) condition ($d = 0.36$ and 0.56, respectively). Obviously, the sample size was small and conclusions should be interpreted cautiously. However, trying to understand the impact of the intervention is important because it shows that interventions may lead to increases in either reading proficiency or language development but not necessarily in both, and it shows that it is possible that improvements in one area could have a negative impact on the other (see the study by Waxman, de Felix, Martinez, Knight, & Padrón, 1994 as described in Gersten & Baker, 2000a, 2000b).

In summary, it appears that ELLs' reading abilities benefit from reading interventions that use explicit and systematic instruction that focuses on frequent opportunities for students to respond in small homogeneous groups. It is not clear whether these types of interventions have a positive impact on overall language development. For Spanish-speaking ELLs, reading instruction in Spanish and English, rather than English only reading instruction, may produce better outcomes in English reading development. This potentially challenging approach for students may also be effective even with ELLs with LD, although more research is needed in this area.

Vocabulary Instruction With ELLs

Through an intervention designed to impact both reading and language development, the study by Echevarria (1995) indirectly addressed vocabulary instruction with ELLs with disabilities. Although vocabulary instruction with ELLs would seem to be a major target for research, only a handful of studies of reasonable quality have been conducted in this area (Shanahan & Beck, 2006).

According to the National Literacy Panel (August & Shanahan, 2006), only three studies on vocabulary have evaluated the effectiveness of explicit vocabulary instruction for ELLs (Carlo et al., 2004; Perez, 1981; Rousseau, Tam, & Ramnarain, 1993; Shanahan & Beck, 2006). The Perez and Carlo et al. studies were randomized controlled trials, and the Rousseau was a single-subject study with ELLs with diagnosed speech and language deficits. All three of these studies demonstrated that explicit vocabulary instruction had a positive impact on reading comprehension for ELLs (Carlo et al., 2004; $d = 0.50$, http://www.whatworks.ed.gov/). In the one study that assessed intervention impact on vocabulary specifically (Carlo et al., 2004), the effect also was positive ($d = 0.43$). Although the number of vocabulary studies with ELLs is small, the extensive research base on vocabulary development with native English speakers indicates that explicit vocabulary instruction improves reading achievement and knowledge of word meanings (for reviews of this literature, see Beck & McKeown, 1991; Blachowicz & Fisher, 2000; Blachowicz, Fisher, Ogle, & Watts-Taffe, 2006; Mezynski, 1983;

NICHD, 2000; Stahl & Fairbanks, 1986). This research on native English speakers provides strong justification that vocabulary instruction should be a significant part of the instructional day for ELLs.

The vocabulary study by Carlo et al. (2004) provides an example of a comprehensive vocabulary instructional routine for ELLs. In the *Vocabulary Improvement Program,* 16 classrooms were randomly assigned to treatment (n = 10) and control (n = 6) conditions. ELLs (n = 142) and English only students (n = 112) participated in the 15-week intervention. The vocabulary routines took 1 week to complete. At the beginning of each week, 10–12 target words were introduced and instruction was provided 4 days during the week for 30–45 minutes each day. Each fifth week was a review of the previous 4 weeks.

On Mondays, ELLs previewed a reading assignment in their native language. On Tuesdays, intervention activities began, with ELLs reading the assignment in English and defining the target vocabulary words in large-group discussion with the teacher. On Wednesdays, the ELLs completed cloze activities (fill in the blanks) in small groups (heterogeneous groups based on language), and on Thursdays, students completed word association, synonym/antonym, and semantic feature analysis activities. On Fridays, intervention activities varied, but the central objective was to promote general word analysis skills, rather than focus specifically on learning the target words.

In the control classrooms, ELLs received instruction normally included in the school curriculum. Findings indicated that a focus on academic words, awareness of multiple word meanings, and morphological analysis not only improved the performance of ELLs but it also led to improvements for the English only students. Further, the variety of oral and written activities that focused on the manipulation and analysis of word meanings also seemed effective.

Typically, the vocabulary instruction provided in research studies is more thorough and explicit than vocabulary instruction often provided in classrooms (National Institute of Child Health and Human Development, 2000). Effective vocabulary instruction includes multiple exposures to target words over several days and across reading, writing, and speaking opportunities. A small but consistent body of intervention research suggests that ELLs should benefit most from rich, intensive vocabulary instruction that emphasizes "student-friendly" definitions, that engages students in the meaningful use of word meanings in different types of language activities, and that provides regular review (Beck & McKeown, 1991; Carlo et al., 2004; Graves, 2006). The goal of this type of rich vocabulary instruction is for students to develop an understanding of word meanings to the point where they can use these words, and related words, in their communication and as a basis for further learning.

In summary, vocabulary instruction that focuses on a deep understanding of words (i.e., multiple meanings, morphological analysis, appropriate use of words in context) will likely benefit ELLs and English only students. The research base is limited, however, and much more research needs to be conducted to determine the most effective interventions. The next section describes studies that have looked at the relation between reading performance and language development in the acquisition of early literacy skills.

Integrating Literacy Instruction and English Language Development

Reading, one of four dimensions of language development (listening, speaking, writing, and reading), requires the reader to translate a visual representation into the orthographic and phonological units that identify words and build a representation of the word in memory. Thus, reading requires the ability to: (a) recognize specific structures of the writing system in which the student is learning to read, and (b) identify words by accessing cognitive processes (word identification processes and meaning and form selection processes). These cognitive processes in turn depend on the reader's general background knowledge, the linguistic structures of the language (phonology, syntax, and morphology), and the lexicon (understanding the meaning of words) (Perfetti, 2000).

In other words, reading is an essential part of comprehensive language proficiency, but at the same time it has unique components (phonological awareness, phonics, and fluency) that can be taught in the absence of oral language proficiency. Vocabulary and comprehension, two additional core components of reading, require oral language proficiency. Several research studies indicate that some early reading skills, such as phonological awareness and aspects of phonics, can be taught without language comprehension serving as a necessary condition for learning these tasks (Chiappe, Siegel, & Wade-Woolley, 2002; Geva & Yaghoub Zadeh, 2006; Lesaux & Siegel, 2003). For example, an English language learner as young as 5 years old can segment and blend sounds in the word "lip," a phonemic awareness task, without necessarily understanding the meaning of the word. Also, a child whose native language is based on the alphabetic system (e.g., Spanish) can recognize letter sounds that are similar in English and Spanish (e.g., almost all consonants) without speaking English (Bialystok, Luk, & Kwan, 2005).

Research indicates that the best predictors of reading achievement for ELLs in English are phonological awareness, print awareness, and alphabetic knowledge (Chiappe et al., 2002; Durgunoglu, Nagy, & Hancin-Bhatt, 1993; Lesaux & Siegel, 2003; Oh, Haager, & Windmueller, 2004).

Further, oral language proficiency is a poor predictor of how well children will learn phonological awareness and phonics. This is because phonological awareness skills (including rhyming, syllable awareness, on-set rhyme recognition, blending and segmenting phonemes) require the auditory recognition and manipulation of sounds, not knowledge of morphology, word meaning, or syntax.

Chiappe et al. (2002) studied whether basic literacy and reading-related skills of ELLs and English only students in kindergarten and first grade differed as a function of proficiency in English. Findings indicated that in kindergarten, ELLs showed weaker performance on measures requiring greater vocabulary and memory demands (e.g., oral cloze test, memory for sentences), but performed as well as English only students on phonological awareness measures such as syllable and phoneme identification, and phoneme deletion. Although the performance of ELLs was below the performance of English only students on phonological awareness tasks at the beginning of the study, by the end of first grade, their performance was comparable to the performance of English only students on skills requiring phonological processing. Phonological processing and spelling explained 46% of the variance in word identification for English only students, and 56% of the variance in word identification for ELLs beyond verbal memory and syntactic knowledge. However, skills requiring syntactic processing and working memory were more difficult for ELLs than English only students. A plausible explanation for the difference is that syntactic awareness and working memory require substantial language proficiency skills whereas phonological awareness skills do not.

Lesaux and Siegel (2003) obtained similar results in their longitudinal study with ELLs from kindergarten to second grade. Participants were ELLs representing 33 different native languages (among them Cantonese, Mandarin, Korean, Spanish, Persian, Polish, and Farsi). Findings indicated that phonological awareness instruction in kindergarten (e.g., syllable and phoneme identification, phoneme deletion, phoneme segmentation and blending, etc.) was as effective for ELLs as for native English speakers.

Although ELLs had difficulty in kindergarten with tasks related to language skills and memory (e.g., pseudoword repetition, memory for letter names and sentences, syntactic awareness), phonological processing was the single best predictor of word reading and comprehension in second grade. Moreover, by second grade, ELLs performed better than native English speakers on word reading tasks, rapid naming, and real word and pseudoword spelling, indicating that language and memory skills were developing simultaneously with other reading skills, but they did not account for a significant percent of the variance explaining word reading.

Understanding the alphabetic principle (i.e., letter-sound correspondence, consonant and vowel digraphs and trigraphs, consonant blends, recognition of prefixes and suffixes) does not require developed oral language proficiency, per se. Students with limited language proficiency can identify letter sounds (and read words that include these letter sounds) without necessarily knowing the meaning of the words they are decoding accurately (Bialystok, Luk, & Kwan, 2005; Droop & Verhoeven, 2003; Geva & Yaghoub Zadeh, 2006).

Droop and Verhoeven (2003) studied the relation between oral language, word decoding, and reading comprehension in Dutch with Turkish and Moroccan speakers and native Dutch speakers in third grade. Findings indicated that Turkish and Moroccan students decoded as efficiently as the native Dutch speakers, but scored lower on reading comprehension and oral language proficiency measures at the word, sentence, and text levels. A disconcerting finding was that vocabulary differences increased over time. Droop and Verhoeven concluded that at the end of third and fourth grade, text comprehension for the Turkish and Moroccan students was much more dependent on vocabulary knowledge and morphosyntactic skills (i.e., knowledge of plurals, verb conjugations, pronoun identification) than for Dutch children.

The ability to read simple material fluently (e.g., building fluent reading on words students have learned to decode accurately) also appears to be a skill that does not depend on strong language proficiency. Geva and Yaghoub Zadeh (2006) studied ELLs and English only students in second grade to examine the role of oral proficiency and underlying cognitive processes in word and text reading. Findings indicate that although language proficiency levels between ELLs and English only students were different, scores on tasks involving word recognition, word reading accuracy, and word attack did not differ between the groups. In fact, ELLs read isolated words significantly faster than English only students. In addition, ELLs read simple texts at or slightly below the level of their oral proficiency with the same efficiency as English only students, indicating that oral proficiency in the second language contributed only marginally to word or simple text reading efficiency. However, when reading materials were more demanding in terms of vocabulary and syntactic structures, oral language proficiency played a stronger role in text comprehension. Additional research is needed to examine the degree of comprehension loss that occurs among ELLs as text complexity increases.

Vocabulary is strongly related to text comprehension, and it appears to be a significant variable in English reading achievement with ELLs (Fitzgerald, 1995; National Reading Panel, 2000). Proctor, Carlo, August, and Snow (2005) investigated the pattern of relations among reading and language measures for Spanish-speaking ELLs in fourth grade. Listening comprehension and vocabulary accounted for the largest amount of variance in predicting reading comprehension ($R^2 = 0.72$). Vocabulary exerted an impact on reading comprehension in two ways. First, it had an indirect impact on reading comprehension through listening comprehension. Second, it had a direct impact on reading comprehension.

The substantial evidence that word reading and reading fluency are strongly correlated with reading comprehension in studies with non-ELLs was not a pattern that held up in the Proctor et al. study (2005). It may be that listening comprehension and vocabulary mediate the impact of word recognition and reading fluency, reducing their influence on reading comprehension. It may also be that this mediation impact is more pronounced with ELLs, particularly in the later grades as text becomes more complex. The less than robust nature of the impact of reading fluency on reading comprehension may also have had something to do with the way reading fluency was measured. Other studies investigating reading fluency, when it is directly measured in text reading and not via word lists, have demonstrated a stronger relation between fluency and comprehension (Baker & Good, 1995; Dominguez de Ramírez & Shapiro, 2006; Wiley & Deno, 2005).

In summary, language development in the early grades does not appear to be a significant contributor to the development of reading skills. As students advance in grades, language development plays a stronger role, particularly when student differences in vocabulary and comprehension skills become more pronounced.

Monitoring Reading Progress of ELLs

If ELLs can make as much progress as English only students in the development of important early literacy skills, then a major component in the implementation of an RTI model becomes conceptually grounded. Measuring RTI—that is, measuring the progress students make to increasingly intense instructional interventions—requires having an anchor or goal against which the adequacy of progress can be evaluated. If we can set the same or similar goals for ELLs and English only students, and have the same or similar expectations for the progress ELLs and English only students make toward achieving early literacy goals, then the system overall will be easier for districts and schools to manage than it would be if there were separate goals and standards of progress for ELLs and English only students. In a system with similar literacy goals for ELLs and English only students in the early grades, it is likely that a greater percentage of ELLs would require more intense instruction early to make sufficient reading progress. The reasons have to do with lower rates of academic achievement generally, academic risk factors associated with socioeconomic status, and the additional challenge ELLs face learning academic content in a second language. However, this more intense and frequent instruction could be provided long before insufficient response to instruction and possible eligibility for special education are considered.

With specific goals and expectations set for the attainment of early literacy skills for ELLs and English only students, an RTI model requires that performance be measured regularly for all students, and for some percentage of students more frequent measures of performance are administered to evaluate how well students are responding to increased levels of intense instruction. When students are not making sufficient progress, interventions are intensified and progress-monitoring data are used to evaluate the impact of these instructional changes (Fuchs et al., this volume).

Few studies have been conducted with ELLs to determine the types of measures that can be used to regularly monitor reading progress (August & Shanahan, 2006). For native English speakers, the evidence for measures that can be used to monitor the development of early literacy skills is much stronger. Perhaps the strongest group of measures for monitoring student progress is based on a procedure called curriculum-based measurement (CBM). CBM was developed in the 1970s in reading, math, writing, and spelling to monitor student acquisition of basic skills. Fuchs (1989) summarized the state of this research 18 years ago and concluded that regular monitoring of student progress using CBM measures produced better student outcomes, and students whose progress was monitored systematically knew more about their own goals and their progress toward those goals. Further, the regular use of these measures helped teachers achieve positive educational outcomes for students with disabilities. In the context of RTI, an important thing about these measures is that they are strong psychometrically, feasible for implementation in school settings, and are constructed specifically to monitor student progress on a regular basis. The most thoroughly researched CBM measures have been in reading.

Four studies have investigated the use of these types of measures with ELLs to monitor student progress over time in reading (Baker & Good, 1995; Dominguez de Ramírez & Shapiro, 2006; Leafstedt, Richards, & Gerber, 2004; Wiley & Deno, 2005). Three of these studies investigated the use of oral reading fluency with ELLs. Baker and Good (1995) monitored the progress of second grade ELLs two times per week for 10 weeks. Passages for monitoring performance were sampled from the reading curriculum used in the district in grade 2. The correlation between oral reading fluency and the reading comprehension subtest of the Stanford Diagnostic Reading Test was statistically not different for ELLs ($r = .73$) compared to English only students ($r = .56$). Most relevant in terms of the value of the measures for monitoring progress was the finding that slope of change over the 10 weeks was reliable specifically for ELLs, indicating the potential value of the measures to register small improvements in reading proficiency over time. A critical assumption of RTI is that measures used to monitor student progress need to be sensitive to small but real changes that occur in student learning or skill development.

In a cross-sectional study, Dominguez de Ramírez and Shapiro (2006) assessed ELLs on oral reading fluency in English and Spanish in grades 1–5. All students made significant growth over time but the growth was greater for English only students. There was no interaction with grade so the differential growth pattern appeared to be true across the grades. Regarding the use of these types of measures to monitor progress, the data indicated slopes were greater for English only students than ELLs, whether the ELLs were being assessed in Spanish or English. ELLs had significantly higher slopes in Spanish than English in grade 1, corresponding to what might be predicted given they were receiving more Spanish literacy instruction in the early grades. As ELLs moved up in grade their slopes were higher in English than Spanish but the differences were not statistically significant. Demographic differences between the ELL and English only groups may have contributed to the outcomes. Less than 50% of English only students were on free or reduced lunch whereas 93% of ELLs were on free or reduced lunch.

Wiley and Deno (2005) assessed ELLs in grades 3 and 5 who were struggling with reading comprehension. Hmong (a language spoken in Laos, Thailand, Burma, Vietnam, and in southern China; http://www.hmongcenter.org/hmonglanguage2.html) was the primary language for 80% of the third grade sample and for 100% of the fifth grade sample. Students were administered two CBM measures—oral reading fluency (ORF) and a maze task—and the Minnesota Comprehensive Assessment (MCA) in reading. For ELLs, ORF was a better overall measure of reading performance than maze in both grades 3 ($r = .61$ vs. $.52$) and 5 ($r = .69$ vs. $.57$). For English only students, ORF correlations were .71 and .57 in grades 3 and 5, respectively. Maze correlations were .73 in both grades 3 and 5.

With the ELL sample, whether ORF or maze was entered first into sequential regression models, the second measure did not account for additional variance on the MCA comprehension measure in either grade 3 or grade 5. With the English only sample, maze contributed additional variance to predicting MCA performance above the variance accounted for by ORF. When maze was entered first, ORF did not contribute additional variance in accounting for the outcomes. This study provides additional evidence that CBM measures of ORF and maze provide a potentially useful approach for screening ELLs for reading problems and monitoring their progress over time. The study also suggests that measures may function somewhat differently for ELLs and English only students. This notion of differential functioning seemed particularly true for the maze CBM measure.

Leafstedt, Richards, and Gerber (2004) implemented a phonological awareness intervention with ELLs in kindergarten that was effective in improving performance on phonological awareness tasks and reading tasks measured by the Woodcock Johnson Tests of Achievement III (Woodcock, McGrew, & Mather, 2001) subtest measures of word reading and pseudoword reading (work attack). Progress monitoring measures in phonological awareness (phonemic segmentation fluency) and pseudoword reading (nonsense word fluency; Good & Kaminski, 2002) were administered biweekly to the intervention group during the 10-week study. Two considerations provide evidence for the use of these types of frequent measures of phonological awareness and alphabetic understanding. First, students were organized by ability groups at pretest based on their word reading scores (the Woodcock Johnson word reading subtest) and teacher recommendation. Performance on a single one-minute administration of phonemic segmentation fluency and nonsense word fluency, as well as multiple administrations over time, corresponded to these ability-grouping decisions. Second, performance scores increased consistently over the course of the intervention. This was a relatively short time period—10 weeks—demonstrating the measures registered small changes in performance, an important issue in RTI approaches.

In summary, CBM measures, especially oral reading fluency, appear to be sensitive to reading growth for ELLs and English only students. Moreover, level of performance on CBM measures such as oral reading fluency in combination with progress monitoring data may be a viable approach to determine level of reading risk for ELLs and responsiveness to intervention (see the "dual discrepancy approach" discussion in chapter 5).

CONCLUSION

In traditional approaches to providing services to students with LD in public school settings, the major emphasis has been on determining whether a child *has* a learning disability, and once confirmed, *placing* the child in special education. The intervention, in effect, is frequently special education placement. Educators, hopeful that special education would prove to be a successful intervention, thought that placement in special education would be viewed favorably by parents and others. However, parents and other stakeholders display a range of perceptions regarding eligibility and placement decisions. For example, "some parents may consider their child's placement in special education for a reading disability as stigmatizing and aversive. Others may view the identical decision as a blessing—as an opportunity for the school to finally respond seriously to their requests to provide intensive reading instruction to their son who has not been learning to read" (p. 50, Gersten & Baker, 2002).

RTI holds many promises for ELLs learning how to read and master other academic content. With RTI, assessment data can be used in school settings for purposes other than special education eligibility determination; the vision is that assessment data will be used to guide instructional support for children in the general education classroom. Although only a handful of studies have been conducted in this area, findings indicate that ELLs in need of support can be identified early, and if provided with additional systematic and explicit instruction in the core components of reading, their rate of growth can parallel the rate of growth of English only students. Moreover, in the early elementary grades, findings summarized in this chapter indicate that language development need not be an obstacle for helping ELLs develop early reading skills such as phonemic awareness and phonics. Language development, however, must be an essential part of teaching ELLs vocabulary and comprehension strategies. Finally, it is important to keep in mind that the ELL population is heterogeneous in terms of native language characteristics and proficiency, academic ability, and demographics. Additional research is needed to understand how these factors influence reading performance and growth among ELLs.

RTI holds the potential to provide more intense instruction earlier for children who need it. The decision to provide 20 more minutes of small group reading instruction per day for a child can and should be, a low-stakes decision, particularly compared to the decision that a child has an LD, which *is* a high-stakes decision. That is, RTI should be more forgiving about potential Type 1 errors, so that more intense instruction is not given to children who may not really need it. Universal screening measures can help tailor instruction for ELLs early. Through regular progress monitoring data collected over time, RTI has the potential to provide educators with frequent feedback on the quality of their efforts to improve instruction and learning outcomes for students.

There are potential downsides of RTI for ELLs. If RTI becomes simply a different procedure for identifying ELLs with LD, it may provide a more defensible means for identifying LD, but it will not be of benefit to students (Messick, 1989). The disproportionate representation of minority students in special education, including ELLs, is a significant national problem, and one of the intended outcomes of RTI is that it ease the problems associated with disproportionate representation. The percentage of children identified as LD has risen consistently each year since 1976, and

LD represents the largest disability category in special education. However, LD classification and growth is not a problem solely with minority students or ELLs. White students, as frequently as Hispanic students or African American students, are just as likely to be identified as LD. These percentages vary substantially from state to state and in some areas of the country overrepresentation is a major problem that should be addressed immediately through RTI or other means. However, many experts believe that disproportionate representation underlies a more fundamental and perhaps serious problem associated with the quality of instruction for ELLs and other groups of students (National Research Council, 2002).

Since the 1970s, data from the NAEP have depicted a large and persistent gap between the academic achievement of White students and Hispanic students (the gap between ELLs specifically and White students is even larger but ELLs as a separate group have only recently begun to be followed on NAEP assessments). Many efforts have been undertaken in the 30 plus years to address this achievement gap. Although these efforts have largely failed, at least when the measure of success is academic achievement, there is some reason for optimism based on recent NAEP data. Analysis of long-term trends (http://nces.ed.gov/nationsreportcard/ltt/results2004/sub_reading_race2.asp) reveals that the achievement gap between Hispanics and Whites in reading has been significantly reduced for 9-year-olds and 17-year-olds (although not for 13-year-olds) over the past 30 years. Between 1998 and 2005, the achievement gap between ELLs and English only students has been reduced for fourth graders but not for eighth graders.

Despite apparent progress in the earlier grades, major problems persist. For instance, the 2005 achievement gap of 35 points in reading between fourth grade ELLs and non-ELLs was greater than the Black-White discrepancy. Some suggest that recent increases in the reading skills of ELLs (despite the large gap) reflect changes in federal policy to hold states more accountable for the academic achievement of all students. Others say this connection between federal policy and achievement scores is misplaced. This debate will continue, as should our careful analysis of performance of ELLs on the NAEP and other assessments; however, RTI models have the potential to help sharpen the instructional focus on ELLs and be part of the effort to improve teaching and learning in both general and special education.

REFERENCES

Anderson, V., & Roit, M. (1998). Reading as a gateway to language proficiency for language-minority students in the elementary grades. In R. M. Gersten & R. T. Jiménez (Eds.), *Promoting learning for culturally and linguistically diverse students* (pp. 42–54). Belmont, CA: Wadsworth.

August, D. (2006). Demographic overview. In D. August & T. Shanahan (Eds.), *Developing literacy in second-language learners: Report of the National Literacy Panel on Language-Minority Children and Youth* (pp. 43–49). Mahwah, NJ: Lawrence Erlbaum Associates.

August, D., & Hakuta, K. (1997). *Improving schooling for language-minority children: A research agenda*. Washington, DC: National Academy Press.

August, D., & Shanahan, L. (2006). *Developing literacy in second-language learners: Report of the National Literacy Panel on Language-Minority Children and Youth*. Washington, DC: National Literacy Panel on Language-Minority Children and Youth.

Baker, S., & Good, R. (1995). Curriculum-based measurement of English reading with bilingual Hispanic students: A validation study with second-grade students. *School Psychology Review, 24*(4), 561–579.

Barrera, M. (2006). Special issue: English language learners struggling to learn to read: Emergent research on linguistic differences and learning disabilities—Roles of definitional and assessment models in the identification of new or second language learners of English for special education. *Journal of Learning Disabilities, 39*(2), 142–157.

Barrera, R. (1983). Bilingual reading in the primary grades: Some questionable views and practices. In T. H. Escobedo (Ed.), *Early childhood bilingual education* (pp. 164–183). New York: Teachers College Press.

Beck, I. L., & McKeown, M. (1991). Conditions of vocabulary acquisition. In R. Barr, M. Kamil, P. Mosenthal & P. D. Pearson (Eds.), *Handbook of reading research* (Vol. 2, pp. 789–814). New York: Longman.

Bialystok, E., Luk, G., & Kwan, E. (2005). Bilingualism, biliteracy, and learning to read: Interactions among languages and writing systems. *Scientific Studies of Reading, 9*(1), 43–61.

Blachowicz, C., & Fisher, P. (2000). Vocabulary instruction. In M. L. Kamil, P. B. Mosenthal, P. D. Pearson, & R. Barr (Eds.), *Handbook of reading research* (Vol. 3, pp. 483–502). Mahwah, NJ: Lawrence Erlbaum.

Blachowicz, C., Fisher, P., Ogle, D., & Watts-Taffe, S. (2006). Vocabulary: Questions from the classroom. *Reading Research Quarterly, 41*(4), 524–539.

Carlo, M. S., August, D., McLaughlin, B., Snow, C. E., Dressler, C., Lippman, D. N., et al. (2004). Closing the gap: Addressing the vocabulary needs of English-language learners in bilingual and mainstream classrooms. *Reading Research Quarterly, 39*(2), 188–215.

Chiappe, P., Siegel, L., & Wade-Woolley, L. (2002). Linguistic diversity and the development of reading skills: A longitudinal study. *Scientific Studies of Reading, 6*(4), 369–400.

Cohen, J. (1988). *Statistical power analysis for the behavioral sciences* (2nd ed.). New York: Academic Press.

Denton, C. A., Anthony, J. L., Parker, R., & Hasbrouck, J. E. (2004). Effects of two tutoring programs on the English reading development of Spanish-English bilingual students. *Elementary School Journal, 104*(4), 289.

Dominguez de Ramírez, R., & Shapiro, E. (2006). Curriculum-based measurement and the evaluation of reading skills of Spanish-speaking English language learners in bilingual education classrooms. *School Psychology Review, 35*(3), 356–369.

Droop, M., & Verhoeven, L. (2003). Language proficiency and reading ability in first- and second-language learners. *Reading Research Quarterly, 38*(1), 78–104.

Durgunoglu, A. Y., Nagy, W. E., & Hancin-Bhatt, B. J. (1993). Cross-language transfer of phonological awareness. *Journal of Educational Psychology, 85*(3), 453–465.

Echevarria, J. (1995). Interactive reading instruction: A comparison of proximal and distal effects of instructional conversations. *Exceptional Children, 61*, 536–552.

Fitzgerald, J. (1995). English-as-a-second-language learners' cognitive reading processes: A review of research in the United States. *Review of Educational Research, 65*(2), 145–190.

Francis, D., Lesaux, N. K., & August, D. (2006). Language of instruction. In D. L. August & T. Shanahan (Eds.), *Developing literacy in a second language: Report of the National Literacy Panel* (pp. 365–410). Mahwah, NJ: Lawrence Erlbaum Associates.

Fuchs, L. (1989). Evaluating solutions: Monitoring progress and revising intervention plans. In M. R. Shinn (Ed.), *Curriculum-based measurement: Assessing special children* (pp. 153–181). New York: Guilford.

Fuchs, L., Fuchs, D., & Zumeta, R. (2007) Responsiveness-to-intervention: A strategy for the prevention and identification of learning disabilities. In E. L. Grigorenko (Ed.), *Educating individuals with disabilities: IDEIA 2004 and beyond* (pp. 115–135). New York: Springer Publishing Company.

Gersten, R., & Baker, S. (2000a). The professional knowledge base on instructional practices that support cognitive growth for English-language learners. In R. M. Gersten & E. P. Schiller (Eds.), *Contemporary special education research: Syntheses of the knowledge base on critical instructional issues. The LEA series on special education and disability* (pp. 31–79). Mahwah, NJ: Lawrence Erlbaum Associates.

Gersten, R., & Baker, S. (2000b). What we know about effective instructional practices for English-language learners. *Exceptional Children, 66*(4), 454–470.

Gersten, R., & Baker, S. K. (2002). The relevance of Messick's four faces for understanding the validity of high-stakes assessments. In G. Tindal & T. M. Haladyna (Eds.), *Large-scale assessment programs for all students: Validity, technical adequacy, and implementation* (pp. 49–67). Mahwah, NJ: Lawrence Erlbaum.

Geva, E., & Yaghoub Zadeh, Z. (2006). Reading efficiency in native English-speaking and English-as-a-second-language children: The role of oral proficiency and underlying cognitive-linguistic processes. *Scientific Studies of Reading, 10*(1), 31–57.

Good, R. H., & Kaminski, R. A. (2002). Nonsense word fluency. In R. H. Good & R. A. Kaminski (Eds.), *Dynamic indicators of basic early literacy skills* (6th ed.). Eugene, OR: Institute for the Development of Educational Achievement.

Graves, M. F. (2006). *The vocabulary book: Learning and instruction.* New York: Teachers College Press, International Reading Association, and National Council of Teachers of English.

Green, E. J. (1997). Guidelines for serving linguistically and culturally diverse young children. *Early Childhood Education Journal, 24*(3), 147–154.

Gunn, B., Smolkowski, K., Biglan, A., & Black, C. (2002). Supplemental instruction in decoding skills for Hispanic and non-Hispanic students in early elementary school: A follow-up. *Journal of Special Education, 36*(2), 69–79.

Hedges, L. V. (1981). Distribution theory for Glass's estimator of effect size and related estimators. *Journal of Educational Statistics, 6*(2), 107–128.

Individuals With Disabilities Education Improvement Act of 2004, Pub. L. No. 108–446, 118 Stat. 2647. Retrieved November 12, 2007, from http://www.nichcy.org/reauth/PL108-446.pdf

Kindler, A. (2002). *Survey of the states' limited English proficient students and available educational programs and services 2000–2001* (Summary Report). Washington DC: National Clearinghouse for English Language Acquisition & Language Instruction Educational Programs.

Klingner, J. K., Artiles, A. J., & Barletta, L. M. (2006). English language learners who struggle with reading: Language acquisition or LD? *Journal of Learning Disabilities, 39*(2), 108–129.

LaCelle-Peterson, M. W., & Rivera, C. (1994). Is it real for all kids? A framework for equitable assessment policies for English language learners. *Harvard Educational Review, 64*(1), 55–75.

Leafstedt, J., Richards, C., & Gerber, M. (2004). Effectiveness of explicit phonological-awareness instruction for at-risk ELLs. *Learning Disabilities Research & Practice,* *19*(4), 252–261.

Lesaux, N., & Siegel, L. (2003). The development of reading in children who speak English as a second language. *Developmental Psychology, 39*(6), 1005–1020.

Lyon, G.R. (1994). *Frames of reference for the assessment of learning disabilities: New views on measurement issues.* Baltimore: Brookes.

Maldonado, J. (1994). Bilingual special education: Specific learning disabilities in language and reading. *Journal of Educational Issues of Language Minority Students, 14,* 127–147.

Messick, S. (1989). Validity. In R.L. Linn (Ed.), *Educational measurement* (3rd ed., pp. 13–103). New York: Macmillan.

Mezynski, K. (1983). Issues concerning the acquisition of knowledge: Effects of vocabulary training on reading comprehension. *Review of Educational Research, 53*(2), 253–279.

National Assessment of Educational Progress. (2005). *The nation's report card: Reading 2005.* Washington, DC: National Center for Education Statistics, U.S. Department of Education.

National Institute of Child Health and Human Development (NICHD). (2000). *Report of the National Reading Panel: An evidence-based assessment of scientific research literature on reading and its implications for reading instruction.* Bethesda, MD: NICHD Clearinghouse.

National Reading Panel. (2000). *Teaching children to read: An evidence-based assessment of the scientific research literature on reading and its implications for reading instruction* (NIH Publication No. 00–4769). Washington, DC: National Institute of Child Health and Human Development.

National Research Council. (1998). *Preventing reading difficulties in young children.* Washington, DC: National Academy Press.

National Research Council. (2002). *Minority students in special and gifted education.* Washington, DC: National Academy Press.

Oh, D., Haager, D., & Windmueller, M. (2004). *Assembling the puzzle of predictability: Validity of the Dynamic Indicators of Basic Early Literacy Skills Assessment with ELLs in kindergarten.* Unpublished manuscript.

Ortiz, A. A., Wilkinson, C. Y., Robertson-Courtney, P., & Kushner, M. I. (2006). Considerations in implementing intervention assistance teams to support English language learners. *Remedial and Special Education, 27*(1), 53–64.

Perez, E. (1981). Oral language competence improves reading skills of Mexican American third graders. *Reading Teacher, 35*(1), 24–27.

Perfetti, Ch. (2000). Comprehending written language: a blueprint of the reader. In C. Brown & Haggort, P. (Eds.), *The neurocognition of language.* Oxford: Oxford University Press.

Perie, M., Grigg, W., & Donahue, P. (2005). *The nation's report card: Reading 2005.* Washington, DC: U.S. Department of Education, National Center for Education Statistics.

Proctor, C.P., Carlo, M., August, D., & Snow, C. (2005). Native Spanish-Speaking children reading in English: Toward a model of comprehension. *Journal of Educational Psychology, 97*(2), 246–257.

Ramírez, J.D. (1992). Executive summary: Longitudinal study of structured English immersion strategy, early-exit and late-exit transitional bilingual education programs for language-minority children. *Bilingual Research Journal, 16*(1 & 2), 1–62.

Rousseau, M. K., Tam, B.K.Y., & Ramnarain, R. (1993). Increasing reading proficiency of language-minority students with speech and language impairments. *Education and Treatment of Children, 16*(3), 254–271.

Rueda, R., & Windmueller, M. P. (2006). Special issue: English language learners struggling to learn to read: Emergent research on linguistic differences and learning disabililities—English language learners, LD, and overrepresentation: A multiple-level analysis. *Journal of Learning Disabilities, 39*(2), 99–108.

Saunders, W. (1999). Improving literacy achievement for ELLs in transitional bilingual programs. *Educational Research and Evaluation, 5*(4), 345–381.

Saunders, W. M., & Goldenberg, C. (1999). Effects of instructional conversations and literature logs on limited- and fluent-English-proficient students' story comprehension and thematic understanding. *Elementary School Journal, 99*(4), 277–301.

Shanahan, T., & August, D. (2007). *Developing reading and writing in second language learners: Lessons from the report of the National Literacy Panel on language-minority children and youth*. New York: National Literacy Panel on Language-Minority Children and Youth.

Shanahan, T., & Beck, I. (2006). Effective literacy teaching for English-language learners. In D. L. August & T. Shanahan (Eds.), *Developing literacy in a second language: Report of the National Literacy Panel* (pp. 415–488). Mahwah, NJ: Lawrence Erlbaum Associates.

Shaywitz, B. A., & Shaywitz, S. E. (1994). Measuring and analyzing change. In G. R. Lyon (Ed.), *Frames of reference for the assessment of learning disabilities: New views on measurement issues* (p. xvii). Baltimore: Brookes.

Slavin, R. E., & Cheung, A. (2004). How do English language learners learn to read? *Educational Leadership, 61*(6), 52.

Stahl, S. A., & Fairbanks, M. M. (1986). The effects of vocabulary instruction: A model-based meta-analysis. *Review of Educational Research, 56*(1), 72–110.

Vaughn, S., Cirino, P. T., Linan-Thompson, S., Mathes, P. G., Carlson, C. D., Hagan, E. C., et al. (2006). Section on teaching, learning, and human development—effectiveness of a Spanish intervention and an English intervention for English-language learners at risk for reading problems. *American Educational Research Journal, 43*(3), 449–489.

Vaughn, S., Linan-Thompson, S., & Hickman, P. (2003). Response to instruction as a means of identifying students with reading/learning disabilities—this examination of a response to treatment model for identifying students with reading/learning disabilities supports its use and identifies several pretest predictors of nonresponse to treatment. *Exceptional Children, 69*(4), 391–411.

Vaughn, S., Mathes, P., Linan-Thompson, S., Cirino, P., Carlson, C., Pollard-Durodola, S., et al. (2006). Effectiveness of an English intervention for first-grade English language learners at risk for reading problems. *Elementary School Journal, 107*(2), 154–180.

Waxman, H. C., de Felix, J. W., Martinez, A., Knight, S. L., & Padrón, Y. (1994). Effects of implementing classroom instructional models on English language learners' cognitive and affective outcomes. *Bilingual Research Journal, 18*(3–4), 1–22.

Wiley, H. I., & Deno, S. L. (2005). Oral reading and maze measures as predictors of success for ELLs on a state standards assessment. *Remedial & Special Education, 26*(4), 207–214.

Woodcock, R. W., McGrew, K. S., & Mather, N. (2001). *Woodcock-Johnson III tests of achievement standard test book*. Itasca, IL: Riverside Publishing Company.

CHAPTER 11

Response to Intervention and Teacher Preparation

Louise Spear-Swerling

Few areas of special education have received more attention than learning disabilities (LD), whether in the scientific community, the educational community, or the popular press. There are many reasons for this interest. First, children with learning disabilities currently constitute the largest category of special education: they represent approximately half of all youngsters receiving special-education services nationally and about 6% of all schoolchildren (Denton, Vaughn, & Fletcher, 2003). Also, learning disabilities have been a particularly controversial area of special education. For example, although virtually all authorities recognize the existence of genuine cases of LD, some investigators have argued that the LD category helps to excuse schools from the responsibility of teaching all children successfully; in this view, classifying struggling students as LD permits schools to locate learning problems solely within children rather than examining and changing school practices that may be inadequate (e.g., Christensen, 1999; Skrtic, 1999).

A third reason for interest in learning disabilities involves the fact that over 90% of children classified as LD prior to fifth grade are identified based primarily on problems in reading (Kavale & Reese, 1992). During the past few decades, a voluminous body of research has developed on how children learn to read, why some children experience difficulty, and what can be done to help them (e.g., Adams, 1990; National Reading Panel, 2000; RAND Reading Study Group, 2002; Stanovich, 2000). This research has vital implications for children with genuine LD, for beginning and struggling readers in general, and for professionals involved with them, including general and special educators, school psychologists, speech/language pathologists, medical professionals, and social workers, among others.

The federal legislation most relevant to learning disabilities is the Individuals With Disabilities Education Improvement Act (P.L. 108–446) of 2004 (IDEIA) as well as accompanying federal regulations published in 2005. This legislation was a major reauthorization and revision of a prior law, the Individuals With Disabilities Education Act (IDEA). IDEIA retains a number of concepts that have been fundamental to the category of LD since its inception: for example, learning disabilities involve difficulties with spoken or written language, and they entail learning problems that cannot be primarily accounted for by other disabilities (e.g., intellectual, sensory, or emotional disabilities) or by lack of opportunity to learn. Several alterations to past procedures for identifying LD also are contained in IDEIA. By far the most groundbreaking change is that schools are given the option to ignore a key previous requirement for identification of LD, a discrepancy between IQ and achievement, and instead to employ response-to-intervention (RTI) approaches to LD identification. Indeed, under IDEIA, states are explicitly prohibited from requiring districts to use IQ-achievement discrepancy criteria.

Successful implementation of RTI models could create extraordinary changes in schools and benefit a wide range of children, not only those with disabilities. However, bringing RTI to scale for millions of schoolchildren involves many challenges (e.g., Denton et al., 2003; Vaughn & Fuchs, 2003). This chapter focuses on one particular and central challenge—how to ensure that both general and special educators are prepared to implement RTI approaches, especially in the area of reading. Although other domains of schooling will also be considered, reading is emphasized here because of the large volume of research evidence on reading, the centrality of reading to school achievement, and prevalence of reading difficulties among youngsters with learning disabilities and other special needs.

The chapter begins with a discussion of the rationale for using RTI models in place of discrepancy criteria for identifying LD. The next section discusses the pedagogical content knowledge necessary to teach reading effectively and the demands of RTI models on the knowledge base and expertise of teachers. The third section of the chapter reviews the growing research literature on teachers' pedagogical content knowledge in reading; the fourth examines preservice elementary teacher preparation in reading. The fifth section considers issues involving RTI approaches in academic domains other than reading. The chapter ends with some conclusions about teacher preparation and professional development in relation to the implementation of RTI models.

RATIONALE FOR USING RTI MODELS

Features of RTI

A basic assumption of virtually all authorities is that genuine learning disabilities are not *caused* by poor instruction or lack of opportunity to learn, although these factors may certainly exacerbate genuine cases of LD. RTI approaches to LD identification, which essentially involve ruling out poor instruction and lack of learning opportunities as primary causes of a child's difficulties, are founded on this assumption. Although RTI models can vary in numerous ways, certain key features are common to all RTI approaches. Children with learning disabilities are conceptualized as those who respond insufficiently to research-based interventions that are generally effective with most youngsters. Interventions involve multiple tiers or levels, with increasing intensity across tiers. Children who fail to make adequate progress even at the most intensive level of intervention are candidates for special education evaluation and placement; those who meet eligibility criteria for LD would be assumed to have genuine learning disabilities.

Because the general education curriculum and instruction constitute the first tier of intervention, the involvement of general educators is imperative in RTI approaches. General education must include universal screening of all children for potential learning problems, as well as ongoing monitoring of all children's progress. Core curriculum, assessment, and instruction must be consistent with scientific evidence on best educational practice. If Tier 1 practices are faulty, then at-risk children may be missed or inappropriately large numbers of youngsters may require intervention. Effective special education practices and knowledgeable special educators also are essential to RTI. Knowledgeable special educators are a key resource in all tiers of intervention, and even with the most successful RTI models, some youngsters can be expected to have genuine learning disabilities and to require direct special education services.

Here is one example of numerous possible ways that an RTI model might be implemented in the primary grades (see, e.g., Reschly, 2003). In general education (Tier 1), a comprehensive curriculum addresses a variety of abilities central to progress in core academic domains, including both phonics and comprehension skills in reading, computational and problem-solving skills in math, and mechanics and content of writing. Instruction in these important component skills is explicit and systematic; children are not expected to infer essential skills and knowledge solely from exposure. General education teachers also provide reasonable differentiation of instruction, for example, through flexible group work with children who need additional instruction in phonics skills or math problem solving. Children's progress in core academic domains is monitored three times a year (fall, winter, and spring), using assessments that are brief and feasible to give to large groups of children. These assessments not only enable the teacher to identify at-risk youngsters early but also ensure that the general education curriculum and instruction enable most children (about 80%) to reach important benchmarks for the grade; were this not the case, curriculum revision or improvements in instruction would be called for. In addition, positive supports for children's behavior are in place, such as clearly stated classroom expectations, positive reinforcement of appropriate behavior, and explicit consequences for inappropriate behavior.

For children at risk based on the screening and progress-monitoring assessments, additional small-group instruction is provided by interventionists (Tier 2), such as general educators with specialized training in literacy or math, the remedial reading teacher, or the special education teacher. About 20% of children may require Tier 2 intervention at any given time, with children grouped based on similar patterns of need (e.g., phonics vs. comprehension in reading or computational skills vs. problem-solving in math); they are seen for about half an hour per day, with instruction supplemental to the general education curriculum. Progress is monitored on a biweekly basis. After about 10 to 18 weeks, children who make inadequate progress in Tier 2 are designated for even more intensive intervention (Tier 3) that involves more instructional time (e.g., an hour per day vs. 30 minutes); a smaller group size (e.g., no more than 2–3 children per group vs. 4–5 per group); and more frequent progress monitoring (e.g., weekly vs. biweekly). About 5% of children may require Tier 3 instruction at any one time. Tier 2 and 3 interventions are research based, to the extent that research exists to inform the selection of interventions; in primary grade reading, this research base is substantial. After another 10 to 18 weeks, children with inadequate progress in Tier 3 are evaluated by a multidisciplinary team which considers their eligibility for special education, including possible learning disabilities services.

Identification of LD Using Discrepancy Criteria

Prior to IDEIA, central to LD identification was the determination of a discrepancy between ability and achievement in at least one of several areas (oral expression, listening comprehension, basic reading, reading comprehension, written expression, math calculation, math reasoning). Ability typically has been measured through an individually administered

IQ test; children with LD have been defined as those whose achievement is low relative to their IQs. The specific amounts of discrepancy required for eligibility for LD services, as well as methods for calculating the discrepancy, have varied across states and school districts. Earlier federal guidelines did require ruling out poor instruction and lack of opportunity to learn as primary causes of learning problems in children evaluated for possible LD; however, instructional and experiential variables rarely, if ever, received the systematic attention characteristic of RTI approaches.

The use of discrepancy criteria has been widely criticized in the scientific community (e.g., Siegel, 1988; Spear-Swerling & Sternberg, 1996; Stanovich, 2000, chapters 17 and 18; Sternberg & Grigorenko, 1999). One serious drawback of discrepancy criteria is that they make early identification of learning problems difficult because it often takes time for children to amass a sufficiently large discrepancy to become eligible for services. Other problems with discrepancy criteria include concerns about the validity of IQ tests as measures of broad ability or potential for learning; failure to correct for regression effects, which leads to over-identification of higher-IQ youngsters and underidentification of lower-IQ children; and lack of evidence to support an educational distinction between low achievers with and without discrepancies. For instance, there is little evidence to support the idea that low achievers with and without IQ discrepancies in reading need different approaches to basic reading instruction or differ in their capacities to benefit from intervention.

Advantages of RTI Approaches

In RTI approaches to LD identification, there is no need to document an IQ-achievement discrepancy or even routinely to administer IQ tests. (However, school personnel can choose to administer an IQ test in cases where they deem it necessary: for example, to rule out broad intellectual disabilities in a youngster being evaluated for possible LD.) Early identification and early intervention are major advantages of RTI models because all youngsters are screened for learning difficulties and intervention begins as soon as a problem is detected. In their emphases on high-quality Tier 1 instruction and timely, research-based interventions, RTI approaches have the potential to benefit a broad range of children, not only those with genuine LD. Furthermore, for the latter, early identification and intervention may lead to better outcomes than if appropriate intervention is delayed until discrepancy criteria are met. In addition, RTI approaches can help to rule out poor instruction as a primary cause of a child's learning problems, as is required under IDEIA for LD identification. RTI approaches may also be less biased in terms of ethnicity, race, and gender than discrepancy approaches to identification of LD (see, e.g., Speece, Case, & Molloy, 2003).

The effectiveness of RTI models depends heavily on well-prepared, knowledgeable teachers, both general and special educators. A high-quality core curriculum and research-based interventions are necessary, but not sufficient, for the success of RTI approaches; the knowledge base and professional expertise of individual teachers also are vital to the implementation of any program or intervention. No domain of school achievement has been studied more extensively than reading, where there is a voluminous research base to inform educational decision making, especially in the early and middle elementary grades. The next section considers what elementary-level general and special educators need to know in order to teach reading well.

PEDAGOGICAL CONTENT KNOWLEDGE FOR TEACHING READING AND FOR IMPLEMENTING RTI MODELS

Teaching reading effectively to diverse groups of youngsters, including those at risk, demands considerable knowledge and skill (Moats, 1999; National Academy of Education, 2005). Among other types of knowledge, teachers of reading need to understand the abilities involved in literacy acquisition and the relationship between oral language and literacy development, not only in native English speakers but also in children learning English as a second language. They must recognize common risk factors for reading difficulties, such as lack of experience with spoken English; limited prior experiences with literacy; a history of preschool language delay or disorder; a disability that impacts language acquisition, such as hearing impairment; or a significant family history of reading problems. Effective teachers must be able to engage and motivate low as well as high achievers and youngsters from a variety of socioeconomic and cultural backgrounds. They need knowledge about a variety of instructional resources, such as children's books, reading programs, and electronic materials, as well as about how to evaluate and use those resources.

To teach both reading and spelling successfully, educators must understand the structure of English, an alphabetic language with complex letter-sound relationships. Reading English words often requires attention not only to single letters, but also to common letter patterns (e.g., the *igh* pattern says long *i* as in *night,* not a blend of the individual sounds for *i, g,* and *h*). Furthermore, many letters and letter patterns can have more than one sound (e.g., *g* can say /g/ as in *go* or /j/ as in *giant,* and *ow* can say long *o* as in *snow* or /ow/ as in *cow*). Vowel sounds are particularly variable in English, although knowledge about common syllable types can help to predict the vowel sound of many syllables. For instance, silent *e* syllables, which end in a vowel-consonant-*e* pattern (e.g., *made* and *broke*), usually have a long vowel sound (i.e., the first vowel letter says its name). In addition, teachers must recognize when words are phonetically irregular, that is, when they violate typical letter-sound relationships; the words *have* and *come* are exceptions to the silent-*e* generalization, so a teacher would not want to use these words as exemplars of the silent-*e* syllable type or encourage children to sound out these words using the silent-*e* rule.

Although many abilities are ultimately important in learning to read, three abilities play central roles in the genesis of learning disabilities and early reading problems: phonemic awareness, word decoding, and reading fluency. Phonemic awareness involves sensitivity to and the ability to manipulate sounds in spoken words, for example, recognizing that the spoken word *bath* contains three sounds, /b/, /a/, and /th/, or being able to blend orally the sounds /f/, /l/, /a/, /p/ into the spoken word *flap*. In an alphabetic language, phonemic awareness is foundational for learning to decode printed words. Word decoding involves using knowledge about common letter-sound relationships (i.e., phonics) to read unfamiliar words.

Reading fluency is the ability to read text not just accurately, but also easily and with a reasonable degree of speed. Lack of fluency tends to impair both comprehension and motivation to read, as well as interfere with struggling readers' abilities to handle marked increases in reading volume as they advance beyond the early grades. Contrary to popular belief in education, skilled readers do not rely on so-called multiple cueing systems such as pictures or sentence context in conjunction with only the first few letters of a word in order to read fluently. Reliance on context to compensate for weak decoding skills is typical of poor or beginning readers; skilled readers pay close attention to all the letters in words but generally do so automatically and without conscious effort (Adams, 1990, 1998).

Difficulties with phonemic awareness, phonics, word decoding, and fluency are extremely common in individuals with learning disabilities involving reading, as well as in struggling readers generally, particularly in the primary grades (Siegel, 1988; Spear-Swerling & Sternberg, 1996; Stanovich, 2000, chapters 5, 7, and 8). For example, in kindergartners, two of the strongest predictors of end-of-first-grade reading achievement are phonemic awareness and knowledge of letter sounds (phonics); children with weaknesses in either or both areas are at high risk of reading failure. Individuals with severe reading difficulties, including genuine learning disabilities, often have lingering problems with fluency, even after successful remediation of phonemic awareness, phonics, and accuracy of word decoding. To meet the needs of at-risk and struggling readers, both general and special educators must understand these key component reading abilities, why they are important in learning to read, and how to assess and develop them. Moreover, because universal screening and progress monitoring are features of all RTI models, educators must know how to use such assessments.

The kind of knowledge outlined above can be termed pedagogical content knowledge, that is, knowledge relevant to teaching a subject effectively to students (Shulman, 1987). Helping teacher candidates acquire the pedagogical content knowledge to teach reading effectively to diverse youngsters is a tall order for teacher preparation programs, especially considering that knowledge alone is insufficient for good teaching, and that elementary and special educators must be prepared to teach a range of domains, not just reading. Given the extensive knowledge base required, continuing professional development is crucial. Nevertheless, it is reasonable to expect preservice teacher preparation to address basic knowledge about the abilities involved in learning to read, the structure of English, and how to identify and help children at risk for reading problems. Furthermore, experienced educators should have a substantial knowledge base in these areas. So, what is the current state of general and special educators' knowledge about reading? An emerging body of research has addressed this question.

RESEARCH ON TEACHERS' PEDAGOGICAL CONTENT KNOWLEDGE

Teachers' Knowledge About Word Structure

Numerous studies have examined teachers' knowledge base about English word structure. Usually these studies have included tasks such as asking participants to count phonemes, or individual sounds, in words (e.g., how many phonemes are in the word *fish*? [3: /f/, /i/, /sh/]); count morphemes, or units of meaning, in words (e.g., how many morphemes are in the word *untie*? [2: un and tie]); identify phonetically irregular words (e.g., which word is irregular: *what, will, when, write*? [what, because most words ending in *at* would be pronounced to rhyme with *cat*]); and classify words by syllable type (e.g., which of the following is a silent-*e* syllable: *she, spoke, bee, toe*? [spoke]). These studies indicate that many elementary-level teachers lack an understanding of English word structure, including both novice and experienced teachers, and special as well as general educators (Bos, Mather, Dickson, Podhajski, & Chard, 2001;

Cunningham, Perry, Stanovich, & Stanovich, 2004; McCutchen, Harry et al., 2002; Moats, 1994; Spear-Swerling, Brucker, & Alfano, 2005). In addition, several studies have documented a link between teachers' word-structure knowledge and the reading achievement of their students (McCutchen, Abbott, & Green, 2002; Moats & Foorman, 2003; Spear-Swerling & Brucker, 2004), providing support for the contention that teachers' knowledge of word structure is important to effective reading instruction.

These studies have also demonstrated that knowledge about word structure, as assessed by the previously mentioned types of tasks, is not merely a natural consequence of high levels of adult literacy. Proficient adult readers can vary somewhat in their word-identification and decoding skills, arguably the skills most related to word-structure knowledge; however, even teacher-education students with strong word-identification and decoding skills perform well below ceiling on tasks requiring them to count phonemes in words, identify syllable types, and detect phonetically irregular words (Spear-Swerling & Brucker, 2006). In fact, literate adults' knowledge of word spellings may create confusion in their understanding of word structure (Ehri & Wilce, 1980). For instance, although the words *much* and *Dutch* end with the same two phonemes (short /u/ and /ch/), adults may be convinced that they hear a /t/ in *Dutch* because they know the word is spelled with the letter *t*. Without information that addresses these misconceptions, teachers may have difficulty interpreting children's reading and spelling errors or may provide inadvertently confusing instruction (Moats, 1994). Returning to the previous example, a youngster who misspells *Dutch* as *Duch* is not failing to hear the phoneme /t/ or lacking phonemic awareness but instead is probably unfamiliar with a specific spelling convention: at the end of a one-syllable word, /ch/ following a short vowel sound often is spelled -*tch* (e.g., *Dutch, hutch, match, scratch, itch,* etc.; *much* is an exception).

Teachers' Knowledge About Reading Development

Compared to investigations of teachers' word-structure knowledge, fewer studies have examined teachers' knowledge about children's reading development: for instance, about the abilities involved in learning to read and about the risk factors for reading difficulties. However, existing studies paint a discouraging picture. As in the case of word structure, these studies suggest serious limitations in the knowledge of both general and special educators, as well as both novice and experienced teachers.

Phonemic awareness in particular appears to be poorly understood by educators, who often confuse it with knowledge of letter sounds or phonics (Bos et al., 2001; Spear-Swerling et al., 2005). As discussed previously, phonemic awareness and phonics are two related but different abilities: Phonemic awareness involves awareness of sounds in *spoken* language whereas phonics pertains to *printed* words. This distinction is not trivial for the implementation of RTI models because assessment and instruction in phonemic awareness are essential for preventing and addressing many children's reading problems. It is difficult to imagine that educators can assess and teach phonemic awareness effectively if they misunderstand what it is.

Teachers' understanding of reading fluency may be somewhat stronger than their understanding of phonemic awareness. In one study (Spear-Swerling et al., 2005), teachers were asked to explain each ability and why it is important. Among fully credentialed teachers with relatively high levels of experience and course preparation for teaching reading (n = 34, with an average of 7.5 years of teaching experience and about five reading-related courses), approximately 75% could explain what reading fluency is and why it is important whereas only 9% could do so for phonemic awareness. Among credentialed teachers with less experience and preparation (n = 51), the percentages who could answer each question correctly were lower, approximately 59% for reading fluency and 4% for phonemic awareness. Furthermore, most teachers could not accurately explain the role of context clues in reading, sometimes alluding to "multiple cueing systems" models of reading. When matched on levels of course preparation and experience, general and special educators did not differ significantly in their performance on any of these questions.

Other kinds of teacher knowledge about reading development also have been examined. McCombes-Tolis and Feinn (in press) surveyed 65 teachers certified to teach at the K–3 elementary level or in special education. Participants were asked to indicate when K–3 children should be expected to develop certain reading competencies; the investigators then compared these results to competencies articulated in the state blueprint for reading achievement. The results indicated that many participants, including both general and special educators, did not know when children should be expected to develop specific reading competencies, such as when children should be expected to read words with common inflectional endings like -*ing* or when they should be expected to know sounds for short vowels.

In addition, many teachers appear to lack knowledge of common characteristics of at-risk readers, as well as of screening and formative assessments in reading. Knowing how to administer screening and formative assessments of reading ability is central to implementing RTI. McCombes-Tolis and Feinn (in press) found that only 51% of elementary-certified teachers, and 63% of special educators, agreed with the statement "I know how to administer and interpret screening and diagnostic measures designed to identify children at risk for reading difficulties." Only 60% of elementary-certified teachers agreed with the statement "I know the common characteristics of children who experience reading difficulties and specific indicators for teacher intervention"; among special educators, 70% agreed. Similarly, when Spear-Swerling et al. (2005) asked highly prepared, experienced teachers to identify three risk factors for reading failure in kindergartners (poor phonemic awareness, lack of knowledge of letter sounds, a history of language delay or disorder, English language learner status, etc.), only 40% could name three risk factors. Moats and Foorman (2003) found that 44% of a sample of third- and fourth-grade teachers (n = 103) had trouble interpreting an oral reading transcript involving a typical elementary-level struggling reader, a youngster who tended to rely on context to compensate for poor decoding, with impaired comprehension as a result.

These gaps in teachers' knowledge do not reflect broad weaknesses in teachers' overall knowledge base or limitations in educators' abilities to learn this information when it is presented. McCutchen, Harry et al. (2002) found that both general and special educators performed much better on measures of their general knowledge and familiarity with children's literature than they did on a survey of word-structure knowledge. Several studies have documented significant improvements in teachers' knowledge, especially knowledge about word structure, after preservice course preparation or professional development focused on such content (e.g., McCutchen, Abbot, & Green, 2002; Spear-Swerling & Brucker, 2003, 2004). Could limitations in many teachers' pedagogical content knowledge about reading reflect a general lack of attention to this knowledge in their preservice preparation? Few studies currently exist on the reading preparation of special educators, but some research has examined the preparation of elementary-level general educators in reading. This research will be considered in the next section.

PRESERVICE ELEMENTARY TEACHER PREPARATION IN READING

Many authorities agree that high-quality preservice teacher preparation in reading must address a range of important literacy competencies; prepare teacher candidates to adapt instruction to meet individual children's needs; link course work to instructional practice; and provide ample supervised field experience (e.g., Brady & Moats, 1997; Hoffman et al., 2005; National Academy of Education, 2005). Some programs do provide prospective teachers with substantial course work in reading, field experiences, and curricula described as comprehensive and attentive to diverse learners (Hoffman et al., 2005). However, relatively few studies have examined specific course content in terms of the pedagogical knowledge outlined here as critical to the implementation of RTI models. A study by the National Council on Teacher Quality (NCTQ, 2006) did consider such content.

The NCTQ examined course outlines from 72 randomly selected education schools across the United States, from institutions varying widely in characteristics such as selectivity, size, minority enrollment, and whether or not they were accredited by NCATE (National Council on Accreditation of Teacher Education). Course outlines came from required reading methods courses taken by prospective elementary teachers. Using information from the syllabus, each course was rated according to the quality of the required textbooks, the nature of assignments, and coverage of five basic components of reading specified in the report of the National Reading Panel (2000): phonemic awareness, phonics, fluency, vocabulary, and comprehension. The NCTQ concluded that many elementary teacher preparation programs do not present research-based information or comprehensive coverage of all important components of reading; the most frequently omitted components were phonemic awareness and fluency. The NCTQ also found the content of many required textbooks, including content about word structure and children's reading development, misleading and inaccurate. Textbooks and course outlines often conveyed a bias against direct, systematic teaching, well-documented as critical for struggling readers and youngsters with learning disabilities, especially in the areas of phonemic awareness, phonics, and word decoding (National Reading Panel, 2000; Spear-Swerling & Sternberg, 1996). In many courses, little information was presented about how to assess children's reading difficulties or intervene early to prevent reading problems. Institutional characteristics such as selectivity or NCATE accreditation did not predict whether a program was likely to include comprehensive, research-based content in the domain of reading.

Recently, a colleague and I (McCombes-Tolis & Spear-Swerling, 2007) examined syllabi from required reading methods courses in our own state. Course outlines came from 9 different institutions and 13 elementary-level teacher preparation programs, including three of the state's largest suppliers of elementary teachers. The institutions, which varied widely with regard to selectivity in admissions, included both public and private schools. Course outlines from all required reading courses in the 13 programs were gathered, with 28 course outlines in total; they were obtained from the state's Department of Higher Education, which had gathered the syllabi in relation to a separate inquiry, via a Freedom of Information request. Course syllabi were analyzed along lines generally similar to those employed by the NCTQ (2006), with the addition of a number of variables of particular interest to us.

Our findings parallel those of the NCTQ in many ways, as well as those of a previous study of reading methods course outlines, which included some highly selective education schools (Steiner & Rozen, 2004). The components of reading most frequently addressed on syllabus course calendars were phonics and comprehension (both on 35.7% of syllabus course calendars); the least frequently addressed component was phonemic awareness (25% of course calendars). Using the rating system of the NCTQ report, at least 50.8% of required textbooks were in the "unacceptable" category, that is, texts that the NCTQ concluded were misleading, inaccurate, or incomplete. Only 14.3% of course outlines made reference to formative assessment, ongoing assessment, progress monitoring, or some related construct. No syllabus referenced the Dynamic Indicators of Basic Early Literacy Skills (DIBELS; see http://dibels.uoregon.edu/), perhaps the most widely used research-based progress monitoring assessments for primary grade reading, and none mentioned RTI. As in the findings of the NCTQ, a school's selectivity in admissions, public vs. private status, or NCATE accreditation did not predict whether an elementary teacher preparation program included comprehensive, research-based content in reading methods course outlines or texts.

Furthermore, there was little focused testing of prospective teachers' knowledge base in the form of tests or quizzes. The mean number of tests and quizzes was 0.71 per syllabus, and 50% of course outlines listed no required tests or quizzes at all. Even assuming that information about topics such as English word structure or reading development was taught, without tests or quizzes, it is hard to understand how teacher educators could assess whether students actually were acquiring that knowledge. Although application assignments such as lesson plans are crucial, gauging teacher candidates' pedagogical content knowledge from such applications is difficult because these applications tap a variety of skills and because a given application can never tap *all* important pedagogical knowledge.

If teacher candidates weren't taking tests, what kinds of assignments were they doing? The three most popular assignments on the course outlines involved a reflective learning journal (46.4% of syllabi), in which teacher candidates write about what they are learning in the course; the administration of a running record, a type of assessment (32% of syllabi); and an observation of a child or lesson (29.6% of syllabi). Some course outlines required other assignments that involve planning an instructional activity: for example, a thematic unit (21.4% of syllabi) about a particular topic, such as ocean life or the food chain. However, only 14.3% of course outlines contained an assignment involving assessment of *any* specific component of reading, such as phonemic awareness, and only 17.9% required a lesson involving any specific component.

Assignments such as planning thematic units or observing children certainly do not lack value; however, they cannot substitute for the use of focused assessments and lesson plans specific to key components of reading, nor do they give teacher candidates a componential, research-based view of the abilities important in learning to read. This componential view is essential for understanding why individual children are experiencing difficulty and for intervening early in the manner fundamental to RTI.

Consider, for example, running records, which involve a teacher's scoring of a child's oral reading of a text. This kind of assessment can help determine whether the particular text being read is at the appropriate level of difficulty for the youngster reading it. However, running records do not provide clear information about *why* a child is having reading difficulties or accurate prediction of risk. For the latter kinds of information, more focused assessments of component skills like phonemic awareness or decoding words in isolation are necessary (Torgesen, 1998). Even worse, running records are often interpreted in terms of so-called multiple cueing systems models of reading, which are not supported by scientific research on reading (see, e.g., Adams, 1998), and which may actually lead teacher candidates to draw erroneous conclusions about the nature of children's reading difficulties.

These findings and others (NCTQ, 2006; Steiner & Rozen, 2004) suggest that one reason why many elementary teachers lack important pedagogical content knowledge in reading is that this knowledge is often inadequately addressed in preservice teacher preparation. Moreover, applications of pedagogical content knowledge involving assessments and lesson planning may be problematic, as in the case of running records, or totally absent. Student teaching experiences sometimes may help to compensate for weak prior course preparation in reading, but student teaching is late in a prospective teacher's education to begin developing critical knowledge and skills.

Obviously, many factors besides course content, as evaluated through course outlines, textbooks, and assignments, can influence teacher candidates' knowledge, and teacher educators certainly may address in classes or in field experiences content that was not written in a course outline. Unfortunately, however, some teacher educators appear to lack the kind of pedagogical content knowledge about reading that is essential for their students (Joshi et al., 2006). Furthermore, licensing exams used to credential both elementary and special educators in many states do not tap this knowledge (e.g., Stotsky, 2006), so prospective teachers who lack it can easily pass the exams. Even with focused preservice course instruction, certain kinds of knowledge, such as that about word structure, may take some time for teacher candidates to acquire (e.g., Spear-Swerling & Brucker, 2003, 2004); very likely, significant time requirements also exist for skills such as interpreting assessments or designing effective lessons. In other words, in some areas, cursory course coverage will be insufficient for prospective teachers to acquire important knowledge and skills. Therefore, it is important to determine how best to prepare teachers. Among the decisions to be made are: what content is most vital to include at the preservice level; how to give focused and rigorous preparation in this content; and how to provide continuing professional development for inservice teachers.

It bears emphasizing that the knowledge highlighted here is not the *only* knowledge important to prospective teachers of reading. Other kinds of knowledge, such as how to create rich literacy environments in the classroom and engage children in literacy activities, are essential as well and may also help to promote children's growth in reading (Hoffman et al., 2005). Even so, to pay more than lip service to meeting the needs of diverse readers, including those at risk or with learning disabilities, preservice teacher preparation cannot give short shrift to content related to word structure, reading development, and early identification.

BEYOND BEGINNING READING

To date, most studies of RTI have focused on primary grade reading. These studies suggest that RTI models can substantially improve reading instruction for general-education youngsters, identify at-risk readers early, and enable many, though not all, at-risk readers to attain grade expectations, at least in the short term (e.g., Speece et al., 2003; Vaughn, Linan-Thompson, & Hickman, 2003; Vellutino et al., 1996). However, to function as an alternative to discrepancy methods of LD identification, RTI must be applicable beyond the early grades: for instance, to youngsters with comprehension-based difficulties whose problems may not emerge before fourth grade (Leach, Scarborough, & Rescorla, 2003), as well as to domains other than reading. Unfortunately, research on applications of RTI at upper grade levels and in domains beyond reading is limited, although some research has begun to emerge in both writing and mathematics (e.g., Berninger & Amtmann, 2003; Fuchs, Fuchs, & Hollenbeck, 2007).

Previous investigators interested in mathematics teaching have distinguished teachers' subject-matter competence (as measured, for example, by completion of advanced math courses) from their pedagogical content knowledge for teaching students (Shulman, 1987). A teacher could be extremely knowledgeable about math but still be unable to explain the subject well to novice learners, an unfortunate phenomenon most students experience at some time in their school careers. Similarly, as noted previously, a high level of literacy skill in teachers (their subject matter competence), although surely essential, does not guarantee high pedagogical content knowledge in reading, such as an understanding of word structure or reading development. In fact, in the absence of pedagogical knowledge, high levels of subject matter competence may actually lead teachers to erroneous conclusions about how to teach students because experts tend to organize their knowledge differently than do novice learners.

For instance, just as teachers' knowledge of word spellings may confound their understanding of word structure and their interpretation of children's errors (as in the example of the word *Dutch*), teachers' expert knowledge in math may confound their understanding of students' math development. Researchers interested in the "expert blind spot" (Nathan & Koedinger, 2000; Nathan & Petrosino, 2003) have shown that secondary teacher candidates with high levels of mathematics knowledge tend to view symbolic reasoning and mastery of decontextualized math equations as prerequisites for story problem solving, a view contradicted by research on students' actual performance patterns. (Students find the story problems easier than they find decontextualized symbolic equations.) This line of research supports the need for teacher preparation involving pedagogical content knowledge in math, such as information about the developmental processes involved in math acquisition and information about early identification, in addition to subject matter competence (see also Rice, 2003). At present, however, there is much less research on mathematics than reading to inform the pedagogical knowledge required of prospective math teachers at different grade levels. Furthermore, the extent to which this knowledge typically is addressed in teacher preparation, or the extent to which it is tapped on teacher licensing exams, has not been well studied.

At upper grade levels, implementing RTI models will require dealing with changing grade expectations, especially those in content areas such as science and social studies (Mastropieri, 2003). Textbook reading makes heavy demands on vocabulary and other language skills, as well as on basic reading skills such as word decoding and fluency; success in science increasingly requires skill in mathematics. Currently there are many unanswered questions about how the core language, literacy, and numeracy deficits typical of learning disabilities would be identified or addressed via RTI models in the context of content subjects. For example, general education instruction in science and social studies frequently involves relatively superficial, fast-paced lecture-style coverage of a wide variety of topics, with minimal opportunities for review or practice and with high expectations for students' independent learning (Mastropieri, 2003). This kind of instruction is not consistent with the recommendations of many professional organizations or with research on the needs of adolescents with learning disabilities (Scruggs & Mastropieri, 2003). If RTI models are to be implemented at upper grade levels and across the curriculum, how will adequate Tier 1 instruction be ensured? Will general educators be prepared to differentiate instruction sufficiently for students who cannot read the textbooks or who lack essential mathematical skills? How will Tiers 2 and 3 be implemented in the context of multiple content areas?

CONCLUSIONS

Even in the domain of primary grade reading, research on teachers' pedagogical content knowledge and on teacher preparation suggests that many general educators will require extensive professional development in order to implement RTI models. Professional development will need to include not only information about specialized interventions and assessments but also more basic knowledge about the abilities important in learning to read, about English word structure, and about the characteristics of at-risk readers. Even fewer studies have examined preservice preparation in reading for special educators than for general educators, although there clearly is research interest in the former (see, e.g., the Center on Personnel Studies in Special Education at www.coe.ufl.edu/copsse/). Nonetheless, research suggests that many special as well as general educators lack pedagogical content knowledge about reading. This situation is very problematic for RTI models because special educators serve as an important resource for general educators in Tier 1 instruction, as well as in subsequent tiers. Moreover, RTI models cannot be expected to eliminate all cases of reading difficulties; rather, special educators must be able to address genuine cases of learning disabilities and other special needs, including the most refractory reading impairments. To do so, they will likely need even greater expertise in reading than general educators.

Although there are some exemplary preservice preparation programs in reading, plainly there is enormous room for improvement in many programs. Better preservice preparation would not eliminate the need for continuing professional development of inservice teachers but would enable professional development efforts to focus on more sophisticated content in relation to RTI, such as effective grouping practices and specialized interventions. Prospective teachers of reading certainly should not become credentialed without a basic understanding of topics such as the structure of English, important reading-related abilities, and early identification of at-risk readers. Thus, licensing exams that include this content are critical.

In teacher preparation and professional development, quality is as important as quantity. Prospective and inservice teachers must complete a reasonable amount of professional preparation in reading because the requisite knowledge base cannot be acquired in just one or two courses. However, preparation involving content contradicted by scientific evidence, such as "multiple cueing systems" models of reading or information that confuses phonemic awareness with phonics, is not helpful. Rather, preservice preparation and professional development must be grounded in the extensive scientific research base that exists in reading. Toward this end, there are many excellent print and electronic resources available to teachers and teacher educators interested in furthering their knowledge about reading (see Spear-Swerling, 2007, for some examples). In particular, numerous texts have been written expressly for prospective teachers of reading by leading scientists of reading, such as Isabel Beck, Louisa Moats, and Marilyn Adams. At present it appears that these books are not often used in teacher preparation (NCTQ, 2006; Steiner & Rozen, 2004), but they could be.

Finally, research to inform RTI models at upper grade levels and in domains beyond reading is at best scanty and at worst nonexistent. However, to implement RTI successfully at these grade levels and in these domains, it seems likely that the need for professional development will be at least as great as in primary grade reading, for both special and general educators, including teachers of content subjects.

Unfortunately, past claims that the LD category gets schools off the hook for teaching all children effectively have held more than a grain of truth. Provisions in IDEIA allowing school districts to use RTI approaches in lieu of discrepancy criteria have the potential to change this situation dramatically, by emphasizing research-based instruction, early identification, and prompt intervention for *all* children. The success of these approaches rests on many factors, not just the expertise of teachers: adequate resources, capable school leadership, and a sound curriculum, to name a few. However, knowledgeable educators are essential. Although limited evidence in many areas of schooling presents serious challenges to the implementation of RTI, reading is the area with the most extensive research base. To be effective, RTI models cannot afford inadequately prepared teachers in the domain of achievement that is best informed by research evidence, most often lacking in struggling students, and most central to school success.

REFERENCES

Adams, M. J. (1990). *Beginning to read: Thinking and learning about print.* Cambridge, MA: MIT Press.

Adams, M. J. (1998). The three-cueing system. In F. Lehr & J. Osborn (Eds.), *Literacy for all: Issues in teaching and learning* (pp. 73–99). New York: Guilford Press.

Berninger, V. W., & Amtmann, D. (2003). Preventing written expression disabilities through early and continuing assessment and intervention for handwriting and/or spelling problems: Research into practice. In H. L. Swanson, K. R. Harris, & S. Graham (Eds.), *Handbook of learning disabilities* (pp. 345–363). New York: Guilford.

Bos, C., Mather, N., Dickson, S., Podhajski, B., & Chard, D. (2001). Perceptions and knowledge of preservice and inservice educators about early reading instruction. *Annals of Dyslexia, 51,* 97–120.

Brady, S., & Moats, L. C. (1997). *Informed instruction for reading success: Foundations for teacher preparation.* A position paper of the International Dyslexia Association. Baltimore: International Dyslexia Association.

Christensen, C. A. (1999). Learning disability: Issues of representation, power, and the medicalization of school failure. In R. J. Sternberg & L. Spear-Swerling (Eds.), *Perspectives on learning disabilities* (pp. 227–249). Boulder, CO: Westview Press.

Cunningham, A. E., Perry, K. E., Stanovich, K. E., & Stanovich, P. J. (2004). Pedagogical content knowledge of K-3 teachers and their knowledge calibration in the domain of early literacy. *Annals of Dyslexia, 54,* 139–167.

Denton, C. A., Vaughn, S., & Fletcher, J. M. (2003). Bringing research-based practice in reading intervention to scale. *Learning Disabilities Research & Practice, 18,* 201–211.

Ehri, L. C., & Wilce, L. S. (1980). The influence of orthography on readers' conceptualization of the phonemic structure of words. *Applied Psycholinguistics, 1,* 371–385.

Fuchs, L. S., Fuchs, D., & Hollenbeck, K. N. (2007). Extending responsiveness to intervention to mathematics at first and third grades. *Learning Disabilities Research & Practice, 22,* 13–24.

Hoffman, J. V., Roller, C., Maloch, B., Sailors, M., Duffy, G., Beretvas, S. N., et al. (2005). Teachers' preparation to teach reading and their experiences and practices in the first three years of teaching. *Elementary School Journal, 105,* 267–287.

Joshi, R. M., Binks, E., Boulware-Gooden, R., Dahlgren, M., Graham, L., Hougen, M., et al. (2006, November). *Why elementary teachers might be inadequately prepared to teach reading.* Paper presented at the Annual Meeting of the International Dyslexia Association, Indianapolis, IN.

Kavale, K. A., & Reese, L. (1992). The character of learning disabilities: An Iowa profile. *Learning Disability Quarterly, 15,* 74–94.

Leach, J. M., Scarborough, H. S., & Rescorla, L. (2003). Late-emerging reading disabilities. *Journal of Educational Psychology, 95,* 211–224.

Mastropieri, M. A. (2003). *Feasibility and consequences of response to intervention: Examination of the issues and scientific evidence as a model for the identification of individuals with learning disabilities.* Paper presented at the National Research Center on Learning Disabilities Symposium on Responsiveness-to-Intervention, Kansas City, MO.

McCombes-Tolis, J., & Feinn, R. (in press). Comparing teachers' literacy-related knowledge to their state's standards for reading. *Reading Psychology.*

McCombes-Tolis, J., & Spear-Swerling, L. (2007). *Are elementary teachers adequately prepared to deliver Tier 1 literacy instruction?* Manuscript in progress.

McCutchen, D., Abbott, R. D., & Green, L. B. (2002). Beginning literacy: Links among teacher knowledge, teacher practice, and student learning. *Journal of Learning Disabilities, 35,* 69–86.

McCutchen, D., Harry, D. R., Cunningham, A. E., Cox, S., Sidman, S., & Covill, A. E. (2002). Reading teachers' knowledge of children's literature and English phonology. *Annals of Dyslexia, 52,* 207–228.

Moats, L. C. (1994). The missing foundation in teacher education: Knowledge of the structure of spoken and written language. *Annals of Dyslexia, 44,* 81–102.

Moats, L. C. (1999). *Teaching reading IS rocket science: What expert teachers of reading should know and be able to do.* Washington, DC: American Federation of Teachers.

Moats, L. C., & Foorman, B. R. (2003). Measuring teachers' content knowledge of language and reading. *Annals of Dyslexia, 53,* 23–45.

Nathan, M. J., & Koedinger, K. R. (2000). Teachers' and researchers' beliefs about the development of algebraic reasoning. *Journal for Research in Mathematics Education, 31,* 168–190.

Nathan, M. J., & Petrosino, A. (2003). Expert blind spot among preservice teachers. *American Educational Research Journal, 40,* 905–928.

National Academy of Education. (2005). *Knowledge to support the teaching of reading: Preparing teachers for a changing world.* San Francisco: Jossey-Bass.

National Council on Teacher Quality (NCTQ). (2006). *What education schools aren't teaching about reading and what elementary teachers aren't learning.* Washington, DC: Author.

National Reading Panel. (2000). *Teaching children to read: An evidence-based assessment of the scientific research literature on reading and its implications for reading instruction.* Washington, DC: National Institutes of Health.

RAND Reading Study Group. (2002). *Reading for understanding: Toward an R&D program in reading comprehension.* Arlington, VA: RAND.

Reschly, D. (2003, December). *What if LD identification changed to reflect research findings?* Paper presented at the National Research Center on Learning Disabilities Symposium on Responsiveness-to-Intervention, Kansas City, MO.

Rice, J. K. (2003). *Teacher quality: Understanding the effectiveness of teacher attributes.* Washington, DC: Economic Policy Institute.

Scruggs, T. E., & Mastropieri, M. A. (2003). Science and social studies. In H. L. Swanson, K. R. Harris, & S. Graham (Eds.), *Handbook of learning disabilities* (pp. 364–379). New York: Guilford.

Shulman, L. S. (1987). Knowledge and teaching: Foundations of the new reform. *Harvard Educational Review, 57,* 1–22.

Siegel, L. S. (1988). Evidence that IQ scores are irrelevant to the definition and analysis of reading disability. *Canadian Journal of Psychology, 42,* 201–215.

Skrtic, T. M. (1999). Learning disabilities as organizational pathologies. In R. J. Sternberg & L. Spear-Swerling (Eds.), *Perspectives on learning disabilities* (pp. 193–226). Boulder, CO: Westview Press.

Spear-Swerling, L. (2007). The research-practice divide in beginning reading. *Theory into Practice, 46,* 301–308.

Spear-Swerling, L., & Brucker, P. (2003). Teachers' acquisition of knowledge about English word structure. *Annals of Dyslexia, 53,* 72–103.

Spear-Swerling, L., & Brucker, P. (2004). Preparing novice teachers to develop basic reading and spelling skills in children. *Annals of Dyslexia, 54,* 332–364.

Spear-Swerling, L., & Brucker, P. (2006). Teacher-education students' reading abilities and their knowledge about word structure. *Teacher Education and Special Education, 29,* 113–123.

Spear-Swerling, L., Brucker, P., & Alfano, M. (2005). Teachers' literacy-related knowledge and self-perceptions in relation to preparation and experience. *Annals of Dyslexia, 55,* 266–293.

Spear-Swerling, L., & Sternberg, R. J. (1996). *Off track: When poor readers become "learning disabled."* Boulder, CO: Westview Press.

Speece, D. L., Case, L. P., & Molloy, D. W. (2003). Responsiveness to general education instruction as the first gate to learning disabilities identification. *Learning Disabilities Research & Practice, 18,* 147–156.

Stanovich, K. E. (2000). *Progress in understanding reading: Scientific foundations and new frontiers.* New York: Guilford Press.

Steiner, D., & Rozen, S. (2004). Preparing tomorrow's teachers: An analysis of syllabi from a sample of America's schools of education. In F. Hess, A. Rotherdam, & K. Walsh (Eds.), *A qualified teacher in every classroom? Appraising old answers and new ideas.* Boston: Harvard Education Press.

Sternberg, R. J., & Grigorenko, E. L. (1999). *Our labeled children: What every parent and teacher needs to know about learning disabilities.* Reading, MA: Perseus Publishing Group.

Stotsky, S. (2006). Why American students don't learn to read very well: The unintended consequences of Title II and teacher testing. Third Education Group Review. *The Journal on Education Policy: A Peer-Reviewed Online Journal, 2,* 1–33. Retrieved November 1, 2006, from www.tegr.org

Torgesen, J. K. (1998). Catch them before they fall. *American Educator, 22,* 32–39.

Vaughn, S., & Fuchs, L. S. (2003). Redefining learning disabilities as inadequate response to instruction: The promise and potential problems. *Learning Disabilities Research & Practice, 18,* 137–146.

Vaughn, S., Linan-Thompson, S., & Hickman, P. (2003). Response to instruction as a means of identifying students with reading/learning disabilities. *Exceptional Children, 69,* 391–409.

Vellutino, F. R., Scanlon, D. M., Sipay, E. R., Small, S., Chen, R., Pratt, A., et al. (1996). Cognitive profiles of difficult-to-remediate and readily remediated poor readers: Early intervention as a vehicle for distinguishing between cognitive and experiential deficits as basic causes of specific reading disability. *Journal of Educational Psychology, 88,* 601–638.

CHAPTER 12

Twice-Exceptional Students

Being Gifted and Learning Disabled —
Implications of the IDEIA

Tonya R. Moon, Catherine M. Brighton, Carolyn M. Callahan,
and Jane M. Jarvis

In 2004 the Individuals With Disabilities Education Act (IDEA) was reauthorized and renamed the Individuals With Disabilities Education Improvement Act (IDEIA). The reauthorization brought about many changes. The purpose of this chapter is to outline areas of alignment and inconsistencies between the reauthorization of IDEA and the best practices in gifted education. The areas reviewed include identification, curriculum and instruction, delivery of services, teacher quality, and parental support. Specific changes in the IDEA legislation that have pointed implications for gifted learning disabled students and for practitioners are highlighted. The chapter will focus specifically on the broad area of gifted students with learning disabilities (GLD) and not other types of gifted students with learning problems such as those with hearing, visual, or motor disabilities, emotional disturbance, or mental retardation. Students with specific learning disabilities (SLD) are the largest subgroup of the 13 specified in IDEIA comprising approximately 52% of the students served in special education settings (Gresham, 2001) and of this group, up to 3.5% may have dual exceptionalities in SLD and gifted (Nielsen, 2002). Consequently, this subgroup of

SLD students warrants specific consideration when investigating the IDEIA legislation.

IMPLICATION OF IDEIA IN THE FIELD OF GIFTED EDUCATION

In considering identifying and serving twice-exceptional students, the implications of IDEIA and the corresponding provisions of NCLB with which IDEIA is aligned are indirect. That is, the legislation does not directly address the instructional needs of students with a diagnosed disability who are also identified as gifted. Even so, potential impacts of IDEIA can be inferred for the education of twice-exceptional students within the classroom setting. In particular, when IDEIA is considered in concert with the lack of federal legislative provisions which mandate identification and/or appropriate services for gifted students, it can be inferred that the dual focus of identification and curricular and instructional modifications is more likely to concentrate on responding to the disability rather than on nurturing identified giftedness.

In order to fully understand the implications that the IDEIA has for the field of gifted education, it is important to establish a working knowledge of what it means to be gifted, learning disabled, and gifted learning disabled (GLD). The intent of this section is to provide that working background based on best practices and research from the fields of gifted education, special education, and the larger field of general education.

Definitions of Giftedness

According to the U.S. Department of Education, the term *gifted and talented* when used with respect to students, children, or youth, means:

> Students, children, or youth who give evidence of high achievement capability in areas such as intellectual, creative, artistic, or leadership capacity, or in specific academic fields, and who need services or activities not ordinarily provided by the school in order to fully develop those capabilities. (Title IX, Part A, Section 9101(22), p. 544)

While states and school districts are not required to use the federal definition, many states use the federal definition or some variation of it. According to the Marland Report (1972), gifted students comprise approximately 3–5% of students in the nation's public schools (Colangelo & Davis, 2003).

Definition of a Specific Learning Disability (SLD)

The definition of SLD was first articulated by the National Advisory Committee on the Handicapped (NACH) in 1968 and remains relatively unchanged in the IDEIA reauthorization, stating:

> The term "specific learning disability" refers to a disorder in one or more of the basic psychological processes involved in understanding or in using language, spoken or written, which may manifest itself in imperfect ability to listen, think, speak, write, spell, or do mathematical calculations. The term includes such conditions as perceptual handicaps, brain injury, minimal brain dysfunction, dyslexia, and developmental aphasia. The term does not include a learning problem which is primarily the result of visual, hearing, or motor handicaps, of mental retardation, of emotional disturbance, or of environmental, cultural, or economic disadvantage.

These regulations state that a student has a diagnosis of SLD if: (a) the child does not achieve adequately for his/her age, or does not meet state-approved grade-level standards in one or more of the following areas, when provided with learning experiences and instruction appropriate for the child's age, or state-approved grade-level standards: oral expression; listening comprehension; written expression; basic reading skills; reading fluency skills; reading comprehension; mathematics calculation; and/or mathematics problem solving; (b) the child does not make sufficient progress to meet age or state-approved grade-level standards in one or more of the areas listed above (e.g., oral expression, basic reading skill) when using a process based on the child's response to scientific, research-based intervention (response to intervention [RTI]); or (c) the child exhibits a pattern of strengths and weaknesses in performance, achievement, or both, relative to age, state-approved grade-level standards, or intellectual development, that is relevant to the identification of a specific learning disability (§300.8). It is important that such pattern not be the result of: a visual, hearing, or motor disability; mental retardation; emotional disturbance; cultural factors; environmental or economic disadvantage; or limited English proficiency (§300.8).

Definition of Twice-Exceptional Students: Gifted and Learning Disabled

Estimates of how many children are gifted with a disability have ranged from a low of 2% to a range of 120,000 to 180,000 (Schnur & Stefanich, 1976). Whitmore and Maker (1985) suggested that actual occurrences of gifted children with disabilities may range between 300,000 to 540,000 or up to 5%. Nielsen's (2002) research suggests that 3.5% of children with LD could also be identified as gifted. Regardless of the estimates, these students remain largely absent in gifted programs throughout the country (Davis & Rimm, 2004).

Research suggests that common academic characteristics of gifted children with learning disabilities may include: high abstract and mathematical reasoning abilities; exceptional abilities in science or geometry; good problem-finding and problem-solving skills; advanced vocabularies; exceptional comprehension of complex systems; difficulties with memorization, computation, phonics, and/or spelling; difficulties with sequential tasks; distractibility and/or disorganization (Baum, Owen, & Dixon, 1991; Nielsen, 2002; Silverman, 2003). Although limited, other empirical research suggests that gifted learning disabled students have superior performance on tasks measuring metacognitive knowledge and skills similar to their gifted peers (Cooper, 1998; Hannah & Shore, 1995). Ferri, Gregg, and Heggoy (1997) note that gifted learning disabled students often have extensive vocabularies and general background knowledge in a content area and tend to be creative and divergent thinkers, but they can be easily distracted and require a significant amount of stimulation.

Ferri et al. (1997) found that college-age women with high cognitive ability tend not to be recognized as having a learning disability as often, or as early, as their male counterparts with similar abilities, suggesting a referral or identification bias. Further, investigating differences in ages, findings indicated that those identified in high school or college tend to have strengths in the verbal domain, whereas students identified in elementary or middle school tend to have stronger performance scores (measured by picture completion, picture arrangement, block design, digit symbol, and object assembly of the [Wechsler Adult Intelligence Scale-Revised]). In summary, the research to date seems to suggest that gifted learning disabled students exhibit a distinctive pattern of high verbal comprehension and abstract thinking with much variability in cognitive scores. Overall, these patterns suggest that students with verbal strengths can compensate more easily in school settings and are more likely to remain unidentified until later in their school careers.

REAUTHORIZATION OF IDEA LEGISLATION

One key purpose of the reauthorization of the IDEA was to bring the public law protecting the educational rights of students with disabilities into alignment with the No Child Left Behind (NCLB; U.S. Department of Education, 2001) legislation. In some instances there are overlaps between the two pieces of legislation and in other instances there are conflicting regulations. The major themes of the NCLB legislation include accountability, parental choice, highly qualified staff, flexibility, and the use of scientifically based methods. The law is predominantly focused on children from poverty, children with special needs, the recruitment and training of teachers and other staff involved in the education of children, academic achievement, pre-kindergarten instruction, and after-school programs. The major purposes of NCLB are: (a) to ensure that all children reach proficiency on state content standards (reading, mathematics, and science) determined by assessments aligned with the standards; (b) to close the achievement gaps between high- and low-performing students, minority and non-minority students, and advantaged and disadvantaged students; and (c) to ensure that all students, including SLD students have access to highly qualified and trained personnel.

The reauthorization of the IDEA legislation increased its focus on connecting to general education and the responsibilities of school systems in meeting the needs of students with disabilities. The major purposes of the IDEIA legislation are (a) to ensure that all children with disabilities have a free and appropriate public education (§301.a); (b) to ensure that the rights of children with disabilities and their parents' rights are protected (§301.b); (c) to provide assistance to educational agencies for the education of students with disabilities (§301.c); and (d) to assist state educational agencies in the implementation of early intervention services (§300.8(c)(10)).

Recognizing that GLD is not specifically mentioned in either IDEIA or NCLB, the existence of these students is not to be overlooked. Although gifted education falls under the purview of special education in only a small number of states, for the majority of states, decisions about all aspects of gifted education are made independently of the more federally regulated special education system. In the absence of federal regulations, there is likely to be marked variation across state education agencies and local education agencies, to the extent that exceptionalities of the twice-exceptional child are concurrently addressed. The following sections outline the degree to which current best practices in gifted education align with IDEIA in terms of identification of gifted children with disabilities and services for gifted children with disabilities.

Assessment and Identification of Gifted Children With Disabilities

While Cohen and Vaughn (1993) conclude "there is little doubt that students who are both gifted and learning disabled exist" (p. 93), research has yet to provide defensible processes to identify such students. The National Association for Gifted Children (NAGC) recognizes three types of students who could be identified as learning disabled: (a) identified gifted students who have subtle learning disabilities; (b) students with a learning disability but whose gift(s) has not been identified; and (c) un-identified students whose gifts and disabilities may be masked by average school achievement (www.nagc.org). The first group of children are those who are typically identified as gifted because of their high achievement or intelligence but, as they grow older, find it difficult to achieve because of their difficulty in completing assignments or in comprehending inde-pendent reading assignments. The second group of students often fails at school and has their weak areas identified as learning disabled. They are first noticed because of what they *cannot* do rather than what they *can* do. Often the focus for these students is on their weaknesses rather than their strengths, thus services are provided for the disability, and the gift(s) are neither identified nor appropriately served. Because of the combina-tion of giftedness and learning disability, the third group of students often goes unnoticed and appears to be of average intelligence. This is due in part to their intelligence compensating for weaknesses, thus making the child appear average.

The IDEIA requires four major components in determining if a child has a specific learning disability (§300.301–311): (a) early intervention; (b) parental and qualified professional staff involvement; (c) documen-tation of observation in the child's normal learning environment; and (d) specific documentation used for eligibility determination. In the field of gifted education, typical identification procedures include standard-ized tests, teacher and/or parent recommendations, and checklists, all of which are problematic in that they are procedures that typically overlook a hidden disability or talent. For example, students with learning dis-abilities may have advanced vocabulary in speaking but be unable to express themselves in writing. Another issue is the lack of gifted students with disabilities included in standardized norming groups thus making comparisons impossible.

One key change in the reauthorized IDEA is the modification of the requirements for identifying children with SLD. States are no longer re-quired to use the discrepancy between the scores from an IQ test and achievement test to determine the existence of an SLD. Rather, states may (but are not required to) utilize alternative problem solving models such as the response to intervention (RTI). Proponents of RTI approaches praise the proactive approach to addressing students' present difficulties rather than the so-called wait to fail approach typical of the discrep-ancy model previously used whereby students must struggle significantly before being eligible for referral and services (Harris-Murri, King, & Rostenberg, 2006; Ofiesh, 2006; Wedl, 2005). See chapter 5 of this book for an in-depth discussion of the details of RTI. In this chapter, we stress the aspects of RTI that are most relevant to our particular discussion of how to best serve GLD students.

Critics of the RTI approach caution that there are still questions unanswered about using problem solving models in identification. Critics argue that use of these models often results in confusion and ultimately in increased numbers of students being identified as having an SLD (Wedl, 2005). Opponents of RTI propose to more rigorously implement existing psycho-educational instruments (Kavale, Holdnack, & Mostert, 2006). The more moderate position suggests a balance between the two approaches, utilizing cognitive assessments and comprehensive evaluations as part of the RTI data-gathering process (Hale, Kaufman, Naglieri, & Kavale, 2006; Ofiesh, 2006).

RTI is a problem solving model, following many of the steps and logic of the scientific method including at least three steps: (a) identifying and defining the educational problem in clear, precise, and observable terms; (b) developing specific interventions that are based on "scientifically-based practices" or if inadequate research is available, based on "promising practices," aimed at reducing the educational concerns; and (c) utilizing progress monitoring to collect frequent and targeted evidence of students' changes (National Research Center on Learning Disabilities, 2002).

Some suggest that early intervention, such as is offered through the alternative RTI approaches, is the process that should be used to identify a learning disability (e.g., Lange & Tompson, 2006; National Joint Committee on Learning Disabilities [NJCLD], 2006). Early intervention has the greatest potential to address the disproportionality issue that has struck special education; it also has the potential to address the needs of students who may otherwise be inaccurately labeled with a learning disability (NJCLD, 2006). Early intervention can also provide services much sooner to students who may, in fact, have a learning disability rather than using the wait to fail model, a characteristic of the discrepancy model, thus benefiting those students identified with LD at a younger age (Ofiesh, 2006; Wedl, 2005).

A review of the literature in the field of gifted and talented yields limited guidelines for the assessment and diagnosis of GLD children. Three sets of authors (Brody & Mills, 1997; Nielsen, 2002; Silverman, 2003) recommend the use of scatter analysis, profile analysis, the use of broad definitions of giftedness and intelligence, and discrepancy definitions. One set of authors (McCoach, Kehle, Bray, & Siegle, 2001) propose a discrepancy model based on the use of IQ tests but recommend against the scatter and profile analysis.

Specific Implications for Identifying GLD Students

The combination of two factors—the IDEIA legislation regarding identification of students with SLD, and the reality that GLD students are an underrepresented population in gifted programs across the country—result in three major implications for identification of GLD students. Without the reconsideration of an identification process for gifted students to be more in alignment with IDEIA legislation, this sub-population of students will continue to remain an underrepresented group in gifted programs.

Implication 1: An identification process should incorporate observation of students in their natural environment (i.e., classroom) by trained observers.

Implication 2: As part of the identification process, alternative approaches such as RTI should be utilized.

Implication 3: Multiple pieces of evidence (formal and informal) should be collected at regular intervals by a variety of qualified, professional staff.

Environmental Context

Research on common characteristics of gifted children with learning disabilities (Nielsen and Higgins, 2005) highlights the need to address educational, social, and affective implications of dual exceptionalities. In the general education classroom, the twice-exceptional student is likely to experience both boredom and frustration, depending on the specific learning situation. Twice-exceptional students may struggle to reconcile the mixed messages, and inconsistent or inappropriate expectations, to which they are exposed by parents, teachers, and peers (Assouline, Nicpon, & Huber, 2006; Coleman, 2001; Dole, 2001) and can have difficulty setting appropriate academic and vocational expectations for themselves (King, 2005). Some studies indicate that gifted students with learning disabilities report feeling socially isolated or struggle with social relationships at school (Vespi & Yewchuck, 1992), and they exhibit lower self-concepts than both students with learning disabilities and students identified as gifted (Waldron, Saphire, & Rosenblum, 1987; Yewchuck & Lupart, 2000). However, the social and affective vulnerabilities are often mediated by the twice-exceptions students' social and educational environments (Reis, Neu, & McGuire, 1995).

Least Restrictive Environment

A defining feature of the IDEIA legislation is the premise that students with disabilities, including students with SLD and consequently GLD students, should be given an appropriate education in the least restrictive environment. Specifically, the legislation requires that:

> To the extent appropriate, children with disabilities are educated with children who are non-disabled; and special classes, separate schooling, or removal from the regular educational environment occurs only if the nature or severity of the disability is such that education in regular classes with appropriate supplementary aids and services cannot be achieved satisfactorily. In determining LRE, the potential harmful effects on the child or on the quality of services needs should be considered. (§300.114)

Further the legislation specifies that, "unless it is specifically stated in the Individualized Education Plan (IEP), the child is educated in the school that he or she would attend if nondisabled ... [the] child is not removed from education in age-appropriate regular classrooms solely because of needed modifications in the general education curriculum" (§300.116).

Based on the degree of the student's disability, there are a wide variety of service delivery models that have the potential to appropriately address both the area(s) of giftedness and the area(s) of the learning disability. Each model is described from the most to least restrictive environment.

Full-Day, Separate Classes

Several schools in both public and private school settings have created intensive, self-contained classes specifically designed for students with the most severe learning disabilities (Hishinuma & Nishimura, 2000; Weinfeld, Barnes-Robinson, Jeweler, & Shevitz, 2002). In the ASSETS school, a private school in Hawaii, the majority of students are identified as gifted learning disabled and receive services in small, self-contained classrooms focused on both acceleration and enrichment to challenge areas of students' strengths while at the same time helping students overcome or compensate for areas of weakness. A key consideration of this type of service delivery option is the provision for interaction with other GLD students, the opportunity to consider both strengths and areas of weakness, and to proactively develop the social and emotional needs such as raising self-esteem, developing coping strategies, increasing persistence with difficult tasks, and sustaining motivation in the face of academic struggles (Hishinuma & Nishimura).

Combination of Part-Day Classes With GLD Students and Part-Day Mainstreaming With General Education Classes

An alternative to the full self-contained program for GLD, the combination model includes up to a half-day of self-contained programming in combination with general education mainstreaming, often in the areas of the students' strengths or areas of interest. These combination programs are the best fit for students with moderate to severe learning disabilities and documented areas of giftedness in one or more area (Nielsen, 2002). One such program in Montgomery County, Maryland, is the GT/LD Center Program, designed for students at any grade level whose educational needs cannot met within their home-based school (Weinfeld et al., 2002). Like the ASSETS program, this approach to service delivery focuses on a balance between developing areas of documented gifts while at the same time providing more intensive support than can be delivered in the student's home school. Because this program is housed within general education school facilities, it provides the opportunities for mainstreaming in as many areas of a student's strength as possible, including extracurricular activities, the arts, as well as lunch and general school initiatives (Weinfeld et al., 2002). This model is aligned with the IDEIA legislation in that it does not alienate students with disabilities from students without disabilities.

Resource Room Within the Home-Based School

A less restrictive option for delivering GLD services is through the combination resource room where students can receive special education support for some part of the day while also participating within the home-based general education setting and remaining with those peers and siblings in the assigned school setting. This service delivery approach is best suited for GLD students with mild to moderate disabilities, or disabilities in one area only (Nielsen, 2002). The challenge of this approach to service delivery is the concentration of other GLD students within that school setting such that they can be grouped together and have opportunities to work with other students of like ability and disability.

General Education Setting With Support of Special Education Staff

The model in which students work in the general education classroom with the support of special education staff delivers services in the least restrictive setting and allows for the most natural educational setting for GLD students. This service delivery model is the best fit for GLD students with mild disabilities (Nielsen, 2002). The challenge of this service approach is the quality of the general education teacher, the access to both qualified special education and gifted education faculty to serve as a resource to the general educator, and the opportunity for the GLD student to interact with other GLD students during the day. The degree of fit for the GLD students depends on the quality of the teacher, the classroom and school climate, and the availability of physical and human resources to facilitate differentiated curriculum and instruction within the general education classroom.

Regardless of the type of service delivery model utilized, the following principles should be addressed:

- Whenever possible, a continuum of service options should be offered within a school or district that allows for GLD students to be served within the least restrictive learning environment;
- The service delivery model should be based upon the philosophy and expectation that GLD students simultaneously possess both gifts and disabilities, and both exceptionalities should be addressed in a strength-based approach;
- GLD services should be built with a continuity of services across all school levels, K–12;
- The GLD program should be part of a well-articulated and aligned gifted program, such that there is agreement of all gifted program elements—definition/philosophy, identification, service delivery model, services, and student assessment;
- Balance of service emphasis supporting both areas of gifts and areas of disability;
- Flexible groupings whenever possible to allow for interactions with other GLD students, LD students, gifted students, and others with similar interests and passions; and
- When age appropriate, GLD students should have access to counseling for career and planning information as well as coping strategies (Brody & Mills, 1997; Nielsen, 2002; Reis & Ruban, 2005; Weinfeld, Barnes-Robinson, Jeweler, & Shevitz, 2002).

Services

Regardless of the service delivery model in place, the specific services provided to GLD students should follow the IDEIA legislation regarding the development, review, and implementation of the individualized education plan (IEP). The legislation mandates that the school-based personnel should consider:

(1) The strengths of the child;
(2) The concerns of the parents for enhancing the education of their child;
(3) The results of the initial or most recent evaluation of the child; and

(4) The academic, developmental, and functional needs of the child. (§300.324)

As this pertains to GLD students, in considering the strengths of the child, educators should consider the area(s) of giftedness as well as those areas that need support and remediation, a practice that is universally endorsed by the gifted education literature (Brody & Mills, 1997; Coleman, 2005; Nielsen, 2002; Reis & Ruban, 2005; Weinfeld, Barnes-Robinson, Jeweler, & Shevitz, 2002).

In the context of small research studies, curricular and instructional approaches designed to simultaneously target the student's areas of talent and interest and to remediate and assist the student to compensate for areas of weakness have consistently shown promise in promoting academic, social and emotional gains for twice-exceptional students, including increased school achievement, creative productivity, persistence, and self-concept (e.g., Baum, 1988; Baum & Olenchak, 2002; Yssel, Margison, Cross, & Merbler, 2005). Positive educational, social, and affective outcomes have been consistent across studies examining classroom, partial pull-out, and self-contained interventions (Newman, 2004). Based on these research findings, Baum, Cooper, and Neu (2001) recommend a "dual differentiation" approach whereby curriculum and instruction are designed to address both the advanced abilities and academic limitations characteristic of the twice-exceptional student.

If the goal of education is to help students develop their potential as well as to become autonomous, self-directed learners, a general principle that would guide the specific curricular and instructional services that GLD students receive would be that they need access to high quality, rigorous curriculum with the appropriate degree of support necessary to ensure their success and development. Much has been said in the learning disabilities literature regarding the use of the term *scaffolding* as a metaphor descriptive of the kind of support learning disabled students require (e.g., Stone, 1998; van der Aalsvoort & Harinck, 2001). The metaphor of scaffolding describes the temporary support that adults provide during the construction of new skills and concepts when the task is beyond the student's capacity, allowing the student to focus on those elements that are within their range of competence (Stone, 1998). That is, the instruction would begin as highly teacher-directed, explicit, and concrete but as students show success with skills and concepts, the teacher would decrease the amount of adult control until the student achieves success with tasks that are student-directed, abstract, and multifaceted.

This scaffolding philosophy can be applied appropriately to the four domains of curricular intervention as identified by Nielsen (2002) in all levels of service delivery from the most restrictive, self-contained GLD setting through the least restrictive, general education placement. These four domains include: (a) Strategies to enhance giftedness, (b) Social and emotional strategies, (c) Compensation strategies for academic problem areas, and (d) Behavior management strategies (pp. 106–108).

For example, specific scaffolded instructional modifications along the placement continuum for the first domain, *enhancing giftedness,* include the use of a broad-based, problem-centered curriculum with decreasing amounts of direct instruction and increasing opportunities for student choice; mentorships with practicing professionals (ideally, with successful GLD adults); and in-depth explorations of content of relevance to the students. For example, the teacher might first introduce a real-world problem such as hikers on a trail needing to find an expedient path through the forest. Initially the teacher would guide the student overtly with structured tasks and concrete questions related to direction and determining distance, but as the student demonstrated proficiency, the teacher would allow for individual student expression, choices, and autonomy.

Although additional research is needed into specific interventions that are effective with the diverse population of twice-exceptional students across educational settings, the research to date indicates that what works for students with disabilities will not necessarily be effective for students with disabilities who are also gifted. That is, a sole focus on the remediation of difficulties arising directly from the student's disability is unlikely to be effective unless the student is also provided with opportunities to work in and develop his or her areas of giftedness. In addition, the twice-exceptional student might benefit from increased guidance in responding to mixed messages about his or her abilities and in setting appropriate goals. While the provisions of IDEIA require interventions based on peer-reviewed research, conclusions from this research are likely to derive from samples of students with specific learning disabilities. Classroom interventions based on such studies might be insufficient or inappropriate to address the academic, social, and affective needs of the GLD student.

Instructional approaches advocated in the field of gifted learning disabilities include the use of:

- Individualized curriculum (Whitmore, 1988);
- Organizational supports including visuals, graphic organizers, diagrams, graphics, pictures, storyboarding, webbing, appointment books (Nielsen, 2002);
- Interactive, hands-on, kinesthetic experiences (Learning Disabilities Association of America, n.d.; Weinfeld et al., 2002);

- Flexibility in classroom routines and structures such as allowing for additional time to complete assignments (Coleman, 2005; Nielsen, 2002); and
- Varied resources, such as books on tape, performance feedback (Nielsen, 2002).

Although RTI is largely utilized as an evidenced-based approach to identify and assign appropriate specialized educational interventions (most often applied in reading) for students who struggle, the problem solving approach has recently been broadened beyond that context to systematically respond to a variety of students' challenges including social and behavioral disorders (Fairbanks, Sugai, Guardino, & Lathrop, 2007); speech disorders (Justice, 2006; Ukrainetz, 2006); and emotional disturbances of culturally and linguistically diverse (CLD) students (Harris-Murri, King, & Rostenberg, 2006), among others. In a similar vein, Tomlinson's discussion of differentiated instruction (1999; 2001) offers a systematic response to students' academic needs in a mixed-ability classroom by the use of ongoing assessment to guide the instructional pace, complexity, and degree of depth; differentiated instruction is often a model utilized for meeting the needs of gifted students in the mixed-ability general education classroom. Although no empirical studies have specifically examined the efficacy of using a problem-solving approach such as RTI with identifying and responding to the needs of GLD students, given the broad application of the model to other areas described above, it stands to reason that the intervention would be applicable. Wedl (2005) suggests that a "Response to Intervention approach is not specifically a special education eligibility tool, rather it is a data-based decision-making system that can be used for all students within the school" (p. 8).

For example, a highly participatory student in an general education, elementary-level math classroom begins to show signs of academic difficulty, such that she fails to complete assignments, shows misunderstandings about the concepts and skills being taught, and demonstrates inaccurate computations and the inability to explain her reasoning with solving a series of problems. When discussing problems informally on the playground the child can provide an insightful explanation of the logic of the problem far beyond the reasoning of the other students in the class; however, when she is asked to provide a written response in a formal classroom setting, the student requires extensive time to complete the assignments and leaves written questions blank.

Given this information and using an RTI approach for assessing and serving GLD students, the general education teacher first *defines the problem*. In this instance, the teacher identifies the specific problems the student encounters, the conditions under which the student most often struggles and succeeds, and other relevant information surrounding this academic difficulty. In this example, the teacher notes that the student struggles when she is provided decontextualized algorithms orally in a whole-class format, when lecture is directly followed by independent practice, or when the assessment of progress demands written responses. The teacher notes that the student typically succeeds and shows progress when the teacher provides one-on-one direct teaching, using concrete materials that the child manipulates to solve the problems orally, and when the math problems—even complex, multifaceted problems—are related to actual problems in the classroom or the family that the student can specifically envision.

The second step of the RTI approach for GLDs is to *develop an intervention plan* that is goal-focused, includes measurable outcomes, and supplies specific strategies for reducing the academic struggles and for increasing student success, specifying the details regarding which individuals will be involved in the intervention and in what ways. Given this information, the intervention for this student includes instructional modifications such as daily small group instruction, alternative methods for direct instruction such as the use of a self-guided contract with frequent mastery checks, the inclusion of authentic problems, and alternative assessments that do not rely exclusively on written responses. In this instance, for the first level of intervention, the classroom teacher is most often the individual to provide the majority of the interventions in the general education setting, noting the specific progress of the student.

The third phase of the RTI approach for the GLD student is to *monitor the progress of the interventions* to determine if additional strategies are to be considered. If the student shows positive growth with the stated interventions, then no further interventions may be required; if the student fails to show expected progress given the systematic interventions, then further study of the student may be required.

At the core, identification of and services for GLD students require differentiation of curriculum, instruction, and assessment at all levels of the service delivery continuum. However, to effectively differentiate, teachers must possess mastery of the content, have proficiency with a wide variety of pedagogical approaches, and have effective classroom leadership skills so as to manage multiple student needs simultaneously (Brighton, Hertberg, Moon, Tomlinson, & Callahan, 2005).

Teachers of the Twice-Exceptional Student

Because one of the primary goals of the reauthorization was to align IDEA with NCLB, the requirement that children with disabilities be served in classrooms with "highly qualified" teachers using evidence-based practices was incorporated into the new legislation with specific requirements relating to special education teachers' education, certification, and competence. The requirements that special education teachers hold a minimum of a bachelor's degree, have full state teacher certification or licensure to teach special education, and be able to demonstrate subject-matter competency in the core academic subjects in which they teach apply to all special education teachers who are responsible for the primary instructional role with students identified as disabled (U.S. Department of Education Office of Special Education Programs, n.d.).

The student who is identified as twice-exceptional with giftedness being one of the dimensions on which exceptionality is documented may receive services in one or more of a variety of educational settings—each requiring specialized attention to ensure that best practice be implemented by teachers whose individual or combined expertise are applied. In the case of the self-contained classroom, the student receives services from a special education teacher and perhaps additional support from a teacher of the gifted, or the teacher may have training and expertise in both groups. In the case of the general education classroom with part-day resource support, the student receives services both from the general educator and the special education teacher, and perhaps also a resource teacher with training in gifted education. In other cases, the twice-exceptional child may be served in a gifted resource room for some period of time each day or week or in a full-time class with a teacher of the gifted receiving support from a special education teacher. In these situations, the special education teacher would likely not serve as the primary instructor in the core academic subject areas (defined as English, reading or language arts, mathematics, science, foreign languages, civics and government, economics, arts, history, and geography). The primary instructor for twice-exceptional children is likely to be the general educator (with or without certification or licensure in gifted education). Although every state has licensure or endorsement requirements for special education teachers, only 26 states have licensure or endorsement requirements for teachers of the gifted (NAGC, 2005). Further, there are no federal statutes comparable to IDEIA that outline required characteristics for "highly qualified" teachers of the gifted. Hence, the requirements of NCLB for general education teachers that would apply to teachers of the twice-exceptional child (except those teaching in the state's public charter schools) include:

- Are fully certified in the state in which they teach (with specifications for alternative licensure routes);
- Hold at least a bachelor's degree;
- New elementary teachers are expected to have demonstrated subject knowledge and teaching skills in reading, writing, mathematics,

and other areas of the basic elementary school curriculum (may be demonstrated by passing "rigorous" state tests, which may be either a state-required state certification test or tests in the specific discipline areas noted);
- New middle or secondary school teachers are expected to demonstrate a high level of competency in each of the academic areas in which they teach by passing "rigorous" state licensure or certification tests or graduate degree or advanced certification or credential;
- Teachers who are *not* new to the profession must be fully certified in the state in which they teach and hold at least a bachelor's degree; and demonstrate competence in all academic subjects taught based on the standards outlined above according to the level taught or through a "highly objective uniform State standard of evaluation" (HOUSSE). (Council for Exceptional Children [CEC], 2005)

In those cases where the special education teacher collaborates with the teacher of the gifted or the classroom teacher by providing consultative services in "designing appropriate learning and performance accommodations and modifications" for the twice-exceptional child based on the identified disability, the special education teacher would not be required to demonstrate the competencies associated with the core academic disciplines. In this case the special education teacher might provide advice on "adjustments to the learning environment, modifications of instructional methods, adaptation of curricula, the use of positive behavioral supports and interventions, or the design, use or implementation of appropriate accommodations to meet the needs of individual children" (H. Report 779, 108th Cong., 2nd Session 171 [2004]). However, when the special education teacher assumes the role of co-teacher or engages in cooperative teaching or team teaching, then the expectations for academic competencies at the level of instruction and in the disciplines taught would be required to designate the special education teacher as "highly qualified" and would be required under the provisions of IDEIA (CEC, 2005).

Teacher Training and Professional Development

In serving in the collaborative role, the teacher training and professional development opportunities that will best serve the special education teacher, the general education teacher, and the teacher of the gifted to better serve the GLD student would include: re-orientation to teaching to strengths of students rather than deficiencies; learning to adjust accommodations to the differing curriculum, instructional strategies, and performance expectations of gifted services; and orientation to the various service models used in the education of gifted and GLD students. Standards for teachers of the gifted jointly developed by the NAGC and the CEC (2006) can provide guidance in supplementing the preparation of special education teachers to assume either collaborative teaching, which falls under the category of consulting, or more direct teaching. These standards encompass how to identify knowledge and skills in the categories of individual learning differences, instructional strategies, learning environments and social interactions, language and communication, instructional planning, assessment, and collaboration. Yell, Shriner, and Katsiyannis (2006) note that compliance with IDEIA also requires the use of academic and behavioral interventions that have been validated in the research literature. Therefore, in creating appropriate curriculum and services for the GLD students, the general education teacher, gifted education teacher, and the special education teacher need to review and synthesize the research in the independent fields of the disability and the research on the particular twice-exceptional construct.

Charter Schools and Private Schools

In some school districts charter schools have been established that either explicitly or implicitly serve gifted students, and hence, may also serve GLD students. To be considered highly qualified in these settings, teachers must meet requirements specified in the state's public charter school law. Private elementary and secondary school teachers providing equitable services to GLD students who have been placed by their parents in private school do not have to meet the qualified special education teacher requirements outlined in section §301.8 of IDEIA.

Parents of Twice-Exceptional Students

Several modifications to the regulations in the area of evaluations, eligibility determinations, individualized education programs, and educational placement relate to parents of twice-exceptional children. The definition of parent in IDEIA has been revised to replace "biological" for "natural" throughout, and a "guardian" is specifically a person generally authorized to act as the child's parent or is authorized to make decisions regarding the child's education. In the category of parental consent, the new law requires the public agency (in most cases school) to make reasonable efforts to obtain informed consent from the parent for initial evaluation and for initial provision of special education and related services. If the parent declines to pursue the evaluation, the public agency may, but is not required, to pursue reevaluation using consent override procedures.

Parents of students who have been evaluated for a disability should be alert to the possibility that the child may be twice-exceptional. Parents who suspect that even though their children are performing on grade level they may have a learning disability should request that problem-solving interventions (e.g., RTI) be part of evaluation for special education and gifted services. The inclusion of the phrase "or (B) the child exhibits a pattern of strengths and weaknesses in performance, achievement, or both, relative to age, State-approved grade-level standards or intellectual development consistent with §300.309(a)(2)(ii)" (Wright, 2006, p. 7) provides a basis for parents to request consideration of the possibility of the child being twice-exceptional. And, if the child *is* identified as twice-exceptional, parents should be assertive in ensuring that the interventions proposed reflect peer-reviewed research on meeting the needs of twice-exceptional students and that the goals and assessments used to measure student progress as part of the IEP process have taken into account expectations the student will make progress in congruence with the dual identification to avoid setting lower expectations than may be appropriate for the student's needs.

OVERALL RECOMMENDATIONS

The field of gifted education constantly struggles with trying to find ways to increase the numbers of underrepresented groups in gifted programs, including GLD students. The IDEIA legislation provides an avenue for reconsidering the identification process and services for gifted students typically implemented in districts across the country. Two overarching recommendations can be made for the field of gifted education regarding identification and services of gifted students, including GLD students:

Recommendation 1: Professional development for in-service teachers and preparation of pre-service teachers should include traits associated with GLD students.

Recommendation 2: State and district leaders should reconsider the process of identifying gifted students as an iterative, ongoing process starting in the general education classroom with the regular education teacher rather than as a once-a-year event. Within the regular education setting, a combination of a discrepancy model and the RTI model can be implemented. Both formal (i.e., standardized assessments) and informal data (e.g., teacher observation, unit-based assessments) have a role to play in identifying the discrepancy between achievement and ability. To avoid the so-called wait to fail model characteristic of using infrequent standardized assessments to determine placement for specialized services, informal data should be used on a more frequent basis to determine potential discrepancies. If the RTI process is in place as part of the district and school culture, then at the first suggestion of a gap between what a student is capable of achieving and the reality of their academic performance, this problem-solving approach would accelerate the process of identifying successful interventions and increasing the student's success. Once the disability is appropriately addressed, then GLD students' gifts are more likely to become evident, thus resulting in increased identification of and services for GLD students.

REFERENCES

Assouline, S. G., Nicpon, M. F., & Huber, D. H. (2006). The impact of vulnerabilities and strengths on the academic experiences of twice-exceptional students: A message to school counselors. *Professional School Counseling, 10*(1), 14–24.

Baum, S. M. (1988). An enrichment program for gifted learning disabled students. *Gifted Child Quarterly, 32,* 226–230.

Baum, S. M., Cooper, C. R., & Neu, T. W. (2001). Dual differentiation: An approach for meeting the curricular needs of gifted students with learning disabilities. *Psychology in the Schools, 38,* 477–490.

Baum, S. M., & Olenchak, R. F. (2002). The alphabet children: GT, ADHD, and more. *Exceptionality, 10,* 77–91.

Baum, S., Owen, S., & Dixon, J. (1991). *To be gifted and learning disabled: From identification to practical intervention strategies.* Mansfield Center, CT: Creative Learning Press.

Brighton, C. M., Hertberg, H., Moon, T. R., Tomlinson, C. A., & Callahan, C. M. (2005). *Feasibility of high-end learning in the middle school classroom.* (Monograph No. 05210). Storrs, CT: National Research Center on the Gifted and Talented.

Brody, L., & Mills, C. J. (1997). Gifted children with learning disabilities: A review of the issues. *Journal of Learning Disabilities, 30,* 282–296.

Cohen, S. S., & Vaughn, S. (1993). Gifted students with learning disabilities: What does the research say? *Learning Disabilities: A Multidisciplinary Journal, 5,* 87–94.

Colangelo, N., & Davis, G. A. (2003). *Handbook of gifted education* (3rd ed.). Boston: Pearson Publications.

Coleman, M. R. (2001). Surviving or thriving? 21 gifted boys with learning disabilities share their school stories. *Gifted Child Today, 24*(3), 56–63.

Coleman, M. R. (2005, Sept./Oct.). Academic strategies that work for gifted students with learning disabilities. *Teaching Exceptional Children,* 28–32.

Cooper, J. M. (1998). An exploratory study of the metacognition of verbally gifted/learning disabled learners with and without reading disabilities. *Dissertation Abstracts International, 58*(12-A), 4559.

Council for Exceptional Children (CEC). (2005). Resources on "highly qualified" requirements for special educators. Retrieved March 20, 2007, from http://www.cec.sped.org/AM/Template.cfm?Section=Home&TEMPLATE=/CM/ContentDisplay.cfm&CONTENTID=1802

Davis, G. A., & Rimm, S. (Eds.). (2004). *Education of the gifted and talented* (5th ed.) Needham Heights, MA: Allyn & Bacon.

Dole, S. (2001). Reconciling contradictions: Identity formation in individuals with giftedness and learning disabilities. *Journal for the Education of the Gifted, 25*(2), 103–137.

Fairbanks, S., Sugai, G., Guardino, D., & Lathrop, M. (2007). Response to intervention: Examining classroom behavior support in second grade. *Exceptional Children, 73,* 288–310.

Ferri, B. A., Gregg, N., & Heggoy, S. J. (1997). Profiles of college students demonstrating learning disabilities with and without giftedness. *Journal of Learning Disabilities, 30,* 552–559.

Gresham, F. (2001, August). *Response to intervention: An alternative approach to identification of learning disabilities.* Paper presented at the Learning Disabilities Summit: Building a Foundation for the Future, Washington, DC.

Hale, J. B., Kaufman, A., Naglieri, J. A., & Kavale, K. A. (2006). Implementation of IDEA: Integrating response to intervention and cognitive assessment methods. *Psychology in the School, 43,* 753–770.

Hannah, C. L., & Shore, B. (1995). Metacognition and high intellectual ability: Insights from the study of learning-disabled gifted students. *Gifted Child Quarterly, 39*(2), 95–109.

Harris-Murri, N., King, K., & Rostenberg, D. (2006). Reducing disproportionate minority representation in special education programs for students with emotional disturbances: Toward a culturally responsive response to intervention model. *Education and Treatment of Children, 29,* 779–799.

Hishinuma, E. S., & Nishimura, S. T. (2000). Parent attitudes on the importance and success of integrated self-contained services for students who are gifted, learning disabled, and gifted/learning disabled. *Roeper Review, 22,* 241–50.

Justice, L. M. (2006). Evidence-based practice, response to intervention, and the prevention of reading difficulties. *Language, Speech, and Hearing Services in Schools, 37,* 284–297.

Kavale, K. A., Holdnack, J. A., & Mostert, M. P. (2006). Responsiveness to intervention and the identification of specific learning disability: A critique and alternative proposal. *Learning Disability Quarterly, 29,* 113–127.

King, E. W. (2005). Addressing the social and emotional needs of twice-exceptional students. *Teaching Exceptional Children, 38*(1), 16–20.

Lange, S. M., & Tompson, B. (2006). Early identification and intervention for children at risk for learning disabilities. *International Journal of Special Education, 21*(3), 108–119.

Learning Disabilities Association of America. (n.d.). *Successful strategies for teaching students with learning disabilities.* Retrieved March 31, 2007, from http://www.ldaamerica.org/aboutld/teachers/understanding/strategies.asp

Marland, S. P., Jr. (1972). Education of the gifted and talented: Report to the Congress of the United States by the U.S. Commissioner of Education (Government Documents Y4.L 11/2: G36). Washington, DC: U.S. Government Printing Office.

McCoach, B., Kehle, T., Bray, M., & Siegle, D. (2007). Best practices in the identification of gifted students with learning disabilities. *Psychology in the Schools, 38,* 403–411.

National Association for Gifted Children (NAGC). (2005). *State of the states (2005-4-2005).* Washington, DC: National Association for Gifted Children.

National Association for Gifted Children and the Council for Exceptional Children. (2006). *NAGC_CEC Teacher knowledge & skill standards for gifted and talented education.* Retrieved March 20, 2007, from http://www.nagc.org/uploadedFiles/Information_and_Resources/NCATE_standards/final%20initial%20standards%20(4.14.06).pdf

National Joint Committee on Learning Disabilities (NJCLD). (2006). Learning disabilities and young children: Identification and intervention. *Learning Disability Quarterly, 30,* 63–73.

National Research Council on Learning Disabilities (NRCLD). (2002). *Specific learning disabilities: Finding common ground. A policy roundtable.* Retrieved February 23, from http://www.ldaamerica.org/legislative/joint_activities/commonground.asp

Newman, T. M. (2004). Interventions work, but we need more! In T. M. Newman & R. J. Sternberg (Eds.), *Students with gifts and learning disabilities* (pp. 235–246). New York: Kluwer.

Nielsen, M. E. (2002). Gifted students with learning disabilities: Recommendations for identification and programming. *Exceptionality, 10,* 93–111.

Nielsen, M. E., & Higgins, L. D. (2005). The eye of the storm: Services and programs for twice-exceptional learners. *Teaching Exceptional Children, 38*(1), 8–15.

Ofiesh, N. (2006). Response to intervention and the identification of specific learning disabilities: Why we need comprehensive evaluations as part of the process. *Psychology in the Schools, 43,* 883–888.

Reis, S. M, Neu, T. W., & McGuire, J. M. (1995). *Talents in two places: Case studies of high ability students with learning disabilities who have achieved.* Storrs, CT: National Research Center on the Gifted and Talented.

Reis, S. M., & Ruban, L. (2005). Services and programs for academically talented students with learning disabilities. *Theory into Practice, 44,* 148–159.

Schnur, J. O., & Stefanich, G. P. (1976). Science for the handicapped gifted child. *Roeper Review, 2*(2), 26–28.

Silverman, L. (2003). Gifted children with learning disabilities. In N. A. Colangelo & G. A. Davis (Eds.), *Handbook of gifted education* (3rd ed., pp. 533–543). Boston: Allyn & Bacon.

Stone, C. A. (1998). The metaphor of scaffolding. Its utility for the field of learning disabilities. *Journal of Learning Disabilities, 31,* 344–364.

Tomlinson, C. A. (1999). *The differentiated classroom: Responding to the needs of all learners.* Alexandria, VA: Association for Supervision and Curriculum Development.

Tomlinson, C. A. (2001). *How to differentiate instruction in mixed-ability classrooms.* Alexandria, VA: Association for Supervision and Curriculum Development.

Ukrainetz, T. A. (2006). The implications of RTI and EBP for SLPs: Commentary on L. M. Justice. *Language, Speech and Hearing Services in Schools, 37,* 298–303.

U.S. Department of Education. (2001). *No Child Left Behind.* Retrieved November 6, 2007, from http://www.ed.gov/policy/elsec/leg/esea02/107-110.pdf

U.S. Department of Education Office of Special Education Programs. (n.d.). IDEA Regulations: Identification of specific learning disabilities. Retrieved March 20, 2007, from http://IDEA.ed.gov

Van der Aalsvoort, G. M., & Harinck, F. J. H. (2001). Scaffolding classroom teaching behavior for use with young students with learning disabilities. *Journal of Classroom Interaction, 36*(2), 29–39.

Vespi, L., & Yewchuck, C. (1992). A phenomenological study of the social/emotional characteristics of gifted learning-disabled children. *Journal for the Education of the Gifted, 16*(1), 55–72.

Waldron, K. A., Saphire, D. G., & Rosenblum, S. A. (1987). Learning disabilities and giftedness: Identification based on self-concept, behavior and academic patterns. *Journal of Learning Disabilities, 20*(7), 422–432.

Wedl, R. J. (2005). *Response to intervention. An alternative to traditional eligibility criteria for students with disabilities.* St. Paul, MN: Education|Evolving.

Weinfeld, R., Barnes-Robinson, L., Jeweler, S., & Shevitz, B. (2002). Academic programs for gifted and talented/learning disabled students. *Roeper Review, 24,* 226–233.

Whitmore, J.R. (1988). Gifted children at risk for learning difficulties. *Teaching Exceptional Children, 20*(4), 10–14.

Whitmore, J.R., & Maker, C.J. (1985). *Intellectual giftedness in disabled persons.* Rockville, MD: Aspen.

Wright, P. W. D. (2006). *Summary of major changes in the regulations.* Retrieved March 20, 2007, from www.wrightslaw.com/idea/law.htm

Yell, M.L., Shriner, J.G., & Katsiyannis, A. (2006, September). Individuals With Disability Education Improvement Act of 2004 and IDEA Regulations of 2006: Implications for educators, administrators, and teacher trainers. *Focus on Exceptional Children, 39,* 1–24.

Yewchuck, C., & Lupart, J.L. (2000). Gifted handicapped: A desultory duality. In K. Heller & H. Passow (Eds.), *International handbook of research and development of giftedness and talent* (pp. 709–726). Oxford, UK: Pergamon.

Yssel, N., Margison, J., Cross, T., & Merbler, J. (2005). Puzzles, mysteries, and Picasso: A summer camp for students who are gifted and learning disabled. *Teaching Exceptional Children, 38*(1), 42–43.

High Stakes Testing and Students With Disabilities

Why Federal Policy Needs to Be Changed

Stuart S. Yeh

In recent years, changes in federal law have ensured that pressure to improve student achievement is directed toward students with disabilities as well as their nondisabled peers. The No Child Left Behind Act of 2001 (NCLB) requires every state receiving federal Title I funds[1] to establish a uniform system of testing students in grades 3 through 8, plus one high school grade, and to sanction schools that do not meet "adequate yearly progress" (AYP) requirements for 2 successive years. These sanctions create high stakes for schools and exert tremendous pressure to raise student achievement. The passage of the Individuals With Disabilities Education Improvement Act of 2004 (IDEIA) reauthorizes the Individuals With

---

1. Title I of the Elementary and Secondary Education Act (ESEA) (Pub.L. 89–10, 79 Stat. 77, 20 U.S.C. Ch.70), a United States federal statute enacted April 11, 1965, authorizes federal funding for schools and school districts that serve a population of students that includes a high percentage (typically around 40%) from low-income families. As a condition of receiving Title I monies, these schools are subject to federal laws including the No Child Left Behind Act.

Disabilities Education Act (IDEA) and aligns IDEA with NCLB, requiring that performance goals for students with disabilities must be aligned with the performance goals established by each state for the purpose of establishing whether a school has achieved AYP.

There are two provisions that provide a modicum of relief. The U.S. Department of Education allows each state to count toward its AYP requirement a small percentage of students who achieve proficient scores using assessments and standards that are more appropriate—but also less challenging—than the regular statewide assessments that all other students must take. Each state may count up to 1% of all tested students, those served under IDEIA with the *most significant* cognitive disabilities, defined as students in any of 13 disability categories who cannot reach grade-level standards even with the best instruction possible. These students take alternate assessments based on *alternate* academic achievement standards (U.S. Department of Education, 2007a, 2007b). In addition, each state may count another 2% of all tested students, those served under IDEIA with *persistent academic disabilities*. These students take alternate assessments based on *modified* academic achievement standards (U.S. Department of Education, 2007a, 2007b). However, the number of disabled students typically exceeds these caps in urban schools. Beyond the caps, any disabled students who do not achieve proficiency according to the same tests and standards that apply to students in regular education are counted against their schools for the purpose of determining whether the schools have met the AYP requirement. Thus, schools where more than 3% of the total student population has disabilities remain under intense pressure to boost achievement.

The implicit theory of action behind the federal law is that increased pressure will provide incentives for school staff to adopt more effective organizational and instructional practices, resulting in improved achievement. This presumes that superior practices are available and that teachers, principals, and superintendents can readily identify and implement them. If this were true, empirical studies would show a relationship between the implementation of accountability and improved student achievement. However, the best available evidence for the impact of accountability policies, involving a sophisticated longitudinal panel study with controls for fixed state effects as well as measures of parental education, school spending, and race, suggests that the implementation of high stakes testing, where consequences are linked to student achievement, results in marginal gains in student achievement, on the order of 0.2 standard deviations (SD) over 4 years or 0.05 SD (roughly 2 weeks of learning) annually (Hanushek & Raymond, 2005). Thus, while the logic of accountability is not implausible, empirical data do not support the hypothesis that large gains in student achievement may be expected simply by applying pressure.

NCLB SANCTIONS

NCLB is due for reauthorization this year (2007), providing an opportunity to change the federal law in ways that improve its potential for raising student achievement, especially for students with disabilities. Perhaps the most critical need for change involves the provisions regarding sanctions. Currently, NCLB requires each state to impose sanctions that increase in severity for every year that a school underperforms:

- after 2 years of failing to make AYP, the school's students must be allowed to transfer to other local schools;
- after 3 years of failing to make AYP, the school's students must be provided with supplemental educational services (typically, after-school tutoring) at no cost to the students;
- after 4 years of failing to make AYP, the school must implement major changes in organization, staffing, curriculum, and instruction (such as the implementation of a comprehensive school reform model);
- after 5 years of failing to make AYP, the school is subject to reconstitution, where staff members must reapply for their jobs and all staff are subject to replacement.

Except for tutoring, however, the research basis supporting each form of sanction is weak and, in some cases, suggests negative effects.

For example, open enrollment is a form of school choice where public school students can apply to public magnet schools outside of their neighborhood, but a recent lottery-based evaluation of open enrollment in the Chicago Public Schools found that this form of school choice reduces 4-year graduation rates and increases the probability that below average students will drop out (Cullen, Jacob, & Levitt, 2006). Students who win lotteries to schools with substantially higher peer quality are more likely to drop out than comparable lottery losers.

Comprehensive school reform (CSR) may be defined as externally developed school improvement programs designed to change the entire organization of schooling, including curriculum, instruction, and administrative practices, with the goal of improving student achievement, especially in schools serving the highest percentages of poor students. Typically, a school will apply for a federal CSR grant that funds the costs of implementation, including staff training. Forty-five percent of all Title I schools, and 80% of the highest-poverty schools, operate a schoolwide program (Heid & Webber, 1999). However, research regarding CSR has found relatively weak effects. Borman, Hewes, Overman, and Brown (2003) synthesized the available research literature and conducted the first meta-analysis of CSR effects. This exhaustive review of 232 studies of achievement, regarding 29 of the most widely implemented CSR models, found a small effect size of 0.12 SD for all studies using comparison groups. Researchers, acknowledging these disappointing results, conceded that "CSR . . . is not the panacea for closing the achievement gap and decreasing high school drop out rates for poor and historically underserved students of color" (Ross & Gil, 2004, p. 170).

Likewise, Malen, Croninger, Muncey, and Redmond-Jones (2002) found that school reconstitution resulted in chaos and confusion, leading to the departure of effective, committed staff, and did not lead to improved student achievement. The researchers suggested that reconstitution was not effective because the underlying theory is incorrect: the notion that reconstitution leads to an influx of more effective and highly committed staff that would redesign underperforming schools, thereby improving student achievement.

Finally, although after-school tutoring can be an effective approach for raising student achievement (Shanahan, 1998), attendance at voluntary programs is poor. Schools that receive Title I funds but do not meet AYP performance goals must arrange free tutoring services and must notify parents in writing that their children are eligible for the free services. However, the U.S. General Accounting Office found that only 19% of eligible students received tutoring services in 2004–2005, the most recent school year for which data are available (Ashby, 2007). Although low participation may partly be attributable to delays in notifying parents, it appears that many students simply do not wish to participate.

Thus, NCLB is not well-designed to improve student achievement, and it is likely that major changes are needed in order to achieve the stated goal: making every student academically proficient by the year 2014. These changes are especially critical in schools where more than 3% of students have disabilities. Together, NCLB and IDEIA are exerting tremendous pressure to raise the achievement of students with disabilities to the level of their nondisabled peers. However, barring the identification of drastically more effective strategies, it is likely that many—if not most—schools will fail to reach this goal.

A PROMISING APPROACH

A more promising approach is curriculum-based measurement (CBM), which involves weekly assessment of student learning through brief (1–5 minute) tests of numeracy and oral reading fluency. Teachers using CBM with students in special education demonstrated improvements in instructional quality and student achievement (Fuchs, Deno, & Mirkin,

1984; Fuchs, Fuchs, Hamlett, & Stecker, 1991; Jones & Krouse, 1988; Wesson, 1991) with an effect size of 0.7 SD (Fuchs, Fuchs, Hamlett, & Stecker, 1991). CBM students liked frequent testing, believed it helped them to learn, saw themselves as more responsible for their learning, and were more likely to attribute their success to personal effort, compared to similar students who were randomly assigned to a control group (Davis, Fuchs, Fuchs, & Whinnery, 1995).

In a quasi-experimental study, Fuchs, Fuchs, and Hamlett (1994) found that CBM helped teachers to manage instructional time efficiently by immediately identifying students who were not making progress and quickly evaluating the efficacy of various intervention strategies. In three experiments, teachers who received computerized CBM skill analyses for their students designed more specific program adjustments, resulting in higher student achievement, compared to teachers who implemented CBM but did not receive the skill analyses (Fuchs, Fuchs, & Hamlett, 1989; Fuchs, Fuchs, Hamlett, & Allinder, 1991; Fuchs, Fuchs, Hamlett, & Stecker, 1990). The development of computer software simplified logistics and training, greatly reduced the time required to implement CBM, and improved teacher satisfaction with the process (Fuchs, Fuchs, Hamlett, & Hasselbring, 1987; Fuchs, Hamlett, Fuchs, Stecker, & Ferguson, 1988). These results suggest that frequent student assessments and rapid feedback of results to teachers may improve teaching effectiveness. However, CBM has not been widely adopted, primarily because many teachers believe that CBM measures of numeracy and oral reading fluency are inadequate measures of performance on higher-order thinking tasks (Allinder & Oats, 1997; Hintze & Shapiro, 1997; Madelaine & Wheldall, 1999; Mehrens & Clarizio, 1993; Wesson, King, & Deno, 1984; Yell, Deno, & Marsten, 1992).

While CBM has not been widely adopted, its modern descendants differ in ways that has improved acceptance among teachers. For example, *Reading Assessment*[2] is a popular program designed to encourage students to read books at appropriate levels of difficulty while alerting teachers to learning difficulties and encouraging teachers to provide individualized tutoring or small group instruction. This is achieved through a system of frequently assessing each student's reading comprehension and monitoring each student's reading level. First, books in the school's library are labeled and shelved according to reading level. Second, students select books to read based on their interests and their reading levels, according to the results of the *STAR Reading* test, a norm-referenced

---

2. *Reading Assessment, Math Assessment,* and the *Rapid Assessment Corporation* are pseudonyms, to avoid the appearance that the author endorses the assessment software. The author is neither affiliated with, nor has received any funding from, the vendor.

computer-adaptive test (Renaissance Learning, n.d.). This helps students to avoid the frustrating experience of choosing a book that is too difficult. After finishing a book, the student takes a computer-based quiz, unique to the book, that is intended to monitor basic reading comprehension (*Rapid Assessment Corporation* has created more than 100,000 quizzes). Similarly, *Math Assessment* is a popular program that provides individualized, printed sets of math problems, a system of assessing student performance on those problems, and a scoring system where students and teachers receive rapid, frequent feedback on student performance upon completion of every set of problems.

Similar to CBM, these programs provide rapid assessment of student progress, assisting teachers in individualizing the curriculum. However, there are key differences between CBM and *Reading* and *Math Assessment*. *Reading Assessment* monitors student progress through a point system that rewards students for reading and comprehending longer, more challenging books, where reading difficulty is measured by the Flesch-Kincaid formula for determining readability. Similarly, *Math Assessment* monitors student progress through math topic strands, as well as accuracy in completing math problems. Thus, it is easier for students to see themselves making progress, compared to CBM, which primarily provides information to teachers regarding oral reading fluency or math numeracy. CBM provides information about the number of words that students are able to read, or the number of math problems that they can complete, rather than the difficulty and length of books that students can read, or the number of math topic strands that have been mastered.

These differences may have important consequences if student engagement depends on whether students can see themselves making progress. It may not be as meaningful for a student to know that she can complete 14 multiplication problems in 5 minutes, as it is to know that she has mastered addition, subtraction, and two-digit multiplication, and is moving forward with division problems. Similarly, it may not be as meaningful for a student to know that he can read 65 words per minute, as it is to know that he is reading longer, more difficult books.

Three meta-analyses have been conducted regarding the effect of feedback on student achievement. These meta-analyses involve studies that experimentally compared the achievement of students who were frequently tested with a group of similar students who received the same curriculum but were not frequently tested. A meta-analysis of 21 experimental studies that focused on studies involving testing found that students who were tested two to five times per week outperformed students who were not frequently tested, with an average effect size of 0.7 SD (Fuchs & Fuchs, 1986), equivalent to raising the achievement of an average nation such as the United States to the level of the top five nations (Black & Wiliam, 1998). When teachers were required to follow rules about using the assessment information to change instruction for students, the average effect size exceeded 0.9 SD (Fuchs & Fuchs, 1986). A second meta-analysis of 40 feedback studies (Bangert-Drowns, Kulik, Kulik, & Morgan, 1991) that included studies involving nontesting feedback (such as praise or criticism), as well as studies involving testing feedback, found that feedback was more effective when it involved testing (effect size = 0.6 SD) and when the feedback was presented immediately after a test (effect size = 0.7 SD). A third meta-analysis of 131 studies that included studies involving nontesting feedback, as well as studies involving testing feedback, found that praise or criticism attenuated the effectiveness of feedback (Kluger & DeNisi, 1996). Emotionally neutral (i.e., testing) feedback that is void of praise or criticism "is likely to yield impressive gains in performance, possibly exceeding 1 SD"—much higher than the average effect size of 0.4 SD when all types of feedback studies were lumped together (Kluger & DeNisi, 1996, p. 278). A recent review of research summarized the results of previous meta-analyses regarding feedback and found an average effect size of 0.79 SD (Hattie & Timperley, 2007).

These results suggest the nature of effective feedback systems: non-judgmental, involving frequent testing (2–5 times per week), presented immediately after a test. Under these conditions, the three meta-analyses of feedback interventions (Bangert-Drowns et al., 1991; Fuchs & Fuchs, 1986; Kluger & DeNisi, 1996) suggest that the effect size for testing feedback is no lower than 0.7 SD. However, the meta-analyses generally involved short implementations of rapid assessment (the average duration across all studies in the three meta-analyses was only 3.4 weeks),[3] and the effectiveness of reading and math assessment in large-scale field trials may differ. Thus, it is useful to examine the best controlled field trials of reading and math assessment.

Two randomized experiments evaluated the effectiveness of the reading assessment program (Nunnery, Ross, & McDonald, 2006; Ross, Nunnery, & Goldfeder, 2004). The first experiment, involving 1,665 Memphis students (a district where 71% of all students are eligible for free/reduced price lunch), found an average effect size of 0.270 SD per

---

3. R. Bangert-Drowns (personal communication, June 7, 2006) estimated that the average duration of the 40 studies in his meta-analysis (Bangert-Drowns et al., 1991) was 1.5 to 2 weeks. D. Fuchs (personal communication, June 8, 2006) estimated that the average duration of the 21 studies in his meta-analysis (Fuchs & Fuchs, 1986) was 10–14 weeks. A. Kluger (personal communication, June 13, 2006) calculated that the average duration of the 131 studies in his meta-analysis (Kluger & DeNisi, 1996) was 17.8 days. Using the midpoints of each range, the weighted average duration of the feedback interventions in the three meta-analyses was 23.9 days, or 3.4 weeks.

grade in grades K through 6, over a 9-month school year (Ross et al., 2004). Using hierarchical linear modeling (a statistical technique that improves precision), the second experiment, involving 978 students (89.9% African American and 83% eligible for free/reduced price lunch) found an average effect size of 0.175 SD per grade in grades 3 through 6, over a 9-month school year (Nunnery et al., 2006). After averaging the grade-level effect sizes across the two studies (where they overlap, in grades 3 through 6), the effect size for reading assessment averaged 0.279 SD per grade in grades K through 6, with an unusually disadvantaged population of students.

The only randomized study of math assessment, involving 1,880 students in grades 2 through 8, in 80 classrooms and 7 states, found an effect size of 0.324 SD over a 7-month period after controlling for treatment integrity (Ysseldyke & Bolt, 2007). The only national, peer-reviewed quasi-experimental evaluation of math assessment, involving 2,202 students in grades 3 through 10, in 125 classrooms in 24 states, found that students in the treatment group gained an average of 0.392 SD per grade over one semester (18 weeks), compared to students not receiving math assessment (at pretest the scores of treatment and comparison students were not significantly different; Ysseldyke & Tardrew, 2007). The mean effect size, across these two studies, is 0.358 SD. Averaging the effect size estimates for reading and math assessment produces an overall effect size of 0.319 SD, or a gain of about 3 months of learning annually.

NCLB, IDEIA, AND HIGH SCHOOL EXIT EXAMS

Ideally, federal policy would be redesigned so that all students reach proficiency by the year 2014. One strategy would be to change federal law to provide funding and support for the implementation of rapid assessment. Over a number of years, this change in policy could have a significant impact. For example, the implementation of rapid assessment in grades 1 through 5 could improve student achievement by 1.5 SD, equivalent to the difference in achievement between an average student and a student scoring at the 96th percentile (that is, above 96% of all students).

However, there is a strong possibility that the implementation of even the very best practices in teaching and learning may be insufficient to boost all students to the level of proficiency (which is determined separately by each individual state). Unless changes are made to the NCLB provisions regarding sanctions, the inevitable outcome is that many schools would eventually be reconstituted, in accordance with federal law—with all of the chaos, confusion, and departure of effective, committed staff that accompanies reconstitution (Malen et al., 2002). However, there is yet another, perhaps more insidious outcome that has largely escaped the attention of policy makers and is likely to have devastating effects on students with disabilities.

It may be difficult for the casual observer to understand how the passage and implementation of NCLB and IDEIA could have anything but positive effects. The goal of improving student achievement for all students is laudable, as are the provisions that hold educators account-able for meeting the needs of students with disabilities. Unfortunately, these federal laws interact with state-mandated high school exit exam requirements to produce a perverse, unintended outcome: the denial of high school diplomas to many students with disabilities.

High School Exit Exams

By the year 2009, half of all states (25) will require students to pass a state test in order to graduate from high school; this requirement will affect 70% of students nationwide (Gayler, Chudowsky, Hamilton, Kober, & Yeager, 2004). The adoption of high stakes testing, where consequences are linked to student performance, aims to make the link between effort and achievement abundantly clear, to motivate students to study harder, and to raise academic standards. The implementation of IDEIA and NCLB means that all students, including those with disabilities, must pass the same state-mandated graduation exams as their nondisabled peers in order to receive a diploma (with the exception of the 3% of all students who are eligible to take alternative assessments).

With few exceptions, the high school exit exams that are now in the process of being implemented will require mastery of material at the high school level in order to encourage students to perform at a much higher level than the previous generation of minimum competency exit exams (Center on Education Policy, 2005, 2006). However, there is wide variation in the difficulty of state exit exams, reflected in wide variations in passing rates. In math, for example, initial passing rates ranged from 36% to 91% across 12 states (Gayler, Chudowsky, Kober, & Hamilton, 2003).

One concern is whether it is equitable to deny a diploma to a stu-dent in one state when the same student would have passed a graduation exam and obtained a diploma in another state. The issue arises because each of the 50 states develops and implements testing systems indepen-dently of each other. The only solution to this issue is to implement a national system of testing. But while there is renewed interest in national testing as a consequence of disparities in state policies, this approach was previously considered and rejected during the debates leading up to the passage of NCLB, primarily because of conflicting ideas about how to design and implement a national testing program (see Jennings, 2000). Educators in Vermont and Kentucky, for example, favored a system of testing involving portfolios of student work, whereas policy makers in other states preferred the reliability and lower cost of multiple choice tests. While available studies had previously suggested that portfolio assessment systems were costly, time-consuming, and did not provide adequate reliability for their intended uses (Koretz, Barron, Mitchell, & Stecher, 1996; Koretz, Stecher, Klein, & McCaffrey, 1994), acceptance of these findings by educators and state policy makers in Vermont and Kentucky lagged for several years.

A second concern is whether the exams are valid; in other words, are the conclusions that are drawn from the results appropriate, useful, and defensible? While exit exams typically include items that test knowledge of algebra and geometry, most students will enter occupations where knowledge of these topics is unnecessary for success. The use of this type of exit exam is not defensible for these students. For college-bound students, however, it may be reasonable to expect knowledge of the critical thinking skills learned through algebra, geometry, and other topics that are commonly tested on high school exit exams. Thus, the implementation of a single state-wide exit exam is ill-suited to the diverse needs of the heterogeneous population of students within each state. Differences among students and their goals suggest a need for a differentiated system of exit exams.

A third concern is that a single exam, with a single level of difficulty, is not the best way to motivate all students to achieve at high levels. An exit exam that is far too difficult for students with cognitive disabilities simply serves to discourage them. Conversely, an exit exam that is easy for advanced students is unlikely to motivate those students to work harder.

These concerns are magnified with regard to students with cognitive disabilities because most, if not all, will struggle to pass an exam that requires mastery of high school level material. Therefore, in many states, any student with a cognitive disability who is not permitted to take an alternative assessment is at risk of failing the state-mandated high school exit exam and is in danger of being denied a high school diploma. It is doubly important to ensure that there are no items on the test that are invalid, meaning not predictive of future success in a range of likely occupations. It is doubly important to ensure that the exam system offers rewards for students who work hard, and does not discourage students because the bar is beyond their reach. And it is doubly important to ensure that standards for graduation that are adequate in one state are also adequate in any other.

It is unfortunate that the current policy debate reduces the complexity of this issue to a simplistic choice of high versus low standards. What has largely escaped most of the combatants is that there are alternatives. It is not necessary to choose between maintaining high standards and awarding diplomas to every student regardless of demonstrated ability.

Differentiated Exams and Multiple Diploma Options

One policy proposal would provide the desired incentive structure for all students to achieve at high levels, while minimizing the risk of denying diplomas unfairly. This would involve the creation of a system of exit exams designed to recognize multiple exit levels of achievement. In New York, for example, students who pass five Regents exams with a score of 65 or above receive a prestigious Regents Diploma, while students who are unable to meet that standard but are able to pass five exams with a score of 55 or above are eligible to receive a local diploma (State Education Department, 2007). This type of system provides a high standard to aim for, and a prestigious reward for those who achieve that standard, yet avoids denying diplomas to large numbers of students who possess basic skills but not knowledge of algebra and geometry.[4] Students who are able to demonstrate mastery of subjects such as algebra and geometry are rewarded for their advanced performance, but mastery of those subjects is not required to obtain a diploma. Thus, students who do not need to know algebra and geometry are not denied a diploma, as long as they can demonstrate the basic competencies needed to obtain a local diploma.

Bishop (1998) analyzed the effects of curriculum-based external exit examination systems, which are exit exam systems that signal multiple levels of achievement. Bishop notes that this feature significantly changes the incentive effects of exit exams. Because higher-achieving students pass minimum competency exams easily, the minimum competency exams motivate only the low-achieving students to work harder. In contrast, exit exam systems that reward students at every level of achievement potentially motivate all students to work harder. After analyzing data from the Third International Math and Science Study (TIMSS), the International Assessment of Educational Progress, and New York's Regents examination system, Bishop concluded that multiple diploma systems and other

---

4. New York has joined the nationwide shift away from basic skills exams. Thus, the current approach is actually less two-tiered than New York's previous approach, where students could obtain a regular diploma by passing the easier Regents Competency Tests but needed to pass the more difficult Regents Examinations to obtain the more prestigious Regents Diploma.

systems that signal multiple levels of achievement significantly improve student achievement and maintain high educational standards.

More recently, after reviewing the effects of alternative testing policies, Bishop, Mane, Bishop, and Moriarty (2001) concluded that "The policy that clearly has the biggest effects on test scores is the hybrid end-of-course/minimum competency exam system that has been in place in New York state since the early 1980s and in North Carolina since about 1991" (p. 310). Bishop et al. explicitly describe New York's system of multiple diplomas as a curriculum-based external exit examination system: "This policy package is also often referred to as a curriculum-based external exit exam system" (p. 310). This statement suggests that research findings regarding these types of systems generalize to multiple diploma systems that are similar to those used by New York.

Thus, a system with multiple levels of incentives that correspond to multiple levels of achievement in a heterogeneous student population is more likely to motivate students at all levels, compared to an exit exam with a single level of difficulty, and is more effective in improving student achievement. Multiple diploma options are currently used on a limited basis by 34 states, primarily with regard to students with disabilities (Johnson & Thurlow, 2003), but federal policy limits the use of differentiated exam systems (effectively limiting multiple diploma options) to 3% of all students. The research by Bishop (1998) and Bishop et al. (2001) suggests that changing this policy to allow all students to pursue multiple diploma options through a differentiated system of testing would motivate all students to strive for high standards and would maximize achievement gains, without discouraging students and denying diplomas unfairly.

Unfortunately, the U.S. Department of Education has interpreted language under section 1111(b)(2)(A) of NCLB to rule out the use of differentiated exam systems for NCLB purposes (except for the allowance regarding 3% of all students). This language specifies that each state must develop and implement "a single, statewide State accountability system" (U.S. Department of Education, 2002a, p. 1445). The U.S. Department of Education ruled that the "use of levels assessments"—including differentiated exam systems—"would not allow all schools and students to be held to the same high standards required by the NCLB Act"; this ruling is based on the presumption that a differentiated exam system would not maintain high standards (CTB/McGraw Hill, 2004; U.S. Department of Education, 2002b, p. 45044). This presumption is inconsistent with Bishop's (1998) and Bishop et al.'s (2001) research, which suggests that a differentiated exam system has the largest effect on student achievement and, thus, is most likely to promote high standards. Currently, there is no research that supports the Department's decision to reject a differentiated testing system. Instead, Education Department officials assert that differentiated exams would not provide a uniform test: "The regulations are very clear in saying all students have to be held to the same standard" (Trotter, 2003, p. 17). Despite the Department's position, it appears that the use of a differentiated exam system is consistent with the spirit as well as the language of the law, suggesting the possibility that the Department could change its policy if desired. What the law requires is a single system of testing in each state. New York provides an example of a single system of testing, but with the type of multiple diploma options that research suggests is most effective in raising achievement. The Department interprets the law in a way that suggests all students must pass the same bar—which would invalidate multiple diploma systems—but that interpretation goes beyond what the law actually says.

There is one highly unsatisfactory alternative. In principle, each state using an exit exam could lower its bar. This would meet the letter of the law and would ensure that no student is denied a diploma unfairly, but it runs counter to the spirit of NCLB to raise academic standards and motivate all students to work harder, and it is unlikely to be implemented.

The implementation of differentiated exam systems would not eliminate the possibility that students with disabilities would be denied diplomas as a result of failing state-mandated tests. However, this policy change would greatly improve the probability that the use of state-mandated graduation exams would be a valid, fair, and defensible use of testing.

CONCLUSION

The lesson of this chapter is that there are two possible changes to federal policy that have strong potential for improving educational outcomes for all children, and especially for children with disabilities. The first change is to replace the current structure of NCLB sanctions with funding and support for systems that rapidly assess student performance in math and reading two to five times per week. These assessments provide valuable performance feedback to students and teachers. The research studies reviewed in this chapter strongly suggest that rapid assessment is far more effective in improving student achievement than the current system of sanctions. The second change is to permit each state to implement a system of differentiated state tests. In states that use high school exit exams, differentiated levels of exit achievement would be linked with a system of multiple diploma options that progressively reward students who are able to reach high bars, while maintaining incentives for students who may be cognitively disabled yet are able to reach basic standards. The research reviewed in this chapter demonstrates that this type of system is more likely to raise achievement and, thus, promote high academic standards.

Unfortunately, neither of these proposals has received much attention. Instead, much effort is being expended either to preserve the existing system of accountability and high stakes testing, under the banner of maintaining high standards, or to argue that NCLB represents an unfunded mandate, with the implication that increased educational spending is the answer. Neither of these approaches will achieve the objective of leaving no child behind. Increased accountability, in the current form of single level high school exit exams, only improves achievement by 0.2 SD over 4 years, or 0.05 SD annually—roughly 2 weeks of learning (Hanushek & Raymond, 2005), while increasing current patterns of educational expenditures by 10% would only increase student achievement by 0.083 SD annually—less than 1 month of learning (Greenwald, Hedges, & Laine, 1996). These meager gains suggest a need to rethink current policies and the alternatives that are being considered.

REFERENCES

Allinder, R. M., & Oats, R. G. (1997). Effects of acceptability on teachers' implementation of curriculum-based measurement and student achievement in mathematics computation. *Remedial and Special Education, 18*(2), 113–120.

Ashby, C. M. (2007). *No Child Left Behind Act: Education actions may help improve implementation and evaluation of supplemental educational services.* Report no. GAO-07-738T. Washington, DC: U.S. General Accounting Office.

Bangert-Drowns, R. L., Kulik, C. C., Kulik, J. A., & Morgan, M. (1991). The instructional effect of feedback in test-like events. *Review of Educational Research, 61*(2), 213–238.

Bishop, J. (1998). *Do curriculum-based external exit exam systems enhance student achievement?* (CPRE Research Report Series RR-40). Philadelphia: Consortium for Policy Research in Education, University of Pennsylvania, Graduate School of Education.

Bishop, J. H., Mane, F., Bishop, M., & Moriarty, J. (2001). The role of end-of-course exams and minimum competency exams in standards-based reforms. In D. Ravitch (Ed.), *Brookings papers on education policy* (pp. 267–345). Washington, DC: Brookings Institution Press.

Black, P., & Wiliam, D. (1998). Assessment and classroom learning. *Assessment in Education, 5*(1), 7–74.

Borman, G. D., Hewes, G. M., Overman, L. T., & Brown, S. (2003). Comprehensive school reform and achievement: A meta-analysis. *Review of Educational Research, 73*(2), 125–230.

Center on Education Policy. (2005). *High school exit exams: Basic features* (Exit Exams Policy Brief No. 1). Washington, DC: Author.

Center on Education Policy. (2006). *State high school exit exams: A challenging year.* Washington, DC: Author.

CTB/McGraw Hill. (2004). *Overview of the U.S. Department of Education's position on the use of computer-adaptive testing.* Retrieved November 26, 2005, from http://www.ctb.com/media/articles/pdfs/AssessmentRelated/Computer_Based_Testing.pdf

Cullen, J. B., Jacob, B. A., & Levitt, S. (2006). The effect of school choice on participants: Evidence from randomized lotteries. *Econometrica, 74*(5), 1191–1230.

Davis, L. B., Fuchs, L. S., Fuchs, D., & Whinnery, K. (1995). "Will CBM help me learn?" Students' perception of the benefits of curriculum-based measurement. *Education and Treatment of Children, 18*(1), 19–32.

Fuchs, L. S., Deno, S. L., & Mirkin, P. K. (1984). The effects of curriculum-based measurement and evaluation on pedagogy, student achievement, and student awareness of learning. *American Educational Research Journal, 21,* 449–460.

Fuchs, L. S., & Fuchs, D. (1986). Effects of systematic formative evaluation: A meta-analysis. *Exceptional Children, 53*(3), 199–208.

Fuchs, L. S., Fuchs, D., & Hamlett, C. L. (1989). Monitoring reading growth using student recalls: Effects of two teacher feedback systems. *Journal of Educational Research, 83,* 103–111.

Fuchs, L. S., Fuchs, D., & Hamlett, C. L. (1994). Strengthening the connection between assessment and instructional planning with expert systems. *Exceptional Children, 61*(2), 138–146.

Fuchs, L. S., Fuchs, D., Hamlett, C. L., & Allinder, R. M. (1991). The contribution of skills analysis to curriculum based measurement in spelling. *Exceptional Children, 57,* 443–452.

Fuchs, L. S., Fuchs, D., Hamlett, C. L., & Hasselbring, T. S. (1987). Using computers with curriculum-based monitoring: Effects on teacher efficiency and satisfaction. *Journal of Special Education Technology, 8*(4), 14–27.

Fuchs, L. S., Fuchs, D., Hamlett, C. L., & Stecker, P. M. (1990). The role of skills analysis in curriculum based measurement in math. *School Psychology Review, 19,* 6–22.

Fuchs, L. S., Fuchs, D., Hamlett, C. L., & Stecker, P. M. (1991). Effects of curriculum-based measurement and consultation on teacher planning and student achievement in mathematics operations. *American Educational Research Journal, 28,* 617–641.

Fuchs, L. S., Hamlett, C. L., Fuchs, D., Stecker, P. M., & Ferguson, C. (1988). Conducting curriculum-based measurement with computerized data collection: Effects on efficiency and teacher satisfaction. *Journal of Special Education Technology, 9*(2), 73–86.

Gayler, K., Chudowsky, N., Hamilton, M., Kober, N., & Yeager, M. (2004). *State high school exit exams: A maturing reform.* Washington, DC: Center on Education Policy.

Gayler, K., Chudowsky, N., Kober, N., & Hamilton, M. (2003). *High school exit exams: Put to the test.* Washington, DC: Center on Education Policy.

Greenwald, R., Hedges, L. V., & Laine, R. D. (1996). The effect of school resources on student achievement. *Review of Educational Research, 66*(3), 361–396.

Hanushek, E. A., & Raymond, M. E. (2005). Does school accountability lead to improved student performance? *Journal of Policy Analysis and Management, 24*(2), 297–327.

Hattie, J., & Timperley, H. (2007). The power of feedback. *Review of Educational Research, 77*(1), 81–112.

Heid, C., & Webber, A. (1999). *School-level implementation of standards-based reform: Findings from the Public School Survey on Education Reform.* Retrieved October 1, 2006, from http://www.ed.gov/pubs/SchoolSurvey/title.html

Hintze, J. M., & Shapiro, E. S. (1997). Curriculum-based measurement and literature-based reading: Is curriculum-based measurement meeting the needs of changing reading curricula? *Journal of School Psychology, 35*(4), 351–375.

Jennings, J. F. (2000). *Why national standards and tests? Politics and the quest for better schools.* Thousand Oaks, CA: Sage.

Johnson, D. R., & Thurlow, M. L. (2003). *A national study on graduation requirements and diploma options for youth with disabilities* (Technical Report No. 36). Minneapolis, MN: University of Minnesota, National Center on Educational Outcomes.

Jones, E. D., & Krouse, J. P. (1988). The effectiveness of data-based instruction by student teachers in classrooms for pupils with mild handicaps. *Teacher Education and Special Education, 11*(1), 9–19.

Kluger, A. N., & DeNisi, A. (1996). The effects of feedback interventions on performance: A historical review, a meta-analysis, and a preliminary feedback intervention theory. *Psychological Bulletin, 119*(2), 254–284.

Koretz, D., Barron, S., Mitchell, K., & Stecher, B. (1996). *Perceived effects of the Kentucky Instructional Results Information System (KIRIS).* Santa Monica, CA: Institute on Education and Training, RAND.

Koretz, D., Stecher, B., Klein, S., & McCaffrey, D. (1994). The Vermont portfolio assessment program: Findings and implications. *Educational Measurement: Issues and Practice, 13*(3), 5–16.

Madelaine, A., & Wheldall, K. (1999). Curriculum-based measurement of reading: A critical review. *International Journal of Disability, Development and Education, 46*(1), 71–85.

Malen, B., Croninger, R., Muncey, D., & Redmond-Jones, D. (2002). Reconstituting schools: "Testing" the "theory of action." *Educational Evaluation and Policy Analysis, 24*(2), 113–132.

Mehrens, W. A., & Clarizio, H. F. (1993). Curriculum-based measurement: Conceptual and psychometric considerations. *Psychology in the Schools, 30*(3), 241–254.

Nunnery, J. A., Ross, S. M., & McDonald, A. (2006). A randomized experimental evaluation of the impact of Accelerated Reader/Reading Renaissance implementation on reading achievement in grades 3 to 6. *Journal of Education for Students Placed At Risk, 11*(1), 1–18.

Renaissance Learning. (n.d.). *STAR Reading: Understanding reliability and validity.* Wisconsin Rapids, WI: Renaissance Learning.

Ross, S. M., & Gil, L. (2004). The past and future of comprehensive school reform: Perspectives from a researcher and practitioner. In C. T. Cross (Ed.), *Putting the pieces together: Lessons from comprehensive school reform research* (pp. 151–174). Washington, DC: National Clearinghouse for Comprehensive School Reform.

Ross, S. M., Nunnery, J., & Goldfeder, E. (2004). *A randomized experiment on the effects of Accelerated Reader/Reading Renaissance in an urban school district: Final evaluation report.* Memphis, TN: Center for Research in Educational Policy, University of Memphis.

Shanahan, T. (1998). On the effectiveness and limitations of tutoring in reading. *Review of Research in Education, 23,* 217–234.

State Education Department. (2007). *Section 100.5 Diploma requirements.* Retrieved April 27, 2007, from http://www.emsc.nysed.gov/part100/pages/1005a.html

Trotter, A. (2003, May 8). A question of direction. *Education Week, 22,* 17–18, 20–21.

U.S. Department of Education. (2002a). *Public Law 107–110, 107th Congress: An Act to close the achievement gap with accountability, flexibility, and choice, so that no child is left behind.* Retrieved October 1, 2007, from http://www.ed.gov/policy/elsec/leg/esea02/107–110.pdf

U.S. Department of Education. (2002b). *Title I—Improving the academic achievement of the disadvantaged: Final rule.* Retrieved October 1, 2007, from http://www.ed.gov/legislation/FedRegister/finrule/2002–3/070502a.pdf

U.S. Department of Education. (2007a). No Child Left Behind: Modified academic achievement standards: Non-regulatory guidance: Draft.

U.S. Department of Education. (2007b). *Raising achievement: Alternate assessments for students with disabilities.* Retrieved April 13, 2007, from http://www.ed.gov/policy/elsec/guid/raising/alt-assess-long.html

Wesson, C. L. (1991). Curriculum-based measurement and two models of follow-up consultation. *Exceptional Children, 57,* 246–257.

Wesson, C. L., King, R. P., & Deno, S. L. (1984). Direct and frequent measurement of student performance: If it's good for us, why don't we do it? *Learning Disabilities Quarterly, 7,* 45–48.

Yell, M. L., Deno, S. L., & Marsten, D. B. (1992). Barriers to implementing curriculum-based measurement. *Diagnostique, 18,* 99–112.

Ysseldyke, J., & Bolt, D. (2007). Effect of technology-enhanced continuous progress monitoring on math achievement. *School Psychology Review, 36*(3), 453–467.

Ysseldyke, J., & Tardrew, S. (2007). Use of a progress-monitoring system to enable teachers to differentiate math instruction. *Journal of Applied School Psychology, 24*(1), 1–28.

CHAPTER 14

Individualized Education Program

Barbara C. Gartin and Nikki L. Murdick

The individualized education program (IEP) as specified by the Individuals With Disabilities Education Improvement Act of 2004 (IDEIA) is considered by many to be the cornerstone for the provision of appropriate educational programs for students with disabilities. The IDEIA is a reauthorization of the older Individuals With Disabilities Education Act (IDEA). For many individuals, "the logic underlying the IEP requirements seems so basic that one would assume the legislation was enacted merely to confirm prevailing practice" (Meyen, 1995, pp. 104–105). In reality, the concept of individualized instruction is based on research in the field of effective education and instructional practices (Kavale & Forness, 1999; Talmadge, 1975; Waxman, Wang, Anderson, & Walberg, 1985). In addition to the research base, courts have found that the IEP is the means by which a free appropriate public education (FAPE) is provided to students with disabilities (*Halderman v. Pennhurst*, 1979; *Mills v. Board of Education of D.C.*, 1972; *PARC v. Pennsylvania*, 1972). The law and regulations posit that the IEP is a product that is developed collaboratively by the IEP team, and thus, it provides a blueprint for a unique educational program specific to the needs of an individual student (Murdick, Gartin, & Crabtree, 2007). Others see the IEP as a process by which a student's strengths and needs are assessed and considered by a team of IDEA identified individuals (Yell, 2006). Additionally, the IEP is seen as the gate by which parents enter into equal participation with the school to ensure that the student with disabilities is provided that educational opportunity.

In this chapter, the historical and legal bases for the inclusion of individualized instruction via the IEP into special education legislation will be discussed. In addition, this chapter will include a description of the process for developing the IEP, a discussion of the concept of parent participation as a requisite factor in the provision of an appropriate education for a child with a disability, and a discussion of the specific changes in the IEP that occurred with the reauthorization in 2004 and their impact on parents, children, and practitioners in the field.

HISTORICAL AND RESEARCH BASES FOR THE IEP

According to Duchnowski and Kutash (1997), a significant issue that continues in the field of special education research is that:

> the link between research and practice in this field has been and continues to be weak (Malouf & Schiller, 1995). Research knowledge has had only a minor effect on education practice even when there has been a significant body of research about important problems of interest to practitioners and policymakers (Huberman, 1990; Shavelson, 1988). (p. 237)

This lack of alignment of research and practice is very apparent when reviewing the research related to IEPs. According to Meyen (1981), "neither individualized instruction nor the development of instructional plans for specific students is new" (p. 44). Educators have consistently attempted to identify the most appropriate means by which to address the needs of students who have not been successful in the heterogeneous general education classroom.

One early method was the removal of students from the general education classroom to a situation where the individual needs of the student could be addressed. During the 1960s, concerns were raised that this method for providing an education was not only ineffective but was actually detrimental to the future of the child (Dunn, 1968; Paul, Berger, Osnes, Martinez, & Morse, 1997). Skrtic, Harris, and Shriner (2005) stated that "a skills-based, 'back-to-basics' instructional approach" (p. 8) was implemented as the dominant education during the 1970s and 1980s in an effort to address the concerns that emerged in the 1960s. This instructional approach used a direct or explicit method of instruction that was often regimented through the use of programmed text materials in either paper or computer-assisted format or through the use of rigid scripts for teachers to follow.

Critics of this form of instruction found that it was difficult to identify student achievement when the results were based on these programs. Critics cited conflicting definitions of what constitutes individualized instruction and the most appropriate method to indicate student success as the cause. Therefore, research results on the use of individualized instruction programs, also known as individualized learning programs, have been mixed. It has been noted that only minor differences in achievement have resulted from this type of programming (Bangert, Kulik, & Kulik, 1983; Horak, 1981), that teachers have difficulty implementing these programs effectively in a heterogeneous classroom (Arlin, 1982; Carlson, 1982; Everhart, 1983), that it is difficult to ascertain which students will be successful with this type of program (Good & Stipek, 1983), that this type of programming results in student boredom and an emphasis on lower order as opposed to higher order thinking skills (Jackson, 1985), and that this type of instruction does not foster generalization (Heshusius, 1995). According to Good and Brophy (2003), these concerns may be ameliorated by an increased use of computerized instruction in conjunction with a significant expansion in the availability of complex computer programs that "provide opportunities for higher-level problem solving, work with complex databases, or simulation activities" (pp. 322–323).

In the research on effective teaching, it was noted that many of the elements recommended in the effective teaching research were incorporated into individualized instructional programs such as Wang's (1981) Adaptive Learning Environments Model; Good, Grouws, and Ebmeier's (1983) Active Mathematics Teaching; and Carnine, Granzen, and Becker's (1988) Direct Instruction model. According to Kavale (1990), "These programs possess considerable specificity, and . . . possess empirical evidence about their impact on student achievement" (p. 51).

The research, though, did not seem to focus on the efficacy of individualizing the instruction for students who were not successful in the general education classroom, as individualization of instruction was understood to be the most appropriate method for students with special needs to be effective. Thus, research focused more on identification of the method by which this individualization should occur. Research on, and the implementation of, individualized programming continued throughout the subsequent decades (Wang, Reynolds, & Walberg, 1990).

It was during this controversial time that the focus on individual civil rights was incorporated into the legislation known as the Education for All Handicapped Children Act of 1975 (EHA). Based on information supplied through congressional hearings Congress found that a significant number of children with disabilities had either been excluded from receiving an education based on their disability or not been receiving appropriate educational services. The major focus of this legislation was to address these issues and "to ensure that all children with disabilities have available to them a free appropriate public education that emphasizes special education and related services designed to meet their unique needs" (Wright & Wright, 2007). The inclusion of an individualized plan for each child was the means selected to fulfill this promise.

DEVELOPMENT OF THE IEP

The IEP is the collaborative result of a group of individuals called the team. The IDEA has always specified the individuals who must be included as members of the team who develop or change the individualized program of a student with a disability. The IEP team includes the parents of the student with a disability. The parents are essential to the planning process and must be included whenever an IEP is to be developed and/or changed. In lieu of the parent, the guardian, foster parent, or appointed surrogate parent must be available to advocate for the child. Other individuals who are to be included on the team are at least one regular education teacher; at least one special education teacher or special service provider; a representative of the local education agency (LEA) who is qualified to provide or supervise the instruction of individuals with disabilities, is knowledgeable about the general education curriculum, and is knowledgeable of the resources available in the local district; a person who is able to interpret the assessment results and their implications; the student when appropriate; and any other individuals who may provide information that is valuable to the program development process (IDEIA, 20 U.S.C. 1414[d][1][B]). The original requisite membership on this team was not changed in the latest reauthorization, although some revisions in wording were included to clarify the description of the members of the IEP team.

According to IDEIA 2006 federal regulations, two additional categories of membership on the IEP team should be included. The first are the transition services participants who must be included when transition concerns are being addressed (IDEIA Regulations, 34 C.F.R. 300.321). For those students who are transitioning from Part C programs, a Part C representative may be included as a member of the team to facilitate the student's smooth transition from preschool to elementary school (IDEIA Regulations, 34 C.F.R. 300.321[f]; Mandlawitz, 2007). According to Turnbull, Huerta, and Stowe (2006), the inclusion of this diverse membership on the IEP team "assures a more robust and holistic evaluation and decision-making processes geared toward 'benefit' in the general curriculum" (p. 47).

Attendance at the IEP meetings had been required for all members of the IEP team. This often caused problems because of scheduling issues with the number of people who were included on the team. A significant change was made to this requirement in the 2004 legislation. According to

IDEIA, with the agreement of the parents of the student with a disability and the school district, an IEP member can be excused from all or part of the meeting if his/her area of expertise is not included on the agenda for that meeting (IDEIA, 20 U.S.C. 1414[d][1][C][i]); IDEIA Regulations, 34 C.F.R. 300.321[a][2]. In addition, if the team member's area of expertise is to be addressed, it is still possible for that individual to be excused from the meeting if the parents and the school district agree in writing and the individual submits a written report of his/her input (IDEIA, 20 U.S.C. 1414[d][1][C][ii]); IDEIA Regulations, 34 C.F.R. 300.321[3] According to Turnbull, Huerta, and Stowe (2006), this provision was included as part of a paperwork reduction plan and in response to concerns of LEAs about the time and cost required for school district personnel to attend numerous meetings.

In addition, when it is difficult to convene all members of the IEP team, IDEIA allows for the use of other methods in lieu of face-to-face meetings (Bartlett, Etscheidt, & Weisenstein, 2007). These other methods include telephone conference calls and videoconferencing and are included as a means to encourage team input and "make the IEP planning process more flexible and convenient for parents and school personnel" (Yell, 2006, p. 280).

In the previous version of IDEA, any changes to the IEP were to be made only when the IEP team had been convened. The 2004 reauthorization of IDEIA changed this requirement. After the annual IEP meeting, changes to the program may be made without the convening of a meeting if the parents and the school district agree to the amendment or modification of the program (Council for Exceptional Children, 2005).

Because parental attendance is so important to the IEP meeting, IDEIA has set forth requirements for notifying the parents concerning IEP meetings and potential changes. The legal requirements for the provision of notice to the parents concerning meetings related to program development for their child with a disability vary by state and district. The legislation requires that notices to the parents be provided in a language that is understandable to the general public. In addition the notice must be provided in the parent's native language or other mode of communication. Any notice of a planned meeting must be provided to the parents in a timely manner, that is, early enough that they can attend (IDEIA Regulations, 34 C.F.R. 300.503). Meeting time and location have always been a concern of both parents and other attendees. Now the legislation indicates that meetings must be scheduled at mutually agreed upon times and places. In addition, the notice must include the purpose of the proposed meeting, the suggested time, the location of the meeting, and a list of those who will participate (IDEIA Regulations, 34 C.F.R. 300.322[a][1]).

GUIDELINES GOVERNING PARENTAL PARTICIPATION

Parental participation in the special education process is a fundamental component of IDEIA. Throughout the history of the IDEA legislation parental participation has been included. Murdick, Gartin, and Crabtree (2007) state that parental participation is "pivotal in the provision of an appropriate education" (p. 27). This principle remains unchanged in the 2004 reauthorization.

The term *parent* has been expanded in the latest reauthorization. Under IDEIA the definition now includes "a biological or adoptive parent of a child, a guardian, a surrogate parent(s) who has been appointed by the LEA, and anyone acting in the place of a parent such as a relative or anyone with whom the child lives" (IDEIA Regulations, 34 C.F.R. 300.30). According to Murdick, Gartin, and Crabtree (2007), IDEIA 2004 expands the definition and rights of "the persons who know the child best" and makes them "full and equal partners with the school" (p. 175).

As participating members of the IEP team, parents have been given the right to agree or disagree with the IEP that has been designed for their child. According to IDEIA:

> an agency that is responsible for making a free appropriate public education available to a child with a disability . . . shall seek to obtain informed consent from the parent of such child before providing special education and related services to the child. (IDEIA, 20 U.S.C. 1414[a][1][D])

If the parents do not consent to the services identified in the IEP for their child, the LEA is not to provide the special education and related services. In such a situation the LEA shall not be considered in violation of the provision of FAPE for the student as long as the LEA has made reasonable efforts to obtain parental consent (Mandlawitz, 2006; Mandlawitz, 2007). According to Turnbull, Huerta, and Stowe (2006):

> IDEA codifies these general rights and at the same time seeks to create, through parental consent, a means whereby parents and educators will be partners with each other and share the decision-making that affects a child's education. (p. 73)

COMPONENTS OF THE IEP SPECIFYING THE 2004 CHANGES

The IEP is a written plan specifying the educational program and related services for each student who is identified as having a disability and is eligible for special education. It is a document that has been developed, reviewed, and revised in accordance with the legal guidelines provided by IDEIA and its regulations and thus provides a blueprint to assist the student in achieving educational success. In addition, the required components of an appropriate IEP were listed in the original authorization of the IDEA legislation. Each of the presently required components will be briefly addressed and any changes will be noted (see Table 14.1 for a list of required components).

Present Level of Academic Achievement and Functional Performance

The components of the IEP are listed in linear order. The first component to be addressed was previously known as the present level of educational performance (PLEP). In an IEP, this section is a summary of the present performance of the student as noted by current evaluations. IDEIA 2004 expanded the focus of this component and renamed it the present level of academic achievement and functional performance (PLAA/FP). The term *academic achievement* generally refers to the student's performance in the typical academic areas of reading, language arts, math, science, and history, while the *level of functional performance* refers to the student's skills or activities that are not considered academic but relate to the student's

TABLE 14.1   Components of the Individualized Education Program (IEP)

Demographic Information

Dates

IEP Team Membership

Present Level of Academic Achievement and Functional Performance (PLAA/FP)

Annual Goals

Special Education and Related Services

Participation in General Education

Participation in State- and District-Wide Assessment

Transition Services

Special Factors

> Behavior, Limited English Proficiency, Visual Impairments, Communication Needs, Assistive Technology Devices and Services

Extended School Year Services

Placement Decision

performances in the routine activities of everyday living. This statement also must include a description of how the disability affects the student's involvement and progress in the general education curriculum, or for preschool children, a description of how the disability affects the child's participation in appropriate activities. If the student has been identified as one who will need to take alternate assessments that are aligned to alternate achievement standards, a description of benchmarks or short-term objectives must also be included in the PLAA/FP (IDEIA, 20 U.S.C. 1414[d][1][A]). As Yell (2006) states, the "PLAAFP is the starting point from which teams develop the IEP and measure its success" (p. 287).

Annual Goals

From the information provided in the PLAA/FP, measurable annual goals, both academic and functional, are to be written so as to provide a projection of the student's progress in the general education curriculum by the end of the academic year. Previously, a requirement was included that benchmarks or major milestones or intermediate short-term objectives be written to accompany the annual goals, but these components are no longer required. The removal of these additional components was a result of the move to reduce required paperwork in the IEP process (Gartin & Murdick, 2005).

The 1997 IDEA required that parents receive reports on their child's progress toward the yearly goals as often as the parents of other children did. This requirement was removed from the legislation in 2004 and replaced with a generic statement that the IEP must include a description of the manner in which the student's annual goals will be measured and a schedule of when periodic reports will be provided to the parents. According to Huefner (2006), this change may be "another way in which Congress intended to reduce paperwork burdens on LEAs" (p. 183).

Special Education and Related Services

Following the development of annual goals, the IEP must include a statement of "special education and related services, the supplementary aids and services and the program modifications or supports" (IDEIA Regulations, 34 C.F.R. 300.34, 300.39[a]). These services must provide a benefit to the child and support the effectiveness of the educational program that is delineated in the IEP. Related services do not stand alone but are a necessary requirement that will support the student and allow for the student to benefit from the IEP that has been developed (Murdick, Gartin, & Crabtree, 2007). Although the IDEIA and its regulations provide a list of the types of services that would be considered as related services, this is not a finite list (IDEIA, 20 U.S.C. 1492[26]; IDEIA Regulations, 34 C.F.R. 300.34[a] & [b]). According to Huefner (2006), these services and supports are those that:

> are needed to help the child (a) achieve his or her annual goals, (b) make progress in the general curriculum, (c) participate in extracurricular and other nonacademic activities, and (d) participate with children without disabilities, as well as children with disabilities, in all these activities. (p. 183)

The IDEIA reauthorization added an additional requirement to this section. Any of the aforementioned services must be "based on peer-reviewed research to the extent practicable" (IDEIA, 20 U.S.C. 1414[d][a][A][i][IV]). Peer-reviewed research generally refers to that research that has been reviewed by qualified reviewers who are knowledgeable and non-biased, thus providing information concerning the effectiveness of the services and supports to those in the field. A concern has arisen that the use of methods not based on peer-reviewed research might be construed as a denial of FAPE. Therefore, it is essential that the selection of services and methods be research driven and that team members be conveyers of current research to the IEP meeting(s).

Participation in General Education

An underlying assumption of IDEIA is that students with disabilities should be participating in general education settings with non-disabled students as often as possible. Previously, the requirement was that the IEP include a section that addressed the amount of time the student with a disability was to spend in general education settings. In the 2004 reauthorization the focus changed to require a decision concerning the amount of time that the student will *not* participate in general education classes with students who are not disabled. This change focuses on the underlying belief that the preferred placement for *all* children is the general education classroom and that any removal from that placement will need to be justified.

In conjunction with this decision, a statement is to be included in the IEP that pinpoints the specific placement on the continuum of alternative placements (CAP) for the delivery of services to the student with a disability. Whichever placement is selected it is required that it be the least restrictive environment for that student. This placement decision must also include a written justification for the student's removal from a less restrictive environment. At this point in the IEP, modifications or accommodations that might be needed to support the student in the general education classroom should be included. This principle of least restrictive environment was set forth in the original IDEA in 1974. Regulations have been modified in some reauthorizations, but there were no changes in this section with the 2004 reauthorization.

Participation in State- and District-Wide Assessments

Since the advent of state- and district-wide assessments required by the No Child Left Behind Act (NCLB) of 2001, a section in the IEP has been added to address the testing requirement. Closely aligned with the decision concerning participation in general education is the decision on whether the student with a disability should be included in state- and district-wide assessments. The assumption is that students, unless otherwise stated, will participate with their peers in the regular assessments used by the school district including those required by their specific state. Thus, the IEP is to include "a statement of any individual appropriate accommodations that are necessary to measure the academic achievement and functional performance of the child on State and districtwide assessments" (IDEIA Regulations, 34 C.F.R. 300.320 [a][6][i]). With the 2004 reauthorization, the previous term "modifications" was replaced by the words "individual appropriate accommodations." The change now aligns the educational language with language in the Rehabilitation Act of 1973 that guarantees access for all persons with disabilities including the subgroup of persons eligible for special education.

If a student is deemed unable to participate in the regular assessments, then the IEP must now include a statement of why this is so. In addition, the team must identify a particular alternate assessment that would be appropriate for assessing the academic achievement and functional performance of that student. This requirement assures that all students, even those with a disability, will be assessed on their progress toward meeting state standards.

Transition Services

For those students with disabilities who are entering middle and secondary educational settings, an important facet of the educational program is the plan for their transition out of school into the community setting. Previously IDEA stated that the identification of transition service needs should begin when the student is age 14. The transition plan was then to be developed for the student no later than age 16 and was to include a statement of interagency responsibilities. The 2004 reauthorization removed the requirements pertaining to students at age 14 and stated that the transition plan should be developed "beginning not later than the first IEP to be in effect when the child is 16, and updated annually" (IDEIA,

20 U.S.C. 1414[d][VIII]). The reference to "interagency responsibilities" was also removed.

Additionally, transition plan components were outlined in the new authorization in 2004. This stated that the transition plan was to include:

1. appropriate measurable postsecondary goals based upon age-appropriate transition assessments related to training, education, employment, and, where appropriate, independent living skills;
2. the transition services (including courses of study) needed to assist the child in reaching those goals. (IDEIA, 20 U.S.C. 1414[d][VIII][aa] & [bb])

Special Factors

When developing the IEP, the team is charged with considering the strengths of the student, the concerns of the parents for their child's education, the results of the most recent as well as past evaluations, and the academic, developmental, and functional needs of the student. All must be considered in order to assure that an appropriate individualized program is developed. Along with these components, the IEP team must consider five special factors related to the behavior of the student, the student's level of English proficiency, the needs of the student who is blind or visually impaired, the needs of the student who has communication impairment, and the student's need for assistive technology devices and services (Gartin & Murdick, 2005; Wright & Wright, 2007).

Behavior

When a student has identified behavioral issues related to the disability, the IEP team must first decide whether the student's behavior impedes his/her learning or the learning of others. If it does, then a functional analysis of behavior is to be conducted. A functional analysis of behavior is a method by which information is gathered about the behavior of an individual including the topography or specific parameters of the behavior, and the events and situations that may influence the occurrence or continuation of the behavior. From this information a hypothesis of the function the behavior serves for the individual is proposed. This functional statement provides the basis for the development of the required behavior intervention plan (BIP) by the IEP team. (See chapter 15 for a more extensive treatment of this topic.) This behavioral program is to address the student's behavioral issues through the use of positive behavioral interventions and supports, and other strategies (IDEIA, 24 U.S.C. 1414[3][B][i]; IDEIA Regulations, 34 C.F.R. 300.324[a][2][(i)]). Positive behavioral interventions and supports is a research-based application of a behavioral-based systems approach to designing environments and services that support the desired behaviors of the persons involved. The only changes in this section were the deletion of the parenthetical "(when appropriate)." According to Turnbull, Huerta, and Stowe (2006), deleting the phrase "when appropriate" not only removes a redundant qualifier but "creates a presumption in favor of using positive behavioral support interventions, strategies, and supports" (p. 49) while still allowing the team the discretion to select other strategies and interventions that may be appropriate.

Students With Limited English Proficiency

With the increasing presence of students with limited English proficiency in our schools, it is imperative that the IEP team evaluate the impact that the student's level of language ability may have on his/her educational success. (See chapter 10 for a more extensive treatment of this topic.) Therefore, IDEIA states that the team must "consider the language needs of the child as such needs relate to the child's IEP" [IDEIA, 24 U.S.C. 1414[3][B][ii]; IDEIA Regulations, 34 C.F.R. 300.324[a][2][ii]). No changes were made related to this factor.

Students With Vision Impairments

In the case of a student who is blind or has vision impairments, the IEP team must consider the student's need for instruction in Braille. This consideration must be based on an "evaluation of the child's reading and writing skills, needs, and appropriate reading and writing media (including an evaluation of the child's future needs for instruction in Braille or the use of Braille)" (IDEIA, 24 U.S.C. 1414[3][B][iii]; IDEIA Regulations, 34 C.F.R. 300.324[a][2][iii]) and must result in a statement of whether or not instruction in Braille or the use of Braille is appropriate for this student. No changes were made to this requirement.

Students With Communication Needs

Students who have communication needs including students who are deaf or hard of hearing require that the IEP team consider their "language and communication needs, opportunities for direct communications with peers and professional personnel in the child's language and communication mode, academic level, and full range of needs, including opportunities for direct instruction in the child's language and communication mode" (IDEIA, 24 U.S.C. 1414[3][B][iv]; IDEIA Regulations, 34 C.F.R. 300.324[a][2][iv]). This factor also had no changes made in the 2004 reauthorization.

Assistive Technology Devices and Services

The final special factor for consideration is the identification of whether the student requires assistive technology devices and services as a supplement to the identified special education and related services [IDEIA, 24 U.S.C. 1414[3][B][v]; IDEIA Regulations, 34 C.F.R. 300.324[a][2][v]). IDEIA defines assistive technology devices "as any item, piece of equipment, or product system . . . that is used to increase, maintain, or improve functional capabilities of a child with a disability" (IDEIA, 20 U.S.C. 1401[1][A]). In addition, IDEIA defines assistive technology service as "any service that directly assists a child with a disability in the selection, acquisition, or use of an assistive technology device" (IDEIA, 20 U.S.C. 1401[2]). No changes were made to this requirement in the 2004 reauthorization.

EXTENDED SCHOOL YEAR

The length of a typical school year is 180 days. Students with disabilities who encounter long absences from educational settings often have difficulty with the retention of content presented in their educational program. That is, they have difficulty retaining this information at the performance level achieved prior to an absence and may not recoup this learning in a timely manner at the beginning of the subsequent school year. Thus, they may continue to regress academically. The issues of retention and recoupment when paired with the 180-day school year limit have been found by the courts to result in a violation of FAPE for students with disabilities (*Armstrong v. Kline*, 1979/1980/1981; *Battle v. Commonwealth*, 1980/ 1981; *GARC v. McDaniel*, 1983/1984). In order for a student's special education program to meet the standards of FAPE, it is mandated that the IEP team consider the student's needs for a program that is longer than the typical 180-day school year. This requirement is known as extended school year (ESY) services and is defined as "special education and related services that are provided to a child with a disability beyond the normal school year of the public agency, in accordance with the child's IEP, and at no cost to the parents of the child" (IDEIA Regulations, 34 C.F.R. 300.106[b]). ESY services must be considered by the team and "must be provided only if a child's IEP Team determines, on an individual basis . . . that the services are necessary for the provision of FAPE to the child" (IDEIA Regulations, 34 C.F.R. 300.106[a][2]). No changes were made to this remedy for those students who regress or experience significant delays in their progress when they are out of school for a specified length of time, such as a summer break (Turnbull, Huerta, & Stowe, 2006).

PLACEMENT DECISION

Basing their decision on the information compiled in each of the previous components of the IEP (PLAA/FP, annual goals, statement of special education and related services, supplementary aids and services, program modifications and supports, participation in general education, participation in state- and district-wide assessments, transition services, and special factors), the IEP team must identify the most appropriate placement for the provision of the special education and related services for the student with a disability. The preferred placement for students is, of course, the least restrictive environment. In other words, students with disabilities are to be educated with students who are not disabled whenever possible, to be placed in educational placements based on their educational needs with that placement as close to the student's home as possible, to be provided access to nonacademic and extracurricular activities, and to be provided with a continuum of placement options with increasing levels of educational supports (Murdick, Gartin, & Crabtree, 2007). It is important to remember that "the decision about placement cannot be made until after the IEP team, which includes the parent, reaches consensus about the child's needs, program, and goals" (Wrightslaw, 2007, p. 3). No changes in the provisions in this section were made in the IDEIA 2004 reauthorization.

ADDITIONAL CHANGES IMPACTING THE IEP

Two additional changes that were made in the IDEIA relating to IEPs have been a cause of much discussion and concern. One is related to IEPs for transfer students and the other is the initiation of multiyear IEPs.

IEPs of Transfer Students

In the past, school districts have questioned the acceptance of IEPs from other districts within the same state and from districts from another state. In lieu of accepting these IEPs, the new district would perform new evaluations, hold new IEP meetings, and construct new IEPs. Although these actions were based on concerns that curricular standards from other districts might not correspond with those of the present district, the result was often a delay in the provision of appropriate educational services for those children.

Two significant provisions were added in 2004 to assist in clarifying this issue. The first addresses the issue of a student with a disability and a current IEP who transfers within the same state and enrolls in that school district within the same school year. In this situation, the district:

> must provide FAPE to the child (including services comparable to those described in the child's IEP from the previous public agency), until the new public agency either—
>
> (1) Adopts the child's IEP from the previous public agency; or
> (2) Develops, adopts, and implements a new IEP that meets the applicable requirements. (IDEIA Regulations, 34 C.F.R. 300.323[e])

Secondly, if the student with a disability and a current IEP is transferring from state to state, then the new district in consultation with the parents:

> must provide the child with FAPE (including services comparable to those described in the child's IEP from the previous public agency), until the new public agency—
>
> (1) Conducts an evaluation . . . (if determined to be necessary by the new public agency); and
> (2) Develops, adopts, and implements a new IEP, if appropriate, that meets the applicable requirements. (IDEIA Regulations, 34 C.F.R. 300.323[f])

To facilitate the process of providing the student with a disability an appropriate education in the new district, the new district must take prompt action to obtain the student's records including copies of the IEP and any other relevant documentation, and the former district must respond in a prompt manner to this request (IDEIA Regulations, 34 C.F.R. 300.323[g]). The additions of these components to this process were included to expedite the provision of appropriate services to the student with a disability.

Multiyear IEPs

A more controversial addition was the inclusion of a pilot project wherein school districts could develop so-called multiyear IEPs. This federal pilot project allowed up to 15 states to propose procedures to develop the "opportunity for long-term planning by offering the option of developing a comprehensive multi-year IEP, not to exceed 3 years, that is designed to coincide with the natural transition points for the child" (IDEIA, 24 U.S.C. 1414[5][A]). This additional component includes a section that assures that parents will not be required to agree to the use of a multiyear IEP for their child, that even if they do agree they may opt out at any time during the 3-year time span, and that a procedure for reviewing the IEP, both at the natural transition points and annually, will be developed. This new component is considered to be another method to reduce paperwork (Gartin & Murdick, 2005). Mandlawitz (2007) notes that "district and parents will most likely find that a multi-year IEP is more appropriate for children with mild to moderate disabilities" (p. 92). Those who oppose this option are concerned that those students who participate in this pilot program will not have an appropriate IEP developed because of the difficulty in projecting achievement rates for a period longer than 1 year.

PROCEDURAL SAFEGUARDS

The IDEIA of 2004 is based on the belief that *all* children with disabilities should be provided with a FAPE. In conjunction with this is the belief that parents are essential partners with the schools in the development and provision of educational programs in which students with disabilities can be successful. The IEP is the method by which the program is designed for each specific child as well as the document prepared to guide the provision of the educational program.

In order to assure that both parents and students are treated fairly in this process, a set of procedures, known as due process procedures or procedural safeguards, are included in the legislation that codifies the due process rights of parents and/or guardians of children with disabilities (IDEIA, 20 U.S.C. 1415). According to Wright and Wright (2007), these procedural safeguards include "the right to participate in all meetings, to examine all educational records, and to obtain an independent educational evaluation (IEE) of the child" (p. 107). In addition, parents are guaranteed the right to written notice whenever the school proposes to initiate a change, or refuses to change the identification, evaluation, or placement of their child (IDEIA, 20 U.S.C. 1415[c]).

DISPUTE RESOLUTION

These rights are meaningless, though, unless the aggrieved party has a forum in which to bring forth any complaints or concerns they might have. The belief that it is the right of any citizen to protest decisions that impact on him or his children is an underpinning of the U.S. Constitution (Murdick, Gartin, & Crabtree, 2007). Thus, the original IDEA legislation (P.L. 94–142) and subsequent reauthorizations include a section that not only delineates the specific due process rights of parents and children but also includes a process by which parents might protest decisions, known as the due process hearing. According to Huefner (2006), these procedural safeguards "are meant to place parents on something of an equal footing with school districts" (p. 206).

Mediation

Mediation is the first procedural option parents and schools have to come together to resolve differences concerning the education of the student with a disability. Mediation, an impartial system that allows disputing parties to meet with an impartial third party to discuss their issues and concerns, was added to the legislation in the 1997 reauthorization of IDEA. The goal of a mediation meeting is to resolve the dispute and develop an agreement instead of proceeding straight to the more adversarial due process hearing. Although it is mandated that the mediation option be provided to parents and they be encouraged to avail themselves of it, they may not be forced to participate in this option.

No changes were made to the procedures in the 2004 reauthorization except to provide for the use of these procedures prior to the filing of a request for due process instead of afterward (Council for Exceptional Children, 2005). But a statement was added that if the dispute is resolved by the mediation, then a written agreement that is legally binding and enforceable in state or federal district court must be signed by the parents and an authorized representative of the LEA (IDEIA, 20 U.S.C. 1415[e][F]). Although the discussions that occur during the mediation session are to be confidential, the requirement that the parties sign a confidentiality pledge was removed (Mandlawitz, 2007).

Mediation is seen as an option for parents and school personnel to address issues and reach consensus without a due process hearing, which can be both an emotionally and financially exhausting experience. According to Murdick, Gartin, and Crabtree (2007), some professionals are concerned that mediation may not be helpful and, in fact, "will neither reduce the adversarial relationship of the parties, nor reduce the number of due process hearings. Instead, it may prolong the timeline for resolution of the disputed issues" (p. 224).

Resolution Process

With IDEIA, an additional requirement was added to the due process complaint procedures (Huefner, 2006). Within 15 days of a parent filing a due process complaint, the school must call a resolution meeting of the parents and other members of the IEP team to allow the parents the opportunity to discuss their complaint, to explain the facts that led to the filing of their complaint, and to provide the LEA with the opportunity to resolve the dispute prior to the due process hearing. If no resolution can be found, then the due process hearing continues. If resolution can occur, then the parents and the school are to sign a legally binding agreement that is enforceable in state or federal district court (IDEIA, 20 U.S.C. 1415[f][1][B][iii]; IDEIA

Regulations, 34 C.F.R. 300.510[d]). According to Mandlawitz (2007) and Richards and Martin (2005), this additional step is another attempt to provide the parents and school with non-adversarial options for resolving disputes. There are concerns with this step, as with the mediation step, that it may only delay the process and increase the hostility between the parents and school personnel instead of reducing it.

Due Process Hearing

According to IDEIA, a due process hearing is a formal meeting between the parents and the school district personnel wherein disputed issues can be resolved by an impartial third party, known as the hearing officer or panel of hearing officers. The hearing officer(s) hear both sides of the dispute, examine the issues, and give a legally binding decision. According to Yell (2006), "Congress deliberately chose an adversarial system for resolving disputes" (p. 346) believing that this would put both parties on an equal footing.

No changes were made in the procedures for a due process hearing. New language was included, though, that disallowed the inclusion of issues in the due process hearing that had not been previously stated. New language was also added that clarified the substantive and procedural requirements that apply to a hearing officer's decision (CEC, 2005). Clarification was also added concerning the timeline for reaching a final decision in a hearing such that:

> the public agency must ensure that not later than 45 days after the expiration of the 30 day period . . .
>
> (1) A final decision is reached in the hearing; and
> (2) A copy of the decision is mailed to each of the parties. (IDEIA Regulations, 34 C.F.R. 300.515[a])

Another change included in the IDEIA regulations is the statement clarifying that both parties may file complaints. Previously school districts were unsure whether they, as well as the parents, had the right to call for due process. Also included was a statute of limitations on the filing of complaints. This limitation was added to reduce the chances that the length of time between the issue and the filing of a complaint would result in a resolution occurring in a timely manner (IDEIA Regulations, 34 C.F.R. 300.511[e]; Mandlawitz, 2007).

Expedited Due Process Hearing

With the inclusion of new discipline policies in the 1997 reauthorization of IDEA, an additional form of the due process hearing was introduced.

This hearing, known as the expedited due process hearing, was included to facilitate decisions concerning discipline procedures and the impact they might have on a child with a disability. The expedited due process hearing occurs when a complaint arises from a disagreement related to the placement of a child in an interim alternative educational setting (IAES). Placement in an IAES is a result of a behavioral incident, or a disagreement over the determination that the child's behavior is not a manifestation of his/her disability (IDEIA, 20 U.S.C. 1415[i][2]; IDEIA Regulations, 34 C.F.R. 300.514[d]). The only change made to this section in the IDEIA was to reduce the time frame for the hearing and subsequent determination from 45 to 30 days (CEC, 2005).

Appeal of Due Process Hearing Decisions

Either party in a due process hearing may appeal the decision of the hearing officer directly to the state education agency (SEA). The SEA must conduct an impartial review of the findings and provide a decision within 30 days of the appeal (IDEIA Regulations, 34 C.F.R. 300.514[b]; 300.515[b]). No changes were made to this provision.

Civil Action

Either parents or LEAs may appeal the due process hearing decision "in any State court of competent jurisdiction or in a district court of the United States without regard to the amount in controversy" (IDEIA Regulations, 34 C.F.R. 300.516[a]). The one caveat to this appeal is that the parties must exhaust all other procedures prior to filing at this level. This option remains the same.

According to Turnbull, Huerta, and Snow (2006), the 2004 IDEIA reauthorization expands the means by which parents can resolve their differences with the schools in a more constructive manner through the options of mediation and mandatory resolution sessions. This codified set of procedures for resolving complaints continues to be an integral part of the legislation.

SUMMARY

The original belief on which the Education for All Handicapped Children Act, now IDEIA, was designed continues to be supported by the latest reauthorization. This belief is the "presumption that students with disabilities will be granted access to and educated in the general education curriculum and will participate in other general education activities"

(Turnbull, Huerta, & Stowe, 2006, p. 66). The changes in the legislation since its initial authorization in 1975 have been based on support for, and clarification of, this principle. This latest reauthorization and its accompanying regulations continue this progression toward full educational opportunity for *all* students, with or without disabilities.

While the entirety of the IEP has stood the test of time, the changes to the individual sections need to be examined in terms of effectiveness and efficacy. For example, the following questions can be asked about significant changes that were made in the IDEIA 2004 reauthorization.

1. At what age is it most effective to design an individualized transition plan? The age for the inclusion of transition services in the IEP has moved from 16 to 14 and now back to 16. Linkage to adult services was added in 1997 and then omitted in 2004.

2. Is it essential that all members of the team be present or can some be allowed to participate only by providing a paper document? And are alternative methods of participation truly addressing the implementation of team participatory decision making? Attendance of all team members at the IEP meeting was initially seen as essential, but now it is considered to be preferable but the requirement of attendance can be met by the provision of alternative methods of participation.

3. Should all students participate in state- and district-wide assessments? Which students can be provided with alternative forms of assessment and what are the criteria for selection of these assessments? The IEP must now include a statement of why the student is unable to participate in the assessment, the name of the specific alternative assessment, and a statement of why this particular assessment is appropriate.

4. Will a 3-year IEP meet the individualized needs of children with disabilities? Throughout the history of IDEA, the concept of the IEP is that of a document that provides a plan for the educational program for 1 academic year. A 3-year IEP is being considered as an option for some students.

These are a few of the areas that need to be examined through research so that future revisions to the IEP and its components become evidence-based.

In this chapter, the research base for utilizing individualized instruction as the focal point in special education legislation was discussed. In addition, a description of the process for developing the IEP and a discussion of the concept of parent participation as a requisite factor in the provision of an appropriate education for a child with a disability was provided. Finally, a discussion of the specific changes in the IEP that occurred with the reauthorization in 2004 and their impact on parents, children, and practitioners in the field was presented. Although the requirement of individualized programming for students with disabilities has been fraught with controversy, it is an established facet of the legislation. And as Yell (2006) states:

> Despite their assessment of the problems with IEPs in the schools today, Bateman and Linden strongly believe that "a well-designed IEP can change a child's schooling experience from one of repeated failure, loss of self esteem, and limited options to one of achievement, directions, and productivity" (p. 2). If IEPs are to become such a tool, special educators must understand how to develop an IEP that is educationally meaningful and legally correct. (p. 275)

REFERENCES

Arlin, M. N. (1982). Teacher responses to student time differences in mastery learning. *American Journal of Education, 90,* 334–352.

Armstrong v. Kline, 476 F. Supp. 583 (E.D. Pa. 1979), *modified and remanded sub nom.,* Battle v. Commonwealth of Pennsylvania, 629 F.2d 259 (3rd Cir. 1980), *on remand,* 513 F. Supp. 425 (E.D. Pa. 1980), *cert denied sub nom,* Scanlon v. Battle, 101 S.Ct. 3123 (1981).

Bangert, R. L., Kulik, J. A., & Kulik, C. C. (1983). Individualized systems of instruction in secondary schools. *Review of Educational Research, 53,* 13–158.

Bartlett, L. D., Etscheidt, S., & Weisenstein, G. R. (2007). *Special education law and practice in public schools* (2nd ed.). Upper Saddle River, NJ: Pearson/Merrill Prentice Hall.

Battle v. Commonwealth of Pennsylvania, 629 F.2d 259 (3rd Cir. 1980), *on remand,* 513 F. Supp. 425 (E.D. Pa. 1980), *cert denied sub nom,* Scanlon v. Battle, 101 S.Ct. 3123 (1981).

Carlson, D. (1982). "Updating" individualism and the work ethic: Corporate logic in the classroom. *Curriculum Inquiry, 12,* 125–160.

Carnine, D., Granzen, A., & Becker, W. (1988). Direct instruction. In J. Braden, J. Zins, & M. Curtis (Eds.), *Alternate educational delivery systems: Enhancing instructional options for all students* (pp. 327–349). Washington, DC: National Association for School Psychologists.

Council for Exceptional Children (CEC). (2005). *What's new in the new IDEA 2004? Frequently asked questions and answers.* Arlington, VA: Author.

Duchnowski, A. J., & Kutash, K. (1997). Future research in special education: A systems perspective. In J. L. Paul, M. Churton, H. Rosselli-Kostoryz, W. C. Morse, K. Marfo, C. Lavely, et al. (Eds.), *Foundations of special education: Basic knowledge informing research and practice in special education* (pp. 236–246). Pacific Grove, CA: Brooks/Cole.

Dunn, L. M. (1968). Special education for the mentally retarded—Is much of it justifiable? *Exceptional Children, 35,* 5–22.

Everhart, R. B. (1983). *Reading, writing, and resistance: Adolescence and labor in a junior high school.* Boston: Routledge and Kegan Paul.

Gartin, B.C., & Murdick, N.L. (2005). IDEA 2004: The IEP. *Remedial and Special Education, 26*(6), 327–331.

Georgia Association for Retarded Citizens (GARC) v. McDaniel, 716 F.2d 1565 (1983), *cert granted,* 469 U.S. 1228, 105 S.Ct. 1228 (1983), 740 F.2d 902 (1984), *vacated,* 468 U.S. 1213 (1984).

Good, T., Grouws, D., & Ebmeier, H. (1983). *Active mathematics teaching.* New York: Longman.

Good, T., & Stipek, D. (1983). Individual difference in the classroom: A psychological perspective. In G. Fenstermacher & J. Goodlad (Eds.), *Individual differences and the common curriculum* (82nd yearbook of the National Society for the Study of Education, Part I). Chicago: University of Chicago Press.

Good, T.L., & Brophy, J.E. (2003). *Looking in classrooms* (9th ed.). Boston: Allyn and Bacon.

Halderman v. Pennhurst, 612 F.2d 84, 124–129 (3rd Cir. 1979).

Heshusius, L. (1995). Holism and special education: There is no substitute for real life purposes and processes. In T.M. Skrtic (Ed.), *Disability and democracy: Reconstructing (special) education for postmodernity* (pp. 166–189). New York: Teachers College Press.

Horak, B. (1981). A meta-analysis of research findings on individualized instruction in mathematics. *Journal of Educational Research, 74,* 249–253.

Huefner, D.S. (2006). *Getting comfortable with special education law: A framework for working with children with disabilities* (2nd ed.). Norwood, MA: Christopher-Gordon.

Individuals With Disabilities Education Improvement Act (IDEIA). (2004). P.L. 108–446 § 1402 *et seq.*

Individuals With Disabilities Education Improvement Act Regulations (IDEIAR). (2006). 34 C.F.R. § 300 *et seq.*

Jackson, P.W. (1985). Private lessons in public schools: Remarks on the limits of adaptive instruction. In M.C. Wang & H.J. Walberg (Eds.), *Adapting instruction to individual differences* (pp. 66–81). Berkeley, CA: McCutchan.

Kavale, K.A. (1990). Differential programming in serving handicapped students. In M.C. Wang, M.C. Reynolds, & H.J. Walberg (Eds.), *Special education research and practice: Synthesis of findings* (pp. 35–55). New York: Pergamon.

Kavale, K.A., & Forness, S.R. (1999). *Efficacy of special education and related services.* Washington, DC: American Association on Mental Retardation.

Mandlawitz, M. (2006). *What every teacher should know about IDEA 2004.* Boston: Pearson/Allyn and Bacon.

Mandlawitz, M. (2007). *What every teacher should know about IDEA 2004 laws and regulations.* Boston: Pearson/Allyn and Bacon.

Meyen, E.L. (1981). *Developing instructional units for the regular and special teacher* (3rd ed.). Dubuque, IA: Wm. C. Brown.

Meyen, E.L. (1995). Current and emerging instructional practices. In E.L. Meyen & T.M. Skrtic (Eds.), *Special education and student disability: An introduction. Traditional, emerging, and alternative perspectives* (pp. 97–138). Denver, CO: Love.

Mills v. Board of Education of District of Columbia, 348 F. Supp. 866 (D.D.C. 1972).

Murdick, N.L., Gartin, B.C., & Crabtree, T. (2007). *Special education law* (2nd ed.). Upper Saddle River, NJ: Pearson/Merrill Prentice Hall.

No Child Left Behind Act (NCLB). 20 U.S.C. § 6301 *et seq.* (2001).

PARC (Pennsylvania Association for Retarded Citizens) v. Pennsylvania, 343 F. Supp. 297 (E.D. Pa. 1972).

Paul, J.L., Berger, N.H., Osnes, P.G., Martinez, Y.G., & Morse, W.C. (1997). *Ethics and decision making in local schools: Inclusion, policy and reform.* Baltimore: Paul H. Brookes.

Rehabilitation Act, 29 U.S.C. § 794 *et seq.* (1973).

Richards, D.M., & Martin, J.L. (2005). *The IDEA amendments: What you need to know.* Horsham, PA: LRP Publications.

Skrtic, T.M., Harris, K.R., & Shriner, J.G. (2005). The context of special education practice today. In T.M. Skrtic, K.R. Harris, & J.G. Shriner (Eds.), *Special education policy and practice: Accountability, instruction, and social challenges* (pp. 1–18). Denver: Love.

Talmadge, H. (Ed.). (1975). *Systems of individualized instruction.* Berkeley, CA: McCutchan.

Turnbull, R., Huerta, N., & Stowe, M. (2006). *The Individuals With Disabilities Education Act as amended in 2004.* Upper Saddle River, NJ: Pearson/Merrill Prentice Hall.

Wang, M.C. (1981). *The Adaptive Learning Environments model.* Pittsburgh, PA: University of Pittsburgh, Learning Research and Development Center.

Wang, M.C., Reynolds, M.C., & Walberg, H.J. (Eds.). (1990). *Special education research and practice: Synthesis of findings.* New York: Pergamon.

Waxman, H.C., Wang, M.C., Anderson, K.A., & Walberg, H.J. (1985). Adaptive education and student outcomes: A quantitative synthesis. *Journal of Educational Research, 78,* 228–236.

Wright, P.W.D., & Wright, P.D. (2007). *Wrightslaw: Special education law* (2nd ed.). Hartfield, VA: Harbor House Law Press.

Wrightslaw (2007). *IDEA 2004 Roadmap to the IEP.* Retrieved June 22, 2007, from http://www.wrightslaw.com/idea/art/iep.roadmap.htm

Yell, M.L. (2006). *The law and special education* (2nd ed.). Upper Saddle River, NJ: Pearson/Merrill Prentice Hall.

Behavior Intervention Plans

Susan Etscheidt and Kerri Clopton

Problematic behavior patterns are increasing dramatically in schools (Walker, Ramsey, & Gresham, 2004), and many teachers face disruptive behaviors on a daily basis (Cipani, 2008). Aggression, non-compliance, disruption, and disinterest in school are increasingly common in nearly all schools (Kauffman, Mostert, Trent, & Pullen, 2006) and disrupt the learning of many students. Behavior problems are a significant concern at the preschool, elementary, middle, and high school levels, and involve students of differing ethnicity, socioeconomic status, and ability. Many students with disabilities require behavioral supports as a component of their educational program. Often, behavioral difficulties interfere with a child's ability to progress and benefit from an individualized education program (IEP). For example, a student with emotional or behavioral disorders may require behavioral supports to improve appropriate social interaction and to decrease aggressive behavior (Larson, 1998). A child with attention-deficit/hyperactivity disorder (ADHD) may require behavioral support to improve attention (Abramowitz & O'Leary, 1991) or decrease non-compliance (Kapalka, 2005). For students with disabilities, the Individuals With Disabilities Education Improvement Act (IDEIA) requires an IEP team to determine if a student requires behavioral supports. For a child whose behavior impedes his or her learning or the learning of others, IEP teams are required to consider positive behavioral interventions, strategies, and other supports to address behavior (20 U.S.C. § 1414(d)(3)(B)(i)). The intent of this provision in the IDEIA was to encourage IEP teams to develop proactive approaches to prevent the challenging behaviors from impacting the child's program and to improve the educational results for students with disabilities.

Although federal law does not specify the components of a behavior intervention plan (BIP), Etscheidt (2006a) suggested five components based on a review of administrative due process and judicial decisions. The components are: (a) BIPs should be developed when the need is clearly evident, (b) the plan should be based on assessment data, (c) the plans should be individualized to meet the specific needs of a child, (d) the plan should include positive behavioral supports, and (e) the plan should be implemented as designed and monitored. In this chapter, each component will be discussed with recommendations and examples.

PLANS DEVELOPED WHEN NEEDED

This first component requires members of IEP teams to be alert to behavior interfering with a child's educational program. Regular educators, special educators or service providers, school psychologists, and other school personnel should observe behaviors that are problematic and meet to discuss those behaviors. These behaviors may include those distracting students from instruction, such as attention difficulties. Students with limited attention or high levels of distractibility may require specific behavioral supports. Other behaviors may include social or interpersonal difficulties, such as inappropriate teacher-student interactions. Students with non-compliant behavior may need plans to increase following directions or completing tasks. Other students may exhibit social or interpersonal behaviors that disrupt the instructional setting. Aggression toward peers or attention-seeking behaviors may also require specific behavior supports. It is important for IEP team members to recognize these interfering behaviors as early as possible, so plans to improve behavior may be developed expediently. Rather than waiting for behavior problems to intensify, school professionals should attempt to identify behavioral difficulties when they first occur. In that way, behavioral problems may be reduced before they accelerate or become resistant to intervention efforts. Early intervention has been frequently recognized as a key to the remediation of behavior problems.

Individual student behavior journals may be helpful to teachers and support personnel in recognizing behaviors that interfere with learning. Briefly recording journal entries that describe problem behavior on a daily basis may lead teachers to quickly recognize the frequency or patterns of certain behaviors. The entries should include a description of the behavior, some information about the context of the setting in which the behavior occurred, and the effect of the behavior on the child, the teacher, or peers. Although not all behaviors require journal records, those behaviors that result in a significant reduction of instructional time or significantly interfere with interpersonal interactions should be captured on a daily basis. Teachers and other school personnel will be able to quickly recognize patterns of behavior that may require intervention plans. Once the need for planning intervention is evident, the next step is to collect assessment data, which will guide the selection of intervention options.

A case from Minnesota illustrates the importance of developing a BIP when the need for such a plan is clearly evident (*Independent School District No. 279, Osseo Area Schools,* 1999). In this case, a 15-year-old student with emotional and behavioral disorders brought the components of a paint gun to school and, as a consequence, was placed in an alternative setting. An administrative law judge determined that the school district failed to develop a BIP despite clear evidence of need. The student had difficulty interacting with other students, difficulty obeying teachers' directions or classroom rules, and other challenging behaviors. The judge concluded that because the "behaviors are serious, have continued over a period of time, and occur in more than one setting" (30 IDELR 645), the school district had an obligation to develop a BIP. In another case, the school district's philosophy that a student's "autistic behaviors should simply be accepted rather than confronted with a behavioral intervention" was determined by a district court to be inconsistent with the IDEIA mandates (*Escambia County Board of Education v. Benton,* 2005). The school district argued that supports for behaviors that were manifestations of the student's disability did not necessitate a behavior plan. However, the court held that the child's self-stimulatory behaviors of self-striking and repetitive chest-beating required his IEP team to plan behavioral supports. These cases illustrate that when behavior is interfering with the learning of a child or others around the child, IEP teams are required to take the necessary steps to develop a BIP. The first step in that planning is to collect assessment data.

PLANS BASED ON ASSESSMENT DATA

Since 1997, the IDEA has required local educational agencies to conduct a functional behavioral assessment (FBA) and implement a BIP prior to disciplinary action that would result in a change of placement (20 U.S.C. § 1415(k)(1)(b)(i-ii)). Since the introduction of these provisions, many IEP teams conduct FBAs to guide the development of BIPs in response to the past and current requirement to "consider, when appropriate, strategies, including positive behavioral intervention strategies and supports" for a student whose behavior impedes his/her learning or that of others (20 U.S.C. § 1414(d)(3)(B)(i)). The peer-reviewed literature has consistently identified the effectiveness of behavioral support plans derived from FBAs (Freeman et al., 2006). The functional assessment process typically involves defining a target behavior; interviewing knowledgeable adults and often the students themselves about occurrences and nonoccurrences of the target behavior; conducting observations of the behavior; developing a hypothesis about the potential function of, and effects of context on, the target behavior; and verifying the hypotheses through the manipulation of environmental variables. The function of a behavior is the purpose or motivation for the student engaging in the problem behavior. The purpose, or motivation, for the behavior may be to gain something such as teacher attention, peer attention, sensory stimulation, or to escape or avoid something, such as undesirable tasks or individuals. For example, a student may engage in inappropriate behavior that leads to removal from class to escape work. The FBA is "a systematic process of identifying problem behaviors and the events that (a) reliably predict occurrences and non-occurrence of those behaviors and (b) maintain the behaviors across time" (Sugai et al., 1999). Research suggests that interventions that are designed to address the function of the target behavior are more effective than those that are not (Meyer, 1999; Newcomer & Lewis, 2004), yet the results of an FBA are often not used in designing interventions (Scott et al., 2005; Van Acker, Boreson, Gable, & Potterton, 2005). Teams must be knowledgeable about the FBA process and the importance of the link between the function of the target behavior and intervention.

The IDEIA does not define a standard for FBA, nor do many state departments of education (Conroy, Katsiyannis, Clark, Gable, & Fox, 2002). Sugai, Horner et al. (1999) indicate that an assessment should at least result in hypotheses statements, observational data that support the stated hypotheses, and a behavior support plan. Hypotheses statements should include "(a) operational definitions of the problem behavior(s), (b) descriptions of the antecedent events that reliably predict occurrence and nonoccurrence of the problem behavior, and (c) descriptions of the consequence events that maintain the problem behavior(s)" (p. 13). As with any assessment, an FBA involves gathering data using multiple methods and multiple sources. Informant methods, direct observation, and functional analysis are assessment methods that may be used in an FBA (O'Neill et al., 1997).

Informant methods may include interviewing the adults who have direct knowledge of the child or gathering information from these individuals using paper and pencil assessment tools such as rating scales. These methods assist in identifying problem behavior and gaining an understanding of the context in which they occur. The FBA process helps determine variables associated with problem behavior by asking questions such as "What is happening before and after the target behavior?," "Are there specific environmental factors that are associated with the behavior?," or "Is the student able to get the same outcome or consequence with a different behavior?" (O'Neill et al., 1997). Interviewing parents and educators can provide information about behaviors that may be consistent across settings.

Instruments, such as the Problem Behavior Questionnaire and the Functional Assessment Interview (FAI; Lewis, Scott, & Sugai, 1994; O'Neill et al., 1997), may also be used to gather pertinent information. The Problem Behavior Questionnaire is an assessment instrument designed to determine the function of a behavior in a general education setting. Teachers are asked to rate the frequency of an occurrence in relation to the target behavior. For example, some of the items address peer reaction to the target behavior. Items address access to and escape/avoidance of peer attention, access to and escape/avoidance of teacher attention, and setting events (Lewis, Scott, & Sugai, 1994). The FAI includes sections that cover defining the target behavior, ecological/setting events, and antecedents and consequences of the target behavior. Questions also explore the "efficiency" of the target behavior as well as behaviors in the student's repertoire that lead to the same consequence. Behaviors that are efficient "(a) require less physical effort, (b) result in quicker and more consistent payoffs, or (c) produce results quickly" (O'Neill et al., 1997, p. 14). For example, a student wanting teacher attention may have learned that yelling is more efficient than raising his hand to ask a question. An appropriate intervention would make yelling no longer efficient (e.g., ignore the behavior) and increase the efficiency of an appropriate behavior that results in teacher attention. The FAI also explores effective reinforcers for the student, communication skills, and past effective and ineffective strategies for working with the student (O'Neill et al., 1997).

When possible and appropriate, information from the child may also be helpful in planning behavioral interventions. Students themselves may be able to assist in identifying the function of the behavior and may identify variables that others may miss (Kinch, Lewis-Palmer, Hagan-Burke, & Sugai, 2001; Reed, Thomas, Sprague, & Horner, 1997). Furthermore, student involvement in the assessment and intervention planning process may increase the student's investment in the plan and ultimately the success of the intervention (Martin & Mithaug, 2003). IEP team members may choose to use available structured interviews such as the Student-Assisted Functional Assessment Interview (Kern, Dunlap, Clarke, & Childs, 1994) or the Student-Directed Functional Assessment Interview Form (O'Neil et al., 1997) or develop their own assessment tools that will provide the needed information. The Student-Assisted Functional Assessment Interview may be completed by the student or with an adult reading the questions and recording the answers. Some of the questions focus on determining the function of the behavior (attention, tangible reinforcement, or escape), while others ask about the situational variables associated with the behavior (the when and why of the behavior). Students are asked about changes that would lead to fewer incidents of the behavior. A number of questions focus on the interests of the child and how much they like specific school subjects. Finally, the interview includes a section focused on obtaining specific information about academic subjects that may assist in understanding the context of the behavior (Kern et al., 1994). For example, a student may indicate that they do not like math because there is too much memorization.

The Student-Directed Interview Functional Assessment Interview Form (Student-FAI) allows the student to list his or her problem behaviors, the contexts where the behaviors occur, and the antecedents and consequences of each behavior. The Student-FAI includes a daily schedule with ratings of level of difficulty with the behaviors in each time period (e.g., classes, hall-time, etc.) for the student to complete. The student's suggestions for ecological changes and/or replacement behaviors are also explored during the Student-FAI (O'Neill et al., 1997).

Direct observation of the target behavior will help clarify or confirm the hypothesis. The focus of the observations is to identify the variables and events leading up to the behavior as well as the consequences of the behavior. The initial hypothesis may or may not be supported by the observation data and new hypotheses may be generated (O'Neill et al., 1997). A number of direct observation methods may be used in the assessment process. An A-B-C (antecedent, behavior, consequence) recording of events provides a narrative that can be analyzed for patterns. These observations are typically 20 to 30 minutes in length and include descriptions of the events and variables surrounding the target behavior. Teachers may be asked to complete a scatter plot indicating when the behavior occurs in order to determine if there are specific times during the day that the behavior is most likely to occur (Knoster & McCurdy, 2002). Tools such as The Functional Assessment Observation Form (O'Neill et al., 1997) may also be used for structured observations. The Functional Assessment Observation Form allows observers to use information obtained through informant methods to develop an individualized tool for observations. The target behaviors, possible antecedents and functions, and the actual consequence of the behavior are labeled in columns and time periods are indicated in rows. The observer numbers each event and numbers are placed in the appropriate rows and columns. For example, if one of the target behaviors is swearing, each time swearing occurs the number of that event is placed in the columns identifying the antecedents and consequences associated with that single event and in the row identifying the appropriate time period. Because each event is numbered, multiple days of observations may be recorded on one form allowing for the identification of patterns across days (O'Neill et al., 1997).

Functional analysis is the third method for gathering data in an FBA. This method involves the "systematic manipulation of specific variables that are or are not associated with the problem behaviors" (O'Neill et al., 1997, p. 6). Antecedents, consequences, and structural variables such as task difficulty are manipulated in a systematic manner in order to determine the relationship between these variables and the behavior. The use of functional analysis requires significant resources and may not be feasible or necessary in most FBAs conducted in school settings. The use of functional analysis is necessary when the other methods have not led to the identification of a pattern of behavior or the hypotheses cannot be confirmed through observational methods. In functional analysis the hypotheses developed by the team are tested (O'Neill et al., 1997). For example, if one hypotheses for a target behavior is "When three or more students join Joey in play in close proximity, Joey becomes verbally aggressive in order to escape the situation," situations would be set up that altered the number of children in close proximity to Joey and his behavior would be observed. Specific situations where Joey would and would not be expected to become verbally aggressive would be set up to determine if escaping the close proximity of others is the function. Similarly, the consequences of a behavior may be manipulated and the occurrence of the behavior in each condition recorded. Data is then analyzed to determine if a clear pattern of behavior exists.

Once data is collected, O'Neill and colleagues (1997) suggest developing a diagram of the problem behavior and the data gathered through the assessment. This diagram should include the contextual variables associated with the problem behavior, such as when or with whom the problem behavior occurred, or the nature of the instructional task. Consequences following the behavior are also noted, such as teacher reprimand or peer response. The diagram should also include the preferred or replacement behaviors. The replacement behavior should result in the same consequence as the target behavior (e.g., teacher attention or peer attention) and should be incompatible with the target behavior (Crone & Horner, 2003; O'Neill et al., 1997). For example, if interview and observation lead to a conclusion or hypothesis that a student's non-compliance was to escape a non-preferred activity, a replacement behavior would be to teach the student to ask for a break prior to beginning the non-preferred task. Asking for a break would be incompatible with task refusal or non-compliance but would still allow for a temporary escape. If based on interviews and observations, a student's verbal outbursts were hypothesized to be teacher attention-seeking, a replacement behavior may be for the student to stand by her desk to signal the teacher to assist her. Once a function of a behavior is hypothesized, replacement behaviors may be identified.

Due to the concerns about the feasibility of implementing FBAs in the school setting, a number of aids are being developed to increase the efficiency of the process. Given the appropriate training and structure, teachers are able to develop a hypothesis regarding the function of the target behavior and assist in developing appropriate interventions (Maag & Larson, 2004; Packenham, Shute, & Reid, 2004). Larson and Maag (1998) developed the Functional Assessment Hypotheses Formulation Protocol in an effort to assist teachers in conducting functional assessment and found it to be effective in guiding the process (Maag & Larson, 2004). It is likely that additional aids will be developed to assist general education teachers in conducting FBAs.

PLANS INDIVIDUALIZED

A review of the assessment results should reveal both quantitative and qualitative data about the behavior of concern. The IEP team should have information about the frequency, duration, and intensity of the behaviors, as well as information about the topography of the behavior. This qualitative data includes information about when the problem behavior occurs, where it occurs, and contexts where it is most and least likely to occur. The assessment results should also provide information about the hypothesized function of the behavior, based on both the interview and observational data. With these data, the members of the IEP team, including the parents, may begin discussing behavior interventions.

The assessment results will provide the planning team with specific information about the child and the problem behavior. Just as the IEP is an individualized plan of a child's educational program, the BIP must also be individualized to meet the child's specific behavioral needs. Similarly, just as the IEP specified goals based on assessment data, the behavior plan should also specify goals based on the FBA. Interventions to achieve those goals may then be planned, and the effectiveness of the interventions monitored. While school- or class-wide behavioral supports may be available, an individualized plan would also include interventions selected specifically for the child. For example, while all children in a second grade classroom may be part of a program designed to increase positive peer interactions through peer mediation, individualized interventions must be planned. Just as the IEP is a plan "for each child with a disability that is developed, reviewed, and revised" (20 U.S.C. § 1402(14)), the behavior plan must also be developed for each child. School- and class-wide supports may be additional, appropriate options but may not replace a plan individualized for the child.

In a case from California, a 13-year-old student with multiple handicaps exhibited challenging behaviors (*Fullerton Elementary School District and Orange County Health Care,* 2004). Her teachers utilized a class-wide system for monitoring behavior and rewarding appropriate behavior. In addition to the class-wide program, the teacher also provided individualized behavioral supports which included a posted schedule, a personal schedule, and a behavioral point chart. When her parents challenged the appropriateness of her program, the hearing officer determined that the program was designed to meet the student's unique needs. In contrast, a case from New York resulted in a finding that the school district failed to provide an appropriate education by using only a class-wide plan for a 9-year-old student with oppositional defiant disorder and ADHD (*Board of Education of the Half Hollow Hills Central School District,* 2003). Instead of an individualized plan, the teacher used a class-wide program where points were given for appropriate behavior and taken away for inappropriate behavior, with rewards provided at the end of the day. Under this class-wide plan, the student's behavior did not improve and he spent a significant amount of time in a "redirection room." The state review officer ruled that an individualized behavior plan should have been developed and provided to the child. Because the child "needed an individualized BIP tailored to meet his individual needs," the officer ruled that the school district failed to offer an appropriate program. These cases illustrate the need for behavior plans to be individualized to meet the child's needs.

PLANS INCLUDE POSITIVE BEHAVIORAL SUPPORTS

The selection of behavioral interventions should be guided by several considerations. First, the IDEIA requires that positive behavioral interventions, strategies, and other supports be developed to address problem behavior (20 U.S.C. § 1414(d)(3)(B)(i)). Therefore, teams should consider positive, supportive interventions rather than reductive techniques that are aversive or punitive. Although in extreme cases of serious self-injury or injury to others certain procedures such as restraint may be selected as emergency interventions. IEP teams should explore positive behavioral supports for students—even those with very challenging behavior. Certain reductive techniques, such as time-out, can be overused (Costenbader & Reading-Brown, 1995) or improperly used. The use of reductive techniques such as time-out should be reserved for significantly disruptive or dangerous behavior. IEP teams should focus on improving appropriate behavior with positive, preventive supports rather than selecting reductive procedures to address inappropriate behavior.

A second guiding consideration is that the interventions selected must be "based on peer-reviewed research to the extent practicable" (20 U.S.C. § 1414(d)(1)(A)(i)(IV)). The legislative history of the IDEIA reveals both the definition and rationale for the inclusion of this phrase. The Department of Education's final regulations for IDEIA 2004 defined peer-reviewed research as research reviewed by qualified and independent reviewers to ensure that the quality of the information meets the standards of the field before the research is published. The inclusion of this provision was to encourage "states, school districts, and school personnel to select and use methods that research has shown to be effective, to the extent that methods based on peer-reviewed research are available" (71 *Fed. Reg.* 46665 (Aug. 14, 2006)). Therefore, behavioral interventions must provide positive support and be supported by research, to the extent practicable.

A variety of positive behavioral supports with empirical efficacy should be explored for inclusion in a child's behavioral plan. Options include reinforcement-based interventions, opportunities to respond, social skill instruction, or self-management (Lewis, Hudson, Richter, & Johnson, 2004). Reinforcement-based interventions include teacher praise or reinforcement for appropriate behavior and ignoring inappropriate responses. An alternative, appropriate behavior that is selected to replace an inappropriate behavior is identified and reinforced on a schedule determined by the IEP team. For example, to improve assignment completion, a child may be given a small icon of a computer each time s/he completes a work task. Once the child has earned 10 icons, s/he may turn them in for 10 minutes of computer time.

Opportunities to respond involve the selection of instructional methods and materials to increase task engagement and decrease disruptive behavior due to instruction or distractibility. Teachers may increase opportunities to respond by "prepping" the student with correct answers prior to instruction, also known as "priming" (DePaepe, Shores, Jack, & Denny, 1996). Opportunities to respond may also be increased by rapid pacing, choral responding or the use of response cards (Sutherland & Wehby, 2001). Clearly, one of the most effective positive behavioral supports is social skill instruction. Social skills are taught to replace inappropriate behaviors and may include commercially available programs or naturalistic approaches. For example, a child may need instruction in how to seek teacher attention in an appropriate manner. A social skill program would involve the teacher modeling the skill, such as raising both hands or standing up next to the desk. The child would then practice the skill with guidance and feedback from the instructor. Opportunities to seek teacher attention in various settings would then be introduced, until the child was independently performing the skill. Social skill instruction is a proven practice (Lo, Loe, & Cartledge, 2002) and is effective in improving interpersonal interactions in preschool through adolescent populations.

Self-management involves teaching students to be aware of their behaviors and to monitor the occurrence of appropriate behaviors. By increasing the child's awareness of behavior and increasing his or her involvement in behavior change, appropriate behaviors are increased. Students may be involved in monitoring task completion, following directions, showing self-control, interacting appropriately with teachers or peers, or a variety of other behaviors. For example, a child's blurting out may be reduced by involving the student in self-monitoring of an alternative, appropriate behavior. A small circle in the shape of a bull's eye could be placed on the child's desk. The child could be instructed to "shoot an arrow into the sky" before speaking. Each time the child "shoots" before talking, s/he draws an arrow on the bull's eye. Teacher and student would schedule meetings to discuss progress in hand-raising before speaking. The child's awareness of the appropriate behavior and involvement in behavior change contribute to the effectiveness of self-monitoring interventions. Self-management interventions also have proven effective for preschool through high school students.

Research has also identified numerous emerging behavioral supports, such as video modeling and priming (Buggey, 1995, 1999, 2005; D'Ateno, Mangiapanello, & Taylor, 2003; Hine & Wolery, 2006; Hundt, 2002; Kinney, Vedora, & Stromer, 2003; Schriebman, Whalen, & Stahmer, 2000). In video modeling, the child watches a video of appropriate behaviors, such as waiting in line. The teacher highlights the behavior during and following the video viewing. The video can be used to prime the child to engage in the behavior, as well as a correction strategy when inappropriate behavior during waiting occurs.

Cognitive strategies have also proven effective in improving behavior (Edmunds, 1999; Fulk, Lohman, & Belfiore, 1997; Wynn-Dancy, 1997). For example, steps or reminders of appropriate behavior such as hands-to-self or sharing can be displayed on a small piece of paper similar to a credit card. The card may be placed so it is always in the child's view or the child may be cued to find the card in situations in which the child should exhibit the appropriate behavior. The card triggers the child to think about the appropriate behavior, thereby increasing the occurrence of that behavior (Edmunds, 1999).

Behavioral contracting (Lassman, Jolivette, & Wehby, 1997) is another effective strategy to improve behavior. The teacher and the child draw up a contract that specifies certain target, appropriate behaviors. The contract includes provisions for how the occurrence of the target behavior will be recognized or rewarded. Both the teacher and student sign the contract to show they agree to the provisions.

Visual schedules (Downing & Peckham-Hardin, 2001; Stromer, Kimball, Kinney, & Taylor, 2006) have been incorporated to improve behavior in students with autism and other developmental disabilities. The schedules display the student's tasks or activities for the day, often on Velcro strips that may be removed as each activity is developed. Visual schedules have been effective in improving both task engagement and transitions between activities.

Social stories have emerged as a highly efficacious method to improve behavior. The story describes a social situation and the behaviors that would be appropriate in that setting. For example, a social story might describe how to ask another student for a toy or preferred object. Although initially used with students with autism, social stories have also been effective with diverse student populations (Delano & Snell, 2006; Glaeser, Pierson, & Fritschmann, 2003; Lorimer, Simpson, Myles, & Ganz, 2002).

Peer supports (Bacon & Bloom, 2000; Tournaki & Criscitiello, 2003; Westerlund, Granucci, Gamache, & Clark, 2006) involve teaching peers to assist students in social or academic settings. Peers may serve as social tutors or social models in improving behavior. The selection of appropriate behavioral supports will depend on the target behavior.

A case from Minnesota addressed the failure of an IEP team to explore positive behavioral supports (*Mounds View Independent School District #621*, 2006). The student, a high school senior, was diagnosed with ADHD and had difficulties following adult directive and completing assignments. The IEP team's plan was to provide a warning to the student and remove him from the classroom for inappropriate behavior. The hearing officer concluded that "the IEP team did not address what type of positive supports and interventions could be utilized to reinforce the behavior they wished the student to have. Each of the interviewed teachers wanted to see the student be more motivated, use his time more effectively, and to take advantage of available help. Positive supports could have addressed ways to focus on acquisition of those skills" (107 LRP 8915). This case illustrates the need for IEP teams to explore positive supports to improve behavior rather than selecting reductive techniques in response to inappropriate behavior.

PLANS IMPLEMENTED AND MONITORED

Once the assessment is completed and positive, appropriate interventions are selected, the interventions must be implemented with integrity. Those individuals responsible for implementing the interventions must ensure that the plan is delivered as written, and attempt to adhere to the intent of the plan. The integrity of an intervention may be maximized by preparing and training the responsible individuals to implement the plan, and by developing performance feedback mechanisms such as observational data and visual graphics (Witt, VanDerHeyden, & Gilbertson, 2004). The likelihood that the plan is implemented with integrity can be increased by integrating a number of elements into the planning process. In selecting the intervention, the team should consider how well the intervention fits in the classroom context as well as the resources that will be needed to implement the intervention, including time, knowledge, and skills. Although the research regarding the connection between treatment acceptability and integrity is mixed, some research suggests a correlation between the feasibility of the intervention and implementation (Odom, McConnell, & Chandler, 1993). The individual responsible for the implementation of the intervention needs to agree with the hypothesis developed by the team and understand the connection between the hypothesized function and the intervention. The consideration of these variables suggests the importance of the teacher's involvement in the assessment and planning process.

The development and use of intervention scripts increase the adherence to the treatment plan. Scripts provide a detailed description of the intervention steps (Telzrow & Beebe, 2002). The involvement of the individual who will implement the intervention in the development of the script, increases the adherence to the script (Allen & Blackston, 2003). Performance feedback on the implementation of the plan also increases treatment integrity (Codding, Feinberg, Dunn, & Pace, 2005; Noell, Duhon, Gatti, & Connell, 2002).

Just as the intervention plan should be clearly specified, so should the plan to monitor the effectiveness of the intervention. The progress monitoring approach should be clearly described in the behavior plan. Decisions regarding the effectiveness of the plan and the need for modification must be based on data and the data must be both reliable and valid. To make good decisions the team must be clear on the behavior that is to be measured and the goal for change. The "who, when, and how" of data collection must be clearly delineated as well as a schedule for the review of the data. Because feedback regarding the implementation of the intervention may increase the integrity with which it is implemented, frequent meetings to evaluate the data may prove helpful in the early period of the plan.

Methods of data collection will depend on the behavior goal. For example, if the goal is to increase positive peer interactions, frequency data may be appropriate. If a behavioral goal is to increase assignment completion, permanent product data may be selected for progress monitoring. If the behavioral goal is to increase task engagement, a time-sampling data collection may be warranted. Numerous options for data collection exist (Etscheidt, 2006b), and the IEP team should select a progress monitoring approach that is a good fit with the behavioral goal.

An evaluation of the data involves comparing the behavior during the baseline to the behavior during the intervention. The data should be analyzed to determine if a change has occurred and if the change is meaningful. Gable, Hendrickson, and Van Acker (2001) suggest that the selected replacement behavior must have both social and functional validity. In order to have social validity the behavior must meet the expectations of others, including parents, teachers, and peers. The behavior has functional validity if it results in the same outcome as the target behavior. If the data do not show a change in the target behavior, the team must determine if the intervention was implemented with integrity. If implemented with integrity, other explanations for the lack of change must be considered, as well as the possibility that the original hypothesis was not correct. At this point, additional assessment may be appropriate. If the plan was not implemented with integrity, the team should discuss the barriers and consider the appropriateness of the intervention given contextual factors (Crone & Horner, 2003).

Once an intervention is deemed effective and the student has met the goals, the team must design a maintenance plan to ensure the continuation of the needed supports. The BIP, like the IEP, must be evaluated on an annual basis. A member of the IEP team may request a more frequent review. A review may be needed if the behavior goals have been met and new goals are needed, adequate progress is not being made, or if the intervention is not addressing the current needs of the student (Gable, Quinn, Rutherford, & Howell, 1998).

Many examples of BIPs are available. For example, the Council for Exceptional Children's Center for Effective Collaboration and Practice (2001) provides BIP forms and samples. Similarly, the National Dissemination Center for Children with Disabilities (NICHCY; 2007) provides guidance for the behavioral assessment, instructions for development of BIPs, and examples of BIPs. Many states and school district also have templates for BIPs.

SUMMARY

The IDEIA contains specific requirements pertaining to student behavior. IEP teams are required to consider positive behavioral supports for children whose behavior is interfering with learning. BIPs should be based on assessment data, be individualized, include positive approaches, and be carefully implemented and monitored. In the selection of positive supports, IEP teams must search for interventions with empirical support of efficacy. The Department of Education has clarified that the reasons for these provisions is to emphasize the need for IEP teams to select positive, preventive, and proven interventions to address children's behavioral needs. Several implications concerning the behavior provisions of the IDEIA may be identified. First, all members of IEP teams must be alerted to responsibilities concerning student behavior. They must recognize interfering behavior, collect and analyze assessment data, select positive and efficacious interventions, and determine plans for progress monitoring. To fulfill these responsibilities, teachers and support personnel must take advantage of professional development opportunities. Such opportunities might include attending conferences, obtaining professional literature, or visiting demonstration programs featuring positive behavioral supports. Second, states or local school districts should consider developing or revising prototypes for behavioral intervention plans based on the five suggested components. For example, in designing or reviewing behavioral intervention forms, a section for progress monitoring should be included. The who, what, where, and when of progress monitoring should be identified, similar to the procedures required for the IEP. Because neither federal law nor regulations specifies the components of a behavioral plan, individual states and districts should develop or refine formats for BIPs that reflect the critical components identified. These formats should be reviewed frequently to determine if additional revisions may be necessary. Finally, members of IEP teams should develop a reservoir of resources pertaining to positive behavior supports. IEP teams should consider interventions from a variety of positive, efficacious options. The reservoir of possible interventions might be arranged by the nature of the behavior, the age of the child, or function of the behavior. An expansive array of intervention options will facilitate the collaborative decision-making envisioned by the IDEIA.

REFERENCES

Abramowitz, A. J., & O'Leary, S. G. (1991). Behavioral interventions for the classroom: Implications for students with ADHD. *School Psychology Review, 20*(2), 220–234.

Allen, S. J., & Blackston, A. R. (2003). Training preservice teachers in collaborative problem solving: An investigation of the impact on teacher and student behavior change in real-world settings. *School Psychology Quarterly, 18*(1), 22–51.

Bacon, E., & Bloom, L. (2000). Listening to student voices: How student advisory boards can help. *Teaching Exceptional Children, 32*(6), 38–43.

Board of Education of the Half Hollow Hills Central School District, 106 LRP 17128 (SEA NY 2003).

Buggey, T. (1995). An examination of the effectiveness of videotaped self-modeling in teaching specific linguistic structures to preschoolers. *Topics in Early Childhood Special Education, 15*(4), 434–58.

Buggey, T. (1999). Look! I'm on TV!": Using videotaped self-modeling to change behavior. *Teaching Exceptional Children, 31*(4), 27–30.

Buggey, T. (2005). Video self-modeling applications with students with autism spectrum disorder in a small private school setting. *Focus on Autism and Other Developmental Disabilities, 20*(1), 52–64.

Cipani, E. (2008). *Classroom management for all teachers: Plans for evidence-based practice* (3rd ed.). Upper Saddle River, NJ: Pearson Education, Inc.

Codding, R. S., Feinberg, A. B., Dunn, E. K., & Pace, G. M. (2005). Effects of immediate performance feedback on implementation of behavior support plans. *Journal of Applied Behavior Analysis, 38*(2), 205–219.

Conroy, M. A., Katsiyannis, A., Clark, D., Gable, R. A., & Fox, J. J. (2002). State Office of Education practices implementing the IDEA disciplinary provisions. *Behavioral Disorders, 27*(2), 98–108.

Costenbader, V., & Reading-Brown, M. (1995). Isolation timeout used with students with emotional disorders. *Exceptional Children, 61,* 353–363.

Council for Exceptional Children. (2001). *Center for Effective Collaboration and Practice: Positive behavioral intervention plan.* Retrieved April 26, 2007, from http://cecp.air.org/fba/problembehavior3/appendixb.htm

Crone, D. A., & Horner, R. H. (2003). *Building positive behavior support systems in schools: Functional behavioral assessment.* New York: Guilford Press.

D'Ateno, P., Mangiapanello, K., & Taylor, B. A. (2003). Using video modeling to teach complex play sequences to a preschooler with autism. *Journal of Positive Behavior Interventions, 5*(1), 5–11.

Delano, M., & Snell, M. E. (2006). The effects of social stories on the social engagement of children with autism. *Journal of Positive Behavior Interventions, 8*(1), 29–43.

DePaepe, P. A., Shores, R. E., Jack, S. L., & Denny, R. K. (1996). Effects of task difficulty on disruptive and on-task behavior of students with severe behavior disorders. *Behavioral Disorders, 21,* 216–225.

Downing, J. E., & Peckham-Hardin, K. D. (2001). Daily schedules: A helpful learning tool. *Teaching Exceptional Children, 33*(3), 62–68.

Edmunds, A. L. (1999). Cognitive credit cards. *Teaching Exceptional Children, 31*(4), 68–73.

Escambia County Board of Education v. Benton, 44 IDELR 272 (SD AL 2005).

Etscheidt, S. (2006a). Behavioral intervention plans: A pedagogical and legal analysis of issues. *Behavioral Disorders, 31*(20), 221–241.

Etscheidt, S. (2006b). Progress monitoring: Legal issues and recommendations for IEP teams. *Teaching Exceptional Children, 38*(3), 56–60.

Freeman, R., Eber, L., Anderson, C., Irvin, L., Horner, R., Bounds, M., et al. (2006). Building inclusive school cultures using school-wide positive behavior support. *Research & Practice for Persons With Severe Disabilities, 31*(1), 4–17.

Fulk, B. M., Lohman, D., & Belfiore, P. J. (1997). Effects of integrated picture mnemonics on the letter recognition and letter-sound acquisition of transitional first grade students with special needs. *Learning Disability Quarterly, 20,* 33–42.

Fullerton Elementary School District and Orange County Health Care Agency, 104 LRP 36039 (SEA CA 2004).

Gable, R. A., Hendrickson, J. M., & Van Acker, R. (2001). Maintaining the integrity of FBA-based interventions in schools. *Education and Treatment of Children, 24*(3), 248–260.

Gable, R. A., Quinn, M. M., Rutherford, R. B., & Howell, K. (1998). Addressing problem behaviors in schools: Use of functional assessments and behavior intervention plans. *Preventing School Failure, 42*(3), 106–119.

Glaeser, B. C., & Pierson, M. R., & Fritschmann, N. (2003). Comic strip conversations: A positive behavioral support strategy. *Teaching Exceptional Children, 36*(2), 14–19.

Hine, J. F., & Wolery, M. (2006). Using point-of-view video modeling to teach play to preschoolers with autism. *Topics in Early Childhood Special Education, 26*(2), 83–93.

Hundt, T. A. (2002). Videotaping young children in the classroom: Parents as partners. *Teaching Exceptional Children, 34*(3), 38–43.

Independent School District No. 279, Osseo Area Schools, 30 IDELR 645 (SEA MN 1999).

Kapalka, G. M. (2005). Avoiding repetitions reduces ADHD children's management problems in the classroom. *Emotional and Behavioural Difficulties, 10*, 269–279.

Kauffman, J. M., Mostert, M. P., Trent, S. C., & Pullen, P. L. (2006). *Managing classroom behavior: A reflective case-based approach.* Boston: MA: Pearson Education, Inc.

Kern, L., Dunlap, G., Clarke, S., & Childs, K. E. (1994). Student-assisted functional assessment interview. *Diagnostique, 19*(2–3), 29–39.

Kinch, C., Lewis-Palmer, T., Hagan-Burke, S., & Sugai, G. (2001). A comparison of teacher and student functional behavior assessment interview information from low-risk and high-risk classrooms. *Education and Treatment of Children, 24*(4), 480–494.

Kinney, E. M., Vedora, J., & Stromer, R. (2003). Computer-presented video models to teach generative spelling to a child with an autism spectrum disorder. *Journal of Positive Behavior Interventions, 5*, 22–29.

Knoster, T. P., & McCurdy, B. (2002). Best practices in functional behavioral assessment for designing individualized student programs. In A. Thomas & J. Grimes (Eds.), *Best practices in schools psychology* (4th ed., Vol. 2, pp. 1007–1028). Bethesda: National Association of School Psychologists.

Larson, J. (1998). Managing student aggression in high schools: Implications for practice. *Psychology in the Schools, 35*(3), 283–295.

Larson, P. J., & Maag, J. W. (1998). Applying functional assessment in general education classrooms: Issues and recommendations. *Remedial and Special Education, 19*(6), 338–349.

Lassman, K. A., Jolivette, K., & Wehby, J. H. (1997). "My teacher said I did good work today!": Using collaborative behavioral contracting. *Teaching Exceptional Children, 31*(4), 12–18.

Lewis, T. J., Hudson, S., Richter, M., & Johnson, N. (2004). Scientifically supported practices in emotional and behavioral disorders: A proposed approach and brief review of current practices. *Behavioral Disorders, 29*(3), 247–259.

Lewis, T. J., Scott, T. M., & Sugai, G. (1994). The problem behavior questionnaire: A teacher-based instrument to develop functional hypotheses of problem behavior in general education classrooms. *Diagnostique, 19*(2–3), 103–115.

Lo, Y., Loe, S. A., & Cartledge, G. (2002). The effects of social skills instruction on the social behaviors of students at risk for emotional or behavioral disorders. *Behavioral Disorders, 27*, 371–385.

Lorimer, P. A., Simpson, R. L., Myles, B. S., & Ganz, J. B. (2002). The use of social stories as a preventative behavioral intervention in a home setting with a child with autism. *Journal of Positive Behavior Interventions, 4*, 53–61.

Maag, J. W., & Larson, P. J. (2004). Training a general education teacher to apply functional assessment. *Education and Treatment of Children, 27*(1), 26–36.

Martin, J. E., & Mithaug, D. E. (2003). Increasing self-determination: Teaching students to plan, work, evaluate, and adjust. *Exceptional Children, 69*(4), 431–446.

Meyer, K. A. (1999). Functional analysis and treatment of problem behavior exhibited by elementary school children. *Journal of Applied Behavior Analysis, 32*(2), 229–232.

Mounds View Independent School District #621, 107 LRP 8915 (SEA MN 2006).

National Dissemination Center for Children with Disabilities (NICHCY). (2007). NICHCY Connections to behavioral assessment, plans, and positive supports. Retrieved April 27, 2007, from http://www.nichcy.org/resources/behavassess.asp

Newcomer, L. L., & Lewis, T. J. (2004). Functional behavioral assessment: An investigation of assessment reliability and effectiveness of function-based interventions. *Journal of Emotional and Behavioral Disorders, 12*(3), 168–181.

Noell, G. H., Duhon, G. J., Gatti, S. L., & Connell, J. E. (2002). Consultation, follow-up, and implementation of behavior management interventions in general education. *School Psychology Review, 31*(2), 217–234.

Odom, S. L., McConnell, S. R., & Chandler, L. K. (1993). Acceptability and feasibility of classroom-based social interaction interventions for young children with disabilities. *Exceptional Children, 60*(3), 226–276.

O'Neill, R. E., Horner, R. H., Albin, R. W., Sprague, J. R., Storey, K., & Newton, J. S. (1997). *Functional assessment and program development for problem behavior: A practical handbook* (2nd ed.). Pacific Grove: Brooks/Cole Publishing Co.

Packenham, M., Shute, R., & Reid, R. (2004). A truncated functional behavioral assessment procedure for children with disruptive classroom behaviors. *Education and Treatment of Children, 27*(1), 9–25.

Reed, H., Thomas, E., Sprague, J. R., & Horner, R. H. (1997). The student guided functional assessment interview: An analysis of student and teacher agreement. *Journal of Behavioral Education, 7*(1), 33–49.

Schriebman, L., Whalen, C., & Stahmer, A. C. (2000). The use of video priming to reduce disruptive transition behavior in children with autism. *Journal of Positive Behavior Interventions, 21*, 3–11.

Scott, T. M., McIntyre, J., Liaupsin, C., Nelson, C. M., Conroy, M., & Payne, L. D. (2005). An examination of the relation between functional behavior assessment and selected intervention strategies with school-based teams. *Journal of Positive Behavior Interventions, 7*(4), 205–215.

Stromer, R., Kimball, J. W., Kinney, E. M., & Taylor, B. A. (2006). Activity schedules, computer technology, and teaching children with autism spectrum disorders. *Focus on Autism and Other Developmental Disabilities, 21*(1), 14–24.

Sugai, G., Horner, R. H., Dunlap, G., Hieneman, M., Lewis, T. J., Nelson, C. M., et al. (1999). *Applying positive behavioral support and functional behavioral assessment in schools. Technical assistance guide 1, version 1.4.3.* Washington, DC: Center on Positive Behavioral Interventions and Support (OSEP). ERIC Document Reproduction Service No. ED443244.

Sutherland, K. S., & Wehby, J. H. (2001). Exploring the relationship between increased opportunities to respond to academic requests and the academic and behavioral outcomes of students with E/BD. *Remedial and Special Education, 22*, 113–121.

Telzrow, C. F., & Beebe, J. J. (2002). Best practices in facilitating intervention adherence and integrity. In A. Thomas & J. Grimes (Eds.), *Best practices in schools psychology* (4th ed., Vol. 1, pp. 503–516). Bethesda: National Association of School Psychologists.

Tournaki, N., & Criscitiello, E. (2003). Using peer tutoring as a successful part of behavior management. *Teaching Exceptional Children, 36*(2), 22–29.

Van Acker, R., Boreson, L., Gable, R. A., & Potterton, T. (2005). Are we on the right course? Lessons learned about current FBA/BIP practices in schools. *Journal of Behavioral Education, 14*(1), 35–56.

Walker, H. M., Ramsey, E., & Gresham, F. M. (2004). *Antisocial behavior in school* (2nd ed.). Belmont, CA: Wadsworth/Thomson Learning.

Westerlund, D., Granucci, E. A., Gamache, P. & Clark, H. B. (2006). Effects of peer mentors on work-related performance of adolescents with behavioral and/or learning disabilities. *Journal of Positive Behavior Interventions, 8*(4), 244–252.

Witt, J. C., VanDerHeyden, A. M., & Gilbertson, D. (2004). Troubleshooting behavioral interventions: A systematic process for finding and eliminating problems. *School Psychology Review, 33*(3), 363–383.

Wynn-Dancy, M. (1997). Accessing long-term memory: Metacognitive strategies and strategic action in adolescents. *Topics in Language Disorders, 18*, 32–44.

PART III

From the Front Lines

Increasing the Academic Performance of Struggling Students and Students With Disabilities in Underperforming Schools

Denise Hexom, Judith Menoher,
Bonnie A. Plummer, and Mary Stone

The purpose of this chapter is to present research we have conducted with underperforming schools during the past 5 years. First it illustrates the complexities of school change within the context of federal and state mandates; describes the plethora of student and teacher issues facing schools; and reviews programs, procedures and practices to affect school reform. Second it examines 33 schools identified by No Child Left Behind (NCLB) mandates as in need of program improvement based on the academic performance of the students. No longer can a school be deemed high performing if students in subgroups (Hispanic, socioeconomically disadvantaged, or disabled) are not proficient in reading/language arts and mathematics. Finally, we analyze a process for facilitating significant school change that increases student academic performance, for all students including students with disabilities.

COMPLEXITIES OF SCHOOL CHANGE

Tailoring America's schools to match the children who attend schools is an ominous task. Most efforts fail because they are built on an inaccurate model of how school organizations function (Reeves, 2006). The purpose of schooling is becoming more complex with district/school organizations unsuited to respond to the cognitive, social, emotional, and physical needs of the children. According to Fullan (2005), the key to enabling school staffs to change is to provide them with new experiences. Many of the current strategies adopted for federal and state reform are based on various assumptions: what students should know and be able to do and what teachers and administrators should know and be able to do. The introduction of accountability in districts/schools provides a baseline for determining the areas where change is required. Schools must also focus on changing the culture and working conditions of the school that will systematically and strategically improve student achievement.

While the issues of performance are paramount to school reform, other areas deserve close attention. Discrepancy in services and support by districts, and often schools within districts, result in inequitable systems. Funding to support textbooks and materials, intervention programs for struggling students and students with disabilities, and assessment systems for monitoring student progress are a few of the variables that affect student, teacher, school, and district performance. The results of inequitable support for education is manifested by the disparity in the performance of students, particularly, those from poverty ("No Small Change," 2005) and those that present unique learning profiles.

The core of the Reauthorization of Title I, NCLB, and Individuals With Disabilities Education Improvement Act (IDEIA) of 2004 is to establish performance targets for every student. These federal guidelines and regulations, based on rigorous scientific research, mandate that education reform efforts must extend not only to general education students but also to students with disabilities as well. These regulations insist on high academic standards and excellence, press for accountability for results at all levels, and require schools to ensure ongoing progress (U.S. Department of Education, Office of Special Education and Rehabilitative Services, 2002).

School reform remains complex and difficult to implement: for example, districts and schools that receive federal Title 1 monies face federal and state sanctions. Federal sanctions include the possibility of neighborhood schools being closed for failure to make significant adequate yearly progress (AYP) as determined by such criteria as participation rates in state administered assessments, graduation rates, and proficiency rates. In addition to school-wide growth targets, each significant subgroup within the school must also meet annual measurable objectives (AMOs). These are defined by proficiency rates in reading/language arts and mathematics. Students with disabilities are identified as one of these subgroups and are required to meet the same AMOs. Further, the state of California requires schools to meet or exceed annual growth targets determined by the Academic Performance Index (API).

Another factor districts/schools need to consider is the qualifications and assignments of school staff. IDEIA and state legislation require proper accreditation of every teacher teaching in either a public or non-public school serving children identified as needing special education services. NCLB requires districts to hire teachers who are certified in the area in which they will teach. According to Perkins-Gough (2005), 48% of the teachers in California, teaching in high-risk, low-performing schools, reported that their schools have high numbers of non-credentialed teachers, compared with only 4% of the teachers in low-risk, high-performing schools. Special education classrooms have even greater difficulty in meeting the tenets of NCLB. According to a recently released government report from the Office of Special Education it is predicted that by the year 2010, there will be a shortage of 7,000 special education teachers. Many of the teachers instructing children with moderate to severe disabilities have never worked with students with disabilities prior to being hired as an intern teacher. Interns are defined as college graduates who have passed subject matter competency, taken three courses, but have not yet completed their full certification requirements for the school or district.

In addition to credentialing issues, the social and economic issues facing California dramatically affects the academic performance of the students. California has the country's largest public school enrollment, with over 6 million students in over 1,000 districts and more than 8,000 schools. Its students are ethnically, linguistically, and socioeconomically diverse: approximately 43% are Latino, 36% White, 12% Asian, 8% African-American, 1% other. Nearly half (47%) are eligible for free or reduced-price lunch, and 25% are designated English language learners (ELL; McLaughlin & Talbert, 2003).

By 2008, it is estimated that over 1,700 schools in California will be identified as in need of program improvement or face the sanctions placed on them by the legislature and California Department of Education. Research institutions and organizations are charged with finding and disseminating research-based practices, which have been deemed effective in turning around schools and dramatically improving student academic achievement. In addition, schools have genuine difficulties responding to the rapidly changing global economy, in terms of the use of technology, work force preparation, and career development. Business is conducted via the Internet yet schools still use paper and pencil with little technology embedded into the curriculum to assist learning and assess academic progress.

Once among the highest-performing states in the nation, California currently ranks among the bottom three states in average reading and mathematics achievement on the National Assessment of Educational Progress. A recent Rand report (Carroll, Reichardt, & Guarino, 2000) stated that California's public education system is widely thought to be ineffective. On the 2005 National Assessment of Educational Progress (NAEP), only 21% of California's fourth graders were proficient in reading and 28% proficient in mathematics. Eighth graders' performance was even lower, with 21% proficient in reading and 22% proficient in mathematics (National Center for Education Statistics, 2005).

There is extreme disparity in California schools; some are the worst in the country (Skinner, 2005). Large class sizes, multiple languages in one classroom, lack of adequate textbooks and materials, and insufficiently trained teachers accelerate the digital divide, achievement gap, and inequities existing in schools. Drop-out rates are on the rise especially for Latino and African American students (Civil Rights Project, 2005). During the 2005–2006 school year over 40,000 high school seniors did not receive a diploma, even after passing all coursework, because they were unable to pass the California High School Exit Exam (CAHSEE).

Students with disabilities at the high school level are failing to graduate in ever increasing numbers and when they do graduate, they are not successful in post secondary education. Over 1,700 schools have been notified of program improvement status due to significant numbers of special education and English learners not meeting the 26.4% proficiency rates in English/language arts and 24.4% in mathematics required by NCLB.

So how does a school or district implement school change? How do teachers and principals collaborate to define and develop a process for working within a complex system? What variables must they consider? What norms for behavior will facilitate the process? How does a school become a learning community versus a group of private practitioners? How do schools support struggling students and students with disabilities?

Littky and Grabelle (2004) and Fullan, Bertani, & Quinn (2004) indicate that the biggest barrier to change seems to be the unlearning needed to let new ideas flourish. New ideas could bring about real, meaningful change that allows teachers, principals, and superintendents to question everything about the structures and the systems of schools as they are currently known. Furthermore, hierarchical models of school organizations are not successful because they assume people will listen to the evidence, learn the new procedure, and follow directions (Reeves, 2006), but changes in behavior do not occur. This means new policies, new language, new structures, and new priorities need to be developed and implemented. Most of all, it means establishing a new commitment to educating all students to be successful.

In 1999 the California State Legislature passed the Public Schools Accountability Act (PSAA). It required a statewide assessment system (STAR) be created, including a California High School Exit Exam (CAHSEE). Additionally, it created a system in which every school would be compared and ranked according to an Academic Performance Index (API), based upon the academic performance of students on both norm-referenced assessments and California Standards Tests (CSTs).

Annual growth targets for each school were established along with academic targets for designated subgroups. Schools failing to meet growth targets for 3 consecutive years were identified as in need of the Immediate Intervention for Underperforming Schools Program (II/USP). Schools received approximately $170 per student for 3 years to support programs, reform initiatives, professional development, and staffing to improve student academic performance. In order to be successful, schools had to meet the growth targets 2 out of the 3 years. If they failed to comply with the mandates, additional state sanctions were enforced by the School Assistance and Intervention Team (SAIT). With NCLB, schools could gain an additional sanction of program improvement (PI), which could result in the principal being released from that school and the school reconstituted.

To assist schools in the initial implementation, ongoing monitoring, and evaluation of the process, county offices, universities, private corporations, and individuals applied to the California Department of Education to become external evaluators. Schools were required to obtain assistance from a state approved external evaluator to facilitate the change processes needed to improve student academic performance. Two of the four authors were external evaluators approved by the California Department of Education. Our work with II/USP, SAIT, and PI schools, is the basis for our ongoing research project. This work began with 3 middle schools and 3 high schools and mushroomed into working with 33 elementary, middle, and high schools over the past 5 years.

The purpose of this ongoing research study is to examine the following research questions within the context of organizational change and systematic and strategic reform.

1. What structures need to be in place to ensure learning for all students?
2. What factors must be present to improve the quality of instruction?

3. How can the school leadership team become a professional learning community? (DuFour, Eaker, & DuFour, 2005; Katzenbach & Smith, 1993).

REVIEW OF THE LITERATURE

The review of the literature centered around five major areas: allocation of instructional time and resources, teacher and principal knowledge and skills, student assessment and monitoring, collaboration time for general and special education teachers, and district office support and expectations. While many entities throughout the United States have conducted research in these areas, the research teams coordinated by EdSource and the Center for the Study of Teaching and Policy have covered these areas thoroughly and have found similar conclusions.

Allocation of Instructional Time and Resources

In an extensive research study in high-performing, high-poverty, high-minority schools, Williams and colleagues (Williams, Kirst, Haertel, Perry, Studier et al., 2005) found that student achievement was a priority with teachers and principals having high expectations for their students. Well-defined plans for instructional improvement were in place with the staff setting measurable goals for exceeding the mandated student subgroup growth targets for improved achievement. Also a coherent standards-based curriculum and instructional program was implemented with the teachers reporting curricular alignment from grade to grade. Classroom instruction was guided by state academic standards and curriculum materials, and instructional resources provided in reading/language arts and mathematics aligned with the state standards. The teachers directly addressed the needs of English learners as well as those of struggling students and students with disabilities. Furthermore, the experienced principals reported the district had clear expectations for student performance that were aligned with the district's adopted curriculum. Also, the district evaluated the principals based on the extent to which instruction in the school aligned with the curriculum.

Teacher and Principal Knowledge and Skills

According to the Center for Study of Teaching and Policy in their *Leading for Learning Sourcebook: Concepts and Examples* (Knapp, Copland, and Talbert, 2003), in order for schools to be successful, leaders must be engaged in three learning agendas: student learning, professional learning, and system learning. The leader's role is to create powerful and equitable learning opportunities. To facilitate this process, five areas of action must occur. First, schools must establish a focus on learning by consistently and publicly focusing their own attention and that of others on learning and teaching. Second, they must build professional communities that value learning by nurturing work cultures that value and support their members' learning. Third, they must develop engaging external environments and secure resources from outside groups that foster students' or teachers' learning. Fourth, they must act strategically and share leadership by distributing leadership across levels and among individuals in different positions. Lastly, they must create coherence by connecting student, professional, and systems learning with one another and with learning goals.

Student academic progress depends on implementation of standards-based curriculum and engaging students in academic tasks. Students' interaction with their work, their teachers, and each other is critical. For this task, developing the opportunity for knowledge and skills attainment is most important (Williams et al., 2003). In a case study of Connecticut's reform process, Wilson, Darling-Hammond, and Berry (2005) found that when there was established policy alignment for the quality of teaching, the areas of professional development, teacher education, teacher and student standards, and assessment functioned as one.

Williams and colleagues (2005) saw effective leadership by the principal as a key to the success of the school as well as the students. They felt that "principal leadership included managing school improvement, driving the reform process, cultivating the school's vision, extensively using student assessment data for a wide variety of schoolwide focus, including evaluation of teacher practice and assistance to struggling students" (p. 20).

Researchers (Knapp, Copland, & Talbert, 2003b) stated the importance of strong leadership: "is that it brings about significant improvement in learning and narrowing of achievement gaps. Yet many school and district administrators report their time is consumed by matters unrelated to learning improvement. Even with enough time to focus, the task leaders face is complex, and it is not always clear what they should be doing to contribute to that goal" (p. 5). These statements sum up the reality of what the principal does as opposed to what they should be doing—improving student learning. This research validates the importance of schools and districts focusing on teaching, learning, and assessing.

Student Assessment and Monitoring

Student assessment and monitoring is an essential piece of the school improvement process. Many researchers have found a correlation to student success when principals, teachers, and the district use assessment to drive instruction. "Through assessment and observation, teachers diagnose student learning strengths and weaknesses, use grouping strategies effectively, and implement other strategies for meeting the needs of all students" (CACC, 2006, p. 3).

Researchers (Williams et al., 2005) studied schools serving low-income students in California. They found increased student achievement when the district and the principal used student assessment data. Frequently, principals and districts used assessment data from multiple sources to evaluate teachers' practices and to identify teachers who needed instructional improvement. Then the data was used to develop strategies to follow up on the progress of selected students and help them reach goals.

The Reading/Language Arts Framework for California Public Schools (Kame'enui et al., 2000) states that ideally, assessment and instruction are linked inextricably within any curriculum. The key to using assessment effectively and efficiently in a program of instruction is to recognize that different types of assessment tools must be used for different purposes. They list entry-level/placement (for grades 4–12), monitoring of progress, and summative assessment as crucial.

Instead of a model based on prevention and intervention, current practice in schools/classrooms is to wait for a child to fail. Too little emphasis is put on prevention, early and accurate identification of learning and behavior problems, and aggressive intervention using research-based approaches. (President's Commission on Excellence in Special Education, 2002).

Collaboration Time for General and Special Education Teachers

Collaboration time for teachers is critical for effective and sustainable change to become institutionalized. This is compounded when regular and special education teachers are encouraged to collaborate, because collaboration between regular and special education teachers is a national priority and a desirable goal in almost every educational environment. "Special education and general education are treated as separate systems but, in fact, share responsibility for the child with disabilities. In instruction, the systems must work together to provide effective teaching and ensure that those with additional needs benefit from strong teaching and instructional methods that should be offered to a child through general education" (Commission on Excellence in Special Education, 2002, p. 7).

However, many teachers experience difficulties when working collaboratively. These difficulties may stem from lack of school/district structures, resistant attitudes, and poor communication. Teachers need time to determine their own personal definitions and understandings of collaborative practices. They also need time to develop relationships with their special education counterparts, and they need time to determine how to best facilitate enhanced collaborative teaching (Murray, 2004). McLaughlin states that in their 10-year study, when they found an effective school, without exception, that school or department has been part of a collaborative professional learning community (McLaughlin & Talbert, 2003).

When teachers and principals establish common ground, clear purpose, effective monitoring, and collaborative processes, improved learning occurs for all students (DuFour, DuFour, Eaker, & Many, 2005).

District Office Support and Expectations

District leadership, accountability, and support appear significantly to influence student achievement. When schools set clear expectations and growth targets, including targets for subgroups of designated students, improved academic performance follows (Williams et al., 2005). By providing schools with achievement data and evaluating principals' performance and teacher practice based on achievement data, schools demonstrate significant growth. Ensuring language arts and math curricula are aligned with state standards and instruction and textbooks are focused on achievement, student achievement improved. This is especially true when the district highlights the expectations of students with disabilities. Compton School District (in Southern California) echoes the key components cited in research as necessary elements to cause their high priority schools to achieve at higher levels. There was a focus in classrooms on standards-based instruction using benchmarks with improved planning systems in place. With staff development at all levels and the building of internal partnerships staff were able to develop knowledge, skills, and attitudes. When performing instructional audits in their high priority schools the district staff looked for key results. Of high importance were explicit lesson delivery, systematic lesson plans, student-centered environment (including school-wide discipline), protection of instruction/time on task, and available instructional materials (Ward, 2000).

Knapp and colleagues (2003b) found the importance of a wider area of activities for the district. They suspect that given their exposure to a wider array of external environments, district administrators and staff might be in a good position to engage potential friends or critics. They recommended that districts educate school board members in building an improvement agenda and engage them as a part of a district learning community. It is important to promote the student and professional learning agenda with the media and influential community groups, join forces with community-based leaders who care about the quality of learning and teaching, and form partnerships with civic or professional groups that focus on learning improvement. Developing allies at the state level and using these contacts to increase flexibility and instructional resources assists in strategically using external requirements and resources to advance a local learning agenda.

Summary

The studies cited found similar results in the areas of allocation of time and resources, teacher and principal knowledge and skills, district office support, collaboration time for teachers, and student assessment and monitoring. Schools that implement the recommendations from these research studies by including all five areas in their school improvement focus, have a much higher chance for success. Schools that attend to the learning of students with disabilities also report high levels of school achievement results. Chrisman in *How Schools Sustain Success* (2005) states that the results of her study support the research studies of Mintrop (2003), Darling-Hammond (1997), and Barth (1990), which suggests that the solutions to improving education lie inside the schoolhouse. Schools and districts can replicate the successful strategies if they are willing to change in critical ways.

RESEARCH DESIGN

During the past 5 years, we have been working with underperforming schools identified by the California Department of Education as in need of immediate assistance to prevent state sanctions. According to federal mandates under NCLB schools not making AYP are classified as in need of program improvement (PI). Many of these schools had the students with disabilities subgroup identified as not meeting proficiency rates in either reading/language arts or mathematics.

This research project was directed at the change processes required to transform a rigid, complex school organization into a focused, high performing learning community accountable for the performance of all children it serves, enabling them to meet all the state and federal mandates. More specifically, it examines the researchers' work with 33 high minority, high poverty, underperforming elementary, middle, and high schools during the past 5 years. The research study is divided into three distinct steps or procedures. These steps include: building school teams who are responsible for analyzing school data and writing action plans; assessing classroom instruction; and monitoring the schools' progress.

These actions took place with most of the schools during a 2- to 4-year period of time.

Description of the Schools

Most schools are located in a large metropolitan area exceeding a population of 550,000. Demographical data reflects a population distribution of 60%–75% Hispanic, 20%–30% White, 5%–10% Black or Asian. English language learners comprise between 30% and 50% of the schools' total populations. Mobility rates range from 21% to 38%. Approximately 70%–80% of the teachers were credentialed, leaving one-third of the teaching staff on emergency permits or participating in an intern program through local universities. Each year 25%–30% of the staff transfer out of the schools. In addition, 85% of the total number of students identified as economically disadvantaged were Hispanic. Student attendance rates fluctuate somewhere between 93% and 96%. Other schools are located in the urban fringe of a mid-sized city in which Hispanic students comprise 68.7% of the school population followed by White 22.6%, African American 3.7%, Asian 2.2%, and American Indian 1.2% of the total population.

Research Questions

We attempted to identify and clarify the following questions:

1. What structures need to be in place to ensure learning for all students including struggling students and students with disabilities?
2. How is accountability for student learning defined?
3. What are the expectations for students, teachers, parents, and principals?
4. What support systems are available for students, teachers, principals, and parents?
5. What must be considered to improve the quality of instruction?
6. How are assessments utilized to monitor progress for students, teachers, principal, and the school as a whole?
7. What is the structure and occurrence of collaboration and time?
8. What is the scope, duration, and occurrence of professional development?
9. How are districts implementing IDEIA?
10. How is the school leadership team transformed from a working group to a high performance team? (Katzenbach & Smith, 1993)

These questions were the focus of the data inquiry in the classrooms, schools, and districts we examined.

Research Design and Data Collection

Major data elements at the school/district were studied, including: schools and districts academic and demographic data, locally administered assessments, curriculum-embedded assessments administered by the teachers, student study team processes, and evidence of response to intervention (RTI) programs.

Then each school completed an Academic Program Survey (APS) to assess their compliance with research-based policies and practices. An example question asked how many minutes were required for students reading 2 or more years below grade level. After the APS was completed the school wrote a 3-year action plan to correct any discrepancies between what they should be doing to promote student learning and what was actually occurring at the school.

The school teams conducted four walk-throughs in every classroom every year to determine the effectiveness of the instruction in terms of student engagement in an academic task or activity. At quarterly monitoring meetings data was reviewed to evaluate the progress the schools were making in implementing the benchmarks of their action plans. Annual meetings focused on analyzing the roadblocks and challenges that effected the successful or lack of successful implementation of the action plan. Revisions to the original plan were made, if appropriate and necessary.

Sample Data Collected

School and District Demographic and Academic Data

An analysis of the schools' and districts' academic and demographic data, locally administered assessments, curriculum-embedded assessments administered by the teachers, student study team processes, and evidence of RTI programs were collected and analyzed to note common themes.

Academic Program Survey

The results of the academic program surveys were examined to determine if verifiable evidence was utilized to support the findings. Developed by the state, essential program components (EPCs) address textbooks and materials, instructional time, principal professional development, teacher credentialing, teacher professional development, monitoring and assessment systems, collaboration time for teachers, use of pacing guides, intervention programs, and fiscal support of the reading/language arts and mathematics programs. Additionally, the least restrictive environment (LRE) self-assessment was completed to determine the districts' readiness to implement the components of IDEIA.

Action Plan Development

The corrective actions and benchmarks of the action plans were reviewed to determine if the actions were substantive and matched the expected outcomes of the process and the results of the APS and LRE.

Classroom Walk-Throughs

We facilitated classroom walk-throughs with school teams, three to four times during the school year. The tool we developed listed elements of effective instruction and described the behaviors teachers would exhibit if that element was in place in the classroom. Reliability and validity was substantiated from its use in over 3,000 classrooms throughout California. In addition, teachers were trained on how to use the tool by referring to the rubric and how to interpret data from the observations.

The Process for Effective Change

Step I. Building School Teams, Analyzing School Data, and Writing Action Plans

The initial step took place over a few days in which the leadership teams and district office staff built relationships with one another, then evaluated the academic programs at their school, including special education and English language instruction. During the course of the week they wrote action plans which addressed the gaps between what was happening at their schools compared to what should be happening, in terms of IDEIA and the California Department of Education's nine essential program components of an effective educational program.

Step II. Assessing Classroom Instruction

The second component empowered the staff at the school to conduct peer reviews of the classroom instruction at their school. The researchers trained the team on how to assess the elements of effective instruction using a modified Likert Scale. The leadership team, in pairs, initially observed every class in the school for a 30-minute time period and recorded what they observed. Each teacher was observed twice during the day to ensure inter-rater reliability. The data was aggregated so no one teacher could be identified. Three more observations occurred throughout the year with new teachers rotating onto the leadership team so they had an opportunity to observe the instructional program at his/her school.

Step III. Monitoring the Schools, Progress

Three to four times during the school year, the leadership teams met with the researchers to demonstrate what progress they had made in implementing the corrective actions of the action plan, based upon the nine essential program components of effective schools. During this time the classroom observations were conducted to see how instruction had improved based upon the data from the initial classroom visits. Often the schools found that direct instruction was not occurring, that classroom management was an issue, and students with disabilities had no access to the core curriculum.

The process is dynamic and each new school we work with adds new perspectives and insights as to the complexities of school change, the realities of staff turnover, new program adoptions, new legislation, and the need for sustained commitment from the district office for substantive improvements.

Preliminary Results

Tables 16.1, 16.2, and 16.3 represent the initial findings from our research. The data is preliminary but it demonstrates that with continued support, monitoring, and trusting relationships, significant progress can be made in high poverty, high minority, and previously underperforming schools. When schools have the support, knowledge, skills, and resources, significant improvement in student academic performance occurs. It is an arduous process in which personal feelings and attitudes must be set aside for the good of the students. Developing schools into professional learning communities takes time, commitment, and a belief system that all adults and children can learn.

SUMMARY OF FINDINGS

A thorough analysis of the data reveal the need for a process to develop a new generation of leaders and decision makers who feel empowered to make the critical changes necessary to turn the schools from dysfunctional entities to collaborative teams focused on improving student academic performance. Moving forward requires careful thought and consideration about what systems, strategies, and concepts must be put into place for the new generation to ensure dramatic increases in student performance.

Allocation of Time and Resources

Standards-Based Textbook and Materials

An analysis of the data indicated that general education students did have enough textbooks and materials but these materials were rarely used on a regular basis. Support materials for English learners and students with

TABLE 16.1   Decile 2 Middle School

| Group | Decile 2 Middle School | | | | | |
| | English Language Arts | | | Mathematics | | |
	Proficient 2002	Proficient 2003	Proficient 2004	Proficient 2002	Proficient 2003	Proficient 2004
Schoolwide	11.3%	20.2%	26.6%	17.6%	19.7%	28.6%
Hispanic	5.2%	9.9%	12.2%	5.2%	7.6%	14.2%
Asian	17.2%	35.1%	47.2%	37.3%	41.8%	52.7%
ELL	9.0%	17.1%	21.8%	15.6%	20.4%	26.0%
SES	8.1%	15.6%	22.3%	15.2%	16.6%	24.5%

TABLE 16.2   Decile 2 High School

| Group | Decile 2 High School | | | | | |
| | English Language Arts | | | Mathematics | | |
	Proficient 2002	Proficient 2003	Proficient 2004	Proficient 2002	Proficient 2003	Proficient 2004
Schoolwide	12.4%	22.4%	33.3%	10.2%	12.7%	32.6%
Hispanic	7.6%	17.3%	28.9%	7.1%	9.3%	26.9%
Asian	13.6%	31.5%	55.5%	21.7%	20.0%	83.3%
ELL	1.8%	11.6%	25.2%	9.6%	8.5%	29.8%
SES	4.2%	15.5%	29.2%	8.0%	11.8%	40.4%

TABLE 16.3   Decile 2 Elementary School

	Decile 2 Elementary School					
	English Language Arts			Mathematics		
Group	Proficient 2004	Proficient 2005	Proficient 2006	Proficient 2004	Proficient 2005	Proficient 2006
Schoolwide	31.3%	37.5%	42.0%	37.9%	45.9%	51.1%
ELL	25.9%	26.2%	33.3%	38.1%	42.6%	52.2%
SpEd	5.9%	9.6%	29.2%	15.9%	27.7%	40.6%
SES	27.8%	34.2%	39.3%	32.8%	43.3%	50.1%

disabilities were not routinely used in the regular classroom and in some cases missing from the resource kits. Staff did not have time to develop an understanding of the content standards nor how to utilize them in tandem with the instructional materials and strategies in their classrooms. Few special education classrooms had core curriculum textbooks or interventions materials available to them.

Time Allocation for Instruction in Reading/Language Arts and Mathematics

The daily classroom schedules did not provide the required time to effectively teach reading/language arts and mathematics. None of the schools met the California Department of Education's (CDE) recommended instructional minutes per day for reading/language arts or mathematics. Instructional time was often fragmented and interrupted with other events occurring in the school.

Intervention Programs

Some schools had some sort of intervention programs in place for students scoring 2 or more years below grade level. However, there was no formalized process to determine how students entered and exited the programs, how staff was trained to instruct the program, and how students were able to master the standards and return to the regular educational program. None of the schools had an RTI program in place nor a clearly defined student study team (SST) process. All the districts/schools were using the discrepancy model to identify students for special education services.

As schools reviewed their procedures for assessing struggling readers and students with disabilities, they began to realize the need for strategic and intensive intervention programs. Schools hired literacy coaches, attended specialized training and/or held student-focused planning meetings to define clearly the procedures for assessing, for placing, and for exiting students from intervention programs. A formalized SST process was developed and implemented, and discussions occurred about how to initiate a RTI program.

Teacher and Principal Knowledge and Skills

Professional Development for Principals and Teachers

Few of the principals and none of the teachers had previously participated in professional development aligned with the adopted textbooks and materials. As a result, instruction was often fragmented and disorganized and not all the components of the program were utilized. When schools became aware of the availability of professional development to assist them in implementing the adopted programs with fidelity, they demonstrated a sense of relief and appreciation. Over 90% of general and special education teachers participated in the summer core curriculum or intervention professional development.

Teacher Collaboration

In most schools teachers had prep times, which were aligned by grade levels or content areas. However, teachers viewed this time to plan for instruction or to meet with students; they did not see it as a time to collaborate with peers around the performance of their students. If collaboration time was listed in the school calendar, no agendas, minutes, or outcomes were noted. Special education teachers had their own departments and did not participate in collaboration meetings with content teachers. Many general education teachers complained they were unaware their students were receiving special education services as there was little dialogue between general and special education teachers.

As teachers/principals reviewed their data, developed pacing guides, and/or compared student performance to state standards, they realized the necessity of ongoing professional development and working together on instructional practices. Special education departments were eliminated and special education teachers joined content area collaboration meetings. This was not an easy accomplishment with significant resistance on all fronts. However, over time, general and special education teachers began to appreciate the unique knowledge and skills of each other and new processes and procedures for effective communication ensued.

Student Assessment and Monitoring

No formalized student assessment systems were in place. Periodically assessments were reviewed but no follow-up took place to determine if students had been retaught those standards they had not yet mastered. Changes in school operations and classroom instruction emerged after curriculum-embedded assessments were built into the school calendar and reviewed every 6–8 weeks. Students with disabilities were also monitored using both the curriculum-embedded assessments and others aligned to their IEPs. As systems were designed to implement RTI, a more formalized process for identifying struggling students was observed.

District Office Support and Expectations

All districts expected their schools to improve and raise student achievement and most districts provided achievement data to the schools. However, few districts evaluated their principals' performance and teacher practice based on the achievement data. Initially the conversation about student performance was only at the school level with periodic updates to the superintendent and the school boards. As these discussions continued the critical role of the district became apparent if underperforming schools were to reach state and federal mandates. Everything from hiring experienced principals to determining budget allocations is directly controlled by the district office staff. As we continue to refine and adapt the process, the district office staff is a key element to successful implementation of the schools' actions plans. In one instance, a district staff member voiced opinions that the principals would not be able to make the necessary changes based on the program improvement plan. Fortunately for the schools, these principals and their teams were able to make the necessary improvements.

RECOMMENDATIONS

Introducing standards, state and federal mandates, and accountability to public schools has been described as one of the biggest changes in America's social system. Holding schools accountable for every student in every school across the country requires a monumental change in attitude and expectations for teachers, principals, superintendents, school boards, and parents. The doubters question the validity of the assumption that all students can learn, that assessments measure performance, and that education must be standards-based.

Change in schools is illusive and problematic in determining how best to ensure its value to the organization. Someone once said that if George Washington returned to the United States that the only place he would recognize would be schools because he could sit down at a desk, open a book, and answer the questions at the end of the chapter. Not so with transportation, health care, communication systems, or the housing industry. They have all responded to the global economy and the so-called flattening of the world. It is essential for the welfare of our democracy for the education system to also adapt and re-engineer itself to meet the vastly different kinds of knowledge, skills, and dispositions students will need in order to survive in tomorrow's world.

As we found in our research, a refocusing on the achievement of all students does change school performance. Setting academic targets for ethnic subgroups and students with disabilities does begin to close the achievement gap. Providing teachers with professional development and collaboration time does improve the quality of teaching and learning.

Have the results and processes been quick and easy? No. It is extremely hard work to retool an entire workforce at the school site and district level. However, we have clearly demonstrated that the goal of educating all students, including students with disabilities, is attainable.

REFERENCES

Barth, R. (1990). *Improving schools from within.* San Francisco: Jossey-Bass.

California Comprehensive Center (CACC) in conjunction with the American Institutes for Research. (2006). *Research summary supporting the nine essential program components and academic program survey: Nine guiding principals for system change.* Sacramento: California Department of Education.

Carroll, S., Reichardt, R., & Guarino, C. (2000). *The distribution of teachers among California school districts and schools.* Santa Monica, CA: Rand Corporation.

Chrisman, V. (2005). How schools sustain success. *Education Leadership, 62,* 16–20.

Civil Rights Project: Harvard University. (2005). Dropouts in California: Confronting graduation rate crisis. *Harvard Education,* Retrieved March 30, 2005, from http://www.civilrightsproject.harvard.edu/news/pressrelease/dropout

Darling-Hammond, L. (1997). *Doing what matters most: Investing in quality teaching.* New York: The National Commission on Teaching and America's Future.

DuFour, R., DuFour, R., Eaker, R., & Many, T. (2005). *Learning by doing: A handbook for professional learning communities at work.* Bloomington, IN: Solution Tree.

DuFour, R., Eaker, R., & DuFour, R. (Eds.). (2005). *On common ground.* Bloomington, IN: National Educational Service.

Fullan, M. (2005). Professional learning communities writ large. In R. Dufour, R. Eaker, & R. Dufour (Eds.), *On common ground* (pp. 209–223). Bloomington, IN: National Educational Service.

Fullan, M., Bertani, A., & Quinn, J. (2004). New lessons for districtwide reform. *Educational Leadership, 61*(6), 42–46.

Kame'enui, E., Simmons, D., Castaneda, L., Astore, M., Abarca, P., Brown, E., et. al. (2000). *Reading/language arts framework for California public schools: Kindergarten through grade twelve.* Sacramento: California Department of Education.

Katzenbach, J. R., & Smith, D. K. (1993). *The wisdom of teams: Creating the high-performance organization.* Boston, MA: Harvard Business School Press.

Knapp, M., Copland, M., & Talbert, J. (2003a). *Leading for learning sourcebook: Concepts and examples.* [[City]]: Center for the Study of Teaching and Policy, University of Washington.

Knapp, M., Copland, M., & Talbert, J. (2003b). *Leading for learning: Reflective tools for school and district leaders.* Seattle: Center for the Study of Teaching and Policy, University of Washington.

Littky, D., & Grabelle, S. (2004). If we love our children more than we love our schools, the systems must change. *Educational Horizons, 82,* 284–289.

McLaughlin, M., & Talbert, J. (2003). *Reforming district: How districts support school reform.* Seattle: Center for the Study of Teaching and Policy, University of Washington.

Mintrop, H. (2003, January 15). The limits of sanctions in low-performing schools: A study of Maryland and Kentucky schools on probation. *Educational Policy Analysis Archives, 11*(3).

Murray, C. (2004). Clarifying collaborative roles in urban high schools. *Teaching Exceptional Children, 36,* 44–51.

National Center for Education Statistics. (2005). NAEP Report 2005. Washinton DC: Institute of Education Sciences.

No small change: Targeting money toward student performance. (2005, January). *Education Week. 24*(17).

Perkins-Gough, D. (2005). A two-tiered education system. *Educational Leadership, 62,* 87–88.

President's Commission on Excellence in Special Education. (2002). *A new era: revitalizing special education for children and their families.* Jessup, MD: U.S. Department of Education.

Reeves, D. (2006). Of hubs, bridges, and networks. *Educational Leadership, 63,* 32–37.

Skinner, R. (2005). State of the states. *Education Week, 24,* 110.

U.S. Department of Education Office of Special Education and Rehabilitative Services. (2002). *A new era: Revitalizing special education for children and their families.* Washington, DC: United States Department of Education.

Ward, R., (2000). *From triage to excellence: Districts supporting school success.* Retrieved from http://www.bayregionssc.org/docs/from_triage_to_excellence.pdf

Williams, T., Kirst, M., Haertel, E., Perrry, M., Studier, C., Brazil, N., et al. (2005). *Similar students, different results: Why do some schools do better? A large-scale survey of California elementary schools serving low-income students.* Mountain View, CA: EdSource.

Wilson, S., Darling-Hammond, L., & Berry, B. (2001) *A case of successful teaching policy: Connecticut's long-term efforts to improve teaching and learning.* Center for the Study of Teaching and Policy, University of Washington. Washington, DC: U.S. Department of Education.

CHAPTER 17

Local Educational Authorities and IDEIA

Linda J. Hawkins and Michael N. Riley

When considering the impact on schools and districts of the Individuals With Disabilities Education Improvement Act (IDEIA), it makes sense to first determine the extent to which the philosophy and requirements of the law are in concert with the philosophy and practices of the institutions. In our school district, we find IDEIA supports and strengthens our mission and our work, it holds us accountable for practices we should engage in whether or not the law existed in the first place, and it pushes us to think more expansively about how we might achieve our goals for students, not just identified students but all students. Unfortunately, this law, like so many other attempts at education reform in the United States, rests on several large and faulty assumptions, and until our profession squares around to the central issues that lie at the heart of education reform in America, it is unlikely IDEIA will produce much change in our schools.

In this chapter we examine IDEIA's potential to improve education; its compatibility with the mission of our school system, the Bellevue School District in Washington State; the assumptions underpinning the act; other issues significant to the delivery of an effective special education program, which remain largely unaddressed by the revised law; the emerging importance of technology; and the chances that IDEIA will achieve its intended purposes.

IDEIA'S PROMISE

Among the changes produced by the law the one getting the most attention is RTI or response to intervention. RTI is intended to become the preferred means for identifying students for special education services, but if successful its implications will be felt well beyond the identification process. Using an RTI approach requires school districts to study student performance frequently; identify students who are not meeting success; provide interventions designed to help these students; measure the effectiveness of these interventions; and provide additional assistance as needed based on results. Districts are expected to deliver a high quality core curriculum, and neither poor curriculum nor poor teaching can be used as justification for students' qualifying for special education. The assessments should be connected directly to the curriculum, and interventions should be designed to improve the students' performance in that curriculum. The data collected should not only measure the students' current status but their improvement over time. The law sends the message that we professionals bear responsibility for the performance of our students, that this responsibility includes taking a scientific approach to both the measurement and treatment components of our work, and that early and ongoing intervention should be standard practice in all classrooms. When teachers share a high quality curriculum, precise assessments, and routine practices for data analysis, the profession should benefit from widespread collaboration, knowledge-sharing, and problem-solving. Across schools and districts, and hopefully even across states and the nation, professionals should be encouraged to work together to improve curriculum, pedagogy, assessments, and intervention strategies.

What's not to like?

Of course the issues are more complex than we have just portrayed them, and there are provisions and implications that practitioners, including us, will find objectionable. However, for the most part, the provisions of the IDEIA, as revised from the Individual Disabilities Education Act (IDEA), are ones we welcome. Allow us to give some context to our views by sharing information about our district.

IDEIA AND BELLEVUE

Sixteen thousand five hundred students attend the Bellevue School District, which is located in an affluent community just outside of Seattle. Fifty-six percent of the students are White; 25% Asian; 8% Hispanic; 8% multi-ethnic; 3% African American. Twenty percent qualify for the federal government's meal program; 25% speak a language other than English as their first, and 8% are enrolled in English as a Second Language (ESL) Program; 10% are in special education. For over a decade, we have declared our mission to be preparing all students for success in college, and we have carried out that goal by trying to help all students achieve success in a top-of-the-line college preparatory curriculum. Because of the national reputation of both the Advanced Placement (AP) Program and the International Baccalaureate (IB) Program, we have held up these two sets of advanced level courses as the culminating experiences in all the relevant disciplines. In the class that graduated in June 2006, just over 80% of the students completed one or more AP or IB courses, and 50% completed four or more.

When we first proclaimed that "all students can be and should be AP/IB students," members of the special education community expressed concern. At the time, which was the 1996–1997 school year, the district administered just under three hundred AP tests to a high school population of 5,000, and only seven tests to Hispanics, two to African Americans, and none to students in ESL or special education programs. It was no surprise, then, that some members of our community assumed the district's goal seemed to ignore, if not discount, students with special needs. Because the goal was in fact intended for *all* students, including those in special education, the special education department studied each of the cases in our special education population and determined that roughly 20% of the group had disabilities severe enough to make college an unrealistic goal. We acknowledged that we needed a different way of expressing high expectations for this 20%, and we began talking about "AP-like experiences" for these students. As one mother said, "For my son, Advanced Placement meant participation in one core class a year throughout high school." For others it meant acquiring a skill set that allowed for independent living.

While tailoring the goals to meet the individual capacities of students in the special education program, we remained insistent that the vast majority of identified students are quite capable of succeeding in some form of higher education. Today, 50% of Bellevue graduates who have received special education services have participated in one or more AP or IB courses. We have ample amounts of anecdotal information to show that many parents, teachers, and administrators now believe disabled students can achieve at very high levels of performance if they have the right level of support. In the spring of 2007, we administered over five thousand AP and IB exams, and all groups of students were solidly represented.

Helping all students achieve success in lofty academic programs and develop the skill and content knowledge necessary for success in college is tough, complex work, and after more than a decade of effort we remain frustrated by our inability to achieve this level of accomplishment with all our students: frustrated, certainly, but still fully committed. We believe success comes with the use of a sophisticated approach, one commensurate with the challenges of the objective. We organize our efforts around four major components.

First, we provide a detailed, coherent, district-wide curriculum. We believe, for instance, that the possibility of students reaching higher level mathematics in high school depends heavily on their experiences with mathematics in the earliest grades and throughout their time in our schools. We spend a considerable amount of our resources developing and refining curriculum in all disciplines.

Second, we measure student progress frequently using district-wide assessments for all grades and disciplines. To return to mathematics as our example, students take common district mathematics assessments for every unit studied from kindergarten through precalculus. Data from the assessments are used to measure the effectiveness of our entire program—curriculum content, curriculum alignment, pedagogy, staff development, even the assessments themselves—as well as the performance of individual students.

Third, we provide support for students who are struggling with mastery of the curriculum as early as possible, as often as needed. Student support consists of a variety of approaches including special classes held during the school day, one-on-one and small group tutoring, after-school programs, and summer programs. Finally, we provide ample support for teachers, with staff development aimed squarely at the successful delivery of the curriculum and meeting the needs of all students as they work to master that curriculum.

While the components of our approach are basic and in all likelihood similar to those used by schools and districts across the nation, we have found through a long and sustained effort that there is a considerable distance between an idea and its consistent and successful implementation. At the heart of our work stands our curriculum, and we have invested a considerable amount of time, money, and human capital in making it as detailed, comprehensive, and coherent as possible. In some areas, we have created programs out of whole cloth because we were so dissatisfied with commercial products that were available to us. In other cases, we purchased a published program but have yet to find a single situation that did not call for extensive work on our part to hit the target we were after. We have similar stories to tell about creating an effective and thorough assessment program, providing the kind of student support that produces high success rates for struggling students, and implementing a staff development program that meets the most significant interests and needs of teachers. The devil, as they say, is in the details.

Our approach in Bellevue seems in perfect concert with RTI. We acknowledge the importance of a high quality core curriculum. We use frequent assessments—and are more than willing to increase their frequency and precision. We analyze data to make determinations about our programs as well as our students' needs. We intervene as well as we know how in order to improve student performance. And we adjust our program—including our methods of supporting students—frequently, continuously searching for improved performance on the part of both professionals and students.

Our wariness and caution about IDEIA spring from our experience implementing this approach. To those who assume that RTI will produce significant and meaningful change quickly, we suggest that positive outcomes will indeed occur but only with a considerable commitment and likely at a pace that is disappointing, and only if the assumptions underlying the act are addressed in an honest and direct fashion.

ASSUMPTION ONE: THE CORE CURRICULUM

IDEIA makes several assumptions that are shaky at best, and chief among these is the belief that schools and districts are already implementing or will soon be implementing a "high quality core curriculum." Our experience, as we indicated above, tells us this will not be accomplished by picking something off the shelf. Further, many districts do not have the financial or human resources to create a high quality program quickly. After 10 years of work, 10 years of placing curriculum development and its consistent implementation at the center of our efforts to improve, it would be fair to describe our program today as incomplete and evolving. America's love affair with local control and teacher autonomy has made curricular coherence a low priority. As Richard Elmore points out, "Educators equate professionalism with autonomy—getting to use their own judgment, to exercise discretion, to determine the conditions of their own work in classrooms and schools" (Fullan, 2007, p. 55).

How important is curricular coherence? We believe that it is essential, that without it not much positive and lasting change occurs in schools. E. D. Hirsch addresses the issue at a national level in many of his works, most recently in *The Knowledge Deficit:*

> No teacher, however capable, can efficiently cope with the huge differences in academic preparation among the students in a typical American classroom—differences that grow with each successive grade. (In other nations, the differences between groups diminish over time, so that they are closer together by grade seven than they were in grade four.)
>
> The chief cause of our schools' inefficiency is precisely this curricular incoherence. At the beginning of the school year, a teacher cannot be sure what the entering students know about a subject, because they have been taught very different topics in prior grades depending on the different preferences of their teachers. (Hirsch, 2006, p. 84)

William Schmidt, who has extensively studied the results and implications of international comparisons in mathematics and science achievement, picks up the same theme in his analysis of science teaching in the United States:

> The picture of the U.S. system that emerges from the TIMSS data is that the U.S. does not have a coherent, focused and rigorous science curriculum that provides all students with a reasonable chance to learn to their potential (Schmidt, McKnight, Cogan, Jakwerth, & Houang, 1999).
>
> Such a result seems inescapable given the nearly 16,000 local school districts, each with its own version of science standards, and textbook manufacturers that strive to meet the standards of as many districts as possible that result in bulky, disconnected textbooks that contain few meaningful connections from one year to another. (Schmidt, 2003, p. 571)

So much of RTI's approach relies on the existence of a high quality core curriculum—it is the curriculum that defines successful student achievement; that is, success *is* mastery of the curriculum; it is from the curriculum that assessments are derived; and it is curriculum that will define the extent to which interventions succeed because interventions are designed to produce student success in the curriculum. The absence of commonly shared core curriculum places RTI itself at serious risk.

There are signs of hope, as Judy Wurtzel reports:

> Many schools and school districts—particularly those serving poor and minority students—are moving towards what is often called "managed instruction," that is, deliberate efforts to align common curriculum and instructional materials, formative and benchmark assessments, extensive professional development, and instructional leaders who support a shared set of instructional practices. Most of the urban districts seeing significant gains at the elementary school level are using some form of managed instruction. (Snipes, Doolittle, & Herlihy 2002; Council of Great City Schools 2004; Bill and Melinda Gates Foundation 2005).
>
> At the high school level, the Advanced Placement and International Baccalaureate programs, available primarily for high performing students, have many characteristics of managed instruction. Yet, few examples of managed instruction exist for low achieving students in urban schools. Recent evaluations of reforming high poverty high schools in urban districts, including American Institute for Research and SRI's evaluation of Gates Foundation supported schools, report that teachers in these schools feel overwhelmed by the demands of creating or selecting their own instructional tools—curriculum and curriculum materials, assessments, etc. (American Institutes for Research and SRI International, 2005, Gates Foundation National School District and Network Grants Program, Year 3 Evaluation Report).

In response, districts including Chicago and Portland, Oregon, and states such as Rhode Island are launching high school redesigns focused squarely on curriculum and instruction. (Wurtzel, n.d., p. 1)

While optimistic, Wurtzel goes on to explain the resistance to this movement, which is substantial, and she argues that it is likely that it will be years before the majority of students in America experience a "high quality core curriculum," as basic as that concept may seem.

ASSUMPTION TWO: RESEARCH-BASED PROGRAMS AND INTERVENTIONS

IDEIA calls for "research-based" interventions, a phrase that chooses to ignore the reality surrounding the quality of research in the profession. Paul Hill, the Director of the Center on Reinventing Public Education at the University of Washington, offers a pointed description of the profession's status along with a suggestion about how the Bill and Melinda Gates Foundation might better spend its money.

> The Gates Foundation's venture-capital approach hasn't worked very well in education because the solutions really aren't there. Though some existing school designs and instructional methods are able to move the needle slightly, even the best of them improve results for disadvantaged students but leave them far below the national average.
>
> A better option would be to acknowledge the primitive state of education methods and the paucity of good ideas about how to educate disadvantaged students effectively, and create grant programs to elicit and develop totally new ideas. (Hill, 2006, p. 34)

While acknowledging recent improvement in education research inspired by the No Child Left Behind Act, Robert Slavin explains how implementation strategies that call for the use of research-based practices can result in disappointment.

> Early on in the "No Child" era, Education Department leaders seemed serious about the "what works" philosophy. But they faced a dilemma in putting it into practice. They felt there was too little high-quality research on too few programs, and too few reviews of research on practical programs, to make confident statements about what works in most arenas. They abandoned the idea of promoting programs with strong evidence of effectiveness and instead applied far lower standards of evidence, promoting programs "based on scientifically-based evidence," meaning that they somehow incorporate elements that have been successfully evaluated, even if the programs themselves have not. (Slavin, 2006, p. 31)

Even today, information on the What Works Clearinghouse Web site (http://www.whatworks.ed.gov/) shows just how few programs have met the test of research-proven effectiveness. Further, while use of research-based methodologies and programs would seem to be supported by common sense, the fact is there is a debate in the education community about whether this focus is even likely to lead to positive school change. As Michael J. Petrilli, previous Associate Assistant Deputy Secretary for Innovation and Improvement at the U.S. Department of Education, explains:

> The whatever-works camp holds a very different world view. They seek to right the system through the classic management model of "tight-loose": Be tight about the results you expect, but loose as to the means. Put differently, the whatever-works camp combines accountability for student learning with flexibility around everything else. This camp aims to create a marketplace of schools, free to experiment, compete, and improve. After all, there's a reason that America has the strongest economy in the world, they assert, and if we can empower educators with significant freedom (in return for getting results), they, too, will rise to the occasion. (Petrilli, 2006, p. 36)

On the whole, our school system values research, and we do our homework before launching initiatives. For many years we have held external validation as an important value, which to us means going beyond the expertise of our own staff to find the best information available. We have developed a number of partnerships—primarily with higher education institutions and national organizations dedicated to education reform—designed to advise us on curriculum development, staff development, and student intervention programs. It is this very focus, however, that makes us realists about the lack of high quality research—and thus lack of high quality research-based programs—in the profession.

In preparing to purchase instructional materials for our special education program, we avoided publishers at the start and worked with special education departments at the University of Oregon, the University of Washington, Columbia University, and others. We asked professors to identify programs for specific disabilities in reading, writing, mathematics, and study skills that appeared from their perspectives to meet research-based criteria. Informed by their higher education colleagues, our special education team read research studies to deepen their knowledge, and only then felt prepared to approach publishers, looking for materials and programs that matched the specific needs of disabled populations. When we found programs that passed muster, we signed on for training and then followed up with our own ongoing staff development and accountability system. While this approach has been successful on many occasions, we have also found that there are specific areas for which there has been no program developed, and we have relied on training staff to develop educational hypotheses, develop and deliver reasonable interventions, monitor progress data, and adjust interventions as needed. We are proud of these efforts but have found the process to be very difficult—time consuming, labor intensive, and expensive. And we would be the first to admit that we are far from having a comprehensive, pre-school to transition, research-based program that meets the needs of all students.

For too long, legislators and, unfortunately, many educators have presumed that the profession already possesses the knowledge and skill it needs to make all students successful. It is this assurance that inspires legislation that calls for the use of preexisting "right" methods. Would that they existed in the amount and quality we desire. Most unfortunate is the fact that a belief in extant solutions prevents an investment in the research and development the profession so desperately needs.

ASSUMPTION THREE: PRECISE AND FREQUENT ASSESSMENTS, DATA ANALYSIS

RTI depends heavily on the use of precise, frequently administered assessments and the classroom teacher's capacity for careful—and frequent—data analysis. The notion that these assessments will measure student performance in the so-called core curriculum is, as we have seen earlier, the first problem. The second is the extent to which assessments exist—even in schools and districts that have a coherent curriculum—at the quality and quantity required for them to provide the information educators will need to make good decisions about individual student needs. In Bellevue, we administer over 400 classroom-based assessments across all the disciplines in the K–12 program. The assessments are the same across the district for a grade level and subject; teachers use common scoring guides to evaluate their students' performance; the data are posted and shared within the entire professional community; and, although this system has only been in place since September 2006, it has inspired focused, helpful, and sometimes heated and frustrating conversations about curriculum, pedagogy, the assessments themselves, the consistency of our scoring—a wealth of topics all worthy of careful attention as we continue to improve our work. The assessments have also alerted us to students who need additional support and given us helpful information in determining the type of intervention students need. More than anything, however, we have learned how little we know about effective test-making (we are not psychometricians); how complex sophisticated data analysis is (we are not statisticians or researchers); and how much guesswork is involved in our attempts to be diagnostic and prescriptive.

We have always believed in holding ourselves accountable for the effectiveness of our curriculum and instruction by using common assessments. However, for years we tried to implement our assessment program without the technology that makes deep data analysis possible in an ongoing way. We collected assessment information from teachers in the earliest years of our curriculum implementation, but our studies were cumbersome, rudimentary and, for the most part, useless. We gathered samples of student work, and they gathered dust in boxes tucked under tables in district offices. We sponsored team meetings with teachers and curriculum developers to analyze student thinking as it was reflected in samples of their work, but we ran out of time and money and always struggled with how to disseminate what was learned in these smaller groups to our entire professional community.

Advancements in technology, in particular software designed to analyze classroom-based assessment data, have made this work much more manageable and useful. However, because this is a relatively new option for schools, detailed assessment-data analysis remains a relatively uncommon practice. Further, even where educators are practiced and proficient in using data to improve instruction, the quality and the frequency of assessments often leave much to be desired.

ASSUMPTION FOUR: IMPLEMENTATION WITH FIDELITY

IDEIA says curriculum and intervention strategies must be administered with *fidelity,* which means teachers must be highly skilled in delivering instruction in the core curriculum both in whole-class and in small-group or individual settings. Teachers and other professionals will also be responsible for making sense of data, for identifying students who need intervention, and for selecting the intervention program or methodology that is most likely to address student needs. In the successful implementation of IDEIA, then, teacher training must be a fundamental component, as it is in almost all education reform efforts. Unfortunately, the effectiveness of staff development is notoriously questionable, not because teachers are not willing, engaged, and capable learners, but typically because the initiatives themselves are often poorly thought out or the training is weak and insufficient.

Michael Fullan in the fourth edition of *The Meaning of Educational Change* does a superb job synthesizing the work of many researchers to explain why teacher training fails more times than it succeeds. Among the issues he identifies is "classroom press," the daily influences on teachers that significantly affect their work. "It draws their focus to day-to-day effects or a short-term perspective; it isolates them from other adults, especially meaningful interaction with colleagues; it exhausts their energy; and it limits their opportunities for sustained reflection" (Fullan, 2007, p. 24). Echoing the concern of others about the profession's fascination with individual autonomy and the resulting lack of coherency, Fullan notes the following.

> Cohen and Hill also found that norms of collaboration among teachers were weak, and that collaboration per se did not necessarily result in improvement. The result for a majority of teachers is lack of consistency and coherence, with few opportunities for what Ball and Cohen and Cohen and Hill call practice-based inquiry and teaching for understanding, in which assessment, curriculum, and opportunities for teachers to learn about connecting assessment and instruction are evident on an ongoing basis. (Fullan, 2007, p. 26)

The difficulty of providing effective professional training for complex skill development—which is what RTI demands—is further exacerbated by teacher turnover, a trend we find especially significant in our district in special education (more on this later). To engage "with fidelity" in the implementation of the core curriculum, the administration of precise and sophisticated assessments, the analysis of a wealth of data, and the selection and use of effective interventions will require a quality and quantity of professional training and support that are quite rare in American schools and districts.

OTHER ISSUES

While RTI is getting the lion's share of attention in the examination of IDEIA, we believe there are several other topics that deserve attention in any serious effort to improve the quality of special education services. We now turn our attention to three of these: increases in cases involving more severe disabilities; issues related to hiring and retaining staff; and funding.

Severe Disabilities

Bellevue, like many school districts across the nation, is experiencing increases in the number of students with more severe disabilities. The number of students in the autism spectrum, for instance, is growing significantly, and these students require labor intensive and time intensive interventions (more on funding issues related to autism will follow). In the 2002–2003 school year, 152 students in our district of 16,000 students were identified with autism; in 2006–2007, 239 students are so identified, marking a 57% increase in only 5 years. While the national incidence of autism is 1 person among every 150, in Bellevue, 1 in every 69 students is autistic. Every school in our district is home to autistic students, and we have recently created several centers to provide more focused resources, including training for both mainstream and special education staff.

Over the past several years we have worked closely with experts at the University of Washington to develop programs that take advantage of the best and most recent research available on autism. We have reaped a number of benefits from this relationship. Our general staff as well as our special educators are much more skilled than they were only a few years ago at recognizing the signs of autism (including Asperger's syndrome), are more adept at discussing the condition with families, and are now experiencing more success in encouraging families to have their children evaluated. At the Kindering Center, a facility for special needs students from birth to age 3 with whom we have had a cooperative relationship for more than a decade, children are now being diagnosed with autism at 18 months, as opposed to age 3. Our autism programs for students of all ages have been marked by well-documented successes.

We are also seeing a significant increase in the number of students with emotional and behavioral disorders. Eleven years ago, the school district provided one classroom each at the elementary, middle, and high school level for students with emotional behavioral disability (EBD). In September of 2007, our EBD population will be taught in six classrooms divided between two elementary schools; two classrooms at two locations for middle school students; and four classrooms and two locations for high schoolers. We also support Bellevue students with emotional disorders at two local hospitals and various residential facilities. Our community is also witnessing an increase in group homes for students who are significantly low functioning and sometimes dangerous.

Increased experience with students with severe disabilities and advancements in the field are enabling us to deliver better services to these students, and we welcome that opportunity. We would also welcome increased attention to these students and their needs by legislators—statewide and national—who provide resources for identified students. As the incidence of severe disabilities increases, so does our need for research, programs that work, and the means to implement those programs.

Hiring, Training, Supporting, and Retaining Staff

In "High Schools Bear Brunt of Teacher Shortage," an article focused on special education staffing in Chicago Public Schools, Leslie Whitaker details the personnel issues known well to anyone familiar with special education programs.

- Nationally, demand for special education teachers has been on the rise for a decade. The number of students classified as learning-disabled is up more than 10%, partly due to more aggressive testing and identification.
- The American Federation of Teachers estimates that in the 2000–2001 school year, up to 60,000 special educations positions nationwide were filled by uncertified teachers. By 2010, jobs for special education teachers are expected to grow as much at 35%.
- Special education jobs accounted for 43% of all unfilled teacher positions in Illinois at the beginning of the 2001–2002 school year.
- The challenges of the special educator's job—mounting paperwork, high case loads, multiple assignments, and contentious relationships with some parents, students, and even mainstream colleagues—encourage special education teachers to transfer to a regular classroom assignment or leave teaching entirely. (Whitaker, 2002, p. 13–14)

Bellevue, like all school districts, has experienced the challenge of hiring and retaining qualified and talented special educators, and we now routinely practice rather extraordinary efforts to meet this challenge. We recruit highly qualified special education employees nationwide throughout the school year. Estimates of turnover in the special education program are made in January, and hiring begins as early as February. "WATeach," an in-state database of potential applicants, is checked daily so that interviews may be set up immediately when a candidate with potential appears. We also support relationships with local universities in order to encourage student teachers to intern in our schools, especially in the areas of early childhood autism and emotional/behavioral disabilities. Student teachers are regularly observed and interviewed, and those showing promise are offered contracts as early as possible. In addition, we encourage promising classified employees to work toward special education certification: Competitive work-study grants have been available through the University of Washington, and staff members have typically continued as part-time paraeducators and received an additional stipend while going to graduate school.

Efforts to retain highly qualified special education staff consist primarily of additional time and compensation for the additional work the job demands. All Bellevue schools release 2 hours early on Wednesdays, allowing time for professional collaboration and program preparation.

Special educators who are responsible for individualized education program (IEP) preparation receive supplemental pay for 2 additional days beyond those provided to regular education staff. Full-time special education staff members receive 6 release days during the year for IDEIA responsibilities. Laptops with server access at work and home are provided to help to streamline paperwork. A new online IEP system has been customized and piloted for over a year, and a system-wide program will be implemented in August 2007. Efforts have been made to reduce caseloads for speech language pathologists over the past 6 years. Related services staff members have access to so-called work-relief funds, which may be used to buy additional support when needed. For example, if a psychologist has a high number of evaluations due, a consultant psychologist, often a retiree, may be hired to assist.

Retired special education staff members are also used to provide mentoring, assistance with paperwork, and support on compliance issues. Special education staff members are both hired and directly supervised by special education administrators who have had extensive teaching and related services experiences as special education practitioners and therefore have the capacity to provide specific and practical suggestions for improvement as well as targeted support.

Still we struggle to both hire and retain the staff we need.

Any legislation meant to improve special education services must address the need for qualified staff, and surely it must go beyond defining what it means to be *highly qualified*. Until the law addresses making the field attractive enough to draw the people we need, the personnel crisis we have all been facing will continue.

Funding

The average cost to educate a student in our district during the 2005–2006 school year was $7,723. The average cost for special education students was an additional $8,015, for a total of $15,738. To provide services for students with autism, we spent another $7,142, bringing the average cost for these students to $22,881. Providing appropriate special education services is expensive, and costs are rising. The sources of funding—the federal and state governments—have been both quick and expansive when describing the type and quality of services students deserve, but much less assertive when providing the means. On September 30, 2004, 11 school districts in the State of Washington filed a law suit against the state, the governor, the superintendent of public instruction, the president of the senate, and the speaker of the house seeking to force the state to fully pay for special education. In January of 2007, a second group of school districts along with a number of local organizations including Washington's PTA, the Urban League, and League of Women Voters, filed a lawsuit in an attempt to force the state to "fulfill its Constitutional duty to fully fund K–12 education." Bellevue is among this second group. Desperate situations call for desperate measures.

Throughout this chapter, we have identified a number of issues that need to be resolved before IDEIA can realize its potential. In brief and at a minimum, we need the following:

- A high quality core curriculum.
- A comprehensive assessment system.
- The tools for conducting sophisticated data analysis.
- Extensive and ongoing teacher training.
- The means for addressing the rising incidence of severe disabilities.
- The conditions for making special education an attractive professional field.

Although it is popular in some circles to claim that we cannot solve the problems in education by "simply throwing money at them," it is clearly the case that the solutions that lie before us will not come cheap. IDEIA points to a promising set of reforms but, like IDEA before it, fails to provide the resources schools and districts need to implement those reforms in a comprehensive and successful way, leaving state governments on the hook, which, in more cases than not, pass on the burden to local districts, many of which do not have the means to meet that burden. The end result, of course, is that children do not receive the service they need, and reform, no matter how intelligent in design and noble in its purpose, fails.

THE EMERGING IMPORTANCE OF TECHNOLOGY

We indicated earlier the important role technology has just recently begun to play in our ability to analyze assessment data. Data for the more than 400 classroom-based assessments the district administers are now routinely posted on the system's District Data Analyzer (DDA), making the data for all assessments—for every course, grade level, teacher, and student—available to every professional in the district. Teachers can now analyze their students' performance in the context of the performance of all students in the district; they can disaggregate the data as they wish in an attempt to find patterns and meaning in the scores; they can identify colleagues who are meeting success in particular areas of the curriculum and seek their advice; they can identify common areas of concern and work together in teams to search for targeted solutions. While the DDA was only made available to our entire professional community in September of 2006 and we are still in the process of learning how to conduct sophisticated analyses and make the best use of what we learn, there is no question that through the use of this tool we are now more data-driven, more well informed about student performance, than we have been at any time in our history. Inspired by the power of data analysis, we are now exploring tools that make the collection of information easier for teachers, which will undoubtedly lead to more frequent and more formative assessments. Our goal, to borrow a phrase from John Bransford (Bransford, Donovan, & Pellegrino, 1999), is to make "student thinking visible."

We have also placed our entire core curriculum online, creating a "Curriculum Web" that allows every professional to have access to every lesson taught in the district. Teachers who are interested in where and how prerequisite skills have been taught to their students can find that information online. Those who want to look ahead to see how the knowledge and skills they are teaching today will be used by their students in the future have that information available to them as well. Most important in the context of this chapter is the ability of teachers to share accommodations, modifications, and interventions that have worked in their classroom with the rest of the Bellevue professional community, thus driving up the individual and collective expertise of that community. As one Bellevue special educator recently commented, "The Curriculum Web is a wonderful tool for teachers. The amount of thought, effort, and collaboration that has been put into it is impressive. I know that special education teachers are very excited about being able to access specific lessons to help their students, as well as the potential for greater communication about students' needs. I hope that the momentum continues to build around including adaptations in the web" (Jared Taylor, personal communication, May 14, 2007). After conducting and publishing a study of the most common adaptations found on Bellevue IEPs, this same special educator described the promise of collaboration inspired by today's technology:

> Providing adaptations often requires looking at the instructional material with a specific student in mind and then making alterations. As we have seen, this can be a cumbersome task; however, looking at the frequencies of adaptations does point out trends that can be incorporated into curriculum development so that students with disabilities and limited English can retain knowledge more effectively. My hope is that, through multidisciplinary collaboration, a series of algorithms or processes can be devised to apply to our curriculum to ensure that we can allow for the greatest number of students to comprehend and

retain instruction, while also accounting for individual differences among students' knowledge and skill levels.

(Jared Taylor, personal communication, May 14, 2007)

Thanks to the access to information the curriculum web provides and our ability to add to and improve our curriculum through the contribution of over 1,200 professionals, we now have the opportunity within our district to conduct research and development at previously unimagined levels.

We have highlighted technology that supports the work of professionals, empowering them to know more about curriculum, instruction, and student performance, and thus improve their overall effectiveness. We would be remiss, however, if we did not also acknowledge how assistive technology is supporting special education students. We estimate that 10% to 15% of our special education students are succeeding in large part because of assistive technology. Because technology can help level the playing field for the disabled, we are committed to staying abreast of developments in the field and using the best of what is available for our students. Here is a sample of some of the ways technology is helping students in Bellevue.

Text Reader Software: This program enables students to see text highlighted as they hear it being read aloud. Core elements of the district's curriculum are available in digital format for use with text reader software.

Alternative Communication: Speech generating devices allow students with little or no speech to communicate.

Assistive Listening: Amplification devices benefit not only hearing impaired students but the general classroom population as well.

Visual Aids: Magnifiers, audio players, screen reading software, and Braille writers help visually impaired students access academic content.

Visual Supports: Pictures and symbols are low-tech methods of improving communication, increasing comprehension and helping with organizational skills. This type of assistive technology is especially effective for students with autism spectrum disorders.

Computer Access: Students with disabilities may use a variety of ways to access computers such as specialized switches, touch screens, or modified keyboards.

Technology is emerging as a powerful force for schools and districts as they pursue the goals that lie at the heart of IDEIA. This is another area where federal and state support would be extremely helpful since most districts have neither the in-house expertise nor funding to take full advantage of the technological resources now available.

IDEIA AND PROMISE OF EDUCATION REFORM

Our pessimism about "the primitive state of education methods and the paucity of good ideas" (Hill, 2006, p. 34) does not make us despair over the chances of IDEIA and, in particular, RTI to make a significant positive difference for many students throughout America. As we have seen in our own district, a sustained focus on curriculum development, frequent assessment, honest and deep analysis of data, ample amounts of student support, and a range of staff development opportunities—all assisted by the power of technology—can lead to improvement in student performance. However, it is also essential to admit that this work is complex and difficult, that the overall expertise of the profession is weak, and that the culture of the profession with its focus on autonomy and its resulting inexperience with meaningful collaboration work against substantial research and development. As we convert to the process of RTI throughout the nation, it would be wise to shed our hubris and focus on collaborative problem-solving. Indeed RTI presents a nationwide common ground and thus a wonderful opportunity for the profession to conduct research and development and find solutions for some of our most intractable problems, but this will occur only if we acknowledge that the assumptions upon which IDEIA relies are faulty and must be addressed before real progress can be made.

REFERENCES

Bransford, J., Donovan, S., & Pellegrino, M. (1999). *How students learn: Brain, mind, experience, and school.* Washington, DC: National Academy Press.

Fullan, M. (2007). *The new meaning of educational change.* New York: Teachers College Press.

Hill, P. (2006). Money, momentum, and the Gates Foundation. *Education Week, 25*(44), 34, 44.

Hirsch, E.D., Jr. (2006). *The knowledge deficit: Closing the shocking education gap for American children.* New York: Houghton Mifflin Company.

Petrilli, M. (2006). What works vs. whatever works: Inside the No Child Left Behind law's internal contradictions. *Education Week, 25*(43), 36, 44.

Schmidt, W. (2003) The quest for a coherent school science curriculum: The need for an organizing principal. *Review of Policy Research, 20*(4), 569–584.

Slavin, R. (2006). Research and effectiveness: A "10 percent solution" that can make evidence-based reform a reality. *Education Week, 26*(8), 34, 40.

Whitaker, L. (2002, December). High schools bear brunt of teacher shortage. *Catalyst, Voices of Chicago School Reform, 14*(4), 13–14.

Wurtzel, J. (n.d.) *Professionalism and prescription: How do they connect to improve teaching and learning?* The Aspen Institute Program on Education and Society, unpublished manuscript.

CHAPTER 18

New Individuals With Disabilities Educational Improvement Act and Psychological Assessment

From Policy to Practice

Michele Goyette-Ewing and Sherin Stahl

In 2004, the United States Congress reauthorized the Individuals With Disabilities Education Improvement Act (IDEIA 2004). Since that time, states, school districts, special educators, and psychologists have been struggling to understand the implications of the reauthorization for the identification of specific learning disabilities (Hale, Kaufman, Naglieri, & Kavale, 2006; Mather & Kaufman, 2006). While states work to interpret the laws, school districts implement them. Professionals both inside and outside of those districts wait to see how these changes will affect both their practice and the children they serve.

The process of interpreting and enacting the federal reauthorization has resulted in polarization, with some professionals advocating for rejecting traditional methods of identifying learning disabilities entirely (e.g., see Bradley, Danielson, & Dolittle, 2005) and others proposing a hybrid of old and new methodologies (Flanagan, Ortiz, Alfonso, & Dynda, 2006; Fletcher, Lyon, Fuchs, & Barnes, 2007; Hale et al., 2006; Wodrich, Spencer, & Daley, 2006). Traditional methods of identifying learning disabilities relied solely on establishing a significant discrepancy between IQ scores and achievement scores. New methodologies suggest learning disabilities can be identified based upon a child's lack of responsiveness to a well-implemented, research-based intervention. Certainly it is in the best interest of children to arrive at common ground on the most efficient, practical, and well-founded approach to identifying children with learning disabilities and providing them with the services that they require in order to best ensure their school success.

The decisions and paradigms arrived at through this process will directly affect the practice of psychological assessment. Psychologists have traditionally been trained to assess individuals' functioning and to use the data they have gathered to make diagnoses and provide recommendations for intervention. The process of assessment can include clinical interviews and gathering standardized data on the individual's behavioral, cognitive, academic, and social-emotional functioning. These data enable a diagnosis to be made. Diagnoses, while not capturing the totality and complexity of an individual, provide a means of communicating between professionals about an individual's strengths and challenges. Such evaluations help to identify the interventions that may be most helpful in meeting those challenges, as well as assessing progress over time. Research should inform the process of how evaluations are conducted and identify the recommendations that are best suited to children experiencing particular difficulties.

Comprehensive evaluations are useful for identifying a child's difficulties as well as for advocating for appropriate services. At the same time, such evaluations are time and resource intensive. Other approaches, such as response to intervention (RTI), provide the promise of alternative avenues for providing children with earlier intervention for targeted problems. Yet for many psychologists, RTI is new and an unknown, and therefore, a source of anxiety and concern. Many questions are raised. What is RTI? How is it conducted? What does RTI mean in terms of psychologists' practice methods? What are the commonalities of implementation across states and school districts? Will RTI be used as a means of denying or delaying children with learning difficulties access to services for which they might once have qualified?

It is the purpose of this chapter to address the changes introduced by IDEIA 2004 that impact psychological practice. The history and research underlying the definition of learning disabilities will be reviewed. Recent proposals recommending a tiered, integrated approach to identification of learning disabilities will be discussed and their implications for application by psychologists will be covered. Finally, a case example which illustrates the tiered approach to identification of learning disabilities will be offered and future questions to be addressed will be raised.

CHANGES INTRODUCED BY THE NEW IDEIA

With the reauthorization of the Individuals With Disabilities Educational Improvement Act in 2004, the legal definition of a specific learning disability has remained unchanged from prior reauthorizations (Mather & Kaufman, 2006). A specific learning disability continues to be defined as "a disorder in one or more of the basic psychological processes involved in using language, spoken or written, which . . . may manifest itself in the imperfect ability to listen, think, speak, read well, or do mathematical calculations" (20 U.S.C. § 1401(30)). Since 1977, the hallmark of a learning disability has been a severe, unexpected discrepancy between achievement and intellectual capacity in one or more of the following areas: (1) oral expression, (2) listening comprehension, (3) written expression, (4) basic reading skills, (5) reading comprehension, (6) math calculation, or (7) mathematical reasoning (U.S. Office of Education, 1977). In fact, the definition has changed little since the 1960s, notwithstanding 40 years of relevant research (Fletcher et al., 2007).

Despite the consistency over time with which learning disabilities have been defined, problems with the ability-achievement discrepancy model have become apparent, and the model has been widely criticized (Fletcher et al., 2007; Francis et al., 2005; Mather & Kaufman, 2006). Sole reliance on the unexpected ability-achievement discrepancy approach has led to systematic problems, including a high rate of false positives in children who do not have specific learning disabilities, as well as a high rate of false negatives in children who do in fact have specific learning disabilities. For example, the ability-achievement discrepancy approach has been shown to result in the overidentification of children with high IQs and average achievement as well as the underidentification of children with lower IQs and below average achievement (Semrud-Clikeman, 2005). Perhaps most importantly, the ability-achievement discrepancy approach has resulted in the delay or total denial of access to special education services for children who showed learning problems in school but whose test scores did not yet indicate a severe enough discrepancy to qualify for services (Dombroski, Kamphaus, & Reynolds, 2004; Mather & Kaufman, 2006). This issue is of particular concern when children are in the early grades and require early intervention yet may not demonstrate an ability-achievement discrepancy due to their young age and limitations in the item density at the lowest levels of the tests that they may have been given.

To address problems such as these, the reauthorization of IDEIA specifically prohibits relying on the use of any single instrument as the sole criterion for the identification of a disability. IDEIA 2004 requires multiple assessment tools that are nondiscriminatory, reliable, and valid (Hale et al., 2006). Important changes to the law mandate that additional information be gathered to support or refute a diagnosis, such as data on classroom performance, information-processing abilities, cognitive capacities, and qualitative data from parents and teachers (Mather & Kaufman, 2006).

Prior to the reauthorization of IDEIA 2004, it was common practice to rely upon the use of an ability-achievement discrepancy formula in diagnosing specific learning disabilities. The new IDEIA permits the continued use of the ability-achievement discrepancy formula, but also permits the alternative strategy of a lack of student response to intervention to be considered as a basis for documenting specific learning disabilities. Thus, the previous reliance on the ability-achievement discrepancy is no longer mandatory (Wodrich, Spencer, & Daley, 2006).

The definition of learning disabilities explicitly excludes learning difficulties that are "primarily the result of visual, hearing, or motor handicaps, or mental retardation, or emotional disturbance, or of environmental, cultural, or economic disadvantage" [20 U.S.C. § 1401(30)]. Therefore, the use of measures of cognitive abilities and adaptive behavior skills continue to be necessary to rule out mental retardation when a child fails to respond to intervention within the school. Other comorbid conditions commonly associated with specific learning disabilities, such as attention-deficit/hyperactivity disorder, must be identified and treated in order to provide the best opportunity for children to take advantage of the interventions provided to them (Fletcher et al., 2007).

WHAT IS RESPONSE TO INTERVENTION?

Response to intervention (RTI) is a term used to describe a system of intervention focused on earlier screening and intervention of children experiencing learning challenges in the classroom (Fuchs, L.S. & Vaugh, 2005). The elements of RTI are "1. Students are provided with 'generally effective' instruction by their classroom teacher; 2. Their progress is monitored; 3. Those who do not respond get something else, or something more, from their teacher or someone else; 4. Again, their progress is monitored; and 5. Those who do not respond either qualify for special education or a special education evaluation" (Fuchs, D., Mock, Morgan, & Young, 2003, p. 159 as cited in Wodrich, Spencer, & Daley, 2006).

There are a number of strengths inherent in the RTI approach. This approach has the advantage of intervening early with close monitoring of student achievement and adjustment of curriculum and teaching methodologies that may be more helpful to the struggling learner. Frequent monitoring of a child's response to the intervention provided allows the teacher to adjust goals for the child, resulting in improved student achievement (Fuchs, L.S., Fuchs, D., & Hamlett, 1989a; Fuchs, L.S,

Fuchs, D., & Hamlett, 1989b; Wesson, 1991). In addition, monitoring progress in RTI provides the opportunity to assess the rate of development for the child who is at risk. Children who are responding to intervention should demonstrate accelerated achievement growth relative to normative expectation, indicating that the remediation is working and the achievement gap is closing (Torgesen, 2000).

When children do not demonstrate accelerated achievement, the efficacy of the intervention must be evaluated. Is the intervention being applied as it was intended? Is the child receiving the intensity of services necessary to facilitate accelerated achievement growth? Does the child require a more comprehensive evaluation to more fully understand his strengths and weaknesses and to rule out language, cognitive, or behavioral factors that may be influencing the efficacy of the intervention approach? To answer questions such as these, the integrity of the intervention as well as the achievement of the child must be monitored and assessed validly, reliably, and with regularity.

Monitoring of progress may be the domain of the teacher, special educator, or of a psychologist, either inside or outside of the school. It can be done using a variety of methods and at a variety of time intervals. Use of norm-referenced tests, particularly those which provide alternative forms, is optimal when assessing a child's response to intervention over a longer period of time. Fletcher et al. (2007) recommend assessing particular aspects of specific learning disabilities with norm-referenced tests and subtests designed to most closely approximate tasks children are asked to perform in school. For example:

Word Recognition: Wide Range Achievement Test—III (WRAT III; Wilkinson, 1993) and the Gray Oral Reading Test—Fourth Edition (GORT-IV; Wiederholt & Bryant, 2001).

Reading Fluency: Test of Word Reading Efficiency (Torgesen, Wagner, & Rachotte, 1999) and the GORT-IV (Wiederholt & Bryant, 2001).

Reading Comprehension: Group Reading Assessment and Diagnostic Education (GRADE; Williams, Cassidy, & Samuels, 2001), or GORT-IV (Wiederholt & Bryant, 2001).

Mathematics: Arithmetic subtest of the Wide Range Achievement Test—III (WRAT III; Wilkinson, 1993), Woodcock-Johnson, 3rd. ed., Applied Problems Subtest (WJ-III ACH; Woodcock, McGrew, & Mather, 2001), Wechsler Individual Achievement Test, 2nd ed., Math Reasoning Subtest, (WIAT II; Wechsler, 2001).

Written Expression: Test of Written Language, 3rd ed. (TOWL-3; Hammill & Larson, 1996) and spelling tests such as the subtests from Woodcock-Johnson Achievement Test, 3rd ed. (WJ-III ACH; Woodcock, McGrew, & Mather, 2001) or Wechsler Individual Achievement, 2nd ed. (WIAT II; Wechsler, 2001).

A common strategy for routinely assessing RTI over shorter periods of time is the use of academic probes drawn directly from local curricula and referred to as curriculum-based measurement (CBM; Wodrich et al., 2006). These probes tend to be fairly brief and vary widely in terms of their reliability, particularly when home grown by each individual teacher or district. Use of CBM probes that are generated at the level of the school district can lead to significant problems with the validity and reliability of the data gathered, particularly when the data are collected by the intervener him or herself which can result in biased findings.

The National Center for Student Progress Monitoring (www. studentprogress.org; as cited in Fletcher et al., 2007) provides technical reviews of CBM tools that have been developed for use by teachers, special educators, and others monitoring student progress. Tools are evaluated and rated in terms of their reliability and validity, availability of alternate forms, sensitivity to student improvement, contribution to improving student learning and teacher planning, and the specification of acceptable rates of improvement. Promising tools include the AIMSWeb (EdInformation, 2007), the Dynamic Indicators of Basic Early Literacy Skills (DIBELS: University of Oregon Center for Teaching and Learning, 2007), EdCheckup (EdCheckup, 2005), Monitoring Basic Skills Progress (MBSP; Fuchs L. S., Hamlett, & Fuchs, D., 1990), and Yearly Progress Pro (McGraw-Hill Digital Learning, 2002) (see National Center for Student Progress Monitoring, 2006). The use of RTI techniques such as these should be an integral part of the systematic prevention, intervention, and identification process of specific learning disabilities (Hale et al., 2006). Use of such techniques allows intervention to begin early, when it is most likely to aid remediation, when the developing brain is most able to lay down new neural connections, which, once formed, may be difficult to reteach (Semrud-Clikeman, 2005). The brain appears most plastic and able to form these connections between the ages of 5 and 8, and for higher level thinking skills between the ages of 12 to 15 (Teeter & Semrud-Clikeman, 1997). Early identification and intervention, therefore, are critical for providing children with the best chance of overcoming their learning challenges.

MODELS COMBINING RTI AND PSYCHOEDUCATIONAL ASSESSMENT

The sole reliance on the ability-achievement discrepancy approach failed to include the close academic monitoring of skills as part of the process of intervention planning. However, reliance on the exclusive use of RTI procedures also would be insufficient. While the RTI approach may indicate that an impairment exists, it is not likely to provide an explanation of the causal factors (Wodrich, Spencer, & Daley, 2006). Comprehensive evaluation of a child's cognitive and academic strengths and weaknesses, in combination with an RTI approach, provides a valuable aid in making recommendations for instruction (Fuchs, L. S. & Vaugh, 2005; Flanagan et al., 2006).

Proponents of a combined approach generally propose a three-tiered model (Fuchs, D. et al., 2003; Hale et al., 2006; Semrud-Clikeman, 2005). In general, at the first level, all children are continuously monitored by the classroom teacher to ensure that they are responding to instruction. Those children who are not responding to instruction are moved to the second level, where they are provided with more or different instruction, and progress is monitored. The intervention at this level is administered by the classroom teacher or in small groups with a learning specialist. Those children who do not demonstrate accelerated growth, despite a well-implemented intervention, move to the third level where a comprehensive evaluation becomes necessary in order to make the best determination of whether a specific learning disability exists.

To be useful, assessments must be tailored to the referral question (Fletcher, Francis, Morris, & Lyon, 2005), contribute to a richer understanding of the child's individual profile of strengths and weaknesses, and provide practical recommendations and intervention strategies. Differential diagnosis is an important component of such assessments and must take into account the cognitive abilities of the individual child (Kaufman, Lichtenberger, Fletcher-Janzen, & Kaufman, 2005). Comprehensive assessment can be used to rule out mental retardation, as required by the federal definition of specific learning disabilities. It can also be used to assess behavioral and emotional factors, such as attention-deficit/hyperactivity disorder, that may explain or contribute to a child's academic challenges. Children who are English language learners may also experience problems with learning in their native language, necessitating assessment in both languages to further elucidate the difficulty. Without gathering comprehensive assessment data to address such questions, it can be difficult to definitively diagnose a child's difficulties and make recommendations tailored to the individual child's cognitive and academic strengths and weaknesses (Fletcher et al., 2007).

While a specific battery of tests is not mandated, the new generation of cognitive and achievement tests provides standardized methods for evaluating the cognitive and academic weaknesses that may contribute to children's academic difficulties (see Semrud-Clikeman, 2005; Flanagan et al., 2006; Flanagan, Ortiz, & Alfonso, 2007). Tests such as the Wechsler Intelligence Scale for Children, 4th ed. (WISC IV; Wechsler, 2003), the Woodcock-Johnson Tests of Cognitive Abilities, 3rd ed. (WJ-III COG;

Woodcock, McGrew, & Mather, 2001), the Das-Naglieri Cognitive Assessment System (CAS; Naglieri & Das, 1997), the Kaufman Assessment Battery for Children, 2nd ed. (KABC-II; Kaufman & Kaufman, 2004), and the Stanford-Binet Intelligence Scales, 5th ed. (SB5; Roid, 2003) are useful for evaluating children's cognitive skills. Academic achievement tests such as the Wechsler Individual Achievement Test, 2nd ed. (WIAT II; Psychological Corporation, 2001), and the Woodcock-Johnson Test of Achievement, 3rd ed. (WJ-III ACH; Woodcock, McGrew, & Mather, 2001) provide standardized methods of evaluating and documenting academic skills.

These tools allow for the measurement of specific academic skills and acquired knowledge. If a child is found to have a deficit in these areas, exclusionary factors must be evaluated (i.e., limited English proficiency, mild mental retardation, behavioral or emotional disturbance). If these exclusionary factors are not found to be the primary cause of the academic skill deficit, then measurement of cognitive abilities, processes, and aptitudes for learning are indicated. The psychologist must look for consistencies between the child's cognitive processing abilities and the academic performance profile that would account for the child's academic underachievement (Semrud-Clikeman, 2005; Flanagan et al., 2006). For example, a child's demonstrated difficulties with phonemic awareness, speed of information processing, and working memory are likely to explain a low basic reading skill level.

A child diagnosed with a specific learning disability should have specific and related academic and cognitive deficits that exist within an otherwise normal ability/processing profile, and the child's difficulties should not be attributable to exclusionary factors (Flanagan et al., 2006). Working memory, attention, executive function, and listening and written comprehension should be assessed, particularly when a child is not responding to intervention (Semrud-Clikeman, 2005). In this way, whether a child meets the federal definition of having a specific learning disability can be determined, and importantly, the underlying processes that result in a child's learning difficulties can be understood so that the best known remediation strategies can be identified and applied.

CASE STUDY

Margaret is a child with a history of a heart defect that was surgically corrected with open heart surgery about one month after birth. She suffered a brief episode of oxygen deprivation in the postoperative period; however, subsequent MRI did not indicate significant untoward effects. She attended preschool and kindergarten at a high quality, developmentally informed child care center. At the conclusion of the kindergarten year, the director of her child care center, her teachers, and her parents felt that she was having problems learning that were primarily developmental in nature. Informal evaluation provided by her teachers indicated that, at 5 1/2, Margaret did not yet recognize some of the numbers 1 through 10 and could not name all of the letters in her name. She had word retrieval difficulties and seemed to have a slow processing speed. Margaret's attention span for group activities could wane. Her fine and gross motor skills were well developed. She could copy sentences in perfect handwriting, but could not name the letters. Beginning phonemic awareness skills were present. Margaret had many strengths—she was a charming, vivacious girl with a love for life who got along well with adults and peers. She followed directions well, sought to please, participated in class, and was motivated to learn. Margaret loved school and books.

At her entry into public school, Margaret's parents elected to have her repeat kindergarten and alerted school personnel to the above issues. No academic problems were reported until January of the first grade. At that time, Margaret was referred for small group Language Arts Support in reading (Tier 2), due to low scores on the Developmental Reading Assessment (DRA; Beaver, 1997), a measure administered individually by her classroom teacher to all children in the class at regular intervals (Tier 1). At that time, her DRA score indicated that she was reading at the preschool level, which was 2 years behind grade-level and 3 years behind age-level. Small group intervention by a language arts specialist outside of the classroom was provided for 1 hour per day, five times per week for a 3-month period.

A reevaluation at the end of the 3-month period indicated that Margaret's performance on the DRA remained at the preschool level, although she had progressed from her initial assessment level. Due to the slow improvement in reading development, which showed progress, but not the accelerated progress that would suggest remediation, Margaret's parents requested a Planning and Placement Team (PPT) meeting to ask for a comprehensive evaluation to assess the possibility of a specific learning disability. Given Margaret's medical and academic history, a comprehensive evaluation was approved and initiated.

Cognitive evaluation conducted by the school psychologist indicated an Average Full Scale IQ on the WISC IV of 108. Achievement test scores on the Woodcock-Johnson III Tests of Achievement, obtained by the resource room specialist, indicated an Average standard score of 91 for Broad Reading, an Average score of 108 for Broad Written Language, and an Average score of 96 for Broad Mathematics.[1] Using

---

1. A stronger evaluation technique would have included co-normed measures (i.e., WISC IV with WIAT II or WJ-III COG with WJ-III ACH; Fletcher et al., 2007; Flanagan et al., 2007) and examination of findings using the Cattell-Horn-Carroll (CHC) Model (see Flanagan & Kaufman, 2004; Flanagan et al., 2007).

an ability-discrepancy model and less current methods of interpreting WISC IV results (see Flanagan & Kaufman, 2004; also Flanagan et al., 2007), Margaret would not have met criteria for a specific learning disability, as the 17-point difference between her Full Scale IQ and her Broad Reading score did not meet the 1.5 standard deviation difference required by the state in which she resided. Had the older model and methods been the sole determinant of eligibility, Margaret would not have been identified at that time.

Using more current methods of test interpretation (Flanagan & Kaufman, 2004), it was determined that Margaret's Full Scale IQ on the WISC IV was not interpretable due to variability in the test profile. Margaret's General Abilities Index of 121 was in the Superior range and her other Index scores were unitary constructs, and therefore, interpretable. Her Verbal Comprehension Index Score of 121 was Superior, her Perceptual Reasoning Index Score of 117 was High Average, her Working Memory score of 86 was Low Average, and her Processing Speed score of 91 was at the low end of the Average range. Further evaluation of memory functioning, using the Wide Range Assessment of Memory and Learning Screen (WRAML; Sheslow & Adams, 1990) provided additional evidence of auditory processing and memory difficulties, with scores ranging from the Extremely Low to Moderately Low range and a Memory Screen Index of 89. Of particular concern was a Verbal Learning score in the Extremely Low range. Findings provided by the speech and language specialist provided further additional evidence of auditory processing difficulties. Mental retardation, executive functioning difficulties, behavioral and attentional difficulties, and status as an English language learner were ruled out.

Margaret's weaknesses in working memory, auditory processing, verbal learning, and processing speed in the context of other intact abilities, when other exclusionary criteria were ruled out, were considered to be indicators that Margaret had a specific learning disability. At the PPT meeting to discuss findings, based on the history, the slow rate of progress despite Tier 2 services, and the evaluation findings, Margaret was classified as having a specific learning disability in reading, and special education services (Tier 3) were initiated. At the start of second grade, Margaret began receiving a research-based, multisensory approach (Orton & Money, 1966) with the resource room special educator specifically targeting her acquisition of phonics, and speech and language services specifically targeted at increasing her auditory memory and rapid retrieval of information. Progress monitoring with the DRA indicated that after 7 months of services, Margaret had achieved an independent level of reading at the second grade level, advancing from early first grade level to late second grade level (nearly 2 academic years of growth over the 7 month period).

At Margaret's annual spring PPT meeting, monitoring results indicated that her level of achievement in reading, although not commensurate with her General Ability Index, her Verbal Comprehension Index, or her age-mates, was at grade level. Therefore, it was determined that she would be returned to Tier 2, Language Arts Support, for further monitoring and assistance as necessary.

This case example shows the potential successes of a combined RTI and psychological assessment approach, particularly as a means of ensuring early intervention and well-targeted intervention strategies. The use of a tiered system to monitor all children in the educational system allowed for fairly early identification of Margaret's lack of progress in reading. The rapid access to Tier 2 services, small group language arts support, allowed for an immediate trial of more intensive reading support and further evaluation of Margaret's progress. When data gathered at this level of intervention did not demonstrate that Margaret's reading skills were being remediated, a comprehensive evaluation of Margaret's strengths and weaknesses provided the professionals working with her an opportunity to specifically identify the areas of learning which required targeted, intensive support while capitalizing on her strengths.

Through the combination of these two approaches Margaret's difficulties in reading were identified early so that she was provided the services she required over a fairly short period of time, at the intensity required to bring her reading to grade level. The example of Margaret also raises questions about how learning disabled children will be identified and served in the later grades, and about what will happen to them after children exit special education services following effective remediation of the specific skill-based deficit that qualified them for services. For while Margaret's reading skills are at grade level, she continues to have learning differences and a profile of strengths and weaknesses that may make future academic work more difficult for her to master (i.e., learning and retaining math facts, learning a second language).

FUTURE QUESTIONS

While the utility of combining the RTI and psychological assessment approaches appears to make the most sense for identifying specific learning disabilities and providing tailored interventions to young children, less is known about how this new approach will impact older children. RTI approaches are skills-focused and do not emphasize generalized learning or abstract thinking. While emphasis on skills is appropriate for the early grades, it is less appropriate for children in the later grades, such as Grade 4 and higher (Semrud-Clikeman, 2005). Studies with middle school and high school children are needed to determine the appropriateness of the model for children of this age (Semrud-Clikeman, 2005). Will we be using a wait-to-fail approach with these older children, if we depend on RTI as the primary tool for determining a learning disability? Should we begin to incorporate screenings of characteristics associated with higher risk for not responding to intervention, such as working memory, attention, and executive functioning, in our RTI strategies (Semrud-Clikeman, 2005), particularly for these older children?

While much attention has been paid to diagnosing and serving children with specific learning disabilities, less attention has been directed at what happens when children diagnosed as learning disabled achieve thresholds for exiting special education services. How will these thresholds be identified? Will these children continue to be monitored? Who will be responsible for monitoring? Will the regularity of that monitoring be more frequent than for children who have never been diagnosed as learning disabled? Clearly, there are many questions still to be addressed as the field progresses.

CONCLUSION

The ways in which diagnoses are defined and policies, such as IDEIA 2004, are enacted can profoundly affect the lives of individual children and has important implications for psychological assessment and all professionals who serve children and their families. For the professionals who serve children directly it is of utmost importance to develop a coherent, integrated way of approaching the identification of children with learning disabilities, so that we can continue to work together to diagnose, serve, and advocate for them. For those who conduct research, developing shared diagnostic procedures allows research to use a common language and interventions to be evaluated more readily, promoting the rapidity with which effective approaches to identifying and helping children with learning disabilities can be brought to the field. For policy makers, the implications of policy revisions and the ways that they are interpreted and implemented need to take into account an integration of multiple perspectives in order to use what is known about how to best serve children. Without many professionals working together toward a common vision using the best each has to offer, we may end up with a fractured community not doing its best by the children and families whom they wish to serve.

REFERENCES

Beaver, J. (1997). *Developmental reading assessment.* Parsippany, NJ: Celebration Press.

Bradley, R., Danielson, L., & Dolittle, J. (2005). Response to intervention. *Journal of Learning Disabilities, 38,* 485–486.

Dombroski, S. C., Kamphaus, R. W., & Reynolds, C. R. (2004). After the demise of the discrepancy: Proposed learning disabilities diagnostic criteria. *Professional Psychology: Research and Practice, 35,* 364–372.

EdCheckup, Inc. (2005). *EdCheckup.* Retrieved June 28, 2007, from http://www.edcheck up.com

EdInformation, Inc. (2007). *AIMSweb progress monitoring and response to intervention system.* Retrieved June 29, 2007, from http://www.aimsweb.com

Flanagan, D. P., & Kaufman, A. S. (2004). *Essentials of WISC IV assessment.* Hoboken, NJ: John Wiley & Sons.

Flanagan, D. P., Ortiz, S. O., & Alfonso, V. C. (2007). *Essentials of cross battery assessment* (2nd ed.). Hoboken, NJ: John Wiley & Sons.

Flanagan, D. P., Ortiz, S. O., Alfonso, V. C., & Dynda, A. M. (2006). Integration of response to intervention and norm referenced tests in learning disability identification: Learning from the Tower of Babel. *Psychology in the Schools, 43*(7), 807–824.

Fletcher, J. M., Francis, D. J., Morris, R. D., & Lyon, G. R. (2005). Evidence-based assessment of learning disabilities in children and adolescents. *Journal of Clinical Child and Adolescent Psychology, 34,* 506–522.

Fletcher, J. M., Lyon, G. R., Fuchs, L. S., & Barnes, M. A. (2007). *Learning disabilities: From identification to intervention.* New York: The Guilford Press.

Francis, D. J., Fletcher, J. M., Stuebing, K. K., Lyon, G. R., Shaywitz, B. A., & Shaywitz, S. E. (2005). Psychometric approaches to the identification of learning disabilities: IQ and achievement scores are not sufficient. *Journal of Learning Disabilities, 38,* 98–108.

Fuchs, D., Mock, D., Morgan, P. L., & Young, C. L. (2003). Responsiveness-to-intervention: Definitions, evidence, and implications for the learning disabilities construct. *Learning Disabilities Research and Practice, 27,* 157–171.

Fuchs, L. S., & Vaugh, S. R. (2005). Response-to-intervention as a framework for identification of learning disabilities. *Trainer's Forum: Periodical of the Trainers for School Psychologists, 25,* 12–19.

Fuchs, L. S., Fuchs, D., & Hamlett, C. L. (1989a). Effects of alternative goal structures within curriculum-based measurement. *Exceptional Children, 55,* 429–438.

Fuchs, L. S., Fuchs, D., & Hamlett, C. L. (1989b). Effects of instrumental use of curriculum-based measurement to enhance instructional programs. *Remedial and Special Education, 102,* 43–52.

Fuchs, L. S., Hamlett, C. L., & Fuchs, D. (1990). *Monitoring basic skills progress.* Austin, TX: PRO-ED.

Hale, J. B., Kaufman, A., Naglieri, J. A., & Kavale, K. A. (2006). Implementation of IDEA: Integrating response to intervention and cognitive assessment methods. *Psychology in the Schools, 42*(7), 753–770.

Hammill, D. D., & Larson, S. (1996). *Test of written language-III.* Austin, TX: PRO-ED.

Individuals With Disabilities Education Improvement Act of 2004 (IDEA), Pub. L. No. 108–446, 118 Stat. 2647 (2004). [Amending 20 U.S.C. §§ 1400 et. Seq.].

Kaufman, A. S., & Kaufman, N. L. (2004). *Kaufman assessment battery for children* (2nd ed.). Circle Pines, MN: American Guidance Press.

Kaufman, A. S., Lichtenberger, E. O., Fletcher-Janzen, E., & Kaufman, N. L. (2005). *Essentials of the K-ABC II assessment.* New York: Wiley.

Mather, N., & Kaufman, N. (2006). Introduction to the special issue, part two: It's about the *what*, the *how well*, and the *why. Psychology in the Schools, 43*, 829–834.

McGraw-Hill Digital Learning. (2002). *Yearly Progress Pro*. Retrieved June 28, 2007, from www.mhdigitallearning.com/prod_tour.jsp

Naglieri, J. A., & Das, J. P. (1997). *Cognitive assessment system*. Itasca, IL: Riverside Publishing Co.

National Center for Student Progress Monitoring. (2006). *Review of progress monitoring tools*. Retrieved June 28, 2007, from www.studentprogress.org/chart/chart.asp

Orton, J. D., & Money, J. (1966). *The Orton-Gillingham approach*. Baltimore, MD: Orton Dyslexia Society.

Psychological Corporation. (2001). *Wechsler individual achievement test* (2nd ed.). San Antonio, TX: Author.

Roid, G. H. (2003). *Stanford-Binet intelligence scales* (5th ed.). Itasca, IL: Riverside Publishing Co.

Semrud-Clikeman, M. (2005). Neuropsychological aspects for evaluating learning disabilities. *Journal of Learning Disabilities, 38*, 563–568.

Sheslow, D., & Adams, W. (1990). *Wide range assessment of memory and learning*. Wilmington, DE: Wide Range Inc.

Teeter, P. A., & Semrud-Clikeman, M. (1997). *Child neuropsychological assessment and intervention*. Boston, MA: Allyn & Bacon.

Torgesen, J. K. (2000). Individual responses in response to early interventions in reading: The lingering problem of treatment resisters. *Learning Disabilities Research and Practice, 15*, 55–64.

Torgesen, J. K., Wagner, R. K., & Rachotte, C. (1999). *Test of word reading efficiency*. Austin, TX: PRO-ED.

U.S. Office of Education. (1977). Assistance to states for education for handicapped children: Procedures for evaluating specific learning disabilities. *Federal Register, 42*, G1082–G1085.

University of Oregon Center for Teaching and Learning. (2007). *Official DIBELS Homepage*. Retrieved June 28, 2007, from http://dibels.uoregon.edu

Wechsler, D. (2001). *Wechsler Intelligence Scale for children: Administration and scoring manual*. (4th ed.). San Antonio: TX: Psychological Corporation.

Wesson, C. L. (1991). Curriculum-based measurement and two models of follow-up consultation. *Exceptional Children, 57*, 246–257.

Wiederholt, J. L., & Bryant, B. R. (2001). *Gray oral reading test* (4th ed.). Austin, TX: PRO-ED.

Wilkinson, G. (1993). *Wide range achievement tests—3*. Wilmington, DE: Wide Range.

Williams, K. T., Cassidy, J., & Samuels, S. J. (2001). *Group reading assessment and diagnostic education*. Circle Pines, MN: American Guidance Service.

Wodrich, D. L., Spencer, M. L. S., & Daley, K. B. (2006). Combining RTI and psychoeducational assessment: What we must assume to do otherwise. *Psychology in the Schools, 43*, 797–806.

Woodcock, R. W., McGrew, K. S., & Mather, N. (2001). *Woodcock-Johnson III tests of cognitive abilities and tests of achievement*. Itasca, IL: Riverside.

Reading Assessment and IDEIA

The Science Made Practical

Saylor Heidmann

WHY WE NEED RTI

Like other reading educators I have long been frustrated with the so-called wait-to-fail model for identifying students in need of intensive remedial reading instruction. We have known which children need more instruction, and we have known about the research-based methods and materials that work with these children. Yet, without the comprehensive testing that documented a significant difference between tested cognitive skills and achievement, these children did not qualify for the research-based instruction. Even after the testing has been completed, there is not enough of a difference to refer the children for the appropriate intervention. Many children have been referred to me for assessment to document the nature of their reading disorders. Their parents have described them as no longer enjoying school. The children come home tired and frustrated. Every night after dinner there are the homework battles. The parents accurately describe their children as having reading problems; they do not read as well as they talk, think, and solve problems. However, there is not a psychometrically significant difference between their tested intelligence and reading skills, so the children have not been able to receive additional research-based literacy training. When I go to the schools to make the case for appropriate educational plans, the school personnel tell me that they agreed with the need for intervention, but they cannot offer it because the student does not qualify. Many caring teachers have quietly whispered to me, "I know that Johnny needs the help, so I just take him along with the special education group that I'm teaching."

With the 2004 reauthorization of the Individuals With Disabilities Education Improvement Act (IDEIA), school districts are no longer required to use IQ-achievement discrepancies to determine whether or not a student has a learning disability, and they are not required to identify a student as having a reading disability in order to offer tutorial services. IDEIA even provides for 15% of a district's special education funding to be used for assessment, materials, and other services for unidentified students. School districts have the option to implement a process that carefully documents how a student responds to scientific research-based instruction as part of the evaluation process (IDEIA: P.L. 108–446). This process is commonly known as the response to intervention (RTI) model. Reading assessment is used to identify those children who might have or are having difficulty and then to determine which research-based interventions are most effective for the situation. Children who are at-risk are now identified in kindergarten before they have had a chance to fail. These identified children get extra reading instruction in addition to the regular classroom instruction. Those students who do not respond to intensive scientific research-based remedial reading instruction are identified as reading disabled and receive appropriate accommodations and modifications so that they can learn other essential academic skills. This chapter particularizes the International Reading Association's three-tiered RTI model.

THE INTERNATIONAL READING ASSOCIATION'S RTI MODEL

The International Reading Association has proposed a well-designed three-tiered RTI model that provides a scaffold to build upon. The International Reading Association's three-tiered RTI model (2007) emphasizes a "coherent instruction plan that provides coordinated reading lessons every day for every student at every level of instruction" (http://www. reading.org/resources/issues/focus). The first level is the universal tier—a preventative process for all students. At this level all students are screened three times a year in order to make sure that they do not fall behind. The second level is the selective tier, where at-risk students who have not responded to a research-based reading program have 30 minutes additional reading instruction each day in groups of five or fewer. At this level students' progress should be monitored each week. If they do not rapidly meet the benchmarks, they are placed in the intensive tier. Remediation at the intensive level happens one-to-one or in groups of two or three with instructional time and curriculum that is in addition to Tiers 1 and 2.

THE UNIVERSAL TIER IS FOR ALL CHILDREN

The assessment at this tier is brief norm-referenced measures administered for all children at all grade levels. If significantly more than 20% of the students are identified, the first step should be an evaluation of the components and methods of the core reading program. The core program must use evidence-based methods and materials. If these are not in place, the reading program should be changed so that it emphasizes direct instruction in phonological awareness, word recognition, fluency, vocabulary, and comprehension using methods and materials that have been proven to be effectual. If these research-based methods and materials are not effective with 80% of the students, the next changes to consider are increasing the time spent on direct instruction and reducing the size of the instructional group. At least 1 hour of daily direct literacy instruction in small groups is recommended for all students. The final essential change would be focused staff development that includes modeling lessons, providing coaching, and ongoing support. The most effective professional development model provides consultation directly to the teachers within the classroom setting.

The universal tier assessment protocol should include measures of phonological awareness and word identification at the kindergarten and first grade levels and measures of word identification and fluency from second grade on. Word identification assessment should include phonetic decoding skills and knowledge of frequently used phonetically irregular words. Although reading comprehension is clearly the goal of all reading instruction, there is an abundance of compelling evidence that word identification and fluency measures are highly correlated with reading comprehension measures (Carlise & Rice, 2002; Fletcher, Lyon, Fuchs, & Barnes, 2007; Hosp & Fuchs, 2005). Many valid and reliable screening procedures are available for universal tier assessment and progress monitoring and are reviewed on the U.S. Office of Special Education's National Center on Student Progress Monitoring Web site (htpp://www. studentprogress.org). These benchmark screening procedures should be administered three times yearly; a schedule that would maximize the opportunity for general education intervention would be the first weeks in October, January, and April (2007). Any student who has not achieved the benchmark level on two successive screenings would be referred to the selective tier.

THE SELECTIVE TIER PROVIDES TIME-LIMITED ADDITIONAL INSTRUCTION

The selective tier is designed for the students who need only a small instructional boost to meet the benchmark goals. Students receiving remediation through the selective tier have additional differentiated instruction that parallels the essential components of the core-reading program. Selective tier instruction should be 30 minutes in addition to the time spent in the universal tier for a total of 90 minutes daily. The instruction group should comprise five or less. The kindergarten and first grade children have additional phonological awareness instruction and practice. Students in the higher grades have additional instruction and practice in the areas where they have not yet mastered the benchmark skills. The goal of the selective tier is rapid response to the additional targeted instruction. Student progress should be monitored with weekly assessment using alternative versions of the screening tools that are used at the universal level. Although school districts may define *rapid* in many different ways, students should remain in the selective tier for at least 4 weeks (10 hours of additional instruction for a total of 30 hours) and not more than 6 weeks (15 hours of additional instruction for a total of 45 hours). If the students are making measurable progress, 4 weeks of intervention help consolidate the skills before they return to the core curriculum. If the students have not achieved the benchmark goals within 6 weeks (15 hours of additional instruction for a total of 45 hours), they should be moved to the intensive tier.

THE INTENSIVE TIER IS THE HALLMARK OF THE RTI MODEL

The intensive tier begins with norm-referenced assessments to define the remediation methods and materials. The children are no longer using the core reading program. Instead, they are using an evidence-based reading program that is fine-tuned to their specific literacy profile. In order to define their profile, the students are assessed using many different norm-referenced and curriculum-based assessments. These assessments, taken together with the results of the progress monitoring measures from the selective tier, define their remedial program. The first stage of this assessment process is brief norm-referenced assessment of word identification, fluency, and reading and listening comprehension skills. Subtests from academic achievement batteries that have alternative forms, such as the Kaufman Test of Educational Achievement, Second Edition, (Kaufman & Kaufman, 2004) and the Woodcock-Johnson Tests of Achievement, Third

Edition, (Woodcock, McGrew & Mather, 2007), would be good choices for this first stage. (See Table 19.1.)

The children who evidence weaknesses at the word level have additional assessment of their phonological awareness skills with measures such as the Comprehensive Test of Phonological Processing (Wagner, Torgesen, & Rahotte, 1999) and analysis of their phonetic decoding and encoding skills with measures such as the Word Identification and Spelling Test (Wilson & Felton, 2004; see Table 19.2). Students whose skills break down at the word level and who also evidence difficulty with listening comprehension complete a receptive vocabulary assessment to determine the need for oral vocabulary instruction. Students with intact skills at the word level complete both a receptive vocabulary measure and an informal reading inventory to delineate appropriate metacognitive strategic training.

DIAGNOSTIC TUTORING USING EVIDENCE-BASED METHODS AND MATERIALS

The second phase of the intensive tier is diagnostic tutoring to determine which evidence-based methods and materials can best remediate the weaknesses identified by the diagnostic assessment. The instruction is either one-on-one or in groups of two or three children of the same age who have the same identified weaknesses. The daily instructional time is in addition to the time that the students have spent in both the core reading program and the additional instruction at the selective tier (i.e.,

TABLE 19.1 Intensive Tier: First Stage Literacy Assessments

	Kaufman Test of Educational Achievement, Second Edition	*Woodcock-Johnson Tests of Achievement, Third Edition*
Word Identification	Letter/Word Recognition	Word Identification
Fluency	Word Recognition Fluency Decoding Fluency	Reading Fluency
Reading Comprehension	Reading Comprehension	Passage Comprehension
Listening Comprehension	Listening Comprehension	Story Recall Following Directions

TABLE 19.2   Intensive Tier: Second Stage Literacy Assessments

Pattern of Strengths and Weaknesses	Recommended Assessments
1. Weak Word Identification Skills and Intact Listening Comprehension Skills	Phonological Awareness Assessment Phonetic Decoding/Encoding Assessment
2. Weak Word Identification Skills and Weak Listening Comprehension Skills	Phonological Awareness Assessment Phonetic Decoding/Encoding Assessment Receptive Vocabulary Assessment
3. Intact Word Identification Skills and Weak Listening and/or Reading Comprehension Skills	Receptive Vocabulary Assessment Informal Reading Inventory (Note Fluency Assessment from First Stage)

2 hours of direct literacy instruction). The tutor develops a program that targets the areas of weakness that are shown on the assessment.

The children whose sole difficulty is at the word level are given direct instruction in phonological awareness until they have mastered the prerequisite skills needed to learn to segment and blend words efficiently as demonstrated on a norm-referenced assessment. At the same time they have direct instruction in the phonetic decoding and encoding patterns that have been identified on the norm-referenced assessment. These students should use comprehensive sequential evidence-based methods and materials from programs such as Project Read (Greene & Enfield, 1997) or Phono-Graphix (McGuinness & McGuinness, 1998). To train for encoding, students practice spelling words that they have learned in exercises that are formulated so that the students spell the word correctly. For fluency training, students repeat readings of the words that they have learned in lists, phrases, and sentences.

The children who have both weak word identification skills and weak listening comprehension skills need the phonological awareness and phonetic decoding and encoding instruction described above as well as vocabulary and comprehension instruction at the *oral level*. This instruction might be planned and coordinated with the instruction provided by a speech/language pathologist. Their vocabulary instruction could use the methods and materials such as those recommended in *Bringing Words to Life* (Beck, McKeown, & Kucan, 2002) and *LETRS Module 4: The Mighty Word* (Moats, 2005). Their comprehension instruction should include making predictions and connections with texts that are read to them. Hearing and discussing picture books is appropriate for the younger children; hearing and discussing illustrated nonfiction texts works well with the older students.

Students who do not have difficulty at the word level but still struggle with reading comprehension may have weak fluency skills. If so, they need intensive fluency practice with materials that emphasize repeated readings such as *Great Leaps* (Campbell & Mercer, 1998). Most students with intact word identification skills and weak comprehensive skills require vocabulary instruction such as those described above. In addition, they require intensive instruction in metacognitive strategies such as figurative language, sentence and text structures, inference, and comprehension monitoring. Instruction in metacognitive strategies should use well-structured methods and materials, such as those recommended in *LETRS Module 5: Digging for Meaning* (Moats, 2005).

PROGRESS MONITORING OF ACHIEVEMENT AT THE INTENSIVE TIER

Students who are receiving instruction at the intensive tier should have their progress monitored weekly with curriculum-based measures (CBMs). For example, the students who are working on segmentation and blending tasks could complete timed tests of segmentation and blending; speed would indicate relative mastery of the tasks. Students' word identification skills could be assessed with phonetically based parallel word lists; again speed of word identification would indicate relative mastery. Students working on vocabulary tasks could receive measures that directly assess knowledge of the words taught. Comprehension skills could be assessed with alternative passages from informal reading inventories. More frequent progress monitoring gives a better indication of the students' learning rates. If the student is not making discernible progress, the tutorial program should be reviewed and adjusted.

After the students have completed 6–8 weeks of intensive diagnostic tutoring, they should again be assessed with the norm-referenced measures, whenever possible using alternative forms of the intensive tier: first stage assessments (see Table 19.1). The results of these evaluations taken together with the results of the multiple CBMs determine next steps to be taken. The students who have made steady progress on CBMs and show some measurable progress on the norm-referenced measures can return to the selective tier; however, their progress should continue to be monitored with weekly CBMs. The students who have made steady progress on the CBMs but no measurable gains on the intensive tier, first stage norm-referenced measures should continue with another 6–8 weeks of diagnostic tutoring. The students who have not made gains on either the CBMs or the first stage norm-referenced assessments also need to continue with diagnostic tutorial services; however, their program should be carefully reviewed with adjustments made to accelerate their rate of learning.

SPECIAL EDUCATION CLASSIFICATION

All students who remain in the intensive tier after two diagnostic tutorial cycles are classified as learning disabled in reading. Special education students should then be referred for additional evaluation that considers such disabilities as mental retardation, attention-deficit/hyperactivity disorder, and communication disorders. Special education students should also receive accommodations and modifications so that they can be successful in as many mainstream classes as possible.

RTI BEGINS IN KINDERGARTEN

At the universal tier, all of the children are briefly screened during the first month of school using a norm-referenced measure such as the Dynamic Indicators of Basic Early Literacy Skills (Good & Kaminski, 2004). Following 60 hours of evidence-based literacy instruction, the kindergarten children's prerequisite literacy skills would again be assessed 12 weeks later, in December or January. The children who do not achieve the benchmark level move to the selective tier and form a tutorial group. These students receive additional small group instruction for the next 4–6 weeks, an additional 30–45 hours of instruction. The students who are now at the benchmark level could return to the regular kindergarten program. But they would not be forgotten because the next universal tier assessment point would be the regularly scheduled screening 6 weeks later. Those students who were not successful at the selective tier would then move on to the diagnostic assessment stages of the intensive tier. They would then receive 60–80 more hours of diagnostic tutorial instruction that is tailored exactly to their pattern of strengths and weaknesses. After 6–8 weeks of diagnostic tutoring, they would again be assessed with norm-referenced tests. If they have not met grade-level expectations, they would be classified as special education students and would receive a comprehensive diagnostic evaluation. (See Table 19.3.)

By using this model, students have a literacy program that fits their needs as they enter first grade. The students who begin and remain in the core reading program continue to build on the skills that they attained in kindergarten. The children who had some additional small group instruction in the selective tier also have the prerequisite skills to learn in

TABLE 19.3 RTI Kindergarten Model: Yearly Calendar

	Universal Assessment	Universal Program	Selective Assessment	Selective Program	Intensive Assessment	Intensive Program
Sep		Core Program				
Oct	DIBELS	Core Program: Differentiated as needed				
Nov		Core Program: Differentiated as needed				
Dec		Core Program: Differentiated as needed				
Jan	DIBELS	Core Program	Weekly CBM	Core plus 30 minutes in small groups		
Feb		Core Program	Weekly CBM	Core plus 30 minutes in small groups		
Mar		Core Program	Weekly CBM DIBELS	Return to universal or move to intensive	Norm-referenced and CBM literacy assessments	Diagnostic tutorial (2 hours)
Apr	DIBELS	Core Program	Weekly CMB	New students may be added	Weekly CBM	Diagnostic tutorial (2 hours)
May		Core Program	Weekly CMB	Core plus 30 minutes	Norm-referenced literacy assessment	Return to selective or continue with intensive
Jun		Core Program	Weekly CBM DIBELS	Return to universal or forward to intensive	Norm-referenced and CBM literacy assessments	Return to selective or place in special education

a first grade core reading program. Some of the children who had been in the intensive tier return to the selective tier core reading program so that they can have the extra support of additional instruction in a small group. And the few children who remain in the intensive tier have the comprehensive evaluations, accommodations, modifications, and intensive tutoring that they require as special education students.

Vincent is an excellent example of the efficacy of the RTI model at the kindergarten level. Vincent was referred to me toward the end of his kindergarten year because he had not made much progress in literacy skills. Vincent had some early language acquisition problems during his preschool years but had made progress with individual lessons from a speech-language therapist. By the end of kindergarten, his teachers and his parents were both expressing concern with his beginning reading skills.

Vincent and I worked together for some diagnostic reading sessions during the summer between kindergarten and first grade. He evidenced some beginning phonological awareness skills and was able to blend words when they were read to him as individual phonemes. Although he was slow to respond, he accurately matched all the pictures with the same initial sounds and many with the same ending sounds. In contrast to these two tasks, Vincent had significant difficulty on the elision subtest when he had to listen to words and repeat them without one of the consonant sounds (e.g., "Say *cup*. Now say it again without the /k/.") Vincent had the most success when he used manipulatives for phonological awareness activities during the diagnostic tutorial. On an Elkonin task, he quickly and accurately segmented and blended words while moving discs for each sound. He was then able to complete elision tasks when I moved one disc for each sound.

Vincent accurately gave letter names and sounds for several consonants on the Kaufman Test of Educational Achievement, Second Edition (KTEA-II), letter and recognition subtest and decoded three three-letter short vowel words but could not read on other words. He was more successful on the KTEA-II reading comprehension subtest because there were illustrations to match with the words. Vincent was able to write single letters and some three-letter words on the KTEA-II spelling and written expression subtests. However, he evidenced significant sound-letter confusions when he was unsure of the words. For example:

Word dictated	Vincent's spelling
play	qap
look	log
see	L(reversed)o

Vincent also attempted to write his last name but gave up after reversing the first letter and transposing the next two.

Vincent completed several literacy activities during the diagnostic tutorial. He first practiced words that he would later encounter in a decodable text by reading word cards and then tossing them into a tray. The words were color-coded with phonetically irregular words printed in red. At this point in the lesson, Vincent segmented each sound before accurately blending the phonetically regular words but was having difficulty remembering the irregular words. Vincent reviewed the words with speed drills that listed each word several times. He was proud that he was able to reread a speed drill in half the initial time. Vincent also spelled the words using plastic letters before reading the decodable text slowly and accurately. Vincent selected a few pages to practice reading smoothly. Vincent practiced some other decodable words and played a final game with all of the words that he had been working on. Although he was clearly focused on winning the game, Vincent read all of the frequently practiced words automatically and fluently. He did not read the less-practiced words automatically and continued to have difficulty with the irregular words.

Vincent's parents took the results of my evaluation to his school where his team decided that he would have daily instruction at the intensive level for most of first grade. He worked on different phonological awareness tasks for the first few minutes of each daily lesson, using manipulatives especially for deletion and substitution tasks. Most of Vincent's tutorial program focused on phonetic decoding and encoding instruction. He continued to learn and practice sound-letter matches using visual and manipulative aids. New matches were added when he was at least 85% accurate with the ones that had been previously introduced. In order to build automaticity and fluency, Vincent practiced the most frequently occurring words that he could decode and encode in different formats, especially games. Vincent reviewed and practiced these reading skills by reading decodable texts that were comprised of the words that he had learned. Vincent continued to work on comprehension skills with the speech/language clinician as they discussed illustrated texts that were read aloud to him.

Vincent's parents brought him for another reading assessment during the summer after first grade. He had made enough progress during the year that his teaching team thought that he should be placed in the universal tier. Indeed Vincent had made a great deal of progress. His word identification and comprehension skills were solidly commensurate with his grade level; however, he still confused many words when the passages were more challenging. For example, he read *balloon* as *bone* in a passage and could not answer any comprehension questions. Vincent also read very slowly, both silently and orally. As his teaching team reported, Vincent has made excellent progress in first grade; however, he is not yet ready to return to the universal tier. He should remain in the intensive tier until the assessments show that he has learned more phonetic decoding skills and all of his reading is automatic and fluent.

RTI FOR UPPER ELEMENTARY STUDENTS

For children who may have difficulties with more advanced literacy skills, the universal tier of the RTI model also includes a safety net: they continue to be assessed briefly three times yearly. As in the kindergarten model, students are assigned to the selective tier if they have not attained the benchmark level at two assessment points. And if additional time in small group instruction with the core reading program is not effective, they move rapidly to the intensive tier. The three times a year brief assessment component of the RTI model takes no longer than the referral system of the discrepancy model, and in many instances can be a significantly shortened process.

Isabel was referred to me by her parents because she appeared to have lost interest in school. They reported that she enjoyed learning new facts and concepts and that she really liked first and second grade. She began third grade with enthusiasm, but then became reluctant to attend school. She was happy on the weekend, but she got headaches every Sunday evening. She had many friends in school, and her teacher was as puzzled as her parents. When I assessed her reading skills at the beginning of fourth grade, I found that many were well above her age and grade level; however, she had not developed a full range of reading strategies. Although she could slowly recognize a large pool of words, she would often have to try out different sound patterns until she found a real word that matched. Her errors were usually substitutions of other words that had many similar sounds. Isabel had much more difficulty reading nonsense words on a pseudoword decoding assessment because she could not rely on this trial-and-error approach. On this measure, Isabel sometimes reversed sounds and added sounds that were not in the words. These phonetic decoding weaknesses also impacted Isabel's speed of reading complicated texts. On the WJ-III reading fluency subtest, she read and understood short sentences with adequate speed. On the KTEA-II word recognition fluency subtest she read the easy words very quickly and pondered over the harder ones. Predictably, Isabel had the most difficulty reading nonsense words in a timely manner on the decoding fluency subtest. Isabel read the passages on the KTEA-II reading comprehension subtest to herself, so it was not possible to assess her accuracy. An analysis of her passage reading accuracy was possible, however, because she chose to read the questions aloud. She sometimes stumbled over words, sometimes omitted words, and sometimes repeated phrases to gain an understanding of the questions. In spite of these difficulties, Isabel was able to read complicated passages and correctly answer both literal and inferential comprehension questions about her reading. Isabel's written expression skills mirrored her reading skills. She made many spelling errors because she reversed sounds and confused vowel patterns. Isabel had very well-developed writing skills. On the written expression subtest she wrote grammatically correct complex sentences and a succinct retelling of the story. Most of her errors were mistakes were either misspellings or omissions of internal sentence punctuation.

Isabel's school used a discrepancy model to determine eligibility for extra help, so she did not qualify. Instead she worked with me after school for an hour each week. We worked on syllable types and multisyllable decoding. Isabel especially enjoyed the decoding games that we played with nonsense words and the speed drills with multisyllable real words. She worked hard and made remarkable gains. By spring of her fourth grade year, her reading fluency was in the high average range when compared to other students at her grade level. She loved school and was reading in every spare minute. When I saw her after school had ended, she proudly told me that she had read nine books in 2 weeks and "could not wait" for *Harry Potter* to be released.

CLASSIFICATION OF MIDDLE AND HIGH SCHOOL STUDENTS

Although not a prevention model at later elementary, middle, and high school levels, RTI also meets the IDEIA recommendations as a way to identify students as reading disabled without using the discrepancy model. There are many children who have been floundering in mainstream classrooms as they continue to fall short of grade-level expectations. They have learned how to read, but they frequently do not meet the reading proficiency levels determined by their districts and state standards. Yet they are close enough, so they move on to the next grade without the prerequisite skills to be successful.

Marie was referred for testing by her pediatrician. She was near the end of fourth grade, and her parents were concerned because she had difficulties getting along with her classmates. She had received low grades in all aspects of language arts since first grade but had not had any assessments or supportive services. My assessment showed that all of Marie's language arts skills were below grade-level expectations. Although she could recognize many commonly used words, the only phonetic word patterns that she could read with greater than 85% accuracy were single syllable words with short vowels and the vowel–consonant–silent-*e* pattern. She was able to read some words with *r*-controlled vowels and common vowel teams; however, she had not mastered these patterns. Although Marie had difficulty on both reading and listening comprehension measures, her answers on the reading comprehension measure reflected problems with word identification as well as comprehension. Marie was better able to answer questions about the passages that were read to her, yet she still had difficulty with several literal and inferential questions. Marie's correct and incorrect answers seemed to be due to question analysis and not the difficulty of the passages. Marie wrote cohesive, grammatically correct answers to the single sentence prompts. She had more difficulty with a longer passage, writing one run-on sentence in response to a story-retelling prompt. Based on this assessment, I recommended tutorial intervention that included direct instruction of phonetically regular decoding and encoding patterns. I also suggested daily instruction in comprehension strategies beginning with oral discussions of texts that are read to her so that she could learn the strategies without the burden of decoding the words. Finally I recommended written language instruction that again began with oral discussion and moved gradually through sentence stems and teacher-provided scaffolding toward independent writing skills. Because Marie could not read grade-level texts, I suggested accommodations and modifications for her school program so that she could learn the facts and concepts that her classmates were learning and alternative assessment methods so that she could demonstrate her knowledge.

Following my assessment, Marie was assessed by the school psychologist, learning disabilities teacher, and literacy specialist. The school psychologist's evaluation found that Marie had average cognitive skills with no significant differences among the various subtests. The learning disabilities teacher found that Marie's math skills were in the average range and her reading skills were at the low end of the average range. The literacy specialist's evaluations confirmed the specific difficulties that Marie was having with phonetic decoding and comprehension. Because there was not a significant difference between Marie's tested cognitive and achievement skills, she did not qualify for additional literacy instruction. If the school had been using an RTI model, Marie could have entered the fifth grade in the selective tier and received 4–6 weeks of focused instruction in the core reading program. If this had not been successful, she would have been moved into the intensive tier and received tutorial instruction that would have been designed to remediate her specific weaknesses. If she had not responded at the intensive tier, she would have been identified as learning disabled and received accommodations and modifications so that she could be successful in her content area classes.

PROGRAM PLANNING FOR OLDER STUDENTS

At the later grades, the RTI model can also be used to delineate a comprehensive program for children who have already been identified as reading disabled. Sometime the remediation program does not match the student's individual learning style. Most often, though, the program is appropriate, but it lacks the intensity that is needed to help the student gain sufficient skills to learn within the mainstream classroom.

For example, Will is a sixth-grade student who had been identified as having a reading disability based on the discrepancy model. His tested cognitive skills were in the high average range, yet his reading skills fell into the low end of the average range. He had been receiving 2 hours each week of direct instruction in word identification and fluency skills and 4 hours each week of classroom support. His general education modifications and accommodations have been limited to extended time and no spelling penalty on tests and quizzes. However, norm-referenced assessment with alternate forms of the Kaufman Test of Educational Achievement, Second Edition, indicated that this was not an appropriate level of service for Will. (See Table 19.4.)

Following this evaluation, Will began receiving an additional half hour of reading instruction each week, and he listened to audio texts to help him learn concepts and facts in science and social studies. His end-of-year testing did not indicate any improvement, so he was placed in an alternative program that is specifically designed for learning disabled students where he will receive intensive instruction throughout each school day.

Sam is another example of the use of RTI to fine-tune a literacy program. Sam has been identified as a reading-disabled fourth grader because of the very significant discrepancy between his tested superior cognitive skills and his tested average literacy skills. He has made progress in word identification skills, but his fluency and reading comprehension skills are still not commensurate with grade-level expectations. (See Table 19.5.)

Based on this evaluation, Sam will receive intensive word identification and fluency remediation as well as regular education modifications

TABLE 19.4   Intensive Tier: Norm-Referenced Progress Monitoring

	Standard Score/ Percentile Rank End of Sixth Grade	Standard Score/ Percentile Rank Middle of Seventh Grade
KTEA-II Word Recognition	84/14	81/10
KTEA-II Word Recognition Fluency	78/7	76/5
KTEA-II Nonsense Word Decoding	99/47	87/19
KTEA-II Decoding Fluency	87/19	79/8
KTEA-II Reading Comprehension	80/9	85/16

TABLE 19.5   Intensive Tier: Norm-Referenced Progress Monitoring

	Standard Score January Third Grade	Standard Score End of Fourth Grade
KTEA-II Word Recognition	86/18	93/32
KTEA-II Word Recognition Fluency	n/a	94/34
KTEA-II Nonsense Word Decoding	81/10	92/30
KTEA-II Decoding Fluency	n/a	87/19
KTEA-II Reading Comprehension	105/63	103/58
WJ-III Reading Fluency	n/a	89/23

and accommodations. Both his classroom teacher's reports and the results of his cognitive testing indicate that he does not need remediation in reading comprehension strategies; he has difficulties because he can not identify the words in a fast and accurate manner and not because he has any language comprehension weaknesses.

RTI IS A CHILD-CENTERED COLLABORATIVE MODEL

The RTI model includes different deployment of school personnel and increased collaboration among all educators. A school that employs an effective RTI model does not require additional personnel, and their schedules can be realigned so that they can be more effective in their work with children. At the universal tier level, reading consultants help to select the evidence-based core reading programs that make it possible for 80% of the children to achieve benchmarks three times a year. Reading consultants also coach and model lessons of best practices for the classroom teachers. The reading consultants can also teach the additional 30-minute small group lessons and complete the weekly progress monitoring with the students in the selective tier. Special educators and reading consultants (and perhaps speech/language pathologists as well) may be the diagnostic tutors at the intensive level, even though the students have not yet been classified as special education students. Since the ultimate goal of RTI is *prevention,* this model ultimately provides more time for special educators to concentrate intense instruction with fewer students.

In addition to being a prevention model, RTI provides a forum for general educators, reading specialists, and special educators to work together. In the RTI model, children with reading difficulties are not placed in special education, instead all of their teachers assess and teach them. All educators can be deployed for assessment and instruction at the universal and selective tiers; reading specialists and special educators can be deployed for assessment and instruction at the selective and intensive tiers. When all educators work together they can share common focus: teaching kids how to read.

REFERENCES

Beck, I. L., McKeown, M. G., & Kucan. L. (2002). *Bringing words to life: Robust vocabulary instruction*. New York: Guilford Press.

Campbell, K., & Mercer, C. D. (1998). *Great Leaps*. Gainesville, FL: Diarmuid.

Carlisle, J. F., & Rice, M. S. (2002). *Improving reading comprehension: Research-based principles and practices*. Baltimore: York Press.

Fletcher, J. M., Lyon, G. R., Fuchs, L. S., & Barnes, M. A. (2007). *Learning disabilities: From identification to intervention*. New York: The Guilford Press.

Good, R. H., & Kaminski, R. (2004). *Dynamic indicators of basic early literacy skills*. Longmont, CA: Sophis West.

Greene, V. E., & Enfield, M. L. (1997). *Project read*. Bloomington, MN: Language Circle.

Hosp, M. K., & Fuchs, L. S. (2005). Using CBM as an indicator of decoding word reading, and comprehension: Do the relations change with the grade? *School Psychology Review, 34*, 9–26.

International Reading Association. RtI: Response to intervention. Retrieved [January 2007] from http://www.reading.org/resources/issues.focus_rti.html

Kaufman, A., & Kaufman, N. (2004). *Kaufman test of educational achievement* (2nd ed.). Circle Pines, MN: American Guidance Service.

McGuinness, C., & McGuinness, G. (1998). *Reading reflex: The foolproof phono-graphix method for teaching your child to read*. New York: Fireside.

Moats, L. (2005). *Language essentials for teachers of reading and spelling*. Longmont, CA: Sophis West.

National Center on Student Progress Monitoring. (2006). Retrieved April 2007, from http://www.studentprogress.org3/chart/chart.asp

Wagner, R., Torgesen, J., & Rashotte, C. (1999). *Comprehensive test of phonological processing*. Austin, TX: Pro-Ed.

Wilson, B., & Felton, R. H. (2004). *Word identification and spelling test*. Austin, TX: Pro-Ed.

Woodcock, R. W., McGrew, K. S., & Mather, N. (2007). *Woodcock-Johnson tests of achievement* (3rd ed.). Rolling Meadows, IL: Riverside Publishing.

CHAPTER 20

How Private Practice Should Respond to IDEIA 2004

Eric R. Arzubi

IDEIA 2004 represents the latest version of special education law, which continues to evolve as researchers and practitioners uncover new and, hopefully, more effective ways of promoting school success among children of all abilities. Given the flaws in the identification of learning disabilities using the widespread IQ-achievement discrepancy model, IDEIA 2004 opens the door to the more dynamic response-to-intervention (RTI) paradigm (Fuchs, Fuchs, Mock, Morgan, & Young, 2003). In theory, RTI is designed to identify learning disabilities in children before the children fall too far behind in the classroom. Additionally, educators hope that the new model will help them readily and accurately identify emotional, cognitive, and behavioral dysfunctions among students (Albers, Glover, & Kratochwill, 2007). Until state governments and school districts decide on the details of RTI, debate over its ultimate incarnation will continue.

In the meantime, what is private practice doing to improve its ability to identify and treat children who are at risk for or are now experiencing school failure? After all, IDEIA 2004 will seek to drive changes in school systems, not in the offices of pediatricians, private psychologists, child and adolescent psychiatrists, or among tutors. Children spend about a third of their waking hours until the age of 18 years in school and performing school-related tasks. School represents the most important platform for child development outside the home (Noam & Hermann, 2002). At their best, schools are made up of teams of professionals including teachers, special educators, educational psychologists, and collaborating community-based mental health clinicians. IDEIA 2004 is an attempt to make sure that these teams use the best possible protocols for identifying and treating children at risk for school failure during the crucial developmental years.

In the community, there is no organizational structure to force collaboration and the use of best practices among private practitioners from different pediatric disciplines. Anxious parents hoping to understand their children's school struggles gather up as much educational and developmental history as they can remember or find, and bounce from pediatrician to psychologist to child psychiatrist—if they can find one—in search of answers. These professionals, acting as independent agents, approach the problem with different tools and biases, often differing in their diagnoses and treatment plans. Parents are left to sift through the data and make the ultimate decisions in treatment. Additionally, parents are forced to educate themselves quickly in order to play the role of case manager and advocate because it is rare that anyone will do it for them; case management is beyond the scope of services delivered by psychologists or psychiatrists, and pediatricians are often too busy. If effective treatment requires the service of more than one specialist, parents are forced to coordinate and schedule care on their own, while ensuring that the schools are doing their part by way of accommodations and educational interventions.

IDEIA 2004 is designed to improve the educational and developmental environment in schools for children at risk for failure. This chapter serves to underscore the urgency for community-based practitioners to employ best practices in the educational and developmental care of children. Specifically, this is a call for private clinicians and learning specialists to develop more collaborative relationships in order to coordinate the care of children who are chronically struggling in the classroom. The shift away from the IQ-discrepancy model in schools also represents an opportunity for private practitioners to update their methods in light of emerging research on learning disabilities and on treatment of chronic conditions. Better care coordination, enhanced practitioner communication, and an emphasis on dynamic, performance-driven assessments and treatments could lead to improved mental health and educational outcomes in children and better professional relationships across pediatric disciplines.

In some special education cases, identification and treatment or accommodation can be fairly straightforward. Federal law provides funding for special education services to children who are eligible under one or more of the following disability categories: autism, specific learning disability, speech or language impairments, emotional disturbance, traumatic brain injury, visual impairment, hearing impairment, deafness, mental retardation, deaf-blindness, multiple disabilities, orthopedic impairment, and other health impairment. Among these categories, it may be easier to identify the student who is blind than the one who is struggling with schoolwork due to an internalizing behavioral disorder. An unfortunate traumatic brain injury represents a discrete event that may lead to cognitive dysfunctions, while the existence of a specific learning disability is sometimes more subtle and difficult to recognize. There is no need to develop an RTI model for children with suspected orthopedic impairments; these children are readily identified and the methods of support are often clear.

I am calling for the improvement of services in the private sector for children whose sources of school struggles are not immediately obvious or easily identified. There is always going to be a demand for these services, and we have a professional responsibility for them to be effective and well coordinated. Even if school-based RTI turns out to be successful beyond district officials' wildest dreams, many parents will continue to demand a second opinion and will obtain it using a practitioner of their choice in the private sector. Some parents may not even wait until their child has been shepherded through each tier in the school's RTI algorithm; they reserve the right to request a comprehensive evaluation at any point throughout the RTI cycle.

While the schools' ability to identify learning disabilities evolves, shouldn't private practitioners look beyond methods and instruments that support the IQ-discrepancy model?

A PREVIEW

Any well-trained teacher will encourage readers to preview the material they are going to read as a way to boost comprehension. To that end, here is a brief synopsis of the discussion to follow.

I discovered the dynamic relationship between learning and behavior while tutoring hundreds of K–12 students at a learning center that I founded in Connecticut. A special relationship with one of my students underscored the importance of nurturing the link between learning and behavior while coordinating the care of different pediatric practitioners. Nearly a quarter of U.S. children are at risk for school failure, which can be a chronic problem caused by a myriad of medical and psychosocial conditions. Moreover, children suffering from school failure are more likely to experience a deterioration of physical and mental health, making this a serious public health concern. Because the antecedents and consequences of learning dysfunctions affect more than one domain in children, a collaborative, multidisciplinary approach to assessment and treatment is imperative. Community-based specialists, who often act as independent agents, could be encouraged to cooperate in the interest of patient care, but that is unlikely to happen on its own. I recommend the creation of the developmental care clinic, a team-based model that allows practitioners from several disciplines to work under one roof. The different practitioners may include psychologists, learning specialists, and child psychiatrists, among others. The assessment and management of a child with attention-deficit/ hyperactivity disorder (ADHD) provides a useful test case to challenge the effectiveness of the developmental care clinic model. A discussion of the child with ADHD reveals several hurdles that may be faced by private practice as it grapples with the changes in the identification of learning disabilities introduced by IDEIA 2004. Improved communication and coordination across specialties as part of a developmental care clinic could represent a promising response by the private sector to the changes in special education law; however, the model will likely evolve as we learn more about the efficacy of RTI and the ability of professionals from different specialties to work together.

DOCTOR MEANS TEACHER

In December 2000, I started tutoring Westport, Connecticut, middle and high school children across all school subjects. At that time, I was completing my premed requirements through the postbaccalaureate program at Columbia University ahead of my eventual enrollment at the Yale School of Medicine in 2003. My tutoring work helped me uncover a passion for working with children and adolescents at the intersection of learning and behavior. This passion, shared by my wife, inspired us to open a learning center called Raging Knowledge, and it prompted me to seek out mentors at the Yale Child Study Center when I arrived for my first semester at the School of Medicine. My wife managed the learning center while I attended classes and completed my clinical training.

Over the last 7 years, Raging Knowledge has provided learning support to over 1,000 struggling K–12 students. The sources of school struggles have varied greatly, including dyslexia, ADHD, depression, anxiety, and chronic illness. I sought out formal and informal training to improve my understanding of the expansive psychological and neuropsychological reports that accompanied many of my new students on their first tutoring appointment. I also completed a course in the Orton-Gillingham method of literacy instruction to better appreciate the subtleties of reading and writing skills acquisition among children. The coursework, combined with my rapidly growing experience with learning-disabled students, opened my eyes to the dynamic relationship between learning and behavior among children. Furthermore, I was surprised by the inability of parents to find conclusive explanations and effective interventions for their children's school struggles, no matter how many professionals and specialists they consulted.

I recently finished my third year of medical school, a year in which I was exposed to clinical practice and instruction for about 60 hours weekly. I did my best to learn lessons from encounters with patients and medical staff. While the hospital certainly does not provide a flawless model for clinical care, I was struck by the structure and rigor with which good hospital-based physicians communicated with one another about patients. When discussing or writing about patients, physicians often follow a template best described as a SOAP note. The note is made up of four elements in the following order: (a) *Subjective* information gathered from the patient describing symptoms; (b) *Objective* data collected from observations and tests; (c) *Assessment* of the problem and possible diagnoses; (d) *Plan* for treatment and follow-up. The importance given to the structure and content of clinical communication is impressive. It facilitates collaboration among hospital-based physicians and it improves the coordination of multidisciplinary care. This year's experience reinforced a lesson about the effectiveness of good communication and the importance of collaboration that I had learned from working with one of my most challenging students, Emily, at our learning center.

CAN TUTORING SAVE A LIFE?

"Raging Knowledge saved my life." Those words, uttered to my wife by a former student last year, represent to me the most powerful evidence that learning and behavior are inextricably linked. When I become a child and adolescent psychiatrist, I will never forget the power of an educational intervention and the importance of collaborative multidisciplinary care.

Emily's mother pulled me aside one afternoon in 2002 after dropping off her sixth grade son for tutoring at our learning center. "I don't know what to do about Emily," she pleaded. "Her grades are dropping, she's always sad and she is cutting herself." Emily's mother explained that she was in therapy and was taking several psychiatric medications but little had improved.

I offered to give Emily, a freshman in high school, learning support free of charge because I knew that her family could not afford intensive tutoring services for both children. It was only our third year of providing support services to struggling K–12 students and I had never encountered a case like this. Several highly trained professionals had already evaluated and treated Emily; I was hoping to give her an incremental boost in self-esteem by helping her to find some success in school. As an aspiring pediatric mental health clinician, I was also hoping that Emily would teach me about her experience as an adolescent in the 21st century.

I was given permission to speak to her therapist and psychiatrist so that I could better understand her ADHD and depression. Throughout her childhood, Emily had been to several psychologists who had administered batteries of tests and written what amounted to nearly 100 pages of reports detailing her performance on countless cognitive and behavioral subtests.

I read the reports in hopes of gaining an even deeper understanding of Emily's learning and behavioral profiles; however, I found the reports to be jargon-filled and difficult to understand. Emily's parents, both of whom were highly educated, had spent thousands of dollars on these assessments and were frustrated because they still didn't know how to help their daughter. The bulk of the reports were dedicated to detailing the nature of her deficits, with a few lines at the end of each one outlining some very vague recommendations.

I spoke with the last psychologist who had tested Emily and found her to be very helpful. She spent time explaining the results of the testing and what they uncovered about Emily's behavioral and cognitive functioning. Additionally, we discussed some specific educational interventions that could benefit Emily, and the psychologist shed some light on some of the strengths that could be exploited during our therapeutic relationship. Now, why couldn't this have all been spelled out in the report in plain English in the first place?

I had the privilege to work with Emily for over 2 years. She had become a different person by the time she finished the eleventh grade and prepared to apply to art schools. Her depression had started to lift, she was no longer self-injurious and her motivation to do well in school had increased dramatically. I assumed that my role in her transformation had been minimal; either the combination of psychotherapy and medication finally took effect, or time had taken over, carrying her from a difficult developmental stage into a new, more promising one.

"Raging Knowledge saved my life," she insisted. What had made such a difference to Emily? Had it been our work on organizational skills? Was it her improved ability to write a well-structured essay? Was it the nature of our tutoring relationship?

When I heard about Emily's words, I suspected that integrating academic interventions into the overall care of a child was fundamental to improving both educational and mental health outcomes. Also, without knowing it, I had become Emily's case manager; I had loosely coordinated her educational and emotional care by communicating with educators, clinicians, and her family. I had learned that being Emily's tutor opened the door for me to provide her and her family the support she was not receiving from other practitioners. Emily and her family had let me into their lives, allowing me to make a big impact on her developmental trajectory. Fortunately, I didn't ruin that golden opportunity.

THE CASE FOR COORDINATED CARE

The private sector care for children struggling with school failure can be improved immediately by delivering coordinated, multidisciplinary assessment and treatment services. Based on the experience of my many students, it seems that the quality of educational and developmental care remains somewhat patchy and uncoordinated. Psychologists, pediatricians, child psychiatrists, education specialists, and other pediatric practitioners continue to operate as independent agents, rarely coordinating their patients' care. I have not met many educators who have a good understanding of child psychology and psychiatry, nor have I met many clinicians who appreciate the nuances of educational assessments and interventions. It is reminiscent of the traditional tale of the six blind men and the elephant; each person examines a separate part, resulting in six different explanations for the same phenomenon. Parents, many of which are unfamiliar with the differences among the cultures and vernaculars of each field, are forced to act as their child's case manager and school advocate.

Coordinating educational and developmental care is a straightforward way to improve academic and mental health outcomes among struggling school children. Researchers, clinicians, and educators are spending a lot of time and resources debating the quality of special education services because it represents an important public health issue. Over 25% of U.S. children are at risk for school failure and accompanying social, emotional, and behavioral problems (Noam & Hermann, 2002). School success is good for you. It boosts self-esteem, enhances self-efficacy, and supports healthy cognitive and social development. Untreated, chronic school failure is detrimental to children's emotional, cognitive, and physical development. School failure can hurt self-esteem, interfere with social functioning, and prompt unhealthy behaviors in children and adolescents (Noam & Hermann, 2002). Mel Levine, MD, a developmental pediatrician at the University of North Carolina School of Medicine, describes the far-reaching impact of learning dysfunctions:

> Needless suffering occurs when children grow up disappointing themselves and the adults who care about them. Often they do so because

they perform inadequately in school. Unfortunately, these children come to question their own worthiness, as they gaze about and compare themselves to others.

So much is at stake. Children who experience too much failure early in life are exquisitely vulnerable to a wide range of complications. When these students are poorly understood, when their specific problems go unrecognized and untreated, they are especially prone to behavioral and emotional difficulties that are more severe than the learning problems that generated them. (Levine, 2002)

Coordinated, multidisciplinary care is imperative because the cause of learning dysfunctions in children almost always involves more than one domain (Byrd, 2005). The causes of school failure can be linked to several areas of functioning, including the educational, behavioral, and affective; cognitive and developmental; and environmental and medical domains (Levine, 2002). Unless the source of a learning dysfunction is limited to one domain, the assessment and treatment of the problem is preferably performed using a coordinated, team-based approach. A list of the possible causes of school failure is presented in Table 20.1 (Byrd, 2005).

Learning disabilities and emotional-behavioral dysfunctions must be approached in a coordinated, multidisciplinary way because they are chronic conditions. A chronic condition is defined as one that affects a patient for more than 12 months in at least one of three ways: functional limitations, dependence on compensatory mechanisms, or service use beyond routine care (Burns, Sadof, & Kamat, 2006). The specifics of school struggles among children with learning disabilities or emotional-behavioral dysfunctions illustrate all three in that these students may experience mental or emotional delays, take prescription medication, regularly visit a mental health clinician, or use special education services.

While there have been repeated calls for the improved coordination of care for patients with chronic conditions, the quality of the studies supporting improved outcomes is questionable. Unfortunately, there are only observational studies and demonstration programs to show that coordinated care improves outcomes; however, the lack of double-blind, randomized trials shouldn't preclude improved communication among pediatric practitioners. It is important to note that the treatment of chronic conditions in children is particularly challenging since ongoing cognitive and physical development introduce another layer of complexity (Burns et al., 2006). Capable clinicians and educators must understand normal child development as well as the ways in which learning and emotional-behavioral dysfunctions alter the developmental trajectory of children.

TABLE 20.1   Conditions and Factors Associated With School Failure

Endogenous Factors	
Chronic disease	*Learning disability*

Chronic disease
-Anemia
-Asthma
-Obstructive sleep apnea
 syndrome
-Cystic fibrosis
-Crohn disease
-Lupus
Acute conditions causing school absences
Sensory impairment
-Vision
-Hearing
Perinatal conditions
-Prematurity
-Fetal alcohol syndrome
-In utero drug exposure
-Maternal conditions that affect
 pregnancy
  -Seizures
  -Depression
  -Phenylketonuria
  -Maternal tobacco use
  -Maternal hypothyroidism
Neurologic disorders
-Brain injury
  -Meningitis
  -Perinatal insult
  -Traumatic brain injury
  -Radiation (e.g., following brain
  tumor)
-Tic disorders
  -Tourette syndrome
-Seizure disorders
-Toxic exposures: lead

Learning disability
-Developmental speech and
language disorder
  -Phonological disorder
  -Expressive language
  disorder
  -Developmental receptive
  language disorder
  -Mixed receptive-expressive
  -Stuttering
-Learning disorders (LD)
  -Developmental reading
  disorder
  -Written expression disorder
  -Mathematics disorder
-LD not otherwise specified:
  combination of reading,
  writing, or math disorders
Other developmental disorders
-Mental retardation
-Communication disorders
-Attention-deficit/hyperactivity
 disorder
-Autistic spectrum disorders
Genetic disorders: Fragile X
syndrome
Endocrine disorders: hypo and
hyperthyroidism
Psychiatric disorders
-Mood disorders
-Sleep disorder
-Disruptive behavior disorder
  -Oppositional defiant disorder
  -Conduct disorder
  -Obsessive-compulsive disorder
-Anxiety disorder
  -Phobia
  -Panic
  -Separation anxiety disorder
-Substance abuse

Continued

TABLE 20.1   Conditions and Factors Associated With School Failure
(Continued)

Exogenous Factors	

Family
-Divorce/separation/conflict
-Poverty
-Frequent moves
-Substance abuse
-Depression
-Attitudes toward school/education
  -Low level of family support for
  the student
  -Inadequate accommodation for
  studies at home
-Neglect/Abuse
Environmental
-Neighborhood/housing
-TV/computers
Peers
-Peer pressures for low
performance
-Substance abuse
	Competing priorities: excessive
	extramural activities
	-Social
	-Work
	-Sports
	School
	-Mismatch between student and
	teacher
	-Unrealistic expectations
	-Inadequate school environment
	  -Violence/safety
	  -Classroom size
	Transitions
	-Third grade
	-Elementary to middle school
	Increasing in testing standards
	without increasing educational
	support
	Excessive testing

If educators and clinicians can agree that a well-integrated, multi-disciplinary model of care is ideal, what should it look like? The current system of care leaves a lot of room for improvement. It is fragmented, requiring patients and their families to do much of the work to integrate care across specialties.

THE DEVELOPMENTAL CARE CLINIC

If the goal is to promote communication and collaboration among local practitioners from different specialties, then, in theory, improved communication could be achieved if they made more of an effort to pick up the phone and speak to one another, or if they determined a regular place and time in the community to meet and review cases. Because each private practitioner represents an individual practice with a separate schedule, fee structure, and insurance relationships, ongoing weekly contact is unlikely to be sustained and the care of shared patients will not be coordinated. Some have suggested that the pediatrician, a child's primary caregiver and the clinician most likely to have nurtured a longitudinal patient relationship, play the role of the case manager to facilitate communication (Burns et al., 2006). In reality, many pediatricians are already overextended by the responsibilities that accompany the delivery of primary care. Asking a busy pediatrician to coordinate the educational, psychiatric, and developmental care of a child suffering from school failure seems unreasonable.

The simplest way to foster communication, collaboration, and coordination is to put educational and mental health practitioners under one roof. Learning and behavior are inextricably linked, so why should educational and mental health services be separate in practice? This perspective is not unique. Gil Noam, PhD, is the executive director of the Program in Education, Afterschool & Resiliency (PEAR) at Harvard University and an associate professor at Harvard Medical School and McLean Hospital in Boston, MA. He developed a school-based prevention and intervention model for young adolescents in Boston called Responsive Advocacy for Life and Learning in Youth (RALLY). In a paper describing the program's theoretical framework, Dr. Noam explained that "RALLY strives to overcome the traditional distinctions between mental health and educational practice in work with at-risk children" (Noam & Hermann, 2002). The blurring of the line dividing educational and mental health services is appealing because poor school experiences and academic failure represent both an antecedent and a consequence of emotional-behavioral dysfunctions.

There are far-reaching practical implications for overcoming existing distinctions between mental health and educational practice. Again and again, we see that, when confronted with a patient suffering from school failure, the pediatrician makes a referral to the child psychiatrist, who makes a referral for testing to the psychologist, who ultimately makes a referral to the education specialist for targeted academic interventions. Of course, this scenario doesn't always represent the end of the service chain; the child often bounces between practitioners as parents attempt to confirm the diagnosis and tweak interventions. Furthermore, the resulting private sector assessment will likely be shared with school officials, leading to debates over accommodations or special education services that need to be coordinated with everyone in and out of school. Parents, who often have more than one child to care for, become overwhelmed by the scheduling demands of going from practitioner to practitioner and by the amount of information they are required to assimilate in hopes of making well-informed decisions.

We wish to turn Raging Knowledge into a new model for the delivery of private educational and mental health services; when the two areas of care become fully integrated, we will call it a developmental care clinic (DCC). For now, we offer tutoring, educational assessments, case management services, interpretive services for existing neuropsychological reports, applied behavioral analysis, and parent support groups. To deliver this array of services, our staff is made up of professionals with varying backgrounds. We have a learning specialist who has a PhD in behavioral neuroscience and is working on her master's degree in clinical social work, and we have a pediatric neuropsychologist who assesses children and interprets any existing psychological reports. Our reading specialist has a master's degree in literacy and language education and a master's degree in human development. We employ a behavioral specialist who is a certified applied behavioral analyst with 13 years of experience working with children on the autism spectrum. An experienced middle school counselor is trained to run our parent groups, and we have two math and science specialists, one of which earned a master's degree in chemistry and the other graduated with a bachelor's degree in mathematics with plans to enroll in medical school in 2008. We assembled this staff partly based on their academic and professional backgrounds, but mostly because of their demonstrated passion for teaching and community service.

The future DCC will be staffed to provide the following services to children and their families (see Figure 20.1):

1. Case Management
2. School Advocacy
3. Neuropsychological Testing
4. Clinical Psychology
5. Behavioral Therapy
6. Child and Adolescent Psychiatry
7. Educational Testing
8. Tutoring
9. Speech and Language Therapy
10. Parent Support and Education Groups

The case manager, equipped with the training and experience to appreciate the intricacies of educational and mental health care, will play the most important role at the DCC. Children and their families will communicate mostly with their assigned case manager, who will coordinate and integrate all services, both within the DCC and among outside professionals, including community pediatricians and school staff. If performed effectively, the work of the case manager will represent the most important step in overcoming the distinction between mental health and educational practice. Ultimately, the goal of the DCC is to improve academic and mental health outcomes by optimizing the dynamic relationship between learning and behavior among children.

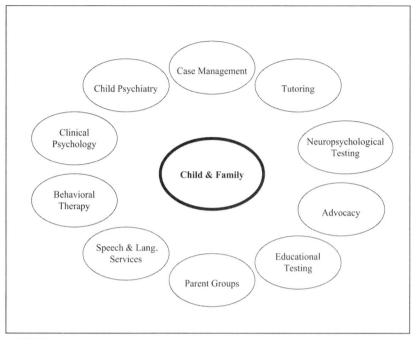

FIGURE 20.1   Developmental care clinic services.

ADHD VS. LEARNING DISABILITY:
A TEST CASE FOR THE DCC

The assessment and treatment of a child with suspected ADHD provides an illustrative example of the way that the DCC can provide comprehensive, integrated care for children at risk for school failure. ADHD, a neurobehavioral disorder, is the most prevalent pediatric behavioral disorder in the United States, affecting as much as 5% of all children (Daly, Creed, Xanthopoulous, & Brown, 2007). Additionally, ADHD is associated with problems in school. Many studies report a comorbid learning disability in about 50% of cases, with reading disabilities listed as particularly rampant among those children (Riccio & Jemison, 1998). The *Diagnostic and Statistical Manual of Mental Disorders (DSM-IV)* represents the gold standard in medicine for diagnostic manuals to identify psychiatric disorders. The *DSM-IV* lists several school-related problems among its criteria for the diagnosis of ADHD, including making careless mistakes in schoolwork or leaving it unfinished, displaying reluctance to complete homework, losing school-related implements, leaving a classroom at inappropriate times, and blurting answers in class out of turn.

ADHD and learning disabilities present a diagnostic puzzle for everyone; both educators and clinicians find it difficult to untangle the two diagnoses. Teachers who are concerned that students may have ADHD often ask parents to send their children to pediatricians for an evaluation before taking advantage of well-qualified school professionals to screen for possible learning dysfunctions. Pediatric visits to address concerns over ADHD are frequent. About 10% of all pediatric visits are related to behavior, half of which are for suspected problems in attention (Byrd, 2005). A recent review of diagnostic practices among pediatric primary care physicians, including both pediatricians and family practice physicians, revealed that most doctors are still not following best practices as defined by published guidelines of the American Academy of Pediatrics (AAP) when diagnosing ADHD (Chan, Hopkins, Perrin, Herrerias, & Homer, 2005). While 88.2% of pediatricians reported using information from both parents and teachers to make the diagnosis, only 9.4% made use of that information while considering *DSM-IV* criteria and screening for coexisting conditions, such as conduct disorders, tic disorders, or learning disabilities. AAP guidelines include the collection of parent and teacher information, the use of *DSM-IV* criteria, and screening for coexisting disorders (Chan et al., 2005).

Researchers have been calling for a multidisciplinary approach to the diagnosis and treatment of ADHD for some time.

> Collaboration and comprehensive assessment are needed initially in the assessment process to identify co-occurring deficits. Furthermore, collaboration and consultation should continue throughout the intervention planning and implementation to ensure that interrelated deficits in language areas and basic reading skills are effectively addressed. Through active collaboration, the educational outcome of students with co-occurring AD/HD, linguistic deficits, and early reading difficulties may be improved. (Riccio & Jemison, 1998)

In private practice, the DCC will be in an ideal position to support the assessment process initiated by the pediatrician. Assuming that the pediatrician is doing her best to follow AAP guidelines, the DCC, using the services of its education specialist and child and adolescent psychiatrist, can screen for related or comorbid conditions, including learning disabilities and emotional-behavioral dysfunctions. The pediatrician can refer her patient to the DCC after performing a complete history and physical exam, both of which help practitioners rule out, or eliminate, the possibility of an underlying acute or chronic physical illness.

IDEIA 2004 has shifted the paradigm for the identification of children with learning disabilities, and practices at the DCC must reflect that shift. In order to screen for learning disabilities in the child with attention-related difficulties, DCC practitioners must consider the methods used by the student's school district. The analysis of the school district's process for identifying learning disability also raises questions that all private practitioners will need to consider in the context of IDEIA 2004:

- Has RTI been implemented in the school district yet?
- If so, what services and evaluations are associated with each RTI tier?
- Where in the RTI cycle is the student who has been referred?
- What if the school district does not use RTI? Should we fall back on the IQ-discrepancy model with which the school is more familiar?
- What if the district uses RTI, but the student has not yet experienced failure and his mother wants a comprehensive assessment anyway?

Until RTI practices have been fully standardized, the assessment for learning disabilities is likely to involve a combination of diagnostic tutoring sessions and neuropsychological testing. It will likely take some time before schools and parents get comfortable with the idea of diagnosing a learning disability based on a child's response to teaching alone. Diagnostic tutoring is essentially a version of RTI in which the DCC delivers evidence-based instruction in one of three basic academic skills—reading, writing, or mathematics—and tracks the child's ability to learn.

This scenario uncovers additional challenges for private practice following the implementation of IDEIA 2004. First, who is going to perform the evaluations? A highly skilled tutor who has the training to administer evidence-based assessments as part of an RTI protocol, or a pediatric neuropsychologist who also has the background to perform educational interventions as part of the evaluation process? Perhaps instructors and assessors will need to collaborate and train one another, while following the rules that govern the purchase and use of each published assessment. Secondly, families have no way of knowing who is or is not a qualified tutor with the ability to provide evidence-based instruction. Most specialties providing educational and mental health care for children have organized professional organizations, which offer ongoing training and publish guidelines for each field's so-called best practices. Furthermore, teacher certification cannot guarantee appropriate training, as much of the work in private practice is different than in the classroom, involving one-on-one instruction with a focus on very specific skills. Also, there is evidence that teacher training programs don't always provide their graduates with some of the knowledge required to deliver appropriate instruction. Until there is a board certification program for tutors, a well-run DCC can screen job candidates to ensure that they have the proper toolbox to assess and treat children with learning disabilities.

After a child has been diagnosed with ADHD and a comorbid reading disability using an effective assessment protocol and guidance from the case manager, the DCC will be in a position to provide several treatment options. With the family's consent, the staff psychiatrist could prescribe one of the medications that have been proven to reduce core symptoms, such as hyperactivity, impulsivity, and inattentiveness; however, not all children respond well to medication and some families prefer psychosocial interventions to address ADHD. Interestingly, one of the most effective and well-studied interventions in pediatric mental health is parent training. For ADHD, training parents is an approach designed to empower them with strategies to manage contingencies in the relationships with their children by emphasizing behavior modification, cues and consequences, reward systems, and discipline (Daly et al., 2007). Other interventions that have been proven to improve behavioral outcomes in children with ADHD include targeted classroom management strategies and computer programs designed to boost working memory (Daly et al., 2007). The DCC will have the ability to access a richer pool of interventions in the treatment of ADHD than the independent community practitioner.

The child's reading disability will be treated at the DCC by a learning specialist who has been trained to provide instruction by supporting all five reading sub-skills, including phonemic awareness, phonics, vocabulary, fluency, and reading comprehension. Instruction at the DCC will be coordinated with the student's schoolteachers by the case manager, ensuring that interventions are translating into school success. Moreover, the DCC will track progress throughout the intervention cycle to demonstrate improvement in each of the sub-skills and in reading as an overall skill.

The DCC will make service delivery and coordination more practical for parents who can drop off their children at one location for assessments and interventions. Additionally, the quality of care is likely to improve because practitioners will see each other regularly, prompting more communication and coordination. The DCC protocol will limit record-keeping to only one comprehensive, multispecialty chart per child with a standardized method for recording educational and clinical information. For example, DCC educational and mental health practitioners could all adopt the SOAP-note method for detailing occurrences and observations from each patient visit, while conforming to state and federal laws that govern the content of these records. By tracking this valuable information in one place and in the same format, practitioners will have better access to data on which they can base decisions, and parents will no longer have to be saddled with hundreds of pages of reports to manage. Furthermore, providing educational and clinical services as part of a well-organized, multidisciplinary group can be more stimulating for professionals: Clinicians can learn more about education and educators can learn more about clinical work. These opportunities for cross-training improve everyone's ability to help children and their families.

CONCLUSION

Changes in the identification and treatment of children with learning disabilities in schools heralded by IDEIA 2004 should serve as a welcome opportunity for private practitioners in education and mental health to examine critically their clinical approach to care and make changes where necessary. The magnitude of some changes may create some discomfort among professionals, but that feeling will pale in comparison to the suffering produced by chronic school failure among children who are being supported with ineffective approaches to developmental care. Changes in education law do not require private practitioners to implement RTI, and specialty-specific professional organizations can only publish guidelines and recommendations for so-called best practices among their members in this regard. The legislative change now gives everyone the choice of using RTI or the IQ-discrepancy model, which is falling out of favor. An organized, multidisciplinary approach to children who are at risk for or who are already experiencing school failure emerges as the best option for practitioners dedicated to providing the best in educational and mental health care. The lines separating educational and mental health practice are likely to continue fading, and professionals from each field should prepare to continue working together. The DCC provides a structure for collaboration that can improve the communication and coordination of care. Moreover, it will simplify the lives of those parents who are now overwhelmed with the responsibility of playing the roles of record-keeper, case manager, and school advocate.

REFERENCES

Albers, C. A., Glover, T. A., & Kratochwill, T. R. (2007). Editorial: Where are we, and where do we go now? Universal screening for enhanced educational and mental health outcomes. *Journal of School Psychology, 45*, 257–263.

Burns, J. J., Sadof, M., & Kamat, D. (2006). The adolescent with a chronic illness: How to manage treatment issues and provide specialized services in this population. *Pediatric Annals, 35*(3), 207–216.

Byrd, R. S. (2005). School failure: Assessment, intervention, and prevention in primary pediatric care. *Pediatrics in Review, 26*, 233–243.

Chan, E., Hopkins, M. R., Perrin, J. M., Herrerias, C., & Homer, C. J. (2005). Diagnostic practices for attention deficit hyperactivity disorder: A national survey of primary care physicians. *Ambulatory Pediatrics, 5,* 201–208.

Daly, B. P., Creed, T., Xanthopoulous, M., & Brown, R. T. (2007). Psychosocial treatments for children with attention deficit/hyperactivity disorder. *Neuropsychology Review, 17*(1), 73–89.

Fuchs, D., Fuchs, L. S., Mock, D., Morgan, P. L., & Young, C. L. (2003) Responsiveness-to-intervention: Definitions, evidence, and implications for the learning disabilities construct. *Learning Disabilities Research and Practice, 18,* 157–171.

Levine, M. (2002). *Educational care: A system for understanding and helping children with learning differences at home and in school* (2nd ed.). Cambridge: Educators Publishing Service.

Noam, G. G., & Hermann, C. A. (2002). Where education and mental health meet: Developmental prevention and early intervention in schools. *Development and Psychopathology, 14,* 861–875.

Riccio, C. A., & Jemison, S. J. (1998). ADHD and emergent literacy: Influence of language factors. *Reading & Writing Quarterly, 14*(1), 43–58.

CHAPTER 21

The Road Just Started

Concluding Remarks From the Editor

Elena L. Grigorenko

On Tuesday, January, 20, 2004, the 108th Congress of the United States of America gathered at its second session in the city of Washington to reauthorize the Individuals With Disabilities Education Act (http://thomas. loc.gov/cgi-bin/query/C?c108:./temp/ˉc108xcRKgA). The stated outcome of this gathering was: "Be it enacted by the Senate and House of Representatives of the United States of America in Congress assembled," *it* being the Individuals With Disabilities Education Improvement Act of 2004 (IDEIA 2004) or, alternatively, the Individuals With Disabilities Education Act of 2004 (IDEA 2004).

The significance of the reenactment of IDEA is virtually impossible to understate provided that, for example, in the fall of 2005, 6,813,656 children aged 3–21 were being served under IDEIA (https://www.ideadata. org/tables29th/ar_1–1.xls). Also of note is that the cost of educating a child with special educational needs is about twice as high as that of a typically developing child (http://www.csef-air.org/publications/seep/ national/AdvRpt1.PDF).

The majority of the children served in 2005 were served under the categories of specific learning disabilities (45.5% of all eligible children) and speech and language impairment (18.9% of all eligible children).

The reauthorization of IDEA is closely linked to No Child Left Behind (NCLB) (see Introduction). The linkages are many, but the most pronounced ones are related to the issues of accountability, progress

monitoring, and the desired dominance of preventive rather than reme-
diative pedagogical practices.

This volume explores the fundamental importance of IDEIA for educating children in the United States, the costs of educating children with
special needs, the distribution of disabilities within the subpopulation
of children with special needs, the close connection between IDEIA and
NCLB, the recent reauthorization of IDEIA, and the ongoing discussions
regarding the upcoming reauthorization of NCLB.

This book is designed to review, at multiple levels, the experiences
related to the enactment of IDEIA in 2004. The book presents the context for and the innovative characteristics of IDEIA. It then discusses a
range of theoretical, methodological, and research issues linked to the introduction and dissemination of IDEIA's innovations. Finally, the volume
samples various accounts from the field, illustrating the incorporation of
IDEIA into states, districts, schools, and private practices.

Specifically, the volume first attempts to introduce the broad, not only
national but also international context of IDEIA. Dabie Nabuzoka discusses the issues pertaining to both classical and modern traditions of educating children with special needs around the world. He presents general issues of terminology and the classification of disabilities, their presentations
as well as the difficulties of differentiating disabilities from underachievement, especially in disadvantaged children; and he presents issues related
to assessment and intervention and their contextual validities and effectiveness. In the last part of his chapter, Nabuzoka comments on the links
between research and services in special education, and thus sets the stage
for the second part of the book, which is primarily research-oriented.

Andrea Kayne Kaufman follows Nabuzoka, bringing up the links
between IDEIA and NCLB (following the theme brought forward by
Barbara Foorman in her introduction to the volume) and rigorously reviewing these links and the innovations of IDEIA. Kaufman briefly presents the context and content of the major themes of the new IDEIA,
specifically, issues of (a) teacher qualifications; (b) the minority achievement gap; (c) the identification of children with special needs; (d) the delivery of special education services; (e) progress monitoring; (f) the rights
of students; and (g) due process.

In her chapter, Mary Konya Weishaar takes a very applied perspective on the innovations introduced by IDEIA by putting the reader in the
position of a special education professional who is to deliver services
under the three different realizations of the law (1975, 1990, and 2004).
In these scenarios, the official legal language of Kaufman's chapter is
translated into the applied language of a teacher. Reading this chapter,
one sees the disconnect between what is written in the law and what
needs to happen in the real enactment of it—not in the buildings of Congress, but in the reality of American classrooms.

The chapters by Kaufman and Weishaar are enormously helpful in setting up the context for what follows in the volume: a discussion of the research pertaining to these innovations. This research, covered in the next 12 chapters, constitutes the largest portion of the book. All of these chapters, in different voices and with different words, ask more or less the same questions: (a) Is there enough evidence to introduce the innovations, cited by Kaufman and Weishaar into IDEIA; and (b) What does the research show with regard to the viability of these innovations since the reauthorization of IDEIA?

One of the so-called golden threats of both IDEIA and NCLB relates to the concept of *evidence-based practice*. Ronnie Detrich offers an excellent introduction to the tensions surrounding this concept and the large-scale debate concerning the role of scientific research in educational policy. The chapter provides a broad overview of not only the policy-related issues but also the fundamental components of the concept of evidence-based practice. Detrich takes the reader through a brief discussion of the nature of evidence, types of evidence, methods of obtaining evidence and judging its strength, and approaches to standards of evidence. The chapter stresses the direct impact of NCLB and IDEIA as movers and shakers of educational research that call not only for the development of research-informed interventions but also for the shortening of the time span between the initial efficacy research of a particular intervention and its validation as an evidence-based practice. This means that the policies not only call for more research but for research conducted at higher speeds. Detrich concludes the chapter by taking the discussion to the junction of IDEIA and evidence-based practice; this is where the concept of response to intervention (RTI) enters the volume in its full force and remains a major idea throughout, shaping the discussion around issues of eligibility, intervention, and progress monitoring.

As mentioned above, the majority of the children served under the IDEIA are served under the categories of specific learning disabilities (SLD) and speech and language impairments (S&LI); together students in this category constitute approximately 65% of all children with special educational needs. Correspondingly, it is of no surprise that the field of specific education is dominated by questions pertaining to the needs and qualifications of this group of children. As noted by Foorman, RTI is cited in IDEIA as a generic concept linking evaluation procedures and research-based interventions for all children; thus, this concept's application covers much more than SLDs and S&LIs. Yet, given that these two categories are entry points for services for the majority of children with special needs, the concept of RTI is particularly present in the research and practice involving children with SLDs and S&LIs.

The chapter by Lynn S. Fuchs, Doug Fuchs, and Rebecca O. Zumeta takes the reader in depth into the RTI-related discussions in the field. They offer a thoughtful overview of RTI, setting the stage for a number of subsequent chapters. Written by experts on RTI, this contribution questions a number of the strong and weak aspects of the concept and serves as a trigger for specific discussion in the chapters to follow.

The tensions between various identification approaches are further investigated in the next three chapters. In chapter 6, Peggy McCardle, Chandra Keller-Allen, and Tanya Shuy bring into the focus issues in identification for SLDs as they relate to English language learners (ELLs). The authors, observing that the subpopulation of ELLs has doubled between 1994/1995 and 2004/2005, with language minority students forming the fastest growing subgroup of children among various subpopulations of public school students, argue that today's practice of identification and service does not meet the unique needs of ELLs. Their argument unfolds around the utilization of RTI as a potential aid to addressing the special needs of ELLs.

The concept of RTI is also central in the chapter by Jack A. Naglieri and Alan S. Kaufman. This chapter focuses specifically on the identification of children with SLD and comments on the usability of two assessments paradigms, one of RTI and the other of psychological processes. Naglieri and Kaufman provide a comprehensive overview of the inspirations and difficulties associated with the utilization of the IDEIA's RTI-based approaches in today's everyday practices, as well as the similarities and dissimilarities between the objectives and outcomes of RTI- and psychological processes–based approaches.

Chapter 8, written by Jennifer H. Lindstrom, Elizabeth D. Tuckwiller, and Daniel P. Hallahan, brings the variety of issues concerning identification and assessment, discussed in the three previous chapters, together. Here, they present a discussion of the process of identification, starting with pre-referral events, going through various models of assessment for identification purposes and the underlying the importance of clinical judgment in the eligibility decision-making process. A particular feature of this chapter is a focus on issues of educating children with attention-deficit/hyperactivity disorder. In addition, their chapter revisits the issue of the new features of IDEIA, bringing up changes regarding Individualized Education Program (IEP) and the participation of children with special needs in high-stake tests. Both issues are mentioned in brief here and are further examined in chapters 13 and 14.

The so-called flip side of the coin as it pertains to RTI—namely, its instructional side—enters the flow of the discussion in chapter 9, by David J. Chard, Leanne R. Ketterlin-Geller, and Asha Jitendra. These authors explore the instructional part of RTI using the teaching of mathematics as an example. Here again, the readers sees a discussion of research-informed interventions and evidence-based teaching practices. Similarly, chapter 10, written by Scott K. Baker and Doris Luft Baker, deals with issues of teaching, specifically teaching of ELLs.

The instruction-oriented nature of the two preceding chapters prepares the reader for the discussion of aspects of teacher preparation that need to be adjusted when RTI is introduced in the classroom. Louise Spear-Swerling offers the reader her views on the matter in chapter 11, which contains detailed illustrations of the links between teaching literacy, teacher knowledge of the fundamentals of literacy and teaching literacy, and the implementation of RTI.

Chapter 12, written by Tonya R. Moon, Catherine M. Brighton, Carolyn M. Callahan, and Jane M. Jarvis, comments on yet another subpopulation of school children directly impacted by IDEIA, that is, of children who are twice-exceptional, with SLDs and gifts.

The issue of quality of teaching and related issues of accountability, as captured by high stakes testing, is central to chapter 13, written by Stuart S. Yeh. The discussion, once again, revolves around the connections between IDEIA and the NCLB, but now with the major accent of the discussion being placed on high school exit exams that, by 2009, students in half of all the states (or 70% of all students) will most likely be required to take.

Two other domains of changes of IDEIA, brought up in passing in a number of the volume's chapters, are central to the following two chapters. Chapter 14, the contribution by Barbara C. Gartin and Nikki L. Murdick, reviews changes in provisions regarding Individualized Education Program (IEP). Chapter 15, by Susan Etscheidt and Kerri Clopton, presents and discusses changes as they pertain to Behavior Intervention Plans (BIPs). These two chapters complete the second part of the book and bring the reader to the next major set of IDEIA-related issues discussed in this volume, specifically, those concerning the practical experiences of implementing IDEIA.

The third part of the book, "From the Front Lines," opens with a contribution from Denise Hexom, Judith Menoher, Bonnie A. Plummer, and Mary Stone. The focus here is an analysis of underperforming rural and urban schools in the state of California. In this chapter, once again, NCLB and IDEIA meet and are analyzed hand in hand.

Chapter 17 brings the discussion from the state level to the district level, presenting a case of the implementation of both NCLB and IDEIA in a well-performing district. This contribution is provided by Linda J. Hawkins and Michael N. Riley and comes from the Bellevue school district in Washington State.

The following three chapters, chapters 18–20, all present views of IDEIA by professionals who are at the front lines, working with students with special needs: psychologists (Michele Goyette-Ewing and Sherin

Stahl), an educator (Saylor Heidmann), and a private tutor (Eric R. Arzubi). All three chapters provide first-hand examples and illustrations of the impact of IDEIA on the lives of specific children.

Here, I have tried to supply a simple road map that captures the range and complexity of the various topics discussed in this volume. The book is multilayered and multifaceted and provides a diversity of positions and views on IDEIA. The volume was conceived in such a way that, collectively, all chapters can present the reader with an overview of the field and, individually, can stand alone. Correspondingly, there is an inevitable amount of overlap in referencing IDEIA and NCLB and their central concepts. Yet, possibly remarkably so, the interpretations of the same language of the law can be as diverse as the positions of the authors offering them.

From my point of view, this book is especially valuable now as states and districts around the country consider aligning their practices with the changes in IDEIA. In addition, the volume is valuable as we observe and reflect on debates preceding the reauthorization of NCLB. The main conclusion from the discourse in the book is that although, allegedly, many concepts of IDEIA were research-informed, they were not, strictly speaking, evidence-based. We now stand at the very beginning of the road of implementing IDEIA, along which relevant evidence can be and possibly will be accumulated. And this book, I hope, can serve as a guidebook, an initial map for the road ahead, by offering an overview of both the current successes and the difficulties in bringing IDEIA into the reality of the classroom.

Concluding this brief commentary, I would like to extend my gratitude to the authors for being so responsive to deadlines and so open to incorporating comments. I have learned a tremendous amount in working on this book, and I hope that readers will feel the same as they read it.

Index

MIGUEL VARGAS MARTIN

Lecture Notes in Computer Science 5230

Commenced Publication in 1973
Founding and Former Series Editors:
Gerhard Goos, Juris Hartmanis, and Jan van Leeuwen

Editorial Board

David Hutchison
Lancaster University, UK

Takeo Kanade
Carnegie Mellon University, Pittsburgh, PA, USA

Josef Kittler
University of Surrey, Guildford, UK

Jon M. Kleinberg
Cornell University, Ithaca, NY, USA

Alfred Kobsa
University of California, Irvine, CA, USA

Friedemann Mattern
ETH Zurich, Switzerland

John C. Mitchell
Stanford University, CA, USA

Moni Naor
Weizmann Institute of Science, Rehovot, Israel

Oscar Nierstrasz
University of Bern, Switzerland

C. Pandu Rangan
Indian Institute of Technology, Madras, India

Bernhard Steffen
University of Dortmund, Germany

Madhu Sudan
Massachusetts Institute of Technology, MA, USA

Demetri Terzopoulos
University of California, Los Angeles, CA, USA

Doug Tygar
University of California, Berkeley, CA, USA

Gerhard Weikum
Max-Planck Institute of Computer Science, Saarbruecken, Germany

Richard Lippmann   Engin Kirda
Ari Trachtenberg (Eds.)

Recent Advances
in Intrusion Detection

11th International Symposium, RAID 2008
Cambridge, MA, USA, September 15-17, 2008
Proceedings

 Springer

Volume Editors

Richard Lippmann
Lincoln Laboratory
Massachusetts Institute of Technology
Lexington, MA, USA
E-mail: lippmann@ll.mit.edu

Engin Kirda
Institut Eurecom
Sophia-Antipolis, France
E-mail: engin.kirda@eurecom.fr

Ari Trachtenberg
Boston University
Boston, MA, USA
E-mail: trachten@bu.edu

Library of Congress Control Number: 2008934305

CR Subject Classification (1998): K.6.5, K.4, E.3, C.2, D.4.6

LNCS Sublibrary: SL 4 – Security and Cryptology

ISSN	0302-9743
ISBN-10	3-540-87402-X Springer Berlin Heidelberg New York
ISBN-13	978-3-540-87402-7 Springer Berlin Heidelberg New York

Springer is a part of Springer Science+Business Media

springer.com

© Springer-Verlag Berlin Heidelberg 2008
Printed in Germany

Typesetting: Camera-ready by author, data conversion by Scientific Publishing Services, Chennai, India
Printed on acid-free paper   SPIN: 12511846   06/3180   5 4 3 2 1 0

Preface

On behalf of the Program Committee, it is our pleasure to present the proceedings of the 11th International Symposium on Recent Advances in Intrusion Detection (RAID 2008), which took place in Cambridge, Massachusetts, USA on September 15–17.

The symposium brought together leading researchers and practitioners from academia, government and industry to discuss intrusion detection research and practice. There were six main sessions presenting full-fledged research papers (rootkit prevention, malware detection and prevention, high performance intrusion and evasion, web application testing and evasion, alert correlation and worm detection, and anomaly detection and network traffic analysis), a session of posters on emerging research areas and case studies, and two panel discussions ("Government Investments: Successes, Failures and the Future" and "Life after Antivirus - What Does the Future Hold?").

The RAID 2008 Program Committee received 80 paper submissions from all over the world. All submissions were carefully reviewed by at least three independent reviewers on the basis of space, topic, technical assessment, and overall balance. Final selection took place at the Program Committee meeting on May 23rd in Cambridge, MA. Twenty papers were selected for presentation and publication in the conference proceedings, and four papers were recommended for resubmission as poster presentations.

As a new feature this year, the symposium accepted submissions for poster presentations, which have been published as extended abstracts, reporting early-stage research, demonstration of applications, or case studies. Thirty-nine posters were submitted for a numerical review by an independent, three-person subcommittee of the Program Committee based on novelty, description, and evaluation. The subcommittee chose to recommend the acceptance of 16 of these posters for presentation and publication.

The success of RAID 2008 depended on the joint effort of many people. We would like to thank all the authors who submitted papers, whether accepted or not. We would also like to thank the Program Committee members and additional reviewers, who volunteered their time to carefully evaluate the numerous submissions. In addition, we would like to thank the General Chair, Rob Cunningham, for handling the conference arrangements, Ari Trachtenberg for handling publication, Jon Giffin for publicizing the conference, Anup Ghosh for finding sponsors for the conference, and MIT Lincoln Lab for maintaining the conference website. Finally, we extend our thanks to The Institute for Information Infrastructure Protection (I3P), Symantec Corporation, IBM, and MIT Lincoln Laboratory for their sponsorship of student scholarships.

June 2008

Richard Lippmann
Engin Kirda

Organization

RAID 2008 was organized by MIT Lincoln Laboratory and held in conjunction with VIZSEC 2008.

Conference Chairs

Conference Chair	Robert Cunningham (MIT Lincoln Laboratory)
Program Chair	Richard Lippmann (MIT Lincoln Laboratory)
Program Co-chair	Engin Kirda (Eurecom / Technical University of Vienna)
Publications Chair	Ari Trachtenberg (Boston University)
Publicity Chair	Jon Giffin (Georgia Tech)
Sponsorship Chair	Anup Ghosh (George Mason University)

Program Committee

Michael Bailey	University of Michigan
Michael Behringer	Cisco
Herbert Bos	Vrije Universiteit
David Brumley	Carnegie Mellon University
Tzi-cker Chiueh	State University of New York at Stony Brook
Andrew Clark	Queensland University of Technology
Robert Cunningham	MIT Lincoln Lab
Ulrich Flegel	SAP Research
Debin Gao	Singapore Management University
Anup Ghosh	George Mason University
Jonathon Giffin	Georgia Institute of Technology
Thorsten Holz	University of Mannheim
Jaeyeon Jung	Intel
Engin Kirda	Institute Eurecom
Kwok-Yan Lam	Tsinghua University
Zhuowei Li	Microsoft
Richard Lippmann	MIT Lincoln Laboratory
Raffael Marty	Splunk
Benjamin Morin	Supélec
Rei Safavi-Naini	University of Calgary
R. Sekar	State University of New York at Stony Brook
Robin Sommer	ICSI and LBNL
Salvatore Stolfo	Columbia University
Toshihiro Tabata	Okayama University
Ari Trachtenberg	Boston University

Vijay Varadharajan   Macquarie University
Andreas Wespi   IBM Zurich Research Laboratory
Diego Zamboni   IBM Zurich Research Laboratory
Jianying Zhou   Institute for Infocomm Research

Steering Committee

Marc Dacier (Chair)   EURECOM, France
Hervé Debar   France Télécom R&D, France
Deborah Frincke   Pacific Northwest National Lab, USA
Ming-Yuh Huang   The Boeing Company, USA
Erland Jonsson   Chalmers, Sweden
Wenke Lee   Georgia Tech, USA
Ludovic Mé   Supélec, France
Alfonso Valdes   SRI International, USA
Giovanni Vigna   University of California, Santa Barbara, USA
Andreas Wespi   IBM Research, Switzerland
S. Felix Wu   UC Davis, USA
Diego Zamboni   IBM Research, Switzerland
Christopher Kruegel   University of California, Santa Barbara, USA /
                            Technical University of Vienna, Austria

Additional Reviewers

Hirotake Abe   Toyohashi University of Technology
Manos Antonakakis   Georgia Tech
Venkat Balakrishnan   Macquarie University
Ulrich Bayer   Technical University of Vienna
Leyla Bilge   Technical University of Vienna
Damiano Bolzoni   University of Twente
Gabriela Cretu   Columbia University
Italo Dacosta   Georgia Tech
Loic Duflot   DCSSI
Thomas Dullien   Zynamics
Jose M. Fernandez   École Polytechnique de Montréal
Vanessa Frias-Martinez   Columbia University
Jochen Haller   SAP Research
Philip Hendrix   Harvard University
Yoshiaki Hori   Kyushu University
Kyle Ingols   MIT Lincoln Laboratory
Florian Kerschbaum   SAP Research
Hyung Chan Kim   Columbia University
Andreas Lang   University of Magdeburg
Pavel Laskov   Fraunhofer FIRST & University of Tuebingen
Timothy Leek   MIT Lincoln Laboratory

Zhenkai Liang	National University of Singapore
Ludovic Mé	Supélec
Chee Meng	Tey
Philip Miseldine	SAP Research
Andreas Moser	Technical University of Vienna
Jon Oberhide	University of Michigan
Yoshihiro Oyama	The University of Electro-Communications
Yoshiaki Shiraishi	Nagoya Institute of Technology
Sushant Sinha	University of Michigan
Yingbo Song	Columbia University
Abhinav Srivastava	Georgia Tech
Eric Totel	Supélec
Uday Tupakula	Macquarie University
Shobha Venkataraman	CMU
Peter Wurzinger	Technical University of Vienna
Sachiko Yoshihama	IBM Tokyo Research Laboratory
Weiliang Zhao	Macquarie University

Sponsoring Institutions

The Institute for Information Infrastructure Protection (I3P)
Symantec Corporation
IBM
MIT Lincoln Laboratory

Table of Contents

Web Application Testing and Evasion

Alert Correlation and Worm Detection

Anomaly Detection and Network Traffic Analysis

Posters

Guest-Transparent Prevention of Kernel Rootkits with VMM-Based Memory Shadowing

Ryan Riley[1], Xuxian Jiang[2], and Dongyan Xu[1]

[1] CERIAS and Department of Computer Science, Purdue University
{rileyrd,dxu}@cs.purdue.edu
[2] Department of Computer Science, North Carolina State University
jiang@cs.ncsu.edu

Abstract. Kernel rootkits pose a significant threat to computer systems as they run at the highest privilege level and have unrestricted access to the resources of their victims. Many current efforts in kernel rootkit defense focus on the *detection* of kernel rootkits – after a rootkit attack has taken place, while the smaller number of efforts in kernel rootkit *prevention* exhibit limitations in their capability or deployability. In this paper we present a kernel rootkit prevention system called NICKLE which addresses a common, fundamental characteristic of most kernel rootkits: the need for executing their own kernel code. NICKLE is a lightweight, virtual machine monitor (VMM) based system that transparently prevents unauthorized kernel code execution for unmodified commodity (guest) OSes. NICKLE is based on a new scheme called *memory shadowing*, wherein the trusted VMM maintains a shadow physical memory for a running VM and performs real-time kernel code authentication so that only authenticated kernel code will be stored in the shadow memory. Further, NICKLE transparently routes guest kernel instruction fetches to the shadow memory at runtime. By doing so, NICKLE guarantees that only the authenticated kernel code will be executed, foiling the kernel rootkit's attempt to strike in the first place. We have implemented NICKLE in three VMM platforms: QEMU+KQEMU, VirtualBox, and VMware Workstation. Our experiments with 23 real-world kernel rootkits targeting the Linux or Windows OSes demonstrate NICKLE's effectiveness. Furthermore, our performance evaluation shows that NICKLE introduces small overhead to the VMM platform.

1 Introduction

Kernel-level rootkits have proven to be a formidable threat to computer systems: By subverting the operating system (OS) kernel, a kernel rootkit embeds itself into the compromised kernel and stealthily inflicts damages with full, unrestricted access to the system's resources. Effectively omnipotent in the compromised systems, kernel rootkits have increasingly been used by attackers to hide their presence and prolong their control over their victims.

There have been a number of recent efforts in mitigating the threat of kernel rootkits and they can mainly be classified into two categories: (1) detecting the

R. Lippmann, E. Kirda, and A. Trachtenberg (Eds.): RAID 2008, LNCS 5230, pp. 1–20, 2008.

presence of kernel rootkits in a system [1, 2, 3, 4, 5] and (2) preventing the compromise of OS kernel integrity [6, 7]. In the first category, Copilot [4] proposes the use of a separate PCI card to periodically grab the memory image of a running OS kernel and analyze it to determine if the kernel has been compromised. The work which follows up Copilot [2] further extends that capability by detecting the violation of kernel integrity using semantic specifications of static and dynamic kernel data. SBCFI [3] reports violations of the kernel's control flow integrity using the kernel's control-flow graph. One common attribute of approaches in this category is the *detection* of a kernel rootkit's presence based on certain symptoms exhibited by the kernel *after* the kernel rootkit has already struck. As a result, these approaches are, by design, not capable of *preventing kernel rootkit execution in the first place.*

In the second category, Livewire [6], based on a virtual machine monitor (VMM), aims at protecting the guest OS kernel code and critical kernel data structures from being modified. However, without modifying the original kernel code, an attacker may choose to load malicious rootkit code into the kernel space by either exploiting kernel vulnerabilities or leveraging certain kernel features (e.g., loadable kernel module support in modern OSes). More recently, SecVisor [7] is proposed as a hypervisor-based solution to enforce the W⊕X property of memory pages of the guest machine, with the goal of preventing unauthorized code from running with kernel-level privileges. SecVisor requires modifying kernel source code and needs the latest hardware-based virtualization support and thus does not support closed-source OSes or legacy hardware platforms. Moreover, SecVisor is not able to function if the OS kernel has *mixed* pages that contain both code and data. Unfortunately, such mixed kernel pages do exist in modern OSes (e.g., Linux and Windows as shown in Section 2.2).

To complement the existing approaches, we present NICKLE ("No Instruction Creeping into Kernel Level Executed")[1], a lightweight, VMM-based system that provides an important guarantee in kernel rootkit prevention: *No unauthorized code can be executed at the kernel level.* NICKLE achieves this guarantee on top of legacy hardware and without requiring guest OS kernel modification. As such, NICKLE is readily deployable to protect unmodified guest OSes (e.g., Fedora Core 3/4/5 and Windows 2K/XP) against kernel rootkits. NICKLE is based on observing a common, fundamental characteristic of most modern kernel rootkits: their ability to execute unauthorized instructions at the kernel level. By removing this ability, NICKLE significantly raises the bar for successfully launching kernel rootkit attacks.

To achieve the "NICKLE" guarantee, we first observe that a kernel rootkit is able to access the entire physical address space of the victim machine. This observation inspires us to impose restricted access to the instructions in the kernel space: only *authenticated* kernel instructions can be fetched for execution. Obviously, such a restriction cannot be enforced by the OS kernel itself. Instead,

---

[1] With a slight abuse of terms, we use NICKLE to denote both the system itself and the guarantee achieved by the system – when used in quotation marks.

a natural strategy is to enforce such memory access restriction using the VMM, which is at a privilege level higher than that of the (guest) OS kernel.

Our main challenge is to realize the above VMM-level kernel instruction fetch restriction in a guest-transparent, real-time, and efficient manner. An intuitive approach would be to impose W⊕X on kernel memory pages to protect existing kernel code and prevent the execution of injected kernel code. However, due to the existence of mixed kernel pages in commodity OSes, this approach is not viable for guest-transparent protection. To address that, we propose a VMM-based *memory shadowing* scheme for NICKLE that will work in the face of mixed kernel pages. More specifically, for a virtual machine (VM), the VMM creates two distinct physical memory regions: a *standard memory* and a *shadow memory*. The VMM enforces that the guest OS kernel cannot access the shadow memory. Upon the VM's startup, the VMM performs kernel code authentication and dynamically copies authenticated kernel instructions from the standard memory to the shadow memory. At runtime, any instruction executed in the kernel space must be fetched from the shadow memory instead of from the standard memory. To enforce this while maintaining guest transparency, a lightweight *guest memory access indirection* mechanism is added to the VMM. As such, a kernel rootkit will never be able to execute any of its own code as the code injected into the kernel space will not be able to reach the shadow memory.

We have implemented NICKLE in three VMMs: QEMU[8] with the KQEMU accelerator, VirtualBox [9], and VMware Workstation. Our evaluation results show that NICKLE incurs a reasonable impact on the VMM platform (e.g., 1.01% on QEMU+KQEMU and 5.45% on VirtualBox when running UnixBench). NICKLE is shown capable of transparently protecting a variety of commodity OSes, including RedHat 8.0 (Linux 2.4.18 kernel), Fedora Core 3 (Linux 2.6.15 kernel), Windows 2000, and Windows XP. Our results show that NICKLE is able to prevent and gracefully respond to 23 real-world kernel rootkits targeting the above OSes, without requiring details of rootkit attack vectors. Finally, our porting experience indicates that the NICKLE design is generic and realizable in a variety of VMMs.

2   NICKLE Design

2.1   Design Goals and Threat Model

Goals and Challenges.   NICKLE has the following three main design goals:

First, as its name indicates, NICKLE should prevent any unauthorized code from being executed in the kernel space of the protected VM. The challenges of realizing this goal come from the real-time requirement of prevention as well as from the requirement that the guest OS kernel should not be trusted to initiate any task of the prevention – the latter requirement is justified by the kernel rootkit's highest privilege level inside the VM and the possible existence of zero-day vulnerabilities inside the guest OS kernel. NICKLE overcomes these challenges using the VMM-based memory shadowing scheme (Section 2.2). We

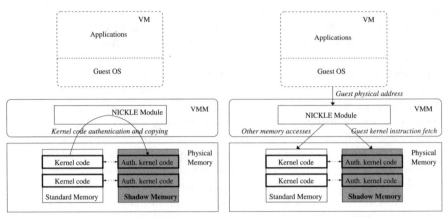

(a) Kernel code authorization and copying   (b) Guest physical address redirection

Fig. 1. Memory shadowing scheme in NICKLE

note that the scope of NICKLE is focused on preventing unauthorized kernel code execution. The prevention of other types of attacks (e.g., data-only attacks) is a non-goal and related solutions will be discussed in Section 5.

Second, NICKLE should not require modifications to the guest OS kernel. This allows commodity OSes to be supported "as is" without recompilation and reinstallation. Correspondingly, the challenge in realizing this goal is to make the memory shadowing scheme transparent to the VM with respect to both the VM's function and performance.

Third, the design of NICKLE should be generically portable to a range of VMMs. Given this, the challenge is to ensure that NICKLE has a small footprint within the VMM and remains lightweight with respect to performance impact. In this paper we focus on supporting NICKLE in software VMMs. However, we expect that the exploitation of recent hardware-based virtualization extensions [10, 11] will improve NICKLE's performance even further.

In addition, it is also desirable that NICKLE facilitate various flexible response mechanisms to be activated upon the detection of an unauthorized kernel code execution attempt. A flexible response, for example, is to cause only the offending process to fail without stopping the rest of the OS. The challenge in realizing this is to initiate flexible responses entirely from outside the protected VM and minimize the side-effects on the running OS.

Threat Model and System Assumption.   We assume the following adversary model when designing NICKLE: (1) The kernel rootkit has the highest privilege level inside the victim VM (e.g., the *root* privilege in a UNIX system); (2) The kernel rootkit has full access to the VM's memory space (e.g., through /dev/mem in Linux); (3) The kernel rootkit aims at stealthily maintaining and hiding its presence in the VM and to do so, the rootkit will need to execute its own (malicious) code in the kernel space. We note that such a need exists in most kernel rootkits today, and we will discuss possible exceptions in Section 5.

Meanwhile, we assume a trusted VMM that provides VM isolation. This assumption is shared by many other VMM-based security research efforts [1, 6, 12, 13, 14, 15]. We will discuss possible attacks (e.g., VM fingerprinting) in Section 5. With this assumption, we consider the threat from DMA attacks launched from physical hosts outside of the scope of this work.[2]

2.2 Enabling Scheme and Techniques

Memory Shadowing. The memory shadowing scheme enforces the "NICKLE" property: For a VM, apart from its standard physical memory space, the VMM also allocates a separate physical memory region as the VM's *shadow memory* (Figure 1) which is transparent to the VM and controlled by the VMM. Upon the startup of the VM's OS, all known-good, authenticated guest kernel instructions will be copied from the VM's standard memory to the shadow memory (Figure 1(a)). At runtime, when the VM is about to execute a kernel instruction, the VMM will transparently redirect the kernel instruction fetch to the shadow memory (Figure 1(b)). All other memory accesses (to user code, user data, and kernel data) will proceed unhindered in the standard memory.

The memory shadowing scheme is motivated by the observation that modern computers define a single memory space for all code – both kernel code and user code – and data. With the VMM running at a higher privilege level, we can now "shadow" the guest kernel code space with elevated (VMM-level) privileges to ensure that the guest OS kernel itself cannot access the shadowed kernel code space containg the authenticated kernel instructions. By doing so, even if a kernel rootkit is able to inject its own code into the VM's standard memory, the VMM will ensure that the malicious code never gets copied over to the shadow memory. Moreover, an attempt to execute the malicious code can be caught immediately due to the inconsistency between the standard and shadow memory contents.

The astute reader may be asking "How is NICKLE functionally different from W⊕X?" In essence, W⊕X is a scheme that enforces the property, "A given memory page will never be both writable and executable at the same time." The basic premise behind this scheme is that if a page cannot be written to and later executed from, code injection becomes impossible. There are two main reasons why this scheme is not adequate for stopping kernel level rootkits:

First, W⊕X is not able to protect mixed kernel pages with both code and data, which do exist in current OSes. As a specific example, in a Fedora Core 3 VM (with the 32-bit 2.6.15 kernel and the NX protection), the Linux kernel stores the main static kernel text in memory range $[0xc0100000, 0xc02dea50]$ and keeps the system call table starting from virtual address $0xc02e04a0$. Notice that the Linux kernel uses a large page size $(2MB)$ to manage the physical memory,[3] which means that the first two kernel pages cover memory ranges

---

[2] There exists another type of DMA attack that is initiated from within a guest VM. However, since the VMM itself virtualizes or mediates the guest DMA operations, NICKLE can be easily extended to intercede and block them.

[3] If the NX protection is disabled, those kernel pages containing static kernel text will be of $4MB$ in size.

$[0xc0000000, 0xc0200000)$ and $[0xc0200000, 0xc0400000)$, respectively. As a result, the second kernel page contains both code and data, and thus must be marked both writable and executable – This conflicts with the W⊕X scheme. Mixed pages also exist for accommodating the code and data of Linux loadable kernel modules (LKMs) – an example will be shown in Section 4.1. For the Windows XP kernel (with SP2), our investigation has confirmed the existence of mixed pages as well [16]. On the other hand, NICKLE is able to protect mixed pages.[4]

Second, W⊕X assumes only one execution privilege level while kernel rootkit prevention requires further distinction between user and kernel code pages. For example, a page may be set executable in user mode but non-executable in kernel mode. In other words, the sort of permission desired is not W⊕X, but W⊕KX (i.e. not writable and kernel-executable at the same time.) Still, we point out that the enforcement of W⊕KX is *not* effective for mixed kernel pages and, regardless, not obvious to construct on current processors that do not allow such fine-grained memory permissions.

Another question that may be asked is, "Why adopt memory shadowing when one could simply guard kernel code by keeping track of the ranges of valid kernel code addresses ?" Indeed, NICKLE is guided by the principle of kernel code guarding, but does so differently from the brute-force approach of tracking/checking kernel code address ranges – mainly for performance reasons. More specifically, the brute-force approach could store the address ranges of valid kernel code in a data structure (e.g., tree) with $O(logN)$ search time. On the other hand, memory shadowing allows us to locate the valid kernel instruction in the shadow memory in $O(1)$ time thus significantly reducing the processing overhead. In addition, memory shadowing makes it convenient to compare the instructions in the shadow memory to those in the standard memory. If they differ (indicating malicious kernel code injection or modification), a number of response actions can be implemented based on the difference (details in Section 3).

Guest Memory Access Indirection. To realize the guest memory shadowing scheme, two issues need to be resolved. First, how does NICKLE fill up the guest shadow memory with authenticated kernel code? Second, how does NICKLE fetch authenticated kernel instructions for execution while detecting and preventing any attempt to execute unauthorized code in the kernel space? We note that our solutions have to be transparent to the guest OS (and thus to the kernel rootkits). We now present the guest memory access indirection technique to address these issues.

---

[4] We also considered the option of eliminating mixed kernel pages. However, doing so would require kernel source code modification, which conflicts with our second design goal. Even given source code access, mixed page elimination is still a complex task (more than just page-aligning data). In fact, a kernel configuration option with a similar purpose exists in the latest Linux kernel (version 2.6.23). But after we enabled the option, we still found more than 700 mixed kernel pages. NICKLE instead simply avoids such complexity and works even with mixed kernel pages.

Guest memory access indirection is performed between the VM and its memory (standard and shadow) by a thin NICKLE module inside the VMM. It has two main functions, kernel code authentication and copying at VM startup and upon kernel module loading as well as guest physical address redirection at runtime (Figure 1).

Kernel Code Authentication and Copying. To fill up the shadow memory with authenticated kernel instructions, the NICKLE module inside the VMM needs to first determine the accurate timing for kernel code authentication and copying. To better articulate the problem, we will use the Linux kernel as an example. There are two specific situations throughout the VM's lifetime when kernel code needs to be authorized and shadowed: One at the VM's startup and one upon the loading/unloading of loadable kernel modules (LKMs). When the VM is starting up, the guest's shadow memory is empty. The kernel bootstrap code then decompresses the kernel. Right after the decompression and before any processes are executed, NICKLE will use a cryptographic hash to verify the integrity of the kernel code (this is very similar to level 4 in the secure bootstrap procedure [17]) and then copy the authenticated kernel code from the standard memory into the shadow memory (Figure 1(a)). As such, the protected VM will start with a known clean kernel.

The LKM support in modern OSes complicates our design. From NICKLE's perspective, LKMs are considered injected kernel code and thus need to be authenticated and shadowed before their execution. The challenge for NICKLE is to *externally* monitor the guest OS and detect the kernel module loading/unloading events in real-time. NICKLE achieves this by leveraging our earlier work on non-intrusive VM monitoring and semantic event reconstruction [1, 14]. When NICKLE detects the loading of a new kernel module, it intercepts the VM's execution and performs kernel module code authentication and shadowing. The authentication is performed by taking a cryptographic hash of the kernel module's code segment and comparing it with a known correct value, which is computed a priori off-line and provided by the administrator or distribution maintainer.[5] If the hash values don't match, the kernel module's code will not be copied to the shadow memory.

Through kernel code authentication and copying, only authenticated kernel code will be loaded into the shadow memory, thus blocking the copying of malicious kernel rootkit code or any other code injected by exploiting kernel vulnerabilities, including zero-day vulnerabilities. It is important to note that neither kernel startup hashing nor kernel module hashing assumes trust in the guest OS. Should the guest OS fail to cooperate, *no* code will be copied to the shadow memory, and any execution attempts from that code will be detected and refused.

Guest Physical Address Redirection. At runtime, the NICKLE module inside the VMM intercepts the memory accesses of the VM *after* the "guest virtual address → guest physical address" translation. As such, NICKLE does not interfere

---

[5] We have developed an off-line kernel module profiler that, given a legitimate kernel module, will compute the corresponding hash value (Section 3.1).

with – and is therefore transparent to – the guest OS's memory access handling procedure and virtual memory mappings. Instead, it takes the guest physical address, determines the type of the memory access (kernel, user; code, data; etc.), and routes it to either the standard or shadow memory (Figure 1(b)).

We point out that the interception of VM memory accesses can be provided by existing VMMs (e.g., QEMU+KQEMU, VirtualBox, and VMware). NICKLE builds on this interception capability by adding the guest physical address redirection logic. First, using a simple method to check the current privilege level of the processor, NICKLE determines whether the current instruction fetch is for kernel code or for user code: If the processor is in supervisor mode (CPL=0 on x86), we infer that the fetch is for kernel code and NICKLE will verify and route the instruction fetch to the shadow memory. Otherwise, the processor is in user mode and NICKLE will route the instruction fetch to the standard memory. Data accesses of either type are always routed to the standard memory.

One might object that an attacker may strive to ensure that his injected kernel code will run when the processor is in user mode. However, this creates a significant challenge wherein the attacker would have to fundamentally change a running kernel to operate in both supervisor and user mode *without changing any existing kernel code*. The authors do not consider such a rootkit to be a possibility without a severe loss of rootkit functionality.

Flexible Responses to Unauthorized Kernel Code Execution Attempts
If an unauthorized execution attempt is detected, a natural follow-up question is, "How should NICKLE respond to an attempt to execute an unauthenticated kernel instruction?" Given that NICKLE sits between the VM and its memory and has a higher privilege level than the guest OS, it possesses a wide range of options and capabilities to respond. We describe two response modes facilitated by the current NICKLE system.

Rewrite mode: NICKLE will dynamically rewrite the malicious kernel code with code of its own. The response code can range from OS-specific error handling code to a well-crafted payload designed to clean up the impact of a rootkit installation attempt. Note that this mode may require an understanding of the guest OS to ensure that valid, sensible code is returned.

Break mode: NICKLE will take no action and route the instruction fetch to the *shadow memory*. In the case where the attacker only modifies the original kernel code, this mode will lead to the execution of the original code – a desirable situation. However, in the case where *new* code is injected into the kernel, this mode will lead to an instruction fetch from presumably null content (containing 0s) in the shadow memory. As such, break mode prevents malicious kernel code execution but may or may not be graceful depending on how the OS handles invalid code execution faults.

3   NICKLE Implementation

To validate the portability of the NICKLE design, we have implemented NICKLE in three VMMs: QEMU+KQEMU [8], VirtualBox [9], and VMware

Workstation[6]. Since the open-source QEMU+KQEMU is the VMM platform where we first implemented NICKLE, we use it as the representative VMM to describe our implementation details. For most of this section, we choose RedHat 8.0 as the default guest OS. We will also discuss the limitations of our current prototype in supporting Windows guest OSes.

3.1   Memory Shadowing and Guest Memory Access Indirection

To implement memory shadowing, we have considered two options: (1) NICKLE could interfere as instructions are executed; or (2) NICKLE could interfere when instructions are dynamically translated. Note that dynamic instruction translation is a key technique behind existing software-based VMMs, which transparently translates guest machine code into native code that will run in the physical host. We favor the second option for performance reasons: By being part of the translator, NICKLE can take advantage of the fact that translated code blocks are cached. In QEMU+KQEMU, for example, guest kernel instructions are grouped into "blocks" and are dynamically translated at runtime. After a block of code is translated, it is stored in a cache to make it available for future execution. In terms of NICKLE, this means that if we intercede during code translation we need not intercede as often as we would if we did so during code execution, resulting in a smaller impact on system performance.

The pseudo-code for memory shadowing and guest memory access indirection is shown in Algorithm 1. Given the guest physical address of an instruction to be executed by the VM, NICKLE first checks the current privilege level of the processor (CPL). If the processor is in supervisor mode, NICKLE knows that it is executing in kernel mode. Using the guest physical address, NICKLE compares the content of the standard and shadow memories to determine whether the kernel instruction to be executed is already in the shadow memory (namely has been authenticated). If so, the kernel instruction is allowed to be fetched, translated, and executed. If not, NICKLE will determine if the guest OS kernel is being bootstrapped or a kernel module is being loaded. If either is the case, the corresponding kernel text or kernel module code will be authenticated and, if successful, shadowed into the shadow memory. Otherwise, NICKLE detects an attempt to execute an unauthorized instruction in the kernel space and prevents it by executing our response to the attempt.

In Algorithm 1, the way to determine whether the guest OS kernel is being bootstrapped or a kernel module is being loaded requires OS-specific knowledge. Using the Linux 2.4 kernel as an example, when the kernel's *startup_32* function, located at physical address 0x00100000 or virtual address 0xc0100000 as shown in the *System.map* file, is to be executed, we know that this is the first

---

[6] We acknowledge the VMware Academic Program for providing the source code. Due to space and licensing constraints, however, the VMware port is not further discussed or evaluated in this work. Some additional discussion of the port is available in our technical report [16].

Algorithm 1. Algorithm for Memory Shadowing and Guest Memory Access Indirection

---

Input: (1) GuestPA: guest physical address of instruction to be executed; (2) ShadowMEM[]: shadow memory; (3) StandardMEM[]: standard memory

1 **if** *!IsUserMode(vcpu)* **AND** *ShadowMEM[GuestPA] != StandardMEM[GuestPA]* **then**
2   **if** *(kernel is being bootstrapped) OR (module is being loaded)* **then**
3   Authenticate and shadow code;
4   **else**
5   Unauthorized execution attempt - Execute response;
6   **end**
7 **end**
8 Fetch, translate, and cache code;

---

instruction executed to load the kernel and we can intercede appropriately. For kernel module loading, there is a specific system call to handle that. As such, the NICKLE module inside the VMM can intercept the system call and perform kernel module authentication and shadowing right before the module-specific *init_module* routine is executed.

In our implementation, the loading of LKMs requires special handling. More specifically, providing a hash of a kernel module's code space ends up being slightly complicated in practice. This is due to the fact that kernel modules are dynamically relocatable and hence some portions of the kernel module's code space may be modified by the module loading function. Accordingly, the cryptographic hash of a loaded kernel module will be different depending on where it is relocated to. To solve this problem, we perform an off-line, a priori profiling of the legitimate kernel module binaries. For each known good module we calculate the cryptographic hash by excluding the portions of the module that will be changed during relocation. In addition, we store a list of bytes affected by relocation so that the same procedure can be repeated by NICKLE during runtime hash evaluation of the same module.

We point out that although the implementation of NICKLE requires certain guest OS-specific information, it does *not* require modifications to the guest OS itself. Still, for a closed-source guest OS (e.g., Windows), lack of information about kernel bootstrapping and dynamic kernel code loading may lead to certain limitations. For example, not knowing the timing and "signature" of dynamic (legal) kernel code loading events in Windows, the current implementation of NICKLE relies on the administrator to designate a time instance when all authorized Windows kernel code has been loaded into the standard memory. Not knowing the exact locations of the kernel code, NICKLE traverses the shadow page table and copies those executable pages located in the kernel space from the standard memory to the shadow memory, hence creating a "gold standard" to compare future kernel code execution against. From this time on, NICKLE can transparently protect the Windows OS kernel from executing any unauthorized kernel code. Moreover, this limited implementation can be made complete when the relevant information becomes available through vendor disclosure or reverse engineering.

3.2 Flexible Response

In response to an attempt to execute an unauthorized instruction in the kernel space, NICKLE provides two response modes. Our initial implementation of NICKLE simply re-routes the instruction fetch to the shadow memory for a string of zeros (break mode). As to be shown in our experiments, this produces some interesting outcomes: a Linux guest OS would react to this by triggering a kernel fault and terminating the offending process. Windows, on the other hand, reacts to the NICKLE response by immediately halting with a blue screen – a less graceful outcome.

In search of a more flexible response mode, we find that by rewriting the offending instructions at runtime (rewrite mode), NICKLE can respond in a less disruptive way. We also observe that most kernel rootkits analyzed behave the following way: They first insert a new chunk of malicious code into the kernel space; then they somehow ensure their code is call'd as a function. With this observation, we let NICKLE dynamically replace the code with return -1;, which in assembly is: mov $0xffffffff, %eax; ret. The main kernel text or the kernel module loading process will interpret this as an error and gracefully handle it: Our experiments with Windows 2K/XP, Linux 2.4, and Linux 2.6 guest OSes all confirm that NICKLE's rewrite mode is able to handle the malicious kernel code execution attempt by triggering the OS to terminate the offending process without causing a fault in the OS.

3.3 Porting Experience

We have experienced no major difficulty in porting NICKLE to other VMMs. The NICKLE implementations in both VMMs are lightweight: The SLOC (source lines of code) added to implement NICKLE in QEMU+KQEMU, VirtualBox, and VMware Workstation are 853, 762, and 1181 respectively. As mentioned earlier, we first implemented NICKLE in QEMU+KQEMU. It then took less than one week for one person to get NICKLE functional in VirtualBox 1.5.0 OSE, details of which can be found in our technical report [16].

4 NICKLE Evaluation

4.1 Effectiveness Against Kernel Rootkits

We have evaluated the effectiveness of NICKLE with 23 real-world kernel rootkits. They consist of nine Linux 2.4 rootkits, seven Linux 2.6 rootkits, and seven Windows rootkits[7] that can infect Windows 2000 and/or XP. The selected rootkits cover the main attack platforms and attack vectors thus providing a good representation of the state-of-the-art kernel rootkit technology. Table 1 shows

---

[7] There is a Windows rootkit named hxdef or Hacker Defender, which is usually classified as a user-level rootkit. However, since hxdef contains a device driver which will be loaded into the kernel, we consider it a kernel rootkit in this paper.

Table 1. Effectiveness of NICKLE in detecting and preventing 23 real-world kernel rootkits (*DKOM*[†] is a common rootkit technique which directly manipulates kernel objects; *"partial"*[‡] means the in-kernel component of the Hacker Defender rootkit fails; *BSOD*[§] stands for "Blue Screen Of Death")

Guest OS	Rootkit	Attack Vector	Outcome of NICKLE Response			
			Rewrite Mode		Break Mode	
			Prevented?	Outcome	Prevented?	Outcome
Linux 2.4	adore 0.42, 0.53	LKM	✓	insmod fails	✓	Seg. fault
	adore-ng 0.56	LKM	✓	insmod fails	✓	Seg. fault
	knark	LKM	✓	insmod fails	✓	Seg. fault
	rkit 1.01	LKM	✓	insmod fails	✓	Seg. fault
	kbdv3	LKM	✓	insmod fails	✓	Seg. fault
	allroot	LKM	✓	insmod fails	✓	Seg. fault
	rial	LKM	✓	insmod fails	✓	Seg. fault
	Phantasmagoria	LKM	✓	insmod fails	✓	Seg. fault
	SucKIT 1.3b	/dev/kmem	✓	Installation fails silently	✓	Seg. fault
Linux 2.6	adore-ng 0.56	LKM	✓	insmod fails	✓	Seg. fault
	eNYeLKM v1.2	LKM	✓	insmod fails	✓	Seg. fault
	sk2rc2	/dev/kmem	✓	Installation fails	✓	Seg. fault
	superkit	/dev/kmem	✓	Installation fails	✓	Seg. fault
	mood-nt 2.3	/dev/kmem	✓	Installation fails	✓	Seg. fault
	override	LKM	✓	insmod fails	✓	Seg. fault
	Phalanx b6	/dev/mem	✓	Installation crashes	✓	Seg. fault
Windows 2K/XP	FU	DKOM[†]	✓	Driver loading fails	✓	BSOD[§]
	FUTo	DKOM	✓	Driver loading fails	✓	BSOD
	he4hook 215b6	Driver	✓	Driver loading fails	✓	BSOD
	hxdef 1.0.0 revisited	Driver	partial[‡]	Driver loading fails	✓	BSOD
	hkdoor11	Driver	✓	Driver loading fails	✓	BSOD
	yyt_hac	Driver	✓	Driver loading fails	✓	BSOD
	NT Rootkit	Driver	✓	Driver loading fails	✓	BSOD

our experimental results: NICKLE is able to detect and prevent the execution of malicious kernel code in *all* experiments using both rewrite and break response modes. Finally, we note that NICKLE in all three VMMs is able to achieve the same results. In the following, we present details of two representative experiments. Some additional experiments are presented in [16].

SucKIT Rootkit Experiment. The SucKIT rootkit [18] for Linux 2.4 infects the Linux kernel by directly modifying the kernel through the /dev/kmem interface. During installation SucKIT first allocates memory within the kernel, injects its code into the allocated memory, and then causes the code to run as a function. Figure 2 shows NICKLE preventing the SucKIT installation. The window on the left shows the VM running RedHat 8.0 (with 2.4.18 kernel), while the window on the right shows the NICKLE output. Inside the VM, one can see that the SucKIT installation program fails and returns an error message *"Unable to handle kernel NULL pointer dereference"*. This occurs because NICKLE (operating in break mode) foils the execution of injected kernel code by fetching a string of zeros from the shadow memory, which causes the kernel to terminate the rootkit installation program. Interestingly, when NICKLE operates in rewrite mode, it rewrites the malicious code and forces it to return −1. However, it seems that SucKIT does not bother to check the return value and so the rootkit installation just fails silently and the kernel-level functionality does not work.

In the right-side window in Figure 2, NICKLE reports the authentication and shadowing of sequences of kernel instructions starting from the initial BIOS

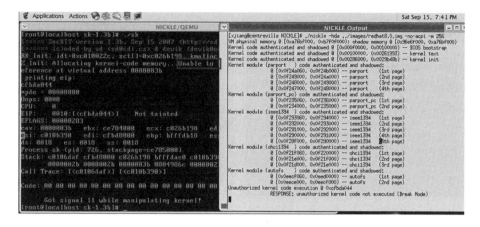

Fig. 2. NICKLE/QEMU+KQEMU foils the SucKIT rootkit (guest OS: RedHat 8.0)

bootstrap code to the kernel text as well as its initialization code and finally to various legitimate kernel modules. In this experiment, there are five legitimate kernel modules, *parport.o*, *parport_pc.o*, *ieee1394.o*, *ohci1394*, and *autofs.o*, all authenticated and shadowed. The code portion of the kernel module begins with an offset of `0x60` bytes in the first page. The first `0x60` bytes are for the kernel module header, which stores pointers to information such as the module's name, size, and other entries linking to the global linked list of loaded kernel modules. This is another example of *mixed kernel pages* with code and data in Linux (Section 2.2).

FU Rootkit Experiment. The FU rootkit [19] is a Windows rootkit that loads a kernel driver and proceeds to manipulate kernel data objects. The manipulation will allow the attacker to hide certain running processes or device drivers loaded in the kernel. When running FU on NICKLE, the driver is unable to load successfully as the driver-specific initialization code is considered unauthorized kernel code. Figure 3 compares NICKLE's two response modes against FU's attempt to load its driver. Under break mode, the OS simply breaks with a blue screen. Under rewrite mode, the FU installation program fails ("Failed to initialize driver.") but the OS does not crash.

4.2   Impact on Performance

To evaluate NICKLE's impact on system performance we have performed benchmark-based measurements on both VMMs – with and without NICKLE. The physical host in our experiments has an Intel 2.40GHz processor and 3GB of RAM running Ubuntu Linux 7.10. QEMU version 0.9.0 with KQEMU 1.3.0pre11 or VirtualBox 1.5.0 OSE is used where appropriate. The VM's guest OS is Redhat 8.0 with a custom compile of a vanilla Linux 2.4.18 kernel and is started inuniprocessor mode with the default amount of memory (256MB for

(a) Under break mode   (b) Under rewrite mode

Fig. 3. Comparison of NICKLE/QEMU+KQEMU's response modes against the FU rootkit (guest OS: Windows 2K)

Table 2. Software configuration for performance evaluation

Item	Version	Configuration	Item	Version	Configuration
Redhat	8.0	Using Linux 2.4.18	Apache	2.0.59	Using the default high-performance configuration file
Kernel	2.4.18	Standard kernel compilation	ApacheBench	2.0.40-dev	-c3 -t 60 <url/file>
			Unixbench	4.1.0	-10 index

Table 3. Application benchmark results

| | QEMU+KQEMU | | | VirtualBox | | |
Benchmark	w/o NICKLE	w/NICKLE	Overhead	w/o NICKLE	w/ NICKLE	Overhead
Kernel Compiling	231.490s	233.529s	0.87%	156.482s	168.377s	7.06%
insmod	0.088s	0.095s	7.34%	0.035s	0.050s	30.00%
Apache	351.714 req/s	349.417 req/s	0.65%	463.140 req/s	375.024 req/s	19.03%

VirtualBox and 128MB for QEMU+KQEMU). Table 2 shows the software configuration for the measurement. For the Apache benchmark, a separate machine connected to the host via a dedicated gigabit switch is used to launch ApacheBench. When applicable, benchmarks are run 10 times and the results are averaged.

Three application-level benchmarks (Table 3) and one micro-benchmark (Table 4) are used to evaluate the system. The first application benchmark is a kernel compilation test: A copy of the Linux 2.4.18 kernel is uncompressed, configured, and compiled. The total time for these operations is recorded and a lower number is better. Second, the insmod benchmark measures the amount of time taken to insert a module (in this case, the *ieee1394* module) into the kernel and again lower is better. Third, the ApacheBench program is used to measure the VM's throughput when serving requests for a 16KB file. In this case, higher is better. Finally, the UnixBench micro-benchmark is executed to evaluate the more fine-grained performance impact of NICKLE. The numbers

Table 4. UnixBench results (for the first two data columns, higher is better)

Benchmark	QEMU+KQEMU			VirtualBox		
	w/o NICKLE	w/NICKLE	Overhead	w/o NICKLE	w/ NICKLE	Overhead
Dhrystone	659.3	660.0	-0.11%	1843.1	1768.6	4.04%
Whetstone	256.0	256.0	0.00%	605.8	543.0	10.37%
Execl	126.0	127.3	-1.03%	205.4	178.2	13.24%
File copy 256B	45.5	46	-1.10%	2511.8	2415.7	3.83%
File copy 1kB	67.6	68.2	-0.89%	4837.5	4646.9	3.94%
File copy 4kB	128.4	127.4	0.78%	7249.9	7134.3	1.59%
Pipe throughput	41.7	40.7	2.40%	4646.9	4590.9	1.21%
Process creation	124.7	118.2	5.21%	92.1	85.3	7.38%
Shell scripts (8)	198.3	196.7	0.81%	259.2	239.8	7.48%
System call	20.9	20.1	3.83%	2193.3	2179.9	0.61%
Overall	106.1	105.0	**1.01%**	1172.6	1108.7	**5.45%**

reported in Table 4 are an index where higher is better. It should be noted that the benchmarks are meant primarily to compare a NICKLE-enhanced VMM with the corresponding unmodified VMM. These numbers are not meant to compare different VMMs (such as QEMU+KQEMU vs. VirtualBox).

QEMU+KQEMU.   The QEMU+KQEMU implementation of NICKLE exhibits very low overhead in most tests. In fact, a few of the benchmark tests show a slight performance gain for the NICKLE implementation, but we consider these results to signify that there is no noticeable slowdown due to NICKLE for that test. From Table 3 it can be seen that both the kernel compilation and Apache tests come in below 1% overheard. The `insmod` test has a modest overhead, 7.3%, primarily due to the fact that NICKLE must calculate and verify the hash of the module prior to copying it into the shadow memory. Given how infrequently kernel module insertion occurs in a running system, this overhead is not a concern. The UnixBench tests in Table 4 further testify to the efficiency of the NICKLE implementation in QEMU+KQEMU, with the worst-case overhead of any test being 5.21% and the overall overhead being 1.01%. The low overhead of NICKLE is due to the fact that NICKLE's modifications to the QEMU control flow only take effect while executing kernel code (user-level code is executed by the unmodified KQEMU accelerator).

VirtualBox.   The VirtualBox implementation has a more noticeable overhead than the QEMU+KQEMU implementation, but still runs below 10% for the majority of the tests. The kernel compilation test, for example, exhibits about 7% overheard; while the UnixBench suite shows a little less than 6% overall. The Apache test is the worst performer, showing a 19.03% slowdown. This can be attributed to the heavy number of user/kernel mode switches that occur while serving web requests. It is during the mode switches that the Virtual-Box implementation does its work to ensure only verified code will be executed directly [16], hence incurring overhead. The `insmod` test shows a large performance degradation, coming in at 30.0%. This is due to the fact that module insertion on the VirtualBox implementation entails the VMM leaving native code execution as well as verifying the module. However, this is not a concern as module insertion is an uncommon event at runtime. Table 4 shows that the worst performing UnixBench test (Execl) results in an overhead of 13.24%. This result is most likely due to a larger number of user/kernel mode switches that occur during that test.

In summary, our benchmark experiments show that NICKLE incurs minimal to moderate impact on system performance, relative to that of the respective original VMMs.

5 Discussion

In this section, we discuss several issues related to NICKLE. First, the goal of NICKLE is to prevent unauthorized code from executing in the kernel space, but not to protect the integrity of kernel-level control flows. This means that it is possible for an attacker to launch a "return-into-libc" style attack within the kernel by leveraging only the existing authenticated kernel code. Recent work by Shacham [20] builds a powerful attacker who can execute virtually arbitrary code using only a carefully crafted stack that causes jumps and calls into existing code. Fortunately, this approach cannot produce *persistent* code to be called on demand from other portions of the kernel. And Petroni et al. [3] found that 96% of the rootkits they surveyed require persistent code changes. From another perspective, an attacker may also be able to directly or indirectly influence the kernel-level control flow by manipulating certain non-control data [21]. However, without its own kernel code, this type of attack tends to have limited functionality. For example, all four stealth rootkit attacks described in [22] need to execute their own code in the kernel space and hence will be defeated by NICKLE. Meanwhile, solutions exist for protecting control flow integrity [3, 23, 24] and data flow integrity [25], which can be leveraged and extended to complement NICKLE.

Second, the current NICKLE implementation does not support self-modifying kernel code. This limitation can be removed by intercepting the self-modifying behavior (e.g., based on the translation cache invalidation resulting from the self-modification) and re-authenticating and shadowing the kernel code after the modification.

Third, NICKLE currently does not support kernel page swapping. Linux does not swap out kernel pages, but Windows does have this capability. To support kernel page swapping in NICKLE, it would require implementing the introspection of swap-out and swap-in events and ensuring that the page being swapped in has the same hash as when it was swapped out. Otherwise an attacker could modify swapped out code pages without NICKLE noticing. This limitation has not yet created any problem in our experiments, where we did not encounter any kernel level page swapping.

Fourth, targeting kernel-level rootkits, NICKLE is ineffective against user-level rootkits. However, NICKLE significantly elevates the trustworthiness of the guest OS, on top of which anti-malware systems can be deployed to defend against user-level rootkits more effectively.

Fifth, the deployment of NICKLE increases the memory footprint for the protected VM. In the worst case, memory shadowing will double the physical memory usage. As our future work, we can explore the use of demand-paging to effectively reduce the extra memory requirement to the actual amount of memory needed. Overall, it is reasonable and practical to trade memory space for elevated OS kernel security.

Finally, we point out that NICKLE assumes a trusted VMM to achieve the "NICKLE" property. This assumption is needed because it essentially establishes the root-of-trust of the entire system and secures the lowest-level system access. We also acknowledge that a VM environment can potentially be fingerprinted and detected [26, 27] by attackers so that their malware can exhibit different behavior [28]. We can improve the fidelity of the VM environment (e.g., [29, 30]) to thwart some of the VM detection methods. Meanwhile, as virtualization continues to gain popularity, the concern over VM detection may become less significant as attackers' incentive and motivation to target VMs increases.

6   Related Work

Rootkit Prevention Through Kernel Integrity Enforcement.   The first area of related work includes recent efforts in enforcing kernel integrity to thwart kernel rootkit installation or execution. Livewire [6], based on a software-based VMM, aims at protecting the guest OS kernel code and critical data structures from being modified. However, an attacker may choose to load malicious rootkit code into the kernel space without manipulating the original kernel code.

SecVisor [7] is a closely related work that leverages new hardware extensions to enforce life-time kernel integrity and provide a guarantee similar to "NICKLE". However, there are two main differences between SecVisor and NICKLE: First, the deployment of SecVisor requires modification to OS kernel source code as well as the latest hardware support for MMU and IOMMU virtualization. In comparison, NICKLE is a guest-transparent solution that supports guest OSes "as is" on top of legacy hardware platforms. In particular, NICKLE does not rely on the protection of any guest OS data structures (e.g., the GDT – global descriptor table). Second, SecVisor is developed to enforce the W⊕X principle for the protected VM kernel code. This principle intrinsically conflicts with mixed kernel pages, which exist in current OSes (e.g., Linux and Windows). NICKLE works in the presence of mixed kernel pages. OverShadow [31] adopts a similar technique of memory shadowing at the VMM level with the goal of protecting application memory pages from modification by even the OS itself. In comparison, NICKLE has a different goal and aims at protecting the OS from kernel rootkits.

To ensure kernel code integrity, techniques such as driver signing [32] as well as various forms of driver verification [5, 33] have also been proposed. These techniques are helpful in verifying the identity or integrity of the loaded driver. However, a kernel-level vulnerability could potentially be exploited to bypass these techniques. In comparison, NICKLE operates at the lower VMM level and is capable of blocking zero-day kernel-level exploitations.

Symptom-Driven Kernel Rootkit Detection. The second area of related work is the modeling and specification of symptoms of a rootkit-infected OS kernel which can be used to detect kernel rootkits. Petroni et al. [4] and Zhang et al. [34] propose the use of external hardware to grab the runtime OS memory image and detect possible rootkit presence by spotting certain kernel code integrity violations (e.g., rootkit-inflicted kernel code manipulation). More recent works further identify possible violations of semantic integrity of dynamic kernel data [2] or state based control-flow integrity of kernel code [3]. Generalized control-flow integrity [23] may have strong potential to be used as a prevention technique, but as yet has not been applied to kernel integrity. Other solutions such as Strider GhostBuster [35] and VMwatcher [1] target the self-hiding nature of rootkits and infer rootkit presence by detecting discrepancies between the views of the same system from different perspectives. All the above approaches are, by design, for the *detection* of a kernel rootkit *after* it has infected a system. Instead, NICKLE is for the *prevention* of kernel rootkit execution in the first place.

Attestation-Based Rootkit Detection. The third area of related work is the use of attestation techniques to verify the software running on a target platform. Terra [13] and other code attestation schemes [36, 37, 38] are proposed to verify software that is being located into the memory for execution. These schemes are highly effective in providing the *load-time* attestation guarantee. Unfortunately, they are not able to provide *run-time* kernel integrity.

7   Conclusion

We have presented the design, implementation, and evaluation of NICKLE, a VMM-based approach that transparently detects and prevents the launching of kernel rootkit attacks against guest VMs. NICKLE achieves the "NICKLE" guarantee, which foils the common need of existing kernel rootkits to execute their own unauthorized code in the kernel space. NICKLE is enabled by the scheme of memory shadowing, which achieves guest transparency through the guest memory access indirection technique. NICKLE's portability has been demonstrated by its implementation in three VMM platforms. Our experiments show that NICKLE is effective in preventing 23 representative real-world kernel rootkits that target a variety of commodity OSes. Our measurement results show that NICKLE adds only modest overhead to the VMM platform.

Acknowledgements. The authors would like to thank the anonymous reviewers for their insightful comments that helped improve the presentation of this paper. This work was supported in part by NSF Grants CNS-0716376, CNS-0716444 and CNS-0546173.

References

[1] Jiang, X., Wang, X., Xu, D.: Stealthy Malware Detection through VMM-Based "Out-of-the-Box" Semantic View Reconstruction. In: Proceedings of the ACM Conference on Computer and Communications Security (CCS 2007) (October 2007)

[2] Petroni Jr., N.L., Fraser, T., Walters, A., Arbaugh, W.A.: An Architecture for Specification-based Detection of Semantic Integrity Violations in Kernel Dynamic Data. In: Proceedings of the 15th USENIX Security Symposium (2006)

[3] Petroni Jr., N.L., Hicks, M.: Automated Detection of Persistent Kernel Control-Flow Attacks. In: Proceedings of the ACM Conference on Computer and Communications Security (CCS 2007) (October 2007)

[4] Petroni, N., Fraser, T., Molina, J., Arbaugh, W.: Copilot: A Coprocessor-based Kernel Runtime Integrity Monitor. In: Proceedings of the 13th USENIX Security Symposium, pp. 179–194 (2004)

[5] Wilhelm, J., Chiueh, T.-c.: A Forced Sampled Execution Approach to Kernel Rootkit Identification. In: Kruegel, C., Lippmann, R., Clark, A. (eds.) RAID 2007. LNCS, vol. 4637, pp. 219–235. Springer, Heidelberg (2007)

[6] Garfinkel, T., Rosenblum, M.: A Virtual Machine Introspection Based Architecture for Intrusion Detection. In: Proc. Network and Distributed Systems Security Symposium (NDSS 2003) (February 2003)

[7] Seshadri, A., Luk, M., Qu, N., Perrig, A.: SecVisor: A Tiny Hypervisor to Guarantee Lifetime Kernel Code Integrity for Commodity OSes. In: Proceedings of the ACM Symposium on Operating Systems Principles (SOSP 2007) (October 2007)

[8] Bellard, F.: QEMU: A Fast and Portable Dynamic Translator. In: Proceedings of the USENIX Annual Technical Conference, FREENIX Track, pp. 41–46 (2005)

[9] Innotek: Virtualbox (Last accessed, September 2007),
http://www.virtualbox.org/

[10] Intel: Vanderpool Technology (2005),
http://www.intel.com/technology/computing/vptech

[11] AMD: AMD64 Architecture Programmer's Manual Volume 2: System Programming, 3.12 edition (September 2006)

[12] Dunlap, G., King, S., Cinar, S., Basrai, M., Chen, P.: ReVirt: Enabling Intrusion Analysis through Virtual Machine Logging and Replay. In: Proc. USENIX Symposium on Operating Systems Design and Implementation (OSDI 2002) (2002)

[13] Garfinkel, T., Pfaff, B., Chow, J., Rosenblum, M., Boneh, D.: Terra: A Virtual Machine-Based Platform for Trusted Computing. In: Proc. of ACM Symposium on Operating System Principles (SOSP 2003) (October 2003)

[14] Jiang, X., Wang, X.: "Out-of-the-Box" Monitoring of VM-Based High-Interaction Honeypots. In: Kruegel, C., Lippmann, R., Clark, A. (eds.) RAID 2007. LNCS, vol. 4637, pp. 198–218. Springer, Heidelberg (2007)

[15] Joshi, A., King, S., Dunlap, G., Chen, P.: Detecting Past and Present Intrusions through Vulnerability-specific Predicates. In: Proc. ACM Symposium on Operating Systems Principles (SOSP 2005), pp. 91–104 (2005)

[16] Riley, R., Jiang, X., Xu, D.: Guest-Transparent Prevention of Kernel Rootkits with VMM-based Memory Shadowing. Technical report CERIAS TR 2001-146, Purdue University

[17] Arbaugh, W.A., Farber, D.J., Smith, J.M.: A Secure and Reliable Bootstrap Architecture. In: Proceedings of IEEE Symposium on Security and Privacy, May 1997, pp. 65–71 (1997)

[18] sd, devik: Linux on-the-fly Kernel Patching without LKM. Phrack 11(58) Article 7

[19] fuzen_op: Fu rootkit (Last accessed, September 2007), http://www.rootkit.com/project.php?id=12

[20] Shacham, H.: The Geometry of Innocent Flesh on the Bone: Return-into-libc without Function Calls (on the x86). In: Proceedings of the ACM Conference on Computer and Communications Security (CCS 2007) (October 2007)

[21] Chen, S., Xu, J., Sezer, E.C., Gauriar, P., Iyer, R.: Non-Control-Data Attacks Are Realistic Threats. In: Proceedings of the 14th USENIX Security Symposium (August 2005)

[22] Baliga, A., Kamat, P., Iftode, L.: Lurking in the Shadows: Identifying Systemic Threats to Kernel Data. In: Proc. of IEEE Symposium on Security and Privacy (Oakland 2007) (May 2007)

[23] Abadi, M., Budiu, M., Erlingsson, U., Ligatti, J.: Control Flow Integrity: Principles, Implementations, and Applications. In: Proc. ACM Conference on Computer and Communications Security (CCS 2005) (November 2005)

[24] Grizzard, J.B.: Towards Self-Healing Systems: Re-establishing Trust in Compromised Systems. Ph.D. Thesis, Georgia Institute of Technology (May 2006)

[25] Castro, M., Costa, M., Harris, T.: Securing Software by Enforcing Data-Flow Integrity. In: Proc. of USENIX Symposium on Operating Systems Design and Implementation (OSDI 2006) (2006)

[26] Klein, T.: Scooby Doo - VMware Fingerprint Suite (2003), http://www.trapkit.de/research/vmm/scoopydoo/index.html

[27] Rutkowska, J.: Red Pill: Detect VMM Using (Almost) One CPU Instruction (November 2004), http://invisiblethings.org/papers/redpill.html

[28] F-Secure Corporation: Agobot, http://www.f-secure.com/v-descs/agobot.shtml

[29] Kortchinsky, K.: Honeypots: Counter Measures to VMware Fingerprinting (January 2004), http://seclists.org/lists/honeypots/2004/Jan-Mar/0015.html

[30] Liston, T., Skoudis, E.: On the Cutting Edge: Thwarting Virtual Machine Detection (2006), http://handlers.sans.org/tliston/ThwartingVMDetection_Liston_Skoudis.pdf

[31] Chen, X., Garfinkel, T., Lewis, E.C., Subrahmanyam, P., Waldspurger, C.A., Boneh, D., Dwoskin, J., Ports, D.R.K.: Overshadow: A Virtualization-Based Approach to Retrofitting Protection in Commodity Operating Systems. In: Proc. of the 13th Conference on Architectural Support for Programming Languages and Operating Systems (ASPLOS 2008) (March 2008)

[32] Microsoft Corporation: Driver Signing for Windows, http://www.microsoft.com/resources/documentation/windows/xp/all/proddocs/en-us/code_signing.mspx?mfr=true

[33] Kruegel, C., Robertson, W., Vigna, G.: Detecting Kernel-Level Rootkits Through Binary Analysis. In: Yew, P.-C., Xue, J. (eds.) ACSAC 2004. LNCS, vol. 3189, pp. 91–100. Springer, Heidelberg (2004)

[34] Zhang, X., van Doorn, L., Jaeger, T., Perez, R., Sailer, R.: Secure Coprocessor-based Intrusion Detection. In: Proceedings of the 10th ACM SIGOPS European Workshop, pp. 239–242 (2002)

[35] Wang, Y.M., Beck, D., Vo, B., Roussev, R., Verbowski, C.: Detecting Stealth Software with Strider GhostBuster. In: Proc. IEEE International Conference on Dependable Systems and Networks (DSN 2005), pp. 368–377 (2005)

[36] Kennell, R., Jamieson, L.H.: Establishing the Genuinity of Remote Computer Systems. In: Proc. of the 12th USENIX Security Symposium (August 2003)

[37] Sailer, R., Jaeger, T., Zhang, X., van Doorn, L.: Attestation-based Policy Enforcement for Remote Access. In: Proc. of ACM Conference on Computer and Communications Security (CCS 2004) (October 2004)

[38] Sailer, R., Zhang, X., Jaeger, T., van Doorn, L.: Design and Implementation of a TCG-based Integrity Measurement Architecture. In: Proc. of the 13th USENIX Security Symposium (August 2004)

Countering Persistent Kernel Rootkits through Systematic Hook Discovery

Zhi Wang[1], Xuxian Jiang[1], Weidong Cui[2], and Xinyuan Wang[3]

[1] North Carolina State University
[2] Microsoft Research
[3] George Mason University

Abstract. Kernel rootkits, as one of the most elusive types of malware, pose significant challenges for investigation and defense. Among the most notable are *persistent kernel rootkits*, a special type of kernel rootkits that implant persistent kernel hooks to tamper with the kernel execution to hide their presence. To defend against them, an effective approach is to first identify those kernel hooks and then protect them from being manipulated by these rootkits. In this paper, we focus on the first step by proposing a systematic approach to identify those kernel hooks. Our approach is based on two key observations: First, rootkits by design will attempt to hide its presence from *all* running rootkit-detection software including various system utility programs (e.g., *ps* and *ls*). Second, to manipulate OS kernel control-flows, persistent kernel rootkits by their nature will implant kernel hooks on the corresponding kernel-side execution paths invoked by the security programs. In other words, for any persistent kernel rootkit, either it is detectable by a security program or it has to tamper with one of the kernel hooks on the corresponding kernel-side execution path(s) of the security program. As a result, given an authentic security program, we *only* need to monitor and analyze its kernel-side execution paths to identify the related set of kernel hooks that could be potentially hijacked for evasion. We have built a proof-of-concept system called HookMap and evaluated it with a number of Linux utility programs such as *ls*, *ps*, and *netstat* in RedHat Fedora Core 5. Our system found that there exist 35 kernel hooks in the kernel-side execution path of *ls* that can be potentially hijacked for manipulation (e.g., for hiding files). Similarly, there are 85 kernel hooks for *ps* and 51 kernel hooks for *netstat*, which can be respectively hooked for hiding processes and network activities. A manual analysis of eight real-world rootkits shows that our identified kernel hooks cover all those used in them.

1 Introduction

Rootkits have been increasingly adopted by general malware or intruders to hide their presence on or prolong their control of compromised machines. In particular, kernel rootkits, with the unique capability of directly subverting the victim operating system (OS) kernel, have been frequently leveraged to expand the basic OS functionalities with additional (illicit) ones, such as providing unauthorized system backdoor access, gathering personal information (e.g., user keystrokes), escalating the privilege of a malicious process, as well as neutralizing defense mechanisms on the target system.

R. Lippmann, E. Kirda, and A. Trachtenberg (Eds.): RAID 2008, LNCS 5230, pp. 21–38, 2008.

In this paper, we focus on a special type of kernel rootkits called *persistent kernel rootkits*. Instead of referring to those rootkits that are stored as persistent disk files and will survive machine reboots, the notion of persistent kernel rootkits here (inherited from [14]) represents those rootkits that will make persistent modifications to run-time OS kernel control-flow, so that normal kernel execution will be somehow hijacked to provide illicit rootkit functionality[1]. For example, many existing rootkits [1,2] will modify the system call table to hijack the kernel-level control flow. This type of rootkits is of special interest to us for a number of reasons. First, a recent survey [14] of both Windows and Linux kernel rootkits shows that 96% of them are persistent kernel rootkits and they will make persistent control-flow modifications. Second, by running inside the OS kernel, these rootkits have the highest privilege on the system, making them very hard to be detected or removed. In fact, a recent report [3] shows that, once a system is infected by these rootkits, the best way to recover from them is to re-install the OS image. Third, by directly making control-flow modifications, persistent kernel rootkits provide a convenient way to add a rich set of malicious rootkit functionalities.

On the defensive side, one essential step to effectively defending against persistent kernel rootkits is to identify those hooking points (or kernel hooks) that are used by rootkits to regain kernel execution control and then inflict all sorts of manipulations to cloak their presence. The identification of these kernel hooks is useful for not only understanding the hooking mechanism [23] used by rootkits, but also providing better protection of kernel integrity [10,14,20]. For example, existing anti-rootkit tools such as [8,16,17] all can be benefited because they require the prior knowledge of those kernel hooks to detect the rootkit presence.

To this end, a number of approaches [14,23] have been proposed. For example, SBCFI [14] analyzes the Linux kernel source code and builds an approximation of kernel control-flow graph that will be followed at run-time by a legitimate kernel. Unfortunately, due to the lack of dynamic run-time information, it is only able to achieve an approximation of kernel control-flow graph. From another perspective, HookFinder [23] is developed to automatically analyze a given malware sample and identify those hooks that are being used by the provided malware. More specifically, HookFinder considers any changes made by the malware as tainted and recognizes a specific change as a hooking point if it eventually redirects the execution control to the tainted attack code. Though effective in identifying specific hooks used by the malware, it cannot discover other hooks that can be equally hijacked but are not being used by the malware.

In this paper, we present a systematic approach that, given a rootkit-detection program, discovers those related kernel hooks that could be potentially used by persistent kernel rootkits to evade from it. Our approach is motivated by the following observation: To hide its presence, a persistent kernel rootkit by design will hide from the given security program and the hiding is achieved by implanting kernel hooks in a number of strategic locations within the kernel-side execution paths of the security program. In other words, for any persistent kernel rootkit, either it is detectable by the security program or it has to tamper with one of the kernel hooks. Therefore, for the purpose of

---

[1] For other types of kernel rootkits that may attack kernel data, they are *not* the focus of this paper and we plan to explore them as future work.

detecting persistent kernel rootkits, it is sufficient to just identify all kernel hooks in the kernel-side execution paths of a given rootkit-detection program.

To identify hooks in the kernel-side execution of a program, we face three main challenges: (1) accurately identifying the right kernel-side execution path for monitoring; (2) obtaining the relevant run-time context information (e.g., the ongoing system call and specific kernel functions) with respect to the identified execution path; (3) uncovering the kernel hooks in the execution path and extracting associated semantic definition. To effectively address the first two challenges, we developed a context-aware kernel execution monitor and the details will be described in Section 3.1. For the third one, we have built a kernel hook identifier (Section 3.2) that will first locate the run-time virtual address of an uncovered kernel hook and then perform OS-aware semantics resolution to reveal a meaningful definition of the related kernel object or variable.

We have developed a prototype called HookMap on top of a software-based QEMU virtual machine implementation [6]. It is appropriate for two main reasons: First, software-based virtualization allows to conveniently support commodity OSes as guest virtual machines (VMs). And more importantly, given a selected execution path, the virtualization layer can be extended to provide the unique capability in instrumenting and recording its execution without affecting its functionality. Second, since we are dealing with a legitimate OS kernel in a clean system, not with a rootkit sample that may detect the VM environment and alter its behavior accordingly, the use of virtualization software will not affect the results in identifying kernel hooks.

To evaluate the effectiveness of our approach, we ran a default installation of Red-Hat Fedora Core 5 (with Linux kernel 2.6.15) in our system. Instead of using any commercial rootkit-detection software, we chose to test with three utility programs, *ls*, *ps* and *netstat* since they are often attacked by rootkits to hide files, processes or network connections. By monitoring their kernel-side executions, our system was able to accurately identify their execution contexts, discover all encountered kernel hooks, and then resolve their semantic definitions. In particular, our system identified 35, 85, and 51 kernel hooks, for *ls*, *ps* and *netstat*, respectively. To empirically evaluate the completeness of identified kernel hooks, we performed a manual analysis of eight real-world kernel rootkits and found that the kernel hooks employed by these rootkits are only a small subset of our identified hooks.

The rest of the paper is structured as follows: Section 2 introduces the background on rootkit hooking mechanisms. Section 3 gives an overview of our approach, followed by the description of HookMap implementation in Section 4. Section 5 presents the experimental results and Section 6 discusses some limitations of the proposed approach. Finally, Section 7 surveys related work and Section 8 concludes the paper.

2 Background

In this section, we introduce the hooking mechanisms that are being used by persistent kernel rootkits and define a number of terms that will be used throughout the paper.

There exist two main types of kernel hooks: *code hooks* and *data hooks*. To implant a code hook, a kernel rootkit typically modifies the kernel text so that the execution of the affected text will be directly hijacked. However, since the kernel text section is

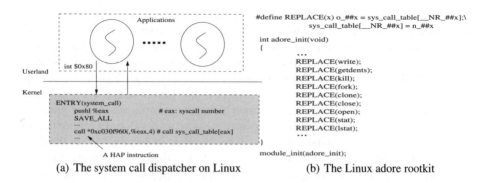

(a) The system call dispatcher on Linux   (b) The Linux adore rootkit

Fig. 1. A HAP instruction example inside the Linux system call dispatcher – the associated kernel data hooks have been attacked by various rootkits, including the Linux adore rootkit [1]

usually static and can be marked as read-only (or not writable), the way to implant the code hook can be easily detected. Because of that, rootkit authors are now more inclined to implant data hooks at a number of strategic memory locations in the kernel space. Data hooks are usually a part of kernel data that are interpreted as the destination addresses in control-flow transition instructions such as *call* and *jmp*. A typical example of kernel data hook is the system call table that contains the addresses to a number of specific system call service routines (e.g., *sys_open*). In addition, many data hooks may contain dynamic content as they are mainly used to hold the run-time addresses of kernel functions and can be later updated because of the loading or unloading of kernel modules. For ease of presentation, we refer to the control-flow transition instructions (i.e., *call* or conditional or un-conditional jumps) whose destination addresses are not hard-coded constants as *hook attach points* (HAPs).

In Figure 1, we show an HAP example with associated kernel data hooks, i.e., the system call table, which is commonly attacked by kernel rootkits. In particular, Figure 1(a) shows the normal system call dispatcher on Linux while Figure 1(b) contains the code snippet of a Linux rootkit – adore [1]. From the control-flow transfer instruction – *call *0xc030f960(,%eax,4)*[2] in Figure 1(a), we can tell the existence of a hook attach point inside the system call dispatcher. In addition, Figure 1(b) reveals that the adore rootkit will replace a number of system call table entries (as data hooks) so that it can intervene and manipulate the execution of those replaced system calls. For instance, the code statement *REPLACE(write)* rewrites the system call table entry *sys_call_table[4]* to intercept the *sys_write* routine before its execution. The corresponding run-time memory location $0xc030f970$ and the associated semantic definition of *sys_call_table[4]* will be identified as a data hook. More specifically, the memory location $0xc030f970$ is calculated as $0xc030f960 + \%eax \times 4$ where $0xc030f960$ is the base address of system call table and $\%eax = 4$ is the actual number for the specific *sys_write* system call. We defer an in-depth analysis of this particular rootkit in Section 5.2.

---

[2] This instruction is in the standard AT&T assembly syntax, meaning that it will transfer its execution to another memory location pointed to by $0xc030f960 + \%eax \times 4$.

Meanwhile, as mentioned earlier, there are a number of rootkits that will replace specific instructions (as code hooks) in the system call handler. For instance, the SucKit [19] rootkit will prepare its own version of the system call table and then change the dispatcher so that it will invoke system call routines populated in its own system call table. Using Figure 1(a) as an example, the rootkit will modify the control-flow transfer instruction or more specifically the base address of the system call table $0xc030f960$ to point to a rootkit-controlled system call table. Considering that (1) implanting a code hook will inflict kernel code modifications, which can be easily detected, and (2) every kernel instruction could be potentially overwritten for code hook purposes, we in this paper focus on the identification of kernel data hooks. Without ambiguity, we use the term kernel hooks to represent kernel data hooks throughout the paper.

Finally, we point out that kernel hooks are elusive to identify because they can be widely scattered across the kernel space and rootkit authors keep surprising us in using new kernel hooks for rootkit purposes [7,18]. In fact, recent research results [23] show that some stealth rootkits use previously unknown kernel hooks to evade all existing security programs for rootkit detection. In this paper, our goal is to systematically discover all kernel hooks that can be used by persistent kernel rootkits to tamper with and thus hide from a given security program.

3   System Design

The intuition behind our approach is straightforward but effective: a rootkit by nature is programmed to hide itself especially from various security programs including those widely-used system utility programs such as *ps*, *ls*, and *netstat*. As such for an infected OS kernel, the provided kernel service (e.g., handling a particular system call) to any request from these security software is likely manipulated. The manipulation typically comes from the installation of kernel hooks at strategic locations somewhere *within* the corresponding kernel-side execution path of these security software. Based on this insight, if we can develop a system to comprehensively monitor the kernel-side execution of the same set of security programs within a clean system, we can use it to exhaustively uncover all kernel hooks related to the execution path being monitored. Figure 2 shows an architectural overview of our system with two main components: *context-aware execution monitor* and *kernel hook identifier*. In the following, we will describe these two components in detail.

3.1   Context-Aware Execution Monitor

As mentioned earlier, our system is built on top of an open-source virtual machine implementation, which brings the convenient support of commodity OSes as guest VMs. In addition, for a running VM, the *context-aware execution monitor* is further designed to monitor the internal process events including various system calls made by running processes. As suggested by the aforementioned insight, we need to only capture those kernel events related to security software that is running inside the VM. Note that the main purpose of monitoring these events is to understand the right execution context inside the kernel (e.g., "which process is making the system call?"). With that, we can

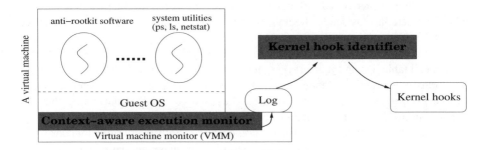

Fig. 2. A systematic approach to discovering kernel hooks

then accurately instrument and record all executed kernel instructions that are relevant to the chosen security software.

However, a challenging part is that modern OS kernels greatly complicate the capture and interpretation of execution contexts with the introduction of "out of order" execution (mainly for improving system concurrency and performance reasons). The "out of order" execution means that the kernel-side execution of any process can be asynchronously interrupted to handle an incoming interrupt request or temporarily context-switched out for the execution of another unrelated process. Notice that the "out of order" execution is considered essential in modern OSes for the support of multi-tasking and asynchronous interrupt handling.

Fortunately, running a commodity OS as a guest VM provides a convenient way to capture those external events [3] that trigger the "out of order" executions in a guest kernel. For example, if an incoming network packet leads to the generation of an interrupt, the interrupt event needs to be emulated by the underlying virtual machine monitor and thus can be intercepted and recorded by our system. The tricky part is to determine when the corresponding interrupt handler ends. For that purpose, we instrument the execution of *iret* instruction to trace when the interrupt handler returns. However, additional complexities are introduced for the built-in support of *nested interrupts* in the modern OS design where an interrupt request (IRQ) of a higher priority is allowed to preempt IRQs of a lower priority. For that, we need to maintain a shadow interrupt stack to track the nested level of an interrupt.

In addition to those external events, the "out of order" execution can also be introduced by some internal events. For example, a running process may voluntarily yield the CPU execution to another process. For that, instead of locating and intercepting all these internal events, we need to take another approach by directly intercepting context switch events occurred inside the monitored VM. The interception of context switch events requires some knowledge of the OS internals. We will describe it in more details in Section 4.

With the above capabilities, we can choose and run a particular security program (or any rootkit-detection tool) inside the monitor. The monitor will record into a local trace

---

[3] Note that the external events here may also include potential debug exceptions caused from hardware-based debugger registers. However, in this work, we do not count those related hooks within the debug interrupt handler.

file a stream of system calls made by the chosen program and for each system call, a sequence of kernel instructions executed within the system call execution path.

3.2   Kernel Hook Identifier

The context-aware execution monitor will collect a list of kernel instructions that are sequentially executed when handling a system call request from a chosen security program. Given the collected instructions, the kernel hook identifier component is developed to identify those HAPs where kernel hooks are involved. The identification of potential HAPs is relatively straightforward because they are the control-flow transfer instructions, namely those *call* or *jmp* instructions.

Some astute readers may wonder "wouldn't static analysis work for the very same need?" By statically analyzing kernel code, it is indeed capable of identifying those HAPs. Unfortunately, it cannot lead to the identification of the corresponding kernel hooks. There are two main reasons: (1) A HAP may use registers or memory locations to resolve the run-time locations of the related kernel hooks. In other words, the corresponding kernel hook location cannot be determined through static analysis. (An example is already shown in Figure 1(a).) (2) Moreover, there exists another complexity that is introduced by the loadable kernel module (LKM) support in commodity OS kernels. In particular, when a LKM is loaded into the kernel, not only its loading location may be different from previous runs, but also the module text content will be updated accordingly during the time when the module is being loaded. This is mainly due to the existence of certain dependencies of the new loaded module on other loaded modules or the main static kernel text. And we cannot resolve these dependencies until at run-time.

Our analysis shows that for some discovered HAPs, their run-time execution trace can readily reveal the locations of associated kernel hooks. As an example, in the system call dispatcher shown in Figure 1(a), the HAP instruction – *call *0xc030f960(,%eax,4)*, after the execution, will jump to a function which is pointed to from the memory location: $0xc030f960 + \%eax \times 4$, where the value of $\%eax$ register can be known at run-time. In other words, the result of the calculation at run-time will be counted as a kernel hook in the related execution path. In addition, there also exist other HAPs (e.g., *call *%edx*) that may directly call registers and reveal nothing about kernel hooks but the destination addresses the execution will transfer to. For that, we need to start from the identified HAP and examine in a backwards manner those related instructions to identify the source, which eventually affects the calculated destination value and will then be considered a kernel hook. (The detailed discussion will be presented in Section 4.2.) In our analysis, we also encounter some control-flow transfer instructions whose destination addresses are hardcoded or statically linked inside machine code. In this case, both static analysis and dynamic analysis can be used to identify the corresponding hooks. Note that according to the nature of this type of hooks (Section 2), we consider them as code hooks in this paper.

Finally, after identifying those kernel hooks, we also aim to resolve the memory addresses to the corresponding semantic definitions. For that, we leverage the symbol information available in the raw kernel text file as well as loaded LKMs. More specifically, for main kernel text, we obtain the corresponding symbol information (e.g., object names and related memory locations) from the related *System.map* file. For kernel modules, we derive the corresponding symbol information from the object files (e.g., by running the *nm* command)[4]. If we use Figure 1(a) as an example, in an execution path related to the *sys_open* routine, the hook's memory address is calculated as *0xc030f974*. From the symbol information associated with the main kernel text, that memory address is occupied by the system call table (with the symbol name *sys_call_table*) whose base address is *0xc030f960*. As a result, the corresponding kernel hook is resolved as *sys_call_table[5]*[5] where 5 is actually the system call number for the *sys_open* routine.

4   Implementation

We have built a prototype system called HookMap based on an open-source QEMU 0.9.0 [6] virtual machine monitor (VMM) implementation. As mentioned earlier, we choose it due to the following considerations: (1) First, since we are dealing with normal OS kernels, the VM environment will not affect the results in the identified kernel hooks; (2) Second, it contains the implementation of a key virtualization technique called dynamic binary translation [6,4], which can be leveraged and extended to select, record, and disassemble kernel instruction sequences of interest; (3) Third, upon the observation of VM-internal process events, we need to embed our own interpretation logic to extract related execution context information. The open-source nature of the VM implementation provides great convenience and flexibility in making our implementation possible. Also, due to the need of obtaining run-time symbols for semantic resolution, our current system only supports Linux. Nevertheless, we point out that the principle described here should also be applicable for other software-based VM implementations (e.g., VMware Workstation [4]) and other commodity OSes (e.g., Windows).

4.1   Context-Aware Execution Logging

One main task in our implementation is that, given an executing kernel instruction, we need to accurately understand the current execution context so that we can determine whether the instruction should be monitored and recorded. Note that the execution context here is defined as the system call context the current (kernel) instruction belongs to. To achieve that, we have the need of keeping track of the lifetime of a system call event. Fortunately, the lifetime of a system call event is well defined as the kernel accepts only two standard methods in requesting for a system call service: *int $0x80* and *sysenter*. Since we are running the whole system on top of a binary-translation-capable VMM, we can conveniently intercept these two instructions and then interpret the associated system call arguments accordingly. For this specific task, we leverage an "out-of-the-box" VM monitoring framework called VMscope [11] as it already allows

---

[4] We point out that the *nm* command output will be further updated with the run-time loading address of the corresponding module. For that, we will instrument the module-loading instructions in the kernel to determine the address at run-time.

[5] The calculation is based on the following: $(0xc030f974 - 0xc030f960)/4 = 5$, where 4 represents the number of bytes occupied by a function pointer.

to real-time capture system calls completely outside the VM. What remains to do is to correlate a system call event and the related system call return event to form its lifetime. Interested readers are referred to [11] for more details.

Meanwhile, we also face another challenge caused by the "out-of-order" execution (Section 3). To address that, we monitor relevant external events (e.g., interrupts) as well as internal events (e.g., context switches) to detect run-time changes of the execution context. The main goal here is to avoid the introduction of "noises" – unnecessary kernel executions – into the execution path for monitoring and analysis. Fortunately, with a software-based VM implementation, we are able to intercept all these external events as they need to be eventually emulated by the underlying VMM. However, an interesting part is to handle the nested interrupts scenario where a shadow interrupt stack should be maintained at the VMM layer to keep track of the nested level of the ongoing interrupt. For the internal events, our prototype sets a breakpoint on a kernel function that actually performs context-switching. On Linux, the related function is called _switch_to and its location is exported by kernel and can be found in the *System.map* file[6].

With the above capabilities, our system essentially organizes the kernel instruction execution into a stream of system calls and each system call contains a sequence of kernel instructions executed within this specific context. Furthermore, to facilitate later identification and analysis of kernel hooks, for each kernel instruction in one particular context, we further dump the memory locations as well as registers, if any, involved in this instruction. The additional information is needed for later kernel hook identification, which we describe next.

4.2 Kernel Hook Identification

Based on the collected sequence of kernel instructions, the kernel hook identifier locates and analyzes those control-flow transfer *call* or *jmp* instructions (as HAP instructions) to uncover relevant kernel hooks. As a concrete example, we show in Table 1 a list of identified HAPs, associated system call contexts, as well as those kernel hooks that are obtained by monitoring kernel-side execution of the *ls* command. Note that a (small) subset of those identified kernel hooks have already been used by rootkits for file-hiding purposes (more in Section 5).

As mentioned earlier, for an HAP instruction that will read a memory location and jump to the function pointed by a memory location, we can simply record the memory location as a kernel hook. However, if an HAP instruction directly calls a register (e.g., *call *%edx*), we need to develop an effective scheme to trace back to the source – a kernel hook that determines the value of the register.

We point out that this particular problem is similar to the classic problem addressed by dynamic program slicing [5,24]: Given an execution history and a variable as the input, the goal of dynamic program slicing is to extract a slice that contains all the instructions in the execution history that affected the value of that variable. As such, for the register involved in an identified HAP instruction, we apply the classic dynamic

---

[6] A different version of *ls* can result in the execution of *sys_getdents64* instead of *sys_getdents*, which leads to one variation in the identified kernel hooks – *sys_call_table[220]* instead of *sys_call_table[141]*. A similar scenario also happens when identifying another set of kernel hooks by monitoring the *ps* command (to be shown in Table 2).

Table 1. File-hiding kernel hooks obtained by monitoring the *ls -alR /* command in RedHat Fedora Core 5

execution path	#	Hook Attach Points (HAPs)		Kernel Hooks
		address	instruction	address
sys_write	1	0xc0102b38	call *0xc030f960(,%eax,4)	sys_call_table[4]
	2	0xc014e5a3	call *0xec(%ecx)	selinux_ops[59]
	3	0xc014e5c9	call *%edi	tty_fops[4]
	4	0xc01c63c6	jmp *0xc02bfb40(,%eax,4)	dummy_con[33]
	5	0xc01fa9d2	call *0xc(%esp)	tty_ldisc_N_TTY.write_chan
	6	0xc01fd4f5	call *0xc8(%ecx)	con_ops[3]
	7	0xc01fd51e	call *0xd0(%edx)	con_ops[5]
	8	0xc01fd5fa	call *%edx	con_ops[4]
	9	0xc01fd605	call *0xc4(%ebx)	con_ops[2]
	10	0xc0204caa	call *0x1c(%ecx)	vga_con[7]
sys_open	1	0xc0102b38	call *0xc030f960(,%eax,4)	sys_call_table[5]
	2	0xc014f024	call *0xf0(%edx)	selinux_ops[60]
	3	0xc0159677	call *%esi	ext3_dir_inode_operations[13] (ext3.ko)
	4	0xc015969d	call *0xbc(%ebx)	selinux_ops[47]
	5	0xc019ea96	call *0xbc(%ebx)	capability_ops[47]
sys_close	1	0xc0102b38	call *0xc030f960(,%eax,4)	sys_call_table[6]
	2	0xc014f190	call *%ecx	ext3_dir_operations[14] (ext3.ko)
	3	0xc014f19a	call *0xf4(%edx)	selinux_ops[61]
sys_ioctl	1	0xc0102b38	call *0xc030f960(,%eax,4)	sys_call_table[54]
	2	0xc015dbcf	call *%esi	tty_fops[8]
	3	0xc015de16	call *0xf8(%ebx)	selinux_ops[62]
	4	0xc01fc5a1	call *%ebx	con_ops[7]
	5	0xc01fc5c9	call *%ebx	tty_ldisc_N_TTY.n_tty_ioctl
sys_mmap2	1	0xc0102b38	call *0xc030f960(,%eax,4)	sys_call_table[192]
	2	0xc0143e0e	call *0xfc(%ebx)	selinux_ops[63]
	3	0xc0143ebc	call *0x2c(%edx)	selinux_ops[11]
	4	0xc0144460	call *%esi	mm→get_unmapped_area
	5	0xc019dc50	call *0x18(%ecx)	capability_ops[6]
	6	0xc019f5d5	call *0xfc(%ebx)	capability_ops[63]
sys_fstat64	1	0xc0102b38	call *0xc030f960(,%eax,4)	sys_call_table[197]
	2	0xc0155f33	call *0xc4(%ecx)	selinux_ops[49]
sys_getdents[6]	1	0xc0102b38	call *0xc030f960(,%eax,4)	sys_call_table[114]
	2	0xc015de80	call *0xec(%ecx)	selinux_ops[59]
	3	0xc015decc	call *0x18(%ebx)	ext3_dir_operations[6] (ext3.ko)
	4	0xc016b711	call *%edx	ext3_dir_inode_operations[3] (ext3.ko)
sys_getdents64	1	0xc0102b38	call *0xc030f960(,%eax,4)	sys_call_table[220]
	2	0xc015de80	call *0xec(%ecx)	selinux_ops[59]
	3	0xc015decc	call *0x18(%ebx)	ext3_dir_operations[6] (ext3.ko)
	4	0xc016b711	call *%edx	ext3_dir_inode_operations[3] (ext3.ko)
sys_fcntl64	1	0xc0102b38	call *0xc030f960(,%eax,4)	sys_call_table[221]
	2	0xc015d7a7	call *0x108(%ebx)	selinux_ops[66]

program slicing algorithm [5] to find out a memory location that is associated with a kernel object (including a global static variable) and whose content determines the register value. To do that, we follow the algorithm by first computing two sets for

```
#line  machine code            instruction           DEF         USE
====   =============           ====================  ========    =====
i-1  : ...
i+0  : 89 c3                   mov    %eax,%ebx       %ebx        %eax
i+1  : 83 ec 04                sub    $0x4,%esp       %esp        %esp
i+2  : 8b 80 c4 00 00 00       mov    0xc4(%eax),%eax %eax        mem[%eax+0xc4], %eax
i+3  : f6 c2 03                test   $0x3,%dl        eflags      %dl
i+4  : 89 04 24                mov    %eax,(%esp)     mem[esp]    %eax
i+5  : 74 0e                   je     c016b713                    eflags
i+6  : 8b 40 24                mov    0x24(%eax),%eax %eax        mem[%eax+0x24], %eax
i+7  : 8b 50 0c                mov    0xc(%eax),%edx  %edx        mem[%eax+0xc],  %eax
i+8  : 85 d2                   test   %edx,%edx       eflags      %edx
i+9  : 74 04                   je     c016b713                    eflags
i+10 : 89 d8                   mov    %ebx,%eax       %eax        %ebx
i+11 : ff d2                   call   *%edx           %eip        %edx
i+12 : ...
```

Fig. 3. Discovering a kernel hook based on dynamic program slicing

each related instruction: one is $DEF[i]$ that contains the variable(s) defined by this instruction, and another is $USE[i]$ that includes all variables used by this instruction. Each set can contain an element of either a memory location or a machine register. After that, we then examine backwards to find out the memory location that is occupied by a kernel object and whose content determines the register value. In the following, we will walk-through the scheme with an example. (For the classic algorithm, interested readers are referred to [5] for more details.)

Figure 3 shows some sequential kernel instructions[7] of a kernel function __mark_inode_dirty that are executed in the sys_getdent64 context of the ls command. In particular, the sequence contains an HAP instruction – call *%edx – at the memory location $0xc016b711$ (line $i + 11$ in Figure 3). Note that since we monitor at run-time, we can precisely tell which memory locations/registers are defined and/or used. As a result, we directly derive the corresponding destination address (contained in the %edx register), which is $0xc885bca0$ – the entry point of a function ext3_dirty_inode within a LKM named ext3.ko. Obviously, it is the destination address the HAP instruction will transfer to, not the relevant kernel hook. Next, our prototype further expands the associated semantics of every executed instruction i to compute the two sets $DEF[i]$ and $USE[i]$ and the results are shown in Figure 3. With the two sets defined for each instruction, we can then apply the dynamic slicing algorithm. Specifically, from the HAP instruction (line $i + 11$), the USE set contains the %edx register, which is defined by the instruction at line $i + 7$. This particular instruction is associated with a USE set having two members: %eax and mem[%eax+0xc]. It turns out the %eax points to the kernel object ext3_dir_inode_operations and $0xc$ is an offset from the kernel object. After identifying the responsible kernel object, the slicing algorithm then outputs ext3_dir_inode_operations[3] as the corresponding kernel hook and terminates. In Table 1, this is the fourth kernel hook identified in the sys_getdent64 context. Note that this particular kernel object is a jump table containing a number of function pointers. The offset $0xc$ indicates that it is the fourth member function in the object as each function pointer is four bytes in size. (The first four member functions in the kernel object are in the offsets of $0x0$, $0x4$, $0x8$, and $0xc$, respectively.)

---

[7] These instructions are in the AT&T assembly syntax, where source and destination operands, if any, are in the reverse order when compared with the Intel assembly syntax.

5 Evaluation

In this section, we present the evaluation results. In particular, we conduct two sets of experiments. The first set of experiments (Section 5.1) is to monitor the execution of various security programs and identify those kernel hooks that can be potentially hijacked for hiding purposes. The second set of experiments (Section 5.2) is to

Table 2. Process-hiding kernel hooks obtained by monitoring the *ps -ef* command in RedHat Fedora Core 5

execution path	# kernel hooks	Details
sys_read	17	sys_call_table[3], selinux_ops[5], selinux_ops[59], capability_ops[5], kern_table[336], timer_pmtmr[2], proc_info_file_operations[2], proc_file_operations[2], proc_sys_file_operations[2], proc_tty_drivers_operations[2], tty_drivers_op[0], tty_drivers_op[1], tty_drivers_op[2], tty_drivers_op[3], proc_inode.op.proc_read, simple_ones[1].read_proc, simple_ones[2].read_proc
sys_write	11	sys_call_table[4], selinux_ops[59], dummy_con[33], tty_fops[4], con_ops[2], con_ops[3], con_ops[4], con_ops[5], vga_con[6], vga_con[7], tty_ldisc_N_TTY.write_chan
sys_open	20	sys_call_table[5], selinux_ops[34], selinux_ops[46], selinux_ops[47], selinux_ops[60], selinux_ops[88], selinux_ops[112], capability_ops[46], capability_ops[47], pid_base_dentry_operations[0], proc_sops[0], proc_sops[2], proc_root_inode_operations[1], proc_dir_inode_operations[1], proc_self_inode_operations[10], proc_sys_file_operations[12] , proc_tgid_base_inode_operations[1], proc_tty_drivers_operations[12], ext3_dir_inode_operations[13] (ext3.ko), ext3_file_operations[12] (ext3.ko)
sys_close	10	sys_call_table[6], selinux_ops[35], selinux_ops[50], selinux_ops[61], pid_dentry_operations[3], proc_dentry_operations[3], proc_tty_drivers_operations[14], proc_sops[1], proc_sops[6], proc_sops[7]
sys_time	2	sys_call_table[13], timer_pmtmr[2]
sys_lseek	2	sys_call_table[19], proc_file_operations[1]
sys_ioctl	5	sys_call_table[54], tty_fops[8], selinux_ops[62], con_ops[7], tty_ldisc_N_TTY.n_tty_ioctl
sys_mprotect	3	sys_call_table[125], selinux_ops[64], capability_ops[64]
sys_getdents[8]	3	sys_call_table[141], selinux_ops[59], proc_root_operations[6]
sys_getdents64	3	sys_call_table[220], selinux_ops[59], proc_root_operations[6]
sys_mmap2	8	sys_call_table[192], selinux_ops[63], selinux_ops[11], capability_ops[6], capability_ops[63], ext3_dir_inode_operations[3] (ext3.ko), ext3_file_operations[11], mm→get_unmapped_area
sys_stat64	16	sys_call_table[195], selinux_ops[34], selinux_ops[46], selinux_ops[47], selinux_ops[49], selinux_ops[88], selinux_ops[112], capability_ops[46], capability_ops[47], ext3_dir_inode_operations[13] (ext3.ko), pid_base_dentry_operations[0], pid_dentry_operations[3], proc_root_inode_operations[1], proc_self_inode_operations[10], proc_sops[0], proc_tgid_base_inode_operations[1]
sys_fstat64	2	sys_call_table[197], selinux_ops[49]
sys_geteuid32	1	sys_call_table[201]
sys_fcntl64	2	sys_call_table[221], selinux_ops[66]

Table 3. Network-hiding kernel hooks obtained by monitoring the *netstat -atp* command in RedHat Fedora Core 5

execution path	# kernel hooks	Details
sys_read	8	sys_call_table[3], selinux_ops[59], seq_ops.start, seq_ops.show, seq_ops.next, seq_ops.stop, proc_tty_drivers_operations[2]
sys_write	12	sys_call_table[4], selinux_ops[59], dummy_con[33], con_ops[2], con_ops[3], con_ops[4], con_ops[5], tty_fops[4], tty_ldisc_N_TTY.write_chan, vga_con[6], vga_con[7], vga_ops[8]
sys_open	19	sys_call_table[5], selinux_ops[34], selinux_ops[35], selinux_ops[47], selinux_ops[50], selinux_ops[60], selinux_ops[61], selinux_ops[112], capability_ops[47], ext3_dir_inode_operations[13] (ext3.ko), pid_dentry_operations[3], proc_root_inode_operations[1], proc_dir_inode_operations[1], proc_sops[0], proc_sops[1], proc_sops[2], proc_sops[6], proc_sops[7], tcp4_seq_fops[12]
sys_close	9	sys_call_table[6], selinux_ops[35], selinux_ops[50], selinux_ops[61], proc_dentry_operations[3], proc_tty_drivers_operations[14], proc_sops[1], proc_sops[6], proc_sops[7],
sys_munmap	2	sys_call_table[91], mm→unmap_area
sys_mmap2	6	sys_call_table[192], selinux_ops[11], selinux_ops[63], capability_ops[6], capability_ops[63], mm→get_unmapped_area
sys_fstat64	2	sys_call_table[197], selinux_ops[49]

empirically evaluate those identified hooks by analyzing a number of real-world rootkits and see whether the used kernel hooks are actually a part of the discovered ones[8].

5.1   Kernel Hooks

In our experiments, we focus on three types of resources that are mainly targeted by rootkits: files, processes, and network connections. To enumerate related kernel hooks, we correspondingly chose three different utility programs – *ls*, *ps*, and *netstat*. These three programs are from the default installation of Red Hat Linux Fedora Core 5 that runs as a guest VM (with $512MB$ memory) on top of our system. Our testing platform was a modest system, a Dell PowerEdge 2950 server with Xeon 3.16Ghz and 4GB memory running Scientific Linux 4.4. As mentioned earlier, the way to choose these programs is based on the intuition that to hide a file (, a process, or a network connection), a persistent kernel rootkit needs to compromise the kernel-side execution of the *ls* (, *ps*, or *netstat*) program.

In our evaluation, we focus on those portions of collected traces that are related to the normal functionality of the security program (e.g., the querying of system states of interest as well as the final result output) and exclude other unrelated ones. For example, if some traces are part of the loading routine that prepares the process memory layout,

---

[8] Different versions of *ps* invokes different system calls to list files under a directory. In our evaluation, the 3.2.7 version of ps uses the *sys_getdents* system call while the version 3.2.3 uses another system call – *sys_getdents64*. Both system calls work the same way except one has a kernel hook *sys_call_table[141]* while another has *sys_call_table[220]*.

we consider them not related to the normal functionality of the chosen program and thus simply ignore them. Further, we assume that the chosen security program as well as those dependent libraries are not compromised. Tables 1, 2, and 3 contain our results, including those specific execution contexts of related system calls. Encouragingly, for each encountered HAP instruction, we can always locate the corresponding kernel hook and our manual analysis on Linux kernel source code further confirms that each identified kernel hook is indeed from a meaningful kernel object or data structure.

More specifically, these three tables show that most identified kernel hooks are part of jump tables defined in various kernel objects. In particular, there are three main kernel objects containing a large collection of function pointers that can be hooked for hiding purposes: the system call table *sys_call_table*, the SELinux-related security operations table *selinux_ops*, as well as the capability-based operations table *capability_ops*. There are other kernel hooks that belong to a particular dynamic kernel object. One example is the function pointer *get_unmapped_area* (in the *sys_mmap2* execution path of Table 2) inside the *mm* kernel object that manages the process memory layout. Note that this particular kernel hook cannot be determined by static analysis.

More in-depth analysis also reveals that an HAP instruction executed in different execution contexts can be associated with different kernel hooks. One example is the HAP instruction located in the system call dispatcher (Figure 1(a)) where around 300 system call service routines are called by the same HAP instruction. A kernel hook can also be associated with multiple HAP instructions. This is possible because a function pointer (contained in a kernel hook) can be invoked at multiple locations in a function. One such example is *selinux_ops[47]*, a kernel hook that is invoked a number of times in the *sys_open* execution context of the *ps* command. In addition, we observed many one-to-one mappings between an HAP instruction and its associated kernel hook. Understanding the relationship between HAP instructions and kernel hooks is valuable for real-time accurate enforcement of kernel control-flow integrity [14].

5.2   Case Studies

To empirically evaluate those identified kernel rootkits, we manually analyzed the source code of eight real-world Linux rootkits (Table 4). For each rootkit, we first identified what kernel hooks are hijacked to implement a certain hiding feature and then checked whether they are a part of the results shown in Tables 1, 2, and 3. It is encouraging that for every identified kernel hook[9], there always exists an exact match in our results. In the following, we explain two rootkit experiments in detail:

The *Adore* Rootkit.   This rootkit is distributed in the form of a loadable kernel module. If activated, the rootkit will implant 15 kernel hooks in the system call table by replacing them with its own implementations. Among these 15 hooks, only three of them are responsible for hiding purposes[10]. More specifically, two system call table en-

---

[9] Our evaluation focuses on those kernel data hooks. As mentioned earlier, for kernel code hooks, they can be scattered over every kernel instruction in the corresponding system call execution path.

[10] The other 12 hooks are mainly used to provide hidden backdoor accesses. One example is the sys_call_table[6] (sys_close), which is hooked to allow the attacker to escalate the privilege to root without going through the normal authorization process.

Table 4. Kernel hooks used by real-world rootkits ([‡] means a code hook)

rootkit	kernel hooks based on the hiding features		
	file-hiding	process-hiding	network-hiding
adore	sys_call_table[141] sys_call_table[220]	sys_call_table[141] sys_call_table[220]	sys_call_table[4]
adore-ng	ext3_dir_operations[6]	proc_root_operations[6]	tcp4_seq_fops[12]
hideme.vfs	sys_getdents64[‡]	proc_root_operations[6]	N/A
override	sys_call_table[220]	sys_call_table[220]	sys_call_table[3]
Synapsys-0.4	sys_call_table[141]	sys_call_table[141]	sys_call_table[4]
Rial	sys_call_table[141]	sys_call_table[141]	sys_call_table[3], sys_call_table[5] sys_call_table[6]
knark	sys_call_table[141] sys_call_table[220]	sys_call_table[141] sys_call_table[220]	sys_call_table[3]
kis-0.9	sys_call_table[141]	sys_call_table[141]	tcp4_seq_fops[12]

tries – *sys_getdents* (sys_call_table[141]) and *sys_getdents64* (sys_call_table[220]) – are hijacked for hiding files and processes while another one – *sys_write* (sys_call_table[4]) – is replaced to hide network activities related to backdoor processes protected by the rootkit. A customized user-space program called *ava* is provided to send hiding instructions to the malicious LKM so that certain files or processes of attackers' choices can be hidden. All these three kernel hooks are uncovered by our system, as shown in Tables 1, 2, and 3, respectively.

The *Adore-ng* Rootkit.   As the name indicates, this rootkit is a more advanced successor from the previous *adore* rootkit. Instead of directly manipulating the system call table, the *adore-ng* rootkit subverts the jump table of the virtual file system by replacing the directory listing handler routines with its own ones. Such replacement allows it to manipulate the information about the *root* file system as well as the */proc* pseudo-file system to achieve the file-hiding or process-hiding purposes. More specifically, the *readdir* function pointer (*ext3_dir_operations[6]*) in the root file system operations table is hooked for hiding attack files, while the similar function (*proc_root_operations[6]*) in the */proc* file system operations table is hijacked for hiding attack processes. The fact that the kernel hook *ext3_dir_operations[6]* is located in the loadable module space (*ext3.ko*) indicates that this rootkit is more stealthier and these types of kernel hooks are much more difficult to uncover than those kernel hooks at static memory locations (e.g., the system call table). Once again, our system successfully identified these stealth kernel hooks, confirming our observation in Section 1. Further, the comparisons between those hooks used by rootkits (Table 4) and the list of hooks from our system (Tables 1, 2, and 3) indicate that only a small subset of them have been used.

6   Discussion

Our system leverages the nature of persistent kernel rootkits to systematically discover those kernel hooks that can potentially be exploited for hiding purposes. However, as a rootkit may implant other kernel hooks for other non-hiding features as its payload, our current prototype is ineffective in identifying them. However, the prototype can be readily re-targeted to those non-hiding features and apply the same techniques to identify those kernel hooks. Also, our system by design only works for persistent kernel rootkits but could be potentially extended for other types of rootkits as well (e.g,. persistent user-level rootkits).

Our current prototype is developed to identify those kernel hooks related to the execution of a chosen security program, either an anti-rootkit software or a system utility program. However, with different programs as the input, it is likely that different running instances will result in different sets of kernel hooks. Fortunately, for the rootkit author, he faces the challenge in hiding itself from all security programs. As a result, our defense has a unique advantage in only analyzing a single instantiated execution path of a rootkit-detection program. In other words, a persistent kernel rootkit cannot evade its detection if the hijacked kernel hooks are not a part of the corresponding kernel-side execution path. There may exist some "in-the-wild" rootkits that take chances in only evading selected security software. However, in response, we can monitor only those kernel hooks related to an installed security software. As mentioned earlier, to hide from it, persistent kernel rootkits will hijack at least one of these kernel hooks.

Meanwhile, it may be argued that our results from monitoring a running instance of a security program could lead to false positives. However, the fact that these kernel hooks exist in the kernel-side execution path suggest that each one could be equally exploited for hooking purposes. From another perspective, we point out that the scale of our results is manageable since it contains tens, not hundreds, of kernel hooks.

Finally, we point out that our current prototype only considers those kernel objects or variables that may contain kernel hooks of interest to rootkits. However, there also exist other types of kernel data such as non-control data [9] (e.g., the *uid* field in the process control block data structure or the doubly-linked process list), which can be manipulated to contaminate kernel execution. Though they may not be used to implement a persistent kernel rootkit for control-flow modifications, how to extend the current system to effectively address them (e.g., by real-time enforcing kernel control flow integrity [10]) remains as an interesting topic for future work.

7   Related Work

Hook Identification.   The first area of related work is the identification of kernel hooks exploitable by rootkits for hiding purposes. Particularly, HookFinder [23] analyzes a given rootkit example and reports a list of kernel hooks that are being used by the malware. However, by design, it does not lead to the identification of other kernel hooks that are not being used but could still be potentially exploited for the same hiding purposes. From another perspective, SBCFI [14] performs static analysis of Linux kernel source code and aims to build a kernel control-flow graph that will be followed by a legitimate kernel at run-time. However, the graph is not explicitly associated with those kernel hooks for rootkit hiding purposes. Furthermore, the lack of run-time information could greatly limit its accuracy. In comparison, our system complements them with the unique capability of exhaustively deriving those kernel hooks for a given security program, which could be potentially hijacked by a persistent rootkit to hide from it.

Hook-based Rootkit Detection.   The second area of related work is the detection of rootkits based on the knowledge of those specific hooking points that may be used by rootkits. For example, existing anti-rootkit tools such as VICE [8], IceSword [16], System Virginity Verifier [17] examine known memory regions occupied by these specific hooking points to detect any illegitimate modification. Our system is designed with a unique focus in uncovering those specific kernel hooks. As a result, they can be naturally combined together to build an integrated rootkit-defense system.

Other Rootkit Defenses.   There also exist a number of recent efforts [12,13,15,20,21] [22] that defend against rootkits by detecting certain anomalous symptoms likely caused by rootkit infection. For example, The Strider GhostBuster system [21] and VMwatcher [12] apply the notion of cross-view detection to expose any discrepancy caused by stealth rootkits. CoPilot [15] as well as the follow-up work [13] identify rootkits by detecting possible violations in kernel code integrity or semantic constraints among multiple kernel objects. SecVisor [20] aims to prevent unauthorized kernel code from execution in the kernel space. Limbo [22] characterizes a number of run-time features that can best distinguish between legitimate and malicious kernel drivers and then utilizes them to prevent a malicious one from being loaded into the kernel. Our system is complementary to these systems by pinpointing specific kernel hooks that are likely to be chosen by stealth rootkits for manipulation.

8   Conclusion

To effectively counter persistent kernel rootkits, we have presented a systematic approach to uncover those kernel hooks that can be potentially hijacked by them. Our approach is based on the insight that those rootkits by their nature will tamper with the execution of deployed rootkit-detection software. By instrumenting and recording possible control-flow transfer instructions in the kernel-side execution paths related to the deployed security software, we can reliably derive all related kernel hooks. Our experience in building a prototype system as well as the experimental results with real-world rootkits demonstrate the effectiveness of the proposed approach.

Acknowledgments

The authors would like to thank the anonymous reviewers for their insightful comments that helped to improve the presentation of this paper. This work was supported in part by NSF Grants CNS-0716376, CNS-0524286, and CCF-0728771.

References

1. The adore Rootkit, `http://lwn.net/Articles/75990/`
2. The Hideme Rootkit,
   `http://www.sophos.com/security/analyses/`
   `viruses-and-spyware/trojhidemea.html`

3. The Strange Decline of Computer Worms,
   `http://www.theregister.co.uk/2005/03/17/f-secure_websec/print.html`
4. VMware, `http://www.vmware.com/`
5. Agrawal, H., Horgan, J.R.: Dynamic Program Slicing. In: Proceedings of ACM SIGPLAN 1990 Conference on Programming Language Design and Implementation (1990)
6. Bellard, F.: QEMU, a Fast and Portable Dynamic Translator. In: Proc. of USENIX Annual Technical Conference 2005 (FREENIX Track) (July 2005)
7. Butler, J.: R$\hat{2}$: The Exponential Growth of Rootkit Techniques,
   `http://www.blackhat.com/presentations/bh-usa-06/BH-US-06-Butler.pdf`
8. Butler, J.: VICE 2.0,
   `http://www.infosecinstitute.com/blog/README_VICE.txt`
9. Chen, S., Xu, J., Sezer, E.C., Gauriar, P., Iyer, R.: Non-Control-Data Attacks Are Realistic Threats. In: Proc. USENIX Security Symposium (August 2005)
10. Grizzard, J.B.: Towards Self-Healing Systems: Re-Establishing Trust in Compromised Systems. Ph.D. thesis, Georgia Institute of Technology (May 2006)
11. Jiang, X., Wang, X.: "Out-of-the-Box" Monitoring of VM-Based High-Interaction Honeypots. In: Kruegel, C., Lippmann, R., Clark, A. (eds.) RAID 2007. LNCS, vol. 4637, pp. 198–218. Springer, Heidelberg (2007)
12. Jiang, X., Wang, X., Xu, D.: "Out-of-the-Box" Semantic View Reconstruction. In: Proceedings of the 14th ACM Conference on Computer and Communications Security (CCS 2007) (October 2007)
13. Petroni, N., Fraser, T., Walters, A., Arbaugh, W.: An Architecture for Specification-Based Detection of Semantic Integrity Violations in Kernel Dynamic Data. In: Proc. of the 15th USENIX Security Symposium (August 2006)
14. Petroni, N., Hicks, M.: Automated Detection of Persistent Kernel Control-Flow Attacks. In: Proc. of ACM CCS 2007 (October 2007)
15. Petroni, N.L., Fraser, T., Molina, J., Arbaugh, W.A.: Copilot - a Coprocessor-based Kernel Runtime Integrity Monitor. In: Proc. of the 13th USENIX Security Symposium (August 2004)
16. PJF. IceSword, `http://www.antirootkit.com/software/IceSword.htm`, `http://pjf.blogcn.com/`
17. Rutkowska, J.: System Virginity Verifier,
   `http://invisiblethings.org/papers/hitb05_virginity_verifier.ppt`
18. Rutkowska, J.: Rootkits vs. Stealth by Design Malware,
   `http://invisiblethings.org/papers/rutkowska_bheurope2006.ppt`
19. sd.: Linux on-the-fly kernel patching without LKM. Phrack 11(58), article 7 of 15 (2001)
20. Seshadri, A., Luk, M., Qu, N., Perrig, A.: SecVisor: A Tiny Hypervisor to Guarantee Lifetime Kernel Code Integrity for Commodity OSes. In: Proc. of the ACM SOSP 2007 (October 2007)
21. Wang, Y., Beck, D., Vo, B., Roussev, R., Verbowski, C.: Detecting Stealth Software with Strider GhostBuster. In: Proc. of the 2005 International Conference on Dependable Systems and Networks (June 2005)
22. Wilhelm, J., Chiueh, T.-c.: A Forced Sampled Execution Approach to Kernel Rootkit Identification. In: Kruegel, C., Lippmann, R., Clark, A. (eds.) RAID 2007. LNCS, vol. 4637, pp. 219–235. Springer, Heidelberg (2007)
23. Yin, H., Liang, Z., Song, D.: HookFinder: Identifying and Understanding Malware Hooking Behaviors. In: Proc. of ISOC NDSS 2008 (February 2008)
24. Zhang, X., Gupta, R., Zhang, Y.: Precise Dynamic Slicing Algorithms. In: Proc. of the IEEE/ACM International Conference on Software Engineering (May 2003)

Tamper-Resistant, Application-Aware Blocking of Malicious Network Connections

Abhinav Srivastava and Jonathon Giffin

School of Computer Science, Georgia Institute of Technology
{abhinav,giffin}@cc.gatech.edu

Abstract. Application-level firewalls block traffic based on the process that is sending or receiving the network flow. They help detect bots, worms, and backdoors that send or receive malicious packets without the knowledge of users. Recent attacks show that these firewalls can be disabled by knowledgeable attackers. To counter this threat, we develop VMwall, a fine-grained tamper-resistant process-oriented firewall. VMwall's design blends the process knowledge of application-level firewalls with the isolation of traditional stand-alone firewalls. VMwall uses the Xen hypervisor to provide protection from malware, and it correlates TCP or UDP traffic with process information using virtual machine introspection. Experiments show that VMwall successfully blocks numerous real attacks—bots, worms, and backdoors—against a Linux system while allowing all legitimate network flows. VMwall is performant, imposing only a 0–1 millisecond delay on TCP connection establishment, less than a millisecond delay on UDP connections, and a 1–7% slowdown on network-bound applications. Our attack analysis argues that with the use of appropriate external protection of guest kernels, VMwall's introspection remains robust and helps identify malicious traffic.

Keywords: Firewall, virtual machine introspection, attack prevention.

1 Introduction

Application-level firewalls are an important component of a computer system's layered defenses. They filter inbound and outbound network packets based on an access policy that includes lists of processes allowed to make network connections. This fine-grained filtering is possible because application-level firewalls have a complete view of the system on which they execute. In contrast, network- or host-level firewalls provide coarse-grained filtering using ports and IP addresses. Application-level firewalls help detect and block malicious processes, such as bots, worms, backdoors, adware, and spyware, that try to send or receive network flows in violation of the fine-grained policies. To be successful, these firewalls must be fast, mediate all network traffic, and accurately identify executing processes.

The conventional design of application-level firewalls has a deficiency that may prevent filtering of malicious traffic. The architectures pass packet information

R. Lippmann, E. Kirda, and A. Trachtenberg (Eds.): RAID 2008, LNCS 5230, pp. 39–58, 2008.

from a kernel-level network tap up to a user-level firewall process that executes alongside malicious software. The firewall is both performant and able to identify the processes attached to a network flow, but it is exposed to direct attack by any malicious software aware of the firewall. Baliga et al. [1] demonstrated the ease of such attacks by manipulating the netfilter framework inside the Linux kernel to remove the hooks to packet filtering functions. Similarly, attackers can disable the Windows Firewall by halting particular services normally running on the system. Once the firewall fails, then all network traffic will be unmediated and the malware can send and receive data at will.

An alternative design isolates firewalls from vulnerable systems to gain protection from direct attack. Virtual machines allow construction of firewall appliances that execute outside of operating systems under attack. Such firewalls dispense with application-level knowledge and filter inbound and outbound packets using coarse-grained rules over IP addresses and port numbers. Attacks can easily evade these firewalls by using allowed ports directly or via tunneling.

This paper leverages the benefits of both application-level firewalls and virtual machine isolation to develop tamper-resistant application-oriented firewalls. Such a firewall needs good visibility of the system so that it can correlate network flows with processes, but it also needs strong isolation from any user-level or kernel-level malware that may be present. We architect an application-level firewall resistant to direct attack from malicious software on the system. Our design isolates the application-level firewall in a trusted virtual machine (VM) and relies on the hypervisor to limit the attack surface between any untrusted VM running malware and the trusted VM. Our firewall, executing in the trusted VM, becomes an application-level firewall by using virtual machine introspection (VMI) [10] to identify the process in another VM that is connected to a suspicious network flow.

Our prototype implementation, VMwall, uses the Xen [2] hypervisor to remain isolated from malicious software. VMwall executes entirely within Xen's trusted virtual machine dom0; it operates with both paravirtualized and fully virtualized domains. A dom0 kernel component intercepts network connections to and from untrusted virtual machines. A user-space process performs introspection to correlate each flow to a sending or receiving process, and it then uses a predefined security policy to decide whether the connection should be allowed or blocked. Policies are straightforward whitelists of known software in the untrusted VM allowed to communicate over the network. To correlate network flows with processes, VMwall's user-space component maps the untrusted operating system's kernel memory into its own address space and uses programmed knowledge of kernel data structures to extract the identity of the process attached to the flow.

VMwall is effective at identifying and blocking malicious network connections without imposing significant performance degradation upon network traffic. Using a Linux system and a collection of known attacks that either send or receive network traffic, we show that VMwall identifies all malicious connections immediately when the first packet is sent or received. In particular, VMwall blocked 100% of the malicious connections when tested against bots, worms, and backdoors, and it correctly allowed all legitimate network traffic. In our design, VMwall only performs introspection for the first packet of a new connection, so network performance remains high. Our tool adds only about 0–1 milliseconds of overhead to the first packet of a session. This is a latency cost to network connection creation that will not impact the subsequent data transfer of legitimate connections.

VMwall looks into the state of the untrusted operating system's memory to find the process bound to a network connection. The system monitors network flows, and it is not an intrusion detection system designed to detect an attack against the OS. Hence, an attacker may try to evade VMwall either by hijacking a process or by subverting the inspected kernel data structures. In Sect. 6.4, we study this problem, provide an in-depth security analysis of VMwall, and suggest appropriate measures to thwart these attacks.

We believe that our tamper-resistant application-oriented firewall represents an appropriate use of virtualization technology for improved system security. We feel that our paper provides the following contributions:

- Correlation between network flows and processes from outside the virtual machine (Sect. 4).
- VMwall, an implementation of a tamper-resistant application-oriented firewall (Sect. 5).
- Evidence that application-aware firewalls outside the untrusted virtual machine can block malicious network connections successfully while maintaining network performance (Sect. 6).

2   Related Work

Prior research has contributed to the development of conventional host-based firewalls. Mogul et al. [21] developed a kernel-resident packet filter for UNIX that gave user processes flexibility in selecting legitimate packets. Venema [29] designed a utility to monitor and control incoming network traffic. These traditional firewalls performed filtering based on restrictions inherent in network topology and assumed that all parties inside the network were trusted. As part of the security architecture of the computer system, they resided in kernel-space and user-space, and hence were vulnerable to direct attack by malicious software.

Administration of firewalls can be cumbersome, and distributed firewalls have been proposed to ease the burden [3, 15]. In distributed firewalls, an administrator manages security policies centrally but pushes enforcement of these policies out to the individual hosts. Although we have not implemented support for distributed management, we expect VMwall to easily fit into this scheme. VMwall policies dictate which processes can legitimately make use of network resources. In a managed environment where administrators are knowledgeable of the software running on the machines in the local network, preparing and distributing VMwall policies from a central location may be an appealing solution.

The recent support for virtual machines by commodity hardware has driven development of new security services deployed with the assistance of VMs [27, 9, 30]. Garfinkel et al. [11] showed the feasibility of implementing distributed network-level firewalls using virtual machines. In another work [10], they proposed an intrusion detection system design using virtual machine introspection of an untrusted VM. VMwall applies virtual machine introspection to a different problem, using it to correlate network flows with the local processes bound to those flows.

Other research used virtual machines for malware detection. Borders et al. [4] designed a system, Siren, that detected malware running within a virtual machine. Yin et al. [33] proposed a system to detect and analyze privacy-breaching malware using taint analysis. Jiang et al. [17] presented an out-of-the-box VMM-based malware detection system. Their proposed technique constructed the internal semantic views of a VM from an external vantage point. In another work [16], they proposed a monitoring tool that observes a virtual machine based honeypot's internal state from outside the honeypot. As a pleasant side-effect of malicious network flow detection and process correlation, VMwall can often identify processes in the untrusted system that comprise portions of an attack.

Previous research has developed protection strategies for different types of hardware-level resources in the virtualized environment. Xu et al. [32] proposed a VMM-based usage control model to protect the integrity of kernel memory. Ta-Min et al. [28] proposed a hypervisor based system that allowed applications to partition their system call interface into trusted and untrusted components. VMwall, in contrast, protects network resources from attack by malware that runs inside the untrusted virtual machine by blocking the illegitimate network connections attempts.

These previous hypervisor-based security applications generally take either a network-centric or host-centric view. Our work tries to correlate activity at both levels. VMwall monitors network connections but additionally peers into the state of the running, untrusted operating system to make its judgments about each connection's validity. Moreover, VMwall easily scales to collections of virtual machines on a single physical host. A single instance of VMwall can act as an application-level firewall for an entire network of VMs.

3   Overview

We begin with preliminaries. Section 3.1 explains our threat model, which assumes that attackers have the ability to execute the real-world attacks infecting widespread computer systems today. Section 3.2 provides a brief overview of Xen-based virtual machine architectures and methods allowing inspection of a running VM's state.

3.1   Threat Model

We assume that attackers have abilities commonly displayed by real-world attacks against commodity computer systems. Attackers can gain *superuser priv-*

ilege from remote. Attackers are external and have no physical access to the attacked computers, but they may install malicious software on a victim system by exploiting a software vulnerability in an application or operating system or by enticing unsuspecting users to install the malware themselves. The software exploit or the user often executes with full system privileges, so the malware may perform administrative actions such as kernel module or driver installation. Hence, malicious code may execute at both user and kernel levels. For ease of explanation, we initially describe VMwall's architecture in Sect. 4 under the assumption that kernel data structure integrity is maintained. This assumption is not valid in our threat model, and Sect. 6.4 revisits this point to describe technical solutions ensuring that the assumption holds.

The installed malware may periodically make or receive network connections. Many examples exist. *Bots* make network connections to a command and control channel to advertise their presence and receive instruction, and they send bulk network traffic such as denial-of-service packets and email spam. *Spyware* programs collect information, such as keystrokes and mouse clicks, and then transmit the confidential data across a network to the attacker. *Worms* may generate network connections to scan the network in search of additional victims suitable for infection. *Backdoors* open holes in machines by listening for incoming connections from the attacker. One common feature of these different classes of attacks is their interest in the network.

In a typical system, malware can directly affect an application-level firewall's execution. The architecture of these malware instances frequently combines a user-level application performing network activity with a kernel-level module that hides the application from the view of host-level security software. The malicious application, likely running with full system privileges, may halt the execution of the firewall. Similarly, the malicious kernel component may alter the hooks used by an in-kernel module supporting the user-level firewall so that the firewall is simply never invoked as data passes to and from the network. Conventional application-level firewalls fail under these direct attacks. Our goal is to develop a system that withstands direct attack from malware at the application layer or the kernel layer.

Our system has requirements for correct execution. As with all requirements, an attacker who is able to violate any requirement is likely able to escape detection. Our two requirements of note center on basic expectations for the in-memory data structures used by the kernel that may be infected by an attack.

First, we expect to be able to find the head of linked data structures, often by extracting a kernel symbol value at boot time. An attacker could conceivably cause our firewall to inspect the incorrect kernel information by replicating the data structure elsewhere in kernel memory and by altering all code references to the original structure to instead refer to the new structure. Our firewall would then analyze stale data. It is not immediately clear that such an attack is plausible; moreover, our tool could periodically verify that code references to the data match the symbol value extracted at boot.

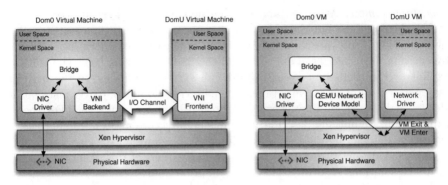

Paravirtualized domain   Fully virtualized domain

Fig. 1. Xen networking architecture

Second, we expect that attacks do not alter the ordering or length of fields in aggregate data structures. Our firewall is preprogrammed with type information about kernel structures, and an attack that alters the structure types would cause our system to read incorrect information from kernel memory. Successfully executing this attack without kernel recompilation appears to be complex, as all kernel code that accesses structure fields would need to be altered to use the attacker's structure layout. As a result, we believe that relying upon known structure definitions is not a limiting factor to our design.

3.2 Virtual Machine Introspection

Our design makes use of virtual machine technology to provide isolation between malicious code and our security software. We use Xen [2], an open source hypervisor that runs directly on the physical hardware of a computer. The virtual machines running atop Xen are of two types: unprivileged domains, called domU or guest domains, and a single fully-privileged domain, called dom0. We run normal, possibly vulnerable software in domU and deploy our application-level firewall in the isolated dom0.

Xen virtualizes the network input and output of the system. Dom0 is the device driver domain that runs the native network interface card driver software. Unprivileged virtual machines cannot directly access the physical network card, so Xen provides them with a virtualized network interface (VNI). The driver domain receives all the incoming and outgoing packets for all domU VMs executing on the physical system. Dom0 provides an Ethernet bridge connecting the physical network card to all virtual network devices provided by Xen to the domU VMs. (Xen offers other networking modes, such as network address translation, that are not used in our work and will not be considered further.) Dom0 uses its virtual bridge to multiplex and demultiplex packets between the physical network interface and éach unprivileged virtual machine's VNI. Figure 1 shows the Xen networking architecture when the virtual machines' network interfaces are connected through a virtual Ethernet bridge. The guest VMs send and receive packets via either an I/O channel to dom0 or emulated virtual devices.

The strong isolation provided by a hypervisor between dom0 and the guest domains complicates the ability to correlate network flows with software executing in a guest domain. Yet, dom0 has complete access to the entire state of the guest operating systems running in untrusted virtual machines. *Virtual machine introspection* (VMI) [10] is a technique by which dom0 can determine execution properties of guest VMs by monitoring their runtime state, generally through direct memory inspection. VMI allows security software to remain protected from direct attack by malicious software executing in a guest VM while still able to observe critical system state.

Xen offers low-level APIs to allow dom0 to map arbitrary memory pages of domU as shared memory. XenAccess [31] is a dom0 userspace introspection library developed for Xen that builds onto the low-level functionality provided by Xen. VMwall uses XenAccess APIs to map raw memory pages of domU's kernel inside dom0. It then builds higher-level memory abstractions, such as aggregate structures and linked data types, from the contents of raw memory pages by using the known coding semantics of the guest operating system's kernel. Our application-level firewall inspects these meaningful, higher-level abstractions to determine how applications executing in the guest VM use network resources.

4   Tamper Resistant Architecture of VMwall

VMwall is our application-level firewall designed to resist the direct attacks possible in our threat model. The architecture of VMwall is driven by the following three goals:

- **Tamper Resistance:** VMwall should continue to function reliably and verify all network connections even if an attacker gains entry into the monitored system. In particular, the design should not rely on components installed in the monitored host as processes or kernel modules, as these have been points of direct attack in previous application-level firewalls.
- **Independence:** VMwall should work without any cooperation from the monitored system. In fact, the system may not be aware of the presence of the firewall.
- **Lightweight Verification:** Our intent is to use VMwall for online verification of network connections to real systems. The design should allow for efficient monitoring of network traffic and correlation to applications sending and receiving that traffic.

Our firewall design satisfies these goals by leveraging virtual machine isolation and virtual machine introspection. Its entire software runs within the privileged dom0 VM, and it hooks into Xen's virtual network interface to collect and filter all guest domains' network packets. Since the hypervisor provides strong isolation among the virtual machines, this design achieves the first goal of tamper-resistance.

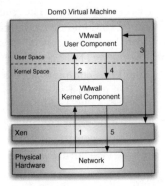

Fig. 2. VMwall's high-level architecture. (1) Packets inbound to and outbound from a guest domain are processed by dom0. (2) The VMwall kernel component intercepts the packets and passes them to a user-space component for analysis. (3) The user-space component uses virtual machine introspection to identify software in a guest domain processing the data. (4) The user-space component instructs the kernel component to either allow or block the connection. (5) Packets from allowed connections will be placed on the network.

In order to provide application-level firewalling, VMwall must identify the process that is sending or receiving packets inside domU. VMwall correlates packet and process information by directly inspecting the domU virtual machine's memory via virtual machine introspection. It looks into the kernel's memory and traverses the data structures to map process and network information. This achieves our second design goal of independence, as there are no components of VMwall inside domU. Our introspection procedure rapidly analyzes the kernel's data structures, satisfying the third goal of lightweight verification.

The high-level design of VMwall has two components: a kernel module and user agent, both in dom0 (Fig. 2). The VMwall kernel component enforces a per-packet policy given by the user agent and either allows or drops each packet. The user agent determines policy by performing introspection to extract information about processes executing in guest VMs and evaluating the legitimacy of those processes. Sections 4.1 and 4.2 present detailed information about the two components.

4.1 Kernel Component

VMwall's kernel component is a module loaded inside the dom0 Linux kernel. It intercepts all network packets to or from untrusted virtual machines and uses security policies to decide whether each packet should be allowed or dropped. Interception occurs by hooking into Xen's network bridge between the physical interface card and virtual network interface. When the kernel component intercepts a packet, it checks a rule table to see if a firewall rule already exists for the packet, as determined by the local endpoint IP address and port. If so, it takes the allow or block action specified in the rule. If there is no rule, then it

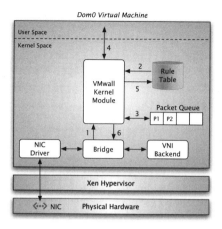

Fig. 3. VMwall's kernel module architecture. (1) Packets inbound to and outbound from a guest domain are intercepted and passed to the kernel module. (2) The module receives each packet and looks into its rule table to find the rule for the packet. (3) The kernel module queues the packet if there is no rule present. (4) VMwall sends an introspection request to the user agent and, after the agent completes, receives the dynamically generated rule for the packet. (5) The kernel module adds the rule into its rule table to process future packets from the same connection. (6) The kernel module decides based on the action of the rule either to accept the packet by reinjecting it into the network or to drop it from the queue.

invokes the VMwall user agent to analyze the packet and create a rule. The user agent performs introspection, generates a rule for the packet, and sends this rule back to the kernel module. The kernel module adds this new rule to its policy table and processes the packet. Further packets from the same connection are processed using the rule present in the kernel component without invoking the user agent and without performing introspection.

As kernel code, the kernel component cannot block and must take action on a packet before the user agent completes introspection. VMwall solves this problem for packets of unknown legitimacy by queuing the packets while waiting for the user agent's reply. When the user agent sends a reply, the module adds a rule for the connection. If the rule's action is to block the connection, then it drops all the packets that are queued. Otherwise, it re-injects all the packets into the network.

Figure 3 presents the kernel module's complete architecture. It illustrates the steps involved in processing the packet inside the kernel. It shows the queue architecture, where packets are stored inside the kernel during introspection.

4.2   User Agent

The VMwall user agent uses virtual machine introspection to correlate network packets and processes. It receives introspection requests from the kernel component containing network information such as source port, source IP address,

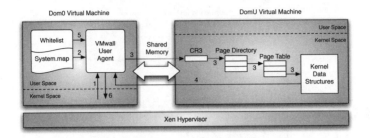

Fig. 4. VMwall's user agent architecture. (1) The VMwall user agent receives the introspection request. (2) The user agent reads the System.map file to extract the kernel virtual addresses corresponding to known kernel symbols. (3) The user agent uses Xen to map the domU kernel memory pages containing process and network data structures. (4) VMwall traverses the data structures to correlate network and process activity. (5) The agent searches for the recovered process name in the whitelist. (6) The user agent sends a filtering rule for the connection to the VMwall kernel module.

destination port, destination IP address, and protocol. It first uses the packet's source (or destination) IP address to identify the VM that is sending (or receiving) the packet. When it finds the VM, it then tries to find the process that is bound to the source (or destination) port.

VMwall's user agent maps a network port to the domU process that is bound to the port, shown in Fig. 4. As needed, it maps domU kernel data structures into dom0 memory. Process and network information is likely not available in a single data structure but instead is scattered over many data structures. VMwall works in steps by first identifying the domU kernel data structures that store IP address and port information. Then, VMwall identifies the process handling this network connection by iterating over the list of running processes and checking each process to see if it is bound to the port. When it finds the process bound to the port, it extracts the process' identifier, its name, and the full path to its executable. If the user agent does not find any process bound to the port, it considers this to be an anomaly and will block the network connection.

VMwall uses information about the process to create a firewall rule enforceable by the kernel component. The user agent maintains a whitelist of processes that are allowed to make network connections. When the user agent extracts the name of a process corresponding to the network packet, it searches the whitelist for the same name. VMwall allows the connection if it finds a match and blocks the connection otherwise. It then generates a rule for this connection that it passes to the VMwall kernel component. This rule contains the network connection information and either an allow or block action. The kernel component then uses this rule to filter subsequent packets in this attempted connection.

5   Implementation

We have implemented a prototype of VMwall using the Xen hypervisor and a Linux guest operating system. VMwall supports both paravirtualized and fully-virtualized (HVM) Linux guest operating systems. Its implementation consists of two parts corresponding to the two pieces described in the previous section: the kernel module and the user agent. The following sections describe specific details affecting implementation of the two architectural components.

5.1 Extending Ebtables

Our kernel module uses a modified ebtables packet filter to intercept all packets sent to or from a guest domain. Ebtables [7] is an open source utility that filters packets at an Ethernet bridge. VMwall supplements the existing coarse-grained firewall provided by ebtables. Whenever ebtables accepts packets based on its coarse-grained rules, we hook the operation and invoke the VMwall kernel module for our additional application-level checks. We modified ebtables to implement this hook, which passes a reference to the packet to VMwall.

Ebtables does not provide the ability to queue packets. Were it present, queuing would enable filters present inside the kernel to store packets for future processing and reinjection back into the network. To allow the VMwall kernel module to queue packets currently under inspection by the user agent, we altered ebtables to incorporate packet queuing and packet reinjection features.

5.2 Accessing DomU Kernel Memory

VMwall uses the XenAccess introspection library [31] to accesses domU kernel memory from dom0. It maps domU memory pages containing kernel data structures into the virtual memory space of the user agent executing in the trusted VM. XenAccess provides APIs that map domU kernel memory pages identified either by explicit kernel virtual addresses or by exported kernel symbols. In Linux, the exported symbols are stored in the file named System.map. VMwall uses certain domU data structures that are exported by the kernel and hence mapped with the help of kernel symbols. Other data structures reachable by pointers from the known structures are mapped using kernel virtual addresses. The domU virtual machine presented in Fig. 4 shows the internal mechanism involved to map the memory page that contains the desired kernel data structure.

5.3 Parsing Kernel Data Structures

To identify processes using the network, VMwall must be able to parse high-level kernel data structures from the raw memory pages provided by XenAccess. Extracting kernel data structures from the mapped memory pages is a non-trivial task. For example, Linux maintains a doubly-linked list that stores the kernel's private data for all running processes. The head pointer of this list is stored in the exported kernel symbol init_task. If we want to extract the list of processes running inside domU, we can map the memory page of domU that contains the init_task symbol. However, VMwall must traverse the complete linked list and hence requires the offset to the next member in the process structure. We extract this information offline directly from the kernel source code and use these values

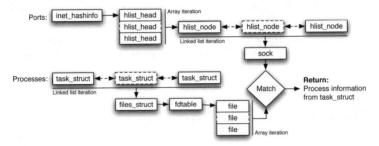

Fig. 5. DomU Linux kernel data structures traversed by the VMwall user agent during correlation of the process and TCP packet information

in the user agent. This source code inspection is not the optimal way to identify offsets because the offset values often change with the kernel versions. However, there are other automatic ways to extract this information from the kernel binary if it was compiled with a debug option [18].

This provides VMwall with sufficient information to traverse kernel data structures. VMwall uses known field offsets to extract the virtual addresses of pointer field members from the mapped memory pages. It then maps domU memory pages by specifying the extracted virtual addresses. This process is performed recursively until VMwall traverses the data structures necessary to extract the process name corresponding to the source or destination port of a network communication. Figure 5 shows the list of the kernel data structures traversed by the user agent to correlate a TCP packet and process information. First, it tries to obtain a reference to the socket bound to the port number specified in the packet. After acquiring this reference, it iterates over the list of processes to find the process owning the socket.

5.4   Policy Design and Rules

VMwall identifies legitimate connections via a whitelist-based policy listing processes allowed to send or receive data. Each process that wants to communicate over the network must be specified in the whitelist *a priori*. This whitelist resides inside dom0 and can only be updated by administrators in a manner similar to traditional application-level firewalls. The whitelist based design of VMwall introduces some usability issues because all applications that should be allowed to make network connections must be specified in the list. This limitation is not specific to VMwall and is inherent to the whitelist based products and solutions [6, 12].

VMwall's kernel module maintains its own rule table containing rules that are dynamically generated by the user agent after performing introspection. A rule contains source and destination port and IP address information, an action, and a timeout value used by the kernel module to expire and purge old rules for UDP connections. In the case of TCP connections, the kernel module purges TCP rules automatically whenever it processes a packet with the TCP `fin` or rst flag set. In an abnormal termination of a TCP connection, VMwall uses the timeout mechanism to purge the rules.

6   Evaluation

The basic requirement of an application-level firewall is to block connections to or from malicious software and allow connections to or from benign applications. We evaluated the ability of VMwall to filter out packets made by several different classes of attacks while allowing packets from known processes to pass unimpeded. We tested VMwall against Linux-based backdoors, worms, and bots that attempt to use the network for malicious activity. Section 6.1 tests VMwall against attacks that receive inbound connections from attackers or connect out to remote systems. Section 6.2 tests legitimate software in the presence of VMwall. We measure VMwall's performance impact in Sect. 6.3, and lastly analyze its robustness to a knowledgeable attacker in Sect. 6.4.

6.1   Illegitimate Connections

We first tested attacks that receive inbound connections from remote attackers. These attacks are rootkits that install backdoor programs. The backdoors run as user processes, listen for connections on a port known to the attacker, and receive and execute requests sent by the attacker. We used the following backdoors:

- **Blackhole** runs a TCP server on port 12345 [22].
- **Gummo** runs a TCP server at port 31337 [22].
- **Bdoor** runs a backdoor daemon on port 8080 [22].
- **OvasOn** runs a TCP server on port 29369 [22].
- **Cheetah** runs a TCP server at the attacker's specified port number [22].

Once installed on a vulnerable system, attacks such as worms and bots may attempt to make outbound connections without prompting from a remote attacker. We tested VMwall with the following pieces of malware that generate outbound traffic:

- **Apache-ssl** is a variant of the Slapper worm that self-propagates by opening TCP connections for port scanning [23].
- **Apache-linux** is a worm that exploits vulnerable Apache servers and spawns a shell on port 30464 [23].
- **BackDoor-Rev.b** is a tool that is be used by a worm to make network connections to arbitrary Internet addresses and ports [20].
- **Q8** is an IRC-based bot that opens TCP connections to contact an IRC server to receive commands from the botmaster [14].
- **Kaiten** is a bot that opens TCP connections to contact an IRC server [24].
- **Coromputer Dunno** is an IRC-based bot providing basic functionalities such as port scanning [13].

Table 1. Results of executing legitimate software in the presence of VMwall. "Allowed" indicates that the network connections to or from the processes were passed as though a firewall was not present.

Name	Connection Type	Result
rcp	Outbound	Allowed
rsh	Outbound	Allowed
yum	Outbound	Allowed
rlogin	Outbound	Allowed
ssh	Outbound	Allowed
scp	Outbound	Allowed
wget	Outbound	Allowed
tcp client	Outbound	Allowed
thttpd	Inbound	Allowed
tcp server	Inbound	Allowed
sshd	Inbound	Allowed

VMwall successfully blocked all illegitimate connections attempted by malware instances. In all cases, both sending and receiving, VMwall intercepted the first SYN packet of each connection and passed it to the userspace component. Since these malicious processes were not in the whitelist, the VMwall user space component informed the VMwall kernel component to block these malicious connections. As we used VMwall in packet queuing mode, no malicious packets were ever passed through VMwall.

6.2   Legitimate Connections

We also evaluated VMwall's ability to allow legitimate connections made by processes running inside domU. We selected a few network applications and added their name to VMwall's whitelist. We then ran these applications inside domU. Table 1 shows the list of processes that we tested, the type of connections used by the processes, and the effect of VMwall upon those connections. To be correct, all connections should be allowed.

VMwall allowed all connections made by these applications. The yum application, a package manager for Fedora Core Linux, had runtime behavior of interest. In our test, we updated domU with the yum update command. During the package update, yum created many child processes with the same name yum and these child processes made network connections. VMwall successfully validated all the connections via introspection and allowed their network connections.

6.3   Performance Evaluation

A firewall verifying all packets traversing a network may impact the performance of applications relying on timely delivery of those packets. We investigated the performance impact of VMwall as perceived by network applications running inside the untrusted virtual machine. We performed experiments both with and

Table 2. Introspection time (μs) taken by VMwall to perform correlation of network flow with the process executing inside domU

Configuration	TCP Introspection Time	UDP Introspection Time
Inbound Connection to domU	251	438
Outbound Connection from domU	1080	445

without VMwall running inside dom0. All experiments were conducted on a machine with an Intel Core 2 Duo T7500 processor at 2.20 GHz with 2 GB RAM. Both dom0 and domU virtual machines ran 32 bit Fedora Core 5 Linux. DomU had 512 MB of physical memory, and dom0 had the remaining 1.5 GB. The versions of Xen and XenAccess were 3.0.4 and 0.3, respectively. We performed our experiments using both TCP and UDP connections. All reported results show the median time taken from five measurements. We measured microbenchmarks with the Linux `gettimeofday` system call and longer executions with the `time` command-line utility.

VMwall's performance depends on the introspection time taken by the user component. Since network packets are queued inside the kernel during introspection, the introspection time is critical for the performance of the complete system. We measured the introspection time both for incoming and outgoing connections to and from domU. Table 2 shows the results of experiments measuring introspection time.

It is evident that the introspection time for incoming TCP connections is very small. Strangely, the introspection time for outgoing TCP connections is notably higher. The reason for this difference lies in the way that the Linux kernel stores information for TCP connections. It maintains TCP connection information for listening and established connections in two different tables. TCP sockets in a listening state reside in a table of size 32, whereas the established sockets are stored in a table of size 65536. Since the newly established TCP sockets can be placed at any index inside the table, the introspection routine that iterates on this table from dom0 must search half of the table on average.

We also measured the introspection time for UDP data streams. Table 2 shows the result for UDP inbound and outbound packets. In this case, the introspection time for inbound and outbound data varies little. The Linux kernel keeps the information for UDP streams in a single table of size 128, which is why the introspection time is similar in both cases.

To measure VMwall's performance overhead on network applications that run inside domU, we performed experiments with two different metrics for both inbound and outbound connections. In the first experiment, we measured VMwall's impact on network I/O by transferring a 175 MB video file over the virtual network via `wget`. Our second experiment measured the time necessary to establish a TCP connection or transfer UDP data round-trip as perceived by software in domU.

We first transferred the video file from dom0 to domU and back again with VMwall running inside dom0. Table 3 shows the result of our experiments. The

Table 3. Time (seconds) to transfer a 175 MB file between dom0 and domU, with and without VMwall

Direction	Without VMwall	With VMwall	Overhead
File Transfer from Dom0 to DomU	1.105	1.179	7%
File Transfer from DomU to Dom0	1.133	1.140	1%

Table 4. Single TCP connection setup time (μs) measured both with and without VMwall inside dom0

Direction	Without VMwall	With VMwall	Overhead
Connection from Dom0 to DomU	197	465	268
Connection from DomU to Dom0	143	1266	1123

median overhead imposed by VMwall is less than 7% when transferring from dom0 to domU, and less than 1% when executing the reverse transfer.

Our second metric evaluated the impact of VMwall upon connection or data stream setup time as perceived by applications executing in domU. For processes using TCP, we measured both the inbound and outbound TCP connection setup time. For software using UDP, we measured the time to transfer a small block of data to a process in the other domain and to have the block echoed back.

We created a simple TCP client-server program to measure TCP connection times. The client program measured the time required to connect to the server, shown in Table 4. Inbound connections completed quickly, exhibiting median overhead of only 268 μs. Outbound connections setup from domU to dom0 had a greater median overhead of 1123 μs, due directly to the fact that the introspection time for outbound connections is also high. Though VMwall's connection setup overhead may look high as a percentage, the actual overhead remains slight. Moreover, the introspection cost occurring at connection setup is a one-time cost that gets amortized across the duration of the connection.

We lastly measured the time required to transmit a small block of data and receive an echo reply to evaluate UDP stream setup cost. We wrote a simple UDP echo client and server and measured the round-trip time required for the echo reply. Note that only the first UDP packet required introspection; the echo reply was rapidly handled by a rule in the VMwall kernel module created when processing the first packet. We again have both inbound and outbound measurements, shown in Table 5. The cost of VMwall is small, incurring slowdowns of 381 μs and 577 μs, respectively.

VMwall currently partially optimizes its performance, and additional improvements are clearly possible. VMwall performs introspection once per connection so that further packets from the same connection are allowed or blocked based on the in-kernel rule table. VMwall's performance could be improved in future work by introducing a caching mechanism to the introspection operation. The VMwall introspection routine traverses the guest OS data structures to perform correlation. In order to traverse a data structure, the memory page that contains the data structure needs to be mapped, which is a costly operation. One possi-

Table 5. Single UDP echo-reply stream setup time (μs) with and without VMwall. In an inbound-initiated echo, dom0 sent data to domU and domU echoed the data back to dom0. An outbound-initiated echo is the reverse.

Direction	Without VMwall	With VMwall	Overhead
Inbound Initiated	434	815	381
Outbound Initiated	271	848	577

ble improvement would be to support caching mechanisms inside VMwall's user agent to cache frequently used memory pages to avoid costly memory mapping operations each time.

6.4   Security Analysis

VMwall relies on particular data structures maintained by the domU kernel. An attacker who fully controls domU could violate the integrity of these data structures in an attempt to bypass VMwall's introspection. To counter such attacks, we rely on previous work in kernel integrity protection. Petroni et al. [26] proposed a framework for detecting attacks against dynamic kernel data structures such as task_struct. Their monitoring system executed outside the monitored kernel and detected any semantic integrity violation against the kernel's dynamic data. The system protected the integrity of the data structures with an external monitor that enforced high-level integrity policies. In another work, Loscocco et al. [19] introduced a system that used virtualization technology to monitor a Linux kernel's operational integrity. These types of techniques ensure that the kernel data structures read by VMwall remain valid.

Attackers can also try to cloak their malware by appearing to be whitelisted software. An attacker can guess processes that are in VMwall's whitelist by observing the incoming and outgoing traffic from the host and determining themselves what processes legally communicate over the network. They can then rename their malicious binary to the name of a process in the whitelist. VMwall counters this problem by extracting the full path to the process on the guest machine. Attackers could then replace the complete program binary with a trojaned version to evade the full path verification. VMwall itself has no defenses against this attack, but previous research has already addressed this problem with disk monitoring utilities that protect critical files [8, 25].

An attacker could hijack a process by exploiting a vulnerability, and they could then change its in-memory image. To address this problem, VMwall userspace process can perform checksumming of the in-memory image of the process through introspection and compare it with previously stored hash value. However, this process is time consuming and may affect the connection setup time for an application.

An attacker could also hijack a connection after it has been established and verified by VMwall as legitimate. They could take control of the process bound to the port via a software exploit, or they could use a malicious kernel module to alter packet data before sending it to the virtual network interface. VMwall can counter certain instances of connection hijacking by timing out entries in its kernel rule table periodically. Subtle hijacking may require deep packet inspection within VMwall.

VMwall's kernel module internally maintains a small buffer to keep a copy of a packet while performing introspection. An attacker may try to launch a denial of service (DoS) attack, such as a SYN flood [5], against VMwall by saturating its internal buffer. VMwall remains robust to such attempted attacks because its buffer is independent of connection status. As soon as VMwall resolves the process name bound to a connection, it removes the packet from the buffer and does not wait for a TCP handshake to complete.

7 Conclusions and Future Work

We set out to design an application-oriented firewall resistant to the direct attacks that bring down these security utilities today. Our system, VMwall, remains protected from attack by leveraging virtual machine isolation. Although it is a distinct virtual machine, it can recover process-level information of the vulnerable system by using virtual machine introspection to correlate network flows with processes bound to those flows. We have shown the efficacy of VMwall by blocking backdoor, bot, and worm traffic emanating from the monitored system. Our malicious connection detection operates with reasonable overheads upon system performance.

Our current implementation operates for guest Linux kernels. VMwall could be made to work with Microsoft Windows operating systems if it can be programmed with knowledge of the data structures used by the Windows kernel. Since VMwall depends on the guest operating system's data structures to perform network and process correlation, it currently cannot be used for Windows-based guest systems. Recently, XenAccess started providing the ability to map Windows kernel memory into dom0 in the same way as done for Linux. If we have a means to identify and map Windows kernel data structures, then network and process correlation becomes possible.

Acknowledgment of Support and Disclaimer. This material is based upon work supported by the Defense Advanced Research Projects Agency and the United States Air Force under contract number FA8750-06-C-0182. Any opinions, findings and conclusions or recommendations expressed in this material are those of the author(s) and do not necessarily reflect the views of the Defense Advanced Research Projects Agency and the United States Air Force.

We thank the anonymous reviewers for their comments that improved the quality of the paper. We thank Steve Dawson of SRI International for his assistance with this project. Portions of this work were performed while Abhinav Srivastava was at SRI International.

References

[1] Baliga, A., Kamat, P., Iftode, L.: Lurking in the shadows: Identifying systemic threats to kernel data. In: IEEE Symposium on Security and Privacy, Oakland, CA (May 2007)

[2] Barham, P., Dragovic, B., Fraser, K., Hand, S., Harris, T., Ho, A., Neugebauer, R., Pratt, I., Warfield, A.: Xen and the art of virtualization. In: 19th ACM Symposium on Operating Systems Principles (SOSP), Bolton Landing, NY (October 2003)

[3] Bellovin, S.: Distributed firewalls. login (November 1999)

[4] Borders, K., Zhao, X., Prakash, A.: Siren: Catching evasive malware. In: IEEE Symposium on Security and Privacy, Oakland, CA (May 2005)

[5] CERT. TCP SYN Flooding and IP Spoofing Attacks. CERT Advisory CS-1996-21 (Last accessed April 4 , 2008),
http://www.cert.org/advisories/CA-1996-21.html

[6] Check Point. ZoneAlarm (Last accessed April 4, 2008),
http://www.zonealarm.com/store/content/home.jsp

[7] Community Developers. Ebtables (Last accessed November 1, 2007),
http://ebtables.sourceforge.net/

[8] Community Developers. Tripwire (Last accessed November 1, 2007),
http://sourceforge.net/projects/tripwire/

[9] Garfinkel, T., Pfaff, B., Chow, J., Rosenblum, M., Boneh, D.: Terra: A virtual machine-based platform for trusted computing. In: ACM Symposium on Operating Systems Principles (SOSP), October 2003, Bolton Landing, NY (2003)

[10] Garfinkel, T., Rosenblum, M.: A virtual machine introspection based architecture for intrusion detection. In: Network and Distributed System Security Symposium (NDSS), San Diego, CA, Feburary (2003)

[11] Garfinkel, T., Rosenblum, M., Boneh, D.: Flexible OS support and applications for trusted computing. In: 9th Hot Topics in Operating Systems (HOTOS), Lihue, HI (May 2003)

[12] Oskoboiny, G.: Whitelist-based spam filtering (Last accessed April 4, 2008),
http://impressive.net/people/gerald/2000/12/spam-filtering.html

[13] Grok. Coromputer Dunno (Last accessed April 4, 2008),
http://lists.grok.org.uk/pipermail/full-disclosure/attachments/
20070911/87396911/attachment-0001.txt

[14] Honeynet Project. Q8 (Last accessed April 4, 2008),
http://www.honeynet.org/papers/bots/

[15] Ioannidis, S., Keromytis, A., Bellovin, S., Smith, J.: Implementing a distributed firewall. In: ACM Conference on Computer and Communications Security (CCS), Athens, Greece (November 2000)

[16] Jiang, X., Wang, X.: Out-of-the-box monitoring of VM-based high-interaction honeypots. In: Kruegel, C., Lippmann, R., Clark, A. (eds.) RAID 2007. LNCS, vol. 4637, pp. 198–218. Springer, Heidelberg (2007)

[17] Jiang, X., Wang, X., Xu, D.: Stealthy malware detection through VMM-based 'out-of-the-box' semantic view. In: 14th ACM Conference on Computer and Communications Security (CCS), Alexandria, VA (November 2007)

[18] LKCD Project. LKCD - Linux Kernel Crash Dump (Last accessed April 4, 2008),
http://lkcd.sourceforge.net/

[19] Loscocco, P.A., Wilson, P.W., Pendergrass, J.A., McDonell, C.D.: Linux kernel integrity measurement using contextual inspection. In: 2nd ACM Workshop on Scalable Trusted Computing (STC), Alexandria, VA (November 2007)

[20] McAfee. BackDoor-Rev.b. (Last accessed April 4, 2008),
     http://vil.nai.com/vil/Content/v_136510.htm
[21] Mogul, J., Rashid, R., Accetta, M.: The packet filter: An efficient mechanism for
     user-level network code. In: ACM Symposium on Operating Systems Principles
     (SOSP), Austin, TX (November 1987)
[22] Packet Storm (Last accessed April 4, 2008),
     http://packetstormsecurity.org/UNIX/penetration/rootkits/
     bdoor.c,blackhole.c,cheetah.c,server.c,ovasOn.c
[23] Packet Storm (Last accessed April 4, 2008),
     http://packetstormsecurity.org/0209-exploits/
     apache-ssl-bug.c,apache-linux.txt
[24] Packet Storm. Kaiten (Last accessed April 4, 2008),
     http://packetstormsecurity.org/irc/kaiten.c
[25] Payne, B.D., Carbone, M., Lee, W.: Secure and flexible monitoring of virtual
     machines. In: 23rd Annual Computer Security Applications Conference (ACSAC),
     Miami, FL (December 2007)
[26] Petroni Jr., N.L., Fraser, T., Walters, A., Arbaugh, W.A.: An architecture for
     specification-based detection of semantic integrity violations in kernel dynamic
     data. In: 15th USENIX Security Symposium, Vancouver, BC, Canada (August
     2006)
[27] Petroni Jr., N.L., Hicks, M.: Automated detection of persistent kernel control-flow
     attacks. In: 14th ACM Conference on Computer and Communications Security
     (CCS), Alexandria, VA (November 2007)
[28] Ta-Min, R., Litty, L., Lie, D.: Splitting interfaces: Making trust between applica-
     tions and operating systems configurable. In: Symposium on Operating System
     Design and Implementation (OSDI), Seattle, WA (October 2006)
[29] Venema, W.: TCP wrapper: Network monitoring, access control and booby traps.
     In: USENIX UNIX Security Symposium, Baltimore, MD (September 1992)
[30] Whitaker, A., Cox, R.S., Shaw, M., Gribble, S.D.: Constructing services with
     interposable virtual hardware. In: 1st Symposium on Networked Systems Design
     and Implementation (NSDI), San Francisco, CA (March 2004)
[31] XenAccess Project. XenAccess Library (Last accessed April 4, 2008),
     http://xenaccess.sourceforge.net/
[32] Xu, M., Jiang, X., Sandhu, R., Zhang, X.: Towards a VMM-based usage control
     framework for OS kernel integrity protection. In: 12th ACM Symposium on Access
     Control Models and Technologies (SACMAT), Sophia Antipolis, France (June
     2007)
[33] Yin, H., Song, D., Egele, M., Kruegel, C., Kirda, E.: Panorama: Capturing system-
     wide information flow for malware detection and analysis. In: ACM Conference on
     Computer and Communications Security (CCS), Arlington, VA (October 2007)

A First Step towards Live Botmaster Traceback

Daniel Ramsbrock[1], Xinyuan Wang[1], and Xuxian Jiang[2]

[1] Department of Computer Science
George Mason University Fairfax, VA 22030, USA
{dramsbro,xwangc}@gmu.edu
[2] Department of Computer Science
North Carolina State University, Raleigh,
NC 27606, USA
jiang@cs.ncsu.edu

Abstract. Despite the increasing botnet threat, research in the area of botmaster traceback is limited. The four main obstacles are 1) the low-traffic nature of the bot-to-botmaster link; 2) chains of "stepping stones;" 3) the use of encryption along these chains; and 4) mixing with traffic from other bots. Most existing traceback approaches can address one or two of these issues, but no single approach can overcome all of them. We present a novel flow watermarking technique to address all four obstacles simultaneously. Our approach allows us to uniquely identify and trace any IRC-based botnet flow even if 1) it is encrypted (e.g., via SSL/TLS); 2) it passes multiple intermediate stepping stones (e.g., IRC server, SOCKs); and 3) it is mixed with other botnet traffic. Our watermarking scheme relies on adding padding characters to outgoing botnet C&C messages at the application layer. This produces specific differences in lengths between randomly chosen pairs of messages in a network flow. As a result, our watermarking technique can be used to trace any interactive botnet C&C traffic and it only requires a few dozen packets to be effective. To the best of our knowledge, this is the first approach that has the potential to allow real-time botmaster traceback across the Internet.

We have empirically validated the effectiveness of our botnet flow watermarking approach with live experiments on PlanetLab nodes and public IRC servers on different continents. We achieved virtually a 100% detection rate of watermarked (encrypted and unencrypted) IRC traffic with a false positive rate on the order of 10^{-5}. Due to the message queuing and throttling functionality of IRC servers, mixing chaff with the watermarked flow does not significantly impact the effectiveness of our watermarking approach.

1 Introduction

Botnets are currently one of the most serious threats to computers connected to the Internet. Recent media coverage has revealed many large-scale botnets worldwide. One botnet [22, 23] has reportedly compromised and controlled over 400,000 computers – including computers at the Weapons Division of the U.S. Naval Air Warfare Center, U.S. Department of Defense Information Systems

R. Lippmann, E. Kirda, and A. Trachtenberg (Eds.): RAID 2008, LNCS 5230, pp. 59–77, 2008.

Agency. Another recently discovered botnet is suspected to have controlled 1.5 million computers around the globe [9]. It has been estimated [20] that more than 5 percent of all computers connected to the Internet have been compromised and used as bots. Currently, botnets are responsible for most spam, adware, spyware, phishing, identity theft, online fraud and DDoS attacks on the Internet.

The botnet problem has recently received significant attention from the research community. Most existing work on botnet defense [1, 2, 3, 6, 11, 14, 15, 18] has focused on the detection and removal of command and control (C&C) servers and individual bots. While such a capability is a useful start in mitigating the botnet problem, it does not address the root cause: the botmaster. For example, existing botnet defense mechanisms can detect and dismantle botnets, but they usually cannot determine the identity and location of the botmaster. As a result, the botmaster is free to create and operate another botnet by compromising other vulnerable hosts. Botmasters can currently operate with impunity due to a lack of reliable traceback mechanisms. However, if the botmaster's risk of being caught is increased, he would be hesitant to create and operate botnets. Therefore, even an imperfect botmaster traceback capability could effectively deter botmasters. Unfortunately, current botmasters have all the potential gains from operating botnets with minimum risk of being caught. Therefore, the botnet problem cannot be solved until we develop a reliable method for identifying and locating botmasters across the Internet. This paper presents a substantial first step towards achieving the goal of botmaster traceback.

Tracking and locating the botmaster of a discovered botnet is very challenging. First, the botmaster only needs to be online briefly to issue commands or check the bots' status. As a result, any botmaster traceback has to occur in real-time. Second, the botmaster usually does not directly connect to the botnet C&C server and he can easily launder his connection through various stepping stones. Third, the botmaster can protect his C&C traffic with strong encryption. For example, Agobot has built-in SSL/TLS support. Finally, the C&C traffic from the botmaster is typically low-volume. As a result, a successful botmaster traceback approach must be effective on low-volume, encrypted traffic across multiple stepping stones.

To the best of our knowledge, no existing traceback methods can effectively track a botmaster across the Internet in real-time. For example, methods [33, 32, 8, 31, 4, 29, 30] have been shown to be able to trace encrypted traffic across various stepping stones and proxies, but they need a large amount of traffic (at least hundreds of packets) to be effective. During a typical session, each bot exchanges only a few dozen packets with the botmaster. Due to this low traffic volume, the above techniques are not suitable for botmaster traceback.

In this paper, we address the botmaster traceback problem with a novel packet flow watermarking technique. Our goal is to develop a practical solution that can be used to trace low-volume botnet C&C traffic in real-time even if it is encrypted and laundered through multiple intermediate hosts (e.g., IRC servers, stepping stones, proxies). We assume that the tracer has control of a single rogue bot in the target botnet, and this bot can send messages in response to a the query from the botmaster. To trace the response traffic back to the botmaster, the rogue bot transparently injects a unique watermark into its response. If the injected watermark can survive the various transformations (e.g., encryption/decryption, proxying) of the botnet C&C traffic, we can trace the watermark and locate the botmaster via monitoring nodes across the Internet. To embed the watermark, we adjust the lengths of randomly selected pairs of packets such that the length difference between each packet pair will fall within a certain range. To track encrypted botnet traffic that mixes messages from multiple bots, we developed a hybrid length-timing watermarking method. Compared to previous approaches [31, 29, 30], our two proposed methods require far less traffic volume to encode high-entropy watermarks. We empirically validated the effectiveness of our watermarking algorithms using real-time experiments on live IRC traffic through PlanetLab nodes and public IRC servers across different continents. Both of our watermarking approaches achieved a virtually 100% watermark detection rate and a 10^{-5} false positive rate with only a few dozen packets. To the best of our knowledge, this is the first approach that has the potential to allow real-time botmaster traceback across the Internet.

The remainder of the paper is structured as follows: Section 2 introduces the botmaster traceback model. Section 3 presents the design and analysis of our flow watermarking schemes. Section 4 describes our experiments and their results, while section 5 discusses limitations and future work. Finally, Section 6 surveys related literature and Section 7 summarizes our findings.

2   Botmaster Traceback Model

According to [17, 21, 28], most botnets currently in the wild are IRC-based. Therefore, we will focus on tracing the botmaster in the context of IRC-based botnets. Nevertheless, our flow watermarking trace approach is applicable to any interactive botnet traffic.

2.1   Botnets and Stepping Stones

Bots have been covered extensively in the existing literature, for example [2, 6, 7, 16, 21] provide good overviews. The typical bot lifecycle starts with exploitation, followed by download and installation of the bot software. At this point, the bot contacts the central C&C server run by the botmaster, where he can execute commands and receive responses from his botnet.

Botmasters rarely connect directly to their C&C servers since this would reveal their true IP address and approximate location. Instead, they use a chain of stepping stone proxies that anonymously relay traffic. Popular proxy software used for this purpose is SSH, SOCKS, and IRC BNCs (such as psyBNC). Since the stepping stones are controlled by the attacker, they do not have an audit trail in place or other means of tracing the true source of traffic. However, there are two properties of stepping stones that can be exploited for tracing purposes: 1) the content of the message (the application-layer payload) is never modified and 2) messages are passed on immediately due to the interactive nature of IRC. Consequently, the relative lengths of messages and their timings are preserved, even if encryption is used. In the case of encryption, the message lengths are rounded up to the nearest multiple of the block size. This inherent length and timing preservation is the foundation of our botmaster traceback approach.

2.2   Tracking the Botmaster by Watermarking Botnet Traffic

Our botmaster traceback approach exploits the fact that the communication between the IRC-based bots and the botmaster is bidirectional and interactive. Whenever the botmaster issues commands to a bot, the response traffic will eventually return to the botmaster after being laundered and possibly trans- formed. Therefore, if we can watermark the response traffic from a bot to the botmaster, we can eventually trace and locate the botmaster. Since the response traffic we are tracking may be mixed with other IRC traffic, we need to be able to isolate the target traffic. With unencrypted traffic, this can be achieved by content inspection, but encrypted traffic presents a challenge which we address with our hybrid length-timing algorithm.

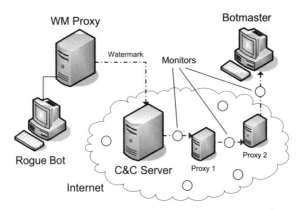

Fig. 1. Botmaster traceback by watermarking the botnet response traffic

Figure 1 shows the overall watermarking traceback model. We assume that we control a rogue bot, which could be a honeypot host that has been compromised and has joined a botnet. The rogue bot watermarks its outgoing PRIVMSG traffic in response to commands from the botmaster. As with any traceback ap- proach, our watermark tracing scheme needs support from the network. Specifi- cally, we assume there are cooperating monitor nodes across the Internet, which will inspect the passing traffic for the specified watermark and report back to us whenever they find it. Note that our approach does not require a global moni- toring capability. If there are uncooperative or unmonitored areas, we would lose one or more links along the traceback path. However, we can pick up the trail again once the watermarked traffic re-enters a monitored area. In general, this appears to be the best possible approach in the absence of a global monitoring capability. We assume that the tracer can securely share the desired watermark with all monitor nodes prior to sending the watermarked traffic. This enables the monitors to report 'sightings' of the watermark in real-time and requires only a single watermarked flow to complete the trace.

3   Length-Based Watermarking Scheme

Our watermarking scheme was specifically designed for a low-traffic, text-based channel such as the one between a bot and its botmaster. This section describes the design and analysis of both the length-only (unencrypted traffic) and the length-timing hybrid algorithms (encrypted traffic). We describe the encoding and decoding formulas for both algorithms and address the issue of false positives and false negatives.

The terms 'message' and 'packet' are used interchangeably since a typical botnet C&C message is usually small (less than 512 bytes) and fits into a single packet).

3.1   Basic Length-Based Watermarking Scheme

Watermark Bit Encoding. Given a packet flow f of n packets $P_1, \ldots, P_n$, we want to encode an l-bit watermark $W = w_0, \ldots, w_{l-1}$ using $2l \leq n$ packets. We first use a pseudo-random number generator (PRNG) with seed s to randomly choose $2l$ distinct packets from $P_1, \ldots, P_n$, we then use them to randomly form l packet pairs: $\langle P_{r_i}, P_{e_i} \rangle$ $(i = 0, \ldots, l-1)$ such that $r_i \leq e_i$. We call packet P_{r_i} a *reference packet* and packet P_{e_i} an *encoding packet*. We further use the PRNG to randomly assign watermark bit w_k $(0 \leq k \leq l-1)$ to packet pair $\langle P_{r_i}, P_{e_i} \rangle$, and we use $\langle r_i, e_i, k \rangle$ to represent that packet pair $\langle P_{r_i}, P_{e_i} \rangle$ is assigned to encode watermark bit w_k.

To encode the watermark bit w_k into packet pair $\langle P_{r_i}, P_{e_i} \rangle$, we modify the length of the encoding packet P_{e_i} by adding padding characters to achieve a specific length difference to its corresponding reference packet P_{r_i}. The padding characters could be invisible (such as whitespace) or visible characters and they can be inserted in random locations within the message. This would make it difficult for the adversary to detect the existence of the padding. Let l_e and l_r be the packet lengths of the watermark encoding and reference packets respectively, $Z = l_e - l_r$ be the length difference, and $L > 0$ be the bucket size. We define the *watermark bit encoding function* as

$$e(l_r, l_e, L, w) = l_e + [(0.5 + w)L - (l_e - l_r)] \bmod 2L \qquad (1)$$

which returns the increased length of watermark encoding packet given the length of the reference packet l_r, the length of the encoding packet l_e, the bucket size L, and the watermark bit to be encoded w.

Therefore,

$$(e(l_r, l_e, L, w) - l_r) \bmod 2L \qquad (2)$$

$$= \{(l_e - l_r) + [(0.5 + w)L - (l_e - l_r)] \bmod 2L\} \bmod 2L$$
$$= \{(0.5 + w)L\} \bmod 2L$$
$$= (w + 0.5)L$$

This indicates that the packet length difference $Z = l_e - l_r$, after l_e is adjusted by the watermark bit encoding function $e(l_r, l_e, L, w)$, falls within the middle of either an even or odd numbered bucket depending on whether the watermark bit w is even or odd.

Watermark Bit Decoding. Assuming the decoder knows the watermarking parameters: PRNG, s, n, l, W and L, the watermark decoder can obtain the exact pseudo-random mapping $\langle r_i, e_i, k \rangle$ as that used by the watermark encoder. We use the following *watermark bit decoding function* to decode watermark bit w_k from the packet lengths of packets P_{r_i} and P_{e_i}

$$d(l_r, l_e, L) = \lfloor \frac{l_e - l_r}{L} \rfloor \bmod 2 \tag{3}$$

The equation below proves that any watermark bit w encoded by the encoding function defined in equation (1) will be correctly decoded by the decoding function defined in equation (3).

$$d(l_r, e(l_r, l_e, L, w), L) \tag{4}$$
$$= \lfloor \frac{e(l_r, l_e, L, w) - l_r}{L} \rfloor \bmod 2$$
$$= \lfloor \frac{(l_e - l_r) \bmod 2L + [(0.5 + w)L - (l_e - l_r)] \bmod 2L}{L} \rfloor \bmod 2$$
$$= \lfloor \frac{(0.5 + w)L}{L} \rfloor \bmod 2$$
$$= w$$

Assume the lengths of packets P_r and P_e (l_r and l_e) have been increased for $x_r \geq 0$ and $x_e \geq 0$ bytes respectively when they are transmitted over the network (e.g., due to padding of encryption), then $x_e - x_r$ is the distortion over the packet length difference $l_e - l_r$. Then the decoding with such distortion is

$$d(l_r + x_r, e(l_r, l_e, L, w) + x_e, L) \tag{5}$$
$$= \lfloor \frac{e(l_r, l_e, L, w) - l_r + (x_e - x_r)}{L} \rfloor \bmod 2$$
$$= w + \lfloor 0.5 + \frac{x_e - x_r}{L} \rfloor \bmod 2$$

Therefore, the decoding with distortion will be correct if and only if

$$(-0.5 + 2i)L \leq x_e - x_r < (0.5 + 2i)L \tag{6}$$

Specifically, when the magnitude of the distortion $|x_e - x_r| < 0.5L$, the decoding is guaranteed to be correct.

Watermark Decoding and Error Tolerance. Given a packet flow f and appropriate watermarking parameters (PRNG, s, n, l, W and L) used by the watermark encoder, the watermark decoder can obtain a l-bit decoded watermark W' using the watermark bit decoding function defined in equation (3). Due to potential distortion of the packet lengths in the packet flow f, the decoded W' could have a few bits different from the encoded watermark W. We introduce a Hamming distance threshold $h \geq 0$ to accommodate such partial corruption of the embedded watermark. Specifically, we will consider that packet flow f contains watermark W if the Hamming distance between W and W': $H(W, W')$ is no bigger than h.

Watermark Collision Probability (False Positive Rate). No matter what watermark W and Hamming distance threshold h we choose, there is always a non-zero possibility that the decoding W' of a random unwatermarked flow happens to have no more than h Hamming distance to the random watermark W we have chosen. In other words, watermark W is reported found in an unwatermarked flow; we refer to this case as a *watermark collision*.

Intuitively, the longer the watermark and the smaller the Hamming distance threshold, the smaller the probability of a watermark collision. Assume we have randomly chosen a l-bit watermark, and we are decoding l-bits from random unwatermarked flows. Any particular bit decoded from a random unwatermarked flow should have 0.5 probability to match the corresponding bit of the random watermark we have chosen. Therefore, the collision probability of l-bit watermark from random unwatermarked flows with Hamming distance threshold h is

$$\sum_{i=0}^{h} \binom{l}{i} (\frac{1}{2})^l \tag{7}$$

We have empirically validated the watermark collision probability distribution with the following experiment. We first use a PRNG and a random seed number s to generate 32 packet pairs $\langle r_i, e_i \rangle$ and pseudo-randomly assign each bit of a 32-bit watermark W to the 32 packet pairs, we then encode the 32 bit watermark W into a random packet flow f. Now we try to decode the watermarked flow f' with 1,000 wrong seed numbers. Given the pseudo-random nature of our selection of the packet pairs, decoding a watermarked flow with the wrong seed is equivalent of decoding an unwatermarked flow, which can be used to measure the watermark collision probability.

The left side of Figure 2 illustrates the number of matched bits from the decoding with each of the 1,000 wrong seed numbers. It shows that the numbers of matched bits are centered around the expected value of 16 bits, which is half of the watermark length. Based on these results and the experimental data in Section 4.2, we can choose a Hamming distance threshold of $h = 4$ (28 bits) as shown on the graph, yielding an expected false positive rate (FPR) of 9.64×10^{-6} according to equation (7). The right side of Figure 2 shows the distributions of the measured and the expected number of matched bits. It illustrates that the distribution of the measured number of matched bits is close to the expected binomial distribution with $p = 0.5$ and $n = 32$.

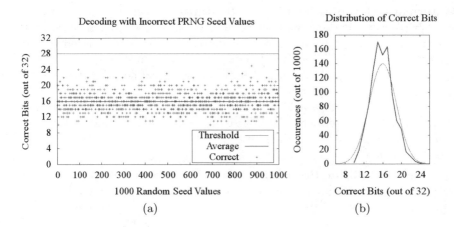

Fig. 2. 32-bit watermark collision probability and distribution

Watermark Loss (False Negative). Our length-only encoding scheme (without the hybrid timing approach) is highly sensitive to having the correct sequence of messages. If any messages are added or deleted in transit, the watermark will be lost in that flow. However, the chance of this happening is very remote since the encoding takes place at the application layer, on top of TCP. By its nature, TCP guarantees in-order delivery of all packets and their contents, so a non-intentional watermark loss is very unlikely.

In the case of active countermeasures, our scheme can tolerate distortion as long as $|x_e - x_r| < 0.5L$, as described by inequality (6). This property is the result of aiming for the center of each bucket when encoding. However, if an active adversary drops, adds, or reorders messages, the watermark will be lost unless additional redundancy is in place or the length-timing algorithm is used.

3.2   Hybrid Length-Timing Watermarking for Encrypted Traffic

By their nature, IRC-based botnets have many bots on one channel at once, many of them joining, parting, or sending data to the botmaster simultaneously. In this case, the watermarked messages from our rogue bot will be mixed with unwatermarked messages from other bots. We call these unwatermarked messages from others *chaff* messages. In order to reliably decode the embedded watermark, we need to filter out chaff messages as much as possible.

When the C&C traffic is unencrypted, it is easy for the watermark decoder to filter out chaff based on the sender nicks in the messages. However, if the traffic is encrypted (e.g., using SSL/TLS), we cannot rely on content inspection to identify chaff messages. To address this new challenge in filtering out chaff, we propose to use another dimension of information – the packet timing – to filter out chaff.

The basic idea is to send the watermark encoding packets at a specific time (e.g., t_i). Assuming the network jitter δ is limited, we can narrow the range of potential packets used for decoding to $[t_{e_i} - \frac{\delta}{2}, t_{e_i} + \frac{\delta}{2}]$. If $\delta > 0$ is small, then the chances that some chaff packet happens to fall within the range $[t_{e_i} - \frac{\delta}{2}, t_{e_i} + \frac{\delta}{2}]$ is small. This means we can decode the watermark correctly even if there are substantial encrypted chaff packets.

Watermark Encoding. The watermark bit encoding process is exactly the same as that of the basic length-based watermarking scheme. The difference is that now we send out each watermarked packet P_{e_i} at a precise time. Specifically, we use the watermark bit encoding function defined in equation (1) to adjust the length of the watermark encoding packet P_{e_i}. We use a pseudo-random number generator PRNG and seed s_t to generate the random time t_{e_i} at which P_{e_i} will be sent out.

An implicit requirement for the hybrid length-timing watermarking scheme is that we need to know when each watermark encoding packet P_{e_i} will be available. In our watermark tracing model, the tracer owns a rogue bot who can determine what to send out and when to send it. Since we have full control over the outgoing traffic, we can use the hybrid length-timing scheme to watermark the traffic in real-time.

Watermark Decoding. When we decode the encrypted botnet traffic, we do not know which packet is a watermark encoding packet P_{e_i}. However, given the PRNG and s_t we do know the approximate time t_{e_i} at which the watermark encoding packet P_{e_i} should arrive. We then use all packets in the time interval $[t_{e_i} - \frac{\delta}{2}, t_{e_i} + \frac{\delta}{2}]$ to decode. Specifically, we use the sum of the lengths of all the packets in the time interval $[t_{e_i} - \frac{\delta}{2}, t_{e_i} + \frac{\delta}{2}]$ as the length of the watermark encoding packet and apply that to the watermark bit decoding function (3).

Due to network delay jitter and/or active timing perturbation by the adversary, the exact arrival time of watermark encoding packet P_{e_i} may be different from t_{e_i}. Fortunately, the decoding can self-synchronize with the encoding by leveraging an intrinsic property of our hybrid length-timing watermarking scheme. Specifically, if the decoding of a watermarked flow uses the wrong offset or wrong seeds (s and s_t), then the decoded l-bit watermark W' will almost always have about $\frac{l}{2}$ bits matched with the true watermark W. This gives us an easy way to determine if we are using the correct offset, and we can try a range of possible offsets and pick the best decoding result.

4   Implementation and Experiment

To validate the practicality of our watermarking scheme, we implemented both the length-only algorithm (unencrypted traffic) and the length-timing hybrid algorithm (encrypted traffic). To let our watermarking proxy interact with a realistic but benign IRC bot, we obtained a sanitized version of Agobot from its source code, containing only benign IRC communication features. We ran the sanitized Agobot on a local machine to generate benign IRC traffic to test the effectiveness of our watermarking scheme across public IRC servers and PlanetLab nodes. At no time did we send malicious traffic to anyone in the course of our experiments.

4.1   Length-Only Algorithm (Unencrypted Traffic)

We implemented the length-only algorithm in a modified open-source IRC proxy server and ran a series of experiments using the sanitized Agobot and public Internet IRC servers. We were able to recover the watermark successfully from unencrypted traffic in all ten of our trials.

Modified IRC Bouncer. To achieve greater flexibility, we added our watermarking functionality to an existing IRC bouncer (BNC) package, psyBNC. Having the watermarking implemented on a proxy server allows us to use it on all bots conforming to the standard IRC protocol. It eliminates the need to have access to a bot's source code to add the watermarking functionality: outgoing traffic is modified by the BNC after the bot sends it.

In order for psyBNC to act as a transparent proxy, it needs to be configured identically to the bot. The information required consists of the C&C server's hostname, the port, and an IRC nick consistent with the bot's naming scheme. This information can be gathered by running the bot and monitoring the outgoing network traffic. In order to trick the bot into connecting to the BNC rather than to the real C&C host, we also need to update our local DNS cache so that a lookup of the C&C server's hostname resolves to the IP of our BNC.

Once it has been configured with this information, the BNC is completely transparent to the bot: when it starts up, the bot is automatically signed into the real C&C server by the BNC. The bot now joins the botnet channel as if it were directly connected and then waits for the botmaster's instructions. All PRIVMSG traffic from the bot to the C&C server (and by extension, to the botmaster) is watermarked by the transparent BNC in between.

Experiment and Results. To test our watermarking scheme, we devised an experiment that emulates the conditions of an Internet-wide botnet as closely as possible. To simulate the botmaster and stepping stones, we used PlanetLab nodes in California and Germany. We used a live, public IRC server in Arizona to act as a C&C host, creating a uniquely-named channel for our experiments. Our channel consisted of two IRC users: the Test Bot was running a copy of the sanitized Agobot and the Botmaster was acting as the botmaster (see Figure 3). As the diagram indicates, all traffic sent by the Test Bot passes through the psyBNC server (WM Proxy) where the watermark is injected. The distances involved in this setup are considerable: the watermarked traffic traverses literally half the globe (12 time zones) before reaching its ultimate destination in Germany, with a combined round-trip time of 292 milliseconds on average (at the time of our experiment).

The objective is to be able to decode the full watermark in the traffic captured at the Stepping Stone and Botmaster. Since only PRIVMSG traffic from the Test Bot is watermarked, all other traffic (chaff) must be filtered out before decoding. Most of this chaff consists of messages from other users on the channel, PING/PONG exchanges, and JOIN/PART notifications from the channel. There could be additional chaff on the same connection if the botmaster is logged into multiple channels on the same IRC server. However, filtering out the chaff is

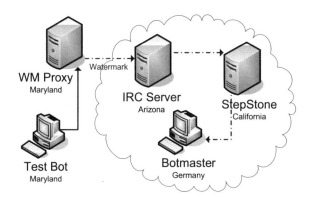

Fig. 3. Experiment setup for unencrypted traffic

trivial in the absence of encryption since all IRC messages contain the sender's nick. Therefore, we can easily isolate the watermarked packets based on the Test Bot's nick.

During our experiments, the psyBNC proxy was configured to inject a 32-bit watermark into a 64-packet stream. To generate traffic from the Test Bot, the Botmaster logged in and issued the `commands.list` command, causing the bot to send a list of all valid bot commands and their descriptions. We captured all traffic leaving the WM Proxy, arriving at the Stepping Stone, and arriving at the Botmaster. In ten trials with different (random) 32-bit watermarks, we were able to correct decode the full 32-bit watermark at all three monitoring locations: the WM Proxy in Maryland, the Stepping Stone in California, and Botmaster in Germany.

4.2   Hybrid Length-Timing Algorithm (Encrypted Traffic)

To test the hybrid length-timing algorithm, we implemented a simple IRC bot that sends length-watermarked messages out at specific intervals. We used a "chaff bot" on the channel to generate controlled amounts of chaff. We were able to recover the watermark with a high success rate, even when high amounts of chaff were present.

Hybrid Length-Timing Encoder. We implemented the hybrid encoding algorithm as a Perl program which reads in a previously length-only watermarked stream of messages and sends them out at specific times. To achieve highly precise timing, we used the `Time::HiRes` Perl package, which provides microsecond-resolution timers. At startup, the program uses the Mersenne Twister PRNG (via the `Math::Random::MT` package) to generate a list of departure times for all messages to be sent. Each message is sent at a randomly chosen time between 2 and 2.35 seconds after the previous message. The 2-second minimum spacing avoids IRC server packet throttling (more details are discussed in Section 4.2).

Hybrid Length-Timing Decoder. The hybrid decoding script was also written in Perl, relying on the PCAP library to provide a standardized network traffic

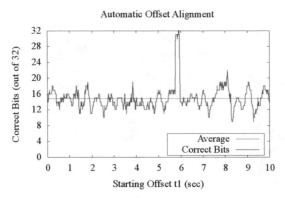

Fig. 4. Offset Self-Synchronization via Offset Sliding-Window

capture mechanism (via the `Net::Pcap` module). The program reads in a stream of packets (either from a live interface or from a PCAP file), then performs a sliding-window offset self-synchronization process to determine the time $t1$ of the first watermarked packet. To find the correct $t1$, the program steps through a range of possible values determined by the `offset`, `max`, and `step` parameters. It starts with $t1$ =`offset`, incrementing $t1$ by `step` until $t1$ =(`offset` + `max`). It decodes the full watermark sequence for each $t1$, recording the number of bits matching the sought watermark W. It then chooses the $t1$ that produced the highest number of matching bits. If there are multiple $t1$ values resulting in the same number of matching bits, it uses the lowest value for $t1$. Figure 4 illustrates the synchronization process, showing that the correct $t1$ is near 6 seconds: 5.92 sec has 32 correct bits. For all incorrect $t1$ values, the decoding rate was significantly lower, averaging 14.84 correct bits.

Experiment and Results. The experiment setup in this case was similar to the unencrypted experiment described in Section 4.1. The three main differences were: 1) a single Source computer producing watermarked traffic on its own replaced the Test Bot and WM Proxy; 2) the connection between the Botmaster and the IRC server (via StepStone) was encrypted using SSL/TLS; and 3) we used a different IRC server because the one in Arizona does not support SSL/TLS connections. The IRC server in this case happens to be located in Germany, but not in the same place as the Botmaster. Please refer to Figure 5 for the full experiment setup. In this configuration, the distances involved are even greater, with the watermarked traffic traversing the equivalent of the entire globe (24 time zones). The combined round-trip time from Source to Botmaster was 482 milliseconds (on average) at the time of our experiment.

To handle encryption, the parameters for the length-only algorithm were adjusted to ensure that the bucket size matched or exceeded the encryption block size. Most SSL/TLS connections use a block size of 128 bits (16 bytes), though 192 and 256 bits are also common. To ensure that each added bucket also causes another encrypted block to be added to the message, the bucket size has to be greater than or equal to the block size. For our experiment, we used a bucket size of 16 bytes, which was sufficient for the 128-bit block size used in the SSL/TLS

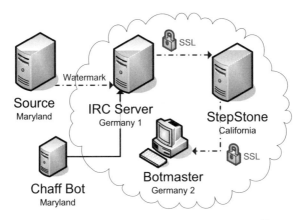

Fig. 5. Experiment setup for encrypted traffic

connection. For compatibility with the larger block sizes (192 and 256 bits), a bucket size of 32 bytes can be used.

For the experiments, the Source produced a stream of 64 packets, containing a randomly generated 32-bit watermark. The Chaff Bot produced a controlled amount of background traffic, spacing the packets at random intervals between 1 and 6 seconds (at least 1 second to avoid throttling). In addition to our Control run (no chaff), we ran five different chaff levels (Chaff 1 to 5). The number refers to the maximum time between packets (not including the minimum 1-second spacing). For example, for the Chaff 1 run, packets were sent at a random time between 1 and 2 seconds. Thus, one packet was sent on average every 1.5 seconds, resulting in a chaff rate of approximately $1/1.5 = 0.667$ packets/sec.

We captured network traffic in three places: 1) traffic from Source and Chaff Bot to IRC Server; 2) traffic arriving at StepStone from IRC Server; and 3) traffic arriving at Botmaster from StepStone. Traffic in all three locations includes both watermark and chaff packets. We decoded the traffic at each location, recording the number of matching bits. For decoding, we used a value of 200 milliseconds for the timing window size δ and a sliding offset range from 0 to 10 seconds. This δ value was large enough to account for possible jitter along the stepping stone chain but small enough to make it unlikely that a chaff packet appears within δ of an encoding packet. We also measured the actual chaff rate based on the departure times of each chaff packet, and these were very close to the expected rates based on an even distribution of random departure times. We repeated this process three times for each chaff level, resulting in a total of 18 runs. Our experiment results are summarized in Table 1, with each column representing the average values from three trials.

We had near-perfect decoding along the stepping-stone chain for all chaff rates of 0.5 packets/sec and below. Only when the chaff rate rose above 0.5 packets/sec did the chaff start having a slight impact, bringing the decoding rate down to an average of 31 bits. The overall average decoding rate at the StepStone and Botmaster was 31.69 bits, or 99.05 percent. The lowest recorded decoding rate

Table 1. Experiment results for encrypted traffic: Recovered watermark bits (out of 32) at each monitoring station along the watermark's path (averaged from three trials)

Monitoring Location	Chaff 1	Chaff 2	Chaff 3	Chaff 4	Chaff 5	Control
Chaff Rate (packets/sec)	0.6719	0.4976	0.4274	0.3236	0.2872	no chaff
Source - Maryland	29.67	30.33	29.67	30.33	30.33	32
StepStone - California	31	32	31.67	31.67	32	32
Botmaster - Germany	31	31.67	32	31.67	31.67	32

during our experiments was 28 bits, so we can use a Hamming distance threshold of $h = 4$ to obtain a 100 percent true positive rate (TPR) and a false positive rate (FPR) of 9.64×10^{-6}.

The most surprising result is that in all cases where chaff was present, the decoding rate was worse at the Source than downstream at the StepStone and Botmaster. After examining the network traces in detail, we realized that this behavior was due to the presence of traffic queuing and throttling on the IRC Server. To avoid flooding, IRC servers are configured to enforce minimum packet spacings, and most will throttle traffic at 0.5 to 1 packets/sec. To confirm this behavior, we sent packets to the IRC Server in Germany at random intervals of 100 to 300 milliseconds. For the first 5 seconds, packets were passed on immediately, but after that the throttling kicked in, limiting the server's outgoing rate to 1 packet/sec. After about 2 minutes, the server's packet queue became full with backlogged packets, and it disconnected our client. Figure 6 illustrates the effect of throttling on the packet arrival times, including the 5-second "grace period" at the beginning.

In the context of our hybrid encoding scheme, IRC message queuing is highly beneficial because it dramatically reduces the chances that chaff and encoding packets will appear close to each other. At the Source, packets appear at the exact intervals they are sent, which could be less than δ and therefore affect decoding. However, this interval will be increased due to queuing by the IRC server. By the time the packets reach the StepStone and Botmaster, they no longer affect decoding because they are more than δ apart. In our experiments, we observed

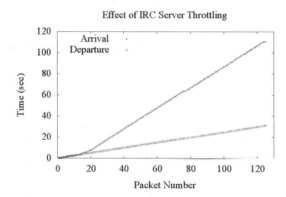

Fig. 6. IRC server throttling causes packets to be spaced apart further upon arrival

that the IRC server introduced a distance of at about 130 milliseconds between packets due to queuing. Since our δ value was 200 milliseconds, this made it unlikely that two packets would arrive in the same slot.

5   Discussion and Future Work

Our experiments show that our watermarking scheme is effective in tracing the botmaster of IRC-based botnets, which are still the predominant type in the wild [17,21,28]. Our watermark can be recovered with a high degree of accuracy even when the watermarked botnet C&C traffic is encrypted across multiple stepping stones and mixed with other flows.

In theory, our flow watermarking technique could be applied to trace any real-time and interactive botnet C&C traffic. Therefore, it could be used to track the botmaster of peer-to-peer (P2P) botnets which have started appearing recently [13]. However, HTTP-based botnets present a much higher level of traceback difficulty: the messages do not get passed from the bot to the botmaster in real-time. They are typically stored on the C&C server until the botmaster retrieves them in bulk, usually over an encrypted connection such as SSH. Due to this, any approach that relies on properties of individual packets (such as length and timing) will be unsuccessful.

When SSH is used as the final hop in a chain of stepping stones, it presents unique challenges. In this case, the botmaster uses SSH to log into a stepping stone, launches a commandline-based IRC client on that host, and uses this IRC client to connect to his botnet (possibly via more stepping stones). In this capacity, SSH is not acting as a proxy, passing on messages verbatim like psyBNC or SOCKS. Instead, it transfers the "graphical" screen updates of the running IRC client, which is not necessarily correlated to the incoming IRC messages. This situation is challenging for our approach because the application-layer content is transformed, altering the relative lengths of packets. We are working on this problem, but we have been unable to explore it in detail. Notice that if SSH is used in a tunnelling capacity (such as port forwarding or a SOCKS proxy) in the middle of a stepping stone chain, this limitation does not apply.

Once the botmaster become aware of the flow watermarking tracing approach, he may want to corrupt the embedded watermark from intermediate stepping stones. However, since the padding characters could be almost any character and they are inserted randomly in the botnet message, it would be difficult for any intermediate stepping stone to identify and remove the padding characters without knowing the original unwatermarked message. The botmaster may be able to detect and identify the padding if he knows exactly what he is expecting for. However, once he receives the watermarked message, the watermarked message has already left the complete trail toward the botmaster. The botmaster could have intermediate stepping stones to perturb the length of the passing botnet messages by adding random padding such as white space. Since the watermark is embedded in the length difference between randomly chosen packets, the negative impact of the padding by the adversary tends to cancel each other. We can further mitigate the negative impact by using redundant pairs of packets to encode the watermark. However, this would increase the number of packets needed. So this is essentially a tradeoff between the robustness and the efficiency.

As previously discussed in Section 2.2, our approach requires at least partial network coverage of distributed monitoring stations. This is a common requirement for network traceback approaches, especially since the coverage does not need to be global. The accuracy of the trace is directly proportional to the number and placement of monitoring nodes.

Our work is a significant step in the direction of live botmaster traceback, but as the title implies, it is indeed a first step. Our future work in this area includes the exploration of several topics, including optimal deployment of monitoring nodes, SSH traffic on the last hop, further data collection with longer stepping stone chains, and traceback experiments on in-the-wild botnets.

6   Related Work

The botnet research field is relatively new, but many papers have been published in the last few years as the botnet threat has accelerated. As one of the first in the botnet arena, the Honeynet Project [1] provided a starting point for future exploration of the problem. A comprehensive study at Johns Hopkins University [21] constructed a honeypot-based framework for acquiring and analyzing bot binaries. The framework can automatically generate rogue bots (drones) to actively infiltrate botnets, which is the first step in injecting a watermark and tracing the botmaster.

Most early botnet work focused on defining, understanding, and classifying botnets. Some examples are papers by Cooke et al. [6], Dagon et al. [7], Ianelli and Hackworth [17], Barford and Yegneswaran [2], and Holz's summary in *Security & Privacy* [16]. Since then, bot detection has become more of a focal point and many techniques have been proposed. Binkley and Singh [3] presented an anomaly-based detection algorithm for IRC-based botnets. Goebel and Holz [11] reported success with their Rishi tool, which evaluates IRC nicknames for likely botnet membership. Karasaridis et al. [18] described an ISP-level algorithm for detecting botnet traffic based on analysis of transport-layer summary statistics. Gu et al. [15] detailed their BotHunter approach, which is based on IDS dialog correlation techniques. They also published a related paper in 2008 [14] where they introduce BotSniffer, a tool for detecting C&C traffic in network traces.

Despite a large amount of literature regarding botnet detection and removal, relatively little work has been done on finding and eliminating the root cause: the botmaster himself. An earlier paper by Freiling et al. [10] describes a manual method of infiltrating a botnet and attempting to locate the botmaster, but the approach does not scale well due to lack of automation.

In the general traceback field, there are two main areas of interest: 1) network-layer (IP) traceback and 2) tracing approaches resilient to stepping stones. The advent of the first category dates back to the era of fast-spreading worms, when no stepping stones were used and IP-level traceback was sufficient. A leading paper in this area is Savage et al. [25], which introduced the probabilistic packet marking technique, embedding tracing information an IP header field. Two years later, Goodrich [12] expounded on this approach, introducing "randomize-and-link" with better scalability. A different technique for IP traceback is the log/hash-based one introduced by Snoeren et al. [26], and enhanced by Li et al. [19].

There are a number of works on how to trace attack traffic across stepping stones under various conditions. For example, [33,34,8,32,31,4,29,30] used inter-packet timing to correlate encrypted traffic across the stepping stones and/or low-latency anonymity systems. Most timing-based correlation schemes are passive, with the exception of the three active methods [31, 29, 30]. Our proposed method is based on the same active watermarking principle used in these three works. However, our method differs from them in that it uses the packet length, in addition to the packet timing, to encode the watermark. As a result, our method requires much fewer packets than methods [31, 29, 30] to be effective.

7 Conclusion

The key contribution of our work is that it addresses the four major obstacles in botmaster traceback: 1) stepping stones, 2) encryption, 3) flow mixing and 4) a low traffic volume between bot and botmaster. Our watermarking traceback approach is resilient to stepping stones and encryption, and it requires only a small number of packets in order to embed a high-entropy watermark into a network flow. The watermarked flow can be tracked even when it has been mixed with randomized chaff traffic. Due to these characteristics, our approach is uniquely suited for real-time tracing of the interactive, low-traffic botnet C&C communication between a bot and its botmaster. We believe that this is the first viable technique for performing live botmaster traceback on the Internet.

We validated our watermarking traceback algorithm both analytically and experimentally. In trials on public Internet IRC servers, we were able to achieve virtually a 100 percent TPR with an FPR of less than 10^{-5}. Our method can successfully trace a watermarked IRC flow from an IRC botnet member to the botmaster's true location, even if the watermarked flow 1) is encrypted with SSL/TLS; 2) passes through several stepping stones; and 3) travels tens of thousands of miles around the world.

Acknowledgments

The authors would like to thank the anonymous reviewers for their insightful comments that helped to improve the presentation of this paper. This work was partially supported by NSF Grants CNS-0524286, CCF-0728771 and CNS-0716376.

References

1. Bächer, P., Holz, T., Kötter, M., Wicherski, G.: Know Your Enemy: Tracking Botnets, March 13 (2005), http://www.honeynet.org/papers/bots/
2. Barford, P., Yegneswaran, V.: An Inside Look at Botnets. In: Proc. Special Workshop on Malware Detection, Advances in Info. Security, Springer, Heidelberg (2006)

3. Binkley, J., Singh, S.: An Algorithm for Anomaly-based Botnet Detection. In: Proc. 2nd Workshop on Steps to Reducing Unwanted Traffic on the Internet (SRUTI), San Jose, CA, July 7, 2006, pp. 43–48 (2006)
4. Blum, A., Song, D., Venkataraman, S.: Detection of Interactive Stepping Stones: Algorithms and Confidence Bounds. In: Jonsson, E., Valdes, A., Almgren, M. (eds.) RAID 2004. LNCS, vol. 3224, pp. 258–277. Springer, Heidelberg (2004)
5. Chi, Z., Zhao, Z.: Detecting and Blocking Malicious Traffic Caused by IRC Protocol Based Botnets. In: Proc. Network and Parallel Computing (NPC 2007). Dalian, China, pp. 485–489 (September 2007)
6. Cooke, E., Jahanian, F., McPherson, D.: The Zombie Roundup: Understanding, Detecting, and Disturbing Botnets. In: Proc. Steps to Reducing Unwanted Traffic on the Internet (SRUTI), Cambridge, MA, July 7, 2005, pp. 39–44 (2005)
7. Dagon, D., Gu, G., Zou, C., Grizzard, J., Dwivedi, S., Lee, W., Lipton, R.: A Taxonomy of Botnets (unpublished paper, 2005)
8. Donoho, D.L., Flesia, A.G., Shankar, U., Paxson, V., Coit, J., Staniford, S.: Multiscale Stepping Stone Detection: Detecting Pairs of Jittered Interactive Streams by Exploiting Maximum Tolerable Delay. In: Wespi, A., Vigna, G., Deri, L. (eds.) RAID 2002. LNCS, vol. 2516, pp. 17–35. Springer, Heidelberg (2002)
9. Evers, J.: 'Bot herders' may have controlled 1.5 million PCs. http://news.com.com/2102-7350_3-5906896.html?tag=st.util.print
10. Freiling, F., Holz, T., Wicherski, G.: Botnet Tracking: Exploring a Root-Cause Methodology to Prevent DoS Attacks. In: Proc. 10th European Symposium on Research in Computer Security (ESORICS), Milan, Italy (September 2005)
11. Goebel, J., Holz, T.: Rishi: Identify Bot Contaminated Hosts by IRC Nickname Evaluation. In: Proc. First Workshop on Hot Topics in Understanding Botnets (HotBots), Cambridge, MA, April 10 (2007)
12. Goodrich, M.T.: Efficient Packet Marking for Large-scale IP Traceback. In: Proc. 9th ACM Conference on Computer and Communications Security (CCS 2002), October 2002, pp. 117–126. ACM, New York (2002)
13. Grizzard, J., Sharma, V., Nunnery, C., Kang, B., Dagon, D.: Peer-to-Peer Botnets: Overview and Case Study. In: Proc. First Workshop on Hot Topics in Understanding Botnets (HotBots), Cambridge, MA (April 2007)
14. Gu, G., Zhang, J., Lee, W.: BotSniffer: Detecting Botnet Command and Control Channels in Network Traffic. In: Proc. 15th Network and Distributed System Security Symposium (NDSS), San Diego, CA (February 2008)
15. Gu, G., Porras, P., Yegneswaran, V., Fong, M., Lee, W.: BotHunter: Detecting Malware Infection Through IDS-Driven Dialog Correlation. In: Proc. 16th USENIX Security Symposium, Boston, MA (August 2007)
16. Holz, T.: A Short Visit to the Bot Zoo. Sec. and Privacy 3(3), 76–79 (2005)
17. Ianelli, N., Hackworth, A.: Botnets as a Vehicle for Online Crime. In: Proc. 18th Annual Forum of Incident Response and Security Teams (FIRST), Baltimore, MD, June 25-30 (2006)
18. Karasaridis, A., Rexroad, B., Hoein, D.: Wide-Scale Botnet Detection and Characterization. In: Proc. First Workshop on Hot Topics in Understanding Botnets (HotBots), Cambridge, MA, April 10 (2007)
19. Li, J., Sung, M., Xu, J., Li, L.: Large Scale IP Traceback in High-Speed Internet: Practical Techniques and Theoretical Foundation. In: Proc. 2004 IEEE Symposium on Security and Privacy. IEEE, Los Alamitos (2004)
20. Naraine, R.: Is the Botnet Battle Already Lost? http://www.eweek.com/article2/0,1895,2029720,00.asp

21. Rajab, M., Zarfoss, J., Monrose, F., Terzis, A.: A multifaceted approach to understanding the botnet phenomenon. In: Proc. 6th ACM SIGCOMM on Internet Measurement, October 25-27, 2006. Rio de Janeiro, Brazil (2006)
22. Roberts, P.F.: California Man Charged with Botnet Offenses,
    http://www.eweek.com/article2/0,1759,1881621,00.asp
23. Roberts, P.F.: Botnet Operator Pleads Guilty,
    http://www.eweek.com/article2/0,1759,1914833,00.asp
24. Roberts, P.F.: DOJ Indicts Hacker for Hospital Botnet Attack,
    http://www.eweek.com/article2/0,1759,1925456,00.asp
25. Savage, S., Wetherall, D., Karlin, A., Anderson, T.: Practical Network Support for IP Traceback. In: Proc. ACM SIGCOMM 2000, September 2000, pp. 295–306 (2000)
26. Snoeren, A., Patridge, C., Sanchez, L.A., Jones, C.E., Tchakountio, F., Kent, S.T., Strayer, W.T.: Hash-based IP Traceback. In: Proc. ACM SIGCOMM 2001, September 2001, pp. 3–14. ACM Press, New York (2001)
27. Symantec. Symantec Internet Security Threat Report – Trends for January 06 - June 06. Volume X (September 2006)
28. Micro, T.: Taxonomy of Botnet Threats. Trend Micro Enterprise Security Library (November 2006)
29. Wang, X., Chen, S., Jajodia, S.: Tracking Anonymous, Peer-to-Peer VoIP Calls on the Internet. In: Proc. 12th ACM Conference on Computer and Communications Security (CCS 2005) (October 2007)
30. Wang, X., Chen, S., Jajodia, S.: Network Flow Watermarking Attack on Low-Latency Anonymous Communication Systems. In: Proc. 2007 IEEE Symposium on Security and Privacy (S&P 2007) (May 2007)
31. Wang, X., Reeves, D.: Robust Correlation of Encrypted Attack Traffic Through Stepping Stones by Manipulation of Interpacket Delays. In: Proc. 10th ACM Conference on Computer and Communications Security (CCS 2003), October 2003, pp. 20–29. ACM, New York (2003)
32. Wang, X., Reeves, D., Wu, S.: Inter-packet Delay Based Correlation for Tracing Encrypted Connections Through Stepping Stones. In: Gollmann, D., Karjoth, G., Waidner, M. (eds.) ESORICS 2002. LNCS, vol. 2502, pp. 244–263. Springer, Heidelberg (2002)
33. Yoda, K., Etoh, H.: Finding a Connection Chain for Tracing Intruders. In: Cuppens, F., Deswarte, Y., Gollmann, D., Waidner, M. (eds.) ESORICS 2000. LNCS, vol. 1895, pp. 191–205. Springer, Heidelberg (2000)
34. Zhang, Y., Paxson, V.: Detecting Stepping Stones. In: Proc. 9th USENIX Security Symposium, pp. 171–184. USENIX (2000)

A Layered Architecture for Detecting Malicious Behaviors

Lorenzo Martignoni[1], Elizabeth Stinson[2], Matt Fredrikson[3], Somesh Jha[3],
and John C. Mitchell[2]

[1] Università degli Studi di Milano
[2] Stanford University
[3] University of Wisconsin

Abstract. We address the *semantic gap* problem in behavioral monitoring by using hierarchical behavior graphs to infer high-level behaviors from myriad low-level events. Our experimental system traces the
execution of a process, performing data flow analysis to identify meaningful actions such as "proxying", "keystroke logging", "data leaking",
and "downloading and executing a program" from complex combinations
of rudimentary system calls. To preemptively address evasive malware
behavior, our specifications are carefully crafted to detect alternative sequences of events that achieve the same high-level goal. We tested eleven
benign programs, variants from seven malicious bot families, four trojans, and three mass-mailing worms and found that we were able to
thoroughly identify high-level behaviors across this diverse code base.
Moreover, we effectively distinguished malicious execution of high-level
behaviors from benign by identifying remotely-initiated actions.

Keywords: Dynamic, Semantic Gap, Malware, Behavior, Data-Flow.

1 Introduction

In the first half of 2007, Symantec observed more than five million active, distinct
bot-infected computers [1]. Botnets are used to perform nefarious tasks, such as:
keystroke logging, spyware installation, denial-of-service (DoS) attacks, hosting
phishing web sites or command-and-control servers, spamming, click fraud, and
license key theft [2,3,4,5,6,7]. Malicious bots are generally installed as applications on an infected (Windows) host and have approximately the same range of
control over the compromised host as its rightful owner. A botmaster can flexibly
leverage this platform in real-time by issuing commands to his botnet. Several
characteristics typical of botnets increase the difficulty of robust network-based
detection; in particular, bots may: exhibit high IP diversity, have high-speed,
always-on connections, and communicate over encrypted channels. Since a botmaster controls both the bots and the command-and-control infrastructure, these
can be arbitrarily designed to evade network-based detection measures.

It is widely recognized that malware defenders operate at a fundamental disadvantage: malware producers can generate malware variants by simple measures
such as packing transformations (encryption and/or compression) and may evade

R. Lippmann, E. Kirda, and A. Trachtenberg (Eds.): RAID 2008, LNCS 5230, pp. 78–97, 2008.

existing AV signatures by systematic means [8]. For the signature purveyors, moreover, analyzing a novel malware instance and creating a detection signature requires substantially greater effort than that required by evasion. The source of this asymmetry is the signature scanners' emphasis on malware's infinitely mutable syntax, rather than on the actions taken by malware. As a result, even the most effective signature-scanners fail to detect more than 30% of malware seen in the wild [9,10]. Therefore, it is essential to develop effective methods that identify the behaviors that make malware useful to their installers.

1.1   Our Approach

We propose, develop, and evaluate a behavior-based approach that targets the high-level actions that financially motivate malware distribution. For bots, these actions include "proxying", "keystroke logging", "data leaking", and "program download and execute." We build representations of these high-level actions hierarchically, taking care to identify only the essential components of each action. The lowest level event in our behavior specifications are system call invocations. Since any specific operating system kernel exports a finite set of operations, we can expect to be able to enumerate all possible ways to interface with that kernel in order to achieve a certain effect (e.g., send data over the network). Since there are a finite number of ways to achieve each high-level action, we can expect to create representations that encode all such ways. Consequently, we can hope to correct the asymmetry present in syntax-based approaches to malware detection.

In this paper we propose and evaluate a behavior-based malware detector that takes as input the behavior specifications introduced above and an event stream provided by our system-wide emulator (Qemu), which monitors process execution. A system-wide emulator provides a rich source of information but infers no higher-level effects or semantics from the observed events. This disconnect between a voluminous stream of low-level events and any understanding of the aggregate effect of those events [13] is referred to as the *semantic gap*. We address the semantic-gap by decomposing the problem of specifying high-level behaviors into layers, making our specifications composable, configurable, less error-prone, and easy to update. Our system compares a monitored process's event stream to behavior specifications and generates an event when there is a match. This generated event may then be used in the specification of a higher-layer behavior.

Fig. 1 provides a subset of the hierarchy of events used to specify our sample target high-level behavior: downloading and executing a program, which is used in malware distribution. Events are represented via rectangles, with directed edges between them indicating dependencies; e.g., the `tcp_client` event depends upon the `sync_tcp_client` and `async_tcp_client` events. At the lowest layer of the hierarchy, $L0$, we identify successful system call invocations. Each $L1$ event aggregates $L0$ events that have a common side effect, as is the case with the $L1$ `net_recv` event which is generated whenever any of the $L0$ events `recv`, `recvfrom`, or `read` occur. Consequently, we can represent "all ways to receive data over the network" using a single event. Events at layers $L2$ and higher identify correlated sequences of lower-layer events that have some

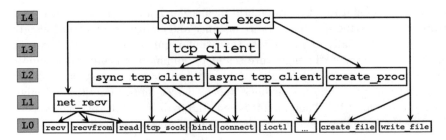

Fig. 1. A subset of the hierarchy of events used to specify download_exec

aggregate, composite effect; e.g., sync_tcp_client identifies when a synchronous TCP socket has been successfully created, bound, and connected upon.

Correlating low-level events generally entails specifying constraints on those events' arguments. In some cases, we need to specify that data used in one event is dependent upon data used in another event. Consequently, Qemu performs instruction-level data-flow analysis (tainting) and exports two related operations: set_tainted designates a memory region tainted with a particular label; and tainted determines whether a memory region contains data received from a particular source (as identified by its taint label). An important class of tainted data is that which is derived from local user input; this *clean data* is used to differentiate locally-initiated from remotely-initiated actions. Both tainted and set_tainted can be used in our behavior specifications; consequently, we can designate novel taint sources without changing our system implementation.

Commonly, malware variants are generated by: (I) applying packing transformations (compression and/or encryption) to a binary, (II) applying instruction-level obfuscation such as nop insertion as in [15], (III) applying source-level obfuscations as in [8], (IV) using a bot-development kit, which provides a point-and-click interface for specifying bot configuration details and builds the requested bot, or (V) directly modifying the source of an existing bot to add novel functionality and/or commands. Our behavioral graphs are insensitive to the type of changes entailed in (I) – (III) since the semantics of a malware's behavior are unchanged. The changes in (IV) also do not affect the bot's implementation of a particular command, only whether that command is available or not. Moreover, since we identify the fundamental system-call signatures for high-level behaviors, even changing the implementation as in (V) without changing the overall semantic effect would not suffice to evade detection.

The contributions of this paper include:

- A behavior-specification language (described in Section 2) that can be used to describe novel, semantically meaningful behaviors.
- A detector (described in Section 3) that identifies when a process performs a specified high-level action, regardless of the process's source-code implementation of the action.
- Our evaluation (described in Section 4) demonstrates that our detector can distinguish malicious execution of high-level behaviors from benign.

2   Representing High-Level Behaviors

In this section, we define our behavior graphs, each of which describes a correlated sequence of events that has some particular semantic effect (such as connect or tcp_client). The graph for a behavior B identifies only the fundamental component events required to achieve B and constrains these events as minimally as possible. Matching a behavior graph generates an event that can be used as a component within another graph; e.g., matching the tcp_client graph generates the tcp_client event, which can be used in specifying other behaviors, such as tcp_proxy. In this way, we compose graphs hierarchically, which enables us to recognize complex process behaviors.

2.1   Behavior Graphs

A *behavior graph* is a directed graph of a form that is adapted from and extends AND/OR graphs [26]. A behavior graph can be thought of as a template; multiple different sequences of events can be bound to this template subject to the edge constraints; binding and matching are described more precisely in sect. 2.1. Fig. 2 contains the behavior graph for our running example, download_exec.

Each behavior graph has a *start point*, drawn as a single point at the top of the graph, internal nodes, and an *output event*, which is represented via a shaded rectangle. Each internal node in the graph has a name, such as create_file, and formal parameters, such as fh0, fname, fname_len, as in fig. 2. Together, a node's name and formal parameters characterize a set of events, namely those events whose name is the same as the node's name. Whereas internal nodes represent input events needed in order to continue graph traversal, the special output event represents an action taken by our system; hence no additional input is required to traverse an edge from a penultimate node to the output event. For example, any sequence of events that matches the graph in fig. 2 up to the create_proc node will also reach the download_exec node and generate a download_exec event. When we match a graph and generate an output event e, the parameters for e are obtained from e's constituent events; e.g., the socket descriptor, rem_ip, and rem_port arguments for the download_exec output event in fig. 2 are obtained from its constituent tcp_client event.

AND-edge sets and OR-edge sets. A behavior graph may have AND-edges and OR-edges. OR-edges are drawn simply as directed edges, while AND-edges are drawn using a horizontal line to form an AND-edge set. In fig. 2, a sequence of events can reach the net_recv node by either of the two OR-edges leading into this node. In contrast, the AND-edges into write_file indicate that both net_recv *and* create_file are required to match this portion of the graph. If a node's in-edge set contains AND-edges and OR-edges, this expresses an OR of ANDs. We use AND-edge sets to identify events which can occur in any relative order but must all precede some other event.

Annihilator and Replicator Nodes. We correlate events by specifying predicates on their parameters; thus, it's important to know when a parameter has

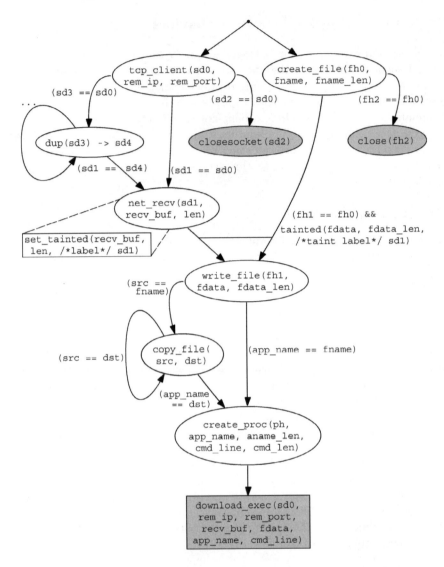

Fig. 2. AND/OR graph for downloading a file and executing it

been destroyed or duplicated. *Annihilator nodes* are used to represent that certain events destroy objects; e.g., calling `closesocket` on a socket descriptor `sd` releases `sd`, rendering it unable to be used in subsequent events. Annihilator nodes are represented via shaded ellipses, as with the `close(fh)` node in fig. 2. The edge from `create_file(fh0, ...)` to `close(fh2)` imposes the condition that `close` cannot be called on the newly-created file handle prior to `write_file(...)` being called on that same handle. Certain events, which we refer to as *replicators*, duplicate objects, such as socket descriptors or files. For example, calling `dup` on a socket descriptor or file handle creates a copy of the passed object; any operation that could be called on the original object can equivalently be called on the duplicate. We represent this via replicator nodes as with `dup(...)` and `copy_file(...)` in fig. 2. Since a replicator operation can be called repeatedly on its own output, replicator nodes contain a self-loop. For succinctness, some annihilators and replicators are excluded from the figures.

Edge Predicates. A directed edge can be labeled with predicates that must be satisfied to traverse the edge. Our system provides three predicate types: argument-value comparison, regular expression matching, and the `tainted` predicate. In *argument-value comparison*, we can apply any of the standard relational operators ($=, \neq, >, <$) to compare an argument value to a constant or to another argument. Fig. 2 contains several argument-value predicates, such as (`sd1 == sd0`) between the `tcp_client` and `net_recv` events. We can also specify that a string or buffer argument value must match a constant *regular expression* as used in the `send_email` behavior graph to identify transmission of SMTP protocol messages (e.g., `MAIL FROM`). The `tainted` predicate identifies data-flow relationships that must hold; we can require that an argument be derived from a general taint source (e.g., the network) or a specific taint source (e.g., a particular network connection). Fig. 2 includes a data-flow dependency; namely, the data written to the newly-created file (`fdata`) must be derived from data received over the specified network connection as indicated by its taint label (`sd1`).

On-reach Actions. Our monitoring system can perform an action in response to reaching a given node. An `on_reach` action is represented in the graph via a rectangle – connected to its corresponding node via dashed lines – containing the action to be performed. Fig. 2 shows that, upon reaching the `net_recv` node, the received buffer will be marked tainted with the taint label `sd1`.

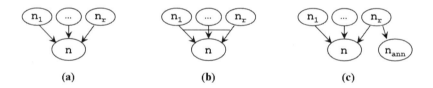

Fig. 3. Graph G with (a) OR-ed edges, (b) AND-ed edges, (c) an annihilator

Summary. A behavior graph defines a set of event sequences that match the graph, and may specify one or more on-reach events that will be generated when events match the graph in certain ways. These properties may be captured precisely in a rigorous definitions that allow us to prove properties of various algorithms. For example, a sequence $E = e_1, e_2, \ldots, e_k$ of events matches a behavior graph G if there is a function f from a subset of the nodes of G to events in E and a substitution S on variables that appear in formal parameters of the graph that satisfy the following conditions:

1. If there is an OR-edge set into a node n with $f(n) \in E$, as illustrated in fig. 3(a), then $\exists i. f(n_i) \in E$.

2. If there is an AND-edge set into a matched node n with $f(n) \in E$, as illustrated in fig. 3(b), then $\forall i.\, f(n_i) \in E$.
3. If there are matched nodes $n_r \to n$ with an annihilator node as illustrated in fig. 3(c), then $\nexists$ event $e \in E$ with $f(n_r) < e < f(n)$ and e matches $ev(n_{ann})$ by any $S' \supseteq S$.
4. If predicate P appears on an edge between nodes n and n' with $f(n) \in E$ and $f(n') \in E$, then the substitution instance $S(P)$ of P is true.

2.2   Behavior-Specification Language

A major contribution of our work is our behavior-specification language and monitoring system. Together, these can be used to specify then identify novel semantically-meaningful behaviors. The substrate consists of the graphs at each layer. Each of the behaviors specified by these graphs is a primitive that can be used in defining additional behaviors. Table 1 contains some primitives from our resulting behavior-specification language. We can describe "log keystrokes then send them in an email" using two of these primitives (keylogging and send_email) and correlating their arguments in a particular way, which illustrates the powerful, high-level expressiveness of our language.

2.3   Graph Construction

We developed our graphs manually and iteratively through domain knowledge and analysis of tens of gigabytes of execution traces, obtained from multiple runs of (I) around fifteen standard applications (including Googletalk, Filezilla, Firefox, putty, mIRC, Internet Explorer, Outlook, Thunderbird, SecureFX, Windows Media Player, SecureCRT, Unreal IRCd, Apple Software Update, Quicktime, etc.), (II) over one hundred specially-crafted programs, and (III) several malicious programs. We present our evaluation of these graphs' coverage in sect. 4.2.

Constructing L0 Graphs. Recall that L0 graphs represent successful system call invocations. The challenges here are as follows, (I) Windows implements the sockets API through a single system call, NtDeviceIoControlFile, (II) we do not have source access to the target OS, and (III) we need to be able to differentiate invocations of listen from invocations of accept and so on. We rely on analysis of process execution traces in order to identify commonalities

Table 1. Some primitives in our resulting behavior-specification language

Event	Arguments
tcp_client	sd, loc_ip, loc_port, rem_ip, rem_port
tcp_server	sd, loc_ip, loc_port, cli_ip, cli_port
net_send	sd, buf, buf_len
net_recv	sd, buf, buf_len
send_email	sd, targ_ip, from_addr, to_addr, data
keylogging	data, data_len

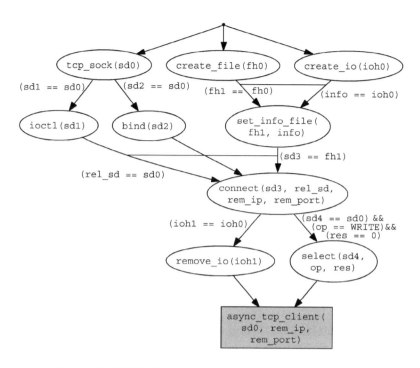

Fig. 4. $L2$ AND/OR graph for an asynchronous TCP client

(in arguments) across all invocations of a sockets function s_1 but which are not present in any invocations of all other sockets functions, s_2, s_3, ..., s_k. These commonalities are the basis of our $L0$ behavior graphs. The coverage of any graph then relies upon the diversity of process traces. Our process traces delineate entry to and return from each sockets function and identify all system calls invoked therein, including each system call's arguments and return value.

For some functions, such as `socket`, we crafted a suite of programs that invoked the function using all possible combinations of valid arguments. The execution of other sockets functions, however, is stateful in that it depends directly upon previous actions performed on the same socket descriptor; e.g. `recv`. Hence, it is not enough to provide different argument combinations to `recv`, we must also precede the invocation of `recv` with different combinations of particular sockets functions, such as `socket`, `bind`, `listen`, `connect`, and so on.

Pending System Call Invocations. A system call *sc* may not immediately return success or failure but rather return `STATUS_PENDING`; `NtWaitForSingleObject` is subsequently invoked on *sc*'s associated event object. We encode this path in our $L0$ graphs so as to identify *eventually successful* system call invocations.

Constructing $L1$ Graphs. Recall that $L1$ graphs aggregate $L0$ events that have a similar side effect. Since the system call interface is finite, we can enumerate the "relevant" effects of each system call and construct an $L1$ graph

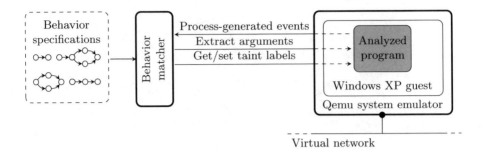

Fig. 5. Architecture of the system

for each such effect, where by "relevant" we mean "of interest". In our case, there were two effects that required $L1$ graphs: net_send and net_recv. These were immediately identifiable through domain knowledge. Note that aggregation graphs can exist at higher layers as well; e.g., we use an $L3$ graph to aggregate async_tcp_client and sync_tcp_client so that we may identify generally **any** tcp_client.

Constructing $L2$ Graphs. The graphs at $L2$ identify correlated sequences of lower-layer events which have some aggregate, composite effect, e.g. create_-write_file. For each target $L2$ behavior, we identify the events essential to that behavior and any dependencies between those constituent events. This identi-fication comes through (I) domain knowledge, such as encoding that in order to connect or listen on a socket, that socket must first have been (explic-itly or implicitly) bound, and (II) analysis of process traces, as used to con-struct the graphs for asynchronous network interaction. Windows exports a rich API for performing asynchronous network interaction, including the standard polling model using select on a socket as well as event-based approaches, such as via WSAEventSelect and WSAAsyncSelect. We are able to represent all of these through a single asynchronous TCP client graph as in fig. 4. This graph was built by examining process traces of existing applications which use the Windows asynchronous API as well as augmenting this analysis with traces of specially-crafted programs designed to capture more execution diversity.

3   System Implementation

Figure 5 depicts the architecture of our system, which has two main components: a system-wide emulator (Qemu) and a behavior matcher. Qemu emulates and traces the execution of analyzed programs in an isolated virtual environment. We use a hybrid emulated/virtualized approach, where the execution of the process under analysis is emulated while the execution of all other processes in the system is virtualized using KQemu [38]. The behavior matcher obtains information about process events from the emulator and attempts to match this input event stream to the behavior graphs. The behavior matcher operates independently of the particular monitoring technique and, as such, could be used in concert with, e.g., a process emulator. We use system-wide rather than process emulation for reasons relating to ease of experiment execution and cleanup. In particular, Qemu offers built-in support for rollback of system state and enables easy isolation of the monitored process from the external world.

3.1 System Emulator

Our system-wide emulator extends Qemu [39], an open-source emulator based on dynamic binary translation, by adding guest-OS-aware virtual machine introspection and taint analysis capabilities [25]. Guest-OS awareness is essential as we must be able to determine: which system call was invoked, which process invoked it, and the format of the system call's argument buffers. Our system currently emulates the IA-32 architecture and supports Microsoft Windows XP.

Process-generated Events. We instrument the code executed in the emulator by hooking the `sysenter` and `sysexit` instructions, which identify, respectively, invocation of and return from system calls. The instrumentation causes the emulator to provide this event stream to the behavior matcher in real-time.

Taint Analysis. The code executed in the emulator is also instrumented to perform taint analysis. In order to propagate taint labels through data dependencies, we extend the semantics of instructions that assign a value to a register or memory location, excluding floating point operations. We set the label of an assignment instruction's destination operand to be the union of the source operands' labels. Instructions instrumented in this manner are referred to as *taint propagation instructions.* To reduce overhead, we perform taint analysis on user-space code only. Our system also includes support for custom taint propagation rules over operations at a higher level than machine code instructions. In particular, we use this support to propagate taint across system calls that participate in hostname resolution; we assign the labels from the input hostname buffer to the location storing the resolved IP address.

Local User Input Tracking. Our local user input tracking module is designed for Win32 GUI applications, which receive messages indicating keyboard or mouse input events. The receiving application invokes its handler for the input event via a call to `DispatchMessage`. Mouse input messages do not provide the data value associated with the event; hence, identifying this data is a challenge. We address this by entering *clean mode* whenever the monitored process is handling receipt of a mouse click or keystroke; we define that period as starting with select invocations of `DispatchMessage` and ending with the corresponding returns. During clean mode, all taint propagation instructions unconditionally set the labels of their destination operands to be the special `clean` label. We present evaluation details related to user input tracking in sect. 4.6.

3.2 Behavior Matcher

At startup, the behavior matcher loads the provided set of behavior graphs. The matcher maintains some state for each graph, including the graph's current set of active nodes. A node n_{act} in graph G is *active* when we have received some event sequence $<ev_1, ev_2, ..., ev_k>$ which causes us to transition from the start state of G to n_{act}. There may be multiple event sequences corresponding to any particular active node; these event sequences (including each event's actual parameters) are also part of a graph's state. For brevity, certain details of the matching algorithm are omitted.

The behavior matcher is notified in real-time by the emulator every time the monitored process invokes or returns from a system call. Given a new event e with name $name_e$, for each behavior graph, the matcher: (I) checks whether there is a transition from an active node to a node n_{new} whose name is the same as $name_e$; if not, discard e, (II) extracts e's actual parameters and binds them to n_{new}'s formal parameters; (III) evaluates the predicates on (n_{act}, n_{new}); if they do not hold, discard e; (IV) if there is an on-reach action associated with n_{new}, then execute it; (V) if there is an edge from n_{new} to this graph's output event, the matcher generates the appropriate synthetic event.

4   Evaluation

This section provides the results of testing our dynamic specification-driven system monitor on seven malicious and eleven benign applications. After describing the experimental setup, we provide results demonstrating our ability to fill the semantic gap. Additionally, in testing the bots and benign applications against seven behavior graphs (referred to as *malspecs*) corresponding to bots' most threatening behaviors, there were no false negatives and seven false positives.

4.1   Experimental Setup

We performed our evaluation of the system in the environment depicted in Fig. 5. The evaluation framework consists of a victim Qemu virtual machine VM_{vict}, which is connected to a second virtual machine VM_{gway}, which is acting as a network gateway. On VM_{vict}, the system-wide emulator monitors the target malicious or benign process. The purpose of VM_{gway} is three-fold: it isolates the emulator from the external network to prevent further infection; it provides a realistic network environment for the execution of network-aware malware; and it hosts the command-and-control (C&C) server used to direct bots' activities.

4.2   Graph Validation

To determine whether our behavior graphs adequately cover semantically -equivalent but programmatically-different execution paths, we ran a diverse suite of applications within our monitoring framework and performed matching against a set of behavior graphs corresponding to generally innocuous actions. The column headings in Table 3 identify the tested behavior graphs. We drove each application's execution via performing the actions described in Table 2.

Table 2. Actions over which benign programs were exercised

Application	Interaction
ftp.exe, FTP Wanderer	Connect to server, authenticate, get a file, get multiple files
Internet Explorer	Access google.com, perform FTP access, download and execute a program.
Outlook Express	Download and read email containing an external image, reply to email, download and execute an attachment.
PuTTy	Connect and authenticate with server, send commands, use as SSH tunnel.
WinSCP, pSCP	Copy a file from server to client (and vice versa) using wildcards, download and execute a program.
SDK Installer	Download and install debugging tools from Microsoft server.
mIRC	Chat on a typical channel, DCC send, DCC get.
Google Talk	Chat, start a voice call, attempt a file transfer.
EasyProxy	Start proxy, route HTTP traffic.

Table 3. Graph validation results. Blank entries indicate that the software did not perform the tested behavior.

	TCP Client	TCP Server	Net Send	Net Recv	Create Proc	Dwnld File	Dwnld & Exec	Send Email	TCP Proxy
ftp.exe	✓	✓	✓	✓		✓			
Internet Explorer	✓		✓	✓	✓	✓	✓		
Outlook Express	✓		✓	✓	✓	✓	✓	✓	
PuTTy	✓	✓	✓	✓		✓			
pSCP	✓		✓	✓		✓			
WinSCP	✓		✓	✓	✓	✓	✓		
FTP Wanderer	✓	✓	✓	✓	✓	✓	✓		
SDK Installer	✓		✓	✓		✓			
mIRC	✓	✓	✓	✓		✓			
Google Talk	✓		✓	✓		✓			
Easy Proxy	✓	✓	✓	✓					✓

Moreover, during process execution, we performed manual analysis of network traffic and OS state in order to obtain "ground truth" about a process's actions. In this way, we were able to determine which behavior specifications any particular process should match at any point in time. Table 3 shows the output of our behavior matcher on each application and for each behavior graph. In all instances, the behavior matcher's output comported with ground truth, demonstrating that our graphs identify the fundamental components of the tested behaviors. Recall that graphs at $L2$ and higher compose lower-layer graphs. Hence, our evaluation was performed over more than forty distinct graphs.

Table 4. Malspecs used for evaluation. Recall that "RI" stands for remotely-initiated. Use of "tainted" in the below refers to data received over the network.

Name	Description
M1 RI Create and Execute File	A file with a tainted name is created, tainted data is written to the file, and a process is created from the file.
M2 RI Net Download	A connection to a tainted address or port is created, a file with a tainted name is created, and tainted data is written to the file.
M3 RI Send Email	A sequence of messages is matched using regular expressions, and found to correspond to an SMTP message sent to a tainted email address.
M4 RI Sendto	A UDP packet is sent to a tainted port or address.
M5 RI TCP Proxy	An application binds to a tainted port number, connects to a tainted address, and relays information from the tainted port to the tainted address.
M6 Keylogging	An application captures keystrokes destined for another process.
M7 Data Leak	An application sends data from either the filesystem or the registry over a network connection.

Table 5. Results on malicious bots. Blank entries denote behaviors not matched because the bot did not implement them; † entries denote behaviors which, when exercised, caused the bot to crash.

	M1	M2	M3	M4	M5	M6	M7
rBot	✓	✓	†	✓	✓		✓
Agobot	✓	✓	✓	✓	✓		✓
DSNX	✓	✓			✓	✓	✓
SpyBot	✓				✓	✓	✓
gSys	✓	✓		✓	✓		✓
rxBot	✓	✓	✓	✓	✓		✓
SDBot	✓	✓		✓	✓		✓

4.3   Specifications of Malicious Behavior

The malicious behavior specifications used in our evaluation (malspecs) reflect the targeted class of malware: bots. We targeted bots because their diverse range of behaviors encompasses the full range of behaviors performed by some other types of malware. Our malspecs (described briefly in Table 4) correspond to the most alarming threats posed by bots [2,3,4,5,6,7], including: malware install (M1, M2), spamming (M3), DoS attacks (M4), proxying (M5), and identity theft (M6, M7). Since bots act at the behest of a remote entity (the botmaster), we describe their actions as *remotely-initiated* (RI), which occurs when the values used to perform an action depend on data received over the network [16].

Table 6. Results on benign applications. "$\overline{\text{UI}}$" refers to an experiment in which user input tracking was not used, and "UI" to one with it enabled.

	M1		M2		M3		M4		M5		M6		M7	
	$\overline{\text{UI}}$	UI	$\overline{\text{UI}}$	UI	$\overline{\text{UI}}$	UI	$\overline{\text{UI}}$	UI	$\overline{\text{UI}}$	UI	$\overline{\text{UI}}$	UI	$\overline{\text{UI}}$	UI
ftp.exe													✓	✓
FTP Wanderer			✓										✓	
Internet Explorer	✓		✓								✓	✓		
Outlook Express	✓		✓										✓	✓
PuTTy													✓	✓
pSCP													✓	✓
WinSCP	✓												✓	✓
SDK Installer			✓											
mIRC			✓										✓	
Google Talk			✓				✓						✓	✓
EasyProxy														

4.4 Malware Results

We evaluated our system against seven malicious bots: rbot, Agobot, DSNX, Spybot, gSys, rxbot, and SDBot. When run in VM_{vict}, the bot connected to its C&C server (hosted in VM_{gway}), received a series of commands, and executed each. Table 5 shows the malspecs matched by each bot. From this, two conclusions can be drawn: first, we can detect when a process performs a high-level, semantically meaningful action, such as **Remotely-Initiated Net Download** (M2); and secondly, a single malspec can be used to identify a malicious behavior in a variety of bots. In one case, a command fed to a bot caused the bot to crash; consequently, we don't have results of executing the `email` command on rBot, which we expected would match **RI Send Email** malspec (M3).

4.5 Benign Application Results

To determine whether our malspecs sufficiently encode the difference between malicious behavior and benign, we tested eleven benign applications against these malspecs. We chose benign applications and actions over which to drive each application by favoring those with the greatest perceived likelihood of triggering a match on at least one malspec. Due to the black-box nature of many Win32 applications, this selection process is imperfect. Since we favored network-intensive applications and since our malspecs define remotely-initiated actions as those which use network-supplied parameters, we expect some false positives.

Table 6 provides the results of evaluating each of our benign programs against the set of malspecs. We ran each program under two scenarios: first, with user-input tracking disabled, which corresponds to the $\overline{\text{UI}}$ column; and second, with user-input tracking enabled, which correspond to the UI column. What this means is that, e.g., GoogleTalk matched M2, M4, and M7 when we performed no user input tracking and only matched M7 when this tracking was enabled.

We note that, in general, we are better able to distinguish malicious from benign when we take local user input into consideration in the manner described in 3.1.

The malspec matched by most benign programs (regardless of whether user input was taken into consideration) is **Leak** (M7). **Leak** identifies when data read from a file or the registry is subsequently sent on the network. This manifests in malicious applications when sensitive user data or product keys are transmitted to the botmaster. The deficiency of this malspec is its coarse granularity; i.e., reading data from *any* file on the system and sending any portion of that causes a match. In actuality, we would prefer to encode that, when an application reads data that *does not belong* to that application, this is considered a breach. So, in a sense, a more finely-tuned **Leak** malspec would retrofit fine-grained access control for applications on Windows systems, enabling application X to read from files and registry keys belonging to X. As proof of concept, we tuned the **Leak** malspec to exclude cookie files and certain registry keys belonging Internet Explorer (IE), which explains why IE does not match M7.

4.6   Tracking Local User Input

Since our benign results make clear the importance of identifying and tracking data which is dependent upon local user input, it is important to understand how often the system is cleaning data in response to local user input (as described in 3.1). If it is the case that our system is in "clean mode" the vast majority of the time, one might question the validity of our distinction between malicious and benign. We identified the number of instructions executed by a benign process over its lifetime as well as the number of instructions executed by that process while it was in *clean* mode. The percent of instructions executed in clean mode for three representative applications was: mIRC, 1%; Outlook, 3%; and IE, 9%. Thus, user-input tracking is performed for a very small portion of a process's lifetime and, hence, our designation of data as clean is conservative.

4.7   Additional Malware

Though our sample malspecs target malicious bots, high-level specifications can be generated to identify other classes of malware. To demonstrate this, we evaluated four Trojans (Bancos, two variants of Banker, and Delf) and three mass-mailing worms (all variants of Bagle) using our previous malspecs plus a new malspec designed to detect self-propagation through email. With no modifications to the **Leak** malspec (M7), each Trojan matched it. To identify self-propagation through email, we modified the **Remotely-Initiated Send Email** malspec (M3). Rather than requiring that the data-flow be from the network to an SMTP message, we specified that the data-flow must be from the code of the executable itself to an SMTP message, which corresponds to a process sending its own code in an email. This demonstrates that specifying signatures for entirely new classes of malware can be straightforward and intuitive.

Table 7. Performance overhead of the system. The **Tainting** column identifies the factor slowdown of running Qemu with tainting over vanilla Qemu. Each MX column identifies the factor slowdown (over vanilla Qemu) of performing both tainting and behavior matching for the given malspec. Startup time is not included and is on the order of ten seconds.

	Tainting	M1	M3	M6
Internet Explorer	5.25	11.53	7.19	5.64
pSCP	7.32	8.08	19.62	7.42
Agobot	3.01	16.40	23.73	16.84
rBot	9.50	11.20	11.08	9.62

4.8   Performance Overhead

We evaluated the performance overhead of our system on a subset of the malicious and benign applications used in the evaluation, including Agobot, rBot, pSCP, and Internet Explorer. We ran each application under three different scenarios: (I) Qemu with no tainting; (II) Qemu with tainting; (III) Qemu with tainting and behavior matching for each of three different malspecs. For each application under each scenario, we measured the amount of wall clock time elapsed between a set of events captured in system logs. We selected events that did not depend on user input, so as to preserve as much determinism as possible.

The **Tainting** column in Table 7 identifies the factor slowdown of using Qemu with tainting over Qemu without tainting, which we refer to as vanilla Qemu. We rely on previous work to determine the overhead of vanilla Qemu relative to native execution, which is substantial: on the order of a 7X to 23X [12]. Each MX column identifies the factor slowdown of performing both tainting and behavior matching for the given malspec. To obtain the total slowdown over native execution, we add the MX value to the numbers in [12]; e.g., running behavior matching using the M3 malspec on rBot exacts an 18X to 34X performance penalty over native execution. Our system yields rich information and would ease the analysis performed in applications which may be less performance sensitive.

5   Limitations and Future Work

Limitations. There are several approaches to evasion that we can imagine attackers would adapt against a system such as ours. In particular, since we identify correlated sequences of system calls, efforts to disrupt our ability to correlate are an obvious choice. This disruption could take the form of splitting the work required to achieve some high-level action across multiple processes or across different instantiations of the same process. Another high-level approach at evasion relates to our assumption that the malicious process interacts with the kernel. Malware that expropriate kernel functionality would disrupt our ability to see and thus correlate their events. For example, an application could use raw sockets and write its own IP and transport-layer headers rather than calling the standard `sockets` functions such as `connect`, `accept`, and so on. Malicious software could also attempt to subvert our user-input tracking. Another approach to evasion relates to breaking our assumption about data-flow; in particular, malware could convert data-flow dependencies into control-flow dependencies thus defeating our mechanism for determining when an action is remotely-initiated. Finally, because we are interposing on a process, we are vulnerable to Time-Of-Check-Time-Of-Use (TOCTOU) bugs as in [24].

Future Work. We are very interested in exploring automated ways of generating the behavior graphs at various layers of the hierarchy. At $L0$, perhaps given source code access, we could ascertain precisely the set of low-level events (and the constraints on those events) that corresponds to each `sockets` operation. Moving up the hierarchy, such access would also presumably enable us to determine all possible sequences of events which achieve some semantic effect, such as `tcp_client`. An alternative approach may be to use symbolic execution to infer these behavior graphs. In this way, we would still achieve our semantic understanding of the aggregate effect of a process's actions but would have more confidence in our coverage than can be obtained through even rigorous testing.

6   Related Work

Behavior-Based Malware Detection. Host-based behavior-based research has been done to identify rootkits, spyware, and bots [22,23,20,19,16]. In [19], Cui *et al* identify *extrusions*: stealthy outgoing network connections made by malicious processes. In the commercial sector, Sana Security's ActiveMDT [21] correlates a process's exhibition of various mostly stateless behaviors to determine whether the process is likely to be malicious. The simple behaviors include: whether a process spawns or terminates other processes, the directory from which a process executes, whether the process attempts to hide, and so on.

Egele *et al* present a method and system for detecting spyware implemented as a Browser Helper Object (BHO) in [30]. The method identifies *malicious information access and processing* when sensitive information flows (such as the list of URLs visited) are written by a BHO to the network, file system, or shared memory. Moreover, they perform static analysis to identify instructions that are control-dependent on sensitive information. Since spyware-writers could prevent the static analysis in [30] from identifying the post-dominator node, they consider failure of their static analysis to be indicative of malicious intent. This control-flow tracking is only performed for BHO code so it's unclear whether such tracking, if applied to general-purpose programs, would blur the ability to distinguish between malicious and benign. Yin *et al* developed a related malware detector, *Panorama* [18], which performs full-system, instruction level tainting and can express more diverse leakage policies than [30]. We can express the behavior identified by these systems using our specification language. As with [18], we do not currently track implicit information flows.

The behavioral specifications developed by Christodorescu *et al* [11] are similar to ours. Our specifications differ in three important ways. First, we use

AND-edges which enables expressing concurrent behaviors. Second, we introduce synthetic event nodes, in order to identify complex behaviors hierarchically. Additionally, the specifications used in Christodorescu's work were generated automatically using data mining techniques, as opposed to the manual techniques we used. This has a few significant implications. Most importantly, their specifications identify sequences of actions which happen to occur in some malicious software; the aggregate effect of such sequences is unknown as is the value to the malware of performing those actions. That is, their specifications may identify *incidental*, rather than fundamental or mission-critical, behaviors as are targeted by our work. Additionally, no effort is made to cover semantically equivalent sequences. Consequently, there may be alternative sequences of system calls which have the same effect as a mined sequence but are not identified in their graphs.

Dynamic Code Analysis. Some systems use emulation to monitor the execution of suspicious executables [27,33,34]; however, rather than attempting to infer high-level behaviors, these systems merely report the numerous low-level events, such as system calls and API invocations, generated during execution. Other research has focused on addressing the shortcomings of dynamic analysis, including using symbolic execution to explore multiple execution paths [31,32].

Semantic Gap Problem. The semantic gap problem was explored by Garfinkel *et al*, as part of an attempt to embed an intrusion detector into a virtual machine monitor [25]. Related systems include honeypots [29,28], where introspective capabilities are used to examine the state of the filesystem in order to detect hidden files. Rather than encoding semantic information about the system, Jones [35] applied implicit techniques to infer relevant state. One notable result was the use of these techniques to detect processes hidden by rootkits [36].

7 Conclusion

Bots are an extremely widespread and serious problem, allowing remote bot masters to direct the activities of millions of compromised hosts. We develop new behavioral monitoring techniques that are effective for identifying meaningful high-level actions, based on hierarchical behavior graphs. Behavior graphs provide a high-level specification language that can be used to describe semantically meaningful behaviors such as "proxying", "keystroke logging", "data leaking", and "downloading and executing a program." To address evasive malware behavior, our specifications are carefully crafted to detect alternate sequences of events that achieve the same goal.

Our experimental emulation-based detector identifies when a process performs a specified high-level actions, regardless of the process's source-code implementation of the action. We tested multiple malicious bots and benign programs and found that we were able to thoroughly identify high-level behaviors across a diverse code base. In addition, we are able to distinguish malicious execution of high-level behaviors from benign ones by distinguishing remotely-initiated from locally-initiated actions.

References

1. Symantec Internet Security Threat Report, Trends for January-June 07, Volume XII (September 2007)
2. Keizer, G.: Bot Networks Behind Big Boos. In: Phishing Attacks. TechWeb (November 2004)
3. Parizo, E.: New bots, worm threaten AIM network. SearchSecurity (December 2005)
4. Naraine, R.: Money Bots: Hackers Cas. In on Hijacked PCs. eWeek (September 2006)
5. Overton, M.: Bots and Botnets: Risks, Issues, and Prevention. In: Virus Bulletin Conference (October 2005)
6. Ianelli, N., Hackworth, A.: Botnets as a Vehicle for Online Crime. CERT Coordination Center (December 2005)
7. Ilett, D.: Most spam generated by botnets, says expert. ZDNet UK (September 22, 2004)
8. Christodorescu, M., Jha, S.: Testing Malware Detectors. In: Proc. of the International Symposium on Software Testing and Analysis (July 2004)
9. SRI Honeynet and BotHunter Malware Analysis Automatic Summary Analysis
10. Jevans, D.: The Latest Trends in Phishing, Crimeware and Cash-Out Schemes. Private correspondence
11. Christodorescu, M., Jha, S., Kruegel, C.: Mining specifications of malicious behavior. In: Proc. of the the 6th Joint Meeting of the European Software Engineering Conference and the ACM SIGSOFT Symposium on the Foundations of Software Engineering (August 2007)
12. NoAH Foundation: Containment Environment Design
13. Chen, P., Noble, B.: When Virtual is Better than Real. In: Proceedings of HotOS-VIII: 8th Workshop on Hot Topics in Operating Systems
14. Petritsch, H.: Understanding and Replaying Network Traffic in Windows XP for Dynamic Malware Analysis. Master's Thesis (February 2007)
15. Christodorescu, M., Jha, S., Seshia, S., Song, D., Bryant, R.: Semantics-Aware Malware Detection. In: IEEE Symposium on Security and Privacy (May 2005)
16. Stinson, E., Mitchell, J.: Characterizing Bots' Remote Control Behavior. In: Proc. of the 4th DIMVA Conference (July 2007)
17. Newsome, J., Song, D.: Dynamic Taint Analysis for Automatic Detection, Analysis, and Signature Generation of Exploits on Commodity Software. In: Network and Distributed Systems Symposium (February 2005)
18. Yin, H., Song, D., Egele, M., Kruegel, C., Kirda, E.: Panorama: capturing system-wide information flow for malware detection and analysis. In: Proc. of the 14th ACM conference on Computer and communications security (October 2007)
19. Cui, W., Katz, R., Tan, W.: BINDER: An Extrusion-based Break-in Detector for Personal Computers. In: Proc. of the 21st Annual Computer Security Applications Conference (December 2005)
20. Kirda, E., Kruegel, C., Banks, G., Vigna, G., Kemmerer, R.: Behavior-based Spyware Detection. In: Proc. of the 15th USENIX Security Symposium (August 2006)
21. United States Patent Application 20070067843 Method and apparatus for removing harmful software: Williamson, Matthew; Gorelik, Vladimir (March 22, 2007)
22. Strider GhostBuster Rootkit Detection

23. Wang, Y., Beck, D., Vo, B., Roussev, R., Verbowski, C.: Detecting Stealth Software with Strider GhostBuster. Microsoft Technical Report MSR-TR-2005-25
24. Garfinkel, T.: Traps and Pitfalls: Practical Problems in System Call Interposition Based Security Tools. In: Network and Distributed System Security (Feburary 2003)
25. Garfinkel, T., Rosenblum, M.: A Virtual Machine Introspection Based Architecture for Intrusion Detection. In: Network and Distributed Systems Symp. (Feburary 2003)
26. Nilsson, N.: Problem-Solving Methods in Artificial Intelligence. McGraw-Hill, New York (1971)
27. Bayer, U., Moser, A., Kruegel, C., Kirda, E.: Dynamic Analysis of Malicious Code. Journal in Computer Virology 2(1) (August 2006)
28. Jiang, X., Xu, D., Wang, X.: Stealthy Malware Detection Through VMM-Based "Out-of-the-Box" Semantic View Reconstruction. In: Proceedings of the 14th ACM Conference on Computer and Communications Security (CCS 2007), Alexandria, VA (November 2007)
29. Jiang, X., Wang, X.: 'Out-of-the-box' Monitoring of VM-based High-Interaction Honeypots. In: Kruegel, C., Lippmann, R., Clark, A. (eds.) RAID 2007. LNCS, vol. 4637, pp. 198–218. Springer, Heidelberg (2007)
30. Egele, M., Kruegel, C., Kirda, E., Yin, H., Son, D.: Dynamic Spyware Analysis. In: Proceedings of Usenix Annual Technical Conference, USA (June 2007)
31. Moser, A., Kruegel, C., Kirda, E.: Exploring Multiple Execution Paths for Malware Analysis. In: Proceedings of IEEE Symposium on Security and Privacy, May 2007, IEEE Computer Society Press, USA (2007)
32. Brumley, D., Hartwig, C., Liang, Z., Newsome, J., Poosankam, P., Song, D., Yin, H.: In: Lee, W., et al. (eds.) Botnet Analysis (2007)
33. Norman Sandbox
34. Willems, C.: Automatic Behaviour Analysis of Malware. Master Thesis. University of Mannheim
35. Jones, S.: Implicit Operating System Awareness in a Virtual Machine Monitor. Ph.D. Thesis, University of Wisconsin - Madison (April 2007)
36. Jones, S., Arpaci-Dusseau, A., Arpaci-Dusseau, R.: VMM-based Hidden Process Detection and Identification using Lycosid. In: ACM International Conference on Virtual Execution Environments (March 2008)
37. Vasudevan, A., Yerraballi, R.: Cobra: Fine-grained Malware Analysis using Stealth Localized-executions. In: Proceedings of IEEE Symposium on Security and Privacy, May 2006, IEEE Computer Society Press, USA (2006)
38. Bellard, F.: QEMU Accelerator (KQEMU)
39. Bellard, F.: QEMU, a Fast and Portable Dynamic Translator

A Study of the Packer Problem and Its Solutions

Fanglu Guo, Peter Ferrie, and Tzi-cker Chiueh

Symantec Research Laboratories

Abstract. An increasing percentage of malware programs distributed in the wild are packed by packers, which are programs that transform an input binary's appearance without affecting its execution semantics, to create new malware variants that can evade signature-based malware detection tools. This paper reports the results of a comprehensive study of the extent of the packer problem based on data collected at Symantec and the effectiveness of existing solutions to this problem. Then the paper presents a generic unpacking solution called Justin (Just-In-Time AV scanning), which is designed to detect the end of unpacking of a packed binary's run and invoke AV scanning against the process image at that time. For accurate end-to-unpacking detection, Justin incorporates the following heuristics: Dirty Page Execution, Unpacker Memory Avoidance, Stack Pointer Check and Command-Line Argument Access. Empirical testing shows that when compared with SymPack, which contains a set of manually created unpackers for a collection of selective packers, Justin's effectiveness is comparable to SymPack for those binaries packed by these supported packers, and is much better than SymPack for binaries packed by those that SymPack does not support.

1   The Packer Problem

1.1   Overview

Instead of directly obfuscating malware code, malware authors today heavily rely on packers, which are programs that transform an executable binary into another form so that it is smaller and/or has a different appearance than the original, to evade detection of signature-based anti-virus (AV) scanners. In many cases, malware authors recursively apply different combinations of multiple packers to the same malware to quickly generate a large number of different-looking binaries for distribution in the wild. The fact that more and more malware binaries are packed seriously degrades the effectiveness of signature-based AV scanners; it also results in an exponential increase in AV signature size, because when an AV vendor cannot effectively unpack a packed threat, it has no choice but to create a separate signature for the threat.

The percentage of malicious programs (malware) and benign applications (goodware) that are packed is hard to measure accurately. The numbers reported vary from vendor to vendor, but it is generally accepted that over 80% of malware is packed. These malware samples are often "wrapped" rather than

R. Lippmann, E. Kirda, and A. Trachtenberg (Eds.): RAID 2008, LNCS 5230, pp. 98–115, 2008.

packed, because many packers alter the original form of input binaries in ways that don't necessarily involve compression.

Not all packed programs are malware. We took a random sample of tens of thousands of executable files that were collected over a period of several months and were packed by packers that Symantec recognizes and knows how to unpack, and ran a set of commercial anti-virus (AV) scanners from multiple vendors against them. About 65% of these executable files are known malware. The remaining 35% most likely falls into the goodware category because these samples were collected more than a year ago and today's AV scanners should be able to capture most malware programs during that period of time. Clearly, the use of packers to protect goodware is quite common too.

The number of known packers is also hard to measure accurately. Symantec has collected a large number of packers - more than 2000 variants in more than 200 families. Among them, Symantec currently can identify nearly 1200 packers spread among approximately 150 families. However, among the 150 packer families Symantec knows about, it can only unpack about 110 of them, which contain approximately 800 members. This means that Symantec has a backlog of approximately 1200 members in 90 families, and this number increases day by day.

Without doubt, UPX [1] remains the most widely used packer. The rest of the list depends on how files are collected, but it always includes the old favorites like ASPack [2], FSG [3], and UPack [4]. In addition to those known packers, analysis of the above randomly sampled file set revealed at least 30 previously unknown packers. Some were minor variations of known packers, but most were custom packers. Amazingly, some of the clean files were packed with these custom packers.

The traditional way an AV vendor such as Symantec handles packers involves the following steps:

1. Recognize a packer's family. This is not as simple as it sounds. There are plenty of packers whose code is constant, and these can be recognized using simple strings. But many packers use polymorphic code to alter their appearance, and some packers intentionally use fake strings from other packers or standard compiler code, in order to fool the recognizers.

2. Identify a packer's version. A packer is classified into an existing version or is assigned to a new version. Being able to identify a packer is essential for successful unpacking, because there can be enough variations among members of the same family such that an unpacker for one member of a family cannot be used for another member for the same family.

3. Create a recognizer. The previous two steps are usually handled by a human, or applications such as neural net programs that have been trained on packers that are assigned to known families. This step, in contrast, is the act of writing a program whose function is solely to recognize that family, and perhaps that particular member/version.

4. Create an unpacker. Unlike the recognizer, whose goal is just to recognize the packer, the unpacker actually performs the reverse actions of the corresponding packer, and restores a packed binary as much as possible to its original form, including its metadata such as PE header for Win32 binaries.

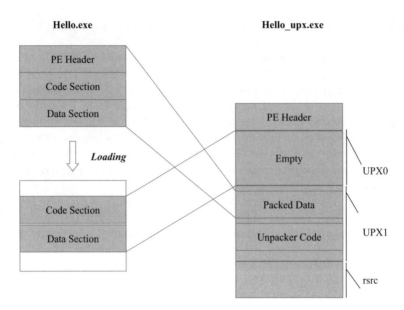

Fig. 1. A diagram that shows how an example program Hello.exe is packed by packer UPX and the layout of the resulting packed binary Hello_upx.exe

It requires a non-trivial amount of efforts to develop packer recognizers and unpackers. As noted above, Symantec has a backlog of approximately 1200 members in 90 families. To add unpacking support for a typical packer takes about six hours, on average. This means that it would take five full-time engineers about six months to clear the backlog if two unpackers are developed per day. However, in the case of complex packers such as Themida [5], it alone may take an experienced engineer up to six months to develop its unpacker. Packers with this level of complexity are not rare.

Due to these obvious disadvantages, the Justin (Just-In-Time AV scanning) solution presented in this paper takes a totally different approach. Justin leverages generic behaviors of unpacking and unpacks arbitrary packers without the need of knowing any information that is specific to the particular packer. Thus Justin doesn't have to go through any steps of the above traditional approach.

1.2   How Packers Work

Let's start with UPX, which arguably is among the most straightforward packers in use today. Figure 1 shows how UPX packs an example program Hello.exe.

When UPX compresses a PE binary, it begins by merging all of its sections into a single section, with the exception of the resource section. The combined data is then compressed into a single section of the resulting packed binary. In Figure 1, the code section and data section of hello.exe is compressed and stored in the Packed Data area of section UPX1 of the resulting binary Hello_upx.exe.

The resulting binary Hello_upx.exe contains three sections. The first section UPX0 is entirely virtual - it contains no physical data and is simply a placeholder.

It reserves the address range when Hello.exe is loaded to memory. At run time, Hello.exe will be restored to section UPX0. The second section contains the Packed Data, followed immediately by the Unpacker Code. The entry point in the PE header of Hello_upx.exe is changed to point directly to the Unpacker Code. The third section contains the resource data, if the original binary had a resource section, and a partial import table, which contains some essential imports from `kernel32.dll` as well as one imported function from every DLL used by the original binary.

The first two sections are set to read/write/execute, regardless of what they were before, and are not changed at run time. Therefore UPX is NX compatible, but it loosens up the protection for the original binary's read-only sections. The third section is simply set to read/write, since no execution should happen within that section.

After unpacking, UPX write-enables the header of the resulting binary, then changes the first two sections of the section table to read-only, and write-protects the header again. This ensures compatibility with some application programs that check in-memory section table instead of the actual section attributes, because these sections are supposed to be non-writable.

More sophisticated packers use a variety of techniques that virus writers use to defeat attempts to reverse-engineer, bypass, and disable the unpackers included in packed binaries. We discuss some of them in the following.

Multi-layer packing uses a combination of potentially different packers to pack a given binary, and makes it really easy to generate a large number of packed binaries from the same input binary. In practice, packed binaries produced by some packers may not be packed again by other packers. Also, the use of multi-layer packing itself could be used as an indication of malware, so the very presence of multiple layers - supported or not - could allow for a heuristic detection.

Anti-unpacking techniques are designed to make it difficult to uncover the logic of an unpacker, and fall into two major categories: passive and active. Passive anti-unpacking techniques are intended to make disassembly difficult, which in turns makes it difficult to identify and reverse the unpacking algorithm. Active techniques are intended to protect the running binary against having the fully unpacked image intercepted and extracted, and can be further classified into three subcategories: *anti-dumping*, *anti-debugging*, and *anti-emulating*. There are several commercial packers, such as Enigma and Themida, which promote their use of all of these techniques.

The simplest way to capture an unpacked image is to dump the address space of a running process. The simplest form of anti-dumping involves changing the value of the image size in the process environment block, and makes it difficult for a debugger to attach to the process or to dump the correct number of pages. More advanced anti-dumping methods include page-level protections, where each page is packed individually and unpacked only when accessed. It can even be packed again afterwards. This technique is used by packers such as Armadillo [6]. Shrinker [7] uses a variation of this method, by unpacking regions when they are accessed, but it is perhaps for performance reasons rather than an anti-dumping mechanism, since the unpacked pages remain in memory.

A very common way to capture an unpacked image is to use a debugger to step through the code, or to set breakpoints at particular locations. Two common forms of anti-debugging involve checking some values that the operating system supplies in the presence of a debugger. The first uses a public API, called `IsDebuggerPresent()`, which returns a Boolean value that corresponds to the presence or absence of a debugger. This technique is defeated by always setting the value to FALSE. The second anti-debugging technique checks if certain bits are set within the `NtGlobalFlag` field. The values of interest are heap tail checking (0x10), heap free checking (0x20), and heap parameter checking (0x40). They get their values from the `GlobalFlag` field of the `HKLM/System/CurrentControlSet/Control/Session Manager` registry key. A debugged process always has these values set in memory, regardless of the values in the registry. This technique can be defeated by clearing the bits in the process environment block.

Another way to capture an unpacked image to use an emulator to execute it in a protected environment. There are many ways to attack an emulator. The most common is to attempt to detect the emulator, since it is very hard to make an emulator whose behavior matches closely to real machine. However, each emulator has different capabilities, so there are multiple methods to detect different emulators [8].

Not all protection methods restore the host to its original form when executed. In particular, wrappers such as VMProtect [9] replace the host code with byte-code, and attach an interpreter to execute that byte-code. The result is that the original host code no longer exists anywhere, making it hard to analyze and essentially impossible to reverse. In addition, the byte-code have different meanings in different files. That is, the value 0x01 might mean "add" in one VMProtect-packed binary, but "xor" in another, and only the corresponding embedded interpreter knows for sure.

2   Unpacking Solutions from the Anti-Virus Industry

The AV industry has developed several approaches to tackle the packer problem, which satisfy different combinations of the following requirements:

- Effective: An ideal unpacker should restore packed binaries to their original form.
- Generic: An ideal unpacker should cover as many different types of packed binaries as possible.
- Safe: Execution of an ideal unpacker should not leave any undesirable side effects.
- Portability: An ideal unpacker should be able to run on multiple operating systems.

The first requirement enables existing signature-based AV scanners to be directly applied to an unpacker's output and detect the embedded malware if applicable. The second requirement decreases the amount of efforts required to keep up with new packers. The third requirement is crucial for at-rest file scanning, where the AV scanner initiates the unpacker and therefore has to be absolutely sure that the unpacker itself does not cause any harm. The final requirement is relevant for in-network scanning, where the unpacker and the AV scanner may need to run on different platforms than that required by the packed binaries.

The first solution to the packer problem is to the traditional way which manually creates recognizers and unpackers by reverse-engineering the unpackers in packed binaries by following steps as outlined in Section 1.1. The Sym-Pack library [10] from Symantec falls into this category. This solution is safe, portable, largely effective but not generic. That is, one needs to develop a packer recognizer and an unpacker for each distinct packer. Given a set of packer recognizers and unpackers, one can classify packed binaries into four categories: (1) packed binaries whose packer can be recognized and that can be unpacked, (2) packed binaries whose packer can be recognized but that cannot be unpacked, (3) packed binaries whose packer cannot be recognized, and (4) non-packed binaries. Assuming all the packers that goodware programs use fall into the first category, then one can black-list all packed binaries belonging to the second and third category. To be able to distinguish between packed and non-packed binaries, one needs a technique to detect packed files generically. This can be done by, for example, calculating the entropy [11] of a particular region of an executable binary that most likely contains compressed data.

However, this general approach of handling packed binaries has several problems. First, it entails significant investments in engineering efforts, and the level of investment required is expected to increase over time as more packers appear in the wild. Second, if goodware decides to use packers in the second and third category above, false positives in the form of blocking legitimate goodware may arise. The same problem may also occur when packer recognizers and unpackers contain design or implementation bugs that, for example, treat variants of packers used by goodware as unknown packers. Finally, this approach requires continuing maintenance for existing packer recognizers and unpackers. Old packers never die. They just get rediscovered and reused, and never quite go away. For example, the self-extractor stub for RAR - the world's second-most popular archiving format after ZIP - is packed by UPX v0.50, which dates from 1999.

The second solution to the packer problem is to run a packed binary inside an emulator for a sufficiently long period of time so that the embedded binary is fully unpacked, and then invoke signature-based AV scanners against the memory image to check if it contains any malware. The x86 Emulator [12] take this approach. This solution is safe, portable and generic, but is not always effective [13] for two reasons. First, a packed binary can terminate itself before the embedded binary is unpacked if it detects that it is running inside an emulator. Second, so far there is no good heuristic to decide when it is safe to stop the emulation run of a packed binary, because it is difficult to distinguish between the following two cases: (1) the embedded binary is benign and (2) the embedded binary is malicious but is not fully unpacked. Another disadvantage of this approach is that it takes a non-trivial amount of effort to develop a high-fidelity and high-performance emulator.

The third solution to the packer problem is to invoke AV scanning against a suspicious running process's memory image either periodically or at certain security-sensitive events. Symantec's Eraser dump [10] takes this approach. This solution is generic, somewhat effective, but neither safe nor portable. Its effectiveness is compromised by the facts that certain information required by AV scanners, such as the entry point, is not available, and that the memory image being scanned is not the same as that of an embedded binary immediately after it is loaded. For example, a malware program may contain an encrypted string in its binary file, and decrypt it at run time. If the encrypted string is part of its signature, periodic memory scanning may fail to detect the malware because the encrypted string is no longer in its memory image.

PolyUnpack [14] is a generic approach to the problem. It detects newly generated code by comparing if the current instruction sequence exists in the original program. Instructions are disassembled and single stepped to achieve the detection. Because both disassembling and single stepping are expensive, this approach incurs significant performance overhead.

Renovo [15] monitors each instruction and tracks if any the memory is overwritten. If any overwritten memory is executed, it is treated as one layer of unpacking. This approach instruments instructions and also incurs significant performance overhead.

OllyBone [16] tracks write and execution too. It improves performance by overloading the user/supervisor bit and exploiting the separation of data TLB and instruction TLB in the X86 architecture. Saffron [17] combines OllyBone's technique with Intel's PIN to build a tool that detects control transfers to dynamically created or modified pages, and dumps memory images at that time.

OmniUnpack [18] also relies on OllyBone for identifying executed pages and invokes AV scanning before every "dangerous" system call. In addition, it incorporates two additional optimizations to reduce the total number of AV scans. First, it invokes an AV scan only when there is a control transfer to a dynamically modified page between the previous and current dangerous system calls. Second, whenever an AV scanner is invoked, it only scans those pages that are modified since the last dangerous system call. OmniUnpack is generic and largely effective, but neither safe nor portable. In particular, the fact that it requires whole-binary scanning is incompatible with almost all existing commercial AV scanners, which scans only a selective portion of each binary. Moreover, it only works for running processes, but is not suitable for at-rest file scanning.

One common heuristic shared among PolyUnpack, Renovo, OllyBone, Saffron, OmniUnpack and Justin (descibed in the next section) is that a necessary condition of the end of unpacking is a control transfer to a dynamically created or modified page. However, there are important differences between Justin and these previous efforts. First, Justin includes a more complete set of heuristics to detect the end of unpacking, including unpacked code region make-up, stack pointer check, and command line argument check. Second, Justin includes several counter-measures that are designed to fend off evasion techniques that existing packers use. Finally, Justin leverages NX support rather than overloads the supervisor/user bit, and is more efficient to track page executions.

3   Justin: Just-in-Time AV Scanning

3.1   Design

Justin is designed to be generic, effective and safe, but is not portable. The key idea of Justin is to detect the end of unpacking during the execution of a packed binary and invoke AV scanning at that instant. In addition to triggering AV scanning at the right moment, Justin also aims to provide the AV scanner a more complete picture about the binary being scanned, specifically its original entry point.

A packed binary logically consists of three components, the unpacker, the packed binary, and the area to hold the output of the unpacker. Different packers arrange these components into different number of PE sections. The section containing the unpacker's output typically is relatively easy to identify because its reserved size is larger than that of its initialized data contained in the binary.

The initial design goal of Justin is to enforce the invariant that no code page can be executed without being scanned first. Its design is relatively straightforward: it first scans a packed binary at load time, runs the binary, keeps track of pages that are dynamically modified or created, and scans any such page when the program's control is transferred to it. This design relies on an AV scanner that does whole-binary scanning, and is not compatible with existing commercial AV scanners, which employ a set of heuristics (e.g., file type) to select a portion of a binary and scan only bytes in that portion.

To work with commercial AV scanners, the design goal of Justin is shifted to detecting the end of unpacking during the execution of a packed binary. In addition, it makes the following two assumptions about packers: (1) The address space layout of the program embedded within a packed binary after it is unpacked is the same as that if the program is directly loaded into memory, and (2) the unpacker in a packed binary completely unpacks the embedded program before transferring control to it. The majority of packers satisfy Assumption (1) because they are supposed to work on commercially distributed executable binaries, which generally do not come with a relocation table. They also satisfy Assumption (2) because they cannot guarantee 100% static disassembly accuracy and coverage [19]. Some packers do perform simple metamorphic transformation to the input binaries before packing them. These packers inherently can evade signature-based AV scanners even without packing and are thus outside the scope of Justin. These two assumptions make it feasible to apply standard file-based AV scanners with selective scanning to a packed binary's memory image at the end of unpacking.

When the unpacker in a packed binary completes unpacking the embedded program, it sets up the import address table, unwinds the stack, and transfers control to the embedded program's entry point. Therefore the necessary conditions for the execution of a packed binary to reach the end of unpacking are

- A control transfer to a dynamically created/modified page occurs.
- The stack is similar to that when a program is just loaded into memory.
- The command-line input arguments are properly set up on the stack.

Accordingly, Justin combines these conditions into a composite heuristic for detecting the end of unpacking during the execution of a packed binary as follows. Given a binary, Justin loads it, marks all its pages as executable but non-writeable, and starts its execution. During the execution, if a write exception occurs on a non-writeable page, Justin marks this page as dirty, turns it into non-executable and writeable and continues; if a execution exception occurs on a non-executable page, Justin invokes an AV scanner to scan the whole memory image, and turns the page into executable and non-writeable if the end-of-unpacking check concludes that the unpacking is not done. Note that the whole memory image is presented as a file and scanned by the AV scanner. This is different from OmniUnpack [18] which only scans dirty pages. By presenting the whole memory image as a file, Justin's output is compatible with existing commercial AV scanners and avoids the problem in which signature straddles page boundaries. For a non-packed binary, because no code page is generated or modified during its execution, it is impossible for an execution exception to occur on a dirty page and no AV scan will be triggered at run time. So the performance overhead of Justin for non-packed binaries is insignificant. The performance overhead of Justin for packed binaries, on the other hand, depends on the number of times in which the program's control is transferred to a newly created page during its execution.

The current Justin prototype leverages virtual memory hardware to identify control transfers to dynamically created pages. More specifically, it manipulates write and execute permissions of virtual memory pages to guarantee that a page is either writeable or executable, but never both. With write protection, Justin can track which pages are modified. With execute protection, Justin can detect which pages are executed. If a binary Justin tracks needs to modify the protection attributes of its pages in ways that conflict with Justin's setting, Justin records the binary's intentions but physically keeps Justin's own setting. If the binary later on queries the protection attributes of its pages, Justin should respond with the binary's intentions, rather than the physical settings.

Whenever a virtual memory protection exception occurs, Justin takes control and first checks if this exception is owing to its setting. If not, Justin simply delivers the exception to the binary being monitored; otherwise Justin modifies the protection attributes according to the above algorithm. To ensure that Justin is the first to respond to an exception, the exception handler component of Justin must be the first in the binary's vectored exception handler list.

To ensure that the original program in a packed binary can execute in the same environment, most unpackers unwind the stack so that when the embedded program is unpacked and control is transferred to it, the stack looks identical to that when the embedded program is loaded into memory directly. For example, assume that the initial ESP at the time when a packed binary is started is 0x0012FFC4, then right after the unpacking is done and the unpacked code is about to be executed, the ESP should point to 0x0012FFC4 again. This rule applies to many unpackers and is widely used in manually unpacking practice. Justin automates this method by recording ESP's value at the entry point of a packed binary, and compares the ESP at every exception in which the program's control is transferred to a dynamically created page. The exception context of an exception contains all CPU registers at the time when the binary raises the exception.

When a PE binary is run with a set of command-line arguments, these arguments are first placed in heap by the loader and later copied to the stack by a piece of compiler-generated code included in the binary at the program start-up time. Based on this observation, one can detect the start of execution of the original binary embedded in a packed binary, which occurs short after the end of unpacking.

3.2   Implementation Details

Justin currently is implemented for Windows only. But the idea will also work on other operating systems. The core logic of Justin is implemented in an exception handler that is registered in every binary at the time when it starts. In addition, Justin contains a kernel component that intercepts system calls related to page protection attribute manipulation and query and "lies" properly so that its page status tracking mechanism is as transparent to the binary being monitored as possible. Justin leverages NX support [20] in modern Intel X86 processors and Windows OS to detect pages that are executed at run time. In theory, it is possible to use other bits such as supervisor bits for this purpose, as is the case with OmniUnpack [18] and OllyBone [16].

Because Justin enforces the invariant that a page is either executable or writeable but not both, it could lead to a live lock for a program that contains an instruction which modifies data in the same page. The live lock is an infinite loop of interleaved execution and write exceptions. To address this issue, Justin checks if a memory-modifying instruction and its target address are in the same page when a write exception occurs. If so, Justin sets the page writeable, single-steps this instruction, and sets the page non-writeable again. This mechanism allows a page to be executable and writeable simultaneously for one instruction, but after that Justin continues to enforce the invariant.

One way to escape Justin's invariant is to map two virtual pages to the same physical page, and set one of them as executable and non-writeable and the other as writeable and non-executable. With this set-up, the unpacker can modify the underlying physical page through the writeable virtual page and jump to the underlying physical page through the executable virtual page, without triggering exceptions. To defeat this evasion technique, Justin makes sure that the protection attributes of virtual pages which are mapped to the same physical page are set in the same way.

Instead of a PE section, an unpacker can put its output in a dynamically allocated heap area. To prevent unpacked binaries from escaping Justin's tracking,

Justin tracks pages in the heap, even when it grows. Similarly when a file is mapped into a process's address space, the mapped area needs to be tracked as well.

An unpacker can also put its output in a file, and spawns a process from the file later on. In this case, Justin will not detect any execution exception, because the generated code is invoked through a process creation mechanism rather than a jump instruction. Fortunately, standard AV scanners can detect this unpacked binary file when it is launched.

After recreating the embedded binary, some packers fork a new process and in the new process jumps to the embedded binary. This evasion technique is effective because page status tracking of a process is not necessarily propagated to all other processes it creates. Justin defeats this technique by tracking the page protection status of a process and that of all of its descendant processes.

Some unpackers include anti-emulation techniques that attempt to determine if they run inside an emulator or are being monitored in any way. Because Justin modifies page protection attributes in ways that may differ from the intentions of these unpackers, sometimes it triggers their anti-emulation techniques and results in program termination. For example, one unpacker detects if a page is writeable by passing a buffer that is supposedly writeable and Justin marks as non-writeable into the kernel as a system call argument. When the kernel attempts to write to the buffer, a kernel-level protection exception occurs and the program terminates. Justin never has a chance to handle this exception because it is a kernel-level exception and never gets delivered to the user level. To solve this problem, Justin intercepts this kernel-level protection exception, modifies the page protection attribute appropriately to allow it to continue, and changes it back before the system call returns.

When Justin detects the end of unpacking, it treats the target address of the control transfer instruction as the entry point of the embedded binary. However, some packers obfuscate the original entry point by replacing the first several instructions at the main entry point with a jump instruction, say Y, to a separate piece of code, which contains the original entry point instructions and a jump back to the instruction following Y. Because an unpacker can only safely replace the first several instructions, Justin can single-step the first several instructions at the supposedly entry point to specifically detect this evasion technique.

Some packers significantly transform an input binary before packing it. In general, these transformations are not always safe, because it requires 100% disassembly accuracy and coverage, which is generally not possible. Therefore, although these packers may evade signature-based AV scanners after Justin correctly produces the unpacked binary, we generally consider these packers to be too unreliable to be a real threat.

4   Evaluation

4.1   Effectiveness of Justin

To assess the effectiveness of Justin, we collect a set of known malware samples that are not packed by any known packers, then use different packers to pack

Table 1. Effectiveness comparison between Justin and manually created unpackers from SymPack when they are used together with an AV scanner

Packers	Packed	Justin Unpack Failure	Justin Detection Failure	Justin Detection	SymPack Detection	Justin Detection Improvement
ASPack	182	4	0	178	182	-4
BeroPacker	178	0	4	174	161	13
Exe32Pack	176	32	0	144	176	-32
Mew	180	1	8	171	171	0
PE-Pack	176	1	0	175	171	4
UPack	181	1	5	175	173	2

them, and run the packed binaries under Justin and Symantec's AV scanner to see if they together can detect these samples. As a comparison, we used the same procedure but replaced Justin with Symantec's SymPack library, which contains a set of unpacker routines created manually by reverse engineering the logic of known packer programs. This experiment tests if Justin can unpack packed binaries to the extent that AV signatures developed for non-packed versions of malware samples still work.

There are totally 183 malware samples used in this study. As shown in Table 1, most packers cannot pack every malware program in the test suite successfully. So only successfully packed malware programs are unpacked. The number of successfully packed malware programs for each packer is listed in Column 2 of Table 1.

Justin cannot unpack certain packed samples. By manually examining each failure case, we identify two reasons. First, some samples simply cannot run any more after being packed. Being a run-time detection technology, Justin cannot unpack something that does not run. From malware detection's standpoint, these packed samples are no longer a threat as they won't be able to cause any harm. Second, the packer Exe32Pack sometimes doesn't really modify the original binary when it produces a packed binary. For these packed binaries, no unpacking occurs at run time and Justin does not have a chance to step in and trigger the AV scan. From malware detection's standpoint, these packed samples are not a problem either. The original program in these samples are in plain-text and AV scanner can detect them without Justin. The number of packed malware programs that Justin fails to unpack is listed in Column 3 of Table 1.

Among those malware samples that Justin successfully unpacks, not all of them can be detected. By manually analyzing these undetected samples, we find that most detection failures arise because signatures developed for non-packed versions of malware programs do not work for their unpacked versions. Although Justin can detect the end of unpacking, the unpacked result it produces is not exactly the same as the original program. Because some AV signatures are too stringent to accommodate these minor differences, they fail to detect Justin's outputs. For the same reasons, none of these undetected samples cannot be detected by SymPack either. The number of unpacked but undetected samples is listed in Column 4 of Table 1.

Overall, Justin's detection rate (Column 5) is slightly higher than SymPack's (Column 6) among the malware samples that can be successfully unpacked, because Justin relies on the unpackers embedded in the packed binaries, which are generally more reliable than the manually created unpackers in SymPack, to capture the execution state of a malware before it starts to run.

To test Justin's generic unpacking capability, we select a set of 13 packers that are not supported by SymPack. Justin can successfully unpack binaries packed by 12 out of these 13 packers. The packer whose packed binaries Justin cannot unpack detects Justin's API call interception and terminates the packed binary's execution without unpacking the original program. We also test a set of malware samples packed by a packer that is not well supported by SymPack against Justin and an AV scanner. The number of these packed malware samples that can be detected by Justin/AV scanner is almost twice the number of SymPack/AV scanner.

To summarize, as long as a packed binary can run and requires unpacking at run time, Justin can unpack it successfully. Moreover, for the same malware samples packed by packers supported in SymPack, the unpacked outputs produced by Justin are more amenable to AV scanning than those produced by SymPack, thus resulting in a higher detection rate than SymPack. Finally, Justin is able to detect twice as many packed malware samples than SymPack when they are packed by packers not supported in SymPack.

4.2   Number of Spurious End-of-Unpacking Detections

When Justin detects an end of unpacking during a packed binary's execution, it invokes the AV scanner to scan the process image at that instant. The main heuristic that Justin uses to detect the end of unpacking is to monitor the first control transfer to a dirty page (called *Dirty Page Execution*). Unfortunately this heuristic triggers many spurious end-of-unpacking detections for binaries packed by certain packers and thus incurs a significant AV scanning overhead even for goodware packed by these packers. The same observation was made by Martignoni et al. [18]. Their solution to this problem is to defer AV scanning until the first "dangerous" system call. Even though this technique drastically decreases the number of spurious end-of-unpacking detections, it also loses the entry-point information, which plays an important role for commercial signature-based AV scanners.

Instead, Justin incorporates three addition heuristics to reduce the number of spurious end-of-unpacking detections. *Unpacker Memory Avoidance* limits the Dirty Page Execution technique to pages that are not likely to contain the unpacker code. *Stack Pointer Check* checks if the current stack pointer at the time of a first control transfer to a dirty page during a packed binary's run is the same as that at the very start of the run. *Command-Line Argument Access* checks if the command-line arguments supplied with a packed binary's run is moved to the stack at the time of a first control transfer to a dirty page. Each of these

Table 2. Comparison among four heuristics in their effectiveness to detect the end of unpacking, as measured by the number of times it thinks the packed binary run reaches the end of unpacking. The last three heuristics, Unpacker Memory Avoidance, Stack Pointer Check and Command-Line Argument Detection, are used together with the first heuristic, which monitors first control transfers to dirty pages.

Packers	Dirty Page Execution	Unpacker Memory Avoidance	Stack Pointer Check	Command-Line Argument Access
ACProtect	186	11	1	2
ASPack	96	12	2	3
ASProtect	1633	12	12	3
Exe32Pack	394	11	1	2
eXPressor	15	11	1	2
FSG	12	12	1	2
Molebox	3707	11	1	2
NsPack	19	11	1	2
Obsidium	not work	14	4	6
PECompact	16	12	2	3
UPack	442084	12	2	3
UPX	11	11	1	2
WWPack	12	11	1	2

three heuristics is meant to work in conjunction with the Dirty Page Execution heuristic.

We apply a set of packers to a set of test binaries, run these packed binaries under Justin, and measure the number of end-of-unpacking detections. Table 2 shows the average number of end-of-unpacking detections for each of these four heuristics. Used together, the three additional heuristics in Justin successfully reduces the number of spurious end-of-unpacking detections to the same level as Martignoni et al. [18], but in a way that still preserves the original program's entry point information.

Although the number of spurious end-of-unpacking detections produced by Unpacker Memory Avoidance is higher than the other two heuristics, it is more reliable and resilient to evasion. If Justin mistakes a normal page as an unpacker page, it will not monitor this page, and the worst that can happen is that Justin loses the original program's entry point if this page happens to contain the original entry point. If Justin mistakes an unpacker page as a normal page, it will monitor this page, and the worst that can happen is additional spurious end-of-unpacking detections. Currently, Justin is designed to err on the conservative side and therefore is tuned to treat unpacker pages as normal pages rather than the other way around.

We test the Stack Pointer Check heuristic using the packers listed in Table 2. Column 4 of Table 2 shows the average number of end-of-unpacking detections for each packer tested is decreased to just one or two for most packers. Unfortunately, this heuristic generates false negatives but no false positive. A false positive occurs when a certain execution point passes the stack pointer check but it is not the end of unpacking. This happens when the unpacker intentionally manipulates the stack pointer to evade this heuristic. None of the packers we tested exhibit this evasion behavior. A false negative happens when Justin thinks an execution point is not the end of unpacking when in fact it is. This happens when the unpacker does not clean up the stack to the exactly same state when the unpacker starts. The unpacker in ASProtect-packed binaries doesn't completely clean up the stack before transferring control to the original binary. It is possible to loosen up the stack pointer check, i.e., as long as the stack pointers are roughly the same, to mitigate this problem, but this is not a robust solution and may cause false positives.

The key idea in Command-Line Argument Access is that when the original binary embedded in a packed binary starts execution, there is a piece of compiler-generated code that will prepare the stack by fetching command-line arguments. Therefore, if at an execution point the command-line arguments supplied to a packed binary's run are already put on the stack, that execution point must have passed the end of unpacking. This command-line argument access behavior exists event if the original binary is not designed to accept any command-line arguments. Because Justin gets to choose the values for command-line arguments, it detects command-line argument access by searching the stack for pointers that point to values that it chooses as command-line arguments.

We test the Command-Line Argument Access heuristic using the packers listed in Table 2. Column 5 of Table 2 list the average number of end-of-unpacking detections for each packer tested, which is generally higher than the Stack Pointer Check heuristic for the following reason. To put command-line arguments on the stack, the original program needs to execute a couple of new generated code pages. The execution of the new generated pages causes one or two more end-of-unpacking detections. Even though its reported number of end-of-unpacking detections is slightly higher, the Command-Line Argument Access heuristic does not generate any false positive or false negative. For example, it can accurately detect the end of unpacking for ASProtect-packed binaries, but the Stack Pointer Check heuristic cannot.

4.3   Performance Overhead of Justin

Justin is designed to work with an AV scanner to monitor the execution of binaries. Its performance penalty comes from two sources: (1) additional virtual memory protection exceptions that are triggered during dirty page tracking, and (2) AV scans invoked when potential ends of unpacking are detected. We packed Microsoft Internet Explorer, whose binary size is 91KB, with a set of packers, ran the packed version, and measured its start-up delay with and without Justin on a 3.2GHz Pentium-4 machine running Windows XP. The start-up delay is defined as the interval between when the IE process is created and when it calls the Win32 API CreateWindowEx function, which creates the first window. The start-up time excludes the program load time, which involves disk access, so

Table 3. The average additional start-up delays for Microsoft Internet Explorer (IE) when it is packed by a set of packers and run under Justin and an AV scanner. The additional delay is dominated by AV scanning, which is mainly determined by the number of AV scans invoked during a packed binary's run.

Packers	Number of AV Scans	Original Delay (msec)	Extra Delay (msec)	Extra Delay %
ACProtect	2	46	4.2	9.1
ASProtect	3	62	9.0	14.6
eXPressor	2	62	5.5	8.8
FSG	2	62	4.2	6.8
Molebox	2	31	4.2	13.5
NsPack	2	46	4.5	9.9
Obsidium	6	31	12.1	38.7
PECompact	3	62	5.8	9.3
UPX	2	31	4.1	13.1

that we can focus on the CPU overhead. After the first window is created, a packed GUI application must have been fully unpacked, and there will not be any additional protection exceptions or AV scans from this point on. The AV scanner used in this study runs at 40 MB/sec on the test machine, and is directly invoked as a function call.

Table 3 shows the base start-up delay and the additional start-up delay for IE when it is packed by a set of packers and runs under Justin and an AV scanner. Overall, the absolute magnitude of the additional start-up delay is quite small. Justin only introduces several milliseconds of additional delay under most packers. The largest additional delay occurs under Obsidium and is only around 12 msec. At least for IE, the additional start-up delay that Justin introduces is too small to be visible to the end user.

Most of the additional start-up delay comes from AV scanning, because the additional delay becomes close to zero when the AV scan operation is turned into a no-op. This is why the additional start-up delay correlates very well with the number of AV scans invoked. More specifically, the additional start-up delay for a packer is the product of the AV scanning speed, the number of scans, and the size of the memory being scanned. Because the amount of memory scanned in each AV scan operation may be different for binaries packed by different packers, the additional delay is different for different packers even though they invoke the same number of AV scans.

We also try other GUI programs such as Microsoft NetMeeting, whose binary is around 1 MB, and the additional delay results are consistent with those associated with IE. The performance overhead associated with additional protection exceptions is still negligible. Because of a larger binary size, the performance cost of each AV scan is higher. On a typical Windows desktop machine, more than 80% of its executable binaries is smaller than 100 KB. This means that the additional start-up delay when they are packed and run under Justin will be similar to that of IE and thus not noticeable. Finally, for legitimate programs that are not packed, no AV scanning will be triggered when they run under Justin, so there is no performance overhead at all.

5 Conclusion

Packer poses a serious problem for the entire AV industry because it significantly raises the bar for signature-based malware detection. Existing solutions to the packer problem do not scale because they require either expensive manual reverse engineering efforts or creation of separate signatures for variants of the same malware. In this paper, we report the result of a detailed study of the packer problem and its various solutions described in the literature, taking into account practical requirements and design considerations when integrating such solutions with commercial AV products. In particular, we describe a solution to the packer problem called Justin (JUST-IN-time AV scanning), which aims to detect the end of unpacking during the execution of a packed binary in a packer-independent way and invoke AV scanning against the binary's run-time image at that moment. Towards that end, Justin incorporates the following heuristics: first control transfer to dirty pages, avoiding tracking unpacker pages, checking for stack unwinding, and detection of command-line input argument access. More concretely, this paper makes the following contributions to the field of malware detection:

- A detailed analysis of the extent of the packer problem and the packing and evasion technologies underlying state-of-the-art packers,
- A set of heuristics that collectively can effectively detect the end of unpacking during the execution of packed binaries without any a priori knowledge about their packers,
- A comprehensive set of countermeasures against anti-unpacking evasion techniques built into modern packers, and
- A fully working Justin prototype and a thorough evaluation of its effectiveness and performance overhead.

Overall, Justin's effectiveness at detecting packed malware is excellent and its performance overhead for packed goodware is minimal. However, this paper will not be the final chapter on the packer problem. If anything, experiences tell us that the packer community will sooner or later shift to a different set of tactics to evade Justin's detection techniques. So the search for better solutions to the packer problem is expected to continue for the next few years.

References

1. Oberhumer, M.F., Molnár, L., Reiser, J.F.: UPX: the Ultimate Packer for eXecutables (2007), http://upx.sourceforge.net/
2. ASPACK SOFTWARE, ASPack for Windows, (2007), http://www.aspack.com/aspack.html

3. bart, FSG: [F]ast [S]mall [G]ood exe packer, (2005),
   http://www.xtreeme.prv.pl/
4. Dwing, WinUpack 0.39final, (2006), http://dwing.51.net/
5. Oreans Technology, Themida: Advanced Windows Software Protection System,
   (2008), http://www.oreans.com/themida.php
6. Silicon Realms, Armadillo/SoftwarePassport (2008),
   http://www.siliconrealms.com/
7. Blinkinc,Shrinker 3.4, (2008), http://www.blinkinc.com/shrinker.htm
8. Ferrie, P.: Attacks on Virtual Machines. In: Proceedings 9th Annual AVAR International Conference (2006)
9. VMProtect, VMProtect (2008), http://www.vmprotect.ru/
10. Symantec Corporation (2008), http://www.symantec.com/
11. Lyda, R., Hamrock, J.: Using entropy analysis to find encrypted and packed malware. IEEE Security and Privacy 5(2), 40–45 (2007)
12. Prakash, C.: Design of X86 Emulator for Generic Unpacking. In: Proceedings of 10th Annual AVAR International Conference (2007)
13. Tan, X.: Anti-unpacker Tricks in Malicious Code. In: Proceedings of 10th Annual AVAR International Conference (2007)
14. Royal, P., Halpin, M., Dagon, D., Edmonds, R., Lee, W.: Polyunpack: Automating the hidden-code extraction of unpack-executing malware. In: ACSAC 2006: Proceedings of the 22nd Annual Computer Security Applications Conference on Annual Computer Security Applications Conference, pp. 289–300 (2006)
15. Kang, M.G., Poosankam, P., Yin, H.: Renovo: A hidden code extractor for packed executables. In: Proceedings of the 5th ACM Workshop on Recurring Malcode (WORM) (Oct. 2007)
16. Stewart, J.: OllyBonE v0.1, Break-on-Execute for OllyDbg (2006),
    http://www.joestewart.org/ollybone/
17. Quist, D., Valsmith,: Covert Debugging: Circumventing Software Armoring. In: Proceedings of Black Hat USA (2007)
18. Martignoni, L., Christodorescu, M., Jha, S.: OmniUnpack: Fast, Generic, and Safe Unpacking of Malware. In: 23rd Annual Computer Security Applications Conference (ACSAC) (2007)
19. Nanda, S., Li, W., chung Lam, L., cker Chiueh, T.: BIRD: Binary Interpretation using Runtime Disassembly. In: Proceedings of the 4th IEEE/ACM Conference on Code Generation and Optimization (CGO 2006) (2006)
20. NX bit, http://en.wikipedia.org/wiki/NX_bit

Gnort: High Performance Network Intrusion Detection Using Graphics Processors

Giorgos Vasiliadis, Spiros Antonatos, Michalis Polychronakis,
Evangelos P. Markatos, and Sotiris Ioannidis

Institute of Computer Science, Foundation for Research and Technology – Hellas,
N. Plastira 100, Vassilika Vouton, GR-700 13 Heraklion, Crete, Greece
{gvasil,antonat,mikepo,markatos,sotiris}@ics.forth.gr

Abstract. The constant increase in link speeds and number of threats poses challenges to network intrusion detection systems (NIDS), which must cope with higher traffic throughput and perform even more complex per-packet processing. In this paper, we present an intrusion detection system based on the Snort open-source NIDS that exploits the underutilized computational power of modern graphics cards to offload the costly pattern matching operations from the CPU, and thus increase the overall processing throughput. Our prototype system, called *Gnort*, achieved a maximum traffic processing throughput of 2.3 Gbit/s using synthetic network traces, while when monitoring real traffic using a commodity Ethernet interface, it outperformed unmodified Snort by a factor of two. The results suggest that modern graphics cards can be used effectively to speed up intrusion detection systems, as well as other systems that involve pattern matching operations.

Keywords: GPU, pattern matching, intrusion detection systems, network security, SIMD, parallel programming.

1 Introduction

Network security architectures such as firewalls and Network Intrusion Detection Systems (NIDS) attempt to detect break-in attempts by monitoring the incoming and outgoing traffic for suspicious payloads. Most modern network intrusion detection and prevention systems rely on a set of rules that are compared against network packets. Usually, a rule consists of a filter specification based on packet header fields, a string that must be contained in the packet payload, the approximate or absolute location where that string should be present, and an associated action to take if all the conditions of the rule are met.

Signature matching is a highly computationally intensive process, accounting for about 75% of the total CPU processing time of modern NIDSes [2,7]. This overhead arises from the fact that most of the time, every byte of every packet needs to be processed as part of the string searching algorithm that searches for matches among a large set of strings from all signatures that apply for a particular packet. For example, the rule set of Snort [26], one of the most widely used

R. Lippmann, E. Kirda, and A. Trachtenberg (Eds.): RAID 2008, LNCS 5230, pp. 116–134, 2008.

open-source NIDS, contains about 10000 strings. Searching every packet for all of these strings requires significant resources, both in terms of the computation capacity needed to process a packet, as well as the amount of memory needed to store the rules.

Several research efforts have explored the use of parallelism for improving the packet processing throughput [25,8,14,4,37]. Specialized hardware devices can be used to inspect many packets concurrently, and such devices include ASICs and Network Processors. Both are very efficient and perform well, however they are complex to modify and program. Moreover, FPGA-based architectures have poor flexibility since most of the approaches are usually tied to a specific implementation.

As Graphics Processing Units (GPUs) are becoming increasingly powerful and ubiquitous, researchers have begun exploring ways to tap their power for non-graphic or general-purpose (GPGPU) applications. The main reason behind this evolution is that GPUs are specialized for computationally-intensive and highly parallel operations—required for graphics rendering—and therefore are designed such that more transistors are devoted to data processing rather than data caching and flow control [23]. The release of software development kits (SDKs) from big vendors, like NVIDIA[1] and ATI,[2] has started a trend of using GPUs as a computational unit to offload the CPU.

In addition, many attempts have been made to use graphics processors for security purposes, including cryptography [11], data carving [20] and intrusion detection [17]. Specifically, it has been shown that GPU support can substantially increase the performance of digital forensics software that relies on binary string searches [20]. Jacob and Brodley were the first that tried to use the GPU as a pattern matching engine for NIDS in PixelSnort [17]. They used a simplified version of the Knuth-Morris-Pratt (KMP) algorithm [18], however, their performance results indicated marginal improvement.

In this paper, we explore how GPUs can be used to speed up the processing throughput of intrusion detection systems by offloading the string matching operations to the GPU. We show that single pattern matching algorithms, like KMP, do not perform well when executed on the GPU, especially when using an increased number of patterns. However, porting multi-pattern matching algorithms, like the Aho-Corasick algorithm can boost overall performance by a factor of three. Furthermore, we take advantage of DMA and the asynchronous execution of GPUs to impose concurrency between the operations handled by the CPU and the GPU. We have implemented a prototype intrusion detection system that effectively utilizes GPUs for pattern matching operations in real time.

The paper is organized as follows: In the remainder of the Introduction we will give an overview of the GPU architecture that we used for this research. In Section 2 we will briefly present a survey of related work. Section 3 and 4 presents our prototype architecture and the implementation details respectively.

---

[1] http://developer.nvidia.com/object/cuda.html
[2] http://ati.amd.com/technology/streamcomputing/index.html

In Section 5 we evaluate our implementation and we compare with the previous work. Finally, in Section 6 we present some conclusions as well as some ideas for future work.

1.1   Overview of the GeForce 8 Series Architecture

In this Section we briefly describe the architecture of the NVIDIA GeForce 8 Series (G80) cards, which we have used for this work, as well as the programming capabilities it offers through the Compute Unified Device Architecture (CUDA) SDK. The G80 architecture is based on a set of multiprocessors, each of which contains a set of *stream processors* operating on SIMD (Single Instruction Multiple Data) programs. When programmed through CUDA, the GPU can be used as a general purpose processor, capable of executing a very high number of threads in parallel.

A unit of work issued by the host computer to the GPU is called a *kernel*, and is executed on the device as many different *threads* organized in *thread blocks*. Each multiprocessor executes one or more thread blocks, with each group organized into *warps*. A warp is a fraction of an *active group*, which is processed by one multiprocessor in one batch. Each of these warps contains the same number of threads, called the *warp size*, and is executed by the multiprocessor in a SIMD fashion. Active warps are time-sliced: A thread scheduler periodically switches from one warp to another to maximize the use of the multiprocessors' computational resources.

Stream processors within a processor share an instruction unit. Any control flow instruction that causes threads of the same warp to follow different execution paths reduces the instruction throughput, because different executions paths have to be serialized. When all the different execution paths have reached a common end, the threads converge back to the same execution path.

A fast *shared memory* is managed explicitly by the programmer among thread blocks. The *global*, *constant*, and *texture memory spaces* can be read from or written to by the host, are persistent across kernel launches by the same application, and are optimized for different memory usages [23]. The constant and texture memory accesses are cached, so a read from them costs much less compared to device memory reads, which are not being cached. The texture memory space is implemented as a read-only region of device memory.

GPGPU programming on G80 series and later is feasible using the CUDA SDK. CUDA consists of a minimal set of extensions to the C language and a runtime library that provides functions to control the GPU from the host, as well as device-specific functions and data types. CUDA exposes several hardware features that are not available via the graphics API. The most important of these features is the read and write access to the shared memory shared among the threads, and the ability to access any memory location in the card's DRAM through the general memory addressing mode it provides. Finally, CUDA also offers highly optimized data transfers to and from the GPU.

2   Related Work

Pattern matching is the most critical operation that affects the performance of network intrusion detection systems. Pattern matching algorithms can be classified into single- and multi-pattern algorithms.

In single pattern matching algorithms, each pattern is searched in a given text individually. This means that if we have k patterns to be searched, the algorithm must be repeated k times. Knuth-Morris-Pratt [18] and Boyer-Moore [6] are some of the most widely used single pattern matching algorithms. Knuth-Morris-Pratt is able to skip characters when a mismatch occurs in the comparison phase using a partial-match table for each pattern. Each table is built by preprocessing every pattern separately. Boyer-Moore is the most widely used single-pattern algorithm. Its execution time can be sublinear if the suffix of the string to be searched for appears infrequently in the input stream, due to the skipping heuristics that it uses.

Multi-pattern string matching algorithms search for a set of patterns in a body of text simultaneously. This is achieved by preprocessing the set of patterns and building an automaton that will be used in the matching phase to scan the text. The automaton can be thought of as a state machine that is represented as a trie, a table or a combination of the two. Each character of the text will be searched only once. Multi-pattern matching scales much better than algorithms that search for each pattern individually. Multi-pattern string matching algorithms include Aho-Corasick [1], Wu-Manber [36] and Commentz-Walter [10].

Most Network Intrusion Detection Systems (NIDS) use finite automata and regular expressions [26,24,16] to match patterns. Coit *et al.* [9] improved the performance of Snort by combining the Aho-Corasick keyword trie with the skipping feature of the Boyer-Moore algorithm. Fisk and Vaghese enhance the Boyer-Moore-Horspool algorithm to simultaneously match a set of rules. The new algorithm, called Set-wise Boyer-Moore-Horspool [15], was shown to be faster than both Aho-Corasick and Boyer-Moore for sets with less than 100 patterns. Tuck *et al.* [31] optimized the Aho-Corasick algorithm by applying bitmap node and path compression.

Snort from version 2.6 and onwards uses only flavors of the Aho-Corasick for exact-match pattern detection. Specifically, it contains a variety of implementations that are differentiated by the type of the finite automaton they use (NFA or DFA), and the storage format they use to keep it in memory (full, sparse, banded, trie, *etc.*). It should be mentioned, however, that the best performance is achieved with the full version that uses a deterministic finite automaton (DFA) at the cost of high memory utilization [30].

To speed-up the inspection process, many IDS implementations are based on specialized hardware. By using content addressable memory (CAM), which is suitable to perform parallel comparison for its contents against the input value, they are very well suited for use in intrusion detection systems [37,38]. However they have a high cost per bit.

Many reconfigurable architectures have been implemented for intrusion detection. Most approaches involve building an automaton for a string to be searched, generating a specialized hardware circuit using gates and flip-flops for the automaton, and then instantiating multiple such automata in the reconfigurable chip to search the streaming data in parallel. However, the circuit implemented on the FPGA to perform the string matching is designed based on the underlying hardware architecture to adjust to a given specific rule set. To adjust to a new rule set, one must program a new circuit (usually in a hardware description language), which is then compiled down through the use of CAD tools. Any changes in the rule set requires the recompilation, regeneration of the automaton, resynthesis, replacement and routing of the circuits which is a time consuming and difficult procedure.

Sidhu and Prasanna implemented a regular expression matching architecture for FPGAs [28]. Baker *et al.* also investigated efficient pattern matching as a signature based method [4]. In [13], the authors used hardware bloom filters to match multiple patterns against network packets at constant time. Attig *et al.* proposed a framework for packet header processing in combination with payload content scanning on FPGAs [3].

Several approaches attempt to reduce the amount of memory required to economically fit it in on-chip memory [4,31,14]. However, the on-chip hardware resource consumption grows linearly with the number of characters to be searched. In [29], the authors convert a string set into many tiny state machines, each of which searches for a portion of the strings and a portion of the bits of each string.

Other approaches involve the cooperation with network processors in order to pipeline the processing stages assigned to each hardware resource [8], as well as the entire implementation of an IDS on a network processor [5,12]. Computer clusters have also been proposed to offload the workload of a single computer [19,34,33,27]. The cost however remains high, since it requires multiple processors, a distribution network, and a clustered management system.

On the contrary, modern GPUs have low design cost while their increased programmability makes them more flexible than ASICs. Most graphic cards manufacturers provide high-level APIs that offer high programming capabilities and are further ensure forward compatibility for future releases, in contrast with most FPGA implementations that are based on the underlying hardware architecture and need to be reconfigured whenever a change occurs in the rule set. Furthermore, their low design cost, the highly parallel computation and the potential that are usually underutilized, especially in hosts used for intrusion detection purposes, makes them suitable for use as an extra low-cost coprocessor for time-consuming problems, like pattern matching.

The work most related to ours is PixelSnort [17]. It is a port of the Snort IDS that offloads packet matching to an NVIDIA 6800GT. The GPU programming was complicated, since the 6800GT did not support a general purpose programming model for GPUs (as the G80 used in our work). The system encodes Snort rules and packets to textures and performs the string searching using the KMP algorithm on the 16 fragment shaders in parallel. However, PixelSnort *does not* achieve *any* speed-up under normal-load conditions. Furthermore, PixelSnort

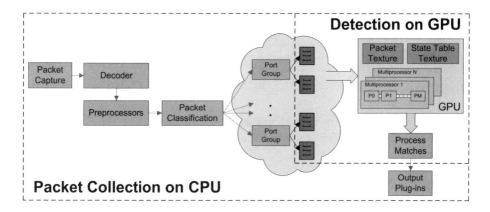

Fig. 1. Overall architecture of Gnort

did not have any multi-pattern matching algorithms ported to GPU. This is a serious limitation since multi-pattern matching algorithms are the default for Snort. In a more recent work, Marziale *et al.* [20] evaluated the effectiveness of offloading the processing of a file carving tool to the GPU. The system was implemented on the G80 architecture and the results show that GPU support can substantially increase the performance of digital forensics software that relies on binary string search.

3   Architecture

The overall architecture of Gnort, which is based on the Snort NIDS, is shown in Figure 1. We can separate the architecture of our system in three different tasks: the transfer of the packets to the GPU, the pattern matching processing on the GPU, and finally the transfer of the results back to the CPU.

3.1   Transferring Packets to the GPU

The first thing to consider is how the packets will be transferred from the network interface to the memory space of the GPU. The simplest approach would be to transfer each packet directly to the GPU for processing. However, due to the overhead associated with a data transfer operation to the GPU, batching many small transfers into a larger one performs much better than making each transfer separately [23]. Thus, we have chosen to copy the packets to the GPU in batches.

Snort organizes the content signatures in groups, based on the source and destination port numbers of each rule. A separate detection engine instance is used to search for the patterns of a particular rule group. Table 1 shows the number of rules that come with the latest versions of Snort and are enabled by default, as well as the number of groups in which they are organized. We use a separate buffer for temporarily storing the packets of each group. After a packet has been classified to a specific group, it is copied to the corresponding buffer.

Table 1. Snort Data Structures

Snort version	# Groups	# Rules
2.6	249	7179
2.7	495	8719
2.8	495	8722

Whenever the buffer gets full, all packets are transferred to the GPU in one operation. In case a buffer is not yet full after 100ms, its packets are explicitly transferred to the GPU.

The buffers are allocated as a special type of memory, called page-locked or "pinned down" memory. Page-locked memory is a physical memory area that does not map to the virtual address space, and thus cannot be swapped out to secondary storage. The use of pinned down memory results to higher data transfer throughput between the host and the device [23]. Furthermore, the copy from page-locked memory to the GPU is performed using DMA, without occupying the CPU. Thus, the CPU can continue working and collecting the next batch of packets at the same time the GPU is processing the packets of the previous batch.

To further improve parallelism, we use a double buffering scheme. When the first buffer becomes full, it is copied to a texture bounded array that can be read later by the GPU through the kernel invocation. While the GPU is performing pattern matching on the packets of the first buffer, the CPU will copy newly arrived packets in the second buffer.

3.2   Pattern Matching on the GPU

Once the packets have been transferred to the GPU, the next step is to perform the pattern matching operation. We have ported the Aho-Corasick algorithm [1] to run on the graphics card. The Aho-Corasick algorithm seems to be a perfect candidate for SIMD processors like a GPU. The algorithm iterates through all the bytes of the input stream and moves the current state to the next correct state using a state machine that has been previously constructed during initialization phase. The loop lacks any control flow instructions that would probably lead to thread divergence.

In our GPU implementation, the deterministic finite automaton (DFA) of the state machine is stored as a two-dimensional array. The dimensions of the array are equal to the number of states and the size of the alphabet (256 in our case), respectively, and each cell consists of four bytes. The first two bytes contain the next state to move, while the other two contain an indication whether the state is a final state or not. In case the state is final, the corresponding cell will contain the unique identification number (*ID*) of the matching pattern, otherwise zero. A drawback of this structure is that state machine tables will be sparsely populated, containing a significant number of zero elements and only a few non-zero elements. However, the use of more efficient storage structures, like those proposed in [22], are much more complex to map in the memory space of a GPU.

During the initialization phase, the state machine table of each rule group is constructed in host memory by the CPU, and is then copied to texture memory that is accessible directly from the GPU. At the searching phase, all state machine tables reside only in GPU memory. The use of GPU texture memory instead of generic GPU memory has the benefit that memory fetches are cached. A cache hit consumes only one cycle, instead of several hundreds in case of transfers from generic device memory. Since the Aho-Corasick algorithm exhibits strong locality of references [12], the use of texture memory for storing the state machine tables boosts GPU execution time about 19%.

We have implemented two different parallelization methods for the Aho-Corasick searching phase. In the first, each packet is splitted into fixed equal parts and each thread searches each portion of the packet in parallel. In the second, each thread is assigned a whole packet to search in parallel. Both techniques have advantages and disadvantages that will be discussed in Section 4.

3.3   Transferring the Results to the CPU

Every time a thread matches a pattern inside a packet, it reports it by appending it in an array that has been previously allocated in the device memory. The reports for each packet will be written in a separate row of the array, following the order they were copied to the texture memory. That means that the array will have the same number of rows as the number of packets contained in the batch. Each report is constituted by the *ID* of the pattern that was matched and the index inside the packet where it was found.

After the pattern matching execution has finished, the array that contains the matching pairs is copied to the host memory. Before raising an alert for each matching pair, the following extra cases should be examined in case they apply:

- *Case-sensitive patterns.* Since Aho-Corasick cannot distinguish between capital and low letters, an extra, case-sensitive, search should be made at the index where the pattern was found.
- *Offset-oriented rules.* Some patterns must be located in specific locations inside the payload of the packet, in order for the rule to be activated. For example, it is possible to look for a specified pattern within the first 5 bytes of the payload. Such ranges are specified in Snort with special keywords, like `offset`, `depth`, `distance`, etc. The index where the match was found is compared against the offset to argue if the match is valid or not.
- *Patterns with common suffix.* It is possible that if two patterns have the same suffix will also share the same final state in the state machine. Thus, for each pattern, we keep an extra list that contains the "suffix-related" *ID*s in the structure that holds its attributes. If this list is not empty for a matching pattern, the patterns that contained in the list have to be verified to find the actual matching pattern.

4   Implementation

We have implemented Gnort on the GeForce 8 Series architecture using CUDA. NVIDIA states that programs developed for the GeForce 8 series will also work without modification on all future NVIDIA video cards.

To facilitate concurrent execution between the host and the device, we associate GPU execution into streams. A *stream* is a sequence of operations that execute in order. It is created by the host and in our case includes the copying of the packets to the device memory, the kernel launch, and the transfer of the results back to the host memory. While the stream is executing, the CPU is able to collect the next batch of packets. The CPU work includes the execution flow of Snort to capture, decode, and classify the incoming packets, as well as the extra packet copies to the page-locked memory buffer that we have introduced.

The page-locked memory buffers that are used to collect the packets in batches are allocated by the CUDA runtime driver. The driver tracks the relevant virtual memory ranges and automatically accelerates calls to functions that are used to copy data to the device. The copying of the buffers to the device is asynchronous and is associated to the stream. The device memory where the packets are copied is bound to a texture reference of type **unsigned char** and dimensionality 2. Texture fetches are cached using a proprietary 2D caching scheme and cost only one clock cycle when a cache hit occurs; otherwise a fetch can take 400 to 600 clock cycles. The cache size for texture fetches is 8 KB per multiprocessor. Only the packet payloads are copied to the device, and each payload is stored in a separate row of fixed size. The actual length of the payload is stored in the first two bytes of the row.

The state machine tables that are used for each group of rules are stored in a texture reference of type **unsigned short** and dimensionality 2. CUDA does not support dynamic allocation of textures yet. To overcome this limitation, all state table arrays are copied to the device at start-up and each of them is dynamically bound to the texture reference, every time a batch of packets have to be matched against.

Once the packets have been copied to the texture bound array, the kernel is initiated by the host to perform the pattern matching. The 8-Series (G8X)—as well as the 9-Series (G9X) which was recently released—contain many independent multiprocessors, each comprising eight processors that run on a SIMD fashion. However, every multiprocessor has an independent instruction decoder, so they can run different instructions.

The Aho-Corasick algorithm performs multi-pattern search, which means that all patterns of a group are searched concurrently. We have explored two different approaches for parallelizing the searching phase by splitting the computation in two ways: assigning a single packet to each multiprocessor at a time, and assigning a single packet to each stream processor at a time. The two approaches are illustrated in Figure 2.

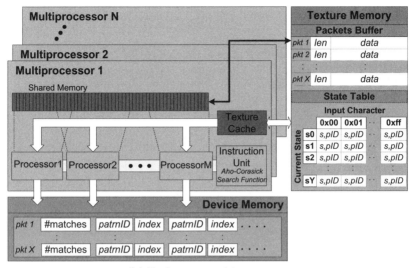

(a) Packet per multiprocessor

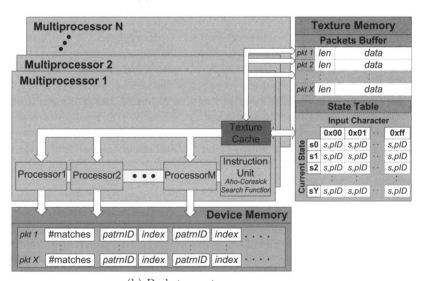

(b) Packet per stream processor

Fig. 2. Different pattern matching parallelization approaches. In (a), a different packet is processed by each multiprocessor. All stream processors in the multiprocessor search the packet payload concurrently. In (b), a different packet is processed by each stream processor independently of the others.

4.1   Assigning a Single Packet to each Multiprocessor

In this approach, each packet is processed by a specific thread block, executed by one multiprocessor. The number of threads in the thread block that searchthe packet payload is fixed and equal to the warp size (currently 32). Even though each multiprocessor consists of eight stream processors, the warp size ensures that the multiprocessor's computational resources are maximized by hiding arithmetic pipeline and memory delays.

Each thread searches a different part of the packet, and thus the packet is divided in 32 equal chunks. The 32 chunks of the packet are processed by the 32 threads of the wrap in parallel. To correctly handle matching patterns that span consecutive chunks of the packet, each thread searches in additional X bytes after the chunk it was assigned to search, where X is the maximum pattern length in the state table. To reduce further communication costs due to the overlapping computations, each packet is also copied to the shared memory of the multiprocessor (besides the texture memory)—all threads copy a different chunk in parallel, so this additional copy does not add significant overhead.

An advantage of this method is that all threads are assigned the same amount of work, so execution does not diverge, which would hinder the SIMD execution. Moreover, the texture cache is entirely used for the state tables, as shown in Figure 2(a). A drawback of this approach is that extra processing is needed for the chunk overlaps, especially in case of small packets.

4.2 Assigning a Single Packet to each Stream Processor

In this approach, each packet is processed by a different thread. The number of blocks that are created is equal to the number of multiprocessors the GPU has, so all are working. Each thread block processes X/N packets using an equal number of threads, where X is the number of packets in the batch sent to the GPU, and N is the number of multiprocessors. However, the maximum number of threads that can be created per block is currently 512. So if the number of threads per thread block is greater, more thread blocks are created to keep the number of threads under this limit. The disadvantage of this method is that the amount of work per thread will not be the same since packet sizes will vary. This means that threads of a warp will have to wait until all have finished searching the packet that was assigned to them. However, no additional computation will occur since every packet will be processed in isolation.

Whenever a match occurs, regardless of the implementation used, the corresponding *ID* of the pattern and the index where the match was found are stored in an array allocated in device memory. Each row of the array contain the matches that were found per packet. We use the first position of each row as a counter to know where to put the next match. Every time a match occurs, the corresponding thread increments the counter and writes the report where the counter points to. The increment is performed using an atomic function supplied by CUDA, to overcome possible race conditions for the first parallelization method.

5 Evaluation

In this section, we explore the performance of our implementation. First, we measure the scalability of the various algorithms for different number of patterns and packet sizes, and how they affect overall performance. We then examine how these algorithms perform in a realistic scenario as a function of the traffic load.

In our experiments we used an NVIDIA GeForce 8600GT card, which contains 32 stream processors organized in 4 multiprocessors, operating at 1.2GHz with 512 MB of memory. The CPU in our system was a 3.40 GHz Intel Pentium 4 processor with 2 GB of memory.

In order to directly compare with prior work, we re-implemented the KMP algorithm on the NVIDIA G80 GPU architecture using CUDA. In our implementation, the patterns to be searched, and the partial-match tables that KMP uses, are stored in two 2D texture arrays. Each packet is assigned to a different thread block, while each thread in a block is responsible for searching a specific pattern in the entire packet. This way, each warp of threads performs pattern matching against each packet in parallel, as long as the number of patterns is equal with the number of processors. If the number of patterns is greater than 512, the pattern matching is bundled in groups of 512 patterns each time, due to the limitation of the 512 threads that can be created per block.

We also did a GPU implementation of the Boyer-Moore algorithm, which performs better than KMP. The patterns to be searched, as well as the bad-character shift tables, are stored in two 2D texture arrays similarly to the KMP implementation. Each packet is assigned to a different thread block, while each thread in a block is responsible for searching a specific pattern in the whole packet.

For all experiments conducted, we disregard the time spent in the initialization phase of Snort as well as the logging of the alerts to the disk. Even though it only takes less than just a few seconds to load the patterns and build its internal structures in all cases, there is no practical need to include this time in our graphs. For all experiments we measure the performance of the default Snort using the full Aho-Corasick implementation. We conducted experiments with other implementations as well, however they performed worse in every case. Some information on the different implementations of Aho-Corasick that Snort uses can be found in [30].

5.1 Microbenchmarks

We start by investigating the effect that the size of the batch of packets that are transferred to the GPU has on the overall system performance. We used a synthetic payload trace that contains 1344330 UDP packets with random payload, each 800 bytes in length. The detection engine was disabled, so no execution would take place on the GPU. This way, we measured the time needed for the packets to transferred to the device in batches using the double buffer technique described in Section 3. The times include the capture, decode and classification phases performed by Snort as well as the copying of each packet to our buffer. Table 2 shows the time needed for a packet to copied to the memory of the device for various buffer sizes. We can see that the cost per packet increased as the size of the buffer decreased. For bigger sizes the cost remained somewhat constant. This may be due to the PCI startup overhead of each transaction. As

Table 2. Transfer times per packet as a function of the buffer size for 800-bytes packets

Buffer size (# packets)	Transfer time (ms)
4	0.035547
32	0.008218
512	0.004626
1024	0.004472
4096	0.004326
32768	0.004296

the size of the buffer increases, the number of transaction decreases, resulting in lower startup overheads. For all subsequent experiments we used a buffer of 1024 packets size, which we think is optimal considering the available memory of the host computer we used for the evaluation.

In the next experiment we evaluated how each detection algorithm scales with the number of patterns. We created Snort rules of randomly generated patterns which size varied between 5 and 25 bytes and gave as input to Snort a payload trace that contains UDP packets with random payload, each of 800 bytes in length. All rules are matched against every packet. This is the worst case scenario for a pattern matching engine, as in most cases each packet has to be checked only against a few hundred rules. Figures 3 and 4 show the maximum throughput achieved for single- and multi-pattern matching algorithms respectively, to perform string searches through rule-sets of sizes 10 up to 4000 rules. As shown in Figure 3, single pattern algorithms do not scale as the rule-set size increases. Performance of the CPU implementations of both KMP and BM decreases linearly with the number of patterns. KMP achieves nearly 100 Mbit/s for 10 patterns but its performance for 4000 patterns drops under 1 Mbit/s. BM presents better results but still for a large number of patterns it can only achieve up to 5 Mbit/s. The GPU implementation of these algorithms boosts their performance by up to an order of magnitude. For the case of 50, 100 and 250

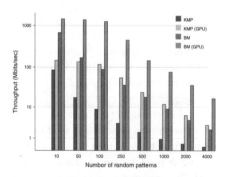

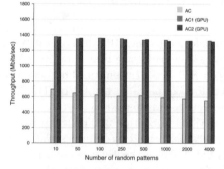

Fig. 3. Throughput sustained for single-pattern matching algorithms

Fig. 4. Throughput sustained for multiple-pattern matching algorithms

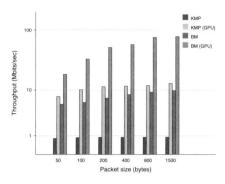 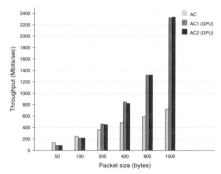

Fig. 5. Throughput sustained for single-pattern matching algorithms

Fig. 6. Throughput sustained for multiple-pattern matching algorithms

patterns we can see that GPU versions of algorithms are an order of magnitude faster than the CPU ones, while for the case of 4000 patterns the improvements reaches a factor of 3.

An interesting observation is that the throughput of the GPU implementations for both KMP and BM remained constant for up to 100 patterns. Even though there are 32 processors available, the thread scheduler can pipeline threads execution to effectively utilizes available resources. To verify it, we changed the kernels to return immediately performing a null computation and we observed the same behavior. Performance of the system remained constant for up to 100 patterns and then began decreasing linearly.

In the case of Aho-Corasick algorithm, the throughput remains constant independently of the number of patterns, a behavior expected for a multi-pattern approach. The results are shown in Figure 4. For the CPU implementation, Aho-Corasick achieves nearly 600 Mbit/s throughput, while the GPU implementation reaches up to 1.4 Gbit/s, yielding a 2.4 times improvement. Our two different approaches for implementing Aho-Corasick (displayed as AC1 and AC2 in the graph) do not present significant differences in performance.

Figures 5 and 6 show the throughput achieved for various UDP packet sizes. Snort was loaded with 1000 random patterns which size varied between 5 and 25 bytes. Each packet contains random data, a property that favors the BM algorithm as it will skip most of the payload. CPU implementations of KMP and BM presented a stable performance of around 1 and 10 Mbit/s respectively, independently of the packet size. Their GPU implementations yield a speedup from 2 up to 10 times. The throughput of Aho-Corasick reached over 2.3 Gbit/s for 1500-byte packets, giving a total speed-up of 3.2 compared to the respective CPU implementation. It is important to notice that it is worthless to process small packets on GPU. As it can be seen in Figure 6, for small packet sizes (under 100), the CPU implementation performs better than the GPU. However, for sizes larger than 100 bytes, the GPU implementation outperforms the CPU one in all cases.

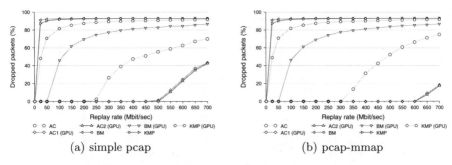

(a) simple pcap

(b) pcap-mmap

Fig. 7. Packet loss ratio as a function of the traffic speed

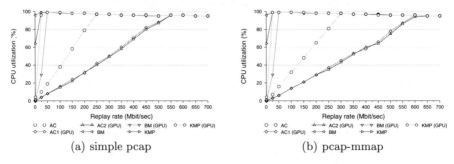

(a) simple pcap

(b) pcap-mmap

Fig. 8. CPU utilization as a function of the traffic speed

5.2   Macrobenchmarks

In this section we present the evaluation of our prototype implementation using real rules from the current Snort rule set on real network traffic. Our experimental environment consists of two PCs connected via a 1 Gbit/s Ethernet switch. The first PC is equipped with a NVIDIA GeForce 8600GT card and runs our modified version of Snort, while the second is used for replaying real network traffic traces using tcpreplay [32]. We used a full payload trace captured at the access link that connects an educational network with thousands of hosts to the Internet. By rewriting the source and destination MAC addresses in all packets, the generated traffic can be sent to the first PC.

We ran Snort with a custom configuration in which preprocessors and regular expression pattern matching were disabled, as both processes are executed only on the CPU. Snort loaded 5467 rules that contain about 7878 content patterns.

Figure 7 shows the packet loss ratio while replaying the trace at different speeds for two versions of pcap: the default one [21] and the pcap-mmap [35]. The pcap-mmap is a modified version of libpcap that implements a shared memory ring buffer to store captured packets. In this fashion user-space applications are able to read them directly, without trapping to kernel mode and copying them to a user buffer. The use of pcap-mmap gave both unmodified Snort and our system an increase of 50 to 100 Mbit/s to the overall performance. We can

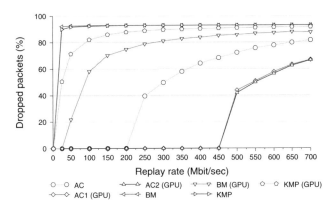

Fig. 9. Packet loss ratio as a function of the traffic speed under heavy CPU load

see that conventional Snort cannot process all packets in rates higher than 300 Mbit/s, so a significant percentage of packets is being lost. On the other hand, our GPU-assisted Snort is twice as fast as the original one. Packet loss for our approach starts at 600 Mbit/s, a 200% improvement to the processing capacity of Snort. The two different GPU implementations of the Aho-Corasick algorithm achieve almost the same performance. For completeness, in Figure 8, we plot the corresponding CPU utilization. Packet loss starts when CPU reaches 100% utilization.

Figure 9 plots the packets dropped by the kernel when CPU was overloaded synthetically. We used a simple program in an infinite tight loop, performing basic math operations to increase CPU usage to 100%. Snort was executing simultaneously. We observe that the performance decreased even when the matching process was executing on GPU. This can be explained by the fact that as the CPU controls the execution of the GPU, by overloading the former the execution flow is affected directly. However, performance degradation did not converge to that of default Snort, in contrast with [17].

6   Conclusions

In this paper, we presented Gnort, an intrusion detection system that utilizes the GPU to offload pattern matching computation. We ported the classic Aho-Corasick algorithm to run on the GPU exploiting the SIMD instructions. Our prototype system was able to achieve a maximum throughput of 2.3 Gbit/s, while in a real world scenario outperformed conventional Snort by a factor of two.

As future work we plan on eliminating the extra copy we introduced in order to transfer the packets to the GPU in batches. One way to accomplish this, is to transfer the packets directly from the kernel buffer. This would require that the buffer will be allocated from the application and will be shared between the user and kernel spaces. We believe that by modifying the pcap-mmap, that already implements this shared buffer capability, we can benefit from the lack of copies of both from kernel to user space as well as the one to our defined buffer. An even more efficient way would be to DMA directly the packets from the NIC to the GPU, without occupying the CPU at all. Currently, this is not supported but it may be in the future.

Finally, we plan on utilizing multiple GPUs instead of a single one. Modern motherboards support dual GPUs, and there are PCI Express backplanes that support multiple slots. We believe that building such *"clusters"* of GPUs will be able to support multiple Gigabit per second Intrusion Detection Systems.

Acknowledgments

This work was supported in part by the project CyberScope, funded by the Greek Secretariat for Research and Technology under contract number PENED 03ED440 and by the Marie Curie Actions - Reintegration Grants project PASS. G. Vasiliadis, S. Antonatos, M. Polychronakis, E. P. Markatos and S. Ioannidis are also with the University of Crete.

References

1. Aho, A.V., Corasick, M.J.: Efficient string matching: an aid to bibliographic search. Communications of the ACM 18(6), 333–340 (1975)
2. Antonatos, S., Anagnostakis, K., Markatos, E.: Generating realistic workloads for network intrusion detection systems. In: Proceedings of the 4th ACM Workshop on Software and Performance (January 2004)
3. Attig, M., Lockwood, J.: A framework for rule processing in reconfigurable network systems. In: Proceedings of the 13th Annual IEEE Symposium on Field-Programmable Custom Computing Machines (FCCM 2005), Washington, DC, USA, 2005, pp. 225–234. IEEE Computer Society Press, Los Alamitos (2005)
4. Baker, Z.K., Prasanna, V.K.: Time and area efficient pattern matching on FPGAs. In: Proceedings of the 2004 ACM/SIGDA 12th International Symposium on Field Programmable Gate Arrays (FPGA 2004), pp. 223–232. ACM, New York (2004)
5. Bos, H., Huang, K.: Towards software-based signature detection for intrusion prevention on the network card. In: Valdes, A., Zamboni, D. (eds.) RAID 2005. LNCS, vol. 3858, pp. 102–123. Springer, Heidelberg (2006)
6. Boyer, R.S., Moore, J.S.: A fast string searching algorithm. Communications of the Association for Computing Machinery 20(10), 762–772 (1977)
7. Cabrera, J.B.D., Gosar, J., Lee, W., Mehra, R.K.: On the statistical distribution of processing times in network intrusion detection. In: 43rd IEEE Conference on Decision and Control, December 2004, pp. 75–80 (2004)
8. Clark, C., Lee, W., Schimmel, D., Contis, D., Kone, M., Thomas, A.: A hardware platform for network intrusion detection and prevention. In: Proceedings of the 3rd Workshop on Network Processors and Applications (NP3) (2004)
9. Coit, C., Staniford, S., McAlerney, J.: Towards faster string matching for intrusion detection or exceeding the speed of Snort. In: Proceedings of DARPA Information Survivability Conference & Exposition II (DISCEX 2001) (June 2001)
10. Commentz-Walter, B.: A string matching algorithm fast on the average. In: Proceedings of the 6th International Colloquium on Automata, Languages and Programming, pp. 118–131.

11. Cook, D.L., Ioannidis, J., Keromytis, A.D., Luck, J.: Cryptographics: Secret key cryptography using graphics cards. In: Proceedings of RSA Conference, Cryptographer's Track (CT-RSA), pp. 334–350 (2005)
12. de Bruijn, W., Slowinska, A., van Reeuwijk, K., Hruby, T., Xu, L., Bos, H.: SafeCard: a Gigabit IPS on the network card. In: Zamboni, D., Krügel, C. (eds.) RAID 2006. LNCS, vol. 4219, pp. 311–330. Springer, Heidelberg (2006)
13. Dharmapurikar, S., Krishnamurthy, P., Sproull, T.S., Lockwood, J.W.: Deep packet inspection using parallel bloom filters. IEEE Micro 24(1), 52–61 (2004)
14. Dharmapurikar, S., Lockwood, J.: Fast and scalable pattern matching for content filtering. In: Proceedings of the 2005 ACM symposium on Architecture for networking and communications systems (ANCS 2005), pp. 183–192. ACM, New York (2005)
15. Fisk, M., Varghese, G.: Applying fast string matching to intrusion detection. Technical Repor In preparation, successor to UCSD TR CS2001-0670, University of California, San Diego (2002)
16. C. IOS. IPS deployment guide, http://www.cisco.com
17. Jacob, N., Brodley, C.: Offloading IDS computation to the GPU. In: Security Applications Conference on Annual Computer Security Applications Conference (ACSAC 2006), Washington, DC, USA, pp. 371–380. IEEE Computer Society, Los Alamitos (2006)
18. Knuth, D.E., Morris, J., Pratt, V.: Fast pattern matching in strings. SIAM Journal on Computing 6(2), 127–146 (1977)
19. Kruegel, C., Valeur, F., Vigna, G., Kemmerer, R.: Stateful intrusion detection for high-speed networks. In: Proceedings of the IEEE Symposium on Security and Privacy, May 2002, pp. 285–294 (2002)
20. Lodovico Marziale, G.G.R.I., Roussev, V.: Massive threading: Using GPUs to increase the performance of digital forensics tools. Digital Investigation 1, 73–81 (2007)
21. McCanne, S., Leres, C., Jacobson, V.: libpcap. Lawrence Berkeley Laboratory, Berkeley, http://www.tcpdump.org/
22. Norton, M.: Optimizing pattern matching for intrusion detection (July 2004), http://docs.idsresearch.org/OptimizingPatternMatchingForIDS.pdf
23. NVIDIA. NVIDIA CUDA Compute Unified Device Architecture Programming Guide, version 1.1,
http://developer.download.nvidia.com/compute/cuda/1_1/
NVIDIA_CUDA_Programming_Guide_1.1.pdf
24. Paxson, V.: Bro: A system for detecting network intruders in real-time. In: Proceedings of the 7th conference on USENIX Security Symposium (SSYM 1998), Berkeley, CA, USA, p. 3. USENIX Association (1998)
25. Paxson, V., Sommer, R., Weaver, N.: An architecture for exploiting multi-core processors to parallelize network intrusion prevention. In: Proceedings of the IEEE Sarnoff Symposium (May 2007)
26. Roesch, M.: Snort: Lightweight intrusion detection for networks. In: Proceedings of the 1999 USENIX LISA Systems Administration Conference (November 1999)
27. Schaelicke, L., Wheeler, K., Freeland, C.: SPANIDS: a scalable network intrusion detection loadbalancer. In: CF 2005: Proceedings of the 2nd conference on Computing frontiers, pp. 315–322. ACM, New York (2005)
28. Sidhu, R., Prasanna, V.: Fast regular expression matching using FPGAs. In: IEEE Symposium on Field-Programmable Custom Computing Machines (FCCM 2001) (2001)

29. Tan, L., Brotherton, B., Sherwood, T.: Bit-split string-matching engines for intrusion detection and prevention. ACM Transactions on Architecture and Code Optimization 3(1), 3–34 (2006)
30. The Snort Project. Snort users manual 2.8.0,
    http://www.snort.org/docs/snort_manual/2.8.0/snort_manual.pdf
31. Tuck, N., Sherwood, T., Calder, B., Varghese, G.: Deterministic memory-efficient string matching algorithms for intrusion detection. In: Proceedings of the IEEE Infocom Conference, pp. 333–340 (2004)
32. Turner, A.: Tcpreplay, http://tcpreplay.synfin.net/trac/
33. Vallentin, M., Sommer, R., Lee, J., Leres, C., Paxson, V., Tierney, B.: The NIDS cluster: Scalable, stateful network intrusion detection on commodity hardware. In: Kruegel, C., Lippmann, R., Clark, A. (eds.) RAID 2007. LNCS, vol. 4637, pp. 107–126. Springer, Heidelberg (2007)
34. Watanabe, K., Tsuruoka, N., Himeno, R.: Performance of network intrusion detection cluster system. In: Proceedings of The 5th International Symposium on High Performance Computing (ISHPC-V) (2003)
35. Wood, P.: libpcap-mmap, http://public.lanl.gov/cpw/
36. Wu, S., Manber, U.: A fast algorithm for multi-pattern searching. Technical Report TR-94-17 (1994)
37. Yu, F., Katz, R.H., Lakshman, T.V.: Gigabit Rate Packet Pattern-Matching Using TCAM. In: Proceedings of the 12th IEEE International Conference on Network Protocols (ICNP 2004), Washington, DC, USA, October 2004, pp. 174–183. IEEE Computer Society, Los Alamitos (2004)
38. Yusuf, S., Luk, W.: Bitwise optimised CAM for network intrusion detection systems. In: Proceedings of International Conference on Field Programmable Logic and Applications, pp. 444–449 (2005)

Predicting the Resource Consumption of Network Intrusion Detection Systems

Holger Dreger[1], Anja Feldmann[2], Vern Paxson[3,4], and Robin Sommer[4,5]

[1] Siemens AG, Corporate Technology
[2] Deutsche Telekom Labs / TU Berlin
[3] UC Berkeley
[4] International Computer Science Institute
[5] Lawrence Berkeley National Laboratory

Abstract. When installing network intrusion detection systems (NIDSs), operators are faced with a large number of parameters and analysis options for tuning trade-offs between detection accuracy versus resource requirements. In this work we set out to assist this process by understanding and predicting the CPU and memory consumption of such systems. We begin towards this goal by devising a general NIDS resource model to capture the ways in which CPU and memory usage scale with changes in network traffic. We then use this model to predict the resource demands of different configurations in specific environments. Finally, we present an approach to derive site-specific NIDS configurations that maximize the depth of analysis given predefined resource constraints. We validate our approach by applying it to the open-source Bro NIDS, testing the methodology using real network data, and developing a corresponding tool, `nidsconf`, that automatically derives a set of configurations suitable for a given environment based on a *sample* of the site's traffic. While no automatically generated configuration can ever be optimal, these configurations provide sound starting points, with promise to significantly reduce the traditional trial-and-error NIDS installation cycle.

1 Introduction

Operators of network intrusion detection systems (NIDSs) face significant challenges in understanding how to best configure and provision their systems. The difficulties arise from the need to understand the relationship between the wide range of analyses and tuning parameters provided by modern NIDSs, and the resources required by different combinations of these. In this context, a particular difficulty regards how resource consumption intimately relates to the specifics of the network's traffic—such as its application mix and its changes over time—as well as the internals of the particular NIDS in consideration. Consequently, in our experience the operational deployment of a NIDS is often a trial-and-error process, for which it can take weeks to converge on an apt, stable configuration.

In this work we set out to assist operators with understanding resource consumption trade-offs when operating a NIDS that provides a large number of tuning options. We begin towards our goal by devising a general NIDS resource model to capture the ways in which CPU and memory usage scale with changes in network traffic. We then use

R. Lippmann, E. Kirda, and A. Trachtenberg (Eds.): RAID 2008, LNCS 5230, pp. 135–154, 2008.
© Springer-Verlag Berlin Heidelberg 2008

this model to predict the resource demands of different configurations for specific environments. Finally, we present an approach to derive site-specific NIDS configurations that maximize the depth of analysis given predefined resource constraints.

A NIDS must operate in a *soft real-time* manner, in order to issue timely alerts and perhaps blocking directives for intrusion prevention. Such operation differs from *hard* real-time in that the consequences of the NIDS failing to "keep up" with the rate of arriving traffic is not catastrophe, but rather *degraded performance* in terms of some traffic escaping analysis ("drops") or experiencing slower throughput (for intrusion prevention systems that forward traffic only after the NIDS has inspected it). Soft real-time operation has two significant implications in terms of predicting the resource consumption of NIDSs. First, because NIDSs do not operate in hard real-time, we seek to avoid performance evaluation techniques that aim to prove compliance of the system with rigorous deadlines (e.g., assuring that it spends no more than T microseconds on any given packet). Given the very wide range of per-packet analysis cost in a modern NIDS (as we discuss later in this paper), such techniques would severely reduce our estimate of the performance a NIDS can provide in an operational context. Second, soft real-time operation means that we also cannot rely upon techniques that predict a system's performance solely in terms of aggregate CPU and memory consumption, because we must also pay attention to *instantaneous* CPU load, in order to understand the degree to which in a given environment the system would experience degraded performance (packet drops or slower forwarding).

When modeling the resource consumption of a NIDS, our main hypothesis concerns *orthogonal decomposition*: i.e., the major subcomponents of a NIDS are sufficiently independent that we can analyze them in isolation and then extrapolate aggregate behavior as the composition of their individual contributions. In a different dimension, we explore how the systems' overall resource requirements correlate to the volume and the mix of network traffic. If orthogonal decomposition holds, then we can systematically analyze a NIDS' resource consumption by capturing the performance of each subcomponent individually, and then estimating the aggregate resource requirements as the sum of the individual requirements. We partition our analysis along two axes: type of analysis, and proportion of connections within each class of traffic. We find that the demands of many components scale directly with the prevalence of a given class of connections within the aggregate traffic stream. This observation allows us to accurately estimate resource consumption by characterizing a site's traffic "mix." Since such mixes change over time, however, it is crucial to consider both short-term and long-term fluctuations.

We stress that, by design, our model does *not* incorporate a notion of detection quality, as that cannot reasonably be predicted from past traffic as resource usage can. We focus on identifying the types of analyses which are *feasible* under given resource constraints. With this information the operator can assess which option promises the largest gain for the site in terms of operational benefit, considering the site's security policy and threat model.

We validate our approach by applying it to Bro, a well-known, open-source NIDS [7]. Using this system, we verify the validity of our model using real network data, and develop a corresponding prototype tool, nidsconf, to derive a set of configurations suitable for a given environment. The NIDS operator can then examine these configurations and select one that best fits with the site's security needs. Given a relatively small *sample* of a site's traffic, `nidsconf` performs systematic measurements on it, extrapolates a set of possible NIDS configurations and estimates their performance and resource implications. In a second stage the tool is also provided with a longer-term connection-level log file (such as produced by NetFlow). Given this and the results from the systematic measurements, the tool can project resource demands of the NIDS' sub-components without actually running the NIDS on long periods of traffic. Thus the tool can be used not only to derive possible NIDS configurations but also to estimate when, for a given configuration and a given estimation of traffic growth, the resources of the machine running the NIDS will no longer suffice. While we do not claim that `nidsconf` always produces optimal configurations, we argue that it provides a sound starting point for further fine-tuning.

We structure the remainder of this paper as follows. In §2 we use an example to demonstrate the impact of resource exhaustion. In §3 we introduce our approach, and validate its underlying premises in §4 by using it to predict the resource usage of the Bro NIDS. In §5 we present our methodology for predicting the resource consumption of a NIDS for a specific target environment, including the automatic derivation of suitable configurations. We discuss related work in §6 and conclude in §7.

2 Impact of Resource Exhaustion

We begin with an examination of how resource exhaustion affects the quality of network security monitoring, since this goes to the heart of the problem of understanding the onset and significance of degraded NIDS performance. We do so in the context of the behavior of the open-source Bro NIDS [7] when it runs out of available CPU cycles or memory.

CPU Overload. The primary consequence of CPU overload are packet drops, and thus potentially undetected attacks. As sketched above, a NIDS is a *soft real-time* system: it can buffer packets for a certain (small) amount of time, which enables it to tolerate sporadic processing spikes as long as traffic arriving in the interim fits within the buffer. On average, however, processing needs to keep up with the input stream to avoid chronic overload and therefore packets drops. To understand the correlation between packet drops and CPU load, we run the Bro NIDS live on a high-volume network link (see §4) using a configuration that deliberately overloads the host CPU in single peaks. We then correlate the system's CPU usage with the observed packet drops.

Figure 1 shows the real-time (Y-axis) that elapses while Bro processes each second of network traffic (X-axis). The vertical lines denote times at which the packet capture facility (libpcap) reports drops; the corresponding CPU samples are shown with a *filled* circle.

The NIDS can avoid drops as long as the number of processing outliers remains small—more precisely, as long as they can be compensated by buffering of captured packets. For example, the 20MB buffer used in our evaluations enabled us to process an extreme outlier—requiring 2.5 s for one real-time second worth of network traffic—without packet drops. Accordingly, we find that the first packet drop occurs only after a spike in processing real time of more than 4s. Closer inspection shows that the loss

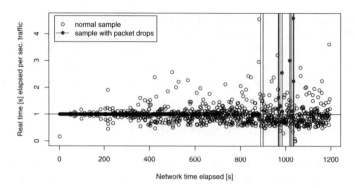

Fig. 1. Relation between elapsed real-time and packet drops

does not occur immediately during processing the "expensive" traffic but rather six network seconds later. It is only at that point that the buffer is completely full and the *lag* (i.e., how far the NIDS is behind in its processing) exceeds 5.5s. Such a large amount of buffering thus makes it difficult to predict the occurrence of drops and their likely magnitude: *(i)* the buffer can generally absorb single outliers, and *(ii)* the buffer capacity (in seconds) depends on the traffic volume yet to come. But clearly we desire to keep the lag small.

Memory Exhaustion. When a stateful NIDS completely consumes the memory available to it, it can no longer effectively operate, as it cannot store additional state. It can, however, try to reclaim memory by expiring existing state. The challenges here are *(i)* how to recognize that an exhaustion condition is approaching prior to its actual onset, *(ii)* in the face of often complex internal data structures [3], and then *(iii)* locating apt state to expire that minimizes the ability for attackers to leverage the expiration for evading detection.

One simple approach for limiting memory consumption imposes a limit on the size of each internal data structure. Snort [8], for example, allows the user to specify a maximum number of concurrent connections for its TCP preprocessor. If this limit is reached, Snort randomly picks some connections and flushes their state to free up memory. Similarly, Snort addresses the issue of variable stream reassembly size by providing an option to limit the total number of bytes in the reassembler. Bro on the other hand does not provide a mechanism to limit the size of data structures to a fixed size; its state management instead relies on timeouts, which can be set on a per-data structure basis, and with respect to when state was first created, or last read or updated. However, these do not provide a guarantee that Bro can avoid memory exhaustion, and thus it can crash in the worst case. Bro does however include extensive internal memory instrumentation [3] to understand its consumption, which we leverage for our measurements.

Memory consumption and processing lag can become coupled in two different ways. First, large data structures can take increasingly longer to search as they grow in size, increasing the processing burden. Second, in systems that provide more virtual memory than physical memory, consuming the entire physical memory does not crash the system but instead degrades its performance due to increased paging activity. In the worst case, such systems can thrash, which can enormously diminish real-time performance.

3   Modeling NIDS Resource Usage

In this section we consider the high-level components that determine the resource usage of a NIDS. We first discuss the rationale that leads to our framing of the components, and then sketch our resulting distillation. The next section proceeds to evaluate the framework against the Bro NIDS.

3.1   The Structure of NIDS Processing

Fundamental to a NIDS's operation is tracking communication between multiple network endpoints. All major NIDS's today operate in a *stateful* fashion, decoding network communication according to the protocols used, and to a degree mirroring the state maintained by the communication endpoints. This state naturally grows proportional to the number of active connections[1], and implementations of stateful approaches are naturally aligned with the network protocol stack. To reliably ascertain the semantics of an application-layer protocol, the system first processes the network and transport layers of the communication. For example, for HTTP the NIDS first parses the IP header (to verify checksums, extract addresses, determine transport protocol, and so on) and the TCP header (update the TCP state machine, checksum the payload), and then reassembles the TCP byte stream, before it can finally parse the HTTP protocol.

A primary characteristic of the network protocol stack is its extensive use of *encapsulation*: individual layers are independent of each other; while their input/output is connected, there ideally is no exchange of state between layers. Accordingly, for a NIDS structured along these lines its protocol-analyzing components can likewise operate independently. In particular, it is plausible to assume that the total resource consumption, in terms of CPU and memory usage, is the sum of the demands of the individual components. This observation forms a basis for our estimation methodology.

In operation, a NIDS's resource usage primarily depends on the characteristics of the network traffic it analyzes; it spends its CPU cycles almost exclusively on analyzing input traffic, and requires memory to store results as it proceeds. In general, network packets provide the only sustained stream of input during operation, and resource usage therefore should directly reflect the volume and content of the analyzed packets.[2]

We now hypothesize that for each component of a NIDS that analyzes a particular facet or layer of network activity—which we term an *analyzer*—the relationship between input traffic and the analyzer's resource demands is linear. Let t_0 be the time when NIDS operation begins, and P_t the number of input packets seen up to time $t \geq t_0$. Furthermore, let C_t be the *total* number of transport-layer connections seen up to time t, and c_t the number of connections *currently active* at time t. Then we argue: *Network-layer* analyzers operate strictly on a per-packet basis, and so should require $O(P_t)$ CPU time, and rarely store state. (One exception concerns reassembly of IP fragments; however, in our experience the memory required for this is

---

[1] For UDP and ICMP we assume flow-like definitions, similar to how NetFlow abstracts packets.

[2] In this work, we focus on stand-alone NIDSs that analyze traffic and directly report alerts. In more complex setups (e.g., with distributed architectures) resource consumption may depend on other sources of input as well.

negligible even in large networks.) *Transport-layer* analyzers also operate packet-wise. Thus, their amortized CPU usage will scale as $O(P_t)$. However, transport-layer analyzers can require significant memory, such as tracking TCP sequence numbers, connection states, and byte streams. These analyzers therefore will employ data structures to store all currently active connections, requiring $O(max(c_t))$ memory. For stream-based protocols, the transport-layer performs payload reassembly, which requires memory that scales with $O(max(c_t \cdot m_t))$, where m_t represents the largest chunk of unacknowledged data on any active connection at time t (cf. [1]). Finally, *application-layer* analyzers examine the payload data as reconstructed by the transport layer. Thus, their CPU time scales proportional to the number of connections, and depends on how much of the payload the analyzer examines. (For example, an HTTP analyzer might only extract the URL in client requests, and skip analysis of the much larger server reply.) The total size of the connection clearly establishes an upper limit. Accordingly, the state requirements for application analyzers will depend on the application protocol and will be kept on a per-connection basis, so will scale proportional to the protocol *mix* (how prevalent the application is in the traffic stream) and the number of connections c_t.

In addition to protocol analyzers, a NIDS may perform *inter-connection* correlation. For example, a scan detector might count connections per source IP address, or an FTP session analyzer might follow the association between FTP client directives and subsequent data-transfer connections. In general, the resource usage of such analyzers can be harder to predict, as it will depend on specifics of the analysis (e.g., the scan detector above requires $O(C_t)$ CPU and memory if it does not expire any state, while the FTP session analyzer only requires CPU and memory in proportion to the number of FTP client connections). However, in our experience it is rare that such analyzers exceed CPU or memory demands of $O(C_t)$, since such analysis quickly becomes intractable on any high-volume link. Moreover, while it is possible that such inter-connection analyzer may depend on the results of other analyzers, we find that such analyzers tend to be well modular and decoupled (e.g., the scan detector needs the same amount of memory independent of whether the NIDS performs HTTP URL extraction or enables FTP session-tracking).

3.2   Principle Contributors to Resource Usage

Overall, it appears reasonable to assume that for a typical analyzer, resource usage is *(i)* linear with either the number of input packets or the number of connections it processes, and *(ii)* independent of other analyzers. In this light, we can frame two main contributors to the resource usage of a NIDS:

1. The specific analyzers enabled by the operator for the system's analysis. That these contribute to resource usage is obvious, but the key point we want to make is that most NIDSs provide options to enable/disable certain analyzers in order to trade off resource requirements. Yet NIDSs give the operators almost no concrete guidance regarding the trade-offs, so it can be extremely hard to predict the performance of a NIDS when enabling different sets of analyzers. This difficulty motivated us to build our tool `nidsconf` (per §5.2) that provides an understanding of resource usage trade-offs to support configuration decisions.

2. The traffic *mix* of the input stream—i.e., the prevalence of different types of application sessions—as this affects the number of connections examined by each type of analyzers.

The above reasoning need not hold universally. However, we examined the architecture of two popular open source NIDS, Snort and Bro, and found that their resource consumption indeed appears consistent with the model discussed above. We hypothesize that we can characterize most operational NIDSs in this fashion, and thus they will lend themselves well to the kind of performance prediction we outline in §5. To support our claims, we now explore the resource usage of the Bro NIDS in more depth.

4   Example NIDS Resource Usage

To assess our approach of modeling a NIDS's resource demands as the sum of the requirements of its individual analyzers, and scaling linearly with the number of application sessions, we now examine an example NIDS. Among the two predominant open-source NIDSs, Snort and Bro, we chose to examine Bro for two reasons: *(i)* Bro provides a superset of Snort's functionality, since it includes both a signature-matching engine and an application-analysis scripting language; and *(ii)* it provides extensive, fine-grained instrumentation of its internal resource consumption; see [3] for the specifics of how the system measures CPU and memory consumption in real-time. Snort does not provide similar capabilities. For our examination we have to delve into details of the Bro system, and we note that some of the specifics of our modeling are necessarily tied to Bro's implementation. While this is unavoidable, as discussed above we believe that similar results will hold for Snort and other modern NIDSs.

For our analysis we captured a 24-hour *full* trace at the border router of the Münchener Wissenschaftsnetz (MWN). This facility provides 10 Gbps upstream capacity to roughly 50,000 hosts at two major universities, along with additional research institutes, totaling 2-4 TB a day. To avoid packet drops, we captured the trace with a high-performance Endace DAG card. The trace encompasses 3.2 TB of data in 6.3 billion packets and 137 million connections. 76% of all packets are TCP. In the remainder of this paper, we refer to this trace as `MWN-full`.

4.1   Decomposition of Resource Usage

We first assess our hypothesis that we can consider the resource consumption of the NIDS's analyzers as independent of one another. We then check if resource usage generally scales linearly with the number of connections on the monitored network link.

Independence of Analyzer Resource Usage. For our analysis we use Bro version 1.1, focusing on 13 analyzers: *finger, frag, ftp, http-request, ident, irc, login, pop3, portmapper, smtp, ssh, ssl,* and *tftp*. To keep the analyzed data volume tractable, we use a 20-minute, TCP-only excerpt of `MWN-full`, which we refer to as `Trace-20m`,

We run 15 different experiments. First, we establish a base case (BROBASE), which only performs generic connection processing. In this configuration, Bro only analyzes connection control packets, i.e., all packets with any of the TCP flags SYN, FIN or

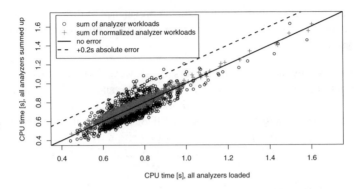

Fig. 2. Scatter plot of accumulated CPU usages vs. measured CPU usage

RST set. This suffices for generating one-line summaries of each TCP connection in the trace. BROBASE thus reflects a minimal level of still-meaningful analysis. Next, we run a fully loaded analysis, BROALL, which enables all analyzers listed above, and by far exceeds the available resources. Finally, we perform 13 additional runs where we enable a single one of the analyzers on top of the BROBASE configuration. For each test, Bro is supplied with a trace prefiltered for the packets the configuration examines. This mimics live operation, where this filtering is usually done in the kernel and therefore not accounted to the Bro process.

We start with examining CPU usage. For each of the 13 runs using BROBASE plus one additional analyzer, we calculate the contribution of the analyzer as the difference in CPU usage between the run and that for the BROBASE configuration. We then form an estimate of the time of the BROALL configuration as the sum of the contributions of the individual analyzers plus the usage of the BROBASE configuration. We term this estimate BROAGG.

Figure 2 shows a scatter plot of the measured CPU times. Each point in the plot corresponds to the CPU time required for one second of network input. The circles reflect BROAGG (Y-axis) versus BROALL (X-axis), with five samples between 1.7s and 2.6s omitted from the plot for legibility. We observe that there is quite some variance in the matching of the samples: The mean relative error is 9.2% (median 8.6%) and for some samples the absolute error of BROAGG's CPU time exceeds 0.2s (20% CPU load). There is also a systematic bias towards slight underestimation by BROAGG, with about 64% of its one-second intervals being somewhat lower than the value measured during that interval for BROALL.

To understand the origin of these differences, we examine the relative contribution of the individual analyzers. We find that there are a number of analyzers that do not add significantly to the workload, primarily due to those that examine connections that are not prevalent in the analyzed network trace (e.g., *finger*). The resource consumption with these analyzers enabled is very close to that for plain BROBASE. Furthermore, due to the imprecision of the operating system's resource accounting, two measurements of the same workload are never exactly the same; in fact, when running the BROBASE configuration ten times, the per-second samples differ by $M_R = 18$ msec on average. This means that if an analyzer contributes very little workload, we cannot soundly distinguish its contribution to CPU usage from simple measurement variation. The fluctuations of all individual runs with just one additional analyzer may well accumulate to the total variation seen in Figure 2.

To compensate for these measurement artifacts, we introduce a normalization of CPU times, as follows. For each single-analyzer configuration, we first calculate the differences of all its CPU samples with respect to the corresponding samples of BROBASE. If the mean of these differences is less than the previously measured value of M_R then we instead predict its load based on aggregation across 10-second bins rather than 1-second bins. The '+' symbols in Figure 2 show the result: we both reduce overall fluctuation considerably, and no sample of BROAGG exceeds BROALL by more than 0.2s. The mean relative error drops to 3.5% (median 2.8%), indicating a good match. As in the non-normalized measurements, for most samples (71%) the CPU usage is extrapolated to slightly lower values than in the actual BROALL measurement. The key point is we achieve these gains solely by aggregating the analyzers that introduce very light additional processing. Thus, we conclude that *(i)* these account for the majority of the inaccuracy, *(ii)* correcting them via normalization does not diminish the soundness of the prediction, and *(iii)* otherwise, analyzer CPU times do in fact sum as expected.

Turning to memory usage, we use the same approach for assessing the additivity of the analyzers. We compute the difference in memory allocation between the instance with the additional analyzer enabled versus that of BROBASE. As expected, summing these differences and adding the memory consumption of BROBASE yields 465 MB, closely matching the memory usage of BROALL (461 MB).

Overall, we conclude that we can indeed consider the resource consumption of the analyzers as independent of one another.

Linear Scaling with Number of Connections. We now assess our second hypothesis: that a NIDS resource consumption scales linearly with the number of processed connections. For this evaluation, we run Bro with identical configurations on traces that differ mainly in the number of connections that they contain at any given time. To construct such traces, we randomly subsample an input trace using per-connection sampling with different sampling factors, run Bro on the subtrace, and compare the resulting resource usage in terms of both CPU and memory. To then extrapolate the resource usage on the full trace, we multiply by the sample factor.

To sample a trace with a sample factor P, we hash the IP addresses and port numbers of each packet into a range $[0; P - 1]$ and pick all connections that fall into a particular bucket. We choose a prime for the sample factor to ensure we avoid aliasing; this approach distributes connections across all buckets in a close to uniform fashion as shown in [11]. For our analysis we sampled Trace-20m with sampling factors $P = 7$ (resulting in STRACE7) and $P = 31$ (resulting in STRACE31).

CPU Usage. Figure 3 shows a scatter plot of the CPU times for BROBASE on Trace-20m without sampling, vs. extrapolating BROBASE on STRACE7 (circles) and STRACE31 (triangles). We notice that in general the extrapolations match well, but are a bit low (the mean is 0.02 sec lower). Unsurprisingly, the fluctuation in the deviation from the originally measured values grows with the sampling factor (further measurements not included in Figure 3 with sampling factors between 7 and 31 confirm this).

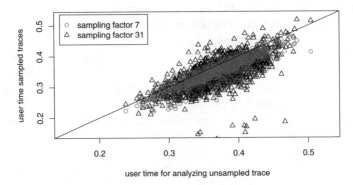

Fig. 3. Scatter plot of BROBASE configuration on sampled traces vs. non-sampled trace

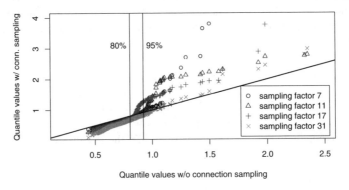

Fig. 4. QQ plot of analyzer workload without sampling vs. with different sampling factors

Naturally, the measured CPU times are very small if only a few connections are analyzed. For example, in the unsampled trace Bro consumes on average 370 msec for one second of network traffic when analyzing all the connections. With a sampling factor of 31, we would expect consumption to drop to $370/31 = 12$ msec, at which point we are at the edge of the OS's accounting precision. In fact, however, we find that extrapolation still works fairly well: for sample factor 31, the median of the extrapolated measurements is only 28 msec lower than the median of the measurements for the full trace. We have verified that similar observations hold for other segments of MWN-full, as well as for other traces.

Next we check if this finding still holds for more complex configurations. To this end, the QQ-plot in Figure 4 compares the distribution of CPU times for BROALL (i.e., 13 additional analyzers) on the full Trace-20m (X-axis) vs. sub-sampled traces

Table 1. Memory scaling factors: 10 BROBASE runs (left) / 10 BROALL runs (right)

Sampling factor	1	7	11	17	31	Sampling factor	1	7	11	17	31
Memory ratio	1	7.0	11.0	16.6	30.7	Memory ratio	1	3.64	4.87	6.30	9.34

(Y-axis, with sample factors of 7, 11, 17, and 31). Overall, the majority of the samples match fairly well, though with a bias for smaller values towards underestimation (left of the 80th percentile line), and with unstable upper quantiles (usually overestimates).

Memory Usage. Turning to memory consumption, for each sampling factor we conducted 10 runs with BROBASE on `Trace-20m`, measuring the maximum consumption figures on the sampled traces as reported by the OS.[3] Table 1 (left) shows the ratio between the memory consumption on the entire trace versus that for the sampled traces. Ideally, this figure would match the sampling factor, since then we would extrapolate perfectly from the sample. We see that in general the ratio is close, with a bias towards being a bit low. From this we conclude that for BROBASE, predicting memory use from a sampled trace will result in fairly accurate, though sometimes slightly high, estimates.

As discussed in Section 3, we would not expect memory usage of application-layer analyzers to always scale linearly with the number of connections, since some analyzers accumulate state not on a per-connection basis but rather according to some *grouping* of the connections (e.g., Bro's HTTP analyzer groups connections into "sessions"). In such cases the memory estimate we get by scaling with the connection sample factor can be a (potentially significant) overestimation. This effect is visible in Table 1 (right), which shows the same sort of analysis as above but now for BROALL. We see that the extrapolation factors can be off by more than a factor of three. By running each analyzer separately, we identified the culprits: both the HTTP and SSL analyzers associate their state per session, rather than per connection. However, we note that at least the required memory never *exceeds* the prediction, and thus we can use the prediction as a conservative upper bound.

In summary, we find that both CPU and memory usage can generally be predicted well with a model linear in the number of connections. We need to keep in mind however that it can overestimate the memory demand for some analyzers.

5   Resource Prediction

After confirming that we can often factor NIDS resource usage components with per-analyzer and per-connection scaling, we now employ these observations to derive suggestions of reasonable configurations for operating in a specific network environment.

We start by devising a methodology for finding a suitable configuration based on a snapshot of an environment's network traffic. Then we turn to estimating the *long-term* performance of such a configuration given a coarser-grained summary of the network traffic that contains the time-of-day and day-of-week effects. The latter is crucial, as traffic characteristics, and therefore resource consumption, can change significantly over time.

5.1   From Traffic Snapshots to Configurations

In this section we consider the degree to which we can analyze a short sample trace from a given environment in order to identify suitable NIDS configurations, in terms of

---

[3] As in the case of CPU usage, we find inherent fluctuation in memory usage as well: running instances under identical conditions exhibits some noticeable, though not huge, variation.

maximizing the NIDS's analysis while leaving enough "head room" to avoid exhausting its resources. More generally, we wish to enable the network operator to make informed decisions about the prioritization of different types of analysis. Alternatively, we can help the operator decide whether to upgrade the machine if the available resources do not allow the NIDS to perform the desired analysis.

We stress that due to the variability inherent in network traffic, as well as the measurement limitations discussed in §4, no methodology can aim to suggest an *optimal* configuration. However, automating the process of exploring the myriad configuration options of a NIDS provides a significant step forward compared to having to assess different configurations in a time-consuming, trial-and-error fashion.

Capturing an Appropriate Trace. Our approach assumes access to a packet trace from the relevant network with a duration of some tens of minutes. We refer to this as the *main analysis trace*. At this stage, we assume the trace is "representative" of the busiest period for the environment under investigation. Later in this section we explore this issue more broadly to generalize our results.

Ideally, one uses a *full* packet trace with all packets that crossed the link during the sample interval. However, even for medium-sized networks this often will not be feasible due to disk capacity and time constraints: a 20-minute recording of a link transferring 400 Mbit/s results in a trace of roughly 60 GB; running a systematic analysis on the resulting trace as described below would be extremely time consuming. In addition, full packet capture at these sorts of rates can turn out to be a major challenge on typical commodity hardware [9].

We therefore leverage our finding that in general we can decompose resource usage on a per-connection basis and take advantage of the connection sampling methodology discussed in Section 4. Given a disk space budget as input, we first estimate the link's usage via a simple libpcap application to determine a suitable sampling factor, which we then use to capture an accordingly sampled trace. We can perform the sampling itself using an appropriate kernel packet filter [2], so it executes quite efficiently and imposes minimal performance stress on the monitoring system.

Using this trace as input, we then can scale our results according to the sample factor, as discussed in §4, while keeping in mind the most significant source of error in this process, which is a tendency to overestimate memory consumption when considering a wide range of application analyzers.

Finding Appropriate Configurations. We now leverage our observation that we can decompose resource usage per analyzer to determine analysis combinations that do not overload the system when analyzing a traffic mix and volume similar to that extrapolated from the captured analysis trace. Based on our analysis of the NIDS resource usage contributors (§3.2) and its verification (§4), our approach is straight-forward. First we derive a baseline of CPU and memory usage by running the NIDS on the sampled trace using a minimal configuration. Then, for each potentially interesting analyzer, we measure its additional resource consumption by individually adding it to the minimal configuration. We then calculate which combinations of analyzers result in feasible CPU and memory loads.

The main challenge for determining a suitable level of *CPU* usage is to find the right trade-off between a good detection rate (requiring a high average CPU load) and leaving sufficient head-room for short-term processing spikes. The higher the load budget, the more detailed the analysis; however, if we leave only minimal head-room then the system will likely incur packet drops when network traffic deviates from the typical load, which, due to the long-range dependent nature of the traffic [12] will doubtlessly happen. Which trade-off to use is a *policy decision* made by the operator of the NIDS, and depends on both the network environment and the site's monitoring priorities. Accordingly, we assume the operator specifies a target CPU load c together with a quantile q specifying the percentage of time the load should remain below c. With, for example, $c = 90\%$ and $q = 95\%$, the operator asks our tool to find a configuration that keeps the CPU load below 90% for 95% of all CPU samples taken when analyzing the trace.

Two issues complicate the determination of a suitable level of *memory* usage. First, some analyzers that we cannot (reasonably) disable may consume significant amounts of memory, such as TCP connection management as a precursor to application-level analysis for TCP-based services. Thus, the option is not whether to enable these analyzers, but rather how to *parameterize* them (e.g., in terms of setting timeouts). Second, as pointed out in §4, the memory requirements of some analyzers do not scale directly with the number of connections, rendering their memory consumption harder to predict.

Regarding the former, parameterization of analyzers, previous work has found that connection-level timeouts are a primary contributor to a NIDS's memory consumption [3]. Therefore, our first goal is to derive suitable timeout values given the connection arrival rate in the trace. The main insight is that the NIDS needs to store different amounts of state for different connection types. We can group TCP connections into three classes: *(i)* failed connection attempts; *(ii)* fully established and then terminated connections; and *(iii)* established but not yet terminated connections. For example, the Bro NIDS (and likely other NIDSs as well) uses different timeouts and data structures for the different classes [3], and accordingly we can examine each class separately to determine the corresponding memory usage. To predict the effect of the individual timeouts, we assume a constant arrival rate for new connections of each class, which is reasonable given the short duration of the trace. In addition, we assume that the memory required for connections within a class is roughly the same. (We have verified this for Bro.) This then enables us to estimate appropriate timeouts for a given memory budget.

To address the second problem, analyzer memory usage which does not scale linearly with the sampling factor, we can identify these cases by "subsampling" the main trace further, using for example an additional sampling factor of 3. Then, for each analyzer, we determine the total memory consumption of the NIDS running on the subsampled trace and multiply this by the subsampling factor. If doing so yields approximately the memory consumption of the NIDS running the same configuration on the main trace, then the analyzer's memory consumption does indeed scale linearly with the sampling factor. If not, then we are able to flag that analysis as difficult to extrapolate.

5.2   A Tool for Deriving NIDS Configurations

We implemented an automatic configuration tool, `nidsconf`, for the Bro NIDS based on the approach discussed above. Using a sampled trace file, it determines a set of Bro configurations, including sets of feasible analyzers and suitable connection timeouts. These configurations enable Bro to process the network's traffic within user-defined limits for CPU and memory.

We assessed `nidsconf` in the MWN environment on a workday afternoon with a disk space budget for the sampled trace of 5 GB; a CPU limit of $c = 80\%$ for $q = 90\%$ of all samples; a memory budget of 500 MB for connection state; and a list of 13 different analyzers to potentially activate (mostly the same as listed previously, but also including *http-reply* which examines server-side HTTP traffic).

Computed over a 10-second window, the peak bandwidth observed on the link was 695 Mbps. A 20-minute full-packet trace would therefore have required approximately 100 GB of data. Consequently, `nidsconf` inferred a connection sampling factor of 23 as necessary to stay within the disk budget (the next larger prime above the desired sampling factor of 21). The connection-sampled trace that the tool subsequently captured consumed almost exactly 5 GB of disk space. `nidsconf` then concluded that even by itself, full HTTP request/reply analysis would exceed the given c and q constraints. Therefore it decided to disable server-side HTTP analysis. Even without this, the combination of all other analyzers still exceeded the constraints. Therefore, the user was asked to chose one to disable, for which we selected *http-request*. Doing so turned out to suffice. In terms of memory consumption, `nidsconf` determined that the amount of state stored by three analyzers (HTTP, SSL, and the scan detector) did not scale linearly with the number of connections, and therefore could not be predicted correctly. Still, the tool determined suitable timeouts for connection state (873 secs for unanswered connection attempts, and 1653 secs for inactive connections).

Due to the complexity of the Bro system, there are quite a few subtleties involved in the process of automatically generating a configuration. Due to limited space, here we only outline some of them, and refer to [2] for details. One technical complication is that not all parts of Bro are sufficiently instrumented to report their resource usage. Bro's scripting language poses a more fundamental problem: a user is free to write script-level analyzers that consume CPU or memory in unpredictable ways (e.g., not tied to connections). Another challenge arises due to individual connections that require specific, resource-intensive analysis. As these are non-representative connections any sampling-based scheme must either identify such outliers, or possibly suggest overly conservative configurations. Despite these challenges, however, `nidsconf` provides a depth of insight into configuration trade-offs well beyond what an operator otherwise can draw upon.

5.3   From Flow Logs to Long-Term Prediction

Now that we can identify configurations appropriate for a short, detailed packet-level trace, we turn to estimating the *long-term* performance of such a configuration. Such extrapolation is crucial before running a NIDS operationally, as network traffic tends to exhibit strong time-of-day and day-of-week effects. Thus, a configuration suitable for a short snapshot may still overload the system at another time, or unnecessarily forsake some types of analysis during less busy times.

For this purpose we require long-term, coarser-grained logs of connection information as an abstraction of the network's traffic. Such logs can, for example, come from

NetFlow data, or from traffic traces with tools such as tcpreduce [10], or perhaps the NIDS itself (Bro generates such summaries as part of its generic connection analysis). Such connection-level logs are much smaller than full packet traces (e.g., $\ll 1\%$ of the volume), and thus easier to collect and handle. Indeed, some sites already gather them on a routine basis to facilitate traffic engineering or forensic analysis.

Methodology. Our methodology draws upon both the long-term connection log and the systematic measurements on a short-term, (sampled) full-packet trace as described above. We proceed in three steps: First, we group all connections (in both the log and the packet trace) into classes, such that the NIDS resource usage scales linearly with the class size. Second, for different configurations, we measure the resources used by each class based on the packet trace. In the last step, we project the resource usage over the duration of the connection log by scaling each class according to the number of such connections present in the connection log.

In the simplest case, the overall resource usage scales linearly with the *total* number of connections processed (for example, this holds for TCP-level connection processing without any additional analyzers). Then we have only one class of connections and can project the CPU time for any specific time during the connection log proportionally: if in the packet trace the analysis of N connections takes P seconds of CPU time, we estimate that the NIDS performing the same analysis for M connections uses $\frac{P}{N}M$ seconds of CPU time. Similarly, if we know the memory required for I concurrent connections at some time T_1 for the packet trace, we can predict the memory consumption at time T_2 by determining the number of active connections at T_2.

More complex configurations require more than one connection class. Therefore we next identify how to group connections depending on the workload they generate. Based on our observation that we can decompose a NIDS's resource requirements into that of its analyzers (§3), along with our experience validating our approach for Bro (§4), we identified three dimensions for defining connection classes: duration, application-layer service, and final TCP state of the connection (e.g., whether it was correctly established). Duration is important for determining the number of active connections in memory at each point in time; service determines the analyzers in use; and the TCP state indicates whether application-layer analysis is performed.

As we will show, this choice of dimensions produces resource-consumption predictions with reasonable precision for Bro. We note, however, that for other NIDSs one might examine a different decomposition (e.g., data volume per connection may have a strong impact too). Even if so, we anticipate that a small number of connection classes will suffice to capture the principle components of a NIDS's resource usage.

Predicting Long-Term Resource Use. We now show how to apply our methodology to predict the long-term resource usage of a NIDS, again using Bro as an example. We first aggregate the connection-level data into time-bins of length T, assigning attributes reflecting each of the dimensions: TCP state, service, and duration. We distinguish between five TCP states (attempted, established, closed, half-closed, reset), and consider 40 services (one for each Bro application-layer analyzer, plus a few additional well-known service ports, plus the service "other"). We discretize a connection's duration D by assigning it to a duration category $C \leftarrow \lfloor log_{10}D \rfloor$. Finally, for each time-bin we count the number of connections with the same attributes.

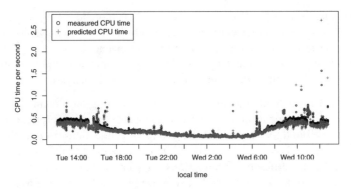

Fig. 5. Measured CPU time vs. predicted CPU time with BROBASE

Simple CPU Time Projection. To illustrate how we then project performance, let us first consider a simple case: the BROBASE configuration. As we have seen (§4), for this configuration resource consumption directly scales with the total number of connections. In Figure 5 we plot the actual per-second CPU consumption exhibited by running BROBASE on the complete MWN-full trace (circles) versus the per-second consumption projected by using connection logs plus an independent 20-minute trace (crosses). We see that overall the predicted CPU time matches the variations in the measured CPU time quite closely. The prediction even correctly accounts for many of the outliers. However, in general the predicted times are somewhat lower than the measured ones with a mean error of -25 msec of CPU time per second, and a mean relative error of -9.0%.

CPU Time Projection for Complex Configurations. Let us now turn to predicting performance for more complex configurations. We examine BROALL⁻, the BROALL configuration except with *ssl* deactivated (since the analyzer occasionally crashes the examined version of Bro in this environment). In this case, we group the connections into several classes, as discussed above. To avoid introducing high-variance effects from minimal samples, we discard any connections belonging to a service that comprises less than 1% of the traffic. (See below for difficulties this can introduce.) We then predict overall CPU time by applying our projection first individually to each analyzer and for each combination of service and connection state, and then summing the predicted CPU times for the base configuration and the predicted additional CPU times for the individual analyzers.

Figure 6 shows the resulting predicted CPU times (crosses) and measured BROALL⁻ CPU times (circles). Note that this configuration is infeasible for a live setting, as the required CPU regularly exceeds the machine's processing capacity. We see, however, that our prediction matches the measurement fairly well. However, we underestimate some of the outliers with a mean error of -29 msec of CPU time and a mean relative error of -4.6%. Note that the mean relative error is smaller than for predicting BROBASE performance since the absolute numbers of the measured samples are larger for the complex configuration.

Above we discussed how we only extrapolate CPU time for connections that contribute a significant portion (> 1%) of the connections in our base measurement. Doing

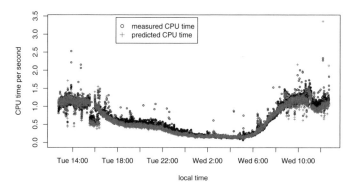

Fig. 6. Measured CPU time vs. predicted CPU time with BROALL⁻

so can result in underestimation of CPU time when these connection types become more prominent. For example, during our experiments we found that SSH and Telnet connections did not occur frequently in the 20-minute trace on which the systematic measurements are performed. Yet the long-term connection log contains sudden surges of these connections (likely due to brute-force login attempts). `nidsconf` detects such cases and reports a warning, but at this point it lacks sufficient data to predict the CPU time usage, since it does not have an adequate sample in the trace from which to work.

Memory Projection. Our approach for predicting *memory* consumption is to derive the number of active connections per class at any given time in the connection log, and then extrapolate from this figure to the overall memory usage. However, Bro's resource profiling is not currently capable of reporting precise per-connection memory usage for application-layer analyzers, so here we limit ourselves to predicting the *number* of TCP connections in memory, rather than the actual memory consumption. To do so, we draw upon the dimensions of connection *duration* and *state*. These two interplay directly since Bro keeps its per connection state for the lifetime of the connection plus a timeout that depends on the state. To determine the relevant timeout, we use the states discussed above (attempted, established, etc.), binning connections into time intervals of length T and then calculating their aggregate memory requirements.

However, a problem with this binning approach arises due to connections with durations shorter than the bin size (since we use bin sizes on the order of tens of seconds, this holds for the majority of connections). Within a bin, we cannot tell how many of these are *concurrently* active. Therefore, we refine our basic approach, as follows. We pick a random point in the base trace and compute the average number N of short-lived connections per second occurring in the trace up to that point. We also measure the number F of these short-lived connections instantaneously in memory at the arbitrary point. Let N_i be the number of short-lived connections per second for each bin i in the connection log. Assuming that F is representative, we can then scale N_i/N by F to estimate the number of short-lived connections concurrently active in each bin.

Figure 7 shows the results of our prediction for the number of established connections in memory (crosses) assuming Bro's default inactivity timeout of 300s, along with the the actual number of in-memory connections when running on MWN-full (circles).

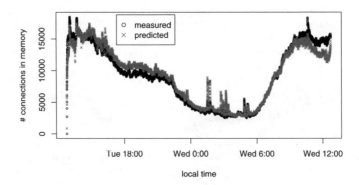

Fig. 7. Predicted number of established connections in memory for `MWN-full`

We observe that the prediction matches the measurements well, with a mean relative error of +5.0%. While not shown on the plot, we obtain similar prediction results for other classes of connections, e.g., unanswered connection attempts.

6   Related Work

Numerous studies in the literature investigate IDS detection quality, generally analyzing the trade-off between false positives and false negatives. Some studies [6,4,5] take steps towards analyzing how the detection quality and detection coverage depends on the cost of the IDS configuration and the attacks the network experiences. Gaffney and Ulvila [4] focus on the costs that result from erroneous detection, developing a model for finding a suitable trade-off between false positives and false negatives dependent on the cost of each type of failure. In contrast, Lee et al. [6,5] focus on developing and implementing high-level cost models for operating an IDS, enabling dynamic adaptation of a NIDS's configuration to suit the current system load. The models take as input both metrics of the benefits of a successful detection and (self-adapting) metrics reflecting the cost of the detection. Such metrics may be hard to define for large network environments, however. To adapt to the cost metrics, they monitor the performance of their prototype systems (Bro and Snort) using a coarse-grained instrumentation of packet counts per second. As was shown by Dreger et al. [3], this risks oversimplifying a complex NIDS. While the basic idea of adapting NIDS configurations to system load is similar to ours, we focus on predicting resource usage of the NIDS depending on both the network traffic and the NIDS configuration.

In the area of general performance prediction and extrapolation of systems (not necessarily NIDSs), three categories of work exam *(i)* performance on different hardware platforms, *(ii)* distribution across multiple systems, and *(iii)* predicting system load. These studies relate to ours in the sense that we use similar techniques for program decomposition and for runtime extrapolation. We omit details of these here due to limited space, but refer the reader to [2] for a detailed discussion. In contrast to this body of work, our contributions are to predict performance for *soft* real-time systems, both at a fine-grained resolution (prediction of "head room" for avoiding packet drops) and over long time scales (coupling a short, detailed trace with coarse-grained logs to extrapolate performance over hours or days), with an emphasis on memory and CPU trade-offs available to an operator in terms of depth of analysis versus limited resources.

7 Conclusion

In this work we set out to understand and predict the resource requirements of network intrusion detection systems. When initially installing such a system in a network environment, the operator often must grapple with a large number of options to tune trade-offs between detection rate versus CPU and memory consumption. The impact of such parameters often proves difficult to predict, as it potentially depends to a large degree on the internals of the NIDS's implementation, as well as the specific characteristics of the target environment. Because of this, the installation of a NIDS often becomes a trial-and-error process that can consume weeks until finding a "sweet spot."

We have developed a methodology to *automatically* derive NIDS configurations that maximize the systems' detection capabilities while keeping the resource load feasible. Our approach leverages the modularity likely present in a NIDS: while complex systems, NIDSs tend to be structured as a set of subcomponents that work mostly independently in terms of their resource consumption. Therefore, to understand the system as a whole, we can decompose the NIDS into the main contributing components. As our analysis of the open-source Bro NIDS shows, the resource requirements of these subcomponents are often driven by relatively simple characteristics of their input, such as number of packets or number and types of connections.

Leveraging this observation, we built a tool that derives realistic configurations for Bro. Based on a short-term, full-packet trace coupled with a longer-term, flow-level trace—both recorded in the target environment—the tool first models the resource usage of the individual subcomponents of the NIDS. It then simulates different configurations by adding together the contributions of the relevant subcomponents to predict configurations whose execution will remain within the limits of the resources specified by the operator. The operator can then choose among the feasible configurations according to the priorities established for the monitoring environment. While no automatically generated configuration can be optimal, these provide a sound starting point, with promise to significantly reduce the traditional trial-and-error NIDS installation cycle.

Acknowledgments

We would like to thank Christian Kreibich for his feedback and the fruitful discussions that greatly helped to improve this work. We would also like to thank the Leibnitz-Rechenzentrum München. This work was supported by a grant from the Bavaria California Technology Center, and by the US National Science Foundation under awards STI-0334088, NSF-0433702, and ITR/ANI-0205519, for which we are grateful. Any opinions, findings, conclusions or recommendations expressed in this material are those of the authors or originators and do not necessarily reflect the views of the National Science Foundation.

References

1. Dharmapurikar, S., Paxson, V.: Robust TCP Stream Reassembly In the Presence of Adversaries. In: Proc. USENIX Security Symposium (2005)
2. Dreger, H.: Operational Network Intrusion Detection: Resource-Analysis Tradeoffs. PhD thesis, TU München (2007), http://www.net.in.tum.de/~hdreger/papers/thesis_dreger.pdf
3. Dreger, H., Feldmann, A., Paxson, V., Sommer, R.: Operational Experiences with High-Volume Network Intrusion Detection. In: Proc. ACM Conference on Computer and Communications Security (2004)
4. Gaffney Jr., J.E., Ulvila, J.W.: Evaluation of Intrusion Detectors: A Decision Theory Approach. In: Proc. IEEE Symposium on Security and Privacy (2001)
5. Lee, W., Cabrera, J.B., Thomas, A., Balwalli, N., Saluja, S., Zhang, Y.: Performance Adaptation in Real-Time Intrusion Detection Systems. In: Proc. Symposium on Recent Advances in Intrusion Detection (2002)
6. Lee, W., Fan, W., Miller, M., Stolfo, S.J., Zadok, E.: Toward Cost-sensitive Modeling for Intrusion Detection and Response. Journal of Computer Security 10(1-2), 5–22 (2002)
7. Paxson, V.: Bro: A System for Detecting Network Intruders in Real-Time. Computer Networks 31(23–24), 2435–2463 (1999)
8. Roesch, M.: Snort: Lightweight Intrusion Detection for Networks. In: Proc. Systems Administration Conference (1999)
9. Schneider, F., Wallerich, J., Feldmann, A.: Packet Capture in 10-Gigabit Ethernet Environments Using Contemporary Commodity Hardware. In: Proc. Passive and Active Measurement Conference (2007)
10. tcp-reduce, http://ita.ee.lbl.gov/html/contrib/tcp-reduce.html
11. Vallentin, M., Sommer, R., Lee, J., Leres, C., Paxson, V., Tierney, B.: The NIDS Cluster: Scalable, Stateful Network Intrusion Detection on Commodity Hardware. In: Proc. Symposium on Recent Advances in Intrusion Detection (2007)
12. Willinger, W., Taqqu, M.S., Sherman, R., Wilson, D.V.: Self-Similarity Through High-Variability: Statistical Analysis of Ethernet LAN Traffic at the Source Level. IEEE/ACM Transactions on Networking 5(1) (1997)

High-Speed Matching of Vulnerability Signatures

Nabil Schear[1], David R. Albrecht[2], and Nikita Borisov[2]

[1] Department of Computer Science
[2] Department of Electrical and Computer Engineering
University of Illinois at Urbana–Champaign
{nschear2,dalbrech,nikita}@uiuc.edu

Abstract. Vulnerability signatures offer better precision and flexibility than exploit signatures when detecting network attacks. We show that it is possible to detect vulnerability signatures in high-performance network intrusion detection systems, by developing a matching architecture that is specialized to the task of vulnerability signatures. Our architecture is based upon: i) the use of high-speed pattern matchers, together with control logic, instead of recursive parsing, ii) the limited nature and careful management of implicit state, and iii) the ability to avoid parsing large fragments of the message not relevant to a vulnerability.

We have built a prototype implementation of our architecture and vulnerability specification language, called VESPA, capable of detecting vulnerabilities in both text and binary protocols. We show that, compared to full protocol parsing, we can achieve 3x or better speedup, and thus detect vulnerabilities in most protocols at a speed of 1 Gbps or more. Our architecture is also well-adapted to being integrated with network processors or other special-purpose hardware. We show that for text protocols, pattern matching dominates our workload and great performance improvements can result from hardware acceleration.

1 Introduction

Detecting and preventing attacks is a critical aspect of network security. The dominant paradigm in network intrusion detection systems (NIDS) has been the *exploit signature*, which recognizes a particular pattern of misuse (an *exploit*). An alternative approach is to use a *vulnerability signature*, which describes the *class* of messages that trigger a vulnerability on the end system, based on the behavior of the application. Vulnerability signatures are exploit-generic, as they focus on how the end host interprets the message, rather than how the particular exploit works, and thus can recognize polymorphic and copycat exploits.

Exploit signatures are represented using byte-string patterns or regular expressions. Vulnerability signatures, on the other hand, usually employ protocol parsing to recover the semantic content of the communication and then decide whether it triggers a vulnerability. The semantic modeling allows vulnerability signatures to be both more general and more precise than exploit signatures. However, this comes at a high performance cost. To date, vulnerability signatures have only been considered for user on end hosts, severely limiting their deployment.

R. Lippmann, E. Kirda, and A. Trachtenberg (Eds.): RAID 2008, LNCS 5230, pp. 155–174, 2008.
© Springer-Verlag Berlin Heidelberg 2008

In our work, we observe that full and generic protocol parsing is *not necessary* for detecting vulnerability signatures. Using custom-built, hand-coded vulnerability signature recognizers, we show that these signatures can be detected 3 to 37 times faster than the speed of full protocol parsing. Therefore, there is no *inherent* performance penalty for using vulnerability signatures instead of exploit signatures.

Motivated by this, we design an architecture, called VESPA[1], for matching vulnerability signatures at speeds adequate for a high-performance enterprise NIDS, around 1 Gbps. We build our architecture on a foundation of fast string and pattern matchers, connected with control logic. This allows us to do deep packet inspection and model complex behavior, while maintaining high performance. We also minimize the amount of implicit state maintained by the parser. By avoiding full, in-memory semantic representation of the message, we eliminate much of the cost of generic protocol parsing. Finally, in many cases we are able to eliminate the recursive nature of protocol analysis, allowing us to skip analysis of large subsections of the message.

We have implemented a prototype of VESPA; tests show that it matches vulnerability signatures about three times faster than equivalent full-protocol parsing, as implemented in binpac [1]. Our architecture matches most protocols in software at speeds greater than 1 Gbps. Further, we show that our text protocol parsing is dominated by string matching, suggesting that special-purpose hardware for pattern matching would permit parsing text protocols at much higher speeds. Our binary protocol parsing is also well-adapted to hardware-aided implementation, as our careful state management fits well with the constrained memory architectures of network processors.

The rest of this paper is organized as follows: Section 2 gives some background on vulnerability signatures and discusses the context of our work. Sections 3 and 4 describe the design of VESPA and the vulnerability signature language. We present the implementation details of VESPA in Section 5. Section 6 contains a performance evaluation of our prototype. We discuss some future directions in Section 7 and related work in Section 8. Finally, Section 9 concludes.

2   Background

2.1   Vulnerability Signatures

Vulnerability signatures were originally proposed by Wang et al. [2] as an alternative to traditional, exploit-based signatures. While exploit signatures describe the properties of the exploit, vulnerability signatures describe how the vulnerability gets triggered in an application. Consider the following exploit signature for Code Red [3]:

```
urlcontent:"ida?NNNNNNNNNNNNN..."
```

The signature describes how the exploit operates: it uses the ISAPI interface (invoked for files with extension ".ida") and inserts a long string of N's, leading to a buffer overflow. While effective against Code Red, this signature would not match Code Red II [4]; that variant used X's in place of the N's. A vulnerability signature, on the other hand, does not specify how the worm works, but rather how the application-level vulnerability is triggered. An extract from the CodeRed signature in Shield [2] is:

---

[1] VulnErability Signature Parsing Architecture.

```
c = MATCH_STR_LEN(>>P_Get_Request.URI,"id[aq]\?(.*)$",limit);
IF (c > limit)
  # Exploit!
```

This signature captures *any* request that overflows the ISAPI buffer, making it effective against Code Red, Code Red II, and any other worm or attack that exploits the ISAPI buffer overflow. In fact, this signature could well have been written before the release of either of the Code Red worms, as the vulnerability in the ISAPI was published a month earlier [5]. Thus, while exploit signatures are reactive, vulnerability signatures can proactively protect systems with known vulnerabilities until they are patched (which can take weeks or months [6]).

2.2 Protocol Parsing

Traditionally, exploit signatures are specified as strings or regular expressions. Vulnerability signatures, on the other hand, involve some amount of protocol parsing. Shield [2] used a language for describing C-like binary structures, and an extension for parsing text protocols. The follow-on project, GAPA [7], designed a generic application-level protocol analyzer to be used for matching vulnerability signatures. GAPA represented both binary and text protocols using a recursive grammar with embedded code statements. The generated GAPA parser, when guided by code statements, performed context-sensitive parsing. GAPA aimed to provide an easy-to-use and safe way to specify protocols and corresponding vulnerabilities.

Binpac [1], another protocol parser, was designed to be used in the Bro intrusion detection system [8]. Binpac is similar to GAPA: both use a recursive grammar and embedded code for parsing network protocols, and both are intended to minimize the risks of protocol parsing. Binpac, however, is designed only for parsing, with other parts of Bro performing checks for alarms or vulnerabilities. Binpac uses C++ for its embedded code blocks, and compiles the entire parser to C++ (similar to yacc), whereas GAPA uses a restricted, memory-safe interpreted language capable of being proven free of infinite loops. Binpac trades some of GAPA's safety for parsing speed; consequently, it achieves speeds comparable to hand-coded parsers written for Bro.

Since the implementation of GAPA is not freely available, we use binpac as our prototypical generic protocol parser generator in comparing to our work. Binpac is significantly faster than GAPA, yet it is not able to parse many protocols at speeds of 1 Gbps (though sparing use of binpac, where most data passing through the NIDS is not analyzed, can be supported.)

2.3 Vulnerability Complexity

Although Shield and GAPA used protocol parsing for vulnerability signatures, Brumley et al. suggest that vulnerability signatures could be represented across a spectrum of complexity classes [9]. They consider the classes of regular expressions, constraint satisfaction languages, and Turing machines, and provide algorithms to derive automatic vulnerability signatures of each class. As increasingly complex specifications of signatures are used, the precision of signature matching improves.

We make a different observation: most vulnerability signatures can be matched *precisely* without full protocol parsing. And such precise matching can be carried out at much greater speeds. In Table 1, we compare the performance of binpac to hand-coded implementations of several vulnerability signatures. We wrote the hand-coded implementations in C and designed them to match one specific vulnerability only. These would fall into the Turing machine class according to Brumley et al., but they are optimized for speed. Notice that the hand-coded implementations operate about *3x to 37x faster* than equivalent binpac implementation.

Table 1. The throughput (Mbits/s) of binpac parsers vs. hand-coded vulnerability matchers

Protocol	binpac	hand-coded
CUPS/HTTP	5,414	20,340
DNS	71	2,647
IPP	809	7,601
WMF	610	14,013

To see why this is the case, consider the following CUPS vulnerability (CVE-2002-1368 [10]). CUPS processes the IPP protocol, which sends messages embedded inside HTTP requests. CUPS would crash if a negative `Content-Length` were specified, presenting a denial-of-service opportunity. Our binpac implementation to check for this vulnerability is based on the binpac HTTP specification, which parses the HTTP header into name–value pairs. We add a constraint that looks for header names that match `Content-Length` and verifies that a non-negative value is used. Our hand-coded implementation, on the other hand, is built upon an Aho–Corasick [11] multi-string matcher, which looks for the strings "`Content-Length:`" and "`\r\n\r\n`" (the latter indicating the end of the headers). If "`Content-Length:`" is found, the following string is parsed as an integer and checked for being non-negative.

The parsers operate with equal precision when identifying the vulnerability, yet the hand-coded approach performs much less work per message, and runs more than 3 times as quickly. Of course, not all vulnerabilities can be matched with a simple string search. However, what this vulnerability demonstrates is that an efficient vulnerability signature matching architecture must be able to handle such simple vulnerabilities quickly, rather than using heavy-weight parsing for all vulnerabilities, regardless of complexity. The architecture will surely need to support more complex constructs as well, but they should only be used when necessary, rather than all the time. We next present a new architecture for specifying and matching vulnerability signatures that follows this principle. Our architecture shares some of the goals of binpac and GAPA; however, it puts a stronger focus on performance, rather than generality (GAPA) or ease-of-authoring (binpac).

3   Design

To make vulnerability signatures practical for use in network intrusion detection systems, we developed VESPA, an efficient vulnerability specification and matching architecture. The processes of writing a protocol specification and writing a vulnerability signature are coupled to allow the parser generator to perform optimizations on the generated code that specialize it for the vulnerabilities the author wishes to match.

Our system is based on the following design principles:

- Use of fast matching primitives
- Explicit state management
- Avoiding parsing of irrelevant message parts

Since text and binary protocols require different parsing approaches, we describe our design of each type of parser and how we apply the design principles listed above. We first give a brief outline of how the system works, and then go into detail in the subsequent sections on how our approach works.

We use fast matching primitives—string matching, pattern matching (regular expressions), and binary traversal—that may be easily offloaded to hardware. The signature author specifies a number of matcher primitive entries, which correspond to fields needed by the signature to evaluate the vulnerability constraint. Each matcher contains embedded code which allows the matching engine to automatically extract a value from the result of the match. For example, the HTTP specification includes a string matcher for "Content-Length:", which has an extraction function that converts the string representation of the following number to a integer.

Along with each matcher, the author also specifies a handler function that will be executed following the extraction. The handlers allow the signature author to model the protocol state machine and enable additional matchers. For example, if a matcher discovers that an HTTP request message contains the POST command, it will in turn enable a matcher to parse and extract the message body. We also allow the author to define handlers that are called when an entire message has been matched.

The author checks vulnerability constraints inside the handler functions. Therefore constraint evaluation can be at the field level, intra-message level, and inter-message level. Depending on the complexity of the vulnerability signature, the author can choose where to evaluate the constraint most efficiently.

3.1   Text Protocols

We found that full recursive parsing of text protocols is both too slow and unnecessary for detecting vulnerabilities. However, simple string or regular expression matching is often insufficient to express a vulnerability constraint precisely in cases where the vulnerability depends on some protocol context. In our system, we combine the benefits of the two approaches by connecting multiple string and pattern matching primitives with control logic specialized to the protocol.

Matching Primitives. To make our design amenable to hardware acceleration we built it around simple matching primitives. At the core, we use a fast multi-string matching algorithm. This allows us to approximate the performance of simple pattern-based IDSes for simple vulnerability signatures. Since our system does not depend on any specific string matching algorithm, we have identified several well-studied algorithms [11,12] and hardware optimizations [13] that could be employed by our system.

Furthermore, hardware-accelerated regular expression matching is also becoming a reality [14]. As discussed later, this would further enhance the signature author's ability to locate protocol fields.

Minimal Parsing and State Managment. We have found that protocol fields can be divided into two categories: core fields, which define the structure and semantics of the protocol, and application fields, which have meaning to the application, but are not necessary to understand the rest of the message. An example of a core field is the Content-Length in HTTP, as it determines the size of the message body that follows in the protocol, whereas a field such as Accept-Charset is only relevant to the application.

Our approach in writing vulnerability signatures is to parse and store only the core fields, and the application fields relevant to the vulnerability, while skipping the rest. This allows us to avoid storing irrelevant fields, focusing our resources on those fields that are absolutely necessary.

Although many text protocols are defined in RFCs using a recursive BNF grammar, we find that protocols often use techniques that make identification of core fields possible without resorting to a recursive parse. For example, HTTP headers are specified on a separate line; as a result, a particular header can be located within a message by a simple string search. Header fields that are not relevant to a vulnerability will be skipped by the multi-string matcher, without involving the rest of the parser. Other text protocols follow a similar structure; for example, SMTP uses labeled commands such as "MAIL FROM" and "RCPT TO", which can readily be identified in the message stream.

3.2 Binary Protocols

While some of the techniques we use for text protocol parsing apply to binary protocols as well, binary protocols pose special challenges that must be handled differently from text.

Matching Primitives. Unlike text protocols, binary protocols often lack explicit field labeling. Instead, a parser infers the meaning of a field from its position in the message—relative to either the message start, or to other fields. In simple cases, the parser can use fixed offsets to find fields. In more complicated cases, the position of a field varies based on inter-field dependencies (e.g., variable-length data, where the starting offset of a field in a message varies based on the length of earlier fields), making parsing data-dependent. Thus, parsers must often traverse many or all of the preceding fields. This is still simpler than a full parse, since the parser only examines the lengths and values of structure-dependent fields.

Since binary protocols are more heavily structured than text protocols, we need a matching primitive that is sufficiently aware of this structure while still maintaining high performance. We call this type of parser a binary traverser.

Designing an efficient binary protocol traverser is difficult because binary protocol designs do not adhere to any common standard. In our study of many common binary protocols, we found that they most often utilize the following constructs: C structures, arrays, length-prefixed buffers, sentinel-terminated buffers, and field-driven case evaluation (switch). The binpac protocol parser generator uses variations on these constructs as building blocks for creating a protocol parser. We found binpac to have sufficient expressive power to generate parsers for complex binary protocols. However, binpac parsers perform a full protocol parse rather than a simple binary traversal, so we use a modification to improve their performance.

Minimal Parsing and State Management. We reduced overhead of original binpac parsers for state management and skipped parsing unimportant fields. Because binpac carefully separates the duties of the protocol parser and the traffic analysis system which uses it, we were able to port binpac specifications written for the Bro IDS to our system. We retain the protocol semantics and structure written in the Bro versions but use our own system for managing state and expressing constraints. While we feel that additional improvements may be made in generating fast binary traversers, we were able to obtain substantial improvements in the performance of binpac by optimizing it to the task of traversal rather than full parsing. Furthermore, the binpac language provides exceptional expressiveness for a wide range of protocols, allowing our system to be more easily deployed on new protocols.

3.3 Discussion

By flattening the protocol structure, we can ignore any part of a message which does not directly influence properly processing the message or matching a specific vulnerability. However, some protocols *are* heavily recursive and may not be flattened completely without significantly reducing match precision. We argue that it is rarely necessary to understand and parse *each and every* field and structural construct of a protocol message to match a vulnerability. Consider an XML vulnerability in the skin processing of Trillian (CVE-2002-2366 [10]). An attacker may gain control of the program by passing an over-length string in a `file` attribute, leading to a traditional buffer overflow. Only the `file` attribute, in the `prefs/control/colors` entity can trigger the vulnerability, while instances of `file` in other entities are not vulnerable. To match this vulnerability with our system, the signature author can use a minimal recursive parser which only tracks entity open and close tags. The matcher can use a stack of currently open tags to tell whether it is in the `prefs/control/colors` entity and match `file` attributes which will cause the buffer overflow. The generated parser is recursive but only for the specific fields that are needed to match the vulnerability. This type of signature is a middle-ground for our system—it will provide higher performance than a full parser while requiring the user to manipulate more state than a simpler vulnerability.

In rare cases it may be necessary to do full protocol parsing to properly match a vulnerability signature. While our system is designed to enhance the performance of simpler vulnerability signatures, it is still able to generate high-performance full recursive parsers. The drawback to our approach versus binpac or GAPA in this situation is that the user must manage the parser state manually, which may be error prone.

We do not yet address the problem of protocol detection. However, our system can be integrated with prior work [15] in an earlier stage of the intrusion detection system.

```
1       parser HTTP_Request {
2           dispatch () %{   deploy(vers);    deploy(is_post);    deploy(crlf);    }%
3
4       int vers = str_matcher "HTTP/1."
5           handler handle_vers()
6               %{    end = next_whitespace(rest);
7                     vers = str_to_int(rest,end);    }%
8
9       handle_vers() %{   // handle differently depending on version ... }%
10
11      bool is_post = str_matcher "POST"
12          handler handle_post()
13              %{   is_post=true;    }%
14
15      handle_post() %{    if(is_post) { deploy(content_length);  }    }%
16
17      int content_length = str_matcher "Content-Length:"
18          handler handle_cl()
19              %{   end = next_line(rest);
20                   content_length = str_to_int(rest,end);    }%
21
22      handle_cl() %{    if(this->content_length < 0) { // EXPLOIT! }
23                       else  { deploy(body); }        }%
24
25      bool crlf = str_matcher "\r\n\r\n" ||  "\n\n"
26              %{ // do nothing explicit here }%
27
28      Buffer body = extended_matcher crlf
29          handler handle_body()
30              %{    body = Buffer(rest,this->content_length);
31                    stopMachine();    }%
32
33      handle_body() %{  // process body using another layer   }%
34      }
```

Fig. 1. Sample Specification for HTTP Requests (simplified)

Furthermore, the high-speed matching primitives used by VESPA may also be used to match protocol detection signatures.

4 Language

We have developed a vulnerability signature expression language for use with our system. We give an example vulnerability specification for the CUPS negative content length vulnerability in Figure 1.

Writing a signature involves specifying the matchers for the core fields of the protocol message and then specifying additional matchers to locate the vulnerability. We specify a single protocol message using a *parser* type. The code generator maps this message parser to a C++ class that will contain each state field as a member variable. Inside a message parser, the vulnerability signature author defines handler function declarations and field variable declarations with matching primitives. The author can specify additional member variables that are not directly associated with a matcher using member_vars %{ ... }%.

Each underlying matching primitive always searches for *all* the requested strings and fields with which the matcher is initialized. For example, an HTTP matcher might

search for "`Content-Type:`" in a message even though this string should only be expected in certain cases. This allows the primitive matcher to run in parallel with the
state machine and constraint evaluation, though we have not yet implemented this. It
also prevents the matching primitives from needing to back up to parse a newly desired field. We provide a utility for keeping track of which fields the matcher should
expect and perform extraction and which to ignore. This state is controlled using the
`deploy(var)` function. This function may be called from any handler function, and
initially by the `dispatch` function. `deploy` marks a variable as expected in a state mask
stored inside the parser. This will cause the matcher to execute the variable extraction
function and handler when it is matched. A handler function may in turn enable additional matchers (including re-enabling itself) using the `deploy` function. The parser
ignores any primitive match that is not set to be active using `deploy`.

The parser automatically calls the `dispatch` function each time the parser starts
parsing a new protocol message. This allows the author to define which fields should
be matched from the start of parsing. It also allows the initialization of member variables created using `member_vars`. Conversely, the parser automatically calls `destroy`
to allow any resources allocated in `dispatch` to be freed.

4.1   Matcher Primitives

Protocol fields and matcher primitives are the heart of a vulnerability specification. The
format of matcher primitive specification is:

```
var_type symbol = matching_primitive meta-data
        handler handler_func_name()
        %{
                // embedded C++ code to extract the value
        }%
```

The `var_type` specifies the storage type of the field; e.g., `uint32`. The symbol is the
name of the field that will be stored as a member of the C++ parser class. There are
three types of matching primitives.

1. `str_matcher` (string matcher primitive): The meta-data passed to this matcher are a
   string or sequence of strings separated by ||, and this instructs the underlying multi-
   string matching engine to match this string and then execute its extraction function.
   It supports matching multiple different strings that are semantically identical using
   or ("||").
2. `bin_matcher` (binary traversal primitive): The meta-data passed to this matcher are
   the file name of a binpac specification. This is followed by a colon and the name of a
   binpac `record` type. The meta-data end with the name of a field inside that `record`
   that the author wishes to extract (*e.g.*, IPP.binpac: IPP_Message.version_num). The
   generated binpac parser will then call back to our system to perform the extraction
   and run the handler for the requested field.
3. `extended_matcher` (extension to another matcher): This construct allows us to
   perform additional extractions after matching a single string or binary field. This is
   often useful when multiple fields are embedded after a single match. It also allows

the author to specify a different extraction function depending on which state is expected. The meta-data passed to this primitive are the name of another variable that uses a standard matching primitive.

Each variable match also specifies an extraction function within braces, %{ and }%, which extracts a relevant field from the message. We have provided a number of helper functions that the author can use in the extraction function, such as string conversion and white space elimination. In a string matcher extraction function, there are two pre-defined variables the signature author can use and modify: rest and end. The rest variable points to the first byte of input after the string that was matched. The parser also defines end, which allows the extraction function to store where the extraction ends. Extended matchers run immediately following the extraction function of the string matcher on which they depend and in the same context. Hence, any changes to the state of rest and end should be carefully accounted for in extended matcher extraction functions.

There are two additional functions that the author can use inside the extraction function of a string matcher: stopMachine() and restartMachine(ptr). These functions suspend and restart pattern matching on the input file. This is useful, for example, to prevent the system from matching spurious strings inside the body of an HTTP message. The restartMachine(ptr) function restarts the pattern matching at a new offset specified by ptr. This allows the matcher to skip portions of the message.

4.2 Handlers

Each matcher may also have an associated handler function. The handler function is executed after the extraction and only if the matcher is set to be active with deploy. The signature author defines the body of the handler function using C++ code. In addition to calling the deploy function, handler bodies are where vulnerability constraints can be expressed. We do not yet address the reporting mechanism when a vulnerability is matched. However, since any C++ code may be in the handler, the author may use a variety of methods, such as exceptions or integer codes. The author may also use the handler functions to pass portions of a protocol message to another parser to implement layering and encapsulation.

While structurally different from existing protocol parser generators like GAPA and binpac, our language is sufficiently expressive to model many text and binary protocols and vulnerabilities. Porting a protocol specification from an RFC or an existing spec in another language (like binpac or GAPA) is fairly straightforward once the author understands the protocol semantics.

5 Implementation

5.1 Compiler

We designed a compiler to generate machine-executable vulnerability signature matchers from our language. We implemented the compiler using the Perl programming language. Our implementation leverages the "Higher Order Perl" [16] Lexer and Parser classes, which kept down the implementation complexity: the entire compiler is 600 lines. Approximately 70% of the compiler code specifies the lexical and grammatical structures of our language; the balance performs symbol rewriting, I/O stream management, and boilerplate C++ syntax.

Our compiler operates on a single parser file (e.g., `myparser.p`), which defines a signature matcher. The generated code is a C++ class which extends one of the parser super classes. The class definition consists of two files (following the example above, `myparser.h` and `myparser.cc`), which jointly specify the generated parser subclass.

5.2 Parser Classes

Generated C++ classes for both binary and text parsers are structurally very similar, but differ in how they interface with the matching primitives. We have optimized the layout and performance of this code. We use inlined functions and code whenever possible. Many extraction helper functions are actually macros to reduce unnecessary function call overhead. We store the expected state set with `deploy` using a bit vector.

For string matchers, we use the sfutil library from Snort [17], which efficiently implements the Aho–Corasick (AC) algorithm [11]. Because the construction of a keyword trie for the AC algorithm can be time-consuming, we generate a separate reusable class which contains the pre-built AC trie. Our text matcher is not strongly tied to this particular multi-string matching implementation, and we have also prototyped it with the libSpare AC implementation [18].

We use binpac to generate a binary traverser for our parsers. As input, the compiler expects a binpac specification for the binary protocol. This should include all the `record` types in the protocol as well as the basic `analyzer`, `connection`, and `flow` binpac types. We then use the `refine` feature of binpac to embed the extraction functions and callbacks to our parser. Since binpac does simple extractions automatically, it is often unnecessary to write additional code that processes the field before it is assigned. Like the AC algorithm for text parsers, the binary parser is not heavily tied to the binary traversal algorithm or implementation. For a few protocols, we have developed hand-coded replacements for binpac binary traversal.

5.3 Binary Traversal-Optimized Binpac

We have made several modifications to the binpac parser generator to improve its performance for binary traversal. The primary enhancement we made is to change the default model for the in-memory structures binpac keeps while parsing. The original binpac allocated a C++ class for each non-primitive type it encountered while parsing. This resulted in an excessive number of calls to `new`, even for small messages. To alleviate this problem, we changed the default behavior of binpac to force all non-primitive types to be pre-allocated in one object. We use the `datauint` type in binpac to store all the possible subtypes that binpac might encounter. To preserve binpac semantics, we added a new function, `init(params...)`, to each non-primitive type in binpac. The `init` function contains the same code as the constructor, and we call it wherever a new object would have been created. It also accepts any arguments that the constructor takes to allow fields to be propagated from one object to another. We restrict binpac specifications to be able to pass only primitive types from object to object. While this reduces our compatibility with existing binpac specifications, it is easy to change them to support this limitation.

Some objects in binpac *must* be specified using a pointer to a dynamically created object and cannot be pre-allocated. For example, in the Bro DNS binpac specification, a DNS_name is composed of DNS_labels. A DNS_label type also contains a DNS_name object if the label is a pointer to another name. This circular dependency is not possible with statically sized classes. We added the *&pointer* attribute modifier to the binpac language to allow the author to specifically mark objects that must be dynamically allocated.

The final modification we made to binpac was to change the way that it handled arrays of objects. The original version of binpac created a vector for each array and stored each element separately. Because binary traversal only needs to access the data as it is being parsed, we do not need to store the entire array, only the current element. We eliminated the vector types entirely and changed binpac to only store the current element in the array using a pre-allocated object. If the author needs to store data from each element in the array, he must explicitly store it outside of binpac in the VESPA parser class using a handler function.

6 Evaluation

We evaluated VESPA with vulnerabilities in both text and binary protocols. We implemented matchers for vulnerabilities in the HTTP, DNS, and IPP protocols. We searched for exploitable bugs in network-facing code, focusing especially on scenarios where traditional exploit signatures would fail. Like Cui et al. did with GAPA [19], we found the process of writing a vulnerability signature for a protocol very similar to writing one for a file format. Thus, we used our system develop to a binary parscr for thc Windows Meta-file Format (WMF).

We ran all our experiments on an Ubuntu 7.10 Linux (2.6.22-14-x86_64) system with a dual-core 2.6 GHz AMD Athlon 64 processor and 4GB of RAM (our implementation is single-threaded so we only utilized one core). We ran the tests on HTTP and DNS on traces of real traffic collected from the UIUC Coordinated Science Laboratory network. We collected WMF files from freely available clipart websites. Since we did not have access to large volumes of IPP traffic, we tested using a small set of representative messages. We repeated the trace tests 10 times, and we repeated processing the IPP messages 1 million times to normalize any system timing perturbations. We show the standard deviation of these runs using error bars in the charts.

6.1 Micro-benchmarks of Matching Primitives

To evaluate the performance of using fast string matching primitives, we implemented our parser using two different implementations of the Aho–Corasick (AC) algorithm and compared their performance (Figure 2a). We used the sfutil library, which is part of the Snort IDS [17], and the Spare Parts implementation of AC [18]. We used those base implementations to search for the same strings as our vulnerability matcher does, but without any of the control logic or constraint checking. We found that for either AC implementation, the performance of a basic HTTP vulnerability matcher (which handles optional bodies and chunking) was very close to that of the string matching primitive.

The performance of string matching alone approximates (generously) the performance of a simple pattern-based IDS. If the vulnerability signature is simple enough to be expressed using a simple string match (e.g., the IPP vulnerability for a negative Content-Length), our system is able to match it with comparable performance to a pattern based IDS.

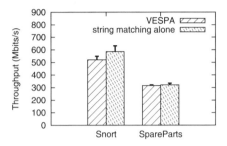

Parser Type	Bytes allocated	Num calls to new
DNS (binpac)	15,812	539
DNS (traversal)	2,296	14
IPP (binpac)	1,360	33
IPP (traversal)	432	6
WMF (binpac)	3,824	94
WMF (traversal)	312	6

(a) Comparison between string matching primitive and parsing for HTTP requests

(b) Dynamic memory usage for a single message for standard binpac vs. binary traversal

Fig. 2. Micro-benchmarks

We next investigated the performance of binary traversal in binpac. One of the primary changes we made to binpac was to change its default memory and allocation behavior. We instrumented the original version of binpac and a parser built with our binary traversal-optimized version to assess the effectiveness of this change (Figure 2b). We saw an overall reduction in memory usage despite pre-allocating types that may not be present in the message. We were also able to cut the number of calls to new by a substantial factor for all three binary protocols we implemented. Our IPP and WMF traversers do not contain any explicit pointer types (specified with &pointer), so the number of allocated blocks is constant for *any* protocol message. The number of times the DNS parser calls the new allocator is proportional to the number of name pointers in the message.

6.2   Signature Matching Performance

We evaluated the throughput of our vulnerability signature matching algorithms compared to the binpac parser generator. Binpac is the most efficient freely available automated protocol parser generator. We do not evaluate against GAPA because it has not been publicly released. Furthermore, binpac far exceeds GAPA in performance because it directly generates machine code rather than being interpreted [1]. Since binpac is not specifically designed for vulnerability signatures, we added vulnerability constraint checking to the binpac protocol specifications. In each of the following sections we describe the protocol and vulnerabilities we tested against. We show the results in Figure 3.

HTTP/IPP. The Common Unix Printing System (CUPS), with its protocol encapsulation and chunk-capable HTTP parser, illustrates several design choices which confound exploit-signature writers. The vulnerability given in CVE-2002-0063 [10] occurs because of the way the Internet Printing Protocol (IPP) specifies a series of textual key–value pairs, called attributes. The protocol allows attribute lengths to vary, requiring the sender to use a 16-bit unsigned integer to specify the length of each attribute. CUPS reads the specified number of bytes into a buffer on the stack, but the buffer is only 8192 bytes long, allowing an attacker to overflow the buffer and execute arbitrary code with the permissions of the CUPS process. A signature for this attack must check that each attribute length is less than 8192. IPP is a binary protocol but it is encapsulated inside of chunked HTTP for transport. Attackers can obfuscate the exploit by splitting it across an arbitrary number of HTTP chunks, making it very hard to detect this attack with pattern-based signatures. We also tested the negative content length vulnerability that we have discussed previously.

We designed a text-based vulnerability signature matcher for HTTP. In addition to vulnerabilities in HTTP itself, many protocols and file formats which are encapsulated inside of HTTP also have vulnerabilities. We use VESPA to match the `Content-Length` vulnerability in CUPS/IPP, as well as to extract the body of the message to pass it to another layer for processing. We support standard and chunked message bodies and pass them to a null processing layer. Unfortunately, we were unable to make a direct comparison to binpac for chunked HTTP messages due to a bug in binpac's buffering system: binpac will handle such a message but fail to extract data from each individual chunk. Despite this, we found that VESPA was considerably faster than the equivalent binpac parser. Since much of the HTTP message body is ignored by both VESPA and binpac, the throughputs we observed are very high because the size of the body contributes to the overall number of bytes processed. We also measured the message processing rates for various types of HTTP messages and found them to be adequate to process the traffic of a busy website (Table 2).

We implemented a binary IPP vulnerability matcher to be used in conjunction with our HTTP parser. The VESPA IPP matcher ran four times as fast as the binpac version, largely due to the improved state management techniques we described earlier. We also developed a hand-coded drop-in replacement for our binpac binary traverser of the IPP protocol. Using this replacement, we were able to achieve an order of magnitude improvement over the performance of the binpac binary traversal (see Table 1).

Table 2. HTTP Message Rate

HTTP Message Type	Message Rate (msgs per sec)
Requests	370,005
Responses	196,897
Chunked	41,644
Overall	314,797

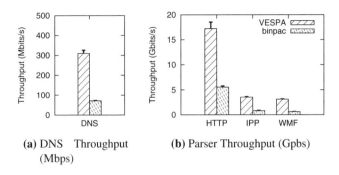

(a) DNS   Throughput
(Mbps)

(b) Parser Throughput (Gpbs)

Fig. 3. Vulnerability Signature Matcher Performance

Therefore, our architecture stands to benefit from further improvements of the base matching primitives of binary traversal as well.

DNS. The DNS protocol includes a compression mechanism to avoid including a common DNS suffix more than once in the same message. Parsing these compressed suffixes, called name pointers, is best done with a recursive parser, but doing so introduces the possibility of a "pointer cycle," where a specially-crafted message can force a parser to consume an infinite amount of stack space, leading to a denial of service [20].

DNS name pointers can occur in many different structures in DNS, so the binary traversal must parse and visit many of the fields in the protocol. Therefore, parsing DNS is usually much slower than other protocols. Indeed, DNS is the worst-performing of our vulnerability signature matchers, though it is still several times faster than binpac, as can be seen in Figure 3. Pang et al. suggest that this is due to an inherent difficulty of parsing DNS, pointing to the comparable performance of their hand-implemented parser to binpac [1]. We have found this not to be the case, as our hand-implemented DNS parser that finds pointer cycles can operate at nearly 3 Gbps (see Table 1). As part of our future work, we will investigate what part of our current design is responsible for the much worse performance of DNS; our hope is that we will be able to achieve speeds in excess of 1 Gbps with an automatically-generated parser.

WMF. Vulnerabilities are increasingly being found in file formats (so called "data-driven attacks") rather than just network messages. The WMF format allows specification of a binary "abort procedure," called if the rendering engine is interrupted. Attackers began to misuse this feature in late 2005, using the abort handler for "drive-by downloads," where an attacker could run arbitrary code on a victim's computer by simply convincing them to render a WMF, requiring only a website visit for clients using Internet Explorer (CVE-2005-4560 [10]).

This vulnerability has been problematic for intrusion detection systems, Snort in particular. Snort normally processes only the first few hundred bytes of a message when looking for vulnerabilities; however, a WMF vulnerability can be placed at the end of a very large media file. However, matching the Snort rule set over an entire message exhausts the resources of most intrusion detection systems, requiring most sites to resort to a convoluted configuration with two Snort processes running in concert. Our architecture allows for a much cleaner approach: after an HTTP header has been parsed, the WMF vulnerability matcher would be called in the body handler, while other string matchers and handlers would be turned off. Figure 3 shows that WMF files can be parsed at multi-gigabit rates, so this would not put a significant strain on the CPU resources of the NIDS.

7   Future Directions

Although our prototype shows that high-performance vulnerability signature matching is possible in software, to achieve speeds in excess of 1 Gbps for all protocols, a hardware-accelerated approach is likely needed. Our plan is to use hardware implementations of fast pattern-matching algorithms [14,21] to replace the software implementations. This should dramatically increase the performance of text protocol parsing, as discussed in Section 6.1. We will also investigate the use of network processors, such as the Intel IXP family [22], to bring vulnerability processing closer to the network interface, and to exploit the inherent parallelism in matching signatures. Previous work has shown that using network processors can be nearly two orders of magnitude faster than similar implementations in software [23]. Network processors achieve such speedups in part by using a complex memory hierarchy; our careful management of limited state makes our architecture well-adapted to being ported to a network processor.

There are also performance gains yet to be realized in software matching as well. Our hand-coded matchers for vulnerabilities in binary protocols, in particular, are significantly fasters than those implemented using VESPA (see Table 1). The extra performance is likely due to eliminating the abstractions that ensue from representing a binary protocol structure in binpac. Our future work includes faster implementation of those abstractions, as well as the design of abstractions better suited to fast matching. One challenge that we will face is the fact that binary protocols exhibit much less consistency of design than text protocols.

Our eventual goal is to create a network intrusion *prevention* system (NIPS), which will sit as a "bump in the wire" and filter attacking traffic. In addition to throughput, another challenge that a NIPS will face is reducing latency, since, unlike intrusion detection systems, filtering decisions must be complete before the traffic can be forwarded to its destination. Furthermore, a NIPS must be able to recognize a large collection of vulnerability signatures at once. Our use of multi-pattern search as a base primitive will make parallel matching of several signatures easier to implement, but our design will need to incorporate constructs that will allow the reuse of common components (e.g., HTTP Content-Length extraction) between multiple signatures.

Authoring of effective signatures is a complex and error-prone process; this is true for exploit signatures, and more so for vulnerability signatures. Although our architecture was optimized for performance, rather than ease of authorship, we have found that expressing vulnerability constraints using VESPA was not appreciably more difficult than using binpac or GAPA. However, as we gain more experience with VESPA, we plan to improve the interface between the programmer and our architecture by, for example, introducing more reusable constructs and modularity. We also plan to develop better architectures for testing vulnerability signatures, to ensure that they do not generate false positives or false negatives.

Finally, automatic generation of vulnerability signatures can make them useful for not only known vulnerabilities, but new ones just observed ("zero-day"). Previous work has used annotated protocol structure [24,19], program analysis [9,25], or data flow analysis [26] to automatically generate vulnerability signatures. We will explore to what extent these approaches may be used to automatically generate signatures in our architecture. This will present a significant challenge to an automated approach, given that our architecture relegates more of state management to the programmer.

8 Related Work

8.1 Pattern Matching

The Wu–Manber [12], Boyer–Moore [27], and Aho–Corasick [11] algorithms provide fast searching for multiple strings. Their superior performance has made them natural candidates for IDS pattern-matching; in addition to our system, Snort [17] uses Aho–Corasick to match static strings.

Although slower than string matching, regular expression-based matching provides considerably more expressive power. Regular-expression matching is well-studied in the literature; broadly, deterministic matching (e.g., flex [28]) offers linear time but exponential space complexity, while nondeterministic matching (e.g., pcre [29]) offers linear space but exponential time complexity. Smith et al. attempt to combine the advantages of deterministic and nondeterministic matching using Extended Finite Automata [30]. Rubin et al. have developed protomatching to heuristically reduce matching complexity by discarding non-matching packets as quickly as possible, while keeping a low memory footprint [31]. Special-purpose hardware achieves sustained pattern matching at 4 Gbps [14]. Clark et al. [13] used application-specific FPGA cores to exploit the parallelism inherent in searching for many patterns simultaneously in a single body of text.

8.2 Vulnerability Signatures

The Shield project at Microsoft Research [2] pioneered the idea of vulnerability signatures; Borisov et al. extended the idea with a generic protocol parser generator [7]. Brumley et al. explained the complexity of various approaches to matching [9].

The binpac project at UC Berkeley and the International Computer Science Institute [1] focused on implementing a yacc-like tool for generating efficient protocol parsers from high-level definitions. binpac abstracts away much error-inducing complexity (e.g., network byte ordering). Its performance for many protocols is adequate for many intrusion detection tasks, but the VESPA architecture significantly improves on it, as shown in our evaluation.

The ongoing NetShield project [32] shares our goals of high-speed vulnerability signature detection. It has resulted in novel techniques for fast binary traversal, as well as efficient multi-signature matching, which may provide promising approaches for addressing some of the same challenges in VESPA.

8.3   Intrusion Detection

Intrusion detection requires attention to both algorithmic efficiency, and systems / implementation issues. Ptacek and Newsham [33] have detailed several strategies for evading intrusion detection by shifting packet TTLs, among others. Snort [34,17] and Bro [8], two popular IDS platforms, have addressed many systems-level issues, but are intended only to detect, not prevent intrusion. So-called intrusion prevention systems go further, by being deployed inline with the forwarding path; these systems take a more active stance against hostile traffic by dropping malicious or otherwise anomalous packets. The SafeCard [35] project used an Intel IXP network processor to perform intrusion protection in real-time up to 1 Gbps. It used high-speed matching of regular expressions, as well as an early implementation of Prospector [26] signatures, finding vulnerabilities within HTTP headers. The project shows that special-purpose hardware is a promising direction for high-performance intrusion prevention systems.

9   Conclusion

We have proposed an architecture, called VESPA, for fast matching of vulnerability signatures. VESPA relies on the fact that full protocol parsing is often not necessary to match vulnerability signatures and as a result is able to match signatures several times faster than existing work. We have built a prototype implementation of our architecture, and we showed that we can match vulnerabilities in many protocols at speeds in excess of 1 Gbps, thus demonstrating that vulnerability signatures are practical for high-performance network intrusion detection systems. We plan to continue to improve the performance of our system by improved implementation of base primitives and hardware acceleration, and to develop a full-fledged implementation of a high-performance network intrusion prevention system based on vulnerability signatures.

Acknowledgments

We would like to thank David Nicol and William Sanders for their guidance on this project and the anonymous referees for their suggestions on an earlier version of this draft. This work was supported by NSF grant CNS 06–27671.

References

1. Pang, R., Paxson, V., Sommer, R., Peterson, L.: binpac: A yacc for Writing Application Protocol Parsers. In: Proceedings of the Internet Measurement Conference (2006)
2. Wang, H.J., Guo, C., Simon, D.R., Zugenmaier, A.: Shield: Vulnerability-Driven Network Filters for Preventing Known Vulnerability Exploits. In: ACM SIGCOMM Computer Communications Review (2004)
3. CERT: "Code Red" Worm Exploiting Buffer Overflow in IIS Indexing Service DLL. CERT Advisory CA-2001-19 (July 2001),
   www.cert.org/advisories/CA-2001-19.html
4. Friedl, S.: Analysis of the New "Code Red II" Variant (August 2001),
   http://www.unixwiz.net/techtips/CodeRedII.html

5. Microsoft: Unchecked Buffer in ISAPI Extension Could Enable Compromise of IIS 5.0 Server. Microsoft Security Bulletin MS01-033 (June 2001), www.microsoft.com/technet/security/bulletin/ms01-023.mspx

6. Rescorla, E.: Security Holes... Who Cares?. In: Paxson, V. (ed.) USENIX Security Symposium (August 2003)

7. Borisov, N., Brumley, D.J., Wang, H.J., Dunagan, J., Joshi, P., Guo, C.: A Generic Application-Level Protocol Parser Analyzer and its Language. In: Proceedings of the 14th Annual Network and Distributed System Security Symposium (2007)

8. Paxson, V.: Bro: A System for Detecting Network Intruders in Real-time. Comput. Netw. 31(23-24), 2435–2463 (1999)

9. Brumley, D., Newsome, J., Song, D., Wang, H., Jha, S.: Towards Automatic Generation of Vulnerability-Based Signatures. In: Proceedings of the 2006 IEEE Symposium on Security and Privacy (2006)

10. CVE: Common Vulnerabilities and Exposures, http://cve.mitre.org/

11. Aho, A.V., Corasick, M.J.: Efficient String Matching: an Aid to Bibliographic Search. Commun. ACM 18(6), 333–340 (1975)

12. Wu, S., Manber, U.: A Fast Algorithm for Multi-Pattern Searching. Technical Report TR-94-17, Department of Computer Science, University of Arizona (1994)

13. Clark, C., Lee, W., Schimmel, D., Contis, D., Koné, M., Thomas, A.: A Hardware Platform for Network Intrusion Detection and Prevention. In: Proceedings of the Third Workshop on Network Processors and Applications (2004)

14. Brodie, B.C., Taylor, D.E., Cytron, R.K.: A Scalable Architecture For High-Throughput Regular-Expression Pattern Matching. In: ISCA, pp. 191–202 (2006)

15. Dreger, H., Feldmann, A., Mai, M., Paxson, V., Sommer, R.: Dynamic Application-layer Protocol Analysis for Network Intrusion Detection. In: USENIX-SS 2006: Proceedings of the 15th conference on USENIX Security Symposium, Berkeley, CA, USA, p. 18. USENIX Association (2006)

16. Dominus, M.J.: Higher Order Perl: Transforming Programs with Programs. Morgan Kaufmann, San Francisco (2005)

17. Sourcefire, Inc.: Snort, www.snort.org

18. Watson, B.W., Cleophas, L.: SPARE Parts: a C++ Toolkit for String Pattern Recognition. Softw. Pract. Exper. 34(7), 697–710 (2004)

19. Cui, W., Peinado, M., Wang, H.J., Locasto, M.E.: ShieldGen: Automatic Data Patch Generation for Unknown Vulnerabilities with Informed Probing. In: Pfitzmann, B., McDaniel, P. (eds.) IEEE Symposium on Security and Privacy, May 2007, pp. 252–266 (2007)

20. NISCC: Vulnerability Advisory 589088/NISCC/DNS (May 2005), http://www.cpni.gov.uk/docs/re-20050524-00432.pdf

21. Clark, C.R., Schimmel, D.E.: Scalable Pattern Matching for High-Speed Networks. In: IEEE Symposium on Field-Programmable Custom Computing Machines (FCCM), Napa, California, pp. 249–257 (2004)

22. Intel: Intel Network Processors, www.intel.com/design/network/products/npfamily/index.htm

23. Turner, J.S., Crowley, P., DeHart, J., Freestone, A., Heller, B., Kuhns, F., Kumar, S., Lockwood, J., Lu, J., Wilson, M., Wiseman, C., Zar, D.: Supercharging PlanetLab: A High Performance, Multi-application, Overlay Network Platform. SIGCOMM Computing Communications Review 37(4), 85–96 (2007)

24. Liang, Z., Sekar, R.: Fast and Automated Generation of Attack Signatures: A Basis for Building Self-protecting Servers. In: Meadows, C. (ed.) ACM Conference on Computer and Communications Security, November 2005, pp. 213–222. ACM, New York (2005)

25. Brumley, D., Wang, H., Jha, S., Song, D.: Creating Vulnerability Signatures Using Weakest Pre-conditions. In: Proceedings of the 2007 Computer Security Foundations Symposium, Venice, Italy (July 2007)
26. Slowinska, A., Bos, H.: The Age of Data: Pinpointing Guilty Bytes in Polymorphic Buffer Overflows on Heap or Stack. In: Samarati, P., Payne, C. (eds.) Annual Computer Security Applications Conference (December 2007)
27. Boyer, R.S., Moore, J.S.: A Fast String Searching Algorithm. Commun. ACM 20(10), 762–772 (1977)
28. Flex: The Fast Lexical Analyzer, http://www.gnu.org/software/flex
29. PCRE: Perl Compatible Regular Expression Library, http://www.pcre.org
30. Smith, R., Estan, C., Jha, S.: XFA: Faster Signature Matching with Extended Automata. In: Proceedings of the 2008 IEEE Symposium on Security and Privacy (2008)
31. Rubin, S., Jha, S., Miller, B.P.: Protomatching Network Traffic for High Throughput Network Intrusion Detection. In: Proceedings of the 13th ACM conference on Computer and communications security (2006)
32. Li, Z., Xia, G., Tang, Y., He, Y., Chen, Y., Liu, B., West, J., Spadaro, J.: NetShield: Matching with a Large Vulnerability Signature Ruleset for High Performance Network Defense (manuscript) (2008)
33. Ptacek, T.H., Newsham, T.N.: Insertion, Evasion, and Denial of Service: Eluding Network Intrusion Detection. Technical report, Secure Networks, Inc., Suite 330, 1201 5th Street S.W, Calgary, Alberta, Canada, T2R-0Y6 (1998)
34. Roesch, M.: Snort—Lightweight Intrusion Detection for Networks. In: Parter, D. (ed.) Proceedings of the 1999 USENIX LISA Systems Administration Conference, Berkeley, CA, USA, November 1999, pp. 229–238. USENIX Association (1999)
35. de Bruijn, W., Slowinska, A., van Reeuwijk, K., Hruby, T., Xu, L., Bos, H.: SafeCard: A Gigabit IPS on the Network Card. In: Proceedings of the 9th International Symposium On Recent Advances in Intrusion Detection (2006)

Swarm Attacks against Network-Level Emulation/Analysis

Simon P. Chung and Aloysius K. Mok⋆

Department of Computer Sciences,
University of Texas at Austin, Austin TX 78712, USA
{phchung,mok}@cs.utexas.edu

Abstract. It is always assumed that if the attackers can achieve their goal by exploiting a vulnerability once, they won't exploit it twice. This assumption shapes our view of what attacks look like, and affects the design of many security systems. In this work, we propose the swarm attack, in which the attacker deliberately exploits the same vulnerability multiple times, each intended to carry out only a small part of the attack goal. We have studied eight systems that detect attacks using network-level emulation/analysis, and find them surprisingly vulnerable to attacks based on this strategy.

Keywords: Decoder detection; network-level emulation; network IDS; evasion; swarm attacks.

1 Introduction

In its simplest, most common form, a control hijacking attack works as follow: the attacker sends in **one single malicious input** with the proper "protocol frame" to trigger the targeted vulnerability, together with **a self contained payload** that will achieve the attacker's goal once executed. When the malicious input is processed, certain control data structure will be overwritten, and this results in **an almost instant transfer of control** to the attacker's payload. We believe many security systems are designed with this simple model of attacks in mind, and it is usually implicitly assumed that the attacker gains nothing by making the attack more complicated (or less "efficient"). In other word, if they can get all their attack code executed with one instance of control hijacking, they will not divide their code into multiple pieces and execute them through multiple exploitations of the vulnerability. Similarly, the attacker will overwrite the piece of control data that leads to the control hijacking with the minimum delay.

In this paper, we propose the attack strategy where the attacker violates the above assumption and be deliberately "inefficient" in their attacks, and study the implications of such strategy to systems that try to locate executable code within network traffic and determine if those are attack payload. We call our proposed attack **the swarm attack**, and will refer to target systems described

---

⋆ The research reported here is supported partially by a grant from the Office of Naval Research under contract number N00014-03-1-0705.

R. Lippmann, E. Kirda, and A. Trachtenberg (Eds.): RAID 2008, LNCS 5230, pp. 175–190, 2008.

above **network-level emulation/analysis systems**. Surprisingly, we find that by deliberately dividing the attack code into many pieces and have each executed through a different exploitation of the same vulnerability, the attacker can evade at least seven out of the eight network-level emulation/analysis systems that we have studied [1,3,13,14,15,21,24,25] (we believe the third one, [13], may detect our attack if specifically trained to, but can only do so at the cost of high false positives). The design of our attack is simple; the attack will be divided into n+1 instances of control hijacking. Each of the first n instances will have a small payload to write part of the real decoder to a predetermined area in the attacked process' address space, and the $(n+1)^{st}$ instance will direct the hijacked control to the decoder we just constructed. Under this attack, the number of unencoded instructions in each attack instance can be reduced to below 10, and all these unencoded payload will appear to serve no useful purpose for an attack. Note that the need to have multiple instances of control hijacking on the target system places certain constraints on our swarm attack. However, we will argue in Scct. 4.1 that the attack can be used against many vulnerable network servers, and there are techniques to overcome this constraint even if the target system is single-threaded. Finally, we believe if network-level emulation/analysis systems continue to consider traffic separately, such small, simple payload will be very hard to detect with low false positives; the payload behavior is so simple that the chance of finding such behavior in random data by coincidence is non-negligible.

The rest of the paper will be organized as follow: in Sect. 2, we will present related work in the area of network-level emulation/analysis based detection, and attacks against other types of network intrusion detection systems. In Sect. 3, we will present the details of the proposed swarm attack, and address some practical issues that may arise in the implementation of the attack in Sect. 4. Analysis of how the proposed attack evade network-level emulation/analysis will be given in Sect. 5, and in Sect. 6, we will discuss whether it is possible to improve existing systems to detect the attack. Finally, we conclude in Sect. 7.

2   Related Work

There are generally three approaches for network intrusion detection, and the most traditional of which is signature matching. The second approach is anomaly detection, which compares properties of observed traffic against properties of known good traffic. Network anomaly detection systems usually treat the traffic under analysis as a bag of bytes, and use statistical methods to determine if this bag of bytes appears to be an attack. For example, PAYL [23] distinguishes normal traffic from attacks based on byte frequency distribution. The last approach, which we call the network-level emulation/analysis, is the focus of our work. The main idea behind this approach is to locate executable code within the incoming traffic, and analyze the extracted code to determine if it is random data that coincidentally appears to be syntactically correct machine instructions or actual attack code. We note that any useful attack strategy must be able to defeat all three kinds of detectors. However, in this work, we will focus on evading systems based on network-level emulation/analysis, which is the least attacked among the three approaches. As for the evasion of the other two mechanisms, we will rely on existing techniques against them.

2.1   Analyzing Code within Network Traffic

The earliest network-level emulation/analysis systems are designed specifically for buffer overflow attacks. In particular, they are designed to detect the sled in these attacks; since the attacker does not know the exact address where their payload will be found, the hijacked control is usually directed to an area filled with NOPs that precedes the actual payload. This technique allows the attack to succeed even though the attackers only have a rough estimate of where their payload will be located on the stack or the heap, and the area of NOP is called the sled. Sled-detection systems are usually very simple. For example, [21] scans through the incoming traffic and declares it as malicious if it finds 30 or more consecutive valid instructions in the traffic. Similarly, [1] considers the incoming traffic malicious if it contains an instruction sequence that spans at least 230 bytes, with each of its suffix also being a valid instruction sequence.

The obvious problem with sled-detection is that not all attacks contain sleds. In fact, with the use of register springs, many buffer overflow attacks can avoid using sled. Thus a second generation of detection systems is developed to identify "meaningful" code within network traffic. For example, [24] will classify incoming traffic as malicious if: (1) it contains two or more separate instruction sequences for function calls (including the instructions for placing arguments on the stack and the actual control transfer), or (2) it contains a sequence of 14 or more "useful" instructions that does not cause any data flow anomaly (i.e. they define data values once before use). As another example, [3] defines malicious traffic as one that contains either obvious library/system calls (identified by hardcoded jump target and interrupt instructions after initializing eax), return/indirect control transfer with target address being properly set up by preceding instructions found in the traffic, or a proper loop structure that appears to be a decoding routine in polymorphic shellcode. The weakness of this second generation of systems is that they are not very effective against polymorphic shellcode, in which only the decoder appears as valid instructions in the network traffic, and the rest of the attack code is encoded. To address this problem, systems are designed to target properties specific to the decoding routines of polymorphic shellcode. The most commonly used property is the presence of GetPC code, which allows a position-independent shellcode to find out its own location, as well as the address of the payload to be decoded. In both [14,25], the presence of GetPC code (e.g. call, fnstenv) is used both as a precondition for further analysis, and an indicator of the beginning of the decoding routine. With this location of the GetPC code, [25] confirms that the identified code is indeed a decoder if it is self modifying and involves a loop which contains indirect write instructions with target addresses that are different in each iteration. On the other hand, after identifying the GetPC code, [14] characterizes the decoder by a significant number (6 or more) of reads from different locations within the analyzed traffic itself. A machine learning based approach is used in [13], where a neural network is employed to determine if a sequence of instructions is a decoder, based on the frequency at which different types of instructions appears in that sequence. Even though [13] shows that neural network trained with decoder from one polymorphic engine can identify decoder routines from another polymorphic engine, we believe retraining is necessary if there is a drastic change in the decoding algorithm. Finally, as an extension of [14], [15] argued that some non-self-contained polymorphic shellcode does not have any GetPC code or reads to bytes within the traffic itself. [15] thus proposed two new properties for identifying polymorphic shellcode: writing to a significant number of different memory locations, and then executing those locations that has been written to.

2.2 Evading Signature-Based and Statistics-Based Detectors

Polymorphic shellcode, which is the focus of many systems described in the previous section, is originally designed to evade signature-based defenses. The idea is simple, to avoid being matched by signatures generated based on previous instances of the same attack, the attacker will make every attack instance appears differently. This goal is usually achieved by having the attack code encoded by some very simple "keyed-encryption" algorithm, and has the code for each attack instance encoded under a different key. In order to allow correct execution of the attack code, we need to attach a decoder to each attack instance, provide it with the correct key and execute it to decode the real payload. This way, only the decoding routine will remain constant throughout all attack instances. To avoid the decoder from being targeted by signature-matching, various "polymorphic"[1] engines have been developed to make the routine slightly different in every attack instance. Common techniques for achieving this goal include instruction substitution [6,10] and insertion of junk instructions [10].

Even though the encoding of the actual payload, together with the metamorphism applied on the decoder will successfully evade a signature-based detector, the resulting attack instances may still have very different properties from normal traffic, and thus can be detected by some kind of anomaly detection. In [8], a technique is proposed to encode the payload so that it will have the same byte frequency distribution as the observed normal traffic, and evade anomaly detection systems based on byte frequency (e.g. PAYL [23]). The idea is extended in [7] so that encoded payload (using either xor-based or byte-substitution-based encoding) which satisfies any normal traffic profile (expressed in a finite-state machine) can be found.

The difficulties of detecting the decoder of a polymorphic attack with either a signature-based or statistical-based approach are also demonstrated in [20], but in an unconventional way. Instead of showing concrete ways to defeat the studied defenses, [20] only presents an "existential proof", showing that n-byte sequences that exhibit decoder-like behavior are distributed over a very large

---

[1] Which are actually "metamorphic" engines.

span of all possible n-byte sequences, and uses this as an evidence to suggest the actual decoder population may have a similar span, and thus it will be very difficult to characterize all of them with signatures or statistical model. What is of interest are the properties [20] used to define decoder behavior: self-writing (containing instructions that write to nearby locations) and self-modification (containing instructions that write to nearby locations using values read from another nearby location). This further illustrates the general perception of what decoders should look like, and can be very useful when we design our attack to evade systems that detect instruction sequences which appear to be decoding routines.

2.3   Other Related Attacks

In general, attacks for evading data-non-executable defenses can achieve the same goal as ours; they carry out the attack without executing (or placing) any code within the network traffic, thus there will be nothing for network-level emulation/analysis systems to detect. However, these attacks are usually much more difficult to construct than those that use highly obfuscated/polymorphed shellcode. For example, [18] makes extensive use of the ret-to-libc technique, and allows the attacker to "execute" arbitrary code by chaining up "gadgets", each being code fragment within libc which contains instructions for achieving some primitive binary-level operations (e.g. data movement), followed by a return instruction that will pass the control to the next gadget. However, there seems no easy way to automatically locate all the gadgets needed for some set of primitive operations, and these gadgets can only be invoked by using hard-coded addresses, which may harm the portability of the resulting attack, and can provide a lot of materials for signature matching. As for the non-control-data attack in [2], the logic of the attacked program is altered through the manipulation of its critical data, and such attacks cannot be designed without intimate knowledge of the internals of the victim program, as well as the whereabouts of its critical data. Once again, it is unclear to us whether [2] can be effective against signature-based or statistics-based defenses. Furthermore, standard techniques (like [6,8,10]) for evading detection, that mostly focus on code morphing/encoding, are not applicable to attacks against data-non-executable, since they don't involve any code at all. Finally, an attack of similar flavor but different objective to ours is [17], where a technique for evading signature-based detection systems is presented. The idea in [17] is similar to ours in the sense that evasion is achieved through breaking up the attack into many small pieces, and inserting some useless pieces in between (though the attacks generated by [17] still exploit the target vulnerability only once).

To conclude our discussion of related work, we note that techniques for evading the three types of detection systems can be easily combined; while the technique in [7] only works for certain types of encryption/decryption routine, both the technique we are going to present and the metamorphism employed in [6,10] can work on any kind of decoders. Thus, [7] will determine the decryption routine we can use, and provide an encrypted payload that can blend in with normal traffic, our swarm attack will modify the routine to remove any behavior expected of a decoder (or any non-polymorphic malicious code), and the metamorphism will be applied to the modified routine so that it appears differently in every attack instance.

3   Swarm Attack against Network-level Emulation/Analysis

As we have mentioned in the introduction, the idea of swarm attack against network-level emulation/analysis systems is to modify a control hijacking attack so that the decoder in its polymorphic shellcode will not appear in any attack traffic. We achieve this goal by creating the decoder inside the attacked process' address space using multiple instances of the attack, with each attack instance writing a small part of the decoder at the designated location. When we have finished building the decoder, we will send in one last attack instance which serves two purposes; first of all, it will hijack the control of the attacked process to start executing the decoder, and secondly, it will carry the encoded actual payload.

Note that the decoder under this swarm attack will have to be modified to locate the actual payload (which may not be found using the same method as in the original exploit where both the decoder and the encoded payload appear in the same attack traffic). However, this is not a serious difficulty; we can construct our last attack instance by modifying the original self-contained exploit so that the encoded payload is placed at where the decoder will have appeared in the original case. As such, the decoder can locate the payload based on how we direct the hijacked control to the right location in our original attack. If a hardcoded address is used in the original exploit, the decoder in the swarm attack will locate the payload using this same hardcoded value. If the original attack used a register spring, the address of the payload will be found in the register involved (remember that the last attack instance is constructed from the original attack by replacing the decoder with the encoded payload; if the register points to the beginning of the decoder in the old attack, it will point to the encoded payload in the new one).

Now let's consider the design of the attack instances responsible for building the decoder. If the vulnerability exploited allows writing arbitrary value to arbitrary address (e.g. a format string vulnerability), our task is trivial: we only have to build exploits to write the right value to the right place. Also, in this case, we can avoid putting any executable code into traffic generated, and it would be quite impossible for a detector based on network-level emulation/analysis to identify this attack. However, care must be taken to have some of the attack instances write to slightly overlapping addresses; otherwise, the attack instances responsible for building up the decoder may become easy target for signature matching. For example, suppose the vulnerability allows us to overwrite 4 bytes at a time, and the first four bytes of the decoder we are building are $b_1b_2b_3b_4$; if we build the decoder by always writing to non-overlapping bytes, we will always have an attack instance that contains the bytes $b_1b_2b_3b_4$. To avoid this problem, we can have one attack instance writing $b_1 r_1 r_2 r_3$ to address i, and the next instance writing $b_2 r_4 r_5 r_6$ to address i+1, so on so forth. Since we know $r_1 r_2 r_3$ will be overwritten by the second attack instance, we can put random values there. Of course, the byte b_1 will still appear in the first attack instance of every swarm attack that employs the same decoder, but this property that involves only one byte will not be very useful to the defender.

If the exploited vulnerability only allows direct control hijacking (e.g. stack based buffer overflow), the design of the attack instances which build up the decoder is much more interesting. In this case, we will need to put some executable code into each attack instance, and have each instance hijack the control to execute its attached code and write the correct value to the right address. As opposed to the previous case, the attack traffic will now contain some executable code. In order to evade detection by network-level emulation/analysis systems, we need to craft the code visible to these systems carefully. Nonetheless, we note that the task to be performed by this code snippet is very simple, and should not involve much behavior that is typically considered "decoder-like" (e.g. no GetPC or self-modification, minimal read/write). Thus the design should be quite easy. We have also taken care to have a design that is easily polymorphed, and does not have long sequence of bytes that remains constant over different attack instances, or always appears in an instance responsible for writing a particular part of the decoder. This precludes using the bytes we want to write as immediate operands or reading it directly from the attack traffic; i.e. we have to somehow "generate" what we are writing as a product of executing some instructions, and we used the xor operation for this purpose. We note that this design also allows us to use decoder that contains bytes forbidden for successful exploitation of the vulnerability (e.g. the presence of byte 0x00 is not allowed in many exploits). Similar constraints apply to the target of the write operations, and the same approach can be used for "generating" it in our attack. The code we have designed for building the decoder is given in Fig. 1.

As we can see on the left of Fig 1, we assume the initial value of ebp is under our control, which is true for almost all stack-based buffer overflows. Also, as shown in the right part of Fig. 1, by using some very simple metamorphism (replacing registers, using slightly different instructions and randomizing exxOffset, exxMask, ebpMask and ebpOffset) , we can achieve such degree of polymorphism that no two instances of the code we have for building the decoder will share any common byte sequence that is more than one byte long. Further polymorphism/metamorphism is possible by re-ordering some of the instructions, or inserting junk instructions. Finally, note that the last instruction in our code snippet will put the execution into a dead-loop. This is only necessary when we cannot crash the attacked thread without killing the entire process. In case we are attacking a serve-type process that handles thread failure gracefully, we can simply put some junk bytes after the instructions that write the value to the right location. This way, the code snippet will look even more innocuous to network-level emulation/analysis systems, since they all assume the attacker will not crash the target.

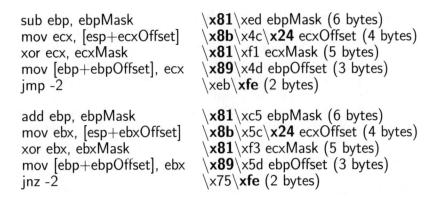

Fig. 1. Two possible versions of the attack code for building the decoder. All ebpMask, exxOffset, exxMask and ebpOffset are variable. The binary representation of the code are given on the right, with bytes that remain the same despite the use of different registers/operations highlighted. Note that condition used in the "jnz -2" is set by the xor. Since we know the result of that xor operation, we can choose the right kind of conditional branch, and there are many different condition codes that we can use in this branch instruction.

We have tested our swarm attack by modifying an exploit against a stack based buffer overflow in the Savant web server [11]. In our experiments, we used as our decoder a simple 27-byte routine which xor each DWORD of the encoded payload with a fixed key, and this requires 7 attack instances to build up the decoder, and one last instance to execute it. As for the real payload, we used a 198 byte shellcode that starts notepad.exe. More complicated shellcode are easily accommodated, we only choose this one for its very visible result (which makes it easy to determine that the attack is successful). As of the location of the decoder, we choose to build it at the end of Savant's data area. This makes our attack quite portable across machines running different versions of Windows, as long as Savant is loaded at the same place. However, since the address of this data area starts with 0x00, we cannot use a hardcoded address in the last attack instance to jump to the decoder. Instead, we execute a small (2-instruction, 8-byte long) code snippet in this last attack instance to "generate" the address of the decoder in some register (the same way we "generate" the target address for the write in the instances responsible for building the decoder) and jump to this address using a register indirect control transfer. By transferring the hijacked control to the decoder using a small, easily poly/meta-morphed payload in the last attack instance, we can also avoid the hardcoded address for the decoder from appearing in every swarm attack and being used as a signature. We believe this "trampoline" payload in the last attack instance is necessary if we cannot have too much variation in the location where we place the decoder. Finally, we report that all our experiments successfully lead to the execution of the decoded payload and launch notepad as expected.

4   Practical Concerns

In this section, we will address some possible difficulties that may arise during the implementation of the swarm attack. Our main focus is, given an exploit that allows us to execute arbitrary code on the attacked machine, what are the extra problems that we will have to face in order to build a swarm attack based on this exploit?

4.1   Multiple Exploitations

The biggest constraint in implementing a swarm attack is that we need a vulnerability that can be exploited multiple times, with the effect of each exploitation being persistent and visible to all later exploitations until the actual payload execution starts. The above constraint is automatically satisfied if the target is a multi-threaded program that will continue to function (i.e. accept further traffic/input) while under attack, and we note that many network servers have this nice property. We believe even the simplest of such servers will be multi-threaded (especially true under the Windows environment), and it is very likely that the port concerned will be freed to accept further traffic once the processing of the incoming request starts. In case we are attacking a single-threaded program (or one with only one thread performing the vulnerable processing), swarm attacks are still possible if:

1. the vulnerable program processes multiple inputs that may cause the control hijacking
2. we can have a way to continue the normal processing in the attacked process after accomplishing the current step in the decoder construction process.

Since we believe the first of the above conditions will be satisfied by many programs (and there is very little we can do otherwise), we will focus on ways to restore normal processing of the target program after each attack instance in our swarm attack. Though it first appears very complicated, we find this task quite achievable for the most common types of exploits.

If the targeted vulnerability is a stack buffer overflow, techniques similar to the "error-virtualization" in [19] can be applied to "return to normal execution" after an attack instance has accomplished its goal. The idea is to prevent the attacked process from crashing by rolling the execution forward to the point where some function x higher up in the "call tree" than the vulnerable function returns a value that signifies failure/error, with the caller of function x equipped to handle the error. This technique should be feasible in many cases because the attackers usually have very accurate knowledge of the size of the few activation records on the top of the stack when the injected code starts execution, and thus can properly adjust the stack for the return. Also note that such "recovery" from the attack can be achieved with very few instructions; it only involves an addition to esp, a single write (if we need to fake a return value) and a return. Furthermore, since the return address used does not come with the attack traffic, most network-level emulation/analysis systems will ignore the return (e.g. [3]), considering it to have too high a chance of crashing the process to be any part of a robust attack. The only system that may find this recovery suspicious is [24], which specifically looks for "push-call" patterns. However, two such patterns are needed to trigger an alert in [24], and we will only have one in our attacks. Another very favorable scenario appears when the control hijacking occurs within code that handles exceptions; in this case, the attacker simply executes an invalid instruction, and the attacked program will return to normal execution. Unlikely as it may sound, there is indeed one real life example of this favorable situation: the ANI vulnerability in Windows XP/Vista [16].

Format string vulnerabilities are also very suitable for a swarm attack: their exploitations generally do not contaminate any of the target program's data structures "by accident"; once the vulnerable function has finished processing the malicious format string, it will return properly. Thus the target program can usually carry on with its normal execution after every attack instance in a swarm attack built on top of a format string vulnerability (e.g. we have confirmed that it is possible to exploit the format string vulnerability in the wu-ftpd server [22] multiple times, through a single connection to the server). Finally, we admit that the feasibility of a swarm attack is more questionable in the case of a heap buffer overflow; in many cases, the corruption in the heap will crash the attacked program shortly. However, the technique in [9] may be improving the situation.

4.2   Where to Put the Decoder?

Another difficulty that we may face when implementing a swarm attack is that we need to find an area in the attacked process' address space that: (1) will be reliably writable in every instance of the program, even if it's running on different OSs, using different versions of libraries, and (2) will remain untouched until the decoding of the real payload is completed.

In most scenarios, the first condition can be easily satisfied given the original exploit for control hijacking. In particular, if the original exploit used a register spring to direct the hijacked control, we can easily derive an address within the data area of the module which holds the exploited register spring instruction (this is true even when some address space layout randomization is applied, if only the base of a module is randomized). In this case, we will argue that having to find a writable location to place the decoder does not make the swarm attack any more difficult to implement than the original. However, if the original exploit used a hardcoded address (which is less common nowadays), a different approach is needed. One solution is to use another hardcoded address (as we did in our experiments on Savant). Given our success in finding register springs that remain at the same address throughout various versions of OS/library, finding hardcoded addresses that are writable across different target machines should be very feasible. Another possibility is to see if any register is pointing to some global data area at the time of control hijacking.

As of storing the decoder in an area that will not be modified until we've finished building it, we note that since memory protection is applied at the granularity of a page, the last parts of many writable regions are never used (they do not correspond to any variable/data structure in the underlying program). Thus, the last part of all writable regions should be very good starting point in our search for places to hold the decoder, and we can always test the target program to "estimate" if it is safe to store the decoder at one of these candidate areas. Some other possible locations for persistent storage of injected code have been proposed in Sect. 3.1 of [12].

5   How Swarm Attacks Evade?

5.1   Sled-Detection Systems

To see how our swarm attack evades the sled-detection systems described in Sect. 2.1, we note that our attack against Savant used a register spring, and contains no sled. Thus the only executable code that a sled-detection system can find is that for building the decoder or transferring the control to the decoder.

Recall that [21] considers incoming traffic malicious if it contains a valid sequence of 30 instructions or more. For the swarm attack against Savant, the attack instances for building up the decoder consists of 6 instructions, with one to jump over junk bytes (not shown in Fig. 1 since it is specific to the attack against Savant), 4 for actually writing part of the decoder to the right place, and one that puts the execution in dead loop. As for the last attack instance that transfers control to the decoder we've built, it consists of one instruction to jump over junk bytes, one for setting up the target of the jump and one for the jump itself. Finally, note that [21] counts jumps targeting address outside the attack traffic as two instructions; any other jump instructions will be counted as one, and a jump targeting instructions that appear earlier in the instruction sequence will mark the end of that sequence. Obviously, [21] will not be able to discover any valid sequence that contains more than 6 instructions in all our attack instances, and thus will pass them all as benign. Similarly, [1] tries to locate the longest byte sequence in traffic such that any suffix of the sequence is a valid chain of instructions, and consider the traffic as malicious if the longest of such sequences found is 230 byte or longer. The longest sequence that [1] can find in our attack will be of 22 byte long (with 2 bytes for jumping over junk, and 20 bytes as shown in Fig. 1). Thus, the swarm attack will evade [1] also.

5.2   "Meaningful Code" Detection

As for systems that try to detect code that appears to serve some "meaningful" purpose in an attack, recall that [24] looks for push-call sequences and instructions that do not cause any data flow anomaly. All attack instances in our swarm attack contain no push-call sequence (there will be one if we try to continue with normal execution after the attack using the method described in Sect. 4.1), and contains at most 6 "useful" instructions. Since the number of useful instructions needed for [24] to sound the alarm is 10, [24] will not be able to detect our attack. As for [3], the detector only considers control transfers at the end of every chain of basic blocks it identifies with static analysis of the incoming traffic. As such, only the jump that forms a dead loop in the earlier attack instances and the jump to the decoder in the last instance will be used by [3] to determine whether the traffic is malicious. Since an empty loop is considered benign, and register indirect jumps are only malicious to [3] if they target instructions within the analyzed traffic, our attack will certainly evade [3].

5.3   Decoder Detection

As we've mentioned in Sect. 2.1, almost all network-level emulation/analysis systems designed to specifically detect decoders in polymorphic shellcode will only consider incoming traffic malicious if it contains some GetPC code. Since our attack does not contain any such code, it will evade all detection systems that use GetPC as a precondition for further analysis. For the sake of argument, even if some GetPC code is added to our attack instances, they still won't be sufficiently "decoder like" to be detected. For example, [25] requires a loop containing indirect writes for traffic to be classified as malicious, but the only loop in our attack instances is empty. As for [14], more than 6 reads to different locations within the analyzed traffic have to be found before it will be flagged as an attack, while our attack instances perform at most one read operation.

The successful evasion of [13] by our swarm attack is less certain. When presented traffic from our swarm attack, we believe [13] will successfully identify the code involved (either for building the decoder or for executing the decoder). Whether [13] can detect our attack will then be determined by its model for a shellcode decoder (i.e. the frequency at which different types of instructions appear in a decoder), and in the worst case, if [13] is trained to recognize code in our attack instances, it is quite likely that our attack will be detected. However, we can always polymorph our attack to introduce noise for the classification in [13] (i.e. introduce various types of instructions). Furthermore, it is questionable if [13] can maintain a low false positive if it's trained to recognize the small "decoder" in our attack (we will elaborate on this point in Sect. 6).

Finally, [15] used a negative heuristic that if the code recovered from the traffic contains fewer than 8 write instructions, it will be considered benign. Since all our attack instances contain only one write operation, they will all successfully bypass [15].

6   Can Network-Level Emulation/Analysis Detects Swarm Attacks?

In this section, we will try to answer the following question:

Can network-level emulation/analysis systems be improved to detect the swarm attack we've proposed?

The answer to this question depends on our ability to characterize the kind of write operations that allows one to build the decoder, as well as the amount of false positives that will result from our best characterization of such "useful writes". We focus our discussion on characterizing the write operations used for building the decoder because it is the most essential feature of the visible payload in a swarm attack. The way of generating both the value to be written and the target address can be easily changed to evade detection, and as we will argue below, we maybe able to design swarm attacks in which these values are not "generated" by any instructions. As of the payload for the control transfer to the decoder in the last attack instance, we note that it may not be necessary in some swarm attacks. If we can build the decoder at many different places, we can have the last instance of attack direct the hijacked control to a hardcoded address (without executing any code), and still evade signature-based detection targeting that hardcoded value; due to the large number of choices we have for this address, any signature targeting a particular address will be useless. Even if it turns out that the executable payload in the last instance is unavoidable, we believe the difficulties in the characterization of this small payload, as well as the false positives resulting from detecting it, will be similar to that of the "useful write" discussed below.

Let's start our discussion by considering our attack against the Savant server once again. In the attack code in Fig. 1, the write operations involved have some very specific properties; in particular, both the value written and the address to write are direct products of previous instructions. However, we can easily avoid the dynamic generation of the former by using immediate values instead. This is especially true if we can afford to construct the decoder with more attack instances. For example, if we can double the number of attack instances used in building the decoder, we can specify the values to be written as immediate operands, and still leave no constant byte sequence for signature-based detection. This is because we can "write" each 4-byte of the decoder using two attack instances, the first writes an immediate value to the target location directly, and the second performs some arithmetic/bitwise operation between another immediate value and the previously written value, such that the result of the operation will be the right value for the decoder. This way, we can avoid having the values written in useful writes from being defined in previous instructions. To push the idea even further, if we can afford to build the decoder one byte at a time, and if we have control over an extra register when the control hijacking occurs, we can simply put the value to write in the register we control. As such, the value written will appear entirely undefined to the network-level emulation/analysis. When coupled with the overlapping-writes technique in Sect. 3, there will only be one byte that's constant across all attack instances responsible for building a particular part of the decoder.

If it turns out that there are so many locations in the attacked process' address space where the decoder can be safely built, we can avoid generating the target of the write operations used in building the decoder also; instead, we can include the immediate value of the write target in our attacks and still be able to evade any signature-matching by building the decoder at different place in different attacks. In fact, from our experience with attacking Savant, at least the least significant two bytes of the address where we place our decoder can show a high level of entropy, leaving only the most significant two bytes useful for signature matching (if we leave the write target unencoded in our attack instances). Thus, it is possible to design our attack such that the "useful writes" we use for building the decoder will appear to have both the value and the address written undefined to the network-level emulation/analysis.

It is also quite unlikely that we can keep the false positives of the network-level emulation/analysis low while we try to detect attack code as simple as those in the swarm attack. We based this pessimistic prediction on two pieces of data from [15]:

1. when tested against artificial binary data, the system in [15] found that 0.01% of the data writes to 8 unique addresses, and contain one control transfer to one of those written locations.
2. almost 1% of random binary/printable data will contain code that writes to a certain address and then an instruction that jumps to it.

We note that if we phrase a "useful write" in a swarm attack as "defining certain register and then use it as the target of a register indirect write", the behavior involved in the second item will be quite similar to a useful write in terms of the level of sophistication: both involve two related operations. Thus, it is not unreasonable to use the figure given to predict the level of false positives resulted from detecting traffic that contains one "useful write" operation.

7 Conclusions

In this paper, we have studied an attack strategy where the attacker deliberately makes his attack less efficient; instead of achieving their goal through one instance of control hijacking, they hijack the control of the target process multiple times, and achieve some minimal objective in each hijacking. Surprisingly, such swarm attack is very effective in evading detection systems that are based on network-level emulation/analysis, which is the least challenged approach for network intrusion detection. The swarm attack evades these systems by exposing a very small, simple piece of code in each attack instance, and slowly building up a decoder somewhere in the attacked process' memory using this minimal payload. Once the decoder is complete, one last instance of attack will be launched to carry the encoded payload and hijack the control to execute the decoder. We argue that since the exposed code in the swarm attack can be made so short and simple, it would be virtually impossible to detect such attack without incurring a high false positive. We have also noted that the need to hijack the control of the attacked process multiple times may constraint the type of vulnerabilities that can be exploited in a swarm attack, but we believe vulnerabilities in network servers are generally suitable for us, and there are techniques to exploit vulnerabilities that are less favorable to our swarm attacks.

As we have mentioned in the introduction, many security systems are built based on the assumption that the attackers will gain nothing by being inefficient and make their attacks "unnecessarily complicated". Thus, the swarm attack can have significant impact to other systems too. For example, a similar "multi-threaded" attack as the one we have presented can open up new avenue for mimicry attacks against system-call based IDS: in this new attack, not only can the attacker insert null calls into the sequence of system calls observed by the IDS, he can also issue system calls from another thread that's at a more favorable state. Our preliminary analysis also shows that some form of swarm attack can have significant impact on intrusion prevention systems which analyze information collected from the attacked host. In particular, with separation of the attack traffic that overwrites the targeted control structure and that hijacks the control using those contaminated structures, together with careful control of the time delay between the two parts of the attack, an attacker can make IPSs like Vigilante [5] vulnerable to allergy attacks [4], or force them into generating signatures/execution filters that are useless in stopping attacks. In our future work, we plan to further experiment with the swarm attacks against these two types of systems, and study their real impact.

References

1. Akritidis, P., Markatos, E.P., Polychronakis, M., Ananostakis, K.: Stride: Polymorphic sled detection through instruction sequence analysis. In: Proceedings of the 20th IFIP International Information Security Conference (IFIP/SEC 2005), Chiba, Japan (May 2005)
2. Chen, S., Xu, J., Sezer, E.C., Gauriar, P., Iyer, R.K.: Non-control data attacks are realistic threats. In: Proceedings of the 14th conference on USENIX Security Symposium (USENIX Security 2005), Madison (July 2005)
3. Chinchani, R., Van Den Berg, E.: A fast static analysis approach to detect exploit code inside network flows. In: Valdes, A., Zamboni, D. (eds.) RAID 2005. LNCS, vol. 3858, pp. 284–308. Springer, Heidelberg (2006)
4. Chung, S.P., Mok, A.K.: Allergy Attack Against Automatic Signature Generation. In: Zamboni, D., Krügel, C. (eds.) RAID 2006. LNCS, vol. 4219, pp. 61–80. Springer, Heidelberg (2006)
5. Costa, M., Crowcroft, J., Castro, M., Rowstron, A., Zhou, L., Zhang, L., Barham, P.: Vigilante: End-to-end containment of internet worms. In: Proceedings of 20th ACM Symposium on Operating Systems Principles, Brighton (October 2005)
6. Detristan, T., Ulenspiegel, T., Malcom, Y., von Underduk, M.S.: Polymorphic shellcode engine using spectrum analysis. In: Phrack, vol. 11 (2003)
7. Fogla, P., Lee, W.: Evading network anomaly detection systems: Formal reasoning and practical techniques. In: Proceedings of the 13th Conference on Computer and Communication Security (CCS 2006), Virginia (October 2006)
8. Fogla, P., Sharif, M., Perdisci, R., Kolesnikov, O., Lee, W.: Polymorphic blending attacks. In: Proceedings of 15th USENIX Security Symposium Abstract (USENIX Security 2006), Vancouver (July 2006)
9. jp. Advanced Doug lea's malloc exploits,
   http://doc.bughunter.net/buffer-overflow/ advanced-malloc-exploits.html
10. K2. ADMmutate documentation (2003),
    http://www.ktwo.ca/ADMmutate-0.8.4.tar.gz

11. mati@see security.com. Savant 3.1 Web Server Buffer Overflow Tutorial, `http://www.securinfos.info/english/security-whitepapers-hacking-tutorials/Savant-BO-tutorial.pdf`
12. Parampalli, C., Sekar, R., Johnson, R.: A practical mimicry attack against powerful system-call monitors. In: Proceedings of the ACM Symposium on Information, Computer and Communications Security (ASIACCS 2008), Tokyo (March 2008)
13. Payer, U., Teufl, P., Lamberger, M.: Hybrid engine for polymorphic shellcode detection. In: Julisch, K., Krügel, C. (eds.) DIMVA 2005. LNCS, vol. 3548, pp. 19–31. Springer, Heidelberg (2005)
14. Polychronakis, M., Anagnostakis, K.G., Markatos, E.P.: Network-level polymorphic shellcode detection using emulation. In: Büschkes, R., Laskov, P. (eds.) DIMVA 2006. LNCS, vol. 4064, pp. 54–73. Springer, Heidelberg (2006)
15. Markatos, E.P., Anagnostakis, K.G., Polychronakis, M.: Emulation-Based Detection of Non-self-contained Polymorphic Shellcode. In: Kruegel, C., Lippmann, R., Clark, A. (eds.) RAID 2007. LNCS, vol. 4637, pp. 87–106. Springer, Heidelberg (2007)
16. Determina Security Research. Windows Animated Cursor Stack Overflow Vulnerability, `http://www.determina.com/security.research/vulnerabilities/ani-header.html`
17. Rubin, S., Jha, S., Miller, B.: Automatic generation and analysis of nids attacks. In: Proceedings of the Annual Computer Security Applications Conference 2004 (ACSAC 2004), California (December 2004)
18. Shacham, H.: The geometry of innocent flesh on the bone: Return-into-libc without function calls (on the x86). In: Proceedings of the 14th Conference on Computer and Communication Security (CCS 2007), Virginia (October 2007)
19. Sidiroglou, S., Locasto, M.E., Boyd, S.W., Keromytis, A.D.: Building a reactive immune system for software services. In: Proceedings of the USENIX Annual Technical Conference 2005, California (April 2005)
20. Song, Y., Locasto, M.E., Stavrou, A., Keromytis, A.D., Stolfo, S.J.: On the infeasibility of modeling polymorphic shellcode. In: Proceedings of the 13th Conference on Computer and Communication Security (CCS 2007), Virginia (October 2007)
21. Toth, T., Kruegel, C.: Accurate buffer overflow detection via abstract payload execution. In: Wespi, A., Vigna, G., Deri, L. (eds.) RAID 2002. LNCS, vol. 2516. Springer, Heidelberg (2002)
22. US-CERT. Vulnerability Note VU#29823: Format string input validation error in wu-ftpd site_exec() function, `http://www.kb.cert.org/vuls/id/29823`
23. Wang, K., Cretu, G., Stolfo, S.J.: Anomalous payload-based worm detection and signature generation. In: Valdes, A., Zamboni, D. (eds.) RAID 2005. LNCS, vol. 3858, pp. 227–246. Springer, Heidelberg (2006)
24. Wang, X., Pan, C.C., Liu, P., Zhu, S.: Sigfree: A signature-free buffer overflow attack blocker. In: Proceedings of 15th USENIX Security Symposium Abstract (USENIX Security 2006), Vancouver (July 2006)
25. Zhang, Q., Reeves, D.S., Ning, P., Iyer, S.P.: Analyzing network traffic to detect self-decryption exploit code. In: Proceedings of the 2nd ACM Symposium on InformAtion, Computer and Communications Security (ASIACCS 2007), Singapore (March 2007)

Leveraging User Interactions for In-Depth Testing of Web Applications

Sean McAllister[1], Engin Kirda[2], and Christopher Kruegel[3]

[1] Secure Systems Lab, Technical University Vienna, Austria
sean@seclab.tuwien.ac.at
[2] Institute Eurecom, France
kirda@eurecom.fr
[3] University of California, Santa Barbara
chris@cs.ucsb.edu

Abstract. Over the last years, the complexity of web applications has grown significantly, challenging desktop programs in terms of functionality and design. Along with the rising popularity of web applications, the number of exploitable bugs has also increased significantly. Web application flaws, such as cross-site scripting or SQL injection bugs, now account for more than two thirds of the reported security vulnerabilities.

Black-box testing techniques are a common approach to improve software quality and detect bugs before deployment. There exist a number of vulnerability scanners, or fuzzers, that expose web applications to a barrage of malformed inputs in the hope to identify input validation errors. Unfortunately, these scanners often fail to test a substantial fraction of a web application's logic, especially when this logic is invoked from pages that can only be reached after filling out complex forms that aggressively check the correctness of the provided values.

In this paper, we present an automated testing tool that can find reflected and stored cross-site scripting (XSS) vulnerabilities in web applications. The core of our system is a black-box vulnerability scanner. This scanner is enhanced by techniques that allow one to generate more comprehensive test cases and explore a larger fraction of the application. Our experiments demonstrate that our approach is able to test more thoroughly these programs and identify more bugs than a number of open-source and commercial web vulnerability scanners.

1 Introduction

The first web applications were collections of static files, linked to each other by means of HTML references. Over time, dynamic features were added, and web applications started to accept user input, changing the presentation and content of the pages accordingly. This dynamic behavior was traditionally implemented by CGI scripts. Nowadays, more often then not, complete web sites are created dynamically. To this end, the site's content is stored in a database. Requests are processed by the web application to fetch the appropriate database entries and present them to the user. Along with the complexity of the web sites, the use

R. Lippmann, E. Kirda, and A. Trachtenberg (Eds.): RAID 2008, LNCS 5230, pp. 191–210, 2008.
© Springer-Verlag Berlin Heidelberg 2008

cases have also become more involved. While in the beginning user interaction was typically limited to simple request-response pairs, web applications today often require a multitude of intermediate steps to achieve the desired results.

When developing software, an increase in complexity typically leads to a growing number of bugs. Of course, web applications are no exception. Moreover, web applications can be quickly deployed to be accessible to a large number of users on the Internet, and the available development frameworks make it easy to produce (partially correct) code that works only in most cases. As a result, web application vulnerabilities have sharply increased. For example, in the last two years, the three top positions in the annual Common Vulnerabilities and Exposures (CVE) list published by Mitre [17] were taken by web application vulnerabilities.

To identify and correct bugs and security vulnerabilities, developers have a variety of testing tools at their disposal. These programs can be broadly categorized as based on black-box approaches or white-box approaches. White-box testing tools, such as those presented in [2, 15, 27, 32], use static analysis to examine the source code of an application. They aim at detecting code fragments that are patterns of instances of known vulnerability classes. Since these systems do not execute the application, they achieve a large code coverage, and, in theory, can analyze all possible execution paths. A drawback of white-box testing tools is that each tool typically supports only very few (or a single) programming language. A second limitation is the often significant number of false positives. Since static code analysis faces undecidable problems, approximations are necessary. Especially for large software applications, these approximations can quickly lead to warnings about software bugs that do not exist.

Black-box testing tools [11] typically run the application and monitor its execution. By providing a variety of specially-crafted, malformed input values, the goal is to find cases in which the application misbehaves or crashes. A significant advantage of black-box testing is that there are no false positives. All problems that are reported are due to real bugs. Also, since the testing tool provides only input to the application, no knowledge about implementation-specific details (e.g., the used programming language) is required. This allows one to use the same tool for a large number of different applications. The drawback of black-box testing tools is their limited code coverage. The reason is that certain program paths are exercised only when specific input is provided.

Black-box testing is a popular choice when analyzing web applications for security errors. This is confirmed by the large number of open-source and commercial black-box tools that are available [1, 16, 19, 29]. These tools, also called web vulnerability scanners or fuzzers, typically check for the presence of well-known vulnerabilities, such as cross-site scripting (XSS) or SQL injection flaws. To check for security bugs, vulnerability scanners are equipped with a large database of test values that are crafted to trigger XSS or SQL injection bugs. These values are typically passed to an application by injecting them into the application's HTML form elements or into URL parameters.

Web vulnerability scanners, sharing the well-known limitation of black-box tools, can only test those parts of a web site (and its underlying web application) that they can reach. To explore the different parts of a web site, these scanners frequently rely on built-in web spiders (or crawlers) that follow links, starting from a few web pages that act as seeds. Unfortunately, given the increasing complexity of today's applications, this is often insufficient to reach "deeper" into the web site. Web applications often implement a complex workflow that requires a user to correctly fill out a series of forms. When the scanner cannot enter meaningful values into these forms, it will not reach certain parts of the site. Therefore, these parts are not tested, limiting the effectiveness of black-box testing for web applications.

In this paper, we present techniques that improve the effectiveness of web vulnerability scanners. To this end, our scanner leverages input from real users as a starting point for its testing activity. More precisely, starting from recorded, actual user input, we generate test cases that can be replayed. By following a user's session, fuzzing at each step, we are able to increase the code coverage by exploring pages that are not reachable for other tools. Moreover, our techniques allow a scanner to interact with the web application in a more meaningful fashion. This often leads to test runs where the web application creates a large number of persistent objects (such as database entries). Creating objects is important to check for bugs that manifest when malicious input is stored in a database, such as in the case of stored cross-site scripting (XSS) vulnerabilities. Finally, when the vulnerability scanner can exercise some control over the program under test, it can extract important feedback from the application that helps in further improving the scanner's effectiveness.

We have implemented our techniques in a vulnerability scanner that can analyze applications that are based on the Django web development framework [8]. Our experimental results demonstrate that our tool achieves larger coverage and detects more vulnerabilities than existing open-source and commercial fuzzers.

2   Web Application Testing and Limitations

One way to quickly and efficiently identify flaws in web applications is the use of vulnerability scanners. These scanners test the application by providing malformed inputs that are crafted so that they trigger certain classes of vulnerabilities. Typically, the scanners cover popular vulnerability classes such as cross-site scripting (XSS) or SQL injection bugs. These vulnerabilities are due to input validation errors. That is, the web application receives an input value that is used at a security-critical point in the program without (sufficient) prior validation. In case of an XSS vulnerability [10], malicious input can reach a point where it is sent back to the web client. At the client side, the malicious input is interpreted as JavaScript code that is executed in the context of the trusted web application. This allows an attacker to steal sensitive information such as cookies. In case of a SQL injection flaw, malicious input can reach a database query and modify the intended semantics of this query. This allows an attacker to obtain sensitive information from the database or to bypass authentication checks.

By providing malicious, or malformed, input to the web application under test, a vulnerability scanner can check for the presence of bugs. Typically, this is done by analyzing the response that the web application returns. For example, a scanner could send a string to the program that contains malicious JavaScript code. Then, it checks the output of the application for the presence of this string. When the malicious JavaScript is present in the output, the scanner has found a case in which the application does not properly validate input before sending it back to clients. This is reported as an XSS vulnerability.

To send input to web applications, scanners only have a few possible injection points. According to [26], the possible points of attack are the URL, the cookie, and the POST data contained in a request. These points are often derived from form elements that are present on the web pages. That is, web vulnerability scanners analyze web pages to find injection points. Then, these injection points are fuzzed by sending a large number of requests that contain malformed inputs.

Limitations. Automated scanners have a significant disadvantage compared to human testers in the way they can interact with the application. Typically, a user has certain goals in mind when interacting with a site. On an e-commerce site, for example, these goals could include buying an item or providing a rating for the most-recently-purchased goods. The goals, and the necessary operations to achieve these goals, are known to a human tester. Unfortunately, the scanner does not have any knowledge about use cases; all it can attempt to do is to collect information about the available injection points and attack them. More precisely, the typical workflow of a vulnerability scanners consists of the following steps:

– First, a web spider crawls the site to find valid injection points. Commonly, these entry points are determined by collecting the links on a page, the action attributes of forms, and the source attributes of other tags. Advanced spiders can also parse JavaScript to search for URLs. Some even execute JavaScript to trigger requests to the server.
– The second phase is the audit phase. During this step, the scanner fuzzes the previously discovered entry points. It also analyzes the application's output to determine whether a vulnerability was triggered.
– Finally, many scanners will start another crawling step to find stored XSS vulnerabilities. In case of a stored XSS vulnerability, the malicious input is not immediately returned to the client but stored in the database and later included in another request. Therefore, it is not sufficient to only analyze the application's immediate response to a malformed input. Instead, the spider makes a second pass to check for pages that contain input injected during the second phase.

The common workflow outlined above yields good results for simple sites that do not require a large amount of user interaction. Unfortunately, it often fails when confronted with more complex sites. The reason is that vulnerability scanners are equipped with simple rules to fill out forms. These rules, however, are not suited well to advance "deeper" into an application when the program enforces constraints on the input values that it expects. To illustrate the problem, we briefly discuss an example of how a fuzzer might fail on a simple use case.

The example involves a blogging site that allows visitors to leave comments to each entry. To leave a comment, the user has to fill out a form that holds the content of the desired comment. Once this form is submitted, the web application responds with a page that shows a preview of the comment, allowing the user to make changes before submitting the posting. When the user decides to make changes and presses the corresponding button, the application returns to the form where the text can be edited. When the user is satisfied with her comment, she can post the text by selecting the appropriate button on the preview page.

The problem in this case is that the submit button (which actually posts the message to the blog) is activated on the preview page only when the web application recognizes the submitted data as a valid comment. This requires that both the name of the author and the text field of the comment are filled in. Furthermore, it is required that a number of hidden fields on the page remain unchanged. When the submit button is successfully pressed, a comment is created in the application's database, linked to the article, and subsequently shown in the comments section of the blog entry.

For a vulnerability scanner, posting a comment to a blog entry is an entry point that should be checked for the presence of vulnerabilities. Unfortunately, all of the tools evaluated in our experiments (details in Section 5.2) failed to post a comment. That is, even a relatively simple task, which requires a scanner to fill out two form elements on a page and to press two buttons in the correct order, proved to be too difficult for an automated scanner. Clearly, the situation becomes worse when facing more complex use cases.

During our evaluation of existing vulnerability scanners, we found that, commonly, the failure to detect a vulnerability is not due to the limited capabilities of the scanner to inject malformed input or to determine whether a response indicates a vulnerability, but rather due to the inability to generate enough valid requests to reach the vulnerable entry points. Of course, the exact reasons for failing to reach entry points vary, depending on the application that is being tested and the implementation of the scanner.

3   Increasing Test Coverage

To address the limitations of existing tools, we propose several techniques that allow a vulnerability scanner to detect more entry points. These entry points can then be tested, or fuzzed, using existing databases of malformed input values. The first technique, described in Section 3.1, introduces a way to leverage inputs that are recorded by observing actual user interaction. This allows the scanner to follow an actual use case, achieving more depth when testing. The second technique, presented in Section 3.2, discusses a way to abstract from observed user inputs, leveraging the steps of the use case to achieve more breadth. The third technique, described in Section 3.3, makes the second technique more robust in cases where the broad exploration interferes with the correct replay of a use case.

3.1 Increasing Testing Depth

One way to improve the coverage, and thus, the effectiveness of scanners, is to leverage actual user input. That is, we first collect a small set of inputs that were provided by users that interacted with the application. These interactions correspond to certain use cases, or workflows, in which a user carries out a sequence of steps to reach a particular goal. Depending on the application, this could be a scenario where the user purchases an item in an on-line store or a scenario where the user composes and sends an email using a web-based mail program. Based on the recorded test cases, the vulnerability scanner can replay the collected input values to successfully proceed a number of steps into the application logic. The reason is that the provided input has a higher probability to pass server-side validation routines. Of course, there is, by no means, a guarantee that recorded input satisfies the constrains imposed by an application at the time the values are replayed. While replaying a previously recorded use case, the scanner can fuzz the input values that are provided to the application.

Collecting input. There are different locations where client-supplied input data can be collected. One possibility is to deploy a proxy between a web client and the web server, logging the requests that are sent to the web application. Another way is to record the incoming requests at the server side, by means of web server log files or application level logging. For simplicity, we record requests directly at the server, logging the names and values of all input parameters.

It is possible to record the input that is produced during regular, functional testing of applications. Typically, developers need to create test cases that are intended to exercise the complete functionality of the application. When such test cases are available, they can be immediately leveraged by the vulnerability scanner. Another alternative is to deploy the collection component on a production server and let real-world users of the web application generate test cases. In any case, the goal is to collect a number of inputs that are likely correct from the application's point of view, and thus, allow the scanner to reach additional parts of the application that might not be easily reachable by simply crawling the site and filling out forms with essentially random values. This approach might raise some concerns with regards to the nature of the captured data. The penetration tester must be aware of the fact that user input is being captured and stored in clear text. This is acceptable for most sites but not for some (because, for example, the unencrypted storage of sensitive information such as passwords and credit card numbers might be unacceptable). In these cases, it is advisable to perform all input capturing and tests in a controlled testbed.

Replaying input. Each use case consists of a number of steps that are carried out to reach a certain goal. For each step, we have recorded the requests (i.e., the input values) that were submitted. Based on these input values, the vulnerability scanner can replay a previously collected use case. To this end, the vulnerability scanner replays a recorded use case, one step at a time. After each step, a fuzzer component is invoked. This fuzzer uses the request issued in the previous step to test the application. More precisely, it uses a database of malformed values to replace the valid inputs within the request sent in the previous step. In other words, after sending a request as part of a replayed use case, we attempt to fuzz this request. Then, the previously recorded input values stored for the current step are used to advance to the next step. This process of fuzzing a request and subsequently advancing one step along the use case is repeated until the test case is exhausted. Alternatively, the process stops when the fuzzer replays the recorded input to advance to the next page, but this page is different from the one expected. This situation can occur when a previously recorded input is no longer valid.

When replaying input, the vulnerability scanner does not simply re-submit a previously recorded request. Instead, it scans the page for elements that require user input. Then, it uses the previously recorded request to provide input values for those elements only. This is important when an application uses cookies or hidden form fields that are associated with a particular session. Changing these values would cause the application to treat the request as invalid. Thus, for such elements, the scanner uses the current values instead of the "old" ones that were previously collected. The rules used to determine the values of each form field aim to mimic the actions of a benign user. That is, hidden fields are not changed, as well as read-only widgets (such as submit button values or disabled elements). Of course security vulnerabilities can also be triggered by malicious input data within these hidden fields, but this is of no concern at this stage because the idea is to generate benign and valid input and then apply the attack logic to these values. Later on, during the attacking stage, the fuzzer will take care that all parameters will be tested.

Guided fuzzing. We call the process of using previously collected traces to step through an application *guided fuzzing*. Guided fuzzing improves the coverage of a vulnerability scanner because it allows the tool to reach entry points that were previously hidden behind forms that expect specific input values. That is, we can increase the depth that a scanner can reach into the application.

3.2 Increasing Testing Breadth

With guided fuzzing, after each step that is replayed, the fuzzer only tests the single request that was sent for that step. That is, for each step, only a single entry point is analyzed. A straightforward extension to guided fuzzing is to not only test the single entry point, but to use the current step as a starting point for fuzzing the complete site that is reachable from this point. That is, the fuzzer can use the current page as its starting point, attempting to find additional entry points into the application. Each entry point that is found in this way is then tested by sending malformed input values. In this fashion, we do not only increase the depth of the test cases, but also their breadth. For example, when a certain test case allows the scanner to bypass a form that performs aggressive input checking, it can then explore the complete application space that was previously hidden behind that form. We call this approach *extended, guided fuzzing*.

Extended, guided fuzzing has the potential to increase the number of entry points that a scanner can test. However, alternating between a comprehensive fuzzing phase and advancing one step along a recorded use case can also lead to problems. To see this, consider the following example. Assume an e-commerce application that uses a shopping cart to hold the items that a customer intends to buy. The vulnerability scanner has already executed a number of steps that added an item to the cart. At this point, the scanner encounters a page that shows the cart's inventory. This page contains several links; one link leads to the checkout view, the other one is used to delete items from the cart. Executing the fuzzer on this page can result in a situation where the shopping cart remains empty because all items are deleted. This could cause the following steps of the use case to fail, for example, because the application no longer provides access to the checkout page. A similar situation can arise when administrative pages are part of a use case. Here, running a fuzzer on a page that allows the administrator to delete all database entries could be very problematic.

In general terms, the problem with extended, guided fuzzing is that the fuzzing activity could interfere in undesirable ways with the use case that is replayed. In particular, this occurs when the input sent by the fuzzer changes the state of the application such that the remaining steps of a use case can no longer be executed. This problem is difficult to address when we assume that the scanner has no knowledge and control of the inner workings of the application under test. In the following Section 3.3, we consider the case in which our test system can interact more tightly with the analyzed program. In this case, we are able to prevent the undesirable side effects (or interference) from the fuzzing phases.

3.3   Stateful Fuzzing

The techniques presented in the previous sections work independently of the application under test. That is, our system builds black-box test cases based on previously recorded user input, and it uses these tests to check the application for vulnerabilities. In this subsection, we consider the case where the scanner has some control over the application under test.

One solution to the problem of undesirable side effects of the fuzzing step when replaying recorded use cases is to *take a snapshot* of the state of the application after each step that is replayed. Then, the fuzzer is allowed to run. This might result in significant changes to the application's state. However, after each fuzzing step, the application is *restored* to the previously taken snapshot. At this point, the replay component will find the application in the expected state and can advance one step. After that, the process is repeated - that is, a snapshot is taken and the fuzzer is invoked. We call this process *stateful fuzzing*.

In principle, the concrete mechanisms to take a snapshot of an application's state depend on the implementation of this application. Unfortunately, this could be different for each web application. As a result, we would have to customize our test system to each program, making it difficult to test a large number of different applications. Clearly, this is very undesirable. Fortunately, the situation is different for web applications. Over the last years, the model-view-controller (MVC) scheme has emerged as the most popular software design pattern for applications on the web. The goal of the MVC scheme is to separate three layers that are present in almost all web applications. These are the data layer, the presentation layer, and the application logic layer. The data layer represents the data storage that handles persistent objects. Typically, this layer is implemented by a backend database and an object (relational) manager. The application logic layer uses the objects provided by the data layer to implement the functionality of the application. It uses the presentation layer to format the results that are returned to clients. The presentation layer is frequently implemented by an HTML template engine. Moreover, as part of the application logic layer, there is a component that maps requests from clients to the corresponding functions or classes within the program.

Based on the commonalities between web applications that follow an MVC approach, it is possible (for most such applications) to identify general interfaces that can be instrumented to implement a snapshot mechanism. To be able to capture the state of the application and subsequently restore it, we are interested in the objects that are created, updated, or deleted by the object manager in response to requests. Whenever an object is modified or deleted, a copy of this object is serialized and saved. This way, we can, for example, undelete an object that has been previously deleted, but that is required when a use case is replayed. In a similar fashion, it is also possible to undo updates to an object and delete objects that were created by the fuzzer.

The information about the modification of objects can be extracted at the interface between the application and the data layer (often, at the database level). At this level, we insert a component that can serialize modified objects and later restore the snapshot of the application that was previously saved. Clearly, there are limitations to this technique. One problem is that the state of an application might not depend solely on the state of the persistent objects and its attributes. Nevertheless, this technique has the potential to increase the effectiveness of the scanner for a large set of programs that follow a MVC approach. This is also confirmed by our experimental results presented in Section 5.

Application feedback. Given that stateful fuzzing already requires the instrumentation of the program under test, we should consider what additional information might be useful to further improve the vulnerability scanning process.

One piece of feedback from the application that we consider useful is the *mapping of URLs to functions.* This mapping can be typically extracted by analyzing or instrumenting the controller component, which acts as a dispatcher from incoming requests to the appropriate handler functions. Using the mappings between URLs and the program functions, we can increase the effectiveness of the extended, guided fuzzing process. To this end, we attempt to find a set of forms (or URLs) that all invoke the same function within the application. When we have previously seen user input for one of these forms, we can reuse the same information on other forms as well (when no user input was recorded for these forms). The rationale is that information that was provided to a certain function through one particular form could also be valid when submitted as part of a related form. By reusing information for forms that the fuzzer encounters, it is possible to reach additional entry points.

When collecting user input (as discussed in Section 3.1), we record all input values that a user provides on each page. More precisely, for each URL that is requested, we store all the name-value pairs that a user submits with this request. In case the scanner can obtain application feedback, we also store the name of the program function that is invoked by the request. In other words, we record the name of the function that the requested URL maps to. When the fuzzer later encounters an unknown action URL of a form (i.e., the URL where the form data is submitted to), we query the application to determine which function this URL maps to. Then, we search our collected information to see whether the same function was called previously by another URL. If this is the case, we examine the name-value pairs associated with this other URL. For each of those names, we attempt to find a form element on the current page that has a similar name. When a similar name is found, the corresponding, stored value is supplied. As mentioned previously, the assumption is that valid data that was passed to a program function through one form might also be valid when used for a different form, in another context. This can help in correctly filling out unknown forms, possibly leading to unexplored entry points and vulnerabilities.

As an example, consider a forum application where each discussion thread has a reply field at the bottom of the page. The action URLs that are used for submitting a reply could be different for each thread. However, the underlying function that is eventually called to save the reply and link it to the appropriate thread remains the same. Thus, when we have encountered one case where a user submitted a reply, we would recognize other reply fields for different threads as being similar. The reason is that even though the action URLs associated with the reply forms are different, they all map to the same program function. Moreover, the name of the form fields are (very likely) the same. As a result, the fuzzer can reuse the input value(s) recorded in the first case on other pages.

4   Implementation Details

We developed a vulnerability scanner that implements the techniques outlined above. As discussed in the last section, some of the techniques require that a web application is instrumented (i) to capture and restore objects manipulated by the application, and (ii) to extract the mappings between URLs and functions. Therefore, we were looking for a web development framework that supports the model-view-controller (MVC) scheme. Among the candidates were most popular web development frameworks, such as Ruby on Rails [7], Java Servlets [28], or Django [8], which is based upon Python. Since we are familiar with Python, we selected the Django framework. That is, we extended the Django framework such that it provides the necessary functionality for the vulnerability scanner. Our choice implies that we can currently only test web applications that are built using Django. Note, however, that the previously introduced concepts are general and can be ported to other development frameworks (i.e., with some additional engineering effort, we could use our techniques to test applications based upon other frameworks).

Capturing web requests. The first task was to extend Django such that it can record the inputs that are sent when going through a use case. This makes it necessary to log all incoming requests together with the corresponding parameters. In Django, all incoming requests pass through two middleware classes before reaching the actual application code. One of these classes is a URL dispatcher class that determines the function that should be invoked. At this point, we can log the complete request information. Also, the URL dispatcher class provides easy access to the mapping between URLs and the functions that are invoked.

Replaying use cases. Once a use case, which consists of a series of requests, has been collected, it can be used for replaying. To this end, we have developed a small test case replay component based on twill [30], a testing tool for web applications. This component analyzes a page and attempts to find the form elements that need to be filled out, based on the previously submitted request data.

Capturing object manipulations. Our implementation uses the Django middleware classes to attach event listeners to incoming requests. These event listeners wait for signals that are raised every time an object is created, updated, or deleted. The signals are handled synchronously, meaning that the execution of the code that sent the signal is postponed until the signal handler has finished. We exploit this fact to create copies of objects before they are saved to the backend storage, allowing us to later restore any object to a previous state.

Fuzzer component. An important component of the vulnerability scanner is the fuzzer. The task of the fuzzer component is to expose each entry point that it finds to a set of malformed inputs that can expose XSS vulnerabilities. Typically, it also features a web spider that uses a certain page as a starting point to reach other parts of the application, checking each page that is encountered.

Because the focus of this work is not on the fuzzer component but on techniques that can help to make this fuzzer more effective, we decided to use an existing web application testing tool. The choice was made for the "Web Application Attack and Audit Framework," or shorter, w3af [31], mainly because the framework itself is easy to extend and actively maintained.

5   Evaluation

For our experiments, we installed three publicly available, real-world web applications based on Django (SVN Version 6668):

- The first application was a blogging application, called Django-basic-blog [9]. We did not install any user accounts. Initially, the blog was filled with three articles. Comments were enabled for each article, and no other links were present on the page. That is, the comments were the only interactive component of the site.
- The second application was a forum software, called Django-Forum [23]. To provide all fuzzers with a chance to explore more of the application, every access was performed as coming from a privileged user account. Thus, each scanner was making requests as a user that could create new threads and post replies. Initially, a simple forum structure was created that consisted of three forums.
- The third application was a web shop, the Satchmo online shop 0.6 [24]. This site was larger than the previous two applications, and, therefore, more challenging to test. The online shop was populated with the test data included in the package, and one user account was created.

We selected these three programs because they represent common archetypes of applications on the Internet. For our experiments, we used Apache 2.2.4 (with pre-forked worker threads) and mod_python 3.3.1. Note that before a new scanner was tested on a site, the application was restored to its initial state.

5.1 Test Methodology

We tested each of the three aforementioned web applications with three existing web vulnerability scanners, as well as with our own tool. The scanners that we used were Burp Spider 1.21 [5], w3af spider [31], and Acunetix Web Vulnerability Scanner 5.1 (Free Edition) [1]. Each scanner is implemented as a web spider that can follow links on web pages. All scanners also have support for filling out forms and, with the exception of the Burp Suite Spider, a fuzzer component to check for XSS vulnerabilities. For each page that is found to contain an XSS vulnerability, a warning is issued. In addition to the three vulnerability scanners and our tool, we also included a very simple web spider into the tests. This self-written spider follows all links on a page. It repeats this process recursively for all pages that are found, until all available URLs are exhausted. This web spider serves as the lower bound on the number of pages that should be found and analyzed by each vulnerability scanner.

We used the default configuration for all tools. One exception was that we enabled the form filling option for the Burp Spider. Moreover, for the Acunetix scanner, we activated the "extensive scan feature," which optimizes the scan for mod_python applications and checks for stored XSS.

When testing our own tool, we first recorded a simple use case for each of the three applications. The use cases included posting a comment for the blog, creating a new thread and a post on the forum site, and purchasing an item in the online store. Then, we executed our system in one of three modes. First, guided fuzzing was used. In the second run, we used extended, guided fuzzing (together with application feedback). Finally, we scanned the program using stateful fuzzing.

There are different ways to assess the effectiveness or coverage of a web vulnerability scanner. One metric is clearly the number of vulnerabilities that are reported. Unfortunately, this number could be misleading because a single program bug might manifest itself on many pages. For example, a scanner might find a bug in a form that is reused on several pages. In this case, there is only a single vulnerability, although the number of warnings could be significantly larger. Thus, the number of unique bugs, or vulnerable *injection points*, is more representative than the number of warnings.

Another way to assess coverage is to count the number of *locations* that a scanner visits. A location represents a unique, distinct page (or, more precisely, a distinct URL). Of course, visiting more locations potentially allows a scanner to test more of the application's functionality. Assume that, for a certain application, Scanner A is able to explore significantly more locations than Scanner B. However, because Scanner A misses one location with a vulnerability that Scanner B visits, it reports fewer vulnerable injection points. In this case, we might still conclude that Scanner A is better, because it achieves a larger coverage. Unfortunately, this number can also be misleading, because different locations could result from different URLs that represent the same, underlying page (e.g., the different pages on a forum, or different threads on a blog).

Finally, for the detection of vulnerabilities that require the scanner to store malicious input into the database (such as stored XSS vulnerabilities), it is more important to create many different database objects than to visit many locations. Thus, we also consider the number and diversity of different (database) objects that each scanner creates while testing an application.

Even though we only tested for XSS vulnerabilities, many other attacks can be performed against web applications. XSS is a very common and well understood vulnerability and, therefore, we selected this type of attack for our testing. However, the techniques presented in this paper apply to other injection attacks as well (for example, SQL injection and directory traversal attacks).

5.2   Experimental Results

In this section, we present and discuss the results that the different scanners achieve when analyzing the three test applications. For each application, we present the number of locations that the scanner has visited, the number of reported vulnerabilities, the number of injection points (unique bugs) that these reports map to, and the number of relevant database objects that were created.

Blogging application. Table 1 shows the results for the simple blog application. Compared to the simple spider, one can see that all other tools have reached more locations. This is because all spiders (except the simple one) requested the root of each identified directory. When available, these root directories can provide additional links to pages that might not be reachable from the initial page. As expected, it can be seen that extended, guided fuzzing reaches more locations than guided fuzzing alone, since it attempts to explore the application in breadth. Moreover, there is no difference between the results for the extended,

Table 1. Scanner effectiveness for blog application

	Locations	POST/GET Requests	Comments	XSS Warnings		Injection Points	
				Reflected	Stored	Reflected	Stored
Spider	4	4	-	-	-	-	-
Burp Spider	8	25	0	-	-	-	-
w3af	9	133	0	0	0	0	0
Acunetix	9	22	0	0	0	0	0
Use Case	4	4	1	-	-	-	-
Guided Fuzzing	4	64	12	0	1	0	1
Extended Fuzz.	6	189	12	0	1	0	1
Stateful Fuzz.	6	189	12	0	1	0	1

guided fuzzing and the stateful fuzzing approach. The reason is that, for this application, invoking the fuzzer does not interfere with the correct replay of the use case.

None of the three existing scanners was able to create a valid comment on the blogging system. This was because the posting process is not straightforward: Once a comment is submitted, the blog displays a form with a preview button. This allows a user to either change the content of the comment or to post it. The problem is that the submit button (to actually post the message) is not part of the page until the server-side validation recognizes the submitted data as a valid comment. To this end, both comment fields (name and comment) need to be present. Here, the advantage of guided fuzzing is clear. Because our system relies on a previously recorded test case, the fuzzer can correctly fill out the form and post a comment. This is beneficial, because it is possible to include malicious JavaScript into a comment and expose the stored XSS vulnerability that is missed by the other scanners. Concerning the number of injection points, which are higher for some tested scanners, it has to be noted that this is caused by the way in which some scanners attempt to find new attack points. When discovering a new URL, these scanners also issue requests for all subdirectories of the injection point. Depending on the application, this might lead to the discovery of new pages (injection points), redirects, or page-not-found errors. As our fuzzer focuses on following use cases, we did not implement this heuristics for our scanner (of course, it could be easily added).

Forum application. For the forum application, the scanners were able to generate some content, both in the form of new discussion threads and replies. Table 2 shows that while Burp Spider [5] and w3af [31] were able to create new discussion threads, only the Acunetix scanner managed to post replies as well. w3af correctly identified the form's action URL to post a reply, but failed to generate valid input data that would have resulted in the reply being stored in the database. However, since the vulnerability is caused by a bug in the routine that validates the thread title, posting replies is not necessary to identify the flaw in this program.

Table 2. Scanner effectiveness for the forum application

	Locations	POST/GET Requests	Threads Created	Replies Created	XSS Warnings Reflect	Stored	Inject. Points Reflect	Stored
Spider	8	8	-	-	-	-	-	-
Burp Spider	8	32	0	0	-	-	-	-
w3af	14	201	29	0	0	3	0	1
Acunetix	263	2,003	687	1,486	63	63	0	1
Use Case	6	7	1	2	-	-	-	-
Guided Fuzzing	16	48	12	22	0	1	0	1
Extended Fuzz.	85	555	36	184	0	3	0	1
Stateful Fuzz.	85	555	36	184	0	3	0	1

Both the number of executed requests and the number of reported vulnerabilities differ significantly between the vulnerability scanners tested. It can be seen that the Acunetix scanner has a large database of malformed inputs, which manifests both in the number of requests sent and the number of vulnerabilities reported. For each of the three forum threads, which contain a link to the unique, vulnerable entry point, Acunetix sent 21 fuzzed requests. Moreover, the Acunetix scanner reports each detected vulnerability twice. That is, each XSS vulnerability is reported once as reflected and once as stored XSS. As a result, the scanner generated 126 warnings for a single bug. w3af, in comparison, keeps an internal knowledge base of vulnerabilities that it discovers. Therefore, it reports each vulnerability only once (and the occurrence of a stored attack replaces a previously found, reflected vulnerability).

The results show that all our techniques were able to find the vulnerability that is present in the forum application. Similar to the Acunetix scanner (but unlike w3af), they were able to create new threads and post replies. Again, the extended, guided fuzzing was able to visit more locations than the guided fuzzing alone (it can be seen that the extended fuzzing checked all three forum threads that were present initially, while the guided fuzzing only analyzed the single forum thread that was part of the recorded use case). Moreover, the fuzzing phase was not interfering with the replay of the use cases. Therefore, the stateful fuzzing approach did not yield any additional benefits.

Online shopping application. The experimental results for the online shopping application are presented in Tables 3 and 4. Table 3 presents the scanner effectiveness based on the number of locations that are visited and the number of vulnerabilities that are detected, while Table 4 compares the number of database objects that were created by both the Acunetix scanner and our approaches. Note that the Acunetix scanner offers a feature that allows the tool to make use of login credentials and to block the logout links. For this experiment, we made two test runs with the Acunetix scanner: The first run (#1) as anonymous user and the second test run (#2) by enabling this feature.

Both w3af and Acunetix identified a reflected XSS vulnerability in the login form. However, neither of the two scanners was able to reach deep into the

Table 3. Scanner effectiveness for the online shopping application

	Locations	POST/GET Requests	XSS Warnings Reflected	XSS Warnings Stored	Injection Points Reflected	Injection Points Stored
Spider	18	18	-	-	-	-
Burp Spider	22	52	-	-	-	-
w3af	21	829	1	0	1	0
Acunetix #1	22	1,405	16	0	1	0
Acunetix #2	25	2,564	8	0	1	0
Use Case	22	36	-	-	-	-
Guided Fuzzing	22	366	1	8	1	8
Extended Fuzz.	25	1,432	1	0	1	0
Stateful Fuzz.	32	2,078	1	8	1	8

Table 4. Object creation statistics for the online shopping application

Object Class	Acunetix #1	Acunetix #2	Use Case	Guided Fuzzing	Extended Fuzzing	Stateful Fuzzing
OrderItem	-	-	1	1	-	2
AddressBook	-	-	2	2	-	7
PhoneNumber	-	-	1	3	-	5
Contact	1	-	1	1	1	2
CreditCardDetail	-	-	1	1	-	2
OrderStatus	-	-	1	1	-	1
OrderPayment	-	-	1	1	-	2
Order	-	-	1	1	-	2
Cart	2	1	1	1	3	3
CartItem	2	1	1	1	5	5
Comment	-	-	1	21	11	96
User	1	-	1	1	1	1

application. As a result, both tools failed to reach and correctly fill out the form that allows to change the contact information of a user. This form contained eight stored XSS vulnerabilities, since none of the entered input was checked by the application for malicious values. However, the server checked the phone number and email address for their validity and would reject the complete form whenever one of the two values was incorrect.

In contrast to the existing tools, guided fuzzing was able to analyze a large part of the application, including the login form and the user data form. Thus, this approach reported a total of nine vulnerable entry points. In this experiment, we can also observe the advantages of stateful fuzzing. With extended, guided fuzzing, the fuzzing step interferes with the proper replay of the use case (because the fuzzer logs itself out and deletes all items from the shopping cart). The stateful fuzzer, on the other hand, allows to explore a broad range of entry points, and, using the snapshot mechanism, keeps the ability to replay the test case. The number of database objects created by the different approaches (as shown in Table 4) also confirms the ability of our techniques to create a large variety of different, valid objects, a result of analyzing large portions of the application.

Discussion. All vulnerabilities that we found in our experiments were previously unknown, and we reported them to the developers of the web applications. Our results show that our fuzzing techniques consistently find more (or, at least, the same amount) of bugs than other open-source and commercial scanners. Moreover, it can be seen that the different approaches carry out meaningful interactions with the web applications, visiting many locations and creating a large variety of database objects. Finally, the different techniques exhibit different strengths. For example, stateful fuzzing becomes useful especially when the tested application is more complex and sensitive to the fuzzing steps.

6   Related Work

Concepts such as vulnerability testing, test case generation, and fuzzing are well-known concepts in software engineering and vulnerability analysis [3, 4, 11]. When analyzing web applications for vulnerabilities, black-box fuzzing tools [1, 5, 31] are most popular. However, as shown by our experiments, they suffer from the problem of test coverage. Especially for applications that require complex interactions or expect specific input values to proceed, black-box tools often fail to fill out forms properly. As a result, they can scan only a small portion of the application. This is also true for SecuBat [16], a web vulnerability scanner that we developed previously. SecuBat can detect reflected XSS and SQL injection vulnerabilities. However, it cannot fill out forms and, thus, was not included in our experiments.

In addition to web-specific scanners, there exist a large body of more general vulnerability detection and security assessment tools. Most of these tools (e.g., Nikto [19], Nessus [29]) rely on a repository of known vulnerabilities that are tested. Our tool, in contrast, aims to discover unknown vulnerabilities in the application under analysis. Besides application-level vulnerability scanners, there are also tools that work at the network level, e.g., nmap [14]. These tools can determine the availability of hosts and accessible services. However, they are not concerned with higher-level vulnerability analysis. Other well-known web vulnerability detection and mitigation approaches in literature are Scott and Sharp's application-level firewall [25] and Huang et al.'s [13] vulnerability detection tool that automatically executes SQL injection attacks. Moreover, there are a large number of static source code analysis tools [15, 27, 32] that aim to identify vulnerabilities.

A field that is closely related to our work is automated test case generation. The methods used to generate test cases can be generally summarized as random, specification-based [20, 22], and model-based [21] approaches. Fuzzing falls into the category of random test case generation. By introducing use cases and guided fuzzing, we improve the effectiveness of random tests by providing some inputs that are likely valid and thus, allow the scanner to reach "deeper" into the application.

A well-known application testing tool, called WinRunner, allows a human tester to record user actions (e.g., input, mouse clicks, etc.) and then to replay these actions while testing. This could be seen similar to guided fuzzing, where inputs are recorded based on observing real user interaction. However, the testing with Win-Runner is not fully-automated. The developer needs to write scripts and create check points to compare the expected and actual outcomes from the test runs. By adding automated, random fuzzing to a guided execution approach, we combine the advantages provided by a tool such as WinRunner with black-box fuzzers. Moreover, we provide techniques to generalize from a recorded use case.

Finally, a number of approaches [6, 12, 18] were presented in the past that aim to explore the alternative execution paths of an application to increase the analysis and test coverage of dynamic techniques. The work we present in this paper is analogous in the sense that the techniques aim to identify more code to test. The difference is the way in which the different approaches are realized, as well as their corresponding properties. When exploring multiple execution paths, the system has to track constraints over inputs, which are solved at branching points to determine alternative paths. Our system, instead, leverages known, valid input to directly reach a large part of an application. Then, a black-box fuzzer is started to find vulnerabilities. This provides better scalability, allowing us to quickly examine large parts of the application and expose it to black-box tests.

7   Conclusions

In this paper, we presented a web application testing tool to detect reflected and stored cross-site scripting (XSS) vulnerabilities in web applications. The core of our system is a black-box vulnerability scanner. Unfortunately, black-box testing tools often fail to test a substantial fraction of a web application's logic, especially when this logic is invoked from pages that can only be reached after filling out complex forms that aggressively check the correctness of the provided values. To allow our scanner to reach "deeper" into the application, we introduce a number of techniques to create more comprehensive test cases. One technique, called guided fuzzing, leverages previously recorded user input to fill out forms with values that are likely valid. This technique can be further extended by using each step in the replay process as a starting point for the fuzzer to explore a program more comprehensively. When feedback from the application is available, we can reuse the recorded user input for different forms during this process. Finally, we introduce stateful fuzzing as a way to mitigate potentially undesirable side-effects of the fuzzing step that could interfere with the replay of use cases during extended, guided fuzzing. We have implemented our use-case-driven testing techniques and analyzed three real-world web applications. Our experimental results demonstrate that our approach is able to identify more bugs than several open-source and commercial web vulnerability scanners.

Acknowledgments

This work has been supported by the Austrian Science Foundation (FWF) under grant P-18764, the FIT-IT project SECoverer (Detection of Application Logic Errors in Web Applications), and the Secure Business Austria Competence Center.

References

[1] Acunetix. Acunetix Web Vulnerability Scanner (2008),
http://www.acunetix.com/

[2] Balzarotti, D., Cova, M., Felmetsger, V., Jovanov, N., Kirda, E., Kruegel, C., Vigna, G.: Saner: Composing Static and Dynamic Analysis to Validate Sanitization in Web Applications. In: IEEE Security and Privacy Symposium (2008)

[3] Beizer, B.: Software System Testing and Quality Assurance. Van Nostrand Reinhold (1984)

[4] Beizer, B.: Software Testing Techniques. Van Nostrand Reinhold (1990)

[5] Spider, B.: Web Application Security (2008), http://portswigger.net/spider/

[6] Cadar, C., Ganesh, V., Pawlowski, P., Dill, D., Engler, D.: EXE: Automatically Generating Inputs of Death. In: ACM Conference on Computer and Communication Security (2006)

[7] Hannson, D.: Ruby on Rails (2008), http://www.rubyonrails.org/

[8] Django. The Web Framework for Professionals with Deadlines (2008), http://www.djangoproject.com/

[9] Basic Django Blog Application,
http://code.google.com/p/django-basic-blog/

[10] Endler, D.: The Evolution of Cross Site Scripting Attacks. Technical report, iDEFENSE Labs (2002)

[11] Ghezzi, C., Jazayeri, M., Mandrioli, D.: Fundamentals of Software Engineering. Prentice-Hall International, Englewood Cliffs (1994)

[12] Godefroid, P., Klarlund, N., Sen, K.: DART. In: Programming Language Design and Implementation (PLDI) (2005)

[13] Huang, Y., Huang, S., Lin, T.: Web Application Security Assessment by Fault Injection and Behavior Monitoring. In: 12th World Wide Web Conference (2003)

[14] Insecure.org. NMap Network Scanner (2008), http://www.insecure.org/nmap/

[15] Jovanovic, N., Kruegel, C., Kirda, E.: Pixy: A Static Analysis Tool for Detecting Web Application Vulnerabilities (Short Paper). In: IEEE Symposium on Security and Privacy (2006)

[16] Kals, S., Kirda, E., Kruegel, C., Jovanovic, N.: SecuBat: A Web Vulnerability Scanner. In: World Wide Web Conference (2006)

[17] Mitre. Common Vulnerabilities and Exposures, http://cve.mitre.org/

[18] Moser, A., Kruegel, C., Kirda, E.: Exploring Multiple Execution Paths for Malware Analysis. In: IEEE Symposium on Security and Privacy (2007)

[19] Nikto. Web Server Scanner (2008), http://www.cirt.net/code/nikto.shtml

[20] Offutt, J., Abdurazik, A.: Generating Tests from UML Specifications. In: Second International Conference on the Unified Modeling Language (1999)

[21] Offutt, J., Abdurazik, A.: Using UML Collaboration Diagrams for Static Checking and Test Generation. In: Evans, A., Kent, S., Selic, B. (eds.) UML 2000. LNCS, vol. 1939, pp. 383–395. Springer, Heidelberg (2000)

[22] Offutt, J., Liu, S., Abdurazik, A., Ammann, P.: Generating Test Data from State-based Specifications. In: Journal of Software Testing, Verification and Reliability (2003)
[23] Poulton, R.: Django Forum Component,
http://code.google.com/p/django-forum/
[24] Satchmo, http://www.satchmoproject.com/
[25] Scott, D., Sharp, R.: Abstracting Application-level Web Security. In: 11th World Wide Web Conference (2002)
[26] WhiteHat Security. Web Application Security 101 (2005),
http://www.whitehatsec.com/articles/webappsec101.pdf
[27] Su, Z., Wassermann, G.: The Essence of Command Injection Attacks in Web Applications. In: Symposium on Principles of Programming Languages (2006)
[28] Sun. Java Servlets (2008), http://java.sun.com/products/servlet/
[29] Tenable Network Security. Nessus Open Source Vulnerability Scanner Project (2008), http://www.nessus.org/
[30] Twill. Twill: A Simple Scripting Language for Web Browsing (2008),
http://twill.idyll.org/
[31] Web Application Attack and Audit Framework,
http://w3af.sourceforge.net/
[32] Xie, Y., Aiken, A.: Static Detection of Security Vulnerabilities in Scripting Languages. In: 15th USENIX Security Symposium (2006)

Model-Based Covert Timing Channels: Automated Modeling and Evasion

Steven Gianvecchio[1], Haining Wang[1], Duminda Wijesekera[2], and Sushil Jajodia[2]

[1] Department of Computer Science
College of William and Mary, Williamsburg, VA 23187, USA
{srgian,hnw}@cs.wm.edu
[2] Center for Secure Information Systems
George Mason University, Fairfax, VA 22030, USA
{dwijesek,jajodia}@gmu.edu

Abstract. The exploration of advanced covert timing channel design is important to understand and defend against covert timing channels. In this paper, we introduce a new class of covert timing channels, called model-based covert timing channels, which exploit the statistical properties of legitimate network traffic to evade detection in an effective manner. We design and implement an automated framework for building model-based covert timing channels. Our framework consists of four main components: filter, analyzer, encoder, and transmitter. The filter characterizes the features of legitimate network traffic, and the analyzer fits the observed traffic behavior to a model. Then, the encoder and transmitter use the model to generate covert traffic and blend with legitimate network traffic. The framework is lightweight, and the overhead induced by model fitting is negligible. To validate the effectiveness of the proposed framework, we conduct a series of experiments in LAN and WAN environments. The experimental results show that model-based covert timing channels provide a significant increase in detection resistance with only a minor loss in capacity.

Keywords: covert timing channels, traffic modeling, evasion.

1 Introduction

A covert channel is a "communication channel that can be exploited by a process to transfer information in a manner that violates a system's security policy" [1]. There are two types of covert channels: covert storage channels and covert timing channels. A covert storage channel manipulates the contents of a storage location (e.g., disk, memory, packet headers, etc.) to transfer information. A covert timing channel manipulates the timing or ordering of events (e.g., disk accesses, memory accesses, packet arrivals, etc.) to transfer information. The focus of this paper is on covert timing channels.

The potential damage of a covert timing channel is measured in terms of its capacity. The capacity of covert timing channels has been increasing with the

R. Lippmann, E. Kirda, and A. Trachtenberg (Eds.): RAID 2008, LNCS 5230, pp. 211–230, 2008.

development of high-performance computers and high-speed networks. While covert timing channels studied in the 1970s could transfer only a few bits per second [2], covert timing channels in modern computers can transfer several megabits per second [3]. To defend against covert timing channels, researchers have proposed various methods to detect and disrupt them. The disruption of covert timing channels manipulates traffic to slow or stop covert timing channels [4,5,6,7,8]. The detection of covert timing channels mainly uses statistical tests to differentiate covert traffic from legitimate traffic [9,10,11,12,13]. Such detection methods are somewhat successful, because most existing covert timing channels cause large deviations in the timing behavior from that of normal traffic, making them relatively easy to detect.

In this paper, we introduce model-based covert timing channels, which endeavor to evade detection by modeling and mimicking the statistical properties of legitimate traffic. We design and develop a framework for building model-based covert timing channels, in which hidden information is carried through pseudo-random values generated from a distribution function. We use the inverse distribution function and cumulative distribution function for encoding and decoding. The framework includes four components, filter, analyzer, encoder, and transmitter. The filter profiles the legitimate traffic, and the analyzer fits the legitimate traffic behavior to a model. Then, based on the model, the encoder chooses the appropriate distribution functions from statistical tools and traffic generation libraries to create covert timing channels. The distribution functions and their parameters are determined by automated model fitting. The process of model fitting proves very efficient and the induced overhead is minor. Lastly, the transmitter generates covert traffic and blends with legitimate traffic.

The two primary design goals of covert timing channels are high capacity and detection resistance. To evaluate the effectiveness of the proposed framework, we perform a series of LAN and WAN experiments to measure the capacity and detection resistance of our model-based covert timing channel. We estimate the capacity with a model and then validate the model with real experiments. Our experimental results show that the capacity is close to that of an optimal covert timing channel that transmits in a similar condition. In previous research, it is shown that the shape [9, 10] and regularity [11, 12] of network traffic are important properties in the detection of covert timing channels. We evaluate the detection resistance of the proposed framework using shape and regularity tests. The experimental results show that both tests fail to differentiate the model-based covert traffic from legitimate traffic. Overall, our model-based covert timing channel achieves strong detection resistance and high capacity.

There is an arms race between covert timing channel design and detection. To maintain the lead, researchers need to continue to improve detection methods and investigate new attacks. The goal of our work is to increase the understanding of more advanced covert timing channel design. We anticipate that our demonstration of model-based covert timing channels will ultimately lead to the development of more advanced detection methods.

The remainder of the paper is structured as follows. Section 2 surveys related work. Section 3 provides background information on covert timing channels and describes two base cases in their design. Section 4 details the design and implementation of the proposed framework. Section 5 validates the effectiveness of the model-based covert timing channel through live experiments over the Internet. Finally, we conclude the paper and discuss future directions in Section 6.

2   Related Work

To defend against covert timing channels, researchers have proposed different solutions to detect and disrupt covert traffic. The disruption of covert timing channels adds random delays to traffic, which reduces the capacity of covert timing channels but reduces the network performance as well. The detection of covert timing channels is mainly accomplished using statistical tests to differentiate covert traffic from legitimate traffic. While the focus of earlier work is on the disruption of covert timing channels [4,5,6,7,8], more recent research has begun to investigate the design and detection of covert timing channels [9,10,11,12,14].

Kang et al. [5] designed a device, known as "The Pump," which reduces the capacity of covert timing channels by disrupting the timing of communication. This device increases the number of errors by randomly manipulating the timing values. The basic version of "The Pump" is designed to address covert timing channels within systems. A network version was later designed and developed [6,7]. Giles et al. [8] studied the disruption of covert timing channels from a game theoretic perspective. The authors takes the point of view of both the jammer and the covert timing channel, and discusses the strategies for both optimal jammers and optimal input processes. Fisk et al. [4] investigated the concept of Active Wardens in relation to covert channels. The authors introduced the quantity of Minimal Requisite Fidelity (MRF), which is the minimum fidelity needed to support the communication channel, and proposed a system to identify and eliminate unneeded fidelity in traffic that could be used for covert channels.

Cabuk et al. [11] designed and implemented a simple covert timing channel and showed that the regularity of the covert timing channel can be used in its detection. To disrupt the regularity, the authors tried two approaches. The first is to change the timing intervals, which is still successfully detected. The second is to introduce noise in the form of legitimate traffic. However, the covert timing channel is still sometimes detected, even with 50% of the inter-packet delays being legitimate traffic. This covert timing channel has similar regularity test scores to Fixed-average Packet Rate (FPR) and OPtimal Capacity (OPC) (described in Section 3) but transmits information more slowly.

Berk et al. [9, 10] proposed a scheme for detecting binary and multi-symbol covert timing channels. The detection method measures the distance between the mean and modes, with a large distance indicating a potential covert timing channel. The detection test assumes a normal distribution for the inter-packet delays and, as a result, is not applicable to the covert timing channels we discussed. The authors used the Arimoto-Blahut algorithm [15, 16] in the binary case without considering the cost. In contrast, we use the Arimoto-Blahut algorithm in the multi-symbol case but with a cost constraint, to formulate the optimal input distribution for FPR.

Shah et al. [12] developed a keyboard device, called *JitterBug*, to create a loosely-coupled covert channel capable of leaking information typed on a keyboard over the network. Such a covert timing channel takes advantage of small delays in key-presses to affect the inter-packet delays of a networked application. As a result, the keyboard slowly leaks information to an observer outside of the network. The authors showed that the initial scheme leaves a regular pattern in the inter-packet delays, which can be removed by rotating the position of the window. The JitterBug transmits information much more slowly than our model-based covert timing channel, but does so under tighter constraints on the transmission mechanism.

Borders et al. [17] developed a system, called *Web Tap*, to detect covert tunnels in web traffic based on header fields, inter-request delays, request sizes, capacity usage, request regularity, and request time. Such a system is successful in detecting several spyware and backdoor programs. However, the technique used by our model-based covert timing channel to mimic the inter-request delays and request regularity of traffic, could be used by spyware and backdoor programs to evade the Web Tap.

While some recent research has taken steps to better hide covert timing channels [11, 12], these works focus on removing regularity rather than making the covert timing channel look like legitimate traffic. Moreover, removing regularity is the last step in the covert channel design process, instead of a consideration up front. In contrast, our framework is designed from the ground up to provide high detection resistance. As a result, the proposed model-based covert timing channel is able to provide much stronger detection resistance than most practical implementations of covert timing channel presented in the literature.

There are recent works on using timing channels to watermark traffic [18, 19] and on detecting such timing-based watermarks [20]. Wang et al. [18] developed a robust watermarking scheme for tracing encrypted attack traffic through stepping stones. The scheme, through the use of redundancy, can resist arbitrarily large timing perturbations, if there are a sufficient number of packets to watermark. Peng et al. [20] investigated how to detect such watermarks, as well as methods for removing or duplicating the watermarks. Yu et al. [19] developed a sophisticated technique for hiding watermarks by disguising them as pseudo-noise. There are some interesting differences between timing-based watermarking and traditional covert timing channels, such as the fact that the defender, not the attacker, uses the timing channel in the watermarking schemes.

3 Background

In this section, we describe basic communication concepts and relate them to covert timing channels. Then, based on these concepts, we formulate two base cases in covert timing channel design. The basic problem of communication, producing a message at one point and reproducing that message at another point, is the same for both overt and covert channels, although covert channels must consider the additional problem of hiding communication.

3.1   Basic Communication Concepts

The capacity of a communication channel is the maximum rate that it can reliably transmit information. The capacity of a covert timing channel is measured in bits per time unit [21]. The capacity in bits per time unit C_t is defined as:

$$C_t = \max_X \frac{I(X;Y)}{E(X)},$$

where X is the transmitted inter-packet delays or input distribution, Y is the received inter-packet delays or output distribution, $I(X;Y)$ is the mutual information between X and Y, and $E(X)$ is the expected time of X.

The mutual information measures how much information is carried across the channel from X to Y. The mutual information $I(X;Y)$ is defined as:

$$I(X;Y) = \begin{cases} \sum_X \sum_Y P(y \mid x)P(x)\log\frac{P(y|x)P(x)}{P(x)P(y)}, \text{(discrete)} \\ \int_X \int_Y P(y \mid x)P(x)\log\frac{P(y|x)P(x)}{P(x)P(y)}\, dx\, dy, \text{(continuous)} \end{cases}$$

The noise, represented by the conditional probability in the above definitions, is defined as:

$$P(y \mid x) = f_{noise}(y, x),$$

where f_{noise} is the noise probability density function, x is the transmitted inter-packet delays, and y is the received inter-packet delays.

The noise distribution f_{noise} is the probability that the transmitted inter-packet delay x results in the received inter-packet delay y. The specific noise distribution for inter-packet delays is detailed in Section 5.2.

3.2   Base Cases in Design

The two main goals of covert timing channel design are high capacity and detection resistance. There are few examples of practical implementations of covert timing channels in the literature, so we begin to explore the design space in terms of both capacity and detection resistance. The focus of our model-based covert timing channel is to achieve high detection resistance. In the following section, we formulate two base cases in covert channel design as comparison to the model-based covert timing channel.

The first case, optimal capacity, transmits as much information as possible, sending hundreds or more packets per second. Such a design might not be able to achieve covert communication, but is useful as a theoretical upper bound. The second case, fixed average packet rate, sends packets at a specific fixed average packet rate, encoding as much information per packet as possible. The fixed average packet rate is mainly determined by the packet rate of legitimate traffic.

Optimal Capacity Channel. The first design, OPtimal Capacity (OPC), uses the discrete input distribution that transmits information as fast as possible. The optimal capacity is dependent on the optimal distance between two symbols. The first symbol is (approximately) zero and the second symbol is non-zero, so the use of more symbols (i.e., four or eight) will introduce more non-zero symbols and decrease the symbol rate. The use of smaller distances between the two symbols increases the symbol rate and the error rate. The optimal distance is the point at which the increase in error rate balances the increase in symbol rate.

The code operates based on two functions. The encode function is defined as:

$$F_{encode}(s) = d_s = \begin{cases} 0, & s = 0 \\ d, & s = 1 \end{cases}$$

where s is a symbol, d_s is an inter-packet delay with a hidden symbol s, and d is the optimal distance between the two symbols. The decode function is defined as:

$$F_{decode}(d_s) = s = \begin{cases} 0, & d_s < \frac{1}{2}d \\ 1, & \frac{1}{2}d \le d_s \end{cases}$$

where d_s is an inter-packet delay with a hidden symbol s.

Channel Capacity: The channel capacity of OPC is dependent on the optimal input distribution and noise. The input distribution is defined as:

$$P(x) = \begin{cases} p, & x = d \\ 1 - p, & x = 0 \\ 0, & \text{otherwise} \end{cases}$$

where p is the probability of the symbol $s = 1$, and $1 - p$ is the probability of the symbol $s = 0$.

Therefore, the capacity of OPC is the maximum of the mutual information with respect to the parameters d and p of the input distribution over the expected time $d \cdot p$:

$$C_t = \max_{d,p} \frac{1}{d \cdot p} \sum_X \sum_Y P(y \mid x)P(x)\log\frac{P(y \mid x)P(x)}{P(x)P(y)}.$$

Fixed-Average Packet Rate Channel. The second design, Fixed-average Packet Rate (FPR), uses the input distribution that encodes as much information per packet as possible with a constraint on the average cost of symbols. The cost is measured in terms of the time required for symbol transmission. Therefore, the optimal input distribution is subject to the constraint on the average packet rate, i.e., the cost of symbol transmission.

The optimal input distribution for FPR is computed with the Arimoto-Blahut algorithm generalized for cost constraints [16]. The Arimoto-Blahut algorithm computes the optimal input distribution for capacity in bits per channel usage. The capacity in bits per channel usage C_u is defined as:

$$C_u = \max_X I(X;Y).$$

In general, C_u and C_t do not have the same input distribution X. However, if the input distribution is constrained so that $E(X) = c$ (where c is a constant), then the optimal input distribution X is optimal for both C_u and C_t, and $C_u = C_t \cdot c$. Thus, FPR transmits as much information per packet (channel usage) and per second (time unit) as possible with a fixed average packet rate. We use the Arimoto-Blahut algorithm to compute the optimal input distribution for FPR. The capacity results for FPR, based on the Arimoto-Blahut algorithm, are detailed in Section 5.

4   The Framework

The covert timing channel framework, as shown in Figure 1, is a pipeline that filters and analyzes legitimate traffic then encodes and transmits covert traffic. As the output of the pipeline, the covert traffic mimics the observed legitimate traffic, making it easy to evade detection. The components of the framework include filter, analyzer, encoder, and transmitter, which are detailed in the following paragraphs.

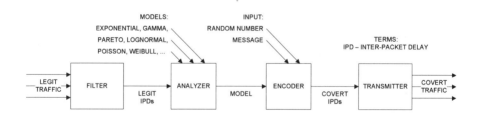

Fig. 1. Framework for building model-based covert timing channels

The filter monitors the background traffic and singles out the specific type of traffic to be mimicked. The more specific application traffic the filter can identify and profile, the better model we can have for generating covert traffic. For example, FTP is an application protocol based on TCP, but generating a series of inter-packet delays based on a model of all TCP traffic would be a poor model for describing FTP behaviors. Once the specified traffic is filtered, the traffic is further classified into individual flows based on source and destination IP addresses. The filter then calculates the inter-packet delay between subsequent pair of packets from each flow, and forwards the results to the analyzer.

The analyzer fits the inter-packet delays in sets of 100 packets with the Exponential, Gamma, Pareto, Lognormal, Poisson, and Weibull distributions. The

Table 1. The scores for different models for a sample of HTTP inter-packet delays

model	parameters	root mean squared error
Weibull	0.0794, 0.2627	0.0032
Gamma	0.1167, 100.8180	0.0063
Lognormal	-4.3589, 3.5359	0.0063
Pareto	3.6751, 0.0018	0.0150
Poisson	11.7611	0.0226
Exponential	11.7611	0.0294

fitting process uses maximum likelihood estimation (MLE) to determine the parameters for each model. The model with the smallest root mean squared error (RMSE), which measures the difference between the model and the estimated distribution, is chosen as the traffic model. The model selection is automated. Other than the set of models provided to the analyzer, there is no human input. The models are scored based on root mean squared errors, as shown in Table 1. The model with the lowest root mean squared error is the closest to the data being modeled. Since most types of network traffic are non-stationary [22], the analyzer supports piecewise modeling of non-stationary processes by adjusting the parameters of the model after each set of 100 covert inter-packet delays. The analyzer refits the current model with new sets of 100 packets to adjust the parameters. The analyzer can take advantage of a larger selection of models to more accurately model different types of application traffic. For example, if we know that the targeted traffic is well-modeled as an Erlang distribution, we will add this distribution to the set of models. For each of the current models, the computational overhead is less than 0.1 milliseconds and the storage overhead for the executable is less than 500 bytes, so the induced resource consumption for supporting additional models is not an issue.

The filter and analyzer can be run either offline or online. In the offline mode, the selection of the model and parameters is based on traffic samples. The offline mode consumes less resources, but the model might not represent the current network traffic behavior well. In the online mode, the selection of the model and parameters is based on live traffic. The online mode consumes more resources and requires that the model and parameters be transmitted to the decoder with the support of a startup protocol, but the model better represents the current network traffic behavior. The startup protocol is a model determined in advance, and is used to transmit the online model (1 byte) and parameters (4-8 bytes) to the decoder.

The encoder generates random covert inter-packet delays that mimic legitimate inter-packet delays. The input to the encoder includes the model, the message, and a sequence of random numbers. Its output is a sequence of covert random inter-packet delays. The message to be sent is separated into symbols. The symbols map to different random timing values based on a random code that distributes symbols based on the model.

Using a sequence of random numbers $r_1, r_2, ..., r_n$., we transform the discrete symbols into continuous ones. The continuization function is

$$F_{continuize}(s) = (\frac{s}{|S|} + r) \bmod 1 = r_s,$$

where S is the set of possible symbols, s is a symbol and r is a Uniform(0,1) random variable. The corresponding discretization function is:

$$F_{discretize}(r_s) = |S| \cdot ((r_s - r) \bmod 1) = s,$$

where r_s is a Uniform(0,1) random variable with a hidden symbol s.

The encoder and decoder start with the same seed and generate the same sequence of random numbers, $r_1, r_2, ..., r_n$. To maintain synchronization, the encoder and decoder associate the sequence of symbols with TCP sequence numbers, i.e., s_1 with the first TCP sequence number, s_2 with the second TCP sequence number, and so on. [1] Therefore, both the encoder and decoder have the same values of r through the sequence of symbols. The inverse distribution function F_{model}^{-1} takes a Uniform(0,1) random number as input and generates a random variable from the selected model as output. The sequence of transformed random numbers $r_{s1}, r_{s2}, ..., r_{sn}$ is used with the inverse distribution function to create random covert inter-packet delays $d_{s1}, d_{s2}, ..., d_{sn}$. The encode function is:

$$F_{encode} = F_{model}^{-1}(r_s) = d_s,$$

where F_{model}^{-1} is the inverse distribution function of the selected model. The decode function is:

$$F_{decode} = F_{model}(d_s) = r_s,$$

where F_{model} is the cumulative distribution function of the selected model, and d_s is a random covert inter-packet delay with a hidden symbol s.

The transmitter sends out packets to produce the random covert inter-packet delays $d_{s1}, d_{s2}, ..., d_{sn}$. The receiver then decodes and discretizes them to recover the original symbols $s_1, s_2, ..., s_n$.

4.1   Model-Based Channel Capacity

The model-based channel capacity is also dependent on the input distribution and noise. The input distribution is defined as:

$$P(x) = f_{model}(x)$$

where f_{model} is the probability density function of the selected model.

Therefore, the capacity of the model-based channel is the mutual information over the expected time $E(X)$:

$$C_t = \frac{1}{E(X)} \int_X \int_Y P(y \mid x) P(x) \log \frac{P(y \mid x) P(x)}{P(x) P(y)}.$$

---

[1] With this mechanism, repacketization can cause synchronization problems, so other mechanisms such as "bit stuffing" [12] could be useful for synchronization.

4.2   Implementation Details

We implement the proposed framework using C and MATLAB in Unix/Linux environments. The components run as user-space processes, while access to tcpdump is required. The filter is written in C and runs tcpdump with a user-specified filtering expression to read the stream of packets. The filter processes the traffic stream and computes the inter-packet delays based on the packet timestamps. The analyzer is written in MATLAB and utilizes the fitting functions from the statistics toolbox for maximum likelihood estimation.

The encoder is written in C, and uses random number generation and random variable models from the Park-Leemis [23] simulation C libraries. The transmitter is also written in C, with some inline assembly, and uses the Socket API. The timing mechanism used is the Pentium CPU Time-Stamp Counter, which is accessed by calling the RDTSC (Read Time-Stamp Counter) instruction. The RDTSC instruction has excellent resolution and low overhead, but must be calibrated to be used as a general purpose timing mechanism. The usleep and nanosleep functions force a context switch, which delays the packet transmission with small inter-packet delays, so these functions are not used.

5   Experimental Evaluation

In this section, we evaluate the effectiveness of a model-based covert timing channel built from our framework. The OPC and FPR covert timing channels, discussed in Section 3, are used as points of comparison. In particular, we examine the capacity and detection resistance of each covert timing channel.

5.1   Experimental Setup

The defensive perimeter of a network, composed of firewalls and intrusion detection systems, is responsible for protecting the network. Typically, only a few specific application protocols, such as HTTP and SMTP, are commonly allowed to pass through the defensive perimeter. We utilize outgoing HTTP inter-packet delays as the medium to build model-based covert timing channels, due to the wide acceptance of HTTP traffic for crossing the network perimeter. We refer to the model-based HTTP covert timing channel as MB-HTTP.

Testing Scenarios. There are three different testing scenarios in our experimental evaluation. The first scenario is in a LAN environment, a medium-size campus network with subnets for administration, departments, and residences. The LAN connection is between two machines, located in different subnets. The connection passes through several switches, the routers inside the campus network, and a firewall device that protects each subnet.

The other two scenarios are in WAN environments. The first WAN connection is between two machines, both are on the east coast of the United States but in different states. One is on a residential cable network and the other is on

Table 2. The network conditions of each test scenario

	LAN	WAN E-E	WAN E-W
distance	0.3 miles	525 miles	2660 miles
RTT	1.766ms	59.647ms	87.236ms
IPDV	2.5822e-05	2.4124e-03	2.1771e-04
hops	3	18	13
IPDV - inter-packet delay variation			

a medium-size campus network. The second WAN connection is between two machines on the opposite coasts of the United States, one on the east coast and the other on the west coast. Both machines are on campus networks.

The network conditions for different experiment scenarios are summarized in Table 2. The two-way round-trip time (RTT) is measured using the ping command. We compute the one-way inter-packet delay variation based on the delays between packets leaving the source and arriving at the destination. The inter-packet delay variations of the three connections span three orders of magnitude, from 1×10^{-3} to 1×10^{-5}. The LAN connection has the lowest inter-packet delay variation and the two WAN connections have higher inter-packet delay variation, as expected. The WAN E-E connection is shorter and has smaller RTT time than the WAN E-W connection. However, WAN E-E has higher inter-packet delay variation than WAN E-W, due to more traversed hops. This implies that the inter-packet delays variation is more sensitive to the number of hops than the physical distance and RTT between two machines.

Building MB-HTTP. We install the components of the framework on the testing machines. The filter distinguishes the outgoing HTTP traffic from background traffic. The analyzer observes 10 million HTTP inter-packet delays, then fits the HTTP inter-packet delays to the models, as described in Section 4. The fitting functions use maximum likelihood estimation (MLE) to determine the parameters for each model. The model with the best root mean squared error (RMSE), a measure of the difference between the model and the distribution being estimated, is chosen as the traffic model.

For the HTTP inter-packet delays, the analyzer selects the Weibull distribution based on the root mean squared error. Note that HTTP inter-packet delays have been shown to be well approximated by a Weibull distribution [22]. The Weibull probability distribution function is:

$$f(x, \lambda, k) = \frac{k}{\lambda}(\frac{x}{\lambda})^{(k-1)} e^{-(\frac{x}{\lambda})^k}.$$

The parameters, which vary for each set of 100 packets, have a mean scale parameter λ of 0.0371 and a mean shape parameter k of 0.3010. With these parameters, the mean inter-packet delay is 0.3385, approximately 3 packets per second.

Table 3. The mean packets per second and mean inter-packet delay for OPC

channel	LAN		WAN E-E		WAN E-W	
	PPS	IPD	PPS	IPD	PPS	IPD
OPC	12,777.98	7.87e-05	137.48	7.31e-03	1,515.56	6.63e-04
PPS - mean packets per second, IPD - mean inter-packet delay						

Formulating OPC and FPR. The average packet rate for FPR is fixed at $\frac{1}{0.3385} = 2.954$ packets per second, based on the average packet rate of HTTP traffic. We use the Arimoto-Blahut algorithm to compute the optimal input distribution, with the average packet rate of 2.954 as the cost constraint. The optimal input distribution balances high cost symbols with low probabilities and low cost symbols with high probabilities, such that the average cost constraint is satisfied. The constraint can be satisfied for infinitely large symbols with infinitely small probabilities, and hence, the optimal input distribution decays exponentially to infinity. The results of the Arimoto-Blahut algorithm, as the number of intervals increases, reduce to an Exponential distribution with an inverse scale parameter of $\lambda = 2.954$. The Exponential probability distribution function is:

$$f(x, \lambda) = \lambda e^{-\lambda x}.$$

We compute the optimal distance between packets for OPC based on the noise distribution. The optimal distance between packets and the average packet rate for OPC is shown in Table 3. For connections with higher inter-packet delay variation, OPC increases the time elapse between packets to make the inter-packet delays easier to distinguish, and, as a result, lowers the average number of packets per second.

5.2   Capacity

The definition of capacity allows us to estimate the capacity of each covert timing channel based on the network conditions of each connection. In previous research [24], the inter-packet delay differences have been shown to be well-modeled by a Laplace distribution. The probability density function of the Laplace distribution is:

$$f(x, \mu, b) = \frac{1}{2b} e^{-\frac{|x-\mu|}{b}}.$$

The setting of the scale parameter b is based on the inter-packet delay variation for each connection. The variation of the Laplace distribution is $\sigma^2 = 2b^2$. Therefore, we set b to:

$$b = \sqrt{\frac{1}{2}\sigma^2},$$

where σ^2 is the inter-packet delay variation for each connection.

Table 4. The theoretical capacity of each covert timing channel

channel	LAN CPP	LAN CPS	WAN E-E CPP	WAN E-E CPS	WAN E-W CPP	WAN E-W CPS
MB-HTTP	9.39	27.76	4.12	12.19	6.84	20.21
FPR	12.63	37.32	6.15	18.17	9.59	28.35
OPC	0.50	6395.39	0.50	68.80	0.50	758.54
CPP - capacity per packet, CPS - capacity per second						

The results, in terms of capacity per packet and capacity per second, are shown in Table 4. While OPC has the highest capacity, it is the least efficient in terms of capacity per packet. Furthermore, with the large number of packets per second, it can be easily detected by most intrusion detection systems.

The capacity of MB-HTTP is 67% to 74% of that of FPR, with larger differences for connections with high inter-packet delay variation than for those with low inter-packet delay variation. The Weibull distribution has a larger proportion of very small values than the Exponential distribution. As a result, MB-HTTP uses more small values than FPR and benefits more from lower inter-packet delay variation.

The theoretical capacity is somewhat optimistic. The model only considers the noise introduced after packets leave the transmitter. With the real covert timing channels, noise is introduced before packets leave the transmitter. The transmitter is sometimes not able to transmit at the appropriate times, due to slow processing, context switches, etc. Thus, the actual distance between packets can increase or decrease from the intended distance as the packets are transmitted.

Empirical Capacity. To evaluate the channel capacity in practice, we run covert timing channels on each connection. The channels are configured to transmit 16,000 random bits of information. For FPR and MB-HTTP, the number of bits encoded per packet is set to 16 (i.e., $2^{16} = 65,536$ different values), while OPC transmits a single bit per packet.

During these tests, we measure the bit error rate of each covert timing channel from the most significant bit to the least significant bit of each packet. The most significant bit represents a large part of the inter-packet delay, where the least significant bit represents a small part of the inter-packet delay. While flipping the most significant bit causes a difference in seconds or tenths of seconds, changing the least significant bit means a difference only in milliseconds or microseconds. In other words, the higher the number of bits encoded per packet, the smaller the precision of the lowest order bits. Interestingly, encoding at 16 bits per packet and decoding at 8 bits per packet produces the most significant 8 bits of the 16 bit code.

To determine the transmission rate with error correction, we measure the empirical capacity of each bit as a binary symmetric channel. The binary symmetric channel is a special case where the channel has two symbols of equal probability.

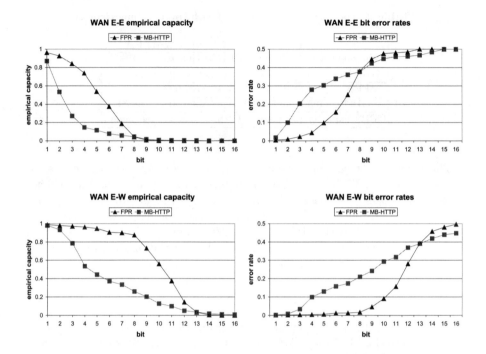

Fig. 2. The empirical capacity and bit error rates for WAN E-E and WAN E-W

The capacity of a binary symmetric channel is:

$$C = I(X;Y) = 1 - (p \log p + q \log q),$$

where p is the probability of a correct bit and $q = 1 - p$ is the probability of an incorrect bit.

The empirical capacity and bit error rate for each bit, from the most significant to the least significant, are shown in Figure 2. The empirical capacity per bit degrades as the bit error rates increase. The total capacity of the channel is the summation of the capacity for each bit. For MB-HTTP, the bit error rate increases somewhat linearly. For FPR, the bit error rate accelerates gradually, eventually overtaking the bit error rates of MB-HTTP, though at this point the capacity per bit is insignificant.

The empirical capacity of each covert timing channel is shown in Table 5. The empirical capacity of MB-HTTP is still about 46% to 61% of that of FPR, somewhat lower than the case in the theoretical model. This is because a larger proportion of MB-HTTP traffic has small inter-packet delays than that of FPR, and small inter-packet delays are more sensitive to noise caused by transmission delays (i.e., slow processing, context switches, etc.) than large inter-packet delays, which is not represented in the theoretical model.

Table 5. The empirical capacity of each covert timing channel

channel	LAN		WAN E-E			WAN E-W
	ECPP	ECPS	ECPP	ECPS	ECPP	ECPS
MB-HTTP	6.74	19.93	2.15	6.35	5.18	15.31
FPR	10.95	32.35	4.63	13.67	9.37	27.69
OPC	0.85	10,899.62	0.66	91.28	0.98	1,512.53
ECPP - empirical capacity per packet, ECPS - empirical capacity per second						

5.3   Detection Resistance

The detection resistance, as described in Section 3, is estimated based on the shape and regularity tests. To examine the shape of the distribution, we use the Kolmogorov-Smirnov test [25], which is a non-parametric goodness-of-fit test. To examine the regularity of the traffic, we use the regularity test [11], which studies the variance of the traffic pattern. In this section, we detail these two tests and show the detection resistance of MB-HTTP against both tests.

Shape Tests. The two-sample Kolmogorov-Smirnov test determines whether or not two samples come from the same distribution. The Kolmogorov-Smirnov test is distribution free, meaning the test is not dependent on a specific distribution. Thus, it is applicable to a variety of types of traffic with different distributions. The Kolmogorov-Smirnov test statistic measures the maximum distance between two empirical distribution functions.

$$KSTEST = \max \mid S_1(x) - S_2(x) \mid,$$

where S_1 and S_2 are the empirical distribution functions of the two samples.

In our experiments, we test a large set of legitimate inter-packet delays against a sample of either covert or legitimate inter-packet delays. The large set is a training set of 10,000,000 HTTP inter-packet delays. The training set is used to represent the normal behavior of the HTTP protocol.

The test score by comparing the two sets is used to determine if the sample is covert or legitimate. A small score indicates that the behavior is close to normal. However, if the test score is large, i.e., the sample does not fit the normal behavior of the protocol, it indicates a potential covert timing channel.

Table 6. The mean and standard deviation of the Kolmogorov-Smirnov test scores

sample size	LEGIT-HTTP		MB-HTTP		FPR		OPC	
	mean	stdev	mean	stdev	mean	stdev	mean	stdev
100x 2,000	.193	.110	.196	.093	.925	.002	.999	.000
100x 10,000	.141	.103	.157	.087	.925	.001	.999	.000
100x 50,000	.096	.088	.122	.073	.924	.000	.999	.000
100x 250,000	.069	.066	.096	.036	.924	.000	.999	.000

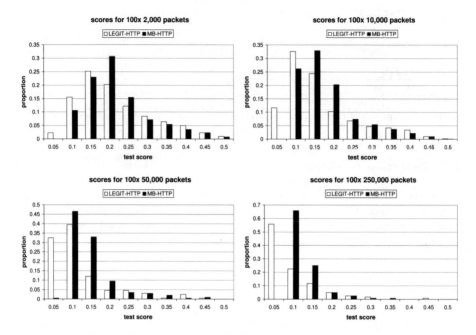

Fig. 3. The distribution of Kolmogorov-Smirnov test scores

The Kolmogorov-Smirnov test is run 100 times for each of 2,000, 10,000, 50,000, and 250,000 packet samples of legitimate and covert traffic from each covert timing channel. The mean and standard deviation of the test scores are shown in Table 6. For FPR and OPC, the mean scores are over 0.90 and the standard deviations are extremely low, indicating that the test can reliably differentiate both covert timing channels from normal HTTP traffic. By contrast, the mean scores for MB-HTTP samples are very close to those of legitimate samples. The mean scores are for 100 tests, which in total include as many as 25 million (250,000 x 100) inter-packet delays. The distribution of individual test scores is illustrated in Figure 3.

The detection resistance based on the Kolmogorov-Smirnov test is shown in Table 7. The targeted false positive rate is 0.01. To achieve this false positive rate, the cutoff scores—the scores that decide whether samples are legitimate or

Table 7. The false positive and true positive rates for the Kolmogorov-Smirnov test

		LEGIT-HTTP	MB-HTTP	FPR	OPC
sample size	cutoff	false pos.	true pos.	true pos.	true pos.
100x 2,000	$KSTEST \geq .66$	.01	.01	1.00	1.00
100x 10,000	$KSTEST \geq .65$	.01	.01	1.00	1.00
100x 50,000	$KSTEST \geq .41$	.01	.01	1.00	1.00
100x 250,000	$KSTEST \geq .21$	.01	.02	1.00	1.00

covert—are set at the 99th percentile of legitimate sample scores. The true positive rates, based on the cutoff scores, are then shown for each covert timing channel. Since the true positive rates in all 100 tests are 1.00, the Kolmogorov-Smirnov test detects FPR and OPC easily. However, the true positive rates for MB-HTTP are approximately the same as the false positive rates. The Kolmogorov-Smirnov test cannot differentiate between MB-HTTP and legitimate samples. Such a result can be explained based on the distribution of individual test scores, which is shown in Figure 3. While the mean scores of MB-HTTP traffic in Table 6 are slightly higher than those of LEGIT-HTTP, the distributions of individual scores overlap so that the false positive rate and true positive rate are approximately equal.

Regularity Tests. The regularity test [11] determines whether the variance of the inter-packet delays is relatively constant or not. This test is based on the observation that for most types of network traffic, the variance of the inter-packet delays changes over time. With covert timing channels, the code used to transmit data is a regular process and, as a result, the variance of the inter-packet delays remains relatively constant over time.

In our experiments, we test the regularity of a sample of either covert or legitimate inter-packet delays. The sample is separated into sets of w inter-packet delays. Then, for each set, the standard deviation of the set σ_i is computed. The regularity is the standard deviation of the pairwise differences between each σ_i and σ_j for all sets $i < j$.

$$regularity = STDEV(\frac{|\sigma_i - \sigma_j|}{\sigma_i}, i < j, \forall i, j)$$

The regularity test is run 100 times for 2,000 packet samples of legitimate and covert samples from each covert timing channel. The window sizes of $w = 100$ and $w = 250$ are used. The mean regularity scores are shown in Table 8. If the regularity is small, the sample is highly regular, indicating a potential covert timing channel.

Table 8. The mean of the regularity test scores

sample size	LEGIT-HTTP	MB-HTTP	FPR	OPC
100x 2,000 w=100	43.80	38.21	0.34	0.00
100x 2,000 w=250	23.74	22.87	0.26	0.00

The mean regularity scores for OPC are 0.0 for both tests, indicating regular behavior. There are two values, each with 0.5 probability. Therefore, the standard deviation within sets is small $\sigma = 0.5d = 3.317e - 4$, and there is no detectable change in the standard deviation between sets. The mean regularity score for FPR is small as well, showing that the test is able to detect the regular behavior. While the standard deviation of FPR, which is based on the Exponential distribution, is $\sigma = \lambda = 0.3385$, the code is a regular process, so the variance of the inter-packet delays remains relatively constant.

The mean regularity scores for MB-HTTP are close to those of legitimate samples. This is because the parameters are recalibrated after each set of 100 packets, as described in Section 4. The parameters of the distribution determine the mean and standard deviation, so adjusting the parameters changes the variance after each set of 100 inter-packet delays. As a result, like legitimate traffic, the variance of the inter-packet delays appears irregular.

Table 9. The false positive and true positive rates for the regularity test

		LEGIT-HTTP	MB-HTTP	FPR	OPC
sample size	cutoff	false pos.	true pos.	true pos.	true pos.
100x 2,000 w=100	$reg. \leq 6.90$	.01	.00	1.00	1.00
100x 2,000 w=250	$reg. \leq 5.20$	.01	.00	1.00	1.00

The detection resistance based on the regularity test is shown in Table 9. The targeted false positive rate is 0.01. The cutoff scores are set at the 1st percentile of legitimate sample scores, in order to achieve this false positive rate. The true positive rates, based on the cutoff scores, are then shown for each covert timing channels. The regularity test is able to detect FPR and OPC in all 100 tests. The resulting true positive rates for MB-HTTP are approximately the same as the false positive rate. Basically, the test is no better than random guessing at detecting MB-HTTP.

6   Conclusion

We introduced model-based covert timing channels, which mimic the observed behavior of legitimate network traffic to evade detection. We presented a framework for building such model-based covert timing channels. The framework consists of four components: filter, analyzer, encoder, and transmitter. The filter characterizes the specific features of legitimate traffic that are of interest. The analyzer fits the traffic to several models and selects the model with the best fit. The encoder generates random covert inter-packet delays that, based on the model, mimic the legitimate traffic. The transmitter then manipulates the timing of packets to create the model-based covert timing channel.

Using channel capacity and detection resistance as major metrics, we evaluated the proposed framework in both LAN and WAN environments. Our capacity results suggest that model-based covert timing channels work efficiently even in the coast-to-coast scenario. Our detection resistance results show that, for both shape and regularity tests, covert traffic is sufficiently similar to legitimate traffic that current detection methods cannot differentiate them. In contrast, the Kolmogorov-Smirnov and regularity tests easily detect FPR and OPC.

Our future work will further explore the detection of model-based covert timing channels. There are other non-parametric goodness-of-fit tests, such as the Anderson-Darling and Cramer-Von Mises tests [25], that are less general than the Kolmogorov-Smirnov test but might be more effective in measuring certain types of traffic. We will also further consider the regularity test at different levels of granularity. We believe that a scheme capable of detecting model-based covert timing channels will be effective in detecting other types of covert timing channels as well.

Acknowledgments

We would like to thank Cheng Jin and Lachlan Andrew at CalTech for assisting us in the coast-to-coast experiments. We also thank the anonymous reviewers for their insightful comments. This work was partially supported by NSF grants CNS-0627340 and CNS-0627493.

References

1. Department of Defense, U.S.: Trusted computer system evaluation criteria (1985)
2. Lampson, B.W.: A note on the confinement problem. Communications of the ACM 16(10) (October 1973)
3. Wang, Z., Lee, R.: Covert and side channels due to processor architecture. In: Jesshope, C., Egan, C. (eds.) ACSAC 2006. LNCS, vol. 4186, Springer, Heidelberg (2006)
4. Fisk, G., Fisk, M., Papadopoulos, C., Neil, J.: Eliminating steganography in internet traffic with active wardens. In: Proc. of the 2002 International Workshop on Information Hiding (October 2002)
5. Kang, M.H., Moskowitz, I.S.: A pump for rapid, reliable, secure communication. In: Proc. of ACM CCS 1993 (November 1993)
6. Kang, M.H., Moskowitz, I.S., Lee, D.C.: A network version of the pump. In: Proc. of the 1995 IEEE Symposium on Security and Privacy (May 1995)
7. Kang, M.H., Moskowitz, I.S., Chincheck, S.: The pump: A decade of covert fun. In: Srikanthan, T., Xue, J., Chang, C.-H. (eds.) ACSAC 2005. LNCS, vol. 3740. Springer, Heidelberg (2005)
8. Giles, J., Hajek, B.: An information-theoretic and game-theoretic study of timing channels. IEEE Trans. on Information Theory 48(9) (September 2002)
9. Berk, V., Giani, A., Cybenko, G.: Covert channel detection using process query systems. In: Proc. of FLOCON 2005 (September 2005)
10. Berk, V., Giani, A., Cybenko, G.: Detection of covert channel encoding in network packet delays. Technical Report TR2005-536, Department of Computer Science, Dartmouth College, Hanover, NH., USA (August 2005)
11. Cabuk, S., Brodley, C., Shields, C.: IP covert timing channels: Design and detection. In: Proc. of ACM CCS (October 2004)
12. Shah, G., Molina, A., Blaze, M.: Keyboards and covert channels. In: Proc. of the 2006 USENIX Security Symposium (July–August, 2006)
13. Gianvecchio, S., Wang, H.: Detecting covert timing channels: An entropy-based approach. In: Proceedings of the 2007 ACM Conference on Computer and Communications Security (October 2007)
14. Luo, X., Chan, E.W.W., Chang, R.K.C.: Cloak: A ten-fold way for reliable covert communications. In: Biskup, J., López, J. (eds.) ESORICS 2007. LNCS, vol. 4734, pp. 283–298. Springer, Heidelberg (2007)

15. Arimoto, S.: An algorithm for computing the capacity of arbitrary discrete memoryless channels. IEEE Trans. on Information Theory 18(1) (January 1972)
16. Blahut, R.E.: Computation of channel capacity and rate-distortion functions. IEEE Trans. on Information Theory 18(4) (July 1972)
17. Borders, K., Prakash, A.: Web tap: Detecting covert web traffic. In: Proc. of ACM CCS 2004 (October 2004)
18. Wang, X., Reeves, D.S.: Robust correlation of encrypted attack traffic through stepping stones by manipulation of interpacket delays. In: Proc. of ACM CCS 2003 (October 2003)
19. Yu, W., Fu, X., Graham, S., Xuan, D., Zhao, W.: Dsss-based flow marking technique for invisible traceback. In: Proc. of the 2007 IEEE Symposium on Security and Privacy, Washington, DC, USA (May 2007)
20. Peng, P., Ning, P., Reeves, D.S.: On the secrecy of timing-based active watermarking trace-back techniques. In: Proc. of the 2006 IEEE Symposium on Security and Privacy (May 2006)
21. Moskowitz, I.S., Kang, M.H.: Covert channels - here to stay? In: Proc. of the 1994 Annual Conf. on Computer Assurance (June 1994)
22. Cao, J., Cleveland, W.S., Lin, D., Sun, D.X.: On the nonstationarity of internet traffic. In: Proc. of SIGMETRICS/Performance 2001 (June 2001)
23. Leemis, L., Park, S.K.: Discrete-Event Simulation: A First Course. Prentice-Hall, Upper Saddle River (2006)
24. Zheng, L., Zhang, L., Xu, D.: Characteristics of network delay and delay jitter and its effect on oice over IP (VoIP). In: Proc. of the 2001 IEEE International Conf. on Communications (June 2001)
25. Duda, R., Hart, P., Stork, D.: Pattern Classification. Wiley-Interscience, New York (2001)

Optimal Cost, Collaborative, and Distributed Response to Zero-Day Worms - A Control Theoretic Approach

Senthilkumar G. Cheetancheri[1,*], John-Mark Agosta[2], Karl N. Levitt[1], Felix Wu[1], and Jeff Rowe[1]

[1] Security Lab, Dept. of Computer Science, Univ. of California, One Shields Ave., Davis, CA - 95616, USA
{cheetanc,levitt,wu,rowe}@cs.ucdavis.edu
[2] Intel Research. 2200, Mission College Blvd., Santa Clara, CA - 95052, USA
{john.m.agosta}@intel.com

Abstract. Collaborative environments present a happy hunting ground for worms due to inherent trust present amongst the peers. We present a novel control-theoretic approach to respond to zero-day worms in a signature independent fashion in a collaborative environment. A federation of collaborating peers share information about anomalies to estimate the presence of a worm and each one of them independently chooses the most cost-optimal response from a given set of responses. This technique is designed to work when the presence of a worm is uncertain. It is unique in that the response is dynamic and self-regulating based on the current environment conditions. Distributed Sequential Hypothesis Testing is used to estimate the extent of worm infection in the environment. Response is formulated as a Dynamic Programming problem with imperfect state information. We present a solution and evaluate it in the presence of an Internet worm attack for various costs of infections and response.

A major contribution of this paper is analytically formalizing the problem of optimal and cost-effective response to worms. The second contribution is an adaptive response design that minimizes the variety of worms that can be successful. This drives the attacker towards kinds of worms that can be detected by other means; which in itself is a success. Counter-intuitive results such as leaving oneself open to infections being the cheapest option in certain scenarios become apparent with our response model.

Keywords: Worms, Collaboration, Dynamic Programming, Control Theory.

1 Introduction

Computer worms are a serious problem. Particularly in a collaborative environment, where the perimeter is quite secure but there is some amount of trust and implicit security within the environment. Once a worm breaks the perimeter

---

[*] Corresponding Author.

R. Lippmann, E. Kirda, and A. Trachtenberg (Eds.): RAID 2008, LNCS 5230, pp. 231–250, 2008.

defense, it essentially has a free run within the collaborative environment. An enterprise environment is a typical example of a network with this 'crunchy on the outside – chewy on the inside' characteristic. In this paper, we try to leverage the collaboration to collectively defend against such worm attacks. Dealing with known worms is a solved problem – signatures to be used by Intrusion Prevention Systems(IPSs) are developed to prevent further infections, and patches are developed to fix vulnerabilities exploited by these worms. Dealing with unknown worms – worms that exploit zero-day vulnerabilities or vulnerabilities for which patches have either not been generated or not applied yet – is still a research question. Several ingenious proposals to detect them automatically exist. Many sophisticated counter measures such as automatic signature generation and distribution [17,13,16,20] and automatic patch generation to fix vulnerabilities [18] have also been developed.

Often times, even if automated, there is not much time to either generate or distribute signatures or patches. Other times, system administrators are skeptical about applying patches. During instances when response based on the above mentioned techniques are not feasible, the only option left is to either completely shut-down the vulnerable service or run it risking infection. It is usually preferred to shut-down the service briefly until a mitigating response is engineered manually.

However, making a decision becomes hard when one is not certain if there is really a worm, and if the service being offered is vulnerable to it. It is not desirable to shut-down a service only to realize later that such an action was unwarranted because there is no worm. However, suspending the service in an attempt to prevent infection is not considered bad. Intuitively, it is desired to suspend the service briefly until it is clear whether there is an attack or not. Balancing the consequences of providing the service risking infection against that of not providing the service is of the essence.

This paper captures this intuition and devises an algorithm using Dynamic Programming(DP) techniques to minimize the overall cost of response to worms. Cost is defined as some mathematical expression of an undesirable outcome.

These algorithms use information about anomalous events that are potentially due to a worm from other co-operating peers to choose optimal response actions for local application. Such response can be later rolled-back in response to changes to the environment such as a curtailed worm. Since peers decide to implement response independently, the response is completely decentralized.

We surprisingly found that in certain scenarios, leaving oneself open to infection by the worm might be the least expensive option. We also show that these algorithms do not need large amounts of information to make decisions. One of the key achievements here is that we use weak Intrusion Detection Systems(IDSs) as sensors that have high false positive rates. By corroborating alerts raised by them with other collaborating sensors, we are able to minimize the false positives and achieve better fidelity in detecting worms.

2   Dynamic Programming

This section provides a brief introduction to the theory behind Dynamic Programming [6]. DP as applied to the current problem balances the low costs presently associated with operating a system against the undesirability of high future costs. The basic model of such a system is dynamic and discrete with an associated cost that is additive over time. The evolution of such a system can be described as:

$$x_{k+1} = f_k(x_k, u_k, w_k), \quad k = 0, 1, \ldots, N-1 \; , \tag{1}$$

where k indexes discrete time, x_k is the state of the system and summarizes past information that is relevant for future optimization, u_k is the control or decision variable to be selected at time k, w_k is a random parameter, also called disturbance or noise depending on the context, N is the horizon or the number of times control is applied and f_k is the mechanism by which the state is updated. The cost incurred at time k is denoted by $g_k(x_k, u_k, w_k)$, which is a random function because it depends on w_k. The goal is to minimize the total *expected cost*

$$J_\pi(x_0) = \mathop{E}_{w_k} \left\{ g_N(x_N) + \sum_{k=0}^{N-1} g_k(x_k, u_k, w_k) \right\} \; .$$

This is achieved by finding a sequence of functions called the *policy* or *control law*, $\pi = \{\mu_0, \ldots, \mu_{N-1}\}$, where each $\mu_k(x_k) \to u_k$ when applied to the system takes it from state x_k to x_{k+1} and minimizes the total *expected cost*. In general, for a given π, we use $J_k(x_k)$ to denote the *cost-to-go* from state x_k at time k to the final state at time N.

Dynamic Programming Algorithm: The optimal total cost is given by $J_0(x_0)$ in the last step of the following algorithm, which proceeds backwards in time from period $N-1$ to period 0:

$$J_N(x_N) = g_N(x_N), \tag{2}$$

$$J_k(x_k) = \min_{u_k} \mathop{E}_{w_k} \left\{ g_k(x_k, u_k, w_k) + J_{k+1}(x_{k+1}) \right\}, \quad k = 0, 1, \ldots, N-1 \; . \tag{3}$$

2.1   Imperfect Information Problems

DP problems as described above have perfect information about the state of the system, x_k. Often, x_k cannot be determined accurately; only an estimate,

$$z_k = h_k(x_k, v_k) \; , \tag{4}$$

can be made, where h_k is a sensor that maps x_k and a random disturbance v_k, into an observation, z_k. Such problems are solved by reformulating them into a perfect state information problem by introducing an augmented state variable I_k, which is a vector of the past observations and controls applied.

$$I_{k+1} = (I_k, z_{k+1}, u_k), \quad k = 0, 1, \ldots, N-2 \; ,$$

$$I_0 = z_0 \; . \tag{5}$$

3 Response Formulation with Imperfect State Information

In this section we formulate the computer worm response problem as a DP problem with imperfect state information. We assume that there could be only one worm and that the worm is a random scanning worm. We also assume that there is a sensor, such as an IDS albeit not very accurate. This DP formulation tells us which control should be applied to minimize the costs incurred until the worm detection process is complete.

3.1 Problem Statement

System Evolution: Consider a machine that provides some service. This machine needs to be operated for N steps or N time units. This machine can be in one of two states, P or $\overline{P}$, corresponding to the machine being in proper(desired state) or improper(infected by a worm) state respectively. During the course of operating the machine, it goes from state P to $\overline{P}$ with a certain probability λ and remains in state P with a probability $\overline{\lambda} = (1-\lambda)$. If the machine enters state $\overline{P}$, it remains there with probability 1. The infectious force λ, is an unknown quantity and depends on how much of the Internet is infected with the worm, if at all a worm is present.

Sensor: The machine also has a *sensor*, which inspects the machine for worm infections. However, it cannot determine the exact state of the machine. Rather, it can only determine the state of a machine with a certain probability. There are two possible observations; denoted by G (good, probably not infected) and B(bad, probably worm infected). Alternatively, instead of infections, we can imagine that the *sensor* looks for infection attempts and anomalies. The outcome would then indicate that there is probably a worm on the Internet (B) or not (G) as opposed to whether the host machine is infected or not. It is this latter interpretation we adopt for the rest of this paper. For the time being, let us assume that the inspections happen proactively at random intervals and also when alerts are received from peers. We also assume that the *sensor*'s integrity is not affected by the worm.

Controller: The machine also includes a *controller* that can continue(C) or stop(S) operating the machine. The machine cannot change states by itself if it is stopped. Thus the *controller* can stop the machine to prevent a worm infection and start it when it deems it safe to operate the machine. There are certain costs involved with each of these actions under different conditions as described in the next paragraph. The controller takes each action so that the overall cost of operating the machine for N steps is minimized.

Costs: Continuing(C) to operate the machine when it is in state P costs nothing. It is the nominal. We incur a cost of τ_1 for each time step the machine is stopped(S) irrespective of whether it is infected or not, and a cost τ_2 for each step an infected machine is operated. One might argue that τ_1 and τ_2 should be

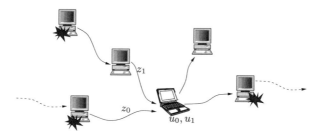

Fig. 1. Alert Sharing Protocol. The laptop is our machine of interest. It uses information, z_0 and z_1, from different chains to choose, actions, u_0 and u_1. It may or may not have seen an anomaly while the machines shown with a blast have seen an anomaly.

the same because an infected machine is as bad as a stopped machine. If that argument is true, the problem becomes trivial and it can be stated right away that the most cost effective strategy is to operate the machine uninterrupted until it is infected. On the contrary, we argue that operating an infected machine costs more as it can infect other machines also. Hence, $\tau_2 > \tau_1$.

Alert Sharing Protocol: Since a computer worm is a distributed phenomenon, inspection outcomes at one machine is a valid forecast of the outcome from a later inspection at another identical machine. (This is an assumption we make to develop the formulation and will be relaxed later on when we discuss a practical application.) Hence, a collection of such machines with identical properties seek to co-operate and share the inspection outcomes. Under this scheme, an inspection outcome at one machine is transmitted to another co-operating peer chosen randomly. The *controller* on the randomly chosen machine uses such received messages to select the optimal control to apply locally. This has the effect of a machine randomly polling several neighbors to know the state of the environment. This gives the uninfected machines an opportunity to take actions that prevent infection. Refer to Fig. 1. In addition to the inspection outcome, peers share information about the anomaly observed in what we call an *anomaly vector* – the structure, form and generation of which we leave undefined. Any two peers observing the same anomaly generate identical *anomaly vector*s.

Goal: Now, the problem is to determine the policy that minimizes the total expected cost of operating the machine for N time periods in an environment that could possibly be infected with a worm. DP problems are generally plagued with state space explosion with increasing number of stages to the horizon. However, since we solve the DP formulation of our problem offline, the value of N does not have any impact on the operational efficiency of the model. Moreover, DP problems can be solved approximately, or analytically for larger Ns significantly reducing the computational needs of the original formulation. The rest of this section develops the formulation for the current problem and provides a solution for $N = 3$. Computer generated results for larger Ns are presented and discussed in later sections.

3.2   Problem Formulation

The above description of the problem fits the general framework of Sect. 2.1, "Problems with imperfect state information." The state, control and observation variables take values as follows:

$$x_k \in \{P, \overline{P}\}, \quad u_k \in \{C, S\}, \quad z_k \in \{G, B\} \ .$$

The machine by itself does not transit from one state to another. Left to itself, it remains put. It is transferred from P to $\overline{P}$ only by a worm infection, a random process – an already infected victim chooses this machine randomly. The evolution of this system follows (1), and is shown in Fig. 2. The function f_k of (1) can be derived from Fig. 2 as follows:

$$\begin{aligned}
P(x_{k+1} = P \mid x_k = P, u_k = C) &= \overline{\lambda}, \\
P(x_{k+1} = \overline{P} \mid x_k = P, u_k = C) &= \lambda, \\
&\vdots \\
P(x_{k+1} = \overline{P} \mid x_k = \overline{P}, u_k = S) &= 1 \ .
\end{aligned} \tag{6}$$

The random disturbance, w_k is provided by λ and is rolled in x_k. λ is the infectious force, a function of the number of the machines infected on the Internet. Assuming the machine initially starts in state P, the probability distribution of x_0 is

$$P(x_0 = P) = \overline{\lambda}, \qquad P(x_0 = \overline{P}) = \lambda \ . \tag{7}$$

(This assumption is for exposition only. In practice, we do not have to know the initial state the machine starts in.) Recollect that the outcome of each inspection of the machine is an imperfect observation of the state of the system. Thus,

$$\begin{aligned}
P(z_k = G \mid x_k = \overline{P}) &= \mathrm{fn}, \\
P(z_k = B \mid x_k = \overline{P}) &= (1 - \mathrm{fn}), \\
P(z_k = G \mid x_k = P) &= (1 - \mathrm{fp}), \\
P(z_k = B \mid x_k = P) &= \mathrm{fp} \ ,
\end{aligned} \tag{8}$$

where fp and fn are properties of the *sensors* denoting the false positive and false negative (miss) rates.

Assuming the cost function remains the same regardless of time, the sub-script k can be dropped from g_k. We define the cost function as follows:

$$\begin{aligned}
g(P, C) &= 0, & g(\overline{P}, C) &= \tau_2, \\
g(P, S) &= g(\overline{P}, S) = \tau_1, \\
g(x_N) &= 0.
\end{aligned} \tag{9}$$

$g(x_N) = 0$ because u_N is chosen with accurate knowledge of the environment, (i.e) whether there is a worm or not. If there is a worm, $u_N = S$, else $u_N = C$.

Our problem now is to find functions $\mu_k(I_k)$ that minimize the total expected cost

$$\mathop{E}_{x_k, z_k} \left\{ g(x_N) + \sum_{k=0}^{N-1} g\big(x_k, \mu_k(I_k)\big) \right\} \ .$$

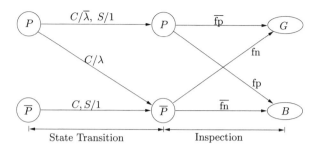

Fig. 2. The left half of the figure shows the state transition probabilities for each action. For example, the system goes from state P to P with a probability of $\overline{\lambda}$ when action C is applied. The right half of the figure shows the observation probabilities for each state. For example, when the system is in state P, the sensors output a G with a probability of $\overline{\text{fp}}$.

We now apply the DP algorithm to the augmented system (refer Sect. 2.1). It involves finding the minimum cost over the two possible actions, C and S, and has the form:

$$
J_k(I_k) = \min_{\{C,S\}} \Bigg[\Big(P(x_k = P \,|\, I_k, C) \cdot g(P,C) + P(x_k = \overline{P} \,|\, I_k, C) \cdot g(\overline{P},C) \Big)
$$
$$
+ \mathop{E}_{z_{k+1}} \Big\{ J_{k+1}(I_k, C, z_{k+1}) \,|\, I_k, C \Big\} ,
$$
$$
\Big(P(x_k = P \,|\, I_k, S) \cdot g(P,S) + P(x_k = \overline{P} \,|\, I_k, S) \cdot g(\overline{P},S) \Big)
$$
$$
+ \mathop{E}_{z_{k+1}} \Big\{ J_{k+1}(I_k, S, z_{k+1}) \,|\, I_k, S \Big\} \Bigg] \quad (10)
$$

where $k = 0, 1, \ldots N - 1$ and the terminal condition is $J_N(I_N) = 0$. Applying the costs (9), and noticing that $P(x_k = P \,|\, I_k, S) + P(x_k = \overline{P} \,|\, I_k, S)$ is the sum of probabilities of all elements in a set of exhaustive events, which is 1, we get

$$
J_k(I_k) = \min_{\{C,S\}} \Bigg[\tau_2 \cdot P(x_k = \overline{P} \,|\, I_k, C) + \mathop{E}_{z_{k+1}} \Big\{ J_{k+1}(I_k, C, z_{k+1}) \,|\, I_k, C \Big\} ,
$$
$$
\tau_1 + \mathop{E}_{z_{k+1}} \Big\{ J_{k+1}(I_k, S, z_{k+1}) \,|\, I_k, S \Big\} \Bigg] . \quad (11)
$$

This is the required DP formulation of response to worms. Next, we demonstrate a solution derivation to this formulation for $N = 3$.

3.3   Solution

Here we show a solution assuming that we expect to know with certainty about the presence of a worm at the receipt of the third message, that is, $N = 3$. The same procedure can be followed for larger Ns.

With that assumption, control u_2 can be determined without ambiguity. If the third message says there is a worm, we set $u_2 = S$, else we set it to C. This also means that the cost to go at that stage is

$$J_2(I_2) = 0 \ . \qquad \text{(Terminal Condition)}$$

Penultimate Stage: In this stage we determine the cost $J_1(I_1)$. Applying the terminal condition to the DP formulation (11), we get

$$J_1(I_1) = \min \left[\tau_2 \cdot P(x_1 = \overline{P} \mid I_1, C) , \ \tau_1 \right] \ . \qquad (12)$$

The probabilities $P(x_1 = \overline{P} | I_1, C)$ can be computed using Bayes' rule and (6–8), assuming the machine starts in state P. (See Sect. B for exposition.) The cost for each of the eight possible values of $I_1 = (z_0, z_1, u_0)$ under each possible control, $u_1 \in \{C, S\}$ is computed using (11). Then, the control with the smallest cost is chosen as the optimal one to apply for each z_1 observed. The *cost-to-go*, $J_1(I_1)$, thus calculated are used for the zeroth stage.

Stage 0: In this stage we determine the cost $J_0(I_0)$. We use (11) and values of $J_1(I_1)$ calculated during the previous stage to compute this cost. As before this cost is computed for each of the two possible values of $I_0 = (z_0) = \{G, B\}$, under each possible control, $u_1 = \{C, S\}$. Then, the control with the smallest cost is chosen as the optimal one to apply for the observed state of the machine. Thus we have,

$$J_0(I_0) = \min \left[\tau_2 \cdot P(x_0 = \overline{P} \mid I_0, C) + \underset{z_1}{E}\left\{ J_1(I_1) \mid I_0, C \right\} , \right.$$
$$\left. \tau_1 + \underset{z_1}{E}\left\{ J_1(I_1) \mid I_0, S \right\} \right] \ . \qquad (13)$$

The optimal cost for the entire operation is finally given by

$$J^* = P(G)J_0(G) + P(B)J_0(B) \ .$$

We implemented a program that can solve the above formulation for various values of $\lambda, \mathrm{fp},$ and fn. A sample rule-set generated by that program is given in Table 1. Armed with this solution, we now show a practical application.

4   A Practical Application

4.1   Optimal Policy

Table 1 shows the optimal policies for a given set of operational parameters. The table is read bottom up. At start, assuming the machine is in state P, the optimal action is to continue, C. In the next time step, stage 0, if the observation is B, the optimal action is to stop, S. If $z_0 = B$ is followed by $z_1 = G$, the optimal action is to operate the machine, C. This is denoted by the second line in

Table 1. An optimal policy table

$\lambda = 0.50,$	$\mathrm{fp} = 0.20,$	$\mathrm{fn} = 0.10$	
	$\tau_1 = 1,$	$\tau_2 = 2$	
	I_k	J_k	u_k
Stage 1	(G, G, S)	0.031	C
	(B, G, S)	0.720	C
	(G, B, S)	0.720	C
	(B, B, S)	1.000	S
	(G, G, C)	0.270	C
	(B, G, C)	1.000	S
	(G, B, C)	1.000	S
	(B, B, C)	1.000	S
Stage 0	(G)	0.922	C
	(B)	1.936	S
Start		1.480	C

stage 1. This shows that an undesirable response is rolled back when the environment is deemed not dangerous. In a practical application, such a table will be looked up for a given λ and observation to choose the optimal action. Note that the first, third, sixth and eighth states are unreachable because, for the given z_0, the control u_0 mentioned in the vector is never applied if the system operates in good faith.

4.2   Choosing λ

The value of λ varies with the extent of infection in the Internet. Given we are uncertain that there is a worm in the Internet, λ cannot be determined with any accuracy. Rather, only estimates can be made. Hence the distributed Sequential Hypothesis Testing developed earlier is used to estimate λ [9].

Given a sequence of observations $y = \{y_0, y_1, \ldots, y_n\}$, made by a sequence of other participating nodes, and two contradicting hypotheses that there is a worm on the Internet(H_1) and not(H_0), the former is chosen when the likelihood ratio $L(y)$ of these hypotheses is greater than a certain threshold η [9]. This threshold η is determined by the performance conditions required of the algorithm. Assuming the observations are independent, $L(y)$ and η are defined as follows:

$$L(y) = \prod_{i=1}^{n} \frac{P(y_i|H_1)}{P(y_i|H_0)}, \quad \eta = \frac{DD}{DF}, \tag{14}$$

where DD is the minimum desired detection rate and DF is the maximum tolerable false positive rate of the distributed Sequential Hypothesis Testing(dSHT) algorithm. We define each of the above probabilities as follows:

$$P(y_k = B \mid H_1) = [\lambda(1 - \mathrm{fn}) + (1 - \lambda)\,\mathrm{fp}],$$
$$P(y_k = G \mid H_1) = [(\lambda\,\mathrm{fn}) + (1 - \lambda)(1 - \mathrm{fp})],$$

$$P(y_k = B \mid H_0) = \text{fp} \,, \tag{15}$$
$$P(y_k = G \mid H_0) = (1 - \text{fp}) \ .$$

The first equation in the above set is the probability of observing a B given hypothesis H_1 is true. It is the sum of probability of getting infected (λ) times the probability of detection, and the probability of not getting infected $(1 - \lambda)$ times the probability of false positives. The others in (15) are defined similarly.

For a received sequence of observations, a node calculates $L(\boldsymbol{y})$ for several values of λ – say for ten different values in steps of 0.1 starting at 0.1. The lowest λ for which the $L(\boldsymbol{y})$ exceeds η is then taken as the current levels of infection and used in determining the optimal response. The reason for choosing discrete values of λ will be apparent shortly.

An observation at a node can be conveyed to another by transmitting the observation vector, $\boldsymbol{y} = \{y_0\}$. The recepient can add its own observation to this vector making it $\boldsymbol{y} = \{y_0, y_1\}$. Such a sequence accumulates information leading to larger vectors with each hop. Given $L(\boldsymbol{y})$ in (14) is essentially a digest of such vectors, no node has to transmit a whole vector. Instead, it suffices to transmit just one number, $L(\boldsymbol{y})$. A recepient can update the received $L(\boldsymbol{y})$ using (14), (15), and its own observations. It is indeed a conundrum to estimate λ using (15), which is a function of λ itself. This problem is solved as described in the previous paragraph – the lowest λ for which $L(\boldsymbol{y})$ exceeds η is taken as the current operating λ.

In operational practice, a policy in the form of a table is calculated offline for several candidate values of λ. Each row in these tables gives a u_k for a given I_k. For each new λ estimated, the corresponding table is consulted to choose u_k given I_k, where I_k is the node's own past observations and corresponding actions. Thus, each node only receives a likelihood ratio of the worm's presence from its peers and also has to remember only its own I_k. Limiting the number of such tables is the reason for choosing discrete λs in the preceeding paragraphs.

4.3   Larger Ns

As N increases, the dimensions of I_k increases, which in turn increases the number of the calcuations involved exponentially. This problem can be overcome by reducing I_k to smaller dimensions containing only the *Sufficient Statistics* yet summarizing all essential contents of I_k as far as control is concerned. There are many different functions that can serve as *sufficient statitics*. The one we use here is the conditional probability distribution $P_{x_k \mid I_k}$ of the state x_k, given the information vector I_k [6]. Discrete-time stochastic systems can be described by the evolution

$$P_{x_{k+1} \mid I_{k+1}} = \Phi_k \left(P_{x_k \mid I_k}, u_k, z_{k+1} \right), \tag{16}$$

where Φ_k is a function that estimates the probalistic state of the system $P_{x_k \mid I_k}$ based on $P_{x_{k-1} \mid I_{k-1}}$, z_k and u_{k-1}, and can be determined from the data of the problem [5]. Figure 3 explains this concept. The actuator $\overline{\mu}_k$ then selects the optimal response based on $P_{x_k \mid I_k}$.

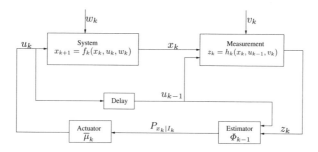

Fig. 3. The controller split into an *Estimator* and an *Actuator*. The *Estimator* Φ_{k-1} estimates the probabilistic state of the system $P_{x_k|I_k}$ while the *Actuator* $\bar{\mu}_k$ picks the appropriate control u_k.

This re-formulation makes it easy to apply the response model for larger Ns. We implement this model and evaluate it in a simulation. The evaluation and the results are discussed in the next section.

5 Evaluation

The sufficient statistics formulation discussed in the previous section was implemented and evaluated with a discrete event simulation. The simulation consisted of a world of 1000 participants with 10% of the machines being vulnerable. We set the number of stages to operate the machine, $N = 4$ to calculate the rule-sets. Note that $N = 4$ is used only to calculate the rule-sets but the machines can be operated for any number of steps. N is essentially the number of past observations and actions that each machine remembers. The local IDSes were set to have a false positive and false negative rates of 0.1. These characteristics of the local IDS is used to calculate the probability of infection, λ with a desired worm detection rate of 0.9 and failure rate of 0.1. In all the following experiments, we used a random scanning worm that scans for vulnerable machines once every unit-time.

5.1 Experiments

Parameters of Evaluation: A set of experiments was designed to understand the effect of various parameters on the effectiveness of the model in controlling the spread of the worm. The only free variable we have here is the ratio τ_2/τ_1. There is no one particular parameter that can measure or describe the effectiveness of the response model. Rather, the effectiveness is described by the number of vulnerable machines that are not infected and of those the number that provide service, i. e. in state C.

Algorithm: The algorithm for the discrete-event simulation is as follows. At each time cycle.

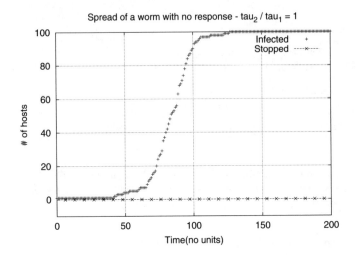

Fig. 4. No machines are stopped when the cost of being infected is the same as cost of shutting down the machine. fp = fn = 0.1, $DD = 0.9, DF = 0.1$

- all infected machines attempt one infection,
- all machines that had an alert to share, share the likelihood ratio that there is a worm on the Internet with another randomly chosen node,
- and all vulnerable machines that received an alert earlier take a response action based on the information received and the current local observations.

Results: In the first experiment, we want to make sure that we have a worm that behaves as normal random scanning worm and validate the response model for

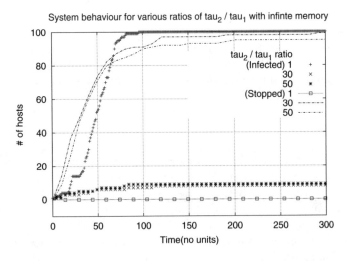

Fig. 5. When nodes are set to remember infection attempts forever, they never back-off their defensive posture. Once entered the S state, a machine stays there. fp = fn = 0.1, $DD = 0.9, DF = 0.1$.

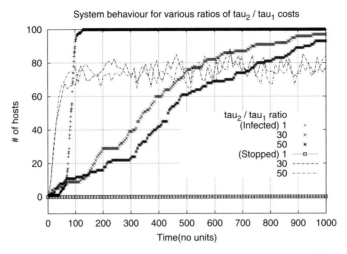

Fig. 6. Higher costs of being infected invoke stricter responses. fp = fn = $0.1, DD =$ $0.9, DF = 0.1$.

the degenerate cases. We verify this by providing no response. This response can be achieved by setting the cost ratio to 1 – the cost of stopping the service is the same as getting infected. In this scenario, we expect the response model not to take any defensive measures against suspected infection attempts. As expected, we see in Fig. 4, that none of the machines are stopped (S state). The worm spreads as it would spread when there is no response in place. This validates our worm and also our response model.

As another sanity check we set the machines to remember infection attempts forever. Under this policy, once a machine enters the S state, it remains in that state forever. We see that in this case (Fig. 5) the number of machines infected are very low except when $\tau_2/\tau_1 = 1$.

In the next experiment, we try to understand the behavior of our response model in various situations. Since the only free variable is the ratio τ_2/τ_1, we repeat the previous experiment with various values for that ratio. The results for this set of experiments is shown in Fig. 6. This graph shows behavior of our response model in three different tests. There are two different curves for each test indicating the number of vulnerable machines being infected and the number of machines that are stopped. We can see that when the ratio is 1, the number of machines that are in S state is 0. As the ratio τ_2/τ_1 rises, the response becomes stricter. We see that the number of machines in the stopped(S) state is higher when the cost of being infected is higher. Also the worms spreads significantly slower than without any response in place or with a lower τ_2/τ_1 ratio.

5.2   Effects of Increasing N

The experiments shown earlier in this section were all conducted with $N = 4$. An interesting question to ask here, "What happens if we increase the value of

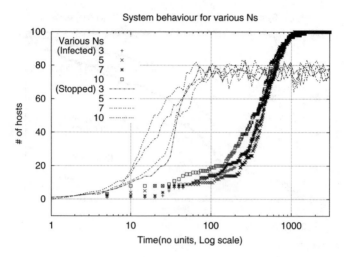

Fig. 7. Larger Ns do not contribute much to improve performance due to the small number of dimensions to the state, $x_k \in \{P, \overline{P}\}$. fp = fn = $0.1, DD = 0.9, DF = 0.1$

N?". Fig. 7 shows the performance of the system for various values of N while holding the ratio of τ_2/τ_1 constant at 30. The set of sigmoidal curves that increase monotonically trace the growth of the worm, while the other set of curves trace the number of nodes that are shut-down at any given instant. We notice that there is no appreciable slowing of the worm with increased values of N – all the worm growth curves are bunched up together. This is due to the small number of dimensions to the state, $x_k \in \{P, \overline{P}\}$. A larger observation space does not contribute much to improve the performance of the system.

6   Conclusion

This section concludes this paper by reflecting on the strengths and weaknesses of the approach discussed so far. Assumptions are identified. Arguments are made for the choice of certain design and evaluation decisions. Where appropriate, future directions are provided to address the limitations identified.

6.1   Limitations and Redress

There are several topics in this paper yet to be addressed. There are issues to be addressed from three different perspectives – one, problems that would arise during the practical adoption of this model; two, in the evaluation; and three, in the model itself.

Adoption Impediments: This is a collaborative response model. As with any collaborative effort, there is a host of issues such as privacy, confidentiality, non-repudiation, etc, that will need to be addressed during practical adoption. Thankfully, these are issues for which there are solutions available already through cryptography and IPSEC. In a co-operative or collaborative environment, we expect these issues to be either easily resolved or already addressed. Regardless, co-operation amongst various entities on the Internet such as amongst different corporate networks pose more legal, political, and economic problems than technical. In such cases where sharing anomaly information with networks outside of the corporation is not feasible, applying this response model within the corporate network itself can provide valuable protection.

Assigning realistic values to τ_1 and τ_2 is another major impediment to adoption. However, that is a separate problem requiring independent study. There are indeed prior work that attempt to assign costs to various responses that can be used [14,4]. Whereas, this paper focusses on optimizing those costs for overall operation of a system.

Evaluation Issues: Integral and faithful scaling down of the Internet is a difficult problem [22], which makes evaluating worm defenses more so [8]. At one extreme we have realistic evaluation possible only on the Internet, which is infeasible. At the other extreme, we have pure mathematical models. In between these two extremes, we have simulations such as the one used in this paper and emulation as used in one of our previous studies for worm detection [9].

With the availability of data about Internet traffic during worm outbreaks, it may be possible to evaluate the defense model on a network testbed such as Emulab [23] or DETER [3] by replaying the traffic for a scaled down version of the Internet. Such an experiment would need the available data to be carefully replayed with tools such as TCP Replay,TCP Opera [12], etc. This is a future task. Nevertheless, such emulation experiments can only scale up to a certain level and after that we would have to resort to mathematics or simulations to extrapolate the results to Internet scales.

We avoid emulation experiments by choice. Emulations can provide details about exploit behavior, traffic patterns, etc. As important as those issues are, they lie outside the scope of our present interest and are considered for later study. Focus for this paper is primarily on the cost optimization models. As mentioned in the previous paragraph, experiment population sizes are limited in emulations while simulations can support larger number of nodes. Given that stochastic processes are involved in our model, we need a large population to achieve fidelity in results. Consequently, simulations form a natural choice for our experiments.

An issue to be studied is the behavior of this model in the face of false alarms and isolated intrusions. For example, consider one and only participant raising an alarm for an isolated event and several other participants choosing the S control. We would like to know when these participants would apply the C control. Trivially, we can set a time-out for the defense to be turned-off. However, the time-out should be chosen carefully and probably be dynamic to guard against exposing oneself to slow-worm attacks.

In our experiments we have showed only one worm operating at a time. While this might seem like a limitation of the model, it is not. As mentioned in Sect. 3.1, there is an *anomaly vector* associated with each suspected worm incident. When multiple worms operate simultaneously, each will be associated with a different *anomaly vector*. In operational practice, we expect a different process to be associated with each *anomaly vector* so multiple worms can be handled independently and concurrently.

Limitations and Extensions to the Model: When there is a cost to sampling packets, this model can be extended to optimally stop the sampling process and declare either that there is a worm or that there is no worm – essentially a distributed worm detector. Interestingly, this extension would lead us to the distributed Sequential Hypothesis Testing that we discussed in our previous paper [9].

One of the assumptions in our model is that the worm is a random scanning worm. This model will not work against more intelligent worms such as hit-list or flash worms but will likely be moderately successful against sub-net scanning worms [19]. Evaluating and extending the model against such other kinds of worms is a future work.

Integrity of the sensors, and absence of wilful malfeasance are assumed in our model. After all, in the real world we do assume the safety and security of the firewalls and IDSes we use. Nevertheless, if a few of the sensors are compromised by the attackers, we expect the stochastic nature of our model to act as a cushion absorbing some of the ill-effects. This needs to be evaluated. If numerous sensors are affected, our assumption about collaboration is not valid any more and the results are undefined.

Actions such as C and S if applied frequently could lead to a very unstable system. We need to evaluate this factor in light of ambient anomaly levels in different environments. This is a problem with the model itself. However, this can be alleviated to some extent during adoption in various ways. For example, the set of response options, $\{C, S\}$, can be made larger by introducing several levels of reduced functionality. This will however increase the complexity of the DP formulation but can be tolerated as we solve the formulation offline.

When all participants behave identically each participant knows exactly how the others will behave. In such a scenario, each one can make a better decision about the optimal control to be applied taking into account the others' behavior. For example, if participant A determines that the optimal policy to be applied is S, it now knows that all other participants will also apply the same control. Then, there is no need for A to apply S. Instead A could apply C as there is no opportunity for a worm to spread when all others participants are stopped. The problem now enters the realm of *game theory*.

6.2   Strengths

One question that needs to be answered for any defensive technique is this: "If the attacker knows about the approach being used for defense, will s/he be able to write a new generation of worms that can overcome the defense?"

There are two different goals that an attacker with knowledge about our system can try to achieve. One, try to circumvent the defense and spread the worm. Two, trick the defense into over-reacting.

The second goal cannot be achieved because of the dynamic and self-regulating nature of our approach, which is based on the current environmental conditions as depicted in Fig. 3. The attacker may force our system to react to an initial stimulus that is not a true worm, but once the stimulus has reduced, the defence pulls back too. If the sensors are compromised, however, the results are undefined as mentioned in the previous section. However, compromising sensors are extraneous to the model and is not a tenable argument against the model.

To achieve the first goal, the worm needs to either spread very slowly such that information about anomalous incidents are forgotten by the participants, or attack pre-selected victims that may not be alerted by its peers. However, since the alerts are shared with randomly chosen peers while the worm is spreading, there can be no effective pre-selection that can overcome the defense. Whereas a slow spreading worm might be successful to a certain extent.

Nevertheless, we believe that a slow spreading worm can be identified by other means such as manual trouble-shooting prompted by the ill-effects of the worm; unless the worm installs a time-bomb that is set to trigger after the worm has spread to most vulnerable nodes. We also believe that such slow worms will be circumvented by routine maintenance patches – most worms we know so far have exploited only known, but unpatched, vunlerabilities.

Moreover, there is a heightened awarness about security issues amongst the information technology community than ever before. Laws related to data security are being tightened and enforced more vigorosly than in the past. Patch generation and deployment techniques have advanced tremendously recently. In such an environment, we expect that steps to patch or workaround known vulnerabilities will be taken with more urgency than ever before effectively thwarting extremely slow worms discussed in the preceeding paragraphs.

Thus, the worm has a very narrow window between spreading too slow and spreading too fast – the window where our response mechanism works to thwart the worm. In conclusion, to answer the question above, knowledge of our approach does not provide much value to the attacker or new generation of worms.

6.3   Summary

This paper presents a novel control-theoretic approach toward worm response. We showed how to formalize a response strategy as a Dynamic Programming problem and solve this formulation to yield a practically applicable response solution. This formalization has been one of the key contributions of this paper. We show how this model severely curtails the worm options available to attackers. Several interesting directions in which this work could be extended are identified.

Acknowledgments. We would like to thank Branislav Kveton of Intel Research and Jed Crandall of University of New Mexico for providing early critique on the work.

References

1. Anagnostakis, K.G., et al.: A cooperative immunization system for an untrusting internet. In: Proc. of IEEE ICON, October 2003, pp. 403–408 (2003)
2. Anagnostakis, K.G., Greenwald, M.B., Ioannidis, S., Keromytis, A.D.: Robust reactions to potential day-zero worms through cooperation and validation. In: Katsikas, S.K., López, J., Backes, M., Gritzalis, S., Preneel, B. (eds.) ISC 2006. LNCS, vol. 4176, pp. 427–442. Springer, Heidelberg (2006)
3. Bajcsy, R., et al.: Cyber defense technology networking and evaluation. Commun. of the ACM 47(3), 58–61 (2004)
4. Balepin, I., Maltsev, S., Rowe, J., Levitt, K.: Using specification-based intrusion detection for automated response. In: Vigna, G., Krügel, C., Jonsson, E. (eds.) RAID 2003. LNCS, vol. 2820, pp. 136–154. Springer, Heidelberg (2003)
5. Bertsekas, D.P., Shreve, S.E.: Stochastic Optimal Control: The Discrete Time Case. Academic Press, N.Y (1978)
6. Bertsekas, D.P.: Dynamic Programming and Optimal Control, 3rd edn., vol. 1. Athena Scientific (2005)
7. Cai, M., Hwang, K., Kwok, Y.-K., Song, S., Chen, Y.: Collaborative internet worm containment. IEEE Security and Privacy 4(3), 34–43 (2005)
8. Cheetancheri, S.G., et al.: Towards a framework for worm defense evaluation. In: Proc. of the IPCCC Malware Workshop on Swarm Intelligence, Phoenix (April 2006)
9. Cheetancheri, S.G., Agosta, J.M., Dash, D.H., Levitt, K.N., Rowe, J., Schooler, E.M.: A distributed host-based worm detection system. In: Proc. of SIGCOMM LSAD, pp. 107–113. ACM Press, New York (2006)
10. Costa, M., et al.: Vigilante: end-to-end containment of internet worms. In: Proc. of the SOSP, pp. 133–147. ACM Press, New York (2005)
11. Dash, D., Kveton, B., Agosta, J.M., Schooler, E., Chandrashekar, J., Bachrach, A., Newman, A.: When gossip is good: Distributed probabilistic inference for detection of slow network intrusions. In: Proc. of AAAI, AAAI Press, Menlo Park (2006)
12. Hong, S.-S., Felix Wu, S.: On Interactive Internet Traffic Replay. In: Valdes, A., Zamboni, D. (eds.) RAID 2005. LNCS, vol. 3858, pp. 247–264. Springer, Heidelberg (2006)
13. Kim, H.-A., Karp, B.: Autograph: Toward automated, distributed worm signature detection. In: Proc. of the USENIX Security Symposium (2004)
14. Lee, W., Fan, W., Miller, M., Stolfo, S.J., Zadok, E.: Towards cost-sensitive modeling for intrusion detection and response. J. of Computer Security 10(1,2) (2002)
15. Malan, D.J., Smith, M.D.: Host-based detection of worms through peer-to-peer cooperation. In: Proc. of the WORM, pp. 72–80. ACM Press, New York (2005)
16. Newsome, J., Karp, B., Song, D.: Polygraph: Automatically generating signatures for polymorphic worms. In: Proc. of the IEEE Symposium on Security and Privacy, pp. 226–241. IEEE, Los Alamitos (2005)
17. Singh, S., Estan, C., Varghese, G., Savage, S.: Automated worm fingerprinting. In: Proc. of OSDI, San Francisco, CA (December 2004)
18. Sidiroglou, S., Keromytis, A.D.: Countering network worms through automatic patch generation. IEEE Security and Privacy 3(6), 41–49 (2005)
19. Staniford, S., Paxson, V., Weaver, N.: How to Own the Internet in Your Spare Time. In: Proc. of the Summer USENIX Conf., Berkeley, August 2002. USENIX (2002)

20. Wang, K., Cretu, G., Stolfo, S.J.: Anomalous payload-based worm detection and signature generation. In: Proc. of RAID. ACM Press, New York (2005)
21. Wang, K., Stolfo, S.J.: Anomalous payload-based network intrusion detection. In: Proc. of RAID, September 2004. ACM Press, New York (2004)
22. Weaver, N., Hamadeh, I., Kesidis, G., Paxson, V.: Preliminary results using scale-down to explore worm dynamics. In: Proc. of WORM, pp. 65–72. ACM Press, New York (2004)
23. White, B., et al.: An integrated experimental environment for distributed systems and networks. In: OSDI, Boston, December 2002, pp. 255–270. USENIX (2002)
24. Zou, C.C., Gao, L., Gong, W., Towsley, D.: Monitoring and early warning for internet worms. In: Proc. of the CCS, pp. 190–199. ACM Press, New York (2003)

A   DP Example

We provide a short, classical inventory control example to help readers unfamiliar with DP to formulate a DP problem. This is an example from Bertsekas [6].

Consider the problem of stocking store shelves for N days. The state of the system is denoted by the quantity (x_k) of a certain item available on the store shelves at the beginning of a day. Shelves are stocked(with u_k units) at day break while demand(w_k) for the item is stochastic during the day. Both w_k and u_k are non-negative. There is no change overnight. It is clear that this system evolves according to:

$$x_{k+1} = \max(0, x_k + u_k - w_k).$$

While there is an upper bound of, say, 2 units on the stock that can be on the shelves, demand in excess of stocks is lost business. Say, the storage costs for a day is $(x_k + u_k - w_k)^2$ implying penalty for both lost business and for excess inventory at the end of the day. Assuming the purchase cost incurred by the store is 1 per unit stock, the operating cost per day is

$$g_k(x_k, u_k, w_k) = u_k + (x_k + u_k - w_k)^2.$$

The terminal cost at the end of N days is assumed to be 0. Say the planning horizon N is 3 days and the initial stock $x_0 = 0$. Say, the demand w_k has the same probability distribution for all three days and is given by

$$p(w_k = 0) = 0.1 \qquad p(w_k = 1) = 0.7 \qquad p(w_k = 2) = 0.2.$$

The problem now is to determine the *optimal policy* for reordering of stocks so as to minimize the total operational cost. Applying (3), the DP algorithm for this problem is

$$J_k(x_k) = \min_{\substack{0 \le u_k \le 2-x_k \\ u_k=0,1,2}} \mathop{E}_{w_k} \left\{ u_k + (x_k + u_k - w_k)^2 + J_{k+1}(x_{k+1}) \right\}, \qquad (17)$$

where $k = 0, 1, 2$, and x_k, u_k, w_k can take the values of $0, 1, 2$ while the terminal condition $J_3(x_3) = 0$.

Now starting with $J_3(x_3) = 0$ and solving (17) backwards for $J_2(x_k)$, $J_1(x_k)$ and $J_0(x_k)$ for $k = 0, 1, 2$, we find that the *optimal policy* is to reorder one unit if the shelves are empty and nothing otherwise.

B   Applying Bayes' Rule

The probabilities, $P(x_1 = \overline{P} \mid I_1, C)$ for (12) can be calculated using Bayes' rule and (6–8). We show the calculations for one of them here for exposition.

$$P(x_1 = \overline{P} \mid G, G, S)$$

$$= \frac{P(x_1 = \overline{P}, G, G, \mid S)}{P(G, G, \mid S)}$$

$$= \frac{\displaystyle\sum_{i=\{P,\overline{P}\}} P(G|x_0 = i) \cdot P(x_0 = i) \cdot P(G|x_1 = \overline{P}) \cdot P(x_1 = \overline{P}|x_0 = i, u_0 = S)}{\displaystyle\sum_{i=\{P,\overline{P}\}} \sum_{j=\{P,\overline{P}\}} P(G|x_0 = i) \cdot P(x_0 = i) \cdot P(G|x_1 = j) \cdot P(x_1 = j|x_0 = i, u_0 = S)}$$

$$= \frac{(\overline{fp} \cdot \overline{\lambda} \cdot fn \cdot 0) + (fn \cdot \lambda \cdot fn \cdot 1)}{(\overline{fp} \cdot \overline{\lambda} \cdot \overline{fp} \cdot 1) + (\overline{fp} \cdot \overline{\lambda} \cdot fn \cdot 0) + (fn \cdot \lambda \cdot \overline{fp} \cdot 0) + (fn \cdot \lambda \cdot fn \cdot 1)}$$

On the Limits of Payload-Oblivious Network Attack Detection

M. Patrick Collins[1] and Michael K. Reiter[2]

[1] RedJack
michael.collins@redjack.com[*]
[2] Department of Computer Science,
University of North Carolina at Chapel Hill
reiter@cs.unc.edu

Abstract. We introduce a methodology for evaluating network intrusion detection systems using an *observable attack space*, which is a parameterized representation of a type of attack that can be observed in a particular type of log data. Using the observable attack space for log data that does not include payload (*e.g.*, NetFlow data), we evaluate the effectiveness of five proposed detectors for bot harvesting and scanning attacks, in terms of their ability (even when used in conjunction) to deter the attacker from reaching his goals. We demonstrate the ranges of attack parameter values that would avoid detection, or rather that would require an inordinately high number of false alarms in order to detect them consistently.

Keywords: network intrusion detection, ROC curve, evaluation.

1 Introduction

We address the problem of evaluating network intrusion detection systems, specifically against scan and harvesting attacks. In the context of this work, a harvesting attack is a mass exploitation where an attacker initiates communications with multiple hosts in order to control and reconfigure them. This type of automated exploitation is commonly associated with worms, however, modern bot software often includes automated buffer-overflow and password exploitation attacks against local networks[1]. In contrast, in a scanning attack, the attacker's communication with multiple hosts is an attempt to determine what services they are running; *i.e.*, the intent is reconnaissance.

While harvesting attacks and scanning may represent different forms of attacker *intent* (*i.e.*, reconnaissance vs. host takeover), they can appear to be similar phenomena in traffic logs. More specifically, a single host, whether scanning

---

[*] This work was done while the author was affiliated with the CERT/NetSA group at the Software Engineering Institute, Carnegie Mellon University.

[1] A representative example of this class of bot is the Gaobot family, which uses a variety of propagation methods including network shares, buffer overflows and password lists. A full description is available at http://www.trendmicro.com/vinfo/virusencyclo/default5.asp?VName=WORM_AGOBOT.GEN.

R. Lippmann, E. Kirda, and A. Trachtenberg (Eds.): RAID 2008, LNCS 5230, pp. 251–270, 2008.
© Springer-Verlag Berlin Heidelberg 2008

or harvesting, will open communications to an unexpectedly large number of addresses within a limited timeframe. This behavior led to Northcutt's observation that in the absence of payload—either due to the form of log data, encryption or simply a high connection failure rate—methods for detecting these attacks tend to be threshold-based [19]. That is, they raise alarms after identifying some phenomenon that exceeds a threshold for normal behavior.

Historically, such IDS have been evaluated purely as alarms. Lippmann *et al.* [16] established the standard for IDS evaluation in their 1998 work on comparing IDS data. To compare intrusion detectors, they used ROC curves to compare false positive and false negative rates among detectors. Since then, the state of the practice for IDS evaluation and comparison has been to compare IDS' ROC curves [9].

The use of ROC curves for IDS evaluation has been criticized on several grounds. For our purposes, the most relevant is the *base rate fallacy* described by Axelsson [2]. Axelsson observes that a low relative false positive rate can result in a high number of actual false positives when a test is frequently exercised. For NIDS, where the test frequency may be thousands or tens of thousands of per day, a false positive rate as low as 1% may still result in hundreds of alarms.

In this paper, we introduce an alternative method of evaluating IDS that focuses on an IDS' capacity to frustrate an attacker's goals. In order to do so, we develop a model for evaluating IDS that captures the attacker's payoff over an *observable attack space*. The observable attack space represents a set of attacks an attacker can conduct as observed by a particular logging system. The role of logging in the observable attack space is critical; for example, NetFlow, the logging system used in this paper, does not record payload. As such, for this paper, we define an observable attack space that classifies attacks by the attacker's *aggressiveness* (the number of addresses to which they communicate in a sample period) and their *success* (the probability that a communication opened to an address actually contacts something).

To evaluate the payoff, we construct a *detection surface*, which is the probability of detection over the observable attack space, and then apply a *payoff function* to this detection surface. The payoff function is a function representing the rate at which an attacker achieves the strategic goal of that attack, which is either occupying hosts (in a harvesting attack) or scouting network composition (in a scanning attack).

We use the payoff function to evaluate the impact of various IDS on attacker strategy. We can model payoff as a function of the number of viable hosts in a network that an attacking bot communicates with — the more hosts a bot can contact without being detected, the higher his payoff. We show in this paper that several methods which are good at raising alarms primarily identify low-payoff attacks; with these detectors, an attacker can achieve a high payoff simply by limiting his behavior.

By combining detection surfaces with a payoff function, we are able to compare IDS with greater insight about their relative strengths and weaknesses. In particular, we are able to focus on the relationship between detection capacity and attacker payoff. Instead of asking what kind of false positive rate we get for a specific true positive rate, we are able to relate false positive rates to the attacker goals. By doing so, we are able to determine how high a false positive rate we must tolerate in order to prevent an attacker from, say, substantially compromising a network via a harvesting attack. Our work therefore extends the ROC framework into a model of the attacker's own goals. By doing so, we can reframe questions of IDS designs by evaluating their impact on attacker behavior, on the grounds that a rational attacker will attempt to maximize payoff.

Using this approach, we compare the efficacy of five different detection techniques: client degree (*i.e.*, number of addresses contacted); protocol graph size and protocol graph largest component size [6]; server address entropy [15]; and Threshold Random Walk [11]. We train these systems using traffic traces from a large (larger than /8) network. Using this data, we demonstrate the configurations of aggressiveness and success rate with which an attack will go undetected by any of these techniques. Furthermore, we show that when configured to be sufficiently sensitive to counter attackers' goals, these anomaly detection systems will result in more than ten false alarms per hour, even when alarms are limited to occur only once per 30-second interval.

To summarize, the contributions of this paper are the following. First, we introduce a new methodology for evaluating NIDS that do not utilize payload. Second, we apply this methodology to evaluate several attack detection methods previously in the literature, using data from a very large network. And third, we demonstrate via this evaluation the limits that these techniques face in their ability to prevent attackers from reaching harvesting or scanning goals.

The remainder of this paper is structured as follows. §2 is a review of relevant work in IDS evaluation and anomaly detection. §3 describes the IDS that we evaluate in this paper, and how we configure them for analysis. §4 describes the observable attack space and detection surface. §5 describes the first of our two attack scenarios, in this case the acquisition of hosts by an attacker with a hit list. §6 describes the second scenario: reconnaissance by attackers scanning networks. §7 concludes this work.

2   Previous Work

Researchers have conducted comparative IDS evaluations in both the host-based and network-based domains. In the host-based domain, Tan and Maxion [25,17] developed an evaluation methodology for comparing the effectiveness of multiple host-based IDS. Of particular importance in their methodology is the role of the data that an IDS can actually analyze, an idea further extended in Killourhy *et al.*'s work on a defense-centric taxonomy [13]. The methods of Tan and Maxion and of Killourhy *et al.* informed our experimental methodology and the concept of an observable attack space. However, their approach is focused on host-based IDS and they consequently work with a richer dataset then we believe feasible for NIDS.

A general approach to evaluating IDS was proposed by Cárdenas *et al.* [4], who developed a general cost-based model for evaluating IDS based on the work of Gaffney and Ulvila [8] and Stolfo *et al.* [24]. However, these approaches all model cost from a defender-centric viewpoint — the defensive mechanism is assumed to have no impact on the attacker. In contrast, our models treat the attacker as economically rational, meaning that the attacker attempts to maximize payoff within the rules given by the model.

The general problem of NIDS evaluation was first systematically studied by Lippmann *et al.* [16]. Lippmann's comparison first used ROC curves to measure the comparative effectiveness of IDS. The ROC-based approach has been critiqued on multiple grounds [18,9,2]. Our evaluation model is derived from these critiques, specifically Axelsson's [2] observations on the base-rate fallacy. Our work uses a ROC-based approach (specifically, comparing Type I and Type II errors) as a starting point to convert the relative error rates into payoffs.

3   IDS Construction and Training

In the context of this work, an *IDS* is an anomaly detection system that compares the current state of a network against a model of that network's state developed from historical data. In this section, we describe our candidate IDS, and our method for training and configuring them. This section is divided as follows: §3.1 describes the raw data, §3.2 describes the types of IDS used, and §3.3 describes the detection thresholds used for our IDS.

3.1   Raw Data

Every IDS in this paper is trained using a common data source over a common period of time. The source data used in this paper consists of unsampled NetFlow records[2] generated by internal routers in a large (in excess of 16 million distinct IP address) network. For training and evaluation, we use SSH traffic.

NetFlow records approximate TCP sessions by grouping packets into *flows*, sequences of identically addressed packets that occur within a timeout of each other [5]. NetFlow records contain size and timing information, but no payload. For the purposes of this paper, we treat NetFlow records as tuples of the form (clntip, srvip, succ, stime).

The elements of this tuple are derived from the fields available in CISCO NetFlow. The clntip, srvip, succ and stime fields refer, respectively, to the client address, server address, whether a session was successful, and the start time for the session. Since SSH is TCP based, we rely on the port numbers recorded in the original flow record both for protocol identification and classifying the role a particular address played in the flow. Any flow which is sent to or from TCP port 22 is labeled an SSH flow, srvip is the address corresponding to that port

---

[2] CISCO Systems, "CISCO IOS NetFlow Datasheet", http://www.cisco.com/en/US/ products/ps6601/products_data_sheet0900aecd80173f71.html, last fetched October 8th, 2007.

and clntip the other address[3]. stime, the start time, is derived directly from the corresponding value in the flow record, and is the time at which the recording router observed the flow's earliest packet.

The succ element is a binary-valued descriptor of whether the recorded flow describes a legitimate TCP session. succ is 0 when the flow describes a TCP communication that was not an actual session (e.g., the target communicated with a nonexistent host), 1 when the flow describes a real exchange between a client and a server.

succ is an inferred property in the sense that it can be truly determined only by the receiving host — a sufficiently perverse attacker could generate one side of a session without the others' involvement. *In situ*, we can approximate succ using other flow properties, such as the number of packets in the flow or TCP flag combinations. In our work on IDS training [7], we approximate succ by setting it to 1 when a flow has 4 or more packets, on the grounds that a TCP session has at least 3 packets of overhead. Other methods for calculating succ include looking for indicators such as total payload, the presence of ACK flags, or aggregate measures such as Binkley and Singh's TCP work weight [3].

In our simulations we generate the succ values as part of the process of generating attack flows. During the simulations, attackers choose their targets from a hit list generated from the training data; the attack's success rate determines how many addresses come from this hit list, and how many addresses are chosen from a pool of dark addresses. For flows communicating with the hit list, succ = 1, and for flows communicating with the pool of dark addresses, succ = 0.

IDS properties are generated using 30 second (s) samples of traffic data. We refer to a distinct sample as a *log file*, Λ, consisting of all the flows $\lambda_1 \ldots \lambda_l$ whose stime values occur in the same 30s period. The use of 30s periods comes from our previous work on protocol graphs [6].

3.2 IDS State Variables

In the context of this paper, an IDS is a threshold-based alarm that triggers if a value derived from a log file Λ exceeds a threshold derived from a set of training data. Each IDS in this paper is based around a single *state variable* which, when evaluated against a log file produces a scalar *state value*. For this paper, we evaluate the state of a log file using five distinct state variables: g, c, h, d and r. Each state variable is used by one IDS; we will refer to each IDS by its state variable (e.g., "g is an IDS").

$g(\Lambda)$ and $c(\Lambda)$ are, respectively, the total graph size and the largest component size of a *protocol graph* constructed from Λ. A protocol graph, described in our previous work on hit-list detection, is an undirected graph constructed from a log of traffic for a single protocol over a limited observation period [6]. In a protocol graph, the nodes represent hosts communicating using that protocol, and the links represent that a communication between these two hosts happened during

---

[3] We constrain the flows used in this paper to flows which used an ephemeral port between 1024 and 5000.

that time. In a protocol graph, the graph size is equivalent to the total number of hosts communicating using a particular protocol. The largest component size is the size of the largest connected component of the graph.

$h(\Lambda)$ is the entropy of server addresses in Λ. This metric is derived from work by Lakhina *et al.* [15] on mining traffic features. The entropy is defined as:

$$h(\Lambda) = - \sum_{i \in \mathsf{srvs}(\Lambda)} \left(\frac{|\{\lambda \in \Lambda | \lambda.\mathsf{srvip} = i\}|}{|\Lambda|} \right) \log_2 \left(\frac{|\{\lambda \in \Lambda | \lambda.\mathsf{srvip} = i\}|}{|\Lambda|} \right) \quad (1)$$

where $\mathsf{srvs}(\Lambda) = \bigcup_{\lambda \in \Lambda} \lambda.\mathsf{srvip}$ is the set of all server addresses observed in the log file. During a harvesting attack, an attacker will increase $|\mathsf{srvs}(\Lambda)|$, which reduces the probability of any one server being the target of a communication and therefore increases the entropy.

$d(\Lambda)$, the maximum degree of Λ, is the number of servers with which the busiest client in Λ communicated. $d(\Lambda)$ is arguably the simplest form of scan detection and consequently has been used by a variety of anomaly detection systems, notably GrIDS [23] and Bro [20].

$r(\Lambda)$ is the maximum *failed connection run* observed in Λ. A failed connection run is a sequence of flow records $\lambda_1 \ldots \lambda_n$ where each λ in the run has the same client address and $\lambda_i.\mathsf{succ} = 0$. This method is used by TRW scan detection [11] to determine if an address is actively scanning. We use the maximum failed connection run measure to indicate whether TRW would have detected at least one attack during the sample period.

3.3   IDS Thresholds

In order to calculate detection thresholds for four of the IDS we consider (g, c, h and d), we first must train the IDS using log files of benign traffic from the monitored network. However, SSH traffic is prone to constant scanning [1] which, unless aggressively filtered, will result in artificially high thresholds.

To address the problem of constant clumsy scanning, we use a two-stage filtering method developed in previous work [7]. This approach is based on our previous observations that certain graph attributes of major protocols (graph size and largest component size) can be modeled using a Gaussian distribution when the traffic logs describing those attributes do not contain attacks [6]. Using these results, we use a stateless filter that eliminates records where $\mathsf{succ} = 0$. The resulting log files are then tested using the Shapiro-Wilk normality test [22] to identify those log files where the observed graph and largest component size are outside the expected range for a Gaussian distribution.

The initial training data consisted of 7,200 log files for the five business days between February 11–15, 2008. Source data was chosen exclusively from 1200GMT to 2359GMT for each day, a period corresponding to peak activity for the network. After filtering, the resulting set consisted of 5,619 log files from a source set of 7,200.

Table 1. Summary of Gaussian state variables in SSH training set

State variable x	Range	$\mu_X \pm \sigma_X$
g		299.27±42.49
c		35.13±21.32
h		6.88±0.35

Applying this filtering technique in order to isolate benign traffic yields a vector $\Lambda_1 \ldots \Lambda_m$ of log files, each representing benign traffic in a 30s interval. State values are calculated for each log file in this vector; we refer to the resulting vector of state values using the same subscript notation, $e.g.$, $r(\Lambda_i) = r_i$. We refer to the complete vector of values for a vector of log files by the corresponding capital letter $(e.g., G = \{g(\Lambda_1) \ldots g(\Lambda_m)\})$.

We examined the H and D distributions in the filtered data to see if they could be modeled via a Gaussian distribution. (Our previous work already established that G and C are Gaussian for the monitored network [6].) Using the Shapiro-Wilk statistic (W) [22], we found that H had $W = 0.97$ and negligible p-value, and so we treated entropy as Gaussian. D had a Shapiro-Wilk statistic of $W = 0.77$ with negligible p-value, and consequently was not considered Gaussian.

Table 1 summarizes the Gaussian state variables, $i.e.$, g, c, and h. This table shows the summary data (left hand column), the mean and standard deviation (right side) and a sparkline for each data set. The sparkline is a time series plot of the activity over the training period. We plot the mean and shade an area one standard deviation from the mean in each sparkline.

For these three state variables, we can use (2) to calculate the detection threshold. For a given false positive rate, FPR, the corresponding threshold for a Gaussian IDS x is given by:

$$\theta_x = \mu_X + \sqrt{2}\mathrm{erf}^{-1}(\mathsf{FPR})\sigma_X \tag{2}$$

where erf is the error function [14], μ_X is the arithmetic mean of the vector of observations X, and σ_X is the standard deviation of the same vector.

The detection threshold for d is computed differently since, as shown above, d is not normally distributed over the sample space. We use d's maximum observed value over the benign log files as the detection threshold:

$$\theta_d = \max(D) \tag{3}$$

The detection threshold for r is prescribed by Jung $et\ al.$ to be

$$\theta_r = \frac{\beta \ln \frac{\beta}{\alpha} + (1 - \beta) \ln \frac{1-\beta}{1-\alpha}}{t_1 \ln \frac{t_1}{t_0} + (1 - t_1) \ln \frac{1-t_1}{1-t_0}} \tag{4}$$

Here, α and β are user-configured thresholds for the maximum false positive rate (α) and the minimum true positive rate (β). For this work, we set $\beta = 1 - \alpha$, and set α to our acceptable FPR (see below). t_0 and t_1 are, respectively, the probabilities that a normal user will successfully communicate with a target, and the probability that a randomly scanning attacker will successfully communicate with a target. Per these definitions, t_0 and t_1 depend on a variety of factors including the density of targets in the network, the type of protocol involved, and dynamic addressing, some of which are difficult to accurately evaluate for the monitored network due to our limited view of it. However, Jung's simulation analysis of TRW [10] suggest that choices of t_0 and t_1 have relatively little impact on performance. As such, we generally adopt Jung's original values of $t_0 = 0.8$ and $t_1 = 0.2$ and will examine the impact of alternative θ_r values in §5.2.

Recall that based on our previous work on graph-based anomaly detection [6], we monitor traffic over 30s periods. This 30s period governs the effective response time of the entire intrusion detection and response mechanism — an IDS sends out at most one alert in a period, and defenders respond to changes at that time. If we constrain the *aggregate* false positives for *all* of the detectors to one false alarm per eight hours (*i.e.*, the duration of a typical network analyst's shift), this yields a combined rate of 0.1% for the five IDS together. We solve for individual false positive rates FPR using

$$0.001 = 1 - (1 - \text{FPR})^5 \qquad (5)$$

Plugging this value of FPR into (2) yields detection thresholds $\theta_g = 447$, $\theta_c = 110$, and $\theta_h = 8.105$, and setting $\alpha = \text{FPR}$ in (4) yields $\theta_r = 6$. We also use the value $\theta_d = 150$, computed directly from (3). These are the thresholds we use in our evaluations in subsequent sections. Equation 5 treats each IDS as a statistically independent. While not true, this simplifies our exploratory analysis.

4   Observable Attack Spaces and Detection Probability

In §3, we developed and configured a combined IDS based around five different state variables: graph size g, largest component size c, server address entropy h, maximum client degree d and maximum failed connection run r. In doing so, we specifically configured these systems to yield a low false positive rate, resulting in one false positive per eight-hours as predicted by our training data. Now that we have developed this hybrid IDS, we can evaluate its efficacy for deterring attackers.

In order to do this, we develop a method for describing attacker utility which we call the *observable attack space* (OAS). An observable attack space describes the range of attacks that an attacker can conduct *as observed by a particular logging mechanism*. In this section, we develop an observable attack space common to our logging system (NetFlow) and our five candidate IDS. Using this approach, we model the aggregate *detection surface* of the OAS and use this to evaluate both our combined IDS and the constituent IDS individually.

This section is structured as follows. §4.1 describes OAS, IDS and the estimation of detection surfaces. §4.2 then compares the effectiveness of our five detection methods both in aggregate and as individual detection schemes.

4.1   OAS and Detection Surface

The type of log data that an IDS uses strongly impacts the types of attacks that an IDS can detect. An example of this is the impact of choosing NetFlow. NetFlow is a compact representation of traffic that is viable to collect on large networks, but since it lacks payload, signature-matching techniques are not possible with this log format. An observable attack space is therefore a parameterized representation of all possible forms of a particular attack, as observable using a particular form of log data. For this work, the observable attack space has two attributes: *aggressiveness* (a) and *success* (s). The aggressiveness is a natural number describing the number of distinct addresses with which the attacker communicates in the observation period. The success of an attack is the fraction of these communications that were successful, and is within the range $[0, 1]$.

When conducting simulations, we limit a to the range of $(0, \theta_d)$ because we treat the d IDS as deterministic — it will trigger if *and only if* $a \geq \theta_d$. In doing so, we ignore the possibility that during an attack, a benign host contacts more than θ_d addresses, thus "accidentally" causing a true detection even though $a < \theta_d$. This treatment also presumes that the attack is launched from a bot that is not also contributing benign traffic at the same time, *i.e.*, $a < \theta_d$ implies that the bot host does, in fact, contact fewer than θ_d addresses in a 30s interval. The other IDS' chances of detecting attacks are not so directly dependent on an attack's characteristics within the OAS.

Consider a particular IDS $x \in \{g, c, h, r\}$. Given an arbitrary log file of control data Λ^{ctl} that we are confident does not contain an attack, $\mathcal{P}^x_{\text{det}}(a, s)$ is the probability that the IDS x raises an alarm for the log file resulting from Λ^{ctl} merged with an attack Λ^{atk} with aggressiveness a and success s. That is,

$$\mathcal{P}^x_{\text{det}}(a, s) = \mathbb{P}\left[x(\Lambda^{\text{atk}} \cup \Lambda^{\text{ctl}}) \geq \theta_x\right] \tag{6}$$

where the probability is taken with respect to the selection of Λ^{ctl} and the generation of Λ^{atk} with aggressiveness a and success rate s. For a particular IDS x, the *detection surface of x* is the surface of values $\mathcal{P}^x_{\text{det}}(a, s)$ for $a \in (0, \theta_d)$ and $s \in [0, 1]$.

More specifically, to estimate the probability of detection and the corresponding detection surface, we evaluate the distribution of state variables for normal behavior merged with randomly generated attacks meeting the aggressiveness and success requirements specified by a and s. For this paper, we limit our simulations to $a \in \{10, 20, 30, 40, \ldots, 140\}$ (recall $\theta_d = 150$) and $s \in \{0.1, 0.2, 0.3, \ldots, 1.0\}$. At each point, we conduct 100 simulations, each using one of fifty randomly selected 30s periods from the week of February 18–22 (the week following that used for training) for Λ^{ctl}. Λ^{atk} is randomly generated for

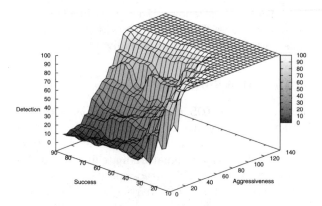

Fig. 1. Detection surface ($\mathcal{P}^{\text{all}}_{\text{det}}(a, s)$, as a percentage) for combined IDS

each simulation. Λ^{atk} contains a unique records, where each record has the same client address, and a different server address. The composition of the server addresses is a function of s: $a \cdot s$ addresses are chosen from a hit list of internal SSH servers identified in the training data[4] in order to approximate hit-list attacks; the remainder are sent to addresses with no listening server. We then merge Λ^{atk} with a randomly selected control log Λ^{ctl} and then calculate the state variables.

Four of the IDS examined by this paper (g, c, h, and d) are unaffected by the order of log records within the monitored 30s period. The fifth, r, is order-sensitive, however, in that TRW triggers an alert if any host is observed making more than θ_r failed connections *in a row*. This order sensitivity is a weakness, since an attacker can interleave scanning with connections to known hosts in order to avoid a failed connection run greater than θ_r [12]. To address this particular exploit, we randomly permute the records originating in each 30s interval. After this permutation, r is calculated for each host in the network.

Figure 1 plots the detection surface for all the IDS combined. As this figure shows, the combined detection mechanism generally increases proportionally to the aggressiveness of the attack and inversely relative to the success of the attack. Furthermore, the detection mechanisms tend to vary more as a function of the aggressiveness than due to the success rate.

The effectiveness of the aggregate IDS may be considered low, in the sense that an attacker with a relatively small hit list ($a = 40, s = 0.5$) can communicate with the network with little fear of detection. However, we should note that the attacks represented by this OAS are the most subtle space of attacks available. Our own experience indicates that the majority of attacks are orders of magnitude more aggressive than these hypothetical SSH scans, at which point *any* IDS will identify them. This latter point is particularly critical. As Figure 1 shows, once $a \geq 100$, the combined IDS will raise an alarm.

---

[4] This hit list is composed of all internal addresses in the training data which had one flow originating from them on port 22 and with a payload of greater than 1kB.

4.2   Detection Surface Comparison

In addition to the detection surface for the aggregate IDS, we have also calculated the detection surfaces for each component IDS in this system. We can use these results to evaluate the comparative effectiveness of each IDS.

Figure 2 plots detection surfaces for each IDS $x \in \{g, c, h, r\}$ as *contour plots*. A contour plot maps a 3-dimensional surface into a 2-dimensional representation using *contour lines*. Each contour line represents the axis coordinates where the surface takes on its labeled value.

These plots show that the most successful individual IDS are c and r : these IDS are the only ones to have significant ($\geq$ 10%) detection rates over the majority of the OAS. In contrast, the h IDS has a very *low* detection rate, less than 6% over the entire OAS. Of particular interest with c and r is their relative disconnectedness to each other: r's detection rate is dependent on s and less dependent on a. Conversely, c is largely independent of s, while a plays larger role in detection.

These IDS are calibrated to have an effective false positive rate of zero. As a result, they are largely insensitive to anomalies and have a relatively low detection rate. In addition, as noted above, the attacks represented here are extremely subtle. More aggressive attackers would be identified and eliminated *regardless* of the detection strategy used — by the time an attacker communicates with $\theta_d = 150$ addresses, the d IDS will raise an alarm, making other approaches effectively moot.

This phenomenon is partly observable in our models in Table 1. Recall that, for example, the model of graph size g, was 299 ± 42.47 hosts. If $g(\Lambda) = 299$ for some log file Λ, then an attacker will not trigger an anomaly until he has communicated with at least 149 hosts, at which point he is close to triggering d as well as g.

5   Modeling Acquisition

In §4.2 we examined the efficacy of the detection mechanisms purely as detectors: for a fixed false positive rate, we calculated the effective true positive rate. In this section, we use the detection surface in Figure 1 to examine the impact of IDS on *acquisition attacks*. We evaluate the efficacy of the detection surface by building a mathematical model for attacker payoff during an acquisition attack. Applying this model to the surface, we can determine how many hosts an attacker can expect to take over, and from these results determine how effective an IDS has to be in order to keep attackers from taking over hosts.

This section is divided as follows: §5.1 describes our model for acquisition attacks. §5.2 compares IDS efficiency using our payoff function. §5.3 considers the problem of IDS evaluation from a different perspective — instead of calculating efficiency in terms of true and false positives, we determine the minimum false positive rate required to counter an attacker.

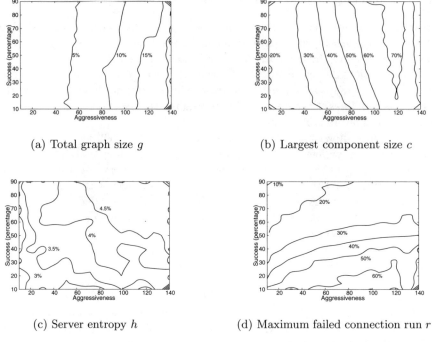

(a) Total graph size g

(b) Largest component size c

(c) Server entropy h

(d) Maximum failed connection run r

Fig. 2. Detection surfaces ($\mathcal{P}_{\det}^x(a, s)$, as a percentage) for individual IDS

5.1   Acquisition Payoff Model

We define an acquisition attack as a game between two parties who are competing for ownership of a single network. The two parties in the game are the *attacker*, who attempts to take over hosts on the network, and the *defender*, who attempts to prevent takeover of hosts on the network. In this game, the attacker uses a single *bot* to perform a series of *attempts*, during each of which the bot communicates with multiple hosts within the network using a *hit list* acquired previous to the attack.

In each attempt, the attacker communicates with some number of addresses (specified by the attacker's a), each of which has s chance of succeeding. For the purposes of the simulations, a successful attack is one that communicates with a real host, and a failed attack is one that communicates with a nonexistent host. That is, we assume that if an attacker talks with a host, the attacker takes the host over. The *payoff* of an attempt, $\mathcal{H}_{\text{acq}}$, is the expected number of hosts with which the attacker communicates during an attempt.

The goal of the defender is to minimize $\mathcal{H}_{\text{acq}}$, and the goal of the attacker to maximize the same. To do so, the defender deploys an IDS x, and so the probability of detecting a particular attempt with aggressiveness a and success rate s is $\mathcal{P}_{\det}^x(a, s)$. We assume that once the defender successfully identifies an

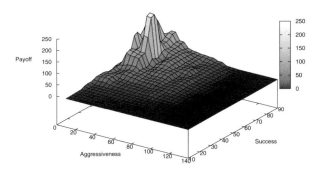

Fig. 3. Payoff $\mathcal{H}_{\text{acq}}^{\text{all}}(a, s, k_{\text{max}}^{\text{all}}(a, s))$ for acquisition attacks for combined IDS

attacker, it will block the attacker's bot, ending all further acquisition attempts by that bot. Furthermore, the defender will then recover all of the hosts that the bot communicated with during the game.

We note that this model assumes that the attacker and defender are perfect. That is, the probability that an attacker takes over a host that it contacts, and the probability that a defender correctly identifies an occupied host after being notified of an attack, are both one. The model can be modified by incorporating additional probabilities for measuring the attacker's takeover success per host contact and the defender's vigilance.

Let owned be a random variable indicating the number of hosts taken over, and let alarmed be the event that the bot is detected. Below, we assume that the probability of detection in each attempt is independent. If such is the case, then we can derive the payoff for an attack comprised of k attempts and for an IDS x as:

$$\mathcal{H}_{\text{acq}}^{x}(a, s, k) = \mathbb{E}\,[\text{owned}]$$
$$= \mathbb{P}\,[\text{alarmed}]\,\mathbb{E}\,[\text{owned} \mid \text{alarmed}] + \mathbb{P}\,[\neg\text{alarmed}]\,\mathbb{E}\,[\text{owned} \mid \neg\text{alarmed}]$$
$$= (1 - \mathcal{P}_{\text{det}}^{x}(a, s))^{k}(ask) \tag{7}$$

The last step follows by taking $\mathbb{E}\,[\text{owned} \mid \text{alarmed}] = 0$, since we presume that if the defender detects an attacker during an attempt, then the defender recovers *all* of the hosts the attacker has communicated with using that particular bot. Note that the attacker maximizes his payoff by maximizing k subject to $\mathcal{H}_{\text{acq}}(a, s, k) - \mathcal{H}_{\text{acq}}(a, s, k - 1) > 0$ or, in other words,

$$k < \frac{1 - \mathcal{P}_{\text{det}}^{x}(a, s)}{\mathcal{P}_{\text{det}}^{x}(a, s)} \tag{8}$$

We denote this value of k by $k_{\text{max}}^{x}(a, s)$.

Figure 3 plots the payoff over the observed attack space using (7) with the maximum k satisfying (8). As this figure shows, aggressive attacks have a minimal payoff, a result that can be expected based on Figure 1. Above approximately $a \geq 80$, the attacker is consistently identified and stopped regardless of their success rate.

This behavior is the result of the interaction of two detectors: c and r. As s increases, the probability of the attacker combining previously separate components of the protocol graph increases, increasing the likelihood of detection by the c IDS. As the attacker's success rate decreases, he is more likely to generate a sufficiently long failed connection run to trigger the r detector. The other detectors will identify attackers, however their effectiveness is limited for attacks that are this subtle — an attacker who does disrupt g or h will typically already have disrupted d.

5.2   Calculating IDS Efficiency

We can use (7) to also calculate a comparative efficiency metric for IDS. The volume under the surface specified by (7) is the ability of the attacker to take over hosts in the presence of a particular IDS. The *efficiency* of an IDS x is therefore the indicator of how much x reduces an attacker's payoff. We can express IDS efficiency as the ratio between the number of hosts an attacker expects to take over in the presence of an IDS x and the number of hosts the attacker can take over (in the same number of attempts) in that IDS' absence.

$$\mathcal{E}^x_{\text{acq}} = 1 - \frac{\sum_{a \in (0, \theta_d)} \sum_{s \in (0,1]} \mathcal{H}^x_{\text{acq}}(a, s, k^x_{\max}(a, s))}{\sum_{a \in (0, \theta_d)} \sum_{s \in (0,1]} ask^x_{\max}(a, s)} \qquad (9)$$

The subtraction in (9) is included simply to provide an intuitive progression for efficiency: if $\mathcal{E}$ is greater for IDS A than IDS B, then A is a better IDS than B. Based on (9), we can calculate an efficiency of 0.14 for g, 0.0099 for h, 0.73 for c and 0.22 for r. The effectiveness of the combined detector is 0.80.

Using Equation 9 we can examine the impact of alternative values for θ_r. Recall from §3.3 that θ_r is based on models of normal behavior and attacker behavior that can vary as a function of the protocol, the density of the observed network and other behaviors. Without revisiting the model, we can simply change the values of θ_r and examine how that changes the efficiency. In this case, we find that for $\theta_r = 3$, 4, and 5, $\mathcal{E}^x_{\text{acq}} = 0.50$, 0.37, and 0.29, respectively. The most interesting result from these calculations is the relatively low efficiency of r as an IDS for acquisition attacks, despite its relatively good true positive rates (Figure 2). Because the detection mechanism relies on attacker failures, it is better at detecting attacks which have a relatively low s. IDS r is therefore very good at detecting attacks with low payoff.

We expect that the comparative efficiency of these IDS will differ from one protocol to the next. g and h are affected by the aggregate traffic for one protocol, e.g., the total number of hosts using a particular protocol. Conversely, r relies exclusively on per-host behavior. Consequently, using protocols with more clients or servers (such as HTTP) should result in less g and h efficiency, while r should have the same efficiency regardless of protocol.

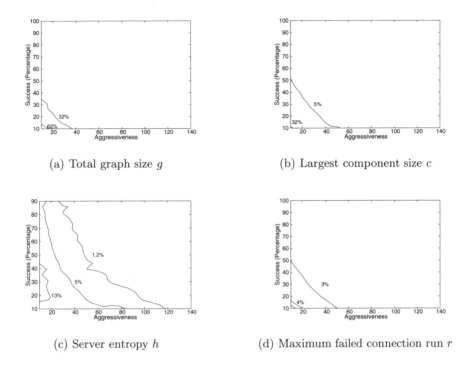

(a) Total graph size g (b) Largest component size c

(c) Server entropy h (d) Maximum failed connection run r

Fig. 4. False positive rates required to limit $\mathcal{H}_{\mathrm{acq}}^{x}(a, s, k) = 1$

5.3   Determining a Minimum False Positive Rate

As Figure 3 implies, even with all the detection mechanisms operating, attackers can still acquire a high rate of return with a sufficiently subtle hit-list attack. In this section, we will now address the question of detection from a different perspective: how high a false positive rate do we have to tolerate in order to prevent the attacker from seriously compromising the monitored network?

To do so, we invert (7) so that instead of calculating the attacker's payoff as a function of detectability, we calculate the probability of detection as a function of payoff. Solving for $\mathcal{P}_{\mathrm{det}}^{x}(a, s)$ in (7) yields

$$\mathcal{P}_{\mathrm{det}}^{x}(a, s) = 1 - \sqrt[k]{\frac{\mathcal{H}_{\mathrm{acq}}^{x}(a, s, k)}{ask}} \tag{10}$$

Suppose the defender wishes to minimize $\mathcal{P}_{\mathrm{det}}^{x}(a, s)$ (and hence also the false alarm rate) while restricting $\mathcal{H}_{\mathrm{acq}}^{x}(a, s, k) \leq 1$, and so the attacker wishes to maximize $\mathcal{P}_{\mathrm{det}}^{x}(a, s)$ in order to achieve $\mathcal{H}_{\mathrm{acq}}^{x}(a, s, k) = 1$. The attacker does so by choosing k so as to minimize $(ask)^{-1/k}$, for any a and s.

Using this strategy, we calculate the detection probability required to identify and stop attackers at points within the OAS. To calculate the resulting detection thresholds for each IDS, we use our simulated attacks with parameters a and s to calculate the threshold needed to filter off $\mathcal{P}_{\text{det}}^x(a, s)$ of the attacks when overlaid on our training data.

The results of these runs are given in Figure 4. These figures are contour plots over the OAS as before. However, the contours for the figure are the false positive rates that would result from this analy-

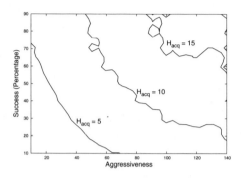

Fig. 5. Values of a and s for which $\mathcal{H}_{\text{acq}}^c(a, s, k)$ can be limited to at most the specified value, using a threshold $\theta_c = \mu_C + 3.5\sigma_C$

sis. For the g, c and h detectors, these values are calculated using (2). For r, this value is calculated by using (4).

As Figure 4 indicates, anomaly detection systems that are capable of defending against subtle attacks will require extremely high false positive rates. Recall that our measurement system conducts a test every 30s; for every 1% false positive rate we accept, we pay 10 alerts per eight-hour shift. As such, this figure indicates that the false positive rates for building systems that can limit the attacker to $\mathcal{H}_{\text{acq}}^x(a, s, k) \leq 1$ are much higher than we can consider accepting.

One way to avoid such high false positive rates would be to not place such a stringent limit of $\mathcal{H}_{\text{acq}}^x(a, s, k) \leq 1$. For example, if the defender insists on a near-zero false positive rate, we can determine if there is a higher threshold for the payoff that can accommodate this rate, such as $\mathcal{H}_{\text{acq}}^x(a, s, k) \leq 5$. Figure 5 shows this for the c IDS, for $\mathcal{H}_{\text{acq}}^c(a, s, k) \in \{5, 10, 15\}$. Specifically, each contour line shows the values of a and s for which $\mathcal{H}_{\text{acq}}^c(a, s, k)$ can be limited to at most the specified value, using a threshold $\theta_c = \mu_C + 3.5\sigma_C$, which is large enough to ensure a false positive rate very close to zero. As this figure shows, the defender can effectively impose an upper limit on the attacker's payoff, but unfortunately this limit must be rather large ($\mathcal{H}_{\text{acq}}^c(a, s, k) = 15$) in order to cover the majority of the attack space.

From Figures 4 and 5, we conclude that in order for an anomaly detection system to be a viable deterrent to host compromise, it must either use finer resolution data than NetFlow, develop mechanisms for coping with a high false positive rate, or permit higher attacker payoff than would be ideal.

6   Modeling Reconnaissance

In this section, we develop an alternative attack scenario, *reconnaissance*, where the attacker scouts out the network with his bots. In each attack, he communicates with addresses to simply determine the presence of hosts at certain addresses. The reconnaissance scenario differs from the acquisition scenario by the attacker's knowledge and goals. Specifically, the attacker's goal is to contact as many addresses as possible within a short period. To do so, the attacker uses a *chaff hit list* consisting of hosts that the attacker already knows about, and a target space of addresses to probe. The chaff hit list reduces the attacker's probability of detection by lowering his failure rate. However, it also reduces the attacker's payoff by requiring him to "sacrifice" a certain number of targets every round.

Let alarmed $= i$ be the event that the bot is detected at the end of attempt i (and before attempt $i + 1$); as before, an attempt is comprised of contacting a addresses with success rate of s (in this case, owing to the chaff hit list). Let scanned denote a random variable indicating the number of scans that one bot performs successfully (*i.e.*, determines whether the scanned address has a listening service or not), not counting the "chaff" that it introduces to avoid detection. Note that we suppose that the number of listening services the bot finds is sufficiently small that it does not relieve the bot from introducing a fraction s of chaff scans. We also presume that the probability the bot is detected in each attempt is independent.

$$\mathcal{H}_{\text{rec}}^x(a, s) = \mathbb{E}\left[\text{scanned}\right]$$

$$= \sum_{i=1}^{\infty} \mathbb{P}\left[\text{alarmed} = i\right] \mathbb{E}\left[\text{scanned} \mid \text{alarmed} = i\right]$$

$$= \sum_{i=1}^{\infty} \left((1 - \mathcal{P}_{\text{det}}^x(a, s))^{i-1} \mathcal{P}_{\text{det}}^x(a, s)\right) (ia(1 - s))$$

$$= a(1 - s) \frac{\mathcal{P}_{\text{det}}^x(a, s)}{1 - \mathcal{P}_{\text{det}}^x(a, s)} \sum_{i=1}^{\infty} i(1 - \mathcal{P}_{\text{det}}^x(a, s))^i$$

$$= a(1 - s) \frac{\mathcal{P}_{\text{det}}^x(a, s)}{1 - \mathcal{P}_{\text{det}}^x(a, s)} \frac{1 - \mathcal{P}_{\text{det}}^x(a, s)}{\mathcal{P}_{\text{det}}^x(a, s)^2}$$

$$= a(1 - s) \frac{1}{\mathcal{P}_{\text{det}}^x(a, s)} \tag{11}$$

Applying (11) to the detection matrix over our OAS results in the payoff plot shown in Figure 6. This figure plots the aggregate payoff over the OAS for reconnaissance. Of particular note with this result is that it demonstrates that a sufficiently motivated and subtle attacker can scan a network by subtly exploiting attacks with high s rates. In this case, the attacker can slowly scan the network for an extended period — the observed peak at the $a = 20$ segment of the graph implies that the attacker scans for 25 minutes before being detected.

However, the attacker can achieve just as effective results by aggressively scanning the network. Recall that the effective aggressiveness of the attacker is bound by θ_d to less than 150 nodes. In the reconnaissance scenario, the attacker faces

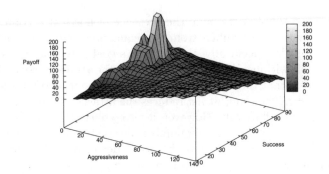

Fig. 6. Payoff $\mathcal{H}_{\text{rec}}^{\text{all}}(a, s)$ for reconnaissance attacks for combined IDS

no penalty for scanning at a higher aggressiveness rate, since the defender can only block an address. Consequently, this plot can continue out to whatever the practical upper limit for a is, a result which would correspond to the aggressive scanning we observe right now.

7   Conclusion

In this paper we have developed a new method for evaluating the performance of IDS based on an observable attack space, specifically the view of a harvesting or scanning attack that is available in flow logs that lack payload data. Our approach complements ROC-based analysis by enabling the creation of detection surfaces — models of an IDS' ability to detect different attacks. Moreover, we augment this analysis with a payoff-based metric. By incorporating payoffs, we are better able to characterize the deterrence offered by an IDS. In particular, instead of describing the detection of a system in terms of pure false positive and false negative rates, we are able to use payoff functions to calculate the gain that an attacker can expect from a certain type of attack. This also enables us to determine how high a false positive rate we must endure in order to limit the attacker's payoff to a target value.

Future work will focus on expanding the OAS approach to address different scenarios and parameters. First, our previous work on graph-based intrusion detection [6] considered the possibility of multiple bots being active simultaneously, and extending our OAS to account for this is a natural direction of future work. Second, generalizing from 30-second traffic samples to an approach considering multiple sample durations may provide additional detection capability [21]. Third, this work outlines two initial attack scenarios: harvesting and reconnaissance. However, a variety of other attacks may be considered and evaluated. In particular, different scanning strategies (such as topological scanning), bot command and-control, and DDoS attacks all merit further investigation and similar payoff-based evaluation.

Several useful and, in some cases, discouraging results fall out of our analysis techniques as applied to SSH traffic observed on a very large network. For example, in §4.2 our analysis elucidated the complementary capabilities of detection using the size c of the largest component of a protocol graph [6] and the TRW scan detector r [11]. Consequently, there is good reason to use both simultaneously. Moreover, we showed that these detectors significantly outperform the server address entropy detector h, the graph-size detector g, and the degree-based detector d, for the stealthy attacks that form our observable attack space. That said, using our payoff analysis for acquisition attacks, we showed in §5.2 that r detection is primarily effective at detecting acquisition attacks with low payoff for the attacker, and so its utility for acquisition attacks is less compelling. In addition, we showed in §5.3 that to severely limit the attacker's acquisitions, the false positive rates that would need to be endured by any of the detectors we considered would be significant and, for a network of the size we studied, impractical. We showed how to derive more relaxed payoff limits that would enable near-zero false positive rates for an IDS.

References

1. Alata, E., Nicomette, V., Kaaniche, M., Dacier, M., Herrb, M.: Lessons learned from the deployment of a high-interaction honeypot. In: Proceedings of the 2006 European Dependable Computing Conference (2006)
2. Axelsson, S.: The base rate fallacy and the difficulty of intrusion detection. ACM Transactions on Information and System Security 3(3), 186–205 (2000)
3. Binkley, J.: An algorithm for anomaly-based botnet detection. In: Proceedings of the 2006 USENIX Workshop on Steps for Reducing Unwanted Traffic on the Internet (SRUTI) (2006)
4. Cárdenas, A., Baras, J., Seamon, K.: A framework for evaluation of intrusion detection systems. In: Proceedings of the 2006 IEEE Symposium on Security and Privacy (2006)
5. Claffy, K., Braun, H., Polyzos, G.: A parameterizable methodology for internet traffic flow profiling. IEEE Journal on Selected Areas in Communications 13(8), 1481–1494 (1995)
6. Collins, M.P., Reiter, M.: Hit-list worm detection and bot identification in large networks using protocol graphs. In: Kruegel, C., Lippmann, R., Clark, A. (eds.) RAID 2007. LNCS, vol. 4637, pp. 276–295. Springer, Heidelberg (2007)
7. Collins, M.P., Reiter, M.K.: Anomaly detection amidst constant anomalies: Training IDS on constantly attacked data. Technical Report CMU-CYLAB-08-006, Carnegie Mellon University, CyLab (2008)
8. Gaffney, J., Ulvila, J.: Evaluation of intrusion detectors: A decision theory approach. In: Proceedings of the 2001 IEEE Symposium on Security and Privacy (2001)
9. Gates, C., Taylor, C.: Challenging the anomaly detection paradigm, a provocative discussion. In: Proceedings of the 2006 New Security Paradigms Workshop, pp. 22–29 (2006)
10. Jung, J.: Real-Time Detection of Malicious Network Activity Using Stochastic Models. PhD thesis, Massachuesetts Institute of Technology (2006)

11. Jung, J., Paxson, V., Berger, A.W., Balakrishnan, H.: Fast portscan detection using sequential hypothesis testing. In: Proceedings of the 2004 IEEE Symposium on Security and Privacy (2004)
12. Kang, M., Caballero, J., Song, D.: Distributed evasive scan techniques and countermeasures. In: Hämmerli, B.M., Sommer, R. (eds.) DIMVA 2007. LNCS, vol. 4579, pp. 157–174. Springer, Heidelberg (2007)
13. Killourhy, K., Maxion, R., Tan, K.: A defense-centric taxonomy based on attack manifestations. In: Proceedings of the 2004 Conference on Dependable Systems and Networks (DSN) (2004)
14. Kreyszig, E.: Advanced Engineering Mathematics, 9th edn. J. Wiley and Sons, Chichester (2005)
15. Lakhina, A., Crovella, M., Diot, C.: Mining anomalies using traffic feature distributions. In: Proceedings of the 2005 Conference on Applications, Technologies, Architectures, and Protocols for Computer Communications (SIGCOMM), pp. 217–228 (2005)
16. Lippmann, R., Fried, D., Graf, I., Haines, J., Kendall, K., McClung, D., Weber, D., Webster, S., Wyschogrod, D., Cunningham, R., Zissman, M.: Evaluating intrusion detection systems: The 1998 DARPA off-line intrusion detection evaluation. In: Proceedings of the DARPA Information Survivability Conference and Exposition (2000)
17. Maxion, R., Tan, K.: Benchmarking anomaly-based detection systems. In: Proceedings of the 2000 Conference on Dependable Systems and Networks (DSN) (2000)
18. McHugh, J.: Testing intrusion detection systems: A critique of the 1998 and 1998 DARPA intrusion detection system evaluations as performed by Lincoln Laboratory. ACM Transactions on Information and Systems Security 3(4), 262–294 (2000)
19. Northcutt, S.: Network Intrusion Detection: An Analyst's Handbook. New Riders (1999)
20. Paxson, V.: Bro: A system for detection network intruders in real time. In: Proceedings of the 2008 Usenix Security Symposium (1998)
21. Sekar, V., Xie, Y., Reiter, M.K., Zhang, H.: A multi-resolution approach for worm detection and containment. In: Proceedings of the 36th International Conference on Dependable Systems and Networks, June 2006, pp. 189–198 (2006)
22. Shapiro, S., Wilk, M.: An analysis of variance test for normality (complete samples). Biometrika 52(3–4), 591–611 (1965)
23. Staniford-Chen, S., Cheung, S., Crawford, R., Dilger, M., Frank, J., Hoagland, J., Levitt, K., Wee, C., Yip, R., Zerkle, D.: GrIDS – A graph-based intrusion detection system for large networks. In: Proceedings of the 19th National Information Systems Security Conference, pp. 361–370 (1996)
24. Stolfo, S., Fan, W., Lee, W., Prodromidis, A., Chan, P.: Cost-based modeling for fraud and intrusion detection: Results from the JAM project. In: Proceedings of the 2000 DARPA Information Survivability Conference and Exposition (2000)
25. Tan, K., Maxion, R.: The effects of algorithmic diversity on anomaly detector performance. In: Proceedings of the 2005 Conference on Dependable Systems and Networks (DSN) (2005)

Determining Placement of Intrusion Detectors for a Distributed Application through Bayesian Network Modeling

Gaspar Modelo-Howard, Saurabh Bagchi, and Guy Lebanon

School of Electrical and Computer Engineering, Purdue University
465 Northwestern Avenue, West Lafayette, IN 47907 USA
{gmodeloh,sbagchi,lebanon}@purdue.edu

Abstract. To secure today's computer systems, it is critical to have different intrusion detection sensors embedded in them. The complexity of *distributed* computer systems makes it difficult to determine the appropriate configuration of these detectors, i.e., their choice and placement. In this paper, we describe a method to evaluate the effect of the detector configuration on the accuracy and precision of determining security goals in the system. For this, we develop a Bayesian network model for the distributed system, from an attack graph representation of multi-stage attacks in the system. We use Bayesian inference to solve the problem of determining the likelihood that an attack goal has been achieved, *given* a certain set of detector alerts. We quantify the overall detection performance in the system for different detector settings, namely, choice and placement of the detectors, their quality, and levels of uncertainty of adversarial behavior. These observations lead us to a greedy algorithm for determining the optimal detector settings in a large-scale distributed system. We present the results of experiments on Bayesian networks representing two real distributed systems and real attacks on them.

Keywords: Intrusion detection, detector placement, Bayesian networks, attack graph.

1 Introduction

It is critical to provide intrusion detection to secure today's distributed computer systems. The overall intrusion detection strategy involves placing multiple detectors at different points of the system, at network ingress or combination points, specific hosts executing parts of the distributed system, or embedded in specific applications that form part of the distributed system. At the current time, the placement of the detectors and the choice of the detectors are more an art than a science, relying on expert knowledge of the system administrator.

The impact of the choice is significant on the accuracy and precision of the overall detection function in the system. The detectors are of different qualities, in terms of their false positive (FP) and false negative (FN) rates, some may have overlapping functionalities, and there may be many possible positions for

R. Lippmann, E. Kirda, and A. Trachtenberg (Eds.): RAID 2008, LNCS 5230, pp. 271–290, 2008.
© Springer-Verlag Berlin Heidelberg 2008

deploying a detector. Therefore the entire space of exploration is large and yet not much exists today to serve as a scientific basis for the choices. This paper is a step in that direction.

In the choice of the number of detectors, more is not always better. There are several reasons why an extreme design choice of a detector at every possible network point, host, and application may not be ideal. First, there is the economic cost of acquiring, configuring, and maintaining the detectors. Detectors are well-known to need tuning to achieve their best performance and to meet the targeted needs of the application (specifically in terms of the false positive-false negative performance balance). Second, a large number of detectors would mean a large number of alert streams under attack as well as benign conditions. These could overwhelm the manual or automated process in place to respond to intrusion alerts. Third, detectors impose a performance penalty on the distributed system that they are meant to protect. The penalty arises because the detectors typically share the computational cycles and the bandwidth along with the application. Fourth, a system owner may have specific security goals, e.g., detecting a security goal may be very important and requires high sensitivity, while another may need to be done with less tolerance for false positives.

The problem that we address in this paper is, given the security goals in a system and a model for the way multi-stage attacks can spread in the system, how can we automatically and based on scientific principles, select the right set of detectors and their placements. Right is determined by an application-specific requirement on the true positive (TP) - true negative (TN) rate of detection in the system. We explore the space of the configuration of the individual detectors, their placement on the different hosts or network points, and their number.

Our solution approach starts with attack graphs, which are a popular representation for multi-stage attacks [9]. Attack graphs are a graphical representation of the different ways multi-stage attacks can be launched against system. The nodes depict successful intermediate attack goals with the end nodes representing the ultimate goal of an attack. The edges represent the relation that one attack goal is a stepping stone to another goal and will thus have to be achieved before the other. The nodes can be represented at different levels of abstraction, thus the attack graph representation can bypass the criticism that detailed attack methods and steps will need to be known a priori to be represented (which is almost never the case for reasonably complex systems). Research in the area of attack graphs has included automation techniques to generate these graphs [11], [25], to analyze them [14], [21], and to reason about the completeness of these graphs [14].

We model the probabilistic relation between attack steps and the detectors using the statistical Bayesian network formalism. Bayesian network is particularly appealing in this setting since it enables computationally efficient inference for the unobserved nodes—the attack goals—based on the observed nodes—the detector alerts. The important question that Bayesian inference can answer for us is, given a set of detector alerts, what is the likelihood that an attack goal has been achieved. Further the Bayesian network can be relatively easily created from an attack graph structure for the system, which we assume is given by existing methods.

We design an algorithm to systematically perform Bayesian inference and determine the accuracy and precision for determining that attack goals have been achieved. The algorithm then chooses the number, placement, and choice of detectors that gives the highest value of an application-specific utility function. We apply our technique to two specific systems—a distributed e-commerce system and a Voice-over-IP (VoIP) system and demonstrate the optimal choice under different conditions. The conditions we explore are different qualities of detectors, different level of knowledge of attack paths, and different threshold settings by the system administrator for determining if an attack goal is reached. Our exploration also shows that the value of a detector for determining an attack step degrades exponentially with distance from the site of the attack.

The rest of this document is organized as follows. Section 2 introduces the attack graphs model and provides a brief presentation of inference in Bayesian networks. Section 3 describes the model and algorithm used to determine an appropriate location for detectors. Section 4 provides a description of the systems used in our experiments. Section 5 presents a complete description of the experiments along with their motivations to help determine the location of the intrusion detectors. Section 6 presents related work and section 7 concludes the paper and discusses future work.

2   Background

2.1   Attack Graphs

An attack graph is a representation of the different methods by which a distributed system can be compromised. It represents the intermediate attack goals for a hypothetical adversary leading up to some high level attack goals. The attack goal may be in terms of violating one or more of confidentiality, integrity, or availability of a component in the system. It is particularly suitable for representing multi-stage attacks, in which a successful attack step (or steps) is used to achieve success in a subsequent attack step. An edge will connect the antecedent (or precondition) stage to the consequent (or postcondition) stage. To be accurate, this discussion reflects the notion of one kind of attack graph, called the exploit-dependency attack graph [11], [14], [25], but this is by far the most common type and considering the other subclass will not be discussed further in this paper.

Recent advances in attack graph generation have been able to create graphs for systems of up to hundreds and thousands of hosts [11], [25].

For our detector-location framework, exploit-dependency attack graphs are used as the base graph from which we build the Bayesian network. For the rest of this paper, the vertex representing an exploit in the distributed system will be called an attack step.

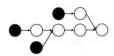

Fig. 1. Attack graph model for a sample web server. There are three starting vertices, representing three vulnerabilities found in different services of the server, from where the attacker can elevate the privileges in order to reach the final goal of compromising the password file.

2.2   Inference in Bayesian Networks

Bayesian networks [13] provide a convenient framework for modeling the relationship between attack steps and detector alerts. Using Bayesian networks we can infer which unobserved attack steps have been achieved based on the observed detector alerts.

Formally, a Bayesian network is a joint probabilistic model for n random variables $(x_1, \ldots, x_n)$ based on a directed acyclic graph $G = (V, E)$ where V is a set of nodes corresponding to the variables $V = (x_1, \ldots, x_n)$ and $E \subseteq V x V$ contains directed edges connecting some of these nodes in an acyclic manner. Instead of weights, the graph edges are described by conditional probabilities of nodes given their parents that are used to construct a joint distribution $P(V)$ or $P(x_1, \ldots, x_n)$.

There are three main tasks associated with Bayesian networks. The first is inferring values of variables corresponding to nodes that are unobserved given values of variables corresponding to observed nodes. In our context this corresponds to predicting whether an attack step has been achieved based on detector alerts. The second task is learning the conditional probabilities in the model based on available data which in our context corresponds to estimating the reliability of the detectors and the probabilistic relations between different attack steps. The third task is learning the structure of the network based on available data. All three tasks have been extensively studied in the machine learning literature and, despite their difficulty in the general case, may be accomplished relatively easily in the case of a Bayesian network.

We focus in this paper mainly on the first task. For the second task, to estimate the conditional probabilities, we can use characterization of the quality of detectors [20] and the perceived difficulty of achieving an attack step, say through risk assessment. We consider the fact that the estimate is unlikely to be perfectly accurate and provide experiments to characterize the loss in performance due to imperfections. For the third task, we rely on extensive prior work on attack graph generation and provide a mapping from the attack graph to the Bayesian network.

In our Bayesian network, the network contains nodes of two different types $V = V_a \bigcup V_b$. The first set of nodes V_a corresponds to binary variables indicating whether specific attack steps in the attack graph occurred or not. The second set of nodes V_b corresponds to binary variables indicating whether a specific detector issued an alert. The first set of nodes representing attack

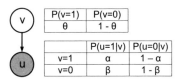

Fig. 2. Simple Bayesian network with two types of nodes: an observed node (u) and an unobserved node (v). The observed node correspond to the detector alert in our framework and its conditional probability table includes the true positive (α) and false positive (β).

steps are typically unobserved while the second set of nodes corresponding to alerts are observed and constitute the evidence. The Bayesian network defines a joint distribution $P(V) = P(V_a, V_b)$ which can be used to compute the marginal probability of the unobserved values $P(V_a)$ and the conditional probability $P(V_a|V_b) = P(V_a, V_b)/P(V_b)$ of the unobserved values given the observed values. The conditional probability $P(V_a|V_b)$ can be used to infer the likely values of the unobserved attack steps given the evidence from the detectors. Comparing the value of the conditional $P(V_a|V_b)$ with the marginal $P(V_a)$ reflects the gain in information about estimating successful attack steps given the current set of detectors. Alternatively, we may estimate the suitability of the detectors by computing classification error rate, precision, recall and Receiver Operating Characteristic (ROC) curve associated with the prediction of V_a based on V_b.

Note that the analysis above is based on emulation done prior to deployment with attacks injected through the vulnerability analysis tools, a plethora of which exist in the commercial and research domains, including integrated infrastructures combining multiple tools.

Some attack steps have one or more detectors that specifically measure whether an attack step has been achieved while other attack steps do not have such detectors. We create an edge in the Bayesian network between nodes representing attack steps and nodes representing the corresponding detector alerts. Consider a specific pair of nodes $v \in V_a, u \in V_b$ representing an attack step and a corresponding detector alert. The conditional probability $P(v|u)$ determines the values $P(v = 1|u = 0), P(v = 0|u = 1), P(v = 0|u = 0), P(v = 1|u = 1)$. These probabilities representing false negative, false positive, and correct behavior (last two) can be obtained from an evaluation of the detectors quality.

3   System Design

3.1   Framework Description

Our framework uses a Bayesian network to represent the causal relationships between attack steps and also between attack steps and detectors. Such relationships are expressed quantitatively, using conditional probabilities. To produce

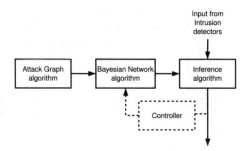

Fig. 3. A block diagram of the framework to determine placement of intrusion detectors. The dotted lines indicate a future component, controller, not included currently in the framework. It would provide for a feedback mechanism to adjust location of detectors.

the Bayesian network[1], an attack graph is used as input. The structure of the attack graph maps exactly to the structure of the Bayesian network. Each node in the Bayesian network can be in one of two states. Each attack stage node can either be achieved or not by the attacker. Each detector node can be in one of two states: alarm generated state or not. The leaf nodes correspond to the starting stages of the attack, which do not need any precondition, and the end nodes correspond to end goals for an adversary. Typically, there are multiple leaf nodes and multiple end nodes.

The Bayesian network requires that the sets of vertices and directed edges form a directed acyclic graph (DAG). This property is also found in attack graphs. The idea is that the attacker follows a monotonic path, in which an attack step does not have to be revisited after moving to a subsequent attack step. This assumption can be considered reasonable in many scenarios according to experiences from real systems.

A Bayesian network quantifies the causal relation that is implied by an edge in an attack graph. In the cases when an attack step has a parent, determined by the existence of an edge coming to this child vertex from another attack step, a conditional probability table is attached to the child vertex. As such, the probability values for each state of the child are conditioned by the state(s) of the parent(s). In these cases, the conditional probability is defined as the probability of a packet from an attacker that already achieved the parent attack step, achieving the child attack step. All values associated to the child are included in a conditional probability table (CPT). As an example, all values for node u in Figure 2 are conditioned on the possible states of its parent, node v. In conclusion, we are assuming that the path taken by the attacker is fully probabilistic. The attacker is following a strategy to maximize the probability of success, to reach the security goal. To achieve it, the attacker is well informed about the vulnerabilities associated to a component of the distributed system

---

[1] Henceforth, when we refer to a node, we mean a node in the Bayesian network, as opposed to a node in the attack graph. The clarifying phrase is thus implied.

and how to exploit it. The fact that an attack graph is generated from databases of vulnerabilities support this assumption.

The CPTs have been estimated for the Bayesian networks created. Input values are a mixture of estimates based on testing specific elements of the system, like using a certain detector such as IPTables [12] or Snort [28], and subjective estimates, using judgment of a system administrator. From the perspective of the expert (administrator), the probability values reflect the difficulty of reaching a higher level attack goal, having achieved some lower level attack goal.

A potential problem when building the Bayesian network is to obtain a good source for the values used in the CPTs of all nodes. The question is then how to deal with possible imperfect knowledge when building Bayesian networks. We took two approaches to deal with this issue: (1) use data from past work and industry sources and (2) evaluate and measure in our experiments the impact such imperfect knowledge might have.

For the purposes of the experiments explained in section 5, we have chosen the junction tree algorithm to do inference, the task of estimating probabilities given a Bayesian network and the observations or evidence. There are many different algorithms that could be chosen, making different tradeoffs between speed, complexity, and accuracy. Still, the junction tree engine is a general-purpose inference algorithm well suited for our experiments since it works under our scenario: allows discrete nodes, as we have defined our two-states nodes, in direct acyclic graphs such as Bayesian networks, and does exact inference. This last characteristic refers to the algorithm computing the posterior probability distribution for all nodes in network, given some evidence.

3.2   Algorithm

We present here an algorithm to achieve an optimal choice and placement of detectors. It takes as input (i) a Bayesian network with all attack vertices, their corresponding CPTs and the host impacted by the attack vertex; (ii) a set of detectors, the possible attack vertices each detector can be associated with, and the CPTs for each detector with respect to all applicable attack vertices.

Input: (i) Bayesian network $BN = (V, CPT(V), H(V))$ where V is the set of attack vertices, $CPT(V)$ is the set of conditional probability tables associated with the attack vertices, and $H(V)$ is the set of hosts affected if the attack vertex is achieved.

(ii) Set of detectors $D = (d_i, V(d_i), CPT[i][j])$ where d_i is the ith detector, $V(d_i)$ is the set of attack vertices that the detector d_i can be attached to (i.e., the detector can possibly detect those attack goals being achieved), and $CPT[i][j] \; \forall j \in V(d_i)$ is the CPT tables associated with detector i and attack vertex j.

Output: Set of tuples $\theta = (d_i, \pi_i)$ where d_i is the ith detector selected and π_i is the set of attack vertices that it is attached to.

DETECTOR-PLACEMENT (BN, D)
1   System-Cost $= 0$
2   Sort all $(d_i, a_j), a_j \in V(d_i), \forall i$ by BENEFIT(d_i, a_j). Sorted list $= L$
3   Length$(L) = N$
4   for $(i = 1 to N)$
5   System-Cost $=$ System-Cost $+$ COST(d_i, a_j)
6   /* COST(d_i, a_j) can be in terms of economic cost, cost due
         to false alarms and missed alarms, etc. */
7   if (System-Cost $>$ Threshold τ) break
8   if $(d_i \in \theta)$ add a_j to $\pi_i \in \theta$
9   else add $(d_i, \pi_i = a_j)$ to θ
10   end for
11   return θ

BENEFIT (d, a)
     /* This is to calculate the benefit from attaching detector d
     to attack vertex a */
1   Let the end attack vertices in the BN be $F = f_i, i = 1, \ldots, M$
2   For each f_i, the following cost-benefit table exists
3   Perform Bayesian inference with d as the only detector
     in the network and connected to attack vertex a
4   Calculate for each f_i, the precision and recall, call them,
     Precision(f_i, d, a), Recall(f_i, d, a)
5   System-Benefit $= \sum_{i=1}^{M}$ [Benefit$_{f_i}$(True Negative) $\times$ Precision(f_i, d, a)
                                    $+$ Benefit$_{f_i}$(True Positive) $\times$ Recall(f_i, d, a)]
6   return System-Benefit

The algorithm starts by sorting all combinations of detectors and their associated attack vertices according to their benefit to the overall system (line 2).
The system benefit is calculated by the BENEFIT function. This specific design
considers only the end nodes in the BN, corresponding to the ultimate attack
goals. Other nodes that are of value to the system owner may also be considered.
Note that a greedy decision is made in the BENEFIT calculation each detector
is considered singly. From the sorted list, (detector, attack vertex) combinations
are added in order, till the overall system cost due to detection is exceeded (line
7). Note that we use a cost-benefit table (line 2 of BENEFIT function), which is
likely specified for each attack vertex at the finest level of granularity. One may
also specify it for each host or each subnet in the system.

The worst-case complexity of this algorithm is $O(dv\, B(v, CPT(v)) + dv \log(dv)$
$+ dv)$, where d is the number of detectors and v is the number of attack vertices. $B(v, CPT(v))$ is the cost of Bayesian inference on a BN with v nodes and
$CPT(v)$ defining the edges. The first term is due to calling Bayesian inference
with up to d times v terms. The second term is the sorting cost and the third
term is the cost of going through the for loop dv times. In practice, each detector
will be applicable to only a constant number of attack vertices and therefore the

dv terms can be replaced by a constant times d, which will be only d considering order statistics.

The reader would have observed that the presented algorithm is greedy-choice of detectors is done according to a pre-computed order, in a linear sweep through the sorted list L (the for loop starting in line 4). This is not guaranteed to provide an optimal solution. For example, detectors d_2 and d_3 taken together may provide greater benefit even though detector d1 being ranked higher would have been considered first in the DETECTOR-PLACEMENT algorithm. This is due to the observation that the problem of optimal detector choice and placement can be mapped to the 0-1 knapsack problem which is known to be NP-hard. The mapping is obvious, consider $D \times A$ (D: Detectors and A: Attack vertices). We have to include as many of these tuples so as to maximize the benefit without the cost exceeding, the system cost of detection.

4   Experimental Systems

We created three Bayesian networks for our experiments modeling two real systems and one synthetic network. These are a distributed electronic commerce (e-commerce) system, a Voice-over-IP (VoIP) network, and a synthetic generic Bayesian network that is larger than the other two. The Bayesian networks were manually created from attack graphs that include several multi-step attacks for the vulnerabilities found in the software used for each system. These vulnerabilities are associated with specific versions of the particular software, and are taken from popular databases [6], [23]. An explanation for each Bayesian network follows.

4.1   E-Commerce System

The distributed e-commerce system used to build the first Bayesian network is a three tier architecture connected to the Internet and composed of an Apache web server, the Tomcat application server, and the MySQL database backend. All servers are running a Unix-based operating system. The web server sits in a de-militarized zone (DMZ) separated by a firewall from the other two servers, which are connected to a network not accessible from the Internet. All connections from the Internet and through servers are controlled by the firewall. Rules state that the web and application servers can communicate, as well as the web server can be reached from the Internet. The attack scenarios are designed with the assumption that the attacker is an external one and thus her starting point is the Internet. The goal for the attacker is to have access to the MySQL database (specifically access customer confidential data such as credit card information node 19 in the Bayesian network of Figure 4).

As an example, an attack step would be a portscan on the application server (node 10). This node has a child node, which represents a buffer overflow vulnerability present in the rpc.statd service running on the application server (node 12). The other attack steps in the network follow a similar logic and represent other phases of an attack to the distributed system. The system includes four

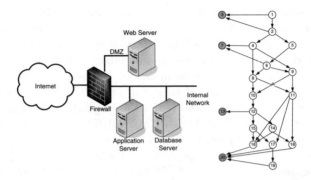

Fig. 4. Network diagram for the e-commerce system and its corresponding Bayesian network. The white nodes are the attack steps and the gray nodes are the detectors.

detectors: IPtables, Snort, Libsafe, and a database IDS. As shown in Figure 4, each detector has a causal relationship to at least one attack step.

4.2   Voice-over-IP (VoIP) System

The VoIP system used to build the second network has a few more components, making the resulting Bayesian network more complex. The system is divided into three zones: a DMZ for the servers accessible from the Internet, an internal network for local resources such as desktop computers, mail server and DNS server, and an internal network only for VoIP components. This separation of the internal network into two units follows the security guidelines for deploying a secure VoIP system [18].

The VoIP network includes a PBX/Proxy, voicemail server and software-based and hardware-based phones. A firewall provides all the rules to control the traffic between zones. The DNS and mail servers in the DMZ are the only accessible hosts from the Internet. The PBX server can route calls to the Internet or to a public-switched telephone network (PSTN). The ultimate goal of this multi-stage

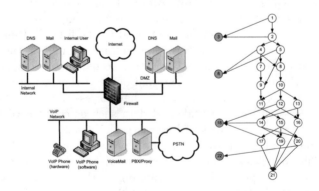

Fig. 5. VoIP system and its corresponding Bayesian network

	Attack = True	Attack = False
Detection = True	TP	FP
Detection = False	FN	TN

$$Recall = \frac{TP}{TP + FN} \qquad Precision = \frac{TP}{TP + FP}$$

Fig. 6. Parameters used for our experiments: True Positive (TP), False Positive (FP), True Negative (TN), False Negative (FN), precision, and recall

attack is to eavesdrop on VoIP communication. There are 4 detectors Iptables, and three network IDSs on the different subnets.

A third synthetic Bayesian network was built to test our framework for experiments where a larger network, than the other two, was required. This network is shown in Figure 7(a).

5   Experiments

The correct number, accuracy, and location of the detectors can provide an advantage to the systems owner when deploying an intrusion detection system. Several metrics have been developed for evaluation of intrusion detection systems. In our work, we concentrate on the precision and recall. Precision is the fraction of true positives determined among all attacks flagged by the detection system. Recall is the fraction of true positives determined among all real positives in the system. The notions of true positive, false positive, etc. are shown in Figure 6. We also plot the ROC curve which is a traditional method for characterizing detector performanceit is a plot of the true positive against the false positive.

For the experiments we create a dataset of 50,000 samples or attacks, based on the respective Bayesian network. We use the Matlab Bayesian network toolbox [3] for our Bayesian inference and sample generation. Each sample consists of a set of binary values, for each attack vertex and each detector vertex. A one (zero) value for an attack vertex indicates that attack step was achieved (not achieved) and a one (zero) value for a detector vertex indicates the detector generated (did not generate) an alert. Separately, we perform inference on the Bayesian network to determine the conditional probability of different attack vertices. The probability is then converted to a binary determination whether the detection system flagged that particular attack step or not, using a threshold. This determination is then compared with reality, as given by the attack samples which leads to a determination of the systems accuracy. There are several experimental parameters which specific attack vertex is to be considered, the threshold, CPT values, etc. and their values (or variations) are mentioned in the appropriate experiment. The CPTs of each node in the network are manually configured according to the authors experience administering security for distributed systems and frequency of occurrences of attacks from references such as vulnerability databases, as mentioned earlier.

5.1   Experiment 1: Distance from Detectors

The objective of experiment 1 was to quantify for a system designer what is the gain in placing a detector close to a service where a security event may occur. Here we used the synthetic network since it provided a larger range of distances between attack steps and detector alerts.

The CPTs were fixed to manually determined values on each attack step. Detectors were used as evidence, one at a time, on the Bayesian network and the respective conditional probability for each attack node was determined. The effect of the single detector on different attack vertices was studied, thereby varying the distance between the node and the detector. The output metric is the difference of two terms. The first term is the conditional probability that the attack step is achieved, conditioned on a specific detector firing. The second term is the probability that the attack step is achieved, without use of any detector evidence. The larger the difference is, the greater is the value of the information provided by the detector. In Figure 7(b), we show the effect due to detector corresponding to node 24 and in Figure 7(c), we consider all the detectors (again one at a time). The effect of all the detectors shows that the conclusions from node 24 are general.

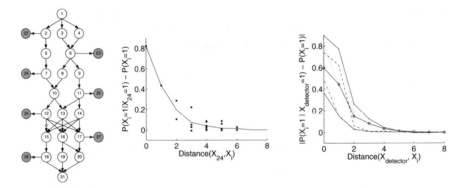

Fig. 7. Results of experiment 1: Impact of distance to a set of attack steps. (a) Generic Bayesian network used. (b) Using node 24 as the detector (evidence), the line shows mean values for rate of change. (c) Comparison between different detectors as evidence, showing the mean rate of change for case.

The results show that a detector can affect nodes inside a radius of up to three edges from the detector. The change in probability for a node within this radius, compared to one outside the radius, can be two times greater when the detector is used as evidence. For all Bayesian networks tested, the results were consistent to the three edges radius observation.

5.2   Experiment 2: Impact of Imperfect Knowledge

The objective of experiment 2 was to determine the performance of the detection system in the face of attacks. In the first part of the experiment *(Exp 2a)*, the

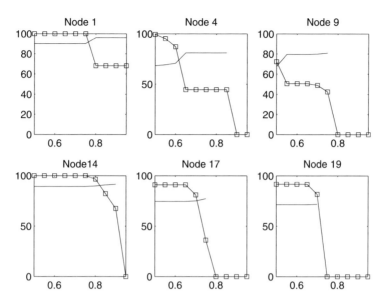

Fig. 8. Precision and recall as a function of detection threshold, for the e-commerce Bayesian network. The line with square markers is recall and other line is for precision.

effect of the threshold, that is used in converting the conditional probability of an attack step into a binary determination, is studied. This corresponds to the practical situation that a system administrator has to make a binary decision based on the result of a probabilistic framework and there is no oracle at hand to help. For the second part of the experiment *(Exp 2b)*, the CPT values in the Bayesian network are perturbed by introducing variances of different magnitudes. This corresponds to the practical situation that the system administrator cannot accurately gauge the level of difficulty for the adversary to achieve attack goals. The impact of the imperfect knowledge is studied through a ROC curve.

For Exp 2a, precision and recall were plotted as a function of the threshold value. This was done for all the attack nodes in the Bayesian network and the results for a representative sample of six nodes are shown in Figure 8. We used threshold values from 0.5 to 0.95, since anything below 0.5 would imply the Bayesian network is useless in its predictive ability.

Expectedly, as the threshold is increased, there are fewer false positives and the precision of the detection system improves. The opposite is true for the recall of the system since there are more false negatives. However, an illuminating observation is that the precision is relatively insensitive to the threshold variation while the recall has a sharp cutoff. Clearly, the desired threshold is to the left of the cutoff point. Therefore, this provides a scientific basis for an administrator to set the threshold for drawing conclusions from a Bayesian network representing the system.

In experiment 2b we introduced variance to the CPT values of all the attack nodes, mimicking different levels of imperfect knowledge an admin may

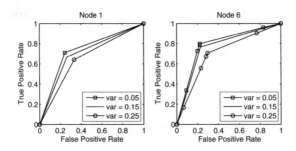

Fig. 9. ROC curves for two attack steps in e-commerce Bayesian network. Each curve corresponds to a different variance added to the CTP values.

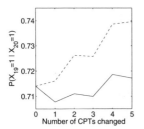
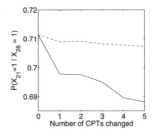

Fig. 10. Impact of deviation from correct CPT values, for the (a) e-commerce and (b) generic Bayesian networks

have about the adversary's attack strategies. When generating the samples corresponding to the attacks, we used three variance values: 0.05, 0.15, and 0.25. Each value could be associated with a different level of knowledge from an administrator: expert, intermediate, and nave, respectively. For each variance value, ten batches of 1,000 samples were generated and the detection results were averaged over all batches.

In Figure 9, we show the ROC curves for nodes 1 and 6 of the e-commerce system, with all four detectors in place. Expectedly, as the variance increases, the performance suffers. However, the process of Bayesian inference shows an inherent resilience since the performance does not degrade significantly with the increase in variance. For node 1, several points are placed so close together that only one marker shows up. On the contrary, for node 6, multiple well spread out TP-FP value pairs are observed. We hypothesize that since node 1 is directly connected to the detector node 3, its influence over node 1 dominates that of all other detectors. Hence fewer number of sharp transitions are seen compared to node 6, which is more centrally placed with respect to multiple detectors.

Experiment 2c also looked at the impact of imperfect knowledge when defining the CPT values in the Bayesian network. Here we progressively changed the CPT values for several attack steps in order to determine how much we would deviate from the correct value. We used two values 0.6 and 0.8 for each CPT cell (only two are independent) giving rise to four possible CPT tables for each node. We plot the minimum and maximum conditional probabilities for a representative attack node for a given detector flagging. We change the number of CPTs that we perturb from the ideal values. Expectedly as the number of CPTs changed increases, the difference between the minimum and the maximum increases, but the range is within 0.03. Note that the point at the left end of the curve for zero CPTs changed gives the correct value.

Both experiments indicate that the BN formalism is relatively robust to imperfect assumptions concerning the CPT values. This is an important fact since it is likely that the values determined by an experienced system administrator would still be somewhat imperfect. Overall, as long as the deviation of the assumed CPTs from the truth is not overwhelming, the network performance degrades gracefully.

5.3   Experiment 3: Impact on Choice and Placement of Detectors

The objective of experiment 3 was to determine the impact of selecting the detectors and their corresponding locations. To achieve this, we ran experiments on the e-commerce and the VoIP Bayesian networks to determine a pair of detectors that would be most effective. This pair, called the optimal pair, is chosen according to the algorithm described in Section 3.2. The performance of the optimal pair is compared against additional pairs selected at random. We show the result using the ROC curve for the two ultimate attack goals, namely node 19 and node 21 in the e-commerce and the VoIP systems.

To calculate the performance of each pair of detectors, we created 10,000 samples from each Bayesian network, corresponding to that many actual attacks. Then we performed Bayesian inference and calculated the conditional probability of the attack step, given the pair of detectors. We determined the true positive rate and false positive rate by sweeping across threshold values.

Results show that the pair of detectors determined from the algorithm performs better than the other randomly selected pairs. Figure 11a shows the situation in which a single detector (d_{20}) attached to two attack nodes (x_{19}, x_{18}) performs better than two detectors $(d_{13}$ and d_7, or d_{12} and $d_3)$. The placement of the detector d_{20} affects the performance. This can be explained by the fact that node 18 is more

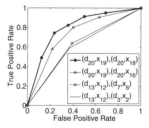
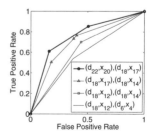

Fig. 11. ROC curves for detection of attack steps, using pairs of detectors, in the e-commerce network (left) and the VoIP network (right)

highly connected in the attack graph and therefore attaching detector d_{20} to that node, rather than node 16, provides better predictive performance.

There is a cost of adding detectors to a system, but there is also a cost of having a detector attached to more attack nodes, in terms of the bandwidth and computation. Thus adding further edges in the Bayesian network between a detector node and an attack node, even if feasible, may not be desirable. For the VoIP network, detector pair d_{22} and d_{18} performs best. This time two separate detectors outperform a single high quality detector (d_{18}) connected to two nodes.

Further details on all experiments performed, including all the probability values used for the Bayesian networks, are available at [22]. These are omitted here due to space constraints and the interested party is welcome to further read. All the experiments validate the intuition behind our algorithm that the greedy choice of the detectors also gives good results when multiple detectors are considered together and over the entire Bayesian network.

6   Related Work

Bayesian networks have been used in intrusion detection to perform classification of events. Kruegel et al. [17] proposed the usage of Bayesian networks to reduce the number of false alarms. Bayesian networks are used to improve the aggregation of different model outputs and allow integration of additional information. The experimental results show an improvement in the accuracy of detections, compared to threshold-based schemes. Ben Amor et al. [4] studied the use of nave Bayes in intrusion detection, which included a performance comparison with decision trees. Due to similar performance and simpler structure, nave Bayes is an attractive alternative for intrusion detection. Other researchers have also used nave Bayesian inference for classifying intrusion events [29].

To the best of our knowledge, the problem of determining an appropriate location for detectors has not been systematically explored by the intrusion detection community. However, analogous problems have been studied to some extent in the physical security and the sensor network fields.

Jones et al. [15] developed a Markov Decision Process (MDP) model of how an intruder might try to penetrate the various barriers designed to protect a physical facility. The model output includes the probability of a successful intrusion and the most likely paths for success. These paths provide a basis to determine the location of new barriers to deter a future intrusion.

In the case of sensor networks, the placement problem has been studied to identify multiple phenomena such as determining location of an intrusion [1], contamination source [5], [27], and atmospheric conditions [16]. Anjum et al. [1] determined which nodes should act as intrusion detectors in order to provide detection capabilities in a hierarchical sensor network. The adversary is trying to send malicious traffic to a destination node (say, the base node). In their model, only some nodes called tamper-resistant nodes are capable of executing a signature-based intrusion detection algorithm and these nodes cannot be compromised by an adversary. Since these nodes are expensive, the goal is to minimize the number of such nodes and the authors provide a distributed approximate algorithm for this based on minimum cut-set and minimum dominating set. The solution is applicable to a specific kind of topology, widely used in sensor networks, namely clusters with a cluster head in each cluster capable of communicating with the nodes at the higher layer of the network hierarchy.

In [5], the sensor placement problem is studied to detect the contamination of air or water supplies from a single source. The goal is to detect that contamination has happened and the source of the contamination, under the constraints that the number of sensors and the time for detection are limited. The authors show that the problem with sensor constraint or time constraint are both NP-hard and they come up with approximation algorithms. They also solve the problem exactly for two specific cases, the uniform clique and rooted trees. A significant contribution of this work is the time efficient method of calculating the sensor placement. However, several simplifying assumptions are made—sensing is perfect and no sensor failure (either natural or malicious) occurs, there is a single contaminating source, and the flow is stable.

Krause et al. [16] also point out the intractability of the placement problem and present a polynomial-time algorithm to provide near-optimal placement which incurs low communication cost between the sensors. The approximation algorithm exploits two properties of this problem: submodularity, formalizing the intuition that adding a node to a small deployment can help more than adding a node to a large deployment; and locality, under which nodes that are far from each other provide almost independent information. In our current work, we also experienced the locality property of the placement problem. The proposed solution learns a probabilistic model (based on Gaussian processes) of the underlying phenomenon (variation of temperature, light, and precipitation) and for the expected communication cost between any two locations from a small, short-term initial deployment.

In [27], the authors present an approach for determining the location in an indoor environment based on which sensors cover the location. The key idea is to ensure that each resolvable position is covered by a unique set of sensors, which then serves as its signature. They make use of identifying code theory to reduce the number of active sensors required by the system and yet provide unique localization for each position. The algorithm also considers robustness, in terms of the number of sensor failures that can be corrected, and provides solutions in harsh environments, such as presence of noise and changes in the structural topology. The objective for deploying sensors here is quite different from our current work.

For all the previous work on placement of detectors, the authors are looking to detect events of interest, which propagate using some well-defined models, such as, through the cluster head en route to a base node. Some of the work (such as [16]) is focused on detecting natural events, that do not have a malicious motive in avoiding detection. In our case, we deal with malicious adversaries who have an active goal of trying to bypass the security of the system. The adversaries' methods of attacking the system do not follow a well-known model making our problem challenging. As an example of how our solution handles this, we use noise in our BN model to emulate the lack of an accurate attack model.

There are some similarities between the work done in alert correlation and ours, primarily the interest to reduce the number of alerts to be analyzed from an intrusion. Approaches such as [24] have proposed modeling attack scenarios to correlate alerts and identify causal relationships among the alerts. Our work aims to closely integrate the vulnerability analysis into the placement process, whereas the alert correlation proposals have not suggested such importance.

The idea of using Bayes theorem for detector placement is suggested in [26]. No formal definition is given, but several metrics such as accuracy, sensitivity, and specificity are presented to help an administrator make informed choices about placing detectors in a distributed system. These metrics are associated to different areas or sub-networks of the system to help in the decision process.

Many studies have been done on developing performance metrics for the evaluation of intrusion detection systems (IDS), which have influenced our choice of metrics here. Axelsson [2] showed the applicability of estimation theory in the intrusion detection field and presented the Bayesian detection rate as a metric for the performance of an IDS. His observation that the base rate, and not only the false alarm rate, is an important factor on the Bayesian detection rate, was included in our work by using low base rates as part of probability values in the Bayesian network. The MAFTIA Project [8] proposed precision and recall to effectively determine when a vulnerability was exploited in the system. A difference from our approach is that they expand the metrics to consider a set of IDSes and not only a single detector. The idea of using ROC curves to measure performance of intrusion detectors has been explored many times, most recently in [7], [10].

Extensive work has been done for many years with attack graphs. Recent work has concentrated on the problems of generating attack graphs for large networks and automating the process to describe and analyze vulnerabilities and system components to create the graphs. The NetSPA system [11] uses a breath-first technique to generate a graph that grows almost linearly with the size of the distributed system. Ou et al. [25] proposed a graph building algorithm using a formal logical technique that allows to create graphs of polynomial size to the network being analyzed.

7   Conclusions and Future Work

Bayesian networks have proven to be a useful tool in representing complex probability distributions, such as in our case of determining the likelihood that an attack goal has been achieved, given evidence from a set of detectors. By using attack graphs and Bayesian inference, we can quantify the overall detection performance in the systems by looking at different choices and placements of detectors and the detection parameter settings. We also quantified the information gain due to a detector as a function of its distance from the attack step. Also, the effectiveness of the Bayesian networks can be affected by imperfect knowledge when defining the conditional probability values. Nevertheless, the Bayesian network exhibits considerable resiliency to these factors as our experiments showed.

Future work should include looking at the scalability issues of Bayesian networks and its impact on determining the location for a set of detectors in a distributed system. The probability values acquisition problem can be handled by using techniques such as the recursive noisy-OR modeling [19] but experimentation is required to determine its benefits and limitations for our scenario.

Acknowledgments. Gaspar Modelo-Howard was partly supported by an IFARHU-SENACYT Scholarship from the Republic of Panama. Saurabh Bagchi was partly supported in this work by an endowment grant from Purdue's Center for Education and Research in Information Assurance and Security (CERIAS).

References

1. Anjum, F., Subhadrabandhu, D., Sarkar, S., Shetty, R.: On Optimal Placement of Intrusion Detection Modules in Sensor Networks. In: 1st IEEE International Conference on Broadband Networks, pp. 690–699. IEEE Press, New York (2004)
2. Axelsson, S.: The base-rate fallacy and the difficulty of intrusion detection. ACM Trans. Inf. Syst. Secur. 3-3, 186–205 (2000)
3. Bayes Net Toolbox for Matlab, http://www.cs.ubc.ca/~murphyk/Software
4. Ben Amor, N., Benferhat, S., Elouedi, Z.: Naive Bayes vs decision trees in intrusion detection systems. In: 19th ACM Symposium on Applied computing, pp. 420–424. ACM Press, New York (2004)
5. Berger-Wolf, T., Hart, W., Saia, J.: Discrete Sensor Placement Problems in Distribution Networks. J. Math. and Comp. Model. 42, 1385–1396 (2005)
6. Bugtraq Vulnerability Database, http://www.securityfocus.com/vulnerabilities
7. Cardenas, A., Baras, J., Seamon, K.: A Framework for the Evaluation of Intrusion Detection Systems. In: 27th IEEE Symposium on Security and Privacy, p. 15. IEEE Press, New York (2006)
8. Dacier, M. (ed.): Design of an Intrusion-Tolerant Intrusion Detection System. Research Report, Maftia Project (2002)
9. Foo, B., Wu, Y., Mao, Y., Bagchi, S., Spafford, E.: ADEPTS: Adaptive Intrusion Response using Attack Graphs in an E-Commerce Environment. In: International Conference on Dependable Systems and Networks, pp. 508–517 (2005)
10. Gu, G., Fogla, P., Dagon, D., Lee, W., Skoric, B.: Measuring Intrusion Detection Capability: An Information-Theoretic Approach. In: 1st ACM Symposium on Information, Computer and Communications Security, pp. 90–101. ACM Press, New York (2006)
11. Ingols, K., Lippmann, R., Piwowarski, K.: Practical Attack Graph Generation for Network Defense. In: 22nd Annual Computer Security Applications Conference, pp. 121–130. IEEE Press, New York (2006)
12. IPTables Firewall, http://www.netfilters.org/projects/iptables
13. Jensen, F.: Bayesian Networks and Decision Graphs. Springer, Heidelberg (2001)
14. Jha, S., Sheyner, O., Wing, J.: Two Formal Analyses of Attack Graphs. In: 15th IEEE Computer Security Foundations Workshop, pp. 49–63. IEEE Press, New York (2002)

15. Jones, D., Davis, C., Turnquist, M., Nozick, L.: Physical Security and Vulnerability Modeling for Infrastructure Facilities. Technical Report, Sandia National Laboratories (2006)
16. Krause, A., Guestrin, C., Gupta, A., Kleinberg, J.: Near-optimal Sensor Placements: Maximizing Information while Minimizing Communication Cost. In: 5th International Conference on Information Processing in Sensor Networks, pp. 2–10. ACM Press, New York (2006)
17. Krügel, C., Mutz, D., Robertson, W., Valeyr, F.: Bayesian Event Classification for Intrusion Detection. In: 19th Annual Computer Security Applications Conference, pp. 14–23. IEEE Press, New York (2003)
18. Kuhn, D., Walsh, T., Fires, S.: Security Considerations for Voice Over IP Systems. Special Publication 800-58, National Institute of Standards and Technology (2005)
19. Lemmer, J., Gossink, D.: Recursive Noisy OR - A Rule for Estimating Complex Probabilistic Interactions. IEEE Trans. Syst. Man. Cybern. B. 34, 2252–2261 (2004)
20. Lippmann, R., et al.: Evaluating Intrusion Detection Systems: The 1998 DARPA Off-line Intrusion Detection Evaluation. In: 1st DARPA Information Survivability Conference and Exposition, pp. 81–89 (2000)
21. Mehta, V., Bartzis, C., Zhu, H., Clarke, E., Wing, J.: Ranking Attack Graphs. In: Zamboni, D., Krügel, C. (eds.) RAID 2006. LNCS, vol. 4219, pp. 127–144. Springer, Heidelberg (2006)
22. Modelo-Howard, G.: Addendum to Determining Placement of Intrusion Detectors for a Distributed Application through Bayesian Network Modeling, http://cobweb.ecn.purdue.edu/ dcsl/publications/ detectors-location_addendum.pdf
23. National Vulnerability Database, http://nvd.nist.gov/nvd.cfm
24. Ning, P., Cui, Y., Reeves, D.: Constructing Attack Scenarios through Correlation of Intrusion Alerts. In: 9th ACM Conference on Computers & Communications Security, pp. 245–254 (2002)
25. Ou, X., Boyer, W., McQueen, M.: A Scalable Approach to Attack Graph Generation. In: 13th ACM Conference on Computer & Communications Security, pp. 336–345 (2006)
26. Peikari, C., Chuvakin, A.: Security Warrior. O'Reilly, New York (2004)
27. Ray, S., Starobinski, D., Trachtenberg, A., Ungrangsi, R.: Robust Location Detection with Sensor Networks. IEEE J. on Selected Areas in Comm. 22, 1016–1025 (2004)
28. Snort Intrusion Detection System, http://www.snort.org
29. Valdes, A., Skinner, K.: Adaptive, Model-based Monitoring for Cyber Attack Detection. In: Debar, H., Mé, L., Wu, S.F. (eds.) RAID 2000. LNCS, vol. 1907, pp. 80–92. Springer, Heidelberg (2000)

A Multi-Sensor Model to Improve
Automated Attack Detection

Magnus Almgren[1], Ulf Lindqvist[2], and Erland Jonsson[1]

[1] Department of Computer Science and Engineering
Chalmers University of Technology
SE-412 96 Göteborg, Sweden
[2] Computer Science Laboratory
SRI International
333 Ravenswood Ave
Menlo Park, CA 94025, USA

Abstract. Most intrusion detection systems available today are using a single audit source for detection, even though attacks have distinct manifestations in different parts of the system. In this paper we investigate how to use the alerts from several audit sources to improve the accuracy of the intrusion detection system (IDS). Concentrating on web server attacks, we design a theoretical model to automatically reason about alerts from different sensors, thereby also giving security operators a better understanding of possible attacks against their systems. Our model takes sensor status and capability into account, and therefore enables reasoning about the absence of expected alerts. We require an explicit model for each sensor in the system, which allows us to reason about the quality of information from each particular sensor and to resolve apparent contradictions in a set of alerts.

Our model, which is built using Bayesian networks, needs some initial parameter values that can be provided by the IDS operator. We apply this model in two different scenarios for web server security. The scenarios show the importance of having a model that dynamically can adapt to local transitional traffic conditions, such as encrypted requests, when using conflicting evidence from sensors to reason about attacks.

Keywords: intrusion detection, alert reasoning.

1 Introduction

The accuracy of an intrusion detection system (IDS), meaning the degree to which the security officer can trust the IDS to recognize attacks and at the same time not produce false alarms, can be considered the most important property of an IDS (a general definition of detector accuracy can be found in [19]). However, many IDSs do not provide a very high degree of accuracy, because of two common shortcomings. First, the IDS tends to rely on a single detection method applied to a single audit source such as network packets, which is not sufficient to accurately recognize all types of attacks. Second, many IDSs have a propensity for producing

R. Lippmann, E. Kirda, and A. Trachtenberg (Eds.): RAID 2008, LNCS 5230, pp. 291–310, 2008.
© Springer-Verlag Berlin Heidelberg 2008

massive amounts of alerts, many of which are irrelevant or false. Over time, the security officer monitoring the alerts from the IDS could learn which types of alerts can be safely ignored, and even which combinations of alerts indicate a more serious incident.

A significant amount of research has been conducted to improve the accuracy of IDSs. Some of that work has been focused on the implementation of detectors, such as speed improvements or techniques to detect obfuscated attacks. Other work has been focused on alert processing techniques in the form of alert aggregation and correlation, such as root-cause analysis. Diversity has been proposed as a principle to be adopted to improve detection coverage. One form of diversity is to use a combination of detection techniques, for example, signature-based detection combined with statistical anomaly detection. Another form of diversity is to simultaneously use input from different audit streams, for example, network packets and application event logs.

While diversity is a promising approach to increasing IDS accuracy, complementary sensors are currently not widely developed or deployed. This happens because without automated procedures to take advantage of multiple diverse alert sources and make the correct inferences, the burden on the security officer will increase rather than decrease, especially in the cases of conflicting sensor reports. This paper proposes and investigates a model upon which such automated reasoning can be based, ultimately presenting the security officer with actionable and highly accurate information about ongoing attacks, and reducing the need for operator experience and expertise.

The model presented in this paper is applied to the output of traditional correlators—we assume that these techniques preprocess the alert stream and present us with an aggregated set of related alerts concerning an attack (see Section 7 for a discussion of correlation techniques). We propose a model to combine the alerts from several intrusion detection systems using different audit sources. We show how our model can resolve seemingly conflicting evidence about possible attacks as well as properly account for transient failure modes of the sensors in the system, such as the network IDS being blind when analyzing encrypted traffic.

Our approach would benefit from sensors having an intrinsic knowledge of their own detection capability as well as having modes to specifically monitor the outcomes of certain attacks. However, our approach also works with traditional sensors. By using correlated alerts as input, we benefit from previous research into correlation. As we present them with further refined information, the security officers can spend their time actively protecting the system instead of trying to understand the mixed message from intrusion detection sensors.

The rest of the paper is organized as follows. In Section 2 we describe the notation used in the paper and outline the problem we are investigating. We then formally describe the assumptions and requirements we need before we introduce our decision framework in Section 3. We use two scenarios to exemplify the model, and these are presented in Section 4. The test bed and the experiments

are described in Section 5. We summarize our findings in Section 6 and discuss
related work in Section 7. The paper is concluded in Section 9.

2   Theory

2.1   Notation

We use the term *sensor* to denote a component that monitors an event stream
(audit source) for indications of suspicious activity according to a detection algorithm and produces alerts as a result. A simple IDS, such as a typical deployment
of the popular tool Snort, in most cases constitutes a single sensor. We therefore
use the terms *sensor* and *IDS* interchangeably in this paper. More advanced
IDS deployments could be composed of several sensors that feed into a common
alerting framework.

Let us assume that we use a set of intrusion detection sensors, S, to detect
attacks, and in particular the attack, $\mathcal{A}$. A sensor S_i may alert for ongoing
attacks but sometimes gives false alerts. We denote such alerts by $_{\mathcal{A}}a_j^i$, where
each sensor may give several alerts for each attack (j-index). If S_i is present in
the system and alerts for the attack $\mathcal{A}$, we denote this by $S_i : {}_{\mathcal{A}}a_j^i$. For simplicity,
we are going to concentrate on a single attack in the discussion below, so the
index $\mathcal{A}$ is not shown explicitly. When the attack $\mathcal{A}$ does not trigger any alert
in the sensor S_i, we denote this by $S_i : \neg_{\mathcal{A}}a_j^i$ or simpler as $S_i : \neg a_j^i$. To simplify
the discussion, we show only the missing alerts that are actually relevant for the
current situation. Finally, a sensor may temporarily be missing in a system or
a specific sensor may not work as intended. Following the same notation as for
alerts, we denote such a malfunctioning or missing sensor with $\neg S_i$. Observing
this state directly is very difficult in current intrusion detection systems, and
often we can only indirectly assume that a sensor is not working correctly. For
example, a heartbeat message may tell us that a network IDS is still running,
but if the traffic is encrypted, the sensor cannot properly analyze it.

Following this notation, we have the four separate cases shown in Table 1.
Each alert for these cases may be true or false, but if the sensor is not working
(iii and iv) we treat all alerts as being false, as they would only coincidentally
be true. We consider case (iv) to be uncommon with more sophisticated sensors, but if it happens the security officer will investigate the (false) alert and
discover the malfunctioning sensor. Finally, as the sensor status cannot directly
be observed, cases (i) and (iv) would look similar to a security operator without
further investigation, as would cases (ii) and (iii).

2.2   Example with Two Sensors

Now consider a particular system with two sensors S_1 and S_2, where each sensor
can output a single alert for the $\mathcal{A}$-attack (we drop the j-index in this example).

Table 1. The four possible sensor / alert states

(i) S_i: a_j^i S_i is working correctly and outputs alert a_j^i.

(ii) S_i:$\neg a_j^i$ S_i is working correctly and has not found any signs that warrant the output of alert a_j^i.

(iii) $\neg S_i$:$\neg a_j^i$ S_i is not working correctly and does not output alert a_j^i regardless of the attack status.

(iv) $\neg S_i$: a_j^i S_i is not working correctly but still outputs an alert regardless of the attack status, for example, when traffic is encrypted but happens to contain a pattern that triggers the alert a_j^i.

Table 2. An example using two sensors with one alert each

$\neg a^1$	$\neg a^2$	(2a)
a^1	a^2	(2b)
$\neg a^1$	a^2	(2c)
a^1	$\neg a^2$	(2d)

As hinted earlier, the sensor status is seldom directly measured, so with such a setup only the four cases shown in Table 2 can be directly observed.

The interpretations of (2a) (i.e., the first case in Table 2) and (2b) are straightforward. In the first case, no sensor reports anything so we do not investigate further. In the second case, both sensors warn for an attack and for that reason it is worth investigating further. However, cases (2c) and (2d) are interesting, as only one of the two sensors reports the possible ongoing attack. How should these two cases be interpreted?

Clearly, we need more information to draw any conclusions for cases (2c) and (2d). The burden of collecting this extra information, and using it to reason about the attack status for these cases, has often fallen on the security operator. In our opinion, many correlator techniques have so far taken a simplified but safe view: if any sensor reports an attack, it should be treated as an attack, i.e., the security operator needs to investigate this issue manually. The problem we are investigating is whether we can improve the automatic analysis and provide a more refined answer to the security operator. In the remainder of this section, we describe some reasons for why traditional correlation technologies may have used the simplified view described above. These reasons are used as a basis for the discussion in Section 3, where we set up the necessary framework to provide a model that aids the security operator by solving cases with seemingly conflicting evidence.

2.3   The Problem of Conflicting Evidence

In Section 2.2, we showed the possible outputs of two sensors, which in certain cases may be conflicting. Here, we discuss how to interpret those cases of conflicting sensor output. This discussion serves as a background to understand the requirements of our model that we introduce in Section 3.

No Complementary Sensors Deployed. First we note that in many typical environments, cases (2c) and (2d) described above may not be very common, because the same type of sensor is duplicated across the network to allow for some partial redundancy in the monitoring capacity. For example, a company may have two instances of Snort analyzing almost the same traffic. In this case, the only reason the identical sensors would disagree is if one is broken. Thus, the only recourse is to interpret both (2c) and (2d) as a sign of an attack. We would like to point out that even though it may be common to have only one type of sensor, research shows the benefits of using several different sensors for attack detection ([3]).

Ambiguity between 'No Attack' and a Broken Sensor. Even when we use different types of sensors we are still faced with the problem of what a missing alert means. The sensor state is often unknown, and as we showed in Table 1, a sensor reporting no alert may signify one of two conditions: $S_i : \neg a^i$ or $\neg S_i : \neg a^i$. In the first case, the sensor is working as intended and does not detect any signs of an attack. In the second case, the sensor is broken, and for that reason it cannot reliably detect attacks. Not only is it difficult to determine the stationary state of a sensor through direct observation, but the conditions for when a sensor may detect attacks may also change dynamically; a network IDS is blind to the single encrypted web request, or a request that is routed around it, and so on. Not knowing the sensor state, the operator cannot confidently disregard an alert just because only one sensor produced it.

Detailed Sensor Alert Information Missing. Let us say that we do know that both sensors are working as intended but they report conflicting evidence as in (2c). Without any detailed information about the particulars of a sensor and its proclivity to produce false alerts, one cannot automatically decide which sensor to believe. One might not even know that a^1 is missing in (2c). Unless we have a sensor model, this decision must be left to the human operator.

Generality Has Been Prioritized. Many correlation techniques try to group alerts belonging to the same attack to make the security operator's task easier. As correlation techniques have been developed after most intrusion detection techniques, the developers of correlation techniques have not had much influence on the operation of IDS sensors; instead, the focus has been to work with *any* sensor.

3   Intrusion Detection Sensor Model

We first describe our assumptions and our requirements. With these clearly in mind, we then describe our proposed model and its advantages and disadvantages.

3.1   Assumptions and Requirements

As shown in the previous section, we need more information to be able to handle cases with conflicting information from different sensors. We make the following assumption in our work:

Assumption 1. *We assume that the absence of a particular alert may constitute evidence that an attack is not taking place.* At first glance this assumption may look strange, but this is already the case in any IDS deployment today; with no alert, one assumes that all is well and one does not follow up with an investigation (this is case (2a) in Section 2.2).

We can then formulate the following requirements.

Requirement 1. *We require a sensor model, which tells us whether an alert for a particular attack is in the set of possible alerts that this sensor can produce.* Such a model could possibly be created by automatic tools [15].

Requirement 2. *Furthermore, we require that this sensor model describe the sensor's accuracy with respect to detecting a particular attack.* Knowing the sensor's accuracy helps us resolve cases with conflicting evidence.

Requirement 3. *We require sensors to have some degree of functional independence.* Additional identical sensors analyzing the same event stream do not provide added value beyond redundancy. However, independence is a difficult requirement to satisfy and to verify. More work is needed to develop different types of sensors and to measure the functional independence between them.

Requirement 4. *We require knowledge of the sensor status to draw the correct conclusion.* There are two reasons why a sensor may not produce an alert; the sensor is either functioning normally and has concluded that an attack is not in progress, or the sensor is malfunctioning. Only in the former case should we consider a missing alert to be evidence that an attack is not occurring. The sensor model needs to describe under what conditions a sensor will not work (for example, when it encounters encrypted traffic).

Now let us return to case (2c) described in Section 2.2 with conflicting information: $\neg a^1$, a^2. Using *assumption 1* above (and knowing to look for the missing alert from *req. 1*), we can conclude that one of the sensors is not reliable in this case. There are two possible interpretations:

– *An attack is indeed in progress*
  - S_1 is not working correctly, and therefore did not produce an alert, or
  - the attack detection mechanism in S_1 does not cover all variants of this attack.
– *There is no attack in progress*
  - S_2 is not working correctly and produced this alert as a result of malfunctioning, or
  - the attack detection mechanism in S_2 falsely concluded that an attack was in progress based on its analysis of the audit source (a traditional false alarm).

Thus, we are faced with first deciding if all sensors are working in the system (*req. 4*). Clearly, if a sensor is malfunctioning in an easily discernible way, we

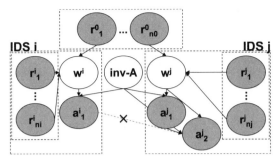

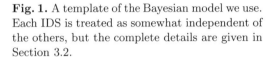

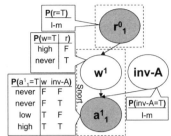

Fig. 1. A template of the Bayesian model we use. Each IDS is treated as somewhat independent of the others, but the complete details are given in Section 3.2.

Fig. 2. An example of the model using Snort with the rule for detecting the *phf attack* (sid=1762). We use conditional probability tables with labels (where l-m stands for low-medium), which are later replaced with actual probabilities.

can differentiate between these situations. However, if all sensors seem to work correctly we need to weigh the evidence given by one sensor for this particular attack against the evidence given by another sensor (*req. 2*). Simply put, if it is known that S_2 is prone to false alarms for this particular attack, while S_1 is more accurate, we can ignore the combined alert for now. This analysis is possible only if the sensors are somewhat independent (*req. 3*). Thus, our model needs to account for the sensor status (and its known weaknesses) as well as the detection capability of the sensor (rule) for this particular attack.

3.2   Model Description

We use a Bayesian framework to model the sensors and their interdependence. Such a framework has several advantages, and among them is the intuitive mix between the graphical model with the underlying formal reliance on probability. The model is shown in Figure 1. As shown, the model consists of a series of nodes and the directional connections between these nodes. The model can graphically be represented as a DAG (directionally acyclic graph). The nodes represents variables, and the edges between nodes signify a dependence between these particular variables. There are efficient algorithms to calculate the posterior probability of a variable, given the observed evidence of other variables.

We use the model to find out whether an attack that should be further investigated (node **investigate-A**) is occurring, based on evidence in the form of alerts (nodes a_*^*) collected from a set of intrusion detection sensors. Based on several parameters and observations (nodes r_*^*), a sensor may accurately detect an attack or fail to do so, and this is accounted for in the model (nodes w^*). The value of each node may be observed in some circumstances (for example, a specific alert is triggered). In this particular application domain, some nodes will probably almost always be observed while some others will never be observed. In Figure 1, the observable nodes are shaded, while the white nodes are seldom observed directly.

To summarize, in the model we use four types of nodes:

Node inv-A is used to determine if the ongoing attack is serious enough to be further investigated. Obviously, the value of this node is never directly observed.

Nodes a_*^* signify whether we have received particular alerts, and thus serve as the basis to calculate the node *inv-A*.

Nodes w^* model the sensor status, as a missing alert may mean two different conditions: no attack or a broken sensor. These nodes cannot directly be observed.

Nodes r_*^* are used to calculate the sensor status (nodes w^*) in a fashion similar to how the nodes a_*^* are used to calculate *inv-A*. These nodes are often observed and populated with particular observations from the sensor environment.

The nodes are informally organized into groups based on which intrusion detection system they belong to. Keeping each IDS as isolated from others as possible leads to a simpler model and below we elaborate on this topic and describe the dotted edge with the x found in Figure 1.

Even though each IDS has its own particular failure modes, some observations are important to several IDSs. For that reason, there are both *global* (r^0) and *local* r-nodes. Furthermore, some of the r-nodes report transient observations while others may report more stationary conditions where a value is *sticky*, i.e., remains until explicitly changed. We describe the implementation in further detail in Section 5. Below we expand on the features of the model.

Parameter Estimation. As with any other probability model, one needs to estimate parameters for each node. This is difficult, but there are several reasons why we believe it is feasible for our model.

Using Independence Assumptions: the model takes advantage of the independence assumptions visible in the graphical structure and thus reduces the number of estimates that are necessary as compared with a full joint distribution without explicit independence assumptions.

Robust Parameter Estimation: furthermore, it is many times enough to capture the ratio between the parameters while their actual values are less important [5].

Local Parameters: the model parameters are expressed as something the security officer is already familiar with, e.g., false positives and false negatives for each rule.

We envision that most of these parameters have reasonable default values that can be estimated by the IDS vendor, and that the security officer then only needs to fine-tune the settings at the local site. It is possible that some of this fine-tuning can be performed by machine learning algorithms based on current traffic seen at the site.

Problematic Interdependence between IDSs. We would like to highlight the problem concerning independence assumptions. Clearly, the model in Figure 1 is simplified. Keeping a simple and modular structure introduces some incorrect independence assumptions. For example, let us assume that IDS i and IDS j are both signature-based IDSs. IDS i has one alert for $\mathcal{A}$ while IDS j has two alerts. In Figure 1, we show that the two alerts from IDS j are dependent, but that the alert from IDS i is independent of the others. In reality, it is likely that a_2^j is dependent on, for example, a_1^i as indicated in Figure 1 with the dotted line with the x. Even different commercial IDSs many times use similar signatures to detect attacks. As will be seen in the examples shown in Section 4, we sometimes ignore this particular dependence. The reasons are the following:

- First, a model may work very well despite some broken independence assumptions; consider for example the Naive Bayes model, which works surprisingly well despite being very inaccurate in terms of independence assumptions [11].
- Second, excluding the inter-IDS dependence simplifies the model. If we include these dependencies between IDSs, it would mean that the inclusion of a new IDS to the whole system would necessitate a re-evaluation of many parameters (and thus invalidate the opportunity to have pre-set default values).
- Third, estimating this dependence is difficult. Someone would have to be an expert on both IDSs to be able to set the level of dependence between two alerts.

For these reasons, we sometimes explicitly ignore the inter-IDS dependencies even though we acknowledge that they exist. Thus, we balance the simplicity of the model against its accuracy.

3.3   Model Example: Estimating the Parameters

In Figure 2 we show a simplified example of the model, where we have limited the number of nodes to make it more understandable. In this case, we concentrate on the *phf attack* [12]. The background and execution of the attack can be found in Almgren et al. [3]. By sending a request to run the vulnerable cgi script *phf* and including the newline character in hex encoding (%0a), the attacker may be able to execute arbitrary commands. The script passes control to the shell without removing the newline character, which has special meaning to the shell.

The open-source IDS Snort has several potential ways to detect this attack ([3]). For example, one can use *rule 1762*, which detects the string "/phf" matched with a newline character within the URI. Snort is a network-based IDS, and for that reason it cannot detect attacks in encrypted traffic (among other things).

Now let us consider how to estimate the necessary parameters for the model shown in Figure 2. The structure is given from Figure 1 and we have restricted each node to be either *true (T)* or *false (F)*. Even though one can give probability distributions over each node, we use *conditional probability tables* (CPTs) in this paper. A full joint probability distribution would need 16 parameters, but taking advantage of the independence shown in the figure, we are left with only 8 parameters. As we will show, several of these parameters are easy to specify and we can also use some conditional independence not visible in the structure. For example, there is no need to compare the effectiveness of different IDSs, but all values are set in relation to the current IDS and the underlying attack it tries to detect. In principle, one needs to consider the following three areas: the underlying risk of the attack, the likelihood of IDS degrading tricks, and the false positive / false negative rate. These are discussed in detail below.

Underlying Risk of the Attack. Starting with *inv-A*, being the node that signifies whether the attack is serious enough to warrant an investigation, we need to set a value for the probability $P(inv\text{-}A = \mathrm{T})$, known as the *prior probability* in a Bayesian model. We consider this to be the most difficult value to specify in the model. Axelsson [4] has discussed the problems of setting certain parameters for an anomaly detection system. If false positives are more acceptable than false negatives one should exaggerate the risk of the attack, which we have done in our example.

Likelihood of IDS Degrading Tricks. In Section 3.2, we introduced the *r*-nodes for observations that may affect the IDS's detection capability. For a network-based IDS, this may include encrypted traffic, different types of obfuscating techniques, a heartbeat message, and so on. In Figure 2, we have only one such node, r_1^0. This node signifies whether the web request is encrypted (a typical failure mode for a network IDS). Thus, we estimate how often the web requests are encrypted.

We can then move on to w^1, a node that signifies whether the sensor is working correctly but which is never directly observed. If the traffic is encrypted, we consider it very unlikely that the sensor is working. However, the sensor may fail for conditions other than encrypted traffic, and thus we let this be reflected in the estimate for $P(w^1|\neg r_1^0)$.

False Positive / False Negative Rate. For the node a_1^1, which signifies whether the sensor outputs an alert from rule 1762, the first two parameters are easy to set. When the sensor is not working (the first two rows), we do not expect to see any alerts. Formally, a_1^1 is conditionally independent of *inv-A*, given that the sensor is broken ($\neg w^1$). For the last two rows, we need to determine the value of these parameters:

The false positive rate, $P(a_1^1|w^1, \neg inv\text{-}A)$, i.e., the probability that the alert is triggered when there is no attack.

The power, $P(a_1^1|w^1, inv\text{-}A)$, i.e., how likely the attack will trigger the rule 1762 in Snort. This is easily calculated from the *false negative rate* (FNR) of the rule: $1 - \mathrm{FNR}$.

Both of these values are well known to the security officer and already indirectly used when manually deciding whether an alert is worth extra examination. If the alert comes from a rule that has many false alarms, the security officer will probably not follow up unless there is further evidence.

To summarize, we need to specify eight parameters, but because of the domain and the inherent structure we are left with four values that the security officer is already familiar with. These values can be estimated by the IDS vendor, and then fine-tuned at the local site. As we specified in Section 3.2, parameter estimation for Bayesian networks is quite robust and a correct absolute number is seldom necessary as long as the magnitude of the numbers correspond. To emphasize this fact, we have used a set of predefined ranges to define our model: `never`, `low`, `low-medium`, `medium`, `medium-high`, `high`, and `always`. In Section 5 we replace these labels with their corresponding numerical probabilities and show that the model is robust against some error when estimating these values. When running the examples with real traffic, one would rather tune the values according to knowledge of the network environment and the specifics of the actual alert rule.

4   Example Scenarios

We use two scenarios to exemplify the model. We limit our discussion to attacks directed at web servers and related software. The web server is a complex piece of software, often outside the perimeter defense and accessible to anyone in the world. To complicate matters, the web server often forwards requests to inside resources (legacy databases) that were never designed with a robust security model. Being the analogy of the front door to a company, numerous attacks have been directed toward web servers and the resources with which they communicate. There also exist open-source web server alternatives that are mature enough to allow direct instrumentation (to collect security-relevant events). We use the basic *phf attack* to illustrate the principles of our model (see Section 3.3).

Example 1 is how we foresee the typical use of our model: using several complementary sensors together to increase the accuracy of the system as a whole. This is also the easiest application of the models, as the parameters can be reused.

Example 2 shows a deployment that is fairly common among users of IDSs, with one sensor on the outside of a firewall and another one on the inside. Even though it is more complicated than the typical use of our model (example 1), one can easily foresee how some of the settings could automatically be set by an automatic tool.

4.1   Example 1: Two Sensors Using Different Audit Streams

In this scenario we deploy two sensors using different audit sources (Figure 3). The first is the networked-based IDS Snort used previously, and the other one is developed by us and called *webIDS* in this paper. *webIDS* uses events from within the web server for its analysis. It is a variant of the system described by Almgren et al. [2], i.e., a signature-based system using pattern matching similar to that in Snort.

Using two complementary systems improves the attack detection capability, as shown by Almgren [3]. The Snort system uses rule 1762 described above, while the webIDS has the following rule for this scenario:

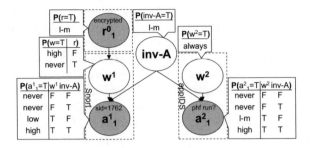

Fig. 3. Model for using Snort together with a sensor within the web server (example 1)

webIDS 1: detects whether the phf program is run successfully by the web server.

Clearly, this rule will have some false positives if the phf program is normally used in the environment. However, an alert from webIDS 1 coupled with an alert from Snort 1762 means that an attack was launched and the script executed successfully.

The model is shown in Figure 3. Adding independent IDSs to the model does not change the already-existing parts. For that reason, the Snort part remains the same and we reuse the values from Figure 2. We only need to add parameters for w^2 and a_1^2. To simplify the model, we assume that the webIDS is very resistant to failures and set $P(w^2 = \mathrm{T})$ to be close to one (always). We define the CPT for a_1^2 in a similar fashion as was done for a_1^1 in Section 3.3. Note that we exclude any dependency between the IDSs to simplify the model.

4.2 Example 2: Two Sensors on Opposite Sides of a Firewall Proxy

In this scenario we monitor an internal web server, protected by a firewall / web proxy. We use one instance of Snort (S_2) to monitor traffic outside the proxy and another instance of Snort for the inside traffic (S_1). The resulting model is shown in Figure 4. The proxy *should* block all web-related traffic. As long as the proxy works as expected, we expect that all attacks are blocked. Thus, even if S_2 reports about attacks, these can safely be ignored as long as S_1 is quiet. However, if S_1 is broken or taken offline, one should ensure that the proxy is working as expected.

In this scenario, we want to show how two (identical) versions of Snort still can be seen as somewhat independent given that they analyze different traffic streams and thus are used in collaboration in our model.

We show the resulting model in Figure 4. For this scenario, we made several changes compared to the model shown in Figure 2. First, we replaced the type of failure observation node from an observation of encrypted traffic to an observation of a heartbeat message. This change is done to show that one should use a diversity of r-nodes, even though we restrict them in this paper for clarity. Having S_1 inside of the proxy implies that alerts from this sensor are more serious than alerts from a sensor without a filtering proxy (as the one in Example 1, shown in Figure 3).

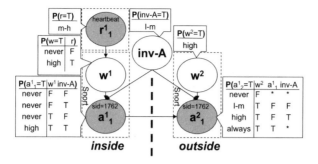

Fig. 4. Model for using two versions of Snort with one outside a proxy and the other one inside (example 2)

Thus, we lowered the probability for $P(a_1^1|w^1, \neg inv\text{-}A)$, meaning that we expect fewer false alarms (in the sense that they are not worth further investigation) from this sensor. For this example, we say that all alerts from the inside sensor should be investigated.

Furthermore, we have added an explicit dependence between a_1^1 and a_1^2. As we run two versions of Snort, we expect that any alert-raising traffic on the inside also exists outside, i.e., S_1 sees a subset of all the traffic passing by S_2. The CPT for a_1^2 is shown in the figure. We omitted special r-nodes for w^2 to keep the model simple and to the point.

5   Experiment

We base the simulations and experiments on the two examples described in Section 4. We first simulated the models presented in Figure 3 and Figure 4, and then we implemented the models on our test bed. As described above, we concentrate on the *phf attack* described in Section 3.3. Even though this may seem limiting at first glance, it clearly illustrates the principles of our approach. Other attacks can easily be added later.

5.1   Experiment Setup

The models for Example 1 and Example 2 each have three observable nodes. The test series used for the simulations are shown in Table 3. When we refer to the different experiments, we replace the x in the first column with the corresponding example number. As we noted in Section 2.1, we consider case (iv) in Table 1 uncommon with modern sensors. For example, as Snort cannot rebuild the HTTP transaction for an encrypted request, the string matching on the URI fails for rule 1762 and Snort does not produce an alert. Hence, the case TT* for example 1 is unusual in practice and is not included in the test series. Similar reasoning goes for FT* for example 2.

Table 3. Results of the simulation of example 1 and example 2

Exp #	Example 1				Example 2		
	P(inv-A$\mid r_1^1 a_1^1 a_2^1$)	P($w^1\mid$...)	Comment		P(inv-A$\mid r_1^1 a_1^1 a_2^1$)		P($w^2\mid$...)
x-1	0.01	FFF	0.89	no attack / script run	0.02	TFF	0.87
x-2	0.20	FFT	0.80	normal phf (no attack)	0.19	TFT	1.00
x-3	0.30	FTF	0.99	phf attack against server without the script	0.96	TTF	0.08
x-4	0.91	FTT	1.00	attack and script run	0.96	TTT	1.00
x-5	0.05	TFF	0.01	broken sensor, but no script invocation	0.08	FFF	0.84
x-6	0.54	TFT	0.01	broken sensor, and script run	0.54	FFT	1.00

As our focus is on alert reasoning, normal traffic causing no alerts is quite uninteresting. Normal web traffic can be used to track down false alarms on a sensor-per-sensor basis, but it adds little to our analysis of reasoning with the available alerts. Rather, the analysis of these false alarms would be used to tune the parameter estimation of our model. For these reasons, we do not use any normal web requests in our experiment.

In the Comment column in Table 3, we explain what the node status implies and we use this as a basis to decide what type of traffic to use in the experiment for that particular case. Based on the observable events, we then calculate the posterior probability for node *inv-A*. In a real system, we would most likely collapse this posterior to either *investigate* or *do not investigate* using a decision function. In this paper, we use a simple decision function with a threshold parameter, $0 \leq \tau \leq 1$, where all values that are less than τ are not considered worthy of investigation. We let $\tau = 0.5$, thus choosing the most probable class.

For the simulation and the experiment, we map our labels to actual probabilities. Instead of a range (represented by our labels), a Bayesian network needs an actual probability (as we have shown in Section 3.3). Thus, we collapse the ranges and let never, low, low–medium, medium, medium–high, high, and always map to the following values (in order): [0.01, 0.1, 0.25, 0.5, 0.75, 0.9, 0.99]. These values could be fine-tuned. However, in Section 5.4 we show that such fine-tuning is not always necessary because the model is robust against minor estimation errors.

5.2   Simulation

We simulated the models used in Examples 1 and 2 by setting the observable nodes (columns 3 and 7) to a specific value and then calculating the posterior probability for the other nodes. The simulation results of Examples 1 and 2 are presented in Table 3. Each experimental series is prefixed with the scenario number when we discuss it in the text.

5.3   Experiment

We implemented the two scenarios in our test bed. The implementation used the SMILE reasoning engine [10].

For Example 1, we ran *normal phf requests* and *attack phf requests* past a Snort sensor to a web server that either *had a script called phf installed,* or *no such script.* We repeated the experiment with *encrypted traffic.* The alerts were collected, and analyzed by our reasoning engine. The results correspond to the values shown in Table 3.

For Example 2, we sent normal phf requests and attack phf requests to a web proxy. The proxy either forwarded the result to a web server (proxy broken) or returned a message stating that the script did not exist (proxy working correctly). We used two versions of Snort to monitor the traffic. The first version monitored the traffic to the proxy, while the second monitored the traffic to the web server. We added a special rule to simulate a heartbeat for Snort. We simulated the failure of the inside Snort sensor by simply killing the process. All alerts were collected and analyzed. The results correspond to the values shown in Table 3. Not shown in the table is $P(w^1 = T | \ldots)$ for Example 2. These values are similar to the ones shown in column 4 for Example 1. For example, when there is no heartbeat the probability of S_1 working is only 0.01.

Based on our decision function, we would thus further investigate case *1-4* and case *1-6* for Example 1 and case *2-3*, case *2-4*, and case *2-6* for Example 2.

5.4   Sensitivity Analysis

One weakness of the model is the difficulty of accurately estimating the parameters. For that reason, we exhaustively perturbed each estimate in the models by 20% and then recalculated the probability for node *inv-A*. In Example 1, we have 13 independent parameters and the option of subtracting or adding 20% to each estimate gives a total of 2^{13} test cases. For each test case, we then compared the outcome of the decision function (i.e., *investigate* or *do not investigate*) with the outcome from the unperturbed network. There was no difference, implying that the model is relatively robust against estimation errors.

6   Discussion

Column 2 and column 6 in Table 3 show the probability of having a serious attack that needs investigation, given the observable evidence in the network. In a real system, as we specified above, we would most likely collapse the values to *investigate* or *do not investigate* using a decision function. Now let us go through the results in detail.

6.1   Analysis of Scenario 1

In the upper half of Table 3 for Scenario 1, we do not encrypt the requests. Thus, both sensors work and we require alerts from both sensors to investigate the attack. If only the web sensor raises an alert, (*1-2*), no attack code was detected by Snort and it was most likely a normal request. This is reflected in the relatively low value of $P(\text{inv-A}|\ldots)$ for this case. The same holds for case *1-3*. Here, only Snort raises an alert so no phf script was run on the server and thus the attack did not propagate within the web server. If both sensors alert, we should investigate further as illustrated by the high value for case *1-4*.

In the lower part of Table 3, we encrypt all requests. There is no alert, but observed encrypted traffic is not regarded as very sensitive, and thus case *1-5* is rather low. However, note that it is five times that of case *1-1* as we have only one working sensor. If we have an alert from the webIDS when the traffic is encrypted (case *1-6*), the system indicates that we should investigate further. The missing alert from Snort is either because there is no attack, or because Snort is not working. Looking closer at the model for this case, we can determine that $P(w^1 = T|\ldots) = 0.01$, i.e., that the Snort IDS cannot properly analyze the request.

6.2   Analysis of Scenario 2

Now let us have a look at the results for Scenario 2 in Table 3. In the upper half of the table, we receive a heartbeat from the Snort sensor placed inside the proxy, meaning that it should work. When we have no alert (case *2-1*) or when only the outside sensor raises an alert (case *2-2*), the risks are relatively low as indicated in Table 3. Case *2-3*, on the other hand, is interesting. We have an alert only on the inside, which seems impossible as the outside Snort sensor should see all traffic that the inside sensor can see. The only explanation, properly deducted in the model, is that the outside sensor is broken ($P(w^2 = T|\ldots) = 0.08$). The alert should be investigated as indicated in the table, and sensor 2 should most likely be restarted. In case *2-4*, we have alerts from both sensors and thus the alert should be investigated.

In the lower part of Table 3, there is no heartbeat from the Snort sensor placed inside the proxy. For that reason, an alert from the outside sensor is deemed to be much more serious, as can be seen for case *2-6*. In this case, the lack of alert from the inside sensor is explained by a broken sensor (S_1) as there is no longer a heartbeat (not explicitly shown in the table but discussed in Section 5.3).

6.3   Summary

The interesting cases are thus how the model can directly adapt to changes in the environment. The evaluation of case *1-2* is very different from case *1-6*, despite the fact that we in both these cases have an alert only from the webIDS. The same goes for case *2-2* and case *2-6*. The model can also make predictions for when a sensor is broken, as in case *1-5*, case *1-6*, case *2-3*, case *2-5*, and case *2-6*.

The examples we used were designed to illustrate the basic principles of our model while being easy to understand. In real operational settings, the models would be slightly more complex. For example, when using Snort, it would be prudent to have indicators of both encrypted traffic (as in Example 1) and heartbeats (as in Example 2). It would be easy to modify the model to incorporate information from two such nodes. One can also imagine using the results from a vulnerability scan to adjust the weight of the evidence—indications of an attack for which the target is not vulnerable would be given lower weight.

7 Related Work

Several research groups have presented correlation techniques that are able to cluster related alerts, thus presenting the security operator with sets of related alerts belonging to (it is hoped) a single attack. Even though these techniques reduce the number of alerts the security officer needs to consider at a single time, they do not alleviate the actual analysis of the alerts to decide whether an attack is in progress. As we stated in Section 1, we find our approach complementary and we even assume that such a traditional correlator preprocesses the data before it is given to the model presented in this paper. See the excellent overview given by Kruegel et al. [14] and the references therein.

Other correlation efforts have tried to recognize predefined attack scenarios (Debar et al. [9]) or correlating based on the capabilities gained by the attacker from each attack step (Ning et al. [18], Cheung et al. [6], Cuppens et al. [7], and Zhou et al. [23]). Even though some of these approaches account for an imperfect alert stream with missed attack steps, they do not resolve conflicting evidence or model the IDS failure modes as we do. Our approach increases the accuracy of the alert stream and would thus also increase the performance of these higher-level correlation efforts.

Other researchers have focused on using several sensors to collect information about attacks. Abad et al. [1] use a data mining approach to correlate information from different logs on a single host. The underlying ideas are similar to those of our approach. However, we include negative information (no alert) when judging whether an attack is in progress and also try to explain the missing information.

Dagorn [8] discusses a cooperative intrusion detection system for web applications. Thresholds are avoided and instead a Bayesian framework is used, where each node has a twin to measure its confidence level. In our approach, we use a much more constrained view of the sensors and their capabilities but in return we can then reason more about alerts we have.

Tombini et al. [20] combine an anomaly-based IDS with a misuse IDS. They have an enlightening discussion concerning combinations of alerts from the two systems but they focus on a serial combination of the IDSs as opposed to our approach, and they do not consider sensor failure.

Morin et al. [17] introduce a formal model for correlation and discuss some scenarios where this model can be used. Even though Morin et al. describe the need to solve inconsistencies in the output from several IDSs, they do not show any model to do so. Morin et al. [16] also show an application of Chronicles to IDS. However, in this paper they explicitly state that they only use available alerts. In our approach, we also take advantage of false negatives.

Kruegel et al. [13] describe an IDS for analyzing operating system calls to detect attacks against programs. They use the same decision framework from artificial intelligence (i.e., Bayesian networks) as we do, but explore a different problem from the one presented here.

The two approaches most similar to ours are Yu et al. [21] and Zhai et al. [22]. The former tries to predict the intruder's next goal with hidden colored petri nets. They infer missing alerts and reason about alerts using an exponentially weighted Dempster-Shafer theory of confidence. They do not, as we do, explicitly model an IDS weakness to use missing alerts as evidence against an ongoing attack.

Zhai et al. [22] use Bayesian networks to combine event-based evidence (intrusion detection alerts) with state-based evidence (observations in the environment) by chaining them together in a causal structure. Even though their model considers false negatives in a limited way, they do not account for the failure modes of the IDS and thus cannot explain why or how an attack was missed. A consequence is that they also do not use true negatives as evidence against an attack in the same way we do.

Finally, we would like to mention tools such as Thor (Marty [15]). An extension to Thor, for example, would automate the need to manually build correlation tables and set the parameters that are needed for our model.

8   Future Work

We would like to extend the sensor models we have started to build. We would also like to run the system in more challenging environments to learn more about its limitations and how the model can be improved. For example, we have considered adding a general *threat* node. This would allow the system to increase its sensitivity in certain scenarios and lower it in others, based on input from the security operator. In addition, we would like to investigate how to build a sensor that is better tailored to the requirements posed by our model.

9   Conclusions

We have proposed and investigated an intrusion detection model that can analyze alerts from several audit sources to improve the detection accuracy of the intrusion detection system (IDS) as a whole. Our model, expressed in the form of a Bayesian network, can resolve seemingly conflicting evidence collected from different audit sources, thus making it different from other cluster-based correlation approaches. We explicitly model the transitory state of the IDS sensor and can therefore reason about the case when an alert is not produced (a negative) in addition to the case when an alert is produced (a positive).

We validate our model in two scenarios in our test bed. We show that not only can the model correctly reason about evidence collected from several audit sources, but it can also point out when a sensor seems to have failed.

Acknowledgments. The authors are grateful for valuable comments from our colleagues Daniel Hedin, Marina Papatriantafilou, David Sands and Alfonso Valdes. This material is based upon work supported by the Swedish Emergency Management Agency.

References

1. Abad, C., Taylor, J., Sengul, C., Yurcik, W., Zhou, Y., Rowe, K.: Log correlation for intrusion detection: A proof of concept. In: ACSAC 2003: Proceedings of the 19th Annual Computer Security Applications Conference, p. 255. IEEE Computer Society, Los Alamitos (2003)
2. Almgren, M., Debar, H., Dacier, M.: A lightweight tool for detecting web server attacks. In: Tsudik, G., Rubin, A. (eds.) Network and Distributed System Security Symposium (NDSS 2000), San Diego, USA, Feburary 3–4, 2000, pp. 157–170. Internet Society (2000)
3. Almgren, M., Jonsson, E., Lindqvist, U.: A comparison of alternative audit sources for web server attack detection. In: Erlingsson, Ú., Sabelfeld, A. (eds.) 12th Nordic Workshop on Secure IT Systems (NordSec 2007), October 11–12, pp. 101–112. Reykjavík University, Iceland (2007)
4. Axelsson, S.: The base-rate fallacy and its implications for the difficulty of intrusion detection. In: Proceedings of the 6th ACM Conference on Computer and Communications Security, November 1999. Kent Ridge Digital Labs (1999)
5. Breese, J., Koller, D.: Tutorial on Bayesian Networks. Internet (1997), http://robotics.stanford.edu/~koller/BNtut/BNtut.ppt
6. Cheung, S., Lindqvist, U., Fong, M.W.: Modeling multistep cyber attacks for scenario recognition. In: DARPA Information Survivability Conference and Exposition (DISCEX III), Washington, DC, April 22–24, 2003, vol. I, pp. 284–292 (2003)
7. Cuppens, F., Miege, A.: Alert correlation in a cooperative intrusion detection framework. In: Proceedings of the IEEE Symposium on Security and Privacy, Oakland, CA, May 2002, pp. 202–215. IEEE Press, Los Alamitos (2002)
8. Dagorn, N.: Cooperative intrusion detection for web applications. In: Pointcheval, D., Mu, Y., Chen, K. (eds.) CANS 2006. LNCS, vol. 4301, pp. 286–302. Springer, Heidelberg (2006)
9. Debar, H., Wespi, A.: Aggregation and correlation of intrusion-detection alerts. In: RAID 2000: Proceedings of the 4th International Symposium on Recent Advances in Intrusion Detection, pp. 85–103. Springer, Heidelberg (2001)
10. Decision Systems Laboratory, University of Pittsburgh. SMILE reasoning engine for graphical probabilistic model (2008), http://dsl.sis.pitt.edu
11. Domingos, P., Pazzani, M.: On the optimality of the simple Bayesian classifier under zero-one loss. Machine Learning 29(2-3), 103–130 (1997)
12. Hernan, S.V.: 'phf' CGI script fails to guard against newline characters. CERT/CC; Internet (January 2001), http://www.kb.cert.org/vuls/id/20276
13. Kruegel, C., Mutz, D., Robertson, W., Valeur, F.: Bayesian event classification for intrusion detection. In: ACSAC 2003: Proceedings of the 19th Annual Computer Security Applications Conference, p. 14. IEEE Computer Society, Los Alamitos (2003)
14. Kruegel, C., Valeur, F., Vigna, G.: Intrusion Detection and Correlation. Advances in Information Security, vol. 14. Springer, Heidelberg (2005)

15. Marty, R.: Thor - a tool to test intrusion detection systems by variations of attacks. Master's thesis, Swiss Federal Institute of Technology (ETH), Institut für Technische Informatik und Kommunikationsnetze (TIK), Zurich, Switzerland (2002), http://www.raffy.ch/projects/ids/thor.ps.gz

16. Morin, B., Debar, H.: Correlation of intrusion symptoms: An application of Chronicles. In: Vigna, G., Jonsson, E., Kruegel, C. (eds.) RAID 2003. LNCS, vol. 2820, pp. 94–112. Springer, Heidelberg (2003)

17. Morin, B., Mé, L., Debar, H., Ducassé, M.: M2D2: A formal data model for IDS alert correlation. In: Wespi, A., Vigna, G., Deri, L. (eds.) RAID 2002. LNCS, vol. 2516, pp. 115–137. Springer, Heidelberg (2002)

18. Ning, P., Cui, Y., Reeves, D.S.: Analyzing intensive intrusion alerts via correlation. In: Wespi, A., Vigna, G., Deri, L. (eds.) RAID 2002. LNCS, vol. 2516, pp. 74–94. Springer, Heidelberg (2002)

19. Swets, J.A.: Measuring the accuracy of diagnostic systems. Science 240(4857), 1285–1293 (1988)

20. Tombini, E., Debar, H., Mé, L., Ducassé, M.: A serial combination of anomaly and misuse IDSes applied to HTTP traffic. In: ACSAC 2004: Proceedings of the 20th Annual Computer Security Applications Conference (ACSAC 2004). IEEE Computer Society, Los Alamitos (2004)

21. Yu, D., Frincke, D.: Improving the quality of alerts and predicting intruder's next goal with hidden colored petri-net. Comput. Netw. 51(3), 632–654 (2007)

22. Zhai, Y., Ning, P., Iyer, P., Reeves, D.S.: Reasoning about complementary intrusion evidence. In: ACSAC 2004: Proceedings of the 20th Annual Computer Security Applications Conference, Washington, DC, USA, pp. 39–48. IEEE Computer Society, Los Alamitos (2004)

23. Zhou, J., Heckman, M., Reynolds, B., Carlson, A., Bishop, M.: Modeling network intrusion detection alerts for correlation. ACM Trans. Inf. Syst. Secur. 10(1), 4 (2007)

Monitoring SIP Traffic Using Support Vector Machines

Mohamed Nassar, Radu State, and Olivier Festor

Centre de Recherche INRIA Nancy - Grand Est
615, rue du jardin botanique, 54602
Villers-Lès-Nancy, France

Abstract. We propose a novel online monitoring approach to distinguish between attacks and normal activity in SIP-based Voice over IP environments. We demonstrate the efficiency of the approach even when only limited data sets are used in learning phase. The solution builds on the monitoring of a set of 38 features in VoIP flows and uses Support Vector Machines for classification. We validate our proposal through large offline experiments performed over a mix of real world traces from a large VoIP provider and attacks locally generated on our own testbed. Results show high accuracy of detecting SPIT and flooding attacks and promising performance for an online deployment are measured.

1 Introduction

The voice over IP world is facing a large set of threats. SPAM on email systems takes a new and very annoying form on IP telephony advertising. This threat is known as SPIT (Spam over Internet Telephony). However, SPIT is not the only threat vector. The numerous software flaws in IP phones and servers affect their reliability and open the door to remotely attack previously unseen in the "stable" world of telecommunication operators (PSTN), which was based on mutual trust among few peers. Leveraging the IP to support voice communications exposes this service (voice) to the known denial of service attacks that can be easily implemented by service or network request flooding on the Internet. Resource exhaustion thus automatically finds its place against SIP proxies and back-to-back user agents, which are essential to support this critical infrastructure. The list of potential threats is huge and ranges from VoIP bots (that could spread by malware and perform distributed attacks, perform SPIT or toll fraud), to eavesdropping and Vishing (similar attack to the Phishing are using VoIP as the transport vehicle) [1].

Securing VoIP infrastructures constitutes one of the major challenges for both the operational and research communities because security by design was not a key component in the early phases of both VoIP research and development. VoIP-specific security solutions are currently required by the market because the research and standardization efforts are still trying hard to address the issues of securing and monitoring VoIP infrastructures.

R. Lippmann, E. Kirda, and A. Trachtenberg (Eds.): RAID 2008, LNCS 5230, pp. 311–330, 2008.
© Springer-Verlag Berlin Heidelberg 2008

Our work fits into these efforts and addresses a new monitoring approach for VoIP specific environments. Our monitoring scheme is based on Support Vector Machines for efficient classification. We continuously monitor a set of 38 features in signaling time slices and use these features as the raw input to the classification engine. A threshold based alarm generator is placed on top of the classification engine. We show that the system is both efficient and accurate and study the impact of the various features on the efficiency.

We start the presentation with a short survey on VoIP security with focus on flooding attacks and SPIT. We then give a functional description of our monitoring solution together with the definition of the 38 features computed in our system for classification (section 3). In section 4, we provide a short mathematical background of the SVM learning machine model used in the monitoring process. Offline traces inspection is presented in section 5 where we also describe the data set. Section 6 demonstrates the performances of our approach to detect different types of attacks. Related work is addressed in section 7. Section 8 concludes the paper and enumerates some future work.

2   The Threat Model

2.1   Flooding Attacks

Denial of service attacks can target the signaling plane elements (e.g. proxy, gateway, etc.) with the objective to take them down and produce havoc in the VoIP network. Such attacks are launched by either flooding the signaling plane with a large quantity of messages, malformed messages or executing exploits against device specific vulnerabilities.

The authors of [2] categorize some of these attacks based on the request URI and perform a comparative study of these ones against popular open source VoIP equipment. We adopt the same categorization, i.e.:

- UDP flooding: Since the vast majority of SIP systems use UDP as the transport protocol, a large amount of random UDP packets are sent in an attempt to congest the network bandwidth. Such attacks produce a high packet loss. Legitimate call signaling has thus a reduced probability to reach the target and to be processed.
- INVITE flooding with a valid SIP URI: The attacker calls one user/phone registered at a server/proxy. The proxy relays the calls to the phone. If the proxy is stateful it will manage a state machine for every transaction. The phone is quickly overloaded by the high rate of calls and is no more able to terminate the calls. As a result, the server is allocating resources for a long time and it will run out of memory.
- INVITE flooding with a non existent SIP URI: If the attacker doesn't know a valid SIP URI registered on the target, it can send calls to an invalid address. The proxy/server responds with an error response like "user not found". When the attack rate is higher than the server capabilities, the resources are exhausted. This type of flooding is less disturbing than the previous one but

the target CPU is loaded with useless transactions and legitimate requests may be rejected.

- INVITE flooding with an invalid IP domain address: The attacker calls a user with a rogue IP address of the destination domain. The target is led to connect several times to an unreachable host/network while keeping the state of the current SIP transaction. This attack is efficient on some proxies like OpenSER [2].
- INVITE flooding with an invalid domain name: The attacker calls a user with a false destination domain name. The target is trapped to send DNS requests to resolve the domain name. The target may issue different DNS types (A, AAAA, SRV, NAPTR, ENUM) and repeat them multiple times. In the same time, the target is managing the transactions waiting for a valid DNS response to proceed. Memory is quickly exhausted. The effect of this attack on the performance of OpenSER is shown in Fig. 1. The impact is evaluated in terms of duration, number of messages exchanged and final state of sessions or transactions. The behavior of the server can be divided in two successive phases. In the first phase, the first few requests are correctly handled (REJECTED) but the session duration is increasing and the proxy is slowing down. The number of messages is increasing because of response retransmissions (no ACK is sent by the attacker). In the second phase, the proxy is no more able to handle the requests (still in CALLSET state) so the proxy is taken down. The take down time is about 20 seconds for an attack having just one INVITE/s rate.
- INVITE flooding with an invalid SIP URI in another domain: The attacker calls a user/phone located in another domain than the target's one. The target relays all requests to the server/proxy of the other domain. The latter replies with an error response. In this way, multiple targets are hit at the same time and cascading failures occur.
- INVITE flooding with a valid SIP URI in another domain: The attacker calls a user/phone registered in another domain. The target relays all requests to the server/proxy of the other domain which sends them to the phone. The phone gets quickly out of service and maintaining the state by the intermediary servers will exhaust the resources from all the servers in the forwarding chain.
- INVITE/REGISTER flooding when authentication is enabled: The attacker sends INVITE or REGISTER messages and then stops the handshaking process. The proxy/registrar responds with a challenge and waits for the request to be send again with the proper authentication credentials. This process is costly for the proxy/registrar in term of computing (generating challenges and nonces) and memory (dialogs/transaction state machines).

2.2 Social Threats and SPIT

Social threats are attacks ranging from the generation of unsolicited communications which are annoying and disturbing for the users to more dangerous data stealing (Vishing) attacks. The threat is classified as social since the term

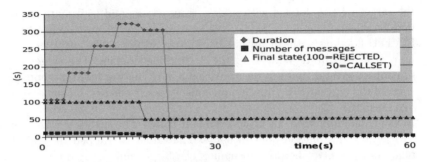

Fig. 1. OpenSER Response to an INVITE Flooding with Invalid Domain Name

"unsolicited" depends on user-specific preferences. This makes this kind of attack difficult to identify. An example of this is a threat commonly referred to as SPam over Internet Telephony (SPIT). This threat is similar to spam in the email systems but is delivered by means of voice calls. This leverages the cheap cost of VoIP when compared with legacy phone systems. It's currently estimated that generating VoIP calls is three order of magnitude cheaper than generating PSTN calls. Such SPIT calls can be telemarketing calls that sell products. A subtle variant of SPIT is the so-called Vishing (VoIP phishing) attack, which aims either to make the callees dial expensive numbers in order to get the promised prize or to collect personal data redirecting the users towards an Interactive Voice Responder (IVR) pretended to be trusted. Most of these attacks are going to be generated by machines (bot-nets) programmed to do such a job. Unsolicited communications (like SPIT or Vishing) are, from a signalling point of view, technically correct transactions. It is not possible to determine from the INVITE message (in the case of SIP) if a VoIP transaction is SPIT or not. From a technical point of view, the challenge is actually higher since the content is not available to help in the detection until the phone rings (disturbing the user) and the callee answers the call. For this reason, techniques successfully used against e-mail spam like text filtering are hardly applicable in the VoIP sphere. Even if a transaction is identified as unsolicited how to handle such a transaction highly depends on the legal environment in the country of the caller.

3   Our Monitoring Solution

When facing the mentioned threats, monitoring of the signalling traffic can detect anomalous situations and prevent them. The monitoring scheme can be quite simple and flexible to support different techniques. Thus, our approach follows these principles. As shown in Fig. 2, we track SIP messages in a queue of predefined size. Once the queue is full, this slice of messages is used to compute a vector of statistics/features. The classifier decides if a vector represents a certain anomaly and issues an alarm event if necessary. This approach is based on a learning phase in which couples (vector, class Id) have been used to feed the engine for learning. This learning process can be made on the fly during the operational phase of the monitoring system by allowing it to update the prediction model over time. Finally, an event correlator or decider has to filter and correlate the events. It generates an alarm for a group of events if they trigger one of the rules/conditions. e.g. if the number of events of type i bypasses a certain threshold in a period of time t.

The architecture is modular and enables experimenting with different classification and artificial intelligence techniques ranging from statistics and information theory to pattern classification and machine learning. The pace of the system t_{pace} is the time it takes to make a decision about one slice without accounting for the time needed by the event correlation stage. This time is composed of two components: the analysis time of the processor and the machine time of the classifier. The design achieves real time pace if t_{pace} is less than the size of the slice S divided by the arrival rate of messages λ:

$$t_{pace} = t_{analysis} + t_{machine}$$
$$t_{pace} < \frac{S}{\lambda}$$

We define in the following the important features that characterize a slice of SIP traffic and motivate why we collect them. We divide these features in four groups:

- **General Statistics:** are number of requests, number of responses, number of requests carrying an SDP (Session Description Protocol) body, average inter requests arrival time, average inter response arrival time and average inter requests arrival time for requests having SDP bodies; these statistics represent the general shape of the traffic and indicate the degree of congestion. The fraction of requests carrying SDP bodies (normally INVITE, ACK or UPDATE) is a good indicator because it will not exceed a certain threshold. An excessive use of re-INVITE or UPDATE for media negotiation or maybe QoS theft increases the number of SDP bodies exchanged and decrements the average inter-arrival of them. Flooding attacks are associated with peaks of all these statistics.

- **Call-Id Based Statistics:** are number of Call-Ids, average of the duration between the first and the last message having the same Call-Id, the average number of messages having the same Call-Id, the number of different senders (the URI in the From header of a message carrying a new Call-Id) and the number of different receivers (the URI in the To header of a message carrying a new Call-Id). Similar to the Erlang model used in the telecommunication networks, where the arrival rate of calls and the average duration of a call characterize the underling traffic, the arrival rate of Call-Ids (can be starting a call or any kind of SIP dialog) and the interval time of messages having the same Call-Ids, can be used to characterize the overlay SIP traffic. Nevertheless, we notice that non-INVITE dialogs have shorter durations and fewer number of messages than INVITE dialogs. Thus their Call-Id statistics can be taken as different features.

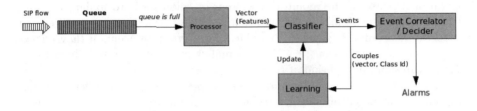

Fig. 2. Real-time Online SIP Traffic Monitoring

- **Distribution of Final State of Dialogs/Call-Ids:** Since we are using a limited number of messages in the traffic analysis unit, dialogs can be partitioned into two or several units/slices. The final state of a dialog at the analysis moment is considered and this one is not necessarily the final state when all the messages of the dialog can be taken into account. The following states are defined: NOTACALL: for all non-INVITE dialogs, CALLSET: for all calls/INVITE dialogs that do not complete the initiation, CANCELED: when the call is cancelled before it is established, REJECTED: for all redirected or erroneous sessions, INCALL: when the call is established but not realized yet, COMPLETED: for a successful and ended call and RESIDUE: when the dialog does not start with a request. This latter is a residual of messages in a previous slice. In a normal situation where the size of the unit is large enough, NOTACALL, COMPLETED and REJECTED (in busy or not found situations) dominate this distribution. Major deviations may indicate an erroneous situation.

- **Distribution of SIP Requests:** are INVITE, REGISTER, BYE, ACK, OPTIONS, CANCEL, UPDATE, REFER, SUBSCRIBE, NOTIFY, MESSAGE, INFO, PRACK. Although the first five types represent the main methods used in SIP, every other type may point out a specified application running above. The number of REGISTER sent by a user within a time interval is indirect proportional to the period of registration (`expires` parameter or `Expires` header). Obviously, the total number of REGISTER messages is proportional to the number of users of the domain and inversely proportional to the average period of registration among all users. The existence of SUBSCRIBE and NOTIFY messages indicates SIP presence services. Instant messaging can also be revealed by MESSAGE requests. REFER requests may reveal a SIP peer to peer application or some call transfer running above. INFO requests are normally used to carry out of band DTMF tones within PSTN-VoIP calls. Finally, PRACK requests may reveal VoIP to PSTN activity.

- **Distribution of SIP Responses:** are Informational, Success, Redirection, Client Error, Server Error, Global Error. An unexpected high rate of error responses is a good indication for error situations.

Among the different scientific approaches in the area of classification (Bayesian networks, decision trees, neural networks), we have chosen the support vector machines approach for their superior ability to process high dimensional data [3,4]. SVM is a relatively novel (1995) technique for data classification and exploration. It has demonstrated good performance in many domains like bioinformatics and pattern recognition (e.g. [5] and [6]). SVM has been used in network-based anomaly detection and has demonstrated better performance than neural networks in term of accuracy and processing proficiency [7]. In the next section, we give a short description of the SVM concept and methodology.

4   Support Vector Machines

Principle. Given a set of couples $S = (\overrightarrow{x_l}, y_l)_{1 \leq l \leq p}$, with $y_l \in \{-1, +1\}$, which denotes the correct classification of the training data, the SVM method tries to distinguish between the two classes by mean of a dividing hyperplane which has as equation $\overrightarrow{w}.\overrightarrow{x} + b = 0$. If the training data are linearly separable, the solution consists in maximizing the margin between the two hyperplanes, $\overrightarrow{w}.\overrightarrow{x} + b = +1$ and $\overrightarrow{w}.\overrightarrow{x} + b = -1$, such that for all points either $\overrightarrow{w}.\overrightarrow{x} + b \geq +1$ (1) or $\overrightarrow{w}.\overrightarrow{x} + b \leq -1$ (2). This is equivalent to minimizing the module $|\overrightarrow{w}|$ because the distance between the two mentioned hyperplanes is $2/|\overrightarrow{w}|$. The resulting quadratic problem where the conditions (1) and (2) are aggregated is formulated as:

Find $\overrightarrow{w}$ and b to minimize $\frac{1}{2}\overrightarrow{w}.\overrightarrow{w}$
so that $y_l(\overrightarrow{w}.\overrightarrow{x_l}) + b \geq 1 \forall (\overrightarrow{x_l}, y_l) \in S$

The non linear separation has a similar formulation except that we replace the dot product by a non-linear kernel function. The kernel function takes the data set to a transformed feature space where it searches the optimal classifier. The transformation may be non-linear and the transformed space high dimensional. The maximum-margin hyperplane in the high-dimensional feature space may be non-linear in the original input space. The following kernels can be used :

- linear $K_l(\overrightarrow{x}, \overrightarrow{z}) = \overrightarrow{x}.\overrightarrow{z}$
- polynomial $K_d(\overrightarrow{x}, \overrightarrow{z}) = (\gamma \overrightarrow{x}.\overrightarrow{z} + r)^d$, $\gamma > 0$
- radial basis function $k_{rbf}(\overrightarrow{x}, \overrightarrow{z}) = exp(-\gamma|\overrightarrow{x} - \overrightarrow{z}|^2)$ where $\gamma > 0$
- sigmoid $k_s(\overrightarrow{x}, \overrightarrow{z}) = tanh(\gamma \overrightarrow{x}.\overrightarrow{z} + r)$, $\gamma > 0$ and $r < 0$

The C-SVC (C parameter - Support Vector Classification) approach is particularly interesting when the training data is not linearly separable.

C-SVC. For the general case where the data S is not separable, the solution allows some points to be mislabeled by the separating hyperplane. This method, so called soft margin, is expressed by the introduction of slack variables ξ_l where ξ_l measures the degree of misclassification of a point x_l. The objective function is then increased by a function which penalizes non-zero ξ_l, and the optimization becomes a trade off between a large margin, and a small error penalty.

$$\boxed{\begin{array}{l} \text{Find } \overrightarrow{w}, \text{ b and } \xi \text{ to minimize } \frac{1}{2}\overrightarrow{w}.\overrightarrow{w} + C\sum_{l}\xi_{l} \\ \text{so that } \begin{cases} y_{l}(\overrightarrow{w}.\overrightarrow{x_{l}}) + b \geq 1 - \xi_{l}, \forall(\overrightarrow{x_{l}}, y_{l}) \in S \\ \xi_{l} \geq 0, \forall l \end{cases} \end{array}}$$

5   Monitoring SIP

We aim to detect anomalies within a SIP traffic capture, demonstrate the accuracy of the learning machine to identify attacks and non-attacks and distinguish between different types of attacks. We have performed an extensive analysis on offline VoIP traces in order to assess the performance of our approach.

We use the popular LibSVM tool [8] which contains several algorithms for classification and regression. In addition, the tool provides support for multiclass classification and probability estimates (so a test vector x_i seems to be of class i with a probability p_i) as well as support for one class SVM training. LibSVM is bound to other several tools such as an algorithm that performs a grid search over the SVM parameters space and optimizes their values by cross validation (divide the data into n subsets, for i going from 1 until n, learn over all the subsets except subset number i then test over subset number i). At the end, we can measure the test accuracy for each subset. The aggregation of all results is the accuracy given by the selected parameters. In Fig. 3 we illustrate this tool's flow. The data we use in this study originates from two different sources. The first source is traffic from a real-world VoIP provider and it is supposed to be completely normal. The second source is signaling traffic from a small test-bed installed by us to generate different forms of SIP attacks. We have three types of data files: clean and normal trace, clean attack trace, and mixed trace which is a normal trace where attack is injected.

To be processed by the SVM tool, each data file is cut into slices and entered into the analyzer. For each slice, the analyzer evaluates a set of predefined features (38 variables are defined in our study) and builds a vector for the LibSVM. All vectors are assembled in one file and annotated as either attack vector or normal vector. In Fig. 4, this process is shown for a mixed trace.

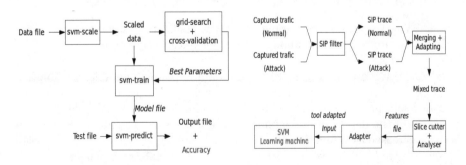

Fig. 3. SVM Flow Chart   **Fig. 4.** Analysis Flow Chart

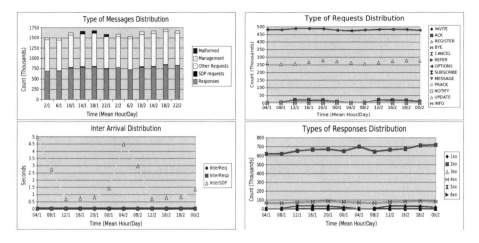

Fig. 5. Long Term Statistics over Real World Traces

5.1 Normal Traffic

The input data is a SIP trace from a two days continuous capture at a real world VoIP provider server. We performed a preliminary long term analysis of the traces with a two hours step. We depict the results in the four charts of Fig. 5. If we consider the distribution of different SIP messages, we can remark the following:

- The two main components of the traffic are the OPTIONS messages in the first place and then the REGISTER messages.
- Some methods are absent from the capture such a MESSAGE, PRACK and UPDATE.
- Some methods like NOTIFY have constant statistics over all periods of the day which reveal SIP devices remaining always connected and periodically sending notifications.
- The three main components of the call signalling (INVITE, BYE and ACK) have practically constant ratios over all the slots, with an average ratio $\#INVITE/\#BYE = 2.15$ and $\#INVITE/\#ACK = 0.92$.

Response distribution is dominated by the 2nd response class (most of them belong to OPTIONS and REGISTER transactions). 3xx, 5xx and 6xx are very rare while informational responses (1xx) follow INVITE messages because they are exclusively used in INVITE transactions (the average ratio $\#INVITE/\#1xx = 0.59$ can be explained by the fact that a call probably regroups one 100 Trying and one 180 Ringing so two 1xx responses). Average inter-request arrival and average inter-response arrival seem to be constant over all periods and they are about 20 ms. While average inter-request carrying SDP bodies which are exchanged in call dialogs move inversely to the quadruple (INVITE-BYE-ACK-1xx) curve, they reach 3s in quiet hours and decrease to 0.5s in rush hours.

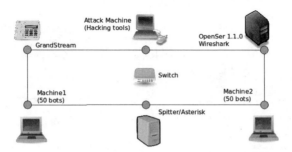

Fig. 6. Testbed of Attack Generation

5.2   The Testbed

The testbed consists of one OpenSER server and three other machines: the first machine plays the role of the attacker and uses a number of hacking tools (scanning, flooding, SPIT). The two other machines play the role of victims where one hundred SIP bots are equally distributed and running. The bots are programmable SIP agents and are controlled by an IRC channel[1]. All SIP bots and a GrandStream hardphone are registered to the OpenSER server and all machines belong to the same domain. Traces of attacks performed by the attacker machine are collected at the OpenSER server.

6   Performance and Accuracy

All experiments are done in a machine which has an Intel Pentium 4 CPU 3.40GHz and 2GB RAM memory running a Linux kernel 2.6.18-1. In term of performance, experiments show that a file containing 2449 slices/vectors of 38 features takes between 196 and 994 ms in the SVM prediction stage (depending on the used kernel).

Coherence Test

The first question we addressed was how many of the normal traces are self-similar and consistent. For example, is traffic from 22:00 to 02:00 from a day similar to traffic of the same period in another day? To test the coherence between two given traces, we used the following procedure: the analyzer evaluates feature vectors from each trace. Vectors are then labeled with respect to the origin trace and scaled. We make a 2-fold training test over all the vectors. In a 2-fold test, training is done over one part of the file and the testing is performed over the second. We define the coherence to be indirect proportional to the resulting accuracy of the 2-fold cross training. As long as the SVM can not distinguish between the two traces, they are tagged to the same class. In Table 1, we summarize some results:

---

[1] http://www.loria.fr/~nassar/readme.html

Table 1. Coherence Test for two Successive Days

Day 1	06-10	10-14	14-18	18-22
Day 2	06-10	10-14	14-18	18-22
Accuracy(%)	55.91	53.72	52.83	56.90

Table 2. Coherence Test for Different Periods of the Same Day

Day 1	02-06	02-06	02-06	02-06	22-02
Day 1	06-10	10-14	14-18	18-22	22-02
Accuracy(%)	51.82	62.79	63.72	63.76	60.80

We tested the coherence of a period with respect to other periods. In Table 2, we show the results of the same procedure for a period of 2-6 of Day 1 compared to other periods of the same day. SVM is not able to label 50% of vectors in the correct class while proceeding with the same period of two successive days and 40% of vectors during different periods of the same day. The second table reveals that period 02-06 is more coherent with neighboring periods (06-10 and 22-02) than with other periods of the day. In conclusion, the coherence of the data is acceptable.

Multi-Class Detection Experiment

We also tested SVM's ability to distinguish between different classes of traffic: for instance traces coming form different VoIP platforms. We built a group of four traces, each representing a different traffic class : normal traffic, a burst of flooding DoS, a trace generated by the KIF stateful fuzzer [9], and a trace generated by an unknown testbed as shown in Table 3. The size of the analyzed slice is fixed to 30 messages. After analysis, a 2-fold training/testing cross test is performed over all respectively labeled vectors (2449 vectors). The test Accuracy is defined as the percentage of correctly classified vectors over all test vectors. When the RBF (Radial Basis Function) kernel is used with default parameters ($C=1$ and $\gamma = 1/38$), the accuracy is 98.24%.

Table 3. Multi-Class SIP Traffic Data Set

Trace	Normal	DoS	KIF	Unknown
SIP pkts	57960	6076	2305	7033
Duration	8.6(min)	3.1(min)	50.9 (min)	83.7(day)

Comparison between Different Kernel Experiments

The RBF kernel is a reasonable first choice if one can assume that the classes are not linearly separable and because it has few numerical settings (small number of

Table 4. Testing Results for Different Kernels

Kernel	Parameters	Accuracy(%)	Time(ms)
Linear	$C = 1$	99.79	196
Polynomial	$C = 1$; $\gamma = 1/38$; $r = 0; d = 3$	79.09	570
Sigmoid	$C = 1$; $\gamma = 1/38$; $r = 0$	93.83	994
RBF	$C = 1$; $\gamma = 1/38$	98.24	668
Linear	$C = 2$	99.83	157
RBF	$C = 2$; $\gamma = 0.5$	99.83	294

parameters, exponential function bounded between 0 and 1). On the other hand, linear and RBF kernels have comparable performance if the number of features is significantly higher than the number of instances or if both are to large [8]. Therefore, we have tested all kernels with their default parameters over our dataset. The accuracy (defined as the percentage of correctly classified messages over all the test results) for 2-fold cross and machine dependent running time are shown in Table 4. The last two lines of the table are for RBF and linear kernels after parameter selection. Machine running time is given for comparison purpose only and it is averaged over ten runs. RBF and linear kernels have clearly better accuracy and execution time. We expect that RBF kernel will bypass linear kernel performance when dealing with larger sets of data.

Size of SIP Slice Experiment

The analyzer window is an important parameter in the feature evaluation process. The size of the slice can be fixed or variable with respect to other monitoring parameters. In this experiment, we report the accuracy of our solution, when changing the size of the analyzed slice. The results shown in Table 5 were obtained using a 5-fold cross test using a RBF kernel and the default parameters. The time the analyzer takes to process the packets is critical in online monitoring. This is the reason why we show the analysis time of the overall trace: (note that values are for comparison purpose). As expected, the accuracy improves with larger window size, which incurs an increased analysis time.

Feature Selection

The 38 features are chosen based on domain specific knowledge and experience, but other features might be also relevant. The selection of highly relevant features is essential in our approach. In the following experiments, we rank these features with respect to their relevance. We can thus reduce the number of features by gradually excluding less important features from the analysis. In Table 6, the

Table 5. Testing Results for Different Kernels

Window size	5	15	30	60	90	120	150
Accuracy (%)	95.4	99.32	99.30	99.67	99.63	100	100
Analysis Time (min)	1.12	2.40	2.56	4.31	6.39	7.42	8.51

Table 6. Results for Decreasing Size of Features Set

# of features	38	31	18	12	7
Accuracy (%)	99.30	99.39	98.90	98.65	98.22
Machine Time (s)	1.85	1.59	1.42	1.28	0.57

results of a preliminary experiment, where we exclude one group of features at each column in the following order: the distribution of final state of dialogs, the distribution of SIP requests, the distribution of SIP responses, and the Call-Id based statistics are given. The last column of the table represents only the general statistics group of features. Experiments use a 5-fold cross test over our data set with RBF kernel and its default parameters. The test accuracy is the percentage of correctly classified vectors over all the vectors in the test data set.

Although we notice a sudden jump between 12 and 7 features, the associated accuracy is not strictly decreasing as a function of number of features used. It is thus reasonable to inquire on the dependencies among the features.

Detection of Flooding Attacks

We have used the Inviteflood tool [2] to launch SIP flooding attacks. We have used INVITE flooding with an invalid domain name (which is the most impacting on the OpenSER server). We have generated five attacks at five different rates, where each attack lasts for one minute. After adaptation (we assume that one machine of the real world platform is performing the attack), each one minute attack period is injected into a normal trace of two hours duration. The time of the attack is fixed to five minutes after the start of the two hours period. Each mixed trace is then analyzed and labeled properly (positively along the period of attack and negatively in all the remaining time).

We have trained the system with the mixed trace (flooding at 100 INVITE/s - normal trace) in the learning stage. This means that 100 INVITE messages arc taken as a critical rate (the rate we consider as threshold to launch an alarm).

As shown in Fig. 7 (for simplification and clarity sake a slice is sized to only three packets), we take the period of attack and we calculate the corresponding SVM estimation. The estimated probability is the average of the estimated probabilities for the elementary slices composing the attack traffic. This granular probability is given by the LibSVM tool and is useful for both the probability estimate option in both learning and testing stages. We define the detection accuracy as the percentage of vectors correctly classified as attack over all vectors of the attack period. The results are in Table 7: the detection accuracy-1 is obtained without a parameter selection (Default parameters : $C = 1$, $\gamma = 1/38$,

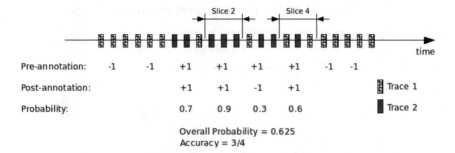

Fig. 7. Attack Detection in a Mixed Trace

Table 7. Attack Estimation for Different Rates of Flooding

Flooding Rate (INVITE/s)	0.5	1	10	100	1000
Detection Accuracy-1 (%)	0	0	5.47	67.57	97.36
Detection Accuracy-2 (%)	0	1.48	30.13	88.82	98.24
Pr(Normal)	0.96	0.95	0.73	0.24	0.07
Pr(Attack)	0.04	0.05	0.27	0.76	0.93

training accuracy: 90.95), detection accuracy-2 and calculated probabilities are after parameter selection ($C = 32$, $\gamma = 0.5$, training accuracy is of 93.93). We tested the coherence of a period with respect to other periods. In Table 2, we show the results of the same procedure for a period of 2-6 of Day 1 compared to other periods of the same day.

Even though stealthy attacks cannot to be detected, the results show a promising opportunity to fine-tune the defensive solution. The threshold rate can be learnt by a dual trace : the ongoing normal/daily traffic and a stress condition where the server was troubleshooted or was noticed to be under-operating. In this way, SVM is promising for an adaptive online monitoring solution against flooding attacks.

Detection of SPIT Attacks

SPIT mitigation is one of the open issues in VoIP security today. Detection of SPIT alone is not sufficient if it is not accompanied by a prevention system. In-depth search in the suspicious traffic is needed to build a prevention system to block the attack in the future. Elements like IP source and URI in the SIP headers can be automatically extracted.

To generate SPIT calls, we used a well known tool which is the Spitter/ Asterisk tool [2]. Spitter is able to generate call instances described in a ".call" file using the open source Asterisk PBX. The rate of simultaneous concurrent calls can also be specified as an option of the attack. We profiled our programmable bots to receive SPIT calls. Once an INVITE is received, the bot chooses randomly between three different responses :

- the first choice is to ring for a random time interval between one and six seconds and then to pick up the phone. This emulates two cases : a voice mail which is dumping a message or a human which is responding. The bot then listens during a random time between five and ten seconds and hangs up,
- the second choice is to respond with 'Busy',
- the last choice is to ring for some time and then to send a redirection response informing the caller that the call has to be directed to another destination (destination that we assume to not be served by this proxy). Other similar scenarios like forking (by the proxy) or transferring (by the bot) can also be supported.

We have performed two experiments with two different hit rates. The former is a partial SPIT: Spitter targets the proxy with hundred destinations and among these only ten are actually registered bots. In this case the hit rate is just 10%. This emulates the real world scenario where attackers are blindly trying a list of extensions. The latter is a total SPIT: we assume that attackers knew already the good extensions so the hit rate is 100%. This emulates the real world scenario where attackers knew already the good extensions either by a previous enumerating attack or from a web crawler.

In the partial SPIT experiment (SPIT not covering all the domain extensions, hit rate < 100 %), we send four successive campaigns with respectively one, ten, fifty and hundred concurrent calls. In the first campaign, Spitter does not start a dialog before the previous dialog is finished. In the second campaign, ten dialogs go on at the same time and only when a dialog is finished, a new dialog is started.

The four resulting traces (duration about two minutes each) are injected - after adaptation (we assume that one agent of the real trace is performing the attack against the hundred other agents) - in four different normal traces (duration of two hours each). The traces are then cut into slices of thirty messages and analyzed. These are annotated positively for the period of attack and negatively in all the remaining duration. The mixed trace with fifty concurrent calls SPIT is used in the training stage. The SVM prediction results are shown in Table 8. True positives are the percentage of vectors correctly classified as attack over all the vectors of the attack period. True negatives are the percentage of vectors correctly classified as normal over all the vectors of the normal period. These results should be considered under the larger umbrella of event correlation. For instance, the example with ten concurrent calls:

- Most of the two hours traffic is normal and is correctly detected (47436 slices).
- 16 out of the 766 slices that compose the attack traffic are detected. This means that we have ten correct events in a period of two minutes, because the detection of one slice is highly relevant to all ongoing traffic around this slice.

In addition, the attacks are partial since they target a small fraction of the users of the VoIP server (more than 3000 users are identified in the two hours period).

Table 8. Detection of Partial SPIT in Four Mixed Traces With Different Intensities

# of Concurrent Calls	True Positives (%)	True Negatives (%)
RBF; C= 1; $\gamma = 1/38$; Training accuracy = 99.0249		
1	0 (0/3697)	
10	1.30 (10/766)	
50	10.01 (62/619)	100
100	18.31 (102/557)	
Linear ; C=1 ; Training accuracy = 99.0197		
1	0 (0/3697)	
10	2.09 (16/766)	
50	10.66 (66/619)	100
100	19.39 (108/557)	

We agree that a stealthy SPIT of the magnitude of one concurrent call is never detected, but in the case of hundred concurrent calls, one over five positives is successfully detected when training was done using a half of this intensity attack.

With the help of a set of deterministic event correlation rules, our online monitoring system is able to detect the attacks efficiently:

Predicate	SPIT intensity
10 distributed positives in a 2 minutes period	Low
Multiple Series of 5 Successive Positives	Medium
Multiple Series of 10 Successive Positives	High

Table 9. Detection of Full SPIT in Four Mixed Traces With Different Intensities

# of Concurrent calls	1	10	50	100
RBF; C= 1; $\gamma = 1/8$; Training accuracy = 98.9057				
True Positives	0.03	3.05	12.18	23.41
	2/7015	15/492	85/698	184/786
True Negatives	100			

In the full SPIT experiment, we request the hundred bots to register with the proxy. Spitter hits all the bots in four successive campaigns with increasing intensity. Results are slightly better than in the partial SPIT experiment (Table 9). Partial SPIT generates an abnormal traffic at the same level as full SPIT does.

7   Related Works

VoIP security is a recent research domain that emerged over the last few years with the increasing use of this technology by enterprises and individuals. Combating SPIT and DoS is the subject of many research proceedings. Quittek et al. [10] apply hidden Turing tests and compare the resulting patterns with typical human communication patterns. Passing these tests causes significant resource consumption in the SPIT generation side. The authors of [11] propose a call rank mechanism based on call duration, social networks and global reputation to filter SPIT calls. Other ideas include a progressive and multi (short term -long term) grey level algorithm [12] and incorporating active stack fingerprinting [13].

The authors of [14] design application and transport sensors to protect enterprise networks from VoIP DoS attacks based on previous works on TCP DoS protection and study different recovery algorithms. The authors of [15] modify the original state machine of SIP transactions to detect transaction anomalies and apply different thresholds to detect flooding attacks. More adaptive to such attacks is the work of Sengar et al. [16] where the Hellinger distance between learning and testing periods is used to detect TCP SYN, SIP INVITE and RTP floods. Their approach shows good performances. There have many papers in the community on generic intrusion detection methods [17,18,19] without to extend to the fine tuned session, dialog, transaction related parameters found in SIP. Over the past, many security related applications have leveraged machine learning techniques and the reader is referred to [20] and [21] for an overview.

The closest work to ours is the study of [22] where the authors have presented a traffic behavior profiling methodology and demonstrated its applications in problem diagnosis and anomaly detection. Our work is more oriented towards attack detection and classification rather than proposing a global and multi level profiling methodology. We have addressed the VoIP specific event correlation and honeypots in previous published work [23] and [24], which did not cover SIP-level monitoring.

8   Conclusion and Future Works

As attacks on VoIP are popping-up in different forms with increasing impact on both the users and infrastructure, more monitoring and security management is needed. In this paper, we proposed an online monitoring methodology based on support vector machines. Our idea is to cut the ongoing signalling (SIP) traffic into small slices and to extract a vector of defined features characterizing each slice. Vectors are then pushed into a SVM for classification based on a learning model. We then use a deterministic event correlator to raise an alarm when suspicious and abnormal situations occur.

We validated our approach by offline tests over a set of real world traces and attacks which are generated in our customized testbed and inserted in the normal traffic traces. Results showed a real time performance and a high accuracy of detecting flooding and SPIT attacks especially when coupled with efficient event correlation rules. Detection of other types of attacks are future work.

Unsupervised learning techniques are appealing because they don't need a priori knowledge of the traffic and can detect new and previously unknown attacks. We consider currently to redefine and reorder our set of features based on different features selection algorithms. We will extend the current event correlation and filtering algorithm in order to reveal attack strategies and improve intrusion prevention/detection accuracy.

Acknowledgment. We would like to thank Mr Dorgham Sisalem and Mr. Sven Ehlert, both from Fraunhofer Institute in Berlin for their comments and feedback on discussing the analysis of SIP traces.

References

1. VoIPSA: VoIP security and privacy threat taxonomy. Public Realease 1.0 (October 2005), http://www.voipsa.org/Activities/VOIPSA_Threat_Taxonomy_0.1.pdf
2. Endler, D., Collier, M.: Hacking Exposed VoIP: Voice Over IP Security Secrets and Solutions. McGraw-Hill Professional Publishing, New York (2007)
3. Vapnik, V.N.: The nature of statistical learning theory. Springer, New York (1995)
4. Vapnik, V.: Statistical Learning Theory, New York (1998)
5. Guyon, I., Weston, J., Barnhill, S., Vapnik, V.: Gene selection for cancer classification using support vector machines. Mach. Learn. 46(1-3), 389–422 (2002)
6. Romano, R.A., Aragon, C.R., Ding, C.: Supernova recognition using support vector machines. In: ICMLA 2006: Proceedings of the 5th International Conference on Machine Learning and Applications, Washington, DC, USA, pp. 77–82. IEEE Computer Society, Los Alamitos (2006)
7. Mukkamala, S., Janoski, G., Sung, A.: Intrusion detection: Support vector machines and neural networks. The IEEE Computer Society Student Magazine 10(2) (2002)
8. Chang, C.C., Lin, C.J.: LIBSVM: a library for support vector machines (2001), http://www.csie.ntu.edu.tw/~cjlin/libsvm
9. Abdelnur, H.J., State, R., Festor, O.: KiF: a stateful SIP fuzzer. In: IPTComm 2007: Proceedings of the 1st international conference on Principles, systems and applications of IP telecommunications, pp. 47–56. ACM, New York (2007)
10. Quittek, J., Niccolini, S., Tartarelli, S., Stiemerling, M., Brunner, M., Ewald, T.: Detecting SPIT calls by checking communication patterns. In: IEEE International Conference on Communications (ICC 2007) (June 2007)
11. Balasubramaniyan, V.A., Ahamad, M., Park, H.: CallRank: Combating SPIT using call duration, social networks and global reputation. In: Fourth Conference on Email and Anti-Spam (CEAS 2007). Mountain View, California (2007)
12. Shin, D., Shim, C.: Progressive multi gray-leveling: A voice Spam protection algorithm. IEEE Network 20
13. Yan, H., Sripanidkulchai, K., Zhang, H., Shae, Z.Y., Saha, D.: Incorporating active fingerprinting into SPIT prevention systems. In: Third annual security workshop (VSW 2006), June 2006, ACM Press, New York (2006)
14. Reynolds, B., Ghosal, D.: Secure IP Telephony using Multi-layered Protection. In: Proceedings of The 10th Annual Network and Distributed System Security Symposium, San Diego, CA, USA (February 2003)
15. Chen, E.: Detecting DoS attacks on SIP systems. In: Proceedings of 1st IEEE Workshop on VoIP Management and Security, San Diego, CA, USA, April 2006, pp. 53–58 (2006)
16. Sengar, H., Wang, H., Wijesekera, D., Jajodia, S.: Detecting VoIP Floods using the Hellinger Distance. Transactions on Parallel and Distributed Systems (acepted for future publication, September 2007)

17. Valdes, A., Skinner, K.: Adaptive, model-based monitoring for cyber attack detection. In: Debar, H., Mé, L., Wu, S.F. (eds.) RAID 2000. LNCS, vol. 1907, pp. 80–92. Springer, Heidelberg (2000)
18. Denning, D.E.: An intrusion-detection model. In: IEEE Symposium on Security and Privacy, April 1986, pp. 118–133. IEEE Computer Society Press, Los Alamitos (1986)
19. Krügel, C., Toth, T., Kirda, E.: Service specific anomaly detection for network intrusion detection. In: SAC 2002: Proceedings of the 2002 ACM symposium on Applied computing, pp. 201–208. ACM Press, New York (2002)
20. Ning, P., Jajodia, S.: Intrusion Detection in Distributed Systems: An Abstraction-Based Approach. Springer, Heidelberg (2003)
21. Maloof, M.: Machine Learning and Data Mining for Computer Security: Methods and Applications. Springer, Heidelberg (2005)
22. Kang, H.J., Zhang, Z.L., Ranjan, S., Nucci, A.: Sip-based voip traffic behavior profiling and its applications. In: MineNet 2007: Proceedings of the 3rd annual ACM workshop on Mining network data, pp. 39–44. ACM, New York (2007)
23. Nassar, M., State, R., Festor, O.: Intrusion detections mechanisms for VoIP applications. In: Third annual security workshop (VSW 2006), June 2006. ACM Press, New York (2006)
24. Nassar, M., State, R., Festor, O.: VoIP honeypot architecture. In: Proc. of 10 th. IEEE/IFIP Symposium on Integrated Management. (June 2007)

Table 10. Appendix: List of features

Number	Name	Description
		Group 1 - General Statistics
1	Duration	Total time of the slice
2	NbReq	# of requests / Total # of messages
3	NbResp	# of responses / Total # of messages
4	NbSdp	# of messages carrying SDP / Total # of messages
5	AvInterReq	Average inter arrival of requests
6	AvInterResp	Average inter arrival of responses
7	AvInterSdp	Average inter arrival of messages carrying SDP bodies
		Group 2 - Call-ID Based Statistics
8	NbSess	# of different Call-IDs
9	AvDuration	Average duration of a Call-ID
10	NbSenders	# of different senders / Total # of Call-IDs
11	NbReceivers	# of different receivers / Total # of Call-IDs
12	AvMsg	Average # of messages per Call-ID
		Group 3 - Dialogs Final State Distribution
13	NbNOTACALL	# of NOTACALL/ Total # of Call-ID
14	NbCALLSET	# of CALLSET/ Total # of Call-ID
15	NbCANCELED	# of CANCELED/ Total # of Call-ID
16	NbREJECTED	# of REJECTED/ Total # of Call-ID
17	NbINCALL	# of INCALL/ Total # of Call-ID
18	NbCOMPLETED	# of COMPLETED/ Total # of Call-ID
19	NbRESIDUE	# of RESIDUE/ Total # of Call-ID
		Group 4 - Requests Distribution
20	NbInv	# of INVITE / Total # of requests
21	NbReg	# of REGISTER/ Total # of requests
22	NbBye	# of BYE/ Total # of requests
23	NbAck	# of ACK/ Total # of requests
24	NbCan	# of CANCEL/ Total # of requests
25	NbOpt	# of OPTIONS / Total # of requests
26	Nb Ref	# of REFER/ Total # of requests
27	NbSub	# of SUBSCRIBE/ Total # of requests
28	NbNot	# of NOTIFY/ Total # of requests
29	NbMes	# of MESSAGE/ Total # of requests
30	NbInf	# of INFO/ Total # of requests
31	NbPra	# of PRACK/ Total # of requests
32	NbUpd	# of UPDATE/ Total # of requests
		Group 5 - Responses Distribution
33	Nb1xx	# of Informational responses / Total # of responses
34	Nb2xx	# of Success responses / Total # of responses
35	Nb3xx	# of Redirection responses / Total # of responses
36	Nb4xx	# of Client error responses / Total # of responses
37	Nb5xx	# of Server error responses / Total # of responses
38	Nb6xx	# of Global error responses / Total # of responses

The Effect of Clock Resolution on Keystroke Dynamics

Kevin Killourhy and Roy Maxion

Dependable Systems Laboratory
Carnegie Mellon University
5000 Forbes Ave,
Pittsburgh PA, 15213
{ksk,maxion}@cs.cmu.edu

Abstract. Keystroke dynamics—the analysis of individuals' distinctive typing rhythms—has been proposed as a biometric to discriminate legitimate users from impostors (whether insiders or external attackers). Anomaly detectors have reportedly performed well at this discrimination task, but there is room for improvement. Detector performance might be constrained by the widespread use of comparatively low-resolution clocks (typically 10–15 milliseconds).

This paper investigates the effect of clock resolution on detector performance. Using a high-resolution clock, we collected keystroke timestamps from 51 subjects typing 400 passwords each. We derived the timestamps that would have been generated by lower-resolution clocks. Using these data, we evaluated three types of detectors from the keystroke-dynamics literature, finding that detector performance is slightly worse at typical clock resolutions than at higher ones (e.g., a 4.2% increase in equal-error rate). None of the detectors achieved a practically useful level of performance, but we suggest opportunities for progress through additional, controlled experimentation.

Keywords: Anomaly detection; Insider-attack detection; Keystroke dynamics; Digital biometrics.

1 Introduction

Compromised passwords, shared accounts, and backdoors are exploited both by external attackers and insiders. Lists of default passwords and password-cracking programs are a staple in the toolbox of external attackers. In a study of insider attacks (i.e., those conducted by people with legitimate access to an organization), Keeney et al. [11] found that the majority of insiders exploited shared or compromised passwords, as well as backdoor accounts. However, if we had some sort of "digital fingerprint" with which to identify exactly who is logging into an account, and to discriminate between the *legitimate user* of an account and an *impostor*, we could significantly curb the threats represented by both insiders and external attackers. Of the various potential solutions to this problem, one technique that has been popular within the research community is

R. Lippmann, E. Kirda, and A. Trachtenberg (Eds.): RAID 2008, LNCS 5230, pp. 331–350, 2008.

keystroke dynamics—the analysis of individual typing rhythms for use as a bio-metric identifier. Compared to other biometric data, typing times are relatively easy to collect. When a user logs into a computer by typing his or her password, the program authenticating the user could save not just the characters of the password, but the time at which each key was pressed and released. One could imagine a keystroke-dynamics detection algorithm that analyzes these typing times, compares them to a known profile of the legitimate user of the account, and makes a decision about whether or not the new typist is an impostor. In fact, detectors have been designed to use typing rhythms as a biometric, not just during password entry (which is our focus in this work), but also for free-text typing [17].

In terms of accuracy, the European standard for access-control systems (EN-50133-1) specifies a false-alarm rate of less than 1%, with a miss rate of no more than 0.001% [3]. In other words, in order for a keystroke-dynamics detector to be practical, it must correctly identify a legitimate user 99% of the time, and it must correctly identify an impostor 99.999% of the time. At this point, no proposed detector has obtained such numbers in repeated evaluations. When a detector comes up short in evaluation, the common strategy is to go back to the drawing board and try a new detector. However, it may be possible to boost the performance of an existing detector by giving it better data.

Imagine the effect that timing noise might have on a detector. With enough noise, subtle differences between typists will be masked, and even a good detector will be ineffective. One obvious source of noise comes from the resolution of the clock supplying timestamps for each keystroke. For instance, our testing shows that the clock used by Microsoft Windows XP to timestamp keystroke-event messages [15] (which we call the *Windows-event clock*) has a resolution of 15.625 milliseconds (ms), corresponding to 64 updates per second. Figure 1 shows how the clock resolution affects the calculation of keydown–keydown digram latencies. Specifically, if every time reported by the clock is a multiple of 15.625 ms (truncated to the nearest millisecond), then all latencies will appear to fall in bands separated by 15 ms. The calculated latencies could differ from the true latencies by as much as the resolution of the clock (approximately ± 15 ms). If two typists differ in their typing times by less than 15 ms, then the difference could be lost. This investigation empirically measures the effect of clock resolution on the performance of a detector. Specifically, we look at whether the performance of a detector can be boosted by increasing the resolution of the clock, and whether or not detectors are robust to low-resolution clocks.

2   Background and Related Work

Detectors for discriminating between users' and impostors' keystroke dynamics have been investigated for over 30 years. They were first considered in 1977 by Forsen et al. [6], who distinguished a legitimate user from an impostor on the basis of how each one typed the user's name. In 1980, Gaines et al. [7] compared

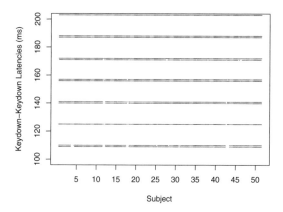

Fig. 1. The spacing between each horizontal band of keystroke latencies reveals that the Windows-event clock has a resolution of 15.625 milliseconds. Any fine-grained differences between the subjects are masked when all latencies are coarsened to a nearby multiple of the clock resolution. Data are keydown–keydown digram latencies (between 100 and 200 ms) recorded by the 15.625 ms resolution clock when each of 51 subjects typed a password 400 times. Double bands occur because Windows reports the timestamps as a whole number of milliseconds, sometimes rounding up and sometimes rounding down.

several users' keystrokes on a transcription task. Both studies presented positive findings, but cautioned that their results were only preliminary.

Joyce and Gupta [10] were some of the earliest researchers to study the keystroke dynamics of passwords. They developed a detector that compared typing characteristics of a new presentation of a password against the average (mean) typing characteristics of the legitimate user. Cho et al. [4] developed and compared two new detectors, inspired by techniques from machine learning. One was based on the nearest-neighbor algorithm, and the other used a multilayer perceptron. A full survey of keystroke-dynamics detectors has been conducted by Peacock et al. [17], but we focus here on the work of Joyce and Gupta, and Cho et al. Their work shows a diversity among available detection techniques, and our investigation uses detectors similar to theirs.

In terms of timing considerations, Forsen et al. and Gaines et al. collected data on a PDP-11. Forsen et al. reported times in 5-millisecond intervals, while Gaines et al. reported millisecond accuracy. Both Joyce and Gupta, and Cho et al. collected data on a Sun workstation. Cho et al. specified that they used X11, which provides keystroke timestamps with a 10 ms resolution. The X11 clock is typically used by researchers on UNIX-based platforms, while Windows users typically use the Windows-event clock (e.g., Sheng et al. [19]). Our testing shows that the timestamps reported through this clock have a 15.625 ms resolution (see Figure 1).

3   Problem and Approach

Keystroke-dynamics detectors—programs designed to distinguish between a legitimate user and an impostor on the basis of typing rhythms—will almost certainly be affected by the resolution of the clock that is used for timing the keystrokes. However, the extent of this effect has never been quantified or measured. In this work, we investigate the effect that clock resolution has on the performance of keystroke-dynamics detectors. We hope to boost detector performance by using better clocks, and to quantify the error introduced by typical clocks.

3.1   Investigative Approach

Our approach is outlined in the following four steps:

1. **Password-data collection:** We choose a password, and we implement a data-collection apparatus that records high-resolution timestamps. We recruit subjects to type the password. We collect keystroke timestamps simultaneously with a high-resolution clock and with a typical low-resolution clock.
2. **Derived clock resolutions:** We coarsen the high-resolution timestamps, in order to calculate the timestamps that would be generated by a range of lower-resolution clocks; we derive password-timing data at a range of resolutions.
3. **Detector implementation:** We develop three types of keystroke-dynamics detectors similar to those reported in the literature: a mean-based detector, a nearest-neighbor detector, and a multilayer perceptron.
4. **Performance-assessment method:** We construct evaluation data sets from our password timing data, and we use them to measure the performance of the three detectors. We verify the correctness of our derivations (in step 2) by comparing a detector's performance on derived low-resolution data to its performance on data from a real clock operating at that resolution. Finally, we examine how the performance changes as a function of clock resolution.

In the end, we are able to quantify the effect that clock resolution has on several diverse detectors. We show a small but significant improvement from using high-resolution clocks. We describe the four steps of our investigation in Sections 4–7.

3.2   Controlling for Potential Confounding Factors

Our approach departs from typical keystroke-dynamics evaluations, where realism is considered to have higher importance than control. A reason for designing a controlled experiment is to remove *confounding factors*—variables that may distort the effect of the variable of interest on the experimental outcome [5].

In our investigation, the variable of interest is the clock resolution, and the experimental outcome is the performance of a detector. The clock might affect detector performance because it subtly changes the keystroke times analyzed by the detectors. All other factors that change these keystroke times are potential confounding factors that might obscure or distort this effect. They might change a detector's performance, or even change *how clock resolution affects the detector's performance.* The presence of such a factor would compromise our investigation by offering an alternative explanation for our results.

Ideally, we would test all potential confounding factors, to see whether they actually do confound the experiment. However, to do so would require an exponential amount of data (in the number of factors). Practically, we control for potential confounding factors by keeping them constant.

4 Password-Data Collection

The first step in our investigation was to collect a sample of keystroke-timing data using a high-resolution clock. We chose a single password to use as a typing sample. Then we designed a data-collection apparatus for collecting subjects' keystrokes and timestamps. Finally, we recruited 51 subjects, and collected the timing information for 400 passwords from each one (over 8 sessions).

4.1 Choosing a Password

Password selection is the first potential confounding factor we identified. Some passwords can be typed more quickly than others. The choice of password may affect a subject's keystroke times, distorting the effect of clock resolution. To control for the potential confounding factor, we chose a single fixed but representative password to use throughout the experiment.

To make the password representative of a typical, strong password, we employed a publicly available password generator [21] and password-strength checker [13]. We generated a 10-character password containing letters, numbers, and punctuation and then modified it slightly, interchanging some punctuation and casing to better conform with the general perception of a strong password. The result of this procedure was the following password:

.tie5Roanl

The password-strength checker rates this password as strong because it contains at least 8 characters, a capital letter, a number, and punctuation. The best rating is reserved for passwords with at least 14 characters, but we decided to maintain a 10-character limit on our password so as not to exhaust our subjects' patience. (Other researchers used passwords as short as 7 characters [4].)

4.2 Data-Collection Apparatus

We wrote a Windows application that prompts a subject to type the password 50 times. Of course, in the real world, users do not type their password 50 times in a row; they might only type it a few times each day. However, the amount of practice a subject has at typing a particular password represents another potential confounding factor (see Section 3.2). Practiced typists are usually faster, and the amount of practice a subject has may affect his or her keystroke times.

By having our subjects type the password in fixed-length sessions, we controlled how much (and under what circumstances) our subjects became practiced at typing the password.

The application displays the password in a screen along with a text-entry field. In order to advance to the next screen, the subject must type the 10 characters of the password correctly in sequence and then type Return. If the subject makes a mistake, the application immediately detects the error, clears the text-entry field, and after a short pause, it prompts the subject to type the password again. For instance, if a subject typed the first three characters of the password correctly (.ti) but mistyped the fourth (w instead of e), the application would make the subject type the whole password over again. In this way, we ensure that the subject correctly types the entire password as a sequence of exactly 11 keystrokes (corresponding to the 10 characters of the password and the Return key). Forcing subjects to type the password without error is a typical constraint when analyzing keystroke dynamics [4, 19].

When a subject presses or releases a key, the application records the event (i.e., whether a key was pressed or released, and what key was involved), and also the time at which the event occurred. Two timestamps are recorded: one is the timestamp reported by the 15.625 ms resolution Windows-event clock; the other is the timestamp reported by a high-resolution external reference clock. The resolution of the reference clock was measured to be 200 microseconds by using a function generator to simulate key presses at fixed intervals. This clock reported the timestamps accurately to within ±200 microseconds. We used an external reference instead of the high-precision performance counter available through Windows [16] because of concerns that factors such as system load might decrease the accuracy of the timestamps.

The data collection application was installed on a single laptop with no network connection and with an external keyboard. We identified keyboard selection as another potential confounding factor (see Section 3.2). If subjects used different keyboards, the difference might affect their keystroke times. We control for the potential confounding factor by using one keyboard throughout the experiment.

4.3   Running Subjects

We recruited 51 subjects, many from within the Carnegie Mellon Computer Science Department, but some from the university at large. We required that subjects wait at least 24 hours between each of their 8 sessions, so each session was recorded on a separate day (ensuring that some day-to-day variation existed within our sample). All 51 subjects remained in the study, contributing 400 passwords over the 8 sessions.

Our sample of subjects consisted of 30 males and 21 females. We had 8 left-handed and 43 right-handed subjects. We grouped ages by 10-year intervals. The median group was 31–40, the youngest group was 11–20, and the oldest group was 61–70. The subjects' sessions took between 1.25 minutes and 11 minutes, with the median session taking 3 minutes. Subjects took between 9 days and 35

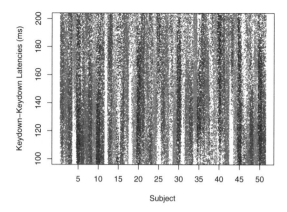

Fig. 2. The absence of horizontal bands demonstrates that the high-resolution clock has a resolution of less than 1 millisecond (200 microseconds, specifically). The keystrokes are the same as in Figure 1, but the latencies in this figure are based on the high-resolution clock.

days to complete all 8 sessions. The median length of time between the first and last session was 23 days.

5   Derived Clock Resolutions

The second step in our investigation was to use the high-resolution data to reconstruct the data that would have been collected with lower-resolution clocks. We developed a procedure to derive the timestamp of a low-resolution clock from the corresponding timestamp of a high-resolution clock.

First, we examine the keydown–keydown latencies based on the high-resolution timestamps. The latencies are shown in Figure 2. Compare these latencies to the equivalent latencies from Figure 1. Whereas the horizontal bands in Figure 1 reveal that the Windows-event clock cannot capture any timing variation smaller than 15.625 milliseconds, the absence of such bands in Figure 2 demonstrates that very subtle variations (smaller than 1 millisecond) can be captured by the high-resolution clock.

Next, to determine what would have happened if the data had been collected with a lower-resolution clock, we need to artificially decrease the resolution of this clock. Consider how timestamps are normally assigned to keystroke events:

1. The operating system is notified of the pending key event by an interrupt from the keyboard controller.
2. The operating system reads the key event from the keyboard device into memory.
3. During the handling of the key event, the operating system queries a clock for the current time.
4. The timestamp returned by the clock is included in the description of the keystroke event and is delivered to any applications waiting on the event.

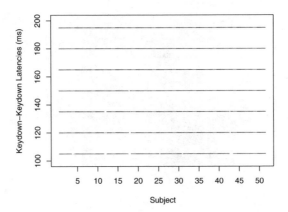

Fig. 3. The presence of horizontal bands 15 ms apart suggests that the derived 15 ms clock exhibits the same behavior as a real clock with a 15 ms resolution. The keystrokes are the same as in Figures 1 and 2, but the derived 15 ms clock was used to calculate the latencies. The bands resemble those of the real 15.625 ms clock in Figure 1, but without double bands because the 15 ms clock resolution has no fractional part being rounded to a whole millisecond.

For example, if we have a clock with a resolution of 15 ms (i.e., it is updated every 15 ms), then the timestamp returned by the clock will be divisible by 15 ms. Specifically, it will be the largest multiple of 15 ms smaller than the actual time at which the clock was queried. In general, if the clock was queried at time $t_{\text{hi-res}}$, and we want to reproduce the behavior of a lower-resolution clock (with a resolution of r), the low-resolution timestamp would be

$$t_{\text{lo-res}} \leftarrow \lfloor t_{\text{hi-res}}/r \rfloor \times r$$

where $\lfloor x \rfloor$ is the largest integer smaller than x (floor function).

Finally, with this formula and the high-resolution data, we can derive the timestamps that would have been collected with lower-resolution clocks. For instance, Figure 3 shows keystroke latencies calculated from a clock with a derived 15 ms resolution. Note the similarity to Figure 1, which shows latencies calculated from a real Windows-event clock with a 15.625 ms resolution. (The fractional part of the real clock's resolution accounts for the slight differences.)

One limitation of this procedure is that we can only derive clock resolutions that are evenly divisible by that of our high-resolution clock. This criteria allows the small but non-zero inaccuracy of our high-resolution clock to be absorbed into the inaccuracy of the lower-resolution clock. For instance, we should be able to accurately derive a 1 ms clock resolution since 1 ms is evenly divisible by 200 microseconds (the resolution of the high-resolution clock). However, we could not accurately derive a 1.5 ms clock resolution (or a 15.625 ms resolution) because it is not evenly divided. Regardless of this limitation, the accuracy of results obtained with these derived clock resolutions will be established by comparing detector performance on derived 15 ms resolution data to that on the 15.625 ms resolution Windows-event clock data. We derive data at the following 20 clock resolutions:

Milliseconds: 1 2 5 10 15 20 30 50 75 100 150 200 500 750

Seconds: 1 2 5 10 15 30

The specific resolutions were chosen arbitrarily, but with the intent of including a range of typical values (on the first line), and a range of extremely low-resolution values (on the second line) in order to identify the point at which detector performance degrades completely. In total, we have data at 22 different clock resolutions: the 20 derived clocks, the high-resolution clock, and the 15.625 ms resolution Windows-event clock.

6   Detector Implementation

The third step in our investigation was to create detectors to test using our data. We identified three different types of detector from the literature, and implemented a detector of each type:

1. a mean-based detector,
2. a nearest-neighbor detector, and
3. a multilayer-perceptron detector.

By ensuring that we have diversity in the set of detectors we evaluate, we can examine whether or not an observed effect is specific to one type of detector or more generally true for a range of detectors.

6.1   Detector Overview

We constrained our attention to detectors that behave similarly in terms of their input and output. For instance, each of our detectors must analyze password-timing data, and aims to discriminate between a legitimate user and an impostor. Each of the detectors expects the password data to be encoded in what is called a *password-timing vector*. A password-timing vector is a vector of hold times and intervals. A hold time is the difference between the key-press timestamp and the key-release timestamp for the same key. An interval time is the (signed) difference between the key-release timestamp of the first key in a digram and the key-press timestamp of the second key.

The password-timing vector is 21 elements long for the password we chose (.tie5Roanl). Each element is either a hold time for one of the 11 keys in the password (including the Return key), or the interval between one of the 10 digrams, arranged as follows:

Index	Element name
1	Hold(period)
2	Interval(period-t)
3	Hold(t)
4	Interval(t-i)
5	Hold(i)
⋮	⋮
19	Hold(l)
20	Interval(l-Return)
21	Hold(Return)

where Hold(period) is the hold time of the period key, and Interval(period-t) is the interval between the period key-release and the t key-press.

Each detector has two phases: training and testing. During training, a set of password vectors from a legitimate user is used to build a *profile* of that user. Different detectors build this profile in different ways, but the objective of a successful detector is to build a profile that uniquely distinguishes the user from all other typists (like a fingerprint). During testing, a new password-timing vector (from an unknown typist) is provided, and the detector compares the new vector against the profile. The detector produces an *anomaly score* that indicates whether the way the new password was typed is similar to the profile (low score) or different from the profile (high score). The procedure by which this score is calculated depends on the detector.

In practice, the anomaly score would be compared against some pre-determined threshold to decide whether or not to raise an alarm (i.e., whether or not the password-typing rhythms belong to an impostor). However, in our evaluation, we will use these scores directly to assess the detector's performance.

The three detectors are implemented using the R statistical programming environment (version 2.4.0) [18]. The nearest-neighbor detector leverages an implementation of Bentley's *kd*-trees [1] by Mount and Arya [14]. The multilayer perceptron uses the neural-network package AMORE [12].

6.2   Mean-Based Detector

A mean-based detector models a user's password-timing vectors as coming from some known distribution (e.g., a multidimensional normal distribution) with an unknown mean. During training, the mean is estimated, and during testing, a new password-timing vector is assigned an anomaly score based on its distance from this mean. Joyce and Gupta [10] used a detector that fits this description, and the detector we implemented is similar to theirs, but not precisely the same.[1]

During training, our mean-based detector estimates the mean vector and the covariance matrix of the training password-timing vectors. The mean vector is a 21-element vector, whose first element is the mean of the first elements of the training vectors, whose second element is the mean of the second elements of the training vectors, and so on. Similarly, the covariance matrix is the 21-by-21-element matrix containing the covariance of each pair of elements in the 21-element training vectors. These mean and covariance estimates comprise the user's profile.

During testing, the detector estimates the *Mahalanobis distance* of the new password-timing vector from the mean vector of the training data. The

---

[1] Our detector differs from that proposed by Joyce and Gupta in both its mean-vector calculation and the distance measure used. We calculated the mean vector using all the training data while Joyce and Gupta preprocessed the data to remove outliers. We used the Mahalanobis distance while Joyce and Gupta used the Manhattan distance. Our mean-based detector was intended to be simple (with no preprocessing) while still accommodating natural variances in the data (with the Mahalanobis distance).

Mahalanobis distance is a measure of multidimensional distance that takes into account the fact that a sample may vary more in one dimension than another, and that there may be correlations between pairs of dimensions. These variations and correlations are estimated using the correlation matrix of the training data. More formally, using the matrix notation of linear algebra, if $\mathbf{x}$ is the mean of the training data, $\mathbf{S}$ is the covariance matrix, and $\mathbf{y}$ is the new password-timing vector, the Mahalanobis distance (d) is:

$$d \leftarrow (\mathbf{x} - \mathbf{y})^{\mathsf{T}} \mathbf{S}^{-1} (\mathbf{x} - \mathbf{y})$$

The anomaly score of a new password-timing vector is simply this distance.

6.3   Nearest-Neighbor Detector

Whereas the mean-based detector makes the assumption that the distribution of a user's passwords is known, the nearest-neighbor detector makes no such assumption. Its primary assumption is that new password-timing vectors from the user will resemble one or more of those in the training data. Cho et al. [4] explored the use of a nearest-neighbor detector in their work, and we attempted to re-implement their detector for our investigation.

During training, the nearest-neighbor detector estimates the covariance matrix of the training password-timing vectors (in the same way as the mean-based detector). However, instead of estimating the mean of the training data, the nearest-neighbor detector simply saves each password-timing vector.

During testing, the nearest-neighbor detector calculates Mahalanobis distances (using the covariance matrix of the training data). However, instead of calculating the distance from the new password-timing vector to the mean of the training data, the distance is calculated from the new password-timing vector to each of the vectors in the training data. The distance from the new vector to the nearest vector from the training data (i.e., its nearest neighbor) is used as the anomaly score.

6.4   Multilayer-Perceptron Detector

Whereas the behaviors of the mean-based and nearest-neighbor detectors allow for an intuitive explanation, the multilayer perceptron is comparatively opaque. A multilayer perceptron is a kind of artificial neural network that can be trained to behave like an arbitrary function (i.e., when given inputs, its outputs will approximate the function's output). Hwang and Cho [8] showed how a multilayer perceptron could be used as an anomaly detector by training it to *auto-associate*—that is, to behave like a function that reproduces its input as the output. In theory, new input that is like the input used to train the network will also produce similar output, while input that is different from the training input will produce wildly different output. By comparing the input to the output, one can detect anomalies. Cho et al. [4] used an auto-associative multilayer perceptron to discriminate between users and impostors on the basis of password-timing vectors. We attempted to re-implement that detector.

During training, the password-timing vectors are used to create an auto-associative multilayer perceptron. This process is a standard machine-learning procedure, but it is fairly involved. We present an overview here, but we must direct a reader to the works by Hwang, Cho, and their colleagues for a comprehensive treatment [4, 8]. A skeleton of a multilayer perceptron is first created. The skeleton has 21 input nodes, corresponding to the 21 elements of the password-timing vector, and 21 output nodes. In general, a multilayer-perceptron network can have a variety of structures (called hidden nodes) between the input and the output nodes. In keeping with earlier designs, we had a single layer of 21 hidden nodes. This skeleton was trained using a technique called back-propagation to auto-associate the user's password-timing vectors. We used the recommended learning parameters: training for 500 epochs with a 1×10^{-4} learning rate and a 3×10^{-4} momentum term.[2]

During testing, the new password-timing vector is used as input to the trained multilayer perceptron, and the output is calculated. The Euclidean distance of the input to the output is computed and used as the anomaly score.

7   Performance-Assessment Method

Now that we have three detectors and data at a variety of clock resolutions, the final step is to evaluate the detectors' performance. First, we convert the data to password-timing tables. Then we devise a procedure for training and testing the detectors. Last, we aggregate the test results into overall measures of each detector's performance at each clock resolution.

7.1   Creating Password-Timing Tables

As mentioned in Section 5, we have 22 data sets that differ only in the resolution of the clock used to timestamp the keystroke events: the high resolution clock, the 15.625 ms Windows-event clock, and the 20 derived clocks. For each clock, we have timing information for 51 subjects, each of whom typed the password (.tie5Roanl) 400 times.

We extract password-timing tables from the raw data. Hold times and digram intervals are calculated. We confirm that 50 password-timing vectors are extracted from each one of a subject's 8 sessions, and that a total of 20,400 password-timing vectors are extracted (50 passwords × 8 sessions × 51 subjects).

7.2   Training and Testing the Detectors

Consider a scenario in which a user's long-time password has been compromised by an impostor. The user is assumed to be practiced in typing her password,

---

[2] Note that our learning rate and momentum are 1000 times smaller than those reported by Cho et al. This change accounts for a difference in units between their password-timing vectors and ours. (We record in seconds; they used milliseconds.)

while the impostor is unfamiliar with it (e.g., typing it for the first time). We measure how well each of our three detectors is able to detect the impostor, discriminating the impostor's typing from the user's typing in this scenario.

We start by designating one of our subjects as the legitimate user, and the rest as impostors. We train and test each of the three detectors as follows:

1. We train the detector on the first 200 passwords typed by the legitimate user. The detector builds a profile of that user.
2. We test the ability of the detector to recognize the user herself by generating anomaly scores for the remaining 200 passwords typed by the user. We record these as *user scores*.
3. We test the ability of the detector to recognize impostors by generating anomaly scores for the first 5 passwords typed by each of the 50 impostors. We record these as *impostor scores*.

This process is then repeated, designating each of the other subjects as the legitimate user in turn. After training and testing a detector for each combination of subject, detector, and clock-resolution data set, we have a total of 3,366 sets of user and impostor scores (51 subjects × 3 detectors × 22 data sets).

It may seem that 200 passwords is an unrealistically large amount of training data. However, we used 200 passwords to train because we were concerned that fewer passwords might unfairly cause one or more detectors to under-perform (e.g., Cho et al. [4] trained the multilayer perceptron on up to 325 passwords). Likewise, an unpracticed impostor might seem unrealistic. If he knew that his keystroke dynamics would be scrutinized, he might practice first. However, as we argued in Section 4.2, the amount of practice a subject has had represents a potential confounding factor. Consequently, all impostors in our experiment were allowed the same level of practice. Our intuition was that the effect of clock resolution on detector performance might be seen most clearly with unpracticed impostors, and so we used their data (with plans to use practiced impostors' data in future investigations).

7.3   Calculating Detector Performance

To convert these sets of user and impostor scores into aggregate measures of detector performance, we used the scores to generate a graphical summary called an ROC curve [20], an example of which is shown in Figure 4. The hit rate is the frequency with which impostors' passwords generate an alarm (a desirable response), and the false-alarm rate is the frequency with which the legitimate user's passwords generate an alarm (an undesirable response). Whether or not a password generates an alarm depends on how the threshold for the anomaly scores is chosen. Over the continuum of possible thresholds to choose, the ROC curve illustrates how each one would change hit and false-alarm rates. Each point on the curve indicates the hit and false-alarm rates at a particular threshold.

The ROC curve is a common visualization of a detector's performance, and on the basis of the ROC curve, various cost measures can be calculated. Two common measures are the *equal-error rate* and the *zero-miss false-alarm rate*.

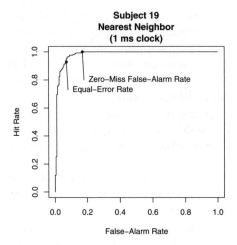

Fig. 4. An example ROC curve depicts the performance of the nearest-neighbor detector with subject 19 as the legitimate user and data from the derived 1 ms resolution clock. The curve shows the trade-off between the hit rate and false-alarm rate. The proximity of the curve to the top-left corner of the graph is a visual measure of performance.

The equal-error rate is the place on the curve where the false-alarm rate is equal to the miss rate (note that miss rate = 1 − hit rate). Geometrically, the equalerror rate is the false-alarm rate where the ROC curve intersects a line from the top-left corner of the plot to the bottom right corner. This cost measure was advocated by Peacock et al. [17] as a desirable single-number summary of detector performance. The zero-miss false-alarm rate is the smallest false-alarm rate for which the miss rate is zero (or, alternatively, the hit rate is 100%). Geometrically, the zero-miss false-alarm rate is the leftmost point on the curve where it is still flat against the top of the plot. This cost measure is used by Cho et al. [4] to compare detectors.

For each combination of subject, detector, and clock resolution, we generated an ROC curve, and we calculated these two cost measures. Then, to obtain an overall summary of a detector's performance at a particular clock resolution, we calculated the average equal-error rate and the average zero-miss false-alarm rate across all 51 subjects. These two measures of average cost were used to assess detector performance.

8   Results and Analysis

A preliminary look at the results reveals that—while the equal-error rate and the zero-miss false-alarm rate differ from one another—they show the same trends with respect to different detectors and clock resolutions. Consequently, we focus on the equal-error-rate results and acknowledge similar findings for the zero-miss false-alarm rate.

Table 1. The average equal-error rates for the three detectors are compared when using (1) the high-resolution clock, (2) the derived 15 ms resolution clock, and (3) the 15.625 ms Windows-event clock. The numbers in parentheses indicate the percent increase in the equal-error rate over that of the high-resolution timer. The results from the 15 ms derived clock very closely match the results with the actual 15.625 ms clock.

| Clock | Detectors | | |
	Mean-based	Nearest Neighbor	Multilayer Perceptron
(1) High-resolution	0.1100	0.0996	0.1624
(2) Derived 15 ms resolution	0.1153 (+4.8%)	0.1071 (+7.5%)	0.1631 (+0.4%)
(3) 15.625 ms Windows-event	0.1152 (+4.7%)	0.1044 (+4.8%)	0.1634 (+0.6%)

The accuracy of our results depends on our derived low-resolution timestamps behaving like real low-resolution timestamps. Our first step is to establish the validity of the derived clock data by comparing a detector's performance on derived low-resolution data to its performance on data from a real clock operating at that resolution. Then we proceed to examine our primary results concerning the effect of clock resolution on detector performance.

8.1   Accuracy of the Derived Clock

Table 1 shows the average equal-error rate for each of the three detectors, using the high-resolution clock, the derived 15 ms resolution clock, and the real 15.625 ms resolution Windows-event clock. In addition to the equal-error rates, the table includes a percentage in parentheses for the derived clock and the Windows-event clock. This percentage indicates the percent increase in the equal-error rate over that from the high-resolution clock.

To verify the correctness of the results using the derived low-resolution clocks, we compare the second and third rows of Table 1. The results are almost exactly the same except for the nearest-neighbor detector. Since the nearest-neighbor detector is not robust to small changes in the training data, it is not surprising to see a comparatively large difference between the derived 15 ms clock and the real 15.625 ms clock. The similarity in the results of the other two detectors indicate that the derived clock results are accurate.

Even if we had been able to directly derive a 15.625 ms clock (impossible because of the limitations of the derivation procedure described in Section 5), small differences between the derived and real timestamps would still cause small differences in detector performance (e.g., differences resulting from small delays in how quickly the real clock is queried).

8.2   Effects of Clock Resolution on Detector Performance

Figure 5 depicts the effect of clock resolution on the average equal-error rate of the three detectors. Each panel displays a curve for each of the three detectors, but at different scales, highlighting a different result.

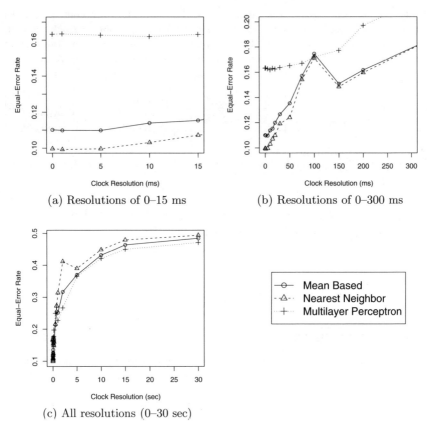

(a) Resolutions of 0–15 ms   (b) Resolutions of 0–300 ms

(c) All resolutions (0–30 sec)

Fig. 5. The equal-error rates of the three detectors increase as clock-resolution goes from fine to coarse. Panel (a) depicts the minor but significant change in performance resulting from a transition from the high-resolution clock to typical 15 ms clocks. Panel (b) shows how the error jumps significantly when the clock resolution is between 50 ms and 300 ms. Panel (c) characterizes the variation in detector performance over the full range of derived clock resolutions from 1 ms to 30 seconds (where the detector does no better than randomly guessing).

Panel (a) shows the effect of clock resolutions in the range of 0–15 ms on the equal-error rate. These are resolutions that we see in practice (e.g., in Windows and X11 event timestamps). We observe some increase in the equal-error rate for the mean-based and nearest-neighbor detectors, even from the 1 ms clock to the 15 ms clock. The change from the 1 ms clock to the 15 ms clock does not seem to have much effect on the multilayer perceptron (which could be because that detector's performance is already comparatively poor, rather than because the multilayer perceptron is more robust to lower-resolution clocks). The parenthetical percentages in Table 1 quantify the change from high resolution to typical resolutions. When the detectors use the 15 ms clock, their equal-error rate is an average of 4.2% higher than with the high-resolution clock. While this loss may not seem significant, keystroke dynamics needs near-perfect accuracy to be practical (1% false-alarm rate and 0.001% miss rate according to the European standard for access control [3]), so every possible boost in performance will help.

Panel (b) examines the effect of clock resolution beyond the 15 ms range. The graph reveals that the equal-error rates of the mean-based and nearest-neighbor detectors increase sharply after a resolution of 50 ms, and all three detectors' equal-error rates increase together after a resolution of 150 ms. While such low-resolution clocks are not used for keystroke dynamics, we can consider clock resolution to be one of many factors that might affect a detector. (Other factors include bus contention, system load, and even networking delays.) This panel suggests that these detectors are not particularly robust to noise in the form of low clock resolution. By extrapolation, it suggests that tens of milliseconds of noise from any of these sources (or any combination thereof) could be a problem.

Panel (b) also reveals a peak in the equal-error rate of the mean-based and nearest-neighbor detectors at a resolution of 100 ms. The cause of the peak is not obvious; it could be an artifact of our particular subjects' typing characteristics and would disappear with more or different subjects. More typing data and analysis would be necessary to determine whether such peaks appear consistently for a particular detector and clock resolution, but the existence of a peak does suggest that the effects of factors like clock resolution are not always easy to predict.

Panel (c) demonstrates the effect of very-low-resolution clocks on the equal-error rate of a detector. All three detectors' equal-error rates tend to 0.5, which is the theoretically worst possible equal-error rate (akin to random guessing). That the equal-error rate goes to 0.5 is not surprising, but it is surprising that the equal-error rate converges so slowly to 0.5. With a 1-second resolution, the three detectors all have equal-error rates of about 0.3. While not great, it is certainly better than randomly guessing. It is surprising that key-hold times and digram intervals retain some (weakly) discriminative information even when expressed as a whole number of seconds. It may be that the features being used to discriminate users from impostors are present only because our impostors are unpracticed; they type the password a few seconds more slowly than a practiced user would. It is possible that a curve for practiced impostors would be steeper, more quickly ascending to 0.5 (to be investigated in future work).

9   Discussion

Based on these findings, we take away two messages from this investigation, each of which suggests a trajectory for the future. First, we have demonstrated that clock resolution does have an effect on the performance of keystroke-dynamics detectors, and as a result, we should consider the potential deleterious effects of timing noise. Fortunately, the effect appears to be small for the typical clock resolutions we see in practice, but we do get a small boost in performance by using a high-resolution clock. However, clock-resolution granularity is not the only factor that affects keystroke timestamps. Given these results, it seems almost certain that other forms of noise (e.g., system load) will cause similar problems. In the long term, we should try to eliminate noise from our timestamps, but in the short term we should at least acknowledge and account for its presence by carefully evaluating our timing mechanisms (e.g., by measuring and reporting clock resolution).

Second, even with the high-resolution timestamps, our detectors' performance is less than ideal. The best performance we obtained was a 9.96% equal-error rate for the nearest-neighbor detector, which is a long way from a 1% false-alarm rate and a 0.001% miss rate. We were surprised, since the detectors we used are similar to those that have performed well in the literature (e.g., by Joyce and Gupta [10], and by Cho et al. [4]). However, it would be improper to compare our results directly to those in the literature, because there are significant differences between our experimental method and theirs. The most obvious difference is our control of potential confounding factors (e.g., password selection and practice effect).

We speculate that experimental control is indeed responsible for the poorer performance of our detectors. Furthermore, we advocate the control of potential confounding factors in future experiments. Why? While realistic but uncontrolled experiments can demonstrate that a detector does well (or poorly), controlled experiments are necessary to reveal a causal connection between experimental factors (e.g., password choice or practice) and detector performance. If we are to use keystroke dynamics as a biometric, causal factors must be identified—*why it works* is as important as *whether it works*. For instance, it would be significant to discover that, regardless of other factors, every typist has an immutable, intrinsically identifiable quality to his or her typing. It would also be significant (but unfortunate) to find that a detector's performance depends primarily on the number of times an impostor practiced a password, and that with enough practice, any impostor could pass for a legitimate user.

We intend to conduct a survey of other detectors proposed in the literature to see whether performance remains poor on our data. We also observe that these detection algorithms tend to treat typing data as arbitrary points in a high-dimensional space, ignoring the fact that the data are observations about fingers typing. Perhaps better results can be obtained by building a detector that relies upon a model of user typing (such as those proposed by Card et al. [2] or John [9]).

10   Summary and Conclusion

The goal of this work is to investigate the effect that clock resolution has on the performance of keystroke-dynamics detectors, in part to determine if a high-resolution clock would boost performance. We collected data at a high resolution, and derived data at lower resolutions. We implemented three detectors and evaluated their performances over a range of clock resolutions. We found that a high-resolution clock does provide a slight performance boost, and conversely, clocks with a typical 15 ms resolution increase the equal-error rate by an average of 4.2%. Based on results using very-low-resolution clocks, we found that detectors are not particularly robust to timing noise. Finally, we discovered that none of the detectors achieved a practically useful level of performance, and identified significant opportunities for progress through controlled experimentation.

Acknowledgements

The authors are grateful to Rachel Krishnaswami for her insightful comments and helpful advice, and to Patricia Loring for running the experiments that provided the data for this paper. Fahd Arshad and Rob Reeder were responsible for the instrumentation that presented stimuli to participants. Thanks also to several anonymous reviewers for their comments.

This work was supported by National Science Foundation grant numbers CNS-0430474 and CNS-0716677, and by the Army Research Office through grant number DAAD19-02-1-0389 (Perpetually Available and Secure Information Systems) to Carnegie Mellon University's CyLab. The views and conclusions contained in this document are those of the authors, and should not be interpreted as representing the official policies, either expressed or implied, of any sponsoring institution, the U.S. government, or any other entity.

References

[1] Bentley, J.L.: Multidimensional binary search trees used for associative searching. Communications of the ACM 18(9), 509–517 (1975)

[2] Card, S.K., Moran, T.P., Newell, A.: The keystroke-level model for user performance time with interactive systems. Communications of the ACM 23(7), 396–410 (1980)

[3] CENELEC. European Standard EN 50133-1: Alarm systems. Access control systems for use in security applications. Part 1: System requirements, Standard Number EN 50133-1:1996/A1:2002, Technical Body CLC/TC 79, European Committee for Electrotechnical Standardization (CENELEC) (2002)

[4] Cho, S., Han, C., Han, D.H., Kim, H.-I.: Web-based keystroke dynamics identity verification using neural network. Journal of Organizational Computing and Electronic Commerce 10(4), 295–307 (2000)

[5] Dodge, Y.: Oxford Dictionary of Statistical Terms. Oxford University Press, New York (2003)

[6] Forsen, G., Nelson, M., Staron Jr., R.: Personal attributes authentication techniques. Technical Report RADC-TR-77-333, Rome Air Development Center (October 1977)

[7] Gaines, R.S., Lisowski, W., Press, S.J., Shapiro, N.: Authentication by keystroke timing: Some preliminary results. Technical Report R-2526-NSF, RAND Corporation (May 1980)

[8] Hwang, B., Cho, S.: Characteristics of auto-associative MLP as a novelty detector. In: Proceedings of the IEEE International Joint Conference on Neural Networks, Washington, DC, July 10–16, 1999, vol. 5, pp. 3086–3091 (1999)

[9] John, B.E.: TYPIST: A theory of performance in skilled typing. Human-Computer Interaction 11(4), 321–355 (1996)

[10] Joyce, R., Gupta, G.: Identity authentication based on keystroke latencies. Communications of the ACM 33(2), 168–176 (1990)

[11] Keeney, M., Kowalski, E., Cappelli, D., Moore, A., Shimeall, T., Rogers, S.: Insider threat study: Computer system sabotage in critical infrastructure sectors. Technical report, U.S. Secret Service and CERT Coordination Center/SEI (May 2005), http://www.cert.org/archive/pdf/insidercross051105.pdf

[12] Limas, M.C., Meré, J.O., Gonzáles, E.V., Martinez de Pisón Ascacibar, F.J., Espinoza, A.P., Elias, F.A.: AMORE: A MORE Flexible Neural Network Package (October 2007), http://cran.r-project.org/web/packages/AMORE/index.html

[13] Microsoft. Password checker (2008),
http://www.microsoft.com/protect/yourself/password/checker.mspx

[14] Mount, D., Arya, S.: ANN: A Library for Approximate Nearest Neighbor Searching (2006), http://www.cs.umd.edu/~mount/ANN/

[15] Microsoft Developer Network. EVENTMSG structure (2008),
http://msdn2.microsoft.com/en-us/library/ms644966(VS.85).aspx

[16] Microsoft Developer Network. QueryPerformanceCounter function (2008),
http://msdn2.microsoft.com/en-us/library/ms644904(VS.85).aspx

[17] Peacock, A., Ke, X., Wilkerson, M.: Typing patterns: A key to user identification. IEEE Security and Privacy 2(5), 40–47 (2004)

[18] R Development Core Team. R: A Language and Environment for Statistical Computing. R Foundation for Statistical Computing, Vienna, Austria (2008)

[19] Sheng, Y., Phoha, V., Rovnyak, S.: A parallel decision tree-based method for user authentication based on keystroke patterns. IEEE Transactions on Systems, Man, and Cybernetics 35(4), 826–833 (2005)

[20] Swets, J.A., Pickett, R.M.: Evaluation of Diagnostic Systems: Methods from Signal Detection Theory. Academic Press, New York (1982)

[21] PC Tools. Security guide for windows—random password generator (2008),
http://www.pctools.com/guides/password/

A Comparative Evaluation of Anomaly Detectors under Portscan Attacks

Ayesha Binte Ashfaq, Maria Joseph Robert, Asma Mumtaz,
Muhammad Qasim Ali, Ali Sajjad, and Syed Ali Khayam

School of Electrical Engineering & Computer Science
National University of Sciences & Technology (NUST)
Rawalpindi, Pakistan
{ayesha.ashfaq,47maria,45asma,mqasim.ali,ali,khayam}@niit.edu.pk

Abstract. Since the seminal 1998/1999 DARPA evaluations of intrusion detection systems, network attacks have evolved considerably. In particular, after the CodeRed worm of 2001, the volume and sophistication of self-propagating malicious code threats have been increasing at an alarming rate. Many anomaly detectors have been proposed, especially in the past few years, to combat these new and emerging network attacks. At this time, it is important to evaluate existing anomaly detectors to determine and learn from their strengths and shortcomings. In this paper, we evaluate the performance of eight prominent network-based anomaly detectors under malicious portscan attacks. These ADSs are evaluated on four criteria: accuracy (ROC curves), scalability (with respect to varying normal and attack traffic rates, and deployment points), complexity (CPU and memory requirements during training and classification,) and detection delay. These criteria are evaluated using two independently collected datasets with complementary strengths. Our results show that a few of the anomaly detectors provide high accuracy on one of the two datasets, but are unable to scale their accuracy across the datasets. Based on our experiments, we identify promising guidelines to improve the accuracy and scalability of existing and future anomaly detectors.

1 Introduction

With an increasing penetration of broadband Internet connectivity and an exponential growth in the worldwide IT infrastructure, individuals and organizations now rely heavily on the Internet for their communication and business needs. While such readily-available network connectivity facilitates operational efficiency and networking, systems connected to the Internet are inherently vulnerable to network attacks. These attacks have been growing in their number and sophistication over the last few years [1]. Malware, botnets, spam, phishing, and denial of service attacks have become continuous and imminent threats for today's networks and hosts [1], [2]. Financial losses due to these attacks are in the orders of billions of dollars[1]. In addition to the short-term revenue losses for

---

[1] Economic losses to recover from the CodeRed worm alone are estimated at $2.6 billion [3].

R. Lippmann, E. Kirda, and A. Trachtenberg (Eds.): RAID 2008, LNCS 5230, pp. 351–371, 2008.
© Springer-Verlag Berlin Heidelberg 2008

businesses and enterprises, network attacks also compromise information confidentiality/integrity and cause disruption of service, thus resulting in a long-term loss of credibility.

Since the CodeRed worm of 2001, malware attacks have emerged as one of the most prevalent and potent threats to network and host security[2]. Many network-based anomaly detection systems (ADSs) have been proposed in the past few years to detect novel network attacks [4]–[23]. Since malicious portscans are the vehicle used by malware and other automated tools to locate and compromise vulnerable hosts, some of these anomaly detectors are designed specifically for portscan detection [4]–[11], [19], while other detectors are more general-purpose and detect any anomalous traffic trend [12]–[18], [20]. Most of the network-based anomaly detectors model and leverage deep-rooted statistical properties of benign traffic to detect anomalous behavior. A variety of theoretical frameworks–including stochastic, machine learning, information-theoretic and signal processing frameworks–have been used to develop robust models of normal behavior and/or to detect/flag deviations from that model. However, very little effort has been expended into comparative evaluation of these recent ADSs for the portscan detection problem.

In this paper, we evaluate and compare eight prominent network-based anomaly detectors on two public portscan datasets. The objectives of this study are: 1) to quantify and compare the accuracies of these detectors under varying rates of attack and normal traffic and at different points of deployment; 2) to identify promising traffic features and theoretical frameworks for portscan anomaly detection; 3) to investigate the accuracy of contemporary anomaly detectors with respect to their complexity and detection delay; 4) to identify a set of promising portscan detection guidelines that build on the strengths and avoid the weaknesses of the evaluated anomaly detectors; and finally 5) to provide an open-source library of anomaly detection tools that operate on public and labeled datasets, and can be used for repeatable performance benchmarking by future detectors[3].

The anomaly detectors compared in this work were proposed in [4], [7], [8], [12], [15], [18], [20] and [21]. These ADSs are chosen because they employ very different traffic features and theoretical frameworks for anomaly detection. Moreover, most of these detectors are frequently used for performance benchmarking in the intrusion detection research literature [6], [9]–[11], [13], [14], [16], [17], and [19]. Some of these ADSs have been designed for and evaluated at endpoints while others have been tailored towards organization/ISP gateways. Similarly, some detector are designed for portscan detection, while others are general-purpose ADSs. This diversity allows us to determine how much, if any, performance improvement is provided by portscan ADSs over general-purpose ADSs.

---

[2] From 2006 to 2007, the total number of malicious code attacks reported by Symantec DeepSight™ showed a phenomenal increase of 468% [1].

[3] Background and attack datasets are available at [24] and [25]. ADS implementations are also available at [25].

For performance evaluation of the anomaly detectors, we use two independently-collected datasets with complementary strengths. The first dataset is an enterprise traffic dataset collected at the edge router of the Lawrence Berkeley National Lab (LBNL) [24]. Attack traffic in this dataset mostly comprises high-rate background traffic and low-rate outgoing scans. The second dataset comprises traffic data collected at network endpoints in home, university and office settings. Background traffic rates of these endpoints are relatively low as compared to the LBNL dataset, but the endpoint attack data contains relatively high-rate outgoing scan traffic.

We evaluate these ADSs on four criteria: accuracy, scalability, complexity and detection delay. Accuracy is evaluated by comparing ROC (false alarms per day versus detection rate) characteristics of the ADSs. Scalability is evaluated with respect to different background and attack traffic rates. Since the two datasets used in this study are collected at different network entities and contain attacks with different characteristics, evaluation over these datasets allows us to compare the scalability of the proposed ADSs under varying traffic volumes. Complexity is evaluated in terms of time and memory required during training and classification steps of each ADS. Detection delay is evaluated separately for high- and low-rate attacks.

Our results show that some of the evaluated anomaly detectors provide reasonable accuracy with low detection delay. However, these detectors do not provide sustained accuracy on both the datasets. For instance, the Maximum Entropy detector [20] provides very high accuracy at the endpoints, but cannot provide the same level of accuracy at the edge router. Similarlyl, the credit-based TRW algorithm [8] provides reasonably high accuracy at endpoints, while its original counterpart, the TRW algorithm [7], outperforms all other algorithms at the edge router. The rate limiting detector [4], [5] that has been designed for malware detection fails to provide high accuracy at endpoints or routers. In summary, the detectors are unable to scale their accuracies for different points of network deployment.

To improve scalability and detection accuracy, we further evaluate two anomaly detectors, namely the Maximum Entropy and the PHAD detectors. These two detectors are somewhat unique because they allow more degrees of freedom in their feature spaces; i.e. they have higher dimensional feature spaces than the other detectors. Using these two detectors, we show that a promising approach to improve the accuracy of a detector is to operate it across a high dimensional feature space and/or over multiple time windows. We refer to these accuracy improving extensions as Space-Time (ST) variants of the original detectors.

2   Related Work

In this section, we focus on prior IDS/ADS evaluation studies. Details of anomaly detectors used in this work are deferred to subsequent sections.

Performance evaluation of IDSs received significant attention from the industry and academia in the late 1990's [30]–[45]. However, in the past few years, only four studies have performed comparative comparison of anomaly detectors

[26]–[29]. Similarly, very few prior studies have performed ROC analysis of the evaluated IDSs. Still fewer studies have made their evaluation datasets available online.

DARPA-funded IDS evaluation studies by the MIT Lincoln Lab in 1998 and 1999 represent a shift in the IDS evaluation methodology [33], [38]. Datasets used in these studies were made publicly available [39] and the ROC method used in these studies has since become the de facto standard for IDS accuracy evaluation. While some shortcomings of the DARPA evaluation have been highlighted [47], [48], in the absence of other benchmarks, the results and datasets of this study have been used extensively in subsequent works. In the present paper's context, the DARPA dataset is somewhat dated.

The four recent ADS evaluation studies focus on specific types of detectors and attacks [26]–[29]. The study by Wong et al. [26] is most relevant in the present context. Wong et al. [26] evaluated four variants of the rate limiting detector under portscan attacks at two different network points [4]–[11]. Two findings of this study are pertinent to the present work: 1) classical rate limiting is not an effective technique for portscan detection, and 2) rate limiting can operate on aggregate-level DNS traffic and hence can potentially scale to core-level deployments. Attack and background traffic data used in this study are not publicly available.

A comparative evaluation of bio-inspired anomaly detection algorithms was performed recently [27]. This work proposed to improve the accuracy of bio-inspired anomaly detectors by providing intelligent and discriminant features as inputs to the detectors' classification algorithms. The experimental results indicated that the use of intelligent features significantly improves the true positive and false positive rates of bio-inspired classifiers.

Ingham and Inoue [28] compared seven IITTP anomaly detection techniques under real-world attacks reported at public databases. These authors report the same evaluation difficulties that were faced by us: 1) Some anomaly detectors are not described completely; 2) Implementation source code is not available; and 3) labeled data used for algorithm evaluation are not publicly available. Consequently, the authors in [28] make their implementation and attack data publicly available "to encourage further experimentation". We subscribe to the same viewpoint and therefore all data and implementation used in this project are available online [25]. Lazarevic et al. performed a comparative analysis of four data mining based anomaly detection techniques in [29]. The live network traffic data used by this study is not publicly available.

3   Evaluation Datasets

We wanted to use real, labeled and public background and attack datasets to measure the accuracy of the evaluated anomaly detectors. Real and labeled data allow realistic and repeatable quantification of an anomaly detector's accuracy, which is a main objective of this work. Moreover, as defined in the introduction, another objective is to evaluate the accuracy or scalability of the anomaly detectors under different normal and attack traffic rates and at different points of deployment in the network. This evaluation objective is somewhat unique to this effort, with [26] being the only other study that provides some insight into host versus edge deployments.

Different network deployment points are responsible for handling traffic from varying number of nodes. For instance, an endpoint requires to cater for only its own traffic, while an edge router needs to monitor and analyze traffic from a variety of hosts in its subnet. In general, as one moves away from the endpoints towards the network core, the number of nodes, and consequently the traffic volume, that a network entity is responsible for increase considerably. We argue that if an algorithm that is designed to detect high- or low-rate attacks at a particular point of deployment, say an edge router, scales to and provides high accuracy at other traffic rates and deployment points, say at endpoints, then such an algorithm is quite valuable because it provides an off-the-shelf deployment option for different network entities. (We show later in this paper that some existing algorithms are able to achieve this objective.)

To test the anomaly detectors for scalability, we use two real traffic datasets that have been independently-collected at different deployment points. The first dataset is collected at the edge router of the Lawrence Berkeley National Laboratory (LBNL), while the second dataset is collected at network endpoints by our research lab[4]. In this section, we describe the data collection setups and the attack and background traffic characteristics of the LBNL and the endpoint datasets.

3.1   The LBNL Dataset

LBNL Background Traffic: This dataset was obtained from two international network locations at the Lawrence Berkeley National Laboratory (LBNL) in USA. Traffic in this dataset comprises packet-level incoming, outgoing and internally-routed traffic streams at the LBNL edge routers. Traffic was anonymized using the tcpmkpub tool; refer to [49] for details of anonymization.

LBNL data used in this study is collected during three distinct time periods. Some pertinent statistics of the background traffic are given in Table 1. The average remote session rate (i.e., sessions from distinct non-LBNL hosts) is approximately 4 sessions per second. The total TCP and UDP background traffic rate in packets per second is shown in column 5 of the table. A large variance can be observed in the background traffic rate at different dates. This variance will have an impact on the performance of volumetric anomaly detectors that rely on detecting bursts of normal and malicious traffic.

The main applications observed in internal and external traffic are Web (HTTP), Email and Name Services. Some other applications like Windows Services, Network File Services and Backup were being used by internal hosts;

---

[4] We also wanted to use a traffic dataset collected at a backbone ISP network; such datasets have been used in some prior studies [15]–[17]. However, we could not find a publicly available ISP traffic dataset.

Table 1. Background Traffic Information for the LBNL Dataset

Date	Duration(mins)	LBNL Hosts	Remote Hosts	Backgnd Rate(pkt/sec)	Attack Rate(pkt/sec)
10/4/04	10min	4,767	4,342	8.47	0.41
12/15/04	60min	5,761	10,478	3.5	0.061
12/16/04	60min	5,210	7,138	243.83	72

details of each service, information of each service's packets and other relevant description are provided in [50].

LBNL Attack Traffic: Attack traffic was isolated by identifying scans in the aggregate traffic traces. Scans were identified by flagging those hosts which unsuccessfully probed more than 20 hosts, out of which 16 hosts were probed in ascending or descending order [49]. Malicious traffic mostly comprises failed incoming TCP SYN requests; i.e., TCP portscans targeted towards LBNL hosts. However, there are also some outgoing TCP scans in the dataset. Most of the UDP traffic observed in the data (incoming and outgoing) comprises successful connections; i.e., host replies are received for the UDP flows. Table 1 [column 6] shows the attack rate observed in the LBNL dataset. Clearly, the attack rate is significantly lower than the background traffic rate. Thus these attacks can be considered low rate relative to the background traffic rate. (We show later that background and attack traffic at endpoints exhibit the opposite characteristics.)

Since most of the anomaly detectors used in this study operate on TCP, UDP and/or IP packet features, to maintain fairness we filtered the background data to retain only TCP and UDP traffic. Moreover, since most of the scanners were located outside the LBNL network, to remove any bias we filter out internally-routed traffic. After filtering the datasets, we merged all the background traffic data at different days and ports. Synchronized malicious data chunks were then inserted in the merged background traffic.

Since no publicly available endpoint traffic set was available, we spent up to 14 months in collecting our own dataset on a diverse set of 13 endpoints. Complexity and privacy were two main reservations of the participants of the endpoint data collection study. To address these reservations, we developed a custom tool for endpoint data collection. This tool was a multi-threaded MS Windows application developed using the `Winpcap` API [51]. (Implementation of the tool is available at [25].) To reduce the packet logging complexity at the endpoints, we only logged some very elementary session-level information of TCP and UDP packets. Here a *session* corresponds to a bidirectional communication between two IP addresses; communication between the same IP address on different ports is considered part of the same network session. To ensure user privacy, the source IP address (which was fixed/static for a given host) is not logged, and each session entry is indexed by a one-way hash of the destination IP with the hostname. Most of the detectors evaluated in this work can operate with this level of data granularity.

Table 2. Background Traffic Information for Four Endpoints with High and Low Rates

Endpoint ID	Endpoint Type	Duration(months)	Total Sessions	Mean Session Rate(/sec)
3	Home	3	373, 009	1.92
4	Home	2	444, 345	5.28
6	Univ	9	60, 979	0.19
10	Univ	13	152, 048	0.21

3.2   Endpoint Dataset

Statistics of the two highest rate and the two lowest rate endpoints are listed in Table 2[5]. As can be intuitively argued, the traffic rates observed at the endpoints are much lower than those at the LBNL router. In the endpoint context, we observed that home computers generate significantly higher traffic volumes than office and university computers because: 1) they are generally shared between multiple users, and 2) they run peer-to-peer and multimedia applications. The large traffic volumes of home computers are also evident from their high mean number of sessions per second. For this study, we use 6 weeks of endpoint traffic data for training and testing. Results for longer time periods were qualitatively similar.

To generate attack traffic, we infected VMs on the endpoints by the following malware: `Zotob.G`, `Forbot-FU`, `Sdbot-AFR`, `Dloader-NY`, `SoBig.E@mm`, `MyDoom.A@mm`, `Blaster`, `Rbot-AQJ`, and `RBOT.CCC`; details of the malware can be found at [52]. These malware have diverse scanning rates and attack ports/applications. Table 3 shows statistics of the highest and lowest scan rate worms; `Dloader-NY` has the highest scan rate of 46.84 scans per second (sps), while `MyDoom-A` has the lowest scan rate of 0.14 sps, respectively. For completeness, we also simulated three additional worms that are somewhat different from the ones described above, namely `Witty`, `CodeRedv2` and a fictitious TCP worm with a fixed and unusual source port. `Witty` and `CodeRedv2` were simulated using the scan rates, pseudocode and parameters given in research and commercial literature [52], [53].

Endpoint Background Traffic: The users of these endpoints included home users, research students, and technical/administrative staff. Some endpoints, in particular home computers, were shared among multiple users. The endpoints used in this study were running different types of applications, including peer-to-peer file sharing software, online multimedia applications, network games, SQL/SAS clients etc.

Endpoint Attack Traffic: The attack traffic logged at the endpoints mostly comprises outgoing portscans. Note that this is the opposite of the LBNL dataset, in which most of the attack traffic is inbound. Moreover, the attack traffic rates

---

[5] The mean session rates in Table 2 are computed using time-windows containing one or more new sessions. Therefore, dividing total sessions by the duration does not yield the session rate of column 5.

Table 3. Endpoint Attack Traffic for Two High- and Two Low-rate Worms

Malware	Release Date	Avg. Scan Rate(/sec)	Port(s) Used
Dloader-NY	Jul 2005	46.84 sps	TCP 135,139
Forbot-FU	Sept 2005	32.53 sps	TCP 445
MyDoom-A	Jan 2006	0.14 sps	TCP $3127 - 3198$
Rbot-AQJ	Oct 2005	0.68 sps	TCP 139,769

(Table 3) in the endpoint case are generally much higher than the background traffic rates (Table 2). This characteristic is also the opposite of what was observed in the LBNL dataset. This diversity in attack direction and rates provides us a sound basis for performance comparison of the anomaly detectors evaluated in this study [7], [8].

For each malware, attack traffic of 15 minutes duration was inserted in the background traffic of each endpoint at a random time instance. This operation was repeated to insert 100 non-overlapping attacks of each worm inside each endpoint's background traffic.

4   Anomaly Detection Algorithms

In this section, we focus on network-based anomaly detectors and compare the anomaly detectors proposed in [4], [7], [8], [12], [15], [18], [20], and [21]. Most of these detectors are quite popular and used frequently for performance comparison and benchmarking in the ID research community. Improvements to these algorithms have also been proposed in [6], [9]–[11], [13], [14], [16], [17], [19], and [26][6].

Before briefly describing these detectors, we highlight that some of these detectors are designed specifically for portscan detection, while others are general-purpose network anomaly detectors. More generically, based on the taxonomy of [54], the algorithms evaluated in this study can be subdivided into the ADS categories shown in Fig. 1. Clearly, the evaluated ADSs are quite diverse in their traffic features as well as their detection frameworks. These ADSs range from very simple rule modelling systems like PHAD [12] to very complex and theoretically-inclined self-Learning systems like the PCA-based subspace method [15] and the Sequential Hypothesis Testing technique [7]. This diversity is introduced to achieve the following objectives: a) to identify promising traffic features and theoretical frameworks for portscan anomaly detection; b) to investigate the accuracy, complexity and delays of these anomaly detectors under different attack and normal traffic scenarios and at different points of deployment in the network; and c) to identify a set of promising portscan detection guidelines that build on the strengths and avoid the weaknesses of the evaluated anomaly detectors.

---

[6] Some promising commercial ADSs are also available in the market now [22], [23]. We did not have access to these ADSs, and therefore these commercial products are not evaluated in this study.

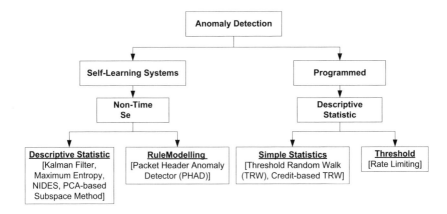

Fig. 1. Taxonomy of the anomaly detectors evaluated in this work [54]

Due to space constraints, we do not provide detailed descriptions of the evaluated algorithms. We instead focus on the algorithm adaptation and parameter tuning for the datasets under consideration. Readers are referred to [4], [7], [8], [12], [15], [18], [20], and [21] for details of the algorithms. For techniques operating on fixed-sized time windows, we use a window of 20 seconds. All other parameters not mentioned in this section are the same as those described in the algorithms' respective papers.

4.1   Rate Limiting

Rate limiting [4], [5] detects anomalous connection behavior by relying on the premise that an infected host will try to connect to many different machines in a short period of time. Rate limiting detects portscans by putting new connections exceeding a certain threshold in a queue. An alarm is raised when the queue length, η_q, exceeds a threshold. ROCs for endpoints are generated by varying $\eta_q = \mu + k\sigma$, where μ and σ represent the sample mean and sample standard deviation of the connection rates in the training set, and $k = 0, 1, 2, \ldots$ is a positive integer. Large values of k will provide low false alarm and detection rates, while small values will render high false alarm and detection rates. In the LBNL dataset, connection rate variance in the background traffic is more than the variance in the attack traffic. Therefore, to obtain a range of detection and false alarm rates for the LBNL dataset, we use a threshold of $\eta_q = w\mu$, with a varying parameter $0 \geq w \leq 1$, and the queue is varied between 5 and 100 sessions.

4.2   Threshold Random Walk (TRW) Algorithm

The TRW algorithm [7] detects incoming portscans by noting that the probability of a connection attempt being a success should be much higher for a benign host than for a scanner. To leverage this observation, TRW uses sequential hypothesis testing (i.e., a likelihood ratio test) to classify whether or not a remote host is a scanner. We plot ROCs for this algorithm by setting different values of false alarm and detection rates and computing the likelihood ratio thresholds, η_0 and η_1, using the method described in [7].

4.3 TRW with Credit-Based Rate Limiting (TRW-CB)

A hybrid solution to leverage the complementary strengths of Rate Limiting and TRW was proposed by Schechter et al. [8]. Reverse TRW is an anomaly detector that limits the rate at which new connections are initiated by applying the sequential hypothesis testing in a reverse chronological order. A credit increase/decrease algorithm is used to slow down hosts that are experiencing unsuccessful connections. We plot ROCs for this technique for varying η_0 and η_1 as in the TRW case.

4.4 Maximum Entropy Method

This detector estimates the benign traffic distribution using maximum entropy estimation [20]. Training traffic is divided into $2,348$ packet classes and maximum entropy estimation is then used to develop a baseline benign distribution for each packet class. Packet class distributions observed in real-time windows are then compared with the baseline distribution using the Kullback-Leibler (K-L) divergence measure. An alarm is raised if a packet class' K-L divergence exceeds a threshold, η_k, more than h times in the last W windows of t seconds each. Thus the Maximum Entropy method incurs a detection delay of at least $h \times t$ seconds. ROCs are generated by varying η_k.

4.5 Packet Header Anomaly Detection (PHAD)

PHAD learns the normal range of values for all 33 fields in the Ethernet, IP, TCP, UDP and ICMP headers [12]. A score is assigned to each packet header field in the testing phase and the fields' scores are summed to obtain a packet's aggregate anomaly score. We evaluate PHAD-C32 [12] using the following packet header fields: source IP, destination IP, source port, destination port, protocol type and TCP flags. Normal intervals for the six fields are learned from 5 days of training data. In the test data, fields' values not falling in the learned intervals are flagged as suspect. Then the top n packet score values are termed as anomalous. The value of n is varied over a range to obtain ROC curves.

4.6 PCA-Based Subspace Method

The subspace method uses Principal Component Analysis (PCA) to separate a link's traffic measurement space into useful subspaces for analysis, with each subspace representing either benign or anomalous traffic behavior [15]. The authors proposed to apply PCA for domain reduction of the Origin-Destination (OD) flows in three dimensions: number of bytes, packets, IP-level OD flows. The top k eigenvectors represent normal subspaces. It has been shown that most of the variance in a link's traffic is generally captured by 5 principal components [15]. A recent study showed that the detection rate of PCA varies with the level and method of aggregation [55]. It was also concluded in [55] that it may be impractical to run a PCA-based anomaly detector over data aggregated at the level of OD flows. We evaluate the subspace method using the number of TCP flows aggregated in 10 minutes intervals. To generate ROC results, we changed the number of normal subspace as $k = 1, 2, \ldots, 15$. Since the principal components capture maximum variance of the data, as we increase k, the dimension of the residual subspace reduces and fewer observations are available for detection. In other words, as more and more principal components are selected as normal subspaces, the detection and false alarm rates decrease proportionally. Since there is no clear detection threshold, we could not obtain the whole range of ROC values for the subspace method. Nevertheless, we evaluate and report the subspace method's accuracy results for varying number of principal components.

4.7 Kalman Filter Based Detection

The Kalman filter based detector of [18] first filters out the normal traffic from the aggregate traffic, and then examines the residue for anomalies. In [18], the Kalman Filter operated on SNMP data to detect anomalies traversing multiple links. Since SNMP data was not available to us in either dataset, we model the traffic as a 2-D vector X_t. The first element of X_t is the total number of sessions (in the endpoint dataset) or packets (in the LBNL dataset), while the second element is the total number of distinct remote ports observed in the traffic. We defined a threshold, η_f on the residue value r to obtain ROC curves. Thresholding of r is identical to the rate limiting case. An alarm is raised, if $r < -\eta_f$ or $r > \eta_f$.

4.8 Next-Generation Intrusion Detection Expert System (NIDES)

NIDES [21] is a statistical anomaly detector that detects anomalies by comparing a long-term traffic rate profile against a short-term, real-time profile. An anomaly is reported if the Q distribution of the real-time profile deviates considerably from the long-term values. After specific intervals, new value of Q are generated by monitoring the new rates and compared against a predefined threshold, η_s. If $\Pr(Q > q) < \eta_s$, an alarm is raised. We vary η_s over a range of values for ROC evaluation.

5   Performance Evaluation

In this section, we evaluate the accuracy, scalability, complexity and delay of the anomaly detectors described in the last section on the endpoint and router datasets.

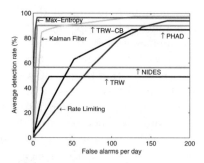

Fig. 2. ROC analysis on the endpoint dataset; each ROC is averaged over 13 endpoints with 12 attacks per endpoint and 100 instances per attack

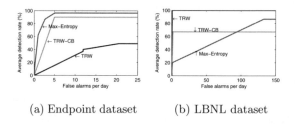

(a) Endpoint dataset   (b) LBNL dataset

Fig. 3. Comparison of the Maximum Entropy, TRW and TRW-CB algorithms

5.1   Accuracy and Scalability Comparison

In this section, we present ROC analysis on the endpoint dataset. The following section explains the scalability experiments in which ROC analysis is performed on the LBNL dataset and the results are compared with the endpoint experiments.

Averaged ROCs for the Endpoint Dataset: Fig. 2 provides the averaged ROC analysis of the anomaly detection schemes under consideration. Clearly, the Maximum Entropy detector provides the highest accuracy by achieving near 100% detection rate at a very low false alarm rate of approximately 5 alarms/day. The Maximum Entropy detector is followed closely by the credit-based TRW approach. TRW-CB achieves nearly 90% detection rate at a reasonable false alarm rate of approximately 5 alarms/day. The original TRW algorithm, however, provides very low detection rates for the endpoint dataset. Results of these three schemes are shown more clearly in Fig. 3(a). Based on these results, the Maximum Entropy algorithm provides the best accuracy on endpoints, while TRW provides the best detection on LBNL dataset.

The Kalman Filter approach is also quite accurate as it provides up to 85% detection rates at a reasonably low false alarm cost. Rate Limiting, although designed to detect outgoing scanning attacks, provides very poor performance. This result substantiates the results of [26] where very high false positive rates

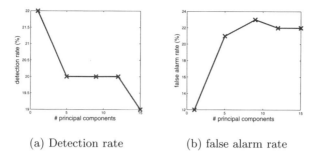

(a) Detection rate   (b) false alarm rate

Fig. 4. Detection and false alarm rates for the subspace method [15]

for high detection rates were reported for classical rate limiting. Hence, we also deduce that rate limiting is ineffective for portscan detection at endpoints.

PHAD does not perform well on the endpoint data set. The detection is accompanied with very high false alarm rates. NIDES achieve reasonable detection rates at very low false alarm rates, but is unable to substantially improve its detection rates afterwards. PHAD relies on previously seen values in the training dataset for anomaly detection. Therefore, if a scanner attacks a commonly-used port/IP then PHAD is unable to detect it. On similar grounds, if the malicious traffic is not bursty enough as compared to background traffic then NIDES will not detect it, irrespective of how much the detection threshold is tuned.

Due to the thresholding difficulties for the subspace method explained in Section 4, in Fig. 4 we report results for this technique for varying values of selected principal components. The highest detection rate of 22% is observed at $k = 2$ principal components. This already low detection rate decreases further at $k = 5$ and drops to 0% at $k = 15$. False alarm rates show the opposite trend. Thus the subspace method fails to give acceptable accuracy on the endpoint dataset.

The ROC results for the endpoint dataset are somewhat surprising because two of the top three detectors are general-purpose anomaly detectors (Maximum Entropy and Kalman Filter), but still outperform other detectors designed specifically for portscan detection, such as the TRW and the Rate Limiting detectors. We, however, note that this analysis is not entirely fair to the TRW algorithm because TRW was designed to detect incoming portscans, whereas our endpoint attack traffic contains mostly outgoing scan packets. The credit-based variant of TRW achieves high accuracy because it leverages outgoing scans for portscan detection. Thus TRW-CB combines the complementary strengths of rate limiting and TRW to provide a practical and accurate portscan detector for endpoints. This result agrees with earlier results in [26].

ROCs for Low- and High-Rate Endpoint Attacks: To evaluate the scalability of the ADSs under high- and low-rate attack scenarios, Fig. 5 plots the ROCs for the highest rate (`Dloader-NY`) and lowest rate (`MyDoom-A`) attacks in the endpoint dataset. It can be observed that for the high-rate attack [Fig. 5(a)] Maximum Entropy, TRW, TRW-CB and Kalman Filter techniques

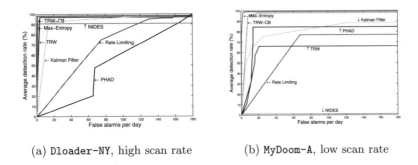

(a) `Dloader-NY`, high scan rate   (b) `MyDoom-A`, low scan rate

Fig. 5. ROC curves for the lowest and highest rate attack in the endpoint dataset; results averaged over 12 endpoints with 100 instances of each attack

provide excellent accuracy by achieving 100% or near-100% detection rates with few false alarms. NIDES' performance also improves as it achieves approximately 90% detection rate at very low false alarm rates. This is because the high-rate attack packets form bursts of malicious traffic that NIDES is tuned to detect. Rate Limiting and PHAD do not perform well even under high attack rate scenarios.

Fig. 5(b) shows that the accuracies of all detectors except PHAD and Maximum Entropy degrade under a low-rate attack scenario. Maximum Entropy achieves 100% detection rate with false alarm rate of 4-5 alarms/day. TRW-CB recovers quickly and achieves a near-100% detection rate for a daily false alarm rate around 10 alarms/day. NIDES, however, shows the biggest degradation in accuracy as its detection rate drops by approximately 90%. This is because low-rate attack traffic when mixed with normal traffic does not result in long attack bursts. TRW's accuracy is also affected significantly as its detection rate drops by about 35% as compared to the high-rate attack. PHAD does not rely on traffic rate for detection, and hence its accuracy is only dependent on the header values observed during training.

Averaged ROCs for the LBNL Dataset: Fig. 6 shows the ROCs for the LBNL dataset. Comparison with Fig. 3 (a) and (b) reveals that the Maximum Entropy detector is unable to maintain its high accuracy on the LBNL dataset; i.e., the Maximum Entropy algorithm cannot scale to different points of network deployment. TRW's performance improves significantly as it provides a 100% detection rate at a negligible false alarm cost. TRW-CB, on the other hand, achieves a detection rate of approximately 70%. Thus contrary to the endpoint dataset, the original TRW algorithm easily outperforms the TRW-CB algorithm on LBNL traces. As explained in Section 3.1, the LBNL attack traffic mostly comprises failed incoming TCP connection requests. TRW's forward sequential hypothesis based portscan detection algorithm is designed to detect such failed incoming connections, and therefore it provides high detection rates. Thus on an edge router, TRW represents a viable deployment option.

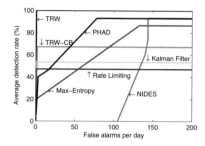

Fig. 6. ROC analysis on the LBNL dataset

Table 4. Complexity Comparison of the Anomaly Detectors

	Rate Limiting	TRW	TRW-CB	Max Entropy	NIDES	PHAD	Subspace Method	Kalman Filter
Training Time(sec)	48.58	37948.42	23185.11	50.06	2.01	17650.52	34111.89	16.56
Detection Time(sec)	15961.75	31339.43	18226.38	22.79	5.4	25082.45	15939.27	12.58
Training Memory(KB)	22789.04	21110.86	25104.67	57223.39	3590.95	48100.35	68851.71	34515.98
Detection Memory(KB)	14667.4	49087.78	67545.53	66930.06	4013.08	42262.46	16685.93	60314.65

Kalman Filter detector's accuracy drops as it is unable to achieve a detection rate above 60%. PHAD provides very high detection rates, albeit at an unacceptable false alarm rate. Other detectors' results are similar to the endpoint case. (Results for the subspace method were similar to those reported earlier and are skipped for brevity.) It can be observed from Fig. 6 that all algorithms except TRW fail to achieve 100% detection rates on the LBNL dataset. This is because these algorithms inherently rely on the high burstiness and volumes of attack traffic. In the LBNL dataset, the attack traffic rate is much lower than the background traffic rate. Consequently, the attack traffic is distributed across multiple time windows, with each window containing very few attack packets. Such low density of attack traffic in the evaluated time-windows remains undetected regardless of how much the detection thresholds are decreased.

5.2 Complexity and Delay Comparison

Table 4 lists the training and classification time taken by the anomaly detectors as well as their training and run-time memory requirements. These numbers are computed using the `hprof` tool. The first observation from the table is that, contrary to common intuition, complexity does not translate directly into accuracy of an anomaly detector. For instance, the Maximum Entropy detector, while providing the highest accuracy on endpoints, has orders of magnitude lower training and run-time complexity than many other detectors. NIDES is by far the least complex algorithm requiring only a few seconds for training and execution. However, NIDES' low accuracy makes it an unsuitable choice for practical

Table 5. Detection Delay of the Anomaly Detectors

	Rate Limiting	TRW	TRW-CB	Max Entropy	NIDES	PHAD	Subspace Method	Kalman Filter
MyDoom (msec)	310	510	40	215000	∞	900	79	377
Dloader-NY (msec)	140	320	20	56000	0.086	990	23	417
LBNL (msec)	660	660	290	86000	330	330	∞	800

deployments. The Kalman Filter based detector is also extremely low complexity. Thus despite its low accuracy at edge routers, it is still a viable deployment option at network endpoints.

The credit-based TRW algorithm has slightly lower complexity than the originally-proposed TRW algorithm. Since TRW-CB also provides better accuracy than TRW at endpoints, it is a good deployment option for systems without significant complexity constraints. Rate Limiting, while having low complexity, is not a practical deployment option because of its poor accuracy. The subspace method and PHAD have high complexity requirements, but still render very poor accuracy.

Table 5 provides the detection delay for each anomaly detector. On the endpoint dataset, delay is reported for the highest and the lowest rate attacks, while on the LBNL dataset this delay is computed for the first attack that is detected by an anomaly detector. A delay value of ∞ is listed if an attack is not detected altogether. It can be observed that detection delay is reasonable (less than 1 second) for all the anomaly detectors except the Maximum Entropy detector which incurs very high detection delays. High delays are observed for the Maximum Entropy detector because it waits for perturbations in multiple time windows before raising an alarm. Among other viable alternatives, TRW-CB provides the lowest detection delays for all three experiments. Detection delay for the TRW is also reasonably low.

6   Summary, Discussion and Future Work

6.1   Summary

In this paper, we evaluated eight prominent network-based anomaly detectors using two portscan traffic datasets having complementary characteristics. These detectors were evaluated on accuracy, scalability, complexity and delay criteria. Based on the results of this paper, we now rephrase and summarize our deductions pertaining to the main objectives of this study:

- Which algorithms provide the best accuracy under varying rates of attack and normal traffic and at different points of deployment? Under the varying attack and background traffic rates observed in the two datasets, a general-purpose Maximum Entropy Detector [20] and variants of the Threshold Random Walk (TRW) algorithm [7], [8] provided the best overall performance under most evaluation criteria. In this context, TRW is suitable for deployment at routers, while TRW-CB and Maximum Entropy are suitable for deployment at endpoints.

- What are the promising traffic features and theoretical frameworks for portscan anomaly detection? The Maximum Entropy and TRW detectors use statistical distributions of failed connections, ports and IP addresses. Furthermore, based on the results of the Maximum Entropy detector on endpoints, a histogram-based detection approach, in which baseline frequency profiles of a set of features is compared with real-time feature frequencies, appears very promising.
- Does complexity improve accuracy? Complexity has no relation with the accuracy of an algorithm. Intelligence of traffic features and detection frameworks determine the accuracy of an algorithm.
- What detection delays are incurred by the anomaly detectors? If an attack is detected, detection delay is less than 1 second for all anomaly detectors, except the Maximum Entropy Estimation method which incurs very large delays.
- What are promising portscan detection guidelines that build on the strengths and avoid the weaknesses of the evaluated anomaly detectors? From the high detection rates of the Maximum Entropy and PHAD detectors, it appears that using a higher dimensional feature space facilitates detection, without compromising complexity. On the other hand, relying on specific traffic features (e.g., rate, connection failures, etc.) can degrade accuracy as the attack and background traffic characteristics change. In summary, a number of statistical features used in an intelligent histogram-based classification framework appear promising for portscan anomaly detection.

6.2   Discussion

Based on our comparative analysis and deductions, we further evaluate Maximum Entropy and PHAD detectors. Both these detectors have a high dimensional feature space, thereby allowing us to improve their accuracy by evaluating them in feature space and/or time. For instance, recall that PHAD operates on a high dimensional feature space and detects an anomaly when a certain number of features in a packet are perturbed. Thus PHAD leverages its large feature space to achieve high detection rates, but the high false alarm rates render the detector useless. To reduce PHAD's false alarms, in addition to operating the PHAD detector in its feature space, we also operate it in time and an alarm is raised only when an anomaly is observed in multiple time windows/packets. This Space-Time (ST) strategy should reduce the false alarm rate of PHAD.

Maximum Entropy, on the other hand, operates across multiple time windows before raising an alarm. Such a strategy results in very low false alarm rates, but compromises the detection rate and delay, as seen in Fig. 6 and Table 5. Extending this algorithm across its high dimensional feature space should improve its detection rate and delay. Thus, instead of waiting for h windows before making

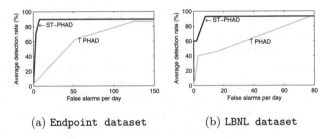

(a) Endpoint dataset   (b) LBNL dataset

Fig. 7. ROC comparison of PHAD and its Space-Time variant (ST-PHAD)

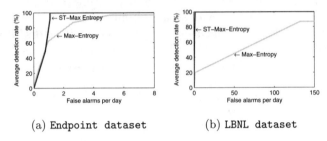

(a) Endpoint dataset   (b) LBNL dataset

Fig. 8. ROC comparison of Maximum Entropy and its Space-Time variant (ST-Max-Entropy)

Table 6. Detection Delay of the ST variants of Maximum Entropy and PHAD

	ST-Max Entropy	ST-PHAD
MyDoom (msec)	157	900
Dloader-NY (msec)	100	990
LBNL (msec)	333	330

a decision, we modified the Maximum Entropy method to raise an alarm if the K-L divergence of l packet classes in a given time-window exceed η_k.

Figs. 7 and 8 show a comparative analysis of the original and the Space-Time variants of PHAD and Maximum Entropy. It can be seen that evaluating PHAD across multiple time windows using a high dimensional feature space clearly improves the accuracy of the detector. Similarly, evaluating Maximum Entropy across its feature space instead of its original time domain design considerably improves the accuracy and detection delay of the detector.

Table 6 provides the detection delay for the Space-Time variants of Maximum Entropy detector and PHAD. It can be observed that the detection delay for ST variant of the Maximum Entropy detector is dramatically lower than the original algorithm. This is because the ST variant of the Maximum Entropy detector does not wait for multiple anomalous windows before raising an alarm. For PHAD, the detection delay remains unaltered because the ST-PHAD variants simultaneously operates in space and time.

6.3   Future Work

The preliminary results of this section show that operating an anomaly detector in space and time can improve the detector's accuracy and delay. In a future work, we will report detailed results on this finding.

Acknowledgements

This work is supported by the National ICT R&D Fund, Ministry of Information Technology, Government of Pakistan. The information, data, comments, and views detailed herein may not necessarily reflect the endorsements of views of the National ICT R&D Fund.

The authors would like to thank Aamir Shafi for providing unrestricted access to the Solaris cluster for our experiments.

References

1. Symantec Internet Security Threat Reports I–XI (January 2002–January 2008)
2. McAfee Corp., McAfee Virtual Criminology Report: North American Study into Organized Crime and the Internet (2005)
3. Computer Economics: Economic Impact of Malicious Code Attacks (2001), http://www.computereconomics.com/cei/press/pr92101.html
4. Williamson, M.M.: Throttling viruses: Restricting propagation to defeat malicious mobile code. In: ACSAC (2002)
5. Twycross, J., Williamson, M.M.: Implementing and testing a virus throttle. In: Usenix Security (2003)
6. Sellke, S., Shroff, N.B., Bagchi, S.: Modeling and automated containment of worms. In: DSN (2005)
7. Jung, J., Paxson, V., Berger, A.W., Balakrishnan, H.: Fast portscan detection using sequential hypothesis testing. In: IEEE Symp. Sec. and Priv. (2004)
8. Schechter, S.E., Jung, J., Berger, A.W.: Fast detection of scanning worm infections. In: Jonsson, E., Valdes, A., Almgren, M. (eds.) RAID 2004. LNCS, vol. 3224, pp. 59–81. Springer, Heidelberg (2004)
9. Weaver, N., Staniford, S., Paxson, V.: Very fast containment of scanning worms. In: Usenix Security (2004)
10. Chen, S., Tang, Y.: Slowing Down Internet Worms. In: IEEE ICDCS (2004)
11. Ganger, G., Economou, G., Bielski, S.: Self-Securing Network Interfaces: What, Why, and How. Carnegie Mellon University Technical Report, CMU-CS-02-144 (2002)
12. Mahoney, M.V., Chan, P.K.: PHAD: Packet Header Anomaly Detection for Indentifying Hostile Network Traffic. Florida Tech. technical report CS-2001-4 (2001)
13. Mahoney, M.V., Chan, P.K.: Learning Models of Network Traffic for Detecting Novel Attacks. Florida Tech. technical report CS-2002-08 (2002)
14. Mahoney, M.V., Chan, P.K.: Network Traffic Anomaly Detection Based on Packet Bytes. In: ACM SAC (2003)
15. Lakhina, A., Crovella, M., Diot, C.: Characterization of network-wide traffic anomalies in traffic flows. In: ACM Internet Measurement Conference (IMC) (2004)

16. Lakhina, A., Crovella, M., Diot, C.: Diagnosing network-wide traffic anomalies. In: ACM SIGCOMM (2004)
17. Lakhina, A., Crovella, M., Diot, C.: Mining anomalies using traffic feature distributions. In: ACM SIGCOMM (2005)
18. Soule, A., Salamatian, K., Taft, N.: Combining Filtering and Statistical methods for anomaly detection. In: ACM/Usenix IMC (2005)
19. Zou, C.C., Gao, L., Gong, W., Towsley, D.: Monitoring and early warning of Internet worms. In: ACM CCS (2003)
20. Gu, Y., McCullum, A., Towsley, D.: Detecting anomalies in network traffic using maximum entropy estimation. In: ACM/Usenix IMC (2005)
21. Next-Generation Intrusion Detection Expert System (NIDES), http://www.csl.sri.com/projects/nides/
22. Peakflow-SP and Peakflow-X, http://www.arbornetworks.com/peakflowsp, http://www.arbornetworks.com/peakflowx
23. Cisco IOS Flexible Network Flow, http://www.cisco.com/go/netflow
24. LBNL/ICSI Enterprise Tracing Project, http://www.icir.org/enterprise-tracing/download.html
25. WisNet ADS Comparison Homepage, http://wisnet.niit.edu.pk/projects/adeval
26. Wong, C., Bielski, S., Studer, A., Wang, C.: Empirical Analysis of Rate Limiting Mechanisms. In: Valdes, A., Zamboni, D. (eds.) RAID 2005. LNCS, vol. 3858, pp. 22–42. Springer, Heidelberg (2006)
27. Shafiq, M.Z., Khayam, S.A., Farooq, M.: Improving Accuracy of Immune-inspired Malware Detectors by using Intelligent Features. In: ACM GECCO (2008)
28. Ingham, K.L., Inoue, H.: Comparing Anomaly Detection Techniques for HTTP. In: Kruegel, C., Lippmann, R., Clark, A. (eds.) RAID 2007. LNCS, vol. 4637, pp. 42–62. Springer, Heidelberg (2007)
29. Lazarevic, A., Ertoz, L., Kumar, V., Ozgur, A., Srivastava, J.: A Comparative Study of Anomaly Detection Schemes in Network Intrusion Detection. In: SIAM SDM (2003)
30. Mueller, P., Shipley, G.: Dragon claws its way to the top. In: Network Computing (2001), http://www.networkcomputing.com/1217/1217f2.html
31. The NSS Group: Intrusion Detection Systems Group Test (Edition 2) (2001), http://nsslabs.com/group-tests/intrusion-detection-systems-ids-group-test-edition-2.html
32. Yocom, B., Brown, K.: Intrusion battleground evolves, Network World Fusion (2001), http://www.nwfusion.com/reviews/2001/1008bg.html
33. Lippmann, R.P., Haines, J.W., Fried, D.J., Korba, J., Das, K.: The 1999 DARPA OffLine Intrusion Detection Evaluation. Comp. Networks 34(2), 579–595 (2000)
34. Durst, R., Champion, T., Witten, B., Miller, E., Spagnuolo, L.: Testing and Evaluating Computer Intrusion Detection Systems. Comm. of the ACM 42(7), 53–61 (1999)
35. Shipley, G.: ISS RealSecure Pushes Past Newer IDS Players. In: Network Computing (1999), http://www.networkcomputing.com/1010/1010r1.html
36. Shipley, G.: Intrusion Detection, Take Two. In: Network Computing (1999), http://www.nwc.com/1023/1023f1.html
37. Roesch, M.: Snort – Lightweight Intrusion Detection for Networks. In: USENIX LISA (1999)

38. Lippmann, R.P., Fried, D.J., Graf, I., Haines, J.W., Kendall, K.R., McClung, D., Weber, D., Webster, S.E., Wyschogrod, D., Cunningham, R.K., Zissman, M.A.: Evaluating Intrusion Detection Systems: The 1998 DARPA Off-Line Intrusion Detection Evaluation. In: DISCEX, vol. (2), pp. 12–26 (2000)
39. DARPA-sponsored IDS Evaluation (1998 and 1999). MIT Lincoln Lab, Cambridge, www.ll.mit.edu/IST/ideval/data/data_index.html
40. Debar, H., Dacier, M., Wespi, A., Lampart, S.: A workbench for intrusion detection systems. IBM Zurich Research Laboratory (1998)
41. Denmac Systems, Inc.: Network Based Intrusion Detection: A Review of Technologies (1999)
42. Ptacek, T.H., Newsham, T.N.: Insertion, Evasion, and Denial of Service: Eluding Network Intrusion Detection. Secure Networks, Inc. (1998)
43. Aguirre, S.J., Hill, W.H.: Intrusion Detection Fly-Off: Implications for the United States Navy. MITRE Technical Report MTR 97W096 (1997)
44. Puketza, N., Chung, M., Olsson, R.A., Mukherjee, B.: A Software Platform for Testing Intrusion Detection Systems. IEEE Software 14(5), 43–51 (1997)
45. Puketza, N.F., Zhang, K., Chung, M., Mukherjee, B., Olsson, R.A.: A Methodology for Testing Intrusion Detection Systems. IEEE Trans. Soft. Eng. 10(22), 719–729 (1996)
46. Mell, P., Hu, V., Lippmann, R., Haines, J., Zissman, M.: An Overview of Issues in Testing Intrusion Detection Systems. NIST IR 7007 (2003)
47. McHugh, J.: The 1998 Lincoln Laboratory IDS Evaluation (A Critique). In: Debar, H., Mé, L., Wu, S.F. (eds.) RAID 2000. LNCS, vol. 1907, Springer, Heidelberg (2000)
48. Mahoney, M.V., Chan, P.K.: An Analysis of the 1999 DARPA/Lincoln Laboratory Evaluation Data for Network Anomaly Detection. In: Vigna, G., Krügel, C., Jonsson, E. (eds.) RAID 2003. LNCS, vol. 2820, pp. 220–237. Springer, Heidelberg (2003)
49. Pang, R., Allman, M., Paxson, V., Lee, J.: The Devil and Packet Trace Anonymization. In: ACM CCR, vol. 36(1) (2006)
50. Pang, R., Allman, M., Bennett, M., Lee, J., Paxson, V., Tierney, B.: A First Look at Modern Enterprise Traffic. In: ACM/USENIX IMC (2005)
51. Winpcap homepage, http://www.winpcap.org/
52. Symantec Security Response, http://securityresponse.symantec.com/avcenter
53. Shannon, C., Moore, D.: The spread of the Witty worm. IEEE Sec & Priv 2(4), 46–50 (2004)
54. Axelsson, S.: Intrusion Detection Systems: A Survey and Taxonomy. Technical Report 99-15, Chalmers University (2000)
55. Ringberg, H., Rexford, J., Soule, A., Diot, C.: Sensitivity of PCA for Traffic Anomaly Detection. In: ACM SIGMETRICS (2007)

Advanced Network Fingerprinting

Humberto J. Abdelnur, Radu State, and Olivier Festor

Centre de Recherche INRIA Nancy - Grand Est
615, rue du jardin botanique
Villers-les-Nancy, France
{Humberto.Abdelnur,Radu.State,Olivier.Festor}@loria.fr
http://madynes.loria.fr

Abstract. Security assessment tasks and intrusion detection systems do
rely on automated fingerprinting of devices and services. Most current
fingerprinting approaches use a signature matching scheme, where a set
of signatures are compared with traffic issued by an unknown entity. The
entity is identified by finding the closest match with the stored signatures.
These fingerprinting signatures are found mostly manually, requiring a
laborious activity and needing advanced domain specific expertise. In
this paper we describe a novel approach to automate this process and
build flexible and efficient fingerprinting systems able to identify the
source entity of messages in the network. We follow a passive approach
without need to interact with the tested device. Application level traffic is captured passively and inherent structural features are used for
the classification process. We describe and assess a new technique for
the automated extraction of protocol fingerprints based on arborescent
features extracted from the underlying grammar. We have successfully
applied our technique to the Session Initiation Protocol (SIP) used in
Voice over IP signalling.

Keywords: Passive Fingerprinting, Feature extraction, Structural syntax inference.

1 Introduction

Many security operations rely on the precise identification of a remote device
or a subset of it (e.g. network protocol stacks, services). In security assessment
tasks, this fingerprinting step is essential for evaluating the security of a remote
and unknown system; especially network intrusion detection systems might use
this knowledge to detect rogue systems and stealth intruders. Another important
applicability resides in blackbox devices/application testing for potential copyright infringements. In the latter case, when no access to source code is provided,
the only hints that might detect a copyright infringement can be obtained by
observing the network level traces and determine if a given copyright protected
software/source code is used unlawfully.

The work described in this paper was motivated by one major challenge that
we had to face when building a Voice over IP (VoIP) specific intrusion detection

R. Lippmann, E. Kirda, and A. Trachtenberg (Eds.): RAID 2008, LNCS 5230, pp. 372–389, 2008.
© Springer-Verlag Berlin Heidelberg 2008

system. We had to fingerprint VoIP devices and stacks in order to detect the presence of a rogue system on the network. Typically, only some vendor specific devices should be able to connect, while others and potentially malicious intended systems had to be detected and blocked. We decided that an automated system, capable to self-tune and self-deploy was the only viable solution on the long run. Therefore, we considered that the ideal system has to be able to process captured and labeled network traffic and detect the structural features that serve as potential differentiators. When searching for such potential features, there are some natural candidates: the type of individual fields and their length or the order in which they appear. For instance, the presence of login headers, the quantities of spaces after commas or the order presented in the handshake of capabilities. Most existing systems use such features, but individual signatures are built manually requiring a tedious and time consuming process.

Our approach consists in an automated solution for this task, assuming a known syntax specification of the protocol data units. We have considered only the signalling traffic - all devices were using Session Initiation Protocol [1] (SIP) - and our key contribution is to differentiate stack implementations by looking at some specific patterns in how the message processing code has been designed and developed. This is done in two main steps. In the first step, we extract features that can serve to differentiate among several stack implementations. These features are used in a second phase in order to implement a decisional process. This approach and the supporting algorithms are presented in this paper.

This paper is organized as follow. Section 2 illustrates the overall architecture and operational framework of our fingerprinting system. Section 3 shows how structural inference, comparison and identification of differences can be done based on the underlying grammar of a given specified protocol. Section 4 introduces the training, calibration and classification process. We provide an overview of experimental results in Sect.5 using the signalling protocol (SIP) as an application case. Section 6 describes the related work in the area of fingerprinting as well as the more general work on structural similarity. Finally, Sect.7 points out future works and concludes this paper.

2   Structural Protocol Fingerprinting

Most known application level and network protocols use a syntax specification based on formal grammars. The essential issue is that each individual message can be represented by a tree like structure. We have observed that stack implementers can be tracked by some specific subtrees and/or collection of subtrees appearing in the parse trees. The key idea is that structural differences between two devices can be detected by comparing the underlying parse trees generated for several messages. A structural signature is given by features that are extracted from these tree structures. Such distinctive features are called fingerprints. We will address in the following the automated identification of them.

If we focus for the moment one individual productions (in a grammar rule), the types of signatures might be given by:

- Different **contents** for one field. This is in fact a sequence of characters which can determinate a signature. (e.g. a prompt or an initialization message).
- Different **lengths** for one field. The grammar allows the production of a repetition of items (e.g. quantity of spaces after a symbol, capabilities supported). In this case, the length of the field is a good signature candidate.
- Different **orders** in one field. This is possible, when no explicit order is specified in a set of items. A typical case is how capabilities are advertised in current protocols.

We propose a learning method to automatically identify distinctive structural signatures. This is done by analyzing and comparing captured messages traces from the different devices. The overview of the learning and classification process is illustrated in Fig.1.

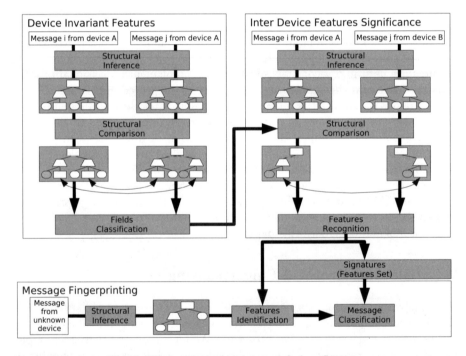

Fig. 1. Fingerprinting training and classification

The upper boxes in Fig.1 constitute the training period of the system. The output is a set of signatures for each device presented in the training set. The lowest box represents the fingerprinting process. The training is divided in two phases:

Phase 1 (*Device Invariant Features*). In this phase, the system automatically classifies each field in the grammar. This classification is needed to identify which fields may change between messages coming from the same device.

Phase 2 (*Inter Device Features Significance*) identifies among the Invariant fields of each implementation, those having different values for at least two group of devices. These fields will constitute part of the signatures set.

When one message has to be classified, the values of each invariant field are extracted and compared to the signature values learned in the training phase.

3   Structural Inference

3.1   Formal Grammars and Protocol Fingerprinting

The key assumption made in our approach is that an Augmented BackusNaur Form (ABNF) grammar [2] specification is a priori known for a given protocol. Such a specification is made of some basic elements as shown in Fig.2.

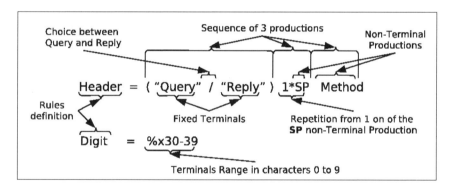

Fig. 2. Basic elements of a grammar

- A **Terminal** can represent a fixed string or a character to be chosen from a range of legitimate characters.
- A **Non-Terminal** is reduced using some rules to either a Terminal or a Non-Terminal.
- A **Choice** defines an arbitrary selection among several items.
- A **Sequence** involves a fixed number of items, where the order is specified.
- A **Repetition** involves a sequence of one item/group of items, where some additional constraints might be specified.

A given message is parsed according to the fields defined in the grammar. Each element of the grammar is placed in an n-ary tree which obeys the following rules:

- A **Terminal** becomes a leaf node with a name associated (i.e. the terminal that it represents) which is associated to the encountered value in the message.
- A **Non-Terminal** is an internal node associated to a name (i.e. the non-terminal rule) and it has a unique child which can be any of the types defined here (e.g. Terminal, non-Terminal, Sequence or Repetition).
- A **Sequence** is an internal node that has a fixed number of children. This number is in-line with the rules of the syntax specification.
- A **Repetition** is also an internal node, but having a number of children that may vary based on the number of items which appear in the message.
- A **Choice** does not create any node in the tree. However, it just marks the node that has been elected from a choice item.

It is important to note that even if sequences and repetitions do not have a defined name in the grammar rules, an implicit name is assigned to them that uniquely distinguishes each instance of these items at the current rule.

Figure 3 shows a Toy ABNF grammar defined in (a), messages from different implementation compliant with the grammar in (b/c) and (d) the inferred structure representing one of the messages in (d).

With respect to the usage, fields can be classified in three categories:

- **Cosmetics Fields:** these fields are mandatory and do not really provide a value added interest for fingerprinting purposes. The associated values do not change in different implementations.
- **Static Fields:** are the fields which values never change in a same implementation. These values do however change between different implementations. Obviously, these are the type of fields which may represent a signature for one implementation.
- **Dynamic Fields:** these fields are the opposite of static fields and do change their values in relation to semantic aspects of the message even in a single implementation.

An additional sub-classification can be defined for Dynamic and Static fields:

- **Value Type** relates to the String reduction of the node (i.e. the text information of that node),
- **Choice Type** relates to the selected choice from the grammar,
- **Length Type** corresponds to the number of items in a Repetition reduction,
- **Order Type** corresponds to the order in which items of a Repetition reduction appear.

Even if one implementation may generate different kind of values for the same field, such values could be related by a function and then serve as a feature. Therefore, a **Function Type** can be also defined to be used to compute the value from a node of the tree and return an output useful for the fingerprinting. Essentially, this type is used for manually tuning the training process.

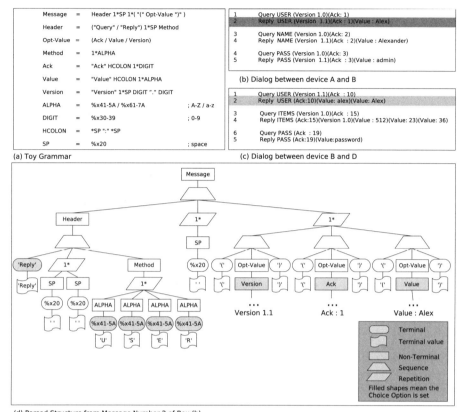

(a) Toy Grammar

(b) Dialog between device A and B

(c) Dialog between device B and D

(d) Parsed Structure from Message Number 2 of Box (b)

Fig. 3. Parsed Structure Grammar

3.2 Node Signatures and Resemblance

Guidelines for designing a set of tree signatures (for a tree or a sub-tree) should follow some general common sense principles like:

- As more items are shared between trees, the more similar their signatures must be.
- Nodes that have different tags or ancestors must be considered different.
- In cases where the parent node is a Sequence, the location order in the Sequence should be part of the tree signature.
- If the parent node is a repetition, the location order should not be part of the tree signature, order will be captured later on in the fingerprinting features.

The closest known approach is published by D. Buttler in [3]. This method starts by encoding the tree in a set. Each element in the set represents a partial path from the root to any of the nodes in the tree. A resemblance method defined by A. Broder [4] uses the elements of the set as tokens. This resemblance is based on shingles, where a shingle is a contiguous sequence of tokens from the document. Between documents D_i and D_j the resemblance is defined as:

$$r(D_i, D_j) = \frac{|S(D_i, w) \bigcap S(D_j, w)|}{|S(D_i, w) \bigcup S(D_j, w)|} \tag{1}$$

where $S(D_i, w)$ creates the shingles of length w for the document D_i.

Definition 1. *The **Node Signature** function is defined to be a Multi-Set of all partial paths belonging to the sub-branch of the node.*

The *partial paths* start from the current node rather than from the root of the tree, but still goes through all the nodes of the subtree which has the current element as root like it was in the original approach. However, partial paths obtained from fields classified as *Cosmetics* are excluded from this Multi-Set. The structure used is a Multi-Set rather than a Set in order to store the quantity of occurrences for specific nodes in the sub-branch. For instance, the number of spaces after a specific field can determinate a signature in an implementation.

Siblings nodes in a Sequence items are fixed and representative. Sibling nodes in a Repetition can be made representative creating the partial paths of the Multi-Set and using the respective position of a child.

Table 1 shows the *Node Signature* obtained from the node *Header* at the tree of Fig. 3 (d).

Definition 2. *The **Ressemblance** function used to measure the degree of similarity between two nodes is based on the (1). The $S(N_i, w)$ function applies the Node Signature function over the node N_i.*

Using $w = 1$ allows to compare the number of items these nodes have in common though ignoring their position for a repetition.

3.3   Structural Difference Identification

Algorithm 1 is used to identify differences between two nodes which share the same ancestor path in the two trees,

where the functions *Tag*, *Value*, *Type* return the name, value and respectively the type of the current node. Note that $Tag(node_a) = Tag(node_b) \Rightarrow Type(node_a) = Type(node_b)$.

The function **Report_Difference** takes the type of difference to report and the corresponding two nodes. Each time the function is called, it creates one structure that stores the type of difference, the partial path from the root of the tree to the current nodes (which is the same for both nodes) and a corresponding value. For differences of type 'Value' it will store the two terminal values, for 'Choice' the two different Tags names, for 'Length' the two lengths and for 'Order' the matches.

The function **Identify_Children_Matches** identifies a match between children of different repetition nodes. The similitude between each child from $node_a$ and $node_b$ (with n and m children respectively) is represented as a matrix, M, of size $n \ x \ m$ where:

Table 1. Partial paths obtained from Fig.3 (d)

Partial Paths	Occurrences
Header.0.'Reply'	1
~~Header.0.'Reply'.'Reply'~~	1
Header.1.?	2
~~Header.1.?.SP~~	2
~~Header.1.?.SP.%x20~~	2
~~Header.1.?.SP.%x20.' '~~	2
Header.2.Method.?	4
~~Header.2.Method.?.ALPHA.~~	4
Header.2.Method.?.ALPHA.%x41-5A	4
Header.2.Method.?.ALPHA.%x41-5A.'U'	1
Header.2.Method.?.ALPHA.%x41-5A.'S'	1
Header.2.Method.?.ALPHA.%x41-5A.'E'	1
Header.2.Method.?.ALPHA.%x41-5A.'R'	1

(~~strikethrough~~) Strikethrough paths are the ones considered as cosmetics.
(?) Quotes define that the current path may be any of the repetition items.

Algorithm 1. Node differences Location

---

procedure NODEDIFF($node_a$, $node_b$)
    if $Tag(node_a) = Tag(node_b)$ **then**
        if $Type(node_a) = TERMINAL$ **then**
            if $Value(node_a) != Value(node_b)$ **then**
                $Report\_Difference('Value', node_a, node_b)$
            end if
        else if $Type(node_a) = NON-TERMINAL$ **then**
            $NODEDIFF(node_a.child_0, node_b.child_0))$ ▷Non_Terminals have
                                                      ▷an unique child
        else if $Type(node_a) = SEQUENCE$ **then**
            for $i = 1..\#node_a$ **do**   ▷In a Sequence
                $NODEDIFF(node_a.child_i, node_b.child_i)$ ▷$\#node_a = \#node_b$
            end for
        else if $Type(node_a) = REPETITION$ **then**
            if not $(\#node_a = \#node_b)$ **then**
                $Report\_Difference('Length', node_a, node_b)$
            end if
            $matches := Identify\_Children\_Matches(node_a, node_b)$
            if $\exists\ (i,j) \in matches : i != j$ **then**
                $Report\_Difference('Order', node_a, node_b)$
            end if
            forall $(i,j) \in matches$ **do**
                $NODEDIFF(node_a.child_i, node_b.child_j)$
            end for
        end if
    else
        $Report\_Difference('Choice', node_a, node_b)$
    end if
end procedure

$$M_{i,j} = resemblance(node_a.child_i, node_b.child_j)$$

To find the most adequate match, a greedy matching assignment based on the concept of Nash Equilibrium [5] is used. Children with the biggest similarity are bound. If a child from $node_a$ shares the same similarity score with more than one child from $node_b$, some considerations have to be added respecting their position in the repetitions.

Figure 4 illustrates an example match, assuming that the following matrix was obtained using the *Resemblance* method with the path "Message.2.?". The rows in the matrix represent the children from the subtree in (a) and the columns the children from subtree (b).

$$M = \begin{pmatrix} .00 & .00 & .00 \\ .33 & .00 & .00 \\ .00 & .61 & .90 \end{pmatrix}$$

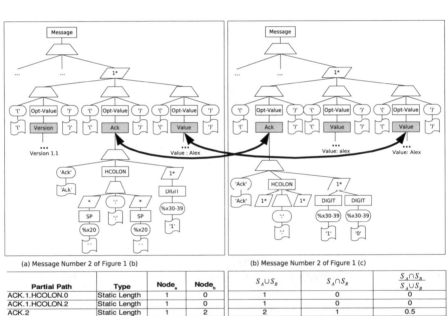

(a) Message Number 2 of Figure 1 (b)

(b) Message Number 2 of Figure 1 (c)

Partial Path	Type	Node$_a$	Node$_b$
ACK.1.HCOLON.0	Static Length	1	0
ACK.1.HCOLON.2	Static Length	1	0
ACK.2	Static Length	1	2
ACK.2.(?).DIGIT.%x30-39	Static Value	'1'	'1'
ACK.2.(?).DIGIT.%x30-39	Static Value		'0'

$S_A \cup S_B$	$S_A \cap S_B$	$\dfrac{S_A \cap S_B}{S_A \cup S_B}$
1	0	0
1	0	0
2	1	0.5
1	1	1
1	0	0
6	2	0.33

(c) Node Signatures from the **Ack** nodes

(d) Shingle information from the **Ack** nodes where $S_a = S(N_a, 1)$ and $S_b = (N_b, 1)$

Fig. 4. Performed match between sub-branches of the tree

All the compared children share some common items besides the choice nodes (colored). Those common items are *Cosmetics* nodes, which are required in the message in order to be compliant with the grammar. Note that, besides the *Cosmetic* fields, the first item of the subtree (a) does not share any similarity with any of the other nodes. It should therefore not match any other node.

4   Structural Features Extraction

4.1   Fields Classification

One major activity that was not yet described is how non-invariant fields are identified. The process is done by using all the messages coming from one device and finding the differences between each two messages using Algorithm 1. For each result, a secondary algorithm (Algorithm 2) is run in order to fine tune the extracted classification.

Algorithm 2. Fields Classification Algorithm

---

procedure FieldClassification($differences_{a,b}$)
    forall $diff \in differences_{a,b}$ **do**
        if $diff.type ==' Value')$ **then**
            $Classify\_as\_Dynamic('Value', diff.path)$
        else if $diff.type ==' Choice'$ **then**
            $Classify\_as\_Dynamic('Choice', diff.path)$
        else if $diff.type ==' Length'$ **then**
            $Classify\_as\_Dynamic('Length', diff.path)$
        else if $diff.type ==' Order'$ **then**
            if not $(\forall\ (i, j), (x, z) \in diff.matches :$
                $(i < x \wedge j < z) \vee (i > x \wedge j > z))$ **then**
                ▷Check if a permutation exists between the matched items.
                $Classify\_as\_Dynamic('Order', diff.path)$
            end if
        end if
    end for
end procedure

The **Classify_as_Dynamic** functions store in the global list, **fieldClassifications**, a tuple with the type of the found difference (e.g. 'Value', 'Choice', 'Length' or 'Order') and the partial path in the tree structure that represents the node in the message.

This algorithm recognizes only the fields that are *Dynamic*. The set of *Static* fields will be represented by the union of all the fields not recognized as *Dynamic*.

Assuming a training set *Msg_set*, of messages compliant with the grammar as

$$Msg = \bigcup_{i=0}^{n} msg\_set_i$$

where n is quantity of devices and msg_set_i is the set of messages generated by device i, the total number of comparisons computed in this process is

$$cmps_1 = \sum_{i=0}^{n} \frac{|msg\_set_i| * (|msg\_set_i| - 1)}{2} \qquad (2)$$

4.2   Features Recognition

Some features are essential for an inter-device classification. In contrast to the Fields Classification, this process compares all the messages from the training set sourced from different devices. All the *Invariant* Fields -for which different implementations have different values- are identified. Algorithm 3 recognizes these features. Its inputs are the *fieldClassifications* computed by the Algorithm 2, the Devices Identifier to which the compared message belongs as well as the set of differences found by Algorithm 1 between the messages.

Algorithm 3. Features Recognition Algorithm

---

procedure featuresRecognition($fieldClassifications$, $DevID_{a,b}$, $differences_{a,b}$)
   forall $diff \in differences_{a,b}$ **do**
     if not $(diff.type, diff.path) \in fieldClassifications$ **then**
       if $diff.type ==$ $'Value'$ **then**
         $addFeature('Value',$ $diff.path,$ $DevID_{a,b},$ $diff.value_{a,b})$
       else if $diff.type ==$ $'Choice'$ **then**
         $addFeature('Choice',$ $diff.path,$ $DevID_{a,b},$ $diff.name_{a,b})$
       else if $diff.type ==$ $'Length'$ **then**
         $addFeature('Length',$ $diff.path,$ $DevID_{a,b},$ $diff.length_{a,b})$
       else if $diff.type ==$ $'Order'$ **then**
        if $(\exists\ (x,z) \in diff.matches : x \neq z)$ **then**
         $addFeature('Order',$ $diff.path,$ $DevID_{a,b},$
                           $diff.match,$ $diff.children\_nodes_{a,b})$
        end if
       end if
     end if
   end for
end procedure

The **add_Feature** function stores in a global variable, **recognizedFeatures**, the partial path of the node associated with the type of difference (i.e. Value, Name, Order or Length) and a list of devices with their encountered value. However, the 'Order' feature presents a more complex approach, requiring minor improvements.

Assuming the earlier Msg_set set, this process will do the following number of comparisons:

$$cmps_2 = \sum_{i=0}^{n} |msg\_set_i| * \sum_{j=i+1}^{n} |msg\_set_j| \qquad (3)$$

From the *recognizedFeatures* only the *Static* fields are used. The recognized features define a sequence of items, where each one represents the field location path in the tree representation and a list of Device ID with their associated value.

The Recognized Features can be classified in:

- Features that were found with each device and at least two distinct values are observed for a pair of devices,
- Features that were found in some of the devices for which such a location path does not exists in messages from other implementations.

4.3   Fingerprinting

The classification of a message uses the tree structure representation introduced in section 3.1. The set of recognized features obtained in section 4 represents all the partial paths in a tree structure that are used for the classification process.

In some cases, the features are of type *'Value'*, *'Choice'* or *'Length'*. Their corresponding value is easily obtained. However, the case of an *'Order'* represents a more complex approach, requiring some minor improvements

Figure 5 illustrates some identified features for an incoming message.

Field path	Feature associated	
	Type	Value
Message.2	Static Order	Version, Ack, Value
Message.2.?.1.Opt-Value.Version.1	Static Length	1
Message.2.?.1.Opt-Value.Version.4.DIGIT.%x30-39	Static Value	'1'

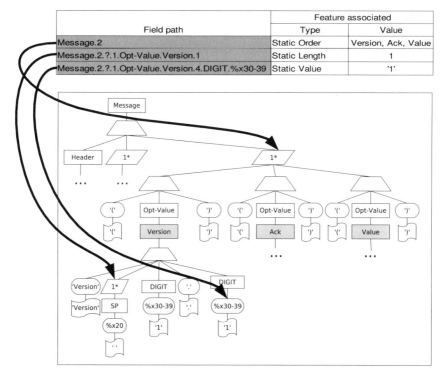

Fig. 5. Features Identification

Once a set of distinctive features is obtained, some well known classification techniques can be leveraged to implement a classifier. In our work, we have leveraged the machine learning technique described in [6].

5   Experimental Results

We have implemented the Fingerprinting Framework approach in Python. A scannerless Generalized Left-to-right Rightmost (GLR) derivation parser has been used (Dparser[7]) in order to solve ambiguities in the definition of the grammar. The training function could easily be parallelized.

We have instantiated the fingerprinting approach on the SIP protocol. The SIP messages are sent in clear text (ASCII) and their structure is inspired from HTTP. Several primitives - REGISTER, INVITE, CANCEL, BYE and OPTIONS - allow session management for a voice/multimedia call. Some additional extensions do also exist -INFO, NOTIFY, REFER, PRACK- which allow the support of presence management, customization, vendor extensions etc.

We have captured 21827 SIP messages from a real network, summarized in Table 2.

Table 2. Tested equipment

Device	Software/Firmware version
Asterisk	v1.4.4
Cisco CallManager	v5.1.1
Cisco 7940/7960	vP0S3-08-7-00
	vP0S3-08-8-00
Grandstream Budge Tone-200	v1.1.1.14
Linksys SPA941	v5.1.5
Thomson ST2030	v1.52.1
Thomson ST2020	v2.0.4.22
SJPhone	v1.60.289
	v1.60.320
	v1.65
Twinkle	v0.8.1
	v0.9
Snom	v5.3
Kapanga	v0.98
X-Lite	v3.0
Kphone	v4.2
3CX	v1.0
Express Talk	v2.02
Linphone	v1.5.0
Ekiga	v2.0.3

The system was trained with only 12% of the 21827 messages. These messages were randomly sampled. However, a proportion between the number of collected messages and the number used for the training was kept; they ranged from 50 to 350 messages per device. Table 3 shows the average and total time obtained for the comparisons of each training phase and for the message classification process (i.e. message fingerprinting). During both Phase 1 and 2, the comparisons were distributed over 10 computers ranging from Pentium IV to Core Duo. As it was expected, the average comparison time per message in Phase 2 was lower than in the previous phase, since only the invariant fields are compared. To evaluate the training, the system classified all the sampled messages (i.e. 21927 messages) in only in one computer (Core Duo @ 2.93GHz).

Table 3. Performance results obtained with the system

Type of Action	Average time per action	Number of actions computed	Total computed time
Msg. comparisons for Phase 1	632 milisec	296616	5 hours[1]
Msg. comparisons for Phase 2	592 milisec	3425740	56 hours[1]
Msg. classification	100 milisec.	21827	40 minutes

[1] Computed time using 10 computers.

172 features were discovered among all the different types of messages. These features represent items order, different lengths and values of fields where non protocol knowledge except its syntax grammar had been used. Between two different devices the distance of different features ranges between 26 to 95 features, where most of the lower values correspond to different versions of the same device. Usually, up to 46 features are identified in one message.

Table 4 summarizes the sensitivity, specificity and accuracy. The results were obtained using the test data set.

Table 4. Accuracy results obtained with the system

	True Positive	False Positive	Positive Predictive Value
Classification	18881	20	0.998
	False Negative	**True Negative**	**Negative Predictive Value**
	2909	435780	0.993
	Sensitivity	**Specificity**	**Accuracy**
	0.866	0.999	0.993

In this table we can observe that the results are very encouraging due to the high specificity and accuracy. However, some observations can be made about the quantity of false negatives. About 2/5 of them belong to only one implementation (percentage that represents 50% of its messages), 2/5 belongs to 3 more device classes (representing 18% of their messages), the final 1/5 belongs to 8 classes (representing 10% of their messages) and the 7 classes left do not have false negatives. This issue can be a consequence of the irregularity in the quantity from the set of messages in each device. Three of the higher mentioned classes had been used in our test-bed to acquire most features of SIP. A second explanation can be that in fact many of those messages do not contain valuable information (e.g. intermediary messages). Table 5 shows all the 38 types of messages collected in our test with information concerning their miss-classification (i.e. False Negatives).

Finally, we created a set of messages which have been manually modified. These modifications include changing the User-Agent, Server-Agent and references to device name. As a result, deleting a few such fields did not influence

Table 5. False Negative classification details

Type of Message	False Negatives	Message quantity	Miss percentage
200, 100, ACK	1613	9358	17%
	(710, 561, 347)	(4663, 1802, 2893)	(15%, 31%, 11%)
501, 180, 101 BYE, 486	824	3414	24%
	$\begin{pmatrix} 257,\ 215,\ 148 \\ 104,\ 100 \end{pmatrix}$	$\begin{pmatrix} 385,\ 1841,\ 148 \\ 892,\ 176 \end{pmatrix}$	$\begin{pmatrix} 65\%,\ 11\%,\ 100\% \\ 11\%,\ 67\% \end{pmatrix}$
489, 487, 603 202, 480, 481 380, 415, 400	213	636	33%
	$\begin{pmatrix} 84,\ 57,\ 28 \\ 21,\ 13,\ 6 \\ 2,\ 1,\ 1 \end{pmatrix}$	$\begin{pmatrix} 84,\ 230,\ 118 \\ 52,\ 42,\ 18 \\ 2,\ 38,\ 51 \end{pmatrix}$	$\begin{pmatrix} 100\%,\ 24\%,\ 23\% \\ 40\%,\ 30\%,\ 33\% \\ 100\%,\ 2\%,\ 2\% \end{pmatrix}$
INVITE, OPTIONS REGISTER, CANCEL SUBSCRIBE	117	5694	2%
	$\begin{pmatrix} 38,\ 34 \\ 25,\ 19 \\ 1 \end{pmatrix}$	$\begin{pmatrix} 3037,\ 628 \\ 1323,\ 297 \\ 409 \end{pmatrix}$	$\begin{pmatrix} 1\%,\ 5\% \\ 1\%,\ 6\% \\ .00\% \end{pmatrix}$
INFO, REFER PRACK, NOTIFY PUBLISH	0	2223	0%
		$\begin{pmatrix} 1830, 163 \\ 117, 77 \\ 36 \end{pmatrix}$	
11 other Response Codes	0	492	0%

the decision of the system; neither did it changing their banners to another implementation name. However, as more modifications were done, less precise the system became and more mistakes were done.

6   Related Work

Fingerprinting became a popular topic in the last few years. It started with the pioneering work of Comer and Lin [8] and is currently an essential activity in security assessment tasks. Some of the most known network fingerprinting operations are done by NMAP [9], using a set of rules and active probing techniques. Passive techniques became known mostly with the P0F [10] tool, which is capable to do OS fingerprinting without requiring active probes. Many other tools like (AMAP, XProbe, Queso) did implement similar schemes.

Application layer fingerprinting techniques, specifically for SIP, were first described in [11,12]. These approaches proposed active as well as passive fingerprinting techniques. Their common baseline is the lack of an automated approach for building the fingerprints and constructing the classification process. Furthermore, the number of signatures described are minimal which leaves the systems easily exposed to approaches as the one described by D. Watson et al. [13], that can fool them by obfuscation of such observable signatures. Recently, the work by J. Caballero et al. [6] described a novel approach for the automation of Active Fingerprint generation which resulted in a vast set of possible signatures. It is one of the few automatic approaches found in the literature and it is based in finding a set of queries (automatically generated) that identify different responses in the different implementations. While our work addresses specifically the automation for passive fingerprinting, we can imagine this two complementary approaches working together.

There have been recently similar efforts done in the research community aiming however at a very different goal from ours. These activities started with practical reverse engineering of proprietary protocols [14] and [15] and a simple application of bioinformatics inspired techniques to protocol analysis [16]. These initial ideas matured and several other authors reported good results of sequence alignment techniques in [17], [18], [19] and [20]. Another major approach for the identification of the structure in protocol messages is to monitor the execution of an endpoint and identify the relevant fields using some tainted data [21], [22]. Recently, work on identifying properties of encrypted traffic has been reported in [23,24]. These two approaches used probabilistic techniques based on packet arrivals, interval, packet length and randomness in the encrypted bits to identify Skype traffic or the language of conversation. While all these complementary works addressed the identification of the protocol building blocks or properties in their packets, we assumed a known protocol and worked on identifying specific implementation stacks.

The closest approach to ours, in terms of message comparison, it is the work developed by M. Chang and C. K.Poon [25] for collection training SPAM detectors. However, in their approach as they focus in identifying human written sentences, they only consider the lexical analysis of the messages and do not exploit an underlying structure.

Finally, two other solutions have been proposed in the literature in this research landscape. Flow based identification has been reported in [26], while a grammar/ probabilistic based approach is proposed in [27] and respectively in [28].

7   Conclusions

In this article we described a novel approach for generating fingerprinting systems based on the structural analysis of protocol messages. Our solution automates the generation by using both formal grammars and collected traffic traces. It detects important and relevant complex tree like structures and leverages them for building fingerprints. The applicability of our solution lies in the field of intrusion detection and security assessment, where precise device/service/stack identification are essential. We have implemented a SIP specific fingerprinting system and evaluated its performance. The obtained results are very encouraging. Future work will consist in improving the method and applying it to other protocols and services. Our work is relevant to the tasks of identifying the precise vendor/device that has generated a captured trace. We do not address the reverse engineering of unknown protocols, but consider that we know the underlying protocol. The current approach does not cope with cryptographically protected traffic. A straightforward extension for this purpose is to assume that access to the original traffic is possible. Our main contribution consists in a novel solution to automatically discover the significant differences in the structure of

388 H.J. Abdelnur, R. State, and O. Festor

protocol compliant messages. We will extend our work towards the natural evolution, where the underlying grammar is unknown.

The key idea is to use a structural approach, where formal grammars and collected network traffic are used. Features are identified by paths and their associated values in the parse tree. The obtained results of our approach are very good. This is due to the fact that a structural message analysis is performed. Most existing fingerprinting systems are built manually and require a long lasting development process.

References

1. Rosenberg, J., Schulzrinne, H., Camarillo, G., Johnston, A., Peterson, J., Sparks, R., Handley, M., Schooler, E.: SIP: Session Initiation Protocol (2002)
2. Crocker, D.H., Overell, P.: Augmented BNF for Syntax Specifications: ABNF (1997)
3. Buttler, D.: A Short Survey of Document Structure Similarity Algorithms. In: Arabnia, H.R., Droegehorn, O. (eds.) International Conference on Internet Computing, pp. 3–9. CSREA Press (2004)
4. Broder, A.Z.: On the Resemblance and Containment of Documents. In: SEQUENCES 1997: Proceedings of the Compression and Complexity of Sequences 1997, Washington, DC, USA, p. 21. IEEE Computer Society, Los Alamitos (1997)
5. Nash, J.F.: Non-Cooperative Games. The Annals of Mathematics 54(2), 286–295 (1951)
6. Caballero, J., Venkataraman, S., Poosankam, P., Kang, M.G., Song, D., Blum, A.: FiG: Automatic Fingerprint Generation. In: The 14th Annual Network & Distributed System Security Conference (NDSS 2007) (February 2007)
7. DParser, http://dparser.sourceforge.net/
8. Comer, D., Lin, J.C.: Probing TCP Implementations. In: USENIX Summer, pp. 245–255 (1994)
9. Nmap, http://www.insecure.org/nmap/
10. P0f, http://lcamtuf.coredump.cx/p0f.shtml
11. Yan, H., Sripanidkulchai, K., Zhang, H.: Incorporating Active Fingerprinting into SPIT Prevention Systems. In: Third Annual VoIP Security Workshop (June 2006)
12. Scholz, H.: SIP Stack Fingerprinting and Stack Difference Attacks. Black Hat Briefings (2006)
13. Watson, D., Smart, M., Malan, G.R., Jahanian, F.: Protocol scrubbing: network security through transparent flow modification. IEEE/ACM Trans. Netw. 12(2), 261–273 (2004)
14. Open Source FastTrack P2P Protocol (2007), http://gift-fasttrack.berlios.de/
15. Fritzler, A.: UnOfficial AIM/OSCAR Protocol Specification (2007), http://www.oilcan.org/oscar/
16. Beddoe, M.: The Protocol Informatics Project. Toorcon (2004)
17. Gopalratnam, K., Basu, S., Dunagan, J., Wang, H.J.: Automatically Extracting Fields from Unknown Network Protocols. In: Systems and Machine Learning Workshop 2006 (2006)
18. Wondracek, G., Comparetti, P.M., Kruegel, C., Kirda, E.: Automatic Network Protocol Analysis. In: Proceedings of the 15th Annual Network and Distributed System Security Symposium (NDSS 2008) (2008)

19. Newsome, J., Brumley, D., Franklin, J., Song, D.: Replayer: automatic protocol replay by binary analysis. In: CCS 2006: Proceedings of the 13th ACM conference on Computer and communications security, pp. 311–321. ACM, New York (2006)
20. Cui, W., Kannan, J., Wang, H.J.: Discoverer: automatic protocol reverse engineering from network traces. In: SS 2007: Proceedings of 16th USENIX Security Symposium on USENIX Security Symposium, Berkeley, CA, USA, pp. 1–14. USENIX Association (2007)
21. Brumley, D., Caballero, J., Liang, Z., Newsome, J., Song, D.: Towards automatic discovery of deviations in binary implementations with applications to error detection and fingerprint generation. In: SS 2007: Proceedings of 16th USENIX Security Symposium on USENIX Security Symposium, Berkeley, CA, USA, pp. 1–16. USENIX Association (2007)
22. Lin, Z., Jiang, X., Xu, D., Zhang, X.: Automatic Protocol Format Reverse Engineering through Context-Aware Monitored Execution. In: 15th Symposium on Network and Distributed System Security (2008)
23. Bonfiglio, D., Mellia, M., Meo, M., Rossi, D., Tofanelli, P.: Revealing skype traffic: when randomness plays with you. SIGCOMM Comput. Commun. Rev. 37(4), 37–48 (2007)
24. Wright, C.V., Ballard, L., Monrose, F., Masson, G.M.: Language identification of encrypted VoIP traffic: Alejandra y Roberto or Alice and Bob? In: SS 2007: Proceedings of 16th USENIX Security Symposium on USENIX Security Symposium, Berkeley, CA, USA, pp. 1–12. USENIX Association (2007)
25. Chang, M., Poon, C.K.: Catching the Picospams. In: Hacid, M.-S., Murray, N.V., Raś, Z.W., Tsumoto, S. (eds.) ISMIS 2005. LNCS (LNAI), vol. 3488, pp. 641–649. Springer, Heidelberg (2005)
26. Haffner, P., Sen, S., Spatscheck, O., Wang, D.: ACAS: automated construction of application signatures. In: MineNet 2005: Proceedings of the 2005 ACM SIGCOMM workshop on Mining network data, pp. 197–202. ACM, New York (2005)
27. Borisov, N., Brumley, D.J., Wang, H.J.: Generic Application-Level Protocol Analyzer and its Language. In: 14th Symposium on Network and Distributed System Security (2007)
28. Ma, J., Levchenko, K., Kreibich, C., Savage, S., Voelker, G.M.: Unexpected means of protocol inference. In: IMC 2006: Proceedings of the 6th ACM SIGCOMM conference on Internet measurement, pp. 313–326. ACM, New York (2006)

On Evaluation of Response Cost for Intrusion Response Systems
(Extended Abstract)

Natalia Stakhanova[2], Chris Strasburg[1], Samik Basu[1],
and Johnny S. Wong[1]

[1] Department of Computer Science, Iowa State University, USA
{cstras,sbasu,wong}@cs.iastate.edu
[2] Faculty of Computer Science, University of New Brunswick, Canada
natalia@unb.ca,
nStakhanova@gmail.com

Abstract. In this work we present a structured and consistent methodology for evaluating cost of intrusion responses. The proposed approach provides consistent basis for response evaluation across different systems while incorporating security policy and properties of specific system environment. The advantages of the proposed cost model were evaluated via simulation process.

The proliferation of complex and fast-spreading intrusions against computer systems brought new requirements to intrusion detection and response, demanding the development of sophisticated and automated intrusion response systems. In this context, the cost-sensitive intrusion response models have gained the most interest mainly due to their emphasis on the balance between potential damage incurred by the intrusion and cost of the response. However, one of the challenges in applying this approach is defining consistent and adaptable measurement of these cost factors on the basis of policy of the system being protected against intrusions.

We developed a structured and consistent methodology for the evaluation of intrusion response cost based on three parameters: (a) *the impact of a response on the system* that quantifies the negative effect of the response on the system resources, (b) *the response goodness* that measures the ability of the corresponding response to mitigate damage caused by the intrusion to the system resources and (c) *the operational cost of a response in a given environment*.

Within this methodology, we assess response impact with respect to resources of the affected system. Our model takes into account the relative importance of the system resources determined through the review of the system policy goals according to the following categories: *confidentiality, availability* and *integrity*. One of the important steps in this process is the analysis of the system resources. Based on this analysis, the evaluation algorithm assesses the *response goodness* in terms of the resources protected by the response, the *response damage* in terms of the resources impaired by the action and the *operational cost* with respect to its environmental impact.

This methodology does not substitute the response selection process in case of detected intrusion, but rather allows to evaluate the available responses on the consistent basis. The proposed methodology includes the following steps:

R. Lippmann, E. Kirda, and A. Trachtenberg (Eds.): RAID 2008, LNCS 5230, pp. 390–391, 2008.

1. **The system classification:** The first step in quantifying the cost of a response involves determining the characteristics of the computing environment where the response will be deployed which includes evaluating system security policy priorities, defining level of tolerable risk, etc.

2. **The system policy goals:** The next step is to determine the importance of the system policy goals, and subsequently, to assess the potential risks according to the following categories: *confidentiality, availability* and *integrity*.

3. **The system resources:** System resources can be broadly viewed as the system assets (e.g., host, network, etc.), services provided by the system (e.g., HTTP, file system) and users served by the system. The analysis of system resources includes the enumeration of the available resources and their classification according to the importance for the system policy goals.

4. **The intrusion responses:** The responses are deployed to either counter possible attacks and defend the system resources or regain secure system state. Thus, the selection of applicable responses primarily depends on the identified system resources.

5. **The response operational cost:** The assessment of operational cost is generally independent from the system policy. We assess the involved operational expenses on the basis of three requirements: *human resources* , i.e., administrator time, *system resources*, i.e., storage, network bandwidth, processor time, etc., and *direct expenses* i.e., data processing fees by a third party, subscription service fees, cost of components replacement, etc.

6. **The response goodness:** Often the detection mechanism of the intrusion detection system (IDS) provides administrators with a set of alerts indicating potential attacks rather than a specific intrusion. When this situation arises, the response needs to be deployed preemptively on the basis of high likelihood of possible intrusions. In these cases, the response goodness is evaluated based on the number of possible intrusions it can potentially address, and consequently, the number of resources that can be protected by the response.

7. **The response impact on the system:** The impact of a response on the system is evaluated based on the defined system goals and their importance. The impact assessment process for a specific response includes three steps: (1) identifying the system resources affected by each response, (2) for each resource determining the priority of responses based on their effect on the resource, and (3) computing the negative impact of the responses on the associated resource using the ordering obtained in step 2. Eventually, the impact of a response on the system as a whole is an aggregation of the response's impact on the system resources.

The proposed methodology for assigning response costs essentially presents the first roadmap for defining *standardized metrics* for response cost evaluation. These response metrics provide a *consistent basis* for evaluation across systems, while allowing the response cost to be *adapted with respect to the security policy and properties of specific system environment*. Importantly, this approach is *practically implementable* in a real-world environment, making response cost assessment accessible to system administrators with a range of system expertise.

WebIDS: A Cooperative Bayesian Anomaly-Based Intrusion Detection System for Web Applications
(Extended Abstract)

Nathalie Dagorn

Laboratory of Algorithmics, Cryptology and Security (LACS), Luxembourg
& ICN Business School, France
nathalie.dagorn@icn-groupe.fr,
nathalie.dagorn@orange.fr
http://www.uni.lu/
http://www.icn-groupe.fr/

Abstract. This paper presents WebIDS, a learning-based anomaly detection system for Web applications aiming at improving the decision process, reducing the number of false positives, and achieving distributed detection.

Keywords: Anomaly detection, Correlation, Web application.

1 Introduction

Attacks on Web applications and services have been increasing dramatically for the last years. Related approaches in intrusion detection are still rare. The major challenges anomaly-based systems have to solve in the field are the improvement of the decision process, the reduction of the high number of (false) alarms caused by unusual activities, and the recent need of distributed intrusion detection. At the crossing of these research areas, the aim of our work is to propose an efficient distributed anomaly detection system dedicated to the security of Web applications.

2 Our Proposal: WebIDS

WebIDS analyzes HTTP GET requests as logged by Apache Web servers. The analysis process is based on a multi-model approach [5] implementing ten statistical algorithms: attribute length, attribute character distribution, structural inference, token finder, attribute presence or absence, attribute order, access frequency, inter-request delay, invocation order, and anomaly history (which allows, among others, keeping track of alarms). The system requires no special configuration (autonomous learning). A non-naive Bayesian network is used as a decision process [3], classifying the events more accurately and incorporating information about confidence in the models. At the root node, a specification of the event classification [6] distinguishes between a normal state and five Web attack states (authentication, XSS, command execution, denial of service, and other attack). The system is improved after each log analysis by filtering out false positives using an alarm clustering technique [2]. As part of the anomaly

R. Lippmann, E. Kirda, and A. Trachtenberg (Eds.): RAID 2008, LNCS 5230, pp. 392–393, 2008.

history model, a cooperation feature enables the system to achieve alarm and event correlation [4]. The Intrusion Detection Message Exchange Format (IDMEF) [1] is used for sharing alarm information between systems.

3 Experimental Results

WebIDS has been implemented in an IT company based in Luxembourg and showed good detection rates (sensitivity of 96.02 %, specificity of 99.99 %, and reliability of 99.94 %). The false positive rate (0.01422 %) is lower than the rates observed for similar systems. Nevertheless, these results must be mitigated because only a small number of anomalies could be observed by WebIDS over the experimental period, and the comparison with existing systems is not based on the same dataset.

4 Conclusion and Future Work

As a conclusion, we can state that the cooperative anomaly-based intrusion detection system proposed is both innovative and efficient. By improving the decision process, reducing the false positive rate and enabling cooperation between systems, it meets the defined challenges. As a follow-up to this research, the deployment of WebIDS in a more widely distributed environment is currently considered. Some functional and technical improvements are being carried out for that purpose.

References

1. Debar, H., Curry, D., Feinstein, B.: The Intrusion Detection Message Exchange Format. Internet Draft IETF (2005), http://www.ietf.org/internet-drafts/draft-ietf-idwg-idmef-xml-14.txt
2. Julisch, K.: Using Root Cause Analysis to Handle Intrusion Detection Alarms. PhD Thesis, University of Dortmund, Germany (2003)
3. Kruegel, C., Mutz, D., Robertson, W., Valeur, F.: Bayesian Event Classification for Intrusion Detection. In: 19th Annual Computer Security Applications Conference. IEEE Computer Society Press, New York (2003)
4. Kruegel, C., Valeur, F., Vigna, G.: Intrusion Detection and Correlation - Challenges and Solutions. In: Advances in Information Security, vol. 14. Springer, Heidelberg (2005)
5. Kruegel, C., Vigna, G., Robertson, W.: A Multi-Model Approach to the Detection of Web-Based Attacks. Computer Networks 48(5), 717–738 (2005)
6. Valdes, A., Skinner, K.: Adaptive, Model-Based Monitoring for Cyber Attack Detection. In: 3rd International Symposium on Recent Advances in Intrusion Detection, pp. 80–92. Springer, Heidelberg (2000)

Evading Anomaly Detection through Variance Injection Attacks on PCA

(Extended Abstract)

Benjamin I.P. Rubinstein[1], Blaine Nelson[1], Ling Huang[2],
Anthony D. Joseph[1,2], Shing-hon Lau[1], Nina Taft[2], and J. D. Tygar[1]

[1] UC Berkeley
{benr,nelsonb,adj}@cs.berkeley.edu, mrvulcanpaypal@gmail.com
[2] Intel Research, Berkeley
hling@cs.berkeley.edu, nina.taft@intel.com

Abstract. Whenever machine learning is applied to security problems, it is important to measure vulnerabilities to adversaries who poison the training data. We demonstrate the impact of variance injection schemes on PCA-based network-wide volume anomaly detectors, when a single compromised PoP injects chaff into the network. These schemes can increase the chance of evading detection by sixfold, for DoS attacks.

1 Motivation and Problem Statement

We are broadly interested in understanding vulnerabilities associated with using machine learning in decision-making, specifically how adversaries with even limited information and control over the learner can subvert the decision-making process [1]. An important example is the role played by machine learning in dynamic network anomography, the problem of inferring network-level Origin-Destination (OD) flow anomalies from aggregate network measurements. We ask, can an adversary generate OD flow traffic that misleads network anomography techniques into misclassifying anomalous flows? We show the answer is yes for a popular technique based on Principal Components Analysis (PCA) from [2].

The detector operates on the $T \times N$ link traffic matrix $\mathbf{Y}$, formed by measuring N link volumes between PoPs in a backbone network, over T time intervals. Figure 1 depicts an example OD flow within a PoP-to-PoP topology. Lakhina et al. observed that the rows of the normal traffic in $\mathbf{Y}$ lie close to a low-dimensional subspace captured by PCA using $K = 4$ principal components. Their detection method involves projecting the traffic onto this normal K-dimensional subspace; large (small) residuals, as compared with the Q-statistic, are called *positive* anomalies (*negative* normal traffic).

2 Results and Future Work

Consider an adversary launching a DoS attack on flow f in week w. Poisoning aims to rotate PCA's K-dimensional subspace so that a false negative (FN) occurs during the attack. Our *Week-Long* schemes achieve this goal by adding high variance chaff at the compromised origin PoP, along f, throughout week $w - 1$.

R. Lippmann, E. Kirda, and A. Trachtenberg (Eds.): RAID 2008, LNCS 5230, pp. 394–395, 2008.

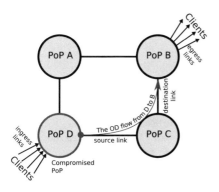

FNR vs. Relative Link Traffic Increase

Fig. 1. Point-of-presence (PoP)-level granularity in a backbone network, and the links used for data poisoning

Fig. 2. *Week-Long* attacks: test FNRs are plot against the relative increase to the mean link volumes for the attacked flow

Figure 2 presents results for two chaff methods. Both methods add chaff c_t to each link in f at time t, depending on parameter θ: *Scaled Bernoulli* selects c_t uniformly from $\{0, \theta\}$; *Add-More-If-Bigger* adds $c_t = (y_o(t) - \overline{y_o})^\theta$ where $y_o(t)$ and $\overline{y_o}$ are the week $w - 1$ origin link traffic at time t and average origin link traffic, respectively. We evaluated these methods on data from Abilene's backbone network of 12 PoPs. For each week 2016 measurements were taken, each averaged over 5 minute intervals, for each of 54 virtual links—15 bi-directional inter-PoP links and the PoPs' ingress & egress links.

The attacker's chance of evasion is measured by the FN rate (FNR). We see that the *Add-More-If-Bigger* chaff method, which exploits information about origin link traffic, achieves greater FNR increases compared to *Scaled Bernoulli*. The baseline FNR of 4% for PCA on clean data, can be doubled by adding on average only 4% additional traffic to the links along the poisoned flow. The FNR can be increased sixfold to 24% via an average increase of 10% to the poisoned link traffic. In our *Boiling Frog* strategies, where poisoning is increased slowly over several weeks, a 50% chance of successful evasion can be achieved with a modest 5% volume increase from week-to-week over a 3 week period [3].

We have verified that simply increasing the number of principal components is not useful in protecting against our attacks [3]. In future work we will evaluate counter-measures based on Robust formulations of PCA, and will devise poisoning strategies for increasing PCA's false positive rate.

References

1. Barreno, M., Nelson, B., Joseph, A.D., Tygar, J.D.: The security of machine learning. Technical Report UCB/EECS-2008-43, UC Berkeley (April 2008)
2. Lakhina, A., Crovella, M., Diot, C.: Diagnosing network-wide traffic anomalies. In: Proc. SIGCOMM 2004, pp. 219–230 (2004)
3. Rubinstein, B.I.P., Nelson, B., Huang, L., Joseph, A.D., Lau, S., Taft, N., Tygar, J.D.: Compromising PCA-based anomaly detectors for network-wide traffic. Technical report UCB/EECS-2008-73, UC Berkeley (May 2008)

Anticipating Hidden Text Salting in Emails
(Extended Abstract)

Christina Lioma[1], Marie-Francine Moens[1], Juan-Carlos Gomez[1],
Jan De Beer[1,*], Andre Bergholz[2], Gerhard Paass[2], and Patrick Horkan[3]

[1] Katholieke Universiteit Leuven, Belgium
{christina.lioma,sien.moens,juancarlos.gomez}@cs.kuleuven.be,
jan.debeer@be.ibm.com
[2] Fraunhofer IAIS, Germany
{andre.bergholz,gerhard.paass}@ais.fraunhofer.de
[3] Symantec, Ireland
patrick_horkan@symantec.com

Abstract. Salting is the intentional addition or distortion of content,
aimed to evade automatic filtering. Salting is usually found in spam
emails. Salting can also be hidden in phishing emails, which aim to steal
personal information from users. We present a novel method that detects
hidden salting tricks as visual anomalies in text. We solely use these salting tricks to successfully classify emails as phishing (F-measure >90%).

1 Introduction

Given a text and a user who reads this text, *hidden text salting* is any modification of text content that cannot be seen by the user, e.g., text written in
invisible colour, or in zero font size. Hidden text salting can be applied to any
medium and content genre, e.g. emails or MMS messages, and can be common in
fraudulent *phishing* emails [3]. We present a novel method for detecting hidden
text salting and using it to recognise phishing emails.

Related research has focused on filtering email spam. Early spam filters used
human-coded ad-hoc rules, often optimized by machine learning, e.g. spamassassin. Such filters were easy to fool, hard to maintain, and outperformed by filters
using visual features, e.g. embedded text in images [4]. Recently, statistical data
compression has been used to build separate models for compressed ham and
spam, and then classify emails according to which model they fit better when
compressed [2]. None of these studies addresses hidden salting directly.

2 Hidden Text Salting Detection

Given an email as input, a text production process, e.g. a Web browser, creates
an internal parsed representation of the email text and drives the rendering of
that representation onto some output medium, e.g. a browser window. We tap
into this rendering process to detect hidden content (= manifestations of salting).

---

* Jan De Beer is no longer at K.U.Leuven.

R. Lippmann, E. Kirda, and A. Trachtenberg (Eds.): RAID 2008, LNCS 5230, pp. 396–397, 2008.

Methodology. We intercept requests for drawing text primitives, and build an internal representation of the characters that appear on the screen. This representation is a list of attributed *glyphs* (positioned shapes of individual characters). Then, we test for *glyph visibility* (are glyphs seen by the user?) according to these conditions: (1) *clipping:* glyph drawn within the bounds of the drawing clip, which is a type of 'spatial mask'; (2) *concealment:* glyph not concealed by other shapes; (3) *font colour:* glyph's colour contrasts with the background colour; (4) *glyph size:* large enough glyph size and shape. We compute a visibility score for each feature and consolidate their product into a single confidence score, parameterised by an empirically-tuned penalty factor. The lower the final glyph visibility score, the stronger the indication of hidden text salting.

Evaluation. We use the above salting tricks as features for classifying emails as ham or phishing in a real-life corpus that contains 16,364 ham and 3,636 phishing emails from 04/2007-11/2007. The corpus is protected by non-disclosure privacy-preserving terms. We use a standard Support Vector Machine (SVM) classifier with 10-fold cross validation. We obtain 96.46% precision, 86.26% recall, and 91.07% F-measure. The best classification feature, found in 86% of all phishing emails, is font colour. State-of-the-art phishing classification reaches F-measures of 97.6% (with random forests [3]) up to 99.4% (with SVMs [1]) when using known discriminative features, such as url length & longevity, HTML & Javascript information on the 2002-2003 spamassassin corpus & a public phishing corpus (these corpora are described in [3]). We use **only salting features**. If we also combine these known discriminative features, performance may improve.

3   Conclusions

We detect hidden text salting in emails as hidden visual anomalies in text, unlike existing methods which target spam in general. We show that hidden text salting is used in phishing emails, and that phishing emails can be identified based on hidden text salting features alone. Our method can be used as improved content representation in filtering, retrieval or mining.

Acknowledgments. Partly funded by project EU-FP6-IST-027600-ANTI-PHISH.

References

1. Bergholz, A., Paass, G., Reichartz, F., Strobel, S., Chang, J.-H.: Improved phishing detection using model-based features. In: Conf. on Email and Anti-Spam (CEAS) (2008)
2. Bratko, A., Cormack, G., Filipic, B., Lynam, T., Zupan, B.: Spam filtering using statistical data compression models. J. of Mach. Learn. Res. 7, 2673–2698 (2006)
3. Fette, I., Sadeh, N., Tomasic, A.: Learning to detect phishing emails. In: International World Wide Web Conference (WWW), pp. 649–656 (2007)
4. Fumera, G., Pillai, I., Roli, F.: Spam filtering based on the analysis of text information embedded into images. J. of Mach. Learn. Res. 7, 2699–2720 (2006)
5. Kirda, E., Kruegel, C.: Protecting users against phishing attacks. The Computer Journal 49(5), 554–561 (2006)

Improving Anomaly Detection Error Rate by Collective Trust Modeling

(Extended Abstract)

Martin Rehák[1], Michal Pěchouček[1], Karel Bartoš[2,1], Martin Grill[2,1],
Pavel Čeleda[3], and Vojtěch Krmíček[3]

[1] Department of Cybernetics, Czech Technical University in Prague
mrehak@labe.felk.cvut.cz, pechouc@labe.felk.cvut.cz
[2] CESNET, z. s. p. o.
bartosk@labe.felk.cvut.cz, grillm@labe.felk.cvut.cz
[3] Institute of Computer Science, Masaryk University
celeda@ics.muni.cz, vojtec@ics.muni.cz

Abstract. Current Network Behavior Analysis (NBA) techniques are based on anomaly detection principles and therefore subject to high error rates. We propose a mechanism that deploys trust modeling, a technique for cooperator modeling from the multi-agent research, to improve the quality of NBA results. Our system is designed as a set of agents, each of them based on an existing anomaly detection algorithm coupled with a trust model based on the same traffic representation. These agents minimize the error rate by unsupervised, multi-layer integration of traffic classification. The system has been evaluated on real traffic in Czech academic networks.[1]

Network Behavior Analysis attempts to detect the attacks against computer systems by analyzing the network traffic (flow/session) statistics. We present a mechanism that efficiently combines several anomaly detection algorithms in order to significantly reduce their error rate, especially in terms of false positives. The mechanism is based on **extended trust modeling**, a method from the multi-agent field [1], which generalizes traditional trust modeling by introduction of generalized identities and situation representation. The traditional trust models are principally used to identify dishonest partners engaged in repetitive interactions, such as supply chain management.

Traditionally, the alerts from multiple sources are grouped to improve the quality of classification and reduce the number of events presented to the user [2]. Other approaches concentrate on the improvement of several distinct intrusion detection methods, differentiated by the set of traffic features these methods work on [3]. In our work [4], we extend the latter by introducing the collective extended trust modeling as a supplementary layer which further improves the quality of classification.

The system (Fig. 1) receives the flow data in batches, typically covering between 2-5 minutes of network traffic. The data is processed by several anomaly

[1] This material is based upon work supported by the International Technology Center - Atlantic of the US Army under Contract No. W911NF-08-1-0250. Also supported by Czech Min. of Education grants 6840770038 (CTU) and 6383917201 (CESNET).

R. Lippmann, E. Kirda, and A. Trachtenberg (Eds.): RAID 2008, LNCS 5230, pp. 398–399, 2008.
© Springer-Verlag Berlin Heidelberg 2008

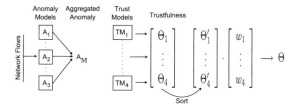

Fig. 1. Detection process overview

detection algorithms, and each algorithm determines an **anomaly value** for each of the flows. The anomaly value is a real number in the $[0, 1]$ interval, with the values close to 0 corresponding to normal flows and the values around 1 being reserved for anomalous flows.

The anomalies provided by individual anomaly detectors are averaged to obtain a single **joint anomaly** for each flows. At this stage, our algorithm differentiates from the existing approaches by introducing another processing layer, based on extended trust modeling. Flow description and joint anomaly value is processed by several trust models. Each of these models represents the flows in a distinct feature space, aggregates them into clusters, and assigns **trustfulness** to these clusters. The trustfulness of the cluster (again in the $[0, 1]$ interval) is aggregated from the joint anomaly of the flows (from all past data sets) that were previously assigned to the cluster.

The system than uses the trustfulness provided for each flow (aggregated from the trustfulness of the close clusters) as its output. Use of trustfulness in lieu of single-file dependent anomaly, together with the order-weighted combination of the results between the models, filters most of the false positives, and significantly reduces the error rate of the mechanism.

We validate [4] our technique on the NetFlow data from the university network (with botnet/P2P traffic, buffer overflow attempts) and empirically show that its use successfully reduces the rate of false positives, while not impacting the false negatives ratio. The false positives are reduced by the factor of 10-20 when compared to the individual anomaly detection methods, and by the factor of 2-4 when compared to joint anomalies.

References

1. Rehak, M., Pechoucek, M.: Trust modeling with context representation and generalized identities. In: Klusch, M., Hindriks, K.V., Papazoglou, M.P., Sterling, L. (eds.) CIA 2007. LNCS (LNAI), vol. 4676, pp. 298–312. Springer, Heidelberg (2007)
2. Valeur, F., Vigna, G., Kruegel, C., Kemmerer, R.A.: A comprehensive approach to intrusion detection alert correlation. IEEE Transactions on Dependable and Secure Computing 01, 146–169 (2004)
3. Giacinto, G., Perdisci, R., Rio, M.D., Roli, F.: Intrusion detection in computer networks by a modular ensemble of one-class classifiers. Information Fusion 9, 69–82 (2008)
4. Rehak, M., Pechoucek, M., Grill, M., Bartos, K.: Trust-based classifier combination for network anomaly detection. In: Cooperative Information Agents XII. LNCS(LNAI), Springer, Heidelberg (to appear, 2008)

Database Intrusion Detection and Response
(Extended Abstract)*

Ashish Kamra and Elisa Bertino

Purdue University
akamra@ecn.purdue.edu, bertino@cs.purdue.edu

Why is it important to have an intrusion detection (ID) mechanism tailored for a database management system (DBMS)? There are three main reasons for this. First, actions deemed malicious for a DBMS are not necessarily malicious for the underlying operating system or the network; thus ID systems designed for the latter may not be effective against database attacks. Second, organizations have stepped up data vigilance driven by various government regulations concerning data management such as SOX, GLBA, HIPAA and so forth. Third, and this is probably the most relevant reason, the problem of *insider threats* is being recognized as a major security threat; its solution requires among other techniques the adoption of mechanisms able to detect access anomalies by users internal to the organization owning the data.

Our approach to an ID mechanism tailored for a DBMS consists of two main elements: an anomaly detection (AD) system and an anomaly response system. We have developed algorithms for detecting anomalous user/role accesses to a DBMS [2]. Our approach considers *two* different scenarios. In the first scenario, it is assumed that the DBMS has a Role Based Access Control (RBAC) model in place. Our AD system is able to determine role intruders, that is, individuals that while holding a specific role, behave differently than expected. The problem in this case is treated as a supervised learning problem. The roles are used as classes for the classification purpose. For every user request under observation, its role is predicted by a classifier. If the predicted role is different from the role associated with the query, an anomaly is detected. In the second case, the same problem is addressed in the context of a DBMS without any role definitions. In such setting, every request is associated with the user that issued it. We build user-group profiles based on the SQL commands users submit to the database. The specific methodology used for anomaly detection is as follows. The training data is partitioned into clusters using standard clustering techniques. A mapping is maintained for every user to its representative cluster (RC). For a new query under observation, its RC is determined by examining the user-cluster mapping. For the detection phase, two different approaches are followed. In the first approach, the classifier is applied in a manner similar to the supervised case with the RCs as classes. In the second approach, a statistical test is used to identify if the query is an outlier in its RC. If the result of the statistical test is positive, the query is marked as an anomaly.

---

* The work reported here has been partially supported by the NSF grant 0712846 "IPS: Security Services for Healthcare Applications".

R. Lippmann, E. Kirda, and A. Trachtenberg (Eds.): RAID 2008, LNCS 5230, pp. 400–401, 2008.

In order to build profiles, the log-file entries need to be pre-processed and converted into a format that can be analyzed by the detection algorithms. Therefore, each entry in the log file is represented by a basic data unit that contains five fields, and thus it is called a *quiplet*. The abstract form of a quiplet consists of five fields (*SQL Command, Projection Relation Information, Projection Attribute Information, Selection Relation Information and Selection Attribute Information*). Depending on the level of details required, the quiplets are captured from the log file entries using *three* different representation levels. Each level is characterized by a different amount of recorded information. For details, we refer the reader to [2]. Our approach towards a DBMS specific AD mechanism has several advantages. By modeling the access patterns of users based on the SQL command syntax, the insider threat scenario is directly addressed. Our approach is able to capture users/roles that access relations not conforming to their normal access pattern. Second, the three different granularity levels of representation proposed in the scheme offer alternatives for space/time/accuracy overhead. Third, the profiles themselves can be used by the security administrators to refine existing access control policies of the DBMS or define new ones.

The second element of our approach addresses a common shortcoming of all other DBMS-specific ID mechanisms, that is, a limited number of possible anomaly response options. In all such mechanisms, the response is either *aggressive*, thus dropping the malicious request, or *conservative*, thus simply raising an alarm while letting the malicious request go through. So what more can a DBMS do to respond to a database access anomaly signaling a possible intrusion? Consider an AD system in place for a DBMS. AD systems are useful for detecting novel zero-day attacks, but they are also notorious for generating a large number of false alarms. Taking an aggressive action on every alarm can result in potential denial of service to legitimate requests, while only logging the alarms will nullify the advantages of the AD mechanism. We address these problems using a two-pronged approach [1]. First we propose the notion of *database response policies* that specify appropriate response actions depending on the details of the anomalous request. Second we propose more fine-grain response actions by introducing the concept of *privilege states* in the access control system. For example, as we discuss in [1], the privilege corresponding to an anomalous action may be moved into a *suspended* state until a remedial action, such as a 2nd-factor authentication, is executed by the user. We have implemented a policy language and extended the PostgreSQL DBMS with an engine supporting the enforcement of the response policies. We have also extended the access control mechanism of PostgreSQL to support privilege states. Initial performance evaluation shows that our approach is very efficient.

References

1. Kamra, A., Bertino, E., Nehme, R.: Responding to anomalous database requests. In: Proceedings of Secure Data Management (SDM) (to appear, 2008)
2. Kamra, A., Bertino, E., Terzi, E.: Detecting anomalous access patterns in relational databases. VLDB Journal (2008)

An Empirical Approach to Identify Information Misuse by Insiders
(Extended Abstract)

Deanna D. Caputo, Greg Stephens, Brad Stephenson, Megan Cormier,
and Minna Kim

The MITRE Corporation[*]
{dcaputo,gstephens,stephenson}@mitre.org

Abstract. Rogue employees with access to sensitive information can easily abuse their access to engage in information theft. To help differentiate malicious from benign behavior, this study measures how participants, given a common search topic, seek information. This study uses double-blind procedures, a stratified sample, and carefully designed control and experimental conditions. We seek to validate previously identified network indicators (ELICIT), find new host-based behaviors, and consider other human attributes that affect the information-use of malicious insiders by comparing their behavior to equivalent non-malicious users.

Keywords: insider threat, detection, malicious users, misuse.

1 Introduction

Malicious insiders who abuse their privileges to steal valuable information remain largely invisible to current detection methods that rely on rule-breaking behavior. To effectively detect this misuse, one must observe how trusted insiders interact with information and differentiate innocuous from malicious patterns of information-use.

In prior work[1], we developed ELICIT, a network-based system designed to help analysts detect insiders who operate outside the scope of their duties but within their privileges. The current research uses the same approach, observing information-use and applying user and information context. This study will evaluate ELICIT's detectors across a different participant pool while adding host-based monitoring, and

[*] This material is based upon work supported by the U.S. Department of Homeland Security under Grant Award Number 2006-CS-001-000001, under the auspices of the Institute for Information Infrastructure Protection (I3P) research program. The I3P is managed by Dartmouth College. The views and conclusions contained in this document are those of the authors and should not be interpreted as necessarily representing the official policies, either expressed or implied, of the U.S. Department of Homeland Security, the I3P, or Dartmouth College.

[1] Maloof, M.A., and Stephens, G.D. "ELICIT: A system for detecting insiders who violate need-to-know." Recent Advances in Intrusion: 146-166.

R. Lippmann, E. Kirda, and A. Trachtenberg (Eds.): RAID 2008, LNCS 5230, pp. 402–403, 2008.
© Springer-Verlag Berlin Heidelberg 2008

considering baseline human behavior as well as individual differences in a controlled environment.

Envision a labyrinth where people enter the maze (an information landscape) at different locations (intentions) yet seek the same prize (information). Can one's path to the prize tell us where they started from? We hypothesize that the information gathering patterns of maliciously motivated users will differ in predictable ways from those of benignly motivated users. For example, malicious insiders may attempt to hide their bad behavior by interleaving it with separate innocuous information gathering sessions whereas benign users may focus on a single information gathering session.

2 Methods

There will be a minimum of 50 participants in this study. They will all be MITRE employees and the sample will be stratified by seniority in the company.

The experimental procedure is double-blind to guard against bias and placebo effects. Participants are randomly assigned to one of two conditions: Benign User (control) or Malicious User. Participants are recruited under the cover story that we are monitoring computer use while testing the latest anti-keylogging software. Deception is necessary so they are all unaware that we are studying insider threat behaviors. Participants complete a pre-questionnaire asking for biographical data and other behavioral questions of interest.

Each participant receives a study laptop running software that monitors their information-use behavior. They are randomly assigned one of two scenarios, based on their condition, explaining a role and task. Both conditions are tasked to search the MITRE intranet and deliver the most valuable information found, on an identical topic, onto a CD and are informed that it will be evaluated by subject matter experts (creating a performance demand). Each participant is given up to 10 hours to play the role and complete the task over a 7 day period. Participants complete a post-questionnaire about their experience, the role, the task, and other behaviors of interest.

The two scenarios were designed to be completely balanced, except for the experimental variable—*user intent*. Both roles describe a person who has fallen on hard financial times and must complete the task in order to improve their financial situation. In the benign condition, the person joins a high profile team and good performance on that team will lead to a promotion and pay increase. In the malicious condition, the person accepts a new, higher paying job. The offer is conditional on bringing inside information from his old employer that would provide the new employer a competitive advantage.

Monitoring is done using the network-based ELICIT sensors and the host-based product Verdasys' Digital Guardian. Together, the sensors monitor information-use events including file/directory reads, writes, moves, and deletes. They also monitor search engine queries, cut-and-pastes, application launches, and URLs visited. Events will be analyzed to measure statistical differences in information usage for each condition. We will apply previously determined ELICIT indicators where appropriate, and look for new behavior patterns in network and host activity. Participant responses to pre-/post-experiment questionnaires will be analyzed across conditions.

Page-Based Anomaly Detection in Large Scale Web Clusters Using Adaptive MapReduce (Extended Abstract)

Junsup Lee[1] and Sungdeok Cha[2]

[1] The Attached Institute of ETRI, Daejeon, Republic of Korea
jslee@dependable.kaist.ac.kr
[2] Department of CSE, Korea University, Seoul, 136-701, Republic of Korea
scha@korea.ac.kr

Abstract. While anomaly detection systems typically work on single server, most commercial web sites operate cluster environments, and user queries trigger transactions scattered through multiple servers. For this reason, anomaly detectors in a same server farm should communicate with each other to integrate their partial profile. In this paper, we describe a real-time distributed anomaly detection system that can deal with over one billion transactions per day. In our system, base on Google MapReduce algorithm, an anomaly detector in each node shares profiles of user behaviors and propagates intruder information to reduce false alarms. We evaluated our system using web log data from www.microsoft.com. The web log data, about 250GB in size, contains over one billion transactions recorded in a day.

Anomaly detection systems are often considered impractical solutions because of two major limitations. One is a difficulty of collaboration among anomaly detectors from web servers. The other limitation is real-time consideration. Existing systems fail to deliver real-time performance and often require expensive computational cost during training and evaluation. Conventional ADSs implicitly assume that all activities related to an event have been completed before the event may be inspected. To satisfy such assumption, the systems usually have timing windows to ensure that an event is not inspected until complete information is available. Consequently, the systems fail to satisfy real-time constraints.

To overcome these issues, we developed a page-based anomaly detection system (PADS). The PADS keeps track of access patterns on each service object such as web page and generate models per pages. In this page-profile based ADS, compare with other user-based ADS, timing windows are unnecessary during operation. An anomaly detector in each node, base on Google MapReduce algorithm [1], shares self-learned profiles and propagates intruder information to reduce false alarms.

The PADS architecture employs a combination of self-learning and profile-based anomaly detection techniques. Self-learning methodology enables the PADS to study the usage and traffic patterns of web service objects over time. In

R. Lippmann, E. Kirda, and A. Trachtenberg (Eds.): RAID 2008, LNCS 5230, pp. 404–405, 2008.
© Springer-Verlag Berlin Heidelberg 2008

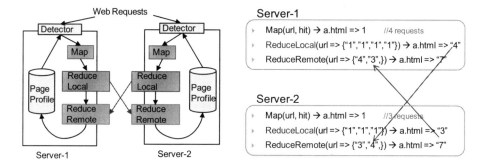

Fig. 1. Overview of PADS, Example of MapReduce in PADS (Page hit)

our model, profiles that summarize statistical features (such as exchanged bytes, query related behavior and HTTP traffic features using Chebyshev inequality, relative frequency and clustering method) per web service objects (e.q., html, asp, aspx, mspx and so on). Because popular web sites do experience legitimate and sometimes unexpected surge on particular web pages, the PADS automatically specifies access thresholds per web pages to understand unusual patterns that may occur during legitimate web query operations.

To keep pace with the latest usage and traffic pattern per web pages, each PADS node in a server farm propagates the profiles to other nodes using adaptive MapReduce technique[2]. We redesigned the technique which aware memory and network traffic. Using MapReduce algorithm, user requests are summarized into page profiles and share with other server simultaneously (Fig 1). According to our experiment on Microsoft web log data, the PADS only generate 4.44% of network traffic compare with sharing all requests among servers. In a half hour, a server receives 0.42 million requests on average. In the meantime, only 7.2 thousand page profiles are produced by LocalReduce. While total size of these profiles is 3.6MB, all requests are 81MB relatively.

In our system, each web page profile is generated dynamically by the system initially and subsequently updated and shared with other servers in real time by Google MapReduce algorithm. Currently, we are evaluating PADS using a web log data from 'www.microsoft.com'. While every web servers maintain same latest web page profiles which is about million, communication overhead between nodes is dramatically low.

References

1. Dean, J., Ghemawat, S.: Mapreduce: Simplified data processing on large clusters. Operating Systems Design and Implementation, 137–149 (2004)
2. Ranger, C., Raghuraman, R., Penmetsa, A., Bradski, G., Kozyrakis, C.: Evaluating MapReduce for Multi-core and Multiprocessor Systems. In: Proceedings of the 13th Intl. Symposium on HPCA, Phoenix, AZ (February 2007)

Automating the Analysis of Honeypot Data
(Extended Abstract)

Olivier Thonnard[1], Jouni Viinikka[2], Corrado Leita[1], and Marc Dacier[3]

[1] Institut Eurecom
olivier.thonnard@rma.ac.be, Corrado.Leita@eurecom.fr
[2] France Telecom R&D
jouni.viinikka@orange-ftgroup.com
[3] Symantec Research Labs, France
dacier@eurecom.fr

Abstract. We describe the on-going work towards further automating the analysis of data generated by a large honeynet architecture called Leurre.com and SGNET. The underlying motivation is helping us to integrate the use of honeypot data into daily network security monitoring. We propose a system based on two automated steps: *i)* the detection of relevant attack events within a large honeynet traffic data set, and *ii)* the extraction of highly similar events based on temporal correlation.

Keywords: Honeypots, Internet threats analysis, malicious behavior characterization.

1 Introduction

We look to identify and characterize certain large-scale phenomena that are active on the Internet by detecting similarities across network attack traces in an automated manner. The analyzed data is extracted from datasets collected through Leurre.com [4] and SGNET honeypot deployments [5]. By automating our analysis, it should help us to integrate the use of honeypot data into daily network security monitoring. To achieve this we need to identify relevant periods of activity on the sensors shortly after they occurred. These periods of activity are analyzed to detect temporal and spatial similarities within the observed attack processes.

In [2] the authors highlighted the usefulness of analyzing temporal correlations between different attacks collected through a honeynet, e.g. to highlight synchronized attack patterns which are part of a very same phenomenon, or to discover stealthier attack phenomena related to botnet propagation schemes or "multi-headed" attack tools [3].

Once groups of similar attack events are revealed, we can perform a more in-depth analysis of those specific groups so as to characterize them with respect to other relevant attack features, e.g. by analyzing the spatial and temporal characteristics of the attackers, or by looking at other meta-information obtained from the SGNET sensors, such as shellcode or malware characteristics when the attacks have led to a successful upload of shellcode commands and malicious binaries.

Thanks to the extensive characterization of those similar attack events, we seek to discover other types of similarities across attack events, even when they occurred at different periods of time. As a result, this process should facilitate the identification of possible root causes for new attack phenomena. The characterization and correlation steps may currently require some manual or semi-automated work.

R. Lippmann, E. Kirda, and A. Trachtenberg (Eds.): RAID 2008, LNCS 5230, pp. 406–407, 2008.

2   Analysis Process

The main idea of our ongoing effort consists to automatically i) detect relevant attack events within a large honeynet traffic data set shortly after it has been collected, and ii) group highly similar temporal events by relying on *clique* algorithms and appropriate similarity metrics.

We propose to use in step i) an approach based on non-stationary autoregressive (NAR) modeling using Kalman fixed-lag smoothers [1] and in step ii) we use clique algorithms described in [2,6].

The strengths of the detection algorithm are its capability to flag the beginnings of activity periods and isolated activity peaks. Our initial results show that the algorithm is effective when applied to the three different types of time series identified in [2], i.e. ephemeral spikes, sustained bursts and continous patterns. The shortcomings are related to detection of the end of an activity period, the association of the end to the beginning, and the risk of an activity peak begin masked by closely preceding peak. We look to improve these aspects of the detection algorithm.

Then, to correlate the identified attack events, we use an approach based on *maximal cliques* [6], which are able to group all events having important similarities in an unsupervised manner. The main advantage of this approach is that the number of groups (or cliques) does not need to be specified before executing the clustering, and many different feature vectors and similarity distances can be used transparently. We currently use two different techniques: *i)* the dominant sets approach developed by Pavan and Pelillo[7], and *ii)* the quality-based clustering developed in [2]. While the first approach provides a real approximation of the maximum clique problem (known to be NP-hard), the second approach is more pragmatic and is mainly focused on finding cliques having a high quality garantee with a low computational overhead. The choice of one or another clique algorithm depends on the intrinsic characteristics of the data set, as well as the *feature vectors* used in the data mining process.

References

1. Viinikka, J., Debar, H., Mé, L., Lehikoinen, A., Tarvainen, M.: Processing intrusion detection alert aggregates with time series modeling. Information Fusion Journal (2008); Special Issue on Computer Security (to appear)
2. Thonnard, O., Dacier, M.: A Framework for Attack Patterns Discovery in Honeynet Data. In: Digital Forensic Research Workshop (DFRWS) (2008)
3. Pouget, F., Urvoy-Keller, G., Dacier, M.: Time signatures to detect multi-headed stealthy attack tools. In: 18th Annual FIRST Conference, Baltimore, USA (2006)
4. The Leurre.com Project, http://www.leurrecom.org
5. Leita, C., Dacier, M.: SGNET: a worldwide deployable framework to support the analysis of malware threat models. In: Proceedings of EDCC 2008, 7th European Dependable Computing Conference, Kaunas, Lithuania, May 7-9 (2008)
6. Pouget, F., Dacier, M., Zimmerman, J., Clark, A., Mohay, G.: Internet attack knowledge discovery via clusters and cliques of attack traces. Journal of Information Assurance and Security 1(1) (March 2006)
7. Pavan, M., Pelillo, M.: A new graph-theoretic approach to clustering and segmentation. In: Proceedings of IEEE Conference on Computer Vision and Pattern Recognition (2003)

Anomaly and Specification Based Cognitive Approach for Mission-Level Detection and Response*

(Extended Abstract)

Paul Rubel[1], Partha Pal[1], Michael Atighetchi[1], D. Paul Benjamin[2], and Franklin Webber[1]

[1] BBN Technologies, Cambridge MA 21038, USA
prubel@bbn.com, ppal@bbn.com, matighet@bbn.com, franklin@eutaxy.net
[2] Pace University, 1 Pace Plaza, New York NY 10038, USA
benjamin@pace.edu

Abstract. In 2005 a survivable system we built was subjected to red-team evaluation. Analyzing, interpreting, and responding to the defense mechanism reports took a room of developers. In May 2008 we took part in another red-team exercise. During this exercise an autonomous reasoning engine took the place of the room of developers. Our reasoning engine uses anomaly and specification-based approaches to autonomously decide if system and mission availability is in jeopardy, and take necessary corrective actions. This extended abstract presents a brief summary of the reasoning capability we developed: how it categorizes the data into an internal representation and how it uses deductive and coherence based reasoning to decide whether a response is warranted.

1 The Basic Idea

Requiring experts to manage a system's defenses is an expensive undertaking, even assuming that such operators can be found. With faster CPUs, more RAM, faster and higher capacity networks we can transfer this tedious work to a reasoning engine. Our reasoning engine uses the mission concept (a model of how the system functions in a particular context) and sensor inputs, generated while the mission runs, to autonomously defend the system.

1.1 Challenges and Solution Approach

The main challenge is making sense of the low level observables reported by the survivability architecture in the context of the current system and mission, and then deciding what and when remedial actions should be taken. Additionally, we want the reasoning to accommodate new systems and missions.

At the center of our reasoning engine is a general reasoner, bracketed by system specific adapter logic. The input adapter takes alerts and turns them into **accusations**. The general reasoner then uses these accusations to make

---

* This research was funded by DARPA under Navy Contract No. N00178-07-C-2003.

R. Lippmann, E. Kirda, and A. Trachtenberg (Eds.): RAID 2008, LNCS 5230, pp. 408–410, 2008.

hypotheses and passes **claims** and hypotheses to the output adapter where they are evaluated in the mission context and may be acted upon.

Accusations are abstract alerts, expressive enough to enable a wide range of responses while not overwhelming the reasoner with unnecessary distinctions. Accusations come in five types: value (wrong data), omission, flood, timing (right message at the wrong time), and policy (not following a specification). From these accusations the reasoning engine generates four types of hypotheses, which are potential explanations of the accusation: dead host, corrupt host, flooded host, or communication is broken between hosts. A single accusation may create multiple hypotheses. For example, we assume that the sender may be corrupt so accusing a host of not sending a reply creates a dead hypotheses about the accused as well as a corrupt hypothesis about the accuser.

In order for a hypothesis to be acted upon, there needs to be sufficient support to turn that hypothesis into a claim. Claim selection relies upon four main techniques: deductive reasoning, coherence search[1], mission knowledge, and heuristic techniques. Deductive reasoning takes the current hypotheses and system knowledge and attempts to logically prove hypotheses. Coherence search takes multiple accusations, each supporting hypotheses, and aggregates the support. In this way a single source will likely not turn a hypothesis into a claim but a collection of accusations may. Mission knowledge is used to include or exclude some options. For example, if a host is corrupt but is critical to the mission a reboot may initially be preferred to permanently blocking its network traffic. Finally, we use heuristics to choose claims when the other techniques have failed to come up with any workable claims but yet actions still need to be taken.

2 Evaluation

In May of 2008 our system was subjected to an external red-team evaluation. One goal was to effectively respond to 50% of attacks. Preliminary results delivered immediately after the exercise showed 89% of the attacks were detected, and of those detected, 69% were responded to effectively. Additional analysis is ongoing.

3 Conclusion

Application of cognitive/knowledge based tools, especially in the area of specification and anomaly-based detection and response, at the mission level, is a promising way to extend the reach of current intrusion detection technology and enhance the overall accuracy of true detection. One issue, still left unresolved, is the needed speed of cognitive processing component. Our goal was to respond in 250ms. In some cases we achieved that target during evaluation, but in others our reasoning took multiple seconds, a problem which needs further refinement.

References

1. Freuder, E., Wallace, R.: Partial constraint satisfaction. Artificial Intelligence, special issue on constraint-based reasoning 58(1-3), 21–70 (1992)

Monitoring the Execution of Third-Party Software on Mobile Devices

(Extended Abstract)

Andrew Brown and Mark Ryan

School of Computer Science, University of Birmingham, UK. B15 2TT
{A.J.Brown, M.D.Ryan}@cs.bham.ac.uk

Abstract. The current security model for a third-party application running on a mobile device requires its user to trust that application's vendor and whilst mechanisms exist to mediate this relationship, they cannot guarantee complete protection against the threats posed. This work introduces a security architecture that prevents a third-party application deviating from its intended behaviour, defending devices against previously unseen malware more effectively than existing security measures.

In 2002, mobile device capabilities were expanded to permit users to install applications from sources other than the cellular network operator and they now mirror those of more traditional hosts. 2004 saw the first malware aimed at mobile devices hit and today over four hundred known entities exist. By 2009, it is estimated that 200 million "smart" mobile devices will be in operation, setting the scene for widespread malware infection.

Mobile device architectures commonly utilise code signing, discretionary access controls and signature-based anti-virus software to secure third-party software installations. Digitally signing code can confirm its author and guarantee that it has not been altered since it was signed, but does not guarantee the quality or security of code that the application will execute: determined attackers will go to many lengths to obtain a signature for their code. Access controls contribute to a systematic security framework, but are inflexible: default settings tend to leave the device vulnerable to numerous attacks and applying stricter controls impedes program functionality. Mobile anti-virus software can only detect *known* malware entities whose signatures exist in a virus dictionary and attack recovery simply deletes an application's executable files.

We propose an architecture for mediating third-party software that uses *execution monitors*, which operate in parallel (as a separate thread) with the target application in order to analyse and mitigate the events it invokes. This enables full regulation of the target's interaction with its host's resources, preventing and recovering from harmful behaviour in real-time. As most end-users do not have the technical capability to specify or deploy such monitors, we have developed ABML – a high-level policy language in which they can express *a priori* judgements about the type of application downloaded, which are translated by our compiler into a monitor specification. An ABML policy contains a set of rules which reason about temporally-ordered application events, sets of local

R. Lippmann, E. Kirda, and A. Trachtenberg (Eds.): RAID 2008, LNCS 5230, pp. 410–411, 2008.

and global variables, and can be categorised by the class of application it is applied to (e.g., an *editor*, a *browser*, a *game*, a *messenger*).

A policy is compiled into Java source code and then enforced on application bytecode by the Polymer [1] engine. This executes on the JVM and monitors calls the application makes to the Java ME and native device libraries (Fig. 1). Policy violations are recovered from by weaving a set of recovery events into application bytecode, which are derived from a rule at compile-time. Where a policy denies its triggering event, that event can be removed from the target's instruction stream and execution can continue. Our language is equipped with constructs that more precisely identify the context of an event, leading to more fine-grained application control. It can therefore mitigate some forms of information-

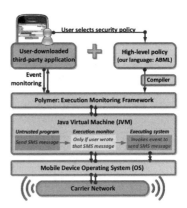

Fig. 1. System architecture

flow and ensure that only data which is not deemed sensitive is transmitted by the application to the device's carrier network. In addition, our architecture ensures that an attacker cannot write application code to bypass our security measures and control the operating system directly. Third-party applications can only gain access to native device functions whilst an ABML policy is being enforced on them.

We have proven this concept using the BlackBerry 8800-series mobile device, although our work is cross-platform (for it to work on other types of device, ABML's libraries are re-mapped to the APIs of the target platform). An example attack we recently studied allowed an application to intercept and forward SMS messages to an attacker and could occur despite that application being signed. Device access controls queried the user on the target's first attempt to send an SMS, but where the user agreed to this prompt, an SMS 'channel' to the attacker was created. Our countermeasure to this stated: *"the target may send an SMS message only if the data that message contains was entered manually by the user, and the recipient of that message exists as a contact in the user's personal information manager (PIM)"*. In order to enforce such a policy, a monitor must precisely identify the context in which the triggering event occurred: *was the data contained in that SMS message typed by the user? At some time after the entry of this data, did the user press "send" in reference to this message? and is that message to be sent to recipient in the device's PIM?* Where any of these conditions evaluates to false, the device's operating system never receives the command to send that SMS message and the application continues executing.

Reference

1. Bauer, L., Ligatti, J., Walker, D.: Composing security policies with Polymer. In: PLDI 2005: Proceedings of the 2005 ACM SIGPLAN conference on Programming language design and implementation, New York, USA, pp. 305–314 (2005)

Streaming Estimation of Information-Theoretic Metrics for Anomaly Detection* (Extended Abstract)

Sergey Bratus, Joshua Brody, David Kotz, and Anna Shubina

Institute for Security Technology Studies
Department of Computer Science, Dartmouth College, USA
sergey@cs.dartmouth.edu, jbrody@cs.dartmouth.edu,
dfk@cs.dartmouth.edu, ashubina@cs.dartmouth.edu

Abstract. Information-theoretic metrics hold great promise for modeling traffic and detecting anomalies if only they could be computed in an efficient, scalable way. Recent advances in streaming estimation algorithms give hope that such computations can be made practical. We describe our work in progress that aims to use streaming algorithms on 802.11a/b/g link layer (and above) features and feature pairs to detect anomalies.

Information-theoretic statistics applied to monitoring of network traffic can be useful in detecting changes in its character [7,5,4]. These metrics make few assumptions about what constitutes normal and abnormal traffic (e.g., [3]), and so should do well at adapting to traffic characteristics of specific networks, realizing the "home network advantage" of prior knowledge that defenders have over outside attackers.

However, necessary computations place a heavy load on both the sensor CPU and RAM. Thus, scalability of methods that rely on precise real-time computations of entropy and other related statistics remains a challenge. Luckily, a new class of streaming algorithms produce practically usable estimated results with much smaller requirements to CPU and RAM [6,2]. They have the potential to allow information-theoretic metrics to be scalably used in practice.

Several experimental systems (including Wi-Fi link layer anomaly detectors being developed at Dartmouth) apply entropy of pre-selected packet or session features to produce alerts. Such mechanisms rely on the idea that a change in the character of a feature distribution is suspicious. In our experience, watching a set of features as if they were independent is highly prone to false positives. A change in the entropy of a feature may be due to factors such as normal business day and other workflow cycles. Even the simplest cases of single protocol features require, e.g., some modeling of when a particular protocol is normally expected to be in use.

* This research program is a part of the Institute for Security Technology Studies, supported by Intel Corporation, NSF grant CCF-0448277, and by Award number NBCH2050002 from the U.S. Department of Homeland Security, Science and Technology Directorate. Points of view in this document are those of the authors and do not necessarily represent the official position of the U.S. Department of Homeland Security, Intel Corporation, or any other sponsor.

R. Lippmann, E. Kirda, and A. Trachtenberg (Eds.): RAID 2008, LNCS 5230, pp. 412–414, 2008.

Conditional entropy between pairs of features are likely to provide a better metric of normal use, because it relies on tracking the average "predictability" of one feature given the knowledge of another. Such relationships are more likely to persist through diurnal cycles, because they are less related to volumes of traffic.

Unusual use of protocol fields is characteristic of many exploits, but sophisticated attackers take pains to disguise it, as IDSes might be watching for it. It is much harder to disguise unusual payloads in such a way that does not introduce unusual statistical effects in pairs of protocol features. Note that rule-based IDS evasion techniques themselves (e.g., [8]) can produce just such effects.

Streaming estimation algorithms open up the possibility of a scalable sampling-based system that allows tracking of joint distributions, and thus of mutual information-type statistics. Furthermore, the sampling scheme used in the estimation algorithm can be adjusted dynamically depending on how much precision is meaningful and practicable for a particular network.

The 802.11a/b/g link layer is feature-rich and complex. Besides the frame type and subtype fields, the link layer header may contain one to four MAC address fields, eight bit flags, and two 16-bit fields, frame sequence number and duration (the distribution of which has been shown[1] to identify wireless chipset–driver combination as a distinctive fingerprint).

Thus this link layer allows a range of interesting attacks and related statistical distibution anomalies. We distinguish between the four levels of features, based on the sensor RAM and CPU requirements to follow them: (a) PHY layer errors as calculated and reported by the firmware, (b) frequency of basic events, such as observing deauthentication frames, (c) single header field values' frequency distributions, and (d) joint and conditional distributions of pairs of features. Anomalies in (a) may indicate inteference or jamming, and (b) frequency serves as good indicators of various DoS-type flooding and resource consumption attacks, whereas (c) and especially (d) expose other attacks that involve unusual headers and payloads.

References

1. Cache, J.: Fingerprinting 802.11 implementations via statistical analysis of the duration field. Uninformed Journal 5(1) (September 2006)
2. Chakrabarti, A., Cormode, G., McGregor, A.: A near-optimal algorithm for computing the entropy of a stream. In: SODA 2007: Proceedings of the eighteenth annual ACM-SIAM symposium on Discrete algorithms, pp. 328–335 (2007)
3. Gu, G., Fogla, P., Dagon, D., Lee, W., Skoric, B.: Towards an information-theoretic framework for analyzing intrusion detection systems. In: Gollmann, D., Meier, J., Sabelfeld, A. (eds.) ESORICS 2006. LNCS, vol. 4189, pp. 527–546. Springer, Heidelberg (2006)
4. Gu, Y., McCallum, A., Towsley, D.: Detecting anomalies in network traffic using maximum entropy estimation. In: IMC 2005: Proceedings of the 5th ACM SIG-COMM conference on Internet measurement, pp. 1–6 (2005)

5. Lakhina, A., Crovella, M , Diot, C.: Mining anomalies using traffic feature distributions. In: SIGCOMM 2005: Proceedings of the 2005 Conference on Computer Communication, pp. 217–228. ACM, New York (2005)
6. Lall, A., Sekar, V., Ogihara, M., Xu, J., Zhang, H.: Data streaming algorithms for estimating entropy of network traffic. SIGMETRICS Performance Evaluation Review 34(1), 145–156 (2006)
7. Lee, W., Xiang, D.: Information-theoretic measures for anomaly detection. In: Proc. of the 2001 IEEE Symposium on Security and Privacy, pp. 130–143 (2001)
8. Ptacek, T.H., Newsham, T.N.: Insertion, evasion, and denial of service: Eluding network intrusion detection, January 1998. Secure Networks, Inc. (1998)

Bots Behaviors vs. Human Behaviors on Large-Scale Communication Networks (Extended Abstract)

Wei Lu[1,2] and Ali A. Ghorbani[1]

[1] Faculty of Computer Science, University of New Brunswick, Fredericton,
NB Canada
[2] Department of Electrical and Computer Engineering, University of Victoria,
BC Canada
{wlu,ghorbani}@unb.ca

Abstract. In this paper we propose a hierarchical framework for detecting and characterizing any types of botnets on a large-scale WiFi ISP network. In particular, we first analyze and classify the network traffic into different applications by using payload signatures and the cross-associations for IP addresses and ports. Then based on specific application community (e.g. IRC, HTTP, or Peer-to-Peer), we present a novel temporal-frequent characteristic of flows that leads the differentiation of malicious behaviors created by bots from normal network traffic generated by human beings. We evaluate our approach with over 160 million flows collected over five consecutive days on a large-scale network and preliminary results show the proposed approach successfully detects the IRC botnet flows from over 160 million flows with a high detection rate and an acceptable low false alarm rate.

1 Problem Statement, State of the Art and Contributions

Detecting botnets behaviors on large-scale networks is a very challenging problem. This is because: (1) botnets are often hidden in existing applications, and thus their traffic volume is not that big and is very similar with normal traffic behaviors; (2) identifying network traffic into different applications becomes more challenging and is still an issue yet to be solved due to traffic content encryption and the unreliable destination port labeling method. The observation on a large-scale WiFi ISP network over a half year period showed that even exploring the flow content examination method, there are still about 40% network flows that cannot be classified into specific applications. Investigating such a huge number of unknown traffic is very important since they might stand for the abnormalities in the traffic, malicious behaviors or simply the identification of novel applications.

Current attempts on detecting botnets are mainly based on honeypots, passive anomaly analysis and traffic application classification. The anomaly analysis for detecting botnets on network traffic is usually independent of the traffic content and has the potential to find different types of botnets. However, anomaly

R. Lippmann, E. Kirda, and A. Trachtenberg (Eds.): RAID 2008, LNCS 5230, pp. 415–416, 2008.
© Springer-Verlag Berlin Heidelberg 2008

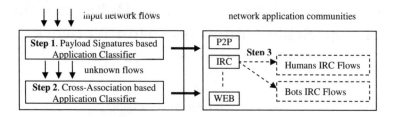

Fig. 1. The proposed hierarchical framework for botnets detection

detection tends to generate a large volume of false alarms traditionally when deployed on a large-scale communication network. The traffic application classification based botnets detection focuses on classifying traffic into IRC traffic and non-IRC traffic, offering a potential to reduce number of false alarms, but can detect IRC based botnets only.

In this paper, we focus on traffic classification based botnets detection. Instead of labeling and filtering traffic into non-IRC and IRC, we propose a hierarchical framework illustrated in Fig. 1 for discriminating malicious behaviors generated by any types of bots from normal behaviors generated by human beings. The major contributions of this work include: (1) a novel application discovery approach for classifying traffic into different network application communities (e.g. P2P, Chat, Web, etc.) on a large-scale WiFi ISP network, in which the input flows are first labeled through payload signatures (i.e. Step 1 of Fig.1) and unknown flows are then labeled through the cross-associations of IP addresses and port numbers (i.e. Step 2 of Fig.1); (2) a novel temporal-frequent metric based on N-gram (frequent characteristic) of flow payload over a time period (temporal characteristic) for discriminating bots behaviors from humans behaviors on a large-scale network (i.e. Step 3 of Fig.1).

2   Preliminary Evaluation Results and Conclusions

We implement a prototype system for the proposed hierarchical framework and then evaluate it on a large-scale WiFi ISP network over five consecutive business days. Our traffic classification approach can classify the unknown IRC flows into the IRC application community with a 100% classification rate on the five days evaluation. The detection rate for differentiating bots IRC traffic from normal human beings IRC traffic is 100% on four days testing, while an exception happens on the third day's testing on which our prototype obtained a 77.8% detection rate with a 3.1% false alarm rate. The best evaluation over the five days testing is a 100% detection rate with only 1.6% false alarm rate. Moreover, the preliminary evaluation results show that the average standard deviation of bytes frequency over the 256 ASCIIs on the flow payload is an important metric to indicate normal human IRC traffic and malicious IRC traffic generated by machine bots. In the near future, we will conduct an experimental evaluation with the web based botnets and new appeared P2P botnets.

Anomalous Taint Detection

(Extended Abstract)[*]

Lorenzo Cavallaro[1] and R. Sekar[2]

[1] Department of Computer Science, University of California at Santa Barbara, USA
sullivan@cs.ucsb.edu
[2] Department of Computer Science, Stony Brook University, USA
sekar@cs.sunysb.edu

Abstract. We propose *anomalous taint detection*, an approach that combines fine-grained taint tracking with learning-based anomaly detection. Anomaly detection is used to identify behavioral deviations that manifest when vulnerabilities are exercised. Fine-grained taint-tracking is used to target the anomaly detector on those aspects of program behavior that can be controlled by an attacker. Our preliminary results indicate that the combination increases detection accuracy over either technique, and promises to offer better resistance to mimicry attacks.

1 Introduction

A number of approaches have been developed for mitigating software vulnerabilities. Of these, learning-based anomaly detection has been popular among researchers due to its ability to detect novel attacks. Although the basic assumption behind anomaly detection, which states that attacks manifest unusual program behaviors, is true, the converse does not hold: unusual behaviors are not necessarily attacks. As a result, anomaly detection techniques generally suffer from a high rate of false positives, which impact their practical deployment.

Recently, fine-grained taint-tracking has become popular in software vulnerability defense. Its strength lies in its ability to reason about the degree of control exercised by an attacker on data values within the memory space of a vulnerable program. This enables the development of security policies that can, with high confidence, detect dangerous uses of such "tainted" data in security-critical operations. This technique is capable of defeating a wide range of attacks, including code injection, command injection and cross-site scripting[1]. Its main drawback is the requirement for manual policy development, which can be hard for some classes of attacks, e.g., non-control data attacks[2] and directory traversals.

We propose a new taint-based approach in this paper that avoids the need for policies by leveraging an anomaly detector. By targeting the anomaly detector on tainted data

---

[*] This research was supported in part by an NSF grant CNS-0627687, and performed while the first author was a PhD student from Università degli Studi di Milano, Italy visiting Stony Brook University.

[1] See, for instance, XU, BHATKAR and SEKAR, *"Taint-enhanced Policy Enforcement: a Practical Approach to Defeat a Wide Range of Attacks,"* USENIX Security Symposium, 2006.

[2] These attacks corrupt security-critical data without subverting control-flow. Chen *et al.* (*"Non-Control-Data Attacks Are Realistic Threats,"* USENIX Security Symposium, 2005) showed that they can achieve the same results as code injection attacks, while evading many code injection defenses.

R. Lippmann, E. Kirda, and A. Trachtenberg (Eds.): RAID 2008, LNCS 5230, pp. 417–418, 2008.

and/or events, our approach can avoid a large fraction of false positives that occur due to benign anomalies, i.e., behavioral deviations that are not under the attacker's control.

2 Anomalous Taint Detection

Our starting point is a system-call based program behavior model, e.g., the one used by Forrest *et al.* ("A Sense of Self for Unix Processes," IEEE Security and Privacy '96). We enhance this model with information about system call arguments and taint. As in Bhatkar *et al.* ("Dataflow Anomaly Detection," IEEE Security and Privacy '06), this learning technique leverages the control-flow context provided by system-call models.

Our technique learns information about system calls (or other interesting functions) and their arguments at multiple granularity. At a coarse granularity, it learns whether an event's argument is tainted. At a finer granularity, it learns whether structure fields (or array elements) are tainted. Furthermore, we also generate application-specific taint-enhanced profiles, such as expected maximum and minimum argument lengths, structural inference with character class mapping, and longest common prefix models.

We briefly illustrate our technique[3] using a format-string vulnerability existing in the WU-FTPD program. This program elevates its privileges temporarily, and then uses the following code snippet to revert its privilege to that of a normal user. Chen *et al.* demonstrated a non-control data attack that overwrites pw->pw_uid field with zero. As a result, the server does not revert to user privilege.

```
1    FILE *getdatasock(...) {
2        ...
3        seteuid(0);
4        setsockopt(...);
5        ...
6        seteuid(pw->pw_uid);
7        ...
8    }
```

Our approach can detect this attacks in two ways. First, the attack causes this seteuid's argument to be tainted, whereas the argument is untainted under normal operation. Second, the attack causes deviations in the structure of a (tainted) argument to a printf-like function. While the latter method is tied to the specifics of the underlying vulnerability, the former technique is able to detect the effect of corruptions that may be caused by other vulnerabilities as well.

By leveraging on taint information, our approach is less vulnerable to mimicry-like attacks than, for instance, a learning-based anomaly detection approach which relies *only* on statistical properties of the observed data, e.g., Mutz *et al.* ("Anomalous System Call Detection," ACM TISSEC 2006). With a purely learning-based approach, if a limited number of authenticated users were observed during training, then a mimicry attack would be possible that may allow an attacker to impersonate any one of these users.

We have been able to detect other non-control data attacks described by Chen *et al.* using models that reason about the structure and/or lengths of tainted arguments. Our future work is aimed at (a) extending the technique to work on other attack types that require application-specific taint policies (e.g., directory traversals), and (b) deriving taint policies from the taint-enhanced behavioral models that can provide the basis for preventing (rather than just detecting) exploits.

---

[3] Additional details can be found in CAVALLARO AND SEKAR, *"Anomalous Taint Detection"*, Tech Report SECLAB08-06 at http://seclab.cs.sunysb.edu/pubs.html.

Deep Packet Inspection Using Message Passing Networks
(Extended Abstract)

Divya Jain, K Vasanta Lakshmi, and Priti Shankar

Indian Institute of Science
divya@csa.iisc.ernet.in, kvasanta@csa.iisc.ernet.in,
priti@csa.iisc.ernet.in

Abstract. We propose a solution based on message passing bipartite networks, for deep packet inspection, which addresses both speed and memory issues, which are limiting factors in current solutions. We report on a preliminary implementation and propose a parallel architecture.

1 The Problem, Our Solution and Results

Packet content scanning at high speed is crucial to network security and network monitoring applications. In these applications, the packet payload is matched against a given set of patterns specified as regular expressions to identify specific classes of applications, viruses, protocol definitions, etc. Unfortunately, the speed requirement cannot be met in many existing NFA based payload scanning implementations because of the inefficiency in regular expression matching. Deterministic finite automata (DFAs) for certain regular expression types suffer from state blow up limiting their practical implementation. To solve the problem of state blow up we propose the following two part process.

1. In the first step the regular expressions are divided into subexpressions and these subexpressions of all regular expressions are then categorized into "sub expression modules" depending on their type. These modules are essentially scanners that run on the input and return the positions where the subparts occur in the input. Every regular expression is composed of one of constant strings, closures, length restrictions , a class of characters , a query or a combination of these. Thus the regular expression can be broken down into these components and all components of same type can be combined into a single module. For example all constant strings occurring in all regular expressions will be in one module with a single DFA scanning for constant strings in the input. Many of these components especially closures and length restriction are common to several regular expressions and thus running a single DFA for all of them is beneficial.

2. In the second step we construct *pattern modules* for each regular expression, which collect events consisting of subexpression matches along with matching positions (each such pair termed as an event) generated by the sub expression modules in the first step and string them together to find a match for the actual regular expression. Each such pattern module is modeled as a *timed automaton*. Each subexpression knows which pattern messages it needs to send messages to

R. Lippmann, E. Kirda, and A. Trachtenberg (Eds.): RAID 2008, LNCS 5230, pp. 419–420, 2008.
© Springer-Verlag Berlin Heidelberg 2008

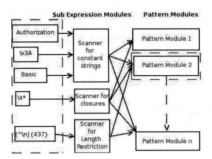

Fig. 1. Fragmenting RE 'Authorization\s*\x3A\s*Basic\s*[^ \n]{437}'

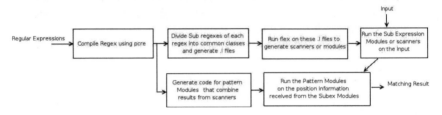

Fig. 2. Block Diagram of our solution

so each timed automaton gets only events of potential interest to it. In a timed automaton each symbol represents a timed event, namely a sub expression of the regular expression along with its "time" or position in the input stream, transitions being based on such events. The timed automaton is triggered when the first subexpression of the regular expression is found in a position buffer maintained for logging these events. The pattern modules are independent of each other and hence can be run in parallel in a hardware setup or on a parallel machine. Currently there is one pattern module per regular expression. As the number of regular expressions is large, in future, we plan to combine multiple regular expressions into single pattern modules based on the subexpressions they share. As a trial setup we have run the implementation for a selected set of 32 regular expressions from more than four thousand such rules that make up SNORT PCRE rulesets. The flex generated scanners are in C and the rest has been implemented in C++. The expressions chosen cover almost all types of regular expressions. The number of states for the traditional DFA for each of the 32 regular expressions ranges from 30 to almost 2^{400} where 400 is the length restriction in one of the expressions. The total number of NFA states for these regular expressions is 11924. In our solution, the total number of states for all DFAs in the sub expression modules is just equal to 533. The number of states in the pattern modules is equal to total sub expressions which is 300. This solution appears scalable though proper parallel communication protocols and a fast simulation of a timed automaton are critical for efficient functioning. We plan to do the simulation of the parallel implementation on the Blue Gene-L machine and later will examine hardware implementations.

System Call API Obfuscation
(Extended Abstract)

Abhinav Srivastava[1], Andrea Lanzi[1,2], and Jonathon Giffin[1]

[1]School of Computer Science, Georgia Institute of Technology, USA
[2]Dipartimento di Informatica e Comunicazione, Università degli Studi di Milano, Italy
{abhinav,giffin}@cc.gatech.edu, andrew@security.dico.unimi.it

Abstract. We claim that attacks can evade the comprehension of security tools that rely on knowledge of standard system call interfaces to reason about process execution behavior. Our attack, called *Illusion*, will invoke privileged operations in a Windows or Linux kernel at the request of user-level processes without requiring those processes to call the actual system calls corresponding to the operations. The Illusion interface will hide system operations from user-, kernel-, and hypervisor-level monitors mediating the conventional system-call interface. Illusion will alter neither static kernel code nor read-only dispatch tables, remaining elusive from tools protecting kernel memory.

1 Illusion Attack

Honeypots and other utilities designed to audit, understand, classify, and detect malware and software attacks often monitor process' behavior at the system call interface as part of their approach. Past research has developed a widespread collection of system-call based systems operating at user or kernel level [1,5,2,4] and at hypervisor level [3]. Employing reference monitors at the system call interface makes intuitive sense: absent flaws in the operating system (OS) kernel, it a non-bypassable interface, so malicious code intending to unsafely alter the system will reveal its behavior through the series of system calls that it invokes.

Current malware increasingly makes use of kernel modules or drivers that help the user-level process perform malicious activities by hiding the process' side effects. For example, the rootkits *adore* and *knark* hide processes, network connections, and malicious files by illegitimately redirecting interrupt or system call handling into their kernel modules. Redirection can alter the semantic meaning of a system call—a problem for any system that monitors system calls to understand the behavior of malware. Jiang and Wang address this class of attack:

> Syscall remapping requires the modification of either the interrupt descriptor table (IDT) or the system call handler routine... [3]

Systems like that of Jiang and Wang assume that protections against illegitimate alteration of the IDT or system call handler will force malicious software to

R. Lippmann, E. Kirda, and A. Trachtenberg (Eds.): RAID 2008, LNCS 5230, pp. 421–422, 2008.

always follow the standard system-call interface when requesting service from the kernel.

Unfortunately, this assumption does not hold true. Malicious code can obfuscate the Windows or Linux system call interface using only legitimate functionality commonly used by kernel modules and drivers. Our *Illusion* attack will allow malicious processes to invoke privileged kernel operations without requiring the malware to call the actual system calls corresponding to those operations. In contrast to prior attacks of the sort considered by Jiang and Wang, Illusion will alter neither static kernel code nor read-only dispatch tables such as the IAT or system call descriptor table (SSDT). During the execution of malware augmented with the Illusion attack, an existing system-call analyzer will see a series of system calls different that those actually executed by the malware.

The Illusion attack is possible because a number of system calls allow *legitimate* dispatch into code contained in a kernel module or driver, and this permits an attacker to alter their semantics. Consider `ioctl`: this system call takes an arbitrary, uninterpreted memory buffer as an argument and passes that argument to a function in a kernel module that has registered itself as the handler for a special file. Benign kernel modules legitimately register handler functions for such files; a malicious module performing the same registration exhibits no behaviors different than the benign code. However, a call to `ioctl` will be directed into the malicious module's code together with the buffer passed to `ioctl` as an argument. In user-space, we marshal a malware's actual system call request into this buffer, and we then use the kernel module to unmarshal the request and invoke the appropriate kernel system call handler function. With this interface illusion in place, the kernel still executes the same operations that the malware instance would have executed without the obfuscation. However, system call monitoring utilities would observe a sequence of `ioctl` requests and would not realize that malicious operations had occurred.

References

1. Forrest, S., Hofmeyr, S.A., Somayaji, A., Longstaff, T.A.: A sense of self for UNIX processes. In: IEEE Symposium on Security and Privacy, Oakland, CA (May 1996)
2. Giffin, J.T., Jha, S., Miller, B.P.: Efficient context-sensitive intrusion detection. In: Network and Distributed System Security Symposium (NDSS), San Diego, CA (February 2004)
3. Jiang, X., Wang, X.: Out-of-the-box monitoring of VM-based high-interaction honeypots. In: Kruegel, C., Lippmann, R., Clark, A. (eds.) RAID 2007. LNCS, vol. 4637, pp. 198–218. Springer, Heidelberg (2007)
4. Krohn, M., Yip, A., Brodsky, M., Cliffer, N., Kaashoek, M.F., Kohler, E., Morris, R.: Information flow control for standard OS abstractions. In: Symposium on Operating System Principles (SOSP), Stevenson, WA (October 2007)
5. Sekar, R., Bendre, M., Dhurjati, D., Bollineni, P.: A fast automaton-based method for detecting anomalous program behaviors. In: IEEE Symposium on Security and Privacy, Oakland, CA (May 2001)

Author Index

Printing: Mercedes-Druck, Berlin
Binding: Stein+Lehmann, Berlin

Lecture Notes in Computer Science

Sublibrary 4: Security and Cryptology

For information about Vols. 1– 4116
please contact your bookseller or Springer

Vol. 4812: P. McDaniel, S.K. Gupta (Eds.), Information Systems Security. XIII, 322 pages. 2007.

Vol. 4784: W. Susilo, J.K. Liu, Y. Mu (Eds.), Provable Security. X, 237 pages. 2007.

Vol. 4779: J.A. Garay, A.K. Lenstra, M. Mambo, R. Peralta (Eds.), Information Security. XIII, 437 pages. 2007.

Vol. 4776: N. Borisov, P. Golle (Eds.), Privacy Enhancing Technologies. X, 273 pages. 2007.

Vol. 4752: A. Miyaji, H. Kikuchi, K. Rannenberg (Eds.), Advances in Information and Computer Security. XIII, 460 pages. 2007.

Vol. 4734: J. Biskup, J. López (Eds.), Computer Security – ESORICS 2007. XIV, 628 pages. 2007.

Vol. 4727: P. Paillier, I. Verbauwhede (Eds.), Cryptographic Hardware and Embedded Systems - CHES 2007. XIV, 468 pages. 2007.

Vol. 4691: T. Dimitrakos, F. Martinelli, P.Y.A. Ryan, S. Schneider (Eds.), Formal Aspects in Security and Trust. VIII, 285 pages. 2007.

Vol. 4677: A. Aldini, R. Gorrieri (Eds.), Foundations of Security Analysis and Design IV. VII, 325 pages. 2007.

Vol. 4657: C. Lambrinoudakis, G. Pernul, A.M. Tjoa (Eds.), Trust, Privacy and Security in Digital Business. XIII, 291 pages. 2007.

Vol. 4637: C. Kruegel, R. Lippmann, A. Clark (Eds.), Recent Advances in Intrusion Detection. XII, 337 pages. 2007.

Vol. 4631: B. Christianson, B. Crispo, J.A. Malcolm, M. Roe (Eds.), Security Protocols. IX, 347 pages. 2007.

Vol. 4622: A. Menezes (Ed.), Advances in Cryptology - CRYPTO 2007. XIV, 631 pages. 2007.

Vol. 4593: A. Biryukov (Ed.), Fast Software Encryption. XI, 467 pages. 2007.

Vol. 4586: J. Pieprzyk, H. Ghodosi, E. Dawson (Eds.), Information Security and Privacy. XIV, 476 pages. 2007.

Vol. 4582: J. López, P. Samarati, J.L. Ferrer (Eds.), Public Key Infrastructure. XI, 375 pages. 2007.

Vol. 4579: B.M. Hämmerli, R. Sommer (Eds.), Detection of Intrusions and Malware, and Vulnerability Assessment. X, 251 pages. 2007.

Vol. 4575: T. Takagi, T. Okamoto, E. Okamoto, T. Okamoto (Eds.), Pairing-Based Cryptography – Pairing 2007. XI, 408 pages. 2007.

Vol. 4567: T. Furon, F. Cayre, G. Doërr, P. Bas (Eds.), Information Hiding. XI, 393 pages. 2008.

Vol. 4521: J. Katz, M. Yung (Eds.), Applied Cryptography and Network Security. XIII, 498 pages. 2007.

Vol. 4515: M. Naor (Ed.), Advances in Cryptology - EUROCRYPT 2007. XIII, 591 pages. 2007.

Vol. 4499: Y.Q. Shi (Ed.), Transactions on Data Hiding and Multimedia Security II. IX, 117 pages. 2007.

Vol. 4464: E. Dawson, D.S. Wong (Eds.), Information Security Practice and Experience. XIII, 361 pages. 2007.

Vol. 4462: D. Sauveron, K. Markantonakis, A. Bilas, J.-J. Quisquater (Eds.), Information Security Theory and Practices. XII, 255 pages. 2007.

Vol. 4450: T. Okamoto, X. Wang (Eds.), Public Key Cryptography – PKC 2007. XIII, 491 pages. 2007.

Vol. 4437: J.L. Camenisch, C.S. Collberg, N.F. Johnson, P. Sallee (Eds.), Information Hiding. VIII, 389 pages. 2007.

Vol. 4392: S.P. Vadhan (Ed.), Theory of Cryptography. XI, 595 pages. 2007.

Vol. 4377: M. Abe (Ed.), Topics in Cryptology – CT-RSA 2007. XI, 403 pages. 2006.

Vol. 4356: E. Biham, A.M. Youssef (Eds.), Selected Areas in Cryptography. XI, 395 pages. 2007.

Vol. 4341: P.Q. Nguyên (Ed.), Progress in Cryptology - VIETCRYPT 2006. XI, 385 pages. 2006.

Vol. 4332: A. Bagchi, V. Atluri (Eds.), Information Systems Security. XV, 382 pages. 2006.

Vol. 4329: R. Barua, T. Lange (Eds.), Progress in Cryptology - INDOCRYPT 2006. X, 454 pages. 2006.

Vol. 4318: H. Lipmaa, M. Yung, D. Lin (Eds.), Information Security and Cryptology. XI, 305 pages. 2006.

Vol. 4307: P. Ning, S. Qing, N. Li (Eds.), Information and Communications Security. XIV, 558 pages. 2006.

Vol. 4301: D. Pointcheval, Y. Mu, K. Chen (Eds.), Cryptology and Network Security. XIII, 381 pages. 2006.

Vol. 4300: Y.Q. Shi (Ed.), Transactions on Data Hiding and Multimedia Security I. IX, 139 pages. 2006.

Vol. 4298: J.K. Lee, O. Yi, M. Yung (Eds.), Information Security Applications. XIV, 406 pages. 2007.

Vol. 4296: M.S. Rhee, B. Lee (Eds.), Information Security and Cryptology – ICISC 2006. XIII, 358 pages. 2006.

Vol. 4284: X. Lai, K. Chen (Eds.), Advances in Cryptology – ASIACRYPT 2006. XIV, 468 pages. 2006.

Vol. 4283: Y.Q. Shi, B. Jeon (Eds.), Digital Watermarking. XII, 474 pages. 2006.

Vol. 4266: H. Yoshiura, K. Sakurai, K. Rannenberg, Y. Murayama, S.-i. Kawamura (Eds.), Advances in Information and Computer Security. XIII, 438 pages. 2006.

Vol. 4258: G. Danezis, P. Golle (Eds.), Privacy Enhancing Technologies. VIII, 431 pages. 2006.

Vol. 4249: L. Goubin, M. Matsui (Eds.), Cryptographic Hardware and Embedded Systems - CHES 2006. XII, 462 pages. 2006.

Vol. 4237: H. Leitold, E.P. Markatos (Eds.), Communications and Multimedia Security. XII, 253 pages. 2006.

Vol. 4236: L. Breveglieri, I. Koren, D. Naccache, J.-P. Seifert (Eds.), Fault Diagnosis and Tolerance in Cryptography. XIII, 253 pages. 2006.

Vol. 4219: D. Zamboni, C. Krügel (Eds.), Recent Advances in Intrusion Detection. XII, 331 pages. 2006.

Vol. 4189: D. Gollmann, J. Meier, A. Sabelfeld (Eds.), Computer Security – ESORICS 2006. XI, 548 pages. 2006.

Vol. 4176: S.K. Katsikas, J. López, M. Backes, S. Gritzalis, B. Preneel (Eds.), Information Security. XIV, 548 pages. 2006.

Vol. 4117: C. Dwork (Ed.), Advances in Cryptology - CRYPTO 2006. XIII, 621 pages. 2006.